Connections

Editorial Board

General Editors

JOEL B. GREEN (The United Methodist Church), Professor of New Testament Interpretation, Fuller Theological Seminary, Pasadena, CA

THOMAS G. LONG (Presbyterian Church (U.S.A.)), Bandy Professor Emeritus of Preaching at Candler School of Theology, Emory University, Atlanta, GA

LUKE A. POWERY (Progressive National Baptist Convention), Dean of Duke University Chapel and Associate Professor of Homiletics at Duke Divinity School, Durham, NC

CYNTHIA L. RIGBY (Presbyterian Church (U.S.A.)), W. C. Brown Professor of Theology, Austin Presbyterian Theological Seminary, Austin, TX

CAROLYN J. SHARP (The Episcopal Church), Professor of Homiletics, Yale Divinity School, New Haven, CT

Volume Editors

ERIC D. BARRETO (Cooperative Baptist Fellowship), Frederick and Margaret L. Weyerhaeuser Associate Professor of New Testament, Princeton Theological Seminary, Princeton, NJ

GREGORY CUÉLLAR (Baptist), Associate Professor of Old Testament, Austin Presbyterian Theological Seminary, Austin, TX

WILLIAM GREENWAY (Presbyterian Church (U.S.A.)), Professor of Philosophical Theology, Austin Presbyterian Theological Seminary, Austin, TX

CAROLYN B. HELSEL (Presbyterian Church (U.S.A.)), Assistant Professor of Homiletics, Austin Presbyterian Theological Seminary, Austin, TX

JENNIFER L. LORD (Presbyterian Church (U.S.A.)), Dorothy B. Vickery Professor of Homiletics and Liturgical Studies, Austin Presbyterian Theological Seminary, Austin, TX

SUZIE PARK (The United Methodist Church), Associate Professor of Old Testament, Austin Presbyterian Theological Seminary, Austin, TX

ZAIDA MALDONADO PÉREZ (The United Church of Christ), Retired Professor of Church History and Theology, Asbury Theological Seminary, Orlando, FL

EMERSON B. POWERY (The Episcopal Church), Professor of Biblical Studies, Messiah College, Mechanicsburg, PA

WYNDY CORBIN REUSCHLING (The United Methodist Church), Professor of Ethics and Theology, Ashland Theological Seminary, Ashland, OH

DAVID J. SCHLAFER (The Episcopal Church), Independent Consultant in Preaching and Assisting Priest, Episcopal Church of the Redeemer, Bethesda, MD

ANGELA SIMS (National Baptist Convention), President of Colgate Rochester Crozer Divinity School, Rochester, NY

DAVID F. WHITE (The United Methodist Church), C. Ellis and Nancy Gribble Nelson Professor of Christian Education, Professor in Methodist Studies, Austin Presbyterian Theological Seminary, Austin, TX

Psalm Editor

KIMBERLY BRACKEN LONG (Presbyterian Church (U.S.A.)), Editor, *Call to Worship: Liturgy, Music, Preaching, and the Arts,* Louisville, KY

Sidebar Editor

RICHARD MANLY ADAMS JR. (Presbyterian Church (U.S.A.)), Director of Pitts Theology Library and Margaret A. Pitts Assistant Professor in the Practice of Theological Bibliography, Candler School of Theology, Emory University, Atlanta, GA

Project Manager

JOAN MURCHISON, Austin Presbyterian Theological Seminary, Austin, TX

Project Compiler

PAMELA J. JARVIS, Austin Presbyterian Theological Seminary, Austin, TX

Year A, Volume 3
Season after Pentecost

Connections
A Lectionary Commentary for Preaching and Worship

Joel B. Green
Thomas G. Long
Luke A. Powery
Cynthia L. Rigby
Carolyn J. Sharp
General Editors

WJK WESTMINSTER
JOHN KNOX PRESS
LOUISVILLE · KENTUCKY

© 2020 Westminster John Knox Press

First edition
Published by Westminster John Knox Press
Louisville, Kentucky

20 21 22 23 24 25 26 27 28 29—10 9 8 7 6 5 4 3 2 1

All rights reserved. No part of this book may be reproduced or transmitted in any form or by any means, electronic or mechanical, including photocopying, recording, or by any information storage or retrieval system, without permission in writing from the publisher. For information, address Westminster John Knox Press, 100 Witherspoon Street, Louisville, KY 40202–1396. Or contact us online at www.wjkbooks.com.

Unless otherwise indicated, Scripture quotations are from the New Revised Standard Version of the Bible, copyright © 1989 by the Division of Christian Education of the National Council of the Churches of Christ in the U.S.A., and are used by permission. Scripture quotations marked CEV are from the Contemporary English Version. Copyright © 1991, 1992, 1995 by American Bible Society. Used by permission. Scripture quotations marked NIV are from *The Holy Bible, New International Version.* Copyright © 1973, 1978, 1984, 2011 by Biblica, Inc.® Used by permission. All rights reserved worldwide. Scripture quotations marked RSV are from the Revised Standard Version of the Bible, copyright © 1946, 1952, 1971, and 1973 by the Division of Christian Education of the National Council of the Churches of Christ in the U.S.A., and are used by permission.

Excerpts from *Celtic Spirituality* from The Classics of Western Spirituality, translated by Oliver Davies, copyright © 1999 by Oliver Davies. Paulist Press, Inc., New York/Mahwah, N.J. Used with permission of Paulist Press. www.paulistpress.com. Excerpt from "Let God's People Sing a New Song: Psalm 149," words and music by Greg Scheer, © 2014 and are used by permission. Available at www.gregscheer.com.

Book and cover design by Allison Taylor

The Library of Congress has cataloged an earlier volume as follows:
Names: Long, Thomas G., 1946- editor.
Title: Connections : a lectionary commentary for preaching and worship / Joel
  B. Green, Thomas G. Long, Luke A. Powery, Cynthia L. Rigby, Carolyn J. Sharp, general
  editors.
Description: Louisville, Kentucky : Westminster John Knox Press, 2018- |
  Includes index. |
Identifiers: LCCN 2018006372 (print) | LCCN 2018012579 (ebook) | ISBN
  9781611648874 (ebk.) | ISBN 9780664262433 (volume 1 : hbk. : alk. paper)
Subjects: LCSH: Lectionary preaching. | Bible—Meditations. | Common
  lectionary (1992) | Lectionaries.
Classification: LCC BV4235.L43 (ebook) | LCC BV4235.L43 C66 2018 (print) |
  DDC 251/.6—dc23
LC record available at https://lccn.loc.gov/2018006372

Connections: Year A, Volume 3
ISBN: 9780664262396 (hardback)
ISBN: 9780664264819 (paperback)
ISBN: 9781611649840 (ebook)

PRINTED IN THE UNITED STATES OF AMERICA

♾ The paper used in this publication meets the minimum requirements of the American National Standard for Information Sciences—Permanence of Paper for Printed Library Materials, ANSI Z39.48-1992.

Most Westminster John Knox Press books are available at special quantity discounts when purchased in bulk by corporations, organizations, and special-interest groups. For more information, please e-mail SpecialSales@wjkbooks.com.

Contents

LIST OF SIDEBARS	xi
PUBLISHER'S NOTE	xiii
INTRODUCING CONNECTIONS	xv
INTRODUCING THE REVISED COMMON LECTIONARY	xvii

Trinity Sunday

Genesis 1:1–2:4a	2
Psalm 8	8
2 Corinthians 13:11–13	10
Matthew 28:16–20	14

Proper 3 (Sunday between May 22 and May 28 inclusive)

Isaiah 49:8–16a	18
Psalm 131	23
1 Corinthians 4:1–5	25
Matthew 6:24–34	29

Proper 4 (Sunday between May 29 and June 4 inclusive)

Deuteronomy 11:18–21, 26–28 and Genesis 6:9–22; 7:24; 8:14–19	33
Psalm 31:1–5, 19–24 and Psalm 46	38
Romans 1:16–17; 3:22b–28	42
Matthew 7:21–29	46

Proper 5 (Sunday between June 5 and June 11 inclusive)

Hosea 5:15–6:6 and Genesis 12:1–9	50
Psalm 50:7–15 and Psalm 33:1–12	55
Romans 4:13–25	58
Matthew 9:9–13, 18–26	63

Proper 6 (Sunday between June 12 and June 18 inclusive)

Exodus 19:2–8a and Genesis 18:1–15 (21:1–7)	68
Psalm 100 and Psalm 116:1–2, 12–19	73
Romans 5:1–8	76
Matthew 9:35–10:8 (9–23)	80

Proper 7 (Sunday between June 19 and June 25 inclusive)

Jeremiah 20:7–13 and Genesis 21:8–21	85
Psalm 69:7–10 (11–15), 16–18 and Psalm 86:1–10, 16–17	91
Romans 6:1b–11	94
Matthew 10:24–39	98

Proper 8 (Sunday between June 26 and July 2 inclusive)

Jeremiah 28:5–9 and Genesis 22:1–14	102
Psalm 89:1–4, 15–18 and Psalm 13	108
Romans 6:12–23	111
Matthew 10:40–42	116

Proper 9 (Sunday between July 3 and July 9 inclusive)

Zechariah 9:9–12 and Genesis 24:34–38, 42–49, 58–67	120
Psalm 145:8–14 and Psalm 45:10–17 or Song of Solomon 2:8–13	126
Romans 7:15–25a	130
Matthew 11:16–19, 25–30	135

Proper 10 (Sunday between July 10 and July 16 inclusive)

Isaiah 55:10–13 and Genesis 25:19–34	139
Psalm 65:(1–8) 9–13 and Psalm 119:105–112	144
Romans 8:1–11	148
Matthew 13:1–9, 18–23	152

Proper 11 (Sunday between July 17 and July 23 inclusive)

Isaiah 44:6–8 and Genesis 28:10–19a	157
Psalm 86:11–17 and Psalm 139:1–12, 23–24	162
Romans 8:12–25	165
Matthew 13:24–30, 36–43	169

Proper 12 (Sunday between July 24 and July 30 inclusive)

1 Kings 3:5–12 and Genesis 29:15–28	173
Psalm 119:129–136 and Psalm 105:1–11, 45b or Psalm 128	178
Romans 8:26–39	182
Matthew 13:31–33, 44–52	187

Proper 13 (Sunday between July 31 and August 6 inclusive)

Isaiah 55:1–5 and Genesis 32:22–31	192
Psalm 145:8–9, 14–21 and Psalm 17:1–7, 15	197
Romans 9:1–5	200
Matthew 14:13–21	205

Proper 14 (Sunday between August 7 and August 13 inclusive)

1 Kings 19:9–18 and Genesis 37:1–4, 12–28	209
Psalm 85:8–13 and Psalm 105:1–6, 16–22, 45b	214
Romans 10:5–15	217
Matthew 14:22–33	222

Proper 15 (Sunday between August 14 and August 20 inclusive)

Isaiah 56:1, 6–8 and Genesis 45:1–15	227
Psalm 67 and Psalm 133	233
Romans 11:1–2a, 29–32	236
Matthew 15:(10–20) 21–28	240

Proper 16 (Sunday between August 21 and August 27 inclusive)

Isaiah 51:1–6 and Exodus 1:8–2:10	245
Psalm 138 and Psalm 124	251
Romans 12:1–8	254
Matthew 16:13–20	258

Proper 17 (Sunday between August 28 and September 3 inclusive)

Jeremiah 15:15–21 and Exodus 3:1–15	262
Psalm 26:1–8 and Psalm 105:1–6, 23–26, 45b	268
Romans 12:9–21	272
Matthew 16:21–28	276

Proper 18 (Sunday between September 4 and September 10 inclusive)

Ezekiel 33:7–11 and Exodus 12:1–14	281
Psalm 119:33–40 and Psalm 149	286
Romans 13:8–14	289
Matthew 18:15–20	294

Proper 19 (Sunday between September 11 and September 17 inclusive)

Genesis 50:15–21 and Exodus 14:19–31	298
Psalm 103:(1–7) 8–13 and Psalm 114 or Exodus 15:1b–11, 20–21	303
Romans 14:1–12	307
Matthew 18:21–35	311

Proper 20 (Sunday between September 18 and September 24 inclusive)

Jonah 3:10–4:11 and Exodus 16:2–15	316
Psalm 145:1–8 and Psalm 105:1–6, 37–45	322
Philippians 1:21–30	325
Matthew 20:1–16	329

Proper 21 (Sunday between September 25 and October 1 inclusive)

Ezekiel 18:1–4, 25–32 and Exodus 17:1–7	334
Psalm 25:1–9 and Psalm 78:1–4, 12–16	340
Philippians 2:1–13	343
Matthew 21:23–32	348

Proper 22 (Sunday between October 2 and October 8 inclusive)

Isaiah 5:1–7 and Exodus 20:1–4, 7–9, 12–20	353
Psalm 80:7–15 and Psalm 19	359
Philippians 3:4b–14	362
Matthew 21:33–46	367

Proper 23 (Sunday between October 9 and October 15 inclusive)

Isaiah 25:1–9 and Exodus 32:1–14	372
Psalm 23 and Psalm 106:1–6, 19–23	377
Philippians 4:1–9	380
Matthew 22:1–14	385

Proper 24 (Sunday between October 16 and October 22 inclusive)

Isaiah 45:1–7 and Exodus 33:12–23	389
Psalm 96:1–9 (10–13) and Psalm 99	395
1 Thessalonians 1:1–10	399
Matthew 22:15–22	403

Proper 25 (Sunday between October 23 and October 29 inclusive)

Leviticus 19:1–2, 15–18 and Deuteronomy 34:1–12	407
Psalm 1 and Psalm 90:1–6, 13–17	412
1 Thessalonians 2:1–8	416
Matthew 22:34–46	420

All Saints

Revelation 7:9–17	424
Psalm 34:1–10, 22	429
1 John: 3:1–3	431
Matthew 5:1–12	435

Proper 26 (Sunday between October 30 and November 5 inclusive)

Micah 3:5–12 and Joshua 3:7–17	440
Psalm 43 and Psalm 107:1–7, 33–37	446
1 Thessalonians 2:9–13	449
Matthew 23:1–12	454

Proper 27 (Sunday between November 6 and November 12 inclusive)

Joshua 24:1–3a, 14–25 and Amos 5:18–24	458
Psalm 78:1–7 and Psalm 70	464
1 Thessalonians 4:13–18	467
Matthew 25:1–13	471

Proper 28 (Sunday between November 13 and November 19 inclusive)

Zephaniah 1:7, 12–18 and Judges 4:1–7	475
Psalm 90:1–8 (9–11), 12 and Psalm 123	481
1 Thessalonians 5:1–11	484
Matthew 25:14–30	488

Proper 29 (Reign of Christ)

Ezekiel 34:11–16, 20–24	493
Psalm 95:1–7a and Psalm 100	498
Ephesians 1:15–23	501
Matthew 25:31–46	506

CONTRIBUTORS	511
AUTHOR INDEX	515
SCRIPTURE INDEX	517
COMPREHENSIVE SCRIPTURE INDEX FOR YEAR A	531

Sidebars

Trinity Sunday:
"Alert the Ears of Your Spirit"   4
Bonaventure

Proper 3: "The Spirit Bestowed
on Us by God"   22
Philip Jacob Spener

Proper 4: "The Light
of Conscience"   41
Dorotheos of Gaza

Proper 5: "The Strangeness
of Christ"   60
Hans Küng

Proper 6: "The Unity Which
Excels Every Unity"   82
"The Broom of Devotion"

Proper 7: "The Way of Life
Lies Here"   88
John Bunyan

Proper 8: "The Call and Courage
to Be Tested"   106
Søren Kierkegaard

Proper 9: "Examine Yourself"   132
Erasmus

Proper 10: "Let Us Attain to God"   154
Augustine

Proper 11: "The Summer
of the Righteous"   159
The Shepherd of Hermas

Proper 12: "On Christ We
Venture All"   180
John Henry Newman

Proper 13: "In Every Respect
Give Thanks"   201
1 Clement

Proper 14: "A Living, Daring
Confidence in God's Grace"   223
Martin Luther

Proper 15: "All Are One Who
Him Receive"   229
Charles Wesley

Proper 16: "The Most
Profitable Lesson"   249
Thomas à Kempis

Proper 17: "Prefer Nothing
to Christ"   270
Benedict

Proper 18: "Let the Last Act
of Life Be Love"   291
Richard Allen

Proper 19: "This Work
of Justice"   313
Robert Russell Booth

Proper 20: "The Beginning
and End of Christ's Work"   319
Dirk Philips

Proper 21: "Share in
Christ's Rest"   338
John Chrysostom

Proper 22: "Following the Will
of God in All Things"   364
Teresa of Avila

Proper 23: "Safety in the Fires"   383
Julia A. J. Foote

Proper 24: "He Rules
by Serving" 391
Jürgen Moltmann

Proper 25: "Everything is Dark
That God Does Not Enlighten" 414
William Law

All Saints: "That Delightful City" 437
James Archer

Proper 26: "The Comprehension
of Sacred Truth" 450
Hilary of Poitiers

Proper 27: "The Assurance
of Faith" 461
Ulrich Zwingli

Proper 28: "God Who
Is Already Seeking Us" 479
Joan Chittister

Proper 29 (Reign of Christ):
"A Communion That
Can Endure" 503
Wilhelm Hermann

Publisher's Note

"The preaching of the Word of God is the Word of God," says the Second Helvetic Confession. While that might sound like an exalted estimation of the homiletical task, it comes with an implicit warning: "A lot is riding on this business of preaching. Get it right!"

Believing that much does indeed depend on the church's proclamation, we offer Connections: A Lectionary Commentary for Preaching and Worship. Connections embodies two complementary convictions about the study of Scripture in preparation for preaching and worship. First, to best understand an individual passage of Scripture, we should put it in conversation with the rest of the Bible. Second, since all truth is God's truth, we should bring as many "lenses" as possible to the study of Scripture, drawn from as many sources as we can find. Our prayer is that this unique combination of approaches will illumine your study and preparation, facilitating the weekly task of bringing the Word of God to the people of God.

We at Westminster John Knox Press want to thank the superb editorial team that came together to make Connections possible. At the heart of that team are our general editors: Joel B. Green, Thomas G. Long, Luke A. Powery, Cynthia L. Rigby, and Carolyn J. Sharp. These gifted scholars and preachers have poured countless hours into brainstorming, planning, reading, editing, and supporting the project. Their passion for authentic preaching and transformative worship shows up on every page. They pushed the writers and their fellow editors, they pushed us at the press, and most especially they pushed themselves to focus always on what you, the users of this resource, genuinely need. We are grateful to Kimberley Bracken Long for her innovative vision of what commentary on the Psalm readings could accomplish, and for recruiting a talented group of liturgists and preachers to implement that vision. Bo Adams has shown creativity and insight in exploring an array of sources to provide the sidebars that accompany each worship day's commentaries. At the forefront of the work have been the members of our editorial board, who helped us identify writers, assign passages, and most especially carefully edit each commentary. They have cheerfully allowed the project to intrude on their schedules in order to make possible this contribution to the life of the church. Most especially we thank our writers, drawn from a broad diversity of backgrounds, vocations, and perspectives. The distinctive character of our commentaries required much from our writers. Their passion for the preaching ministry of the church proved them worthy of the challenge.

A project of this size does not come together without the work of excellent support staff. Above all we are indebted to project manager Joan Murchison. Joan's fingerprints are all over the book you hold in your hands; her gentle, yet unconquerable, persistence always kept it moving forward in good shape and on time. We also wish to thank Pam Jarvis, who skillfully compiled the dozens of separate commentaries and sidebars into this single volume.

Finally, our sincere thanks to the administration, faculty, and staff of Austin Presbyterian Theological Seminary, our institutional partner in producing Connections. President Theodore J. Wardlaw and Dean David H. Jensen have been steadfast friends of the project, enthusiastically agreeing to our partnership, carefully overseeing their faculty and staff's work on it, graciously hosting our meetings, and enthusiastically using their platform to promote Connections among their students, alumni, and friends.

It is with much joy that we commend Connections to you, our readers. May God use this resource to deepen and enrich your ministry of preaching and worship.

WESTMINSTER JOHN KNOX PRESS

Introducing Connections

Connections is a resource designed to help preachers generate sermons that are theologically deeper, liturgically richer, and culturally more pertinent. Based on the Revised Common Lectionary (RCL), which has wide ecumenical use, the hundreds of essays on the full array of biblical passages in the three-year cycle can be used effectively by preachers who follow the RCL, by those who follow other lectionaries, and by nonlectionary preachers alike.

The essential idea of Connections is that biblical texts display their power most fully when they are allowed to interact with a number of contexts, that is, when many connections are made between a biblical text and realities outside that text. Like the two poles of a battery, when the pole of the biblical text is connected to a different pole (another aspect of Scripture or a dimension of life outside Scripture), creative sparks fly and energy surges from pole to pole.

Two major interpretive essays, called Commentary 1 and Commentary 2, address every scriptural reading in the RCL. Commentary 1 explores preaching connections between a lectionary reading and other texts and themes within Scripture, and Commentary 2 makes preaching connections between the lectionary texts and themes in the larger culture outside of Scripture. These essays have been written by pastors, biblical scholars, theologians, and others, all of whom have a commitment to lively biblical preaching.

The writers of Commentary 1 surveyed five possible connections for their texts: the immediate literary context (the passages right around the text), the larger literary context (for example, the cycle of David stories or the passion narrative), the thematic context (such as other feeding stories, other parables, or other passages on the theme of hope), the lectionary context (the other readings for the day in the RCL), and the canonical context (other places in the whole of the Bible that display harmony, or perhaps tension, with the text at hand).

The writers of Commentary 2 surveyed six possible connections for their texts: the liturgical context (such as Advent or Easter), the ecclesial context (the life and mission of the church), the social and ethical context (justice and social responsibility), the cultural context (such as art, music, and literature), the larger expanse of human knowledge (such as science, history, and psychology), and the personal context (the life and faith of individuals).

In each essay, the writers selected from this array of possible connections, emphasizing those connections they saw as most promising for preaching. It is important to note that, even though Commentary 1 makes connections inside the Bible and Commentary 2 makes connections outside the Bible, this does not represent a division between "what the text *meant* in biblical times versus what the text *means* now." *Every* connection made with the text, whether that connection is made within the Bible or out in the larger culture, is seen as generative for preaching, and each author provokes the imagination of the preacher to see in these connections preaching possibilities for today. Connections is not a substitute for traditional scriptural commentaries, concordances, Bible dictionaries, and other interpretive tools. Rather, Connections begins with solid biblical scholarship and then goes on to focus on the act of preaching and on the ultimate goal of allowing the biblical text to come alive in the sermon.

Connections addresses every biblical text in the RCL, and it takes seriously the architecture of the RCL. During the seasons of the Christian year (Advent through Epiphany and Lent through Pentecost), the RCL provides three readings and a psalm for each Sunday and feast day: (1) a first reading, usually from the Old Testament; (2) a psalm, chosen to respond to the first reading; (3) a second reading, usually from one of the New Testament epistles; and (4) a Gospel reading. The first and second readings are chosen as complements to the Gospel reading for the day.

During the time between Pentecost and Advent, however, the RCL includes an additional first reading for every Sunday. There is the usual complementary reading, chosen in relation to the Gospel reading, but there is also a "semicontinuous" reading. These semicontinuous first readings move through the books of the Old Testament more or less continuously in narrative sequence, offering the stories of the patriarchs (Year A), the kings of Israel (Year B), and the prophets (Year C). Connections covers both the complementary and the semicontinuous readings.

The architects of the RCL understand the psalms and canticles to be prayers, and they selected the psalms for each Sunday and feast as prayerful responses to the first reading for the day. Thus, the Connections essays on the psalms are different from the other essays, and they have two goals, one homiletical and the other liturgical. First, they comment on ways the psalm might offer insight into preaching the first reading. Second, they describe how the tone and content of the psalm or canticle might inform the day's worship, suggesting ways the psalm or canticle may be read, sung, or prayed.

Preachers will find in Connections many ideas and approaches to sustain lively and provocative preaching for years to come. But beyond the deep reservoir of preaching connections found in these pages, preachers will also find here a habit of mind, a way of thinking about biblical preaching. Being guided by the essays in Connections to see many connections between biblical texts and their various contexts, preachers will be stimulated to make other connections for themselves. Connections is an abundant collection of creative preaching ideas, and it is also a spur to continued creativity.

JOEL B. GREEN
THOMAS G. LONG
LUKE A. POWERY
CYNTHIA L. RIGBY
CAROLYN J. SHARP
General Editors

Introducing the Revised Common Lectionary

To derive the greatest benefit from Connections, it will help to understand the structure and purpose of the Revised Common Lectionary (RCL), around which this resource is built. The RCL is a three-year guide to Scripture readings for the Christian Sunday gathering for worship. "Lectionary" simply means a selection of texts for reading and preaching. The RCL is an adaptation of the Roman Lectionary (of 1969, slightly revised in 1981), which itself was a reworking of the medieval Western-church one-year cycle of readings. The RCL resulted from six years of consultations that included representatives from nineteen churches or denominational agencies. Every preacher uses a lectionary—whether it comes from a specific denomination or is the preacher's own choice—but the RCL is unique in that it positions the preacher's homiletical work within a web of specific, ongoing connections.

The RCL has its roots in Jewish lectionary systems and early Christian ways of reading texts to illumine the biblical meaning of a feast day or time in the church calendar. Among our earliest lectionaries are the lists of readings for Holy Week and Easter in fourth-century Jerusalem.

One of the RCL's central connections is intertextuality; multiple texts are listed for each day. This lectionary's way of reading Scripture is based on Scripture's own pattern: texts interpreting texts. In the RCL, every Sunday of the year and each special or festival day is assigned a group of texts, normally three readings and a psalm. For most of the year, the first reading is an Old Testament text, followed by a psalm, a reading from one of the epistles, and a reading from one of the Gospel accounts.

The RCL's three-year cycle centers Year A in Matthew, Year B in Mark, and Year C in Luke. It is less clear how the Gospel according to John fits in, but when preachers learn about the RCL's arrangement of the Gospels, it makes sense. John gets a place of privilege because John's Gospel account, with its high Christology, is assigned for the great feasts. Texts from John's account are also assigned for Lent, Sundays of Easter, and summer Sundays. The second-century bishop Irenaeus's insistence on four Gospels is evident in this lectionary system: John and the Synoptics are in conversation with each other. However, because the RCL pattern contains variations, an extended introduction to the RCL can help the preacher learn the reasons for texts being set next to other texts.

The Gospel reading governs each day's selections. Even though the ancient order of reading texts in the Sunday gathering positions the Gospel reading last, the preacher should know that the RCL receives the Gospel reading as the hermeneutical key.

At certain times in the calendar year, the connections between the texts are less obvious. The RCL offers two tracks for readings in the time after Pentecost (Ordinary Time/standard Sundays): the complementary and the semicontinuous. Complementary texts relate to the church year and its seasons; semicontinuous emphasis is on preaching through a biblical book. Both approaches are historic ways of choosing texts for Sunday. This commentary series includes both the complementary and the semicontinuous readings.

In the complementary track, the Old Testament reading provides an intentional tension, a deeper understanding, or a background reference for another text of the day. The Psalm is the congregation's response to the first reading, following its themes. The Epistle functions as the horizon of the church: we learn about the faith and struggles of early Christian communities. The Gospel tells us where we are in the church's time and is enlivened, as are all the texts, by these intertextual interactions. Because the semicontinuous track prioritizes the narratives of specific books, the intertextual connections are not as apparent. Connections still exist, however. Year A pairs Matthew's account with Old Testament readings from the first five books; Year B pairs Mark's account with stories of anointed kings; Year C pairs Luke's account with the prophetic books.

Historically, lectionaries came into being because they were the church's beloved texts, like the scriptural canon. Choices had to be made regarding readings in the assembly, given the limit of fifty-two Sundays and a handful of festival days. The RCL presupposes that everyone (preachers and congregants) can read these texts—even along with the daily RCL readings that are paired with the Sunday readings.

Another central connection found in the RCL is the connection between texts and church seasons or the church's year. The complementary texts make these connections most clear. The intention of the RCL is that the texts of each Sunday or feast day bring biblical meaning to where we are in time. The texts at Christmas announce the incarnation. Texts in Lent renew us to follow Christ, and texts for the fifty days of Easter proclaim God's power over death and sin and our new life in Christ. The entire church's year is a hermeneutical key for using the RCL.

Let it be clear that the connection to the church year is a connection for present-tense proclamation. We read, not to recall history, but to know how those events are true for us today. Now is the time of the Spirit of the risen Christ; now we beseech God in the face of sin and death; now we live baptized into Jesus' life and ministry. To read texts in time does not mean we remind ourselves of Jesus' biography for half of the year and then the mission of the church for the other half. Rather, we follow each Gospel's narrative order to be brought again to the meaning of Jesus' death and resurrection and his risen presence in our midst. The RCL positions the texts as our lens on our life and the life of the world in our time: who we are in Christ now, for the sake of the world.

The RCL intends to be a way of reading texts to bring us again to faith, for these texts to be how we see our lives and our gospel witness in the world. Through these connections, the preacher can find faithful, relevant ways to preach year after year.

JENNIFER L. LORD
Connections Editorial Board Member

Connections

Trinity Sunday

Genesis 1:1–2:4a
Psalm 8

2 Corinthians 13:11–13
Matthew 28:16–20

Genesis 1:1–2:4a

¹In the beginning when God created the heavens and the earth, ²the earth was a formless void and darkness covered the face of the deep, while a wind from God swept over the face of the waters. ³Then God said, "Let there be light"; and there was light. ⁴And God saw that the light was good; and God separated the light from the darkness. ⁵God called the light Day, and the darkness he called Night. And there was evening and there was morning, the first day.

⁶And God said, "Let there be a dome in the midst of the waters, and let it separate the waters from the waters." ⁷So God made the dome and separated the waters that were under the dome from the waters that were above the dome. And it was so. ⁸God called the dome Sky. And there was evening and there was morning, the second day.

⁹And God said, "Let the waters under the sky be gathered together into one place, and let the dry land appear." And it was so. ¹⁰God called the dry land Earth, and the waters that were gathered together he called Seas. And God saw that it was good. ¹¹Then God said, "Let the earth put forth vegetation: plants yielding seed, and fruit trees of every kind on earth that bear fruit with the seed in it." And it was so. ¹²The earth brought forth vegetation: plants yielding seed of every kind, and trees of every kind bearing fruit with the seed in it. And God saw that it was good. ¹³And there was evening and there was morning, the third day.

¹⁴And God said, "Let there be lights in the dome of the sky to separate the day from the night; and let them be for signs and for seasons and for days and years, ¹⁵and let them be lights in the dome of the sky to give light upon the earth." And it was so. ¹⁶God made the two great lights—the greater light to rule the day and the lesser light to rule the night—and the stars. ¹⁷God set them in the dome of the sky to give light upon the earth, ¹⁸to rule over the day and over the night, and to separate the light from the darkness. And God saw that it was good. ¹⁹And there was evening and there was morning, the fourth day.

²⁰And God said, "Let the waters bring forth swarms of living creatures, and let birds fly above the earth across the dome of the sky." ²¹So God created the great sea monsters and every living creature that moves, of every kind, with which the waters swarm, and every winged bird of every kind. And God saw that it was good. ²²God blessed them, saying, "Be fruitful and multiply and fill the waters in the seas, and let birds multiply on the earth." ²³And there was evening and there was morning, the fifth day.

²⁴And God said, "Let the earth bring forth living creatures of every kind: cattle and creeping things and wild animals of the earth of every kind." And it was so. ²⁵God made the wild animals of the earth of every kind, and the cattle of every kind, and everything that creeps upon the ground of every kind. And God saw that it was good.

²⁶Then God said, "Let us make humankind in our image, according to our likeness; and let them have dominion over the fish of the sea, and over the birds of the air, and over the cattle, and over all the wild animals of the earth, and over every creeping thing that creeps upon the earth."

[27]So God created humankind in his image,
 in the image of God he created them;
 male and female he created them.

[28]God blessed them, and God said to them, "Be fruitful and multiply, and fill the earth and subdue it; and have dominion over the fish of the sea and over the birds of the air and over every living thing that moves upon the earth." [29]God said, "See, I have given you every plant yielding seed that is upon the face of all the earth, and every tree with seed in its fruit; you shall have them for food. [30]And to every beast of the earth, and to every bird of the air, and to everything that creeps on the earth, everything that has the breath of life, I have given every green plant for food." And it was so. [31]God saw everything that he had made, and indeed, it was very good. And there was evening and there was morning, the sixth day.

[2:1]Thus the heavens and the earth were finished, and all their multitude. [2]And on the seventh day God finished the work that he had done, and he rested on the seventh day from all the work that he had done. [3]So God blessed the seventh day and hallowed it, because on it God rested from all the work that he had done in creation.

[4]These are the generations of the heavens and the earth when they were created.

Commentary 1: Connecting the Reading with Scripture

The creation story in Genesis 1 is not science but poetry, and it is rooted in faith rather than biological facts. God spoke, and creation happened. The author of Genesis 1 did not debate or defend the divine role and presence but simply assumed that there was a God who created the heavens and the earth. In the beginning was chaos, "without form and void." Then God breathed over the watery mess, and God's *ruach* (breath, wind, or spirit) moved over and separated the waters. God spoke, and the world appeared. God spoke, and divided the day from the night. God spoke, and separated the water from the land. Out of chaos came order and life.

The description of creation is precisely ordered. In the first three days of creation, God made the spaces: day/night (day 1), heaven and the oceans (day 2), earth and seas (day 3). In the next three days, God filled the spaces with the corresponding items: sun, moon, and stars (day 4), birds and sea creatures (day 5), cattle and earth creatures, including humans (day 6). God did not act alone, but shared the divine power to create with the creation itself. God said, "Let the waters bring forth swarms of living creatures." "Let the earth bring forth living creatures of every kind." God gave the animals and the humans the power to create more life. God gave humankind the ability to make the world a safe place for all God's creatures.

This beautiful, poetic story has provoked a great deal of conflict over whether the account should be read literally. Did God create the world in six twenty-four-hour days, a mere six thousand years ago, or did the earth and humanity evolve over millions of years? Genesis does not answer those questions, because it is not a biology textbook or a scientific report. Rather, it is literature—albeit canonical literature—that reflects the views and explanations of those who wrote it and edited it, and continue to read it now. This account communicates truth through story and poetry.

Genesis 1 is the first of two quite different creation narratives, which are difficult to harmonize. Most preachers know this, but it can be a significant insight for those who have been taught that there is a single story. Genesis 1:1–2:4a presents an orderly account of God speaking creation into existence in six

Alert the Ears of Your Spirit

From visible things the soul rises to the consideration of the power, wisdom, and goodness of God, in so far as He is existing, living, intelligent, purely spiritual, incorruptible, and immutable. . . . The origin of things, according to their creation, distinction, and adornment as the work of the six days, proclaims the power of God that produced all things out of nothing, the wisdom of God that clearly differentiated all things, the goodness of God that lavishly adorned all things. . . . Therefore, whoever is not enlightened by such great splendor in created things is blind; whoever remains unheeded of such great outcries is deaf; whoever does not praise God in all these effects is dumb; whoever does not turn to the First Principle after so many signs is a fool. So, open your eyes, alert the ears of your spirit, unlock your lips, and apply your heart that you may see, hear, praise, love, and adore, magnify, and honor your God in every creature, lest perchance the entire universe rise against you. For because of this, the whole world shall fight against the unwise. But on the other hand, it will be a matter of glory for the wise, who can say with the prophet: "For you have given me, O Lord, a delight in your doings, and in the work of your hands I shall rejoice. How great are your works, O Lord! You have made all things in wisdom; the earth is filled with your riches."

Bonaventure, *The Journey to the Mind of God*, trans. Philotheus Boehner, OFM; ed. Stephen F. Brown (Indianapolis: Hackett Publishing, 1993), 9–10.

---

days, culminating in the creation of humanity in God's image. After creation is complete, and pronounced very good, God rests on the seventh day (Gen. 2:2–3). In Genesis 2:4b–3:24, however, God is more hands-on. God sculpts a human out of dirt, and then later, after creating the animals, makes a partner from the first human's rib.

Genesis 1 uses the word "Elohim" for God, while Genesis 2 refers to God as "Yahweh" or "Lord," which likely points to different authorship. The inclusion of two stories suggests that the intent was not to offer an exact record of what happened historically. Instead, the stories reflect two different visions or explanations of how the world came to be and how God was involved.

The variant worldviews reflected in the two accounts of creation may be explained by their different dating. Many scholars think that though placed first, Genesis 1:1–2:4a was the later account, written about 500 BCE, when the Israelites had been exiled to Babylon. The writers tried to show that, despite the destruction of their country, the God of Israel was stronger and better than the gods of Israel's neighbors and captors.

A Babylonian account of creation describes the thunder god, Marduk, who violently kills a water goddess named Tiamat and uses her broken body to form the sky and earth. The biblical God, in contrast, creates through speech, not bloodshed, and out of delight, not destruction. Moreover, the repeated declaration of creation as "good" assured the Israelites that though God appeared to have abandoned them in exile, the world was still good and reliable, and the God who created the world was still very much in charge of it.

Placed as the first narrative of the Bible, Genesis 1:1–2:4a frames the stories that follow by placing the creation story in a larger story about the origins of the world called the Primeval History (Gen. 1–11). The creation account acts as the opening scene to the divine-human trajectory that is evident in Genesis 1–11: God made a very good world, but the human beings made it go wrong. As a result, all relationships were affected: between God and humanity, between humanity and the creation, and between the humans themselves. God sent a flood to destroy it and start again (Gen. 6–9). In Genesis 12, God chooses to bless the broken through Abraham and Sarah and their descendants, the people of Israel. The rest of the Bible expands on these themes. Original goodness was corrupted, and human beings had fallen into murder and misuse of power, but God continued to love and care for and eventually redeem the world.

The placement of this creation story in the lectionary on Trinity Sunday hints of a theological claim not necessarily evident in the text. When God said, "Let us make humankind in our image," did "us" refer to Jesus and the Holy Spirit? Most commentators have argued instead that God was probably referring to a heavenly council of advisors (cf. Job 1–2). The phrase may have also been simply a use of the "royal we," which highlighted the significance of the creation of humanity. On Trinity Sunday, the preacher might lift up God's willingness to collaborate and be in relationship, without trying to find evidence for the Trinity where it does not exist.

Other sermon ideas emerge from this intriguing text. For example, the text could be used for Earth Day to encourage delight in and gratitude for the beauty of the earth. When we are busy, tense, and consumed with technology, we might see the intricate and meticulously ordered world as God's gracious gift to us. God invites us to pay attention to the world, because learning more about the world teaches us about God.

A sermon might explore what it means to be created in the image of God. Creation in God's image does not simply mean that humans are rational or spiritual, but that they are called to imitate God in the care and nurture of creation. All people, whatever their race or gender or class, are created in God's image, which means that each person is to be respected and valued and honored. Forgetting this has led to genocide, war, abuse, and a host of other sins.

God gave humankind dominion over creation, but this responsibility has often been misunderstood as giving humanity the right to strip-mine, to clear cut the rainforest, to dispose of toxic waste in waterways. Instead, dominion means humanity is to care for creation in ways that help the earth and living beings become the best they can be. It is to create safe spaces, not to exploit and dominate.

A sermon might explore the meaning of Sabbath rest. Some people remember Sundays spent being forced to go to church. What if we experienced the Sabbath as a gift instead of demand? What if we let go of our constant need to be productive? What if we took a walk and enjoyed God's creation? What if we stopped trying to control? Rest could be a sign of grace to a weary world. This complex story of the creation of the world opens up space for a rich discussion of our place in it.

LYNN JAPINGA

Commentary 2: Connecting the Reading with the World

As pictured in Genesis 1, creation is an act of holy speech giving order to the universe. What God speaks, God brings forth. God's speech is therefore the sine qua non for emancipation, land, exile, vocation, faith, healing, judgment, and resurrection. It is the medium through which faith is given. God redeems us through the Word; so speech is not simply an information delivery device, communicating meaning by narrowing its possibilities. It is the genesis of all life, expanding possibilities. God's words to Pharaoh, "Let my people go," initiate the exodus. God's words to Israel through the prophets announce the end of kingdoms, and later end the exile and restore the people to new life. Jesus heals primarily with words. "Talitha cum," he says.

The life of the church is centered around the Word, rooting us in the conviction that speech is the primary way that the God of Jesus Christ is revealed to us. Indeed, every preacher knows the shock of hearing testimony from a parishioner who quits a job, forfeits significant wealth, or chooses a different path—all because of the words of a sermon, God's word to us on a particular day and time. Speech matters.

Human beings, by virtue of being made in the image of God, reflect God's creative potential and action. We too speak, create, name, and bless. We have the capacity to speak new worlds into being through the speech that organizes the chaos of activity inside of our brains. It is this human capacity for generating new creation—from art to technology to knowledge itself—that sets us apart from all other creatures. For example, the Declaration of Independence is nothing more than words on a page, yet it brings a new nation into being. The decision of *Brown v. Board of Education* in 1954 is but speech in a document, yet it changes lives and communities. Research shows that one of the most important factors in the development of children is reading to them—speech that literally generates exponential possibilities for their future.

Yet the generative outcomes of human speech are questionable. Some geologists have proposed that the first nuclear explosion (code-named "Trinity") marked a new period in geologic time, the Anthropocene Epoch, meaning the "new human" epoch, characterized by human dominion of the earth. As the selection for Trinity Sunday, Genesis 1 therefore compels us to compare and contrast God's creative powers with our own. What is it that makes God's creative acts unquestionably good—a description that God repeatedly declares of creation (Gen. 1:4, 10, 12, 18, 21, 25, 31)—while our acts are marked by ambiguity? How might we contrast the unquestionably good fruits of God's creation with our own? Perhaps Genesis 1, in all of its beauty and life and in its declarations of "good," not only elucidates the contrast between God's idea of good with that of humans, but also provides a foundational definition for "good" from which all other notions can be judged.

A different focus emerges in the creation of human beings in Genesis 1, which varies from the "rib from Adam" and "garden of Eden" story to come later in Genesis 2. In Genesis 1, the Hebrew word *adam*, meaning "humankind," intimates humanity's close connection to the land, *adamah*. Interestingly, *adam* lacks any explicit reference to gender (1:27). *Adam* is to *adamah* as "earthling" is to "earth." Rather than issues of gender, the language clearly indicates that the text is more concerned with the close connection between humanity and the earth. This is not to dispute that binarisms are found throughout the creation account (light and darkness [1:4], land and sea [1:9–10], day and night [1:14–18], etc.), but that the focus seems to go beyond our simplistic notions of gender.

The text does argue that God creates humanity male and female, but male and female seem to be contained within *adam*," within "the earthling." Superiority of one gender over the other is neither stated nor implied. The text emphasizes humanity's shared connection between genders reflective of our origin from and connection with the earth.

This emphasis suggests several sermon ideas. This idea of the deep relationship between humanity and the earth helps to clarify the earlier problematic declaration by God that humans should "subdue" and "have dominion" over the earth (1:28). Considering that earthlings are made of earth, domination cannot entail irresponsible desecration and destruction, as the earth's demise is that of humanity as well. A wise preacher will do well to reflect on how power given by God is not a free-for-all but comes with accountability to values, commands, and regulations.

Second, the idea that both genders are included in the idea of *adam*, of humanity, hints that gender equality was an original component of the good created order. A sermon possibility might explore how things that lessen this original equality move us away from the harmonious world that God created and intended humanity to inhabit. Lastly, a possible topic worth exploring from the pulpit is the notion of harmony. Harmony is reflected in the description of near idyllic relationships between all living things in Genesis 1. A wise preacher might explore what role the church has in helping the world experience or move closer to this harmony, which God built into creation and has gifted to the world: harmony in family life, harmony in public life between citizens and their leaders, harmony between political parties, harmony between workers and owners, harmony among people and cultures.

A final connection emerges at the conclusion of this pericope, when God rests on the seventh day (2:2–3). Though the command to Sabbath rest is still a full biblical book away, the foundations are laid here at the beginning. Those foundations are rooted in God's action or, rather, absence of action. God rests, and in ceasing from work God "hallowed" the seventh day. In prior verses, creation occurs by God separating matter. Here God separates time itself, setting the seventh day apart from the rest. In her book *Sabbath in the Suburbs*, author MaryAnn

McKibben Dana writes of discovering theologian Karl Barth's statement that "a being is free only when it can determine and limit its activity." Reflecting on her own family's experiment with Sabbath time, McKibben Dana writes, "It seems impossible that restricting our freedom has only increased our feeling of freedom . . . but it has."[1]

This realization is countercultural to the growth-driven world economies that govern so much of our living. We are valued mainly for what we can produce. Beauty and goodness lose value because their contemplation produces no concrete outcomes. God's choice to rest thus challenges the foundations of dominant world orders that overvalue productivity while undervaluing the priceless nature of the earth and its creatures: the stock market with its indices that never reflect the cost of environmental degradation. More locally, God's choice challenges the church when we fail to value nonproductive time together as essential to our life with God: church committees that do not differ in substance from those in government or business, leadership that demotes spiritual formation because it does not contribute to "getting things done." Here in Genesis we learn simply that creation—and we—are complete only when rest is built into the equation. This text invites a revaluation of our use of time, beginning with our use of time in the church.

ANDREW FOSTER CONNORS

---

1. MaryAnn McKibben Dana, *Sabbath in the Suburbs: A Family's Experiment with Holy Time* (St. Louis: Chalice Press, 2012), 151–52.

Trinity Sunday

Psalm 8

¹O LORD, our Sovereign,
 how majestic is your name in all the earth!

You have set your glory above the heavens.
 ²Out of the mouths of babes and infants
you have founded a bulwark because of your foes,
 to silence the enemy and the avenger.

³When I look at your heavens, the work of your fingers,
 the moon and the stars that you have established;
⁴what are human beings that you are mindful of them,
 mortals that you care for them?

⁵Yet you have made them a little lower than God,
 and crowned them with glory and honor.
⁶You have given them dominion over the works of your hands;
 you have put all things under their feet,
⁷all sheep and oxen,
 and also the beasts of the field,
⁸the birds of the air, and the fish of the sea,
 whatever passes along the paths of the seas.

⁹O LORD, our Sovereign,
 how majestic is your name in all the earth!

Connecting the Psalm with Scripture and Worship

God governs the cosmos. This central message of Psalm 8 emerges clearly through the twice-repeated phrase, "O LORD, our Sovereign, how majestic is your name in all the earth!" (Ps. 8:1, 9). The refrain is an exclamation: "How *majestic*!" It can also be understood as a question: "*How* majestic?" The rest of the psalm (vv. 2–8) provides both an answer to the question and an exposition of God's majesty.

To catalog God's majesty, the psalm describes the extreme reaches of the cosmos. Ancient readers would have understood the worldview as the psalm moves from the heavens (vv. 1–3) to the lowest points, "along the paths of the seas" (v. 8). In fact, the psalmist places these elements in a hierarchy. God's glory is "above" the heavens (v. 1). Humans are "a little lower" than God (v. 5). In turn, God puts all things "under" humans (v. 6).

The exposition of these levels of authority begins, appropriately, at the very top. Above the heavens, God sets God's glory (*hod*, v. 1). In Hebrew, "glory" conveys a sense of weightiness and power. For God's glory to reside "above the heavens" (v. 1) suggests that the scale of God's majesty exceeds humans' ability to comprehend it. It stands outside our ability to observe it, higher than anything we can see. It is invisible, but nevertheless palpable within the world, for God protects God's people (v. 2). This paradox of God's glory as both powerful and incomprehensible is expressed through a unique literary image. The sounds of babbling infants are associated with the strength of a fortress (v. 2). For the psalmist, God's glory is ultimately unknowable, like the meaning of baby talk, but also strong enough to repulse an enemy.

Meditating on this paradox of God's glory spurs the psalmist to reflect on humanity in the context of God's creation. In verse 3, the psalmist is moving by increments downward, from above the heavens, through the heavens, and then just a little lower, to the humans whose power lies just below that of the numinous beings. Here the psalmist describes them as "gods" (*elohim*). Many Jewish and Christian traditions have taken this verse as a reference to angelic forces (so the KJV: "Thou hast made him a little lower than the angels").

In many ancient Near Eastern religions, the heavenly bodies like the moon and stars (v. 3) were understood as persons, deities in their own right with agency and volition. It may be that the psalmist, in naming these heavenly forces, is speaking about "gods" in verse 3. In any case, the psalm understands these beings as fashioned by God and thus controlled by God (v. 4). To be sure, the psalm suggests that the heavens are *not* an object of veneration, as in the rest of the ancient world. Rather, God is "above the heavens" (v. 1). The heavenly bodies only give testimony to the greatness of God (cf. Ps. 19:1) who created them.

Like the Priestly account of creation in Genesis 1:1–2:4a, this psalm is concerned with the role of humanity within the hierarchy of the cosmos. In the Priestly account, humans are created last, on the sixth day,. in the image of God (Gen. 1:26). So they represent the Deity in the world, as a proxy for God's cosmic governance. In both Psalm 8 and the Priestly creation account, humans do not have dominion on their own merit, but because of God's overarching authority. Humans have a derived authority. The psalm shows that God has set humans to govern, just as God has set God's glory above the heavens (v. 1) and established the moon and the stars in their proper places (Ps. 8:3).

The Episcopal *Book of Common Prayer* renders the first and last verses of the psalm "O LORD, our Governor, how exalted is your Name in all the world." Today, it is difficult for many listeners to hear the epithet "governor" as anything but a political designation. Most modern English translations opt for different terms like "Sovereign" or "Lord." Yet for liturgical use the language of governance should be preserved whenever possible. Calling God the governor reminds the community of the way divine authority supersedes any political authority on earth. Moreover, the repetition of phrase "our governor" in the refrain of the psalm situates all human forms of domination. All governance, governors, and government pales before God's ultimate authority.

Throughout the history of interpretation of this psalm and Genesis 1:24–31, the description of the dominion of humanity has generated extensive comments. In many homiletical and liturgical uses, Genesis 1:28 and Psalm 8:6 are removed from their context. Doing so often gives the suggestion that humans, having been granted dominion from God, have impunity to act as they see fit, to exploit natural resources for their own benefit without concern for the world.

The context of each of these passages does not support such readings, however. Genesis 1:24–31 suggests a domination of the world that does not include the killing of animals for food. The human diet described in Genesis 1:1–2:4a is entirely vegetarian. Likewise, the description of humans' dominion in Psalm 8 is encircled with the idea of God as governor. Humans govern the world, but God governs them.

So the question for both ancient and modern communities reading this text is this: What kind of governor is God? If human governing reflects God's government, then we are disabused of any notions of destruction and exploitation of the world's resources for our own good. Certainly, our governing should deny the domination of one group of humans over another. Indeed, God's government is of a different sort altogether. In God's government, the most powerful one is the one who gives up power. God's government reverses the expectations for who is valuable and important. As disciples of Jesus Christ, the Son of God, we participate in the paradox of the glory of God. All authority that we have derives from the one who gave up his authority. In our worship of the triune God, we acknowledge and affirm the incompressibility of God's majesty.

JOEL MARCUS LEMON

Trinity Sunday

2 Corinthians 13:11–13

¹¹Finally, brothers and sisters, farewell. Put things in order, listen to my appeal, agree with one another, live in peace; and the God of love and peace will be with you. ¹²Greet one another with a holy kiss. All the saints greet you.

¹³The grace of the Lord Jesus Christ, the love of God, and the communion of the Holy Spirit be with all of you.

Commentary 1: Connecting the Reading with Scripture

Taking leave of those to whom one is close is never easy, whether in person or in writing. The last words that one says or writes in such a situation are hugely significant. They echo long after the parting, lingering in the air and in the heart until the next chance to communicate. In letters, over the composition of which one can take time to reflect, the words attain a particular level of significance.

The words with which Paul concludes his Second Letter to the Corinthians are thus hugely important, offering an insight into the final message with which Paul wishes to leave his addressees. They are especially noteworthy, given they come at the end of a letter in which Paul has sternly rebuked the members of the church in Corinth, a church riven with disputes and divisions, which has failed to heed the gospel Paul has shared with it.

Rather than repeating his admonitions and instructions, however, Paul closes his letter with a series of exhortations and encouragements to the body of Christ in Corinth. The tone is conciliatory, seeking not only to rebuild harmony between himself and his audience but also to further harmony between the rival factions in Corinth. The end of the letter is thus shot through with messages encouraging and invoking the pursuit of peace.

The first encouragement that Paul sounds in this peroration, however, is "Rejoice" (13:11, NIV; NRSV "farewell"). Despite all the earlier censuring and warning, Paul concludes by exhorting the members of the church in Corinth to celebrate. The only reason for this is that there is good news, the good news of Jesus Christ, to which the letter of Paul has earlier repeatedly adverted.

Here is a place where Paul's lesson might usefully be learned in the present. Our churches are regularly factionalized and divided, whether over matters trivial and local or issues major and churchwide. The fallout can be deep and painful, and such disunity can only cause pain and harm to the church and its witness. Yet here too, the first instruction of Paul would be to rejoice, to follow the words of the writer of this week's psalm in declaring: "How majestic is your name in all the earth!" (Ps. 8:1).

This is not a facile instruction, an encouragement to a shallow and escapist joy that is temporary and unfulfilling, that evades the real grief and injustice of conflict, within the church or between the church and others. Rather, Paul's command inspires us to bring forth true joy, that profound joy from God that touches every part of our being, from the surface to the deep, framing all our earthly delights and sorrows.

When Paul moves to further instruction, he offers words aimed at building up the Christian community in Corinth from its current fractured existence to a new integrated whole. Thus he charges the Corinthians to mend their ways, to encourage one another, to agree with one another, and to live in peace. He assures them that the God of love and peace will be with them.

There are three connections that seem important at this point.

The first is to the way in which Paul's instructions are directed at the community *as a whole*. In contrast with the way in which our culture—and, at times, our churches—can tend toward a highly individualistic approach to the Christian life and to Christian instruction, Paul speaks to the church at large. This involves a renewal and edification both of the community as community but also of each member as individual by the community. Even in the church, community is not just a collective noun but a collective task. We are to take care of each other and watch out for each other.

The second is to the way in which Paul's instructions are not directed toward a peace that represents a mere cessation of hostilities. Again, in our own culture and churches, it can be all too easy to declare peace or agreement on the surface without ever embracing genuine reconciliation. For Paul, peace is more than this; it is not simply a cease-fire, but a new alliance, a fresh commitment, a striving together and moving forward in which there is deep common purpose born of and forged by the gospel. Such a peace is not as the world gives, but a peace that only the Lord can give.

The third is to the way in which Paul's instructions are followed by a resolute affirmation that the Corinthians will not be left on their own in their journey, but that the God of love and peace will be with them. In situations of rancor and division, whether in Corinth or around us, the mending of divisive ways is only possible because the God who is in Godself love and peace will be there with us and for us, recreating and restoring our relationships in order that the community of God might reflect God's own peace and love.

God not only desires the community to be at peace. God is the God of peace: the source, meaning, and goal of peace. God promises peace; even in situations where reconciliation seems humanly impossible, it becomes possible by the power of God. Certainly we are called to participate in the work of peace, but it is a work that God inspires, God effects, and God concludes.

Paul ends his letter with a threefold blessing that has passed into common usage in the church. The reference to the grace of Jesus Christ indicates the sheer unmeritedness of the work of reconciliation between God and humanity effected in the cross of Jesus Christ. The reference to the love of God illuminates the ground of this reconciling work in the being of the God whom Paul has already described as the God of peace and love. The reference to the communion of the Holy Spirit highlights the new work being done by God, tearing down barriers between people and creating and sustaining fellowship, both vertically, between the believer and the Spirit, and horizontally, between believers.

What Paul offers here, then, is a compressed summary of the way in which God achieves salvation and of the way in which Christians experience that salvation. The gifts of grace, love, and communion lie at the heart of the Christian life and of the Christian church, in Corinth and today. All these blessings are said to be with *all* the Christians in Corinth, without exception—in spite of the troubles and difficulties in that church, let alone the idolatry and transgressions of its members. Then as now, the promise and presence of God are true for all believers without exception.

This blessing has played a significant role in the history of Christian reflection on God, particularly in discussions of the Trinitarian identity of God. In this respect, it is similar to a text in this week's passage from Matthew: "in the name of the Father and of the Son and of the Holy Spirit" (Matt. 28:19). Some scholars have sought in such passages to find the doctrine of the Trinity, though such attempts seem premature, given that neither text details the relations of Jesus Christ, the Father, and the Spirit in the way that the doctrine does. However, the 2 Corinthians text does clearly articulate a distinction between the three spiritual gifts invoked and their givers, and in this way serves (and did serve) as a starting point for further reflection on the Christian experience of the being of God as triune. Thus at least the roots of that doctrine are nonetheless clearly discernible here.

PAUL T. NIMMO

Commentary 2: Connecting the Reading with the World

These few verses from the very end of 2 Corinthians are included in the lectionary readings for Trinity Sunday for a clear reason: Paul refers to Father, Son, and Holy Spirit in his benediction of this congregation with whom his relationship has often been tense and stormy. These few verses heard alone veil a letter charged with stern admonitions, strong emotions, and Paul's defense of his ministry. Were congregations to hear all of 2 Corinthians 13, they would likely be surprised by the juxtaposition of Paul's warnings to the Corinthians, his clear call for self-examination in regard to faithfulness, his claims to be using his God-given authority to be severe with them, and then these words of prayer for peace, love, and communion (*koinōnia*).

Perhaps the most important learning from these verses is not to convince ourselves that Paul had a concept of the Trinity anything like the postconciliar confessions that shape later theology. The most important word for us comes precisely in the juxtaposition of Paul's blessing in the name of God—Father, Son, and Holy Spirit—and the tension he experiences with these early Christian communities.

Paul knows something very important: without God's Holy Spirit, our koinonia—community, communion, fellowship—is impossible. In the power of God's Holy Spirit, it is possible for us to live together in our differences. Indeed, it strengthens and grows us as Christ's body to live together in our differences.

Even though not all of 2 Corinthians 13 will be read on Trinity Sunday morning, the tension between Paul and the Corinthians (or at least some of them) is implied even within our short passage in verse 11. A string of present imperative verbs reminds the Corinthians and us that much continues to be required of us. The verbs carry the weight of urging folks to continue to rejoice, to continue to put themselves in order as if God's Holy Spirit served as a metaphysical chiropractor to realign this out-of-sync group. They are to continue to be either comforted or admonished by Paul, or both. They are called to share the ethos of Christ and to live in peace. The triune blessing is not somehow to fall upon them, but rather to infuse them and empower all they will yet become.

How much vitality we might identify within our own congregations if we imagine God's unfathomably vast and intimate life flowing among us! The blood of Christ is the blood of God, infusing and enabling our very life.

Krister Stendahl identified the "love" extolled by Paul in 1 Corinthians 13 as a kind of elasticity—the amount of stress and strain a community's relationship could take without breaking. Love must stretch to hold us together precisely when we *feel* least inclined toward it. Love then is a commitment and a gift rather than a feeling. It is this love, twice mentioned in these verses, that is with us, often unrecognized. Love is the field in which we exercise our lives together with all those whom God has called. The Corinthian correspondence highlights the difficulties of such a life together—then and now.

It is hard not to think of all the ways in which our contemporary lives have become disordered, fractious, and out of order. It is so much easier for us to cut off those with whom we disagree by ignoring them, deriding them, or simply moving on. Am I thinking of politics? Racism? Faith communities of various sorts? Am I thinking of family life, marriage, partnerships? Am I thinking of our relationships with medical personnel and retailers? Yes. We go quickly to where we think our best advantages lie. Remaining in the field to rumble it out with someone, being vulnerable to learning that may challenge us or even hurt us, seems a quaint notion.

Yet it is precisely the notion Paul claims as part of the life of a people who are one body. In 2 Corinthians 4:1–2, Paul offers a model for how persons within communities of the faithful are called to live and work together. Again in a few words, Paul highlights our reality: God's mercy and continued engagement with us surround us in our interactions. There is an egalitarian quality to commending the truth before the conscience of everyone: all are called to speak the truth together, all to hear, and finally all to live and act in the sight of God.

It is in such a life that we find ourselves realigned as one body, sharing the peace of God. It takes continuous practice, for each new truth we learn opens us to more and more. God casts a much bigger net of love than any of us can spread out on our own.

What does this look like in real life? In a gripping book, *Enrique's Journey* by Sylvia Nazario, the author tracks people who are desperately trying to escape from Central America, such as one young man who is determined to find the mother who left her family to seek work in the United States. Nazario does not sentimentalize the lives of those left behind, life in the States, or even the life her lead character has to rebuild with his mother when he finds her. Love is the driver, the call to make painful decisions with long-term consequences. It is also the field in which human beings try to live and grow.

A secular, citizens' group launched in 2016, Better Angels, works to bring self-acknowledged "red" and "blue" Americans together to find ways to talk together. It is demanding work, but the goal—to help us hear each other as real people with deep concerns and passions, as people who are capable of love and growth, though we differ in how to express these things—is more than worthy. It is essential.

Our country cannot belong to just one group. The challenges that face us require all of our best thinking, all of our financial contributions, all of our goodwill. How might we speak our truth remembering that we are blessed by God to do so, blessed by God to love even in the midst of tension?

Our congregations likewise are in sore need of that kind of open and honest speech that Paul uses *and* for which he also provides checks and balances in 2 Corinthians 4. The only conformity Paul calls for is to give up the assertion of being right, in order to hear other voices.

If your congregation celebrates the Lord's Supper, that is what you are doing. Communion, the koinonia of the Holy Spirit of God, is grounded in God's blessing in the heart of our differences. God invites us to this feast and gathers us at table so that we all receive, together. We are all in need, together. It is a feast shining with the light of cross and resurrection, reminding us, in-forming us really, that God never gave up on life for God's creatures. Neither do we give up on each other when the going gets tough.

That is what Paul models with this generous benediction by God's power for God's argumentative and self-seeking people—and that would be all of us, sometimes for good reasons, sometimes not! Patiently receiving the blessing of realignment (or a "blood" transfusion), in order to be Christ's body, requires us to hear each other's truth and by small steps learn to embrace one another when we agree *and* when we do not, knowing that God's entire being has chosen to love us and "those others" for the restoration of the world.

SARAH S. HENRICH

Trinity Sunday

Matthew 28:16–20

[16]Now the eleven disciples went to Galilee, to the mountain to which Jesus had directed them. [17]When they saw him, they worshiped him; but some doubted. [18]And Jesus came and said to them, "All authority in heaven and on earth has been given to me. [19]Go therefore and make disciples of all nations, baptizing them in the name of the Father and of the Son and of the Holy Spirit, [20]and teaching them to obey everything that I have commanded you. And remember, I am with you always, to the end of the age."

Commentary 1: Connecting the Reading with Scripture

The Revised Common Lectionary follows the Western liturgical calendar in designating the Sunday after Pentecost as Trinity Sunday. In Year A, the readings express this theme most clearly in Jesus' command to baptize "in the name of the Father, the Son, and the Holy Spirit" (Matt. 28:19, CEV). Luke's references to Baptism in the name of the Lord Jesus Christ in Acts 2:38; 8:16; and 10:48 show that in the first century baptismal customs differed. Paul's response to reports about factions among the Corinthians based on baptismal formulas indicates that sharp divisions could occur (1 Cor. 1:10–17). With the development of Trinitarian theology and the creeds that gave voice to it, Matthew's language became standard for Christians everywhere—even if the shaping of the creeds also gave rise to sharp divisions that continue to affect the body of Christ.

In light of these divisions, one approach to preaching on the Gospel for Trinity Sunday in Year A is to focus on what holds Christians together and affirm the need for continued ecumenical dialogue. In the first century, the phrase "in the name of" defined the limits and boundaries of groups, both in Jewish and Greco-Roman cultural settings.[1] Though Matthew 7:21–23 suggests the community from which the Gospel of Matthew emerged experienced divisions over who evangelized "in the name of the Lord," Jesus' words in the day's Gospel directed his followers to expand their boundaries, not limit them.

The epistle for the day helps us see this, for in his farewell and benediction in 2 Corinthians 13:11–13, Paul uses Trinitarian language to emphasize the attributes of God that inform his appeal for order, unity, and peace within the Corinthian community: "the grace of the Lord Jesus Christ, the love of God, and the communion of the Holy Spirit." He is concerned with defining the community with respect to the nature of God and not with marking its boundaries.

This accords with the immediate context of the baptismal saying in Matthew, Jesus' last words to the disciples. The center of the passage is commonly referred to as the Great Commission (Matt. 28:16–20), a saying that opens another way into preparing a sermon on the day's Gospel. Its core is "making disciples." The means of carrying it out are "baptizing" and "teaching." By placing this commissioning at the end of the Gospel and representing it as Jesus' last words, the author of the Gospel of Matthew emphasizes the importance of the commission; and by declaring that the disciples are to teach obedience to everything Jesus had commanded them, the author sends readers back through the Gospel to discern just what it is Jesus taught.

---

1. See Lars Hartman's article "Baptism" in the *Anchor Bible Dictionary* (New York: Doubleday, 1992), 1:583–94.

Matthew introduces the passage with the observation that when the disciples saw Jesus they "worshiped him," noting, however, that "some doubted" (v. 17). These are not two different groups, believers and doubters. For in Matthew many stories about the disciples link worship and doubt. This is borne out in its account of the stilling of the storm (14:22–33) and the description of the disciples as "you of little faith," in reference to Peter in 14:31 and to the other disciples in 6:30, 8:26, and 17:20. Signficantly, in all of these passages Jesus encourages those of little faith; he does not belittle them. Later the disciples who doubted when they saw the resurrected Jesus were among the disciples who were sent to make disciples. Thus, it should be reassuring for both the preacher and the congregation that worshiping on Trinity Sunday does not require full understanding of Trinitarian theology. Worship that recognizes the grace, love, and communion that define the triune God is more than enough to sustain us both to be and to make disciples—but there is more.

Jesus' very last words in the Gospel for the day express similar reassurance, for they exhort the disciples, "Remember, I am with you always, to the end of the age" (v. 20). Jesus' presence in the community of faith is an important theme in Matthew, as the first prophecy of Jesus' birth, drawn from Isaiah 7:14, makes clear: "'They shall name him Emmanuel,' which means, 'God is with us'" (1:23). In 18:20, Matthew applies the notion of Jesus' abiding presence again, this time in a saying that appears only in Matthew: "For where two or three are gathered in my name, I am there among them."

Referring to Jesus as Emmanuel also introduces us to Matthew's first interweaving of terms that foreshadow the baptismal formula of the Great Commission, for in 1:20–23 we see the work of *the Holy Spirit*, the prophetic word of *the Lord*, and the naming of *the Son*. Matthew uses a similar configuration at the baptism of Jesus in 3:13–17: the *Spirit* of God and God's *heavenly voice*, declaring, "This is *my Son*, the Beloved, with whom I am well pleased" (3:17). It appears yet again in the account of Jesus' temptation in the wilderness (4:1–11), where *the Son* of God, led by *the Spirit*, overcomes temptation by his worship of *the Lord [his] God*.

Finally, in 12:18–21 Matthew quotes Isaiah 42:1–4 and 9, using terms similar to the ones in the Great Commission *and* linking them to a mission to the nations: The Lord declares, "Here is my *pais* ["servant" or "child"], whom I have chosen, my beloved, with whom my soul is well pleased. I will put *my Spirit* upon him"—to "proclaim justice to the Gentiles" and in whose name "the Gentiles will hope."[2] This list of references to three (varying) terms for the identity of God is not meant to suggest Matthew has a fully developed notion of the Trinity, but only that its author is aware of multiple ways God engages the world—and how this informs and sustains discipleship.

Matthew first mentions discipleship immediately after Jesus' baptism and temptation, with Jesus saying to Peter and Andrew, "Follow me, and I will make you fish for people" (4:18–22). Then, after a brief summary of Jesus' first tour through Galilee, Matthew introduces the teachings that define the essence of discipleship, the Sermon on the Mount (chaps. 5–7). "The cost of discipleship" is high in Matthew, as Dietrich Bonhoeffer makes clear in his classic study of the Sermon on the Mount.[3] Instructions on how to fish/make disciples follow in chapter 10, based on Jesus' compassion for the crowds (9:35–38). Then in chapter 13 he explains the parables of the kingdom of heaven, concluding that as scribes "trained for the kingdom of heaven" they must "bring out of [their] treasure what is new and what is old" (13:51–52). In chapter 18 Jesus teaches the disciples about organizing and administering a community of disciples, but here only after teaching them about true greatness in the kingdom of heaven, which means becoming humble like children, welcoming others in his name, not harming little ones, and forgiving brothers and sisters

---

2. The NRSV uses "Gentiles" in 12:18 and 21 and "nations" in 28:19, though the same Greek word appears in all three verses.
3. Dietrich Bonhoeffer, *The Cost of Discipleship* (New York: Touchstone, 1995).

from your heart—all of which complement the themes of the Sermon on the Mount.

Making disciples grows out of being disciples. Matthew makes this clear by placing the Great Commission at the end of the Gospel, *after* his readers (we) have learned what discipleship means.

OLIVER LARRY YARBROUGH

Commentary 2: Connecting the Reading with the World

Many churches throughout the world read Matthew 28:16–20, one of the most well-known passages in the New Testament, on Trinity Sunday. Its inclusion in the lectionary, no doubt, was to provide congregations the opportunity to reflect on and affirm the Christian doctrine of the Trinity. This is apt and fitting, as this special Sunday follows on the heels of Pentecost, where we celebrate the outpouring of the Holy Spirit upon the gathered community, which is recounted in Acts 1:8 and 2:1–4. Like these passages in Acts, Matthew 28:16–20 affirms the continuing and empowering presence of the Holy Spirit following Jesus' ministry and the truth of Jesus' promise that his followers will not ever be left alone. It is, for today's churches, a resounding confirmation of God's enduring presence in a world full of challenge and change, in a time when many churches find themselves navigating new and uncharted territory.

As then, so now, change is underway, and no one can predict precisely what the church will look like in the future. The current growth of churches in the Global South signals an important historic shift, the movement of the center of Christianity from Europe and North America. These constant shifts and changes remind us that the church is formed, shaped, and informed by human diversity and diverse contexts. At the same time, steadily declining church attendance in the United States, and tensions within denominations and between so-called conservatives and progressives underscore particular challenges facing American congregations.

Despite the transformations and challenges, wherever the church is found, it will continue to be called to live into the gospel it proclaims and to address the human need in its midst. Given the many crises that congregations today face, including climate change, hunger, disease, violence, economic and racial injustice, global inequalities, and more, the scale of human need is easily overwhelming. Matthew's assurance of God's presence at the close of the Gospel is a much-needed and very welcome word. A sermon on any of one of these individual crises in light of God's assurances would be worthy topics of discussion at the pulpit. Moreover, considering the increase in isolation and loneliness today, a preacher would do well to reflect on Jesus' assurances of companionship.

Written in a time of great challenge and change itself, the Gospel of Matthew was likely composed in 80–85 CE, in the wake of the Jewish War, an event that culminated in the destruction of the Second Temple in 70 CE. The Gospel of Matthew can therefore be seen, in part, as a response to the cataclysmic losses and devastation incurred by the protracted conflict. Thus this text provides an opportunity to discuss current conflicts—personal, ecclesial, or national—and the role of the people of God in mitigating the suffering. Matthew does not directly address the war or the religious upheaval it generated, but he does place great emphasis on the church's identity and future, an idea that is worthy of thinking about anew. No wonder it is this Gospel that includes Jesus' instructions for how the church (*ecclesia*) is to live. Writing in the aftermath of war, Matthew aims to share the gospel and shore up his readers' certainty about the future.

Thus in his concluding verses Matthew confirms the promise of Jesus' continuing presence with his disciples. The narrative's ending, incorporating what is commonly known as Jesus' Great Commission, is best interpreted in relation to all that precedes it in the narrative: The pericope's reference to Galilee fulfills Jesus' sayings in 26:32 and 28:7; the focus on Jesus' authority in heaven and on earth echoes 11:27;

Jesus' closing words, "And remember, I am with you always, to the end of the age," recalls the Gospel's early reference to Jesus as "'Emmanuel,' which means, 'God is with us'" (Matt. 1:23); his directive to the disciples to "make disciples of all nations" is reminiscent of earlier references to what the whole world will hear and remember (24:14 and 26:13). Matthew's ending thus prompts the reader to recall the entire Gospel as the story of divine presence in a world besieged by the powers that would oppose it.

In so doing, this text pushes us to ask, What in our current context acts as an opposing force to the manifestation of divine presence? More importantly, the text urges us to think about the role of the church in the manifestation of God's continual presence. Just as Matthew's birth narrative includes Herod's brutal massacre (2:16–18), the story of Jesus is immersed, from beginning to end, in violence and injustice. Yet, as Matthew insists, it is rooted in the profound truth of God's ongoing presence, especially in the trenches of human existence. As churches today seek to respond to the overwhelming needs they face, Matthew reminds us that there is nowhere that eludes God's presence. The people of God are never alone as they seek to live into the gospel in the midst of the world.

Matthew's conclusion (28:16–20) is also very much forward looking, functioning as a bridge to what Matthew broadly envisions as the future. In sharp contrast to the Gospel of Mark's original ending, Matthew notes that the disciples did indeed follow Jesus' instruction that they go to Galilee to meet him after the resurrection (28:16, cf. 26:32; 28:7; and 28:9–10). Even when the disciples see Jesus, where some "worshiped him; but some doubted" (28:17), the emphasis focuses less on their response and more on Jesus' authority to commission them to the work for which he has prepared them. His postresurrection appearance thus serves as the validation of all he has done and taught, concluding Jesus' ministry even as it points to the future activity and leadership of his disciples.

Matthew not only underscores Jesus' authority (v. 18); he also illustrates the authority that Jesus confers upon his disciples, such as the curing of disease and sickness (10:1). Most importantly, in 18:18–20, Jesus establishes a circle of followers to carry out his vision for all the world. The one whose name means Emmanuel, or "God is with us" (1:23), is also the one who, having fulfilled the promise to meet the disciples in Galilee, will always be with them, "to the end of the age" (28:20). So this text offers an ideal moment to reflect upon the church's identity as part of Jesus' inner circle, to whom he gives such great power and authority. Indeed, this passage also provides an opportunity for the wise preacher to reflect upon the disconnect between Jesus' great promises and our lived lives, in which loved ones and friends still suffer from and succumb to disease and illness.

This conclusion to Matthew's Gospel serves as a powerful word for Trinity Sunday. As churches throughout the world celebrate the triune God, they acknowledge both the intrarelational nature of the Divine and the relational nature of God's interaction with the community of faith. The name Emmanuel emphasizes that God is with *us*, and Jesus' presence is made known where "two or three are gathered" in his name (18:20). Jesus' followers are neither unflawed nor imbued with any authority of their own. They are called, and they are called *together*. The authority they come to inhabit derives only from Jesus, who abides with them. For according to Matthew, it is Jesus who animates and empowers the church in all its diversity. As congregations live into their calling to proclaim the gospel, they may be assured of the divine presence that will remain ever with them, even in the trenches of responding to the world's great challenges.

MARY F. FOSKETT

Proper 3 (Sunday between May 22 and May 28 inclusive)

Isaiah 49:8–16a   1 Corinthians 4:1–5
Psalm 131   Matthew 6:24–34

Isaiah 49:8–16a

⁸Thus says the LORD:
In a time of favor I have answered you,
 on a day of salvation I have helped you;
I have kept you and given you
 as a covenant to the people,
to establish the land,
 to apportion the desolate heritages;
⁹saying to the prisoners, "Come out,"
 to those who are in darkness, "Show yourselves."
They shall feed along the ways,
 on all the bare heights shall be their pasture;
¹⁰they shall not hunger or thirst,
 neither scorching wind nor sun shall strike them down,
for he who has pity on them will lead them,
 and by springs of water will guide them.
¹¹And I will turn all my mountains into a road,
 and my highways shall be raised up.
¹²Lo, these shall come from far away,
 and lo, these from the north and from the west,
 and these from the land of Syene.

¹³Sing for joy, O heavens, and exult, O earth;
 break forth, O mountains, into singing!
For the LORD has comforted his people,
 and will have compassion on his suffering ones.

¹⁴But Zion said, "The LORD has forsaken me,
 my Lord has forgotten me."
¹⁵Can a woman forget her nursing child,
 or show no compassion for the child of her womb?
Even these may forget,
 yet I will not forget you.
¹⁶See, I have inscribed you on the palms of my hands.

Commentary 1: Connecting the Reading with Scripture

People living in deep despair and grief often lose their ability to envision a more hopeful future for themselves. Isaiah 49:8–16a is addressed to the Israelites who had been carried off to exile in Babylon and forced to live under their political enemies. They lost their land and their homes. Their temple was destroyed. They assumed that God had abandoned them as punishment for their failure to obey the covenant. The prophet, however, announces otherwise. God has not left them. Rather, the Israelites have underestimated the God of Israel. The prophet offers several images of salvation that encourage the Israelites to plan for the future and remain hopeful.

Isaiah 49:8–16 immediately follows a Servant Song, one of a series of prophecies about a Suffering Servant of Yahweh (Isa. 42:1–4; 49:1–6; 50:4–7; 52:13–53:12). As such, Isaiah 49 is bifurcated in terms of gender: it moves from an image of the male Suffering Servant at the beginning of the chapter to that of the suffering maiden, Zion, at the end. Zion, another name for Jerusalem, was frequently imagined in the biblical texts as a female (Hos. 2; Jer. 3:8; Isa. 1:8; 10:32; 16:1; 62:11). With the destruction of Judah, Zion was imagined as a woman bereaved of her children (Isa. 49:21). In the passage for this Sunday, God assures Zion that she and her children have not been forgotten.

The prophet asserts that though the Israelites may be in exile, this is part of God's larger plan to make Israel a light to the nations, a channel for God's salvation to reach to the ends of the earth (49:6). The Israelites may have been tempted to passively wait for God to act. Instead, God invites the Israelites to take initiative and move themselves out of their difficult situation. To the prisoners, God says, "Come out." To those cowering in darkness, God says, "Show yourselves" (v. 9). This is puzzling, because prisoners cannot usually free themselves, and people who feel trapped in darkness cannot simply move into the light upon command. Perhaps the prophet is thinking of people who have been so beaten down, so demoralized, that they prefer the dark, safe place that they know to the risk and challenge of light and freedom. To the Israelites, and to all of us who are afraid, God offers liberation and help.

God also encourages active participation. Use your voice. Come out of the darkness. Tell your story. Resist injustice. Do not allow yourself to be imprisoned by guilt, fear, and shame. It is scary to move into this future, so the prophet assures the Israelites that God will care for them just as sheep are cared for by a loving shepherd. God will give them food and water, protect them from the wind and sun, and lead them on a smooth road (vv. 9–11).

The prophet also encourages the Israelites to rejoice in the Lord's compassion and to trust in God's ability to return them to the promised land. Here, however, the radically hopeful promises for a better future hit the wall of grim present reality. Zion was having none of this: "The LORD has forsaken me, my Lord has forgotten me" (v. 14). To put it more colloquially, the people reply to God, "We are in exile and are miserable! God must have abandoned us. There is no salvation in our future. Do not give us false hope."

God responds to this cry of despair and hopelessness with a powerful image: "Can a woman forget her nursing child, or show no compassion for the child of her womb?" (v. 15). The answer to this powerful image and rhetorical question is obvious. Women who have experienced the uncomfortable, even painful fullness that results when feeding is delayed would have said, "No, we cannot forget!" Women who find after delivery that they love this child more than they ever imagined possible would have said, "No, we cannot forget." So also God's love is equally permanent. God, the mother, cannot forget. God, the mother, will not abandon.

This is a relatively rare example of a feminine image for God in the lectionary. Liturgical language for God, probably reflecting the patriarchal context of the Scriptures, has generally been overwhelmingly male. Words like "King," "Lord," and "Father" can suggest that God is more like a man than a woman, and that women do not reflect the image of God as much as men do. This text offers the opportunity to help people begin to expand the metaphors they use to speak of the Divine. God can be compared to a nursing mother, just as God can be compared to a loving father. Both metaphors say something true about God.

Envisioning God as a mother as Isaiah does here offers a profoundly intimate picture of the Divine as sheltering, nurturing, and giving birth to a child, then feeding and caring for it. It goes against our assumption of a distant, mysterious, demanding, and punishing God. God is both immanent and transcendent, both approachable and mysterious, but the distant God may ironically seem safer and more familiar. A God who is too close for comfort brings her own challenges. We may find that she is as fiercely protective as a dangerous mother bear (Hos. 13:8). We may find that we cannot escape the intensity of her love (Ps. 139:1–18).

Isaiah 49, interestingly, is paired in the lectionary with Psalm 131, which also offers a feminine image of God as a mother of a weaned child. They provide interesting metaphors for different moments in a relationship with God. A nursing child needs the mother for survival and is often eagerly, even desperately, seeking the food she can give. A weaned child takes solid food and is no longer dependent on the mother's body for sustenance. The weaned child is content to sit on the mother's lap without need of anything but her comforting presence. Similarly, there are times when people feel desperate need for divine intervention and help, and other times when they are content to be in a relationship with God based more on gratitude and delight. Both are good and appropriate at different stages of life and spirituality.

The Gospel lection continues the themes of divine immanence, intimacy, and tender care. God is compared to a heavenly father who feeds and clothes his children. Fathers have usually been the ultimate source of these necessities, since they have done the paid work and "brought home the bacon." When it comes to the actual purchase, preparation, and delivery of food and clothing, mothers have been the more common providers.

In a final image of perpetual care and connection in the Isaiah text, God says that the Israelites have been inscribed on the palms of God's hands. Imagine God stretching out her palms to the tattoo artist, to be repeatedly pricked with a needle that would spell out the name of God's own people. God would never forget that tattoo, any more than a mother would forget the infant that she carried and birthed and nursed and raised to independence.

God with a tattoo, God as a mother, God as a father. These metaphors can never capture the fullness of God, but they speak profound truth about the God who will never forget, never give up, never sever the tie to God's people. When it is difficult to hear good news because we feel abandoned, when we cannot sing for joy, when despair and grief make it difficult to envision a hopeful future, these intimate images remind us that we belong to God, who will never let go.

LYNN JAPINGA

Commentary 2: Connecting the Reading with the World

Isaiah's vision of return from exile articulates a future vision of God's restoration, rooted in God's record of faithfulness from the past. One way to think about these various points of location is to organize them into the categories of character, time, and place.

Scholars have long pointed out the difficulty of precisely identifying the Servant in Isaiah 49. Rather than an obstacle to be overcome, this ambiguity opens up the possibility of multiple and diverse connections with the Servant in the text. When we locate ourselves in the role of Servant, emulating (but not erasing) traditional identification of the Servant with Israel, we gain a greater clarity on the process and nature of Christian vocation. Vocation is rooted in the strong verbs of God's activity: I answered you, I helped you, I kept you, I gave you (Isa. 49:8). These verbs authorize the Servant's purpose: "to establish the land, to apportion the heritages," that is, to transform into the kind of shepherd-like leader that eventuates in the homecoming of the people who will return from the suffering of their exile. Just as the word "vocation" is rooted in the verbs "to call" or "to speak," so Christian vocation rises from the voice or call of God.

From the vocation of the Servant flow extraordinary promises—so extraordinary that the heavens and the earth will break into song (v. 13)—for the transformation of the people under the Servant's compassionate charge. According to this passage, when we find our true vocation, not only does God use us to accomplish more than we imagined but also we experience deep joy. This is as true for individual disciples as it is for the church. When the fruits of our vocation contain neither transformation nor joy, we do well to reexamine our calling for signs that God might have us be elsewhere.

Though the Suffering Servant in Isaiah 49 is unidentifiable, the church has seen in the Servant a prefiguration of Jesus. If we follow this reading, Jesus as the Servant brings hope to a sometimes beleaguered church that is apt to echo the words of Zion in verse 14: "the LORD has forsaken me, my Lord has forgotten me." The promises of restoration (49:8ff.) assure the people of God not only of God's steadfast love, but God's commitment to change our present into a different future marked by joy, compassion, and community. Yet even here, the poetry allows for more than just God's established family to find their liberation in God. The prisoners and those who are in darkness (v. 9) receive a word of liberation and inclusion. Isaiah's hope seems to outsize even the best dreams of God's faithful. A sermon could recall points in a local congregation's history when God's blessings surpassed the church's expectations. A different sermon could challenge notions of supersessionism, offering a basis for interfaith generosity through God's blessings that expand beyond the bounds that we recognize or establish.

Another point of connection is Isaiah's notion of time: past, present, and future. The future is the focus of Isaiah, as evidenced by the sheer number of promises that reside there. "They shall feed," "they shall not hunger or thirst," "I will turn all my mountains into a road, and my highways shall be raised up," "I will not forget you," and others. The future is bright and promising. It can be enlightening to examine the life of a congregation to see whether we spend as much time speaking about the future as we do longing for the past or worrying over the present. The future is where possibility resides.

This does not mean that the past is unimportant. Indeed, we can trust that future because of what God has done in the past: "I have answered," "I have helped," "I have kept" and "given" (v. 8). However, the past is not where the church lives. Rather, the present is where most of the activity of human agents occur. It is where the Servant announces good news to the prisoners and those in darkness (v. 9). The volume of human activity certainly pales in comparison to God's movement in the text, reflecting the order of power in the relationship between God and human beings. Even so, the importance of human activity need not be minimized. Human activity is essential to Isaiah's vision, precisely because God calls forth human proclamation and compassionate leadership. The effects of this activity are multiplied exponentially by God's power. Our faithful work in the present is not insignificant. It is validated and vindicated by God's covenantal faithfulness.

These shifts between past, present, and future are not entirely linear. This selection from Isaiah ends in verse 16 with yet another assurance brought to mind from God's activity in the past: "I have inscribed you on the palms of my hands." Rather than completely disentangling past, present, and future, we can observe God's movement through time: the past to remind us of God's promises and the future to assure us of where God is leading, both edifying us to live with joy in the present in spite of our limitations.

A connection with place is also evident in the text. The Servant is assured that the covenant between God and the people for a homeland is secure. God will "establish the land," and "appoint the desolate heritages," which may be a reference to the ruined temple and other places of historic significance to the people. This specificity challenges the church to hear in Isaiah more than simply a heavenly "spiritual" vision detached from the particularly of land and place. Isaiah has in mind a specific land, a specific location, with specific people. The promises of God are realized in the life of human beings. While the images allow for strong metaphors of healing and homecoming, those metaphors are rooted in physical nourishment and restoration: food, springs of water, comfort, compassion, and a child feeding directly from her mother's breast. The promises of God are more than metaphor. These promises must be seen in history, but can also grow beyond it. Particularity is important.

The Spirit Bestowed on Us by God

If one reads the extraordinary examples of glorious virtues which have shone forth in individual Christians, one can only be deeply moved by them. What an ardent love of God it was that caused Christians to hasten toward the most horrible martyrdom rather than be terrified by it when confession of their dear Savior was at stake! How fervent was the love among themselves when they not only called one another by the endearing names of "brother" and "sister" but also lived in such a fraternal fashion that they were ready, if need be, to die for one another! . . . The condition of the early Christian church puts our hot-and-cold condition to shame. At the same time it demonstrates that what we are seeking is not impossible, as many imagine. Hence it is our own fault that we are so far from deserving similar praise. It is the same Holy Spirit who is bestowed on us by God who once effected all things in the early Christians, and he is neither less able nor less active today to accomplish the work of sanctification in us. If this does not happen, the sole reason must be that we do not allow, but rather hinder, the Holy Spirit's work. Accordingly, if conditions are improved, our discussion of this matter will not have been in vain.

Philip Jacob Spener, *Pia Desideria*, trans. and ed. Theodore G. Tappert (Philadelphia: Fortress, 1964), 84–85.

A strong connection point is with the Lord's Prayer, which speaks of daily bread, forgiveness, and God's will that is done "on earth," that is, here in this specific place.

While Isaiah's concept of place is strongly rooted to the specific, the church can also find strong encouragement to embrace the places where congregations are sent. While mission has come to be known in recent years by its Latin root, "sending," perhaps another way to view our vocation is through the metaphor of "homecoming." What would it mean to view the lands where we have been sent as concrete signs of God's covenant to the people? How would we better care for those lands if we viewed them as the actual place to witness and anticipate God's healing blessing? What would it mean for our warming planet and many of our neglected communities if, instead of viewing Isaiah's vision of homecoming as "somewhere else," we anticipated it where we actually live?

A final point of connection is with the pathos of God. This text offers a strong antidote to the Marcionite heresy expressed by many Christians who speak of the Old Testament God as wrathful and judgmental, while the New Testament God is loving and compassionate. Here in Isaiah, God is compared to a breastfeeding mother, the human being least likely to forget her child. This personal, compassion-driven God, who does not forget, is good news to anyone who feels forsaken or forgotten. We have been inscribed on the palms of God's hands (v. 16).

ANDREW FOSTER CONNORS

Proper 3 (Sunday between May 22 and May 28 inclusive)

Psalm 131

¹O LORD, my heart is not lifted up,
  my eyes are not raised too high;
I do not occupy myself with things
  too great and too marvelous for me.
²But I have calmed and quieted my soul,
  like a weaned child with its mother;
  my soul is like the weaned child that is with me.

³O Israel, hope in the LORD
  from this time on and forevermore.

Connecting the Psalm with Scripture and Worship

The lections for this Sunday, Psalm 131 and Isaiah 49:8–16a, call upon images of motherhood to encourage the community to trust in God. Together, these texts invite us to hear the voices of women in prayer and to imagine God as mother.

A Woman's Prayer and Exhortation. A prayer lasting just three verses, Psalm 131 gives us a glimpse into how an ancient Israelite woman would have expressed her faith. The text begins with the psalmist's portrayal of her own disposition (Ps. 131:1–2) and concludes with an address to the community, a call for Israel to rely on Yahweh (v. 3).

Initially, the psalmist characterizes herself by saying who she is not. She does not have a proud heart (v. 1a). Neither does she look about with haughty eyes (v. 1a). She does nothing to suggest that she has an overblown estimation of herself (v. 1b). The verb that NRSV translates "occupy myself" (*hillakti*, v. 1b) comes from the root *hlk*, meaning "to go, walk." Thus, another viable translation would be "to walk around constantly doing things." The psalmist presents a picture of someone moving here and there, striving for unachievable greatness. To be clear, that is *not* who she is. Instead of frantically running around, she rests. Instead of aggrandizing herself, she remains quiet.

The psalmist describes her calmness in verse 2b with a metaphor, one that hinges on the difference between a weaned and a nursing child. Children who have not been weaned will, of course, root around restlessly when with their mothers. They quiet down only when they are nursing and have found nourishment. Weaned children, by contrast, can sit at ease in their mothers' laps Since the child no longer relies on her body for basic sustenance, the child can benefit from her presence in other ways, by embracing her and being embraced by her, by learning from her and receiving other forms of support. So, while the imagery in verse 2b conveys a sense of maternal care, it also suggests a certain level of maturity on the part of the child.

It is worth noting that verse 2b presents many difficulties for translators.[1] Some have suggested that the words of the psalm come from a mother's mouth.[2] Other translations do not go so far in identifying the psalmist as the mother of "the weaned child." Despite these challenges, most

---

1. See Melody D. Knowles, "A Woman at Prayer: A Critical Note on Psalm 131:2b," *Journal of Biblical Literature* 125 (2006): 385–89; and Brent A. Strawn, "A Woman at Prayer (Psalm 131:2b) and Arguments 'from Parallelism,'" *Zeitschrift für die Alttestamentliche Wissenschaft* 124 (2012): 421–26.
2. Strawn, "A Woman at Prayer," 421. See Marianne Grohmann, "The Imagery of the 'Weaned Child' in Psalm 131," *The Composition of the Book of Psalms*, ed. Erich Zenger, Bibliotheca ephemeridum theologicarum lovaniensium 238 (Leuven: Peeters, 2010), 513–22.

scholars agree that this psalm does in fact give us access to a woman's voice in prayer, however fleeting and incomplete.

What starts as a prayer ends as an exhortation, one that stands at odds with the patriarchal milieu of the text and with the psalmist's own self-description in the previous verse. This quiet, reserved woman lifts her voice to address the whole assembly of Israel in verse 3. She encourages everyone to wait on Yahweh, to hope (*yahel*) in God day in and day out. By appending this word of encouragement to her prayer, she suggests that her own disposition—her calmness—can serve as an example for the community to follow. Her demeanor is an expression of her trust in Yahweh.

Imagining God as Mother. Metaphors open up possibilities, creating networks of associations that can surprise and challenge us. Psalm 131 introduces the metaphor of the psalmist as a weaned child. The reader wonders, if the psalmist is the weaned child with its mother, who is its mother? The psalm does not say, at least not directly, yet, as the psalmist affirms her quiet reliance God in verse 3, we are invited to imagine God as mother in the metaphorical world that the psalm creates.

Picturing God as a mother might be unfamiliar for some, accustomed as we are to masculine imagery for God throughout the Bible and the Christian tradition. Yet maternal imagery for God appears in Isaiah 49:14–15 as well, where Israel is not the weaned child, but the nursing child, and Yahweh, Israel's God, appears as its mother.

The prophet asks, "Can a woman forget her nursing child?" The answer, of course, is no. It is painful for a mother not to nurse her child. Her body will not allow her to forget the fruit of her womb. So it is between God and God's people, here described as "Zion" (Isa. 49:14). In the world of images that the prophet creates, God is a mother with engorged breasts longing to nourish the ones whom she loves.

Women's Voices Today. To be sure, there are challenges in highlighting the ways that these texts employ feminine imagery. Because the texts reflect the patriarchal milieu in which they were written, they essentialize womanhood as motherhood. Of course, the experience of motherhood is not universal among women today, nor was it ever. Moreover, the mode of femininity found in Psalm 131 is problematic. It idealizes meekness and quietness as a woman's primary virtue. The text could also be used to tell women to content themselves with their marginal status and never to be concerned with "things too great" or "marvelous." In other words, one could read this text as a warning for women not to transgress the social boundaries that limit them to the sphere of child rearing and other domestic duties.

Yet these texts also work against their patriarchal milieu in subtle but powerful ways. It is important to recognize that the prophet's description of Yahweh as a nursing mother pushed against predominant notions of masculinity and femininity within the ancient Near East. Likewise, in Psalm 131, even as the text affirms an ideal of femininity as quiet and reserved, it upends these ideals by having a woman's voice address all of Israel, encouraging Israel to trust in Yahweh.

Thus we must proceed with care when utilizing these texts in worship. We should highlight their unique portrayals of God and women, while not reinforcing the patriarchy endemic to the ancient world from which the texts emerge. Indeed, we must break down the patriarchy that still exists today. On this Sunday especially, we should not shy away from referring to God as mother. Such references appear in the lectionary readings. We should be sure that women lead worship in all roles, just as a woman leads the worship of God in Psalm 131. This service—and all services for that matter—should include music and hymns composed by women. Many mainline denominations have produced indices of hymns with texts and/or music written by women. So programming this music is not hard. Of course, we should elevate the voices of women within the liturgy. Throughout the centuries, these saints have guided the church's understanding of what it means to trust in God. Women are leading the community of faithful today.

JOEL MARCUS LEMON

Proper 3 (Sunday between May 22 and May 28 inclusive)

1 Corinthians 4:1–5

> [1]Think of us in this way, as servants of Christ and stewards of God's mysteries. [2]Moreover, it is required of stewards that they be found trustworthy. [3]But with me it is a very small thing that I should be judged by you or by any human court. I do not even judge myself. [4]I am not aware of anything against myself, but I am not thereby acquitted. It is the Lord who judges me. [5]Therefore do not pronounce judgment before the time, before the Lord comes, who will bring to light the things now hidden in darkness and will disclose the purposes of the heart. Then each one will receive commendation from God.

Commentary 1: Connecting the Reading with Scripture

What does it mean to be a servant of Christ and a steward of God's mysteries? For the apostle Paul, facing a church in Corinth that was beset by different factions, sexual immorality, and downright idolatry, and that scrutinized and questioned his authority, this is no hypothetical question. Rather, it is a question posed in a volatile and pressing situation where there has been a direct challenge to his ministry. So too for those working in and for churches today, this same question is often posed in the heat of pressure and conflict. Thus now—as then—it is a question that demands clear answers, and Paul's guidance in this regard is as relevant for us as it was for the Corinthians.

Before turning to Paul's insights, however, it is important to acknowledge that Paul's language here is not without conceptual freight. The language of servanthood typically bespeaks a hierarchical relationship in which obedience is demanded and independence of thought, initiative, and action is discouraged. Even where the basic idea is softened into the more gentle language of stewardship, there are attendant risks of disempowerment and dehumanization looming close to the conceptual surface. This language demands careful handling, therefore, in order to make clear the very precise way in which it is here being used by Paul, and the way in which our inherited concepts of servanthood and stewardship are reformed and transformed in the process.

The first connection that we might draw between Paul's time and our own time relates to the one to whom the service is to be addressed, Jesus Christ; and to that over which stewardship is to be exercised, the mysteries of God. This latter term refers to the revelatory events of the life of Jesus Christ, particularly his crucifixion, in which the secret of the reconciliation of God with human beings is hidden. In view, then, is no earthly master or lord, but the eternal Lord of creation. The good news is that this one is the mediator between God and humanity.

The one whom we are called to serve is thus the same one who emptied himself and became a slave for us (Phil. 2:7). Herein lies a radical subversion of our notions of the hierarchy that is at the center of the concept of service: we do not inhabit an ordinary Lord-servant relationship, but a relationship without parallel or likeness. Our Lord, who is the greatest of all lords, comes as a servant who is least of all. Hence our conventional notions of what it means to be a lord or to be a servant are shattered by the event of Jesus Christ and the reversal that event brings. As fuller exploration here might develop, it is precisely in our *service* of Jesus Christ that there arises—paradoxically—our own true *freedom*, a radical freedom of rehumanization and empowerment.

A second connection between the text and our world relates to the qualities considered desirable in a steward. In almost proverbial fashion, Paul declares that stewards must be trustworthy, but this deserves further unpacking. On the one hand, a steward is an important figure, a valued functionary with major responsibility and even privilege. This indicates that as stewards we are answerable for the mysteries of God, having the honor of representing these mysteries to the world. What might this mean for Christians today, to be stewards of such wonders? It would mean proclaiming the gospel in our particular contexts, building up the church and each other in faith, and living a life of witness to the glory of the God revealed in the gospel.

On the other hand, a steward has such responsibility only as is delegated to them. They have no significance or authority of their own, but only as they are the presence and representative of their superior. Their success or failure is measured by only one thing: the extent to which they are held trustworthy by their superior. For us, that means seeking in all things fidelity to the gospel—not our own advancement or reputation—in obedience to Jesus Christ. Our stewardship is not about our wisdom, our eloquence, or our effectiveness, but only about our *faithfulness*.

A third connection between this letter of Paul and the church of today relates to the evaluation of Christian servants. Paul is under no doubt that he is there to serve the church in Corinth. He is also quite clear that his service in this capacity is not to be judged by that church. As he reflects upon his ministry, he declares that the only authority qualified to judge his performance is the Lord, that same Jesus Christ whom he is serving as steward. The time of that judgment will be at the return of that Lord.

Thus, even though the language of accounting and judging in this passage is related to the drama of the courtroom, the irony is that the courtroom to which Paul is referring is no earthly courtroom. We will be judged only by the one who sends us and whom we serve. The judgments of others—whether our congregations, colleagues, friends, or families—are only penultimate. Moreover, we will not ultimately be judged *by ourselves*. We can be our own worst advocates and our own worst critics, and neither is salutary or helpful in the Christian life. There is, of course, a place for self-reflection—just as there is for friendly or collegial evaluation!—but it is neither the first place nor the last place.

The key lesson of this passage is that our service of the gospel will be judged instead by Jesus Christ. This should strike us as both challenge and comfort. It is a challenge because our steward is no ordinary earthly superior, but the Lord of heaven and earth, who rules over all things and who will bring to light the hidden secrets of our hearts and our invisible deeds in the darkness. However, it is also—and to a far greater extent—a comfort, because we will not ultimately be judged by the collection plate or by the attendance roll, by our worst enemies or by our anxious consciences. Instead, we will be judged by the one who gave himself for us, and who justifies us so that we do not need to justify ourselves. This note of grace is made explicit in this week's reading from Isaiah: "The Lord has comforted his people, and will have compassion on his suffering ones. . . . I have inscribed you on the palms of my hands" (Isa. 49:13, 16).

On the day this Lord returns, those stewards who have proven themselves to be trustworthy will receive commendation from God for the faithfulness of their service. In the interim, we are freed from the need to judge (or be judged) by the Judge who was judged in our place.

This lesson is crucial, not only for those in ordained ministry, for whom it may regularly be necessary to go against the grain of popular culture, or to offer a word of criticism that raises hackles, or to venture a prophetic intervention in the face of injustice. It is also crucial for all Christian believers, who are just as surely called to be faithful stewards of the gospel mysteries, yet who also labor in the same, sometimes harsh and inhospitable fields, with the same dedication and selflessness.

PAUL T. NIMMO

Commentary 2: Connecting the Reading with the World

In a recent essay, David Brooks asks the question "What holds America together?" He turns to Walt Whitman (1819–92), who had every reason to be pessimistic about the future of his beloved, war-torn country. Despite noting that there was never "more hollowness at heart than at present, and here in the United States," Whitman still had hope. That hope was that the shared commitment of the American experiment dedicated to the "full flowering" of each person might be rediscovered in a religious and social, even "mystical" purpose. Or faith.[1]

Whitman and Brooks sound a bit like Paul when he wrote to the Corinthians, both longing and demanding that they look to the mystical center and faith in God's purposes to shape their lives, to shape even the way they imagine the world and its realities. In these few verses from 1 Corinthians, Paul wove together three threads: the mysteries at the heart of a Christian's life, trustworthiness in sharing those mysteries in life together, and the ways in which judgment can undermine our confidence when we worry about the wrong judges.

This passage from Paul's First Letter to the Corinthians follows three chapters in which Paul called the Corinthians to a new life as people both sanctified and still in process of being sanctified. The fractiousness and many divisions among the Corinthians, springing straight out of their patronage culture, ran counter to their new reality as one body of Christ. Their lives as sanctified members of Christ's body deteriorated when their shared commitment to God's gifts was no longer at the center. Competition for status, value, and honor was a way of life among the Corinthians and most of the ancient Greco-Roman world. In this letter, part of a web of communication among early Christian communities in and around the newly rebuilt Roman city, competitive strife was front and center. It remained so for decades, at least. Corinthian fractiousness was still a matter of note when Clement of Rome wrote in about 90 CE (*1 Letter of Clement of Rome*, esp. section 46).

Paul insisted that the "mystical center" of the Corinthians' lives was Christ and the "mysteries" of God (1 Cor. 4:1). Paul used the word *mystērion* relatively frequently in 1 Corinthians, precisely as a reminder of the flawed self-perceptions in the Corinthian worshiping communities. In 1 Corinthians 2:1, 7 Paul reminds his hearers that such mysteries, now proclaimed, come only from God. The gift of God's wisdom is not understood, let alone meted out, by "rulers of this age," whose ways are not God's ways. No human can become a patron of these mysteries, of God's wisdom, handing it out to the highest bidder, so to speak. A Christian is a servant of the mysteries or an overseer at best. Self-aggrandizement through claims to be the franchised distributor of God's mysteries is the gravest of errors and makes one "nothing" rather than something (13:2).

In none of our sociopolitical arrangements in the United States are we an overtly patronage culture, but we know something about the importance of "who you know" and the attractions of power. In every arena—be it our country, congregation, family, own self-understandings, schools, or Wall Street—we are smitten by leaders who we believe "can fix it," forgetting that all human "fixing" is limited in scope and effectiveness. Choosing and allying with such leaders offers an old, old model when we forget the "mysteries" at the center of life and our call to steward them. Paul reminds us that such a human model of leadership in which the "fixer" draws us into a web of obligation subverts trustworthiness. Neither self-aggrandizement (forgetting that one is a steward of God's reconciling work) nor allegiance to such a person is our human calling.

Trustworthiness for all of us requires clarity about oneself, thoughtfulness about what is needed for repair or restoration, and willingness to subordinate one's personal popularity to a greater cause. It also requires the ability to see and take whatever small steps are possible toward human thriving, no matter who takes notice and judges.

---

1. David Brooks, "What Holds America Together," *New York Times*, March 19, 2018, https://www.nytimes.com/2018/03/19/opinion/what-holds-america-together.html.

Paul knows about trustworthiness at such a deep level it almost takes us by surprise. For assemblies of worshipers to be commendable (11:2, 17) is for them to abide in the great mysteries of God's love, freely given, of God's Son given to live among us and for us, of God who created all that is calling us all home. When the body is divided by claims to better truth or more powerful leaders or an inside position vis-à-vis God, it no longer discerns the body. It despises the gathering and humiliates others (vv. 22–29).

Trustworthy stewardship of our central truths and values allows all of us to hope to be a part of this body of people. It allows those who have been penalized again and again for marginalized status to continue to hold us all accountable to the truths we affirm. Trustworthiness in stewardship of such truth is at the very heart of a community. When folks are no longer able to trust that values are held in common trust, there are dire repercussions. Recall the deep grief and anger over betrayal by those particular Roman Catholic priests and bishops ordained to protect their people. Keep in mind the traumatized lives of those abused by parents and relatives they trusted to have their well-being at heart. In such cases, "the center cannot hold," and the community crumbles around its wounds.

"Whose judgment matters to us?" we should always be asking. If it is God's judgment that matters—not because we are frightened of it but because we are in a relationship of love and respect with God—that love and respect is at the center of our lives in a complex and diverse world. The regard for self and others founded on God's love of each of us and all of us is the very heart of life together in all our relationships.

Paul writes to move the Corinthian believers to a richer, deeper discernment of how Christ-discipleship speaks to them in their complicated world of diverse social and economic realities. He reminds them of the privilege of belonging to Christ. This is a privilege that fills us, as Brooks says, "with gratitude and humility. That privilege unites us across division and disagreement. It calls forth great energies."[2]

Can acknowledgment of the privilege, the sheer mystery of belonging to God through Christ, unite us in these days? As an epistle lectionary reading appearing only some years here or late in Epiphany (Epiphany 8, Year A), Paul's words may seldom be on our preaching radar. Yet what a powerful reading for emphasizing who Jesus is and how lives bound up in his are different from the lives we often unconsciously live. This passage is powerful proclamation that Jesus the Lord is at the very heart of our lives, neither distant nor neutral. We are empowered and called (sanctified and in the process of being sanctified) to be trustworthy stewards of the great love and mercy God has given us in Christ. Paul reminds us that our lives are truly judged not by the passing standards of the day but only by Christ. Thus, he concisely opens to us our need for repentance, that is, for turning to God again from a world that draws us away.

How does the God-given privilege of being loved and called into new life shape our imaginations today?

SARAH S. HENRICH

---

2. David Brooks, "In Praise of Privilege," *New York Times*, March 26, 2018, https://www.nytimes.com/2018/03/26/opinion/privilege-gun-control-rally.html.

Proper 3 (Sunday between May 22 and May 28 inclusive)

Matthew 6:24–34

²⁴"No one can serve two masters; for a slave will either hate the one and love the other, or be devoted to the one and despise the other. You cannot serve God and wealth.

²⁵"Therefore I tell you, do not worry about your life, what you will eat or what you will drink, or about your body, what you will wear. Is not life more than food, and the body more than clothing? ²⁶Look at the birds of the air; they neither sow nor reap nor gather into barns, and yet your heavenly Father feeds them. Are you not of more value than they? ²⁷And can any of you by worrying add a single hour to your span of life? ²⁸And why do you worry about clothing? Consider the lilies of the field, how they grow; they neither toil nor spin, ²⁹yet I tell you, even Solomon in all his glory was not clothed like one of these. ³⁰But if God so clothes the grass of the field, which is alive today and tomorrow is thrown into the oven, will he not much more clothe you—you of little faith? ³¹Therefore do not worry, saying, 'What will we eat?' or 'What will we drink?' or 'What will we wear?' ³²For it is the Gentiles who strive for all these things; and indeed your heavenly Father knows that you need all these things. ³³But strive first for the kingdom of God and his righteousness, and all these things will be given to you as well.

³⁴"So do not worry about tomorrow, for tomorrow will bring worries of its own. Today's trouble is enough for today."

Commentary 1: Connecting the Reading with Scripture

The Gospel for the day consists of a proverbial saying about serving two masters (Matt. 6:24), sage advice on discerning what matters (vv. 25–33), and an admonition to live in the present—whatever trouble it brings (v. 34). Wisdom sayings like these are drawn from life, distilled to express the essence of experiences humans share and readily recognize. Consequently, they can be as contradictory as human experience. Consider, for example, the proverb "Absence makes the heart grow fonder" and its opposite, "Out of sight, out of mind." They can both be "true," but not at the same time or in all instances. Sometimes the meaning of a saying, proverb, or maxim is clear; at other times it is more like a riddle to be solved. So making sense of wisdom sayings requires determining the moment to which they apply and who is authorized to give them voice. Preaching on the Gospel for the day will require consideration of just such questions, especially with regard to sayings that can be either deeply profound or profoundly empty, depending on who says them, to whom, and when.

In Matthew 6:24a, Jesus' proverb states categorically, "No one can serve two masters," clearly implying one must choose. The sharply contrasting phrases hate/love and devotion/despising in verse 24b suggest the choice reflects one's core values and demands a deeply personal commitment, like the one Jesus makes when tempted in the wilderness (chap. 4). In the application of the parable in verse 24c, however, the choice Matthew presents is not between God and Satan, but between God and wealth. For Matthew, that is, the choice is ethical as much as theological.[1] Strikingly in this saying, the right choice regarding whom one should

---

1. The Greek text preserves the Aramaic term *mammon* in the application of the parable, which for some ancient readers may have suggested a semidivine agent, like Satan in chapter 4.

serve is so obvious that neither Jesus nor Matthew states it: one *must* serve God.

The sage advice about worrying in 6:25–34 intensifies the choice in the proverb about the two masters in verse 24, surprisingly applying it to basic human needs—what you will eat, and what you will drink, and what you will wear (6:31). How can this be? After all, it is one thing to say, "Do not worry about amassing wealth" (as Luke does), and quite another to say, "Do not worry about where your next meal is coming from," as Matthew seems to say.[2]

Preaching on these texts is one of those occasions requiring discernment regarding the moment to which the proverb or sage advice applies and who is authorized to give it voice. A sermon on this text will certainly address the "worries" of the congregation to which it is delivered, whether they derive from a crisis or from the general anxieties of contemporary life. However, a sermon attuned to the profundity of Jesus' teaching in the passage will also be concerned with how a congregation might come to appreciate the "worries" of those whose worries literally concern what they will eat, what they will drink, and what they will wear. The preacher will also tread carefully when the congregation is composed—in whole or in part—of those who have real concerns about what (or when) they will eat. In such cases, the admonition not to worry will sound profoundly empty, if it does not address solutions.

Matthew offers several approaches for preparing a sermon on these issues. The immediate context for approaching them is the Sermon on the Mount, the first and deepest exploration of discipleship in this Gospel. Taking this context into account, the preacher might begin by exploring the language Matthew uses, looking for similarities and differences between key terms and phrases. How, for example, might one compare "*worrying*" (6:25) and "*striving*" (v. 33)? Is one healthy and the other not? Is there a point when "striving" becomes "worrying"? In exploring this, it might help to look at other translations—"being anxious about" (RSV) rather than the NRSV's "worrying about," for example. Similarly, is "striving" different from "seeking" (KJV, RSV), "setting your heart on" (NJB), or phrases such as "being concerned with," "attending to," or "focusing on"? Unfamiliar translations can sometimes give a familiar saying new meaning.

Another approach to the Gospel for the day might lead one to a sermon on the premise that undergirds the whole of verses 25–33: God cares for creation, and it works. Birds do what birds do; flowers do what flowers do; grass does what grass does; and it is all more glorious than Solomon, a king renowned for his splendid living. The passage also presumes that humans are part of the created order, and that God knows we need food, drink, and clothing every bit as much as the birds and lilies. Life may be more than these necessities, but the necessities are part of life, and God provides them. It is worth noting that the Greek term for "life" here is not the generic term *zōē* but the word that connotes what makes one fully human, *psychē*, something like "life-soul." It is that life that is more than food, drink, and clothing. *Worrying* or *being anxious* about it does not do much good; but considering one's life-soul in the context of God's care for creation does, just as looking at (and relating to) the birds of the air and the lilies of the field does.

Related to this approach is the statement in verse 33 that "all these things" will be given to those who "strive first for the kingdom of God and his righteousness." This raises significant questions related to fundamental theological issues well beyond the scope of these brief comments. Within the Gospel reading for the day, however, it is important to note that Jesus says basic needs will be given to those who strive first for the kingdom of God and his righteousness. He does not say God will provide "the abundance of possessions." Similarly, the day's Gospel ends with a matter-of-fact acknowledgment that both today and tomorrow will have a sufficiency of troubles. They too belong to God's created order in Matthew's Gospel. There is no suggestion that striving first for the kingdom of God and his righteousness will change that.

Still, at the beginning of the Sermon on the Mount, the Beatitudes promise a reversal of the

---

2. For Luke's treatment of these passages, see 12:13–31 and 16:1–13.

created order for the poor in spirit, those who mourn, the meek, those who hunger and thirst for righteousness, and those who are persecuted for righteousness' sake. The Gospel of Matthew holds both views in tension, acknowledging the mystery of God's providence.

Whatever approach one takes to the Gospel of the day, the preacher will do well to note that Matthew returns to food, drink, and clothing in the last of the parables of judgment in chapter 25, the parable of the Sheep and Goats. Bearing this parable in mind will ensure that exhortations to strive first for the kingdom of God and his righteousness will call the comfortable to be concerned not only for their own life-souls and basic needs, but also for the needs of those who are hungry, thirsty, naked, sick, in prison, and strangers in the world around them. God's righteousness demands nothing less.

OLIVER LARRY YARBROUGH

Commentary 2: Connecting the Reading with the World

Jesus' teaching in Matthew 6:24–34 falls in the middle of the Sermon on the Mount, considered by many to be both Jesus' most well-known and most challenging instruction. The Sermon on the Mount lays out Jesus' vision of life lived according to God's vision for the world, which Matthew calls the kingdom of heaven. In the midst of what many churches refer to as Ordinary Time, or the period in which Sundays are numbered in order, Jesus' instruction serves to guide Christians through the ins and outs of the everyday.

The teaching that unfolds in Matthew 6 may seem particularly personal for today's readers. Whereas some might initially think that Jesus' words about marriage and divorce in the Sermon on the Mount constitute his most personal teaching, that may very well not be the case. For in today's world, money and financial status are frequently regarded as at least as private a topic as marriage. In congregational contexts, where money often takes on moral, ethical, and theological meaning, some of the most difficult and awkward Sundays are those that address financial stewardship, annual pledges, or capital campaigns. Talking about money in the church requires people to weigh and consider everything that they value and why.

In the Sermon on the Mount, Jesus probes his hearers about this very question. Earlier in Matthew 6, Jesus cautions his listeners to refrain from storing up treasures on earth, which can be easily lost, and instead invites them to "store up for yourselves treasures in heaven. . . . For where your treasure is, there your heart will be also" (Matt. 6:19–21). The contrast that Jesus draws between treasure on earth and that in heaven is inherently a question of values. Rather than valuing the material goods that humans tend to prize most, Jesus exhorts his listeners to focus on the things of heaven, which cannot corrode or be taken away.

The contrast between those that are lasting and those that corrode clearly plays on the distinction between earth and heaven that the Sermon on the Mount assumes. Indeed, the entire Sermon rests on the conviction that the values that correspond with God's vision for the world often oppose conventional wisdom and common understanding of what is desirable and good. Matthew's Gospel argues that those who would be disciples of Jesus are to align their lives with his teaching. For as 6:24 contends, "No one can serve two masters; for a slave will either hate the one and love the other, or be devoted to the one and despise the other. You cannot serve God and wealth."

This is a difficult word to receive in the current context, when so many of the world's economies and global markets place unquestioned priority on profit making and the acquisition of wealth. By suggesting to his hearers that they must choose between "two masters," Jesus makes use of the metaphor of enslavement, well known in antiquity and utilized by the apostle Paul. Here the metaphor deftly illustrates how we are owned by what we most value and serve. As Matthew's parables of the Hidden Treasure (13:44) and the Pearl of Great Price (13:45–46) suggest, the things to which we devote ourselves indicate a lot about who we are.

Acquiring wealth takes time, intention, and sustained energy. What we possess and how we spend our time over the years reveals our deepest commitments and values. In our time, the metaphor may be even more apt than it was in the first century. Money plays a determinative role in contemporary society, and global markets drive so much around the world that shapes whether and how human beings and environments will thrive or wither. Jesus' word is clear. If we serve money, we are not serving God. This direct statement opens up a space to explore both what serving money and what serving God look like in the current context. Moreover, this passage urges us to ponder the difficult question of how the people of God can have a correct relationship with money and wealth.

Clearly, the kingdom of heaven, which Jesus' teaching reveals, stands in sharp contrast to the values and ways of the world. The way of God that Jesus embodies is to be manifest in individual, as well as collective, thinking and doing. For Matthew, it is an order of being that realizes the vision and will of God for all creation, not for God's own sake, but for the good of everyone and everything that is a part of it. Unlike the present age in which we now live, the future will see the complete and unfettered realization of God's way on earth, a way fully revealed in Jesus' teaching and ministry. As Christian discipleship is about imitating Jesus, so is it also about recognizing and living out the way of the kingdom that he teaches and embodies. Discipleship involves more than following specific instructions. It is about embracing the vision that generates Jesus' teaching, in the first place. Discipleship for Matthew is the practice of life itself.

The implication of Jesus' teaching in 6:24 comes to full flower in what follows in 6:25–33 and 34. The topic at first appears to be that anxiety, with the repeated motif of worrying woven throughout the pericope: "do not worry about your life" (v. 25); "And can any of you by worrying add a single hour to your span of life?" (v. 27); "And why do you worry about clothing?" (v. 28); "Therefore do not worry, saying, 'What will we eat?' or 'What will we drink?' or 'What will we wear?'" (v. 31). The concerns that appear in the passage are understandable ones about meeting the basic needs of life, specifically food, drink, and clothing. These are, as all parents know, a baby's very first needs, and they are what all humans depend on for the entirety of their lives. In other words, the concerns that Jesus raises here are fully known to all his hearers.

It is not unusual for readers to take from this passage a sense of shame for worrying at all about such matters and to interpret Jesus' words as a long way of saying, "Don't worry, be happy!" In light of verse 32, "For it is the Gentiles who strive for all these things; and indeed your heavenly Father knows that you need all these things," the passage is commonly read as an admonition to trust God and a rebuke against those who do not. However, Jesus frames his teaching in a way that reveals a different meaning behind his exhortation to not worry. The key to understanding his meaning occurs when Jesus says, "But strive first for the kingdom of God and his righteousness, and all these things will be given to you as well" (v. 33).

The kingdom of God (or heaven) pertains to a new way of being, not just for individuals but also for communities and congregations. Jesus uses the second person plural in 6:33. Striving first for the kingdom of God is a communal act and a collective commitment to the vision that Jesus teaches and realizes in his own being and doing. To seek the kingdom of God is to long for the way of God and to reflect it in our individual and collective lives. Jesus' exhortation not to worry is a call to living as a community that cares for one another and embodies the wisdom and values outlined in the Sermon on the Mount. It is in light of such understanding that we should read Matthew 6:34: "So do not worry about tomorrow, for tomorrow will bring worries of its own. Today's trouble is enough for today."

MARY F. FOSKETT

Proper 4 (Sunday between May 29 and June 4 inclusive)

Deuteronomy 11:18–21, 26–28 and
   Genesis 6:9–22; 7:24; 8:14–19
Psalm 31:1–5, 19–24 and Psalm 46

Romans 1:16–17; 3:22b–28
Matthew 7:21–29

Deuteronomy 11:18–21, 26–28

[18]You shall put these words of mine in your heart and soul, and you shall bind them as a sign on your hand, and fix them as an emblem on your forehead. [19]Teach them to your children, talking about them when you are at home and when you are away, when you lie down and when you rise. [20]Write them on the doorposts of your house and on your gates, [21]so that your days and the days of your children may be multiplied in the land that the LORD swore to your ancestors to give them, as long as the heavens are above the earth. . . .

[26]See, I am setting before you today a blessing and a curse: [27]the blessing, if you obey the commandments of the LORD your God that I am commanding you today; [28]and the curse, if you do not obey the commandments of the LORD your God, but turn from the way that I am commanding you today, to follow other gods that you have not known.

Genesis 6:9–22; 7:24; 8:14–19

[6:9]These are the descendants of Noah. Noah was a righteous man, blameless in his generation; Noah walked with God. [10]And Noah had three sons, Shem, Ham, and Japheth.

[11]Now the earth was corrupt in God's sight, and the earth was filled with violence. [12]And God saw that the earth was corrupt; for all flesh had corrupted its ways upon the earth. [13]And God said to Noah, "I have determined to make an end of all flesh, for the earth is filled with violence because of them; now I am going to destroy them along with the earth. [14]Make yourself an ark of cypress wood; make rooms in the ark, and cover it inside and out with pitch. [15]This is how you are to make it: the length of the ark three hundred cubits, its width fifty cubits, and its height thirty cubits. [16]Make a roof for the ark, and finish it to a cubit above; and put the door of the ark in its side; make it with lower, second, and third decks. [17]For my part, I am going to bring a flood of waters on the earth, to destroy from under heaven all flesh in which is the breath of life; everything that is on the earth shall die. [18]But I will establish my covenant with you; and you shall come into the ark, you, your sons, your wife, and your sons' wives with you. [19]And of every living thing, of all flesh, you shall bring two of every kind into the ark, to keep them alive with you; they shall be male and female. [20]Of the birds according to their kinds, and of the animals according to their kinds, of every creeping thing of the ground according to its kind, two of every kind shall come in to you, to keep them alive. [21]Also take with you every kind of food that is eaten, and store it up; and it shall serve as food for you and for them." [22]Noah did this; he did all that God commanded him. . . .

7:24 . . . And the waters swelled on the earth for one hundred fifty days. . . .

8:14 . . . In the second month, on the twenty-seventh day of the month, the earth was dry. 15Then God said to Noah, 16"Go out of the ark, you and your wife, and your sons and your sons' wives with you. 17Bring out with you every living thing that is with you of all flesh—birds and animals and every creeping thing that creeps on the earth—so that they may abound on the earth, and be fruitful and multiply on the earth." 18So Noah went out with his sons and his wife and his sons' wives. 19And every animal, every creeping thing, and every bird, everything that moves on the earth, went out of the ark by families.

Commentary 1: Connecting the Reading with Scripture

Human beings behave badly. That is the ugly reality behind both lections. In the flood narrative in Genesis 6–9, God is so upset by the broken world that God decides to destroy it and start again. In Deuteronomy, God gives the Israelites a detailed set of instructions for living. Neither strategy produces God's desired effect: a world where people honor God and one another.

In the Genesis text, God decides to wipe out the world and restart with Noah's family. The world is under water for one hundred fifty days according to Genesis 7:24 or forty days and forty nights according to Genesis 7:4. Finally, the land dries out, and humans and animals leave the ark. The lectionary includes a few sanitized excerpts but excludes much of the lengthy and detailed description of the world's destruction in Genesis 6–9. This larger story is also stylistically peculiar, with odd repetitions and contradictions, likely the result of two traditions or sources (J or Yahwist and P or Priestly) being combined.

Some of the best homiletical material is found outside the assigned passage. Note God's deep sorrow and grief (6:6) that the world once pronounced "very good" (1:31) is now too broken and corrupt to tolerate. God resolutely proceeds with the destruction but appears both disappointed and angry.

God does not just destroy, however; he also provides a new beginning. After months of rain, "God remembered" Noah (Gen. 8:1), and as in Genesis 1, the divine breath or wind blows over the waters in order to put the flood waters back in their place. The flood narrative is thus imagined as a redoing of creation in which chaos, as symbolized by the waters, is again constrained by God. "God remembered," just as when God remembered the Israelites and called Moses to deliver them from Egypt (Exod. 2:24). "God remembers" seems to be the turning point when God moves from destruction to restoration. When God remembers, rescue and redemption are not far behind. Divine memory entails divine action.

God also promises that the earth would never again be destroyed with water (Gen. 9:11, 15). Considering that the flood has not altered basic human nature, and that people born after the flood would still behave badly, God's promise hints that though people might not have changed, God has. Indeed, right after the flood, God continues trying to repair the world by calling on Abraham. Perhaps we can read in God's promise a sense of divine resolution to work with the messy world as it is, without resorting to destruction. This suggests that when a city is devastated by a hurricane or flooding, it is not because God is particularly angry with New Orleans or Houston. Rather, these are unfortunate examples of the corruption of the order and perfection of creation. The waters do not always remain in their places, but that is a sign of a broken world, not an angry God.

Though the focus of this narrative is oftentimes on the piety of Noah, sermons about the nature of human suffering emerge easily from this narrative. The flood narrative, disturbingly, is about divine destruction of the entire world, including innocent animals, children, and flora.

A wise preacher might reflect on how the church can make sense of and act in the face of similar suffering and devastation. Indeed, though God promises not to destroy the world again, this text reminds us that God's people need not sit idly by in the face of genocide, warfare, pollution, and oppression—acts that are also world destroying.

When this story is read in the larger literary context of Genesis, the flood narrative shows that God does not give up on the world. Instead, God continually finds new ways to engage with God's people. After the flood, God will make a covenant with Abraham, give the law, and send the prophets. Finally, God will take human flesh and transform the world, not through destruction, but through vulnerability, suffering, and resurrection. God tenaciously and continually attempts to engage with humanity.

The lection from Deuteronomy illustrates one of these divine efforts to work with humanity. Deuteronomy is a series of speeches in which Moses reminds the Israelites of God's covenant, that is, their legal agreement. The law is meant to guide their relationship with God and with each other. It shapes the Israelite community's worship, economy, and community.

In the portions of Deuteronomy included in the lectionary, the first (Deut. 11:18–21) reminds the Israelites to affix the law to their bodies and homes so that it becomes a constant, unforgettable guide in their daily lives, while the second portion (vv. 26–28) warns the Israelites about the gravity of their choice to follow or reject the covenant. If they keep the commandments and follow God, they will be blessed. If they do not, they will be cursed.

This idea that good people will be rewarded and bad people will be punished is a common theme in some parts of the Old Testament, and poses a significant challenge for the preacher. Indeed, this idea directly counters life as we know and live it. People do not always get what they deserve. Blessings and curses are not always distributed in ways that seem connected to behavior. Bad things happen to good people; good things happen to bad people. Indeed, other parts of the Old Testament, such as Job and Ecclesiastes, directly challenge this ordered sentiment found in Deuteronomy.

It might be helpful to think of the book of Deuteronomy as Moses' "last lecture" before he died, or a commencement address delivered to the Israelites as they graduate from the wilderness and enter the promised land. He offers good advice for living. If they do the right things, if they honor God and care for their neighbors, then their vertical and horizontal relationships will be healthy and happy. If they follow God's instructions, worship will be meaningful. If they care for the poor, the community will thrive. Moses encourages the people to obey God because he thinks obedience will lead them to a better life. It was and is good advice, but no single lecture can anticipate and include all the nuances of life and theology. This is not the last word in Moses' theology, or a definitive statement of how the world always works. Good behavior often leads to a happier life, but there is no guarantee.

The law in Deuteronomy is the foundation of an orderly, just, and equitable society. It helps people honor God, each other, and the land. The law is not naive about the reality of chaos and corruption. When people behave badly, the law offers guidance for reconciliation and restoration. The law serves as a check on unbridled self-interest and encourages people to make choices that benefit the whole community.

In the Gospel lection, Matthew 7:21–29, Jesus teaches that merely hearing or repeating his words is not enough. Words require action. Both the Deuteronomic laws and the words of Jesus need to be internalized so that they shape choices and actions.

Respect for law is not the same as blind obedience to law and order. In contemporary society we recognize that laws have sometimes been unjust, but society is held together by a conviction that there should be laws that preserve equal opportunity, equal treatment, and fairness. At best, laws protect the weak and vulnerable from those who would prey upon them. Good laws recognize that all people, even the strangers, are made in God's image.

LYNN JAPINGA

Commentary 2: Connecting the Reading with the World

Unlike the relatively unknown text from Deuteronomy, the flood story in Genesis 6–9 is prevalent as a popularized myth marketed to children. Despite the dramatic and visual aspects of this tale (pairs of animals, flood, giant boat), it is an odd, trauma-inducing story: God destroys the entire world with a flood and saves only the people and animals that can fit in an ark. When understood as myth or a fable, this story hints of a particularly binary understanding of justice: There is right and wrong. Right leads to life and well-being. Wrong leads to destruction.

This reading stems in part from the conditional understanding of the covenant evident in both Deuteronomy and Genesis. God demands obedience, which in turn results in order, justice, and blessing (Deut. 11:27). Disobedience, in contrast, results in a curse (v. 28). Noah—the one who is "righteous" and "blameless" (Gen. 6:9)—is rescued and receives the blessing of life via the ark, while the rest of corrupt humanity receives the curse of death. This theology clearly links external prosperity and well-being with righteousness and proper action. A preacher will need to acknowledge the problematic nature of this conditional theology (i.e., good things happen to good people, bad things happen to bad people), pointing out the various places in the biblical witness where it is contested.

Even so, aspects of conditional theology sound reasonable. It is not a stretch to say that injustice is linked to people's failure to adhere to God's wishes and commandments, which the church summarizes as a twofold requirement to love God and love neighbor (Matt. 22:35–40; Mark 12:28–34; Luke 10:25–28). Indeed, our world offers much evidence that connects human failings to injustice. Racial inequality in public education, for example, leads to greater income inequality. Income inequality, in turn, leads to greater levels of crime and violence, and declines in health and education. This spiral of injustice is undoubtedly the result of our disobedience to the divine command to love God and neighbor. A sermon, therefore, might warn the people of God that disobedience—especially of the central commands to love God and neighbor—leads to some curses that can be avoided. Indeed, a reminder to the church that it has an important role to play in the continual creation of a better, more just universe is always timely.

Though the theology that correct behavior will lead to prosperity and well-being might hold some weight, it helps to recognize that reality subverts and problematizes this idea. Despite the promises in Deuteronomy and Genesis, in our world good people do indeed suffer, and bad people many times escape without punishment. Indeed, the theology that emerges from these texts can be distorted to blame victims for their own misfortune. A wise preacher would do well to discuss the problematic tit-for-tat theology that emerges from these perilous texts. How we so often assume that the unfortunate are wholly responsible for their hardships, and how this assumption results from our deep desire for a just God are worthy topics to address from the pulpit.

Indeed, tempering the tit-for-tat, prosperity gospel–like theology, the biblical texts point to communal, rather than individual obedience as God's chief concern. The Deuteronomy text, for example, is explicitly addressed to the community. In Genesis, moreover, it is the failure of the community that is blamed for God sending the flood. This corporate focus is an important corrective to individualistic notions of faithfulness divorced from love of neighbor. A preacher may wish entirely to deconstruct the prosperity gospel that promises television viewers healing or increased income as inevitable outcomes of an individual believer's faithfulness.

Indeed, we need to discuss corporate responsibility in the church, especially considering that our text concerns a flood. Flooding, which has been occurring with increased frequency as the planet continues to warm, is expected to grow exponentially in the coming decades—a change that would set in motion the movement of millions of people from their homes and the abandonment of entire cities in lower-lying areas. Unlike the flooding in Genesis, the current flooding is human generated. It is caused by us—humanity at large—who, one can argue, have failed in covenantal duties to take care of our world. As Deuteronomy so forcefully reminds us, both blessings and curses will result from our corporate actions.

Connections of this blessing/curse arrangement can be made with the reading of the prior week (Gen. 1:1–2:4a), where humans are given dominion over the earth. As we move more deeply into the liturgical season of Pentecost, the church might explore the power that God issues to human beings at creation, and then again to the church, with greater intensity, with the coming of the Spirit. Perhaps the Spirit's proclamation of a life-saving way of repentance could be understood today not solely in a spiritualized sense but in an existential, planet-healing sense as well. We have wielded God-given power to destroy. The gospel gives us Spirit power to turn around, to repent of our disobedient use of power directed against God's good earth, and to remember that this earth has been entrusted to us since the beginning for our own well-being.

In speaking about human responsibility, we should not gloss over the violence that God carries out in the Genesis text in pursuit of justice. Though humanity seems to "get what is coming to them," a notion that is ubiquitous in film and television narrative today, it is deeply troubling that God orders such wholesale destruction. This disturbing portrayal of God compels us to reflect on violence and abuse done in the name of religion. God-authorized violence continues to fuel abuse and horror by people who justify their own actions in God's name. A sermon might wrestle with how to urge nonviolence while upholding the authority of biblical texts, such as the flood story, that show God engaging in violence. Perhaps God's promise at the end of the flood that God will never attempt to destroy humanity again (Gen. 8:21) hints that this text, rather than serving as authorization for God-ordained violence against humanity, really is a prohibition against righteously fueled violence.

A different connection that can be made is the juxtaposition of the initial description of Noah as "righteous" and "blameless" and the end of the story where one of Noah's sons, Ham, ambiguously dishonors his father (9:18–27). Like most heroes of the Bible and like most families today, Noah's family has problems. Considering that problems are universal and timeless, Noah's story might serve as an interesting starting point for a sermon on relational discord. The idea of a family can be stretched from just nuclear family to discuss issues facing larger families, like the church, the denomination, the country, and the world.

The ending of Noah's story proves that his own covenantal faithfulness does not protect him from curses that find their way into the family. By introducing this curse, the Genesis story seems to raise doubts about the foundational Deuteronomic linkage between obedience and blessing, disobedience and curse. Families have problems. As Genesis states, the "inclination of the human heart is evil from youth" (8:21). This tension between obedience that results in well-being and obedience that does not result in well-being remains unresolved in the Noah story, just as it remains unresolved in the life of faith. It might console the people of God to know that even our greatest heroes in the faith had problems that obedience could not always cure or solve.

ANDREW FOSTER CONNORS

Proper 4 (Sunday between May 29 and June 4 inclusive)

Psalm 31:1–5, 19–24

¹In you, O LORD, I seek refuge;
    do not let me ever be put to shame;
    in your righteousness deliver me.
²Incline your ear to me;
    rescue me speedily.
Be a rock of refuge for me,
    a strong fortress to save me.

³You are indeed my rock and my fortress;
    for your name's sake lead me and guide me,
⁴take me out of the net that is hidden for me,
    for you are my refuge.
⁵Into your hand I commit my spirit;
    you have redeemed me, O LORD, faithful God.
. . . .
¹⁹O how abundant is your goodness
    that you have laid up for those who fear you,
and accomplished for those who take refuge in you,
    in the sight of everyone!
²⁰In the shelter of your presence you hide them
    from human plots;
you hold them safe under your shelter
    from contentious tongues.

²¹Blessed be the LORD,
    for he has wondrously shown his steadfast love to me
    when I was beset as a city under siege.
²²I had said in my alarm,
    "I am driven far from your sight."
But you heard my supplications
    when I cried out to you for help.

²³Love the LORD, all you his saints.
    The LORD preserves the faithful,
    but abundantly repays the one who acts haughtily.
²⁴Be strong, and let your heart take courage,
    all you who wait for the LORD.

Psalm 46

¹God is our refuge and strength,
    a very present help in trouble.
²Therefore we will not fear, though the earth should change,
    though the mountains shake in the heart of the sea;
³though its waters roar and foam,
    though the mountains tremble with its tumult.

⁴There is a river whose streams make glad the city of God,
   the holy habitation of the Most High.
⁵God is in the midst of the city; it shall not be moved;
   God will help it when the morning dawns.
⁶The nations are in an uproar, the kingdoms totter;
   he utters his voice, the earth melts.
⁷The LORD of hosts is with us;
   the God of Jacob is our refuge.

⁸Come, behold the works of the LORD;
   see what desolations he has brought on the earth.
⁹He makes wars cease to the end of the earth;
   he breaks the bow, and shatters the spear;
   he burns the shields with fire.
¹⁰"Be still, and know that I am God!
   I am exalted among the nations,
   I am exalted in the earth."
¹¹The LORD of hosts is with us;
   the God of Jacob is our refuge.

Connecting the Psalm with Scripture and Worship

The lectionary offers two options from the Psalms for this Sunday. Psalm 31 and Psalm 46 have very different literary structures and rhetorical strategies. Yet they present a simple, consistent message. Yahweh is a refuge. Yahweh protects. Yahweh saves. This too is one of the central messages of the Old Testament lessons from Deuteronomy 11:18–21, 26–28 and the flood account found in Genesis 6:9–22; 7:24; 8:14–19.

Psalm 46. Declarations of trust appear throughout Psalm 46. It begins with a claim that God is near during times of trouble (Ps. 46:1). It emphasizes this theme through a refrain, found at the midpoint of the psalm and again at its ending: "The LORD of hosts is with us; the God of Jacob is our refuge" (vv. 7, 11).

As the psalm unfolds, we encounter images of divine power in the midst of chaos. Those in God's presence experience order and blessing (vv. 4–5), while the waters overwhelm everything outside and the very structure of the earth falls apart (vv. 2–3). Political structures also fall apart. Governments and the ground below them dissolve, yet God remains in control (v. 6). In fact, the psalm reveals God as the one who owns all power, both the power to destroy and the power to preserve (v. 8). God's ultimate demonstration of power is to undo the violence of the nations, destroying their weapons, and silencing their warring madness (vv. 9–10).

The lectionary binds Psalm 46 to the story of the flood, stitched together across three chapters in Genesis (6:9–22; 7:24; 8:14–19). This pairing highlights God's control over water as a central image in Psalm 46. The river that runs through the city of God is a poetic expression of God's ability to bring order out of chaos, transforming water as a means of destruction into a source of blessing and salvation (Ps. 46:4). Likewise, in the Genesis flood account, water obliterates the world and also provides a means by which God creates the world anew. Water brings death and life. The richness of this image is alive in the sacrament of baptism, by which one dies with Christ and is raised to new life through God's saving actions.

The imagery of this psalm has inspired composers throughout the centuries. Martin Luther's version of the psalm, known to us today as "A Mighty Fortress is Our God" (c. 1529), is the most well-known along with Bach's famous setting of the hymn in his cantata

BWV 80, "Ein feste Burg ist unser Gott" (ca. 1723). If one decides to utilize one of the many appropriations of Psalm 46 in contemporary Christian music, caution is in order. It is common to hear "Be still and know that I am God" (Ps. 46:10) set musically as a call for one to stop worrying and focus on one's spiritual life. Such an individualistic and interiorized reading is at odds with the immediate context of the psalm. The verse is, in fact, a stern address to the whole world, a command from God's very mouth, for the nations to stop their destructive raging. God ensures his claim of sovereignty by putting an end to all such violence.

Psalm 31. Psalm 31, like many other psalms, alternates between statements of trust and pleas for help. The psalmist is desperate for God to act quickly and deliver him from peril. The word order of the opening phrase underscores the idea that Yahweh alone is the source of the psalmist's hope: "In you, O Lord, I seek refuge" (Ps. 31:1). In Hebrew, the prepositional phrase "in you" (*beka*) appears at the beginning of the sentence, a breach of standard word order. The psalmist modifies the conventional patterns of speech to intensify his confession of trust.

After the opening statement of trust, the psalmist utters a series of four imperative verbs (vv. 1–2), a cascade of entreaties that conveys the extremity of his plight. The psalmist asks that God would snatch him away and save him from this situation, that God would listen to him, and that God would become a strong rock for the psalmist (vv. 1–2).

The psalmist also attempts to elicit a response from God by declaring his trust in God's power to save. The psalmist is here deploying a rhetorical strategy that alternates between two grammatical moods: the indicative and the imperative. He confesses his trust through the indicative mood and frames his request in the imperative mood: "Be a rock refuge for me, a strong fortress to save me [imperative]. For you are my rock and my fortress [indicative]." This interweaving of moods is a formula that we see frequently in modern patterns of speech as well. Princess Leia even employed it in her moment of need: "Help me, Obi Wan Kenobi [imperative]. You're my only hope [indicative]."

Throughout the opening verses of the psalm, we find pleas and faithful declarations woven together:

v. 1a	confession of trust (indicative)
v. 1b–2	petition (imperative)
v. 3a	confession of trust (indicative)
v. 3b–4a	petition (imperative)
v. 5	confession of trust (indicative)

This pattern of alternation has the effect of reinforcing the closeness of the relationship between the speaker and the addressee. The psalmist's complete reliance on Yahweh has a counterpoint in Yahweh's faithfulness to the psalmist. The pleas are simply a statement of trust in a different grammatical form. A direct plea is the truest indication that one believes that God can and will act.

This pattern of petition and confession continues throughout the portions of the psalm not present in the lectionary reading. Imperative verbs requesting God's help are the dominant feature of verses 9, 15–18, while statements of trust appear in verses 6–8, 14. The lectionary reading picks up again in verse 19, in which the psalmist extends his own trust in God as a model of the larger community. All who fear God, like the psalmist, can benefit from God's protection and care (vv. 19–20). The psalmist moves toward a posture of praise. As his prayer comes to a close, he calls on the community to look to God for salvation in the same way that he has (vv. 21–22). The psalm ends, in fact, with an address not to God, but to the community—again through the imperative mood—to rely on Yahweh as the psalmist has done (v. 23).

Here at the end of the psalm, we find a connection to the rhetoric of Deuteronomy 11:18–21, 26–28, another direct address to the community in the imperative mood, outlining what it means to trust in Yahweh. Trusting God requires constant attention to the Word of God, how God has revealed God's order within the world (Deut. 11:18–21). When a people attend to God's Word, blessing is the result (vv. 26–28).

The use of Psalm 31 in worship should reinforce how our patterns of speech reflect our reliance on God. In worship, we move between petitions and confessions of trust. The psalm

The Light of Conscience

Let us be zealous, brothers, to guard our conscience for as long as we are in this world and not to neglect its promptings in anything. And let us not tread it under foot even in the least thing, for you can see that from the smallest things, which of their nature are worth little, we come to despise the great things. When we begin to say, "What is it if I say just these few words? What does it matter if I eat this morsel? What difference if I poke my nose in here or there?" From this way of saying, "What does this or that matter?" a man takes evil and bitter nourishment and begins presently to despise greater and more serious things and even to tread down his own conscience and so, at last destroying it, bit by bit, he falls into danger and finally becomes completely impervious to the light of conscience.

Therefore, brothers, see to it that we do not neglect little things; see to it that we do not despise them as of no account. There are no "little things"—for when it is a question of bad habits, it is a question of a malignant ulcer. Let us live circumspectly, let us give heed to trivial matters when they are trivial, lest they become grave. Doing what is right and what is wrong: both begin from small things and advance to what is great, either good or evil. . . .

In attending to our conscience, we need to consider many different factors. A man needs to satisfy his conscience towards God, towards his neighbor, and towards material things. As regards God: he must not despise God's precepts, even those concerning things which are not seen by men or those things for which one is not accountable to men. A man should obey his conscience in relation to God; for example, did he neglect his prayer? If an evil thought came into his heart, was he vigilant and did he keep control of himself or did he entertain it? He sees his neighbor saying something or doing something; does he suspect it's evil and condemn him? To put it simply, all the hidden things that happen inside us, things which no one sees except God and our conscience, we need to take account of. This is what I mean by our conscience towards God. To respect our conscience towards our neighbor means not to do anything that we think may trouble or harm our neighbor in deed, or word, or gesture, or look. . . . As regards keeping a good conscience in respect of material things: not to use things badly, not to render things useless, not to leave things about, and when we find things left about not to leave them even if they are of small value but to pick them up and put them in their proper place.

Dorotheos of Gaza, *Discourses and Sayings*, trans. Eric P. Wheeler (Kalamazoo, MI: Cistercian Publications, 1977), 105–7.

---

presents multiple moods, both grammatical and emotional. So should our worship.

A number of choral works feature the text of Psalm 31. Henry Purcell's four-voiced anthem "In thee, O Lord, do I put my trust" (1682) requires a strong choir and an audience who might appreciate text painting. Much more accessible to choirs and audience alike, however, is Thomas Tallis's motet "O Lord, in thee is all my trust, Give ear unto my woeful cries" (1565). This piece is not a version of Psalm 31, but it does share the opening line of the psalm. Its text also alternates throughout between confessions of trust and petitions, guided along by a lilting rhythm and clear, satisfying cadences.

JOEL MARCUS LEMON

Proper 4 (Sunday between May 29 and June 4 inclusive)

Romans 1:16–17; 3:22b–28

¹⁶For I am not ashamed of the gospel; it is the power of God for salvation to everyone who has faith, to the Jew first and also to the Greek. ¹⁷For in it the righteousness of God is revealed through faith for faith; as it is written, "The one who is righteous will live by faith." . . .

³:²²ᵇ . . . For there is no distinction, ²³since all have sinned and fall short of the glory of God; ²⁴they are now justified by his grace as a gift, through the redemption that is in Christ Jesus, ²⁵whom God put forward as a sacrifice of atonement by his blood, effective through faith. He did this to show his righteousness, because in his divine forbearance he had passed over the sins previously committed; ²⁶it was to prove at the present time that he himself is righteous and that he justifies the one who has faith in Jesus.

²⁷Then what becomes of boasting? It is excluded. By what law? By that of works? No, but by the law of faith. ²⁸For we hold that a person is justified by faith apart from works prescribed by the law.

Commentary 1: Connecting the Reading with Scripture

These remarkable passages stand at the center of the meaning both of Paul's Letter to the Romans and of the Christian faith as a whole. They have caused intense debate among theologians and exegetes down the centuries, deeply contested at the level of detail. Yet their basic meaning and relevance are luminous and unequivocal, and might be captured in three claims.

"We are all in the same, sinking boat." The claim that all have sinned and fallen short of the glory of God is extraordinary and controversial. It is extraordinary because it runs counter to any narrative of human progress that society may like to tell itself or to any account of personal merit that we may like to present. It is controversial because it functions to erode any sense of difference or superiority between different people or groups of people. Regardless of who we are, where we come from, what we believe or what we have done, we have all failed to honor and glorify the name of God in the way that we should.

This erosion of difference calls into question before God all the distinctions that we like to draw between different groups of people. In Romans, the distinction between Jews and Gentiles was central for Paul; in our day, separatist tendencies are manifest and increasing, whether in the arena of nations, of political groupings, of religions and denominations, or elsewhere. Yet the unerring truth remains: whatever the groups we identify with, we are all united as one in our shortcomings before God.

This idea that we are all irrevocably sinners is one that sometimes struggles to find traction in the proclamation of the church today. It can be seen as unnecessarily pessimistic, contributing to a culture in which people can be suppressed, even oppressed, by feelings of failure and inadequacy. Moreover, the idea there is nothing that we can do to alter this situation can lead to feelings of powerlessness and despondency. It is a teaching of Scripture that invites careful handling and sensitive preaching.

At the same time, sin has a greater constellation of meaning than personal wrongdoing and guilt. A sense of the finitude and brokenness of the human condition abounds everywhere, and lies within the experience of everyone. To encourage Christians to consider their own failures can be made part of an exercise in recognizing wider vistas of human imperfection, and in determining pathways of liberating action, rather than simply in browbeating.

The result of this individual and collective falling short of the calling of God is that we do not stand in the right before God. Our relationship with God is compromised, compromised irrevocably. There is no way out that is within our capabilities. We seem stuck.

"There is a way out of that boat." At the heart of the Christian gospel, and of this letter of Paul, is the great gospel "nevertheless." In musical terms, it is the luminous "*Aber!*" (However!) of the second movement of Brahms's *Requiem*, the unanticipated and glorious moment of transition from the perishability of all flesh to the eternity of the Word of God. Paul declares that despite the universal sinfulness of humanity, a right standing and restored relationship with God, as God originally intended for us in creation, is now once again possible. This is the good news of the gospel: we become righteous before God. In this way the words of the psalmist from this week's lection truly come alive: "God is our refuge and strength, a very present help in trouble" (Ps. 46:1).

We have not merited or earned this; indeed we could not have merited or earned this. Again, here, there is no distinction between different groups of people, whether Jews and Gentiles or whatever. No one can earn or merit this salvation, this removal of sin before God, because the clarion call of this Letter to the Romans is that our right standing with God, our justification, is not achievable by our own works. It is only by faith—by faith all the way down. That faith is itself a gift of God, such that our salvation is a matter of sheer gift—of *grace*.

In turn, this means that boasting is no longer a possibility, for we have no righteousness of our own of which we can boast. Instead, we are called only to receive. That passivity, that quietism at the heart of the first movement of salvation, can be profoundly countercultural in a world that measures the value of people by what they do and what they achieve. It can also be slightly disorienting in a world where we seem to have to fight for everything we have. Yet it is the calm at the center of Christian faith.

"That way is called Jesus Christ." The center of the text from Romans 3 is the confession that our reconciliation with God is achieved through the redemption that is in Christ Jesus. The grace by which we are reconciled to God is not some abstract concept or impersonal force; rather, grace is a dynamic, liberating power identified with the presence and power and person of the one mediator, Jesus Christ. God not only *reveals* but also *effects* our justification in Jesus Christ. The two are accomplished together, grasped by a faith that not only perceives but also trusts.

The cross, Paul observes, is central to this act of atonement. That reconciliation is achieved in this event of violence and shame is explicit in Paul's thinking and is a stumbling block to many. Any account of *how* this takes place is exegetically and theologically contested: themes of a sacrifice in blood, the appeasement of wrath, and the forgiveness of sin run close to the surface of Paul's language in the text. However, what is unambiguous, if sometimes underplayed, is that the initiative of redemption is always absolutely and exclusively that of God.

This means that our justification is not only a matter of ourselves being pronounced righteous in Jesus Christ; our justification is also a matter of God being righteous, revealing his righteousness to the world in both his perduring faithfulness to his creation and his unyielding determination not to tolerate sin forever. It is God in Jesus Christ who purposes and then achieves the transformation of our situation from unrighteousness and enmity with God to peace with God and righteousness. It is our faith that grasps the reality of this transformation.

This, then, is the way of life, the way of righteousness before God. It is not a righteousness that is our own or achieved by our works; it is an alien righteousness that is in Jesus Christ, but that is already shared with us and ascribed to us here, even as the fullness of our salvation is yet awaited. As we travel on this way, we are not ashamed of the message of salvation that it attests. As we journey in faith toward that promised salvation, we recognize that we are not just saved from our sins but are saved for the glorying and honoring of God. As we are blessed to perform this task of witness, then truly, in the words of the Gospel text for this week, we do "the will of my Father in heaven" (Matt. 7:21).

What such witness to God might look like in a given context invites close contextual discernment and reflection. In whatever sphere and manner it takes place, it will be with the purpose of hallowing the name of God, without shame or fear, for the salvation achieved in Jesus Christ.

PAUL T. NIMMO

Commentary 2: Connecting the Reading with the World

This passage from Romans heralds a trifecta of beginnings: it comes at the start of the long season in the church year in which discipleship is often emphasized; it begins a long series of sequential readings in Romans (in the RCL); and it is an introduction to the letter itself. A preacher could take this unique opportunity to dig into Paul's rich letter sequentially. It would be a valuable challenge to unfold the complicated arguments and context of Romans with congregants and get beyond the usual proof texts for theological or denominational predilections. As Paul himself digs deep into God's character, God's covenant, and our hope in God's faithful restoration of all God's creation (including the groaning earth in Rom. 8:22) through the death and resurrection of Jesus the Messiah, Romans can enliven us today.

Romans 1:16–17 is a profound assertion of the gospel. God is faithful to all God has created, all that was once "very good" and that will again be in the harmony of goodness. Paul's vision of God's faithfulness (here God's righteousness) is dynamic. Past, present, and future belong to God. What has been written (Rom. 1:17) stands in the present and assures hearers that there will be life for the just/righteous one who continues to trust in God. A dynamic life in right relationship with God and one another is promised. God's power is out and about among all people (here Jew and Greek) to create faith and bring salvation. Not only is this good news for all humankind. It is very good news about who God is: faithful creator and sustainer and bringer-in of the future.

What an important word here for preachers charged with speaking God's gospel! All of us are beset daily by warnings of catastrophic consequences if we make the "wrong" choices, associate with the "wrong" people, choose the "wrong" attorney general or college or sports drink or pain reliever. Paul reminds us here: we do not make the future. Of course, we can impact it, especially our own, but God continues to care and patiently to bring God's own future to us. That is forgiveness in a nutshell.

In 1989, W. Paul Jones wrote a book to explore five quite different ways in which believers conceive God and God's relationship with them.[1] The typologies, although not perfect, are helpful in trying to show how God, Jesus, church, atonement, communion, and the like are understood by different people. In Romans 3:24–25, Paul use varied language to make Christ's work for us somewhat intelligible. He does not prioritize or explain what Jesus has done: he simply offers "justification," "redemption," and "mercy seat" (*hilastērion*; NRSV note, "place of atonement"). It is as if Paul holds a multifaceted ball in his hands and turns it to get a different view, a different appreciation of God's gift in Christ. Each facet deserves exploration, for folks in the pews will hear differently. So much has been written about justification that my focus here will be on redemption and the "mercy seat."

How do we talk about redemption without trivializing it? At Delphi in Greece there still stands a remnant of a long wall incised painstakingly with name upon name of those who had received their freedom from slavery, a freedom guaranteed to be eternal by the legal fiction that the slave was sold to the Pythian Apollo, the god most honored at Delphi.[2] Transferred from one master to another, the Pythian Apollo would always be a better and less intrusive master than the one from whom the slave was freed.

---

1. W. Paul Jones, *Theological Worlds: Understanding the Alternative Rhythms of Christian Belief* (Nashville: Abingdon, 1989).
2. Notice the reference to a Pythian spirit in Acts 16:16.

Jews and Greeks understood redemption. An accepted interpretation was that God's people were freed by God from slavery to Pharaoh. Redeemed by God, their allegiance was to God, who had justified them, and it set them in a new relationship with Godself.

What does redemption look like? As Romans 6:16–19 argues, we now belong to God. Paul tries to help folks understand their altered status and their altered lives. "Whose are you?" he asks. "To whom do you no longer owe anything?" We are not captive to sin. We owe nothing to all that would separate us from God and one another. We belong to the one who redeemed us. Our master has a character and a will, a yearning for a flourishing creation for which we become obedient stewards. Our new vocation is to serve on behalf of a God who loves all God has made. A wise preacher would see in this message an opportunity to shine a light on the reality of what stewardship of and in creation really means for our corporate and individual lives.

The language of "expiation through faith in his blood" is unclear to many people and potentially misleading. The Greek word is "mercy seat," where blood was sprinkled to atone for the sins of the whole people of God (Exod. 25:17; 30:6 for *hilastērion*). The *Common English Bible* picks the sense of the *hilastērion* as a place of redemption and understand that Christ himself is like that mercy seat, a place where reconciliation occurred. The mercy seat was God's gift of a place for meeting, for reconciliation with God's people, calling them back into the covenant. How can we imagine Jesus as the "place" of reconciliation between God and God's creation? Trusting that we are reconciled to God in Christ, brought into covenant relationship again, ready to start over as God's own, how can we picture it?

On a personal level, all of us have known relationships that have broken down badly. Betrayal between friends, spouses, parents and children, clergy and congregants happens all around us. Every day families deeply hurt by addiction learn that real love must allow an addict to experience the consequences of her or his illness, all the while hoping and praying that the addict might turn and find a place of reconciliation with family or friends. To be reconciled, either to seek to return to relationship or to accept the offer of return to relationship, is very risky. Trust that we are already reconciled people, who have been returned to the God who loves us, makes it more possible for us to live risking the vulnerability of human reconciliation.

The beginnings of reconciliation surround us. In 1993 we all crowded around television sets to see the handshake between Yasser Arafat and Yitzhak Rabin, a first and profound step toward reconciliation in the land known as Israel. Though two years later Rabin was assassinated, the beachhead for peace had been established. In 2018 the leaders of North and South Korea came together. Their handshake is the seed of reconciliation, both real and incomplete. Here too was a place where reconciliation begins.

God lives out the dynamic of patient faithfulness, the power of patient faithfulness, in Christ. Christ's death and life become the occasion, the place, the power for human reconciliation to God. We know we are loved. We have been loved all this time. A wise chaplain once said that "all sin is fundamentally a desperate search for love." Paul proclaims at the beginning of Romans the theme that he will develop throughout the letter. God is faithful to all that God has made and all that God has promised. God's power can bring life out of nothing and has raised Jesus from death, to gather and empower us all for new and eternal covenant life in right relationship, with the one who loves us. We do not need to search any more.

SARAH S. HENRICH

Proper 4 (Sunday between May 29 and June 4 inclusive)

Matthew 7:21–29

> [21]"Not everyone who says to me, 'Lord, Lord,' will enter the kingdom of heaven, but only the one who does the will of my Father in heaven. [22]On that day many will say to me, 'Lord, Lord, did we not prophesy in your name, and cast out demons in your name, and do many deeds of power in your name?' [23]Then I will declare to them, 'I never knew you; go away from me, you evildoers.'
>
> [24]"Everyone then who hears these words of mine and acts on them will be like a wise man who built his house on rock. [25]The rain fell, the floods came, and the winds blew and beat on that house, but it did not fall, because it had been founded on rock. [26]And everyone who hears these words of mine and does not act on them will be like a foolish man who built his house on sand. [27]The rain fell, and the floods came, and the winds blew and beat against that house, and it fell—and great was its fall!"
>
> [28]Now when Jesus had finished saying these things, the crowds were astounded at his teaching, [29]for he taught them as one having authority, and not as their scribes.

Commentary 1: Connecting the Reading with Scripture

The Gospel for the day is composed of the last two segments of the Sermon on the Mount (Matt. 7:21–23 and 24–27) and Matthew's comments on the crowd's response to Jesus' teaching (vv. 28–29). The two segments serve as a warning and as encouragement to those who have heard (or read) the Sermon; the summary gives substance to the claim that Jesus taught with authority—a recurring theme in this Gospel (e.g., 9:2–8; 21:23–27; 28:18). Placing these two segments together as the conclusion to the Sermon on the Mount reveals a tension between them that leads the reader to a deeper understanding of the discipleship that is its core theme. Here the theme is expressed in the relationship between belief and practice, or as the text itself phrases it, between saying (or hearing) and doing.[1] Reflections on this issue appear throughout the New Testament, Christian history, and, in one way or another, in most religious traditions.

Matthew 7:21 and 24–26 appear to make a sharp contrast between saying and doing. The one who does "the will of my Father in heaven" will enter the Father's heavenly kingdom; those who only say, "Lord, Lord," will not. Similarly the one "who hears these words of mine and acts on them" is wise; one who hears and does not act is foolish. Approaching a sermon from this either/or perspective is easy enough. The message would be, "Do not be content with saying/hearing; you must put your words into action."

As important and timely as this may be in many situations, Matthew's version of Jesus' saying in verses 22–23, which is quite different from Luke's in 13:25–27, suggests he sees more to it. It is important to remember that many of the sayings in the Sermon on the Mount also appear in Luke, usually with slightly different phrasing and sometimes in very different settings. Attending to these differences helps the reader discern how each evangelist understands the meaning and application of a saying. Indeed, Matthew 7:22–23 is one of the most challenging of all Jesus' sayings and demands careful, thoughtful consideration in preparing to preach.

The saying begins with a reference to the judgment *on that day*, when "many will say,

---

1. The same Greek verb is translated as "does" in v. 21 and "acts on" in v. 24 and 26.

'Lord, Lord'"; but here the saying takes an unexpected turn. The *sayers* to which it is addressed are *doers.* They have prophesied, cast out demons, and done many deeds of power. They have *done* them "in the name of the Lord." They have performed just the kind of tasks that Jesus authorized for his disciples in chapter 10 when sending them out to proclaim the coming of the kingdom of heaven. So how is it that the saying concludes with Jesus' stinging words, "I never knew you; go away from me, you evildoers"? What more could be expected of them?

Reckoning with Jesus' sayings and parables about judgment in Matthew (and elsewhere) will be part of the preacher's task in addressing these questions, especially since the language in today's Gospel is so close to what we find in some of them. Both segments at the end of the Sermon on the Mount, for example, anticipate the parable of judgment in 25:1–13, first with the phrase "Lord, Lord, open to us" (25:11, echoing 7:22), and then to the Lord's reply, "Truly I tell you, I do not know you" (25:12, recalling 7:23). Similarly, the "wise" and "foolish" bridesmaids hark back to the "wise" and "foolish" builders in 7:24 and 26. Substantively this does not get us very far, since the parable speaks only to being prepared for the unexpected appearance of the bridegroom. The parable of the Separation of the Sheep and Goats in 25:31–46 perhaps gets us further, since it is concerned with doing and not doing, but in 7:21–27, the issue has nothing to do with the hungry, thirsty, sick, imprisoned, and naked that is central to the parable. In fact, the recipients of the deeds in today's Gospel are not mentioned at all. The focus, rather, is entirely on those who perform the deeds. This takes us back to the placement of the segments at the end of the Sermon on the Mount to find clues to understanding Matthew's use of them.

One of these clues is the way Matthew pairs "the will of my Father in heaven" in the first segment (7:11, 21) and "these words of mine" (vv. 24, 26) in the second, with both defining what one should do or act on. For Matthew, doing the Father's will is paramount, though its specific content is rarely specified. It figures in the prayer Jesus teaches his disciples (6:10); here at the conclusion of the Sermon on the Mount (7:21); in Jesus' identification of the disciples as his family because they do "the will of my Father" (12:49–50); in his statement to the disciples that their Father's will is that none of the "little ones should be lost" (18:14); in the parable of the Two Sons (21:28–32), which compares saying and doing; and climactically, three times in Jesus' prayer in Gethsemane (26:36–46).[2]

In the first instance, Jesus' "words" in 7:24 refer to the Sermon on the Mount, which he has just concluded. Matthew's emphasis on Jesus as an authoritative teacher throughout this Gospel demonstrates that he is the one whose words show not only *what* the will of the Father is but also *how* to fulfill it. The Sermon on the Mount is Matthew's showcase for both. This is especially clear in the series of sayings that explain what Jesus means when he says that *doing* and *teaching* the law is what makes one "great in the kingdom of heaven" (5:19–48). Each of these sayings begin with "You have heard it said . . . , but I say to you . . ." and intensifies the commandment cited. Another series of sayings follows, demonstrating that almsgiving, prayer, and fasting are to be carried out in secrecy (6:1–18), since otherwise they become acts of hypocrisy in the quest for public reward, which in Matthew is as much of (if not more of) a danger for disciples as it is for the scribes and Pharisees. Thus, like the rest of the Sermon on the Mount, the concluding segments of the sermon summarize true discipleship as requiring both saying and doing *from one's heart*, which for Matthew is the essence of the law and the prophets.

The other lectionary readings for the day echo the Gospel's concern with judgment, explicitly in the story of the flood in Genesis and the "blessing and curse" in Deuteronomy. Though the lesson from Romans is an example of Paul's wrestling with "faith" and "works," his description of "spiritual worship" in 12:1–15:13 echoes many of the themes in the Sermon on the Mount, notably in the summing up of the

---

2. Matthew's account of Jesus' baptism and the temptation in the wilderness also demonstrates his obedience to God's will (3:13–4:11), though the phrase itself does not appear.

law in the commandment to "love your neighbor as yourself" (Rom. 13:9). James 1:22–2:26 and 3:13–4:17 belong to the same line of interpretation, as does Luke 10:25–42, which uses the parable of the Good Samaritan and Mary's "better part" to illustrate the commandments to love God and one's neighbor.

Christians continue to wrestle with balancing belief and practice, faith and works, contemplation and activism. The Gospel for the day summarizes Matthew's understanding of Jesus' teaching in the Sermon on the Mount, which is the rock on which the wise will build.

OLIVER LARRY YARBROUGH

Commentary 2: Connecting the Reading with the World

This passage at the end of the Sermon on the Mount includes some of the most challenging teaching in the New Testament. It relates a scenario in which those who are earnest in their desire to follow Jesus learn that they have badly missed the mark. The lesson reminds the church to think carefully about what it means to respond to Jesus' teaching.

Early in the Sermon, Jesus famously declares, "For I tell you, unless your righteousness exceeds that of the scribes and Pharisees, you will never enter the kingdom of heaven" (Matt. 5:20). The same austere tone reappears here in Matthew 7:21–23 and 24–27, the concluding words of Jesus' Sermon. Matthew 7:21–29 follows on the heels of 7:13–20, which cautions his hearers to understand that following Jesus' teaching is difficult (vv. 13–14). Moreover, Jesus notes that false prophets will appear, leaving his hearers to judge persons by their fruit rather than by their words (vv. 15–20).

Following this teaching, the focus then turns from being wary of those who would deceive, to the more difficult problem of self-deception. Here Matthew raises critical questions that those who seek to follow in the way of Jesus must consider. Matthew 7:21–23 takes aim not at those who would oppose Jesus, but those very ones who fully understand themselves to be aligned with his teaching. The lesson is a hard, but important, one for the church today. Indeed, a sermon on the topic of self-deception, in terms of both the individual and the church community, would provide an apt and timely lesson.

Matthew 7:21–23 imagines the awful predicament of those who, having performed pious demonstrations of great power in the name of Jesus, are denied inclusion in the kingdom of heaven. Note that their claim that they prophesied, cast out demons, and performed many deeds of power goes unchallenged. The problem is not that they are making false claims or telling tall tales. The problem is that Jesus identifies them as ones who have not done "the will of my Father in heaven" (v. 21).

Many churches say the Lord's Prayer (6:9–13) fairly regularly, if not every Sunday. In speaking the prayer, the congregation affirms its central plea, "Your kingdom come, your will be done, on earth as it is in heaven" (v. 10). Not two distinct supplications, but one, the prayer confirms that the kingdom of heaven on earth is the realization of God's vision for the world. Matthew includes this model prayer, concise and profound in its clarity, as a clear contrast to the verbose prayers of the Gentiles, which are described as "empty phrases" aiming to be heard (6:7).

When congregations utter the prayer that Jesus taught his disciples to pray, they are making Jesus' vision of the way of God their own—an amazing feat that the congregation would do well to be reminded of. What Jesus' final and cautionary teaching in the Sermon on the Mount illustrates is that living in accordance with the kingdom of heaven is about following God's will for the world, as embodied and demonstrated by Jesus. It is not about a piety concerned with grand displays and self-promotion, a fitting topic for discussion at the pulpit. Thus Matthew warns his readers that it is a mistake and an act of self-deception to confuse the will of God with performing acts of power, no matter how benevolent they may be (7:21). So the text encourages us carefully to examine how power and status influence our actions, even those we deem beneficial and selfless.

Rather than ending the Sermon on the Mount with a note of warning, Jesus offers his hearers a closing word of exhortation to help discern the will of God. The story of the wise person who builds a house on rock and the foolish person who builds a house on sand illustrates two responses to Jesus' teaching. The one who both hears Jesus' teaching and acts on it is like the one who builds on a rock foundation. The one who hears Jesus' teaching and fails to act is like the one who builds on sand. Thus Matthew places high value on human response to Jesus' teaching. Deeds do matter, and receptivity that does not lead to response is folly. The response that Matthew calls his readers to is an alignment of their whole person, in word and deed, with Jesus' vision of the kingdom of heaven.

Matthew 7:21–23 may at first strike readers as a harsh lesson, but when the passage is read in the context of the Gospel's understanding of the kingdom of heaven, it takes on new meaning. While the persons in the story who say, "Lord, Lord," are revealed to be mistaken in their expectations, the reader who looks closely at the assumptions that undergird those expectations may find a more welcome word. Even as the story undermines the false equivalence of deeds of power with the doing of God's will, it also overturns the assumption that in order to be aligned with God's purposes, churches must enact visible and dramatic change, or initiate headline-catching ministries. For the transformation to which Matthew's Gospel points does not depend on great displays of power or public acclaim. The persons in Jesus' illustration who said, "Lord, Lord," mistakenly assumed that it did.

The Sermon on the Mount (Matt. 5:3–7:27) includes a good deal of teaching that pertains to right practice. It also instructs Jesus' followers in the way of wisdom, that is, in the attitudes and perspectives that are distinctive to the kingdom of heaven. Together, Jesus' instruction in the Sermon on the Mount calls for disciples to live out and enact the vision of discipleship and community that constitutes the way of God. In direct contrast to our publicity-driven culture, Jesus' teaching directs the reader to contemplate acts of forgiveness, compassion, and righteousness that may or may not generate great attention.

As churches throughout the world seek to respond in faith to the massive changes brought about by technology, migration, shifting geopolitics and world markets, religious and cultural pluralism, climate change, global inequities, and more, it is easy to be overwhelmed. Furthermore, as many American congregations continue to shrink in size, it is easy to also feel irrelevant and to start looking anxiously for ways to show that church matters. In these situations, Jesus' words remind us that the gospel calls the church only to be faithful to God's vision for the world, and the substance of what that can look like is made known through Jesus' teaching, ministry, and person.

The crux of Jesus' teaching is made especially clear in Matthew 5:43–45, the capstone passage in the longer unit that begins in 5:21. Here Jesus says, "You have heard that it was said, 'You shall love your neighbor and hate your enemy.' But I say to you, Love your enemies and pray for those who persecute you. . . . for [God] makes his sun rise on the evil and on the good, and sends rain on the righteous and on the unrighteous." In order to live as children of the God in whose image we are made, we are to reflect the divine compassion and love for all that is demonstrated in our very midst. For it is clearly inarguable that the sun does shine and the rain does fall on everyone. Churches seeking to live rightly need not follow the path of those who cried out, "Lord, Lord." Rather, they are to listen carefully to Jesus' teaching and align themselves, in their being and doing, with the way of God that Jesus reveals.

MARY F. FOSKETT

Proper 5 (Sunday between June 5 and June 11 inclusive)

Hosea 5:15–6:6 and Genesis 12:1–9
Psalm 50:7–15 and Psalm 33:1–12
Romans 4:13–25
Matthew 9:9–13, 18–26

Hosea 5:15–6:6

⁵:¹⁵I will return again to my place
   until they acknowledge their guilt and seek my face.
   In their distress they will beg my favor:

⁶:¹"Come, let us return to the LORD;
   for it is he who has torn, and he will heal us;
   he has struck down, and he will bind us up.
²After two days he will revive us;
   on the third day he will raise us up,
   that we may live before him.
³Let us know, let us press on to know the LORD;
   his appearing is as sure as the dawn;
he will come to us like the showers,
   like the spring rains that water the earth."

⁴What shall I do with you, O Ephraim?
   What shall I do with you, O Judah?
Your love is like a morning cloud,
   like the dew that goes away early.
⁵Therefore I have hewn them by the prophets,
   I have killed them by the words of my mouth,
   and my judgment goes forth as the light.
⁶For I desire steadfast love and not sacrifice,
   the knowledge of God rather than burnt offerings.

Genesis 12:1–9

¹Now the LORD said to Abram, "Go from your country and your kindred and your father's house to the land that I will show you. ²I will make of you a great nation, and I will bless you, and make your name great, so that you will be a blessing. ³I will bless those who bless you, and the one who curses you I will curse; and in you all the families of the earth shall be blessed."
⁴So Abram went, as the LORD had told him; and Lot went with him. Abram was seventy-five years old when he departed from Haran. ⁵Abram took his wife Sarai and his brother's son Lot, and all the possessions that they had gathered, and the persons whom they had acquired in Haran; and they set forth to go to the land of Canaan. When they had come to the land of Canaan, ⁶Abram passed through the land to the place at Shechem, to the oak of Moreh. At that time the Canaanites were in the land. ⁷Then the LORD appeared to Abram, and said, "To your offspring

I will give this land." So he built there an altar to the LORD, who had appeared to him. [8]From there he moved on to the hill country on the east of Bethel, and pitched his tent, with Bethel on the west and Ai on the east; and there he built an altar to the LORD and invoked the name of the LORD. [9]And Abram journeyed on by stages toward the Negeb.

Commentary 1: Connecting the Reading with Scripture

The biblical passages for this Sunday all stress a troubling binarism: law versus faith. Abraham, whose story begins in Genesis 12:1–9, is reimagined as the father of faith in Romans 4:13–25; while Hosea 5:15–6:6; Psalm 50:7–15; and Matthew 9:9–13, 18–26 all declare God's disregard for empty sacrifices or cultic actions. These passages, when taken as a whole, place faith or belief in contradistinction to actions, such as sacrifices or following God's commandments (i.e., the Law). This binarism, which attempts to legitimize Christianity by envisioning it as the religion of faith while simultaneously disparaging and belittling Judaism by stereotyping it as the religion of the Law, is undoubtedly supersessionist. Hence, care must be taken to examine the larger literary context from which these texts were excerpted so as to move beyond these simplistic dichotomies.

It seems odd to declare Abram, who is later called Abraham, the model of faith (see Rom. 4), as the story about this figure in Genesis says frustratingly little about his faith or beliefs. Rather, his story begins with a concrete act: Abraham is suddenly called by God to leave his country, birthplace, and father's house—that is, to immigrate—to an unnamed land that God promises will be shown to him (Gen. 12:1). In an attempt to explain why God calls Abraham so abruptly and without much introduction, midrashic and postbiblical ancient texts transform Abraham into the first anti-idolatrous monotheist. In so doing, ancient interpreters read faith and belief into the patriarch's actions. Abraham's faith is therefore explained and understood by what he did (Heb. 11:8).

Abraham's call begins a section called the patriarchal narratives (Gen. 12–50), which encompass the stories about Israel's first patriarchs, namely, Abraham, Isaac, and Jacob. Despite this paternal designation, the mothers who give birth to the descendants of these patriarchs—the matriarchs—play a crucial, though underappreciated role. Indeed, when Abraham gets the divine call to move, his wife Sarai (who will later be renamed Sarah) goes along with him. As a senior woman with no heir, this journey was riskier and more dangerous for her than for Abraham. Unable to inherit, she would have been left destitute or perhaps even abandoned if her husband were to die en route. In a context with no electricity or police force, one's family, clan, and tribe were the main sources of protection, and being away from family was even more dangerous for a woman.

The history of God's chosen nation, Israel, is marked by such dangerous journeys and movements, both toward and away from the land promised by God. The actions of Abraham and Sarah, the first to undertake this journey, will repeatedly be emulated by their descendants, such as Jacob, Joseph, and the Israelites under the leadership of Moses. So imbued is the history of Israel with this back-and-forth movement to and from the promised land that this movement would take on ever larger symbolic significance. Movements away from the promised land would be aligned with death and exile, while those oriented toward it would be associated with restoration, resurrection, and revival.

Considering the dangers, God promises Abraham a reward for his journey. God declares that those who bless Abraham will be blessed and those who curse him will be cursed, and that by Abraham "all the families of the earth shall bless themselves" (Gen. 12:3). Though this promise of extended blessing later has been interpreted to include the Gentile Christians, it is more likely that it speaks to the significance of Abraham in that region and at that time. Abraham, through his three wives—Sarah, Hagar, and Keturah (Gen. 25)—will be designated as the forefather of various peoples in the ancient Near East. Bespeaking Abraham's lingering influence, the three Abrahamic monotheisms—Judaism, Christianity, and Islam—will all claim descent from this figure.

Abraham remains relevant and important; his story provides multiple themes or ideas that may be of use to the modern preacher. First is the favorable view of migration, understood as conduits through which God's promises and blessings are made manifest. God blesses Abraham precisely because he and his family are willing to immigrate. Migrants, therefore, seem to be elevated in the theological world of the Bible. Second, though rarely remarked upon, it is telling that God calls on two senior citizens (12:4) to undertake the first journey toward the promised land. As the story indicates, no one is ever too old or too anything to receive God's call. Lastly, this narrative shows us that it is not simply belief or faith, but following God's commandments, that is of true importance. Though Abraham is remembered for his faith, his faith inextricably entails action.

This emphasis on action is evident in Hosea 5:15–6:6 as well. Unlike in Genesis, which describes Abraham's faithful deed, Hosea is about the opposite: misdeeds and God's response to them. Hosea, an eighth-century prophet, prophesied in the northern kingdom of Israel (sometimes called the North, Samaria, or, as in this passage, Ephraim, after the main tribe of the North) before its destruction by Assyria in 722 BCE. In the passage for this Sunday, Hosea—again utilizing the exile and return motif—portrays God as patiently waiting for the return of God's chosen people, Israel, whose love is fleeting like dew (Hos. 5:15–6:4). Hosea 6:1–3 describes in beautiful and haunting language how Israel, imagined as a beaten and sick person, will assuredly return to God, who will heal them, revive them, and take care of them.

By extracting this particular portion, however, the lectionary assignments obscure the more challenging prophecies in this book. In stark contrast to the comforting tone of Hosea 6, the previous chapters (Hos. 4–5) detail Israel's misdeeds: "There is no faithfulness or loyalty, and no knowledge of God in the land. Swearing, lying, and murder, and stealing and adultery break out; bloodshed follows bloodshed" (4:1–2). The people are also idolatrous and worship other gods. Israel is so saturated with transgressions that even the religious leadership—the priests and prophets—are complicit (vv. 5–6). Because of all this, "the land mourns, and all who live in it languish; together with the wild animals and the birds of the air, even the fish of the sea are perishing" (v. 3). God therefore will crush and oppress the nation, and make it desolate (5:9, 11).

It is in light of these severe charges that we can now understand God's declaration: "For I desire steadfast love and not sacrifice, the knowledge of God rather than burnt offerings" (6:6). This verse has been deliberately misread as God disparaging action, especially ritual action, and elevating belief and right emotions. However, as Hosea's list of charges clearly shows, actions reflect belief; hence, when God demands steadfast love and knowledge, God is calling for right and ethical action. It is not actions per se but empty actions that are declared to be displeasing to God. In essence, God is saying, What use is going to church every Sunday if you cheat, lie, and rob people during the week?

The sins Hosea charges Israel of committing are eerily reminiscent of what we see today. So the plainest reading of Hosea compels us to reflect upon the ways in which our love and faith toward God, as made manifest through our actions, have been fleeting and empty. Especially convicting is Hosea's statement that the natural world is damaged by and reflects the sins done by humans (4:1–3). Hence, the story of Abraham, despite his being known as the father of faith, and Hosea's damning prophecies underscore how it is through our behavior and deeds that we come to "know the LORD" (6:3).

SONG-MI SUZIE PARK

Commentary 2: Connecting the Reading with the World

The texts from Hosea and Genesis share themes about place and displacement. These are concepts of considerable attention and urgency in our world today. A sermon on these texts could make connections to the ideas of home, work, identity, communication, refugees, and consumerism, as well as the nature of change and the "place to stand" in a world of shifting values. Placed alongside our cultural preoccupations, these texts offer a critique and a promise to people of faith about where to look and whom to trust. Displacement is real in our world, in individual lives, and in the church in its current cultural setting. These texts speak with power and tenderness to each of these connections.

According to a recent report of the United Nations High Commissioner for Refugees, there are 70.8 million forcibly displaced people worldwide, and 37,000 men, women, and children a day are forced to flee their homes because of conflict or persecution.[1] Any treatment of displacement needs to acknowledge the tragedy being lived in real life by people for whom loss of home is not a metaphor. The circumstances in Hosea and Genesis are probably not conflict or persecution, but the voice of the living God, who declares in Hosea 5:15, "I will return again to my place," until the Israelites acknowledge their guilt and seek the face of God again. In Hosea, it is God who feels displaced by the sins of Israel. In Genesis, God calls on the great Israelite patriarch to displace himself so that God can use Abraham to bless the entire world (Gen. 12:3): "Go from your place [country] and your kindred . . . to the land that I will show you" (12:1). Whether by force or by call, how do we understand the gift of place and the loss of place? Moreover, how should the people of God react to issues of immigration and migration, and those who are either called or compelled to mimic our great ancestor, Abraham?

A lack of permanence marks our time. Jobs are fleeting. Relationships can be transactional. We are told that truth is negotiable. Whole nations and groups are treated as disposable. It is into this state of impermanence that the voice of God calls for return to God and movement to a new place of meaning and purpose. A sermon on these texts could explore how out of sync many of us are to this voice of call, return, and sending. How do we learn to discern the voice and call of the living God?

The current cultural moment seems to say that nothing is permanent, so a voice we listen to today may not be one that we need to pay attention to tomorrow. Perhaps nothing shows this more clearly than the contemporary funeral, where tradition and custom are jettisoned to make the service "personal" by all manner of customization. The result too often is a funeral observance that is trivial ("she never knew a stranger") or shallow ("he visited seventy-three countries in his lifetime"). Rather than call on the voice of God to speak into the moment a word of permanence—a word of grace and presence and resurrection—we get a smorgasbord of conventional wisdom that does little to comfort or lift our spirits. How do we trust God's voice? How do we trust that God's voice is the one nonnegotiable voice in our lives?

This sense of impermanence is aggravated by feelings of deep loneliness and isolation in our digitally connected culture. A recent survey conducted by the health care company Cigna reports Americans facing increasingly alarming rates of loneliness.[2] Loneliness, moreover, is toxic and deadly, having the same effect as smoking fifteen cigarettes a day. Yet Hosea's call to "return again to my place" (Hos. 5:15) and the desire "for steadfast love and . . . the knowledge of God" (6:6) depend on a deep connection to God. Similarly, in contrast to isolation, Abram/Abraham's call to go from his known world to a world of purpose and meaning depends on deep trust. What these texts show is that the experience of God's steadfast love and the openness to God's wondrous doings in our lives is the connection offered to a disconnected world. This

---

1. United Nations High Commissioner for Refugees, *Global Trends: Forced Displacement in 2018* (New York: UNHCR, 2018), 2.
2. "Loneliness at Epidemic Levels in America," Cigna, https://www.cigna.com/about-us/newsroom/studies-and-reports/loneliness-epidemic-america.

love and trust is the "place" in a world of severe isolation; it is a permanence our souls seek in a world of seeming impermanence. These texts provide fertile ground to explore these avenues.

In speaking about displacement, the transition of the church from its places of cultural influence and endorsement provides fresh ground for reflection—and proclamation of good news—with these texts. A recent Lilly Endowment project asserted, "When researchers asked each interviewee what they want or hope to hear about God in the sermon, one thing became clear immediately. People are not hearing all they want to know about God from the pulpit."[3] How do we live faithfully in a time of displacement, with God as our one "true place" to provide hope and grounding? How should we too behave like Abram, who willingly heeds God's call to go to a new place, while also acknowledging with honesty that this call for movement is hard and scary? Whatever direction a sermon drawn from these texts takes, the world is thirsty for a clear-throated, openhearted affirmation of the steadfast love and trustworthy call of God.

This affirmation is not "everything is fine, so go your way." God's voice—this holy voice of foundation and permanence—always challenges and confronts as it move us to a new place. That is the point: God is our stability, not a program for renewal or a new, shiny idea. How do we learn, in our fear and grief, to trust God through and through?

Anne Lamott once took her then-two-year-old son to Lake Tahoe, where they rented a condominium by the lake. She put the toddler in his playpen in the pitch dark and went to do some work. A few minutes later she heard knocking from inside the room. Knowing he'd crawled out of his playpen she went to get him, but at the door, she found he'd locked it. He had somehow managed to push the little button on the doorknob. After a moment, it became clear to him that his mother could not open the door, and panic set in. He began sobbing. So his mother ran around like crazy trying everything possible, jiggling the lock and leaving messages for help.

There, in this dark, locked room was this terrified little child. Finally she did the only thing she could: slide her fingers under the door, where there were a few centimeters of space. She kept telling him over and over to bend down and find her fingers. Somehow he did. So they stayed like that for a really long time, connected on the floor, him holding her fingers in the dark—slowly feeling connected, feeling her love, feeling her presence and her care.

In this world of displacement, grace ultimately may well feel like being a two-year-old in the dark, and God is our mother and we are not old enough to speak cogent phrases yet, even in the midst of such panic. She could break down the door if that struck her as being the best way, but instead, by grace, I can just hold onto her fingers under the door.[4]

MARK RAMSEY

---

3. Quoted in Mary Alice Mulligan and Ronald J. Allen, *Make the Word Come Alive: Lessons from Laity* (St. Louis: Chalice Press, 2005), 5.
4. Anne Lamott, *Operating Instructions* (New York: Pantheon, 1993), 88–89.

Proper 5 (Sunday between June 5 and June 11 inclusive)

Psalm 50:7–15

[7]"Hear, O my people, and I will speak,
    O Israel, I will testify against you.
    I am God, your God.
[8]Not for your sacrifices do I rebuke you;
    your burnt offerings are continually before me.
[9]I will not accept a bull from your house,
    or goats from your folds.
[10]For every wild animal of the forest is mine,
    the cattle on a thousand hills.
[11]I know all the birds of the air,
    and all that moves in the field is mine.

[12]"If I were hungry, I would not tell you,
    for the world and all that is in it is mine.
[13]Do I eat the flesh of bulls,
    or drink the blood of goats?
[14]Offer to God a sacrifice of thanksgiving,
    and pay your vows to the Most High.
[15]Call on me in the day of trouble;
    I will deliver you, and you shall glorify me."

Psalm 33:1–12

[1]Rejoice in the LORD, O you righteous.
    Praise befits the upright.
[2]Praise the LORD with the lyre;
    make melody to him with the harp of ten strings.
[3]Sing to him a new song;
    play skillfully on the strings, with loud shouts.

[4]For the word of the LORD is upright,
    and all his work is done in faithfulness.
[5]He loves righteousness and justice;
    the earth is full of the steadfast love of the LORD.

[6]By the word of the LORD the heavens were made,
    and all their host by the breath of his mouth.
[7]He gathered the waters of the sea as in a bottle;
    he put the deeps in storehouses.

[8]Let all the earth fear the LORD;
    let all the inhabitants of the world stand in awe of him.
[9]For he spoke, and it came to be;
    he commanded, and it stood firm.

[10]The LORD brings the counsel of the nations to nothing;
    he frustrates the plans of the peoples.

> [11]The counsel of the LORD stands forever,
>   the thoughts of his heart to all generations.
> [12]Happy is the nation whose God is the LORD,
>   the people whom he has chosen as his heritage.

Connecting the Psalm with Scripture and Worship

Psalm 50:7–15. Psalm 50 is paired with a portion of the scroll of Hosea in which God speaks both as the divine self and for the people. God pines for the beloved nation whose love is fickle and short-lived. "Love me. Know me," God cries. At the same time, God is confident the people will turn . . . and return. They will discover they are alone and in need of help. They will be chastened and remember God's loyalty and promise of rescue. The people's love evaporates, again and again, quickly, like the dew before the rising sun each morning. Yet God is faithful as the sun, as reliable as the arrival of the rains of spring. The theology is as familiar as the metaphors—capricious people, steadfast God—yet our ecological crisis makes the nature imagery crackle. So too in the psalm, although the psalmist's theology and imagery are in tension with those of the prophet. Here, God is content and self-sufficient: "the world and all that is in it is mine" (Ps. 50:12). If I am hungry, I have plenty to consume; I do not need your sacrifices, God asserts. The people, here, are faithful, not fickle: "your burnt offerings are continually before me" (v. 8). The problem is not practice but attitude. All God wants is a thank-you: sacrifice your sense of independence, call on me when you are perplexed, and when I deliver you, tell of my glory.

If one is contemplating preaching on Hosea, it seems important to note the alternative theological commitments of the psalmist. How does Hosea's abandoned lover God jibe with the psalmist's all-powerful creator who stands ready to deliver? If the preacher chooses this path, mention of the psalm verses that do not appear in the lectionary selection might also be warranted; if there are many faithfully fulfilling the commandments, there are also some who deserve divine rebuke, since they lay claim to the covenant but violate its spirit (vv. 16–21). Yet, to these too, at least to those who are ready to set out once again on "the right way," this God is ready to show salvation (vv. 22–23).

A second homiletical choice would be to consider nature, which figures centrally in both the first reading and the psalm. As mentioned above, Hosea equates divine steadfastness with the constancy of cosmic rhythms, and erratic human devotion with morning mist. How does our understanding of the fragility and complexity of ecological and cosmic phenomena illuminate such metaphors today? Further, the prophetic passage ends with burnt offerings, lifeless animal bodies. The psalmist widens the lens to focus on both domestic and untamed species, on birds, and on blood. God has no need of such offerings. Yet mass extinction reigns.

Ken Stone, known for his rereading of Hebrew Bible texts in light of gender and sexuality, now guides us in thinking about the relation of God, sacred texts, and both human and other-than-human animals in his work, *Reading the Hebrew Bible with Animal Studies*.[1] Perhaps this day provides space for contemplation of the flesh and blood that God seems content to do without, but with which our ancestors transacted their lives of faith.

Liturgically, a paraphrase of Psalm 50 might strengthen a call to confession:

> Our God testifies against us: you sacrifice surrogates
>   as you maintain your self-deceptions.
> Your sacrifice of praise is what I desire.
> Call upon me; I will deliver.
> Keep your vows to me and glorify your name.

---

1. See Ken Stone, *Reading the Hebrew Bible with Animal Studies* (Stanford, CA: Stanford University Press, 2017).

Trusting in divine mercy, let us confess
our missteps in silence,
that we might return to paths of
righteousness.

Psalm 33:1–12. The first half of Psalm 33 is paired with a story of Abram, Sarai, and Lot from Genesis 12, which in turn is chosen to illuminate the epistle lection. The psalm covers much ground in twelve verses: a call to praise, a rehearsal of God's attributes, a revisiting of the creation story, and a warning to the nations. It provides both a larger frame into which the emigration of Abram, Sarai, and Lot fits and a sense of why Abram so decisively leaves all he knows for a promise.

Abram is first of the nation that God has chosen as heritage, but his is not the beginning of the story. Nor is it the end. This God chooses Israel—as Abram's descendants will be known—but is concerned with the entire cosmos. This God created the heavens and its hosts, the earth and its seas and all its creatures. So too the love of this God fills, animates, guides, and entices all that lives toward righteousness, toward justice. This God judges all the nations. Abram—and Sarai and Lot—are key, but this is just one episode in the grand story of God's dealing with all that was made, all that was declared, together, "very good."

"Now the LORD said, 'Go.' . . . So Abram went" (Gen. 12:1, 4), without objection or reluctance, from country and kindred, into the unknown. As Paul puts it, "Hoping against hope, [Abram] believed he would become 'the father of many nations,'" since he was "fully convinced that God was able to do what [God] had promised" (Rom. 4:18, 21). Whence Abram's conviction? All we know of Abram is his lineage, the names of his brothers, the relations of his wife and nephew, and that his father moved from Ur to Haran (Gen. 11:26–32). There is no mention of his knowledge of or relation to this God. God has scattered the peoples who were cooperating to build a tower; among whom is Shem, Abram's ancestor. This is all we know. This is Paul's point: Abram simply steps out on faith and so is reckoned righteous.

Finally, these texts reveal complications. Abram, Sarai, and Lot leave home with more than material possessions and livestock; they also lead away "the persons whom they had acquired in Haran" (12:5). The first family is a slaveholding one. Furthermore, we know the land to which they are sent, which is promised as inheritance, is already occupied. Possession and dispossession haunt the narrative. Will the nation that is the offspring of these migrants be happy, or will they face frustration? Will their counsel, their policies, come to nothing?

Liturgically, a reordered paraphrase of the psalm may serve as a call to worship:

Reader 1: Let all the earth fear the Lord; let all the inhabitants of the world stand in awe. For the Lord spoke, and it came to be; our God commanded, and it stood firm.

Reader 2: Sing to our God a new song; play skillfully on the strings, with loud shouts.

Reader 1: For the word of the Lord is upright, and all his work is done in faithfulness. Our God loves righteousness and justice; the earth is full of God's steadfast love.

Reader 2: Praise the Lord with the lyre; make melody to our God with the harp of ten strings.

Reader 1: The Lord brings the counsel of the nations to nothing; he frustrates the plans of the peoples. The counsel of the Lord stands forever, the thoughts of his heart to all generations.

Reader 2: Happy are we whose God is the Lord! We rejoice! We sing praise! Let us worship!

W. SCOTT HALDEMAN

Proper 5 (Sunday between June 5 and June 11 inclusive)

Romans 4:13–25

¹³For the promise that he would inherit the world did not come to Abraham or to his descendants through the law but through the righteousness of faith. ¹⁴If it is the adherents of the law who are to be the heirs, faith is null and the promise is void. ¹⁵For the law brings wrath; but where there is no law, neither is there violation.

¹⁶For this reason it depends on faith, in order that the promise may rest on grace and be guaranteed to all his descendants, not only to the adherents of the law but also to those who share the faith of Abraham (for he is the father of all of us, ¹⁷as it is written, "I have made you the father of many nations")—in the presence of the God in whom he believed, who gives life to the dead and calls into existence the things that do not exist. ¹⁸Hoping against hope, he believed that he would become "the father of many nations," according to what was said, "So numerous shall your descendants be." ¹⁹He did not weaken in faith when he considered his own body, which was already as good as dead (for he was about a hundred years old), or when he considered the barrenness of Sarah's womb. ²⁰No distrust made him waver concerning the promise of God, but he grew strong in his faith as he gave glory to God, ²¹being fully convinced that God was able to do what he had promised. ²²Therefore his faith "was reckoned to him as righteousness." ²³Now the words, "it was reckoned to him," were written not for his sake alone, ²⁴but for ours also. It will be reckoned to us who believe in him who raised Jesus our Lord from the dead, ²⁵who was handed over to death for our trespasses and was raised for our justification.

Commentary 1: Connecting the Reading with Scripture

Romans 4:13–25 has immediate connections to Israel's Scriptures as the apostle Paul invokes the memory of Israel's patriarch, Abraham. According to Paul, Abraham serves as an exemplar of faith par excellence for the Jesus movement, even among non-Jews to whom Paul has been preaching the "good news about Jesus the Christ [the Messiah]." In the first five chapters of Paul's Letter to the Roman believers, faith is key, because without it we cannot experience God's "righteousness," in Greek *dikaiosynē*, also translated "justice." The goal of God's engagement with humanity is that we become "righteous" and "just" like God; faith initiates that journey.

Connections to the Letter to the Romans. Earlier in this letter, Paul expounds on the reality of sin among all, whether Gentile or Jew (Rom. 1:18–2:16). As a result, all humanity needs divine intervention to secure righteousness, because rules and regulations ("law") lack the power to do so (2:17–3:31), "for all have sinned and fall short of the glory of God" (3:23). In Romans 4:1–12, Abraham's story becomes the background for discussing a righteousness made possible by God and faith in God, and not mere human effort ("law"). In Romans 4:13–25, the noun "promise" (*epangelia*) and its verb form appear four times in order to make the simple point that God made a promise (in this case to Abraham) and kept it, albeit ultimately in the person and work of Christ Jesus.

Connections in Romans 4:13–25. The components of God's "promise" to Abraham and to all humanity include "inheritance" of "the world" and reward beyond this world. For Abraham and his "descendants" (literally "seed," *spermati*), the promise is fulfilled not through *nomos* ("law") but through the power of righteousness-making faith. Thus, trust in God makes possible the reality of righteousness and justice, not only for Abraham and his immediate descendants, but for all of humanity, argues Paul.

By contrast, continues Paul, if only being "an adherent of the law" makes one an "heir" of God's promises, faith becomes useless. Paul believes that would contradict the larger witness of Israel's Scriptures regarding the centrality of faith, belief, and trust. Paul has stated in Romans 1–4 that "law" by itself cannot bring about fulfillment of divine promise. Indeed, "law brings wrath" (judgment), because without law we would not be aware of what is wrong and how it is punished (4:15). In contrast, promise can be fulfilled only by belief and trust in the God who fulfills divine promises (v. 16a). Hence, God's promises reflect the grace of God, that is, God's generosity and love for humanity. Faith, therefore, responds to the positive promises of God toward all of humanity. Abraham becomes the exemplar of this dynamic interaction (the "father of us all" [v. 16b]) between promise, faith, and fulfillment, which is for all, Jew and Gentile inclusive.

Connections to Genesis. As happened with Abraham in the book of Genesis, Paul tells us, it is easy to lose faith in a promise when time and physical weariness set in. Paul interprets the narratives about Abraham and Sarah and their difficulty in having children at such advanced ages (Gen. 17:15–22) as instructive for the need to have ongoing faith in the face of evidence to the contrary. Instead of *apistia* (disbelief), Abraham had faith (*pistis*), "fully convinced that God was able to do what [God] had promised" (Rom. 4:21). Abraham believed by "hoping against hope" (v. 18). Thus, concludes Paul, because Abraham and Sarah eventually, in the midst of faithfulness, did have children and descendants, so also even Gentiles would have access to God's promise of righteousness for all, as long as there is patient faith and belief. Such faith in a promise ensured righteousness/justice for all.

A "Logical" Connection. Finally, Paul writes about the "reckoning" or "logic" that comes from believing in God's promises (4:22–25). The "logic" (the root word for "reckoning" is *logos*) of faith is that trusting in the God who fulfills promises leads to one's designation as a "righteous" one. Abraham's faith led, logically in God's reckoning, to his righteousness (*dikaiosynē*). Such reckoning works not only for Abraham, "the father of faith," but for all who believe similarly in the promises of God. The previous experiences of the people Israel, beginning with Abraham, foreshadowed Paul's current day and that of future generations of the faithful: "it will be reckoned to us who believe in [God] who raised Jesus our Lord from the dead," that is, the one "who was handed over to death" because of our own "trespasses."

Resurrection is the final connection to faith, Paul asserts at the end of his argument in Romans 4. The "Lord," Jesus, "was raised" from among "the dead" by God in whom he, and we, put our trust (vv. 24–25). Paul emphasizes that it was God who raised Jesus from the dead to make him "our Lord." The God of Abraham, who promised justification for all, that is, a universal declaration of righteousness based on faith, makes this declaration through a death and through the resurrection from death of that one, the Messiah Jesus, who ultimately becomes "Lord." Justification, the act of being declared righteous and just, lies at the heart of God's promises to humanity.

Connections to Paul Elsewhere. In the larger context of Pauline writings, only in Galatians does Paul describe "justification" more extensively than Romans. There the key passage is Galatians 2:15–21, including these definitive words on justification: "And we have come to believe in Christ Jesus, so that we might be justified by faith in Christ, and not by doing the works of the law, because no one will be justified by the works of the law." This echoes the opening words of Romans 4:13–25: "For the promise that he would inherit the world did not come to Abraham or to his descendants through the law but through the righteousness of faith" (4:13). In both texts, "law" is seen as powerless to effect change in people's lives, but rather serves to point out our shortcomings (cf. Gal. 3:19, 24). Earlier in Romans 4, Paul points out that

The Strangeness of Christ

Jesus is by no means merely an ecclesiastical figure. Sometimes he is even more popular outside the Church than inside it. But, however popular he is, what is immediately evident—when we look at the real Jesus—is his strangeness. And historical analysis, however uncongenial, arduous or even superficial it may seem to some, can help to ensure that this strangeness will not be concealed: that he is not simply fitted into our personal or social requirements, habits, wishful thinking, cherished ideas, that he is not appropriated into the world outlook, moral theories, legal opinions, of Church authorities or theologians, not played down in the Church's rites, creeds and feasts. The all-important point is to let Jesus speak without restriction, whether this is congenial or not. Only in this way can he himself come closer to us in his strangeness. Obviously this does not mean the mechanical repetition of his words, the recital of as many biblical texts as possible, preferably in a long-familiar translation. Nevertheless an interpretation that is relevant in the proper sense of the word is possible only at a certain distance from him. Strictly speaking, I must at the same time keep at a distance from myself, from my own thoughts, ideas, valuations and expectations. Only when it becomes clear what he himself wanted, what hopes he brought for the people of his own time, can it also become clear what he himself has to say to the people of the present time, what hopes he can offer for mankind today and for a future world.

Hans Küng, *On Being a Christian*, trans. Edward Quinn (Garden City, NY: Doubleday, 1976), 166.

Abraham was not justified by the laws around circumcision (Rom. 4:10–12), but rather, as he will argue more extensively in 4:13–15, by his faith in God, who fulfills promises about how one is declared "righteous" (v. 11). Thus, the conclusion repeated in Romans 4:3 and 4:22, echoing the story of Abraham summarized in Genesis 15:6, his faith "reckoned" Abraham as "righteous." So too for believers in Christ, who are "reckoned righteous" by belief in the efficacy of the death and resurrection of Jesus Christ (vv. 24–25).

Connections to Preaching. What themes for preaching arise from the message of Romans 4:13–25? First, in resonance with Israel's traditions and the stories of Abraham and Sarah, the God of Israel keeps promises. Moreover, it is worth preaching about how the faithfulness of God should be reciprocated by faithful people. Indeed, a good sermon about faith and justification would ultimately focus on God's eternal love for humanity. Such love was exhibited in the person and work of Jesus Christ, the one whom Paul argues in this passage was sacrificed for humanity through a painful and shameful death. Nonetheless, preaching on these themes should end with focus not on an ignominious death but, rather, on God's "glorification" of Christ, that is, through "resurrection from the dead" (vv. 24, 25). For today's preacher, the reference to the need for a substitutionary death ("death for our trespasses," v. 25a) will be difficult. Thus, a focus on being "raised for our justification" (v. 25b) will help. Preaching on the "benefits of justification" awaits in the passage that follows (Rom. 5:1–11).

EFRAÍN AGOSTO

Commentary 2: Connecting the Reading with the World

Romans occupies a prominent place in Protestant theology and preaching. It is the epistle by which Martin Luther came to his deep convictions about justification by grace through faith, a theme that shaped the Protestant Reformation in the mid-sixteenth century and beyond. Romans is often viewed as a deeply theological letter with grand themes such as human sin,

God's righteousness and response to sin, justification and salvation, the role of faith, the work that God accomplished through Jesus Christ, the nature and meaning of the Lord's Supper, and the centrality of the resurrection in Christian faith. These are important theological themes that continue to shape the beliefs of the church.

A sole focus, however, on mining this book to prove a theological point might miss the concerns that the apostle Paul had for the Christian communities in Rome. While Romans is deeply theological, it is intensely practical. The practices we see in Romans extend and reflect its theological commitments, even as theological commitments are sharpened and clarified by the challenges experienced by the Christian communities in Rome in the first century in living out their faith.

What clues might we find to the relevance for sermons today of Paul's theological and ecclesial concerns? Like other writings in the New Testament, Paul is addressing the tensions created as Jewish and Gentile Christians come together as a result of their common belief in Jesus Christ. One of these tensions was over the role of the Mosaic Law, often misremembered in the church as wholly negative and nullified by Jesus. The complexities of this tension result in stark dichotomies, such as the perceived conflicts between law and grace, faith and works, the old covenant and the new. Sermons should name these false dichotomies, as Paul does in Romans, where he resolves this tension by reminding readers that faith has always been operative, both before the Law was given to Moses, and even through the Law. The examples that Paul uses for this are Abraham and Sarah. Instead of giving us a theological exposé of faith and righteousness, we are offered examples.

How do Abraham and Sarah illustrate the "righteousness of faith" (Rom. 4:13)? Righteousness through faith is a key theme in Paul's theology. "Righteousness," a word used often in Romans, has textured meanings, depending on context. The context here is a religious one based on the requirements and observance of the Law. True to his own Jewish roots, Paul does not abandon the necessity of righteousness or the Law, especially for the elect Jewish people. Righteousness is still required, but it is now made possible through faith, even for "adherents of the law" (v. 16). Abraham and Sarah are models of this righteousness of faith, our ancestors, *because* of their faith.

From one of our companion lectionary texts, we have a description of this kind of faith. Abraham believed in God's promises, had faith, and set out to an unknown land (Gen. 12:1–9). This stepping out into the unknown becomes a normative expression of faith, marking those "who share the faith of Abraham" (Rom. 4:16–17). The faith demonstrated by Abraham and Sarah relies on the faithfulness of God, with a willingness to step out and follow God into the unknown. This kind of faith pleases God, and God honors it by fulfilling the promises made to Abraham, Sarah, and their descendants (v. 17). Preachers can tell the stories of faithful ancestors in their congregations as a powerful means to demonstrate faith, as opposed to simply defining it. People will remember these stories of faith and be inspired to step out for themselves into unknown territory.

A sermon on this passage should ask, "What does it mean for us today to 'share the faith of Abraham' and Sarah as their heirs?" (vv. 16–17). One area is the role of faith in what seems to be impossible to imagine. Sarah and Abraham were childless, due to old age and the "barrenness of Sarah's womb" (vv. 18–19). Infertility in the ancient world was often seen as a curse, a punishment, particularly against women who failed to provide male heirs and fulfill the gendered expectations of their identities and roles in childbearing.

Perhaps this is not all that different today. Infertility, the inability to produce one's own biological child, continues to be a source of pain, disappointment, and hurt, often exacerbated by the rhetoric of "family values" and the prizing of the nuclear biological family. This often creates experiences of exclusion for those who do not meet these expectations, a burden likely borne by women. The stories in Scripture where infertile women eventually miraculously conceive and bear children—such as Sarah (Gen. 21:1–3), Rebekah (Gen. 25:21), Hannah (1 Sam. 1:12–20), and Elizabeth (Luke 1:5–24)—may add to this pain.

Preachers can ask, "How does faith operate in situations such as these marked by disappointment and unfilled expectations?" Does faith mean that we can or should "name it and claim it" as the solution to a situation such as barrenness? Does having more faith guarantee our desired outcome? These questions challenge our preaching and pastoral practices for persons in congregations struggling with similar situations, particularly the desire for physical healing, where we must choose our words carefully to avoid adding to a person's pain and disappointment. This lectionary text does not suggest that Abraham and Sarah had more faith, were more pious, or prayed harder. Faith is not a magic potion that solves our disappointments and dashed expectations. Faith is predicated on God's faithfulness to us. We share in the faith of Sarah and Abraham by moving forward even in disappointment and unfilled hopes and dreams, not as Stoics but as those whose inheritance is secure because of God's faithfulness.

There is a deeply communal aspect to sharing in the faith of Abraham and Sarah. While not necessarily comforting to those who are personally struggling with infertility or other issues that seem to threaten our identities and well-being, this lectionary text points us to the communal inheritance of our faith. Preachers can remind congregations that we have faith together, and sometimes persons have faith for us when we may not have it ourselves. It is the faith of Abraham and Sarah that ensures our inheritance of the promises of God and its ultimate expression in the resurrection of Jesus Christ (Rom. 4:23–25). While Sarah and Abraham did eventually receive their heir in Isaac, this text seems to suggest that the importance of their faith in the unknown was securing for them many more heirs across time and through history as they became the father and mother of many nations (v. 18). They provide an example for congregations in this unknown time who might be experiencing forms of barrenness in declining attendance, deaths of elderly parishioners, and children who grew up in the context of the church but who no longer actively participate in its inheritance. It may be difficult to "hope against hope," uncertain as to what kind of future there might be, especially with the demographic shifts in some of our churches.

Perhaps this is where faith becomes crucial, as it was for Sarah and Abraham. In reality, faith cannot be easily articulated in a theological treatise or even a sermon. Faith needs to be lived and practiced in the unknown circumstance of our lives and in the ever-present reality of disappointment. Ultimately it is God in whom we have faith, and it is God who reckons us as righteous, not on the basis of more faith, more piety, or praying harder, but out of grace and God's own faithfulness to us.

WYNDY CORBIN REUSCHLING

Proper 5 (Sunday between June 5 and June 11 inclusive)

Matthew 9:9–13, 18–26

⁹As Jesus was walking along, he saw a man called Matthew sitting at the tax booth; and he said to him, "Follow me." And he got up and followed him. ¹⁰And as he sat at dinner in the house, many tax collectors and sinners came and were sitting with him and his disciples. ¹¹When the Pharisees saw this, they said to his disciples, "Why does your teacher eat with tax collectors and sinners?" ¹²But when he heard this, he said, "Those who are well have no need of a physician, but those who are sick. ¹³Go and learn what this means, 'I desire mercy, not sacrifice.' For I have come to call not the righteous but sinners." . . .

¹⁸While he was saying these things to them, suddenly a leader of the synagogue came in and knelt before him, saying, "My daughter has just died; but come and lay your hand on her, and she will live." ¹⁹And Jesus got up and followed him, with his disciples. ²⁰Then suddenly a woman who had been suffering from hemorrhages for twelve years came up behind him and touched the fringe of his cloak, ²¹for she said to herself, "If I only touch his cloak, I will be made well." ²²Jesus turned, and seeing her he said, "Take heart, daughter; your faith has made you well." And instantly the woman was made well. ²³When Jesus came to the leader's house and saw the flute players and the crowd making a commotion, ²⁴ he said, "Go away; for the girl is not dead but sleeping." And they laughed at him. ²⁵But when the crowd had been put outside, he went in and took her by the hand, and the girl got up. ²⁶And the report of this spread throughout that district.

Commentary 1: Connecting the Reading with Scripture

Today's Gospel is set within a broader cycle of healings and controversies in Matthew 9 that highlight Jesus' authority, all based in his hometown of Capernaum (Matt. 4:13; 9:1). As he enters the town, he forgives a paralytic of his sins. Jesus then heals the man as a sign to the scribes that he has the authority both to heal and to forgive (9:1–8). He continues walking until he sees Matthew sitting at the tax booth, there to tax either the fishermen on the coast or the trade traveling the road north from Jerusalem. He tells Matthew to follow him, and the tax collector immediately follows. The call is abrupt, much like his earlier call to the fishermen (4:18–21), and the response brooks no hesitation (8:19–22).

The act of following implies repentance of sins, but the reader can only guess that Matthew amended his life. Indeed, many tax collectors and sinners come to dinner that evening, so Matthew has not left his kind of people for a holier set. Instead, perhaps they all gathered because they were fascinated that a rabbi would associate with someone like them. Sharing a meal together takes Jesus' involvement with this class of people in Capernaum into intimacy and fellowship. Some are abruptly called and others drawn closer into an encounter with Jesus. The preacher might reflect on God's love for us as we are, or how Jesus calls us in different ways, depending on our needs.

The Pharisees have become a stereotype of judgmentalism, but it is important to note the real controversy in this story. The sinners were probably recognizably unsavory characters who lived lives very different from those of observant Jews like Jesus.[1] Furthermore, tax collectors were disparaged as agents of the Roman

---

1. John Nolland, *The Gospel of Matthew* (Grand Rapids: Eerdmans, 2005), 423.

Empire who impoverished the people. This portrayal of Jesus challenges us to think about what it means to love or accept those whose lives are actually offensive to us. The radical answer hinted at in the text is that we are to break bread with them.

Tax collectors will be mentioned a third time in the Gospel when Jesus tells the chief priests and elders that "the tax collectors and the prostitutes are going into the kingdom of God ahead of you" (21:31). If Jesus came to be a physician to the sick—to save people from their sins (1:21)—then perhaps it is dangerous to be too healthy. Indeed, forgiving, healing, calling, cleansing, saving, and restoring intertwine in Matthew 9, suggesting that his mission is to seek out the many "sick" who need his mercy. Preachers might consider how we can "break bread" with those who are offensive to us. Other themes include mercy in the midst of stigma or sickness, God's healing care, and our own healing when we draw close to the Great Physician.

Jesus further responds to the Pharisees' challenge like a rabbi, by telling them to learn better the meaning of mercy and sacrifice in Hosea 6:6. The phrase "mercy, not sacrifice" does not discredit the law or the sacrificial system. It would have been understood as mercy "more so" than sacrifice. This reference to mercy also repeats his teaching in the Sermon on the Mount. After claiming, "Blessed are the merciful," he tells his listeners to love their enemies (5:43–47). Loving our loved ones is not good enough, for "even the tax collectors" love their own (v. 46). Now in chapter 9, we find Jesus putting this teaching into action, showing mercy even to tax collectors, who were thought to barely love others. The sickest of sinners are entering the kingdom before the healthiest of the righteous, and Matthew is the foremost example of this mercy for those who follow Jesus.

The lectionary skips another controversy story about fasting (9:14–17). Then the dinner is finally interrupted a third time by the leader of the synagogue and his desperate need, shifting the reader to another double-miracle story. Mathew has shortened this account considerably from Mark's Gospel, focusing on the faith of the father and the bleeding woman. The girl is already dead, but the father proclaims that if Jesus lays his hand on her, she will live. We sense that Jesus is a holy man who can raise the dead, like Elijah raising the widow's son (1 Kgs. 17:17–24), Elisha raising the Shunammite woman's son (2 Kgs. 4:18–37), or Peter raising Tabitha (Acts 9:36–41). The greatest of God's prophets have this power, and Jesus will list it as one of the proofs to John's disciples that he is the one to come (Matt. 11:4–6).

Jesus immediately follows the father, and in the moving throng a bleeding woman sneaks behind him and lays her own hands on the fringe, or tassels, of his cloak. Tassels were added to an observant religious man's garment to represent God's commandments. It reminds the observant to be holy in memory of God's saving works (Num. 15:38–41). The woman reaches out and touches a symbol of God's covenant and of Jesus' position as bearer of that tradition (imagine a pastor's stole or robes). The lectionary version says that she believes that she will be "made well" but the verb is more particularly "saved." As a woman with an unclean condition, being healed is a broader salvation from her personal and social suffering. Jesus turns to see the woman in her distress, acknowledging her as daughter and proclaiming her well. Faith is this "needing touch," reaching with expectancy, that invariably finds Jesus reaching back in response.[2]

A theme that runs throughout the chapter is that of the controversy around who is inside or outside, sick or well. The scribes, Pharisees, and disciples of John all question Jesus, and he shows himself superior to their knowledge and authority. The professional mourners also mock Jesus, intensifying the difference between his knowledge and that of the people. The leader of the synagogue might have been viewed as an enemy of Matthew's community, since it appears that the community were being persecuted or had already been completely rejected from the synagogue. The term *archōn*, "ruler," might further connote a municipal official, or someone whose

---

2. Frederick Dale Bruner, *The Christbook: A Historical Theological Commentary* (Waco, TX: Word, 1987), 344.

position was religious and political.³ In all of these possibilities, when Jesus works his miracles, we expect to see broader social boundaries crossed: from clean to unclean, from enemy to friend, from lost to restored, from death to life. Breaking through relational and social categories, Jesus challenges us to change how we stigmatize others, and how our categories limit our own possibilities for surprising new life.

The importance of faith is another theme that is woven throughout the chapter. In the lectionary portion, three very different people from very different social and religious positions have faith that Jesus is able to touch their unique needs for healing. Faith is further captured in the readings from Romans (4:13–25) and Genesis (12:1–9) appointed for today. In Genesis 12 Abraham's faith is reckoned to him as righteousness because he believed that God would be faithful to God's promises. Interestingly, as in Matthew, this is not faith in a set of propositions about Divinity but a faithfulness to get up and follow when one is called. Hosea 6:6 is also a lectionary option for this Sunday. This verse will return again in Matthew 12:7 in a controversy about the disciples plucking grain on the Sabbath. Thus, mercy appears to be connected to a practical judgment that responds to real needs in the present.

SONIA E. WATERS

Commentary 2: Connecting the Reading with the World

A wise friend describes therapy as an encounter that takes us out of our misery and places us into our pain. The writer of Matthew too understands the journey from misery to pain—a fact that makes the lectionary form of the passage for this Sunday truly puzzling. In the lectionary, as in our lives and our churches, we glean insight from what we shuttle to the side as much as from what we embrace. The lectionary editors omit the witness to joy at the core of this passage; verses 14–17 simply get the boot. What light might we allow to stream in through this gap?

Falling in Ordinary Time, the "ordinary" daily-ness of the life of faith is a great starting point for a sermon. Focusing on the "excess" verses the lectionary omits from the passage offers a useful mirror for reflection on the needs each of us denies or silences in order to serve in and survive our culture's notions of "ordinary" life and faith. Mired in relationships grown dull and demanding, beset by seemingly endless church commitments and controversies choking out the growth and wonder of ordinary time, relentlessly bombarded with vapid and sensationalist news cycles pressing upon an already fraught and fractured world, we ignore the joy gap to our peril.

At the heart of this passage, in the midst of fear and pain, Jesus witnesses to a joy that bursts life open. The texture of this Jesus joy is another angle into the text: wedding joy; shiny cloth bursting forth against the backdrop of well-worn, familiar garments joy; tipsy new wine joy. The joy offered by Jesus is not a Pollyannaish, "make the best of things and be thankful for each new day," sort of joy. It is not a joy that ignores the grinding structures of our world that elevate and enrich some while turning others into dust. It is a form of joy that is possible only when we face the truth of pain and brokenness.

The faith community to whom Matthew wrote knew what happened to the bridegroom. They knew that he was not just taken away, but murdered. They knew that following that bridegroom put them crosswise with empire, the state authorities and religious power structures that wanted him dead. Matthew's congregation knew that the bridegroom's love was a healing love that so terrified all empires that they nailed that love to a cross and buried it in a tomb.

The church of Matthew knew something else as well: they knew that the bridegroom returned from the tomb and that he dances still, claiming a joy that no tomb can extinguish. There is

---

3. Ulrich Luz, *Matthew 8–20: A Commentary*, trans. James E. Crouch, Hermeneia (Minneapolis: Augsburg Fortress, 2001), 40.

little our world needs more than that sturdy joy. What does Christian joy look, feel, and taste like today? How do we live it with our bodies and not just with our ideas and ideals? Extraordinary joy wrought within the ordinary.

The temptation to shut down our hearts to wonder as we trudge under the ordinary burdens of the day might be another focus for a sermon. Studies in education and psychology increasingly emphasize the imperative of play and the benefits of mindfulness. A sermon might reflect on Christian practices of mindfulness such as centering prayer, suggesting that our life together invites playfulness and presence in each moment God gives us. The joy in the missing verses witnesses to practices of *now*: dancing in the present moment while the bridegroom is with us; opening to joy, even when we know that mourning and emptiness crouch ever near. The Christian liturgical year and a number of historic Christian practices invite us to live in the present moment, acknowledging thoughts and feelings as exactly what they are: a passing experience in an ever-flowing stream.

The diligent, duty-bound faithful who people the pews every Sunday, as well as the brave, curious, and casual who darken the church doors only warily and infrequently, all hunger for a gospel word that rejects the dichotomy of faith lived out through duty versus faith marked by gentle rhythms of presence and participation. This passage invites conversation between the two. It is notable that Jesus does not condemn the practices John's followers accuse Jesus' disciples of neglecting. He does not tell John's groupies we should never fast or mourn. He does not suggest that we put away well-worn and well-loved garments. They remain. Neither does he reject old wineskins. Old and new—"both are preserved" (Matt. 9:17). There is no either/or. Rather, Jesus frames historic and trusted practices in new ways. Joy is the pivot point for his reframing. In stark contrast to the self-righteous questions of John's followers, Jesus celebrates the demands of joy in the midst of all that we know and trust: the good and the bad.

The imperative to take bad news seriously in light of the gospel is another angle into this text. A woman I know in her mid-sixties describes life growing up amid the unrelenting distortions of the late Soviet empire. She vividly remembers the day the world shifted around her: "During Soviet times there was never bad news. Bad news was not allowed. As Glasnost was unfolding, I heard a news story about a cruise ship sinking in the Black Sea. At that moment I knew that everything was changing—bad news was the beginning of good news." Bad news was the beginning of good news for my friend because it opened her world to truth telling that was discouraged in a Soviet order requiring empty, saccharine platitudes spread like frosting over a cake of social disillusionment, fear, human suffering, and exploitation. Bad news broke open space for new imagination in her life. It can do the same for us, inviting expansive hope and fresh possibility to take hold.

Bad news is good news in this Gospel lesson as well. The bad news is that we are all sinners and we are all sick. Jesus bursts like fireworks into the very center of this bad news. He eats with tax collectors and shows up for those who need him. All of us need him. He shows up for all of us. He comes not for the righteous, but for the sinners. He beckons *all* of us to glance up from our tiny tax booths and cubicles, our interminable suffering and exhaustion, even our piercing, life-shattering grief—to follow him.

What is required of us if we wish to be open to this good news? Some of us receive the good news only when we reach a moment of all-encompassing, visceral pain and grief—kneeling before Jesus, desperately begging for his touch of resurrection, for the restoration of relationship, for the return of hope violently ripped from our hands. Others of us journey with the bleeding woman: worn down, depleted, isolated, reaching from within the fog of vulnerability and pain to grab onto the garment of the One whose presence can make us well. Whether by means of high drama or ordinary tenacity, we hear a voice saying, "Follow me," a promise that predator and prey are not the only identities on offer in our world, an invitation to a shared table where Jesus welcomes sinners.

The Christian gift and practice of confession and forgiveness *is* a perfect focus for this passage both liturgically and homiletically. Gordon Cosby, the pastor of the Church of the Savior in Washington, DC, claimed that the great equalizer in society is pain. Pain reaches everyone. It strips us bare. We are all sick. We are all sinners. The leveling ground of pain opens us to encounters that our social structures make impossible in easier places. It is the bad news that is the beginning of good news. Confession and petition crack us open, creating a space where joy may dwell.

DENISE THORPE

Proper 6 (Sunday between June 12 and June 18 inclusive)

Exodus 19:2–8a and
   Genesis 18:1–15 (21:1–7)
Psalm 100 and Psalm 116:1–2, 12–19

Romans 5:1–8
Matthew 9:35–10:8 (9–23)

Exodus 19:2–8a

²They had journeyed from Rephidim, entered the wilderness of Sinai, and camped in the wilderness; Israel camped there in front of the mountain. ³Then Moses went up to God; the LORD called to him from the mountain, saying, "Thus you shall say to the house of Jacob, and tell the Israelites: ⁴You have seen what I did to the Egyptians, and how I bore you on eagles' wings and brought you to myself. ⁵Now therefore, if you obey my voice and keep my covenant, you shall be my treasured possession out of all the peoples. Indeed, the whole earth is mine, ⁶but you shall be for me a priestly kingdom and a holy nation. These are the words that you shall speak to the Israelites."

⁷So Moses came, summoned the elders of the people, and set before them all these words that the LORD had commanded him. ⁸The people all answered as one: "Everything that the LORD has spoken we will do."

Genesis 18:1–15 (21:1–7)

¹⁸:¹The LORD appeared to Abraham by the oaks of Mamre, as he sat at the entrance of his tent in the heat of the day. ²He looked up and saw three men standing near him. When he saw them, he ran from the tent entrance to meet them, and bowed down to the ground. ³He said, "My lord, if I find favor with you, do not pass by your servant. ⁴Let a little water be brought, and wash your feet, and rest yourselves under the tree. ⁵Let me bring a little bread, that you may refresh yourselves, and after that you may pass on—since you have come to your servant." So they said, "Do as you have said." ⁶And Abraham hastened into the tent to Sarah, and said, "Make ready quickly three measures of choice flour, knead it, and make cakes." ⁷Abraham ran to the herd, and took a calf, tender and good, and gave it to the servant, who hastened to prepare it. ⁸Then he took curds and milk and the calf that he had prepared, and set it before them; and he stood by them under the tree while they ate.

⁹They said to him, "Where is your wife Sarah?" And he said, "There, in the tent." ¹⁰Then one said, "I will surely return to you in due season, and your wife Sarah shall have a son." And Sarah was listening at the tent entrance behind him. ¹¹Now Abraham and Sarah were old, advanced in age; it had ceased to be with Sarah after the manner of women. ¹²So Sarah laughed to herself, saying, "After I have grown old, and my husband is old, shall I have pleasure?" ¹³The LORD said to Abraham, "Why did Sarah laugh, and say, 'Shall I indeed bear a child, now that I am old?' ¹⁴Is anything too wonderful for the LORD? At the set time I will return to you, in due season, and Sarah shall have a son." ¹⁵But Sarah denied, saying, "I did not laugh"; for she was afraid. He said, "Oh yes, you did laugh." . . .

²¹:¹The LORD dealt with Sarah as he had said, and the LORD did for Sarah as he had promised. ²Sarah conceived and bore Abraham a son in his old age, at the time of which God had spoken to him. ³Abraham gave the name Isaac to his son whom Sarah bore him. ⁴And Abraham circumcised his son Isaac when he was eight days old, as God had commanded him. ⁵Abraham was a hundred years old when his son Isaac was born to him. ⁶Now Sarah said, "God has brought laughter for me; everyone who hears will laugh with me." ⁷And she said, "Who would ever have said to Abraham that Sarah would nurse children? Yet I have borne him a son in his old age."

Commentary 1: Connecting the Reading with Scripture

The passages for this Sunday center on God's purpose and plan for God's peoples. Genesis 18 and 21 describe the foretelling of the birth of Isaac, the child who will become the ancestor of the nation of Israel, to Sarah, who is elderly and infertile. God's plan for Abraham, Sarah, and Isaac is elucidated in Exodus 19, which describes how their descendants were elected by God to be a priestly kingdom and holy nation. The texts from the New Testament continue this theme by depicting Jesus (Rom. 5:1–8) and his disciples and followers (Matt. 9:35–10:8) as the final iteration of God's promise to create a holy nation and priestly kingdom on earth.

This promise of a special group begins with the selection of an elderly couple by God. Abraham and Sarah are promised land, progeny, and blessing by God in exchange for moving from their homeland to Canaan (Gen. 12). Abraham and Sarah, however, are old, and the birth of a child to Sarah seems unlikely. God, along with two angelic consorts, shows up at Abraham's camp to remind the couple that nothing is too unlikely for God (Gen. 18).

When God and God's divine entourage show up, Abraham and Sarah immediately start preparing a feast for their guests. In verses filled with a string of verbs, the couple bows to their guests, brings water, makes bread, slaughters a calf, and prepares a meal (18:2–8). As then and still now, hospitality was paramount in the Near East—a sentiment affirmed by numerous biblical passages. Leviticus 19:33–34, for example, commands that the Israelites love a *ger*, translated as "guest," "stranger," "foreigner," or even "immigrant," because Israel too was a *ger* in the land of Egypt. Deuteronomy 10:18–19 outright declares that God loves the *ger* and therefore expects God's chosen people to love the *ger* as well. Matthew goes further and states that *inhospitality* to foreigners is a characteristic of those rejected by God (Matt. 25:43). The biblical text is therefore unequivocal that strangers, guests, and foreigners are to be welcomed, cared for, and protected.

The literary context of Genesis 18 affirms the importance of hospitality. After the divine guests finish eating with Abraham and Sarah, they head toward Sodom and Gomorrah, the destruction of which is the topic of the next chapter. The literary context hints that Abraham and Sarah's hospitality in Genesis 18 is placed in contrast to the lack of hospitality exhibited to the angels by the inhabitants of Sodom and Gomorrah in chapter 19. Indeed, despite debates about the exact nature of the sin of Sodom and Gomorrah, Ezekiel 16:49 states that their sin was not just their lack of generosity, but the general mistreatment of those in need: "This was the guilt of your sister Sodom: she and her daughters had pride, excess of food, and prosperous ease, but did not aid the poor and needy." In a world of anti-immigrant sentiment, we do well, therefore, to remember the advice in Hebrews: "Do not neglect to show hospitality to foreigners, for by doing that some have entertained angels without knowing it" (Heb. 13:2, my trans.).

This story, however, is not all seriousness. Rather, humor and joy infuse Genesis 18. In the bizarre back and forth, Sarah, who is eavesdropping in a tent (Gen. 18:10) while the guests are eating, overhears God's promise that she will soon bear a child, and she laughs (v. 12). God, overhearing the laugh and perhaps a bit affronted, asks Abraham why his wife laughed. Sarah retorts to this indirect accusation (all while still in the tent) with a lie that she did not laugh (v. 15). To this, God responds by saying that she *really did* laugh (v. 15). That God would descend to a "no, I did not"/"yes, you did" squabble hints that this narrative is supposed to be funny. The humor is purposeful, in that it provides an etymology for the name of her soon-to-be-born son, Isaac, whose name means "laughter." The humor does not take away, but adds to the truth of God's prophecy, which indeed comes to pass. In Genesis 21, Sarah, despite her age and despite her laughter, finally gives birth to a son. In giving birth to this son, she again laughs, this time with joy (21:6).

This story is rife with sermonic potential. The first concerns humor and levity. In what ways does humor reflect and add to divine truth, and how can we utilize humor, just as the biblical writer does, to better elucidate God's message? Second, the biblical text is filled with stories about infertile women (Rebekah, Rachel, Hannah, Samson's mom) suddenly becoming pregnant. Such stories about miraculous pregnancies can provide hope, but can also mislead struggling women into thinking that their infertility is the result of a lack of faith. Hence, aside from women's reproductive issues, a discussion about how the biblical narratives, especially stories about miracles, can help and also hurt the people of God, is worthy of the pulpit.

While Genesis 18 and 21 describe the birth and promise of the chosen heir, Isaac, as a manifestation of the fulfillment of God's covenant with Abraham, Exodus 19:2–8a describes God's request for a reaffirmation of the covenant by the descendants of Abraham and Isaac. As with Abraham, the covenant (or a legal agreement) is based on deeds and actions. In exchange for Abraham's faithful journey to Canaan, God promised him progeny, land, and blessing. The stories about the Israelites and their settlement on the land of Canaan, described in Exodus and the rest of the Pentateuch, show that God has fully fulfilled this contract with Abraham.

With the descendants of Abraham and Isaac, God points to a deed that has already been accomplished—God's delivery of the Israelites from Egypt (Exod. 19:4)—as "down payment" for the new covenant that has been promised. As with Abraham, however, the Israelites will also receive something for agreeing to this new contract: If the Israelites fulfill their part of the deal, they will become God's "treasured possession out of all the peoples," and a "priestly kingdom and a holy nation" (vv. 5–6). Despite lacking knowledge of the details, the people readily agree (v. 8). This, however, will turn out to be a mistake. The outcome of this agreement will be less successful, as the Israelites, unlike Abraham, repeatedly fail to uphold their end of the deal, eventually leading to the nation's destruction and exile. Bespeaking the everlasting loyalty of God to Israel, however, the nation will eventually be forgiven and be allowed to return to the land promised by God to Israel's forebears.

This cycle of exile and return, of failure leading to recovery and success—all fueled by God's unrelenting loyalty—provides a worthy topic of exploration. What is today's equivalent of exile and return, of failure and recovery? Moreover, the Israelites in Exodus 19 must repeatedly choose to follow God. Like the Israelites, how can we also come back to a place of renewal and reaffirmation of God's covenant? Equally important is a delineation of God's promises: How do we now understand the promise that God's people will be a priestly and holy people? Priests in the ancient world were intermediaries, a bridge between God and the people. How does the church still function as such a bridge? How has it failed in this endeavor? Should it even have this role in our era? Finally, how do we as the people of God remind ourselves, in the midst of difficult and busy lives, that we are and remain God's treasured possession—a people selected by God to fulfill God's wondrous plan in this world?

SONG-MI SUZIE PARK

Commentary 2: Connecting the Reading with the World

"Is anything too wonderful for the LORD?" We might well look out on the world that greets us today and swiftly answer yes. As we face fear, racial strife, abuse, wars and the rumors of wars, a great number of things appear to be too wonderful for even the power and presence of God. We might cry or laugh at the absurdity of such an audacious question promoting God's wonderfulness in a world like ours. Of course, if we laugh, we are in good company with this Genesis text, as Sarah laughs in the face of God's announcement of her imminent pregnancy in her "advanced age."

The establishment of God's covenant with Israel in the Exodus text reflects a similar spirit. God reminds God's people "how I bore you on eagles' wings and brought you to myself" (Exod. 19:4). That is followed immediately by the lavish promise of God: "you shall be my treasured possession" (v. 4), a "priestly kingdom and a holy nation" (v. 6).

One approach to a sermon that brings these texts into our world is to lift up the grief evoked when the words "wonderful" and "treasured" are placed before congregational members living with loved ones who struggle with an addiction (or who are themselves addicted), experiencing the devastating impact of poverty, or feeling the daily sting of racial animus. "Wonderful" and "treasured" feel quite separate from the life of a teenager wrestling with the passage from adolescence to young adulthood or for someone facing retirement without any vision of what comes next.

"Wonderful" and "treasured" do not fill the airways of our national discourse or society's approach to all the problems that those who sit in worship and listen to sermons feel pressing in on them every day: personal job loss in the midst of a "booming economy," loneliness as a national epidemic (and social isolation being reported as most acute among those under thirty), the crisis of addiction that knows no socioeconomic boundaries, teenage sex-trafficking that likewise falls on the young of all sorts of households, as well as the feeling of rage, abandonment, fear, and suspicion, often being stoked by the politics of our time. How does a preacher address "wonderful" and "treasured" in such a context? Of course, how does a preacher not draw deeply from the well of a God who acts to address these very painful issues? Can God be trusted in these contexts to bring the full power and presence of the promise to reach out and address God's creatures as "wonderful" and "treasured"? A sermon on this text would do well to speak to this countercultural truth with pastoral sensitivity and gospel boldness.

I once asked a well-known author of religious/spiritual books about his next book project. He told me it was to be a whodunit—with the twist that it was about a detective searching for the details not of a crime, but of something wonderful. Seeing this author a few years later, I reminded him of the earlier conversation. "I could not pull it off," he said abruptly. "I tried for years to make it work, but devious crime is so much more interesting (and plot driven) than a wonderful act of grace."

A sermon on these texts would do well to go beyond Sarah's laughter to the absurdity—and wonder that lies behind it—that God can do all things in a way we cannot begin to imagine, even when we are lured to think that wonderful acts of grace do not seem compelling in our culture of discord and pain. Wonder and awe are in short supply in our culture. How could a worship service, surrounding proclamation of these texts, create a sense of "wonderfulness" and the joyful absurdity of God's overturning of all reasonable expectations of how our world works? So many people come to worship each week having been marinated in dull, despairing, or distracting conventional wisdom about everything that is perceived as not possible. Liturgically, these texts of promise and covenant yearn for an hour of joyful prayer, holy surprise, heartfelt praise, deep nurture, and a feeling of soaring on eagles' wings.

David Foster Wallace once gave a commencement address, "This Is Water," where he called out our culture's obsession of worshiping false gods—beauty, power, intellect—as well as living as though large, noble, transcendent truths hold no power. "You get to decide what to worship. . . . Everybody worships. The only choice we get is *what* to worship. If you worship money and things, then you will never have enough. Worship your own body and beauty and sexual allure and you will always feel ugly, and when time and age start showing, you will die a million deaths before they finally plant you. . . . Worship power—you will feel weak and afraid, and you will need ever more power over others to keep the fear at bay. Worship your intellect, being seen as smart—you will end up feeling stupid, a fraud, always on the verge of being found out. And so on."[1]

God's covenant and the surprising—wonderful—acts of God dramatically break out of the worship of money, power, appearance, or any other superficiality to reshape the imagination of all who hear these words. Treating these texts as the foundation by which people of faith break the cycle of worshiping "lesser gods" would include connections between the texts and what Wallace so aptly critiques, as well as proclaiming a vision of where these texts lead us—to trust, awe, and devotion to God of the covenant. That God offers a much larger world—of action, imagination, community and hope—through covenant relationship and surprising acts of wonder (as in the announcement of an impending birth to a ninety-year-old) is a stark contrast to the world we are offered by the world. A sermon could build on the "received world" we live in. A world of conflict, division, lower expectations for anything getting better. That world is "what you see is what you get." God is displaying audacious, graceful power in drawing God's followers to believe that wonder is not "beside the point." God is calling creation and creatures "treasured," in stark contrast to the degradation so many human beings feel in a world such as ours. Use of these texts in a sermon should not apologize that we are proclaiming a God of power and presence. That we cannot fully comprehend, along with Abraham and Sarah, how God is doing this unlikely thing is no reason to "tone it down" or use our reason to prove it true. Proclamation is not the same as explanation.

Twentieth-century southern writer Flannery O'Connor, a devout Roman Catholic, was fond of saying "mystery is the great embarrassment to the modern mind." Twenty-first-century minds and hearts are not well accustomed to mystery. Largely, we think technology and expansion of knowledge reduce mystery (which we take to be a good thing). This is precisely why these texts of God's covenant and God's audacious promise of a child, cloaked as they are in the mystery of holiness, are so needed to our modern minds. Stories of God's activity that would lead us to exclaim, "Is anything too wonderful for the Lord?"—this is something we need to draw close to, not to dismantle for examination. These words allow us to give ourselves over in awe and wonder to experience what it is to be treasured by the living God.

MARK RAMSEY

---

1. David Foster Wallace, *This is Water: Some Thoughts, Delivered on a Significant Occasion, about Living a Compassionate Life* (New York: Little, Brown, and Co., 2009), 96-111.

Proper 6 (Sunday between June 12 and June 18 inclusive)

Psalm 100

¹Make a joyful noise to the LORD, all the earth.
 ²Worship the LORD with gladness;
 come into his presence with singing.

³Know that the LORD is God.
 It is he that made us, and we are his;
 we are his people, and the sheep of his pasture.

⁴Enter his gates with thanksgiving,
 and his courts with praise.
 Give thanks to him, bless his name.

⁵For the LORD is good;
 his steadfast love endures forever,
 and his faithfulness to all generations.

Psalm 116:1–2, 12–19

¹I love the LORD, because he has heard
 my voice and my supplications.
²Because he inclined his ear to me,
 therefore I will call on him as long as I live.
. . . .
¹²What shall I return to the LORD
 for all his bounty to me?
¹³I will lift up the cup of salvation
 and call on the name of the LORD,
¹⁴I will pay my vows to the LORD
 in the presence of all his people.
¹⁵Precious in the sight of the LORD
 is the death of his faithful ones.
¹⁶O LORD, I am your servant;
 I am your servant, the child of your serving girl.
 You have loosed my bonds.
¹⁷I will offer to you a thanksgiving sacrifice
 and call on the name of the LORD.
¹⁸I will pay my vows to the LORD
 in the presence of all his people,
¹⁹in the courts of the house of the LORD,
 in your midst, O Jerusalem.
Praise the LORD!

Connecting the Psalm with Scripture and Worship

Psalm 100. The old One Hundredth is so familiar, it is easy to read right over it—or to pick one of the thousands of hymns and choruses based on it and simply sing right through it. The psalm is paired with a story of the escaped slaves, who are now known as the people Israel, reaching the foot of Mount Sinai (Exod. 19:2–8a). In the previous chapter, we learn that they have been traveling for three months. Moses has been their guide and judge—apparently a bit of a micromanager type, hearing every case, deciding every settlement. Father-in-law Jethro helps him delegate, choosing others to adjudicate minor disputes. At Sinai, Moses goes alone up to see God. All the people—and all other-than-human animals—are forbidden to set foot on the mountain, or face death. Moses returns with a sort of collective betrothal invitation from God: "Will you be my people, keep covenant with me, and obey my voice? If so, I will be your God and make you a priestly nation, a special mediating presence between the Divine and all the other peoples—just as Moses serves as go-between from me to you." They people agree: "Everything that the LORD has spoken we will do" (Exod. 19:8a). The stage is set for God to descend upon the mountain and meet the people directly and finalize the covenant through the giving of the law.

This is where the psalm confounds. The covenant is still under negotiation. The wilderness journey continues. There are no gates to enter, no courts in which to praise. Sheep do not choose their shepherd, nor do they listen and consider and agree to a relationship of mutual responsibilities. The key may be the final verse, which addresses the question of "why," as all Israel decides to pledge their troth to this thunderous, liberating divine force: "For the LORD is good," divine love endures, and God is faithful to generation after generation (Ps. 100:5). Such a God, the one who brought them out of bondage and leads them into a new future, is worthy of praise and one to whom it is fitting to bind oneself in covenant.

Along with the Exodus story and Paul's reflections on the economy of salvation, Psalm 100 tempers Jesus' apparent ethnocentrism: "go . . . to the lost sheep of Israel," he tells them, not to Gentiles, nor to Samaritans (Matt. 10:5–6). Both the psalm and the Exodus reading emphasize that God is God of all peoples and nations, of all the earth, but that Israel will have a special role as priestly kingdom and holy nation. Paul notes that Christ died for us "while we still were sinners" (Rom. 5:8). Grace abounds for the ungodly as well as the godly.

Psalm 100 might serve as the basis for an assurance of pardon, thus allowing worshipers to hear the psalm anew:

> Having examined ourselves and brought our failings to mind,
> let us allow grace to revive and renew us.
> For the Lord is good; divine love is steadfast, it endures forever.
> Our God is faithful to all generations.
> Let us, then, rejoice that God pardons,
> that mercy flows . . . even to us.
> So, make a joyful noise! Give thanks! Bless God's holy name!

Psalm 116:1–2, 12–19. This psalm is paired with a story in Genesis about the birth of Isaac. In the first, three visitors appear at Mamre to Abraham and Sarah, who welcome and feed them a bounteous feast: cakes from three measures of choice flour, a good and tender calf, curds, and milk (Gen. 18:1–15). One foretells that when he returns to visit again, Sarah will have had a son. Sarah, well past menopause, laughs. Yet it comes to pass.

Psalm 116, the song of a grateful servant, presents us with another puzzle. Christian ears may hear echoes of the Magnificat: The Lord has been generous to me, has heard my supplications, and bestowed bounty. The hearer cannot help but be moved by the irrepressible gratitude and joy. The singer self-identifies as "the child of your serving girl." Surely, we can appreciate Sarah singing, "What shall I return to the LORD for all his bounty to me," for this child of promise (Ps. 116:12)? For his life—both a miraculous birth and a miraculous intervention upon the altar—Isaac might doubly exclaim, "I will lift up the cup of salvation and call on the name of the Lord" (v. 13).

Hagar too might have declared, "O Lord, I am your servant; . . . you have loosed my bonds" (v. 16)—first in short-lived glee as she escapes Sarah's abuse; later, in horror as she is cast out along with her son to die in the wilderness; and, finally, in consolation as God provides and Ishmael grows strong. Yet, it is Ishmael (is it not?) who is "child of a servant girl," who is servant of the Lord, whose bonds have been loosed and who will make his vows to the Lord (vv. 16, 18). The psalmist might point the preacher to a rereading of the story of the promise of Isaac and then his birth and circumcision through the eyes of a character left unmentioned: Ishmael, Isaac's half brother, who is also a child of promise but slave and outcast and refugee.

In these days of suspicion of adherents of Islam, might we need to remember that we are all related? In these days when refugees are arrested, families torn apart, children put in cages, might we need to remember that both Isaac and Ishmael are saved and blessed . . . in order to be a blessing? In these days when the descendants of those enslaved wonder if their lives matter, might we recall the gratitude of a child of a servant girl for whom God provides water for life from a spring in the desert?

Alternatively, the preacher may take up the question of laughter. God promises, Sarah laughs in incredulity. The angel checks her; Sarah denies. Later, Isaac having been born, she laughs again—and everyone laughs with her. Who can believe such a thing? Who would have said to Abraham that she would nurse a child? Only God. When do we, properly, love the Lord, call upon our God, singing praises . . . just because? When do we laugh, how can the divine promises to us be true? Who are we, to receive unmerited grace? Who will laugh with us, when all these things have come to pass?

Liturgically, the psalm offers language of thanksgiving that reflects our understanding of Eucharist. Even though these words were not created for such a purpose, they might serve as the basis for an invitation to the table:

> Our God has heard our voices, has listened to our supplications;
> for all of God's bounteous gifts, what can we offer in return?
> Let us offer a sacrifice of thanksgiving;
> let us lift up the cup of salvation!
> We are your children, you have loosed our bonds;
> at this table, let us magnify your name . . . and give thanks!

W. SCOTT HALDEMAN

Proper 6 (Sunday between June 12 and June 18 inclusive)

Romans 5:1–8

¹Therefore, since we are justified by faith, we have peace with God through our Lord Jesus Christ, ²through whom we have obtained access to this grace in which we stand; and we boast in our hope of sharing the glory of God. ³And not only that, but we also boast in our sufferings, knowing that suffering produces endurance, ⁴and endurance produces character, and character produces hope, ⁵and hope does not disappoint us, because God's love has been poured into our hearts through the Holy Spirit that has been given to us.

⁶For while we were still weak, at the right time Christ died for the ungodly. ⁷Indeed, rarely will anyone die for a righteous person—though perhaps for a good person someone might actually dare to die. ⁸But God proves his love for us in that while we still were sinners Christ died for us.

Commentary 1: Connecting the Reading with Scripture

Connections to Immediate and Related Context. Romans 5:1–8 is arguably the culminating statement that began with Paul's assertion that he preaches a "gospel" that reflects the power of God: "For I am not ashamed of the gospel; it is the power of God for salvation to everyone who has faith, to the Jew first and also to the Greek" (Rom. 1:16). Such "good news" is necessary because of the sinfulness of humanity (1:18–32), both Jews and non-Jews (2:1–29). Paul posits that all "fall short of the glory of God" (3:23). Even *nomos* ("law") could not eradicate such sin; it could only point it out (4:15; cf. Gal. 3:19). Paul argues consistently throughout the chapters leading up to Romans 5, as well as his Letter to the Galatians, that the real power of the gospel and the forgiveness of sin lies in faith, specifically the faithfulness of Jesus, which connects us to the "righteousness of God," that is, "through faith in Jesus Christ for all who believe" (Rom. 3:22). Paul put it this way in his Letter to the Galatians: "we know that a person is justified not by the works of the law but through faith in Jesus Christ" (Gal. 2:16).

In both Romans and Galatians, Abraham becomes the exemplar of a faithfulness that "justifies" (Gal. 3:6–9; Rom. 4:3–5). Indeed, Paul cites Abraham's story from Genesis to make the claim that applies universally, now in Christ: "For what does the scripture say? 'Abraham believed God, and it was reckoned to him as righteousness'" (Rom. 4:3, citing Gen. 15:6). Such "reckoning" (logical determination) has wide implications, argues Paul: "Now the words, 'it was reckoned to him,' were written not for his sake alone, but for ours also" (4:23–24a). Thus, with Abraham as the exemplar of a faith that justifies all who believe in the power of Jesus' death to forgive sin and his resurrection to declare us just (4:24b–25), Paul is ready to draw out the implications for the life of faith beyond the cross and empty tomb.

Connections to the Benefits of Justification. What are the benefits of justification? Two sets of lists illustrate these at the beginning of Romans 5. The first acknowledges positive benefits (5:1–2); the second turns the negative into a positive (vv. 3–5). "Peace," "access to grace," and "hope" in partnership with God's "glory" represent positive aspects of being declared righteous before God as a result of the faithfulness of Jesus Christ, a faithfulness exhibited in his death and resurrection. We are at peace with God, gain access to divine grace, and secure the hope of new life now and in the future as a result of the resurrection of Christ, which shows

God's glory. All this is made possible because of the faithful obedience of Christ, which is exemplary for our own faithful actions and living, that is, "faith."

Paul acknowledges that complete "glory" (*doxa*) is *not yet* ours. We have a *hope* of glory. Thus Paul reminds us that life this side of "glory" often includes *thlipsis*, suffering or affliction (v. 3). In effect, until the second half of 5:10, in which Paul invokes the language of "reconciliation" through the "life" of the resurrected Christ, Romans 5:3–10a describes the implications of Jesus' death with a rhetorical chain (known as sorites), that is, realities that issue from suffering. Thus "suffering produces endurance [*hypomonēn*], and endurance produces character [*dokimēn*], and character produces hope [*elpida*]" (vv. 3b–4).

In effect, "hope" completes the chain, and so the main point is that suffering in this life, just like the death of Jesus, does not end there. Come what may, there is always hope, just as the death of Jesus issues in resurrection, the ultimate hope. Thus this type of hope "does not disappoint" (v. 5a). Paul turns to the positive side, again, of the results of justification, including the love of God made real through the outpouring of God's Spirit, which is a free gift (v. 5b). Again, just as the death of Jesus and the resurrection of Jesus into our Lord (4:23–25) secures the believer's justification by faith (5:1), justification has positive effects (peace, access, grace, hope, glory). Even the negative effects of our earthly existence (suffering) can build endurance and character until our hope is fulfilled in the glory of God (resurrection). For Paul, such a chain of events and effects is evidence of God's love and the free gift of God's Spirit.

In this shift toward the justifying, positive benefits of love, Spirit, and hope, Paul does not want his audience in the Christian house assemblies of Rome to forget the foundational core of these benefits: the death of Christ. "While we still were sinners Christ died for us," he declares (5:8b). Paul restates the various ways of describing the sinful state of humanity with which this letter began and unfolded (cf. 1:18–32; 3:9–23): "For while we were still weak, at the right time Christ died for the ungodly" (5:6).

Notice the ways in which Paul here describes what he earlier described as "sin": being "weak," being "ungodly." In fact, such a state rarely brings anyone the benefits of love, care, and even attention by others. "Indeed, rarely will anyone die for a righteous person—though perhaps for a good person someone might actually dare to die" (v. 7). What is the difference between a "righteous person" (*dikaiou*) and a "good person" (*agathou*)? Most likely these are Hebraic parallels in which Paul is simply stating that almost never would one be willing to die for even a righteous person, that is, a good person. Yet such is not the case *at all* for God, as manifested in Christ, because "God proves [God's] love for us in that while we still were sinners Christ died for us" (v. 8). Once again a negative (the death of Christ) proves to be a positive; God's love is exhibited for us in that death.

Is this not a form of abuse, in which a loving God allows the death of one on behalf of others? Would not an almighty God rescue all without the death of one? It is just not the way of the world, seems to be the lesson of this passage in Paul. Death is inevitable; the question is, could it be worth something? Would someone die for another? Rarely. In this case, God's love of humanity is evident even through an unwarranted, unnecessary death; the unjust death of Jesus of Nazareth makes possible the life of many, because they saw the love of God in the faithfulness of the man Jesus, whose resurrected life brought hope and reconciliation to all (vv. 9–11).

Connections to Preaching. This passage begins with justification, highlights hope, reflects on death, and just beyond it celebrates reconciliation (vv. 9–11), all themes worthy of sermons each in their own right. A similar pattern is followed by Paul in his most well-known passage on the theme of reconciliation, 2 Corinthians 5:18–21, which reads in part: "In Christ God was reconciling the world to himself, not counting their trespasses against them. . . . For our sake [God] made him to be sin who knew no sin, so that in him we might become the righteousness of God." Justification ("right-wising") based on the faithfulness of Christ, even to the point of death (as in Phil. 2:5–8), is an act of reconciliation, the Creator initiating, with love, the hope of human restoration from sin to a proper relationship with God. Thus any preaching of "justification by faith" should end with clear connections to a reconciled humanity.

EFRAÍN AGOSTO

Commentary 2: Connecting the Reading with the World

Romans 5 continues one of the grand themes of this epistle: justification by faith. While one aspect of justification is forensic, in that it can be interpreted in legal parlance to acquit a person of wrongdoing, or to free someone from the penalty of breaking the law, the foci in our lectionary text are the implications of receiving justification through faith in Christ. This text ought not to encourage smug boasting that views justification as a free pass from the penalties of sin, a kind of "cheap grace" of which Dietrich Bonhoeffer spoke in *The Cost of Discipleship*.[1] Indeed, a possible topic of sermon is the difference between cheap grace and real grace.

One might be reminded when reading this passage in Romans of the *ordo salutis* that characterizes some Protestant theologies. This "order of salvation" starts with regeneration, then conversion, justification, sanctification, and finally glorification. While this order offers important theological language to talk about various dimensions in a doctrine of salvation, it can become artificial and limiting when imposed on scriptural descriptions, such as we find here in Romans 5. Romans 5 does not suggest a particular order of salvation that starts at one point and ends in another, as if this important work of God can be made so linear, tidy, and precise.

Justification by faith does far more than offer us a legal declaration of right standing with God. Justification restores relationship with God so that "we have peace with God through our Lord Jesus Christ" (Rom. 5:1). This provides the means by which a righteous life is formed and lived. Preachers can remind congregations on this Sunday that the purpose of justification is important. We celebrate renewed relationship with God through the grace of Christ and the work of the Holy Spirit.

What are the implications of justification by faith that might be explored in a sermon? First is a shared life with Christ. It may be tempting to emphasize "sharing the glory of God" (v. 2) as an apt reward for justification. However, we must not forget that prior to Christ's glory was Christ's own righteous life and suffering. Jesus' righteous life contributed to his suffering as he challenged injustice, healed the sick and marginalized, and called unlikely persons to follow him, even those who would eventually betray him, as we see in Matthew 9:35–10:8, one of our companion lectionary texts. The kind of righteous life that Christ lived challenged the status quo and those with privileged religious, economic, and political power, who had the means to make sure that he paid the price for these actions, hence bringing about his suffering on the cross (vv. 6–8). A life in relationship to Jesus and committed to his mission will be a life of suffering for righteousness.

A second implication for a sermon focus is that suffering is not something one would normally boast about (v. 3). Glory, yes, but suffering, no. Legal standing with God, yes, but sharing in Christ's suffering, perhaps not. Caution must be taken here in preaching and pastoral care when helping persons understand suffering, lest suffering, in and of itself, becomes glorified. Theodicy is the theological attempt to describe or defend the goodness of God in the face of evil and human suffering. In contexts shaped by the "cause and effect" formula of scientific assumptions, attempts to explain suffering can cause even more pain when we try to identify its causes and effects, especially when its causes are attributed to God and interpreted as forms of judgment or punishment. This text does not justify suffering per se. Sermon preparation that addresses suffering

---

1. Dietrich Bonhoeffer, *The Cost of Discipleship* (New York: Touchstone, 1995).

must be done with sensitivity and caution, lest biblical texts are used to place blame, identify causes, and suggest remedies. This passage does not provide a theological defense that purports to redeem suffering in some way. The passage assumes there will be suffering for those who follow Christ's way and share in his life.

Paul suggests that suffering may produce certain character traits (vv. 3–5). However, these are not guaranteed results. Suffering takes an enormous toll on persons, and its effects are often unpredictable. It is important to acknowledge this in sermons that are addressing suffering. Physical pain and illness can have a debilitating impact on how one can function in everyday tasks, even on a person's will to live. Mental-health disorders cause various degrees of distress for persons and the ones who love and care for them. The infliction of brutal torture at the hands of another calls into question any notion we might have about the human capability for goodness. Broken relationships shatter our trust in others. We all know persons who have experienced suffering in various forms who are bitter, resentful, revengeful, angry, and incapacitated to live lives with any modicum of joy, contentment, or purpose.

The challenge this text presents to us is this: How can suffering produce in us the traits of endurance, character, and hope that do not disappoint us? Perhaps this is a question for a sermon. The challenge of pain and suffering is that they rob us of the ability to see beyond this moment in time. In the context of our quick-fix culture, we seek solutions to solve the problems of pain and suffering, problems that are often complex and even unfixable. We may learn to practice endurance in the midst of distress, a practice that has deep roots in the scriptural practice of crying out to the Lord in our need, noted in Psalm 116:1–2, which is also a lectionary reading this week.

Endurance or steadfastness may become a mark of our character. The word "character" comes to us from the Greek word *charaktēr*, a tool used for etching, making a mark, or stamping an insignia on an object. Think of those you know who have endured suffering. We often see it on their faces or other parts of their body. We might hear it in their voices. These marks we see in their lives often draw us to them. They become sources of wisdom, perspective, and inspiration, helping us see ways in which suffering may produce endurance. They may also remind us of the marks on Jesus' own body, the suffering he endured, and the etchings left on his hands, feet, sides, and brow.

While suffering may produce endurance, and endurance may produce character, character may produce hope. Hope is one of the three theological virtues, along with faith and love. Hope is both a gift from God and a virtue we learn to practice over a lifetime. Hope provides the context for the suffering described in our text today. When there are so few things about which to be hopeful in current circumstances, preachers can offer a gift to congregations in sermons that remind hearers of God's hopeful presence in difficult circumstances.

The hope that God gives, one that does not disappoint, keeps us from the futility and despair that characterizes so much of human suffering. Hope is not just wanting things to be better or different. Hope is not a form of denial about how bad things might be. Rather, hope is a gift from God and a Christian virtue that helps us trust God and God's ability to bring about meaning and life, even in our most dire circumstances. It is God who can bring life out of suffering, as God brought life out of Christ's suffering. This perhaps is the only justification we can provide for suffering.

WYNDY CORBIN REUSCHLING

Proper 6 (Sunday between June 12 and June 18 inclusive)

Matthew 9:35–10:8 (9–23)

9:35Then Jesus went about all the cities and villages, teaching in their synagogues, and proclaiming the good news of the kingdom, and curing every disease and every sickness. 36When he saw the crowds, he had compassion for them, because they were harassed and helpless, like sheep without a shepherd. 37Then he said to his disciples, "The harvest is plentiful, but the laborers are few; 38therefore ask the Lord of the harvest to send out laborers into his harvest."

10:1Then Jesus summoned his twelve disciples and gave them authority over unclean spirits, to cast them out, and to cure every disease and every sickness. 2These are the names of the twelve apostles: first, Simon, also known as Peter, and his brother Andrew; James son of Zebedee, and his brother John; 3Philip and Bartholomew; Thomas and Matthew the tax collector; James son of Alphaeus, and Thaddaeus; 4Simon the Cananaean, and Judas Iscariot, the one who betrayed him.

5These twelve Jesus sent out with the following instructions: "Go nowhere among the Gentiles, and enter no town of the Samaritans, 6but go rather to the lost sheep of the house of Israel. 7As you go, proclaim the good news, 'The kingdom of heaven has come near.' 8Cure the sick, raise the dead, cleanse the lepers, cast out demons. You received without payment; give without payment. 9Take no gold, or silver, or copper in your belts, 10no bag for your journey, or two tunics, or sandals, or a staff; for laborers deserve their food. 11Whatever town or village you enter, find out who in it is worthy, and stay there until you leave. 12As you enter the house, greet it. 13If the house is worthy, let your peace come upon it; but if it is not worthy, let your peace return to you. 14If anyone will not welcome you or listen to your words, shake off the dust from your feet as you leave that house or town. 15Truly I tell you, it will be more tolerable for the land of Sodom and Gomorrah on the day of judgment than for that town.

16"See, I am sending you out like sheep into the midst of wolves; so be wise as serpents and innocent as doves. 17Beware of them, for they will hand you over to councils and flog you in their synagogues; 18and you will be dragged before governors and kings because of me, as a testimony to them and the Gentiles. 19When they hand you over, do not worry about how you are to speak or what you are to say; for what you are to say will be given to you at that time; 20for it is not you who speak, but the Spirit of your Father speaking through you. 21Brother will betray brother to death, and a father his child, and children will rise against parents and have them put to death; 22and you will be hated by all because of my name. But the one who endures to the end will be saved. 23When they persecute you in one town, flee to the next; for truly I tell you, you will not have gone through all the towns of Israel before the Son of Man comes."

Commentary 1: Connecting the Reading with Scripture

The end of chapter 9 marks a transition in Matthew's Gospel. Jesus has left a cycle of healings and controversies in Capernaum and is back on the journey to preach, teach, and heal, reflecting his beginning mission in 4:23. While on the road, he is full of compassion for the crowds who are both without a shepherd and also ripe for the harvest. Matthew 10 solves this dilemma with the commissioning of the Twelve. Jesus then embarks on a special teaching for the disciples and also for all who will preach, teach, and heal in his name.

Jesus' compassion for the shepherd-less crowds fulfills the prophecy in Ezekiel 34, when the prophet claims that God will be the people's shepherd. God will seek the lost, bind up the injured, and feed them with justice (Ezek. 34:16). It also fulfills the claim that Jesus will be a ruler who shepherds Israel (Matt. 2:6) and implies the ever-present criticism, found throughout Matthew, of the religious leaders who have failed the sheep. The mission of Jesus is also attached to the eschatological symbol of the harvest, where the righteous will be gathered together. The number twelve strengthens the association to Israel and its eschatological implications. Going only to the lost sheep suggests that Matthew's community saw itself in line with the history of Israel, as a kind of gathering under a new shepherd.

Matthew first uses the term "disciples" of those to whom Jesus gives authority, and then uses "apostles," which seems a postresurrection term. The use of both terms so close together makes for a fruitful combination. We are gathered as disciples under the teachings of Jesus and then sent out as apostles to do as Jesus does. In fact, his instructions to the disciples are a summary of his own ministry in chapters 5–9: proclaiming, healing, raising, restoring, and exorcising. The ministry will be repeated again in 11:4–5, when John's disciples ask if Jesus is the one to come. The answer is that transformation happens when the kingdom of heaven draws near. Thus, if we need to know what it means to enter into ministry, Matthew offers a clear example to follow. Contemporary Christians might think of "lost sheep" as sinners, but these instructions and the associations to prophecy suggest that spiritual, bodily, and political need are met in this kingdom. Jesus' own ministry addressed the crowd's harassed and helpless state, and he sends the disciples to do the same. Preachers might consider how we are also called to compassion, or identify the crowding needs to which God sends us today.

Authority is a theme throughout Matthew's Gospel, but if the disciples were hoping for earthly authority, they were sadly mistaken. Do not make any provision for the journey, even to the extent of bringing money, extra clothing, or even a staff to protect yourself. Do not accept payment, but depend on others for your food and shelter. Matthew's account may have sought to differentiate the disciples from other wandering philosophers, or these instructions could reflect traditional sayings of itinerant radicals, wandering missionaries who are attested in Acts and also in early Christian writing like the *Didache*.[1]

They certainly challenge the commodification of spiritual leadership and sound similar to the practice of Paul, who tried to support himself so as to not appear a charlatan before the people (Acts 20:34; 1 Thess. 2:9; 2 Thess. 3:8). This wandering life is also another way to live as Jesus did, for he was an itinerant preacher with nowhere to lay his head (Matt. 8:20). It is possible that Matthew's community was started by such preachers or that it sent poor itinerant preachers in mission. Certainly the call to wander for God reaches all the way back to Abraham, and today's reading from Genesis 18 also suggests themes of surprising provision and promise when all hope seemed lost. Preachers could reflect on how Jesus calls believers to minister in vulnerability, depend on God's provision, and follow God's call even when the way seems unclear.

If everything in Matthew can (and most could) be seen as a gloss on the Sermon of the Mount, then we see in this teaching a radical expression of the command to not worry about what you will eat, drink, or wear (Matt. 6:25–33) and to depend on God for daily bread (v. 11). One cannot serve both God and wealth (v. 24), so it is not surprising that the disciples must offer the signs of the kingdom without pay. Later in the Gospel, we hear that the lure of wealth will actually choke away the teachings of Jesus (13:22). Jesus also tells the rich young man to sell all that he has and give to the poor, in order to gain treasure in heaven (19:20–22). Dependence on wealth hampers dependence

---

1. Ulrich Luz, *Studies in Matthew*, trans. Rosemary Selle (Grand Rapids: Eerdmans, 2005), 152.

The Unity Which Excels Every Unity

O holy Jesus,
Gentle friend,
Morning star,
Midday sun adorned,
Brilliant flame of righteousness, life everlasting and eternity,
Fountain ever-new, ever-living, ever-lasting,
Heart's desire of Patriarchs,
Longing of prophets,
Master of Apostles and disciples,
Giver of the Law,
Prince of the New Testament,
Judge of doom,
Son of the merciful Father without mother in heaven,
Son of the true virgin Mary, without father on earth,
True and loving brother,

. . . Receive me at my life's end into heaven in the unity of Patriarchs and prophets, in the unity of Apostles and disciples, in the unity of angels and archangels, in the unity which excels every unity, that is, in the unity of the holy and exalted Trinity, Father, Son, and Holy Ghost.

"The Broom of Devotion," in *Celtic Spirituality*, The Classics of Western Spirituality series, trans. Oliver Davies (New York: Paulist, 1999), 295, 297.

---

on God, and this message has inspired centuries of monastic commitment to poverty, like Anthony, Francis of Assisi, and the Poor Clares. Preachers might note that discipleship is never about self-sufficiency, as the disciples can serve only by accepting service from strangers.

If trust in God's providence were not hard enough, the disciples then hear of persecutions. It is the foreshadowing of what will happen to Jesus, who is put on trial, flogged, and executed. As the Beatitudes tell us, believers are blessed if they are persecuted in Jesus' name (5:11–12). It means that they have faithfully followed Christ. We also sense the bitter break suffered between the Matthean community and the synagogue's leaders. This is suggested later in Jesus' woes against the scribes and Pharisees, when Jesus repeats that they will crucify some, flog others in the synagogue, and pursue others from town to town (23:34–36). Indeed, Peter and John went before the Sanhedrin (Acts 4:1–22), and Paul persecuted the early followers all the way to Damascus (9:1–2). The Roman Empire also periodically martyred Christians. Being lashed or beaten was one of the punishments meted by religious leaders (Deut. 25:1–3; 2 Cor. 11:24–25), and we read of floggings by Roman authorities (Acts 22:24). This history makes today's reading from Romans 5:1–8 all the more profound for preachers. Christians do not possess a saccharine hope, but one produced through bearing the challenges and trials of faithfully following Jesus.

While the followers of Jesus make themselves vulnerable in poverty and persecution, they are certainly not weak in character. If a place does not accept them, it loses their peace. If a village will not hear them, they leave and brush off their responsibility for its final judgment like dust from their feet. When persecution is unbearable, they should flee to the next village. Controversy and persecution are not a sign that the mission has failed. Instead, the believers are told to keep their wits about them, using persecutions strategically for public witness. They are meant to be innocent as doves, when "innocent" literally means "unmixed," simple and without guile.[2] They must also be as wise as the

---

2. Dale Allison and Matthew Davies, *Matthew: A Shorter Commentary* (New York: T. & T. Clark, 2004), 156.

serpent who strikes opportunely and can slither out of anything (Gen. 3:1).

Paul's various adventures in Acts are powerful examples of this dual strategy, and our Romans 5:1–8 reading appointed for today offers a beautiful tribute to both the cost and strength of character built through a life of mission. For individuals and congregations who fear failure, this can be a hopeful message. It is not the height of success or the absence of challenges that matter, but how we grow when we follow the call of Jesus to preach, teach, and heal in his name.

SONIA E. WATERS

Commentary 2: Connecting the Reading with the World

We worship an inefficient, unregulated God. Discipleship is immersion in God's shocking inefficiency, God's unregulated economy, otherwise known as compassion and grace.

In the passage for this Sunday, Jesus "has compassion for the people" and therefore sends out his disciples to minister to them. Like any good teacher or coach, before they go forth to minister, he gives them a pep talk, words of advice that will help them know how to engage with the "lost sheep" (Matt. 10:6). Compassion frames what Jesus sees, his vision of the harvest. It shapes his charge to the disciples (9:36–37). Participation in that harvest is *given* to the disciples; *received* without payment. They live in grace's unrepayable debt (10:8). As modern-day equivalents of these disciples, we might see this passage as chock-full of instructions about what it looks like to be a follower of Jesus today. Four different angles into the text easily suggest themselves: healing as the heart of the gospel; authority; boundaries; and freedom.

Healing. The proximity of proclamation and healing is striking here. Few of us enter the pulpit with the trust that disease and sickness will be cured by our preaching. Yet this passage makes that connection clear: when Jesus taught and preached, disease and sickness *were* healed (9:35). Jesus gives that same power and authority to his followers. What might this mean in our world? Research increasingly suggests that participation in a religious community improves health, providing resources for resilience and support through community.[3] A preacher might delve into this link between the good news of Jesus and healing.

In particular, a wise preacher might explore the role of compassion, just as "Jesus had compassion for them, because they were harassed and helpless, like sheep without a shepherd" (v. 36). In contrast to most Western democracies, in the United States the average life expectancy is shrinking[4] and the suicide rate is rising. One huge driver in these trends is drugs and addiction. New research indicates that the most common cause of addiction is isolation, rather than the more frequently cited reasons of drug availability, moral failing, or biological disease alone.[5] In our increasingly polarized and technology-driven forms of communication and connection, it is not surprising that isolation is increasing.

What are the implications for the church's understanding of what it means to proclaim the gospel in this context? How might the embodied presence of Jesus and his disciples *among* the people—a presence driven by compassion—speak to the power Christ vests in each of us, linking teaching and proclamation to healing and wholeness? Munch's *The Scream* might be a provocative bulletin cover or worship image here. What does the church's witness of compassion look like in a world that is screaming?

---

3. Harold G. Koenig, "Religion, Spirituality, and Health: The Research and Clinical Implications," *ISRN Psychiatry 2012: 278730* (Dec. 16, 2012).
4. Mike Wehner, "Life Expectancy in the United States Continues to Decline, and Officials Know Why," BGR, November 29, 2018; https://bgr.com/2018/11/29/life-expectancy-2017-2018-data-cdc/.
5. Johann Hari, "The Likely Cause of Addiction Has Been Discovered and It's Not What You Think," *Huffington Post*, April 18, 2017.

Authority. Matthew makes bold claims on our behalf in this passage. When Jesus calls out the disciples, he vests them with *authority:* "Cure the sick, raise the dead, cleanse the lepers, cast out demons" (10:8). That's a form of authority most of us would have a hard time mustering on our own. Sermons on the nature of authority are a natural fit here. From whence does this bold authority and power emanate? How do we live with and into the authority Jesus bequeaths to his followers? How does authority operate for Christians? Is it hierarchical? Is Jesus a collaborative leader? How does Jesus entrust that authority to his disciples? How does it vest? What Christian practices empower and guide that authority? Where does accountability lie? How do we take that authority upon ourselves? What is the role of the church in nurturing that authority?

Obedience resulting from coercion (coercive power) and obedience resulting from calibration of internal attitudes (reward power) are two explanations social scientists have traditionally explored in seeking to understand how authority operates in groups. Matthew seems to suggest a different form of authority: authority as response to compassion. Matthew does not describe attitude adjustment among the people thronging for Jesus' touch. He instead proclaims healing. Conversion. New life. Wholeness in response to compassion. Life born of illness, pain, and brokenness noticed and acknowledged. How might this operate in the church?

Boundaries. Of course, any pastor worth her salt will likely feel as if she is going to drown in need in the face of that kind of call to compassion—as will any faithful man or woman listening in the pew. The need is endless. The capacity is limited: "The harvest is plentiful, but the laborers are few" (9:37). It is not surprising that Matthew immediately turns to the question of limits and boundaries: "If anyone will not welcome you or listen to your words, shake off the dust from your feet as you leave that house or town" (10:14). That is, enter, find out who is worthy, stay (be present) until you leave, greet when you enter, invite peace, if peace is not received then be bold enough to claim and embody peace—and *leave.* Given the church's proclivity to indulge wretched behavior in the name of being nice and then to suck people dry with committees, duties, obligations, and moral demands, this gospel word on boundaries and limits bears attention. Inherent to the authority Jesus vests in his disciples is an admonition to trust and to give—and then to set limits when the gift is not received or is abused. Limit setting is not hard just in churches. It is hard in families and work places too. A sermon painting a picture of healthy authority exercised with boundaries and limits would be a gift in most congregations. Few passages in the Bible lend themselves to that sort of sermon more than this one.

Freedom. Limits are not the heart of this passage, though. Limits exist in service of something else: freedom. At its very heart, this passage throbs with the limitless wonder of God's calling and sending. The good news is that Jesus invites us along to do what he does: to proclaim good news. The only suitable response to this wondrous invitation is to follow in vulnerability and to trust that what we receive is freely given and must be freely received and then shared. That is the rhythm of the Christian life.

Living as we do in a transactional culture, this vision of rich and wondrous life is truly radical. A pastor might reflect on the larger world in a sermon, comparing moments of wondrous freedom in giving and receiving to crippling and binding practices of exchange that constantly measure and compare outcome. The church community itself might be a focus for such reflection as well. When someone enters into the fabric of a church, do they experience freedom? Is the gospel freely given and received, or is there an accounting of who gives properly and who does not? Who receives more than she gives?

Every aspect of this passage is marked with fluidity. Nothing is set in stone. All is in motion. This is God on the move in the world. A preacher might point to God on the move in the congregation, or God moving a congregation in crazy, irrational, risking ways into the world God so loves.

DENISE THORPE

Proper 7 (Sunday between June 19 and June 25 inclusive)

Jeremiah 20:7–13 and
   Genesis 21:8–21
Psalm 69:7–10 (11–15), 16–18
   and Psalm 86:1–10, 16–17

Romans 6:1b–11
Matthew 10:24–39

Jeremiah 20:7–13

⁷O LORD, you have enticed me,
   and I was enticed;
you have overpowered me,
   and you have prevailed.
I have become a laughingstock all day long;
   everyone mocks me.
⁸For whenever I speak, I must cry out,
   I must shout, "Violence and destruction!"
For the word of the LORD has become for me
   a reproach and derision all day long.
⁹If I say, "I will not mention him,
   or speak any more in his name,"
then within me there is something like a burning fire
   shut up in my bones;
I am weary with holding it in,
   and I cannot.
¹⁰For I hear many whispering:
   "Terror is all around!
Denounce him! Let us denounce him!"
   All my close friends
   are watching for me to stumble.
"Perhaps he can be enticed,
   and we can prevail against him,
   and take our revenge on him."
¹¹But the LORD is with me like a dread warrior;
   therefore my persecutors will stumble,
   and they will not prevail.
They will be greatly shamed,
   for they will not succeed.
Their eternal dishonor
   will never be forgotten.
¹²O LORD of hosts, you test the righteous,
   you see the heart and the mind;
let me see your retribution upon them,
   for to you I have committed my cause.

¹³Sing to the LORD;
   praise the LORD!
For he has delivered the life of the needy
   from the hands of evildoers.

Genesis 21:8–21

⁸The child grew, and was weaned; and Abraham made a great feast on the day that Isaac was weaned. ⁹But Sarah saw the son of Hagar the Egyptian, whom she had borne to Abraham, playing with her son Isaac. ¹⁰So she said to Abraham, "Cast out this slave woman with her son; for the son of this slave woman shall not inherit along with my son Isaac." ¹¹The matter was very distressing to Abraham on account of his son. ¹²But God said to Abraham, "Do not be distressed because of the boy and because of your slave woman; whatever Sarah says to you, do as she tells you, for it is through Isaac that offspring shall be named for you. ¹³As for the son of the slave woman, I will make a nation of him also, because he is your offspring." ¹⁴So Abraham rose early in the morning, and took bread and a skin of water, and gave it to Hagar, putting it on her shoulder, along with the child, and sent her away. And she departed, and wandered about in the wilderness of Beer-sheba.

¹⁵When the water in the skin was gone, she cast the child under one of the bushes. ¹⁶Then she went and sat down opposite him a good way off, about the distance of a bowshot; for she said, "Do not let me look on the death of the child." And as she sat opposite him, she lifted up her voice and wept. ¹⁷And God heard the voice of the boy; and the angel of God called to Hagar from heaven, and said to her, "What troubles you, Hagar? Do not be afraid; for God has heard the voice of the boy where he is. ¹⁸Come, lift up the boy and hold him fast with your hand, for I will make a great nation of him." ¹⁹Then God opened her eyes and she saw a well of water. She went, and filled the skin with water, and gave the boy a drink.

²⁰God was with the boy, and he grew up; he lived in the wilderness, and became an expert with the bow. ²¹He lived in the wilderness of Paran; and his mother got a wife for him from the land of Egypt.

Commentary 1: Connecting the Reading with Scripture

Being a prophet was a tough job. Prophets were not fortune-tellers, as usually imagined, but messengers of God. As messengers, they were supposed to relay to a community God's interpretation of their society. Prophets therefore functioned as social critics and had the unfortunate task of delivering God's insight and message—usually critical—to the people and to those in power. They, in short, had the job of scolding a community about its mistakes. As a result, they were frequently, though not always (e.g., Isa. 40), the bearers of bad news.

Understandably, prophets and their message were not often well received. No one exemplifies the unfortunate task of being a prophet better than Jeremiah. Jeremiah lived during a difficult and terrifying time in the history of ancient Israel: right before and during the fall of Judah. It was a trying time, and the messages he was tasked to deliver were predictably disheartening. It is no wonder that, in the passage assigned for this Sunday, Jeremiah details the difficulties of his vocation in a disheartening lament. This lament, like those found in the book of Lamentations, is a poem that verbally expresses negative emotions and feelings, such as sorrow or grief. As evident by the presence of lament in the Psalms, they were part of the worship experiences of ancient Israel and the early church.

In this lament, Jeremiah complains that the only messages God gives him to convey to the people are negative ones predicting doom and gloom (Jer. 20:8). This, he complains, makes him incredibly unpopular. He is "ridiculed all day long" and ostracized and mocked by everyone (v. 7, NIV). "All my friends," Jeremiah declares, "are waiting for me to slip" (v. 10). As is evident from Jeremiah's example, being faithful to God can lead to ridicule and ill-treatment from the community, even from friends. This is affirmed by Acts 7:51–53, which states that prophets were regularly persecuted and sometimes even killed.

Despite God's making him very unpopular, Jeremiah states that he cannot resist God. He states that God has deceived him and overpowered him (v. 7). When he tries holding in God's message, it burns within him "like a burning fire shut up in my bones" (v. 9). This pain is relieved only when he prophesies the messages given to him. Chosen and assigned this role before birth (1:4–5), he has little choice but to accept—albeit begrudgingly at times (1:6; 20:9–10)—the task that God has called him to do. Running away, as Jonah attempts to do, was not an option. Hence, despite the suffering, Jeremiah recommits himself to God's service (v. 12).

Jeremiah's lament opens up space for a discussion of difficulties faced by those who currently are called by God to speak and work for moral transformation in society. Who are those in our society who continue the prophetic mission by bravely speaking God's truth to power? How has the church helped or hindered these modern prophets? Jeremiah's lament also brings up questions related to calling. What is our calling, both as individuals and as a community of God? In what ways have we resisted the tasks to which we are called, as Jeremiah tries to do? How can we move from a point of lament and resistance to a point of acceptance and willingness?

Jeremiah's feelings of ostracism and persecution are mirrored by those of Hagar, Abraham's second wife, when she and her son Ishmael are forced out into the desert (Gen. 16, 21). Hagar, the Egyptian slave woman of the infertile Israelite matriarch Sarah, was given to Abraham, Sarah's husband, to act as a surrogate. After being given to Abraham with little say or assent, Hagar immediately conceives. This development in the story is not surprising considering the then-prevailing stereotype of Egyptians and Egypt as the bread basket of the Near East; as overly fertile and overly lusty (e.g., Potiphar's wife). When Hagar conceives, tensions between the women increase, and Sarah mistreats Hagar until she runs away (Gen. 16). During Hagar's first flight, she encounters an angel in the wilderness who instructs her to return to Sarah and to "humble" herself, usually translated as "submit under the hand of Sarah" (v. 9).

Depending on the translation, this command has troubled interpreters. God, instead of telling Hagar to resist, seems to be telling her to submit to slavery and to return to an abusive situation. However, the command to return is countered by the divine recognition of Hagar as the first woman in the Bible whom God talks to directly about her pregnancy. That the first woman to whom God talks is an outsider, a slave, and a foreigner is telling, and hints of God's regard for those in similar positions.

Hagar's troubles do not end, however, with her return. After Sarah bears a child of her own, she rightly fears for the inheritance of her son, Isaac (21:10). As the elder son, Ishmael, the son of Hagar, would normally inherit the lion's share of the inheritance. Things come to a head during Isaac's weaning party, when Sarah, after noticing Ishmael making fun of her son, Isaac (v. 9), forces Abraham to expel Hagar and Ishmael with just meager provisions to the wilderness, an act that entailed certain death.

The verb "isaacing" that describes Ishmael's actions in 21:9 is ambiguous. This word, which underlies Isaac's name, can mean "to play or laugh." However, it can also connote something sexual (26:8). Ishmael might have been making fun of Isaac. The text, however, might be intimating that Ishmael was doing something more serious; if that was the case, some of the blame of Sarah for so viciously throwing out Hagar and Ishmael to the desert is mitigated. As is evident, translation is key to interpretation. However, the fact that both sons come together to bury their father when he dies hints that this family was able to overcome some of their issues in the end (25:9).

This act of family discord, however, will also have lingering effect. Ironically, Hagar's mistreatment at the hands of Israel's ancestor mirrors and foreshadows the mistreatment of the Israelites at the hands of the Egyptian elite recorded

The Way of Life Lies Here

I beheld then, that they all went on till they came to the foot of Hill Difficulty, at the bottom of which was a Spring. There was also in the same place two other ways besides that which came straight from the Gate; one turned to the left hand, and the other to the right, at the bottom of the Hill: but the narrow way lay right up the Hill (and the name of the going up the side of the Hill, is called Difficulty). Christian now went to the Spring and drank thereof to refresh himself, and then began to go up the Hill; saying,

> The Hill though high, I covet to ascend;
> The difficulty will not me offend;
> For I perceive the way to life lies here;
> Come, pluck up, Heart; lets neither faint nor fear:
> Better, tho' difficult, th' right way to go,
> Than wrong, though easy, where the end is wo.

The other two also came to the foot of the Hill. But when they saw that the Hill was steep and high, and that there were two other ways to go; and supposing also, that these two ways might meet again, with that up which Christian went, on the other side of the Hill: Therefore they were resolved to go in those ways (now the name of one of those ways was Danger, and the name of the other Destruction). So the one took the way which is called Danger, which led him into a great Wood; and the other took directly up the way to Destruction, which led him into a wide field full of dark Mountains, where he stumbled and fell, and rose no more.

I looked then after Christian, to see him go up the Hill, where I perceived he fell from running to going, and from going to clambering upon his hands and his knees, because of the steepness of the place. Now about the midway to the top of the Hill, was a pleasant Arbour, made by the Lord of the Hill, for the refreshing of weary Travellers. Thither therefore Christian got, where also he sat down to rest him. Then he pull'd his Roll out of his bosom and read therein to his comfort; he also now began afresh to take a review of the Coat or Garment that was given him as he stood by the Cross. Thus pleasing himself a while, he at last fell into a slumber, and thence into a fast sleep, which detained him in that place until it was almost night, and in his sleep his Roll fell out of his hand. Now as he was sleeping, there came one to him and awakened him saying, Go to the Ant, thou sluggard, consider her ways and be wise; and with that Christian suddenly started up, and sped on his way, and went apace till he came to the top of the Hill.

John Bunyan, *Pilgrim's Progress*, ed. John Brown (Boston: Houghton Mifflin, 1887), 45–46.

---

in Exodus. Indeed, these stories about the conflict between Hagar and Sarah are attempts by biblical writers to explain interethnic conflict. If we are all related to each other, why do we fight with and try to kill each other? The biblical writers, through their narratives, hint that perhaps it has to do with parental favoritism, mistreatment of the less powerful by those with more power, familial abuse, and needless rivalries.

Especially pertinent is the issue of power, particularly as it pertains to ethnicity. Egypt, in the ancient context, should be imagined as encompassing not just modern-day Egypt but also parts of North Africa. Considering Hagar's possible ethnic and social location, Hagar's story has found particular resonance in African American communities.

That Hagar is rescued twice by God, who twice promises her that her descendants will thrive, hints that God has particular regard for those who, like Hagar, are oppressed, powerless, and marginalized. So the stories about Hagar challenge the church to reflect upon the ways in which we have sided *against* the modern-day Hagars and Ishmaels. How have we, like Sarah and Abraham, thrown out the Hagars and

Ishmaels to fend for themselves in the desert? How can we instead act on behalf of the Hagars and Ishmaels by calling out and challenging society when it mistreats the marginalized and powerless? After all, as these stories remind us, the God of Hagar watches and sees the oppression of her descendants (21:17).

SONG-MI SUZIE PARK

Commentary 2: Connecting the Reading with the World

There is a great amount of "happy talk" in our culture and in the culture of many of our churches, at least a great deal of shallowness that finds itself wanting when life gets hard or our world is shaken. These texts from Jeremiah and Genesis not only resist "happy talk" and shallowness. They provide a countercultural model that gives the preacher an opportunity to speak into the world of division, violence, tragedy, and hopelessness. The texts also lead us to see God anew, not as some benign or permissive presence who blesses our lives, but rather a God who calls us and places accountability for that call into our lives. Whatever choices a preacher makes about preaching these texts in this culture, shallow approaches will not work.

The preacher may well find that preaching these texts meets congregational members in the midst of the hardship they are living, their days filled with the strife and difficulty embodied in these texts. Going to the hospital where a child of the church had just died, the pastor asked if she could offer a prayer. "Please do," the grieving mother said evenly, "but when you pray, make sure you yell at your God."

Preaching hard texts is an essential challenge for any congregation—and any preacher. Jeremiah's painful lament over being seduced by God, paired with the account in Genesis of Hagar and Ishmael being sent away, calls us to careful attention to the ways and love of God. If there were ever texts that needed careful weaving into liturgy that displayed honesty and truth-telling, it is these. While the Jeremiah passage ends with the doxological stanza ("Sing to the LORD; praise the LORD! For [God] has delivered the life of the needy from the hands of evildoers" [Jer. 20:13]), the twelve verses that precede that verse exhibit pain, feelings of betrayal, and a near primal scream of loss and lament. Jeremiah accuses God of having enticed him so that he became "a laughingstock all day long" (v. 7), that God forced him to "shout, 'Violence and destruction!'" even when he did not want, even when he tried to hold these words in (vv. 8–9).

How could the prayers for the day that would surround this text echo that painful journey? People in grief or pain or disappointed urgently need models of speech before and with God. How do these texts offer models of how we pray to God in times of extreme hardship? With the news offering reasons to lament practically every day, how does a congregation learn to lament together and continue to give thanks and praise to God? How do we critique the shallowness we see in the face of tragedy ("well, this must be God's will" or "I know we cannot question God") and use what we read in Jeremiah's encounter with God here as a different way forward?

Likewise, while the Genesis account of Hagar's and Ishmael's plight ends with God deploying angels for their care and promising, "I will make a great nation of him" (Gen. 21:18), no one can hear the banishment to the wilderness that precedes that without feeling the pain therein or experiencing doubt as to the nature of the love of God. Sermons on these texts—and especially the worship in which they are preached—would do well to go toward that pain and those doubts and not attempt to bypass them with easy resolution or empty affirmations about God's love. That Jeremiah was both called, affirmed, faithful, *and* in great pain is a theme that a sermon could embrace: the difficulty of holding all those things together in one life.

The "they lived happily ever after" notion of Hollywood exists in many as the goal of life.

When lived life punctures that, when "happily ever after" is not available any more, people need a durable faith in the living God that can carry them deeper and through hardship. The 1980 film *Ordinary People* had as its mantra that "intelligent people can work out their own problems." Then tragedy struck and the family of "intelligent people" was left without recourse. The faithful speech of these texts provides witness that even as one is stripped of all props in life, there is still life and faith and hope.

There is good opportunity with these texts to use visuals to support the struggle that can be experienced in loving God in times of pain. The global news of any given week will provide numerous images of how it is difficult to love God in a world like this: children suffering from poison gas attacks in Syria, refugees struggling through a desert (much like Hagar and Ishmael), isolated figures sitting alone in a nursing home corridor, a long line at a soup kitchen, an emergency room in almost any city late at night.

Classic art has also focused on these biblical images. Rembrandt's *Abraham Dismissing Hagar and Ishmael* (1640) shows Hagar alone in the light, with everyone else in shadows as she is dismissed into the darkness. A very different image by Marc Chagall, *Hagar in the Desert* (1960), shows Hagar attempting to shelter Ishmael as they are isolated and alone and the boy is growing weak. Chagall also has a painting, *Jeremiah's Lamentation* (1956), that offers an image of the Jeremiah 20 text, with Jeremiah alone and crouched with a crowd standing far off. There would be ample opportunities for these and other artistic works—both classic and contemporary—to be put in service of helping the preacher let the congregation feel these texts as well as hear them.

The aim of any sermon or worship service is not to leave a congregation in the depths of these cries—any more than the texts themselves stay with the lament of Jeremiah or the desolate abandonment of Hagar and Ishmael. However, faithful treatment of the emotional and spiritual landscape of these texts will provide ample time to contemplate the character of God's love in light of these words before reaching each text's final verse. There is a difficulty in loving God through all life's hardship and through all the world's pain. That truth is reflected both in these texts, as well as in the lived experience of every single person who will gather in worship to hear them. This truth—and its authentic acknowledgment in sermon and in worship—will nurture deeper spiritual maturity.

These texts allow us to encounter—and practice our response to—these hard truths. A sermon that does not wrap things up or bring everything to a tight conclusion (as hard as that is, before a congregation that probably already has enough "loose ends" in their lives) will reflect the speech of Jeremiah and the difficult account of Hagar and her son. Through both there is assurance of God's steadfast love and care, but that promise is heard through experiences that resist easy resolution or shallow platitudes.

The late novelist John Updike had one of his characters observe, "Westerners have lost whole octaves of passion. We no longer have capacity for full-range of expression—either on the high end or the low end of life's experience. Third-world women can still make an inhuman piercing grieving noise right from the floor of the soul. We struggle to regain that capacity."[1]

These texts point to a way to regain that capacity.

MARK RAMSEY

---

1. John Updike, *Roger's Version* (New York: Alfred A. Knopf, 1986), 273.

Proper 7 (Sunday between June 19 and June 25 inclusive)

Psalm 69:7–10 (11–15), 16–18

⁷It is for your sake that I have borne reproach,
   that shame has covered my face.
⁸I have become a stranger to my kindred,
   an alien to my mother's children.

⁹It is zeal for your house that has consumed me;
   the insults of those who insult you have fallen on me.
¹⁰When I humbled my soul with fasting,
   they insulted me for doing so.
¹¹When I made sackcloth my clothing,
   I became a byword to them.
¹²I am the subject of gossip for those who sit in the gate,
   and the drunkards make songs about me.

¹³But as for me, my prayer is to you, O LORD.
   At an acceptable time, O God,
   in the abundance of your steadfast love, answer me.
With your faithful help ¹⁴rescue me
   from sinking in the mire;
let me be delivered from my enemies
   and from the deep waters.
¹⁵Do not let the flood sweep over me,
   or the deep swallow me up,
   or the Pit close its mouth over me.

¹⁶Answer me, O LORD, for your steadfast love is good;
   according to your abundant mercy, turn to me.
¹⁷Do not hide your face from your servant,
   for I am in distress—make haste to answer me.
¹⁸Draw near to me, redeem me,
   set me free because of my enemies.

Psalm 86:1–10, 16–17

¹Incline your ear, O LORD, and answer me,
   for I am poor and needy.
²Preserve my life, for I am devoted to you;
   save your servant who trusts in you.
You are my God; ³be gracious to me, O Lord,
   for to you do I cry all day long.
⁴Gladden the soul of your servant,
   for to you, O Lord, I lift up my soul.
⁵For you, O Lord, are good and forgiving,
   abounding in steadfast love to all who call on you.
⁶Give ear, O LORD, to my prayer;
   listen to my cry of supplication.

⁷In the day of my trouble I call on you,
    for you will answer me.

⁸There is none like you among the gods, O Lord,
    nor are there any works like yours.
⁹All the nations you have made shall come
    and bow down before you, O Lord,
    and shall glorify your name.
¹⁰For you are great and do wondrous things;
    you alone are God.
. . . .
¹⁶Turn to me and be gracious to me;
    give your strength to your servant;
    save the child of your serving girl.
¹⁷Show me a sign of your favor,
    so that those who hate me may see it and be put to shame,
    because you, LORD, have helped me and comforted me.

Connecting the Psalm with Scripture and Worship

Psalm 69:7–10 (11–15), 16–18. These verses from Psalm 69 are paired with the first part of Jeremiah's impassioned speech in chapter 20. The psalmist speaks as a pious yet persecuted servant. Jeremiah engages in prophetic contest with Pashhur: Who speaks the "word of God," who delivers truth? Pashhur assures that all will be well; Jeremiah warns that Babylon will capture all the wealth of this city and all of Judah's treasures, and the people will be taken into exile and killed. Jeremiah has no love for this message he is given to preach. He tries to stay silent. He curses the day he was born and the one who announced to his father that he had a son (Jer. 20:14–15). Such is his call. Truth unspoken burns right through his bones; he *must* cry: "Violence! Destruction is upon us!" (vv. 8–9). Invasion is inevitable at this point. Rescue will not come in time. Here is a horrifying form of divine providence; punishment is on the way, with restoration at least a generation away.

The psalmist resides in the midst of alienation and humiliation. Continuing to fast and pray, to don sackcloth, to express zeal for God's house, the psalmist also cries out for rescue that does not appear. Only in the final verses of this lament does the reader understand that this cry actually emerges in exile: "For God will save Zion and rebuild the cities of Judah; and his servants shall live there and possess it" (Ps. 69:35). The psalmist is among the captives, surrounded by those who wish harm to the people, mocked by those who deny the power and concern of their God. Distress is all around; death seems imminent. "Make haste to answer me," the psalmist cries. Will deliverance arrive in time?

In our own day, does the preacher emulate Pashhur or Jeremiah or the psalmist? Are we to preach comfort to those in distress, perhaps as their privilege is eroded? Are we to announce destruction based either on divine judgment of the nation's faithlessness or because of divine abandonment? Should we, because we reside as captives in foreign territory, try to sustain the hope—both our own and that of our people—that our cities and our fortunes will be reclaimed?

The answer today—as in the days of ancient Israel—probably depends on one's positioning in relation to the centers of social and religious authority. If one is sure that comfort is needed, one might well ask if "the way things are" is really the way our God wants them to be. If one feels compelled to predict a time of defeat and hardship, one might well ask what additional word can help the people endure it. If one thinks we must languish far from home, one might well ask if dreams of "return" are faithful, since it is also Jeremiah who says, "But seek the welfare of the city where I have sent you into exile, and pray to the LORD on its behalf, for in its welfare you will find your welfare" (Jer. 29:7).

The psalm may serve as a basis for prayers of resilience in difficult days:

> Make haste, O Sustainer, to rescue.
> It is for your sake we bear reproach and suffer insult.
> We lift our prayers to you; we sing your praise.
> In humility, we fast, we trade linen for sackcloth.
> Our zeal is for your justice, our hope in your abundant mercy.
> As waters rise and floods close in,
> Draw near, redeem us, set us free.

Psalm 86:1–10, 16–17. The day's psalm and the story from Genesis with which it appears continue the narrative from the previous week's texts. Psalm 86 as a song of a "child of a servant girl" parallels Psalm 116 in structure but not mood. In Psalm 116, the supplications have been heard, the bonds have been loosed; in Psalm 86, the child awaits rescue. The waiting is confident, to be sure; but the gratitude and joy are tempered by continuing distress. Yes, this God is known and has answered pleas previously. So too this is a God who creates nations, nations who bow to glorify the divine name. As the nations are judged and sustained, so the child will be saved. The child trusts in God, calls to God all day long, and expects an answer, an answer abounding in steadfast love. Rescue will come not only for the child's sake but also to humble the child's enemies: "Show me a sign of your favor, so that those who hate me may see it and be put to shame" (Ps. 86:17). The sign of favor still lingers beyond the horizon.

In the Genesis passage, rescue arrives in the form of a spring of water, a source of life nearby but unseen until God opens Hagar's eyes (Gen. 21:19). She cannot bear to see the boy die, nor can she see that salvation is right at hand. Hagar lifts up her voice and weeps, while the boy fades toward death under a bush next to an empty water skin. Yet the boy's voice reaches the divine ear and moves God to respond with assurance to the mother's anguish: "Do not be afraid. . . . I will make a great nation of him" (vv. 17b–18). It is the voice of the child of a servant girl, this persona of the psalmist, that stirs divine compassion.

Here the enemy is clear. Sarah wishes Hagar and Ishmael dead. to ensure that Isaac is the true son and sole heir. God has other plans. "I will make a nation of him also," God assures Abraham (v. 13). Here Abraham sends his oldest son away with meager provision into a hostile wilderness. Soon, however, God will test Abraham by asking him to sacrifice Isaac on an altar. Then God will call Isaac, Abraham's son, "your son, your only son, the one whom you love" (22:2). Ishmael is forgotten; the trial is divinely ordained. Death looms: a boy alone under a bush, a son tied below the hand of a father wielding a knife. How do our trials and tribulations, which range from trivial to toxic, relate to the banishment of a slave and her son or to a lethal test of loyalty or to a death on a cross? How do our lives relate to a gift of living water, to the rescue of an only son (and the death of a ram), to the promise that "we too might walk in newness of life" as those "united with him in a death like his" (Rom. 6:4–5)? God so often has other plans: "For you are great and do wondrous things" (Ps. 86:10).

One might draw on Psalm 86:1–10 and 16–17 to structure a pastoral prayer in the form of "joys and concerns":

> The psalmist cries: Incline your ear, O Lord,
> and answer me, for I am poor and needy.
> Let us name those whose needs weigh on our hearts and minds today,
> those who are poor, those who are alone,
> those who are ill, those who are dying . . .
>
> The Lord is good and forgiving, abounding in steadfast love.
> In thanksgiving to the giver of all good gifts,
> let us name the blessings we have witnessed,
> the signs of hope that sustain us . . .
> In times of favor and times of distress,
> You are our Help and our Comfort.
> And let all God's people say, Amen.

W. SCOTT HALDEMAN

Proper 7 (Sunday between June 19 and June 25 inclusive)

Romans 6:1b–11

[1b]Should we continue in sin in order that grace may abound? [2]By no means! How can we who died to sin go on living in it? [3]Do you not know that all of us who have been baptized into Christ Jesus were baptized into his death? [4]Therefore we have been buried with him by baptism into death, so that, just as Christ was raised from the dead by the glory of the Father, so we too might walk in newness of life.

[5]For if we have been united with him in a death like his, we will certainly be united with him in a resurrection like his. [6]We know that our old self was crucified with him so that the body of sin might be destroyed, and we might no longer be enslaved to sin. [7]For whoever has died is freed from sin. [8]But if we have died with Christ, we believe that we will also live with him. [9]We know that Christ, being raised from the dead, will never die again; death no longer has dominion over him. [10]The death he died, he died to sin, once for all; but the life he lives, he lives to God. [11]So you also must consider yourselves dead to sin and alive to God in Christ Jesus.

Commentary 1: Connecting the Reading with Scripture

Larger Literary Context in Romans. Paul precedes Romans 6:1–14 with arguably the core description of his gospel: justification for all who believe by the faithfulness of one, Jesus the Christ (Rom. 5:1–11). This is followed by a restatement of earlier descriptions of the sinful state of humanity (e.g., 1:18–32). This time Paul describes this state in terms of two types of humanities: the Adamic and the Christic (5:12–21). The former, the foundational human disobedience represented by Adam, grounded humanity in sin (vv. 12–14); the latter, the Christ event of death and resurrection, eradicates the power of sin through the grace of God (vv. 15–17). Paul summarizes the point as follows: "So that, just as sin exercised dominion in death, so grace might also exercise dominion through justification leading to eternal life through Jesus Christ our Lord" (v. 21). Earlier in the letter, when Paul also argues that the grace of God dealt with human sin through the faithfulness of Christ's death (3:21–26), a possible (or actual) objection was raised: "And why not say (as some people slander us by saying that we say), 'Let us do evil so that good may come'?" (3:8). In comparison to such a hard accusation and response to antinomianism (the notion that if we have no "law," sin will run amok), Paul responds in a measured, but still firm way in the passage before us (6:1b–11).

Immediate Literary Context. Two pointed questions frame Paul's discussion in 6:1–14: "Should we continue in sin in order that grace may abound?" (v. 1b) and "Should we sin because we are not under law but under grace?" (v. 15b). Paul answers each with an emphatic *mē genoito*, "In no way!" To respond to the second, he returns to a discussion of the power of sin over humanity, to which the law was only a temporary answer (vv. 16–23). To respond to the first instance, of doubt about the power of grace over sin, Paul argues for the eradication of the power of sin through both death and resurrection of Christ. Moreover, he uses the ritual of water baptism, which became an early initiation practice among Christian communities (perhaps adapted from Jewish cleansing rituals) and practiced by John the Baptist and Jesus (Matt. 3:13–17; Mark 1:9–11; Luke 3:1–22; John 1:32–34). Paul himself at times tries to downplay the value of baptism as an initiation rite (e.g., 1 Cor. 1:14–17, when it is used against him as someone who rarely baptized and thus was a "lesser leader"). Yet here in Romans, baptism is key.

First, Paul rejects the idea that anyone who understands the meaning of the death of Christ in terms of the end of the power of sin over their lives would ever want to keep on sinning (Rom. 6:2). In effect, argues Paul, that is what baptism signifies, "that all of us who were baptized into Christ were baptized into his death" (v. 3). In baptism, we identify with Christ, both his death and resurrection. Unlike the realm of Adamic sinfulness (5:12–21), Christ's death (crucifixion, 6:6) secures a turning of the ages: the age of Christ and the forgiveness, salvation, and reconciliation (5:9–11) that result from it. Baptism, posits Paul, represents our own personal death, burial, and resurrection (6:4a). Indeed, resurrection of Christ from death, represented when the believer comes out of the baptismal waters, signifies our own new life in Christ, both in the present and in an eschatological future (v. 4b). "Walking" in the "newness of life" has ethical impact for the here and now, not just for a future eschatological resurrection. To "walk" often has ethical implications and expectations for Paul, as in Galatians 5:16: "So I say, walk [*peripateite*] by the Spirit, and you will not gratify the desires of the flesh" (NIV).

Thus the resurrection of Christ, as exemplified by rising from the baptismal waters, symbolizes new life *now* for the believer: "For if we have been united with him in a death like his [through baptism], we will certainly be united with him in a resurrection like his" (6:5). Moreover, *how* we "rise" is as important as the fact that we are resurrected into a new life. We rise into a new life, *leaving behind* the old life of sin. "Our old self was crucified with [Christ]," and "the body of sin" was as well, so we end up no longer "enslaved to sin" (v. 6). All this is represented in our "burial" in the baptismal waters. Paul calls Roman Christ-believers to a life "freed from sin" (v. 7). Otherwise, the only real freedom from sin is when we all die, because our bodies are no longer subject to sinning. In Christ, over time, argues Paul, this freedom from sin, symbolized by our baptism, becomes an increasing reality (v. 8).

The final major point Paul makes in this passage about baptism as symbolic of our new life in Christ is that Christ does not have to die again for this to be our new reality. We may sin again as frail human beings, but our goal lies in being more and more like Christ each and every day. Death has no power over Christ (v. 9), nor should it over us. Even though our mortal body will pass away, death does not have the last word, to paraphrase Paul in another context (1 Cor. 15:51–57).

In short, because Christ died a death that ended the ultimate power of sin "once for all" (Rom. 6:10a), we, like Christ, should live a life dedicated to God (v. 10b). In doing so, we must "consider" (*logizesthe*) ourselves "dead to sin and alive to God in Christ Jesus" (v. 11). Obviously, sin rears its head in the life of Christ-believers again and again. Fear, hate, injustice often show up in our lives and in the lives of our communities, even Christ-following communities that should know better. Paul knew this more than most, as he himself goes on to divulge in Romans 7. Yet that is *not* who we are if we are *in Christ*.

Larger Thematic Connections in Paul: Baptism. Paul's most famous reference to baptism, besides this one in Romans 6, is likely Galatians 3:27–29, where Christ-believers are depicted as being "clothed with Christ" through their baptism (Gal. 3:27), so that religious, social, and gender distinctions are minimized (v. 28). Such baptism "into Christ" ratifies their genuine Abrahamic descent, an inheritance promised by God, but not limited to any other distinctions besides being "in Christ" (v. 29). Thus the language of a baptism into waters, which is like a burial of the old, sinful, human life (Rom. 6:6), echoes new-creation language that Paul invokes elsewhere, such as 2 Corinthians 5:17, where he declares that, "If anyone is in Christ, there is a new creation." While baptism is not in view in that immediate context, certainly being "in Christ" in new and meaningful ways is, and thus a "new creation."

Lectionary and Preaching Connections. In terms of lectionary connections, the texts accompanying Romans 6 in Proper 7 reflect the mercy of God for a lost cause. In particular, the story of Hagar and her son abandoned in the desert depicts God standing with them, providing the necessary sustenance (water!) to ensure an important future. Hence, multiple sermon ideas emerge from Romans 6 and the other texts for this Sunday: God's mercy on the lost, the significance of a new life assured by Christ, the meaning of our baptism, and the question about how to become increasingly like Christ. Sin and death are defeated, but sinning and dying are not over. Their power, nonetheless, does not endure, encouraging words for preaching today.

EFRAÍN AGOSTO

Commentary 2: Connecting the Reading with the World

The Epistle to the Romans played a central role in the theological formation of Protestant thought during the sixteenth-century Reformation. Martin Luther and John Calvin used the book of Romans to establish foundational tenets that have come to characterize various branches of Protestant theology: the impact of sin on humans and the social order, the nature of faith, God's offer of salvation through Christ, and justification before God by faith through grace as a free gift.

Romans was an important epistle for Luther, who, upon reading Romans 1:17 in his monastic cell, came to this realization about the gospel: "For in it the righteousness of God is revealed through faith for faith; as it is written, 'The one who is righteous will live by faith.'"[1] In a letter to Philip Melanchthon, Luther encouraged his friend, because of the surety of this justification by faith, to "be a sinner and let your sins be strong," which we hear in popular parlance as "sin boldly."[2] The danger of redacted quotations such as this can be missed, because Luther also encouraged his friend to let his trust in Christ be stronger because of Christ's victory over sin and death.

Even though Romans was written well over fourteen hundred years prior to Luther's writing, could this human tendency to accept God's free gift with no strings attached lead to a casual view of our sin and an arrogant assumption that God is obligated to forgive humans? This seems to be what Paul suggests when he begins the passage with the rhetorical question, "What then are we to say? Should we continue to sin in order that grace may abound?" (Rom. 6:1). Rhetorical questions are literary devices meant to capture our attention, ones where the answers should be obvious. The answer to this question is found in verse 2: "By no means!" Paul then goes on to explain why this is the right answer, with implications for us who today are reading, preaching, and hearing these words. What might these connections be for sermon preparation on this passage?

First, the free gift of grace we receive from Christ is about new life, not a free pass for sin. It would be important to address this if congregants have assumptions about grace as a free pass. Discipleship in this Pauline perspective mirrors the baptism, life, death and resurrection of Christ (vv. 3–4). The pattern for Christian life is Christ. This is not easily captured by "What would Jesus do?" wristbands and T-shirts, which miss the rich theological context for discipleship.

In the various forms in which it is practiced in Christian traditions, baptism signifies our initiation into a new community and marks our belonging to Christ. When infants are baptized, they are welcomed into a community of faith to whom they belong, one that promises to nurture them in Christian faith and practice. Baptism by immersion in some traditions is an initiation that symbolizes death by going under the water and rising to new life. Either form represents a beginning entry into a shared life with Christ and others in a faith community. This belonging

---

1. Roland H. Bainton, *Here I Stand: A Life of Martin Luther* (Nashville: Abingdon, 1950), 48–49.
2. "Let Your Sins Be Strong: A Letter from Luther to Melanchthon" (Letter No. 99, August 1, 1521), trans. Erika Bullman Flores, www.iclnet.org/pub/resources/text/wittenberg/luther/letsinsbe.txt.

is also a participation in Christ's death and resurrection. As the resurrected Christ defeated sin, evil, and death, so it is possible, according to Paul, that we too can walk in this newness of life, instead of accepting a perpetual condition of sin as an excuse for sinning. In preaching, this passage can offer a reminder of our baptismal vows and perhaps provide space in the worship service for these renewals.

The word "walk" also illuminates a second connection for us in this passage. Over the years, there have been popular Bible-study series that encourage readers to "walk through the Bible." These are important resources to help congregations gain a better understanding of Scripture, the story it tells, and its importance in both personal devotion and congregational identity and mission. However, "walk" in our lectionary text is more closely associated with following a particular way of life and path. In the Hebrew Scriptures, we are to "follow exactly the path that the LORD your God" commanded (Deut. 5:32–33). We are to "walk by the Spirit" (Gal. 5:16 NASB). Of course, we have Jesus' own self-description as "the way, and the truth, and the life" (John 14:6).

Walking in newness of life is a conscious choice on our part, yet it is a choice made available and possible for us by the example of Jesus. In sermons, preachers can ask hearers to visualize and even act out walking along certain paths that illustrate this. Incorporating prayer labyrinths and year-round stations of the cross helps congregants connect with the idea that "walking" is not just good physical exercise but crucial to our spiritual health and growth.

The third connection in today's lectionary text further explains the relationship of Christ's death and resurrection to the "crucifixion of our old self" so that we too might share in Christ's resurrection (Rom. 6:6). This can be troubling language and imagery that could further exacerbate the kinds of self-hatred already experienced by persons in our congregations and communities. Some may have trouble simply believing that God loves them as they are. Crucifixion language is also harsh and violent language, more so when it is used to justify harm to one's self and others. The peril of using this text to shame others about their selves, and to encourage forms of self-hatred, needs to be acknowledged in sermon preparation and pastoral care, lest this text be used as a "text of terror."[3]

To keep from misreading or misusing this text, it is important to note that the crucifixion and death that Paul describes are actions that have already been done to Christ. They are not actions to be done to ourselves or others. We are not commanded to crucify ourselves or to ask others to do the same. Using examples from popular devotional books that refer to "dying to self" and "crucifying one's self" may be ways to help congregants see the harmful ways in which this language is used.

What is the good news offered in this text? This need not evoke morose futility that identifies us as *simul justus et peccator*, or we are at the same time both righteous and a sinner but really, still always a sinner. Our lectionary text indicates otherwise: we are set free from what enslaves us and made alive in Christ. The ending of this text, "dead to sin and alive to God in Christ Jesus" (v. 11), takes us back to its beginning and the pattern for Christian discipleship as walking in "newness of life" (v. 4).

It may be tempting in congregations to assume that persons already know the gospel of Christ, or once they have accepted the gospel, they need not be reminded of its power in their own lives. A wise friend once said there were parts of his life that remained sadly untouched by the good news, and that the gospel of Christ still needed to be preached to him. Persons in our congregations need to hear again and again the good news that is offered in this passage. "Consider yourselves dead to sin and alive to God in Christ Jesus" (v. 11). We cannot hear this good news enough, and sermons are a primary way in which this good news is told in our churches.

WYNDY CORBIN REUSCHLING

---

3. See Phyllis Trible, *Texts of Terror: Literary-Feminist Readings of Biblical Narratives* (Minneapolis: Fortress, 1984).

Proper 7 (Sunday between June 19 and June 25 inclusive)

Matthew 10:24–39

[24]"A disciple is not above the teacher, nor a slave above the master; [25]it is enough for the disciple to be like the teacher, and the slave like the master. If they have called the master of the house Beelzebul, how much more will they malign those of his household!

[26]"So have no fear of them; for nothing is covered up that will not be uncovered, and nothing secret that will not become known. [27]What I say to you in the dark, tell in the light; and what you hear whispered, proclaim from the housetops. [28]Do not fear those who kill the body but cannot kill the soul; rather fear him who can destroy both soul and body in hell. [29]Are not two sparrows sold for a penny? Yet not one of them will fall to the ground apart from your Father. [30]And even the hairs of your head are all counted. [31]So do not be afraid; you are of more value than many sparrows.

[32]"Everyone therefore who acknowledges me before others, I also will acknowledge before my Father in heaven; [33]but whoever denies me before others, I also will deny before my Father in heaven.

[34]"Do not think that I have come to bring peace to the earth; I have not come to bring peace, but a sword.

[35] For I have come to set a man against his father,
and a daughter against her mother,
and a daughter-in-law against her mother-in-law;
[36] and one's foes will be members of one's own household.

[37]Whoever loves father or mother more than me is not worthy of me; and whoever loves son or daughter more than me is not worthy of me; [38]and whoever does not take up the cross and follow me is not worthy of me. [39]Those who find their life will lose it, and those who lose their life for my sake will find it."

Commentary 1: Connecting the Reading with Scripture

Today's Gospel continues Jesus' commissioning of the disciples from last Sunday's lectionary reading. The implications of discipleship have become progressively grimmer across chapter 10, and now Jesus seeks to encourage his followers in the face of persecution and martyrdom. He offers the common proverb that the student is not above the teacher, nor the slave above the master. If the head of the house suffers, so will his whole family. Those who follow Jesus will be maligned and betrayed, and may be forced eventually to carry their cross to their own execution. Thus Matthew foreshadows Jesus' own future in his teaching to the disciples (Matt. 26:47–27:50). If they live as Jesus did, they risk suffering as he did.

Within this threatening landscape, Jesus exhorts his followers to act courageously, continuing the mission for which they were sent. The command to proclaim from dark to light, from secrecy to the housetops, suggests that those who proclaim Jesus should become even bolder in the face of their fear. There is no reason to fear humans, because God is the only one with really fearsome power over our bodies and souls. Thus, after witnessing all of the teaching and wonder-working through chapters 5–9 that suggest power and success, the disciples are brought back to a harsh reality. Those who follow will do what Jesus does, including losing their lives to gain them. Today's reading from Romans 6 adds additional nuance to this death in Christ. It is not just the possibility for dramatic martyrdom but a command for daily living. Preaching themes include facing fear in faith, the challenges of discipleship, and fashioning our lives to Christ's.

God's fearsome power inspires awe, but also comforts through an intimate sense of presence. God sees and cares for insignificant details, much as Jesus actively sees and responds to insignificant people who suffer throughout the Gospel. The sparrow was a humble example, a common and cheap bird sold in the market, and the fare of the poor.[1] We might wonder if Matthew's community might have felt like sparrows—like the poor, the discounted, and the least. If social and religious outcasts were a part of Jesus' ministry, and being poor represented dependence on God (see Proper 6), then this teaching has an interesting connection to sparrows.

In God's economy, you who are poor and dispensable in the eyes of the world are worth far more than you think. This theme expands to today's reading from Genesis 21, where Hagar, the slave of Israel's matriarch, Sarah, is abandoned in the desert. God's promise to Hagar that she will be a mother of a nation shows that God sees the oppressed as worthy and participates in their struggle for survival and liberation.[2]

Jesus continues with a proverb about the numbering of hairs on one's head, yet another saying that suggests God's intimate providence is at work even in situations of suffering. We also are reminded that human knowledge about the fate of sparrows or strands of hair is really quite limited. There is a contrast between what we can see (suffering, fear) and what God sees in us (worthiness, faithfulness). Throughout the lectionary, preaching themes include God's power contrasted to human power, courage and hope, the centrality of the marginalized, and the intimate nearness of God. For the disciples, this near and all-knowing God encourages them to stay committed to the mission in the face of their fear.

What believers choose during the time of trial also has cosmic implications, for to deny Jesus now will mean being denied at the end times. This must have been a popular saying, because it is repeated in 2 Timothy: "if we endure, we will also reign with him; if we deny him, he will also deny us" (2 Tim. 2:12). In Matthew, Jesus also returns to these themes in the separation of sheep and goats at the judgment (Matt. 25:31–46). While this may sound harsh to contemporary ears, for a community in crisis, images of the final judgment may have emboldened courage in the face of threat or pressure to deny Jesus as Lord. At least there would be justice at the end times for what they had suffered (e.g., Ps. 96:13; Rev. 19:1–2). The hope of a future triumph for present faithfulness returns in Mathew 19:27, when Peter reminds Jesus that they have given up everything to follow him. Jesus promises them that they will sit as judges for the twelve tribes of Israel at the eschaton (Matt. 19:28). The eschaton reminds us that, while salvation is a free act of grace, how we conduct ourselves in Jesus' name will someday require an explanation.

For the early church, tribulations occur because Jesus does not usher in the peaceable kingdom but the beginning chaos of the end times. Verses 34–36 reflect Micah 7:4b–7, warning that the end times will set the people into social disarray: one's loved ones cannot be trusted, and one's enemies are of one's own household. Persecution, family discord, and the destruction of social ties are the expected suffering before the messianic age. The new family gathered together by this shepherd is prioritized over earthly loyalties. The lectionary psalms appointed for today evoke a similar feeling of crisis: the fear of being denounced, close friends turning against one, trusting in God to bring about good out of persecution (Ps. 86:14–17). We can almost hear those early Christians saying with the psalmist, "I have become a stranger to my kindred. . . . the insults of those who insult you have fallen on me" (69:8–9).

It is awe inspiring to imagine the personal and social losses that Mathew's community must have experienced in order to make this teaching an encouraging word for them. It is debated

---

1. Ulrich Luz, *Matthew 8–20: A Commentary*, trans. James E. Crouch, Hermeneia (Minneapolis: Augsburg Fortress, 2001), 103.
2. Delores S. Williams, "Hagar in African American Biblical Appropriation," in Phyllis Trible, *Hagar, Sarah, and Their Children: Jewish, Christian and Muslim Perspectives* (Louisville, KY: Westminster John Knox, 2006), 176.

whether they were still a part of the synagogue or had been expelled, though the constant clashes with religious leaders in this Gospel would suggest that a breach had already occurred. They also held the traumatic memory of the fall of the temple in 70 CE, and would have been vulnerable to waves of Roman persecution. It is a community that is embattled and somewhat defenseless, like sparrows. Social rejection becomes a sign of the faith, for "you will be hated by all" on account of Jesus (Matt. 10:22; 24:9). The theme of conflict so prominent in Matthew points toward Jesus' passion while also mirroring the suffering of the early church. Indeed, how to resolve or live with conflict—whether in our world, nation, or church—remains a subject ripe for the preacher's address.

It is important that this lectionary reading be understood as part of the commissioning of the Twelve into the harvest. It is not about personal "crosses" of victimization, oppression, or self-loss. Instead, Jesus is talking about suffering that is the direct result of following Jesus. Unfortunately, today's lectionary stops before the end of the story. If we continue reading, the chapter ends by listing the rewards given to those who welcome and care for these wandering and persecuted missionaries (10:40–42). These are the same rewards offered to the "sheep" in 25:31–40 who care for the members of Jesus' family. Christians embody a new family, and so if any are experiencing suffering for the faith, those around them have a responsibility to receive, nourish, and protect them in their distress.

SONIA E. WATERS

Commentary 2: Connecting the Reading with the World

Many of us are likely familiar with the hymns "His Eye Is on the Sparrow" and "In the Garden." Wary of the perils of individualism and romanticism, we may smile and shake our head. We may need to revisit that response. The longing in many a bereaved family who sing this first song as they bury their loved one provides a marvelous angle into this text. Just as hymns and prayers well up in strength and sustenance during times of trial, so here God's tender love for the sparrow serves as a fulcrum between hard and challenging truths. A possible sermon therefore might explore the dynamic of fear and reassurance within the Christian life.

Too often Christianity in the West propagates the notion that God will always protect us from harm, suggesting that if we fervently follow Jesus, we will attain a life that is both free from pain and suffering and ripe with blessings. That's an odd sort of lie, given the stories we know about Jesus. Here we find a sharp corrective to that illusion. By reminding us that the disciple is not above the teacher, Matthew emphasizes that we receive no extra exemptions and privileges as disciples of Jesus. The snapshot of Christian living he offers is the life of Jesus himself: Jesus suffered; he was falsely accused, persecuted, run out of town, backed to the edge of a cliff, questioned by authorities, and eventually killed. We should expect no less. Our suffering does not mean that we are not beloved by God. It simply means that the power of a life drenched in God's love threatens the powers and principalities of this world.

Reassurance lies at the heart of the passage. In the midst of hard words we are sustained by the promise that when danger and death are near, we can bear down on the presence and power of the Holy One, the one who can "destroy both soul and body in hell" (Matt. 10:28). That one will hold us firm. In following Jesus, we are following the true Messiah, the one whose realm and reality shall one day unfold to claim the entire cosmos.

A sermon on trust therefore emerges naturally from this passage: trust as a creative and constructive act. The ultimate promise on offer is that this one whom we follow remains *trustworthy*. A faithful life therefore uncovers that good news and proclaims it from the housetops (vv. 26–27). In and through Christ, God draws all of us into the great shalom. In trusting and following Christ in the midst of peril and suffering, we not only *receive* that shalom, we *participate in creating it*.

All of that sounds grand and nice, but what about when we really *are* terrified and alone? Matthew joins the other Gospel writers in offering the great reassurance our world needs: Do not be afraid. The *trustworthy* one cares for you and cares for me, and knows the number of hairs on our heads. This reassurance does not magically make the world a better place. Rather, this reassurance grounds us in a love so deep and so wide that it can hold us and propel us when we want to do the brave and faithful thing, but fear that the floor will fall out beneath us if we do. Matthew offers no illusions: the floor may in fact give way. However, like the sparrow, no matter how far we fall, we will never fall beyond God's tenacious love and care.

This reassurance comes *in the midst of*, rather than *instead of*, the pain and struggle around and within us. A sermon that acknowledges the reality of pain in people's lives is a gift. It will naturally pivot to the reassurance that no place of pain is so dark or so scary that God will not go there with us: a child ostracized for being different; a woman passed over because she refuses to mislead clients; nuns hiding Jewish children from the Nazis; churches providing sanctuary; men and women protesting in outrage when children are teargassed at our borders—all claiming with body and action that when church, state, nation, or any other authority fails to respect the glory of God's creation in every person, loyalty to that authority must be rebuffed. The lives of these, along with countless others, loudly proclaim that faith stands in loyalty to Christ alone. This loyalty may not be rewarded by the world. In fact, it may be punished. However, God's eye is on the sparrow. God watches over me . . . and you . . . and all among whom we preach.

None of this is easy. It is messy. It sets us at odds with many of the priorities of our society, our government, even our church. Rarely do we preach on the messiness of faith. This is a good time to do that. These hard words set Christians in conflict with one another, disagreeing on the demands of faithfulness. In this fraught political environment, we have an opportunity to reflect on the nature of faithfulness, and what to do when faithfulness lands people on opposite sides of the political spectrum. What are the marks of true faithfulness? What should a church do when they disagree?

Matthew saves his hardest words for the end: faithfulness to Jesus sows conflict among those we love. Theologian Willie Jennings suggests that the Thanksgiving table, rather than the public square, proffers the most difficult and important location for the hard work of healing our diseased Christian racial imaginations. Formed as we are by our own situation, we are steeped and poached in fear of those we do not know; our families are thick in that formation process. Parents, children, aunts, uncles, and cousins speaking truthfully with one another around a common table feels dangerous to many of us. This is where the Spirit must blow—or separate and divide like a sword. A sermon might wrestle with what it looks like to love an uncle while clearly defining one's understanding of the gospel in contrast to his. What joins us together? How does the love of Jesus allow us to endure fundamental differences that cut like a knife?

The church's call to lament and response is a focus that bears with it a natural liturgical setting within worship, even suggesting a sermon that explores lament and breaks into communal lament, then turns to promise and concludes a congregation's shared doxological response. *Lament* over the hard truths of life and discipleship: we long for peace, but if we follow Jesus, we encounter swords. It is a truth we do not wish to face. We want the world to be otherwise. We lament from that place of pain. *Response* comes from the fulcrum of promise: Do not be afraid. God counts the hairs on our heads. God attends to even the tiniest sparrow. We are of more value than many sparrows.

The call to "fear not" in the gospel is not a requirement to pretend we are not afraid. Far from it. The call to "fear not" is active. In the face of legitimate fear, what does it mean to trust God's love so deeply that we are free to lament and free to respond with faith in God's promises *in the midst of* that fear? How does the sparrow find rest? A sermon might encourage a congregation to embolden one another in the midst of fear by turning to a neighbor in the pew and sharing the song of the sparrow God has given them.

DENISE THORPE

Proper 8 (Sunday between June 26 and July 2 inclusive)

Jeremiah 28:5–9 and Genesis 22:1–14 Romans 6:12–23
Psalm 89:1–4, 15–18 and Psalm 13 Matthew 10:40–42

Jeremiah 28:5–9

⁵Then the prophet Jeremiah spoke to the prophet Hananiah in the presence of the priests and all the people who were standing in the house of the Lord; ⁶and the prophet Jeremiah said, "Amen! May the Lord do so; may the Lord fulfill the words that you have prophesied, and bring back to this place from Babylon the vessels of the house of the Lord, and all the exiles. ⁷But listen now to this word that I speak in your hearing and in the hearing of all the people. ⁸The prophets who preceded you and me from ancient times prophesied war, famine, and pestilence against many countries and great kingdoms. ⁹As for the prophet who prophesies peace, when the word of that prophet comes true, then it will be known that the Lord has truly sent the prophet."

Genesis 22:1–14

¹After these things God tested Abraham. He said to him, "Abraham!" And he said, "Here I am." ²He said, "Take your son, your only son Isaac, whom you love, and go to the land of Moriah, and offer him there as a burnt offering on one of the mountains that I shall show you." ³So Abraham rose early in the morning, saddled his donkey, and took two of his young men with him, and his son Isaac; he cut the wood for the burnt offering, and set out and went to the place in the distance that God had shown him. ⁴On the third day Abraham looked up and saw the place far away. ⁵Then Abraham said to his young men, "Stay here with the donkey; the boy and I will go over there; we will worship, and then we will come back to you." ⁶Abraham took the wood of the burnt offering and laid it on his son Isaac, and he himself carried the fire and the knife. So the two of them walked on together. ⁷Isaac said to his father Abraham, "Father!" And he said, "Here I am, my son." He said, "The fire and the wood are here, but where is the lamb for a burnt offering?" ⁸Abraham said, "God himself will provide the lamb for a burnt offering, my son." So the two of them walked on together.

⁹When they came to the place that God had shown him, Abraham built an altar there and laid the wood in order. He bound his son Isaac, and laid him on the altar, on top of the wood. ¹⁰Then Abraham reached out his hand and took the knife to kill his son. ¹¹But the angel of the Lord called to him from heaven, and said, "Abraham, Abraham!" And he said, "Here I am." ¹²He said, "Do not lay your hand on the boy or do anything to him; for now I know that you fear God, since you have not withheld your son, your only son, from me." ¹³And Abraham looked up and saw a ram, caught in a thicket by its horns. Abraham went and took the ram and offered it up as a burnt offering instead of his son. ¹⁴So Abraham called that place "The Lord will provide"; as it is said to this day, "On the mount of the Lord it shall be provided."

Commentary 1: Connecting the Reading with Scripture

"Do not preach a 'sugar-stick,'" the seminary professor told a preaching class when discussing the sermon that members of the class would present to a congregation considering whether to call them as its pastor. The term refers metaphorically to a feel-good homily that steers clear of the challenging message of the gospel. In this reading for Proper 8, a sugar-stick is just what the prophet Hananiah has offered those gathered in the temple. The historical context is the aftermath of the first Babylonian invasion of 597 BCE, when King Jehoiachin, many of the leading citizens, and much of the temple property had been forcibly removed to Babylon. In Jeremiah 28:1–4 Hananiah prophesies the welcome message that the Babylonian yoke will be broken within two years, bringing about the restoration of all that has been lost. Jeremiah's "Amen to that!" in response turns out to be ironic, as he goes on to remind his audience that the words of the prophets are usually hard, not soft, and that anyone who prophesies peace better hope that events bear them out.

Jeremiah is not wrong; peace is not the first word that comes to the true prophet's lips. In chapter 27 (the immediate context for today's reading), Jeremiah warns his hearers not to listen to those who advise rebellion against Babylon and prophesy peace as a result, "for they are prophesying a lie to you" (Jer. 27:16). The authentic word of the Lord often elicits first a sense of discomfort and dislocation, and only later provides peace. Jeremiah's warning in chapters 27–28 echoes his complaint in 6:14 against those who cry out, "'Peace, peace, when there is no peace'" (cf. Ezek. 13:8–10). When Jesus says, "I have not come to bring peace, but a sword" (Matt. 10:34), he is referring to the same kind of inauthentic peace built on false optimism and human wisdom, rather than genuine hope based on trust in God.

The other thing that makes Hananiah's message inauthentic is that it gives his listeners what they want, rather than what they need, to hear. Another notable prophetic sermon seems to adopt the same strategy, only to turn it on its head. The book of Amos begins with the prophet addressing an audience in the northern kingdom of Israel, working the crowd up with promises that their hated neighbors will receive harsh punishment for their many transgressions (Amos 1:3–2:5). Just when it seems that the sermon has reached its climax and must surely conclude, the prophet delivers the sucker punch: "For three transgressions of *Israel*, and for four, I will not revoke the punishment" (2:6, emphasis mine). In a time when politicians congratulate us for our prejudices and preachers assure us that God hates the same people we do, Jeremiah and Amos can provide the preacher with helpful resources for looking to ourselves, rather than those around us, to discover what has gone wrong.

Opportunities to ask what has gone wrong abound in today's reading from Genesis 22. The great twentieth-century interpreter of the Hebrew Bible, Gerhard von Rad, describes the test to which God subjects Abraham in this passage as an *Anfechtung*, the German word for a soul-shattering temptation or trial.[1] It is the same word that Martin Luther used to describe the period in his life when he was gripped by the fear that God could never forgive him.[2] The preacher might well approach a sermon on this passage as its own kind of *Anfechtung*, given the odd combination of familiarity and moral quandary the passage presents.

The elements of the passage are brief and deceptively simple. We readers know immediately that in the story God is testing Abraham, not actually requiring him to sacrifice Isaac, his beloved son and the fulfillment of God's promise to grant Abraham a bloodline. Abraham, however, does not know what we know, and thus the simple details of the narrative—the divine call, the journey to a strange place, the final preparations for what Isaac surely realized was his death—carry the weight of dread and foreboding. God's last-minute intervention

---

1. Gerhard von Rad, *Genesis: A Commentary*, rev. ed. (Philadelphia: Westminster, 1961), 244–45.
2. Roland Bainton, *Here I Stand: A Life of Martin Luther* (Nashville: Abingdon, 1978), 31.

saves Isaac and resolves the narrative tension of the passage, although not necessarily the questions about divine justice it raises.

To begin to address those questions, the preacher would do well to remember the three words with which the passage opens: "after these things." More than simply the transitional statement we assume it to be, the phrase points us back to episodes in the preceding two chapters, not all of which show up in the lectionary. Genesis 20:1–18 recounts the time when Abraham took up residence in Gerar, a region of the Negev. King Abimelech of Gerar took Sarah for himself, believing (in a strong echo of Gen. 12:10–20) Abraham's cowardly claim that she was his sister. In the next chapter (Gen. 21:8–21) Sarah's jealousy leads her and Abraham to push Hagar and Ishmael out into the desert where, save for God stepping in at the last moment, they surely would have died. Finally, at the end of chapter 21 (vv. 22–34), Abraham offers to Abimelech that which the former owed to God alone: a covenant of loyalty. By the time we arrive at chapter 22, we have to conclude that these escapades might not qualify Abraham to be the great hero of faith we previously assumed, and just might explain why God found it necessary to test Abraham's faithfulness.

The larger context of Genesis 12–50 also provides help in thinking about one of our passage's central questions: Why would Abraham think that God would want him to sacrifice Isaac? Spread throughout these chapters are stories of human misunderstanding and faithlessness, family dysfunction, and personal betrayal. In spite of God's repeated promises to provide Abraham and Sarah with a child, Abraham feels compelled to take the matter of his lineage into his own hands, first by planning to name his servant Eliezer to be his heir (15:2), and then fathering Ishmael by Sarah's slave Hagar (16:1–15). Jacob and his mother Rebekah collude to cheat Esau out of his father's blessing (27:1–40). Jacob's uncle Laban initially reneges on his promise to allow Jacob to marry his younger daughter Rachel (29:15–30). Joseph's brothers conspire to kill him, but wind up selling him into slavery so as to get rid of him and turn a profit at the same time (37:12–36).

Might we not see the sacrifice of Isaac as simply another example of this pattern? Could it be that the test was whether Abraham could rise above the tendency of his family (and of the whole human family) to get it wrong and deal falsely with one another? When God stays Abraham's hand, we see a reflection of all the other epiphanies and interventions by which God delivers the family of Abraham from the consequences of its own folly (cf. 16:7–13; 20:3–7; 21:17–21; 28:10–22).

A final connection that might shed light on Genesis 22 is found in another biblical story of human sacrifice: Jephthah and his daughter (Judg. 11:29–40). Even though Judges makes clear that Jephthah is at fault for the rash vow that requires him to sacrifice his daughter, and even though there is plenty of time for either of them to back out of this unholy arrangement, in the end the unnamed young woman (unlike Isaac) is dead at her father's hand. The preacher might remind the congregation that our daughters still receive far more invitations to this kind of destructive self-denial than do our sons.

ROBERT A. RATCLIFF

Commentary 2: Connecting the Reading with the World

This week's selections include a prophetic speech and an ancestral story. The ancestral stories of Abraham and Sarah (Gen. 12–23), Isaac and Rebekah (Gen. 24 and 26), and Jacob (Gen. 25 and 27–35) are central to the lectionary passages over the next few weeks.

Jeremiah 28:5–9. This text fits amid an ongoing story of prophetic action and prophetic conflict. Considering the memorable story of the prophetic actions of the yoke, first the yoke of wood and then the metal yoke (Jer. 28:12–14), two other stories of prophetic conflict come to mind: Elijah and the prophets of Baal (1 Kgs. 18) and Amos and the priest Amaziah (Amos 7:10–17). Group cohesion and conflict live together. The issues connect to a common enemy or a common vision.

At first glance, the Jerusalem community perceived a common enemy, the enemy from the north. The first Babylonian invasion of Jerusalem in 597 BCE left the survivors disoriented. Nonetheless, they faced two different visions of the future. One prophesied a short trauma. The other offered countertestimony: "Do not listen to the words of the prophets who are saying to you, 'You shall not serve the king of Babylon,' for it is a lie" (Jer. 27:14 RSV).

Prophetic conflict happens when there are different interpretations of God's action in history. In a schismatic world that schematized prophetic conflict, Jeremiah's context allows us to offer three observations. One, it is easy to read Jeremiah 28:6 ironically, a feigned sympathy with the claim of Hananiah. However, when we attend to the laments of Jeremiah concerning the harsh word he was compelled to convey (Jer. 20:7–18), we see his grief for the plight of his people. He wished that his opponent's prophesy could be true, but his word from God meant that it was not. So one should avoid the temptation of allowing the smug rhetoric of religious conflict today to overshadow Jeremiah's pathos for his people. Two, the debate about God's action in history persists in the present and is as real as that of the past. Finally, it is not easy to distinguish true prophets from false ones; in the press of the present prophets, no one carries a sign distinguishing the true from the false.

Jeremiah locates the conflict in a community, the priests and the people standing in the temple of the Lord (28:5). These two groups oppose one another in the community center, in the temple, which defines the "beloved community" of Jeremiah. For the world of Jeremiah these two factions represent the totality of the community; in the twenty-first century these groups would not constitute the entire community. Interpreting the passage invites the reader to ask, What are the publics that shape today's conflict and group cohesion?

Often one reads the second part (v. 6) as ironic, but it may alternatively be read as a gesture of generosity, when Jeremiah says to Hananiah before the priests and the people in the house of the Lord, "Amen! May the LORD do so; may the LORD make the words which you have prophesied come true" (v. 6 RSV). If read in this manner, we see a solidarity between the prophets in their desire to benefit the people.

The gesture gives way to the bad news of the third part of the passage: "But listen now to this word that I speak" (v. 7). The prophet buttresses the statement with a reference to prophetic tradition. In legal terms this would be called a precedent (v. 8). Ultimately the passage ends with Jeremiah announcing that time will reveal the truth.

Sometimes the divergent visions come from subgroups who form one community. The vision of George Wallace—"segregation now, segregation tomorrow, and segregation forever"—perceived the civil rights movement as a moment of racial agitation by well-meaning but misguided whites from the North and benighted black folk from the South. Hananiah stood with George Wallace and Bull Connor arguing a minimalist view of the exile. The civil rights movement perceived itself as more than a Jeremiad moment that would give way to a return to Jim Crow.

Genesis 22:1–14. Test and sacrifice are the two general themes that dominate the Genesis 22 passage, themes that illuminate the message of divine providence in the text. The first sentence frames the narrative as the test or temptation of Abraham. Tests loom large in US culture. Standardized tests have become a gate of relationships and networks. Public school standardized tests determine which schools survive and which schools close or are radically reconfigured. From driving tests to physical examinations, tests shape our lives.

God both promised (Gen. 12:1–3) and tested Abraham. A test is only as real as the stakes are high. "Take your son, your only son, whom you love, Isaac" (22:2, my trans.). If one reads this passage out of its literary context, this verse works. However, in its literary context,

The Call and Courage to Be Tested

Let us then either consign Abraham to oblivion, or let us learn to be dismayed by the tremendous paradox which constitutes the significance of Abraham's life, that we may understand that our age, like every age, can be joyful if it has faith. In case Abraham is not a nullity, a phantom, a show one employs for a pastime, then the fault can never consist in the fact that the sinner wants to do likewise, but the point is to see how great a thing it was that Abraham did, in order that man may judge for himself whether he has the call and the courage to be subjected to such a test. The comic contradiction in the behavior of the orator is that he reduced Abraham to an insignificance, and yet would admonish the other to behave in the same way.

Should not one dare then to talk about Abraham? I think one should. If I were to talk about him, I would first depict the pain of his trial. To that end I would like a leech suck all the dread and distress and torture out of a father's sufferings, so that I might describe what Abraham suffered, whereas all the while he nevertheless believed. I would remind the audience that the journey lasted three days and a good part of the fourth, yea, that these three and a half days were infinitely longer than the few thousand years which separate me from Abraham. Then I would remind them that, in my opinion, every man dare still turn around ere he begins such an undertaking, and every instant he can repentantly turn back. If the hearer does this, I fear no danger, nor am I afraid of awakening in people an inclination to be tried like Abraham. But if one would dispose of a cheap edition of Abraham, and yet admonish everyone to do likewise, then it is ludicrous.

Søren Kierkegaard, *Fear and Trembling*, trans. Walter Lowrie (Garden City, NY: Doubleday, 1954), 63–64.

---

the reader knows that Isaac is not the only son. Every child who was not the favorite son knows the truth of the phrase. Sometimes you can be the only child with siblings. What does it mean to be the favorite son or daughter who is the object of sacrifice? What does it mean to be the other child, the erased child? In the Joseph story this is the role of Reuben (see 37:19–24). For many families this is the girl who is named androgynously for gender-projection reasons. Sometimes this child is so invisible that they are no longer worthy of sacrifice. Isaac represented the most tangible evidence of the promise of progeny (12:1–3).

Søren Kierkegaard's *Fear and Trembling* poses three questions. Is there a teleological suspension of the ethical? Is there an absolute duty to God? Finally, is privatization of religious obligation ethical?[3] The story of the test of Abraham reverberates through Judaism and Christianity. The test comes full circle in the temptation of Jesus (Matt. 4:1–11//Luke 4:1–13). How can we frame questions to capture the way that tests shape the core relationships in our lives?

A second theme is sacrifice (Heb. *'olah*). Genesis 22 appears in the Jewish *Aquedah* tradition, a sacrifice of something dear. Sacrificing what is not dear subverts the sacrifice. When Pharaoh is asked about the scourge of enslavement of the Hebrews in the film *The Prince of Egypt*, Pharaoh replies, "Sacrifices had to be made." The "other" paid the cost of the sacrifice. Could the enslaved Hebrews be the Isaacs of their era?

When slave catchers besieged Margaret Garner, a formerly enslaved woman and her family, she killed her daughter and tried to kill all her children to save them from slavery. The tragedy was an inspiration for Toni Morrison's novel *Beloved*.[4] The promise of freedom is so valued and the terror of enslavement so oppressive that room is made even for the sacrifice of life.

A distressing hierarchy emerges. At the top the obedient parent serves a powerful Deity. Below that is the beloved child worthy of sacrifice. At

---

3. Søren Kierkegaard, *Fear and Trembling*, ed. and trans. Howard V. Hong and Edna H. Hong (Princeton, NJ: Princeton University Press, 1983; orig. 1843), 54–123.
4. Toni Morrison, *Beloved* (New York: Alfred A. Knopf, 1987).

the bottom is the invisible child not worthy of sacrifice. The hierarchy of test and sacrifice problematizes the theme of divine providence in Genesis 22. The passage collapses on itself. The willingness to sacrifice everything means God's providence will subvert the loss of sacrifice.

The prophetic text of Jeremiah draws a challenging picture of prophetic conflict and contested visions. Genesis 22 poses a test and the challenge of sacrifice that ultimately illuminates all relationships to God providing a wager on the providence of God.

STEPHEN BRECK REID

Proper 8 (Sunday between June 26 and July 2 inclusive)

Psalm 89:1–4, 15–18

¹I will sing of your steadfast love, O LORD, forever;
  with my mouth I will proclaim your faithfulness to all generations.
²I declare that your steadfast love is established forever;
  your faithfulness is as firm as the heavens.

³You said, "I have made a covenant with my chosen one,
  I have sworn to my servant David:
⁴'I will establish your descendants forever,
  and build your throne for all generations.'"
. . . .
¹⁵Happy are the people who know the festal shout,
  who walk, O LORD, in the light of your countenance;
¹⁶they exult in your name all day long,
  and extol your righteousness.
¹⁷For you are the glory of their strength;
  by your favor our horn is exalted.
¹⁸For our shield belongs to the LORD,
  our king to the Holy One of Israel.

Psalm 13

¹How long, O LORD? Will you forget me forever?
  How long will you hide your face from me?
²How long must I bear pain in my soul,
  and have sorrow in my heart all day long?
How long shall my enemy be exalted over me?

³Consider and answer me, O LORD my God!
  Give light to my eyes, or I will sleep the sleep of death,
⁴and my enemy will say, "I have prevailed";
  my foes will rejoice because I am shaken.

⁵But I trusted in your steadfast love;
  my heart shall rejoice in your salvation.
⁶I will sing to the LORD,
  because he has dealt bountifully with me.

Connecting the Psalm with Scripture and Worship

Psalm 89:1–4, 15–18. As readers of this volume are aware, the Connections series takes seriously the fact that the framers of the lectionary chose the psalm readings to be responses to the Old Testament lessons. I must confess that their choices are sometimes puzzling and occasionally quite problematic. The choice of Psalm 89:1–4, 15–18 to respond to Jeremiah 28:5–9 seems to be among the most problematic of all. The issue in Jeremiah 28 is false prophecy, Jeremiah versus Hananiah, and verses 5–9 contain one of the two places in the Old Testament that offer a criterion for distinguishing false from true prophecy (see also Deut. 18:21–22). The criterion appears in verse 9, pertaining to "the prophet who prophesies peace." It amounts to wait-and-see: "when the word of that prophet comes true, then it will be known that the LORD has truly sent the prophet." This criterion may serve well for assessing the career of Jeremiah, who predicted the fall of Jerusalem at the hands of the Babylonians, as opposed to Hananiah, who predicted Jerusalem's deliverance. Jerusalem fell in 587 BCE. Jeremiah was right; so, according to the criterion in 28:9, we may conclude "that the LORD has truly sent" Jeremiah.

When one applies the criterion to Psalm 89:1–4, 15–18, as the lectionary seems to invite, then one is led to some interesting and potentially problematic conclusions. True, Psalm 89 is not prophecy, but Psalm 89 is essentially a poetic version of the oracle that the prophet Nathan delivers to David in 2 Samuel 7:1–17. Notice that Psalm 89:3–4 is in quotation marks, and what is being quoted is the prophecy of 2 Samuel 7 (cf. esp. Ps. 89:4 with 2 Sam. 7:13). Psalm 89:15–18 offers more of the Davidic theology, but the psalm concludes with an indication that the promise to David of a "throne for all generations" (Ps. 89:4) has failed. As for the Davidic descendant, God has "spurned and rejected him" (v. 38). God has "renounced the covenant" and has "defiled his crown in the dust" (v. 39). If you apply the criterion of Jeremiah 28:5–9 to Psalm 89, the logical conclusion is that Nathan's prophecy to David was false!

This, of course, is the problematic nature of the lectionary pairing. We should not too quickly dismiss this dilemma. Neither, however, should we conclude that Nathan's prophecy to David was unambiguously false. Rather, the dilemma invites us to consider the possibility that prophecy is more complex than predicting the future. Instead of thinking of prophets as persons who predict the future, we should think of them as persons who attempt to shape the future that God intends. Prophecy becomes a dynamic process, rather than the prediction of a single event that either happens or does not.

From this angle, Jeremiah was right, but not primarily because he correctly predicted the fall of Jerusalem. Rather, he was right because he understood that the fall of an unfaithful Jerusalem would open the way for a renewed relationship between God and God's people. After all, the book of Jeremiah does not end by saying, "I told you so!" It ends by describing the reality of a new covenant, grounded in divine grace and forgiveness (see Jer. 31:31–34). Jeremiah's prophecy contributed to the opening up of a future that God intended.

Similarly, we need not conclude that Nathan's prophecy cited in Psalm 89 was simply false or wrong. Rather, the book of Psalms retains the Davidic language and theology, but it transposes it to a new level. The purpose of the Davidic monarchy was the establishment of the justice and righteousness that God wills (see Pss. 72; 82; 89:14); but in the absence of the Davidic monarchy signaled in Psalm 89, it will be "the faithful" (Ps. 149:1, 5; see "all his faithful ones" in v. 9)—that is, God's whole people—who will carry out "the justice decreed" by God (Ps. 149:9, my trans.). The process of establishing justice continued; Nathan's prophecy was not ultimately discounted nor dismissed; rather, it was expanded. From the Christian point of view, the process of establishing a just world continued and continues in Jesus, "the son of David" (Matt. 1:1; but see also Mark 12:35–37, which indicates some ambiguity surrounding the earliest understandings of Jesus' identity).

Psalm 13. The haunting story of the near-sacrifice of Isaac in Genesis 22:1–14 derives much of its impact and power from the very sparseness of the account. Never are we told what Abraham thought or felt as he and Isaac "walked on together" (Gen. 22:6). Was it anger, fear, terror, sorrow, incredulity, regret? Nor are we told what Abraham thought or felt when he heard the angel call his name and saw the ram in the thicket (vv. 11–13). Was it gratitude, joy, relief, or some inexpressible combination thereof?

Given the sparseness of the account, commentators can hardly avoid speculating on Abraham's state of mind. Perhaps the lectionary's pairing of Psalm 13 with Genesis 22:1–14 is meant to fill in the blanks. In any case, Psalm 13:1–2 may well help one imagine Abraham's thoughts and feelings in Genesis 22:1–10: questioning, apparent abandonment, unsettledness, sorrow. Psalm 13:5–6 may well help one imagine Abraham's thought and feelings in Genesis 22:11–14, especially the joy of life restored.

Beyond the possible psychological dimension, however, it is the word "trusted" (Ps. 13:5) that makes Psalm 13 an appropriate response to this Genesis narrative. In commenting on Psalm 13, James L. Mays offers a compelling analysis of its juxtaposition of the two seemingly contradictory elements—the urgent lament/petition (vv. 1–4) and the jubilant celebration (vv. 5–6)—as follows:

> There is a coherence which holds the apparently separate moments together. God is so much a god of blessing and salvation for the psalmist that he must speak of tribulation and terror as the absence of God. Yet God is so much the God of *hesed* for the psalmist that he can speak to God in the mist of tribulation and terror as the God of his salvation. This is the deep radical knowledge of faith which cannot separate God from any experience of life and perseveres in construing all, including life's worst, in terms of relation to God.[1]

The Abraham cycle of narratives is framed by two episodes that involve situations that are among life's worst, leaving family and home (Gen. 12:1–4) and the potential loss of a child (22:1–14). In both instances, Abraham exhibits what Mays calls "the deep radical knowledge of faith," just as does the psalmist. Abraham is certainly, therefore, *the* exemplar of faith in the Old Testament. Although we have no idea who wrote Psalm 13, we may helpfully imagine the psalm as Abraham's words.

While the journeys of our lives may not be as dramatic as was Abraham's, we too will be confronted with life's worst—not because God is testing us, but simply because we are mortal and finite, and because we live in a sinful world. In his further reflection on Psalm 13, Mays concludes that finally what we learn from the psalm is this: "The agony and the ecstasy belong together as the secret of our identity."[2] To put this insight in explicitly Christian terms, the cross and the resurrection belong together as the secret of our identity. Suffering is neither divine punishment nor evidence that God is absent or has forgotten us. Rather, suffering is an opportunity for us to claim God's help when we need it the most; that is, suffering is an occasion for us to manifest "the deep radical knowledge of faith."

J. CLINTON MCCANN JR.

---

1. James L. Mays, "Psalm 13," *Interpretation* 37 (1983): 282.
2. Mays, "Psalm 13," 282.

Proper 8 (Sunday between June 26 and July 2 inclusive)

Romans 6:12–23

¹²Therefore, do not let sin exercise dominion in your mortal bodies, to make you obey their passions. ¹³No longer present your members to sin as instruments of wickedness, but present yourselves to God as those who have been brought from death to life, and present your members to God as instruments of righteousness. ¹⁴For sin will have no dominion over you, since you are not under law but under grace.

¹⁵What then? Should we sin because we are not under law but under grace? By no means! ¹⁶Do you not know that if you present yourselves to anyone as obedient slaves, you are slaves of the one whom you obey, either of sin, which leads to death, or of obedience, which leads to righteousness? ¹⁷But thanks be to God that you, having once been slaves of sin, have become obedient from the heart to the form of teaching to which you were entrusted, ¹⁸and that you, having been set free from sin, have become slaves of righteousness. ¹⁹I am speaking in human terms because of your natural limitations. For just as you once presented your members as slaves to impurity and to greater and greater iniquity, so now present your members as slaves to righteousness for sanctification.

²⁰When you were slaves of sin, you were free in regard to righteousness. ²¹So what advantage did you then get from the things of which you now are ashamed? The end of those things is death. ²²But now that you have been freed from sin and enslaved to God, the advantage you get is sanctification. The end is eternal life. ²³For the wages of sin is death, but the free gift of God is eternal life in Christ Jesus our Lord.

Commentary 1: Connecting the Reading with Scripture

"The free gift of God is eternal life in Christ Jesus our Lord" (Rom. 6:23). This hopeful statement closes Paul's comparison of the dynamics of sin and grace in the lives of Christians. It sums up the image of a generous, merciful, life-giving God that is carefully constructed in this letter, via a complex theological argument addressed to the Christian community in first-century Rome. Who are these Christians? Why would they elicit such a complex response from Paul?

Romans is arguably the most popular letter in the Pauline corpus. The theology of authors as diverse as Augustine, Abélard, Luther, Melanchthon, and Calvin has been shaped by Paul's argument on the relationship between justification, faith, and the law. Although he developed the theme of justifying faith as union with Christ in Galatians 2:15–21, Romans contains the most thorough exploration of this theme.

To whom was Romans addressed? The letter's greeting describes the Romans as "God's beloved in Rome, who are called to be saints" (1:7). The first-century Roman community, *not* founded by Paul, was at the center of the empire, a location that gave it access to the theological debates that were taking place as Christianity spread throughout the known world. Paul's pastoral concern for the Roman community seems to revolve around the possibility that false teachers could lead them astray: "For such people do not serve our Lord Christ, but their own appetites, and by smooth talk and flattery they deceive the hearts of the simple-minded" (16:18).

Tapping into the Roman Christians' knowledge of Jewish tradition, Paul grounds his argument for inclusion of the Gentiles in the Christian community on justification by faith, as foreseen in the law and the prophets. In the opening prayer, he opens his argument: "The righteous will live by faith" (1:17), a reference to the prophet Habakkuk (Hab. 2:4). Similarly, he refers to his Jewish readers' ancestry in faith by quoting the law: "Abram believed the Lord, and [God] credited it to him as righteousness" (Gen. 15:6 NIV). God promised Abram that he would become the father of *many* nations; thus his experience of God also opened a path for those who were not his direct descendants.

Today's reading, Romans 6:12–23, is located on the "other side" of the high point of Paul's argument for justification by faith. It focuses on living out the reality of justification by choosing which dominion, God or sin, rules and shapes daily life. Paul uses the image of slavery to drive home his argument. Slavery is the abasement of a human person so that they do not have freedom of decision and action in society. In Paul's world, a human being could be born into slavery, surrender themselves or their children to repay debt, or be unwillingly enslaved by the violence of war. Whatever the mode of enslavement, a human being became a "thing," a possession that could be used according to their master's will. Although the law limited the mistreatment of slaves, the result of losing one's agency was dishonor, a form of social death.[1] Social death severed family relationships and isolated a person from their cultural heritage, ancestry, and future progeny. Paul does not use the term "slave" to advocate for social change, but to illustrate the polarity between a life surrendered to sin and a life surrendered to God.

Why does Paul use such an image of hopelessness? Slavery is a "living" death. Feeling, thinking human beings who are enslaved can no longer take their place in the world. They are voiceless, entombed in life, severed from their past, powerless to shape their future. Being a slave to "sin" is analogous to this: feeling, thinking persons are enslaved by the dominion of their "mortal bodies"; they are "slaves to impurity and to greater and greater iniquity" (Rom. 6:12, 19). Righteous persons are also slaves, but to grace. Through faith in the death and resurrection of Christ, they can take their place in the family of believers.

Ironically, Paul exhorts his readers to *choose* one form of slavery over another. A modern reader (and perhaps Paul's readers also), accustomed to the juxtaposition of slavery (evil) vs. freedom (good), would find this exhortation jarring. Paul uses a different polarity: slavery to sin (evil, death) vs. slavery to God, a good that leads to life. A feeling, thinking person lives an obedience from the heart that leads to righteousness (v. 17). In this case "slavery" leads to a greater good: "But now that you have been freed from sin and enslaved to God, the advantage you get is sanctification. The end is eternal life" (v. 22). Death, the result of slavery to sin, becomes life through submission to God. For this reason, Paul urges his readers to present themselves to God "as those who have been brought from death to life, and present your members to God as instruments of righteousness" (v. 13).

How does Romans connect with the other readings from Proper 8? Romans resonates with the readings from Genesis and Matthew through the figure of a truly righteous person. Genesis portrays Abraham as a person whose radical commitment to God includes surrendering even the fruit of God's promises, his son Isaac, to God. "I know that you fear God, since you have not withheld your son, your only son, from me" (Gen. 22:12). This faith or radical commitment overflows the boundaries of a person's life. Abraham's righteousness makes him the father of many nations. Similarly, in Matthew's Gospel, righteousness "flows" toward a person who shows hospitality toward a righteous person: "Whoever welcomes a righteous person in the name of a righteous person will receive the reward of the righteous" (Matt. 10:41b).

The word "righteous" (*dikaios*) describes someone who feels, thinks, and acts in a way that is fully surrendered to the will of God, a connection to Paul's use of slavery in Romans. Inserting Paul's language (Rom. 6:22) into Matthew's statement yields something like this: "Whoever welcomes a slave to God, in the name

---

1. Orlando Patterson, *Slavery and Social Death: A Comparative Study* (Cambridge, MA: Harvard University Press, 1985), 5 and passim.

of someone who is also a slave to God, will receive the reward of those who are fully surrendered to God: eternal life." Union with God is not the only result of full surrender or slavery to God. This type of faith has social implications. In Matthew's Gospel, hospitality is the glue that brings together people who are righteous.

Matthew places the "righteous" in the company of people who represent extremes of the socioreligious hierarchy: the prophet and the "little ones" of his world. Traditionally, both prophets and "little ones" were located on the periphery of social and religious power structures. Prophets critiqued those in power, and "little ones" were oppressed by them. This teaching is set in the context of the disciples, who are sent out to represent Jesus in the world by proclaiming that the kingdom of heaven is at hand, curing the sick, cleansing lepers, and casting out devils (Matt. 10:8). All of these activities are attributed to prophets.

The reward of those who receive the righteous and the "little ones" who are his disciples is to receive in turn the fruits of the prophet. The ministry of the disciples is to proclaim that "the free gift of God is eternal life in Christ Jesus our Lord" (Rom. 6:23). Perhaps, for those who receive them today, the fruits of the prophet are also to proclaim that the kingdom of heaven is at hand, to cure the sick, to cleanse lepers, and to cast out devils. Perhaps the prophet's work is to choose sanctification, but also to overturn the social order.

RENATA FURST

Commentary 2: Connecting the Reading with the World

At baptism and confirmation, many congregations ask both youth and adults to renounce sin and evil. Why? Because life itself convinces us that sin is real and often lethal. The pervasive reality of sin and its dominion over human life connect us with a key feature of this passage. Sin has many faces and disguises as we try to exist without reference to God, run from God, and deny God through our idolatries, indifference, unbelief, disobedience, self-deprecation, and pride. Sin is a powerful parasite that attaches itself to us as it infiltrates our lives in innumerable ways. It appears to have a powerful will of its own that is in relentless opposition to God's power and will. As theologian Paul Tillich testifies, along with the apostle Paul, sin is mysteriously enslaving: "It is our human predicament that a power takes hold of us, that does not come from us but is in us, a power that we hate and at the same time gladly accept. We are fascinated by it; we play with it; we obey it. But we know that it will destroy us if we are not grasped by another power that will resist and control it."[2]

The apostle Paul declares that another power, grace, miraculously frees us from slavery to sin, thus providing a second possible preaching connection. Grace is a gift of freedom from sin's slavery that is beyond our own doing, earning, learning, working, buying, calculating, and personal power. Grace is something we can neither earn nor pay for. Grace is totally free. Grace has been paid for by a person, by God's own human heart of flesh, God's incarnate, crucified, and risen Son, who does a work for us that we cannot do for ourselves.

Surely this is among the most winsome truths touching the lives of persons and their groups. Throughout our pilgrimages, grace intricately connects itself and surprisingly comes forth here and there, baptizing and washing us with fresh hope and unexpected joy, which we had supposed could never cut through life's darkness, mess, ugliness, and stress. Powerful sin will not remain powerful enough to rule us and have controlling dominion over our lives, as we are enabled to live under the liberating rule of grace. This transforming movement from serving our own idolatries to serving righteousness

---

2. Paul Tillich, *The Eternal Now* (New York: Charles Scribner's Sons, 1963), 48.

infuses the heart and soul of our personhood with sanctifying hope and possibility. It is the amazing grace of transformation and renewal, a life-saving exodus from slavery to freedom.

Frequently, such liberating grace speaks profoundly to parents and children. It recalls into our presence Norman Thayer and his daughter Chelsea, played by Henry and Jane Fonda in the film classic *On Golden Pond*. Chelsea finds it almost unbearable that her father has not changed into something other than the controlling, crotchety, condescending old grouch he has always been. Norman finds it almost unbearable that daughter Chelsea has not become more like an all-American son he has longed for all his adult life. Yet miraculously and by the curiously transformative invasion of grace, they receive a power that enables them to accept and forgive one another, blemishes and all.

Such grace nurtures us with soul-searching humor and humility as we look into life's all-too-revealing reflecting pond. An appropriately self-critical anonymous jingle speaks for all of us:

> There is so much good in the worst of us
> And so much bad in the best of us,
> That it hardly becomes any of us
> To talk about the rest of us.

By the redemptive power of grace, we are creatures who forgive and who are forgiven. As Robert Frost explains in his theologically perceptive poem "The Star-Splitter" (1923), we deeply need the abiding grace of one another's forgiving patience.

> If one by one we counted people out
> For the least sin, it wouldn't take us long
> To get so we had no one left to live with.
> For to be social is to be forgiving.

Because we have been baptized into the image of Christ, such grace also fortifies us with a sense of vocational purpose. We can hold fast to the belief that God has warm regard for our individual lives and a sacred calling for our personal abilities. Thus, at their confirmation, I recited these words to our youth (adapted from words of Edward Everett Hale, 1822–1909):

> I am only one but I am one.
> I cannot do everything
> But I can do something.
> What I can do, I ought to do.
> And what I ought to do,
> By the grace of God, I will do.

According to the apostle Paul, a result of the grace that sets us free from the slavery of sin is the *process* of sanctification. This offers another preaching connection. Theologian Daniel L. Migliore describes sanctification as "the process of growth in Christian love." As we are "conformed to the image of Christ," we are released from self-centeredness into a love of God and our neighbors. Migliore lists five "marks of growth" in the ongoing process of sanctification: "*maturing as hearers of the Word of God*"; "*maturing in prayer*"; "*maturing in freedom*" ("*for* the service of God and others"); "*maturing in solidarity*" (our love of all creatures, particularly the poor and outcast); and "*maturing in thankfulness and joy*."[3]

The great womanist visionary theologian Katie Geneva Cannon posed this question about the process of sanctification to each person she mentored: "*What is the work your soul must have?*" Each of us "is born with a purpose," she said. "God wrote it on our hearts in the process of creation."[4] The film *Billy Elliot* beautifully embodies Cannon's important question. Young Billy lives in a tough British mining community where the boys attend boxing class after school, and the girls attend ballet. Because Billy is a terrible boxer who gets pummeled daily, he sneaks into the ballet class, where he discovers that his feet are like wings. However, when his father and older brother discover that Billy yearns to become a ballet dancer, they are humiliated and furious. They brutally try to change Billy, but to no avail.

---

3. Daniel L. Migliore, *Faith Seeking Understanding* (Grand Rapids: Eerdmans, 1991), 177–82.
4. Katie G. Cannon, "Womanist Mentoring—African American Perspectives," in *Mentoring: Biblical, Theological, and Practical Perspectives*, ed. Dean K. Thompson and D. Cameron Murchison (Grand Rapids: Eerdmans, 2018), 124.

Rather, it is they who change. Graciously, indeed lovingly, they grow to support Billy in attending a prestigious dance company and pursuing the work his soul must have. When Billy debuts as a star in the London Ballet Company's performance of *Swan Lake*, his father and brother are in the audience to watch him soar and celebrate the utter electricity of his calling. Thus we behold a true *becoming*, a sanctifying process of growth and maturation.

Sanctification, however, is a maturing process that is finally incomplete in this life. It will be completed, says Paul, in the "eternal life in Christ Jesus our Lord" (Rom. 6:23), risen from the dead. That is why Christians have funerals at the time of death, the time of our radical incompleteness. There we confess, through the power of Christ's resurrection, that the love of God that called us into being in the first place will fulfill our lives with new being when we die. The Holy One who created us and welcomed us at life's beginning will receive us and complete our sanctified growth at life's ending.

DEAN K. THOMPSON

Proper 8 (Sunday between June 26 and July 2 inclusive)

Matthew 10:40–42

⁴⁰"Whoever welcomes you welcomes me, and whoever welcomes me welcomes the one who sent me. ⁴¹Whoever welcomes a prophet in the name of a prophet will receive a prophet's reward; and whoever welcomes a righteous person in the name of a righteous person will receive the reward of the righteous; ⁴²and whoever gives even a cup of cold water to one of these little ones in the name of a disciple—truly I tell you, none of these will lose their reward."

Commentary 1: Connecting the Reading with Scripture

In the middle of Ordinary Time, after the fires of Pentecost have dwindled to a quiet sizzling, we find ourselves near the middle of the Gospel of Matthew. A few dramatic events fill the previous chapter, Jesus healing seemingly anyone, but especially those affected by paralysis, blindness, hemorrhages, even death. He continues on to various cities, teaching, transforming, and touching the people desperately seeking him out. At one point, Matthew tells us, Jesus gazes out to these dense harvest fields and is overwhelmed by the thick crowds who are "harassed and helpless, like sheep without a shepherd" (Matt. 9:36). He makes a decision to send out more laborers, summoning his disciples and launching into a set of instructions and assurances (chap. 10).

The key word in these verses is "welcome," with emphasis on the rewards others will receive when they welcome the disciples, but Jesus makes a subtle switch in the conversation about the nature of reception: from what it means when the people the disciples encounter receive them to what will happen if and when these same people enact the smallest gesture of mercy and kindness toward "one of these little ones" (10:42). The words about welcome, then, are not only about the disciples' comfort and ease in a new community, but also directed at all who might read Matthew's witness.

These words of encouragement come at the end of a larger discourse about the mission set before these would-be followers of Jesus, and what their participation in this work means. The work reorients their identity and purpose. They are no longer simply members of their own individual families and residents of their own respective neighborhoods, but disciples of a teacher. More than any other Gospel, Matthew underscores the ways in which Jesus not only represents divine power and presence, but democratizes this power—and the responsibilities that come with it—in ministry with his disciples. This discourse makes clear that God's power and authority are now at work not only in Jesus but in and through his disciples (10:1). They form a new community as apprentices to Jesus, the teacher, the master, the head of the household, one who asks much of them but promises even more. Their relationship to Jesus now supplants their other relationships. Here we see a glimpse of the expansion of the family of God, when Jesus suggests that the disciples' love for him must extend beyond their love for their family, indeed, beyond their love for their own lives.

At the very least then, discipleship means carrying out and embodying Jesus' mission. Disciples are likened to prophets, the righteous, and little ones, an interesting triad of images that links the disciples to strong prophetic tasks and acts of justice and mercy, even as they are also reminded about their own vulnerability and fragility.

This mission, as an outpouring of welcome, takes on a whole new meaning in light of Matthew's genealogical emphasis on lineages traced through covenant and law. Matthew's account suggests we understand Jesus not in terms of the legitimacy of his lineage but in terms of what

Jesus does and says about the very notion of lineage, that is, fathers and mothers, sons and daughters. In other words, Jesus demarcates new boundaries and expands the structures of all social life, so that even giving a cup of cold water to a little one is analogous to offering refreshment to a disciple of the Holy One. In other words, the work of welcome dissolves traditional networks and engages courageous imagination in ways that help us begin to see, live into, and struggle for a different kind of reality, a reality centered in the community God in Jesus Christ sought to establish in his ministry.

Giving a cup of cold water to a little one: this trivial gesture reverberates with significance and poignancy because Jesus likens these little ones to his disciples.[1] Of course, throughout the Gospel of Matthew these "little ones" play a significant role, whether as examples in Jesus' parables (18:10–14) or as those who possess the kingdom of heaven (19:14). Now we find ourselves on a different trajectory. It is less about the efficacy of our work and how it is perceived and more about who we are in this work and to whom we should orient ourselves as we follow Jesus.

It is no surprise then that later in the Gospel of Matthew we read Jesus' own explicit words: "If any of you put a stumbling block before one of these little ones who believe in me, it would be better for you if a great millstone were fastened around your neck and you were drowned in the depth of the sea" (18:6). Certainly equating the disciples with children is not without its own tension in the Gospel, for instance, when Jesus compares this oblivious generation to children in the market (11:16–17). It is the myriad of representations of children, however, that remind us of the wideness of humanity and the call to broaden our notions of hospitality. This metaphor of children is a key thread in the representation of the kingdom in Matthew's Gospel, and it is again in the context of his emphasis on lineages that we are challenged to rethink the nuances of welcome.

There is resonance with the Genesis 22 passage from the lectionary in the story of the near-sacrifice of Isaac by Abraham's own hand and a reminder of the relationship between lineage and obedience. The two texts share in the question of how God would fulfill God's promises to bring about the blessed nations of the world through Abraham's obedient act of sacrificing Isaac. Still, it connects with the themes of welcome in that God was and is the originator of notions of family and community, even in the most fraught circumstances. Likewise, the connection to the Romans passage suggests an implicit theme of discipleship threaded through obedience in a discourse on freedom. Another relationship, that of the master and slave, is highlighted: "slaves of righteousness" (Rom. 6:18) and "enslaved to God" (6:22). Once again, we see the rupture of the relationships that define humanity, whether the family or the nation or whatever spiritual and theological realities determine relationship with God.

The Genesis passage brings to mind the ways we reify certain narratives in shaping our identity and sense of belonging and relationships. This is especially true of the writer of Hebrews, who includes Abraham, Abel, Enoch, Moses, and others as those who "received approval" (Heb. 11:2). Here too we read of ancestors who did so "by faith." They are examples in which the emphasis is less on pedigree and more on persistence, a clinging to hope in the promises of God's own radical inclusion, and that as a sign of faithfulness. There is recognition that we would not be where we are today without them, and yet the connection to them is not through Matthew's genealogies and other hereditary claims of parentage, but on the way Jesus himself embodied a fracturing of those structures.

So it is in the work to which Jesus calls the disciples and Matthew's fledgling church that we find our purpose and legitimacy in mission. These words are a reminder of those to whom we should orient ourselves in ministry and those with whom we must ultimately identify as we follow after Jesus, that is, the little ones, the least of these, and those who represent the kingdom of heaven.

MIHEE KIM-KORT

---

1. Other translations—NIV, CEB, ESV—equate the "little ones" with the "disciples" (10:42).

Commentary 2: Connecting the Reading with the World

This tenth chapter of Matthew describes Jesus sending out the Twelve to do the mission work of the gospel. Rather than describing this mission as a joyful celebration, where thirsty people give deep thanks for receiving life-giving water, Jesus describes this mission as full of peril, full of resistance, and full of rejection. As he puts it in 10:16, "See, I am sending you into the midst of wolves." The prophetic message of Jesus will not be well received. Often it will be heard as bad news, not good news, and as the verses preceding our verses today indicate, this message has the potential to split families and friends (Matt. 10:34–39).

Part of this story reflects the experience of the church when Matthew was writing this tenth chapter, when there was a great deal of conflict with the established religion and with the governmental authorities. Yet it also reflects the general experience of missionaries in the name of Jesus in all ages. Earlier in Matthew's Gospel, we see an extreme example of this in 8:28–34. Jesus heals two people possessed by demons, but the response of the townspeople is not celebration and welcome but, rather, fear and rejection. They tell Jesus, "Get out of here!"

The instructions of Jesus in this chapter reflect the general experience of prophetic voices: they are often dismissed; they are often rejected; they are sometimes persecuted. Over the centuries, God has sent prophets to proclaim that the God movement is now in our midst. As participants in this movement, we are called to cure the sick, raise those who have given themselves up to death, bring into the center of life those who have been marginalized, and free us all up from our captivity to the demonic powers that distort us as individuals and as communities. This calling will bring us into conflict with the powers that be.

Our verses for today speak both to the emissaries and to those who receive them. Those sent out are reminded that the way is narrow and the journey is long. Rather than seeking a luxury hotel, we should be grateful for a cup of cold water. Those of us in the communities in which these prophets emerge, or to whom these prophets come, are asked to consider that a new word is spoken, that a new view of reality is revealed, that a whole new way of life—a way of love and justice and equity—is proclaimed. Those of us who are recipients of this proclamation are asked to listen, not immediately reject. Those of us recipients who are inclined to reject the prophetic message are asked to consider whether we will be rejecting the power of Jesus in rejecting the message. Will we miss our chance of gaining our new lives because we will not consider whether the prophet is from God?

After the mass shooting took place at Marjory Stoneman Douglas High School in Parkland, Florida, in early 2018, the surviving students, family members, teachers, friends, and allies poured into legislative halls in Florida, in Washington, DC, and around the country. They went into hostile territory, where NRA-influenced legislatures believed that teenagers should have access to assault rifles whose only purpose is to kill human beings in rapid fashion. Like the messengers mentioned in this passage in Matthew, these youth drove the effort to bring a prophetic word to the political leaders. Whether they came in the name of Jesus or not, they were bringing his message. They were exposing our cultural worship of the gun-god Molech, mentioned in Leviticus 20:1–5. Molech is a god that demands child sacrifice, and we have seen the cost of such worship around the country in recent years: our elementary, middle school, and high school children and youth sacrificed to our worship of guns.

Leviticus 20:2 prescribes the death penalty for those who sacrifice their children to Molech. While I do not believe in the death penalty, I do understand the depth of the captivity to death that this prescription implies. It is impossible to worship God while we are worshiping Molech. In those days, the worship of Molech was not always seen as the abomination that it is; rather, it made sense to the worshipers. It kept at bay the dangerous forces of chaos and death. It is no wonder that someone who comes into this kind of atmosphere to proclaim a new way of life, a way that will not require us to sacrifice our children, is seen as a threat and a danger, rather than a messenger of life.

The rewards and the implied warnings of these verses in Matthew remind us that God is always sending prophets into our midst to tell us about our captivity to death and violence and domination. God is always sending missionaries to offer us visions of new life in the household of God. I experienced this firsthand as a child classified as white, growing up in the segregation of the Deep South in the 1940s and 1950s. In white, segregated, southern life, I was taught (and I believed) that God had ordained those classified as white to be supreme and to rule over others. I was taught this, not by cross-burning KKK members, but by loving and decent Christians, who also taught me so much about the love of God. They helped the grace of God seep deep down into my bones. While they taught me about the grace of God, they taught me racism at the same time. Neither they nor I seemed to understand that we were violating the First Commandment, that we had put racial classification before God on our worship list.

When God sent emissaries and prophets into our midst to tell us a new way, a way of justice and equity and mercy, we heard this as bad news, not good news. We offered no welcome, no hospitality, and no cold cup of water. Instead we denied and rejected and expelled, and we still have received no reward, because we did not know the time of our visitation.

Because of our captivity to the power of sin, God will continue to send prophetic voices into our midst. We are in a time of great spiritual hunger, and there will be many voices urging us to go this way and that way, in order to satisfy our hunger. First John 4 tells us to test the voices, so that we will know which ones come from God, and which ones are from the fallen powers (1 John 4:1–6). How do we test them? First John joins the Gospels in telling us that prophets from God will emphasize and will call us into the service of love, justice, equity, and mercy.

The good news is that God will continue to raise prophetic voices in our midst to call us anew into the commonwealth of God. The bad news is that we often will reject these voices as demonic and threatening. The truth is that God is sending missionaries into our lives because we are so hungry for love and wholeness. Let us pray that God's Spirit will give us ears to hear, eyes to see, and hearts to receive, so that we can be converted and transformed and welcomed into the new world of the God movement in our midst, so that we may receive the prophets of God in the name of Jesus.

NIBS STROUPE

Proper 9 (Sunday between July 3 and July 9 inclusive)

Zechariah 9:9–12 and Genesis 24:34–38, 42–49, 58–67
Psalm 145:8–14 and Psalm 45:10–17 or Song of Solomon 2:8–13
Romans 7:15–25a
Matthew 11:16–19, 25–30

Zechariah 9:9–12

⁹Rejoice greatly, O daughter Zion!
    Shout aloud, O daughter Jerusalem!
Lo, your king comes to you;
    triumphant and victorious is he,
humble and riding on a donkey,
    on a colt, the foal of a donkey.
¹⁰He will cut off the chariot from Ephraim
    and the war-horse from Jerusalem;
and the battle bow shall be cut off,
    and he shall command peace to the nations;
his dominion shall be from sea to sea,
    and from the River to the ends of the earth.

¹¹As for you also, because of the blood of my covenant with you,
    I will set your prisoners free from the waterless pit.
¹²Return to your stronghold, O prisoners of hope;
    today I declare that I will restore to you double.

Genesis 24:34–38, 42–49, 58–67

³⁴So he said, "I am Abraham's servant. ³⁵The LORD has greatly blessed my master, and he has become wealthy; he has given him flocks and herds, silver and gold, male and female slaves, camels and donkeys. ³⁶And Sarah my master's wife bore a son to my master when she was old; and he has given him all that he has. ³⁷My master made me swear, saying, 'You shall not take a wife for my son from the daughters of the Canaanites, in whose land I live; ³⁸but you shall go to my father's house, to my kindred, and get a wife for my son.' . . .

⁴²"I came today to the spring, and said, 'O LORD, the God of my master Abraham, if now you will only make successful the way I am going! ⁴³I am standing here by the spring of water; let the young woman who comes out to draw, to whom I shall say, "Please give me a little water from your jar to drink," ⁴⁴and who will say to me, "Drink, and I will draw for your camels also"—let her be the woman whom the LORD has appointed for my master's son.'

⁴⁵"Before I had finished speaking in my heart, there was Rebekah coming out with her water jar on her shoulder; and she went down to the spring, and drew. I said to her, 'Please let me drink.' ⁴⁶She quickly let down her jar from her shoulder, and said, 'Drink, and I will also water your camels.' So I drank, and she also

watered the camels. ⁴⁷Then I asked her, 'Whose daughter are you?' She said, 'The daughter of Bethuel, Nahor's son, whom Milcah bore to him.' So I put the ring on her nose, and the bracelets on her arms. ⁴⁸Then I bowed my head and worshiped the LORD, and blessed the LORD, the God of my master Abraham, who had led me by the right way to obtain the daughter of my master's kinsman for his son. ⁴⁹Now then, if you will deal loyally and truly with my master, tell me; and if not, tell me, so that I may turn either to the right hand or to the left." . . .

. . . ⁵⁸And they called Rebekah, and said to her, "Will you go with this man?" She said, "I will." ⁵⁹So they sent away their sister Rebekah and her nurse along with Abraham's servant and his men. ⁶⁰And they blessed Rebekah and said to her,

"May you, our sister, become
 thousands of myriads;
may your offspring gain possession
 of the gates of their foes."

⁶¹Then Rebekah and her maids rose up, mounted the camels, and followed the man; thus the servant took Rebekah, and went his way.

⁶²Now Isaac had come from Beer-lahai-roi, and was settled in the Negeb. ⁶³Isaac went out in the evening to walk in the field; and looking up, he saw camels coming. ⁶⁴And Rebekah looked up, and when she saw Isaac, she slipped quickly from the camel, ⁶⁵and said to the servant, "Who is the man over there, walking in the field to meet us?" The servant said, "It is my master." So she took her veil and covered herself. ⁶⁶And the servant told Isaac all the things that he had done. ⁶⁷Then Isaac brought her into his mother Sarah's tent. He took Rebekah, and she became his wife; and he loved her. So Isaac was comforted after his mother's death.

Commentary 1: Connecting the Reading with Scripture

The book of Zechariah arrives late, both canonically and chronologically, in the Christian Old Testament (its placement within the Jewish canon is different). Appearing immediately before Malachi, the last of the Old Testament books, Zechariah dates to the period after the exiles' return from Babylon, when Jerusalem and the territory surrounding it were a province of the Persian Empire. On the basis of its disparate styles and outlooks, many scholars have divided Zechariah into two separate literary units: chapters 1–8 and 9–14.[1] Both halves reflect the sense of disappointment with the slow pace of progress in postexilic Jerusalem that Ezra–Nehemiah also describes.

Our reading for Proper 9 falls at a dividing point between two segments of the ninth chapter of Zechariah. The first, verses 1–8, envisions YHWH's triumphant march through Israel's eastern Mediterranean neighborhood, conquering such longtime enemies as Syria and Philistia. The purpose of this invasion becomes clear in verse 8. The Lord has come, not to punish Israel's neighbors but to pacify them, ensuring that they may never again threaten the peace of God's people.

The restoration of Israel and Jerusalem is a frequent theme in the prophets; time and again the promise of divine forgiveness follows closely after the threat of divine judgment (e.g., cf. Jer. 20:4–5 and Jer. 24:4–7). What sets this oracle in Zechariah apart is that judgment has been replaced with the *reversal* of judgment. The Mesopotamian superpowers Assyria and most especially Babylon were the agents of God's judgment, sweeping down from the north to

---

1. Mark McEntire, *A Chorus of Prophetic Voices* (Louisville, KY: Westminster John Knox, 2015), 190.

make war on Israel at YHWH's behest (Jer. 1:14–15; Ezek. 23:24). In Jeremiah 21:5, God's own hand, and not simply that of an intermediary, was to be stretched out against Judah, but in Zechariah 9, the tumult from the north is the sound of YHWH's arm raised against those who would threaten the peace of Jerusalem; instead of an enemy, it is God their deliverer who camps outside the walls.

This is the stage upon which that mysterious figure, the king "triumphant and victorious," arrives in verse 9. The whole of Zechariah 9–14 challenges the interpreter, and 9:9–17 fits the pattern. Is the "king" to whom it refers a member of the house of David? When Genesis 49:10–11 speaks of the rulers of Judah, it associates them with "a donkey's colt." In telling the story of Jesus' entry into Jerusalem, the Gospel of Matthew quotes our passage in Zechariah with a Davidic (and therefore messianic) figure firmly in mind (Matt. 21:5). Yet one can find a strong parallel between our passage and Zephaniah 3:14–15, which also calls upon the reader to sing and rejoice, for "The king of Israel, the Lord, is in your midst." In the end, the homiletical payoff is much the same. Whether it be through human royalty, the Messiah, or God's own self, the cessation of hostility and the dawning of peace is a divine gift and a divine calling.

That calling is not to a general sense of well-being, but rather to specific acts of mercy. Declaring that none of us can enjoy peace until the last one of us finds justice, God intends to rescue the prisoners from the waterless pit and restore to them double (Zech. 9:11–12). Release of the captives stands as one of the great promises of Scripture (Isa. 42:7; Jer. 30:8; Ezek. 34:27; Ps. 146:7; Luke 4:18). The preacher might fruitfully ask here whose captivity we have successfully resisted in our own time.

The question most likely to be asked of the reading for Proper 9 from Genesis 24 is, Why does it jump around the chapter so much? Not all questions about the lectionary are easy to answer, but this choice of verses might be due to the length of Genesis 24, devoted entirely to a leisurely telling of this one story, the search for a wife for Isaac. That the lectionary should choose to summarize it through a judicious use of excerpts is hardly surprising.

Its length notwithstanding, the story is straightforward. Abraham knows he must fulfill his responsibility to his bloodline by securing a good marriage for his son Isaac. To do so, Abraham sends his servant to his family in Mesopotamia to arrange the marriage. The servant (who is never named) arrives at his master's ancestral home in the evening, when the women come to the well to gather water. Having prayed that God would show him the young woman right for his master's son, he immediately sees Rebekah, the daughter of Abraham's relative Bethuel, step down into the well and fill her jar. Her response to the servant's greeting indicates that she is the one he seeks. At her family's home her brother Laban takes over the dual roles of host and chief negotiator in the suit for Rebekah's hand in marriage. Those negotiations conclude successfully, and Rebekah and the servant return to Isaac's home in the Negeb, as our reading tells us. Upon meeting Rebekah, Isaac loves her and makes her his wife.

One thing the preacher might note about this story is its lack of conflict, a fact that becomes evident in comparison to that which comes before and after. With Abraham and Sarah's struggles and disappointments on one side, and Jacob and his sons' chicanery and betrayal on the other, the "courtship" of Isaac and Rebekah stands out as an episode of rare domestic tranquility in the grand narrative of Genesis 12–50.

Another thing that stands out is the singular character of Rebekah, so it is hard to know how we should think of her. Long praised by (male) commentators as a model of humility, her behavior toward Abraham's servant strikes twenty-first-century readers as servile and possibly manipulative. By contrast, readings of Rebekah's role in the conspiracy to deprive Esau of his father's blessing in favor of Jacob (Gen. 27:5–17) have been deeply critical of her as deceptive and controlling, and for favoring one of her children over the other.[2]

A couple of responses to these impressions of Rebekah could help drive a sermon on this

---

2. Lynn Japinga, *Preaching the Women of the Old Testament* (Louisville, KY: Westminster John Knox, 2017), 26.

passage. The first is to draw Genesis 25 into conversation with chapters 24 and 27. In 25:21–27 Rebekah is suffering from the in utero struggle between her two sons. When on her own (not through her husband) she asks YHWH why that is, the Lord lets her know that the two are at odds because "the elder shall serve the younger." Thus God involves Rebekah from the outset in one of the most fundamental elements of the entire biblical story: the election of Israel as God's chosen people.

Second, the preacher might point out that in both chapters 24 and 27, Rebekah employs the means available to her to assert her own agency. When the servant of Abraham shows up to offer a beneficial marriage, she employs the means of the dutiful host and prospective wife. When Isaac is about to give his blessing in chapter 27, she takes on the role of the trickster to make certain that the son *whom God had revealed to her as the heir of promise* will receive it. The fact that she can accomplish her goals only by means we would not choose for ourselves should lead us to ask how today's social context likewise circumscribes the creativity and calling of our daughters and mothers. Giving Rebekah her due may allow us to raise the appropriate questions that lead us to become a more inclusive faith community.

ROBERT A. RATCLIFF

Commentary 2: Connecting the Reading with the World

Zechariah 9:9–12. In the *Simpsons* "Winter Wingding" episode, Homer is determined to see that the whole family enjoys the Springfield Holiday Parade. The episode's title aptly conveys Homer's conviction: "Everybody Loves a Parade." The lectionary readings for Proper 9 fall into the Fourth of July season, which also has its own set of parades. But, Homer aside, "everybody loves a parade" is a cliché and may not even be true. However, it does point to two realities: (1) parades and processionals require sheer numbers for the parading group; (2) a parade requires an audience. Nonetheless, the audience can slip into invisibility, especially if the audience consists of women in a patriarchal culture. On May 6, 1912, women showed up in New York City to march for the right to vote. The use of a parade was a new tactic in the struggle for women's suffrage in the United States. The public nature of the parade prompted some women to refrain from participation, but also meant that it was newsworthy, spreading the message of women's suffrage.

The writer's use of the phrases "daughter of Zion" and "daughter of Jerusalem" (Zech. 9:9, RSV) sometimes refers to a group of women and at other times to daughter cities or villages related to Zion or Jerusalem. This invites the reader to ask how the feminine informs our notion of the city and how the company of women brings a special voice to the faith community of antiquity and informs us today.

A community of women, references to daughters of Zion, provides what can be a transformative metaphor of place. Gloria Naylor's book *The Women of Brewster Place* introduces a group of women who have two things in common: their life in Brewster Place in a walled-in neighborhood, and their gender. Terry McMillan's *Waiting to Exhale* recounts the story of African American women living in Arizona. Amy Tan allows the reader a glimpse of San Francisco and Asian American women in her book *The Joy Luck Club*. Jewish law mandated that the community sequester women during the time of their menstruation; they were together in the "red tent." Anita Diamant through fiction allowed her readers access to the *Red Tent*.[3] Geographically located women often go overlooked in texts such as Zechariah 9.

The phrase "your king comes to you" occurs in Zechariah 9:9 but finds a secondary home in the New Testament (Matt. 21:5 and John 12:15)—so much so that often on Palm Sunday

---

3. Gloria Naylor, *The Women of Brewster Place* (New York: Penguin Books, 1983); Terry McMillan, *Waiting to Exhale* (New York: Viking, 1992); Amy Tan, *The Joy Luck Club* (New York: G. P. Putman's Sons, 1989); Anita Diamant, *The Red Tent* (New York: St. Martin's Press, 1997).

worship leaders forget this quotation's origin in Zechariah. Far from the winter Advent season, the Zechariah passage can have its own day.

The most mundane language—the verb "come" and the noun "king"—engenders a clarion call of hope. The verb captures the hope and the noun captures the object that facilitates the desired transformation. This simple combination of simple noun and verb resonates. Walt Whitman gestures to the growth of the human spirit in his poem "Passage to India": "Finally comes the poet worthy of the name. A true son of God shall come singing his songs." Walter Brueggemann connects the Whitman poem with the prophetic proclamation,[4] whether a poet, a prophet, or a recalibrated king.

The 1978 movie *Comes a Horseman*, starring Jason Robards, Jane Fonda, and Richard Farnsworth, set in the American West in the 1940s, pits the expansionist dreams of a local land baron against the aspirations of a woman rancher trying to retain her way of life. Then comes a horseman. There is no indication that the screenwriter referred to Zechariah at all, but the compelling combination of the mundane verb "come" and a noun, this time a horseman instead of a king, can designate a protagonist of hope.

Zechariah 9 embeds the hope in a slightly reconfigured notion of "king." The parade replaces the warhorse with a donkey (Zech. 9:10). Because of the blood of the covenant (v. 11), the prisoners from the waterless pit, the prisoners of hope (v. 12), will find restoration in the new parade.

Genesis 24:34–38, 42–49, 58–67. The servant takes center stage in the lectionary passage from Genesis. The parade contains two new characters, the slave of Isaac and Rebekah. The Hebrew term for "slave" (Heb. *ebed*) differs from the "chattel" slavery in the history of the United States. This character is not a victim of chattel slavery, nor simply an employee of the company. Often an invisible character in the ancient world, the slave (joined by the maiden) becomes the catalyst of the story.

Rebekah and Isaac's "love story" begins with a problem. Abraham required that his son marry within the clan. Anthropologists call this endogamy, marriage within a limited social group. Endogamous relationships can be based on geography (a state or region) or religious affiliation (Catholic, Protestant, Jewish, evangelical, Muslim) or race/ethnicity. Endogamous marriage occurs so often in contemporary society that colloquial English speakers often refer to this simply as "marriage" and variants of it as "interfaith" or "interracial marriage."

The ancestry stories of Genesis emphasize endogamous marriage, in marked contrast to Moses' marriages in the books of Exodus and Numbers. The concern for endogamy parallels the challenges of the exile and life in the Diaspora. The story outlines the challenge for the diasporic community of how to find an appropriate partner when living among a culturally and religiously diverse group of people. The embedded marriage rules in Genesis 24 provoke the question What are the marriage rules for Christians today?

The role of the servant becomes necessary because of the disappearance of Isaac in the so-called Isaac cycle. Isaac functions as a character in other people's stories. He is the evidence that the divine promise to Abraham and Sarah was fulfilled (Gen. 18–21), the paschal offering for Abraham (Gen. 22). Kierkegaard observes the odd status of Isaac after the failed sacrifice of Isaac. The survivor never talked of the event.[5] However, the story invites the reader of Genesis 24 to imagine more.

The slave's second speech (24:42–48) describes Rebekah's generosity and agency. The story depicts Rebekah as attractive and eligible for marriage, as a virgin (v. 16). The servant responds with gifts of his own, a ring for her nose and bracelets for her arms (v. 47b). The

---

4. Walt Whitman, *Leaves of Grass* (New York: Signet Classic/New American Library, 1955; orig. 1855), 324. See Walter Brueggemann, *Finally Comes the Poet: Daring Speech for Proclamation* (Minneapolis: Fortress, 1989).

5. Søren Kierkegaard, *Fear and Trembling*, ed. and trans. Howard V. Hong and Edna H. Hong (Princeton, NJ: Princeton University Press, 1983; orig. 1843), 14.

slave interprets the generosity of Rebekah as a sign that she is the appropriate partner for Isaac.

Finally, Rebekah speaks her consent. In the twenty-first century the #MeToo movement has crystalized the issue of consent. The role of a woman's consent, unlike in other biblical stories, figures prominently in Genesis 24. There is a "romantic" gesture of reciprocity: Isaac lifts his eyes and Rebekah lifts her eyes (vv. 63–64). Isaac brings Rebekah to the tent of Sarah. Rebekah consoles Isaac on the death of his mother.

The parade for women's suffrage in 1912 made manifest a previously present but invisible community. The Zechariah passage brings to visibility a new horizon of hope. The story of the unnamed slave and Rebekah likewise reconfigures the "romantic" story of endogamous marriage.

STEPHEN BRECK REID

Proper 9 (Sunday between July 3 and July 9 inclusive)

Psalm 145:8–14

⁸The LORD is gracious and merciful,
　　slow to anger and abounding in steadfast love.
⁹The LORD is good to all,
　　and his compassion is over all that he has made.

¹⁰All your works shall give thanks to you, O LORD,
　　and all your faithful shall bless you.
¹¹They shall speak of the glory of your kingdom,
　　and tell of your power,
¹²to make known to all people your mighty deeds,
　　and the glorious splendor of your kingdom.
¹³Your kingdom is an everlasting kingdom,
　　and your dominion endures throughout all generations.

The LORD is faithful in all his words,
　　and gracious in all his deeds.
¹⁴The LORD upholds all who are falling,
　　and raises up all who are bowed down.

Psalm 45:10–17

¹⁰Hear, O daughter, consider and incline your ear;
　　forget your people and your father's house,
　　　¹¹and the king will desire your beauty.
Since he is your lord, bow to him;
　　¹²the people of Tyre will seek your favor with gifts,
　　the richest of the people ¹³with all kinds of wealth.

The princess is decked in her chamber with gold-woven robes;
　　¹⁴in many-colored robes she is led to the king;
　　behind her the virgins, her companions, follow.
¹⁵With joy and gladness they are led along
　　as they enter the palace of the king.

¹⁶In the place of ancestors you, O king, shall have sons;
　　you will make them princes in all the earth.
¹⁷I will cause your name to be celebrated in all generations;
　　therefore the peoples will praise you forever and ever.

Song of Solomon 2:8–13

⁸The voice of my beloved!
　　Look, he comes,

leaping upon the mountains,
    bounding over the hills.
⁹My beloved is like a gazelle
    or a young stag.
Look, there he stands
    behind our wall,
gazing in at the windows,
    looking through the lattice.
¹⁰My beloved speaks and says to me:
"Arise, my love, my fair one,
    and come away;
¹¹for now the winter is past,
    the rain is over and gone.
¹²The flowers appear on the earth;
    the time of singing has come,
and the voice of the turtledove
    is heard in our land.
¹³The fig tree puts forth its figs,
    and the vines are in blossom;
    they give forth fragrance.
Arise, my love, my fair one,
    and come away."

Connecting the Psalm with Scripture and Worship

Psalm 145:8–14. The primary connection between Psalm 145:8–14 and Zechariah 9:9–12 is the repetition of the Hebrew root *mlk*. A noun from this root is translated "king" in Zechariah 9:9, and another noun from the root occurs four times in Psalm 145:11–13, where it is translated "kingdom." Clearly, "kingdom" is the keyword; but the syntax of verses 12–13, as well as the structure of the entire psalm, gives *mlk* and "kingdom" further emphasis. In Hebrew, the final word of verse 12 is "kingdom." Plus, the first two words of verse 13 are "kingdom." Very noticeably, the word appears three times in succession.

Furthermore, Psalm 145 is an acrostic poem; that is, the first verse begins with the first letter of the Hebrew alphabet, and each succeeding verse begins with the next letter, but there is an exception. The Hebrew letter with an n-sound should begin verse 14, but it has been skipped (although the NRSV supplies the missing line from other manuscripts, thus expanding verse 13; see note a). Thus, original readers of the Hebrew would have noticed an irregularity; and if they looked upward, they would have noticed that the preceding three lines (vv. 11–13, from bottom to top) begin with the letters *m*, *l*, *k*, the root of our keyword! All this together suggests that we should pay particular attention to the word "kingdom," as well as to the notion of power that it communicates.

There is another verbal link between these two texts. The word "dominion" in Zechariah 9:10 and Psalm 145:13 is basically synonymous with "kingdom." Like the appearance of "king" or "kingdom" in both texts, the word "dominion" invites attention to the notion of power. So, how and to what end does God exercise power? The prophet and the psalmist point in the same direction. God, who is the king in Zechariah 9:9, rules with humility. The NRSV's "triumphant and victorious" in verse 9 could better be translated "righteous and life-giving." God the king sets things right by destroying the equipment of warfare in verse 10. Thus, God's humble power saves lives, contributing to the *shalom* ("peace," but better "comprehensive well-being") of the nations. In short, God's exercise of power aims for nothing short of world peace (see Ps. 46:9–10; Isa. 2:2–4; Luke 2:14). While Zechariah is a prophetic book, the oracle in 9:9–12 is best understood not as the prediction of a particular event, but rather as a vision of God's intent for all times and places, a vision aimed at shaping the future that God intends (see the essay on Ps. 89:1–4, 15–18 for Year A, Proper 8).

What kind of God exercises power with humility and intends the well-being of all nations? As Psalm 145:8–14 suggests, it is a God who is essentially gracious, merciful, and steadfastly loving (see Exod. 34:6; Pss. 86:15; 103:8). This kind of God rules with "compassion . . . over all that he has made" (Ps. 145:9). "Compassion" represents the same root as "merciful" in verse 8, and one of the nouns from this root means "womb." The implication is that God exercises power as a loving mother. As verse 12 suggests, reinforcing Zechariah 9:10, "all people" are the beneficiaries of God's motherly love, but especially those who most need help (v. 14).

Christian readers will recall that Matthew 21:5 cites Zechariah 9:9 in the account of Jesus' entry into Jerusalem. Even though Zechariah 9:9 was not intended to predict this or any other particular event (see above), to see Jesus as the "fulfillment" of Zechariah 9:9, as Matthew does, is essentially to profess that Jesus embodied in his ministry of compassion the kind of God described in Zechariah 9:9–10 and Psalm 145:8–14. In short, Jesus exercised power humbly, graciously, mercifully, lovingly, aiming at nothing short of peace and life for all the world (see Matt. 11:28–30, part of the Gospel lesson for the day).

Psalm 45:10–17 or Song of Solomon 2:8–13. What connects Genesis 24:34–38, 42–49, 58–67 to both Psalm 45 and Song of Solomon 2 is that all three texts have to do with weddings. Actually, a wedding is not mentioned in Song of Solomon; but the woman and the man are passionately in love and deeply desire each other, and it is possible that the Song originated for use in wedding celebrations.

The superscription of Psalm 45 identifies it as "A love song." It is a celebration of the marriage of a king to the woman addressed in verses 10–13a and described in verses 13b–14 (before the king is addressed again in vv. 16–17, as he was in vv. 2–9). The "I" in verse 17 could be the poet, but perhaps should be understood as God. It may seem strange that the king is to be praised (and for that matter, it may seem strange that Psalm 45 is included in the Psalter); but this makes more sense if one understands that the king's fundamental responsibility was to enact on earth the justice, righteousness, and *shalom* that God wills (see Ps. 45:4, 6; Ps. 72). Hence, a royal wedding that promises an ongoing dynasty (45:16) can be understood as an event that will contribute to the future of the world as God intends it.

Even so, contemporary readers will be disturbed by the portrayal of women in this thoroughly patriarchal text, and rightly so. The marriage described in Psalm 45 is an arranged marriage, and the new queen is becoming the king's possession. Her job is to look pretty and have children. Of course, Genesis 24 and its account of the events leading up to the marriage of Isaac and Rebekah derive from the same cultural context. This marriage too is an arranged marriage, although the narrator suggests that divine guidance is operative; and it seems, according to Genesis 24:50–51, that all parties are agreeable and pleased. Even so, the model of marriage is not one to emulate.

At least both Psalm 45 and Genesis 24 suggest that marriage has more than merely a social significance. Rather, it is an institution in which God can be active and through which God's purposes can be enacted. In short, marriage has a religious significance, a reality that is almost completely lost in our contemporary context, in which even church weddings are viewed almost exclusively as social occasions rather than worship services.

Interestingly and importantly, Song of Solomon actually offers a model of sexuality and marriage that we would do well to emulate. The woman is addressing her partner in Song 2:8–13. Elsewhere, her partner speaks similarly back to her. In short, both partners have voice, and both are free to express what is clearly their mutual desire. The man speaks eloquently and explicitly of his lover in 7:1–9, after which the woman responds in 7:10 with a particularly important affirmation: "I am my beloved's, and his desire is for me." The word "desire" is the same word that occurs in Genesis 3:16 to describe what life under the curse will be like for women: "your desire shall be for your husband, and he shall rule over you." In Song of Solomon, the curse is reversed! Sexuality is not to be an arena for domination, but rather it is to be characterized by equality, mutuality of desire, and the expression of desire. In a culture like ours, where domination and abuse are rampant, it is a shame that the Song of Solomon is virtually ignored, even by the church.

J. CLINTON MCCANN JR.

Proper 9 (Sunday between July 3 and July 9 inclusive)

Romans 7:15–25a

¹⁵I do not understand my own actions. For I do not do what I want, but I do the very thing I hate. ¹⁶Now if I do what I do not want, I agree that the law is good. ¹⁷But in fact it is no longer I that do it, but sin that dwells within me. ¹⁸For I know that nothing good dwells within me, that is, in my flesh. I can will what is right, but I cannot do it. ¹⁹For I do not do the good I want, but the evil I do not want is what I do. ²⁰Now if I do what I do not want, it is no longer I that do it, but sin that dwells within me.

²¹So I find it to be a law that when I want to do what is good, evil lies close at hand. ²²For I delight in the law of God in my inmost self, ²³but I see in my members another law at war with the law of my mind, making me captive to the law of sin that dwells in my members. ²⁴Wretched man that I am! Who will rescue me from this body of death? ²⁵Thanks be to God through Jesus Christ our Lord!

Commentary 1: Connecting the Reading with Scripture

Romans 7 describes the inner struggle of a human being torn between submission to sin and the freedom of life lived with God. The strongly personal tone of this chapter, written as a first-person monologue, draws the reader into an emotionally charged dilemma. While reason dictates one thing, something subverts it, so that the "I" does the things it hates. The subverting power is found in the passions, which Paul identifies with the body and sin. What does this tell us about Paul and his Roman readers?

In Paul's Hellenistic setting, authors used this type of dialogue to explain the moral death of the self, a familiar literary theme. "The depiction of sin here fits with Platonic traditions of personification and metaphor that similarly represent passions and desires as an evil indwelling being that makes war, enslaves, imprisons, and sometimes even metaphorically kills the mind."[1]

These themes are found in Romans 7:15–25: "I see in my members another law at war with the law of my mind, making me captive to the law of sin that dwells in my members" (Rom. 7:23).

By alluding to these literary sources, Paul seems to assume that the Romans have access to the literature of Jewish tradition, as well as the works of pagan writers such as Plato and Plutarch. However, the writer whose work bears the closest resemblance to Paul's is Philo of Alexandria, a Jewish writer with a profound knowledge of Hellenistic culture. Paul's theme of the struggle with passions elicited by sin versus a desire for righteousness, as he developed it in Romans, is echoed in Philo: "And when any one, having conceived an idea of some good . . . hastens to lay hold of it, he then drives his soul forward to a great distance . . . from his anxiety to attain the object of his desires, he is stretched as it were upon the rack, being anxious to lay hold of the thing."[2]

Paul seems to write to a well-connected, literate community, immersed in the Greco-Roman world, yet able to grasp the intricacies of arguments from Jewish tradition.

How does this very personal dialogue fit into the overall argument Paul is building up in the Letter to the Romans? In the letter opening, Paul introduces himself as one Christ "called to be an apostle." He then offers his opening argument: "For I am not ashamed of the gospel; it is

---

1. Emma Wasserman, "Gentile Gods at the Eschaton," *Journal of Biblical Literature* 126, no. 4 (2007): 793–816.
2. Philo, *The Decalogue*, XXVIII, http://www.earlyjewishwritings.com/text/philo/book26.html. Philo's development of similar themes can be found in his treatises *On the Contemplative Life* and *On Virtues*.

the power of God for salvation to everyone who has faith, to the Jew first and also to the Greek. For in it the righteousness of God is revealed through faith for faith; as it is written, 'The one who is righteous will live by faith'" (1:16–17).

Paul then explains the relationship between faith, righteousness, and the law, concluding that all are guilty, both Jews and Gentiles (3:9–20). Sin existed in the world before the law was given to Moses; the function of the law is to reveal sin, not to justify or save. Justification comes through faith, which Paul argues by returning to Abraham's faith in the promises of God (4:18–25). He is using an ancient rule for building arguments; older traditions take precedence over newer ones. Abraham's experience carries greater weight than the law given to Moses.

In chapter 5, Paul explores the contrast between a life of holiness and a life subject to sin. He introduces the image of slavery to contrast obedience to sin and obedience to God. Between chapters 5 and 7, he summarizes the process whereby a person can live freely, without being trapped by the power of sin, by being baptized "into" the death and resurrection of Jesus. In chapter 6, Paul concludes that the life of a Christian is to be "dead to sin and alive to God" (6:11). However, in Romans 7:15–25 Paul seems to interrupt the flow of his argument by going back to review the impact of sin in his personal life. Why does Paul backtrack?

Today's reading reinforces Paul's argument by personalizing the struggle of someone torn between submission to sin and the freedom of life lived with God. This leads to the conclusion: "Wretched man that I am! Who will rescue me from this body of death? Thanks be to God through Jesus Christ our Lord!" (7:25).

How does Romans 7 relate to the other readings in Proper 9? At first glance, relating this very personal theological reflection on human nature and sin to the other readings can seem rather difficult, especially if the reader or preacher recognizes the emphasis on bridal themes in Genesis, Psalm 45, and the Song of Songs. However, the other texts assigned to this day have subtle connections to Paul's argumentation in Romans.

In Zechariah 9:9–12, Jerusalem is a woman who is encouraged by the prophet to celebrate her redemption by God. She represents a *people* restored from the violence that was a direct result of sin or covenant breaking on their part. Zechariah uses images that connect to both Israel and Judah to stress the idea that God will soon establish God's universal dominion:

> He will cut off the chariot from Ephraim
>   and the war-horse from Jerusalem;
> and the battle bow shall be cut off,
>   and he shall command peace to the
>   nations;
> his dominion shall be from sea to sea,
>   and from the River to the ends of the
>   earth.
> As for you also, because of the blood of my
>   covenant with you,
>   I will set your prisoners free from the
>   waterless pit.
> Return to your stronghold, O prisoners of
>   hope;
>   today I declare that I will restore to you
>   double.

This text imagines God as a warrior for peace who banishes violence and war, brings peace to *all* nations, and sets prisoners free. Paul argues that these actions characterize God's dominion over sin in Romans.

Similarly, Psalm 145 celebrates God's dominion, which comes about as a direct result of God's merciful character:

> The Lord is gracious and merciful,
>   slow to anger and abounding in steadfast
>   love.
> The Lord is good to all,
>   and his compassion is over all that he has
>   made. . . .
> Your kingdom is an everlasting kingdom,
>   and your dominion endures throughout
>   all generations.
> The Lord is faithful in all his words,
>   and gracious in all his deeds.
>   (Psalm 145:8, 9, 13)

The teaching of Jesus in Matthew 11 also connects with the themes of Romans. Jesus marvels at the conflicting demands that "this generation," his opponents, requires of prophets or messengers from God: play, dance, fast, eat—and yet they are not satisfied. Their minds are closed to mercy, no matter how it is presented to them. The God who frees, who is merciful, who brings peace in these texts, is the Jesus who

Examine Yourself

To know one's self, is a principal part of wisdom, and was thought by antiquity to be a rule sent from heaven; many illustrious authors have considered it the compendium of wisdom: but among Christians is of no farther weight, than as it accords with the sacred writings. No man should rashly assert that he knows himself; for scarce does any know the constitution of his body, much less the complexion and disposition of his soul. He is a bad soldier, who knows neither his own strength, or that of his enemy. Now man is at war with himself, for in his own breast there arises a troop in array against him. And, without due care, he is in danger of confounding friend and foe, and of treating them accordingly. Therefore . . . you have undertaken to fight against yourself, and there is no prospect of victory, but by a distinct self-knowledge. . . .

I am ashamed of the generality of men professing themselves Christians, who serve their appetites like beasts, and are so far from masters in the art of spiritual warfare, that they do not distinguish between reason and inclination. They think that to be men, it is sufficient to see and feel. They fancy nothing exists, but what falls within the notice of their senses. Whatever they earnestly wish for, they think right. A ready compliance with their passions, they call peace; though it is the greatest slavery, to submit the light of reason to the blind direction of their inclinations. This is that woeful peace, which Christ the true peace-maker came to destroy; kindly setting at variance the father with the son, the husband with the wife, and dissolving all alliances, that spring from a bad principle. . . .

When you have chastised, and crucified the affections and lusts, then you may, uninterrupted, converse with God, and taste that the Lord is gracious. After you have endured the fury and trial of the devil, there follows a still small voice of spiritual consolation. Examine well yourself. *For if ye live after the flesh, ye shall die: but if ye through the spirit do mortify the deeds of the body, ye shall live.* Well, therefore does it behove you to be in the spirit.

Erasmus, *The Christian's Manual*, trans. Philip Wyatt Crowther (London: A. J. Valpy, 1816), 37, 47.

---

says to those who are weary and bowed down: "Come to me, all you that are weary and are carrying heavy burdens, and I will give you rest" (Matt. 11:28). This echoes and connects with Paul's exclamation: "Who will rescue me from this body of death? Thanks be to God through Jesus Christ our Lord!" (Rom. 7:24–25).

These three texts (Zech. 9; Ps. 145; Matt. 11) project hope: whether the struggle is between grace and sin, or whether life or death is personal or national, God is a warrior for peace who will give rest to those who are weary and burdened.

RENATA FURST

Commentary 2: Connecting the Reading with the World

This text is assigned to us in the Ordinary Time of summer, when the liturgical calendar gives way to a cultural cycle of vacations, cookouts, and fireworks. Indeed, this Sunday is very close to the celebration of Independence Day. The lectionary presents the preacher an opportunity in this season by assigning a series of passages from Romans. The epistles can be challenging to preach, because the logic is tightly woven, but preaching in a series gives us a chance to trace the lines of thought from week to week. You can take an extended summer tour through the theological highlands of the New Testament.

Placed alongside Independence Day, one might consider how this text calls into question our freedom, especially at the personal and social dimension. How free are we, really? How free are we to pursue happiness and the flourishing life that we imagine and dream? Paul's introspections would tell us we may not be as free as we think we are: "I do not understand my own actions. For I do not do what I want, but I do the very thing I hate" (Rom. 7:15). Here he professes that the fundamental limit to human freedom lies not in the world out there, but within himself: "I find it to be a law that when I want to do what is good, evil lies close at hand" (v. 21).

There is debate over whether Paul is giving personal testimony, or is using the first person as a rhetorical device to describe the common human condition. Paul's own experience is as a "Pharisee of the Pharisees," who persecuted his Lord even when he was trying his hardest to be righteous. Such experience would prompt testimony like this, yet he speaks to the condition of us all. Why is it I do things I know I should not do? Better yet, why, even when I try my best, is it not enough? Why is it that the me I want to be is always out of reach? Even more to the point, what can I do to change?

These questions are not unique to theology, but are basic questions of self-actualization that are central to counseling practices, self-help books and seminars, and the proliferation of life coaching. One way to look at this is to say we need a stronger will, determination, and formation that can be achieved by wise counsel and better habits. Another way is to say we need to know ourselves better so that we can understand our own actions and, more importantly, the thoughts and feelings behind our actions. Indeed, one could read this passage and conclude that Paul needed a good therapist and coach, and so do the rest of us.

However, I think he is plumbing depths deeper than that. He is coming to the edge of human freedom, out to the point of where we have done our best, and his take on this question is decidedly theological. For Paul, the root of the problem of self-actualization does not lie in weak willpower or dim self-knowledge. Rather, the problem is sin. The sin that Paul describes is not the unintended consequences of our foolish behavior, or our faults and mistakes. Rather, sin is its own power at work in the world. It is the profound root of our failure, even when we are at our best. Whereas the law of God is an agent for good, the law of sin is an agent for evil, and these two laws are "at war" with each other. The human person is caught in the fight, captive within and among ourselves to the law of sin, and thus unable to live out the flourishing existence implanted by God in our hearts and minds.

We do not live in a wider culture that recognizes or often names sin as such, yet the arts do help us wrestle with the tangled web of good and evil. We could reach into classic literature to find connections, but contemporary television has given us unforgettable portrayals. Tony Soprano, the complicated protagonist of the series *The Sopranos*, is born into a crime family but is troubled by the consequences of his violent behavior. He senses he has lost his way, that there is a different life he wants to live. He even goes to therapy to analyze his childhood demons. Ultimately, though, he cannot walk away from his life of violence. On the other hand, Walter White, the protagonist of the series *Breaking Bad*, begins as a sympathetic character and slowly becomes irredeemable. He is diagnosed with cancer and needs to earn money for his family; so he begins his foray into cooking meth. He steadily descends on a path of corruption and destruction until, finally, he is utterly unlovable. Neither of these is a flat moralistic character; both are a mix of vice and virtue, and for both evil lies close at hand.

How do we as individuals and communities come to terms with this law of sin, played out with less drama but no less truth in our own lives? Here we find a liturgical connection to this text that is less about the calendar and more about the order of worship. Confession, far more often than the sermon, is the place in worship where we name the truth that Paul wrestles with in this text: *Merciful God, we confess that we have sinned against you in thought, word, and deed, by what we have done, and what we have left undone.* In other words, not only have we sinned, but our sin is inescapable. We could do no other. We can will what is right, but we cannot do it; we can love the law of God in our minds, but in our lives another law is at work.

We live in a culture where sin is easily characterized as mistakes, and a thing like confession sounds too judgmental. A sermon on a text like this can help us understand why we confess, and must confess, in worship. It is not because we have had an especially bad week, but because we are captive to sin. Moreover, we confess not only the personal dimension of sin, but its corporate and universal nature as well. We confess on behalf of communities and societies, and a humanity that is at war with itself. It takes only a scroll through the newsfeed or a glance at the headlines to realize that Paul's "*I* do not understand my own actions" is also "*we* do not understand our own actions." We cannot do the good we want; instead, we do the wrong we hate.

Fortunately, this lection gives us verse 25, because without it we would be hopeless. Paul's exploration into the deep problem of sin ends with an exasperated cry for help. Like a flash of insight, he understands how the grace of God in Jesus Christ changes everything: "Thanks be to God through Jesus Christ our Lord!" (v. 25). This is the declaration of forgiveness that becomes a declaration of freedom. It is the liberating word that promises we are never hopeless or finally lost; even the worst of us is never irredeemable or unlovable. Even if we descend into utter darkness, even if we can never quite climb into the light, nothing shall separate us from the love of God (8:39). This is the liberating grace that redeems not only our vices but our virtues too. We are set free to joyfully seek the will of God in the confidence that *God* redeems and is making all things new.

PATRICK W. T. JOHNSON

Proper 9 (Sunday between July 3 and July 9 inclusive)

Matthew 11:16–19, 25–30

¹⁶"But to what will I compare this generation? It is like children sitting in the marketplaces and calling to one another,

¹⁷'We played the flute for you, and you did not dance;
we wailed, and you did not mourn.'

¹⁸For John came neither eating nor drinking, and they say, 'He has a demon'; ¹⁹the Son of Man came eating and drinking, and they say, 'Look, a glutton and a drunkard, a friend of tax collectors and sinners!' Yet wisdom is vindicated by her deeds. . . ."

²⁵At that time Jesus said, "I thank you, Father, Lord of heaven and earth, because you have hidden these things from the wise and the intelligent and have revealed them to infants; ²⁶yes, Father, for such was your gracious will. ²⁷All things have been handed over to me by my Father; and no one knows the Son except the Father, and no one knows the Father except the Son and anyone to whom the Son chooses to reveal him.

²⁸"Come to me, all you that are weary and are carrying heavy burdens, and I will give you rest. ²⁹Take my yoke upon you, and learn from me; for I am gentle and humble in heart, and you will find rest for your souls. ³⁰For my yoke is easy, and my burden is light."

Commentary 1: Connecting the Reading with Scripture

Inspired by the play-based curriculum of their nursery school, I used to turn my kitchen over to my children when they were barely toddling around and gurgling a few words at a time. I would get out all the pots and pans, every possible cooking utensil, other paraphernalia, and many large bowls of random ingredients. Uncooked rice grains. Flour. Baking soda. Various shapes of dried pasta noodles. Water. Vinegar. Food coloring. Shrieks of joy and frustration at the experiments we were concocting together punctuated the constant music of spoons clanging on bowls. We would go at it, straining and combining, kneading and splashing, and if there was ever an image for the strange mixing of metaphors that sometimes happens in these Gospel texts, this would be it.

The image of children stands out among the vast assemblage of metaphors in the Gospel of Matthew. We see this even in the beginning in chapter 2, when Jesus is a child and we are told of the horrific massacre of the infants. Jesus blesses the children (Matt. 19:13–15), references children of God in the Beatitudes (5:9), heals a young girl (9:18–25), uses children as an example in the discourse on welcome in (10:42), heals the Canaanite woman's daughter (15:21–28), cures the boy with the demon (17:14–18), and the list goes on.

This is not surprising, as Matthew's focus is on attending to one's roots, the relationships between ancestors and descendants. He makes explicit the line from Jesus to all the familiar characters, with Abraham to King David and then to less familiar names, but nevertheless straight through as the crow flies to "Jacob the father of Joseph the husband of Mary, of whom Jesus was born, who is called the Messiah. So all the generations from Abraham to David are fourteen generations; and from David to the deportation to Babylon, fourteen generations; and from the deportation to Babylon to the Messiah, fourteen generations" (1:16–17).

Matthew has us thinking in terms of generations. In our lectionary passage Jesus begins with a somewhat rhetorical question, "But to what will I compare *this* generation?" (11:16, emphasis mine), and answers with a parable about children who do not respond to the celebrating or to the wailing. In this case, children are a sort of template where we map our expectations and stories, and their responses model something meaningful for us. Are the children in the parable supposed to symbolize John the Baptist and Jesus? John called for mourning and repentance in the face of judgment, whereas Jesus proclaimed joy because of the presence of the kingdom; in both cases their messages encountered unbelief or indifference. We read the possibilities of how "this generation" reacted to their presence by a similar rejection of both: John who neither ate nor drank, and Jesus who did both. They are either demonized or criticized. Should we perhaps read this text and liken "this generation" to the children who play and wail, and suppose the piping and wailing children represent the contentious people surrounding John and Jesus?

Unsurprisingly, there is some slippage here, but that allows for space to see the different possibilities for the work to bring about God's kingdom, and even John and Jesus, supposedly blood kin (though that is less clear in Matthew's account; cf. Luke 1:36) and in at least adjacent lineages, illustrate that for us. There is room for uncertainty, for those questions behind which lie anticipation and hope. Early on in the chapter, after instructing the disciples on their mission in the previous chapter, and presumably sending them on their way, Jesus himself continues on to various cities (Matt. 11:1). From prison John sends his disciples to voice a poignant question, likely on many minds: "Are you the one who is to come?" Jesus' response in this pericope is a picture of the kingdom of heaven: "the blind receive their sight, the lame walk, the lepers are cleansed, the deaf hear, the dead are raised, and the poor have good news brought to them" (11:4–5)—a fitting segue from Jesus' instructions in chapter 10 for what it will look like as the disciples bring that same kingdom to bear in the world.

There is congruence with the lectionary passage of Genesis and the story of Isaac and Rebekah meeting for the first time. After being told all about Isaac and anticipating his arrival, Rebekah seizes on the same question: "Who is the man over there, walking in the field to meet us?" (Gen. 24:65). The Genesis narrative holds a kind of waiting and wondering and hope similar to John the Baptist's question. These are expressions oriented toward a glimmering of the kingdom-come, of the proximity of a bright future and love fulfilled.

The lectionary passage in Matthew skips a section and leads us into Jesus' prayer of thanks for another relationship, that is, between the Father and the Son, and for "wisdom revealed to infants" (Matt. 11:25). It does not belong to the educated or the leadership; after all, look at how they responded to both John the Baptist and Jesus. In usual fashion, Jesus flips the expectations on where wisdom is located and found, and how it is acquired or cultivated; that is, wisdom belongs to the little ones, to "infants," to children, to the descendants, because it is given and revealed to them, specifically, by and through the Son. This is a key thread throughout this strangely mixed passage: the role of wisdom, of intelligence and insight, of perception and application, and how it is "vindicated by her deeds" (v. 19).

Paul gives us the best example of the necessity of wisdom in the Romans lectionary passage, in which he agonizes over not doing what he wants to do and the raging within his "members, another law at war with the law of my mind" (Rom. 7:23). He echoes the thanksgiving prayer Jesus offers in Matthew: for the one who provides wisdom, that is, perception and humility, for the one who will rescue him from the oppression of this "body of death," for the one who provides life and comfort. So it is fitting in many ways that at the end of the Matthew passage we read Jesus' comforting invitation to us: "Come to me . . . and learn from me, and . . . find rest for your souls" (Matt. 11:28–29). These are words not of a conqueror but of a companion. In this we also see that Jesus is the revealer; it teaches us that he is the source of spiritual rest, and it tells us that he is humble and gentle.

The truth of our faith is in the living. To read about feeding the hungry is one thing; to feed them is quite another. So this is an invitation to enact wisdom by redirecting our lives. One discovers the wisdom of Jesus by doing, by adopting his spirit and living his imperatives. This wisdom echoes the familiar passage from Proverbs: "The fear of the Lord is the beginning of wisdom" (Prov. 9:10), because it emphasizes posture and orientation toward the one who will impart wisdom. When Jesus says, "Learn from me," he is calling us not just to read further or to mull over theological ideas, but to incarnate and embody for ourselves the kingdom that he exhibits in his speech and actions. Once again, Jesus upends these social structures around lineages and the relationships between teacher and disciples, parent and child, ancestors and descendants, to show us that wisdom is shared, it knows no bounds or lines, it is healing, and most importantly, it is given and received.

MIHEE KIM-KORT

Commentary 2: Connecting the Reading with the World

Prior to these words in today's passage, Jesus has shared about the powerful and prophetic witness of John the Baptizer. John called the people to turn around and see a whole new reality: the God movement. In this new reality, John indicated that people—in the Lukan portrayal—would share clothes and food with anyone in need (Luke 3:10–11). John's prophecy was a call to change our lifestyle and to work for justice and mercy in order to avoid the judgment of God that was surely coming in this new age. For John the Baptizer, God is coming soon in anger and judgment. The four Gospels indicate that John sees Jesus as the sign that God's inbreaking is imminent.

Jesus seeks to build on the message of John, but he adds a dimension to John's emphasis on avoiding the judgment of God. Jesus emphasizes the radical, unbelievable, and freeing grace of God, and indicates that God wants our passion, not our perfection. This is a dramatic shift from John; indeed, earlier in this chapter (Matt. 11:2–6), John wonders if Jesus really is the one. Jesus notes here that neither the harshness of John nor the joyful proclamation of Jesus has borne fruit. He uses a short parable about children being out of tune with one another and being unable to play together and enjoy their lives. Jesus indicates that the people of his generation have missed the signs of the times; the God movement is breaking into the world and into the life of humanity.

For followers of Jesus in every age, it is important to seek discernment of the signs of the times, to see where God's new energy is breaking into the world and into our lives. We have broken apart in American culture, and preachers and congregations will be asked to look for God's new movement in this time. In his 2005 book *Bury the Chains*, Adam Hochschild narrates the story of twelve people who met in a printing bookshop in London in 1787. They had read the signs of their times, and they made a pact to seek to end the slave trade in England and in the colonies. At the time, it seemed to be an overwhelming project, beyond their capability. Yet they read the signs of the times that God was sending to them and to others. They dedicated themselves to this task, and through God's mercy, England passed the Abolition of the Slave Trade Act in 1807.[1] They heard the music playing and danced in rhythm. The worldly and wise thought that slavery should not and could not be ended, but these twelve believed and proclaimed to many others that the signs that pointed to God's *kairos* made it time to act in human time (*chronos*).

In Matthew's unusual nod to the Johannine view of Jesus, in Matthew 11:25–27, Jesus re-affirms that he is the one to come, that there is no reason to look for another. In Jesus Christ, God has broken into the world to show us a new way of living, a way based on love, justice, and mercy. The time is at hand, and it is time to respond as a child of God, rather than as a child of the fallen powers of the world. Jesus also indicates that you do not have to have a doctoral degree or be a powerful politician or a military

---

1. Adam Hochschild, *Bury the Chains* (Boston: Houghton Mifflin, 2005).

general to respond to this inbreaking. To paraphrase Martin Luther King Jr., you only have to have a heart to serve.

Jesus finishes with famous and strange words: "Come to me, all you that are weary . . . and I will give you rest" (11:28). These words are quoted often at funerals and memorial services, as well they should be. Yet Jesus does not use them as a nod to our mortality and the blessedness of being in the presence of God when we die. He intends them to apply to our lives right now, wherever we find ourselves. The Christian life often seems one of difficulty, with obstacles, sorrow, and suffering. Earlier, in the Sermon on the Mount, Jesus emphasizes that the way is difficult: "For the gate is narrow, and the road is hard that leads to life" (7:14).

These two approaches by Jesus in Matthew seem incongruent. Any of us who have tried the path of Jesus know that it is a difficult road because of our captivity to all the fallen powers in our lives. In Matthew 11, however, Jesus is moving into deeper territory in our individual and collective souls. Jesus sees his mission as one of bringing God's love and joy into our lives. He is not denying the vision of John the Baptizer, the mission of repentance and service and preparation for God's inbreaking. Rather, he is emphasizing that "oughtness" and avoidance of God's judgment are not the main point. Doing what we ought to do is important, as Jesus stresses so emphatically in the Sermon on the Mount; but in these closing verses of Matthew 11 he is pointing his followers, including us, to a more profound understanding.

His emphasis is that the foundational word from God is God's love for us. As Fred Rogers emphasized on *Mister Rogers' Neighborhood*, God wants us to hear at our deepest levels that we are loved. What God wants from us, first and foremost, is our passion rather than our perfection. As I grew up as a white Christian in the segregated South, the God to whom I related was a stern and harsh and judgmental God. Part of that view of God was derived from the white southern orientation toward violence as the proper manner for preserving slavery and later neo-slavery. Violence was at the heart of our lives; because of that, we thought that violence must be at the heart of God. Love, justice, and mercy were seen as weak points, as softness in the real world.

God is certainly shocked at how our lives lie captive to evil, and the warnings and proclamations of John the Baptizer point us to the depth of our captivity. I believe that God is even more grieved at our failure to love—to love God, love neighbor, love ourselves. In Jesus Christ, God is proclaiming and pleading with us to see that our captivity to race and gender and materialism and many other powers is moving us to the unreal world and away from the reality and power of God. As Jesus puts it, we are asked to hear a new message, a message that proclaims that love and justice, rather than violence and death and domination, are at the heart of our lives.

What would it mean to us as individuals and as communities if we came to believe that we are really loved, that love is the center of our lives? What would it mean if we were able to turn our passion toward God, rather than toward so many of the fallen powers?

I think that it would mean what Jesus says in these closing verses: because we are directing our passion toward the God of love, we will find rest for our souls (11:28–30). We will find that our individual lives can be oriented toward gratitude rather than toward anxiety. God's continuing action in the world means that the God movement is always breaking into our lives, dancing for us, pleading with us, insisting to us that our lives depend on receiving the signs of the times in every age: we are loved by the Center of the universe.

NIBS STROUPE

Proper 10 (Sunday between July 10 and July 16 inclusive)

Isaiah 55:10–13 and Genesis 25:19–34
Psalm 65:(1–8) 9–13 and
   Psalm 119:105–112
Romans 8:1–11
Matthew 13:1–9, 18–23

Isaiah 55:10–13

[10] For as the rain and the snow come down from heaven,
   and do not return there until they have watered the earth,
making it bring forth and sprout,
   giving seed to the sower and bread to the eater,
[11] so shall my word be that goes out from my mouth;
   it shall not return to me empty,
but it shall accomplish that which I purpose,
   and succeed in the thing for which I sent it.

[12] For you shall go out in joy,
   and be led back in peace;
the mountains and the hills before you
   shall burst into song,
   and all the trees of the field shall clap their hands.
[13] Instead of the thorn shall come up the cypress;
   instead of the brier shall come up the myrtle;
and it shall be to the LORD for a memorial,
   for an everlasting sign that shall not be cut off.

Genesis 25:19–34

[19] These are the descendants of Isaac, Abraham's son: Abraham was the father of Isaac, [20] and Isaac was forty years old when he married Rebekah, daughter of Bethuel the Aramean of Paddan-aram, sister of Laban the Aramean. [21] Isaac prayed to the LORD for his wife, because she was barren; and the LORD granted his prayer, and his wife Rebekah conceived. [22] The children struggled together within her; and she said, "If it is to be this way, why do I live?" So she went to inquire of the LORD. [23] And the LORD said to her,

   "Two nations are in your womb,
      and two peoples born of you shall be divided;
   the one shall be stronger than the other,
      the elder shall serve the younger."

[24] When her time to give birth was at hand, there were twins in her womb. [25] The first came out red, all his body like a hairy mantle; so they named him Esau. [26] Afterward his brother came out, with his hand gripping Esau's heel; so he was named Jacob. Isaac was sixty years old when she bore them.

²⁷When the boys grew up, Esau was a skillful hunter, a man of the field, while Jacob was a quiet man, living in tents. ²⁸Isaac loved Esau, because he was fond of game; but Rebekah loved Jacob.

²⁹Once when Jacob was cooking a stew, Esau came in from the field, and he was famished. ³⁰Esau said to Jacob, "Let me eat some of that red stuff, for I am famished!" (Therefore he was called Edom.) ³¹Jacob said, "First sell me your birthright." ³²Esau said, "I am about to die; of what use is a birthright to me?" ³³Jacob said, "Swear to me first." So he swore to him, and sold his birthright to Jacob. ³⁴Then Jacob gave Esau bread and lentil stew, and he ate and drank, and rose and went his way. Thus Esau despised his birthright.

Commentary 1: Connecting the Reading with Scripture

Knowing that the prophets at times had to announce the bad news of divine judgment, we can easily understand why passages like today's hope-filled reading from Isaiah constitute some of the most beautiful sections of the Hebrew Bible. The joy that comes from speaking the good news of redemption and restoration fills every line of this passage, and indeed all of the chapter to which it belongs.

Isaiah 55 represents the conclusion of Second Isaiah, the historical setting for which is the defeat of the Babylonian Empire by Cyrus and the Persians, when the possibility of their return home was beginning to dawn on the Jewish exiles in Babylon. Those who composed this portion of the prophetic book knew that hope seemed a risky investment to these children and grandchildren of Jerusalem. The book addresses its skittish audience as an "afflicted one, storm-tossed, and not comforted" (Isa. 54:11). To counter their reluctance to hope, verses 1 and 2 open chapter 55 with the aggressiveness of a street vendor hawking their wares. They invite the reader to a generous feast, offered "without money and without price." Hearing this invitation, the preacher might recall its echoes in the Magnificat's claim that "[God] has filled the hungry with good things" (Luke 1:46–55) and in Jesus' parable of the Great Banquet (Luke 14:15–35). The invitation's openness to all shows up again in verses 3–5, which extend the covenant made with David to anyone who seeks a life devoted to God and God's people.

The reader can rely on this invitation, verses 10–11 assure us, because it is grounded in the divine promise. The preacher would do well to remember the multiple possibilities for the term "word" in verse 11. Among its original readers, it likely referred to the prophetic or covenantal word heard already in this chapter and what precedes. Protestant Christians will be disposed to understand it as the word of God recorded in Scripture and announced in the church's preaching. Even more fundamental to Christian theology, however, is the Word incarnate of the prologue to John's Gospel, who can be most truly said to "accomplish that which I purpose, and succeed in the thing for which I sent [him]" (Isa. 55:11b).

Verses 12 and 13 complete the circle started in chapter 40, the beginning of Second Isaiah. Both passages describe a journey through the wilderness in which the natural order joins in celebrating the return of God's people to the Holy City. While chapter 40 opens with the plaintive assurance that the suffering of God's people has come to an end, chapter 55 closes with God's calm announcement that restored Israel goes forth to a life of plenty and peace.

The chapter's final word is one of implied reversal. Included in the divine punishment of Israel and Judah had been God's intention to make them an example among the nations. In Ezekiel 5:15 God proposes to make them a "mockery and a taunt, a warning and a horror"; in Jeremiah 29:18 they are to become "an object of . . . derision among all the nations." How much different, then—and how much better—is Isaiah 55:13's promise that the life of joy and abundance to which God calls them will forever be a sign and remembrance of divine forgiveness.

Isaiah 55's insistence on the efficacy of the divine promise, culminating in verse 11, finds ratification in the Gospel reading for this Sunday. Just as the prophet insists that God's word does not return empty, Jesus' parable of the Sower (Matt. 13:1–9, 18–23) lets us know that the word planted in the receptive heart yields abundantly.

Our reading from Genesis echoes Isaiah's trust in God's promise, yet adds to it the complex notion of God's choice. Genesis 25 portrays a transition in the narrative of the matriarchs and patriarchs, with a description early in the chapter of Abraham's death. Since Isaac is a minor character, Jacob's emergence later in the chapter represents the beginning of the concluding half of Genesis 12–50's account of the family of Abraham. The preacher might highlight some of the features of the Jacob story by noting their contrasts to what came before. For example, struggle and conflict appear in both parts of the narrative, but they take a different shape. In the Abraham stories, conflict arises *between* one generation and another: Sarah and Abraham's rejection of Ishmael, Abraham's averted sacrifice of Isaac. In the Jacob stories, it happens *within* the same generation, Jacob and Esau, Joseph and his brothers.

Our passage falls into two sections. The first (Gen. 25:19–26) tells the story of Jacob and Esau's conception and birth, focusing on God's declaration that the elder of the two brothers (Esau) will serve the younger (Jacob), and that (by implication) Jacob is the brother through whom God's promises to the family of Abraham will be fulfilled. That God has chosen to bless Abraham's bloodline should come as no surprise at this point (see Gen. 18:19). The surprising element that Genesis 25:19–26 adds is the wholly sovereign nature of that choice. Twins though they might be, the narrator introduces Esau and Jacob in such a way that the reader knows who is more likely the child of promise. In addition to being the firstborn, Esau's physical description seems more imposing. He is also the favorite of his father, himself the promised son. To call Jacob's behavior in this chapter and beyond morally questionable would be an understatement. That he should emerge from the womb gripping his brother's heel surprises us not at all, once we read the rest of story and realize he is continuously grasping for what he wants.

None of that matters. God elects Jacob, and hence Israel. That election announces a theme throughout the Hebrew Bible and the New Testament: God's decision to call and use those whom we would never expect. The preacher might remind the congregation of echoes of that theme heard in the choice of two other younger sons in Genesis: Isaac over Ishmael (17:18–22) and Joseph over his brothers (37:5–8). The theme sounds throughout the Old Testament, as we are reminded frequently of Israel and Judah's weak position in relation to their Egyptian and Mesopotamian neighbors. Matthew and Luke's infancy narratives announce it as well, with a hidden Messiah born of peasant parents and visited by smelly shepherds and crazy magi. It resurfaces in Jesus' assurance that "the last shall be first" (Matt. 19:30; 20:16). It appears in Paul's insistence that God has chosen the "foolish," the "weak," the "low and despised" (1 Cor. 1:27–28).

The second part of our reading from Genesis (25:27–34) stands in creative tension with the first. Whereas verses 19–26 focus on God's choice of Jacob over Esau, verses 27–34 (as well as the subsequent story of the conspiracy to steal Isaac's blessing in chap. 27) show Jacob acting to make himself the son through whom Abraham's promised descendants will arise. The story makes clear that nothing more is at work here than Esau's hasty hunger and Jacob's opportunism. Yet the juxtaposition of this story with the narrative of God's choice of Jacob in utero makes it just as clear that *more* is exactly what is involved. In the midst of these purely human motivations, the scandalous mystery of God's choice of Israel comes to fruition.

ROBERT A. RATCLIFF

Commentary 2: Connecting the Reading with the World

Isaiah 55:10–13. Aristotle claims two things that modernity and postmodernity now contest: the existence of a natural law and that the universe has a purposeful goal. Isaiah 55:10–13 begins with the same presuppositions. Twentieth-century literature and art provide a countertestimony in a movement called magical realism. These writers and artists observe that the natural world sometimes testifies to what the social world tries to obscure. Toni Morrison in her first novel, *The Bluest Eye*, depicts the interplay of natural magic and tragically real events in the lives of the Breedlove family. "Quiet as it's kept, there were no marigolds in the fall of 1941. We thought, at the time, that it was because Pecola was having her father's baby that the marigolds did not grow."[1]

The Isaiah school used nature to signal the new era that only the observant could recognize, an era of the peaceable kingdom when the lion and the lamb lay down together (Isa. 11). The mountains and the valleys respond to divine will, rising and falling accordingly (40:4).

Isaiah 55:10–13 breaks into two interlinked parts: (a) the use of nature as metaphor for the inexorable movement of divine word (vv. 10–11); (b) the "natural" response of celebration. Snow does not occur often in the region around Jerusalem and is an infrequent reference in the Hebrew Bible (Heb. *sheleg*; including Pss. 51:7; 148:8; Job 6:16; 37:6). The snow and rain come down from heaven, provide a service, and disappear. Rain and snow present a pair that stands for precipitation that comes down from heaven as gravity and the God who created gravity mandate.

The creation story presupposes the transformative word of God, divine speech (Gen. 1–2). The Isaianic poet uses the metaphor for divine speech with the phrase "My [divine] word," which finds prominence in the exilic and postexilic period. In contemporary English usage the phrase "my word" still has substantial currency. The simple statement "I gave my word" signals a commitment, a pledge. The use of the phrase in the Isaiah passage seems to convey a similar pledge and promise that provides a liberating force amid the trauma of exile and postexile.

The second movement describes the natural response to God's word (Isa. 55:11–13). The tree metaphor is prominent in Scripture and arts and literature. Both Israelite and Canaanite religions associate sacredness with trees. The writer of Genesis 2–3 builds on the "tree" tradition with the tree of the knowledge of good and evil. The Isaianic school also used the metaphor of trees in the language of new creation in Isaiah 65:22. Indeed, "the trees of the field shall clap their hands" (v. 12). The tree models behavior of exaltation. Shel Silverstein's book *The Giving Tree* (1964) provides another angle on the transformative work of trees. Frank Baum's novel *The Wonderful Wizard of Oz* (1900) introduced the idea of the fighting tree.[2]

Steffie Geiser Rubin grew up with a strong Jewish background in the Bronx. She encountered Moishe Rosen at a Bible study at the University of California Berkeley. He asked her, "What do you think God wants from you?" Her response was to read the four Gospels. After this encounter with the person Moishe Rosen and the testimony to Jesus (Yeshua), Rosen became a Christian believer and completed her undergraduate studies at Simpson Bible College in San Francisco. She also became one of the founding members of Jews for Jesus. She later completed a master's degree in Jewish Studies from Baltimore Hebrew Institute of Towson University. In 1975 Rubin and Stuart Dauermann adapted Isaiah 55:12 into a song, "You shall go out in joy," now found in many denominational hymnals.

This pronouncement contends that the end of certain natural phenomena cannot be stopped. The function or end of rain and snow from the heaven or sky is the nourishing of the land on earth, so that it can be productive. In the Genesis passage, the snow, rain, and the trees seem to know something that eludes Jacob and Esau.

---

1. Toni Morrison, *The Bluest Eye* (New York: Vintage, 1970), xix.
2. Shel Silverstein, *The Giving Tree* (New York: Harper & Row, 1964); L. Frank Baum, *The Wonderful Wizard of Oz* (Chicago: George M. Hill Company, 1900).

Genesis 25:19–34. Form critics classify Genesis 25:19–34 as an etiology, which explains the origin and nature of a person, place, or thing. Readers of this story identify with Jacob, our progenitor. This reading examines the power and privilege of Esau. Jacob and Esau represent two different people groups. The etiology presents a view of each, spiced with broad humor. The Lord said to Rebekah, "Two nations are in your womb," but the unusual element was that "the elder shall serve the younger" (Gen. 25:23). The two nations competed from the moment of delivery. The younger, Jacob, came into the world trying to get there before his twin Esau. His very name means "usurper." Thus the story gives the reader a problem that must be overcome: How can the younger son inherit without killing the older son?

The male head of the household dominated the family structure of ancient Israel. The oldest son inherited everything, a zero-sum game of inheritance. God gave the firstborn status. It was an irrevocable entitlement, privilege, and advantage. An old American Express commercial tagline went "Membership has its privileges." Contemporary parallels in the United States might be gender and race. Being "white" and being "male" have their privileges. Often the advantage is so invisible that the one holding the advantage is not even aware of it.

The etiology of the story understands Esau as hairy, a skillful hunter, and a man of the field (vv. 25, 27a). On the other hand, Jacob is a quiet man who spends most of his time in the tent. The passage takes a moment to locate this conflict in broader family dynamics: Isaac loves Esau and Rebekah loves Jacob. The etiology depicts Esau and his descendants as impetuous, Jacob and his descendants as cunning. The trees of Isaiah 55 are smarter than Esau.

This passage is a one-act play. While Jacob is cooking a stew, the impetuous Esau comes in famished (v. 29). As the firstborn, his is the first speech, the first demand: Give me some of that "red stuff," a play on the red lentil stew. This is also a wordplay on "Esau," the red-haired one from the red land Edom (v. 30). Jacob, the cunning one, understands his advantage and makes an impossible demand: "First sell me your birthright" (v. 31). Many translations render the term "heritage." However, that is too vague and transferable. "Birthright" is a privilege so profound that even to deny it does not dispel it. "Maleness" and "whiteness" might function in comparable ways today.

The simple Esau mistakenly thinks that birthright is a mere idea, a social construct (v. 32), something that he can relinquish on command, but the story accuses Esau of foolishness with the conclusion, "Thus Esau despised his birthright" (v. 34).

Birthright stood so prominent in the culture that it could not be bartered away. The entitlement was so profound that it became invisible to the holder, who felt free to relinquish what can never go away. This is the first of two stories (cf. 27:1–45) that depict Jacob the younger outsmarting Esau the older out of his status as firstborn. Jacob has to flee the area (27:40–45), proving that these stories do not revoke the social practice.

The prophetic passage, Isaiah 55, proclaims God's cosmic restoration, which includes a disenfranchised people. When we read Genesis 25:19–34, we can reevaluate the power of privilege and advantage today.

STEPHEN BRECK REID

Proper 10 (Sunday between July 10 and July 16 inclusive)

Psalm 65:(1–8) 9–13

[1] Praise is due to you,
    O God, in Zion;
and to you shall vows be performed,
    [2] O you who answer prayer!
To you all flesh shall come.
[3] When deeds of iniquity overwhelm us,
    you forgive our transgressions.
[4] Happy are those whom you choose and bring near
    to live in your courts.
We shall be satisfied with the goodness of your house,
    your holy temple.

[5] By awesome deeds you answer us with deliverance,
    O God of our salvation;
you are the hope of all the ends of the earth
    and of the farthest seas.
[6] By your strength you established the mountains;
    you are girded with might.
[7] You silence the roaring of the seas,
    the roaring of their waves,
    the tumult of the peoples.
[8] Those who live at earth's farthest bounds are awed by your signs;
    you make the gateways of the morning and the evening shout for joy.

[9] You visit the earth and water it,
    you greatly enrich it;
the river of God is full of water;
    you provide the people with grain,
    for so you have prepared it.
[10] You water its furrows abundantly,
    settling its ridges,
softening it with showers,
    and blessing its growth.
[11] You crown the year with your bounty;
    your wagon tracks overflow with richness.
[12] The pastures of the wilderness overflow,
    the hills gird themselves with joy,
[13] the meadows clothe themselves with flocks,
    the valleys deck themselves with grain,
    they shout and sing together for joy.

Psalm 119:105–112

¹⁰⁵Your word is a lamp to my feet
    and a light to my path.
¹⁰⁶I have sworn an oath and confirmed it,
    to observe your righteous ordinances.
¹⁰⁷I am severely afflicted;
    give me life, O LORD, according to your word.
¹⁰⁸Accept my offerings of praise, O LORD,
    and teach me your ordinances.
¹⁰⁹I hold my life in my hand continually,
    but I do not forget your law.
¹¹⁰The wicked have laid a snare for me,
    but I do not stray from your precepts.
¹¹¹Your decrees are my heritage forever;
    they are the joy of my heart.
¹¹²I incline my heart to perform your statutes
    forever, to the end.

Connecting the Psalm with Scripture and Worship

Psalm 65:(1–8) 9–13. The first reading, Isaiah 55:10–13, is a portion of the book (Isa. 40–55, usually called Second Isaiah and dated to about the years 540–539 BCE) that asserts God's sovereignty in response to the earlier destruction of Jerusalem in 587 BCE and the subsequent Babylonian exile. Even amid apparent defeat, the God of Israel is still "Creator" (Isa. 40:28; 43:15), "Redeemer" (41:14; 43:14; 44:6; and more—"redeemer" can also be translated "next-of-kin," thus communicating God's intimate relatedness to the people), and "King" (41:21; 43:15; 44:6; see 52:7). Biblically speaking, the primary responsibility of a king was to provide for his people, beginning with feeding them. We know this from Psalm 72, a prayer for the Judean king that asks that the king "be like rain that falls on the mown grass, like showers that water the earth" (Ps. 72:6), and that "there be abundance of grain in the land" (v. 16). Rain, of course, makes the crops grow ("grass" in v. 6 should be understood as a food crop, not a lawn cover), so that people will be able to eat.

The presence of rain is one of the connections between Isaiah 55:10–13 and Psalm 65. Although Psalm 65 does not use the noun translated "rain" in Isaiah 55:10, both texts affirm that God has provided water for the earth (Isa. 55:10; Ps. 65:9–10). In both texts, it is explicit that the watered earth provides food for people, "bread to the eater" (Isa. 55:10; see vv. 1–2) and "grain" that God has "prepared" (Ps. 65:9). In both instances, God's provision is sufficient, indeed abundant (see "satisfied" in Ps. 65:4 and "satisfy" in Isa. 55:2). Such abundant provision is prime evidence of God's gracious sovereignty.

Grace is of the essence in both texts and in both contexts. Psalm 65:3 affirms that God's people have been forgiven, and Isaiah 55:10–13 is immediately preceded by an invitation to "return to the LORD, that he may have mercy on them, and to our God, for he will abundantly pardon" (Isa. 55:7). In this context, what makes God's thoughts and ways "higher" than human thoughts and ways is precisely God's ability and willingness to forgive (vv. 8–9). Putting all this together, we conclude that to be God means to exercise sovereignty or power as grace that sustains the life of God's people (see the Psalms essay for last week, Year A, Proper 9, especially the treatment of Ps. 145:8–14, which is paired with Zech. 9:9–12).

It is not just God's people who are the beneficiaries of God's life-giving and life-sustaining grace. To be sure, the effective "word" that achieves its "purpose" in Isaiah 55:11 (see Isa. 40:8) does promise *shalom* (55:12, "peace," but better "comprehensive well-being") for God's people. From exile, they are being "led back" (v. 12) to a land; and having land means the opportunity to grow food and to eat. God's people also have a mission that involves "the peoples" (v. 4) and "nations that do not know you" (v. 5). Earlier in this portion of the book of Isaiah, the people are cast in the role of a Servant who will somehow be "a light to the nations" (42:6; 49:6), so that God's life-giving and life-sustaining work "may reach to the end of the earth" (49:6). The same expansive, indeed universalistic, reach is evident in Psalm 65, in which God will somehow draw in "all flesh" (Ps. 65:2), and in which God's life-giving and life-sustaining work means that God is "the hope of all the ends of the earth and of the farthest seas" (v. 5).

Quite properly, therefore, the joyful response to God is creation-wide in both Isaiah 55 and Psalm 65. Participants include "the mountains and the hills . . . and all the trees of the field" (Isa. 55:12). According to Psalm 65:12–13, participants include "the pastures of the wilderness . . . the meadows . . . the valleys," all of which "shout and sing together for joy." The profound ecological implications of these descriptions should not be missed. God's worshiping congregation includes not only all people (Isa. 56:3–8; Pss. 67:3, 5; 96:7–9; 100:1; 117:1; 148:11–13), but also nothing short of all creation (Pss. 96:11–13; 98:7–9; 103:20–22; 145:10–12; 148:1–10; 150:6), which is to be accorded the honor and integrity that come from belonging to God. The ethical, theological, and ecological significance of Psalm 65 and Isaiah 55 is expressed beautifully in a hymn by Mary Louise Bringle, "Light Dawns on a Weary World," the refrain of which employs the language of Isaiah. 55:12, along with Isaiah 58:11, which like Psalm 65:9–10 and Isaiah 55:10 mentions being watered.[1]

Psalm 119:105–112. This second psalm for the day is apparently meant to respond to Genesis 25:19–34; however, connections between these two texts are elusive. To be sure, both texts contain the same Hebrew root that is translated "sworn" in Psalm 119:106 and "swear"/"swore" in Genesis 25:33, but the oaths sworn by the psalmist and Esau seem to have nothing in common, so this may not be what the framers of the lectionary had in mind when they paired the two texts.

What they did have in mind is hard to say; but with a little imagination, one might conclude that Psalm 119:111 would have been an appropriate response on Jacob's part when he received the birthright that should not have been his. He had received it at God's behest or decree, and the birthright opened the way for Jacob, who became Israel, to have a "heritage" (Ps. 119:111), a word often associated with the gift of the land.

Israel eventually lost the land, at which point it reorganized itself essentially as a people of the book, that is, as a community constituted by and devoted to God's "word" (vv. 105, 107) or God's *torah* (v. 109, "law," but better "teaching" or "instruction" or "will"). This principle of reorganization gave Jacob/Israel an identity that was enduring; it was and is "forever" (v. 111). Ultimately for Jacob, who became Israel, it would be God's revelation—God's word, teaching, decrees—that would guarantee a future.

One cannot help but wonder, despite the fact that the psalm for the day is supposed to have been chosen as a response to the first reading, whether the framers of the lectionary sometimes wavered and chose the psalm as a response to the Gospel lesson. The Gospel lesson for the day is Matthew 13:1–9, 18–23, the parable of the Sower, whose scattered seed, Jesus says, represents "the word of the kingdom" (Matt. 13:19). The faithful, fruitful respondent

---

1. Mary Louise Bringle, "Light Dawns on a Weary World," in *Glory to God: The Presbyterian Hymnal* (Louisville, KY: Westminster John Knox, 2013), 79.

is "the one who hears the word and understands it" (v. 23). In short, the faithful respondent is the one who embraces, treasures, celebrates, and obeys the word, which is essentially what the psalmist does in Psalm 119:105–112.

The *torah* piety of Psalm 119 was not a narrow legalism, as it is often misconstrued to be. Rather, it involved unwavering trust in God and commitment to God's will. This is essentially what Jesus invited when he announced that "the kingdom of heaven has come near" (Matt. 4:17), and this is why Jesus said, "Do not think that I have come to abolish the law or the prophets; I have come not to abolish but to fulfill" (5:17).

J. CLINTON MCCANN JR.

Proper 10 (Sunday between July 10 and July 16 inclusive)

Romans 8:1–11

¹There is therefore now no condemnation for those who are in Christ Jesus. ²For the law of the Spirit of life in Christ Jesus has set you free from the law of sin and of death. ³For God has done what the law, weakened by the flesh, could not do: by sending his own Son in the likeness of sinful flesh, and to deal with sin, he condemned sin in the flesh, ⁴so that the just requirement of the law might be fulfilled in us, who walk not according to the flesh but according to the Spirit. ⁵For those who live according to the flesh set their minds on the things of the flesh, but those who live according to the Spirit set their minds on the things of the Spirit. ⁶To set the mind on the flesh is death, but to set the mind on the Spirit is life and peace. ⁷For this reason the mind that is set on the flesh is hostile to God; it does not submit to God's law—indeed it cannot, ⁸and those who are in the flesh cannot please God.

⁹But you are not in the flesh; you are in the Spirit, since the Spirit of God dwells in you. Anyone who does not have the Spirit of Christ does not belong to him. ¹⁰But if Christ is in you, though the body is dead because of sin, the Spirit is life because of righteousness. ¹¹If the Spirit of him who raised Jesus from the dead dwells in you, he who raised Christ from the dead will give life to your mortal bodies also through his Spirit that dwells in you.

Commentary 1: Connecting the Reading with Scripture

"There is therefore now no condemnation for those who are in Christ Jesus" (Rom. 8:1). Today's reading from Romans begins with a hopeful conclusion on Paul's discussion of his very personal struggle with the sin at war in his inner self (7:21–25). Romans 8 is the hinge passage that returns the argument to a wider perspective. Paul addresses his readers with the broader, more inclusive "*those* who are in Christ." He then continues, as before, to use polarities or antitheses to draw a picture of what a life lived in the spirit of Christ might look like.

At the heart of this picture of life in the Spirit is yet another antithesis between the law of sin and death and the law of the Spirit (8:2). Paul sets the groundwork for this polarity in previous chapters, beginning with the idea that *all* are guilty even before the law is given by Moses: "Therefore, just as sin came into the world through one man [Adam], and death came through sin, and so death spread to all because *all* have sinned—sin was indeed in the world before the law, but sin is not reckoned [imputed or assigned to someone] when there is no law" (5:12–13, emphasis added). Sin spreads death throughout humanity (Jews and Gentiles) *and the world*. "Israel's special revelation is not the debut of law in the universe, but merely a privileged expansion of what God had made known to the nations through their inventory of nature. Moral goodness was revealed in nature."[1] The law of the Spirit impacts the entire world.

How does this compare to the "law of the Spirit of life in Christ Jesus" (8:2)? In this chapter, the law of the Spirit brings freedom from sin and death (v. 2); when the mind is set on the Spirit, it brings life and peace (v. 6); the Spirit dwells in those who accept it (v. 9); it is life, because of righteousness (v. 10) and will give life to our mortal bodies (v. 11). God's life-giving Spirit sustains the one who walks with God. This "law" is received through the work of God,

---

1. John C. Poirier, "Romans 5:13–14 and the Universality of Law," *Novum Testamentum* 38, no. 4 (1996): 351.

who "condemned sin in the flesh, so that the just requirement of the law might be fulfilled in us, who walk not according to the flesh but according to the Spirit" (vv. 3–4).

The benefits of the law of the Spirit of life for creation appear in a later part of Romans 8: "For the creation waits with eager longing for the revealing of the children of God; . . . in hope that the creation itself will be set free" (vv. 19–21). Romans 1–8 connects the work of salvation to life in the Spirit, in the same way a stone thrown into a still pool creates circles moving out from its point of contact. The power of salvation through Jesus moves outward from the Jews to the Gentiles to all humanity and finally encompasses the entire creation. This is very relevant for today's readers. Concern for nature in the face of global warming can help them move beyond concern for personal or human salvation to creation's inclusion in God's all-encompassing salvation.

How can this reading relate to the others in Proper 10?

Matthew 13, Psalm 65, and Isaiah 55 challenge the preacher to focus on the abundance of life that comes from living in the "law of the Spirit of life" (Rom. 8:2). These three texts contain references or images of abundant life bursting forth and delivering God's people that reach back to connect with very ancient traditions. Isaiah 55 and Matthew 13 both use metaphors deriving from the fertility of nature to illustrate the life-giving power of the Word of God.

Isaiah compares the Word to life-giving rain and snow that brings fertility to a parched land, a cultural metaphor that stretches back and connects with the Canaanite precursors of the ancient Israelites. Nature responds by "giving seed to the sower and bread to the eater" (Isa. 55:10). The creative power of the Word is so great, in fact, that personified nature rejoices: "the mountains and the hills before you shall burst into song, and all the trees of the field shall clap their hands" (v. 12).

Psalm 65 picks up on the idea of nature rejoicing in response to the creative activity of God as an expression of deliverance: "The pastures of the wilderness overflow, the hills gird themselves with joy, the meadows clothe themselves with flocks, the valleys deck themselves with grain, they shout and sing together for joy" (Ps. 65:12–13). For the ancient Israelites, who survived in a world based on subsistence agriculture, abundance in nature protected them against a very precarious existence, where death was just one drought away.

Romans 8 underscores the way salvation impacts creation: nature is free from the cycle of scarcity and poverty that brings suffering. For readers living in circumstances of abundance, who are perhaps out of touch with how nature sustains them, these images can speak to responsibility and care for nature. For those who live in poverty, drought, or scarcity, the images from these readings bring the reassurance that God's involvement in creation will sustain them.

In Matthew 13, the Word of the kingdom of God equates to the seed, which, when it is received under the right conditions (good soil), "brings forth grain, some a hundredfold, some sixty, some thirty" (Matt. 13:8). When Jesus interprets the parable for his disciples, he makes sure that the agricultural image is personalized: "But as for what was sown on good soil, this is the one who hears the word and understands it, who indeed bears fruit and yields, in one case a hundredfold, in another sixty, and in another thirty" (v. 23). Paul's statement that "those who live according to the Spirit set their minds on the things of the Spirit" can be linked to Matthew's Gospel through their common reference to the response of creation to God. The mind who hears the word and understands it lives in the Spirit and gives abundant fruit. Deliverance, abundance, and joy are clearly hallmarks of the activity of God in the human person and in the world.

As we have seen, Romans 8 uses the polarity of the law of sin and death and the Spirit of life in Christ to illustrate the freedom of those who live in Jesus. Paul reminds the reader that the Spirit of God overcomes death (Rom. 8:11) and leads to eternal life. Similarly, Matthew 13, Psalm 65, and Isaiah 55 echo the theme of abundant life bursting forth and delivering God's people found in Romans 8:1–11. They add the dimension of abundant new life for *all* creation. In fact, they anticipate what Paul makes explicit further on, that "the creation itself will be set free from its bondage to decay and will obtain the freedom of the glory of the children of God" (v. 21). This in turn anticipates the themes of creation that also surface in 8:18–39.

Connecting Romans 8 with the other readings in Proper 10, with their joy and care for abundant life in all creation, can help the reader move beyond a human-centered to a creation-centered reading of the entire letter. "Those who live in Christ" (v. 1) is far more inclusive than the community of Roman believers, Paul's primary addressees. It includes all those "who live according to the Spirit [and] set their minds on the things of the Spirit" (v. 5).

RENATA FURST

Commentary 2: Connecting the Reading with the World

The first eleven verses of Romans 8 describe the freedom that is experienced when the Spirit of Christ animates individual Christians, the community of the church, and the world at large. The description includes the contrasting experience of the bondage to sin and death that has been condemned in the destiny of the incarnate Christ. The result is a new power to live without condemnation, because life can be imbued with and guided by the very life of Christ.

A preacher might well find the dynamic of this passage captured in both the text and music of the well-known hymn by Sydney Carter, "I Danced in the Morning." The tune is based on the American folk tune SIMPLE GIFTS, fittingly connecting to the gift of freedom that Paul's own lyrics express. The hymn opens with an allusion to the perichoretic dance of the Godhead in bringing creation into being and quickly brings the dance of divinity to christological focus as it describes its movement from the heights of heaven into a birth in Bethlehem.

Paul affirms something similar when he speaks of God "sending his own Son in the likeness of sinful flesh" (Rom. 8:3), so that we might be freed to "walk not according to the flesh but according to the Spirit" (v. 4). As the Godhead thus moves out of Godself into creation, the result is an indwelling of the Spirit (v. 9), of Christ (v. 10), and of "him who raised Jesus from the dead" (v. 11). Without benefit of later Christian reflections on the perichoretic dancing of the Godhead, Paul affirms the indwelling of God in us that makes possible our walking (and maybe dancing) according to the Spirit of Christ.

For persons living ordinary lives, something extraordinary appears. In these verses Paul describes life, not as being stuck in an existence that he labels walking "according to the flesh," but as a gift of living "according to the Spirit" that has been released into the world with Christ. It is living that does not make the self with its passions, energies, and ambiguities the center of all values, but instead discovers the center of all values in the gracious embrace of Christ Jesus. Thus, we who are caught in the downward, condemnatory spirals of one addiction or another (drugs, alcohol, money, self) hear in Paul's words a summons to find freedom and release by letting go of efforts at self-determination and accepting the Spirit of Christ's readiness to fill us with "life and peace."

Of course, Paul knows that the dance of the Spirit of Christ must struggle against the "things of the flesh" (v. 5). Therefore, facing the addictions that besiege and undermine us is no easy task. Sydney Carter's hymn puts this in vivid language when it reminds us how hard it is to join the dance "with the devil on your back." Yet Paul believes that God, in the death and destiny of Jesus Christ, has decisively condemned and limited the suffocating power of our addictions by the definitive act of raising Christ from the dead (v. 11). So he invites us afresh to this challenge of relying on a power beyond ourselves, beyond that all the world knows, to find the freedom promised. Again, Sydney Carter's lyrics give it exquisite expression when they refer to the resurrecting power of God in Christ.

While Paul opens chapter 8 with the assertion of freedom for those who are "in Christ Jesus" (v. 1). he enriches the picture in 8:9–11 as he speaks of the Spirit of God and Christ "in you." The imagery is of a mutual indwelling, us in Christ and Christ in us. Again, Carter captures the imagery hymnally in a succinct phrase, "I'll live in you, if you'll live in me." The struggle against our fleshly addictions involves the intersection of our will and yearning to be filled with the Spirit of Christ and the will and yearning of Christ to dwell in us with life and peace. Because we know from the gospel proclamation that Christ's will and yearning precede our own, we can be bold to offer ours in return, thereby experiencing the gift of freedom from all that would otherwise condemn us. So, in our individual experience, the dance goes on.

For Christian communities living out their efforts at discipleship, something extraordinary appears as well. Church life in many places is beset by fear of death. That is, congregations that were vital and robust in previous generations see their numbers dwindle, their members age, and their buildings crumble. They discover that the "best practices" of other churches, however earnestly employed, do not seem to stem the receding tide of decay. For such churches, Paul's announcement of freedom from "things of the flesh" is critical and life-giving.

At the very least, such freedom means that "fleshly" standards of church success—from the number of our members to the size of our steeple—can be surrendered. The standard of success is properly found in the experience of life and peace arising from the indwelling Spirit of Christ in the community. Whenever mutual affection and caring support arise within and radiate from Christian communities—large or small—the promised life and peace prevail. Even when one particular form of Christ's community may come to an end—as when a congregation closes its doors—other communities indwelled by Christ generously open theirs. Thus—with reference to Christian community—Paul's promise is confirmed that the indwelling Spirit of the resurrecting God means "he who raised Christ from the dead will give life to your mortal bodies also through his Spirit that dwells in you" (v. 11). Here too the dance goes on.

For the world at large struggling against impending threats of social discord and environmental disruption, the freedom occasioned by the indwelling Spirit of Christ is also implied in this passage. We know from other Pauline writings, most especially Colossians 1:15–20, that the unity of all things is found in Christ. Coupling that with Romans' account of the indwelling of Christ in Christians and Christian communities, we can be bold to hope that the Spirit of Christ will also dwell—however anonymously—in the social fabric of a world rent by division and mutual disregard.

Such a bold hope prompts those of us living explicitly in Christian communities to voice with confidence the unity that undergirds all things and people, a unity that in turn includes the importance of thoughtful concern for all people. Instead of engaging in political rhetoric designed to shout down all opposition, walking by the Spirit in the social order looks to the ways in which the hopes and needs of all might receive just attention.

Finally, when attention is turned to the environmental disruption that threatens the well-being of so much that has unfolded in God's creative purpose, the promise of the indwelling Spirit of Christ gives encouragement to take up the challenge of environmental repair and renewal. For in this domain as well, we may walk "according to the Spirit," confident that Christ's dancing embrace not only of the human part of creation, but also of its vast nonhuman stretches, will make all creation blessed. Thus, in our social dislocation and ecological distress, the dance goes on as well.

D. CAMERON MURCHISON

Proper 10 (Sunday between July 10 and July 16 inclusive)

Matthew 13:1–9, 18–23

¹That same day Jesus went out of the house and sat beside the sea. ²Such great crowds gathered around him that he got into a boat and sat there, while the whole crowd stood on the beach. ³And he told them many things in parables, saying: "Listen! A sower went out to sow. ⁴And as he sowed, some seeds fell on the path, and the birds came and ate them up. ⁵Other seeds fell on rocky ground, where they did not have much soil, and they sprang up quickly, since they had no depth of soil. ⁶But when the sun rose, they were scorched; and since they had no root, they withered away. ⁷Other seeds fell among thorns, and the thorns grew up and choked them. ⁸Other seeds fell on good soil and brought forth grain, some a hundredfold, some sixty, some thirty. ⁹Let anyone with ears listen!" . . .

¹⁸"Hear then the parable of the sower. ¹⁹When anyone hears the word of the kingdom and does not understand it, the evil one comes and snatches away what is sown in the heart; this is what was sown on the path. ²⁰As for what was sown on rocky ground, this is the one who hears the word and immediately receives it with joy; ²¹yet such a person has no root, but endures only for a while, and when trouble or persecution arises on account of the word, that person immediately falls away. ²²As for what was sown among thorns, this is the one who hears the word, but the cares of the world and the lure of wealth choke the word, and it yields nothing. ²³But as for what was sown on good soil, this is the one who hears the word and understands it, who indeed bears fruit and yields, in one case a hundredfold, in another sixty, and in another thirty."

Commentary 1: Connecting the Reading with Scripture

There is a beautiful icon of the sower and the seed parable from the Order of Saint Benedict of Collegeville, Minnesota, created by Aidan Hart. Jesus is the sower in a plain shirt and blue jeans with the traditional golden nimbus around his head. A woven basket hangs around his neck, filled with seeds as he bends slightly forward scattering seeds. A bird searches for seed at the bottom of the icon standing on top of four mounds of soil representing the path, the rocky soil, and the thorny ground, as well as fertile land.

The parable of the Sower is ripe with colorful images and themes as Jesus continues onto various discourses, but this time on parables that speak of the kingdom of heaven. It follows narratives portraying the growing estrangement between Jesus and his contemporaries. Chapter 12 narrates several stories of Jesus' conflicts with the Pharisees, who are now plotting to destroy him (Matt. 12:14) and have accused him of working for Satan (v. 24). By the end of chapter 12, Jesus appears to be at odds even with his own family (vv. 46–50), and at the end of chapter 13, Jesus will be rejected by his hometown (13:54–58). Matthew 13 is the third of five major discourses that give the Gospel its distinctive flavor: dramatic parables where human actions and human decisions engage the hearers, full of stark contrasts and reversals where the stakes are heaven or hell, outer darkness, weeping, and gnashing of the teeth.

At this point Jesus turns to giving special instructions to the disciples, in part because others have rejected his teaching. The lectionary passage focuses on the parable and the parable's interpretation, skipping the verses on the purpose of the parables, where Jesus cites a prophecy from Isaiah and words of blessing for those who see and hear these words. The pericope is generous and capacious, bookended by abundance: "such great crowds gathered around Jesus" (13:2), along with his telling of many parables, and then, at the end, the image of the harvest with plentiful yields, exponential and overflowing the borders (v. 8). The persistence of bounty and joy overflows the text itself as an expression of resistance to the burgeoning conflict and intense drama of the previous chapters. Matthew's Jesus clutches the vision of the kingdom of heaven and is undeterred from his mission; he then instills that same zeal in his disciples.

In light of Jesus' rejection by his hometown (13:54–58), and even his family, the parable exemplifies Matthew's emphasis on the kingdom of heaven as a container for themes of obedience and discipleship as the marker of authentic inclusion in God's family. The world of the kingdom is connected to an eschatological reality already present in mercy and expected in judgment, and it is one to which the disciples, and anyone with ears to listen, are invited and welcomed, and in which they are encouraged to partake, alongside other sowers and laborers.

Jesus' disciples realize the true nature of the kingdom of heaven, as the community of disciples existing between resurrection and the Parousia, as those who are closely identified within the motif of the kingdom of heaven. The kingdom of heaven is a way to talk about the relationship between ethics and eschatology, ministry and mission, the here and now and eternity. We see glimmerings of this relationship in other parables later in the chapter when Jesus compares the kingdom of heaven to ordinary things like weeds and wheat, mustard seeds, yeast, treasures, fishing nets, and pearls. Jesus' teachings orient us to time-beyond while rooting us in the everyday and the mundane.

A close reading of the parable itself yields even more fruit after a thorough engagement of the larger contexts surrounding the passage. The main character in the parable, of course, is the sower. The sower scatters and casts the seeds—"seed" is plural in this version, another indication of that abundance and opposed to Mark's account (Mark 4:1–9, 13–20)—it seems carelessly, recklessly, wasting much of the seed on ground that holds little promise for a fruitful harvest. However, there is a progression, a reminder of the process, that perhaps it takes a few tries, a few hundred tries, not only to get the seeds in the right place but to have the right soil. What is clear is that both are necessary for the harvest.

Jesus' explanation of the parable connects us to what happened when Jesus appeared in Israel, as it also implicitly exhorts believers (who should recognize a bit of themselves in all four groups of seed) to join the fourth sort of hearer, represented by the good seed. Though Jesus appears to invest in disciples who look as unpromising as the hard, rocky, thorny soil, he nevertheless seems to squander his time among them, along with tax collectors and sinners, lepers, demon-possessed, and all manner of outcasts. In doing so, he shows what it means that his profligate sowing of the word will produce a bountiful harvest. These little seeds, these disciples, these that are scattered and cast out of society, become the sanctified means by which Jesus reveals and brings about the kingdom of heaven, one that extends beyond our imagination, but one that is hinted at when all are able to partake in the harvest.

This is the life of the kingdom of heaven, exuberant and copious, and it is connected to the life of the Spirit, vibrant and expansive as in the Romans 8 passage from the lectionary. Paul outlines that it is clearly distinct from living according to the law of sin and death; setting the mind on the Spirit is life and peace (Rom. 8:6). Otherwise, we become like the rich man in Matthew 19:17–22, who could not follow Jesus because in truth he did not own his possessions; they owned him.

While Matthew's Gospel does not demand poverty of all, it does require freedom from whatever hinders obedience. On the other hand, we see some tension with the story of Genesis 25 (where Esau gives up his birthright so easily to his twin, Jacob) and the possibility of thoughtlessly and carelessly holding our possessions when they are the gifts of God. Nevertheless, the thread through all of these readings and the larger biblical canon is the continuous orientation toward the kingdom of heaven and what it looks like to trust, to obey, and to follow in such a way that our hearts are ready to receive both the Word and the Spirit.

Let Us Attain to God

O ye Christians, whose lives are good, ye sigh and groan as being few among many, few among very many. The winter will pass away, the summer will come; lo! the harvest will soon be here. The angels will come who can make the separation, and who cannot make mistakes. We in this time present are like those servants of whom it was said, "Wilt Thou that we go and gather them up?" for we were wishing, if it might be so, that no evil ones should remain among the good. But it has been told us, "Let both grow together until the harvest." Why? For ye are such as may be deceived. Hear finally; "Lest while ye gather up the tares, ye root up also the wheat with them." What good are ye doing? Will ye by your eagerness make a waste of My harvest? The reapers will come, and who the reapers are He hath explained, "And the reapers are the angels." We are but men, the reapers are the angels. We too indeed, if we finish our course, shall be equal to the angels of God; but now when we chafe against the wicked, we are as yet but men. And we ought now to give ear to the words, "Wherefore let him that thinketh he standeth, take heed lest he fall." For do ye think, my Brethren, that these tares we read of do not get up into this seat? Think ye that they are all below, and none above up here? God grant we may not be so. "But with me it is a very small thing that I should be judged of you." I tell you of a truth, my Beloved, even in these high seats there is both wheat, and tares, and among the laity there is wheat, and tares. Let the good tolerate the bad; let the bad change themselves, and imitate the good. Let us all, if it may be so, attain to God; let us all through His mercy escape the evil of this world. Let us seek after good days, for we are now in evil days; but in the evil days let us not blaspheme, that so we may be able to arrive at the good days.

Augustine, "Sermon XXIII, On the Words of the Gospel, Matt. XIII. 19, Where the Lord Jesus Explaineth the Parables of the Sower," in *Saint Augustine: Sermon on the Mount, Harmony of the Gospels, Homilies on the Gospel,* trans. William Findlay, in *Nicene and Post-Nicene Fathers*, series 1, ed. Philip Schaff (Edinburgh: T. & T. Clark, 1888), 6:335.

What is so striking about the icon of the sower of the seed is the image of the sower scattering seeds even onto the text of the Gospel, which surrounds the space on the outside of the borders of the icon. The sower crosses over and enters into a dimension beyond the scope of the parable, suggesting the life-giving power of the word not only to be seed but also to be soil. This power and this work is given to the readers, whether those of the early church or those in the present-day church, to continue to hold these words, these seeds, wherever we go, so that we may participate in the mission of the kingdom of heaven. We are soil; we are seeds; we are sowers too, laboring alongside the one who calls us to that harvest that is ever in front of us.

MIHEE KIM-KORT

Commentary 2: Connecting the Reading with the World

The outstanding science-fiction writer Octavia Butler uses this parable as the title of her 1993 book *Parable of the Sower*, a chilling book about America falling apart in 2025. When I first read it in 1995, it seemed so far away. Recent events like gun violence and the threat of nuclear war have made it seem closer than I wanted to believe. The premise of the book is that American culture has fallen apart, and now there are only walled and heavily armed communities left, isolated and afraid of everyone else. In the book, new voices begin to emerge, voices sowing seeds of a new vision in a world that seems lost and hopeless.

Butler and the author of Matthew's Gospel are well aware that the power of love and the vision of community are sown and grow in very hostile environments. Indeed, our parable today tells us how inefficient this process is: only 25 percent of the seeds sown will succeed. Though this parable could have at least three names—parable of the Sower, parable of the Seed, parable of the Soil—only Matthew names it as the parable of the Sower (Matt. 13:18). These three themes intertwine in this story, but Matthew's emphasis is on the sower and the sowing. Let us keep that focus; that is, we are hearing from Jesus and Matthew about the necessity of our sowing the gospel, the great news of the powerful redeeming love of God.

I grew up in a farming community in Arkansas, and I am familiar with the process, but it never ceases to amaze me. We had an early spring in the Atlanta area this year. I planted some grass seed in a bare patch, covered it with a bit of pine straw, watered it occasionally with recycled "gray" water, and did very little else. The rain and sun produced astonishingly green grass in about eight days, and it was miraculous. The grass is not meant for the punishing heat of an Atlanta summer (like the growth scorched by the sun in Matt. 13:6), but it is a powerful mystery and gift.

Though the failure rate in this parable is three to one, we should never forget the powerful image of the love of God working in our individual lives and in the life of the world. The farmers who originally heard this story would have been familiar with the process (and maybe a bit bored by it), but when they heard the yield in verse 8, their ears would have perked up. Having a yield of 4 to 10 percent would be a good crop year, but yields of 30 and 60 and 100 percent—they want some of that!

This parable knows the struggles and failures of human life and of the attempts to proclaim and share the love of God; it is tough, relentless work, plagued by all the vagaries symbolized in this parable. Yet at its heart this parable is a story of hope and possibility, not because of the expertise of the sower. The sharing of the love of God happens not because of what we do or who we are, but because of who God is and what God is doing. The hearers of this story in every generation are reminded that we are asked to join God in this process of proclaiming the love of God. Most of the time we will never know where or when it will bear fruit, but bear fruit it will.

In the summer of 1955, a woman from Montgomery, Alabama, took a two-week vacation to go to Highlander Folk School near Monteagle, Tennessee. Highlander was founded by several folk, including a Presbyterian named Myles Horton. Its aim was to get people together, especially black people and white people, to talk about and to seek to break down some of the racial barriers in the South. At first the woman was self-conscious and apprehensive. She was unaccustomed to such racial mixing, where everyone called one another "sister" and "brother." She began to warm up some when an African American schoolteacher named Septima Clark took her under her wing.

Septima Clark taught in the segregated schools of South Carolina, but in the summer she was a trainer at Highlander. She encouraged her mentee to begin to live out of gratitude and generosity, rather than fear. In this way, she could become a sower of the seed of love and justice. Her mentee would later write this about the sowing that Septima Clark did in her life: "I am always very respectful and very much in awe of the presence of Septima Clark, because her life story makes the effort that I have made very minute. I only hope that there is a possible chance that some of her great courage and dignity and wisdom has rubbed off on me."[1]

Apparently it did rub off, because four months later, the sowing of the seed of Ms. Clark and Highlander School yielded great fruits after many frustrating failures. On December 1, 1955, that mentee named Rosa Parks refused to give up her seat in a white section of the bus in Montgomery. It was the beginning of the Montgomery bus boycott. It changed her life, and it changed American history. For more than seventy years, African Americans had been "sitting in" on public transportation, seeking to integrate it, without much success. Indeed the infamous *Plessy v. Ferguson* case of 1896, in which the Supreme Court declared "separate but equal" the law of the land, was a decision on a public transportation case in Louisiana. Then,

---

1. Douglas Brinkley, *Rosa Parks* (New York: Penguin Books, 2000), 96–97.

in 1955, the seed sown produced stunning fruit. It yielded 30, 60, 100 percent and it astonished so many people.

This parable understands the struggles of the world and of our efforts to live and to proclaim the stupendous love of God. It realistically states that, at best, we will have a 25 percent success rate, and that we will often not see the fruit that is produced by our sowing of love. Yet it is ultimately a story of hope, a story based in the mysterious and extravagant love of God, a love that is beyond our control and beyond our understanding.

It invites us, and indeed urges us, to join in the sowing of this love. It is a promise to all those who participate, the sowers and the recipients, that God's love will produce fruit and that nothing will be able to prevent this fruition. Though the ground seems rocky, though the time for blossoms and fruit seems long overdue, though there is only a tiny harvest at times (if at all), this parable makes the astonishing claim that God is moving and germinating and producing that which is intended.

As Isaiah 55:10–12 indicates, the word that God sends out will not return to God empty, but will accomplish what God purposes. As the sowing and growing process of this parable indicates, we may experience that fruition only 25 percent of the time, and we will be blessed if we experience that much. This parable is about the astonishing power of God. We should be assured that in the middle of our mess and in the middle of a scary and crazy world, God is working for love and for justice and for equity to prevail in our hearts and in the world.

NIBS STROUPE

Proper 11 (Sunday between July 17 and July 23 inclusive)

Isaiah 44:6–8 and Genesis 28:10–19a
Psalm 86:11–17 and Psalm 139:1–12, 23–24
Romans 8:12–25
Matthew 13:24–30, 36–43

Isaiah 44:6–8

⁶Thus says the LORD, the King of Israel,
  and his Redeemer, the LORD of hosts:
I am the first and I am the last;
  besides me there is no god.
⁷Who is like me? Let them proclaim it,
  let them declare and set it forth before me.
Who has announced from of old the things to come?
  Let them tell us what is yet to be.
⁸Do not fear, or be afraid;
  have I not told you from of old and declared it?
  You are my witnesses!
Is there any god besides me?
  There is no other rock; I know not one.

Genesis 28:10–19a

¹⁰Jacob left Beer-sheba and went toward Haran. ¹¹He came to a certain place and stayed there for the night, because the sun had set. Taking one of the stones of the place, he put it under his head and lay down in that place. ¹²And he dreamed that there was a ladder set up on the earth, the top of it reaching to heaven; and the angels of God were ascending and descending on it. ¹³And the LORD stood beside him and said, "I am the LORD, the God of Abraham your father and the God of Isaac; the land on which you lie I will give to you and to your offspring; ¹⁴and your offspring shall be like the dust of the earth, and you shall spread abroad to the west and to the east and to the north and to the south; and all the families of the earth shall be blessed in you and in your offspring. ¹⁵Know that I am with you and will keep you wherever you go, and will bring you back to this land; for I will not leave you until I have done what I have promised you." ¹⁶Then Jacob woke from his sleep and said, "Surely the LORD is in this place—and I did not know it!" ¹⁷And he was afraid, and said, "How awesome is this place! This is none other than the house of God, and this is the gate of heaven."

¹⁸So Jacob rose early in the morning, and he took the stone that he had put under his head and set it up for a pillar and poured oil on the top of it. ¹⁹He called that place Bethel.

Commentary 1: Connecting the Reading with Scripture

The first book of the Torah is called *bereshit* in Hebrew, based on the first word in the book, which means "beginnings" in terms of the very creation of the world. Perspectives and stories in the book of beginnings coalesce around several key figures—Abraham, Sarah, Isaac, Hagar, Ishmael, Jacob and Esau—and often incorporate social and political undertones. The primary concern of these stories is to invoke Israel's theological imagination and invite new social and political realities. The two readings from the Hebrew Bible for this Sunday, Isaiah 44:6–8 and Genesis 28:10–19a, connect through the story of Jacob, in their canonical order, as they address the experience of migrants traveling to find a home of their own or holding a memory of home as they live in exile in a foreign land.

As you consider the meaning of these passages to their original audience, think carefully about connections that bridge the ancient world with the present day. Where is the Holy One? How does one encounter and recognize God's actions in the midst of decisive and perilous moments in the lives of migrants and those held in captivity? What kind of world does the Holy One create and promise for migrants and captives? How does one understand the identity of being God's chosen people when one is forced to be on the move or to live in exile?

Jacob Dreams of God by His Side. The setting for Jacob's dream at Bethel in Genesis 28:10–19a within the larger literary context of the ancestral stories should not be underestimated. This is the first time that Jacob appears by himself. Earlier chapters in Genesis offer conflicting reasons that Jacob sets out alone. The J (Jahwist) narrative emphasizes Jacob's rivalry with his twin brother Esau: Jacob had acquired Esau's birthright through deception and now flees, fearing his brother's wrath (Gen. 27). The P (Priestly) narrative underscores Rebekah's pivotal role in securing Isaac's blessing for her younger son and focuses on Jacob's duty to fulfill his father's charge and mother's wish that he should not marry a Canaanite woman. He undertakes the journey to Paddan-aram to marry within his own clan, one of the daughters of his mother's brother Laban. Jacob's journey connects with the migration of his ancestors (12:1–8; 13:1–9), as he travels some of the same route along which Abraham and Sarah had migrated, moving from Beersheba to Haran.

In our passage, on his way to Haran Jacob stops to rest in Canaan at a place of familial and religious significance where Abraham "pitched his tent," built an altar, and called upon God (12:8; 13:3–4). Jacob finds there an ordinary stone to use as a pillow, and while he is sleeping, he dreams a remarkable dream. His dream or vision is what scholars call a theophany (appearance of God) and includes both visual and auditory elements.

There is a great deal of debate among biblical scholars about what Jacob *sees* in his dream. Most often the Hebrew word in Genesis 28:12 (*sullam*) is translated "stairway" or "ramp." Since the late nineteenth century, most biblical scholars have agreed that the stairway or ramp resembles that of a Babylonian ziggurat or temple tower. Ziggurats were built to reach toward heaven, and that image connects the story of Jacob's dream to ancient religious practices. Other renderings of this Hebrew term include "ladder," the slope of the hill upon which Bethel was built, a stone staircase, a staircase leading to the top floors of a stately home or palace, or a gate of heaven.[1] The stairway ascends from earth to heaven and the messengers, angels, or heavenly beings (*mal'akîm*) go up and down the stairway.

However, Jacob *hears* the Holy One speak directly to him. Direct speech in the Bible is significant. God does not speak to Jacob through an intermediary, but directly renews with him the covenant promises made to Abraham and Sarah.

In response, Jacob vows to set up an altar and a pillar to honor God's appearance to him there (28:20–22). Jacob's dream has a similar structure to Genesis 32:1–2, about another appearance of

---

1. Michael D. Oblath, "'To Sleep, Perchance to Dream' . . . : What Jacob Saw at Bethel (Genesis 28:10–22)," *Journal of the Study of the Old Testament* 95 (2001): 117–26.

> **The Summer of the Righteous**
> He showed me many trees having no leaves, but withered, as it seemed to me; for all were alike. And he said to me, "Do you see those trees?" "I see, sir," I replied, "that all are alike, and withered." He answered me, and said, "These trees which you see are those who dwell in this world." "Why, then, sir," I said, "are they withered, as it were, and alike?" "Because," he said, "neither are the righteous manifest in this life, nor sinners, but they are alike; for this life is a winter to the righteous, and they do not manifest themselves, because they dwell with sinners: for as in winter trees that have cast their leaves are alike, and it is not seen which are dead and which are living, so in this world neither do the righteous show themselves, nor sinners, but all are alike one to another."
>
> He showed me again many trees, some budding, and others withered. And he said to me, "Do you see these trees?" "I see, sir," I replied, "some putting forth buds, and others withered." "Those," he said, "which are budding are the righteous who are to live in the world to come; for the coming world is the summer of the righteous, but the winter of sinners. When, therefore, the mercy of the Lord shines forth, then shall they be made manifest who are the servants of God, and all . . . shall be made manifest. For as in summer the fruits of each individual tree appear, and it is ascertained of what sort they are, so also the fruits of the righteous shall be manifest, and all who have been fruitful in that world shall be made known."
>
> *Shepherd of Hermas, Similitudes 3–4,* trans. A. Cleveland Coxe, in *The Ante-Nicene Fathers,* repr. ed., ed. Alexander Roberts and James Donaldson (Grand Rapids: Eerdmans, 1979), 2:33.

the Holy One to Jacob upon his return to the land of his birth. In Genesis 35:1–15 Jacob sets up a "pillar of stone" and names the place Bethel (meaning "house of God"). Bethel is referenced for its significance in cultic practices in other ancient literature, including the book of *Jubilees* (part of the Pseudepigrapha) and the Aramaic and Greek *Testaments of Levi.*[2]

"There Is No Other Rock; I Know Not One."

One of the things most often missed in the writings of the prophets is their poetry. Deutero-Isaiah strikes a poetic and lyrical tone, despite the fact that Jerusalem has been destroyed (Isa. 44:26–28; 49:14–23) and the Israelites have been deported to Babylon. No longer is the situation urgent, since the deportation is now a distant memory. The memory of this event forces Israel to confront an identity crisis. What does it mean to be God's chosen people while living in captivity? Chapters 40–55 express Israel's feelings of guilt and mistrust and God's reassurance. Guilt feelings result from their acceptance of the destruction of Jerusalem. They feel that their own shortcomings led to exile. They harbor mistrust for a God who has seemed powerless to save them. God's response is reassurance of forgiveness, and an expression of God's own powerful and loving nature.[3] Several themes emerge as focal points: a new experience of exodus for the Israelites; poetry dedicated to first and last things; God's loving, powerful, and forgiving nature; God's continual acts of creation and justice; and the enduring significance of Jerusalem as the center and citadel of Israel's faith.

Within the literary context of Isaiah, chapter 44 begins with an oracle of salvation and is part of a series of trial speeches (Isa. 41–48). The trial character is evidenced in the repeated questions asked throughout the passage in God's voice: "Who else is like me?" In verses 6–8, the Holy One discredits the Babylonian gods. There is no other god like the God of Israel: "There is no other rock; I know not one" (44:8).

Trial speeches remind ancient Israel of its role as a covenant partner with God. Language used throughout this passage expresses how God acts: making, forming, helping, choosing,

---

2. Joshua Schwartz, "Jubilees, Bethel and the Temple of Jacob," *Hebrew Union College Annual* 56 (1985): 63–85.
3. Johanna W. H. van Wijk-Bos, lecture on Isaiah delivered at Louisville Presbyterian Theological Seminary, Louisville, Kentucky, on April 3, 2013.

pouring, blessing, and calling Israel as witnesses. God promises to pour God's spirit upon Jacob's descendants and offers God's blessing to Jacob's offspring (v. 3).

Themes for Proclamation. Genesis 28:10–19a and Isaiah 44:6–8 connect most directly through the story of Jacob, with whom God directly renews the covenant with Abraham and Sarah. The patriarchs and prophets believed that their relationship with a God in covenant with the whole of creation meant they had certain demands upon them. Both passages represent the perspectives of migrants and captives; emphasize the constancy of God's presence, continual creative activity, and provisions made for the well-being of people and the planet; and call migrants and captives to witness to God's covenant partnership in the midst of social chaos and instability. All of these themes are worthy of significant attention in the twenty-first century.

ELIZABETH HINSON-HASTY

Commentary 2: Connecting the Reading with the World

At the heart of this snippet of poetry in Isaiah 44:6–8 is the image of God as rock. Not only does the image stand out in this bit of Isaiah's text; it is an irresistible word picture in its own right. The metaphor, like the literal reality to which it points, has heft.

Isaiah's God is a very big God, a Brobdingnagian God. Among promising constructive approaches are those that connect Isaiah's images of "bigness" to the church's mission. What is big about the work of God in the world today is not the drive for conquest but the drive for unity. Ours is a big God who goes to great lengths to bring people together and bids us do the same. Isaiah's God highlights the role even of non-Israelite leaders—such as Cyrus—as potential agents in the working out of God's plan for Israel's safety (Isa. 44:28). That vision requires a God big enough to encompass more than God's own chosen ones, one willing to recreate that which has been scattered and restore that which has been lost. This rock appears to be an image of stability in the midst of chaos.

There is no doubt that protection is a primary meaning of the rock image so important to this text: "Do not fear, or be afraid" (v. 8). Few congregations need much help thinking up examples of times and places where God's people were not protected. Are there new ways for this generation of God's people to make sense of God's promise of protection and offer protection to others, not simply protection for themselves?

In her memoir, civil rights activist Rosemarie Freeney Harding writes of the almost mystical sense of protection Clarence Jordan's Koinonia Farm offered those involved in the movement:

> It was a joyful place.... Even though the farm was in a county thick with Klan members who spent years terrorizing the community, we felt safe on the grounds. How do I explain this? Although we may have been apprehensive on the narrow highway as we approached (conscious of the bullets that had been shot into buildings on the farm and the threats against community members), once we walked onto the land at Koinonia, we felt no fear. We could have been surrounded by rattlesnakes—and we were—but we felt safe, protected, as if angels stayed close to us all the time.[4]

As Isaiah might say, there is no rock of protection like God, no, not one (44:8).

In Genesis, the story of Jacob's ladder is heavily laced with references to God's presence (Gen. 28:10–19a). Between verses 13 and 19, six juicy phrases signal the importance of the theme. When combined with the stunning picture of streaming angels and heavenly staircases, the story primes the human heart to reflect wistfully on the deep desire to connect with the Divine.

---

4. Rosemarie Freeney Harding, with Rachel Elizabeth Harding, *Remnants: A Memoir of Spirit, Activism, and Mothering* (Durham, NC: Duke University Press, 2015), 144.

This passage stirs the part of each of us that would dearly love to do what Jacob did: stumble into a place where the Holy happens. Since the Martin Sheen movie *The Way* was released in 2011, an urge has propelled millions out along the highways, byways, and tributaries of the Camino de Santiago. The same desire sends Muslims on annual pilgrimage (*hajj*) to Mecca and underlies Baclaran Wednesdays in Manila, where traffic grinds to a halt for the weekly mass at the National Shrine of Our Mother of Perpetual Help at the Baclaran Church. It sends millions of visitors a year to Mexico City, Portugal, and Lourdes, causes Australians in search of a "thin place" to make the trek to an island off the west coast of Scotland, and countless pilgrims to make their way to the Ramakrishna Mandir in Kolkata, India.

Jacob's famous story suggests three gentle reminders to those who feel the urge to seek out holy ground: (1) surprise, (2) God's larger picture, (3) God's heart for the fugitive.

We do not always recognize a holy place when we come across one. Jacob fell asleep on his, and only after one of the great dreams in the history of dreaming did it dawn on him what kind of place it was. Surely his palm was planted flat against his forehead as he uttered the astonished (or rueful) words, "And I did not know it!" (Gen. 28:16).

Epiphany stories often include an "I was just walking along" theme. They seem to happen in common places—the better to catch us by surprise, perhaps. Contemporary mystic Thomas Merton's famous experience at the corner of Fourth and Walnut in ordinary Louisville, Kentucky, is a good example. His *Conjectures of a Guilty Bystander* tells the story.[5] It was 1958 and the young monk was running errands in the shopping district when he was suddenly overwhelmed with a sense of love for the people around him. The book describes one of the greatest mystical experiences of twentieth-century Christianity.

Poet W. H. Auden tells a similar tale:

One fine summer night in June 1933 I was sitting on a lawn after dinner with three colleagues, two women and one man. We liked each other well enough but we were certainly not intimate friends.... We were talking about everyday matters when, quite suddenly and unexpectedly ... I found myself invaded by a power which, though I consented to it, was irresistible and certainly not mine. For the first time in my life I knew exactly—because, thanks to the power, I was doing it—what it means to love one's neighbor as oneself.[6]

Sometimes, Jacob's story reminds us, it is more a case of the holy ground's finding us than our finding it.

This story is not all about Jacob. This is not a story about a satisfying mystical experience; it is a story about a mystical experience that furthered God's purpose. The fact that Jacob is surprised is a function of his perspective. He thought of himself as a person on the run. He had done x and reaped y and was headed for time in the penalty box—a simple equation. He was, no doubt, thinking his own thoughts as he took off toward Haran. Calculations about ETA, hours of daylight, and the precise location of the next well would have been crowding his mind. He was not thinking of himself as part of a grand plan or heavenly purpose. It likely never occurred to him that God might see him differently, that there might be deep wells in his personal life, or even that he might be a player in one of God's larger stories.

The story also suggests that God has a soft spot for fugitives. Maybe it is the spiritual state that flight causes that God honors. Haste, terror, dread: Jacob experienced them all between Beersheba and Bethel, as refugees do today. Immigration issues, DACA, and the striving of outsiders to get in: all have relevance to this text. The important point of this approach is that in the end it is the fugitive, not the upstanding citizen (or representative of the system), who winds up with the blessing.

JANA CHILDERS

---

5. Thomas Merton, *Conjectures of a Guilty Bystander* (New York: Doubleday, 1965).
6. Alexander McCall Smith, *What W. H. Auden Can Do For You* (Princeton, NJ: Princeton University Press, 2013), 81.

Proper 11 (Sunday between July 17 and July 23 inclusive)

Psalm 86:11–17

¹¹Teach me your way, O LORD,
  that I may walk in your truth;
  give me an undivided heart to revere your name.
¹²I give thanks to you, O Lord my God, with my whole heart,
  and I will glorify your name forever.
¹³For great is your steadfast love toward me;
  you have delivered my soul from the depths of Sheol.

¹⁴O God, the insolent rise up against me;
  a band of ruffians seeks my life,
  and they do not set you before them.
¹⁵But you, O Lord, are a God merciful and gracious,
  slow to anger and abounding in steadfast love and faithfulness.
¹⁶Turn to me and be gracious to me;
  give your strength to your servant;
  save the child of your serving girl.
¹⁷Show me a sign of your favor,
  so that those who hate me may see it and be put to shame,
  because you, LORD, have helped me and comforted me.

Psalm 139:1–12, 23–24

¹O LORD, you have searched me and known me.
²You know when I sit down and when I rise up;
  you discern my thoughts from far away.
³You search out my path and my lying down,
  and are acquainted with all my ways.
⁴Even before a word is on my tongue,
  O LORD, you know it completely.
⁵You hem me in, behind and before,
  and lay your hand upon me.
⁶Such knowledge is too wonderful for me;
  it is so high that I cannot attain it.

⁷Where can I go from your spirit?
  Or where can I flee from your presence?
⁸If I ascend to heaven, you are there;
  if I make my bed in Sheol, you are there.
⁹If I take the wings of the morning
  and settle at the farthest limits of the sea,
¹⁰even there your hand shall lead me,
  and your right hand shall hold me fast.
¹¹If I say, "Surely the darkness shall cover me,
  and the light around me become night,"

¹²even the darkness is not dark to you;
   the night is as bright as the day,
   for darkness is as light to you.
. . . .
²³Search me, O God, and know my heart;
   test me and know my thoughts.
²⁴See if there is any wicked way in me,
   and lead me in the way everlasting.

Connecting the Psalm with Scripture and Worship

Psalm 86:11–17. Like many of us, the writer of Psalm 86 is complicated. In the span of these seven verses, the psalmist manages to petition, praise, protest, and proclaim. The beginning of the psalm tells us the speaker is "poor and needy" (Ps. 86:1). As we read on, it becomes clear that this is someone in trouble, but also someone who is confident God can be trusted to deliver "all who call" for help (v. 5). The vibrant faith of the psalmist interrupts petitions and concerns as the psalm unfolds, praising God's steadfast love and mercy, God's dazzling activities, and God's singularity among the "gods."

In the second half of the psalm, it becomes clear that the trouble the psalmist faces is twofold. On the one hand, there is an external threat: a gang of thugs is out to get, even kill, the psalmist. These "ruffians" do not worship the God who is God, the psalmist points out (v. 14). The psalmist (understandably) would like to see these enemies "put to shame," but how? It is surprising, perhaps, that the psalmist does not ask God to smite the bullies but, instead, requests a sign of God's favor. When haters see that God helps and comforts the one they have persecuted, then, the psalmist imagines, they will experience shame.

The trouble in Psalm 86 is internal as well as external, if we read closely. In verse 11, the psalmist prays for "an undivided heart." What does that mean? Could it be that the tension in the psalm, fluctuating between affirmations of God's steadfast love and requests for the shaming of "the insolent," is evidence of a still bifurcated heart? Is this seeming vengefulness what we would expect from one who worships God with a "whole" heart, the hope that the enemies of God would recognize the absurdity of their ways, feel terrible, and then, perhaps, be transformed? The psalmist leaves this swirl of desire, hope, anger, fear, and praise there for us to ponder, unresolved.

Isaiah 44:6–8 features the prophet voicing God's challenge to would-be opponents; in this text there is also talk of other "gods." As in Psalm 86, there seem to be hostile neighbors milling around just off screen. In response to those aligned with local deities, God declares the singularity we heard the psalmist praise: "I am first, last, and only." Then come words of comfort for anxious exiles as Isaiah's prophecy continues: "Do not fear. You have known of my promises for generations." This leads to a rather unexpected conclusion, as God tells the exiles, "You are my witnesses" (v. 8). Not *should* be, not *could* be, but *are*.

A preacher might relate this assertion to the request of the psalmist in verse 17, the prayer for a sign of God's favor. What if *we* are the signs we have been waiting for? What if the sign of God's favor is the fact that the psalmist is there, witnessing to God's tenacious love, incomprehensible mercy, reluctant anger, in spite of the dangers, toils, and snares within and without?

Because of its frequent shifts in tone, Psalm 86 may best be read by two lectors: one worried, asking for help, perhaps; the other full of thanks and praise. This psalm also offers powerful language to take up in a prayer of confession, particularly the request for an "undivided heart." The cadences for a declaration of forgiveness are there too, in the well-worn eloquence of verse 15, and a hymn like "There's a Wideness in God's Mercy" would flow nicely as a sung response to the confession/forgiveness sequence.

Psalm 139:1–12, 23–24. This psalm and the Genesis reading feature a shared theme: the presence of God. Psalm 139 is, of course, among the "greatest hits" of the Psalter, but one wonders if that popularity has encouraged interpretations that mute the radical nature of its claims. Is this a psalm of assurance: no matter what, God is with you and for you and loves you, just the way you are? Is there, rather, something menacing about this depiction of God's way with us? This God haunts our every moment. Stalks us as we go about our day. Knows everything we are going to do or say before we do. This is a God we can never surprise, a divine helicopter parent who is not willing to give us even a little breathing room. Of course, the psalmist appears to consider this to be a good thing, though there is not much to go on. Verse 6 displays the psalmist's awe at God's omniscience, but that is not quite the same thing as welcoming it.

We leap from a poetic meditation on the inescapability of God in verses 7–12 to the final petition of verses 23–24. Though the psalmist declared in verse 1 that God has already done exhaustive searching and knowing, the concluding prayer suggests there may be more searching and knowing for God to do—or is this just an indication that the psalmist is confident enough to welcome additional scrutiny, on the remote chance something was missed?

The lectionary deftly sidesteps at least two thorny issues by eliminating the description of God's embryonic needlework in verses 13–16 and the psalmist's eager demonstration of "perfect hatred" toward the "wicked" in verses 19–22. Even though it is not included in the reading, the latter hope—that the ever-present God would kill the wicked—may be worth keeping in mind as we consider the companion text from Genesis.

In Genesis 28:10 we meet Jacob on the road, improvising for the night, apparently, choosing a rock for a pillow. He dreams of a spectacular stairway to heaven, but God steals the show, just appearing next to Jacob and talking to him. No ladder needed. God promises that Jacob's children will inherit the ground upon which he sleeps. They will spread in every direction, and in them every family on earth will find blessing.

When Jacob wakes up, he is shocked that God was right there the whole time, and he did not know it. What does he feel? Fear (Gen. 28:17). Does this give us permission to read Psalm 139 with something of the same trepidation?

Either way, one potential point of contact between the two texts is found in God's promise of abiding presence with Jacob and his descendants. God is with and for them, absolutely, but not just with and for *them*. The blessing will extend from the few to the many. Could this include even enemies? This is, perhaps, a word the writer of Psalm 139 is not yet ready to hear, and a preacher might find this contrast a fruitful one to explore.

Psalm 139 is stunning in its rhetoric, and there are many ways to let it shine in worship. It might be read by a well-prepared liturgist, neither theatrically nor impassively. Another effective approach is having a handful of liturgists stationed throughout the worship space, including a few seated within the congregation, taking turns reading the verses. Hearing voices from different places in the room highlights the spatial dimension of the psalm, while having an unexpected voice come from a pew close by is appropriately a bit unsettling. There are several lyrical musical settings that can involve the whole congregation. "You Are before Me, Lord," set to the tune HIGHLAND CATHEDRAL, is particularly lovely.[1]

ANGELA DIENHART HANCOCK

---

1. "You Are before Me, Lord," with words by Ian Pitt-Watson and music by Uli Roever and Michael Korb, can be found in *Psalms for All Seasons: A Complete Psalter for Worship* (Grand Rapids: Calvin Institute of Christian Worship, Faith Alive Christian Resources, and Brazos Press, 2012), 139D.

Proper 11 (Sunday between July 17 and July 23 inclusive)

Romans 8:12–25

[12]So then, brothers and sisters, we are debtors, not to the flesh, to live according to the flesh— [13]for if you live according to the flesh, you will die; but if by the Spirit you put to death the deeds of the body, you will live. [14]For all who are led by the Spirit of God are children of God. [15]For you did not receive a spirit of slavery to fall back into fear, but you have received a spirit of adoption. When we cry, "Abba! Father!" [16]it is that very Spirit bearing witness with our spirit that we are children of God, [17]and if children, then heirs, heirs of God and joint heirs with Christ—if, in fact, we suffer with him so that we may also be glorified with him.

[18]I consider that the sufferings of this present time are not worth comparing with the glory about to be revealed to us. [19]For the creation waits with eager longing for the revealing of the children of God; [20]for the creation was subjected to futility, not of its own will but by the will of the one who subjected it, in hope [21]that the creation itself will be set free from its bondage to decay and will obtain the freedom of the glory of the children of God. [22]We know that the whole creation has been groaning in labor pains until now; [23]and not only the creation, but we ourselves, who have the first fruits of the Spirit, groan inwardly while we wait for adoption, the redemption of our bodies. [24]For in hope we were saved. Now hope that is seen is not hope. For who hopes for what is seen? [25]But if we hope for what we do not see, we wait for it with patience.

Commentary 1: Connecting the Reading with Scripture

Martin Luther said the book of Romans "is really the chief part of the New Testament and the purest Gospel."[1] Basing his view on the central logic of Protestantism, Luther saw this letter as embodying the challenge of Paul's call or conversion, his argument to see Jews and Gentiles as equals, and his lifelong effort to bring unity to his old and new selves. In chapter 8 Paul advances his concept of adoption through faith in Christ, arguing that through grace a redemptive and inclusive faith family is established. For him it is the crux of salvation history—both a present reality and a future promise. It makes Romans essential reading for anyone concerned with Christian identity.

Paul was probably in Corinth when he wrote his letter to the church in Rome. He did not found the congregation and had never been there, but was eager to visit. What he knew about the church probably came from Aquila and Priscilla, who had recently arrived in Corinth among the Jews and Jewish Christians expelled by Emperor Claudius. There is no specific reference here that addresses individuals or local controversies, as in Paul's other letters, except perhaps 14:1–15:6. Romans offers a more general theological argument, setting it apart and inviting intriguing questions of its purpose and its content, although with common themes shared with Galatians.

Paul's work in Asia Minor, Macedonia, and Greece was finished, and he wanted to turn his missionary efforts westward, with Rome as the first stop. A large majority of the members of the church in Rome were Gentile, in contrast to the decidedly Jewish character of the apostolic church in Jerusalem. His anxiety about the latter may have influenced his writing to the former, because before heading to Rome, Paul needed to go back to Jerusalem with a financial collection

---

1. Martin Luther, *Preface to Romans*, in *The Works of Martin Luther* (Grand Rapids: Kregel, 1976; orig. 1552), xiii.

from the Gentiles (Rom. 15:25–28) and assuredly faced another round of hot debates about his mission to the Gentiles. Could it be that this letter was Paul's rehearsal for his presentation to James and the other apostles?

For Paul, becoming a Christian demands a radical reordering of thinking. The old concepts of law, inheritance, indebtedness, life and death, and conversion are turned on their heads. Thus we cannot gloss over the tension Paul's mission and his justification of it created for the early church. How can the history of the chosen people and the Torah be honored, but allow room for the Gentiles to stand on equal ground, without converting to Judaism or being circumcised?

This reading is at the heart of Paul's diatribe on God's righteousness. Building on the example of Abraham (in chap. 4), who was deemed righteous *before* he was circumcised, Paul methodically builds his case for justification by faith alone. The critical distinction for him is the difference between living by the law and living by the Spirit. In Romans 7 he says, "The law is spiritual," but it is captive to the sins of the flesh (7:14): "I can will what is right, but I cannot do it" (v. 18). This dilemma thus sets up his liberating message in chapter 8 of inclusion through Christ's righteousness.

Romans 8:12 begins with "So then," marking the transition from 7:1–8:11 to a life in the Spirit. Verses 14–15 provide the crux of Paul's case about the transformation of believers through baptism: "For all who are led by the Spirit of God are children of God. . . . You have received a spirit of adoption." Here he uses language he used in Galatians 4:5–7, revealing his deep belief in the strength of that insight. If Christians are heirs to the promises of the covenant through the Spirit rather than through observance to the law, there is a solid foundation of hope for the salvation of the Gentiles—now and in the future.

This is a dramatic change in status. In Roman culture an adopted son had the full legal standing as an heir. This is a familiar and accepted concept to his readers, even for the adoption of slaves, and Paul cleverly employs it effectively here. He develops the metaphor even further, saying, "When we cry, 'Abba! Father!' it is that very Spirit bearing witness with our spirit that we are children of God" (8:15–16). "Abba, Father!" is the same phrase Jesus used in the Garden of Gethsemane (Mark 14:36), and its use now for the Gentiles implies an intimacy with God heretofore reserved for the Jews.

The present and future dimensions of Paul's message are seen more clearly in verses 18–25. The acknowledgment of suffering and "labor pains" waiting for adoption is counterbalanced by the message of "eager longing," first fruits, and hope for what lies ahead. In his argument Paul presents a masterful juxtaposition of physical and spiritual birth.

An important opportunity presents itself here for preachers to explore adoption and foster care among the families of the congregation. There are more than 100,000 adoptions in the United States each year and more than two million worldwide. While the story of Moses is an obvious beginning point on this theme, there are good contemporary examples. One can find examples of adoption in many children's films, such as *Kung Fu Panda II* and *Star Wars,* as well as in television, such as in *Sesame Street*'s three-part program "Gina Adopts a Baby." Each addresses the question of becoming part of another family, redefinitions of identity and inclusion, and what it is to be loved. One could even address adoption as a metaphor for inclusion into the varied families and communities of our lives, including the challenges of immigration (a reference to the Ethiopian eunuch in Acts 8:26–40 could work here: "What's to keep me from being baptized?").[2]

The companion lectionary passages provide ample material to weave together a strong reflection on Romans 8 and what it means to be included in the family of the righteous. The Genesis 28 passage on Jacob's ladder fits nicely. It refers to the original covenant and promise to Abraham that Paul has challenged in regard to who qualifies for inheritance. One might even look at the consequences of the trick Jacob played on Esau to receive Isaac's blessing, through which Jacob became the father of the tribes of Israel.

---

2. A good overview of this topic can be found in Trevor J. Burke's *Adopted into God's Family: Exploring a Pauline Metaphor* (Downers Grove, IL: InterVarsity, 2006).

The reading from Psalm 139 is also a good match, particularly for an exploration of the "Abba" passage in Romans 8:15. The intimacy and tenderness of phrases like "O Lord, you have searched me and known me" (Ps. 139:1) lend themselves to a meaningful reflection on the personal nature of our relationship to God. To be known in such a way imparts a sacred dignity that merits unconditional respect. For Paul's concept of adoption to be so fully included in God's family means an unparalleled intimacy—to be as close to God as anyone else.

The sower parable from Matthew (13:24–43) is included in the lectionary readings as well. This surprising inclusion may point back to the end of Matthew 12, where Jesus redefines who his family is, declaring in 12:50 that his family are those who do "the will of my Father in heaven," a designation that embraces a variety of people.

Taken together, the passage from Romans and the lectionary companion selections provide a strong basis for exploring Paul's theology of adoption and inclusion through baptism.

NICK CARTER

Commentary 2: Connecting the Reading with the World

Paul is reflecting on the meaning of the risen Christ in light of the suffering endemic to the human condition and his anticipation that cosmic redemption is near at hand. For now, following the risen Christ means living not in a *different time* but in a *different way* in a world that continues to long for redemption. Empire, then as now, remains alive and well: ethnic and religious hostility, sexual violence, hunger, a violent criminal justice system—and most of all, callous indifference to the relentless oppression of humanity. How can we live "in" but not "of" these injustices?

Paul uses the contrast between flesh and spirit as shorthand to describe two opposing ways of living in the world, a way of life and a way of death (see Deut. 30:15; *Didache*). We can wonder whether "flesh" is a good metaphor for this. Considering how Christians might recover positive meanings of the body and of the earth could itself be an important sermon topic. It has not served Christians to despise bodily existence and feel estranged from the earth. We are creatures of flesh: human existence depends on our bodily creation as part of the natural world. Paul could hardly anticipate the ecological meltdown we now face, the weeping of trees and oceans as whole ecosystems succumb not merely to decay but to active destruction. However, he already understands that it is creation itself, including all of humanity, that is "groaning" for the birth of freedom.

Paul uses "flesh" to evoke a destructive way of life. For him, we are fleshly in the metaphorical sense that we are entangled in systems in which the "works of the flesh" become normative, natural, and even Christian. He implores the Romans to recognize the Spirit bearing witness to their identity as heirs to God's love, because it is only a radical new identity that will empower them to live ethically even while under Rome's rule.

Let us use this as a lens for interpreting our own culture. The 2017 film *The Post* reminds us of a period in our nation's past when a whistleblower revealed that the US government had been engaged in escalating violence and warfare, including bombing politically neutral countries, and lying to citizens and Congress. This "work of the flesh" is a comprehensive moral imagination, a system that occludes reality and reframes immoral behavior as ethically meritorious. That is, the flesh is not just an isolated action (eating food sacrificed to idols). It is an interlocking worldview for interpreting right and wrong. It predetermines our spirituality, our relationships to others, and our participation in religion and nation. The flesh refers to the "way of death": systems of violence, deception, and alienation that infect ethics and religion.

The flesh is not exterior to us, any more than our physical body is something external and alien. It is a part of us; it shapes the way we perceive the world. It is not so much an individual act as the miasma that shapes what our acts will be. The lies the Pentagon Papers revealed were part of the larger lie of a social imagination that made the profitability of war, massacres of villagers, torture, deception, sacrifice of a nation's youth, and all the rest seem heroic.

The "way of the flesh" is a moral universe in which human beings are cut off from each other. Just as I identify most vividly with my own body, the way of the flesh suggests that only I and those like me are important. "They" (e.g., the people of southeast Asia) are not like "us," so their suffering is morally irrelevant. The flesh makes it impossible to recognize others as objects of divine love. Anyone outside my moral imagination is alien, and their suffering is unimportant. This is the way of death.

Paul contrasts this "fleshly" existence with the spirit. He evokes the way of love and compassion—even for enemies—throughout his letters (Rom. 12:9–21; 1 Cor. 13; Phil. 2:1–5; Gal. 5:22–26). In Romans 8, he does not list fruits of the Spirit but rather describes the foundation of these ethical dispositions, so that his readers will remember that they are children of God. In order to banish the works of flesh, we must first remember that we are part of one creation loved by God, destined for freedom.

We may still inwardly await adoption, feeling separated from God and one another, seduced by the lies of our culture. Our deeper truth is that we are already infused with the Spirit, who witnesses to us day and night. When we cry out to Abba/Mother/Beloved, it is the Spirit witnessing *with* us so that we may live into what has already happened. We are already united to the Godhead, "joint heirs with Christ." As Julian of Norwich put it, we are "knit and one'ed with God."[3]

For Paul, this embrace of life in the Spirit is not about individual life after death: it is about the salvation of the entire world—all humanity and the earth itself. As Rosemarie Freeney Harding (one of the great mothers of the civil rights movement) puts it,

"Rights" is an insufficient concept. . . . Your well-being is related to my happiness; is, in fact, my goal. . . . That is simply the way the universe is made. . . . And nothing we do as human beings can destroy that energy in the world. We may be able to harm individual people, but we cannot destroy the life force. It encompasses us and is beyond us. So the Klan brother is really a brother . . . and at some point you will be able to hug him. If not physically, then through the energy of your prayers and compassion for him.[4]

If this seems like a tall order, remember that Paul is inviting us into a completely different universe from the one we know. To wake up to the fact that we are children of God is at the same time to wake up to our common humanity: all creation woven into one broken, beautiful, beloved whole. The system of the flesh separates and deceives. We remain creatures of flesh. We are seduced by the lies of our society and even of religion. We allow hatred to seem noble. We retain callous indifference to the weeping of the earth. For Paul, these sufferings and imperfections are "not worth comparing" to the radiance of the promise. The Spirit crucifies us to the flesh and raises us to a new life in which "love is lord of all."[5] This was strange and seemingly impossible in the first century, and it remains so today, but it is the impossible dream of our faith.

The lectionary readings point us to this life in the Spirit. Like Jacob, we dream of the blessing (Gen. 28:10–19); like Isaiah, we become fearless, remembering that God is our rock (Isa. 44:6–8); and if we read the Wisdom of Solomon, we remember that God's strength is his kindness; her righteousness spares us all (Wis. 12:13, 16–19).

WENDY FARLEY

---

3. Julian of Norwich, "A Revelation of Love," chap. 54 in *The Writings of Julian of Norwich,* ed. Nicholas Watson and Jacqueline Jenkins (University Park, PA: Pennsylvania State University, 2006), 293.

4. Rosemarie Freeney Harding, with Rachel Elizabeth Harding, *Remnants: A Memoir of Spirit, Activism, and Mothering* (Durham. NC: Duke University Press, 2015), 261–62.

5. The phrase is from the song "The Quiet Joys of Brotherhood," lyrics by Richard Fariña.

Proper 11 (Sunday between July 17 and July 23 inclusive)

Matthew 13:24–30, 36–43

²⁴He put before them another parable: "The kingdom of heaven may be compared to someone who sowed good seed in his field; ²⁵but while everybody was asleep, an enemy came and sowed weeds among the wheat, and then went away. ²⁶So when the plants came up and bore grain, then the weeds appeared as well. ²⁷And the slaves of the householder came and said to him, 'Master, did you not sow good seed in your field? Where, then, did these weeds come from?' ²⁸He answered, 'An enemy has done this.' The slaves said to him, 'Then do you want us to go and gather them?' ²⁹But he replied, 'No; for in gathering the weeds you would uproot the wheat along with them. ³⁰Let both of them grow together until the harvest; and at harvest time I will tell the reapers, Collect the weeds first and bind them in bundles to be burned, but gather the wheat into my barn.'" . . .

³⁶Then he left the crowds and went into the house. And his disciples approached him, saying, "Explain to us the parable of the weeds of the field." ³⁷He answered, "The one who sows the good seed is the Son of Man; ³⁸the field is the world, and the good seed are the children of the kingdom; the weeds are the children of the evil one, ³⁹and the enemy who sowed them is the devil; the harvest is the end of the age, and the reapers are angels. ⁴⁰Just as the weeds are collected and burned up with fire, so will it be at the end of the age. ⁴¹The Son of Man will send his angels, and they will collect out of his kingdom all causes of sin and all evildoers, ⁴²and they will throw them into the furnace of fire, where there will be weeping and gnashing of teeth. ⁴³Then the righteous will shine like the sun in the kingdom of their Father. Let anyone with ears listen!"

Commentary 1: Connecting the Reading with Scripture

The second of seven parables Jesus tells in Matthew 13 concerning the "kingdom of heaven" follows the agricultural milieu of the first story. The foundational parable of the Soils (Matt. 13:1–9, 18–23) features four grounds on which sown seed falls. Only one terrain—the cultivated nonthorny, nonrocky "good soil"—proves productive. Jesus applies this farmer's tale to the various ways an individual might receive the "word of the kingdom" (v. 19); the sole commendable response yields "good" and faithful character, evidencing the rule of God on earth as it is in heaven (see 6:10).[1]

In the following parable of the Wheat and Weeds, Jesus continues the theme of disseminating the message of God's reign in the world with decidedly mixed results. In this case, however, the focus falls less on variegated personal responses to God's word (seed), reflecting different receptive attitudes (soils), than on dichotomous group identities within society, the larger "field" of God's work. A quartet of possible engagements with God's word modulates into a duality between "good" and "evil" people, represented in the parable by healthful "wheat" and harmful "weeds."

Such a divide, however, between good and bad crops of people proves not so obvious as it first appears and not so easily managed in the long run. The dramatic suspense of Jesus' story highlights two critical elements: (1) the intrusion of a surreptitious, nocturnal "enemy" who

---

1. In Matthew "kingdom of heaven" refers not to a fixed, discrete celestial locale, but to the all-encompassing, dynamic cosmic realm that advances the righteous rule of God. "Heaven" substitutes for "God," out of respect for the divine name and presence.

aims to corrupt the wheat field by sowing nefarious weeds among the good grain seeds; and (2) the close proximity and intermingling of wheat and weed plants as they begin to sprout and grow *together*. This result poses a crisis demanding delicate handling. While the field workers (slaves), upon discovering the invasive weeds, naturally want to weed them *out* of the property, the landowner blocks such radical uprooting, for fear that good wheat, popping up entangled with the weeds, would also get pulled up. Best, then, to wait until the final harvest, when mature wheat and weed plants can be carefully separated, the former collected in barns and the latter consigned to burning.

Unpacking these scenarios further, consider the enemy's weed-sowing operation. It happens one night, "while everybody was asleep" (13:25) and unaware until the wheat and weed seeds begin to flower. The Greek term for "weed" (*zizanion*) refers to a common botanical species found in Middle Eastern grain fields, the "bearded darnel-grass . . . a strong-growing grass very closely resembling wheat or rye in appearance and from which it is extremely difficult to distinguish in its early stages. . . . Its seeds have very deleterious effects, and even poisonous properties have been ascribed to them."[2] Though the parable does not specify the motive for the enemy's action, it amounts to a kind of vandalism, potentially causing serious damage to the landowner's wheat crop. It may even shade into more vicious intent to harm members of the estate and customers who might consume some of the toxic darnel not properly winnowed from the good grain.

Jesus' explanation of the parable identifies the enemy as the "evil one" or "devil" and the weeds as the devil's evil "children," opposed to the "children of the kingdom," represented by the wheat seeds sown by Jesus himself in his capacity as "Son of Man/Humanity" (vv. 37–39). Here the devil represents a rival sower, in contrast to the soils scenario, which images the "evil one" as a hungry bird snatching the good word (seed) from hard hearts (vv. 4, 19). By clearly marking out the "field" of operation as the "world" (v. 38), including but not restricted to the righteous, Jesus depicts overlapping and interpenetrating spheres of church and society. Matthew is the only Gospel writer who uses the term "church" (see 16:18; 18:17) within the overarching arena of God's cosmic kingdom, where evil still challenges God's righteous rule.

So what should God's faithful people do in this precarious situation? The parable's detail about the servants' sleeping during the enemy's infiltration could suggest a lack of vigilance on their part, something about which Jesus will later warn his disciples (24:36–44; 25:1–13; 26:36–46). In the present case, he places no emphasis on remaining alert to danger or taking any security measures, such as building walls or fences, setting traps, surveilling the enemy, or relocating to a remote safe spot. Jesus simply presents the entwinement of good and bad people (seed) in the world as a fact of life. This is nothing over which to lose sleep or into which one need launch a special investigation. It is going to happen, period: let the weeds be.

While calling for a certain honest acceptance of a mixed good-and-evil world, Jesus is no hopeless fatalist. A judicious "harvest" will ensure the safety (salvation) of the children of God's kingdom and separation (destruction) of evil ones. In other words, the reaping will follow the character of the sown seeds and sowing agents (Son of Man and Evil One): "You reap whatever you sow" (Gal. 6:7; see 6:7–9; Rom. 8:5–14). God's faithful children must *wait* for this harvest at the "end of the age," when the "angels" will carry out God's final judgments and "collect out of his kingdom all causes of sin and all evildoers," consigning them to a fiery furnace, while "the righteous will shine like the sun in the kingdom of their Father" (Matt. 13:38–43). Jesus offers God's people, and indeed all creation, a firm warrant to wait *in hope* for ultimate liberation from debilitating struggles with evil in the present age, as this week's epistle text from Romans 8:12–25 so poignantly confirms (see esp. vv. 22–25).

Matthew's narrative provides more than a distant future hope; it also lodges a radical challenge to God's righteous children in this current mixed era. It is important to notice

---

2. Harold N. Moldenke and Alma L. Moldenke, *Plants of the Bible* (New York: Dover, 1986), 134.

the immediate context of the present parable, wherein Matthew splices two shorter stories (Matt. 13:31–33) between Jesus' description (13:24–30) and explanation (13:36–43) of the wheat/weeds account. In brief, these two snippets about the products of a tiny mustard seed and a pinch of yeast signal the abundant growth of God's realm *in this age* in mysterious ways out of all proportion to our human efforts. This growth principle reinforces the point established in the larger wheat field story, that good grain (God's people) will ultimately thrive and not be throttled by evil influences.

Still, confidence should not be mistaken for complacency. Beyond suggesting in the present parable that his followers not waste energy on targeting enemies and devising schemes to "weed" them out of the world, Matthew's Jesus enjoins them in the Sermon on the Mount to "*love your enemies* and pray for those who persecute you" (Matt. 5:44). True "children of your Father in heaven" appreciate that this Creator-Father "makes his sun rise on the evil and on the good, and sends rain on the righteous and on the unrighteous" (5:45), on the wheat *and* weeds. God longs for all creatures to flourish and realize God's good purposes. Will all reach this goal? Sadly, no—which a final reckoning (reaping) in God's time and according to God's justice will reveal. In the meantime, the good wheat keeps on growing and struggling together with the pesky weeds under the gracious shining of God's sun and splash of God's rain.

F. SCOTT SPENCER

Commentary 2: Connecting the Reading with the World

Jesus teaches his followers by telling stories from everyday life to reveal the wisdom of God's reign. We might think something as glorious as the reign of Israel's God coming into the world would be treated in an elevated manner, something that might seem more worthy of its subject. However, Jesus teaches the way of God's kingdom by telling down-to-earth stories that cannot be understood apart from his down-to-earth life and ministry as "Emmanuel, God with us" (Matt. 1:23). The parables of Jesus thus call attention to the reality of God's reign, the mystery that has been hidden in plain sight since "the foundation of the world" (13:35).

When Jesus speaks in parables, he calls his followers to a change of mind, to the joy of seeing themselves in God's kingdom involving a conversion to, and participation in, God's will for the world, which Jesus reveals in all he says, does, and suffers. An important part of preaching the parables is to do so with the conviction that the church needs to hear them in order to follow Jesus in the way of God's kingdom. The parables, then, in both what they say and how they say it, are gifts of the Holy Spirit that keep Christian people attuned to God's action in, with, and for the sake of the world.

The parable of the Wheat and the Weeds encourages the church to endure patiently in, with, and for a world that in many ways cannot and will not acknowledge the reign of God coming in Jesus and his followers. Moreover, this parable shows us what God's kingdom is like; not just what it was like in the past, or what it will be like in the future, but what it is like now. God's kingdom is present in the world, which is the field where God's people are planted to live, work, pray, suffer, struggle, serve, witness, and finally, in God's good time, surrender their lives wholly to God. We can be confident that it is not necessary to weed out, either from the church or the world, those whom we perceive as resisting and opposing the gospel that we are called to proclaim and live. It is possible to wait actively, knowing that Jesus, the crucified and risen Lord, has sown the church among the nations as a witness to God's patient hope for the world.

However, we preach in a time when Christians are sharply divided over just what God's will for the world might be. Partisan positions are held fiercely and promoted aggressively in ways that too often mirror rather than challenge the world. One long-term consequence of our extended conflicts over doctrinal, moral, and social issues is that fellow Christians, members of the same congregation, denomination, or tradition, are perceived as threats who must be weeded out.

The parable exposes as illusory the idea that it is possible to create a pure or ideal church by "cleaning house." It shows that churches, like the world, are communities made up of both good seeds and bad weeds. Our recent history as Christian people in the world of American culture demonstrates how our fear of the threat posed by weeds, which is often a fear of difference, diminishes the church's life and witness.

It is not uncommon for Christians to weed out those who, in reality, are good seed sown by God in the world. Preaching from the story of the seeds and weeds illumines our hearts and minds to see ourselves and the world in light of God's goodness. The parable counsels more than merely being tolerant of others who are different than ourselves. The parable summons us to recognize and rejoice in the goodness of God in others, a goodness freely given without distinctions.

Another way of stating this is that the created goodness and dignity of all humankind is ultimately deeper and more enduring than our political, intellectual, cultural, and social differences. Rather than seeing the mission of the church as "fixing" itself or "cleaning up" the world according to our passionately held agendas, we are free to proclaim and live the good news of God's reign for the sake of a messy world that appears for many to be a hopeless cause. Moreover, how the church positions itself and responds to the world in its life together is significant if the world is to hear the church's message. This is not a matter of simply "putting our best foot forward" in order to make a good impression on the world by utilizing the best of contemporary public relations and communication strategies. There must be a readiness of heart; a desire to receive what Jesus gives; an attentive receptivity to his gift of discipleship that entails humbly listening, learning, and being led.

As we strive to follow the way of God's kingdom, we might begin by heeding Jesus' exhortations in the Sermon on the Mount. For example: "But I say to you, love your enemies and pray for those who persecute you, so that you may be children of your Father in heaven; for he makes his sun rise on the evil and on the good, and sends rain on the righteous and on the unrighteous" (5:44–45). This is the way of God's people in the world, a community that exists to show forth God's glory by displaying God's goodness spoken and enacted by Jesus.

The good news that can be proclaimed from this parable is that God is at work to redeem and restore the whole creation. Such patient hope, actively waiting upon God in, with, and for the sake of the world, may be the Christian virtue most needed in a time of apocalyptic calls for the church to take up radical action in order to change the world. The parable also offers good insight for preachers to show how the world may perceive the church—if it bothers to pay attention. Outsiders observe Christian people who do not want to wait for and with the God whom they presume to worship and serve, but instead look for ways to take the world and its future into their own hands, seeking to force God's kingdom by the use of violent power. The world, however, sees how the church often seeks to do whatever it takes to make things come out right, even if such impatient action is destructive of the church's call to be a hopeful witness to the coming of God's reign by participating in the way of Jesus.

The parable offers assurance to preachers that—despite the overwhelming threat of all that resists, opposes, and fights against God's kingdom—God's plan for the world will succeed. In the end it will bear much fruit to produce a rich harvest, since God has all the time there is. "The parable describes the coming of the reign of God from the first words onward. That coming includes the sowing, the opponents that cause severe damage, and finally the abundant harvest that is brought forth in spite of all opposition."[3] The good news is that this is already happening in the ordinary, down-to-earth places wherever the church has been planted. The visibility of a patient, hopeful church is necessary if the world is to know what it truly is: God's good creation.

MICHAEL PASQUARELLO III

---

3. Gerhard Lohfink, *Does God Need the Church? Toward a Theology of the People of God*, trans. Linda M. Maloney (Collegeville, MN: Liturgical Press, 1999), 44.

Proper 12 (Sunday between July 24 and July 30 inclusive)

1 Kings 3:5–12 and Genesis 29:15–28
Psalm 119:129–136 and Psalm 105:1–11, 45b or Psalm 128
Romans 8:26–39
Matthew 13:31–33, 44–52

1 Kings 3:5–12

⁵At Gibeon the LORD appeared to Solomon in a dream by night; and God said, "Ask what I should give you." ⁶And Solomon said, "You have shown great and steadfast love to your servant my father David, because he walked before you in faithfulness, in righteousness, and in uprightness of heart toward you; and you have kept for him this great and steadfast love, and have given him a son to sit on his throne today. ⁷And now, O LORD my God, you have made your servant king in place of my father David, although I am only a little child; I do not know how to go out or come in. ⁸And your servant is in the midst of the people whom you have chosen, a great people, so numerous they cannot be numbered or counted. ⁹Give your servant therefore an understanding mind to govern your people, able to discern between good and evil; for who can govern this your great people?"

¹⁰It pleased the Lord that Solomon had asked this. ¹¹God said to him, "Because you have asked this, and have not asked for yourself long life or riches, or for the life of your enemies, but have asked for yourself understanding to discern what is right, ¹²I now do according to your word. Indeed I give you a wise and discerning mind; no one like you has been before you and no one like you shall arise after you."

Genesis 29:15–28

¹⁵Then Laban said to Jacob, "Because you are my kinsman, should you therefore serve me for nothing? Tell me, what shall your wages be?" ¹⁶Now Laban had two daughters; the name of the elder was Leah, and the name of the younger was Rachel. ¹⁷Leah's eyes were lovely, and Rachel was graceful and beautiful. ¹⁸Jacob loved Rachel; so he said, "I will serve you seven years for your younger daughter Rachel." ¹⁹Laban said, "It is better that I give her to you than that I should give her to any other man; stay with me." ²⁰So Jacob served seven years for Rachel, and they seemed to him but a few days because of the love he had for her.

²¹Then Jacob said to Laban, "Give me my wife that I may go in to her, for my time is completed." ²²So Laban gathered together all the people of the place, and made a feast. ²³But in the evening he took his daughter Leah and brought her to Jacob; and he went in to her. ²⁴(Laban gave his maid Zilpah to his daughter Leah to be her maid.) ²⁵When morning came, it was Leah! And Jacob said to Laban, "What is this you have done to me? Did I not serve with you for Rachel? Why then have you deceived me?" ²⁶Laban said, "This is not done in our country—giving the younger before the firstborn. ²⁷Complete the week of this one, and we will give you the other also in return for serving me another seven years." ²⁸Jacob did so, and completed her week; then Laban gave him his daughter Rachel as a wife.

Commentary 1: Connecting the Reading with Scripture

An initial reading of Genesis 29:15–28 and 1 Kings 3:5–12 yields as many contrasts as connections. Genesis 29:15–28 tells the story of Jacob, one who has a reputation for following on someone else's heels, being deceived by his father-in-law and forced to marry Leah, the elder sister of the one he loves. First Kings 3:5–12 relays a dream in which God appears to Solomon and promises to grant anything for which he asks. Solomon asks for a good gift: a "wise and discerning mind" (1 Kgs. 3:12). The contrasts are clear: deception vs. dreams, promises broken vs. promises kept, arrogance vs. wisdom. To explore these connections, the preacher should pay close attention in these passages to the role of women, how God acts, and to whom God appears. God's promises and covenant are unwavering.

Perspectives of Patriarchs and Matriarchs. Genesis 29:15–28 is part of a longer ancestral narrative, Genesis 12–50, that provides the foundational stories of the patriarchal religion of ancient Israel. Feminist commentators observe that the story is told primarily from a male perspective, though women are named and are valued commodities for their potential as wives and mothers.[1] Thus two perspectives emerge within this passage and offer possibilities for preachers. One perspective emphasizes God's paramount concern that Jacob, despite Laban's deception, will realize the promises God made to Abraham and Sarah: land, descendants, and blessing. Another emerges from the perspectives of the matriarchs—Leah and Rachel—whom Laban exchanges as wives to pay Jacob's wages, but who also have their own power and sense of agency.

Jacob first meets Rachel at a well where she waters Laban's flock. He is drawn to her beauty, kisses her, and weeps aloud (Gen. 29:9–14). These are gestures associated with ancient tribal rituals for reunion with one's kin. Jacob's first encounter with Rachel is significant because it recalls the story of his father Isaac's first sight of Rebekah. Rebekah's beauty and hospitality were the signs that she should marry Abraham's and Sarah's son (24:14–16).

After meeting Rachel, Jacob bargains with Laban to marry her in exchange for seven years of his labor. Laban accepts this bargain, but deceives his future son-in-law by sending Leah his elder daughter to the wedding tent. For Laban, the elder daughter Leah should be the first to marry (29:26). Laban uses the feminine form of the Hebrew term for "firstborn" (*bekirah*) that Jacob used when he tricked his father into thinking that he was Esau (27:19). Once Jacob realizes that his father-in-law has tricked him into marrying Leah, he arranges to work for seven more years so he can marry Rachel. The narrative triangulates Jacob and the two sisters and punctuates family strife. The preacher should take care not to overlook Leah's experience in the story: both Laban and Jacob betray her. Ultimately, when God sees that Leah is not favored, God "opens her womb" but leaves Rachel barren (29:31).

Jacob's character connects with Laban's as they share a reputation for deception. Earlier in the narrative, Jacob has tricked his father into giving him Esau's blessing. Biblical scholars point out that Jacob is not the only patriarch with a questionable reputation. However, God works in the midst of deception to ensure that Jacob will receive the covenant promise.

Throughout the story, the roles of Leah and Rachel are defined primarily by their relationships with men (father and husband), but the agency and importance of these women should not be missed. They hold the promise and potential to carry on the family line, giving them great power over husband and father.

Good Leaders Are Wise. Wisdom plays a central role throughout 1 Kings 3 and forms a connecting theme between the introduction of Solomon's reign and the court history of King David and Bathsheba.[2] Solomon's request that

---

1. For an excellent commentary on Leah, Rachel, and other matriarchs, see Susan Niditch, "Genesis," in *The Women's Bible Commentary*, 3rd ed., ed. Carol A. Newsom, Sharon H. Ringe, and Jacqueline E. Lapsley (Louisville, KY: Westminster John Knox, 2012), 27–55.

2. See Carole R. Fontaine, "The Bearing of Wisdom on the Shape of 2 Samuel 11–12 and 1 Kings 3," *Journal for the Study of the Old Testament* 34 (1986): 61–77.

God grant him wisdom could be reminiscent of Egyptian royal ideology. Pharaohs held the title "Lord of Ma'at," goddess and daughter of the sun god Re, associated with the god of wisdom, Thoth, and embodiment of truth, justice, and the cosmic order. There is evidence that the story also alludes to tales told in Egyptian novellas and Ugaritic epic stories.

Solomon is introduced as one who builds an alliance with the Egyptians through marriage. Gibeon, the place where God appears to Solomon, is also significant. Gibeon was a royal city in premonarchic times, a thriving center for religious rituals (Josh. 18:25; 21:17; 2 Sam. 20:8; 2 Chr. 1:3), and associated with the wilderness. In at least one of the historical accounts, Gibeon is named as the place where David wiped out the Philistines from there to Gezer (1 Chr. 14:16).

From a literary perspective, God's appearance to Solomon at Gibeon is critical for two main reasons. First, Solomon is not David's firstborn son. God's appearance to Solomon legitimates his claim to the throne. Second, his father, David, was a decisive leader, but not always one who was wise. Recall that David so desires Bathsheba, another man's wife, that he rapes her (2 Sam. 11; Bathsheba would not have been free to decline a king's advances) and then sends her husband Uriah to the battlefront to be killed, so that Uriah cannot discover the pregnancy that has resulted from the king's violation of Bathsheba.

Another theme worthy of investigation is Bathsheba's role in securing her son's and Israel's future (1 Kgs. 1). Bathsheba is a special figure. Some biblical scholars argue that the bath she takes that attracts David's gaze was not a menstrual bath, which has raised questions about Bathsheba's character, but a ritual of self-purification, thus legitimizing her role as a mother of Israel and a full participant in the narrative.[3] Bathsheba is the daughter of Eliam (2 Sam. 11:3), debatably a non-Israelite; despite her ethnic difference she secures Solomon's (and Israel's) future.

What does Bathsheba's son ask for God to give him? Solomon does not ask for the defeat of his enemies or for wealth. In contrast to his father David's arrogance, lack of gratitude, and lack of a wise and discerning mind, Solomon acknowledges that his authority comes from God and appeals to God for wisdom to lead a people "so numerous they cannot be numbered or counted" (1 Kgs. 3:8).

The main intent of this story is for teaching; wisdom serves as a motivator of action and a way to evaluate the goodness of one's deeds. Solomon receives that which Wisdom confers on those who seek her, things "far more precious than jewels": prudence, knowledge, discretion, and righteousness in the paths of justice (Prov. 8).

Preaching the Connections. One discovers rich possibilities for preaching in the stories of Jacob, Laban, Leah and Rachel, and Solomon's dream. What the characters in the story imagine as the most desirable outcomes for themselves, their families, and their future may not always be the most "wise and discerning" choices. God appears to and works among the least expected—doubters, deceivers, ethnically different—to secure covenant promises.

ELIZABETH HINSON-HASTY

Commentary 2: Connecting the Reading with the World

The 1 Kings passage tells a story meant to validate a new king's regime. On one level, it speaks of systems, nations, and government, of an up-and-comer beginning to play on the world's stage. On another level, it provides colorful examples of a leader's spiritual traits. Themes of humility, covenant, tradition, legacy, and balance wind through each level. Whether a

---

3. See J. D'Ror Chankin-Gould, Derek Hutchinson, David Hilton Jackson, Tyler D. Mayfield, Leah Rediger Schulte, Tammi J. Schneider, E. Winkelman, "The Sanctified 'Adulteress' and Her Circumstantial Clause: Bathsheba's Bath and Self-Consecration in 2 Samuel 11," *Journal for the Study of the Old Testament* 32 (2008): 339–52.

preacher might treat both in the same sermon is an interesting question. It may be that the wise preacher, taking a page from Solomon's book, will have to choose.

Systems. Treating the text at the systemic level forces the preacher to wrestle with the question of what to say about God's involvement in the business of nations. The problem is a common one, especially when treating Old Testament texts. Ancient worldviews of the scope of God's involvement in human life differ sharply from contemporary sensibilities. Contemporary preachers of Old Testament texts often set the question aside entirely, in favor of finding other points of connection with the text. However, it is more difficult to do that here.

The issue of God's involvement in the affairs of state is of particular interest in this text. The passage goes a bit further than some in pressing the issue. It not only assumes God's interest in government; it underscores God's desire to be involved with its leaders. Solomon is rewarded for his listening heart, that is, for being a king who is open to God's direction. Read from one angle, it is the text's primary point.

A sermon that takes this approach would focus on God's desire to be involved in human institutions and grapple directly with the questions that raises. To say that God desires to be involved is not the same thing as saying that God is involved, of course. The passage does not explain why God seems to choose to be involved in some cases and not others. Neither does the text supply a neat answer to the question of how deeply God might get into the red tape and intrigue of national politics. Knee deep? Up to her elbows? Over his head? Viewing it all from a distance?

Nevertheless the story suggests a compelling insight into God's character. God is pictured as listening keenly, anxious to hear what Solomon will request. The God who leans in, who wants to be involved—even in the rough and tumble of the polis—is a God we also know. How else do you explain that here and there and now and then grace breaks into dog-eat-dog and might-makes-right systems?

Examples of such inbreakings include stories drawn from the civil rights era, ranging from those that picture God grieving over Medgar Evers to rejoicing with freedom riders for being sick and tired of being sick and tired with Fannie Lou Hamer. Other nonviolence-movement illustrations include Gandhi's *ahimsa*, Czechoslovakia's Velvet Revolution, and the story of the Liberian women instrumental in putting an end to fourteen years of civil war, told in the 2008 documentary *Pray the Devil Back to Hell.*

A Leader's Traits. Deuteronomy's description of the ideal king plays in the background of this story of Solomon's ascension to the throne, reminding the reader that the good king is someone who neither exalts himself nor "turns aside from [God's] commandment, either to the right or to the left" (Deut. 17:20). The connection provides a possible jumping-off point for an ethical approach to the text. An ideal king—and by extension an ideal nation—would be one that operates with a certain levelness or steadiness of focus and a certain humility. These kings are principled people, the text suggests, and by extension the cultures they help shape may be as well. Examples of leaders known for their humility are readily available, especially when local heroes, congregational leaders, and teachers are included on the list. The book *A Path Appears* tells the poignant and touching story of how Mrs. Grady, a school librarian who exemplifies humility, rescues a rebellious teen even though he makes her cry.[4]

On Genesis. I am sure I have heard more than one Sunday school teacher tell the story of Genesis 29:15–28 wrong. Perhaps upping the ante is just what you have to do to keep squirmy children listening, but I am sure we were taught a more dramatic version of the story. Jacob, our teachers said, worked seven years before being hoodwinked into marrying the wrong woman and then another seven before finally getting to "go into" his true love—a thought that made us squirm for entirely different reasons. Furthermore, on the question of whether Leah had lovely eyes (and a nice personality) or was legally

---

4. Nicholas D. Kristof and Sheryl WuDunn, *A Path Appears: Transforming Lives, Creating Opportunity* (New York: Alfred A. Knopf, 2014), 101–5.

blind, my Sunday school teachers not only opted for weak eyes but added warts and other unsavory details. The added suspense and embroidered details may up the drama a bit, but they do not change the story. It is an old story, about revenge, rivalry, and getting your comeuppance.

Comeuppance. The quickest way into this text is surely to engage the "what goes around comes around" theme. A sermon that takes such an approach may present an opportunity to examine the popular belief more closely.

In chapter 29, Laban does to Jacob what Jacob has done to Isaac in chapter 27, that is, pulls the wool over his eyes. The allusion in verse 26 makes it plain that the writer connects the two incidents. In effect Jacob pays for stealing his brother's birthright. It costs him seven years of labor. The first thing we notice in examining the text from this angle is that seven extra years of labor is not an especially high price for a birthright. Also troubling is the fact that the story gives no indication that the experience brings Jacob to repentance or even a moment of self-awareness. Karmic views begin to look a little thin compared to the Gospel.

An Amused God. The second thing we notice is that the text is rife with punch lines, little shockers, big and medium-sized laughs. When seen in its wider literary context (through chap. 31), today's text turns out to be part of a larger story about wily family members scamming each other. This passage begins to look more like part of a series of humorous stories about craftiness, treachery, double-dealing, and clever deceits. "I am a scamp," you can almost hear Jacob saying. "It is why you like me."

Indeed, God does seem to like Jacob. Read from this angle, the passage paints a picture of a tolerant God, even an amused one, one well acquainted with young men and with blushing brides who sit on the stolen goods protesting demurely about it being their time of the month. This text depicts a God who loves them in spite of, or perhaps because of, their impish ways. "When did religion lose its sense of humor?" this text seems to ask.

Sermons that pursue this approach will find ample room for connection with the current world. Whether it is with congregants' wayward children, faith communities' charismatic leaders, or the individual's inner scamp, everybody knows a Jacob. More importantly, almost everybody needs to be reminded from time to time just how much God loves a good Jacob.

JANA CHILDERS

Proper 12 (Sunday between July 24 and July 30 inclusive)

Psalm 119:129–136

[129] Your decrees are wonderful;
   therefore my soul keeps them.
[130] The unfolding of your words gives light;
   it imparts understanding to the simple.
[131] With open mouth I pant,
   because I long for your commandments.
[132] Turn to me and be gracious to me,
   as is your custom toward those who love your name.
[133] Keep my steps steady according to your promise,
   and never let iniquity have dominion over me.
[134] Redeem me from human oppression,
   that I may keep your precepts.
[135] Make your face shine upon your servant,
   and teach me your statutes.
[136] My eyes shed streams of tears
   because your law is not kept.

Psalm 105:1–11, 45b

[1] O give thanks to the LORD, call on his name,
   make known his deeds among the peoples.
[2] Sing to him, sing praises to him;
   tell of all his wonderful works.
[3] Glory in his holy name;
   let the hearts of those who seek the LORD rejoice.
[4] Seek the LORD and his strength;
   seek his presence continually.
[5] Remember the wonderful works he has done,
   his miracles, and the judgments he has uttered,
[6] O offspring of his servant Abraham,
   children of Jacob, his chosen ones.

[7] He is the LORD our God;
   his judgments are in all the earth.
[8] He is mindful of his covenant forever,
   of the word that he commanded, for a thousand generations,
[9] the covenant that he made with Abraham,
   his sworn promise to Isaac,
[10] which he confirmed to Jacob as a statute,
   to Israel as an everlasting covenant,
[11] saying, "To you I will give the land of Canaan
   as your portion for an inheritance."
. . . .
[45b] Praise the LORD!

Psalm 128

>¹Happy is everyone who fears the LORD,
>   who walks in his ways.
>²You shall eat the fruit of the labor of your hands;
>   you shall be happy, and it shall go well with you.
>
>³Your wife will be like a fruitful vine
>   within your house;
>your children will be like olive shoots
>   around your table.
>⁴Thus shall the man be blessed
>   who fears the LORD.
>
>⁵The LORD bless you from Zion.
>   May you see the prosperity of Jerusalem
>   all the days of your life.
>⁶May you see your children's children.
>   Peace be upon Israel!

Connecting the Psalm with Scripture and Worship

Psalm 119:129–136. Psalm 119 famously and relentlessly celebrates God's teaching, God's "law." The "teaching" in question appears to be a broad category, including not only commandments, but also descriptions of God's will, work, and ways. According to the psalmist, illumination comes by means of remembering, trusting, and anticipating the patterns of God's activity, as well as observing the statutes God provides for human flourishing. To love the concrete expressions of God's will, work, and ways is to love God.

We drop in on this megapsalm in verse 129, with the psalmist delighting in God's decrees. This excerpt contains rich visual tropes: the "unfolding" of God's words gives light (Ps. 119:130); longing for God's commands involves a gaping, panting mouth (v. 131); the heartbreak of God's law ignored results in "streams of tears" (v. 136). The centerpiece of this section is a series of petitions, each of them unpacking the first: that God would turn and be gracious. The psalmist asks God to "keep my steps steady according to your promise" and never to "let iniquity have dominion over me" (v. 133). Perhaps most compelling of all is the request for redemption from "human oppression" in verse 134, an understandable wish in itself; but the psalmist goes a step further, explaining why such relief is needed: "that I may keep your precepts." This idea—that fully living as God intends requires a context free from oppressive structures—is one worth exploring further, perhaps in relation to the 1 Kings text.

Preachers familiar with the escapades of David and his son and successor, Solomon, may experience some resistance when reading the account of the latter's dream in 1 Kings 3:5–12. If we go on only what we find in verses 5–12, David is unimpeachably righteous. Indeed, God loves David precisely because of his virtue, according to Solomon. The new king too looks very impressive. When God shows up in the dream with a test question, "What do you want from me?" Solomon aces it. He praises God, he confesses his inadequacy, he asks for the gift of discernment rather than the more obvious things befitting a monarch. For this, God honors Solomon, granting his request and then some, declaring that no one has been or will be quite like him. Lectionary texts must begin and end somewhere, but the

On Christ We Venture All

What has been now said about the Ascension of our Lord comes to this; that we are in a world of mystery, with one bright Light before us, sufficient for our proceeding forward through all difficulties. Take away this Light, and we are utterly wretched,—we know not where we are, how we are sustained, what will become of us, and of all that is dear to us, what we are to believe, and why we are in being. But with it we have all and abound. Not to mention the duty and wisdom of implicit faith in the love of Him who made and redeemed us, what is nobler, what is more elevating and transporting, than the generosity of heart which risks everything on God's word, dares the powers of evil to their worst efforts, and repels the illusions of sense and the artifices of reason, by confidence in the Truth of Him who has ascended to the right hand of the Majesty on high? What infinite mercy it is in Him, that He allows sinners such as we are, the privilege of acting the part of heroes rather than of penitents? Who are we "that we should be able" and have opportunity "to offer so willingly after this sort?"—"Blessed," surely thrice blessed, "are they who have not seen, and yet have believed!" We will not wish for sight; we will enjoy our privilege; we will triumph in the leave given us to go forward, "not knowing whither we go," knowing that "this is the victory that overcometh the world, even our faith." It is enough that our Redeemer liveth; that He has been on earth and will come again. On Him we venture our all; we can bear thankfully to put ourselves into His hands, our interests present and eternal, and the interests of all we love. Christ has died, "yea rather is risen again, who is even at the right hand of God, who also maketh intercession for us. Who shall separate us from His love? Shall tribulation, or distress, or persecution, or famine or nakedness, or peril, or sword? Nay, in all these things we are more than conquerors, through Him that loved us."

John Henry Newman, "Sermon 18: Mysteries in Religion," in *Parochial and Plain Sermons* (London: Longmans, Green and Co., 1908), 2:215–16.

---

wise preacher will attend to what is missing: the more ambiguous account of Solomon in verses 1–4, as well as the conclusion of God's speech in verses 13–14. There we find that Solomon got his riches after all, and that God's final promise, long life, comes with a condition. The ending to Solomon's story in 1 Kings 11:3–4 dampens the optimism still further.

Psalm 119 can offer the preacher a corrective to any lingering hagiographic tendencies. The psalmist does regularly claim to keep God's decrees, to love God's ways, to despise lawbreakers; but just as frequently prays to be preserved from doing bad things, to be taught again what is good, to be redeemed from the unjust situations that smother faithfulness. Whatever it means to "keep" God's decrees, it is temporary. Wisdom is not an achievement, but a gift, one that can only be sought anew. Solomon was right to ask God for it, and in this, temporarily, he was exemplary.

There are numerous musical settings of different sections of Psalm 119, but one that includes imagery from across the psalm, including this excerpt, is "I Long for Your Commandments."[1] Its tune is well-suited to the petitionary dimensions of the text, and there is a nice allusion to God's table in the final verse, linking word to sacrament.

Psalm 105:1–11, 45b or Psalm 128. A choice of two psalms is offered to accompany the provocative story of Jacob's wedding night in Genesis 29. The first, selected verses from Psalm 105, is categorized as a "historical" psalm, since it recounts Israel's backstory from Joseph's captivity through the postexodus miracles in the desert. The psalm includes a few references to

---

1. "I Long for Your Commandments," with text by Jean Janzen (1991), alt., and music by Heinrich Schütz (1661), may be found in *Glory to God: The Presbyterian Hymnal* (Louisville, KY: Westminster John Knox, 2013), 64.

Jacob, though nearly all of the narrative material is omitted from the reading. It opens with a series of cascading exhortations: give thanks to the Lord, make known God's deeds, sing praises, seek God's presence, remember all God has done (Ps. 105:1–5). Then the reader, addressed as a descendant of Abraham and Jacob, is reminded that God's covenant promise extends for "a thousand generations" (v. 8). Sweet Canaan will belong to the chosen people. The lectionary leaps from this promise in verse 11 to the final verse of the psalm, where we learn (though the lectionary omits this) that God's gifts come with a purpose: in order that Israel might keep God's laws (v. 45a); the lectionary reading concludes with verse 45b: "Praise the Lord!"

In relation to Genesis 29, Psalm 105 offers a broader perspective that might help the preacher navigate the strangeness of the tale: Jacob falls in love, works for years to win Rachel's hand, and then his uncle pulls a fast one, switching the bride. The ensuing domestic unhappiness is not without its bright spots, but this can hardly be the way Jacob imagined God's promise of abundant offspring would play out. Nonetheless, the psalm reminds us, the twelve tribes were established by means of this particular menagerie: Jacob, Leah, Rachel, Zilpah, Bilhah, and even Laban the dishonest. They are all part of the big story of God's way with God's people, unfurled in Psalm 105.

For this reason, it might be worth taking the time to read the whole psalm in worship. One effective way to do this is to make additional use of the exhortations from the opening verses: "give thanks," "make known," "rejoice," "seek," "remember." While one liturgist reads through the psalm, a small Greek chorus of lectors could each take one of these verbs and interject them, one after the other, following each major plot development in the narrative portion of the psalm. This underlines the function of reciting Israel's story in the first place: to prompt praise, proclamation, and prayer.

A second option to pair with Genesis 29 is Psalm 128. The psalmist declares that fear of the Lord will result in professional and domestic bliss, and the first two-thirds of the psalm describes what that looks like. A God-fearer will enjoy the spoils of his labor; he will have a fertile wife and growing children around the dinner table. Only with the last couple of verses does the psalm shift from the assertion of blessing to the prayer for it.

What might this psalm have to offer the preacher of Genesis 29? Perhaps an orientation to Jacob's expectations and a theological puzzle to unravel, or at least name. We learn from Jacob's reaction in Genesis 28:17 that he does fear God, though he is a blessing-thief. It is Laban who enjoys much of the benefit from Jacob's years of work. There is more than one (unhappy) wife in Jacob's household. While children are born, infertility is an ongoing issue. The happiness the psalmist promises is not what Jacob experiences, and what of the women who are caught up in the confusion? A preacher might take this opportunity to bring the psalm and this part of the Jacob cycle into conversation, complicating a too-easy correlation between faith and material/familial blessing. Because of these issues, Psalm 128 should not be read without interpretation. Now, as then, there are God-fearers who long in vain for the dignity of fair wages for their work, or dream of family dinners that have not materialized.

ANGELA DIENHART HANCOCK

Proper 12 (Sunday between July 24 and July 30 inclusive)

Romans 8:26–39

²⁶Likewise the Spirit helps us in our weakness; for we do not know how to pray as we ought, but that very Spirit intercedes with sighs too deep for words. ²⁷And God, who searches the heart, knows what is the mind of the Spirit, because the Spirit intercedes for the saints according to the will of God.

²⁸We know that all things work together for good for those who love God, who are called according to his purpose. ²⁹For those whom he foreknew he also predestined to be conformed to the image of his Son, in order that he might be the firstborn within a large family. ³⁰And those whom he predestined he also called; and those whom he called he also justified; and those whom he justified he also glorified.

³¹What then are we to say about these things? If God is for us, who is against us? ³²He who did not withhold his own Son, but gave him up for all of us, will he not with him also give us everything else? ³³Who will bring any charge against God's elect? It is God who justifies. ³⁴Who is to condemn? It is Christ Jesus, who died, yes, who was raised, who is at the right hand of God, who indeed intercedes for us. ³⁵Who will separate us from the love of Christ? Will hardship, or distress, or persecution, or famine, or nakedness, or peril, or sword? ³⁶As it is written,

> "For your sake we are being killed all day long;
> we are accounted as sheep to be slaughtered."

³⁷No, in all these things we are more than conquerors through him who loved us. ³⁸For I am convinced that neither death, nor life, nor angels, nor rulers, nor things present, nor things to come, nor powers, ³⁹nor height, nor depth, nor anything else in all creation, will be able to separate us from the love of God in Christ Jesus our Lord.

Commentary 1: Connecting the Reading with Scripture

There are at least three important features to this reading, each an essential part of Paul's declaration: his thoughts on the work of the Spirit, understanding God's purposes, and finding meaning in a confusing time.

Though Romans 8:26–27 seems to be a separate thought from what precedes it, it is not. These verses actually continue the theme of previous paragraphs, but shift from the future to the present. Paul says that as children of God, made so through faith in Christ's sacrifice, we can have confidence in our future salvation and assurance for our present challenges. Our "groaning" for the consummation of our adoption acknowledges the eschatological "already but not yet" dilemma of faith. The indwelling of the Spirit offers us something for both realities: it enables us to endure our present suffering, and it gives us hope for what is to come. The Spirit knows our weaknesses and yearnings intimately. Paul even speaks of our need to have the Spirit intercede for us at the deepest level of our yearnings, things we are often unable to recognize or express.

"And God, who searches the heart, knows . . ." (Rom. 8:27) is a beautiful phrase that works nicely with the psalm choices in the lectionary. The intimacy and mindfulness of God is a relational theme Paul shares with the psalmists (Rom. 2:16; 1 Cor. 4:5; Phil. 4:7). Seeing God as a heart-searcher offers a moving image of tenderness and closeness. This stands in contrast to images of a distant and uncaring God and calls us instead to the covenant language of a God who wants to be in relationship (cf. Gen. 9:1–17). That relationship is clearly seen in the lectionary passage from 1 Kings, which portrays the closeness of God to Solomon's deepest yearnings.

Paul positions the Spirit for its work here, a dimension of the Trinity that is often overlooked, but of great meaning to those who suffer. This begs for a word on the place of suffering in the Christian life. Some have argued that suffering is redemptive; in most cases it is not, and Paul's writing does not support that view. Those who are ill, enslaved, or abused do not experience redemption because of their plight. This is a critical distinction that must be made, especially for women and minorities. Only suffering that is accepted freely and without coercion (mental or physical)—in love or for the cause of justice—is redemptive. Such a perspective makes one mindful of Dr. Martin L. King Jr., who said, "We must accept finite disappointment, but never lose infinite hope."[1]

Romans 8:28–30 has been debated through the years, occasionally offering up some bad theology. This is not a Pollyanna passage of blind optimism. Paul is familiar with pain, suffering, and persecution. He is addressing the question of how to live faithfully in the midst of these things. He is suggesting not that God intended these things to happen or that they work for human good but, rather, that God can use them for good.

It may also be productive here to explore God's intentions and the concept of being "called" and set apart, which Paul uses to begin his letters to the Romans, the Corinthians, and the Galatians, as well as in Romans 9:11–17. It is a concept of ordination, not for a few, but for all followers of Christ, to live in a challenging and liminal time that can sustain, justify, and glorify them.

A productive exploration of God's intentions can be seen in this week's lectionary selections from the Genesis story of Jacob and Rachel. Laban tricks Jacob, who tricked Esau. On the face of it, this is an ironic retribution story. Jacob's desire to wed Rachel forces him to defy custom, particularly the birth-order rights and expectations of that society. God's promise is still fulfilled, despite human deception and pain—not because of it.

In 8:28 Paul shifts the focus away from suffering toward an emphasis on the good. Inevitably one asks, "What is good?" It is useful here to concentrate on Paul's idea of "conformation." The highest good for humanity is to love God, to be conformed to the image of Christ, and to be loved by God. God is (and has always been) at work in us seeking to conform us to, or make us like, Christ. We are predestined for God's love.

It is a wide and expansive love that can be seen in Jesus' parables in the lectionary readings, which all seek to answer the question, What is the realm of God like? In them Jesus shows that God is a God of extreme love, who will go to any length on our behalf. In Matthew 13:45–46 Jesus says, "Again, the kingdom of heaven is like a merchant in search of fine pearls; on finding one pearl of great value, he went and sold all that he had and bought it." For Paul this is the miracle of conversion: heirs to God's love, we become full members of the redeemed family. Conversion here is not so much a changing of religion, as it is a change of heart as we respond to God's grace.

Arriving at Romans 8:31, we are struck by the sense that Paul is concluding the argument he has been making since chapter 5, building to an eloquent climax. Like an able lawyer summing up in front of the jury during a high-stakes trial, he speaks with confidence of the case he has made. He posits seven animated questions and emphatic answers, each offering a picture of a loving and gracious God that no force or calamity can defeat.

Paul asks, "If God is for us, who can be against us?" It is his most basic assumption: if God was willing to sacrifice Jesus on our behalf, then there is nothing to prevent God from prevailing against any other foe. The allusion to the binding of Isaac is clear. Where God intervened to stop Abraham from sacrificing Isaac (Gen. 22), God went further and did not intervene in the sacrifice of Jesus. From Isaac's offspring came the people of Israel, but from Christ's

---

1. Martin Luther King Jr., *A Gift of Love: Sermons from Strength to Love and Other Preaching* (Boston: Beacon Press, 2012), 98.

spiritual offspring, through baptism, came a new humanity (see Gal. 3:6–18).

Paul arrives at his closing in verse 35 with a list of sufferings. It does not matter whether this is addressed to the church in Rome or to all the churches he has visited. It could also be a recitation of pain he has personally endured. However one reads the verse, Paul points us to the cross and Christ's suffering and death, and through it to Christ's resurrection, his basis for confidence and hope.

Then Paul reaches the climax of his argument and his entire theology (8:37–39), with one of the greatest statements of assurance ever written.

The message is that misfortunes do not provide any evidence that God has abandoned us, and suffering is not God's final word. Evil exists but it will be overcome. The preacher would do well to help the congregation claim God's love in the face of tragedies such as the mass shootings in Sandy Hook, Las Vegas, and Pittsburgh, and the natural devastations wrought by hurricanes and tsunamis. It is the Christian confession that—in the midst of such tragedies and the ensuing challenges they bring—not even the evil associated with these events can separate us from God's love in Christ Jesus.

NICK CARTER

Commentary 2: Connecting the Reading with the World

Paul believes the world is at a turning point, uniting all humanity in a story of redemption. Things that divide us are passing away. God's cosmic plan for the healing and uniting of all humanity is on the brink of fulfillment. There are two signs of this: (1) the resurrection of Jesus, the first fruit of the death of death and rising to new being; (2) the infusion of the Spirit, encouraging and strengthening us with a faith that nothing can sabotage. God anticipates this cosmic renewal by electing an outpost of Gentiles to recognize how we are to live into the new age. The Anointed One is thus "firstborn within a large family" (Rom. 8:29).

As Karl Barth and Dietrich Bonhoeffer argue, this unprecedented revelation of the election of all humanity to salvation is the end of religion.[2] Christians sometimes have understood this to mean the end of other religions, especially Judaism, but this does not seem to be Paul's point. He does not imagine that Christ's coming creates a Christian church, with creeds, pastors, hymnbooks, national meetings, ordination exams, and the rest. The end of religion means: (1) the ethnic and religious differences among human beings no longer have validity; (2) religious practices and beliefs are valid only in light of the Spirit, not for themselves; (3) salvation is not merely personal but is a cosmic reality that includes all of humanity in a new way of life governed by love and mercy.

Two thousand years later, we might ask, how are we to live within our religion (Christianity) when religion has come to an end? We are in the position of first-century Jews, who (rightly) love their religion and are not eager to overthrow precious practices for the naked nearness of the divine Spirit. How do we live within a religion, and also beyond it? As we see in Romans 9, Paul is sad that Jews have trouble accepting radical faith. I believe he would be no less saddened by Christianity's preference for its religion over radical faith in the outrageous generosity of God.

We are seeing the decline of mainstream Christian churches and seminaries in North America and Europe. Many Christians feel underfed by their tradition; young people are less willing to continue going to church. People feel wounded and rejected, or alienated by dull doctrines, lifeless morality, banal forgiveness. Seminarians' enthusiasm can be snuffed out by a legalistic church. It can feel as if the Spirit has been exiled from our faith.

---

2. I am thinking of Karl Barth's *Letter to the Romans* and Dietrich Bonhoeffer's *Letters and Papers from Prison*. Both of these works decry the dissolution of Christianity into national culture. That is, "religion" is this cultural deployment of religious symbols to justify the dominance of one group by another. Religion in this sense is the opposite of the gospel, which invites us to have faith directly in God and to recognize the unity of all human beings as elected by God's love.

What would it mean for the church to relativize the very things that make Christianity a religion, in favor of the new creation emerging through the inbreaking of the Spirit? How can we continue to witness as the "family" that welcomes the new age? Can we imagine our denomination or congregation becoming open to people we have excluded or alienated? To new practices or styles of worship? New ministries to young people? New relationships to people of other faiths? Can we allow the Spirit to intercede for us when we do not know how to pray?

How will we minister to military veterans suffering from moral injury?[3] Soldiers, addicts, and trauma survivors often find spiritual succor outside anything Christianity has to offer. How might we resist drawing on our playbook of sin and forgiveness, and instead sit and listen to what vital word the Spirit might have for them? What movement of the Spirit could help a community enduring police violence, or a church discovering itself complicit in sexual misconduct? How might worship move from the pews into nature, where we might witness its beauty and commit ourselves to its protection?

Old Testament Professor Yolanda Norton recently preached at a Beyoncé mass that I attended. Some Christians were shocked by the introduction of her music into an Episcopal Communion service. I myself was not familiar with Beyoncé's music. This midweek service, normally drawing fifty people, drew nine hundred. Gay and straight, every color and ethnicity, homeless, affluent, Christian, curious: all gathered at Grace Cathedral and witnessed an explosion of womanist wisdom that left everyone dancing, crying, singing. For a moment the Spirit was unleashed, and the power and beauty of the outcasts were unveiled. "Empire never falls lightly," Norton preached. "Sometimes we call it racism. . . . You call it homophobia; we call it heterosexual aggression; and tonight, we call it empire." Then she concluded: "Rage with love—love alone—undoes empire."[4] The intoxicated joy and weeping of young gay men, the affirming nods of elderly black women testified to the Spirit's "sighs too deep for words"—and to Christ's relentless love that made us all "more than conquerors." Beyond religion, in this land of the Spirit, we all recognized each other as elect.

Churches are finding other ways of living into Paul's vision of the gospel. The Presbyterian Church (U.S.A.) has included the Immigrant's Creed in the 2018 *Book of Common Worship*, a vivid reminder that God chose to become incarnate not only among the poor, but among refugees. One congregation has placed a crèche in its yard, with a fence around Joseph and Mary, graphically illustrating the distance between a biblical and a political response to immigrants.

Paul inspires in us confidence that all humanity is predestined to the glory of a cosmos transfigured by divine goodness that cherishes and celebrates each of us. Whatever makes us feel condemned or alienated is itself rejected by Paul. Whatever makes us condemn others is likewise rejected. He concludes this passage with the stirring words of confidence that in our deepest trials, in our sense of doubt or guilt, in persecution, grief, or oppression, nothing in heaven or earth or below the earth can separate us from the love of God.

These overfamiliar words may seem mere sentimentality. Even when we cannot share this confidence or when we cannot welcome the stranger at our gates or love the enemy or imagine the ecstatic spark of the Divine outside our order of worship, the Spirit sighs within us, perhaps weary of our small vision of religion. The Spirit enflames a deep longing for God's generosity that leaps beyond every boundary we put up.

As Paul acknowledges, humanity is limited by its propensity to sin. What speaks of this sin more clearly than our inability to recognize God's love for humanity and compassion for the earth? Reconsider how religion itself has limited the Spirit's urging. We imagine that we or those

---

3. Shira Maguen and Brett Litz, "Moral Injury in the Context of War," US Department of Veterans Affairs, https://www.ptsd.va.gov/professional/treat/cooccurring/moral_injury.asp; "What Is Moral Injury," Syracuse University, http://moralinjuryproject.syr.edu/about-moral-injury/.

4. Tony Bravo, "Grace Cathedral's Beyoncé Mass Draws Faithful Crowd of 900-Plus," *San Francisco Chronicle* (April 25, 2018), https://www.sfchronicle.com/news/article/Grace-Cathedral-s-Beyonce-Mass-draws-faithful-12865544.php.

we reject—LGBTQ, immigrant, too liberal, too conservative—are condemned by God. We suffer the twin weaknesses of shame for ourselves and denigration of others.

Paul reveals these weaknesses to be mere fantasy. Who can condemn when Christ has shown us how desperately God loves the world? This is the positive version of his point at the beginning of chapter 2: Who are we to condemn one another, if God has judged us righteous? The end of religion is the removal of the veil over God's intention for humanity. It reveals God's unimaginable love and graciousness, a love that may infuse, but is not dependent upon, law, church, or religion itself.

WENDY FARLEY

Proper 12 (Sunday between July 24 and July 30 inclusive)

Matthew 13:31–33, 44–52

³¹He put before them another parable: "The kingdom of heaven is like a mustard seed that someone took and sowed in his field; ³²it is the smallest of all the seeds, but when it has grown it is the greatest of shrubs and becomes a tree, so that the birds of the air come and make nests in its branches."

³³He told them another parable: "The kingdom of heaven is like yeast that a woman took and mixed in with three measures of flour until all of it was leavened. . . .

⁴⁴"The kingdom of heaven is like treasure hidden in a field, which someone found and hid; then in his joy he goes and sells all that he has and buys that field.

⁴⁵"Again, the kingdom of heaven is like a merchant in search of fine pearls; ⁴⁶on finding one pearl of great value, he went and sold all that he had and bought it.

⁴⁷"Again, the kingdom of heaven is like a net that was thrown into the sea and caught fish of every kind; ⁴⁸when it was full, they drew it ashore, sat down, and put the good into baskets but threw out the bad. ⁴⁹So it will be at the end of the age. The angels will come out and separate the evil from the righteous ⁵⁰and throw them into the furnace of fire, where there will be weeping and gnashing of teeth.

⁵¹"Have you understood all this?" They answered, "Yes." ⁵²And he said to them, "Therefore every scribe who has been trained for the kingdom of heaven is like the master of a household who brings out of his treasure what is new and what is old."

Commentary 1: Connecting the Reading with Scripture

Following two substantial agricultural parables about the rule of God in the world (Matt. 13:1–9, 24–30), Jesus presents five shorter tales: two wedged between the wheat/weeds parable, three coming after its explanation. Along with another seed sower (vv. 31–32), Jesus features a baker woman (v. 33), a treasure finder (v. 44), a merchant (vv. 45–46), and fishermen (vv. 47–50). All of these parables illustrate the work of God's kingdom in heaven-and-earth and human responses to it.

In good pedagogical fashion, Jesus wraps up his parable discourse (13:1–50) with a test question to his disciples: "Have you understood all this?" Whether from overconfidence, typical of Peter and others (14:28–30; 16:21–22; 17:4–6; 26:31–35) or from reticence to admit their confusion, Jesus' students answer, "Yes" (13:51). Jesus then commissions them as teacher-scribes who function like household managers (v. 52).

For the sake of thematic affinity, we may group the concluding five parables into two pairs (vv. 31–33/vv. 44–46) plus one (vv. 47–50), before unpacking Jesus' final comments about scribal responsibility (vv. 51–52).

The parables of the Mustard Seed (13:31–32) and the Yeast (13:33) convey elements of *mystery* and *hospitality* integral to God's economy. The mystery angle relates to the amazing growth of God's kingdom from seemingly trivial beginnings. The mustard seed, proverbially known as "the smallest of all seeds," sprouts first into a "shrub" (NRSV) or "garden plant" (NIV) and then "becomes a tree": a remarkable product from an inauspicious source. Likewise, a baker woman "mixes"—or better, "hides," as the Greek term connotes (see KJV, ESV, CEB)—a small amount of yeast into "three measures of flour" (about fifty pounds), causing the entire batch to rise and yield over a hundred loaves of bread. Absent modern knowledge of botany and chemistry, the untraceable processes of growth would seem mysterious indeed.

The salutary work of the yeast particularly surprises, since it is a spoiled, infectious ingredient. Moreover, yeast is a strictly *forbidden* element in the annual Passover meal. Not only is yeast prohibited in baking, evoking Israel's urgent exodus from slavery (there was no time to let leavened bread rise), but all traces of yeast must be eliminated from houses and lands, on penalty of being "cut off from the congregation" (Exod. 12:8–20; 13:3–10). In normal, settled times, however, time and space allow for small amounts of a fungal element with a peculiar symbolic history to enrich the people's lives with delicious, abundant bread. Overall, then, Jesus' parable of the Yeast illustrates God's remarkable *transformative* work for maximal good. In everyday life, God—imaged here, not incidentally, as a domestic working woman[1]—works with and through spoiled "yeast" (like poisonous "weeds" in 13:25) to realize God's flourishing purpose for all creation (see Rom. 8:12–39).

The transformational effects of God's right-making rule on a corrupt society become more evident in the hospitality factor associated with both mustard seed and yeast vignettes. The mustard plant in Israel's land can grow into a modest tree ten to fifteen feet tall with thick enough trunk and branches to sustain small "birds of the air" (13:32).[2] While Matthew's Jesus affirms God's avian creatures as objects of God's care (6:26), he more immediately associates birds with the evil one who snatches God's word (seed) from callous hearts (vv. 4, 19). Accordingly, the mustard tree's sheltering of birds represents the gracious welcome of God's household to outsiders, even to enemies (see 5:43–48; 9:9–13; 11:18–19). Similarly, the baker woman scarcely prepares a hundred loaves for her immediate family; she serves the wider community, perhaps readying for a party or banquet. Though Jesus provides no guest list, the "rotten" pinch of yeast also hints at the open messianic table of God's realm, inclusive of "tax collectors and sinners" (9:10–13) and invitees "both good and bad" (22:8–10).

The next parable pair features themes of *finding* something of utmost value (buried treasure and a precious pearl, vv. 44–45) and *selling* everything to acquire it. The analogy to the "kingdom of heaven" does not mean one must buy a ticket into a "heavenly" venue. In Matthew, "heaven" stands for "God" (as in the English idiom, "Heaven help us"), and "kingdom" represents the orbit of God's dynamic activity, not a static locale. Jesus' point is that human participation in God's cosmic right-making work—"on earth as it is in heaven," 6:10)—is truly worth everything we have. Jesus develops this point further in his encounter with a wealthy inquirer, enjoining the rich man to "sell your possessions, and give the money to the poor" (19:21). God's kingdom is first and foremost a community of care for the least and lowliest ("Blessed are the poor in spirit, for theirs is the kingdom of heaven," 5:3).

Amid the similarity of the two find-and-sell parables, some distinctive elements emerge. Unlike the merchant whose business propels his "search of fine pearls," the person who finds the hidden trove "in a field" seems to stumble upon it (no map marked X). Then he opts to rehide the treasure before buying the field, whereas the merchant purchases the most valuable pearl straightaway. While we can appreciate that people may variously find their way to God, by accident or deliberative quest, the rehiding move seems less appropriate. Why would the finder relocate the treasure, except to keep anyone else from nabbing it? Maybe this concealment links with the baker woman's "hiding" (Jesus uses the same verb in 13:33 and 44) the yeast in the dough for the good of her larger feeding project, hinting that the treasure should also be shared with the wider community.

Lest one think that opportunities for seeking God's kingdom and being transformed are limitless, the final parable reprises the fiery last judgment scene sifting the wheat from the weeds (vv. 37–43), only now the angels separate out good and bad fish (vv. 47–50). The shift

---

1. Barbara E. Reid, "Beyond Petty Pursuits and Wearisome Widows: Three Lukan Parables," *Interpretation* 53 (2002): 284–94.
2. L. W. Koch, "Brassica nigra," in Harold N. Moldenke and Alma L. Moldenke, *Plants of the Bible* (New York: Dover, 1986), 59–62.

from land to sea, from farmer to fishermen, expands the scope of God's creative realm; the net-casting image particularly relates to Jesus' commissioning his disciples to "fish for people" (4:18–22).

So what should Jesus' followers do with his parable discourse? Understand its contents surely (v. 51), but beyond that, they must undertake their own teaching mission as "scribes . . . trained for the kingdom of heaven" (v. 52). Scribes (and Pharisees) represented the chief scriptural-legal scholars in Jewish life, responsible for interpreting the Law (Torah) in contemporary society (see 5:20; 9:3, 11, 14; 23:2–3, 13, 23–29). They trained for this vocation under the mentorship of venerable teachers.

As scribe-scholars in the messianic community, Jesus' disciples, like their master-teacher, must function like a householder "who brings out of his treasure what is new and what is old" (13:52). The verb rendered "bring out/forth" in most English versions typically means "throw/cast out" (*ekballō*).[3] Jesus thus calls his student teachers to clear their minds of preconceived notions in order to grasp fully the power and profundity of his radical instruction about God's inbreaking kingdom.

In Matthew's wider context, however, this fresh realization of God's way in Christ by no means constitutes a rejection or replacement of God's scripturally rooted revelation in the past, but rather a dynamic renewing, a *filling-full* of God's right-making, justice-enacting rule unfolded in the "law and prophets" (5:17–20; see 5:21–48).

F. SCOTT SPENCER

Commentary 2: Connecting the Reading with the World

Matthew 13:31–33, 44–52 provides preachers with vivid, concrete imagery from the teaching of Jesus concerning the kingdom or reign of God in the world. Here preachers will gain much insight for sermons by paying attention to the integral relation between the content and form of the parables and preaching, as Jesus draws from scenes in the world of everyday life that is familiar to his listeners. He depicts the coming of God's reign in ordinary, well-known surroundings. Preachers should not approach the parables as mere "illustrations" of a concept, principle, or application that can be extracted from the stories, images, and conditions spoken by Jesus. To do so reduces preaching from the parables to ideas, principles, or rules to live by, a move that, in practice, actually suggests that God is not active in the world, thus leaving the world to itself.

Abstract preaching renders the church "invisible" to the world. It is not coincidental that the parables of the Treasure and the Merchant are stories of concrete human action in the world that show the full commitment of one's whole self to God. The concrete nature of the parables invites us to preach in a similar manner: to summon the church to living fully in a world ruled by God through the crucified and risen Jesus.

The parables for this Sunday raise an important question that is worth the preacher's attention: how can the power of God and the freedom of human beings be reconciled? Gerhard Lohfink addresses this question clearly:

> How then, does God's omnipotence reach its goal in the world?—only through people and their freedom. It happens only through the fact that people are drawn and moved by *that* which they can desire with their whole hearts and with their whole might. But apparently it is only possible for them to desire in freedom what God also desires if they see, vividly, the beauty of God's cause, so that they experience joy and even passionate desire for the thing that God wills to do in the world, and this passion for God and God's cause is greater than all human self-centeredness.[4]

---

3. Peter Phillips, "Casting Out the Treasure: A New Reading of Matthew 13.52," *Journal for the Study of the New Testament* 31 (2008): 3–24.
4. Gerhard Lohfink, *Does God Need the Church? Toward a Theology of the People of God*, trans. Linda M. Maloney (Collegeville, MN: Liturgical Press, 1999), 47; emphasis in the original.

What is confusing about the parables is the way God's character and activity are imagined in small and insignificant ways. A mustard seed is the size of a pin head, and yet it grows steadily into a bush with branches like a tree. Amazingly, God chooses to begin small, as with the call of Abraham and Sarah, but in God's good time God will accomplish God's plan, reign, and work of salvation in the world.

A similar characteristic of God's work in the world can be seen in the parable of Leaven used in the baking of bread (13:33). Leaven works within the dough quietly, slowly, and steadily, finally bringing about a complete transformation of the dough into something delicious and nourishing.

Preaching from these parables will call the church to endure faithfully in, with, and for a world that does not acknowledge the kingdom coming in Christ. To say the reign of God is hidden does not mean it is nonexistent. God's revelation both conceals and reveals itself in the world. Its smallness and insignificance according to the world's standards are not challenges to be overcome or obstacles to be removed, since God is sovereign and acts through the freedom by which human beings respond to God's humble self-giving act in Jesus.

Discipleship, or *The Cost of Discipleship* as it is commonly known, is the most popular of Dietrich Bonhoeffer's works.[5] While widely seen as a devotional classic, what is often overlooked is that Bonhoeffer wrote *Discipleship* to be a handbook for preachers in the Confessing Church, a small, illegal network of congregations whose confession of the gospel formed the basis for resisting the idolatrous rule of Adolf Hitler and Nazism. Bonhoeffer offers a challenging picture of the preacher's calling to be made small and insignificant in order to be a faithful witness to God's Word spoken in the incarnate, crucified, and risen Christ. In his time, such preaching was perceived as weak and foolish, compared to the impressive and inspiring propaganda communicated by Nazi officials and Germany's political leaders.

Bonhoeffer's comments call attention to the limits of preaching: "But the Word of God is so weak that it suffers to be despised and rejected by people. For the Word, there are such things as hardened hearts and locked doors. The Word accepts the resistance it encounters and bears it." Bonhoeffer admits this is a "cruel insight; nothing is impossible for the idea, but for the gospel there are impossibilities." The Word is weaker than presumably stronger and more effective methods chosen by both politicians and preachers. However, such preaching avoids the resistance, rejection, and suffering that accompany concrete speech and obedience to Christ. Bonhoeffer comments, "They [preachers] should not want to be strong when the Word is weak."[6] "The Word cannot be forced onto the world, since the strength of the Word is its lowliness, the strength of God's mercy which is able to move sinners to repentance from the depths of their hearts."[7]

Hearing the Word and perceiving God's reign in the world evoke great joy, desire, and energy. Jesus points to the conditions in which a common laborer discovers a treasure and a merchant finds a priceless pearl (13:44–46). In both instances, Jesus points to the overwhelming joy and desire out of which the laborer and the merchant act in response to the tangible reality of God's reign, which is sought and received as God's gift.

A sermon from these two parables can be made more concrete, or "worldly," by inviting lay persons to share stories of discovering the joy that comes in seeking and serving God's reign in the world. Rather than through explanation, the joy of participating in God's work in the world is communicated best through testimony that calls attention to the beauty of a life offered faithfully to God in serving others through the shared tasks and responsibilities of everyday life.

The other parable for this Sunday is about a large net capable of drawing a great catch of fish (vv. 47–50). The extraordinary attractiveness of God's reign is capable of drawing many

---

5. Dietrich Bonhoeffer, *Discipleship*, vol. 4 of *Dietrich Bonhoeffer Works*, ed. Geffrey B. Kelly and John D. Godsey, trans. Barbara Green and Reinhard Krauss (Minneapolis: Fortress, 2005).
6. Bonhoeffer, *Discipleship*, 4:130, 187.
7. Bonhoeffer, *Discipleship*, 4:173–74.

people to itself. However, God acts in the world without distinctions, so that the final "catch" of the kingdom is discernible only to God, who is worthy to judge the hearts, loves, and desires of people. God will separate the good fish from the rotten fish. A well-known prayer from Christian tradition gives voice to the disposition that is appropriate for preaching and hearing these parables: "Almighty God, to you all hearts are open, all desires known, and from you no secrets are hid: Cleanse the thoughts of our hearts by the inspiration of your Holy Spirit, that we may perfectly love you, and worthily magnify your holy Name; through Christ our Lord. Amen."

The parables invite preachers to become students of the kingdom (vv. 51–52), leaders who are capable of drawing from the storehouse of God's wisdom, both old and new, past and present, to provide what the church needs to endure faithfully, offering itself to God for the good of the world.

MICHAEL PASQUARELLO III

Proper 13 (Sunday between July 31 and August 6 inclusive)

Isaiah 55:1–5 and Genesis 32:22–31
Psalm 145:8–9, 14–21 and
   Psalm 17:1–7, 15

Romans 9:1–5
Matthew 14:13–21

Isaiah 55:1–5

> ¹Ho, everyone who thirsts,
>   come to the waters;
> and you that have no money,
>   come, buy and eat!
> Come, buy wine and milk
>   without money and without price.
> ²Why do you spend your money for that which is not bread,
>   and your labor for that which does not satisfy?
> Listen carefully to me, and eat what is good,
>   and delight yourselves in rich food.
> ³Incline your ear, and come to me;
>   listen, so that you may live.
> I will make with you an everlasting covenant,
>   my steadfast, sure love for David.
> ⁴See, I made him a witness to the peoples,
>   a leader and commander for the peoples.
> ⁵See, you shall call nations that you do not know,
>   and nations that do not know you shall run to you,
> because of the LORD your God, the Holy One of Israel,
>   for he has glorified you.

Genesis 32:22–31

> ²²The same night he got up and took his two wives, his two maids, and his eleven children, and crossed the ford of the Jabbok. ²³He took them and sent them across the stream, and likewise everything that he had. ²⁴Jacob was left alone; and a man wrestled with him until daybreak. ²⁵When the man saw that he did not prevail against Jacob, he struck him on the hip socket; and Jacob's hip was put out of joint as he wrestled with him. ²⁶Then he said, "Let me go, for the day is breaking." But Jacob said, "I will not let you go, unless you bless me." ²⁷So he said to him, "What is your name?" And he said, "Jacob." ²⁸Then the man said, "You shall no longer be called Jacob, but Israel, for you have striven with God and with humans, and have prevailed." ²⁹Then Jacob asked him, "Please tell me your name." But he said, "Why is it that you ask my name?" And there he blessed him. ³⁰So Jacob called the place Peniel, saying, "For I have seen God face to face, and yet my life is preserved." ³¹The sun rose upon him as he passed Penuel, limping because of his hip.

Commentary 1: Connecting the Reading with Scripture

The preacher beginning to explore Genesis 32:22–31 and Isaiah 55:1–5 should pay careful attention to how both God and the people act within these passages. The story of Jacob and his family crossing the Jabbok and wrestling with God and then God's reassurances to a chosen people struggling with their identity while living in captivity are filled with promises, action, transformation, and healing. God forgives, reassures, calls, speaks, cries out, wrestles with, comforts, and names. The people are equally engaged: questioning, running, walking, moving, crossing, and witnessing. The theological imagination included within these texts offers powerful metaphors for proclamation.

Marked by the Struggle. Traditionally, interpreters of the story of Jacob wrestling with God on his return to the land of his birth focus on the patriarch's personal struggle. Within the larger literary context, the story connects to Jacob's meeting with his brother Esau, which occurs after his deception of their father Isaac. Jacob's confrontation with God shapes his meeting with Esau (Gen. 33:1–17).

Jacob crosses the ford of the Jabbok with his household, his four wives, and eleven children. The location and time of Jacob's struggle are important in that he encounters a mysterious adversary near daybreak, suggesting that the cloak of night will not fully disclose the man's identity. They wrestle, and Jacob refuses to let his assailant go without a blessing. A heavy blow to his hip forever marks Jacob. The one whom Jacob wrestles changes Jacob's name and calls him Israel ("struggle"), "for you have striven with God and with humans, and have prevailed" (32:28).

Jacob asks the man his name but receives no reply. Scholars suggest that God refuses to disclose God's name because it was not common for God to be seen (32:30) and the power of naming in the Hebrew Bible bears with it the power to control. Jacob ultimately knows the One whom he is dealing with and names the place Peniel, meaning "face of God." These interpretations suggest that Jacob truly receives God's blessing when he refuses to let God go.

Other biblical scholars offer another perspective with great possibilities for preaching. One's understanding of this passage expands when the longer story and variety of characters within it are considered. Jacob does not travel alone; Leah, Rachel, Bilhah, Zilpah, and eleven children are with him. The Hebrew terms used to describe the waters the family cross may also be important for interpretation. Jacob crosses the "ford" (Heb. *ma'abar*) of the Jabbok (from the Hebrew root meaning "to empty itself") with his household and then crosses the water again. This second time they cross, the term used (Heb. *hannakhal*) is often translated the "stream."

One consideration worthy of attention is that a stream is thought to be smaller than a ford and easy to step over, which implies that Jacob's entire household could have witnessed the event. Another consideration is that the whole household appears to be crossing the waters at night. These factors raise a variety of hermeneutical questions. Would a male head of the household force his family to cross the river again just to be alone? More important, is Jacob's struggle with God witnessed by his family, thereby including the women and children within the blessing? Is Jacob trying to protect his household or using them as a sort of buffer?[1] There is a disruptive undercurrent here emphasizing the importance of a larger family in securing God's blessing and embodying covenant promises. Both brothers prepare for their meeting as if they anticipate battle, but before Jacob greets Esau face-to-face, he presents his family (33:1). Leah, Rachel, Bilhah, and Zilpah and their children are key to healing wounds.

Poetry of the Prophet and Water for All Who Thirst. Isaiah 55:1–5 continues a familiar theme for Israel: the Davidic covenant and the inclusion of all peoples. Recall the context of Deutero-Isaiah, chapters 40–55. Within these chapters, the author expresses Israel's feelings of

---

1. Serge Frolov, "The Other Side of the Jabbok: Genesis 32 as a Fiasco of Patriarchy," *Journal for the Study of the Old Testament* 91 (2001): 41–59.

guilt for accepting the destruction of Jerusalem; lack of trust in a God who seemed to fail to save them; and God's reassurance of forgiveness, love, and power to create and transform. Read Isaiah 55 in connection with Isaiah 40, as these two chapters serve as bookends for Deutero-Isaiah and include everything significant said about God.

Isaiah 40 opens with a proclamation of God's comforting the people of Israel and raises questions about their mistrust. The Hebrew text is full of language urging plural and singular addressees to convey God's transformative purposes among the people. (Here, the preacher might highlight the many words of speaking, crying out, and lifting up the voice.) There is a sense of urgency in response to God's voice as it invites the movement even of hills, valleys, and mountains. The chapter ends with movement of the people: "they shall mount up with wings like eagles, they shall run and not be weary, they shall walk and not faint" (Isa. 40:31).

Isaiah 55 immediately follows a discussion of Zion (personified Jerusalem) with her children in chapter 54. Some scholars emphasize a style of instruction within Isaiah 55 that is typical of Wisdom literature (Prov. 9:1–5; Sir. 24:18–20). Rich themes for preaching emerge as Zion sings of barrenness, desolation, shame, and forsakenness (Isa. 54) and then celebrates Israel's fullness, coming together, and going out in joy and peace (Isa. 55). Worship leaders could work creatively with these two chapters by inviting congregations to read them responsively or antiphonally in worship.

Other scholars urge preachers to explore more deeply the significance of water imagery in verses 1–5. Isaiah 55 begins by calling the people to "come to the waters." The command reflects themes that had emerged in First Isaiah. First Isaiah remembers events in the last part of the eighth century BCE, when the northern kingdom of Israel has an alliance with Syria, and Judah lives under enormous threat, particularly from Assyria. Isaiah 8:7 says that "the Lord is bringing up against it the mighty flood waters of the River, the king of Assyria and all his glory; it will rise above all its channels and overflow all its banks." The waters, rain, and snow in Isaiah 55 will transform the community in another sense: they bring fullness from emptiness and peace out of distress.

Ultimately, the main idea that cannot be missed is that God's chosen ones are not the only partners in their liberation. God speaks to, draws in, and transforms through love and forgiveness. Even the Persian king Cyrus will participate in liberation of the exiles as he allows them to return home.[2]

Reflecting on the Connections. These passages specifically connect in their descriptions of a God who is forgiving, loving, powerful, and unrelenting, and in the way covenant people wrestle with God, even as they participate in God's acts of healing and liberation. Most important is to explore and emphasize an interpretation that moves beyond the personal and individual. God's forgiveness, powerful nature, and love as described in these passages extend far beyond an individual charismatic leader to family systems, whole communities, and then to all people, even those not known especially as chosen, but who are willing to incline their ears and listen.

ELIZABETH HINSON-HASTY

Commentary 2: Connecting the Reading with the World

On Isaiah. You have to love the expansiveness of a God who shouts, "Ho," who flings wide the doors to the banquet house, tops off the children's milk glasses, splashes around the chardonnay, and extends the terms of David's deal so that everyone is included in its embrace (Isa. 55:1–5). You have to love the lavishness of a God who envisions nations coming on the

---

2. I am indebted here to translation work and commentary presented by Johanna W. H. van Wijk-Bos in a lecture on Isaiah delivered at Louisville Presbyterian Theological Seminary, Louisville, KY, on April 3, 2013.

run and ancient Israel shining like a beacon. It is as if Isaiah believes that God's big business with humankind—the thing the heart of God is most after—is to call people to larger and larger versions of life together, to a big tent and a large life fueled and funded by God.

This is what the people of God celebrate today every time they approach the Communion table. Every time they offer each other the Cup that brims and the Loaf that stretches to feed all. This is what Jesus came for. Died for. This is what his resurrection points us to. This is how the Holy Spirit navigates the twenty-first-century church. Wooing and urging. Planting seeds of the ever-expanding love of God.

In a small Northern California town there lives a saint who knows a good deal about how God's love expands and includes. After a long life of service in her native North Dakota, Jo Gross retired to sunnier climes. Soon she found herself involved in establishing homeless shelters in local congregations around her new community. Looking back on the call that summoned her to what she calls "love in action," she told the story of a visit to New York City's Cathedral of St. John the Divine during the Feast of St. Francis.

> The cathedral was full of animals—all kinds of animals from monkeys to snakes—as well as an elephant and a camel walking down the center aisle. . . . It was a wild and wonderful celebration including Paul Winter on the soprano saxophone playing music from the St. Francis collection. But what really struck me was what happened as the priest lifted the bread for the Eucharist. From the balcony came a thundering drum roll and a blast of trumpets! . . . With this in mind, the next day our group participated in a soup kitchen on the lower east side of Manhattan. In two hours 847 men came off the street and through the line. I was asked to hand out bread as the men left the dining hall. As I held the bread box and watched the hundreds of hands reach in, I heard those words from the day before. A trumpet sounded inside of me and with every heartbeat, the drums began to roll. I knew that through this bread, I was intimately connected to the compassion of Jesus. This was his bread and the bread given to me at the cathedral was the same bread I was giving that day and the same bread broken in all the programs that followed, including that first shelter meal (served in this church).[3]

Sometimes the call is "Ho" (Isa. 55:1), sometimes a trumpet blast, sometimes a voice in the heart—but it is always the call of a big God. A God whose love extended through ancient Israel to "nations that you do not know and nations that do not know you" (v. 5) and a call that continues its love in action today as we invite others to the feast God has prepared.

On Genesis. It could be that the point of Genesis 32:22–31 is simply to explain how ancient Israel got its name. Maybe this text should be preached as a story about a name change, about how Jacob is endowed with the new power that a name change signals. The text may simply represent the work of a writer whose agenda it was to make King David's administration look good. Maybe we should understand this text in Bruno Bettelheim's terms and analyze it the way we analyze fairy tales. In which case, this is a kind of early Harry Potter story—about our desire to win a blessing or a magic agent from a grudging donor. However, it could also be that this is a story about testing. Testing, after all, is a major theme of the Abraham, Isaac, and Jacob stories.

The question this particular testing story raises is about timing. The timing of this test is decidedly odd. After a lifetime of not quite trusting the blessing, Jacob has finally gotten his feet going in the right direction. Why does God test him now? Perhaps the issue is persistence. "I have persisted with this human being," God reasons, "I need to know how far he will persist with me." Or "this human being has tested my persistence, it only seems right that I should find out about his." Or "one thing this human lacks," God may have thought, "is the strength that comes from passing a test." Or even "there is only one more thing I can do to convince him

---

3. Jo Gross, "The Bread Connection," a sermon preached at First Presbyterian Church, San Anselmo, CA, on April 29, 2018.

the blessing is his—to let him think he won it." The text gives us no insight into what God is thinking, just a picture of God wrestling Jacob, building his persistence muscle, and renewing the blessing upon him.

Testing is a way of blessing, the story claims. We know it is true for us too, though we are loath to admit it. Fortunately we have the testimony of those who have traveled the road before us to remind us. For example, there is the word of the great woman leader whose fifty-eight-year crusade may have launched more rotten eggs and tomatoes than had ever been thrown in the history of public speaking. The first breakthrough in her work for women's rights came after twenty years, when New York allowed married women to control their own property. Her ultimate goal, met when women were granted the vote, came a hundred years after Susan B. Anthony's birth and fourteen years after her death.

We could take the word of the grandmother who took a sexually abused eight-year-old into her home in the Deep South, during the Great Depression. The girl would not speak. Every morning for five years, as she braided the traumatized girl's hair, the grandmother would whisper encouragement into the child's ear. Finally the day came that the young Maya Angelou responded to her grandmother's persistence and found her voice.

There is also the testimony of the great contemporary preacher Linda Loving, who describes the long wrestling that prepares her to preach as "a cloud of free-floating anxiety I can never shake and have tried to befriend."[4] She describes finishing preparation in a way that is reminiscent of Jacob at dawn, limping away from the Jabbok. She says, "Finally, I cry. Yes, I do. I spent years thinking I was some kind of wacko who was surely in the wrong business. Then one day it dawned on me (by dawn's early light) that this is simply . . . how I finally surrender the sermon to the grace of God. Then I blow my nose, eat my cereal and go preach."[5] Wrestling with God encourages persistence; persistence enhances human capacity.

JANA CHILDERS

---

4. Linda Carolyn Loving, "Bird's Nest or Hornet's Nest?," in *Birthing the Sermon: Women Preachers on the Creative Process*, ed. Jana Childers (St. Louis: Chalice, 2001), 108.
5. Loving, "Bird's Nest or Hornet's Nest."

Proper 13 (Sunday between July 31 and August 6 inclusive)

Psalm 145:8–9, 14–21

⁸The LORD is gracious and merciful,
　　slow to anger and abounding in steadfast love.
⁹The LORD is good to all,
　　and his compassion is over all that he has made.
. . . .
¹⁴The LORD upholds all who are falling,
　　and raises up all who are bowed down.
¹⁵The eyes of all look to you,
　　and you give them their food in due season.
¹⁶You open your hand,
　　satisfying the desire of every living thing.
¹⁷The LORD is just in all his ways,
　　and kind in all his doings.
¹⁸The LORD is near to all who call on him,
　　to all who call on him in truth.
¹⁹He fulfills the desire of all who fear him;
　　he also hears their cry, and saves them.
²⁰The LORD watches over all who love him,
　　but all the wicked he will destroy.

²¹My mouth will speak the praise of the LORD,
　　and all flesh will bless his holy name forever and ever.

Psalm 17:1–7, 15

¹Hear a just cause, O LORD; attend to my cry;
　　give ear to my prayer from lips free of deceit.
²From you let my vindication come;
　　let your eyes see the right.

³If you try my heart, if you visit me by night,
　　if you test me, you will find no wickedness in me;
　　my mouth does not transgress.
⁴As for what others do, by the word of your lips
　　I have avoided the ways of the violent.
⁵My steps have held fast to your paths;
　　my feet have not slipped.

⁶I call upon you, for you will answer me, O God;
　　incline your ear to me, hear my words.
⁷Wondrously show your steadfast love,
　　O savior of those who seek refuge
　　from their adversaries at your right hand.
. . . .
¹⁵As for me, I shall behold your face in righteousness;
　　when I awake I shall be satisfied, beholding your likeness.

Connecting the Psalm with Scripture and Worship

Psalm 145:8–9, 14–21. Psalm 145 makes several appearances in the lectionary, with different verses taking center stage each time. Here we begin with God's grace, mercy, patience, and steadfast love in verse 8, which sets up a sweeping affirmation of the universal nature of God's care (Ps. 145:9). This account of divine generosity continues in verse 14, where God upholds the stumbling and lifts up the stooped over. Switching to direct address, the psalmist tells God that every hungry creature knows where to look for help, and God gives each the food they need when the time is right (v. 15). Indeed, God fulfills "the desire of every living thing," according to the psalmist, and is thoroughly just and kind (vv. 16–17).

What happens, though, to that indiscriminate care as the psalm continues? The wide-angle lens narrows in verse 18. Now the promise is to those who call on God "in truth," to those who "fear" and "love" God. The Lord will be near to such people, fulfill their longings, hear them, save them, and watch over them; but "the wicked" God will "destroy" (v. 20)—not ignore, not pass over, but annihilate. We pan out again for the final verse, as the psalmist sings that "all flesh" will bless God's name forever (v. 21).

What are we to make of this seeming tension between God's compassion for all living things (including, presumably, the unpleasant ones) and the care reserved for God-fearers? The psalmist somehow affirms both. Devout and wicked alike, apparently, are sustained by God's provision, but there is special attention for the unsteady, those bent low, those who know that they need God's help and say so. Is there any traversing these categories? Can a wicked person call on God and be saved? There is mystery in the relationship between divine and human action in Psalm 145, and in this regard it might be useful to one preaching from Isaiah 55:1–5.

Isaiah's prophecy to Israel in exile invites readers to enter a mystical marketplace where bartering is obsolete—but what, exactly, are we shopping for? Water, wine, milk, and bread, apparently, with "rich food" and nourishing words promised as well (Isa. 55:2–3). This is a place, an event, for hungry, thirsty people, and the speaker assures us that this all-you-can-eat buffet is free. Then why are we told to "come" and "buy" before we can eat (v. 1), and "listen" so that we might live (v. 3)? Why is anything required of us, if the whole point is that there are no price tags on these goods?

Again we are plunged into a paradox: God provides for God's people a bountiful feast, an unshakable covenant, a glorious future, *and* God expects human beings to get up and run toward these gifts as if their lives depend on it. Whatever grace is, it includes both the "all is ready" and the "come, buy and eat" (v. 1). The wise preacher will not try to explain away the mystery but name it with clarity and let it ferment.

Psalm 145 can serve as one illustration of the way Scripture holds together God's unconditional provision and God's relentless call for faith and obedience. A text like Philippians 2:12–13 also comes to mind, and one can detect this dance in the Gospel reading for the day, Matthew 14:13–21, as well. It is Jesus who multiplies the bread and fish that day on the lawn, yes, but he also puts the disciples right to work.

The verses of Psalm 145 alternate between third-person descriptions of God's goodness and first-person prayers addressed to God. For this reason it lends itself to a responsive reading, with a liturgist reciting the third-person verses (vv. 8–9, 14, 17–20) and the congregation voicing the sentences directed to God (vv. 15–16, 21).

Psalm 17:1–7, 15. The alternate set of readings pairs the story of Jacob wrestling with God (Gen. 32:22–31) with portions of Psalm 17. The psalmist is clearly in a difficult situation, falsely accused of some crime and physically threatened. There are hints in the psalm that the writer is holed up in a shrine for the night; a sort of prayer vigil for one, perhaps. What the psalmist wants from God is protection and vindication, but there is something deeper too, which becomes clear by the way the psalm ends.

The opening verses are a fearless appeal, asking God to listen, look, and test the writer, who pleads innocent to all charges: "you will find no wickedness in me" (Ps. 17:3). The psalmist describes a life of faithfulness: no violence, lips free from deceit, steps firmly on God's path. Some have been troubled by the confidence on display here, but it is clear that the psalmist does not make a universal claim to perfect holiness. This is the announcement of specific innocence in relation to particular accusations.

God is named by the psalmist as "savior," specifically of "those who seek refuge from their adversaries" (v. 7). What is the nature of the desired rescue? The omitted verse 13 asks God to get up and confront the predators, overthrowing them. Completely understandable. Yet the final verse of the psalm imagines the psalmist waking up in the morning "satisfied," not (necessarily) because all problems have been solved and enemies subdued, but because "I shall behold your face in righteousness" (v. 15). God's presence is named as the reason joy comes with the dawn, even though it is likely that trouble still awaits.

The Genesis text also describes someone with night terrors. Jacob is on the bank of a river and the brink of a reckoning, with wronged brother Esau getting closer all the time. The strange attack that follows lasts until dawn, and Jacob gets his bum hip and his blessing. What he marvels at, however, is the fact that he got so close to God, "face-to-face," and lived to tell the tale (Gen. 32:30).

Like Psalm 17, this story describes a night of struggle, an individual with some gumption, and a dawn that brings fresh perspective. We might say both of these texts are about someone trying to get God to do something, but they both end with the realization that the truest "blessing" is the encounter with God's own self, God's "face," God's being there. That God allows, even encourages, this sort of persuading, arguing, self-defensiveness from human beings—"innocent" and sneaky alike—is amazing, and Psalm 17 is a resource for a preacher who wants to explore this dimension of the Jacob narrative. Of course, neither of these texts answers all of our questions about what it means to "see God face-to-face"! Nevertheless it would be a fruitful issue to consider in a sermon about wrestling with God: how exactly is God present with those who will not let go of hope, particularly in situations of interpersonal conflict and crisis?

One effective way to pray Psalm 17 in worship is to use a congregational refrain after each set of verses; adding verses 8–9 will help with the flow. A logical grouping of the verses might be: 1–3, 4–7, and finally 8, 9, and 15. For the refrain, the simple Taizé chant "O Lord, Hear My Prayer" works beautifully.[1] Some may want to switch to the alternate chant text after the final set of verses ("The Lord Is My Song") to emphasize the change in tone that comes with verse 15.

ANGELA DIENHART HANCOCK

---

1. "O Lord, Hear My Prayer," with text adapted from Psalm 102:1–2 by the Taizé Community, 1982, 1991; music by Jacques Berthier, 1982. The chant may be found in *Glory to God: The Presbyterian Hymnal* (Louisville, KY: Westminster John Knox, 2013), 471.

Proper 13 (Sunday between July 31 and August 6 inclusive)

Romans 9:1–5

¹I am speaking the truth in Christ—I am not lying; my conscience confirms it by the Holy Spirit— ²I have great sorrow and unceasing anguish in my heart. ³For I could wish that I myself were accursed and cut off from Christ for the sake of my own people, my kindred according to the flesh. ⁴They are Israelites, and to them belong the adoption, the glory, the covenants, the giving of the law, the worship, and the promises; ⁵to them belong the patriarchs, and from them, according to the flesh, comes the Messiah, who is over all, God blessed forever. Amen.

Commentary 1: Connecting the Reading with Scripture

Some have posited that this short section is an interruption in Paul's argument from Romans 1–8 that resumes in chapters 12–16. It is probably better to see chapters 9–11 as an essential and heartfelt examination of the flip side of the same exposition. Here Paul wrestles with the consequences for Jews after his argument for the justification of the Gentiles. While often addressing specific issues in the churches he founded, it is important to see this dimension of Paul's mind, which is always sensitive to the broader consequences of his words. Nowhere is this clearer than in his letter to the church in Rome, a church he did not establish.

Jews were being persecuted in Rome, having been expelled by the imperial order of Emperor Claudius in 48 or 49 CE. Their situation was compounded by the Jewish riots in Alexandria, which led some to fear similar troubles might arise in Rome. For Roman authorities, there was little distinction between Jews and the new sect of Christians. For them, "Christianity" would not have been isolated from the fate of Jews throughout the empire. However, there is some evidence that the new Gentile Christians were anxious to distinguish themselves from the Jews and may have begun to argue for some superiority over them. Added to this dilemma is the ongoing resistance of the Jewish Christians to the inclusive position Paul had taken with regard to the Gentiles.

In order to address these concerns, Paul begins in Romans 9 with an abrupt shift in tone from the soaring heights of the end of chapter 8. Now the mood is solemn and almost oath-like. The reader can feel his heavy heart. It is his witness to the truth. In 9:2 he speaks of his "unceasing anguish" and the presence of a troubled conscience is unmistakable. For the audience of this letter, the shift would have been striking, particularly given that he has not yet said why he is so grief-laden, right on the heels of his glorious words of assurance in 8:37–39.

Preachers can marvel at this masterful change of pace, inviting listeners to a new emotional plane. The idea of a troubled conscience can be explored in several ways, taking cues perhaps from Twain's *Huckleberry Finn* or Shakespeare's *Macbeth*. However, Paul's grief is not driven so much by a sense of having sinned (he is sure he did the right thing), as by the consequences of his position (for those who fail to accept Christ) and fear of misunderstanding. Having a clear conscience is a recurrent theme for Paul (Rom. 9:1; 1 Cor. 8:1–13; Acts 24:16; 25:8), and it reveals that he is sensitive to the impact of what he says and does on those around him, in this case, for Israel and the challenge Christianity presents to individuals and families. Yet Paul's conscience, while anguished, is never wavering; he remains firm.

This passage also provides an opportunity to affirm the place of grief in the midst of our expressions of confidence and hope. Washington Irving supposedly once said: "There is a sacredness in tears. They are not the mark of weakness, but of power. They speak more eloquently than ten thousand tongues. They are the messengers of overwhelming grief, of deep contrition, and of unspeakable love."[1] It is appropriate to recognize that Paul was genuinely distressed over the consequences of his beliefs, particularly the rejection by Jewish Christians, thus leading him to go to great lengths to reconcile those beliefs with them and with Jewish tradition.

What does this inclusive theology mean for Jews, the original recipients of God's covenant? Paul does not directly say this is his purpose, but makes the transition to it by identifying with his religious roots, speaking of "my kindred according to the flesh" (Rom. 9:3). Of no small significance, he then says: "They are Israelites, and to them belong *the adoption*, the glory, the covenants . . ." (v. 4). Whereas in chapter 8 Paul has woven a masterful argument around the concept of adoption to include the Gentiles (8:15, 23), here he says the adoption belongs to the Jews! To his Gentile audience, surely nodding in agreement as they heard the argument prior to these words, this point is certainly unexpected. He then completes his recitation of Jewish distinctiveness—including a reminder of Jesus' Jewishness (v. 5)—ending with an "Amen," almost as a benediction of accepted truth.

The companion lectionary readings offer helpful grounds for exploring Paul's concerns of who is to be a part of the Christian family. The Isaiah passage aligns with Paul's wider message of inclusion. In Isaiah 55:1 God invites "everyone" to participate in the coming restoration and to enjoy abundance without price. The passage from Genesis 32 is well known: Jacob wrestles with the angel, a struggle that ends in something of a draw, and he receives the name Israel as a blessing.

In Every Respect Give Thanks

In our case let the whole body be saved in Christ Jesus, and let each man be subject to his neighbor, to the degree determined by his spiritual gift. The strong must not neglect the weak, and the weak must respect the strong. Let the rich support the poor; and let the poor give thanks to God, because He has given him someone through whom his needs may be met. Let the wise display his wisdom not in words but in good works. The humble person should not testify to his own humility, but leave it to someone else to testify about him. Let the one who is physically pure remain so and not boast, recognizing that it is someone else who grants this self-control. Let us acknowledge, brothers, from what matter we were made; who and what we were, when we came into the world; from what grave and what darkness he who made and created us brought us into this world, having prepared his benefits for us before we were born. Seeing, therefore, that we have all these things from him, we ought in every respect to give thanks to him, to whom be the glory for ever and ever. Amen.

1 Clement 38:1–4, in *The Apostolic Fathers*, ed. Michael W. Holmes (Grand Rapids: Baker, 2004), 71.

The pending meeting with Esau and Jacob's guilt and fear of revenge mark the context for this passage and may provide the necessary connection here. While it is clear that the wrestling is a physical one, there is plenty of reason for Jacob to have wrestled emotionally with God over what he had done and its consequences. The preacher could take the cue from Paul in Romans 9:1–2 and put it in conversation with Jacob's story, exploring how our choices affect others and how that can weigh on us. In Paul's case, we see courage to maintain his beliefs and sensitively reach out to include those he might have excluded. In Jacob's story, we see deception, fear, and then remorse (and, in Esau, a symbol of God's forgiveness and grace).

The selections from the two psalms (Pss. 17 and 145) provide contrasting views of faithfulness and truth—one of human faithfulness to God and the other of God's faithfulness. The first seems to have something to say to Paul's exclamation in Romans 9:1 that he is a

---

1. This quotation is widely attributed to Irving, but it is found without attribution in William C. Brown, ed., *The Mother's Assistant and Young Lady's Friend: July 1843, to July 1844* (Boston: William C. Brown, 1844).

truth-teller: "I am not lying." He is not looking for sympathy. Believing that one is telling the truth is empowering, but to stake that claim is not easy. Paul's position in the face of criticism and persecution takes courage. The poet Maya Angelou once said, "Courage is the most important of all the virtues, because without courage you can't practice any other virtue consistently. You can practice any virtue erratically, but nothing consistently without courage."[2]

The selection from Psalm 145 speaks of a faithful God who cares for "all who are falling" (Ps. 145:14), hungry, and dispossessed. The use of the word "all" here is important for its inclusiveness for everyone who believes in God. Paul's writing invites us to address the issue of "all" and contemporary issues of diversity and social inclusion/exclusion. A global migrant crisis has created staggering challenges for countries once known for their openness—not the least of which is the nation that claims the Statue of Liberty as one of its enduring symbols, remembering the memorable words of Emma Lazarus, "Give me your tired, your poor, your huddled masses yearning to breathe free." As the psalmist cries out, "The LORD is good to all, and [God's] compassion is over all that [God] has made" (v. 9).

NICK CARTER

Commentary 2: Connecting the Reading with the World

This passage begins Paul's long meditation on the relationship between Jews and Gentiles that concludes with the passionate assurance that all Israel will be saved: "as regards election, they are beloved. . . . God has imprisoned all in disobedience so that [God] may be merciful to all" (11:28, 32). There could hardly be a more ringing condemnation of Christian anti-Semitism or exclusivism. Paul is saddened, because he expected that his vision of the crucified and resurrected Messiah bringing an immediate redemption of history would be welcomed by Jews and Gentiles alike.

Few, however, shared Paul's view. Jews remained faithful to the God they knew through Torah obedience; few Gentiles converted. Post-Constantinian Christianity did not realize Paul's dream of a united humanity. This invites us to examine these passages for what they mean for us today, when our situation is vastly different from that of the Roman Empire and Paul's expectation of the transformation of history.

We might begin with Paul's sadness. Things he had hoped for and expected were not happening. It is easy to sympathize with that. Our own hopes for a more just world, the dismantling of racism, the cessation of gun violence, recovery from illness, and less fractious congregational meetings elude us. How do we retain hope when our hopes are constantly frustrated? We believe we know what God should be doing, and it is not happening! Paul helps us connect to the simple sadness of that. We are left with questions about who God is—but perhaps also with questions about our faith.

Paul has to reconsider his understanding of what God is doing in history. He is sad because his ministry is being thwarted, but perhaps he is also sad because he is having to question his assumptions about his new faith. This is a painful moment in Paul's ministry, just as it is in our own moments of frustration. Perhaps it is actually a beautiful moment when a wise and winsome Holy Spirit exposes the smallness of our imagination to us. At these moments, we can feel a kind of freedom from past assumptions; we might feel a freshness that challenges rigid or ossified ways we have understood our faith. Paul thought the Jesus movement would absorb Judaism, but just as God opened a path for Gentiles through the resurrected Christ, God resurrected Palestinian Judaism into rabbinic Judaism, a faith that enabled Jews to survive centuries of persecution and even the Holocaust.

---

2. Maya Angelou, "Commencement Address to the Class of 2008," *Cornell Chronicle* (May 24, 2008).

Paul Tillich argues that the potency of the revelation in Christ is that it empowers us to resist the temptation to make any belief more ultimate than God.[3] H. Richard Niebuhr distinguishes between faith in an always mysterious God and certainty that this or that aspect of our tradition perfectly captures who God is.[4] That we see the great hero of early Christianity struggling with the limits of his zealous certainties is a powerful witness that frees us to do the same. Paul allows a later insight to displace an earlier one. He allows the Spirit to lead him deeper into awareness of God's goodness and reliability. He allows a God who spins galaxies and multiverses to expand his own imagination about what God is doing in history.

We should notice too that Paul speaks vividly of his love for Israel and his appreciation that God's gifts come to the world through Israel. It is through Israel that humanity enters into covenantal relationship. As beloved of God, Israel will not be rejected, just as Gentiles, who have been ignorant of God, are not rejected. Paul speaks from his context, but his insights have implications beyond his own time and place.

Hostility that divides and demeans humanity is as intense as ever. The Southern Poverty Law Center lists over one hundred neo-Nazi groups in this country.[5] We are constantly subjected to hate speech, demeaning depictions of immigrants and refugees, and proposals of walls and travel bans for exclusion based on nationality or religion. How might Paul's wrestling with the unity of humanity and the diversity of belief help us now?

Paul's perspective is cosmic. He describes a narrative of creation and redemption: our journey, from alienation to God's abiding love for us, will not be thwarted. He is bewildered that many Jews wish to continue their faithfulness to Torah while some Gentiles are more receptive to the message of the Messiah, but this puzzlement does not undermine his abiding faith in God's promises or his confidence that "as regards election," all Israel is "beloved" (11:28). He has taken the long view, discerning a pattern of redemption that is being worked out, though in a different way than he had expected.

What if we also looked at diversity and unity from a more intimate point of view? What if the cosmic narrative were being told in each of our lives and in the lives of people whose religion or nationality makes them seem alien or unimportant to us? Films such as *The Visitor* or *El Norte* move beyond ideological caricatures and fear-infused hostility to provide a picture of what real people hope for and what they suffer. *The Visitor* tells of a Syrian immigrant and his mother who have left Syria after the husband/father, a torture victim and political prisoner, died in jail. By the end, the son is falsely accused of jumping over a subway turnstile and deported back to Syria. As she is dying, a character in *El Norte* describes the anguish of many immigrants: "In our own land [Guatemala], we have no home. They want to kill us. In Mexico, there is only poverty. We can't make a home there, either. And here in the north, we aren't accepted. When will we find a home, Enrique? Maybe when we die, we'll find a home."

Paul reassesses what he thinks he knows about Jews and Gentiles. In this he invites us to reassess what we think we know about who is saved, who is important, whose lives matter. Paul is constantly being compelled to sacrifice his certainties and hostilities: first his hostility to Jewish Christians, then to Gentiles, then to Jews who are not willing to give up the Torah. At each stage, his vision and his heart become wider and he glimpses a bit more of how God perceives humanity, how God holds this broken world, groaning for liberation. Paul did not live to see how his writings inspired Christians to become savage persecutors of Jews. He did not grapple with other world religions, each with their own wisdom nourished by the one Wisdom, but perhaps his writings provoke us to continue his journey toward an ever-expanding sense of a humanity united, not by sameness, but by a diversity of gifts—a humanity held in

---

3. Paul Tillich, *Systematic Theology, Volume 1* (Chicago: University of Chicago Press, 1973), 133.
4. H. Richard Niebuhr, *Radical Monotheism and Western Culture* (New York: HarperCollins, 1972), 63.
5. Southern Poverty Law Center; https://www.splcenter.org/fighting-hate/extremist-files/ideology/neo-nazi.

the love revealed by the Son, who invites us to resist attributing to God the smallness of the human heart.

The Genesis reading for today describes Jacob wrestling with an angel. We are reminded to wrestle with the angels of our better natures as we consider Paul's message to us about our relationship to other religious traditions, peoples, cultures, and beliefs. Matthew's Gospel describes Jesus' feeding of the five thousand. Let us hope that there will always be space in our hearts for the whole of humanity, desperately hungry for a healing word.

WENDY FARLEY

Proper 13 (Sunday between July 31 and August 6 inclusive)

Matthew 14:13–21

¹³Now when Jesus heard this, he withdrew from there in a boat to a deserted place by himself. But when the crowds heard it, they followed him on foot from the towns. ¹⁴When he went ashore, he saw a great crowd; and he had compassion for them and cured their sick. ¹⁵When it was evening, the disciples came to him and said, "This is a deserted place, and the hour is now late; send the crowds away so that they may go into the villages and buy food for themselves." ¹⁶Jesus said to them, "They need not go away; you give them something to eat." ¹⁷They replied, "We have nothing here but five loaves and two fish." ¹⁸And he said, "Bring them here to me." ¹⁹Then he ordered the crowds to sit down on the grass. Taking the five loaves and the two fish, he looked up to heaven, and blessed and broke the loaves, and gave them to the disciples, and the disciples gave them to the crowds. ²⁰And all ate and were filled; and they took up what was left over of the broken pieces, twelve baskets full. ²¹And those who ate were about five thousand men, besides women and children.

Commentary 1: Connecting the Reading with Scripture

Matthew's account of Jesus' feeding a large crowd follows two other culinary stories: in the previous chapter, the brief parable of the Baker Woman kneading yeast into a batch of dough (Matt. 13:33); and immediately preceding our focal text, the grisly report of Herod the tetrarch's lavish birthday banquet, which took a macabre turn with John the Baptist's severed head served up on a platter (Matt. 14:1–11). After the party, John's disciples claimed his body, buried it, and "then they went and told Jesus" (v. 12). In response to this news, Jesus "withdrew . . . in a boat to a deserted place by himself" (v. 13), perhaps to grieve for his friend John and to contemplate his own death (see 16:21; 17:22–23; 20:17–19; 26:1–2). However, he enjoys no time alone for reflection, as he finds a throng who "followed him on foot" waiting for him across the Sea of Galilee (vv. 13–14). Despite his longing for privacy in the wake of John's beheading, Jesus promptly responds to the waiting crowd "with compassion," that is, with deep-seated, gut-level sympathy for them, as the Greek term connotes, especially for the infirm who had walked or been carried all this way seeking healing. So, throughout the day, he "cured their sick" (v. 14).

Initially, then, the scene accentuates Jesus' ministry of healing, not feeding; but the two go hand in hand in his concern for the holistic, embodied salvation (health, flourishing) of all persons. By day's end, the crowd Jesus aids naturally has grown hungry. His disciples understand this need and encourage Jesus to dispatch the people from this "deserted place" to surrounding villages so they can buy food (v. 15). Perhaps they also have the ulterior motive of protecting Jesus' need for solitude and their own privileged fellowship with him, apart from the masses.

Jesus will have none of it. He crisply orders the disciples, "You give them something to eat," which frustrates them further, since they can only scrounge up five loaves and two fishes (vv. 16–17). In any case, Jesus takes these meager resources and multiplies them into a munificent feast. He does not perform some magic act, like zapping desert rocks into challah loaves (see 4:2–4), but rather, in a spirit of grateful communion with God the Creator-Father ("he looked up to heaven"), Jesus blesses, breaks, and shares the bounty of God's provision (v. 19). He gives God's children their "daily bread." This poignant communal event thus realizes the

Lord's Prayer (6:11; see 7:7–11), even as it prefigures the eucharistic taking and eating of the Lord's broken body (26:26).

The significance of this mass feeding may be further unpacked in relation to *numerical elements* and *scriptural echoes*. The numbers are important: five loaves and two fishes; twelve baskets of food left over; five thousand men fed, "besides women and children" (14:21). The total number of *seven* loaves and fishes suggests the completeness or fullness of God's creation-week, including "every green plant for food" and all the "fish of the sea" (Gen. 1:10–13, 20–23, 28–31; 2:1–4). A simpler mathematical observation may be the most telling: the paltry amount of available food, in contrast to (1) the lavish birthday spread in Herod's palace and (2) the throngs of hungry people in the desert.

Jesus operates in a different realm than Herod does. Whereas Rome's puppet ruler in Galilee trades in stockpiling the finest goods for his own luxury and protecting his standing among elite guests (14:8–11), the Son of God, the chief agent of God's rule, accumulates nothing for himself (4:1–11; 8:20) and expects the same of his disciples (10:9–13), even though he rightfully claims all the resources of heaven and earth (11:25–27). Rather, Jesus, starting with gratitude for a small portion of God's creational gifts, facilitates the abundant growth of these limited provisions in a magnanimous act of hospitality for guests who have little to offer in return.

No bread-baking women had planned for this "dinner on the grounds" (see 13:33). The last phrase of our text indicates, not surprisingly, that women and children are part of the crowd Jesus has been healing throughout the day. However, the wording, as well as the placement, of this final notation leaves something to be desired: "And those who ate were about five thousand men, *besides* women and children" (14:21; see 15:38). Matthew tacks on as an afterthought those who usually suffer the most in times of economic hardship or deprivation. Preachers may wish to counter this oblique androcentrism by highlighting Matthew's attention to four women in the ancestry of Jesus (1:3, 5–6) and other passages that feature women favorably (8:14–17; 9:18–26; 12:42, 46–50; 13:33; 15:21–28; 20:20–23; 23:37; 25:6–13; 27:19; 28:1–10).[1]

The largesse of Jesus' feeding well over five thousand people is enhanced by everyone's being "filled," with "twelve baskets full" to spare (14:20). Of course, a dozen matches the number of Jesus' disciples (10:1–4). Strategically, Jesus enlists these Twelve, who had first urged him to dismiss the crowd for dinner, to serve the multitude (14:19). This healing and feeding incident turns out to be a memorable seminar in faith and ministry for Jesus' closest followers.

Yet, however much the Twelve might flaunt their special places in God's kingdom (19:27; 20:20–28), they are more representative than distinctive, standing in for all Israel, historically constituted in twelve tribes (19:28). Likewise, Matthew's Jesus not only continues and consummates God's covenants with Abraham and David (1:1, 17, 21–22; 9:27–28; 12:23; 15:22; 20:30–31; 21:9), but also fulfills the Mosaic covenant and reenacts, even as he perfects, Moses' leadership of Israel out of Egyptian slavery and through the Sinai desert (2:13–23; 5:1–2, 17–48).[2] Accordingly, Jesus' feeding the multitude *in the desert* (mentioned twice: 14:13, 15), after crossing a sea, offers a strong scriptural echo of the Lord's providing manna "from heaven" in the wilderness for the grumbling Israelites (Exod. 16:1–12).

Though Moses does not mediate this heavenly fare, he chides the people for their failure to trust God's care (Exod. 16:6–10), thus "testing" the Lord's faithfulness (Exod. 16:4; 17:2; Num. 14:22). Jesus himself passes this wilderness test at the outset of his ministry, trusting in his Father's support rather than acceding to the devil's scheme for conjuring up "loaves of bread" (Matt. 4:1–4). Here the crowd does not complain, but Jesus' disciples are scarcely filled with compassion for the people and faith in God's grace.

---

1. See Amy-Jill Levine, "Gospel of Matthew," in *Women's Bible Commentary*, 3rd ed., ed. Carol. A. Newsom, Sharon H. Ringe, and Jacqueline E. Lapsley (Louisville, KY: Westminster John Knox, 2012), 465–77.
2. Dale C. Allison, *The New Moses: A Matthean Typology* (Minneapolis: Fortress, 1993).

The lesson, however, is clear, not only from the Torah narratives, but also from the prophets. In one of this week's companion lections, Isaiah invites the destitute to experience God's profuse and priceless food-and-word, which cannot be bought for any amount. Good news indeed for desperate people today, as surely as in Isaiah's and Jesus' worlds: "You that have no money, come, buy and eat! . . . Listen carefully to me, and eat what is good, and delight yourselves in rich food. Incline your ear, and come to me; listen, so that you may live. I will make with you an everlasting covenant" (Isa. 55:1–3).

F. SCOTT SPENCER

Commentary 2: Connecting the Reading with the World

Matthew 14 begins with a strong political statement: Herod Antipas, son of Herod the Great, is deeply concerned about the news that has spread about the ministry of Jesus. Herod fears Jesus is John the Baptist raised from the dead, performing miracles and speaking prophetically, which in turn attracts large crowds and wins their approval. Here, in the center of Matthew's Gospel, is a flashback to the birth of Jesus, when the elder Herod, frightened by the news of a child born "King of the Jews," commands the execution of all children under the age of two in and around Bethlehem. At that time, an angel of the Lord appears to Joseph and Mary, telling them to flee to safety in Egypt, where they will remain until Herod's death (Matt. 2:13–16).

Matthew's tale of the two Herods shows how a prominent expression of human power, that of political rulers, will perceive God's reign manifested in the ministry of Jesus as a serious threat to its control of the people they exist to serve. As a vulnerable child, Jesus is led to safety in Egypt. As a vulnerable adult, Jesus withdraws to a deserted place to pray. In both instances, the true "King of the Jews" sees no need to engage with either Herod on his own terms, but follows the leading of the Spirit in order to do the will of the One who sent him. What Jesus does, however, is not simply to retreat into a separate "spiritual world." Jesus lives out his mission in the physical world.

Matthew 14:13–21 provides an opportunity to address the need to show how the authority exercised in the church differs radically from the nature of authority exercised by human rulers. However, this is no small task for a preacher, given the widespread suspicion of institutional life and leadership, including in the church! One dominant narrative of suspicion in the media and culture at large is that church leaders, having assumed the status and privilege of their office, seek to abuse their authority, an abuse that has brought about devastating consequences that have yet to be fully comprehended.

The text invites us to seek a "depoliticization" of the church that shows how the life of God's people is understood in light of the vision provided by the "politics" of God's reign brought by Jesus. The stark contrast between Herod and Jesus is eye-opening, standing in judgment against much that characterizes contemporary political assumptions, arrangements, and practices, including that of the church's own. As reported at the beginning of chapter 14, self-interest drives Herod's reactions, and only the emotion of the crowds constrains him. However, even the "voice of the people" is not enough to prevent him from ordering the death of John the Baptist, as he is enticed by the seductive ways of a young woman who appeals to his pride, vanity, and lust.

Here the preacher would do well to reflect on the response of Jesus to Herod, which should highlight the politics of God's reign that should be practiced by the church in the world. Although Jesus initially withdraws—presumably knowing he will face an ending similar to that of John the Baptist—he quickly turns his attention to the great crowd of ordinary people that gathers around him. What follows is a fully public, even political, account by Matthew that shows in concrete, human terms the nature of God's rule and God's way, made visible in Jesus and shared by his followers.

This is faithful political action, the ordering and building up of a human community generated and guided by Jesus through the power of the Holy Spirit, who rests upon and empowers him. The Spirit is the power of God's future irrupting in the present to create a people whose existence, although still partial and incomplete, points to the final destiny of the world in God's reign. Such community building is what pastors and preachers are authorized to do by witnessing to the work of Jesus through the ministry of the Word in the power of the Spirit.

What makes this story so odd and strange to contemporary ears is that Jesus does not arm himself with the world's effective means of exercising power in order to guarantee success in the struggle with his adversaries. Instead, he withdraws to a "deserted" place, at a distance from Herod and the political center of Israel's life in Jerusalem. Today, the "deserted" place is where our attention may be fully directed to God, a place where we are able to acknowledge our powerlessness and vulnerability before God; that we are utterly dependent upon God's faithful provision and sustaining power. The church withdraws from the world, gathered by the Spirit to worship God in the presence of the risen Lord Jesus.

Worship is often perceived as an escape from the "real" world, in that many Christians demand that the church should become more "engaged" in the world and its problems, struggles, and needs. Worship is not, however, something less or other than the real world; rather, worship trains us to see the world as it really is, as God's good creation, marred by sin, evil, and death, yet loved and sustained by God, who is actively working for its redemption. Worship positions the church to be in the world as a sign, signal, and witness to the reality of God's reign arriving in Jesus, thus showing the world what it truly is: God's gift that is received with gratitude and returned to God in praise. As an act of worship, preaching will speak of and to the world in ways that differ from the world's ways of defining itself. Preaching offers a politics of praise that springs from attentive receptivity to God's abundant self-giving as the source and goal of all things.

Matthew thus highlights the disciples' dependence upon the "political action" of Jesus in exercising the authority of God's reign. "Taking the five loaves and the two fish, he looked up to heaven, and blessed and broke the loaves, and gave them to the disciples, and the disciples gave them to the crowds" (v. 19). Preachers should pay careful attention to Matthew's vivid depiction of God's politics, of the church gathered and situated in the world as a sign and witness to God's superabundance that has come in Jesus. The text prompts us as preachers to look away from ourselves, our plans, programs, and political posturing, and to summon our listeners to receive the gift of God's reign that has embraced the world through Jesus Christ.

What we have been given to proclaim from this narrative is the particular political nature of the church and its authority under the lordship of Jesus Christ, who is himself "God with us" (1:23). This amazing narrative offers a picture of the world as God intends it to be, providentially guided and blessed by Jesus, who rules heaven and earth from a cross rather than a throne. This picture also points to the church as a community whose primary way of being is guided and shaped by the wisdom of the cross, which the world will see as weak and foolish. If preachers desire to make a "political" statement on this Sunday, Matthew 14:13–21 is a good place to begin to show a church as situated in, with, and for the world, as a human community nourished by God's providential care in following the way of Jesus Christ.

MICHAEL PASQUARELLO III

Proper 14 (Sunday between August 7 and August 13 inclusive)

1 Kings 19:9–18 and Genesis 37:1–4, 12–28
Psalm 85:8–13 and Psalm 105:1–6, 16–22, 45b
Romans 10:5–15
Matthew 14:22–33

1 Kings 19:9–18

⁹At that place he came to a cave, and spent the night there.

Then the word of the LORD came to him, saying, "What are you doing here, Elijah?" ¹⁰He answered, "I have been very zealous for the LORD, the God of hosts; for the Israelites have forsaken your covenant, thrown down your altars, and killed your prophets with the sword. I alone am left, and they are seeking my life, to take it away."

¹¹He said, "Go out and stand on the mountain before the LORD, for the LORD is about to pass by." Now there was a great wind, so strong that it was splitting mountains and breaking rocks in pieces before the LORD, but the LORD was not in the wind; and after the wind an earthquake, but the LORD was not in the earthquake; ¹²and after the earthquake a fire, but the LORD was not in the fire; and after the fire a sound of sheer silence. ¹³When Elijah heard it, he wrapped his face in his mantle and went out and stood at the entrance of the cave. Then there came a voice to him that said, "What are you doing here, Elijah?" ¹⁴He answered, "I have been very zealous for the LORD, the God of hosts; for the Israelites have forsaken your covenant, thrown down your altars, and killed your prophets with the sword. I alone am left, and they are seeking my life, to take it away." ¹⁵Then the LORD said to him, "Go, return on your way to the wilderness of Damascus; when you arrive, you shall anoint Hazael as king over Aram. ¹⁶Also you shall anoint Jehu son of Nimshi as king over Israel; and you shall anoint Elisha son of Shaphat of Abel-meholah as prophet in your place. ¹⁷Whoever escapes from the sword of Hazael, Jehu shall kill; and whoever escapes from the sword of Jehu, Elisha shall kill. ¹⁸Yet I will leave seven thousand in Israel, all the knees that have not bowed to Baal, and every mouth that has not kissed him."

Genesis 37:1–4, 12–28

¹Jacob settled in the land where his father had lived as an alien, the land of Canaan. ²This is the story of the family of Jacob.

Joseph, being seventeen years old, was shepherding the flock with his brothers; he was a helper to the sons of Bilhah and Zilpah, his father's wives; and Joseph brought a bad report of them to their father. ³Now Israel loved Joseph more than any other of his children, because he was the son of his old age; and he had made him a long robe with sleeves. ⁴But when his brothers saw that their father loved him more than all his brothers, they hated him, and could not speak peaceably to him. . . .

¹²Now his brothers went to pasture their father's flock near Shechem. ¹³And Israel said to Joseph, "Are not your brothers pasturing the flock at Shechem? Come, I will send you to them." He answered, "Here I am." ¹⁴So he said to him, "Go now, see if it is well with your brothers and with the flock; and bring word back to me." So he sent him from the valley of Hebron.

He came to Shechem, ¹⁵and a man found him wandering in the fields; the man asked him, "What are you seeking?" ¹⁶"I am seeking my brothers," he said; "tell me, please, where they are pasturing the flock." ¹⁷The man said, "They have gone away, for I heard them say, 'Let us go to Dothan.'" So Joseph went after his brothers, and found them at Dothan. ¹⁸They saw him from a distance, and before he came near to them, they conspired to kill him. ¹⁹They said to one another, "Here comes this dreamer. ²⁰Come now, let us kill him and throw him into one of the pits; then we shall say that a wild animal has devoured him, and we shall see what will become of his dreams." ²¹But when Reuben heard it, he delivered him out of their hands, saying, "Let us not take his life." ²²Reuben said to them, "Shed no blood; throw him into this pit here in the wilderness, but lay no hand on him"—that he might rescue him out of their hand and restore him to his father. ²³So when Joseph came to his brothers, they stripped him of his robe, the long robe with sleeves that he wore; ²⁴and they took him and threw him into a pit. The pit was empty; there was no water in it.

²⁵Then they sat down to eat; and looking up they saw a caravan of Ishmaelites coming from Gilead, with their camels carrying gum, balm, and resin, on their way to carry it down to Egypt. ²⁶Then Judah said to his brothers, "What profit is it if we kill our brother and conceal his blood? ²⁷Come, let us sell him to the Ishmaelites, and not lay our hands on him, for he is our brother, our own flesh." And his brothers agreed. ²⁸When some Midianite traders passed by, they drew Joseph up, lifting him out of the pit, and sold him to the Ishmaelites for twenty pieces of silver. And they took Joseph to Egypt.

Commentary 1: Connecting the Reading with Scripture

First Kings 19:9–18. This scene is part of the Elijah story that is the center point of the books of Kings (1 Kgs. 17–19, 21; 2 Kgs. 1–2). It recounts a low moment in Elijah's life, when he flees to the southern city of Beer-sheba from Jezebel, the wife of King Ahab of Israel, who is putting to death the prophets of Yahweh. As Elijah hides, God speaks to him both with words and in silence to reassure him, and then sends him back to continue his prophetic career. The episode is a pivotal moment in Elijah's life that bridges the two sections of Kings that describe his work as God's prophet.

The passage begins with the statement that "the word of the Lord came to him," a phrase that repeats itself like a refrain throughout the Elijah cycle. This is the fourth of its six occurrences, and its frequent appearance highlights Elijah's reliance on divine guidance and assistance (1 Kgs. 17:2, 8; 18:1; 19:9; 21:17, 28). This time the Deity's message takes the form of a question that suggests the prophet is not where he is supposed to be: "What are you doing here, Elijah?" The question is repeated twice, the second time after he has been told to stand on Mount Horeb. Elijah responds to each query with the exact same words before beginning his trek back north.

The scene contains elements that relate to past and future events in Elijah's life. The reference to Mount Horeb recalls his encounter with the four hundred fifty prophets of Baal on Mount Carmel in the previous chapter, when he engages them in a contest that demonstrates the superiority of Israel's Deity over the god they worship. There is an interesting vocabulary connection between the two stories. The Hebrew term translated "voice" that describes the lack of a response from Baal to his prophets' request that he come to their aid (18:29) is also used in the scene on Mount Horeb to describe a "sound" of sheer silence that Elijah identifies with God (19:12). In this way, the power and presence of Yahweh is contrasted with the weakness and absence of Baal. God's charge that Elijah should anoint Elisha as the prophet who will replace him (v. 16) points ahead to 2 Kings 2, where Elijah is transported to heaven in a chariot of fire and Elisha takes up his mantle to succeed him as prophet.

This scene establishes a connection between Elijah and Moses, because Mount Horeb is another name for Mount Sinai, where the Law was revealed after the Israelites had left Egypt. Two events in Moses' life in particular are echoed here. The burning bush episode, also located at Mount Horeb (Exod. 3:1), describes how Moses, like Elijah, is commissioned by God when he is told to go to Pharaoh and demand that the Israelites be set free. Just as Elijah covers his face with his mantle as he stands in God's presence (1 Kgs. 19:13), so too Moses hides his face to avoid looking at the Deity (Exod. 3:6).

This same motif is found later when the Israelites have left Egypt and Moses has another encounter with God near Mount Horeb, during which he is prevented from gazing upon the divine presence (Exod. 33:17–23). The convergence of Elijah, Moses, and a mountain can be seen in the New Testament's accounts of the transfiguration of Jesus, when three of his disciples witness Moses, Elijah, and Jesus together on Mount Tabor. The Gospel of Matthew includes the detail that Jesus' followers were overwhelmed with fear and could not look at what was taking place before them (Matt. 17:1–8; cf. Mark 9:2–8; Luke 9:29–36), which recalls the reluctance of Moses and Elijah to look at God.

Genesis 37:1–4, 12–28. The story of Joseph (Gen. 37–50) brings the Bible's first book to a close, and its opening chapter introduces important themes that will continue to resurface throughout the rest of the story. The favoritism Jacob feels toward Joseph leads to jealousy among his brothers that results in Joseph being sold into Egypt, where he will prosper and, in an ironic twist, ultimately save their lives from a famine.

Most of the events described in the book of Genesis up to now have been set in Canaan, but at this point the focus shifts to Egypt and will remain there until the Israelites begin their long trek homeward that begins in Exodus 12 and is not completed until some forty years later as related in the book of Joshua. The Joseph story serves as a bridge that helps to explain how and why the Israelites relocated to Egypt, from where they were eventually led back to the promised land by Moses at the time of the exodus. The genre, length, and style of the Joseph story are unlike what has been related previously in Genesis, and therefore many scholars believe it may have originally been an independent composition that was inserted here in order to connect the material about the patriarchs and matriarchs with the traditions about Moses.

This passage anticipates a number of other scenes in the Joseph story. Jacob's preference for Joseph is the first of several times a prominent person sees something in him that results in Joseph attaining special honor among his peers. Upon his arrival in Egypt, his master (39:1–6), the chief jailer (39:20–23), and the pharaoh (41:37–45) all promote Joseph and give him a position of authority. The mention of the garment (not a "coat of many colors") given to Joseph that expresses his father's favoritism is the first of a number of references to his clothing throughout the story, which always signal a change in Joseph's status. He is imprisoned when he leaves his garment behind after his master's wife attempts to seduce him (39:11–18). Prior to his meeting with the pharaoh that will set him free, Joseph removes his prison garb and changes clothes (41:14). When the Egyptian ruler promotes Joseph to the position of second in command over the land, the pharaoh dresses him in fine attire and expensive jewelry (41:42).

A further link is established between this opening scene and Joseph's imprisonment because the same Hebrew word is used to describe both the pit into which Joseph's brothers throw him in Canaan (37:24) and the jail cell he occupies in Egypt (41:14). The portion of Genesis 37 that is not included in this reading also contains the first example of a recurring theme in the story. The report of the two dreams Joseph had (37:5–11) sets the stage for the pairs of dreams that his fellow prisoners (40:5–19) and the pharaoh (41:1–36) will have that Joseph is able to interpret.

The events recounted in the Joseph story are rarely mentioned elsewhere in the Bible. The book of Psalms contains a reference to the physical pain Joseph endured when he was sold into Egypt and briefly describes his time in the pharaoh's court (Ps. 105:16–22), but that is the only passage in the Hebrew Bible that directly cites something mentioned in Genesis 37–50. Elsewhere, the term "Joseph" is sometimes used to refer to the people of Israel, particularly those in the northern part of the land (Ps. 80:1; Amos 5:15; 6:6). In the New Testament, Stephen, just prior to his martyrdom, delivers a speech in the book of Acts in which he summarizes what takes place in the Joseph story, beginning with his brothers' jealousy and ending with their being reunited in Egypt and the eventual return of their remains to Canaan (Acts 7:9–16).

JOHN KALTNER

Commentary 2: Connecting the Reading with the World

"Everything happens for a reason." "God is in control." "It is more than a coincidence; someone is watching over you/us." "God's ways are not our ways." Many Christians with good intentions, heavily influenced by determinism, employ statements like these as explanations of natural disasters and human suffering, to offer comfort and to make sense of evil actions. One sentence captures all these expressions: "It was God's will!"

Although these affirmations may contain some level of theological acumen, as explanations for human suffering and natural disasters, they tend to lead us to a distorted understanding of who God is and what God does. Based on this distorted understanding, the Christian church and its leaders present an insensitive response to human suffering.

Obviously we are not the first ones attempting to offer an explanation to tragedies. In fact, history provides a robust account of such responses. For example, Mani argued that the root of the problem is not the presence of tragedies in the world, which are simply symptomatic. The root of the problem is the eternal battle between good and evil, the results of which we experience here on earth. Furthermore, he argues, there is a direct correlation between evil and physical realities and goodness and spiritual expressions. If this explanation is true, then our task is not to discern the origin of evil, but rather to get rid of it, by overcoming physical afflictions as we draw close to God.

Another historical response is found in Augustine. He does not believe in an eternal battle between good and evil; rather, he accounts for evil and tragedies as the result of misuse and abuse of free will. In this way, Augustine dismisses the idea of an eternal battle between good and evil, and sees humans as morally accountable for their actions/decisions. Furthermore, although he ascribes some responsibility to humans for natural disasters (human choices have an effect on the environment), he affirms that nature is no longer perfect, as it was created. Sin has disrupted the environment as well as humanity, and thus natural disasters are linked to sin.

According to Irenaeus, tragedies and disasters are present in order for humans to develop a strong character and maturity. He affirms that the created world, with all these challenges and adversities, provides opportunities for humans to grow stronger, and as we overcome these, we will develop a virtuous character.

Since Joseph's story is quite popular and most readers know the final outcome of it, it is easy to see why some may be led to affirmations like these: "It was God's plan for Joseph to be sold by his brothers." "God can turn suffering into a blessing." Appealing to God's omniscience, these explanations see these terrible events in the life of Joseph as part of God's will and plan. Some may also affirm that in the passage in First Kings, God is plotting vengeance against the Israelites for forsaking God's word and God's prophets and discloses this plot to Elijah. In this situation, God is keenly aware that Elijah fears for his life, and God's response is an easy one: "I will destroy your enemies."

Again, a quick look at these passages would render a self-evident interpretation, and reach these deterministic affirmations. Determinism is defined as: "a theory or doctrine that acts of the will, occurrences in nature, or social or psychological phenomena are causally determined by preceding events or natural laws."[1] Applying this definition to these passages and their face-value interpretation, one may be inclined to affirm that God has a predetermined course of action.

It is essential to ask ourselves these questions: What kind of God is affirmed by these affirmations? What kind of God is depicted in these narratives? Is God playing a chess match and using each of these characters as pieces to accomplish God's ultimate plan, a plan in which some must suffer and experience pain? In answering the above questions, using a deterministic approach, and following the logical conclusion of such reasoning, one would be confronted with a larger question that is loaded with ethical and theological implications: who is morally responsible for evil actions and evil in general?

A closer look at two verses in the story in First Kings would provide some important considerations for our interpretative task. Verses 11–12 (NIV) indicate God's presence in relationship to natural/environmental events:

> The LORD said, "Go out and stand on the mountain in the presence of the LORD, for the LORD is about to pass by." Then a great and powerful wind tore the mountains apart and shattered the rocks before the LORD, but the LORD was not in the wind. After the wind there was an earthquake, but the LORD was not in the earthquake. After the earthquake came a fire, but the LORD was not in the fire. And after the fire came a gentle whisper.

As the body of Christ, we should ask ourselves, Where is God in the midst of suffering?

Are we called to simply proclaim that natural disasters and the suffering they produce are God's will? Are we called to rely on the affirmation that everything happens for a reason without any further theological inquiries? If so, then, what about the declaration of the verses in First Kings, in which Elijah is certain that God's active presence is in the wind, in the earthquake, and in the fire. Yet God is not present in any of these but in "a gentle whisper." Are the stories of Joseph and Elijah captured in these verses trying to provide an explanation for human suffering by simply affirming that God is in control and all the events around their lives were God's plan? Or are they trying to assure readers that God's presence is actively involved and attentive to human suffering? Perhaps these stories also should serve as a warning for us when we move too quickly to affirm "self-evident" conclusions when we rely on face-value readings of Scripture.

If we look at these passages and the lives of Joseph and Elijah, and place these stories in the larger context of Scripture and God's character revealed in the biblical narrative, one could be persuaded at least to be more cautious in making moral claims regarding natural disasters and human suffering, and perhaps develop a more robust understanding of who we are and what is the nature of our proclamation as part of the body of Christ.

HUGO MAGALLANES

---

1. "Determinism," Merriam-Webster; https://www.merriam-webster.com/dictionary/determinism.

Proper 14 (Sunday between August 7 and August 13 inclusive)

Psalm 85:8–13

⁸Let me hear what God the LORD will speak,
 for he will speak peace to his people,
 to his faithful, to those who turn to him in their hearts.
⁹Surely his salvation is at hand for those who fear him,
 that his glory may dwell in our land.

¹⁰Steadfast love and faithfulness will meet;
 righteousness and peace will kiss each other.
¹¹Faithfulness will spring up from the ground,
 and righteousness will look down from the sky.
¹²The LORD will give what is good,
 and our land will yield its increase.
¹³Righteousness will go before him,
 and will make a path for his steps.

Psalm 105:1–6, 16–22, 45b

¹O give thanks to the LORD, call on his name,
 make known his deeds among the peoples.
²Sing to him, sing praises to him;
 tell of all his wonderful works.
³Glory in his holy name;
 let the hearts of those who seek the LORD rejoice.
⁴Seek the LORD and his strength;
 seek his presence continually.
⁵Remember the wonderful works he has done,
 his miracles, and the judgments he has uttered,
⁶O offspring of his servant Abraham,
 children of Jacob, his chosen ones.
 . . . .
¹⁶When he summoned famine against the land,
 and broke every staff of bread,
¹⁷he had sent a man ahead of them,
 Joseph, who was sold as a slave.
¹⁸His feet were hurt with fetters,
 his neck was put in a collar of iron;
¹⁹until what he had said came to pass,
 the word of the LORD kept testing him.
²⁰The king sent and released him;
 the ruler of the peoples set him free.
²¹He made him lord of his house,
 and ruler of all his possessions,
²²to instruct his officials at his pleasure,
 and to teach his elders wisdom.
 . . . .
⁴⁵ᵇPraise the LORD!

Connecting the Psalm with Scripture and Worship

A community who focuses on and regularly recalls God's divine acts and goodness is a community who walks in divine assurance. This is illustrated in Psalms 85 and 105. Psalm 85:8–13 offers a celebration of the personification of God's personal attributes, and presents a transition from lament to listening, culminating in assurance and praise. Opening with a doxological introduction, the reading from Psalm 105 offers a recitation of Israel's past with God. This psalm focuses the attention on God's actions, which are beyond human aptitude, and provides an inventory of miracles to support the opening exhortation. In both accounts, the psalmist depicts God's relationship with God's people as a manifestation of divine power and greatness.

Psalm 85:8–13 portrays God as faithful and steadfast. Beginning in verse 8, there is a transition in the psalm, and the leader implores the community to listen for a word from God, followed by an act of assurance that imagines a world of complete harmony and reconciliation, illustrated through a "well-being in creation grounded in the reliability of the creator who saves."[1] God is the One who promises peace, and whose salvation is near for those who fear God. The attributes presented (faithfulness, righteousness, and peace) speak to God's divine character, which permeates the entire cosmos and brings well-being to the world as a gift from God. This gives the community the assurance that their loving God will deliver on God's promises, God will act in accordance with God's nature and bestow benefits on those who obey God.

Psalm 85:8–13 is a powerful prayer that confidently anticipates a transformational response from God. When paired with the other lectionary texts for the week, Psalm 85:8–13 provides one particular approach for preaching on this Sunday: We are called to be positioned to hear from God with the assurance that God will respond in the fullness of God's divine nature. By focusing on God's attributes of faithfulness, peace, and righteousness, the psalmist makes it clear that even in lament we must listen for God and expect a response that is a gift of wholeness and well-being, because that is God's nature. This is the assurance of our salvation: God is faithful to those who fear and obey God.

Psalm 105:1–6, 16–22, 45b is a strong illustration of God as a God of action. The psalmist praises God for God's wonderful works and acts of judgment, and recalls these works in the specific account of Joseph. Dependent on the Genesis narrative in this week's lectionary texts, Psalm 105 displays God's power to save and preserve God's people. The text opens with a summons to praise God, and the remaining verses (Ps. 105:16–22, 45b) offer the content of that praise. God is the sole focus of this praise, and the recitation of Joseph in Egypt provides an illustration of how God kept God's covenant with Abraham. The psalmist is focusing on God's faithfulness. God is faithful to keep God's covenant and save God's people.

As a hymn of praise, Psalm 105:1–6, 16–22, 45b provides an additional approach for preaching: trust God to be faithful to God's promises. God made a promise to Abraham, Isaac, and Jacob, and the psalmist highlights God honoring this promise. The psalmist (writing after the exile) does not recount Israel's continued failures with God; rather, the psalmist reflects on the ways God works out God's covenant with the ancestors. This reflection is the basis upon which the psalmist compels the community to trust God, to seek the presence and power of God (v. 4), and to trust God based on God's history with Israel. The psalmist's call to remember and trust is key for this approach to preaching, because there are times in the life of the church when we need to be reminded of God's promises to us and our ancestors and God's faithfulness in fulfilling those promises. The particular use of Joseph's narrative further solidifies the psalmist's points by showing the wonderful work of God's restoration in Joseph's life. As a result, Psalm 105 is a clear lesson in divine providence.

Both psalms speak to the faith of Israel and are grounded in the community's historic relationship with God, and can be incorporated

---

1. Walter Brueggemann and William H. Bellinger Jr., *Psalms* (New York: Cambridge University Press, 2014), 369.

into worship services in a variety of ways. Psalm 85:8–13 carries a centered and assured tone in its language and structure. This tone is fitting for use as a prayer for illumination that assures God's response. This can be done with one lead voice allowing the congregation to pray to hear God speak, and the lead voice offering the divine assurance of God's response.

Reader 1: Let me hear what God the Lord will speak, for God will speak to God's people, to the faithful, to those who turn to God in their hearts.

Reader 2: Surely God's salvation is at hand for those who fear the Lord, that God's glory may dwell in the land. Steadfast love and faithfulness will meet; righteousness and peace will kiss each other. Faithfulness will spring up from the ground and righteousness will look down from the sky. The Lord will give what is good, and our land will yield increase. Righteousness will go before him, and will make a path for his steps.

Reader 1: Let me hear what God the Lord will speak, for God will speak to God's people, to the faithful, to those who turn to God in their hearts.

As a prayer for illumination, Psalm 85:8–13 postures the community to hear the sermon with expectant ears, assured that God is going to speak.

If the worship service is using both the Genesis and Romans lections for the week, then Psalm 105:1–6, 16–22, 45b becomes a frame and bridge for the two texts. Psalm 105:1–6, 45b can be offered as a call to worship, opening the service in a format that allows the congregation to respond to the call.

Reader: O give thanks to the Lord, call on God's name, make known God's deeds among the peoples. Sing to the Lord, sing praises to the Lord; tell of all God's wonderful works. Glory in God's holy name; let the hearts of those who seek the Lord rejoice. Seek the Lord and divine strength; seek the Lord's presence continually. Remember the wonderful works God has done, the miracles, and the judgments the Lord has uttered, O offspring of the Lord Abraham, children of Jacob, God's chosen ones.

All: Praise the Lord!

The rest of the psalm text (105:16–22) can be offered as a response to the Genesis reading, and allows the community to be called into worship and encouraged to remember the wonderful works of God, to actually hear an account of those works (Genesis), and then respond by proclaiming the remainder of the psalm, before moving into either the epistle or Gospel text. All of this offers a connection to recalling God's history with God's chosen people and offering praise to God for those wonderful works, knowing God will continue to honor God's promises.

Recitation, remembering, and finding assurance in God's proven acts of faithfulness, righteousness, and peace are at the heart of these psalms, and each calls for a particular response to God. Psalm 85 positions us to hear from God with the assurance that God will answer. Psalm 105 calls us to praise God out of our direct experiences with God, knowing God's actions are divine and God is sure to save.

KHALIA J. WILLIAMS

Proper 14 (Sunday between August 7 and August 13 inclusive)

Romans 10:5–15

⁵Moses writes concerning the righteousness that comes from the law, that "the person who does these things will live by them." ⁶But the righteousness that comes from faith says, "Do not say in your heart, 'Who will ascend into heaven?'" (that is, to bring Christ down) ⁷"or 'Who will descend into the abyss?'" (that is, to bring Christ up from the dead). ⁸But what does it say?

"The word is near you,
 on your lips and in your heart"

(that is, the word of faith that we proclaim); ⁹because if you confess with your lips that Jesus is Lord and believe in your heart that God raised him from the dead, you will be saved. ¹⁰For one believes with the heart and so is justified, and one confesses with the mouth and so is saved. ¹¹The scripture says, "No one who believes in him will be put to shame." ¹²For there is no distinction between Jew and Greek; the same Lord is Lord of all and is generous to all who call on him. ¹³For, "Everyone who calls on the name of the Lord shall be saved."

¹⁴But how are they to call on one in whom they have not believed? And how are they to believe in one of whom they have never heard? And how are they to hear without someone to proclaim him? ¹⁵And how are they to proclaim him unless they are sent? As it is written, "How beautiful are the feet of those who bring good news!"

Commentary 1: Connecting the Reading with Scripture

Connection 1: Immediate Literary Context. In Romans 10:1 Paul returns to his passionate concern for the salvation of his Jewish kindred that began this section of the letter, in 9:1–3. In 9:4–5 he reiterates the divine blessings given to Israel; in 9:6–13 he retells the birth narratives of the patriarchs in support of his understanding of election: Israel's calling into being has always been on the basis of God's freely electing grace and not on any merit in those whom God calls. Paul then amplifies this theme of election in regard to the character of God. Is God unjust? Paul answers the question in an unexpected way: human notions of justice would require punishment, but God exercises God's sovereign freedom by showing mercy to the undeserving, both Israel and also Gentiles (Rom. 9:24–25). Indeed, at this time, the Gentiles are experiencing mercy, while Israel is (temporarily) hardened.

These reflections lead up to the argument in 9:30–33, immediately preceding our passage: Gentiles, with no claim at all, even to seeking God, have attained the righteousness that comes through faith, while Israel, zealously seeking righteousness through the law of Moses, on the basis of works, has not reached its goal. The image is of runners in a race, who stumble on a stone set in the track. The stone is Christ as the object and source of faith (9:33). Here is the contrast between righteousness by faith and righteousness on the basis of works, so frequently associated with Paul's thought. In 10:1–4 he develops this contrast as one between righteousness from God and merely human righteousness; in 10:5–6 he again characterizes the contrast as between righteousness based on law, and righteousness based on faith.

The closing verses of our passage, 10:14–15, need to be read in the context of the immediately following verses, primarily quoting from the Psalms, Deuteronomy, and Isaiah. Yes, says Paul, faith comes from the message of Christ

(10:17); but immediately he asks, "Have they not heard?" and answers, "Yes!" Israel has heard the message, but still has not believed. This raises questions about the relationship between God's sovereign grace and human unbelief, which thread throughout this section of Romans.

Connection 2: Larger Literary Context. Romans 10:1–15 comes roughly halfway through Paul's discussion in Romans 9–11 of God's faithfulness to the promises God has made to Israel. This crucial section of Romans elucidates the theme of divine righteousness that structures the letter as a whole. Romans 1:16–17 proclaims, "For I am not ashamed of the gospel: it is the power of God for salvation to everyone who has faith, to the Jew first and also to the Greek. For in it the righteousness of God is revealed." Romans 1–8 explicates the revelation of God's saving righteousness as deliverance from the power of sin and death; Romans 9–11 explicates the same theme as God's faithfulness to the promises to Israel; Romans 12–15:13 displays the revelation of God's righteousness in the common life of Jews and Gentiles together worshiping "the God and Father of our Lord Jesus Christ" (15:6).

Connection 3: Larger Thematic Context. Romans 9:30–10:13 develops the contrast, first introduced in 3:21–30, between righteousness derived from works of the law, and righteousness based on Christ. Whereas righteousness based on law distinguishes between those who do the law and those who do not, the righteousness based on Christ breaks down all such divisions (3:22, 28–30; 10:12–13); it is given to "all," not just some people (3:23–24; 10:12). This inclusiveness flows from the very character of God revealed in the Shema: "God is one" (3:30), and "the same Lord is Lord of all" (10:12). In 3:21–30 Paul expands on the way in which Gentiles are included by divine faithfulness. In Romans 9–11 he wrestles with God's faithfulness to God's promises to a specific people, Israel.

This theme of divine righteousness cannot be separated from the theme of faith, or trust—both God's trustworthiness enacted in Jesus Christ, and human trust in Christ. The focus is not on human belief as an attitude or disposition, in contrast with human "doing of the law," but rather on the effective action of God in Christ, who alone has power to save (3:24). This divine action, which brings Christ so near that "the word" is in our hearts and on our lips (10:8), in turn gifts human beings with faith, so that we may "confess with the mouth, and believe in the heart" (10:9–10). God's saving action does not override human belief; rather, God activates our trust in Jesus Christ.

In 1:16, Paul introduces the theme of the letter by saying, "I am not *ashamed* of the gospel." This theme of shame resurfaces in the repeated quotation from Isaiah 28:16: "No one who believes in him will be put to shame" (9:33; 10:11). Shame would be the public humiliation of betrayed trust; God is trustworthy, and will not let down or abandon those who rely on Jesus Christ. In Romans 9–11, such trustworthiness is demonstrated by God's faithfulness to Israel.

Connection 4: Lectionary Context. Genesis 37:1–4, 12–28 recounts the jealousy of Joseph's brothers, culminating in their selling him into slavery to a trader who takes him to Egypt. The climax of that story includes Joseph's famous words to his brothers: "Even though you intended to do harm to me, God intended it for good" (Gen. 50:20). Psalm 105:16–22 amplifies the same theme. This affirmation of God's purposes operating even through human disobedience corresponds with the overarching theme of Romans 9–11: Israel's unbelief ultimately serves God's purpose of saving all (Rom. 11:11–32). In Matthew 14:22–33 we see God's divine power and providence embodied and enacted uniquely in Jesus.

Connection 5: Canonical Context. Our passage bristles with quotations from the Old Testament, all read through the lens of faith in Christ. In 10:5–13 Paul calls Moses as a witness to his claim that Christ is the fulfillment and goal of the Mosaic law (10:4): the law points to Christ, and only in Christ is the purpose of the law fulfilled. That is, the law itself testifies against zeal for the law (vv. 1–3) and points away from itself, to Christ! Paul argues this by contrasting the voice of Moses (Lev. 18:5 in Rom. 10:5), with the personified voice of "the righteousness based on faith"; this contrast sets the stage for his quotations from Deuteronomy in 10:6–7.

Deuteronomy 8:17 and 9:4 warn the Israelites against saying in their heart that their conquest of the land was due to their own righteousness. This subliminal warning introduces the quotations from Deuteronomy 30:11–14 in Romans 10:6–8; there the word of the divine commandment becomes the word of faith in Christ, the Messiah who does not need to be brought near, by legal obedience, because he is already present. In Romans 10:11–13 Paul repeats his citation of Isaiah 28:16 in Romans 9:33: no one who believes in Christ will be put to shame. Here this promise grounds Paul's central affirmation that *all*, both Jew and Gentile, are saved through Christ (Rom. 1:16), as the quotation from Joel 2:32 also proclaims.

Sermon Ideas That Emerge from Romans 10:1–15. Paul is remarkably free in his use of Scripture, guided by his central conviction that Jesus Christ is the decisive fulfillment of God's promises. How might Christ as a guiding principle of interpretation also guide our reading of Scripture?

A sermon might explore the ways in which the word of faith is put into our hearts and on our lips, so that faith expresses God's intimate presence already with us.

A sermon might proclaim freedom from shame through reliance on God's gracious and intimate gift of righteousness.

SUSAN GROVE EASTMAN

Commentary 2: Connecting the Reading with the World

The revolutionary nature of this text is striking. Foreshadowing Jesus' oft-repeated words, "You have heard that it was said, but now I say to you," Paul begins with a reference to Moses, reminding the people of their history of earning righteousness by keeping the law. He then introduces a different path to righteousness, one that recognizes the faithfulness of God. God has fulfilled the covenant through Christ, who has now become righteousness for everyone. This righteousness, this salvation, comes to all who believe with their hearts and confess with their lips. This gift of salvation is for Jew *and* Greek alike; indeed, it is for everyone who calls upon the name of the Lord.

Back in Paul's time, his writing would have been considered heretical among the Jewish faithful. Access to God was through the law, and God reserved righteousness for those who kept the law. Any relationship with God depended on strict adherence to the requirements of the law. This new righteousness through faith would have seemed like cheap grace to those who had spent their lives living faithfully before God by keeping the law.

Today, this text still seems unacceptable to many who believe in works righteousness. Many of us want, even demand, a list of things to do that will put us in a right relationship with God. Many believe we *deserve* certain rewards in life because we have earned them through hard work and good living. We want our salvation to depend on our own righteousness. We certainly do not want those who are not living right to be included in the righteousness of God. We are in control of our lives. We can save ourselves. No problem.

No problem, until the reality of our humanity rears its head. Our ultimate trust in ourselves lasts until we come face-to-face with human weakness and our own mortality. This happens in all manner of ways. The death of a loved one, a difficult diagnosis, divorce, job loss, mental illness, deportation of one we love, fear, feelings of inadequacy, anger, addiction: any of these things can jerk us back into the realization that the control we thought we had over our own lives was an illusion. These are the moments, seasons, and journeys that help us remember that God is God and we are not.

Gospel and jazz musician Thomas Andrew Dorsey was only thirty-two when his life fell apart. He was in St. Louis, a soloist at a large revival, when he received word that his wife Nettie had died giving birth to their first child. He rushed home to Chicago, only to find that his baby boy had died as well. Grief consumed him. At some point in his journey of sorrow, knowing that he could not move forward without God's help, recognizing that his trust belonged only with his Lord, he sat at a piano and composed the great hymn "Precious Lord, Take My Hand," in which he wrote, "Through the storm, through the night, lead me on to the light."[1]

In Dorsey's deepest grief, he realized that he could not go on without the help of his loving and faithful God. His utter dependence on God became clear to him, and he called on God in full trust that God would accompany him through his grief, that he was not alone, and that God would comfort, protect, guide, and lead him—to the light, all the way home.

Paul's words to the Romans, "The word is near to you," assure them of this same intimacy. Paul reminds them of God's intimate proximity to us, using words and images from Deuteronomy 30:11–14. God is not in the heavens, distant and remote, waiting for us to make our way to God. God is not beyond the sea (or deep in the abyss). God in Christ is with us, as near to us as hands and feet and the very marrow of our bones, as near to us as our lips and our hearts. What an incredibly comforting word for those who trust in God.

The theme of God's propinquity connects with two other lectionary passages for this Sunday. In 1 Kings 19, Elijah has fled from Jezebel into the wilderness, lost in his self-pity, fear, and loneliness. Hiding in a cave, he realizes God is as near as the sound of silence around him. This knowledge gives him the strength and courage he needs to face his oppressor. He now realizes God is with him, and in fact has never left him, even when his trust in God's presence wavered.

In Matthew 14, Peter climbs out of the disciples' boat to walk across the waters where Jesus walks, but the rough waters frighten him. When he puts his trust in himself, rather than in Jesus, he begins to sink. "Lord, save me," he cries, and Jesus, who alone can be trusted, pulls him up and marvels at the doubt that caused Peter to sink. In these passages, both Elijah and Peter cease to trust in their hearts the one they called Lord with their lips. They rely on their own strength. Their trust in self is misdirected and leads to miserable fear and failure until they locate their trust in the one place it deserves to be.

Paul's words remind us that the righteousness of God is a gift for all in Christ. Our right relationship with God is no longer dependent upon the keeping of the law; rather, it is a gift for all who trust in their hearts and confess with their lips. *Everyone* who trusts in the Lord (those who have come to the realization that God is God and they are not) will be saved. This inclusionary statement was radical in its day and is radical today if we understand its wide-ranging ecclesial implications. As the church, we do not build walls to keep people out. All are invited into this relationship of trust and dependence upon God. This is not dependent upon race or cultural heritage, sexual orientation or gender identity, refugee or immigrant status, age or ability, body art or piercings. God's inclusion in salvation is for *all* who trust in the Lord. God knows no distinction.

Finally, for those who are preachers and teachers, the end of this passage reminds us that God calls us to bear this good news to the people. This is "the word of faith which we preach." It is radical. It is grace. We bear it faithfully when we believe it in our hearts and confess it with our lips. When we acknowledge our total dependence upon this good news for our own lives, we are able to share it as good news for the world.

Martin Luther King Jr. once preached a sermon on the final verses of this passage titled "Without a Preacher." We are left with only

---

1. Thomas A. Dorsey, "Precious Lord, Take My Hand," *Glory to God: The Presbyterian Hymnal* (Louisville, KY: Westminster John Knox Press, 2013), 834.

his outline notes, but we can surmise how he unpacked his last two points: (1) "Without a preacher we would conclude that we could lift ourselves by our own bootstraps," and (2) "Without a preacher we would conclude that man [*sic*] is the center of the universe."[2] The preacher/teacher's vocation is to point to God in Christ, always and only the One who saves us by grace and is as near to us as our hearts and our voices. *Soli Deo Gloria.*

MINDY DOUGLAS

---

2. Martin Luther King Jr., "Without a Preacher," King Papers, Stanford University, https://kinginstitute.stanford.edu/king-papers/documents/without-preacher.

Proper 14 (Sunday between August 7 and August 13 inclusive)

Matthew 14:22–33

[22] Immediately he made the disciples get into the boat and go on ahead to the other side, while he dismissed the crowds. [23] And after he had dismissed the crowds, he went up the mountain by himself to pray. When evening came, he was there alone, [24] but by this time the boat, battered by the waves, was far from the land, for the wind was against them. [25] And early in the morning he came walking toward them on the sea. [26] But when the disciples saw him walking on the sea, they were terrified, saying, "It is a ghost!" And they cried out in fear. [27] But immediately Jesus spoke to them and said, "Take heart, it is I; do not be afraid."

[28] Peter answered him, "Lord, if it is you, command me to come to you on the water." [29] He said, "Come." So Peter got out of the boat, started walking on the water, and came toward Jesus. [30] But when he noticed the strong wind, he became frightened, and beginning to sink, he cried out, "Lord, save me!" [31] Jesus immediately reached out his hand and caught him, saying to him, "You of little faith, why did you doubt?" [32] When they got into the boat, the wind ceased. [33] And those in the boat worshiped him, saying, "Truly you are the Son of God."

Commentary 1: Connecting the Reading with Scripture

The account of Jesus' sea adventure is a fitting continuation of the ongoing Gospel narrative that provides evidence of Jesus' divinity. It also offers directives for Matthew's church as they face the challenges that confront them as followers of the Christ. After employing divine power in the feeding of the five thousand, Jesus goes off alone again to reflect and to commune with God. It is the first time in Matthew that Jesus is recorded as praying, although in the Sermon on the Mount he provided directives for praying (Matt. 6:7–15).

One wonders why the specificity of Jesus' intention, to pray, is important to this story. What is the point of differentiating between Jesus' withdrawal after hearing of John's death, where he leaves the disciples and withdraws to "a deserted place by himself" (14:13), and his similar action after his miraculous work? Is it a call to prayer for the church? Note also the symbolism of Jesus' absence from his disciples, who, as is the case of Matthew's church, must carry out his mission. It is also a message for the whole Christian church that they must carry out their mission without the physical presence of Jesus. Then Jesus comes to the disciples, but, reminiscent of his postresurrection appearances, they do not recognize him and are afraid.

The location of the story seems to be for the purpose of revealing Jesus' divinity, which was brought uncompromisingly to light in the feeding story. Its position makes it the culminating event in a series that gives visibility to his identity as the Son of God. It also addresses the ongoing situation of Matthew's church as they try to carry out their mission in the turbulence visited by their society.

This account seems to point to Jesus' unrecognized presence among the present disciples, who are gripped by fear for their lives as Christians. Matthew's church is caught in the turmoil of a persecuted existence because of their belief in Jesus, and the reality of their fear is a reflection of the fear of the disciples in the boat. Peter's desire to reach Jesus and then falling victim to the choppy waves may also fit with Peter's leadership of the church that requires him to face the prevailing storms that batter the community. Given Matthew's concern for the fledgling Christian church to whom these writings are directed, one wonders also at the purpose for presenting the events with a background that reminds the church of Jesus' physical absence.

Further, when Jesus appears, the disciples are afraid and must be led to peace. How does that affect Matthew's postresurrection congregation, or any congregation? Unlike the feeding story, the demonstration of Jesus' divinity occurs only in the disciples' presence. There are no crowds, and his conversation with them about their lack of faith occurs only within their hearing. So, does Christ act only within the confines of the church, in the presence of his disciples? Then what is the evidence of Christ's presence in the world? The church is being persecuted by outside forces, and internally it is caught in the grip of fear, so Matthew's message is a reminder that, sad as it may be, their situation is not unique, and also that Christ in his divinity offers the assurance that comes from his saving love.

The disciples are battered and fearful, but Peter speaks up and steps out to meet Jesus. Here he represents all who would step out and are challenged in their effort to meet Christ. The connection to the overarching narrative of Matthew's Gospel is the disciples' eventual ability to recognize Jesus' presence in their midst and worship him as the Son of God.

What does it require for one to acknowledge Jesus' presence in turbulent times in the church? When doubts arise, how does the church find assurance in faith that Jesus is present to save? The importance of this story does not rest simply with Peter's actions; Jesus' actions are of major importance. What this story contributes to Matthew's declared Christology is the salvific motif that is evidenced in Peter's cry and Jesus' response. Peter cries out to be saved. Although he is a member of the group who express their doubt about Jesus' identity, he seems to have overcome that doubt with faith. His action models for disciples the need to move beyond fear, to faith openly seeking God's saving grace. It is not simply that Peter sank because he took his eyes off Jesus; it is more noteworthy that Jesus the Christ stands ready to save in the midst of both fear and faith.

Here, unlike in the earlier story (Matt. 8:23–27), once Jesus identifies himself, the disciples no longer question his identity. They acknowledge his divinity, confessing to him, "Truly you are the Son of God" (14:33b). It is this culminating declaration by the disciples, which is often overlooked or considered secondary by preachers, that is of greatest importance to the general meaning and purpose of Matthew's Gospel narrative. In the church, where fear and faith exist together in the midst of the many and varied challenges that shake or even batter the church, the challenge for disciples and the whole church is to make that confession, and continue to step out, trusting in the saving grace of Jesus Christ.

A Living, Daring Confidence in God's Grace

Faith ... is a divine work in us which changes us and makes us to be born anew of God. It kills the old Adam and makes us altogether different men, in heart and spirit and mind and powers; and it brings with it the Holy Spirit. O it is a living, busy, active, mighty thing, this faith. It is impossible for it not to be doing good works incessantly. It does not ask whether good works are to be done, but before the question is asked, it has already done them, and is constantly doing them.

Faith is a living, daring confidence in God's grace, so sure and certain that the believer would stake his life on it a thousand times. This knowledge of and confidence in God's grace makes men glad and bold and happy in dealing with God and with all creatures. And this is the work which the Holy Spirit performs in faith. Because of it, without compulsion, a person is ready and glad to do good to everyone, to serve everyone, to suffer everything, out of love and praise to God who has shown him this grace. Thus it is impossible to separate works from faith, quite as impossible as to separate heat and light from fire. ... Pray God that he may work faith in you. Otherwise you will surely remain forever without faith, regardless of what you may think or do.

Martin Luther, "Preface to the Epistle of St. Paul to the Romans," ed. E. Theodore Bachmann, in *The Works of Martin Luther*, ed. Helmut T. Lehmann (Philadelphia: Fortress, 1960), 35:371–72.

The motif of God's saving love is the overarching theme of these lectionary readings. Just as Jesus reaches out to Peter as he is caught in a situation with the risk of death, God reaches down and saves those who are caught in the death-dealing situations of life. In much the same way, when we are caught in the storms of life that are not entirely of our own making, God responds with saving power when we cry out to God. It is noteworthy that the storm does not cease while Peter is walking on the water, but with his eyes fixed on Jesus, he experiences the faith to believe that he can overcome his fear. In the midst of each storm, there is divine grace that saves when we cry out, and for the church, Christ is the locus of God's salvific love. The readings call the church to remembrance and praise, to make their proclamatory response to that good news, and like the disciples openly confess Jesus is Lord.

That creedal confession was the requirement of Christian disciples in the beginning of the church. It is a matter of faith that reflects the teaching of the prophets, specifically Joel 2:32a, that offers the assurance: "Then everyone who calls on the name of the LORD shall be saved." This is quoted by Peter in his noteworthy Pentecost Day speech (Acts 2:21), making reference to their belief in the lordship of Jesus Christ. As disciples we are called to confess Jesus as Lord in recognition and acceptance of the redemptive sacrifice of Jesus.

Perhaps the church needs to reclaim its confessional nature and put it into action. While confession of sin, more common in today's church, is necessary, the creedal confessions that have taken a back seat to a somewhat facile version of praise and worship might need to be revived. We recognize Jesus as the second person of the Trinity, but given the storms that are raging around the Christian church, there might be a need for the whole church to again confess, like the early Christians, Jesus is Lord.

GENNIFER BENJAMIN BROOKS

Commentary 2: Connecting the Reading with the World

This story about Jesus appearing to his disciples in a boat in a storm-tossed sea is carefully structured to symbolically reflect the situation of the post-Easter church.

In the first place, Jesus is not with his followers. The text states explicitly that this separation is not their choice, but his (Matt. 14:22); and by accenting his aloneness on the mountain (v. 23), it likewise emphasizes their isolation from him. The mountaintop is not a place for teaching as before (chap. 5), but now the site of communion with God in prayer. The result of this arrangement is that the community finds itself alone "below" while Jesus exists apart and "above" in the presence of God. This is, in storied form, the fate of the church in every age: its Lord alive, but not as mundanely accessible as it might like.

The followers are together in the same boat, a symbol that neatly captures the church's collective identity and shared fate: separated from their Lord and weathering on their own the storm of life in a hostile environment. Things are not going well. They are, in the first place, "far from land" (v. 24)—hundreds of yards, too far to easily turn back from their present course. More telling, the boat they share is not "battered" by waves as the NRSV has it, but rather "tortured" or "tormented" (*basanizō*), an interpersonal verb more suited to describing the trials of a human community in the midst of opposition than an inanimate vessel. Finally, we learn that "the wind is against them," a symbol that resonates with our contemporary struggle against the headwinds that resist the life of faith in what Charles Taylor has rightly labeled "a secular age."[1] In short, the boat on the storm-tossed sea is the church in the world, at risk and assailed by the forces of chaos. For reasons beyond the community's

---

1. See James K. A. Smith, *How (Not) to Be Secular: Reading Charles Taylor* (Grand Rapids: Eerdmans, 2014).

control, and through no fault of their own, the situation is dire.

In the midst of such hardship, indeed in the darkest hour of the night (v. 25), the Lord does come to his disciples; but his presence is not familiar or immediately comforting. His immunity to the power of the hostile sea is awesome to behold, but alienating. This Jesus is difficult to recognize, and with the storm's threat shaping their perception, a visitation from beyond their isolation seems as likely to hold menace as comfort. In their terror they take him for a ghost (v. 26). We might say that the presence of Jesus in the midst of the post-Easter church is contested, subtle, and even troubling—a matter for careful discernment rather than unambiguous grounds for triumphalism. The comfort that the Lord offers lies on the other side of the personal risk of embracing a power that is strange to our ordinary senses and sensibilities.

Perhaps the most obvious connection to the life of the church comes at the end of the encounter when Jesus' identity is confirmed and the storm calmed: his followers respond by worshiping him as "the Son of God" (v. 33). If we think of worship as a reverent attitude, it will not seem too out of place for twelve people to manage it on a small boat at sea. However, Matthew's "worship" (*proskyneō*) is a full-bodied devotion that involves falling to the ground in awe and supplication, an activity that points toward the life of "those in the boat" (v. 33), the church on dry ground. Such worship is the proper end of the church's odyssey in the boat.

Before, they had Jesus among them in the familiar way, but they did not know him yet as they should. Only after the difficult passage through separation, danger, terror, and the risky quest to discern the presence of Jesus in their midst, do they have and know him rightly at last and experience the strange peace he offers. Thus, the church's journey in the liminal space between advents is not merely a time to endure until better things, but a unique opportunity to know its Lord now as the one who is worthy of worship.

The connections to ecclesial experience embedded throughout this narrative are clear, yet Matthew's telling, in particular, is also intensely personal in scope. Of the three canonical accounts of this episode, only Matthew depicts Peter's encounter with the ghostly Jesus, with all its resonance for the individual struggle to believe. When Jesus reassures the Twelve that he is no ghost and encourages them to take courage, Peter alone embraces the risk of more fully experiencing the ambiguous presence of the Lord through obedience.

Is he wrong to leave the shelter of the boat and seek something more on his own? "Lord, if it is you, command me to come to you on the water" (v. 28). The challenge is grounded in tentative trust, for if the Lord commands a thing, it surely becomes possible. Jesus, for his part, seems open to what Peter alone is risking: "Come" (v. 29). Of course, the venture ends in failure. It is the wind that does it; seeing it, focusing on it, Peter vacillates and begins to sink into the waters of chaos. After a cry for help, he is saved from drowning, but not from a critical debriefing in the boat: "You of little faith, why did you doubt?" (v. 31).

So perhaps we have our answer: stay in the ecclesial boat and take Jesus' word for it. Do not venture out in search of extraordinary experiences. That is the safest way to believe without getting wet or enduring a humiliating public reprimand about not having enough faith.

Then again, maybe not. Peter's story suggests that you have to get out of the boat in order to fail in such a spectacular, interesting, and generative way. Jesus does not demand that anyone get out of the boat, but he seems as interested as anyone else to see how the venture will end. Even in failure, it does not end in a drowning, but in rescue, and ultimately in grace that swallows up doubt and inspires worship in those who watch from the safety of the boat. On this reading, the scold about "little faith" loses its edge, and we hear in it the good-natured ribbing of one who knows that when it comes to the paradox of faith, a little can go a long way (17:20).

On this reading, Christian faith is not about the certitude and safety of believing "from the boat," but rather about the productive tension between doubt and trust that leads us ever deeper into a mysterious relationship with the Lord who comes to us in the darkness and the storm, who is present to us most palpably just when we risk something and begin to sink. Dietrich Bonhoeffer, whose testimony is all the more compelling because of the real risks he took for faith, summarizes this interpretation in a well-known passage from *The Cost of Discipleship*: "Peter had to leave the ship and risk his life on the sea, in order to learn both his own weakness and the almighty power of his Lord. If Peter had not taken the risk, he would never have learned the meaning of faith."[2]

LANCE PAPE

---

2. Dietrich Bonhoeffer, *The Cost of Discipleship*, rev. ed., trans. R. H. Fuller (New York: Macmillan, 1959), 53.

Proper 15 (Sunday between August 14 and August 20 inclusive)

Isaiah 56:1, 6–8 and Genesis 45:1–15　　Romans 11:1–2a, 29–32
Psalm 67 and Psalm 133　　Matthew 15:(10–20) 21–28

Isaiah 56:1, 6–8

¹Thus says the Lord:
　　Maintain justice, and do what is right,
for soon my salvation will come,
　　and my deliverance be revealed.
. . . .
⁶And the foreigners who join themselves to the Lord,
　　to minister to him, to love the name of the Lord,
　　and to be his servants,
all who keep the sabbath, and do not profane it,
　　and hold fast my covenant—
⁷these I will bring to my holy mountain,
　　and make them joyful in my house of prayer;
their burnt offerings and their sacrifices
　　will be accepted on my altar;
for my house shall be called a house of prayer
　　for all peoples.
⁸Thus says the Lord God,
　　who gathers the outcasts of Israel,
I will gather others to them
　　besides those already gathered.

Genesis 45:1–15

¹Then Joseph could no longer control himself before all those who stood by him, and he cried out, "Send everyone away from me." So no one stayed with him when Joseph made himself known to his brothers. ²And he wept so loudly that the Egyptians heard it, and the household of Pharaoh heard it. ³Joseph said to his brothers, "I am Joseph. Is my father still alive?" But his brothers could not answer him, so dismayed were they at his presence.

⁴Then Joseph said to his brothers, "Come closer to me." And they came closer. He said, "I am your brother, Joseph, whom you sold into Egypt. ⁵And now do not be distressed, or angry with yourselves, because you sold me here; for God sent me before you to preserve life. ⁶For the famine has been in the land these two years; and there are five more years in which there will be neither plowing nor harvest. ⁷God sent me before you to preserve for you a remnant on earth, and to keep alive for you many survivors. ⁸So it was not you who sent me here, but God; he has made me a father to Pharaoh, and lord of all his house and ruler over all the land of Egypt. ⁹Hurry and go up to my father and say to him, 'Thus says your son Joseph, God has made me lord of all Egypt; come down to me, do not delay.

¹⁰You shall settle in the land of Goshen, and you shall be near me, you and your children and your children's children, as well as your flocks, your herds, and all that you have. ¹¹I will provide for you there—since there are five more years of famine to come—so that you and your household, and all that you have, will not come to poverty.' ¹²And now your eyes and the eyes of my brother Benjamin see that it is my own mouth that speaks to you. ¹³You must tell my father how greatly I am honored in Egypt, and all that you have seen. Hurry and bring my father down here." ¹⁴Then he fell upon his brother Benjamin's neck and wept, while Benjamin wept upon his neck. ¹⁵And he kissed all his brothers and wept upon them; and after that his brothers talked with him.

Commentary 1: Connecting the Reading with Scripture

Isaiah 56:1, 6–8. Bible scholars generally agree that the book of Isaiah is a composite work that was written between the eighth and sixth centuries BCE. This passage comes from the end of that time period and is part of a section of the book often called Second Isaiah, which begins in chapter 40 and addresses the concerns of the Israelites during their time of exile in Babylon. According to some scholars, this passage contains the opening words of another section of the book, called Third Isaiah (chaps. 56–66), that anticipates the people's return from exile.

Second Isaiah was written to offer hope and encouragement to a community that was living far from its homeland, so salvation and deliverance are key themes of this part of the book. In fact, both those words are found in the first verse of this passage. The final chapters of Isaiah add an interesting twist to that message, however, in that the promise of salvation is extended to those from whom it was previously denied. This is a revolutionary idea that runs counter to the dominant view of the rest of the Hebrew Bible, which maintains that the Israelites are the chosen people and alone enjoy a privileged relationship with God through the covenant that traces its roots to Abraham.

According to this passage, other groups that had previously been considered outsiders are now on equal footing with the Israelites as part of God's community. Foreigners will observe the Sabbath and be allowed to enter the temple, referred to as "a house of prayer for all peoples," where they will offer sacrifices and praise God (Isa. 56:7). In addition, those among the Israelites who had previously been shunned, called "the outcasts of Israel," are also invited back into the fold, along with others who were marginalized (v. 8). This message of inclusivity and universality can also be seen in the section of the chapter that is not included in this reading but continues the theme and has an important modern-day connection. In verses 3–5, God also invites eunuchs, a group that was never integrated into the life of the community, to participate fully as covenantal partners. Among the gifts God will bestow on eunuchs are "a monument and a name" (*yad vashem*) that will be better than sons and daughters (v. 5). That Hebrew phrase was chosen as the name for Israel's national Holocaust memorial center in Jerusalem, and so Isaiah's words of hope and deliverance continue to be a poignant reminder in our own time.

Isaiah's call to act justly and do what is right is one that is echoed by other biblical prophets (v. 1). Amos speaks out against those who personally profit while oppressing the poor and the needy (Amos 2:6–8). Similarly, Micah urges his people to act justly, speak kindly, and walk humbly with God (Mic. 6:8). The challenge that Isaiah's appeal to inclusivity poses for many is vividly portrayed in the story of the prophet Jonah, who has a hard time coming to terms with God's compassion on the people of Nineveh when they repent and ask forgiveness (Jonah 4).

In the New Testament, Jesus puts into practice Isaiah's message of acceptance when he associates with sinners and other outcasts of society and challenges those who abuse and mistreat them. A portion of this passage from Isaiah is spoken by Jesus in the story of the cleansing of the temple that is told in Mark's Gospel. After expelling the money changers and other merchants from the sacred precinct, Jesus explains his action by quoting from his prophetic forebear, "Is it not written, 'My house shall be called a house of prayer for all the nations'?" (Mark 11:17a).

Genesis 45:1–15. The immediate literary context of this passage is the story of Joseph recounted in Genesis 37–50. Joseph's reunion with his family is something the reader has been anticipating ever since his brothers sold him to Egypt (Gen. 37), and it becomes more likely as they make two trips there in search of food due to a famine in their homeland of Canaan (Gen. 42–44). The true identity of the Egyptian official they have been meeting with during their visits has remained a mystery to them until now, but in this scene they learn what has become of the younger brother they abandoned many years ago.

The Joseph story provides an explanation for how the Israelites ended up in Egypt, and it sets the stage for God's deliverance of the people under Moses' leadership in the book of Exodus that follows. Joseph orders his brothers to return to Canaan and bring their father to him (45:9, 13), and the following chapter contains a detailed list of all of Jacob's offspring who made the trip to Egypt, some sixty-six people, not counting his sons' wives (46:5–27). Many scholars believe the Joseph story originally circulated as a separate composition that was later appended to the book of Genesis to connect the stories of the patriarchs and matriarchs with the traditions associated with Moses.

In this scene Joseph mentions God four times in the space of five verses, and these are the first places in the story that he expresses his belief that the Deity was responsible for his being sold into Egypt. Three times he states that God sent him there so that he might do good (vv. 5, 7, 8), and he then urges his brothers to bring their father to him so he might see for himself how God has elevated Joseph to second-in-command in Egypt (v. 9). In this way, Joseph effectively acknowledges the Deity's role in saving the family while simultaneously preventing his brothers from taking credit for it.

This reunion of brothers recalls another scene of fraternal reconciliation earlier in Genesis 33, when their father Jacob is reunited with his twin brother Esau. That passage calls attention to the fact that Joseph and his brothers were present, and Joseph is the only one who is mentioned by name (33:2). When Esau asks who these many children are, Jacob responds in a way similar to how Joseph will address his brothers years later in Egypt, by crediting God for his offspring (v. 5).

All Are One Who Him Receive

Blest be the dear uniting love
that will not let us part;
our bodies may far off remove,
we still are one in heart.

Joined in one spirit to our Head,
where he appoints we go,
and still in Jesus' footsteps tread,
and do his work below.

O may we ever walk in him,
and nothing know beside,
nothing desire, nothing esteem,
but Jesus crucified!

We all are one who him receive,
and each with each agree,
in him the One, the Truth, we live;
blest point of unity!

Partakers of the Savior's grace,
 the same in mind and heart,
nor joy, nor grief, nor time, nor place,
nor life, nor death can part.

Charles Wesley, "Blest Be the Dear Uniting Love," in *The Poetical Works of John and Charles Wesley*, ed. G. Osborn (London: Wesleyan-Methodist Conference Office, 1868), 2:221.

The reconciliation scene involving the twin brothers also anticipates what will happen at the end of Jacob's life, when he will meet Joseph's two sons for the first time and ask, "Who are these?" and Joseph will respond, "These are my sons, whom God has given me" (48:8–9). In this way, the scene between Joseph and his brothers is the linchpin that connects two other episodes in his family's life that center on the themes of brotherhood, reconciliation, and recognition.

The resettlement of Jacob's family in Egypt due to a famine has key elements in common with a similar journey that Abraham and Sarah make when they also flee Canaan for the same destination and for the same reason (12:10–20).

Another canonical connection can be seen in Psalm 105:16–17, the only other place in the Bible to state explicitly that God sent Joseph to Egypt. A few verses later it is mentioned that Jacob, here referred to as Israel, joined Joseph in Egypt (Ps. 105:23).

In the New Testament's Acts of the Apostles, Stephen gives a speech prior to his martyrdom in which he states that God was with Joseph in Egypt and rescued him from his troubles, and he then goes on to mention the scene in which Joseph reveals his true identity to his brothers and sends for his father and the rest of his family (Acts 7:9–16).

JOHN KALTNER

Commentary 2: Connecting the Reading with the World

The opening verse in Isaiah 56 frames the theological and ethical content of the other two passages, as well as a much larger definition of a word/action that is hotly debated in our communities: justice. Yes, it is obvious and stated clearly in this opening verse that justice should be maintained and that we are required to do what is right—but what does that mean? For years, philosophers, ethicists, and theologians have wrestled with these terms and provided explanations of justice. For example, recent and popular definitions of justice include these: (a) Reinhold Niebuhr's affirmation that "equality is always the regulative principle of justice; and in the ideal of equality there is an echo of the law of love";[1] (b) Paul Tillich's understanding that "all justice is derived from the fundamental principle of the person-to-person encounter";[2] and Karen Lebacqz's grounding of justice in right relationships, not based so much on outcome-oriented goals, but rather in seeking ways to develop, maintain, and promote holistic relationships.

Contemporary debates related to justice are no different. A quick look at the news of the day suggests one will find different groups, with different (and sometimes opposing) political views, picketing and marching before government buildings chanting, "We want justice, we want justice." A quick survey of those asking for justice, of their definitions, practices, and requirements for justice, would reveal a wide array of approaches and theories of justice. Yes, the question remains, What is justice? Furthermore, is there a difference between "secular justice" and "Christian justice"?

First, it is important to note that in the three selected passages, justice is linked to salvation. In the opening verse, justice is connected to God's deliverance and salvation. In the second passage, references to the "holy mountain," "altar," and "house of prayer" are indicative and representative of salvation motifs. Furthermore, in this narrative it is God who gathers and constitutes God's people. Lastly, in the third passage, Joseph does not describe his fate and eventful journey in terms of vengeance or looking for ways to punish his brothers for what they did to him. Instead, Joseph affirms that "God sent me before you to preserve life. . . . God sent me before you to preserve for you a remnant on earth" (Gen. 45:5b, 7a). These affirmations

---

1. Reinhold Niebuhr, *An Interpretation of Christian Ethics* (New York: Harper & Bros., 1935), 108.
2. Paul Tillich, *Love, Power, and Justice* (New York: Oxford University Press, 1954), 79.

speak of salvation, deliverance, and preservation of life. For all these reasons, it is imperative that in our conversations and deliberations regarding justice, we not forget its direct and essential connection to salvation. Obviously, this begs the questions: What is salvation? How does it relate to justice?

Perhaps a good starting point would be to look at the narrative in Isaiah, where an interesting notion is introduced that goes against the expectations of the immediate intended audience. It is not complicated to see that in many instances the people of God in the Old Testament considered themselves, and many occasions rightly so, as exclusive recipients of God's salvation, that is, sole recipients of God's favor and preference. In an interesting fashion, Isaiah, in his definition and parameters of God's people, includes "foreigners"! Without a doubt, this inclusion represents an important plot twist in understanding the identity and nature of God's people and salvation.

Furthermore, the inclusion of foreigners is again emphasized and affirmed in the reference to God's house of prayer, when this house, God's house, is to be called a "house of prayer for *all* peoples" (my emphasis). Again, this reference is a general inclusion that goes beyond the limits, boundaries, and exclusive selection commonly understood at the time. What is more fascinating is that these references are connected to notions of salvation. This explanation would seem contradictory to Joseph's narrative, in which Joseph and his brothers "are saved" simply because they are part of God's people.

However, a closer look at the story would render a broader interpretation, particularly references to Joseph's influence and authority over others, such as "[God] has made me a father to Pharaoh, and lord of all his house and ruler over all the land of Egypt" (v. 8). Obviously, this affirmation offers a much broader scope and includes both groups under the fate and blessing of Joseph's leadership. More importantly, and more directly related to an understanding of justice, is the fact that Joseph's reaction is filled with mercy, grace, and forgiveness.

This stands in clear contrast with current understandings of secular or legal justice. Given his circumstances and all that he endured, many of us would be able to understand and perhaps even justify it if Joseph's reaction was one of seeking some form of retribution for what was done to him (betrayed, attempted murder, sold into slavery). Shockingly there is no sense of revenge or an indication toward retributive justice by Joseph. Rather, his explanation is based on an understanding of salvation as extending God's blessings, grace, and looking for ways to restore everyone involved.

Obviously for the Christian community, soteriology is an integral element in the proclamation of the good news as well as the meaning and practices of justice. These passages seem to point to a distinctive form of justice that is not commonly embraced and practiced in our current debates and liturgies. This form of justice is primarily concerned with restoring relationships with everyone involved, including victims and perpetrators, and thus it is properly labeled as restorative justice.

Restorative justice incorporates the essential components of salvation as presented in the selected passages. For example, restorative justice focuses on the harm that has been done to people and seeks ways to restore damaged relationships, by creating obligations and responsibilities for everyone involved. Salvation through Christ also consists precisely of these elements; it seeks to restore the relationship between God and humans—damaged by sin, self-centered desires and practices—by inviting everyone involved to assume responsibilities for their wrongdoings, not to condemn them but as the starting place on the journey to bring healing and restoration.

In terms of liturgical practices, salvation as *restoration* should be the main focus in every sermon, every song, and every worship expression. We live in a fragmented society and an environment of ideological divisiveness in which victims and aggressors accuse each other of being the opposite—victims calling "the other" aggressor, and vice versa. In these troubled times, the proclamation of good news must include salvation as restorative justice, and liturgical practices should offer such opportunities. For example, during the Eucharist the emphasis on being one body and having one baptism should be the cornerstone of the Christian message, not seeking consensus and full agreement, but rather looking for tangible ways to offer healing, restoration, and justice to everyone involved.

Finally, salvation and justice linked by restoration are perfectly described in Romans, particularly in 5:6–9 and 6:18: "Christ died for us at a time when we were helpless and sinful. No one is really willing to die for an honest person, though someone might be willing to die for a truly good person. But God showed how much he loved us by having Christ die for us, even though we were sinful" (CEV). And "You, having been set free from sin, have become slaves of righteousness." In these verses the all-inclusive love of God is present, as well as a call to live out and embrace God's justice—restoring everyone involved.

HUGO MAGALLANES

Proper 15 (Sunday between August 14 and August 20 inclusive)

Psalm 67

¹May God be gracious to us and bless us
    and make his face to shine upon us,
²that your way may be known upon earth,
    your saving power among all nations.
³Let the peoples praise you, O God;
    let all the peoples praise you.

⁴Let the nations be glad and sing for joy,
    for you judge the peoples with equity
    and guide the nations upon earth.
⁵Let the peoples praise you, O God;
    let all the peoples praise you.

⁶The earth has yielded its increase;
    God, our God, has blessed us.
⁷May God continue to bless us;
    let all the ends of the earth revere him.

Psalm 133

¹How very good and pleasant it is
    when kindred live together in unity!
²It is like the precious oil on the head,
    running down upon the beard,
on the beard of Aaron,
    running down over the collar of his robes.
³It is like the dew of Hermon,
    which falls on the mountains of Zion.
For there the Lord ordained his blessing,
    life forevermore.

Connecting the Psalm with Scripture and Worship

"For there the Lord ordained his blessing" (Ps. 133:3a). Both of the psalms in this week's lectionary readings are centered on God's blessings and call the readers/hearers to focus on and offer praise to God for divine blessings. Psalm 67 is a celebration of God's gracious blessing to Israel and a call to other nations to join Israel in praise for God's abundant goodness to all creation (Ps. 67:3–5). Psalm 133 is a reflection on the blessing God ordains, and the psalmist provides a clear picture of a community in worship that is blessed by God as a result of their unity. While they take different approaches in their poetic petitions of praise, these psalms are consistent in acknowledging that all blessings flow from God and are available to everyone who seeks to know God.

Structurally, Psalm 67 moves in four rhetorical units dominated by the theme of blessing and praise within every element. The psalm opens with a petition parallel to the priestly blessing in Numbers 6:24–26. Beginning with a threefold plea for grace, blessing, and a personal awareness of God's favor, the psalmist gives us a prayer that expresses the desire to have God's ways known to all the world, and invites the hearers to praise God and find joy in God's gracious dealings with humanity and all creation. The consequence of this priestly blessing and posture of praise is that the life-giving power of God will be known in all the world.

Psalm 133 begins with a Wisdom saying about how best to live; central to the saying is the notion of unity.[1] With the message that unity in worship prepares God's people for God's blessing, the psalm uses two similes illustrating the blessing of worship in unity and the blessing of life forevermore. First, the psalmist compares that unity to the anointing of Aaron as high priest, the anointing oil dripping from his head through his beard and onto his robe. The oil consecrated his whole being, not just his head; the unity of the church consecrates the whole church and anoints the whole body of Christ for service.[2] The second simile is the dew of Hermon falling onto the mountains, which is the only precipitation in the country during the dry season. This dew is sufficient to produce a harvest of grapes, and falls everywhere, on the high mountain and on the low mountain. The point the psalmist is making with these similes is that God does not discriminate in a community worshiping in unity. When unity settles in a community—be it family, church, or even a nation—it brings blessing and great joy to everyone.

In both psalms, the blessings are gifts given directly from God and are available to everyone connected to and chosen by God. Psalm 67 praises God's saving power and points to justice and guidance as gifts from God, worthy of gladness and joy. The psalmist expresses a desire for all the nations to participate in praising God. The psalm provides a strong response of praise to Isaiah's call to maintain justice, while echoing the gospel's message of the availability of God's mercy and salvation to all. As children of God, we are to maintain justice because our God is equitable and a guide to all the nations. In the same way, Psalm 133 shows God as the one who gives the gift of unity. It is a divine blessing to the community, making it far more than an achievement. Psalm 133 complements the Genesis account of Joseph's reconciliation with his brothers by illuminating God's necessity of unity.

Both psalms present a particular approach for preaching. Psalm 67's congregational prayer for the blessings of God's ways being known among all the nations is a central theme for preaching. It is a message of inclusivity that makes the knowledge of God accessible to all; and this is a gift from God. Through the salvation of Israel the nations will come to know the Lord's ways as savior. This salvation will reveal God as judge and shepherd of the nations (Ps. 67:4).

In addition, the vivid message of unity in Psalm 133 is a great place for a sermon to begin and compels the sermon to encourage renewal of this kind of full living in the blessings of God enjoyed by a community on the journey together. The reality of Christian life is that our personal identity is directly connected to the community of faith to which we belong, and the picture presented here is one that has a sense of community that has been lost in modern Christian culture.

As petitions and praises for God's blessings upon entire communities, both Psalm 67 and Psalm 133 present opportunities to enhance the congregation's participation in worship. Given the formulaic nature of the prayer of blessing presented in Psalm 67, this psalm can be used as a prayer in response to the sermon. Logistically, this prayer can be offered responsively with the preacher serving as Reader 1.

Reader 1: And in response to God's word, let us pray together.
Reader 2: O God, be gracious to us and bless us and make your divine face shine upon us,
Reader 1: that your way may be known upon earth, your saving power among all the nations.
Reader 2: Let the people praise you, O God; let all the peoples praise you.

---

1. Walter Brueggemann and William H. Bellinger Jr., *Psalms* (New York: Cambridge University Press, 2014), 558.
2. C. Hassell Bullock, *Psalms*, vol. 2, *Psalms 73–150*, ed. Mark L. Strauss and John H. Walton (Grand Rapids: Baker, 2017), 463.

Reader 1: Let the nations be glad and sing for joy, for you judge the peoples with equity and guide the nations upon the earth.
Reader 2: Let the people praise you, O God; let all the peoples praise you.
Reader 1: The earth has yielded its increase; God, our God, has blessed us.
Reader 2: May God continue to bless us; let all the ends of the earth revere the Lord.
All: Amen.

Functioning as a response to the proclamation of the Word, the psalm offers the congregation an opportunity to praise God for what they have heard, to petition God for divine blessing, and to intercede for the world, that God's ways be known to all.

In addition, Psalm 133 can be used as a responsive or antiphonal call to worship, in which one or two alternating voices offer up the entire psalm of praise to begin the service in a joyful tone. Using Psalm 133 as a call to worship focuses the tone of the service on the blessings of the unity among the congregation in worship. This would start a service with an emphasis on unity; a time of sharing peace with one another later in the service would connect to this call to unity.

In summary, both psalms offer praise to God for the blessings of salvation and unity. In Psalm 67, the psalmist presents the gladness for the saving power of God and divine favor upon Israel, which is a life-giving power that all should know and share. Psalm 133 reminds us that the unity found among those worshiping God together is infectious, affecting the whole community and resulting in the blessing of life evermore.

KHALIA J. WILLIAMS

Proper 15 (Sunday between August 14 and August 20 inclusive)

Romans 11:1–2a, 29–32

¹I ask, then, has God rejected his people? By no means! I myself am an Israelite, a descendant of Abraham, a member of the tribe of Benjamin. ²God has not rejected his people whom he foreknew. . . .

. . . ²⁹For the gifts and the calling of God are irrevocable. ³⁰Just as you were once disobedient to God but have now received mercy because of their disobedience, ³¹so they have now been disobedient in order that, by the mercy shown to you, they too may now receive mercy. ³²For God has imprisoned all in disobedience so that he may be merciful to all.

Commentary 1: Connecting the Reading with Scripture

Connection 1: Immediate Literary Context. Paul's opening question, "Has God rejected his people?" immediately follows his lament that Israel, despite the public proclamation of the gospel, has been a "disobedient people" who has not believed (Rom. 10:18–21). Paul answers the question by referring to his own identity as a Jew who believes in Christ; Paul himself is evidence that God has not rejected God's people. The question reprises Paul's anguished concern for his Jewish relatives, in 9:1–5, including their (and his) identity as "Israelites" and children of Abraham (9:7).

The intervening verses leading up to 11:29–32 flesh out the logic of "changing places" that Paul deploys in verses 30–32: just as the Jews were insiders to God's covenant and Gentiles were once outsiders, so now, temporarily, Jews are "outside" and Gentiles are receiving salvation through Christ. This logic undergirds Paul's claim that "God has imprisoned all in disobedience, so that he may be merciful to all" (11:32). The global reach of God's judgment magnifies the all-inclusive scope of God's grace (see also Rom. 5:18; 1 Cor. 15:22).

Connection 2: Larger Literary Context. Romans 11:29–36 concludes Paul's defense of God's purposes for Israel, within the larger drama of salvation (Rom. 9–11). In parallel with Romans 8:31–39 as the climax of 1:18–8:39, and 15:7–13 as the climax of 12:1–15:13, Paul quotes Scripture and ends 9:1–11:35 with a doxology or blessing; in each case God's power and providence are exalted.

Immediately following Romans 11:36, Paul launches into an appeal to the Roman Christians to present their bodies to God as "a living sacrifice" (12:1). This is cultic language, and it is connected to the preceding verses by "therefore." Because God intends the salvation of all, *therefore* present your bodies to God, to be transformed by a renewed mind that can discern God's purposes. The subsequent discussion of mutual respect in the body of Christ builds on the preceding conviction that both enemies and friends have a part to play in God's plan (11:28).

Connection 3: Larger Thematic Context. Paul sees his own story and destiny as representative of God's dealings with Israel. His calling is a sign of God's continued election of the Jews. Furthermore, just as God broke into Paul's life, in the midst of his unbelief and disobedience, so also God will save all Israel in the midst of its unbelief and disobedience. This divine rescue operation demonstrates God's elective grace as undeserved gift (11:35), for Paul, for the Gentiles, and for Israel. Moreover, God's purposes encompass human disobedience as well as obedience. A similar claim is made differently in the Gospels, where even Jesus' enemies crown him king (Mark 15:18, 26, 32). In Romans 11:32, God's sovereignty over unbelief as well as belief means that Gentiles cannot judge Jews for not believing in Jesus; no one can pass judgment on another's faith or lack thereof.

Second, God is faithful to the promises God makes to a specific people in history. The actions of God are not ahistorical timeless truths, but historical events that impact real, embodied human communities. In Romans 4, Paul speaks of God's promises to Abraham, and in Romans 9:6–18 he expounds on Israel's election, grounded in God's freedom to have mercy on the undeserving. This particularity and embodiment contribute, then, to the social enactment of God's all-inclusive righteousness in the practical common life of Jew and Gentile worshiping and working together (12:1–21; 14:1–15:7).

Third, the theme of election and divine promise is balanced by the all-inclusive judgment and mercy of God, which Paul argues forcefully in Romans 2–3, and to which he returns in his discussion of Adam and Christ in 5:12–21: "one man's trespass led to condemnation for all, so one man's act of righteousness leads to justification and life for all" (5:18).

Connection 4: Lectionary Context. Genesis 45:1–15 continues the story of Joseph and his brothers, at the moment when Joseph reveals his identity to his brothers, who have come to Egypt in search of food. The story exemplifies two themes from Romans 11. First is the divine providence that acts through the wrong actions of Joseph's brothers and that acts through the disobedience of Israel, in order to further God's saving purposes. Second is the theme of reconciliation rather than rejection. Joseph could reject his brothers, but he chooses to be reconciled; in 11:11–24 Paul exhorts Gentile Christians not to reject or feel superior to non-Christian Jews. Here he sets the stage for his later appeal: "Welcome one another, therefore, just as Christ has welcomed you" (15:7).

Psalm 133 amplifies this theme of reconciliation beautifully, with its celebration of brothers and sisters who "live together in unity" (Ps. 133:1). Similarly, Romans 15:5–6 entreats God "to grant you to live in harmony with one another." The final blessing, "life forevermore" (Ps. 133:3), echoes the promise of "life from the dead" in Romans 11:15. In both the psalm and Romans, eternal life and human reconciliation go together.

In the Gospel reading, it is a Gentile woman who comes to Jesus for help. Jesus' initial statement that he was sent to the lost sheep of the house of Israel parallels Paul's claim that the gospel was for the Jew first (Rom. 1:16); the Jews are first in election, but the Gentiles are included also. So also in Matthew 15:21–28 Jesus heals the daughter of the Canaanite woman, praising the woman's faith.

Connection 5: Canonical Context. In the present order of the New Testament, Romans, often seen as Paul's magnum opus, comes at the beginning of the collection of Paul's letters and the end of Acts. It moves the canonical reader from a big picture view of the progress of the gospel, to an insider view of the content of that gospel, and it sets the table for the reading of the rest of Paul's letters. Its vision is both personal and cosmic, extending from the anguish of the speaker in Romans 7 to the salvation of all people in 11:32. Within the sweep of this threefold account of God's saving power, delivering all humanity from the lethal effects of Adam's sin and creating a new community in which former enemies join in the worship of God, Romans 9–11 distinctively witnesses to God's abiding faithfulness to Israel. So it is a crucial corrective to texts, particularly in the Gospels of John and Matthew, which over the centuries have resourced Christian persecution of Jews.

Sermon Ideas That Emerge from Romans 11:1–2a, 29–32. The scope of Paul's vision of God's providence pulls the rug out from under human pretensions to judge one another. If even those we consider enemies have their place in God's plan, and if even human disobedience comes within the realm of God's mercy, who are we to judge? Paul expands on this theme in Romans 14, but he lays the groundwork here.

Hope is an overarching theme in Romans (15:13), and it is based on the limitless breadth and depth of the "riches and wisdom and knowledge of God" (11:33). Even when it seems that God has abandoned God's people, Paul finds hope in his very big picture of God.

That picture, and the hope that goes with it, is enlarged by worship together with people who are different from us, across social and cultural divisions.

Paul is not afraid to draw on his own experience of God's call and mercy in order to understand what is happening with his Jewish relatives. He does this in conversation with Scripture, so that Scripture and experience work together in his process of discernment. How might that happen in our churches as we struggle to discern the will of God in new situations?

SUSAN GROVE EASTMAN

Commentary 2: Connecting the Reading with the World

Who are the chosen ones now? In this passage, Paul addresses this question, knowing that it is on the mind of the Gentiles in Rome. They, after all, have received the gift of God's Son as the giver of mercy and Savior of the world, while much of Israel has rejected God's gift. Does this mean that God will now reject Israel? Paul is abundantly clear here: "Absolutely not!" God's covenant with Israel is *irrevocable*. It has always been based on grace and will continue to be. God does not go back on God's promises. Israel's disobedience now is met with mercy, as it always has been.

The disobedience of both Jew and Gentile and the mercy of God for both are unquestionable: "For God has imprisoned all in disobedience so that God may be merciful to all" (Rom. 11:32). Gentiles and Jews alike must not become proud. *All* are grafted into God's love and grace by means of God's mercy toward their disobedience. This passage rejects any form of anti-Semitism or arrogance against the Jews. It demonstrates the captivity to disobedience experienced by all, that God's mercy for all might be undeniable.

Here Paul reminds us that God is mysterious in God's ways while always being faithful and just, full of mercy, and abounding in steadfast love. God's grace is sufficient and God's mercy endures forever. God is eternally faithful to God's creation. All, Jews and Gentiles alike, are grafted into God's love, which is immutable, everlasting, and unconditional.

God's mercy has nothing to do with human worthiness. No one deserves God's grace. Even on our best days, we turn away from God and submit to some form of idolatry. We often believe we have earned God's love through our own goodness, when in reality we fall short of what God intends for us and rely on our own strengths instead of relying upon God.

This is the good news, however: God is merciful to a disobedient people. In Jesus Christ, we are forgiven. God alone deserves our awe and our praise. How then do we as Christians live in response to this passage? How does our understanding of our own disobedience and God's great mercy shape the way we live and move and have our being?

Some Christians begin by acknowledging in communal prayers and worship the ways persons have all sinned and fallen short of God's glory. In these prayers of confession, Christians humbly ask for God's mercy, knowing that God is slow to anger and abounding in steadfast love. This confession precedes one's assurance of God's mercy and forgiveness and the promise of a new beginning that grows out of God's sacrifice in Christ Jesus. In Christ we are washed clean and given new life. By God's grace we are made a new creation, and God's gift of mercy opens a new path before us.

The hymn "Come, Thou Fount of Every Blessing" fits liturgically into our understanding of God's endless and undeserved mercy as "streams of mercy, never ceasing" inspire our "songs of loudest praise" and create in us the desire that grace might, like a fetter, bind our wandering hearts eternally to God. Another hymn, "There's a Wideness in God's Mercy," reminds us that the love and mercy of God extend far beyond the "measure of the mind."

Such knowledge of our own sin and recognition of God's gift of mercy ultimately shape and change our lives. In *Les Misérables* Victor Hugo shares a story of God's mercy revealed and embraced. He tells of Jean Valjean, a hardened prisoner and a man full of hate. After serving nineteen years in prison for stealing bread for his starving niece, Valjean is released from prison. When released, Valjean's rage consumes him. By God's grace he finds his way to the home of a bishop who lets him stay the night. Valjean cannot resist the temptation of the silver candlesticks left on the table, and he flees with them in his bag. Soon captured by the police, he finds himself face-to-face with the one he has wronged, certain that he will be thrown back into prison. Instead, he receives his first glimpse of God's mercy: The bishop tells the police that the candlesticks had been a gift to Valjean, but his true gift was the gift of mercy. In the light of this mercy, Valjean comes face-to-face with the darkness of his own life. Having received mercy, he begins to live with mercy toward others.

Pope Francis tells another story of a conversion by mercy. He was but seventeen, on a train in Buenos Aires, on his way to a school picnic where he was considering proposing to his girlfriend. On the way he passed a church and felt compelled to go in. There he met a young, friendly priest and decided to give his confession. As he did so, he was overwhelmed by a sense of God's power and presence, and most of all, by an understanding of God's mercy for him and for the world. In that moment, God called him to a special vocation of mercy.[1]

Responding to his vocational calling, Pope Francis continues to call Christians to ministries of mercy. When speaking at the Extraordinary Jubilee of God's Mercy in Bogota, Columbia, he encouraged those in attendance to be "amazed by God's mercy," to remember their sin, and not to rest on their own merits. He also called them to act in mercy toward the world:

> We live in a society that is bleeding, and the price of its wounds normally ends up being paid by the most vulnerable. But it is precisely to this society, to this culture, that the Lord sends us. He sends us with one program alone: to treat one another with mercy. To become neighbors to those thousands of defenseless people who walk in our beloved American land by proposing a different way of treating them.[2]

Opportunities to show God's mercy to others abound in this world. Jesus cautioned us not to look upon another with condemnation in our hearts. Instead, we should refrain from judgment, remembering that we have been dealt with mercifully by a gracious and loving God. Recognizing this, we should be the first to dispense such mercy to others. As the woman caught in adultery cowered on the ground awaiting the sting of rocks on her body, Jesus invited those without sin to cast the first stones.

In the end, those who have knowledge of God's endless mercy, in spite of humanity's undeserving, will seek to embrace such a gift with gratitude and a desire to reflect such mercy in our own lives. This mercy shapes our knowledge of God and our knowledge of ourselves. Thomas Merton writes:

> Our knowledge of God is paradoxically not of him as the object of our scrutiny, but of ourselves as utterly dependent on his saving and merciful knowledge of us. It is in proportion, as we are known to him that we find our real being and identity in Christ. We know him in and through ourselves in so far as his truth is the source of our being and his merciful love is the very heart of our life and existence.[3]

MINDY DOUGLAS

---

1. Mary O'Regan, *The Catholic Herald*, March 7, 2014, reposted at http://thepathlesstaken7.blogspot.co.uk/2014/03/pope-franciss-vocation-story.html.
2. "Pope Francis Tells a Fractured World: God's Mercy Gives Hope for Change," Catholic News Agency; https://www.catholicnewsagency.com/news/pope-francis-tells-a-fractured-world-gods-mercy-gives-hope-for-change-30199.
3. Thomas Merton, *Contemplative Prayer* (New York: Image Books, 1971), 83.

Proper 15 (Sunday between August 14 and August 20 inclusive)

Matthew 15:(10–20) 21–28

¹⁰Then he called the crowd to him and said to them, "Listen and understand: ¹¹it is not what goes into the mouth that defiles a person, but it is what comes out of the mouth that defiles." ¹²Then the disciples approached and said to him, "Do you know that the Pharisees took offense when they heard what you said?" ¹³He answered, "Every plant that my heavenly Father has not planted will be uprooted. ¹⁴Let them alone; they are blind guides of the blind. And if one blind person guides another, both will fall into a pit." ¹⁵But Peter said to him, "Explain this parable to us." ¹⁶Then he said, "Are you also still without understanding? ¹⁷Do you not see that whatever goes into the mouth enters the stomach, and goes out into the sewer? ¹⁸But what comes out of the mouth proceeds from the heart, and this is what defiles. ¹⁹For out of the heart come evil intentions, murder, adultery, fornication, theft, false witness, slander. ²⁰These are what defile a person, but to eat with unwashed hands does not defile."

²¹Jesus left that place and went away to the district of Tyre and Sidon. ²²Just then a Canaanite woman from that region came out and started shouting, "Have mercy on me, Lord, Son of David; my daughter is tormented by a demon." ²³But he did not answer her at all. And his disciples came and urged him, saying, "Send her away, for she keeps shouting after us." ²⁴He answered, "I was sent only to the lost sheep of the house of Israel." ²⁵But she came and knelt before him, saying, "Lord, help me." ²⁶He answered, "It is not fair to take the children's food and throw it to the dogs." ²⁷She said, "Yes, Lord, yet even the dogs eat the crumbs that fall from their masters' table." ²⁸Then Jesus answered her, "Woman, great is your faith! Let it be done for you as you wish." And her daughter was healed instantly.

Commentary 1: Connecting the Reading with Scripture

The Christology that undergirds the text reflects a God for all people, and Matthew seems to be putting things in place for confirming Jesus as the fulfillment of that role. Verses 10–20 set the scene for the events to come, namely, the incorporation of Gentiles into the body of Christ. The Matthean community, existing in the midst of a religious society of Judaism, is constantly challenged on their beliefs and its foundation in Jesus Christ as the Son of God. Including that section also facilitates a dialogue between Jewish traditions and the church, regarding acceptable practices. Further, the parable placed in the mouth of Jesus is a literary tactic that serves the purpose of imbuing authority into the community's beliefs and practices.

The scribes and Pharisees as Jesus' questioners put into play the conflict between the synagogues and the fledgling Christian communities, and their definition of true holiness is symptomatic of the challenges faced by Matthew's church. It also brings to the forefront the topic of inclusivity, which is addressed directly in the narrative of Jesus' encounter with a Gentile woman. She challenges Jesus and prevails in her argument for inclusion of her people in Jesus' saving ministry. This gives substance to the doctrinal discussion described earlier and documents the turn that is supposedly taken by Jesus, which brings those persons, previously outcast and excluded, into the realm of his redemptive work.

That the woman addresses Jesus as "Lord" three times is noteworthy, but sometimes overlooked. Her use of the title is an intentional ploy by the writer. It supports Matthew's purpose of convincing the hearers of the need to reach beyond their immediate circle to all persons who would be followers of Christ. The story suggests that there is progressive movement in Jesus' understanding of his role as savior of the world, but since Jesus is one with the Creator, perhaps the intent is to convince the church that there must be movement on their part to reach out to all people. Both the plot of the story and Jesus' actions represent movement from resistance to acceptance.

Jesus has already demonstrated his willingness to embrace those rejected by society. He has touched the untouchable, healing a man with leprosy (Matt. 8:1–4); he has engaged in conversation with the unspeakable, restoring a demon-possessed man to wholeness (8:28–34); and he has permitted the touch of the unclean, healing a hemorrhaging woman (9:20–22). As a consequence, he has already revised the meaning of God's chosen people, enlarged the structure of the children of Abraham, expanded the criteria for those who constitute the children of God, and extended the gift of salvation to all.

This encounter with the Gentile woman, an outsider in every sense, is another marker in the great story of God's redemptive plan for the world. The Canaanite woman's story is not simply about one woman's struggle to be heard; it is the struggle of all people to be seen, and heard, and experience fully God's redemptive love. It is a signpost on the way to Jesus' final act and helps define the ever-widening kingdom of God that rejects exclusion of any. Here Jesus Christ, the instrument of God's redemptive plan, ushers in a new kingdom that dismisses the idea of any being excluded.

The church, as the kingdom of God on earth, is called to emulate Jesus' teaching. In applying this story, focus often rests almost exclusively on Jesus' first response to the woman, and in finding justification for his dismissive response. While that bears attention, what is often bypassed is the acknowledgment of the woman's faith. An important secondary focus of Matthew's Gospel is faith in Jesus Christ. Jesus often questions, calls out, or makes reference to the faith of his disciples and those he encounters on his journey.

The woman's challenge to Jesus is founded on her faith in one that she recognizes as her Lord. Faith in Jesus propels her into his location, fuels her actions, underwrites her determination and perseverance; and it is her faith for which Jesus commends her. This story and others told by Matthew are pointers to faith as essential to discipleship. Jesus' responses to his disciples are generally connected with faith.[1] While the woman's daring rightly garners her much commendation, faith in her Lord is worthy of note, as it offers a model for all who would be disciples. It almost begs the question, does one's belief in the lordship of Jesus Christ move one to faith, or does faith in the working of God move one to proclaim that Jesus is Lord?

While there is no obvious thread that connects this Canaanite woman's story of faith to the other lectionary texts, the theme of restoration arises from her faith-impelled action that leads her to demand the right of full inclusion in God's redemptive plan. Not only is there the restoration of her daughter's health, but it brings to recognition the reality that a restored life originates from faith in Jesus Christ. Further, in claiming her place in the realm of God and standing up for her right to God's bounty, the woman opens the way for others who have known rejection in any form, to claim the right to be restored to the wholeness of life that they have been denied.

Restoration and full inclusion are themes that reside at the heart of Christianity. It holds that God's salvific plan began with Israel's salvation and continues with the Gentiles, so that all are united as the family of God inhabiting the new kingdom of God. In support of this belief, and to overcome challenges put forth, a message of assurance was provided for the Jewish

---

1. For example, see Matt. 8:26b; 14:31b; 16:8b–9a; 17:19–20.

community.[2] The requirement for entry to that kingdom is faith. Through Christ the kingdom of God is redefined, and by faith in Jesus Christ we are restored to wholeness of life and oneness with God. Faith in Jesus Christ is foundational to membership in the body of Christ, and that membership is open to all people.

However, an ongoing challenge for the Christian church is its ability to be the inclusive body of Christ that Jesus sought to model in his acceptance of all people, Paul writes in Galatians 3:28: "There is no longer Jew or Greek, there is no longer slave or free, there is no longer male and female; for all of you are one in Christ Jesus." It is a mandate for the church that is too often overlooked or reinterpreted, in order to exclude particular individuals or groups.

In accepting the Gentile woman, Jesus gives vision to a new society that recognizes both the diversity and the inclusivity that God demonstrated in the creation of human beings. In making all human beings in the image of God, God gave us equality, not with God, but with one another. Separation from God and each other is the result of sin. We who claim Christ as the way to God are privileged through faith in Christ to experience restoration and a renewed life. For each person who comes to Christ, who holds on to faith in the lordship of Jesus Christ, there is a place in the kingdom of God. Like the woman, each one can claim it and experience restoration to the family of God. The model set by the daring Canaanite woman is for all time and all people.

GENNIFER BENJAMIN BROOKS

Commentary 2: Connecting the Reading with the World

This passage, read aloud in Christian worship, is a scandal. In fact, this text might be a good test of who is paying attention during the Gospel reading. (Hint: the people with worried looks were actually listening.) It is not often that we catch Jesus with his compassion down, so to speak. Refusing to answer the plea for help from a desperate mother (Matt. 15:23) is bad enough. Explaining that she and her demon-possessed daughter are like house pets that do not rate highly enough to have a bite of the children's supper (v. 26) is simply shocking. It is hard to imagine Jesus doing or saying something more out of keeping with our idea of him. Even if this is not a coded slur calculated to target the woman's ethnicity or gender, it is plainly an attack on her human dignity, a dismissal of her obvious need, and an affront to the very Beatitudes Jesus proclaimed. This is not the Jesus we think we know.

The cognitive dissonance is so acute that many readers have felt compelled to practice some extratextual speculation in an attempt to explain the discrepancy and fix the problem.

Perhaps this puzzling behavior was a test of faith—one that Jesus knew the woman would pass with flying colors. Maybe we can read a joking tone into Jesus' metaphor about dogs and children. After all, there is nothing funnier than ruthlessly teasing a pleading woman whose child is in desperate need, right? No, even the single-minded and exclusive Jesus of Matthew's telling is preferable to the calculating or clueless versions of Jesus invented in misguided attempts to clean up the mess.

The fact is that Matthew's narrative Christology really is messy. Using stories to witness to Jesus leads to complications, nuances, and paradoxes that would never be tolerated in a clean and tidy doctrinal statement. That is OK, though, because Jesus is a person, not a doctrine. Just last week we saw a Jesus so in tune with the God of the universe that he was able to wield divine power to subdue the chaotic forces of nature (14:22–33). Now we see that same Jesus blinded by tribalism and struggling to recognize the universal scope of his own mission. This all-too-human Jesus cannot magically transcend

---

2. See Rom. 11:1–2a, 29–32, the epistle text for this day.

the limits of the parochial view he inherited, but must learn about God's larger purposes the hard way, by trial and error. Which is the real Jesus? "They both are," Matthew seems to say. "Deal with it."

If we feel compelled to make Jesus into the moral exemplar of every single Gospel story, the lessons to be learned here must surely involve his willingness to leave the familiar and draw close to difference (15:21), his refusal to heed the advice of his followers and simply end the encounter (v. 23), and his capacity for relenting gracefully when it becomes clear that he is on the wrong side of an argument (v. 28). Matthew is crystal clear about one thing: whatever it means to be the "Son of David" (v. 22), it sometimes involves having your mind changed.

But in order to change your mind, you have to put yourself in situations that call for change. In the North American context, many of us are slowly awakening at last to the vast scope of our social and economic privilege. It can be unsettling to realize that racism, sexism, and all the rest are not always the result of bad intentions or explicit bias; sometimes we are clueless in our complicity. What will we do with this uncomfortable realization? The temptation might be to withdraw and insulate ourselves as much as possible from exposure to situations in which we might inadvertently do or say the wrong thing. Perhaps in Jesus' dangerous detour into the district of Tyre and Sidon we can recognize a challenge to risk the uncomfortable transformations that come when we make ourselves vulnerable to new people and situations.

The truth is that, for once, Jesus is not the most compelling character in a Gospel story. The Canaanite woman is the hero of this tale, and if we are to commend boldness, it must surely be hers. She comes into this encounter with the odds stacked heavily against her. Woman in a man's world, Gentile petitioning a Jewish healer, single (?) mother with a dependent child with exceptional needs—she has no reason to think this will end well. Nevertheless, she persists. We recognize in her the courage and resourcefulness that come from having history on one's side, and nothing to lose in the meantime. Maybe we also detect in her the audacity that comes to those who plead not only their own case, but the cause of the vulnerable entrusted to their care.

Whatever the source of her daring, a little name-calling will not dissuade or distract her. In fact, the insult meant to end the debate simply suggests a surprising new angle of attack. Absorbing his parable's offense without comment, she reimagines its central thrust, and turns it back on him. Somehow finding a way through Jesus' carefully arranged defenses, her counterstroke is a masterpiece of subversive humility, absolute trust, and verbal brilliance that he simply cannot resist. He is not accustomed to losing these kinds of engagements, but what can you do?

Like the widow who petitioned for justice in one of the stories Jesus told, this woman will not take no for an answer. She does not naively expect that an inclusive vision will somehow win the day without someone who is willing to take a chance, absorb some blows, and do the hard work of making themselves a nuisance. In this way she sets an example not only for the hard, slow work of justice, but for the mysterious work of prayer. Indeed, her petition sounds very much like the prayer language we learn from the Psalms: "Have mercy on me, Lord!" (v. 22, cf. Ps. 86:3).

Jesus' initial refusal is based on the logic of the zero-sum game. He comes bringing mercy, but there is only so much to go around, and it is meant for Israel. If you give the bread to the dogs, there will not be enough for the children. The Canaanite woman—whether because she is enlightened, or perhaps more likely simply because she is desperate in her motherly need—presses for the alternative possibility. What if mercy does not work that way? What if there is bread to spare (14:13–21)? What if Jesus holds in his hands a surplus that can surprise even him? What if it is possible that at any moment, the hidden extra might spill over unintentionally, like crumbs falling from the lips of careless children? This is her desperate parable prayer, and it is so compelling that for once the spinner of kingdom parables is himself caught up in someone else's shocking vision of the possible. "Woman, great is your faith!" (v. 28).

Our Jesus may be so divine that he cannot learn something crucial from a woman trying desperately to help her daughter, but Matthew's Jesus can and does. What then? We should consider how to rework our Christology to fit this story, rather than stubbornly insisting that the story conform itself to our Christology. One possibility is to consider that the inclusive and demanding message of the kingdom arose, at least in part, organically, through meaningful encounters between Jesus and the people he met. It is not always pretty to see how the kingdom of God sausage gets made. Maybe it is beautiful in a whole new way.

LANCE PAPE

Proper 16 (Sunday between August 21 and August 27 inclusive)

Isaiah 51:1–6 and Exodus 1:8–2:10
Psalm 138 and Psalm 124
Romans 12:1–8
Matthew 16:13–20

Isaiah 51:1–6

¹Listen to me, you that pursue righteousness,
    you that seek the LORD.
Look to the rock from which you were hewn,
    and to the quarry from which you were dug.
²Look to Abraham your father
    and to Sarah who bore you;
for he was but one when I called him,
    but I blessed him and made him many.
³For the LORD will comfort Zion;
    he will comfort all her waste places,
and will make her wilderness like Eden,
    her desert like the garden of the LORD;
joy and gladness will be found in her,
    thanksgiving and the voice of song.

⁴Listen to me, my people,
    and give heed to me, my nation;
for a teaching will go out from me,
    and my justice for a light to the peoples.
⁵I will bring near my deliverance swiftly,
    my salvation has gone out
    and my arms will rule the peoples;
the coastlands wait for me,
    and for my arm they hope.
⁶Lift up your eyes to the heavens,
    and look at the earth beneath;
for the heavens will vanish like smoke,
    the earth will wear out like a garment,
    and those who live on it will die like gnats;
but my salvation will be forever,
    and my deliverance will never be ended.

Exodus 1:8–2:10

¹:⁸Now a new king arose over Egypt, who did not know Joseph. ⁹He said to his people, "Look, the Israelite people are more numerous and more powerful than we. ¹⁰Come, let us deal shrewdly with them, or they will increase and, in the event of war, join our enemies and fight against us and escape from the land." ¹¹Therefore they set taskmasters over them to oppress them with forced labor. They

built supply cities, Pithom and Rameses, for Pharaoh. ¹²But the more they were oppressed, the more they multiplied and spread, so that the Egyptians came to dread the Israelites. ¹³The Egyptians became ruthless in imposing tasks on the Israelites, ¹⁴and made their lives bitter with hard service in mortar and brick and in every kind of field labor. They were ruthless in all the tasks that they imposed on them.

¹⁵The king of Egypt said to the Hebrew midwives, one of whom was named Shiphrah and the other Puah, ¹⁶"When you act as midwives to the Hebrew women, and see them on the birthstool, if it is a boy, kill him; but if it is a girl, she shall live." ¹⁷But the midwives feared God; they did not do as the king of Egypt commanded them, but they let the boys live. ¹⁸So the king of Egypt summoned the midwives and said to them, "Why have you done this, and allowed the boys to live?" ¹⁹The midwives said to Pharaoh, "Because the Hebrew women are not like the Egyptian women; for they are vigorous and give birth before the midwife comes to them." ²⁰So God dealt well with the midwives; and the people multiplied and became very strong. ²¹And because the midwives feared God, he gave them families. ²²Then Pharaoh commanded all his people, "Every boy that is born to the Hebrews you shall throw into the Nile, but you shall let every girl live."

²:¹Now a man from the house of Levi went and married a Levite woman. ²The woman conceived and bore a son; and when she saw that he was a fine baby, she hid him three months. ³When she could hide him no longer she got a papyrus basket for him, and plastered it with bitumen and pitch; she put the child in it and placed it among the reeds on the bank of the river. ⁴His sister stood at a distance, to see what would happen to him.

⁵The daughter of Pharaoh came down to bathe at the river, while her attendants walked beside the river. She saw the basket among the reeds and sent her maid to bring it. ⁶When she opened it, she saw the child. He was crying, and she took pity on him. "This must be one of the Hebrews' children," she said. ⁷Then his sister said to Pharaoh's daughter, "Shall I go and get you a nurse from the Hebrew women to nurse the child for you?" ⁸Pharaoh's daughter said to her, "Yes." So the girl went and called the child's mother. ⁹Pharaoh's daughter said to her, "Take this child and nurse it for me, and I will give you your wages." So the woman took the child and nursed it. ¹⁰When the child grew up, she brought him to Pharaoh's daughter, and she took him as her son. She named him Moses, "because," she said, "I drew him out of the water."

Commentary 1: Connecting the Reading with Scripture

Isaiah 51:1–6. This passage can be divided into two three-verse units that each begin in the same way with a command, "Listen to me" (Isa. 51:1, 4). That command is voiced repeatedly in this section of Isaiah (42:18; 44:1; 46:3, 12; 48:1; 49:1), although the same Hebrew verbal form is sometimes translated as "hear" or "obey." An additional request to "listen to me" is found in verse 7, which means that this passage contains the first two of three consecutive units that begin in identical fashion. These are the last occurrences of the phrase "listen to me" in Isaiah, and its heavy concentration here indicates the theme of listening is a key one in this part of the book.

The addressees of verse 1 are described as "you that pursue righteousness," while those of verse 7 are "you who know righteousness." This suggests that the middle unit (vv. 4–6) provides the key that explains how those who pursue righteousness might attain it. This is supported by the presence of the word "teaching" at the beginning of the second and third units. In verse 4 the people are told to give heed to God's teaching, and in verse 7 they are described as having that teaching in their hearts. The middle section identifies the content of God's teaching in verses 5–6.

Those two verses are bookended by references to God's deliverance and salvation, which will be sent out and endure for all ages. Between those two pairs of terms are double references to the heavens and the earth, which will both fade away and disappear. In addition, humanity will suffer the same fate. The arrangement of verse 6, with the passing nature of the heavens, earth, and humanity literally surrounded by the eternal presence of divine deliverance and salvation, communicates the teaching that leads to righteousness: everything is temporary but God.

That would have been a welcome message for the original audience of this passage, which is a portion of what is often called Second Isaiah. Scholars agree that the book of Isaiah is a composite work that was written between the eighth and sixth centuries BCE. Second Isaiah begins in chapter 40 and addresses the concerns of the Israelites during their time of exile in Babylon. This part of the book was composed to offer hope and encouragement to a community living far from its homeland, and this passage's reminder that God would save and deliver them from their difficult situation is a theme that is repeated frequently in Second Isaiah.

Several elements of this passage recall the opening section of Second Isaiah. The statement that the Lord will comfort Zion (51:3) echoes the double reference to comforting the people that begins this part of the book (40:1). Both chapters also mention the wilderness as a place that God will transform into an inhabitable area (40:3; 51:3). In addition, the temporary nature of human existence is highlighted in both sections (40:6–8, 15–17; 51:6). In this way, the passage resumes and repeats a number of key topics that are introduced in the first chapter of Second Isaiah.

The passage alludes to two of the foundational stories of Genesis. The mention of Abraham and Sarah (51:2) describes the blessing the former received from God (Gen. 12:1–3) and is a rare reference in the Hebrew Bible outside Genesis to a specific event in Abraham's life. If Abraham and Sarah are the rock and quarry mentioned in verse 1, these are unusual metaphors for the couple, not found elsewhere in the biblical corpus. The reference to Eden (Isa. 51:3) recalls the garden story of Genesis 2–3, and the only other place it is mentioned in the book is Isaiah 37:12.

Exodus 1:8–2:10. This passage introduces a central figure into the biblical story, as Moses now becomes the main character in the text until his death in Deuteronomy 34. This passage builds on what has come before it, while also anticipating what is to come. Its first verse mentions the rise of a new king in Egypt who did not know Joseph, thereby establishing a link with the Joseph story in Genesis 37–50. which explains how the Israelites settled in Egypt. The passage also explains how Moses became a member of the household of Pharaoh, who will go on to play an important role later in the Moses story. The text does not specify whether he is the same Egyptian ruler whose daughter finds him on the river, but Moses will encounter another unnamed character identified as the pharaoh when, as an adult, he demands that the Israelites be released, sends plagues on the Egyptians to facilitate their release (Exod. 7–11), and leads his people out of Egypt as they begin their return journey to the promised land (Exod. 12–14).

If the larger literary context is expanded beyond the biblical literature, two other texts from the ancient world have interesting and important connections with the story of Moses' birth. It has affinities with the legend of the birth of King Sargon I, the founder of the Akkadian Empire of Mesopotamia around 2300 BCE. According to that tradition, Sargon's mother abandoned him on the Euphrates River by placing him in a waterproof basket. He was subsequently found and raised by a gardener, and then chosen by the goddess Ishtar to be king. Sargon's ascent from a humble origin to a position of great authority that was bestowed on him by a deity mirrors closely what happens to Moses, and many scholars believe the earlier ancient Near Eastern story may have served as a model for the biblical account of Moses' birth.

Moses' birth story is also present in the sacred text of Islam (Qur'an 28:3–13). Its outline is quite similar to what is found in the biblical version, except for one significant difference; God plays a key role throughout the Islamic account by speaking with Moses' mother, assuring her when she begins to fear for her child, and exercising control over the infant's eating habits. In contrast, the Deity is not mentioned a single time in Exodus 2:1–10, a fact that usually escapes the notice of Bible readers, because they tend to read God into the story.

It is not mentioned again elsewhere in the Hebrew Bible, but some of the circumstances of Moses' birth are recounted or alluded to the New Testament. Matthew's Gospel begins with an infancy narrative that presents Jesus as a second Moses. When King Herod orders the deaths of all children two years of age and younger, Joseph and Mary flee to Egypt with their newborn son until it is safe for them to return to Palestine (Matt. 2). This is one of a number of ways by which Matthew's Christology attempts to link Jesus to Moses.

In his speech in Acts of the Apostles, the first Christian martyr, Stephen, mentions Moses' birth and says that his parents abandoned him after three months but Pharaoh's daughter adopted him and raised him as her own child. Stephen also states that the infant Moses was beautiful in God's eyes, but this detail is not included in Exodus 2 (Acts 7:20–22). The Letter to the Hebrews indicates that Moses' parents did not fear Pharaoh's edict and were motivated by faith when they hid their son for three months after his birth (Heb. 11:23–24). It also reports that they, not God, saw that Moses was beautiful, and this matches what is stated in Exodus 2:2. Even though God is not present in the account of Moses' birth, his story will go on to become one that is centered on the themes of deliverance and salvation, like the Isaiah text.

JOHN KALTNER

Commentary 2: Connecting the Reading with the World

What should we do when everyone seems to be against us? What is a Christian response when we are faced with injustice? Should we remain silent and obey the establishment? Should we raise our voices and denounce injustice? What alternatives do we have? Furthermore, where is God in all of this?

In late 2018, governmental officials quoted Romans 13 to demand obedience to the law of the land, appealing to a simplistic (and distorted) understanding of that passage. After listening to these calls for obedience, I wonder, how would they interpret the selected passages for this week's reading? What would they say of the midwives who blatantly lied and disobeyed the law of the land? How would they explain that a key character in the Old Testament was a product of a law-breaking practice? Romans 13 and other passages have been employed to build a case regarding our Christian responsibility to obey the law and adhere to it.

In recent years these arguments have been used in relation to immigration issues. Some argue that it is morally justifiable to prevent persons from entering the United States without proper documentation. Others argue that immigration practices should reflect a more generous understanding of hospitality and become more welcoming, to reflect Christian values that instruct us to love the neighbor regardless of their immigration status. Of course, many others would offer other approaches that fall between these two positions. This debate, regarding Christian responsibility and obedience to the law of the land, is not new. In fact, the Exodus passage is an excellent example of such moral dilemma, as well as the narrative in Isaiah.

The passage in Isaiah was written to offer consolation and hope to a nation who suffered great affliction. I am certain that at this point the people of God were frustrated and devastated. Without a doubt they felt abandoned. What would be the best way to offer comfort, consolation, and begin the task of rebuilding? In trying to find answers for these questions and in looking at the verses in this portion of

The Most Profitable Lesson

All men naturally desire knowledge; but what availeth knowledge without the fear of God? Indeed, a humble husbandman that serveth God is better than a proud philosopher who, though occupied in studying the course of the stars, neglecteth himself. Whoso knoweth himself is lowly in his own eyes and delighteth not in the praises of men. If I understood all things in the world and had not charity, what would it avail me in the sight of God who will judge me according to my deeds? Cease from an inordinate desire of knowledge, for therein is much distraction and deceit. Learned men are anxious to seem learned to others and to be called wise. Many things there are to know which little or nothing profit the soul; and he is very unwise who minds other things more than those that tend to his salvation. Many words do not satisfy the soul; but a good life giveth ease to the mind, and a pure conscience inspireth great confidence in God.

The more thou knowest and the better thou understandest, the more strictly shalt thou be judged unless thy life be also the more holy. Be not therefore elated in thine own mind because of any art or science, but rather let the knowledge given thee make thee afraid. If thou thinkest that thou understandest and knowest much, yet know that there be many more things which thou knowest not. Affect not to be overwise, but rather acknowledge thine own ignorance. Why wilt thou prefer thyself before others, seeing there be many more learned and more skilful in the Scripture than thou? If thou wouldst know or learn anything profitably, desire to be unknown and to be considered of little worth.

The highest and most profitable lesson is to know truly and despise one's self. It is great wisdom and perfection to think nothing of ourselves and to think always well and highly of others. If thou shouldest see another openly sin or commit some heinous offence, yet oughtest thou not to think the better of thyself; for thou knowest not how long thou shalt be able to stand. We are all frail, but do thou regard none more frail than thyself.

Thomas à Kempis, *The Imitation of Christ,* ed. Brother Leo, FSC (New York: The Macmillan Co., 1959), 3–5.

Isaiah, I immediately noticed the English verbs employed in the imperative commands.

"Listen" and "look" are most prominent. God begins the task of reconstruction by asking those in distress to listen and look. Listen to what God has to say and look to what God has done in the past. Sometimes, when we find ourselves overwhelmed by situations in which we have little or no control, when we feel that everything and everyone is against us, it is important to consider these verbs and to begin our own reconstruction project by listening to God and considering what God has done for us previously.

In this same passage, God's actions are clearly described as intentional acts performed by God on behalf of God's people: "The LORD will comfort Zion"; "he will make her wilderness like Eden, her desert like the garden of the LORD"; "I will bring near my deliverance swiftly." These images of "listen" and "look" are intrinsically connected to the Eucharist. In this liturgical and sacramental practice, we are asked to remember the mighty acts of God; to remember Christ's life, death, and resurrection; and in drinking wine and partaking of the bread, we are indeed listening to God and looking at what God has done to help us rebuild our lives, both individually and communally.

Now let us turn our attention to the Exodus narrative. At first glance there are some obvious connections. The people of God here are also under tremendous distress and enduring extremely difficult conditions. Without a doubt the people of God are oppressed, and the oppressor is clearly identified, but in this case, we do not see any look and listen verbs. What we have here is a couple of subversive stories/actions: the story of the midwives who not only disobeyed the law but also lied about the reasons for their actions, and Moses' mother, who also disobeyed the law and kept her baby boy in hiding. In a male-dominated society and in a highly patriarchal culture, it is important to note that these subversive actions were performed by women and not by men, as the intended audience would have expected.

Is God trying to say here that it is OK to lie and disobey the law? Why did God not say so in the years when God's people were in exile? Why does God take a more proactive role in Isaiah and more passive involvement in the Exodus narrative? Instead of offering concrete answers to these questions, these passages seem to lead to trust in God and God's wisdom, but not in a passive way—rather, in a way that questions and/or challenges the establishment.

These passages indicate that every moral action and/or decision we make should be grounded in trust and dependence in God. In both passages this type of dependence is clearly articulated and embraced by the characters in the stories. This trust in God is not without critical engagement—the ability to read and understand the times and social context in which we find ourselves. The people of God in Isaiah's narrative needed a message of hope and restoration, whereas the people of God in Exodus needed brave and subversive leaders, in this case women. Obviously this begs the question, When should we practice one approach and when the other?

In response to the above question, it is important to consider what our Christian heritage teaches us. In exploring Christian responses to government, one will find varied reactions that include total dependence on God, some in which subversive actions were not only important but crucial. In fact the origins of the Christian church are rooted in precisely this type of dilemma. The simple declaration "Jesus is Lord" was seen and taken as a direct challenge and blatant denial of Roman authority, and for this reason many Christians were put to death.

Yes, some of them went into hiding, while others did not hesitate to make their faith public. These Christians trusted God and had a sense of total dependence, yet some took measures to avoid persecutions, while others did not hesitate to make their confession of faith and disobedience to the law of the land public. Once again, the statement "Jesus is Lord" is not only a political affirmation but also an important theological component of the Eucharist. In this case, as we celebrate Holy Communion, we affirm the lordship of Christ, which is another way to express total dependence on God. In this case, a liturgical setting should be a subversive claim that we as Christians make: our ultimate loyalty is not to a particular state/nation but rather to Christ, and we depend on Christ and Christ alone.

Many before us have responded to the question of loyalty and political involvement. One alternative is a theocratic system, a full Christian endorsement of government, which some would argue was the driving force of the Crusades. An opposite alternative is complete separation from the state, as affirmed, at least in principle, by Anabaptists; in this tradition, the Schleitheim Confession affirms that Christians are not called to serve the government, because in doing so, one is serving the world, and Christians are called to serve not the world but God. Now, it is our responsibility to embrace total dependence on God in a world filled with conflicts and dilemmas.

HUGO MAGALLANES

Proper 16 (Sunday between August 21 and August 27 inclusive)

Psalm 138

¹I give you thanks, O LORD, with my whole heart;
   before the gods I sing your praise;
²I bow down toward your holy temple
   and give thanks to your name for your steadfast love and your faithfulness;
   for you have exalted your name and your word
   above everything.
³On the day I called, you answered me,
   you increased my strength of soul.

⁴All the kings of the earth shall praise you, O LORD,
   for they have heard the words of your mouth.
⁵They shall sing of the ways of the LORD,
   for great is the glory of the LORD.
⁶For though the LORD is high, he regards the lowly;
   but the haughty he perceives from far away.

⁷Though I walk in the midst of trouble,
   you preserve me against the wrath of my enemies;
you stretch out your hand,
   and your right hand delivers me.
⁸The LORD will fulfill his purpose for me;
   your steadfast love, O LORD, endures forever.
   Do not forsake the work of your hands.

Psalm 124

¹If it had not been the LORD who was on our side
   —let Israel now say—
²if it had not been the LORD who was on our side,
   when our enemies attacked us,
³then they would have swallowed us up alive,
   when their anger was kindled against us;
⁴then the flood would have swept us away,
   the torrent would have gone over us;
⁵then over us would have gone
   the raging waters.

⁶Blessed be the LORD,
   who has not given us
   as prey to their teeth.
⁷We have escaped like a bird
   from the snare of the fowlers;
the snare is broken,
   and we have escaped.

⁸Our help is in the name of the LORD,
   who made heaven and earth.

Connecting the Psalm with Scripture and Worship

Thanksgiving and trust are a constant theme throughout the Psalter and are central to both of the psalms for this Sunday, Psalms 124 and 138. In Psalm 124, we witness praise for the Lord's help in times of trouble, which begins with a unique "what-if" scenario (Ps. 124:1–5) that turns to praise for the reality of God's presence (vv. 6–8). The psalmist ruminates about those circumstances that could have materialized into destructive forces if the Lord had not been on their side (vv. 1–2).[1] This reflection presents images of helplessness to indicate the potential dangers faced without God's divine protection. Halfway through, the psalmist shifts to then focus on Israel's reality: the Lord *was* on their side and, as a result, none of what they imagined is possible. Therefore, the community places their trust in God, the one who has made the heaven and the earth.

Psalm 138 offers thanks to God and celebrates God's unfailing love (*hesed*). As in Psalm 124, thanksgiving and petition in worship are the primary themes, with wholehearted thanksgiving for salvation. Employing a form of individual thanksgiving, the psalmist opens the song declaring, "I give you thanks, O Lord, with my whole heart" (Ps. 138:1). This is a personal song of thanksgiving that reflects on the faithfulness of God (vv. 1–3), offers public witness to the ways of God so others may know and praise God (vv. 4–6), and offers an affirmation of trust in the Lord's continued deliverance (vv. 7–8). While this psalm is presented in individual form, it gives opportunity for a communal affirmation that God is the living and acting God who delivers, and it calls the community to openly recall the liberation narrative for all to see and believe.

Founded upon praise for God's trustworthiness, these postexilic psalms illustrate God as the one who delivers from all danger. In Psalm 124, God is the one who has been on Israel's side and delivered them from many points of trial and trouble in their history. In Psalm 138, God is the one who looks on the lowly, and out of steadfast love and faithfulness has been an ever-present protector. These illustrations of God sustain the notion that God can be trusted, because God does not abandon God's own. While Psalm 124 reflects on past actions of God's faithfulness, and Psalm 138's confession comes the midst of a world still filled with trouble, both psalms are great guides to the meaning and practice of thanksgiving by the redeemed.

In the context of the full lectionary texts for this Sunday, these psalms both embody and create a bridge between the testaments. Paired with the account of Moses' birth, Psalm 124 acts as a response of rejoicing for saving Moses' life as a baby to ensure the people's future deliverance. This is merely one example of the many ways God was on Israel's side. In the same way, Psalm 138 parallels Isaiah 51 by presenting a personal account of thanksgiving that mirrors the individual account of God's blessing Abraham and Sarah to bear a child, as well as the communal blessings given to Zion. The concluding declaration that God will fulfill God's purpose, and the petition to not abandon the "work of your hands" further substantiate the prophet's declaration to Israel. In addition, the embodied nature of Psalm 138, illustrating bodily acts of worship, connects to the embodied nature of the Romans 12 passage. Paired together, these texts call for more than cognitive processing of God's blessings and requirements; rather, they demand an action of our entire being. In worship, we are called to offer our whole selves, as seen in the psalm, and in Paul's address to the Romans, our salvation calls us to do the same.

Centered on this theme of fully embodied thanksgiving and trust, Psalm 124 and Psalm 138 offer unique approaches to preaching on this Sunday. First, they are a reminder that there are hazards and dangers on the road of our Christian journey, but we do not face these hazards alone. God is both present with us and acting for us to deliver us from the dangers, both seen and unseen. Therefore, without God, we are completely vulnerable and sure to be done in (Ps. 124). The second approach offered for preaching is that crisis comes in our lives, but

---

1. C. Hassell Bullock, *Psalms*, vol. 2, *Psalms 73–150*, ed. Mark L. Strauss and John H. Walton (Grand Rapids: Baker, 2017), 403.

that does not diminish God's commitment to us or God's trustworthiness. God delivers us and accomplishes divine purpose through us.

Psalm 124 presents several opportunities for use in worship. Given its call and response nature ("Let Israel say"), this psalm can beautifully incorporate a musical element into the worship service by using a cantor to lead the psalm and inviting the congregation to sing the refrain from "If It Had Not Been for the Lord."[2] Here, the cantor sings refrain (v. 1), and the congregation repeats it. The cantor then sings verses 2–5, followed by the congregational refrain, and verses 6–8, followed by the congregational refrain sung twice. This arrangement does not have to limit the hymn to only the refrain; in fact it is a wonderful bonding of the congregation to sing the familiar hymn all the way through after the cantor finishes verses 6–8. Bringing the psalm into the service in this manner provides a truly embodied act of worship through song.

Even though Psalm 138 is written in personal form, it can be shared and recited in worship by the entire community as a litany of thanksgiving. Offering two lead voices to represent diverse parts of the community also allows for the congregation to hear and connect to the psalm as they are reciting the litany. In addition, adding movements to verse 2 offers another opportunity to participate with our full selves. First, the congregation would be asked to stand as they are able to join the litany, and the key movements would include slightly bowing at the waist (this can be done seated as well) when reciting "I bow down"; lifting up at the waist and directing your head upward when reciting "and give thanks to your name"; and then lifting your hands upward to the heavens when reciting "for you have exalted your name." This is just enough movement to ignite a new way to envision the psalm without traumatizing those in the congregation who are averse to moving. Both song and movement in worship can bring a deepened and rich experience to the service through these psalms.

Both these psalms offer opportunities for imaginative worship and preaching. All of it is centered on the understanding that the people of God cannot live life in and of themselves, because the overwhelming nature of life will take them over. Life must be lived in full reliance on God's saving presence, while trusting God to be faithful to complete divine purpose in us, because God's love endures forever.

KHALIA J. WILLIAMS

---

2. This suggestion is inspired by an arrangement of Psalm 124 produced and performed at Candler School of Theology in 2017 by Byron Wratee (current PhD student at Boston College) and John Barnes II (current PhD student at Fordham University). "If It Had Not Been For the Lord" can be found in *The Faith We Sing*, #2053, words and music by Margaret P. Douroux (Nashville: Abingdon, 2000).

Proper 16 (Sunday between August 21 and August 27 inclusive)

Romans 12:1–8

¹I appeal to you therefore, brothers and sisters, by the mercies of God, to present your bodies as a living sacrifice, holy and acceptable to God, which is your spiritual worship. ²Do not be conformed to this world, but be transformed by the renewing of your minds, so that you may discern what is the will of God—what is good and acceptable and perfect.

³For by the grace given to me I say to everyone among you not to think of yourself more highly than you ought to think, but to think with sober judgment, each according to the measure of faith that God has assigned. ⁴For as in one body we have many members, and not all the members have the same function, ⁵so we, who are many, are one body in Christ, and individually we are members one of another. ⁶We have gifts that differ according to the grace given to us: prophecy, in proportion to faith; ⁷ministry, in ministering; the teacher, in teaching; ⁸the exhorter, in exhortation; the giver, in generosity; the leader, in diligence; the compassionate, in cheerfulness.

Commentary 1: Connecting the Reading with Scripture

Connection 1: Immediate Literary Context. In Romans 12:1, Paul turns his attention to the shared life of the church, directly addressing his listeners with an exhortation to present their bodies to God. This command is based on his immediately preceding proclamation of God's inscrutable wisdom, and before that, God's gracious mercy extending to all people, both Jew and Gentile. "Therefore"—because God is trustworthy and will never put us to shame; *therefore*, because God's purposes are so much greater than we can imagine; *therefore*, because God is reconciling all people—give your bodies as a living sacrifice to God. This is a form of worship, says Paul, and it involves a transformation of our minds so that we can begin to understand God's will, mysterious as it is. As is typical of Paul, here body and mind go together, and there can be no bodily surrender to God without a transformation of thinking; nor can there be a mental transformation without affecting the body.

Also typical of Paul's teaching, changes in individual believers are inseparable from their relationships with others, including a right evaluation of their own place in the larger scheme of things. There is no place for a sense of superiority, for competition, or for comparison. The depiction of life in the body of Christ is saturated with the language of gift and grace (which also means "gift" in Greek). Paul exhorts his listeners according to the grace given to him (Rom. 12:3); each person's self-evaluation is also done in accordance with divinely given faith. Furthermore, God gifts each person's place in the interpersonal network of Christ's body. Thus the unity in Christ and the distinctiveness of each person are not human entitlements or achievements or due to innate qualities, but are divinely given and sustained. They are human actions with practical consequences in the day-to-day life of the church.

Connection 2: Larger Literary Context. Romans 12:1 begins a new section of Romans, which focuses on the life of the community of faith. It is linked with Romans 9:15–18, 23–24 by the phrase, "the mercies of God," which echoes God's revelation on Sinai (Exod. 33:19). This focus on divine mercy correlates with the focus on grace in 12:3–6; that language of grace and gift in turn recalls Paul's emphasis on the "free gift" of righteousness and life through Jesus Christ, in 5:15–21.

"Rational worship" (Rom. 12:1), linked with a transformation of the mind, reverses the cognitive impairment that accompanied the primal idolatry (1:28). Paul speaks of a renewing of the mind, making the mind new; such language picks up on the promise of "newness of life" in 6:4. In both 6:12–19 and 12:1–3, Paul assumes a unity of body and mind: Christians are to present the members of the body to God as weapons of righteousness (6:13, 19); they are to present their bodies to God as a living sacrifice (12:1) as their whole mind-set is to be renewed (v. 2). The result is a corporate testing out and demonstration of the will of God in the life of the community.

Romans 12:9–21 expands the depiction of the body of Christ, with a series of imperatives about living out the main theme: genuine love of the brothers and sisters in the faith (vv. 9–10). Such love is the evidence of the victory over evil that Paul so confidently enjoins in 12:21; that victory fulfills the promise in 5:17 that "those who receive the abundance of grace and the free gift of righteousness reign in life through the one man Jesus Christ" (RSV; see also 5:21). The reign of grace is the victory of practical love in mutual service; Paul repeats the call to such love in 13:8–10, insisting that it fulfills the law. In fact, love *welcomes* those who are different from us (14:1; 15:7), and such welcome is displayed by reticence to judge those whose understanding of faithful behavior differs from ours (14:4, 10, 13), and by sensitivity to what might be harmful to their faith (14:15).

Connection 3: Larger Thematic Context. Most striking in this brief passage is the predominance of grace and gift. Here is the social outworking of the theological emphasis on God's overflowing grace in Christ, in Romans 5–6 especially. The quality of connection and reciprocal giving and receiving that Paul depicts in his statement that "you are the body of Christ and individually members of it" has a givenness to it, as something we receive and accept, rather than create and manage; as Shakespeare knew, "the quality of mercy is not strained." Instead of teeth-gritting mutual tolerance, here is an abundance of love, overflowing from God's undeserved grace. So alongside the theme of grace is the theme of love; in human experience, the two go hand in hand.

A second and related theme is the relationship between unity and difference. In merely human communities, what passes for "unity" often comes at the cost of conformity. If there is no disagreement or tension in the community, one wonders who has been silenced or excluded. Paul emphatically stresses that "each one" should not think too highly of himself or herself, and that we are "individually" members of Christ, not simply corporately. The individual believer is never absorbed into the group, but neither is she or he alone. Paul is not interested in conformity (a sign of the present world order or status quo), but in transformation of the whole person and the community.

Connection 4: Lectionary Context. The passage from Exodus begins with the story of Israel's increasing subjection in Egypt, and ends with a promise of divine deliverance in the story of baby Moses. Along the way many characters contribute to that deliverance in quiet and crucial ways: the Hebrew midwives, the mother and sister of Moses, Pharaoh's daughter. Bring on the women! Here are members of a community of faith, with diverse gifts and roles, participating in the larger plan of God, whether or not they know it.

Psalm 124 speaks plainly and eloquently of our absolute dependence on the Lord, who is for us, not against us; in Peter's confession in the Gospel, we learn that Jesus is both Lord and builder of the church.

Connection 5: Canonical Context. Transformation of both mind and body is a central theme in Paul's letters (see esp. Phil. 3:21). Such transformation is always God's work in us, not something we can manage on our own. It is a participation in the mind of Christ (1 Cor. 2:16), again guiding the shared deliberations of the church.

The metaphor of the body of Christ capitalizes on a popular image in Greco-Roman culture of cities as "bodies." Paul appropriates this image in 1 Corinthians 12, again with an eye to countering competition and judgment in the community, and to exalting those who are of low account.

Sermon Ideas That Emerge from Romans 12:1–8. The giftedness of human difference, precisely in terms of gifts to the shared life and worship of the church, opens doors for talking about differences in the church today, including but not limited to differences of race and economic and educational status, and the place of persons with disabilities.

Confidence in God's mercy and grace creates the arena or place in which we can risk surrendering ourselves, our souls and bodies, to God's will. In 5:2–5 Paul speaks of "this grace in which we stand" (v. 2) as a place where we can grow through affliction, in endurance, character, and hope, experiencing the outpoured love of God. Such growth is the kind of transformation Paul envisions in 12:2.

SUSAN GROVE EASTMAN

Commentary 2: Connecting the Reading with the World

Today's text follows Paul's passionate doxology about the mystery and majesty of God, whose wisdom and ways are unsearchable and whose mercy is an irrevocable gift to all (Rom. 11:29, 33–36). *Therefore,* Paul writes to his beloved Romans, *therefore,* as those who have experienced and now claim the gift of grace in Christ, respond to this gift with your whole lives, with your bodies, with your full selves. The days of burnt offerings are past. No longer is your relationship with God dependent upon the purity and excellence of what would have been sacrificed on the altar. Because of Christ, nothing stands between humanity and God.

Paul exhorts the Romans to respond to all that God has done by making their embodied selves a *living* sacrifice, formed and shaped in an active response to grace. He warns them of the temptation to conform to the standards of the world and invites them instead to be transformed, renewed, and connected with the mind of God in such a way that they are able to discern what is good and acceptable and perfect. Such discernment leads to humility and life in beloved community, where all have gifts that are of equal importance to the body of Christ.

Any number of connections can be made with this passage and our lives today. This passage connects personally with readers who wonder, "How am I supposed to live?" and "What am I supposed to do?" Paul first warns against conformity to the world. Today the voices of popular culture are louder than ever and disseminated broadly through television, radio, global advertising, and social media. These messages are often designed to set the standard for how to look, what to drive, where to live, and how to act. Conforming to the world means conforming to the message that greed and acquisition, money and wealth, power and position lead to ultimate happiness. When we conform to these cultural standards, we adopt messages such as "You deserve this" and "You need that." In doing so, we focus not on what God has done for us but on what we can do for ourselves. The antidote to conformity to the world is transformation of the mind to the will of God and to that which is good, acceptable, and perfect.

First, Paul directs his readers: "[Do not] think of yourself more highly than you ought to think" (12:3). Humility in this passage is not about lowliness, meekness, or submissiveness (common definitions of humility) as much as it is a call to recognize that all followers of Jesus have a part (a gift, a function) in the body of Christ that is no more and no less important and valued than anyone else's part. Each person brings particular gifts that become a part of the whole. When all parts function together, the body works the way it should. Humility insists that every part honor every other part equally.

In today's world, however, many perceive humility as a weakness. We see leadership as the assertion of power and believe ourselves to be the most important and indispensable part of the system. Humility has no part in this kind of leadership. In the same way many people see life as a ladder, the goal being to get to the top, regardless of the consequences. For this climber, humility is a hindrance. Paul reminds us not to think too highly of ourselves.

We have all received the gift of God's grace, not as a result of our own efforts, but because of God's goodness and abiding love. Any gifts we receive from God are for the good of the community. Knowledge of God's grace changes the way we live in the world. Instead of living as one climbing a ladder, the follower of Christ lives as one who is part of a body, where all have different, but equally important, roles.

Abraham Lincoln had the ability to identify gifts in those who served in government and to assign them to positions in which their gifts could best serve the commonwealth. He saw himself as one part in a great system of democracy where each individual played a significant part. He served with humility, never needing to put down others in order to elevate himself.

Doris Kearns Goodwin, presidential historian and author of *Team of Rivals: The Political Genius of Abraham Lincoln*, noted the following attributes about Lincoln in a TED talk she gave:

> He possessed an uncanny ability to empathize with and think about other people's point of view. He repaired injured feelings that might have escalated into permanent hostility. He shared credit with ease. He assumed responsibility for the failure of his subordinates. He constantly acknowledged his errors and learned from his mistakes. He refused to be provoked by petty grievances. He never submitted to jealousy or brooded over perceived slights.[1]

Everyone, Lincoln believed, no matter their military rank or station in life, had an important role in building a strong nation and a strong democracy. No one person or committee should shoulder the burden for the whole.

Unfortunately, many church leaders experience burnout because they try to take on too many roles at once. Frequently pastors and church members feel a need to fill multiple roles, while others wait in the wings, hoping for their gifts to be recognized and affirmed. How might we as a Christian community do a better job of claiming the gifts among us and allowing the body to flourish in significant ways that do not lead to burnout, resentment, or underfunctioning?

Paul's focus on humility leads directly into his understanding of the gifts given to members of the body. In order to live well in community, as the body of Christ, all must recognize their own gifts as well as the gifts of others. Today's culture values many different hierarchical and/or competitive leadership models that, while often followed in businesses, corporations, and social clubs, are not appropriate for the Christian church. Humility and the recognition of the variety and importance of all gifts are critical for the full functioning of the body.

Living in community is perhaps the greatest challenge to Christian life. Our churches and communities of faith are made up of people with different gifts, behaviors, actions, and opinions. Some seek to elevate certain gifts and positions while making others feel less important to the body. Paul instructs us not to conform to the ways of the world, where people define others by a hierarchical system of worth; rather, to be transformed so that we might "discern the will of God—what is good, acceptable, and perfect" (12:2). The mind of God builds up the body of Christ and seeks strength in the body through the contributions of all those who have been gifted differently, but who dwell in peace and grace as a full and worthy part of the whole.

Ultimately, Paul wants his readers to understand that we are all saved by grace, and our response to God's grace shapes the way we live in community with one another. New Testament scholar Paul Achtemeier writes: "Life under the lordship of God means a life under the structuring power of grace. That power transforms not only individuals, but the individuals' relationship to the community around them. . . . The task is now to let the structuring power of grace transform that world into the shape of grace."[2]

MINDY DOUGLAS

---

1. Doris Kearns Goodwin, TED2008, "Lessons from Past Presidents"; https://www.ted.com/talks/doris_kearns_goodwin_on_learning_from_past_presidents.
2. Paul Achtemeier, *Romans*, Interpretation (Louisville, KY: John Knox, 1985), 195.

Proper 16 (Sunday between August 21 and August 27 inclusive)

Matthew 16:13–20

> [13]Now when Jesus came into the district of Caesarea Philippi, he asked his disciples, "Who do people say that the Son of Man is?" [14]And they said, "Some say John the Baptist, but others Elijah, and still others Jeremiah or one of the prophets." [15]He said to them, "But who do you say that I am?" [16]Simon Peter answered, "You are the Messiah, the Son of the living God." [17]And Jesus answered him, "Blessed are you, Simon son of Jonah! For flesh and blood has not revealed this to you, but my Father in heaven. [18]And I tell you, you are Peter, and on this rock I will build my church, and the gates of Hades will not prevail against it. [19]I will give you the keys of the kingdom of heaven, and whatever you bind on earth will be bound in heaven, and whatever you loose on earth will be loosed in heaven." [20]Then he sternly ordered the disciples not to tell anyone that he was the Messiah.

Commentary 1: Connecting the Reading with Scripture

The question of Jesus' full identity is a critical one for the disciples, and Matthew seems to prime the pump in determining Jesus' divine identity. Putting one of the recognized names for the Messiah, "the Son of Man," in Jesus' mouth when referring to his identity may be a deliberate tactic. So, is Jesus' question meant to be rhetorical? As a literary device, Jesus' question in Matthew 16:13 seems to be asking not who Jesus is, but about the criteria for the promised Messiah. In effect, Peter has been fed the answer. The structure of the text, in which one of the names for Messiah is present, seems to suggest the idea of Jesus as Messiah instead of representing an actual question about Jesus' messianic identity. The reader is thus prepped to hear Peter's confirming word that Jesus is the Messiah.

One is moved to question whether the interrogation that occurs in the text is being addressed to the disciples or to Matthew's church. Certainly, Jesus must be aware of what is being said about him, in light of his public ministry. Yet the question is still a valid one to be asked of would-be or even current disciples.

The commissioning of Peter seems to come out of nowhere. As a literary device, it facilitates movement of the idea from confessional to instructive. It puts in place an ecclesiology that locates Jesus the Christ as the foundation of the church, and names Peter as his subordinate and official church builder and administrator. So, is this text about Jesus' identity as Messiah, or is it about Peter and his role and place in the origins of the Christian church?

New Testament scholar M. Eugene Boring posits that "Matthew places this scene as the critical mid-point of this extended section, portraying the formation of the church in response to Israel's rejection."[1] From a literary standpoint, this centrality is analogous to the centrality of the Christian convert's formative confession that Jesus is Lord. By using established messianic names (Son of Man, Christ, Son of the living God) the text offers validation for Jesus' divine identity as the foundation of the church. Similarly, it is authoritative for establishing Peter's place in the building of the church. Sandwiched between Peter's confession of Jesus as the Christ and his caution to Jesus about the message he is preaching (16:21–23), the charge to Peter might be looked at, imaginatively, as representative of the responsibility of all who would lead the church.

---

1. M. Eugene Boring, "The Gospel of Matthew," in *The New Interpreter's Bible* (Nashville: Abingdon, 1995), 8:342.

Boring notes that there is scholarly consensus that Jesus' charge to Peter relates to his particular time and place in the formation of the Christian church "and that the position held was unique and unrepeatable."[2] Nevertheless, with a more expansive interpretation, its message could be applied more broadly to all church leaders who assume authority to oversee congregations. They might be inspired by hearing these words as a charge from Jesus to build the church and make disciples for Jesus Christ. Given the current and ongoing challenges facing the church, this text might also offer assurance that evil will not prevail in the face of Christ's promise.

Here, for the first time, Jesus is directly concerned with the beliefs held by the people as a whole and by the disciples in particular, with respect to his identity. Jesus has been exhibiting his divine nature through his ministry publicly among the people and privately with his disciples. Having experienced the results, both groups have offered their conclusions regarding Jesus' true identity, specifically his divinity. The disciples have experienced the human Jesus as they have accompanied him on his journey, and they have seen and experienced signs of his divinity. His questioning of them seems to represent a change in his focus. In response, Peter confesses that Jesus is the Christ. This is followed by Jesus' own confession of his divinity, even as he charges his disciples not to broadcast it. This series of confessions may well set the stage for the church's confession, which is the basis of its faith. Matthew 16:21, the verse that immediately follows this text, begins, "From that time on . . . ," which seems to indicate a turning point in the life and focus of Jesus' ministry.

A short time later, at the transfiguration, God also confesses that Jesus is God's Son (Matt. 17:5–6). Perhaps in the same way that Jesus' confession of his divine persona served as confirmation of Peter's confession, this later confession by God is meant to be the absolute confirmation of Jesus' divine identity. In any event, the theme of confession is a significant motif in Matthew's Gospel, to provide a basis for the confession of converts to their belief in Jesus as Savior and Lord. Unfortunately, the confessions made in today's churches do not follow Peter's model. They wisely decry sin, but they do not proclaim Christ. Confession of Christ is still the linchpin that holds the church together, and a rereading of this text might be helpful in repositioning the church's focus.

There is a thin thread that runs through the four lectionary texts, which moves beyond confession and offers assurance of God's supporting presence in the time of need. In each case, the key to the assurance of God's faithfulness comes as a result of a spoken or unspoken confession of faith in God. Here Peter is assured that his work as builder of Christ's church will not be defeated. In a sense, Matthew's church is exiled from their Jewish roots and needs assurance for their continued life in Christ. For the church in every time, the assurance of God's saving presence and grace is God's promise to all who confess their faith in God.

Jesus' identity as Messiah was a troublesome issue for his opponents. At his baptism, a voice from heaven proclaimed his identity: "This is my Son, the Beloved, with whom I am well pleased" (3:17), but again and again the Pharisees and the Sadducees have tried to disprove it by trying to trip him up with questions pertaining to the Law. On the other hand, demons have recognized him as Son of God (8:29).

Peter's confession was the model for converts to Christianity in both the apostolic and the early church period. Converts' entry into the church was predicated on their ability to verbally confess Christ. Such a confession spoke of the sovereignty of Christ over every aspect of both individuals and the corporate life of the church. The creeds that were developed later focused mainly on the content of faith, with little emphasis placed on individual confessions of belief in Jesus Christ as Lord.

Although it is still the foundation for one's life and the whole Christian church, such a confession is no longer an essential requirement for church membership. The church's confession of the lordship of Jesus Christ has become merely a subset of the more expansive creed that names the triune God as creator, redeemer,

---

2. Boring, *Matthew*, 347.

and sustainer of all people. Most recently in many segments of the church, even the creeds have been treated with disfavor and ignored or rejected. However, the confession of the lordship of Jesus Christ is the basis on which the created order and the church of Jesus Christ rest, but perhaps the disciples of Jesus might be helped to live a more faithful life if they are called to confess openly and live the reality that Jesus is Lord.

GENNIFER BENJAMIN BROOKS

Commentary 2: Connecting the Reading with the World

Who is Jesus? This question posed to the disciples is at the heart of Matthew's Gospel, and is a live question for contemporary faith in a pluralistic context. Who do other people say Jesus is? Who do we in the church say he is? What difference does it make?

Viewed through the lens of the well-developed Christology of the later creeds, it is tempting to superimpose an oversimplified binary structure on the answers given in this text: Do people recognize Jesus as God, or not? However, the answers given in this story do not fit neatly into those categories. The identity ascribed by the people—that in the ministry of Jesus they recognize that same divine power associated with John the Baptist and the prophets of old—is robust and can scarcely be faulted as disparaging Jesus as "merely human." This is not the whole truth to which Matthew testifies, but neither is it deserving of refutation or rebuke. Peter's answer that Jesus is the Messiah (one anointed by God for a special purpose) and the Son of God (a way of expressing his close relationship to God, and the perfect alignment of his actions with the purposes of God) is the ideal confession for Matthew, but it is not the same as simply identifying Jesus with God.

In our own cultural context, there are many who think well of Jesus and his teachings, but do not ascribe to him the full significance that we recognize in the church. For that matter, if the truth were fully known, there are surely considerable differences even within the church about how best to understand and express the identity of Jesus. Must those who recognize in Jesus' life and teachings the purposes of God for the world be pressured to express his identity in terms amenable to orthodoxy? For that matter, are those who say all the right things about Jesus necessarily in tune with what it means to follow Jesus? Several of the details in this story suggest that confessing Jesus is more complicated than simply saying, or even believing, the right things.

In the first place, Jesus blesses Peter for his confession, but the blessing is not a reward for an accomplishment. Rather, Jesus insists that this is not something Peter could have come up with on his own: "flesh and blood has not revealed this to you, but my Father in heaven" (Matt. 16:17). Confessing Jesus rightly is not a puzzle to be solved by the power of the intellect, nor a moral capacity for believing steadfastly even in the face of compelling evidence to the contrary. It is a gift, pure and simple. As a gift, it is not a ground for boasting or criticizing the faith of others, but an awesome responsibility to live into (v. 18). God reveals what needs to be revealed, to whom it needs to be revealed, in order to accomplish all that God wills for the world.

Furthermore, knowing the proper titles for Jesus is not the same as understanding and embracing the way of being in the world his identity demands. The way the lectionary divides this reading (vv. 21–28 constitute a separate lection for the following week), it is easy to lose sight of this aspect of the story. Peter does not truly grasp the identity of Jesus as Messiah and Son, because Peter has not yet understood Jesus as the one who suffers and dies (vv. 21–22).

Perhaps this helps explain why Jesus, even after embracing the answer Peter gives to the question of his identity, is not eager to have him (or the other disciples) as his spokesperson (v. 20). There are situations where even those who have received the gift of knowing the truth about Jesus are not at all clear about what to do with that information. In our own time, the church might do well to spend less time insisting that others acknowledge Jesus with the right language, and more time living into his example of spending himself recklessly for the world he loves, and trusting God to vindicate such obedience in God's own time.

Approaching the homiletical implications of this passage a little differently, the reception history of this text is an interesting window into the way Christian interpretation of the Bible is profoundly shaped by the context and self-interest of the interpreter. For centuries, the debate about this passage has turned on the question of what Jesus was referring to when he promised that he would build the church on "this rock" (v. 18). Roman Catholic interpretation has seen in this story the origin of and justification for the authoritative papal office that extends forward from Peter (the name, conferred here by Jesus, means "rock") in an unbroken line of succession.

Protestant interpreters, resisting the authority of the pope, have insisted that the "rock" Jesus refers to as the foundation of the church has nothing to do with Peter, but points instead to the confession of faith in Jesus as Messiah and Son of God (v. 16). It is fascinating to note that during the Middle Ages, the reading most familiar to Catholic piety (e.g., as found in sermons) was that the "rock" that provides the foundation for the church is Christ himself (cf. 1 Cor. 3:11; 10:4), an interpretation that goes back to Augustine.[3] In other words, it was only under the polarizing pressure of Reformation insistence that the text could not possibly refer to Peter in any way that a Roman Catholic reading first limited to a small circle of theologians and jurists became ubiquitous among the laity, displacing an ancient reading informed by the wider canon and focused on Jesus. This is a bitter irony.

Today, with the ecclesial and political stakes somewhat lowered, the majority of scholars across confessional lines agree that this text clearly points toward Peter as an exceptional figure with exceptional authority in the early church (contra Protestant interpretation), while rejecting the claim that it establishes an office intended to continue by succession in perpetuity (contra Catholic interpretation). In certain preaching contexts, this history of interpretation might helpfully serve as a kind of case study and warning about the way biblical interpretation is distorted by conflict.

Political infighting among Christians leads to misguided readings of biblical texts that age poorly and tend to take the focus off Jesus in the meantime. In hindsight, it seems clear that more valid readings of this text would have emerged from a more generous interpretive disposition toward the other. What interpretive practices can we learn from thinking carefully about the reception history of this text? Rather than thoroughgoing suspicion toward the motives of the other, one might ask what it is that those who read differently are able to see in the text that is obscured from one's own perspective.

Likewise, a healthy suspicion toward one's own reading practices is a virtue. Ask yourself, "What do I and those who are like me have to gain by reading in the way we do? What would we have to lose if we took seriously the readings of others?" Such questions can clarify that much of what we take to be obvious has more to do with what is convenient than what is reasonable. It can be very hard for the eye to see itself, and when it comes to interpreting Scripture, self-criticism is a discipline that must be carefully nurtured.

LANCE PAPE

---

3. For a detailed discussion of the reception history of this passage, see Ulrich Luz, *Matthew 8–20*, Hermeneia (Minneapolis: Augsburg Fortress, 2001), 369–75.

Proper 17 (Sunday between August 28 and September 3 inclusive)

Jeremiah 15:15–21 and Exodus 3:1–15
Psalm 26:1–8 and Psalm 105:1–6, 23–26, 45b
Romans 12:9–21
Matthew 16:21–28

Jeremiah 15:15–21

¹⁵O Lord, you know;
   remember me and visit me,
   and bring down retribution for me on my persecutors.
In your forbearance do not take me away;
   know that on your account I suffer insult.
¹⁶Your words were found, and I ate them,
   and your words became to me a joy
   and the delight of my heart;
for I am called by your name,
   O Lord, God of hosts.
¹⁷I did not sit in the company of merrymakers,
   nor did I rejoice;
under the weight of your hand I sat alone,
   for you had filled me with indignation.
¹⁸Why is my pain unceasing,
   my wound incurable,
   refusing to be healed?
Truly, you are to me like a deceitful brook,
   like waters that fail.

¹⁹Therefore thus says the Lord:
If you turn back, I will take you back,
   and you shall stand before me.
If you utter what is precious, and not what is worthless,
   you shall serve as my mouth.
It is they who will turn to you,
   not you who will turn to them.
²⁰And I will make you to this people
   a fortified wall of bronze;
they will fight against you,
   but they shall not prevail over you,
for I am with you
   to save you and deliver you,
                     says the Lord.
²¹I will deliver you out of the hand of the wicked,
   and redeem you from the grasp of the ruthless.

Exodus 3:1–15

¹Moses was keeping the flock of his father-in-law Jethro, the priest of Midian; he led his flock beyond the wilderness, and came to Horeb, the mountain of God. ²There the angel of the LORD appeared to him in a flame of fire out of a bush; he looked, and the bush was blazing, yet it was not consumed. ³Then Moses said, "I must turn aside and look at this great sight, and see why the bush is not burned up." ⁴When the LORD saw that he had turned aside to see, God called to him out of the bush, "Moses, Moses!" And he said, "Here I am." ⁵Then he said, "Come no closer! Remove the sandals from your feet, for the place on which you are standing is holy ground." ⁶He said further, "I am the God of your father, the God of Abraham, the God of Isaac, and the God of Jacob." And Moses hid his face, for he was afraid to look at God.

⁷Then the LORD said, "I have observed the misery of my people who are in Egypt; I have heard their cry on account of their taskmasters. Indeed, I know their sufferings, ⁸and I have come down to deliver them from the Egyptians, and to bring them up out of that land to a good and broad land, a land flowing with milk and honey, to the country of the Canaanites, the Hittites, the Amorites, the Perizzites, the Hivites, and the Jebusites. ⁹The cry of the Israelites has now come to me; I have also seen how the Egyptians oppress them. ¹⁰So come, I will send you to Pharaoh to bring my people, the Israelites, out of Egypt." ¹¹But Moses said to God, "Who am I that I should go to Pharaoh, and bring the Israelites out of Egypt?" ¹²He said, "I will be with you; and this shall be the sign for you that it is I who sent you: when you have brought the people out of Egypt, you shall worship God on this mountain."

¹³But Moses said to God, "If I come to the Israelites and say to them, 'The God of your ancestors has sent me to you,' and they ask me, 'What is his name?' what shall I say to them?" ¹⁴God said to Moses, "I AM WHO I AM." He said further, "Thus you shall say to the Israelites, 'I AM has sent me to you.'" ¹⁵God also said to Moses, "Thus you shall say to the Israelites, 'The LORD, the God of your ancestors, the God of Abraham, the God of Isaac, and the God of Jacob, has sent me to you':

This is my name forever,
and this my title for all generations."

Commentary 1: Connecting the Reading with Scripture

The Revised Common Lectionary lists two Old Testament passages for Proper 17. The two texts become mutually illuminating as we receive them in light of the wider biblical story. Each describes a movement from the devastation of a person's life to the ongoing divine call by means of the divine Name, a person's life lived within the presence of the one who continuously and eternally is.

We need to abandon romantic images of the shepherd to understand the situation of Moses in Exodus 3:1–15. Shepherding is lowly, unskilled labor. At the beginning of Exodus 3, Moses has paid dearly for his inability to deal with his bicultural life and stresses. Moses' life has moved from the miracle of his preservation as a baby to utter devastation. Exodus 2 details how Moses is not sufficiently Egyptian for the Egyptians nor sufficiently Hebrew for the Hebrews. He murders an Egyptian as his anger overwhelms him.

Moses flees to Midian as a refugee to escape. He marries Zipporah. His father-in-law, Jethro, however, does not award Moses with a position of honor in his household. Jethro sends Moses immediately away from his new bride. Moses finds himself alone. He has ruined his life.

Moses at the beginning of Exodus 3 echoes the lament of Jeremiah in Jeremiah 15. The words of Jeremiah give a language to all those who have found their life devastated by a past event. "Remember me" speaks from the experience of isolation and abandonment. The complaints in Jeremiah 15:15 and 17 culminate in the despair of verse 18: "my wound is horrible; how shall I be healed?" (my translations). The words express the unending suffering of Moses. It exclaims the despair when life seems to have ended in utter catastrophe.

God does not let the story end, however. God has not ended Moses' life. The passage uses the form of the prophetic call. It records the divine commission to Moses (Exod. 3:4–10), Moses' objection of unworthiness (v. 11), and the divine reaffirmation of the call (v. 12). The divine Word calls Moses with his unhealed wound. God offers Moses no promise of healing. The sign that God promises Moses will come only after Moses has returned to Pharaoh and demanded Israel's release to evidence God's faithfulness to God's promise to the ancestors. The call requires Moses to return to the place where he is wanted for murder, to speak for a people who have already rejected him. Moses' vocation, a purpose amid his suffering, comes with only the assurance that God is "with you" (v. 12).

The divine Word also responds with a call in Jeremiah 15:16, 19–20. No promise of healing occurs. The speaker finds comfort in the call of the divine Word: "Your Word is for joy and the favor of my heart" (Jer. 15:16, my trans.). Why? Because the divine Name has "been called upon me" (v. 16). The divine Word calls the speaker even in her or his suffering. The content of the call appears in verses 19–20: to bring forth honor from the unworthy. The divine Word promises only God's presence (v. 20), as in Exodus 3. The divine Word calls the one devastated by life into life. Jeremiah 15:11–21 provides a prophetic Word that details the scriptural call beyond the devastation of sin. Amid wounds that do not heal, God still calls to life. The passages foreshadow the call of Saul to become Paul, the call of the denying Peter to become the Peter upon whom God will build the church.

As the recipient of the divine Word, the prophet announces that God has placed the divine Name upon him (v. 16b). The dialogue between the divine Word and Moses in Exodus 3 also turns to the divine Name. Exodus 3:13 represents the only place in all the Scriptures where a person directly asks God for the divine Name. The movement from devastation to calling requires a revelation of the divine Name by the Word of God. Moses does not go forth on his own credentials. "'I am Be-ing.' And [God] said, 'Thus you will say to the sons of Israel, 'The I Am-ing sent me to you'" (Exod. 3:14, my trans.).

Please forget the old polemics against "static Greek thought" vs. "earthly, concrete Hebrew thought." As throughout the Torah, the Greek offers a literal, even wooden, translation of the Hebrew here. The participial use of "is," as in all participles even today, indicates ongoing action. "To be" works in Exodus 3 as an active verb. The divine Word reveals the divine Name to Moses as ongoing Be-ing, the ongoing, never beginning, never ending, pure Act of Be-ing. The divine Name is *not* "I am an eternal Being" or "I am a Supreme Being." No indefinite article appears in the divine Name. Nowhere do the Scriptures or the classical Christian tradition (for at least its first twelve hundred years) ever name God as "a thing" among other things or "a Being" among "beings." The divine Name given to Moses is the pure verbal action of "Is-ing," the continuous act of existence, the very ongoing activity that is Existence Itself.

Moses receives the divine Name through the Word of God as a gift. God reveals God's name as the unchangeable, ongoing act of existence that the divine Word gives as God's Name. God is with Moses because "God *is*." God never abandons Moses as his life dissolves. God will not abandon Moses when he returns to Pharaoh. God never has abandoned Moses. God cannot deny God's own Life. God's Life is the One from whom are all things, through whom are all things, and to whom are all things. Moses can move from devastation to call because God's

Name, the one who sends Moses, is "I Am-ing." As human life moves from miracle to ruin, God does not change. Creation changes; God does not. "I AM" is the divine Name "forever" (v. 15).

To read Jeremiah 15:15–21 with Exodus 3:1–15 and vice versa bring the divine Name to the center of the day's readings. Most know of the role of the divine Name spoken by the Word of God in the Gospel of John as it relates to Exodus 3. The Apocalypse of John also develops the name. The one on the throne Was-ing, and Is-ing, and Will Be-ing. The divine name has philosophical, theological, and pastoral import. Pseudo-Dionysius and Thomas Aquinas reflected deeply on this central name for God. A name does not describe fully nor list a bundle of qualities contained in that named. It designates without exhausting that which is named. God reveals the divine Name for humans, some of whom find their lives devastated by their inability to handle their lives. Those devastated by life, including ourselves, receive the divine Name to remain in the present, so to speak, to let the past go and live to the future because God's Name is "I am-ing."

Within the larger biblical narrative, we recognize that the divine Word, the Speech of God in the OT, has become flesh and dwelt among us in the one Lord Jesus Christ, the same yesterday, today, and forever. God has revealed God's Life as "I am" in the death and resurrection of the Word. Displacement comes; devastation can ensue. Life can reach a seeming end. God nonetheless still calls by the divine Word through the Holy Spirit. God's constantly full Life calls even devastated human lives into the fullness of God's Life. The divine Name gives us a basis, like Moses, to return to Egypt and speak to the Pharaohs of the world to let God's people go.

JOHN W. WRIGHT

Commentary 2: Connecting the Reading with the World

This text from the prophet Jeremiah goes through different movements, and our attention is drawn to a few ideas that may have resonance for our faith communities today. Perhaps the most significant theological concern for witness and faith development is our understanding of God. The prophet intimates that God knows him intimately (Jer. 15:15a) and that God's words have shaped his identity and given meaning to his life. Jeremiah says: "I am called by your name" (v. 16b).

In our context, both the individual and the faith community are invited to stand with Jeremiah in recognizing that our identity comes from God. We are invited to proclaim God who gives joy and delight and who fashions our vocations so that our activities in the world reflect our identity in God. One does not feed the hungry, or care for the undocumented immigrant or for the environment, because these activities are in vogue but, rather, because our ways of being and doing flow from our identity as God's messengers, voice, or instruments in the world.

In another movement of this passage, Jeremiah seems to expect God to take a more prominent role to deliver him from the wicked and ruthless who persecute him. Worship and faith-development activities must intentionally deal with pain and suffering, grief and loss, exile and abandonment, which are all attributed to God's presence or absence, God's activity or inactivity. Jeremiah described it as unceasing pain and an incurable wound (v. 18a) in a vocation where God is seemingly experienced as a "deceitful brook, like waters that fail" (v. 18b).

In another movement of this passage, we are invited into a space marked by a sense of foreboding and impending doom and destruction, and a cry to be rescued from one's foes. We are reminded here that throughout the worship life of the church, leaders are encouraged to acknowledge the real fears that people face and offer a word, a prayer, or image of salvation in the midst of it.

We have these moments even on the national scene. when we are faced with political strife and incivility, gun violence, terrorism, warfare, and the threat of nuclear annihilation. What can one expect of God in those situations? What is one's personal standing before God? Is God to be understood as one who at any point may sweep us away from the face of the earth? Are God's people to live with a constant belief or fear of divine retribution? Although we may not see God as one who acts in anger or who holds our sins against us, the church is still invited to reckon with how we stand before God to account for our stewardship in the world.

Jeremiah is mindful that the insults and hardships that he suffers are due to his relationship with Yahweh. In the same way, faith communities are invited to examine the nature of their witness as it relates to and reflects their relationship with the Divine. Does ministry flow from a sense of impending doom, performed to assuage the wrath of God? Does ministry truly reflect the divine nature, or is it driven by our personal biases, prejudices, self-interest, and political preferences?

Finally, our spiritual lives may be characterized as feasting on God's word (v. 16a). In a practical sense, worship activities should be conceived and designed in ways that offer joy to those who participate in the liturgy of the faith community. Like Jeremiah, we may become convinced that, in communion with God, the human spirit finds real joy and delight.

In our reading from Exodus, Moses has an encounter with the Divine through supernatural phenomena, a blazing bush that is not consumed. It prompts us to consider what constitutes a personal encounter with the Divine and what value we place on unique, extraordinary, and spectacular moments in our lives. This story has become a template for people of faith who are searching for language and imagery to make a public confession of faith or to share a call story.

In this narrative, our attention is drawn to Moses, at work tending the flock; his father-in-law, the priest of Midian; and Horeb, the mountain of God. In our own context, we may consider the interconnectedness of the social and cultural dimensions of our lives such as work, family, religious practices, and sacred spaces, and their impact on our spiritual journeys. We can only imagine what Moses learned from the priest of Midian, what rituals he witnessed, or how his understanding of family life was shaped in that household. It is likely that, in some cases, we too are influenced by family traditions and religious practices that foster a quest for personal or communal encounters with the Divine. In other cases, we may redefine our understanding of, or relationship to, family or forge a new religious pathway and identity. This may include challenging what is known and/or engaging in dialogue with other religious traditions around us.

Faith communities seek to create spaces and experiences to enable people to encounter the Divine at the mountain of God. As the leader of the people of Israel through their wilderness sojourn, Moses will journey up the sacred mountain repeatedly to meet with God on behalf of the people (Exod. 19:3; 24:15). We have seen mountains as the sacred spaces (John 4:20–21) and have come to speak of having a mountaintop experience (Mark 9:2–9). This may be welcome news for hikers and mountain climbers, but others may find their sacred spaces at the seashore, in botanical gardens, in museums of art or sculpture, or in a library.

In our text, we encounter mystery in the burning bush, a designated sacred space on the mountain of God, and holy ground evoking reverence. These elements may not appear together in our own experience with God. We may experience mystery, but it may not be accompanied by supernatural phenomena. We may also experience holy ground beyond the walls of our houses of worship. In the national conversation, we speak of places such as Gettysburg as a memorial and sacred ground for many.

In stark contrast to the supernatural encounter on the mountain of God is the misery and suffering of the enslaved people of Israel. Moses experienced holy ground because of the presence of the Holy One and it also led to action on behalf of people in bondage. We too experience the Holy One and seek to reflect the holiness of God. The divine mandate, "Be holy, for I am holy" (Lev. 11:44), is translated into both personal and social holiness for people of faith.

For Moses, this sacred encounter was not just personal and private; it was a time of consecration to serve God in the context of a community, the people of God. Sacred spaces may also be designed to call forth action on behalf of those who live in misery and suffering. For us today, our mountaintop experiences or sacred spaces and divine encounters are not just for our edification, but an opportunity to work for the salvation and liberation of a community. For Moses, this moment on holy ground would mark the beginning of divinely initiated and orchestrated venture into liberation and new life for the people of Israel. Holy ground may very well be associated with social justice and activism, communal salvation, and liberation.

LINCOLN E. GALLOWAY

Proper 17 (Sunday between August 28 and September 3 inclusive)

Psalm 26:1–8

¹Vindicate me, O LORD,
   for I have walked in my integrity,
   and I have trusted in the LORD without wavering.
²Prove me, O LORD, and try me;
   test my heart and mind.
³For your steadfast love is before my eyes,
   and I walk in faithfulness to you.

⁴I do not sit with the worthless,
   nor do I consort with hypocrites;
⁵I hate the company of evildoers,
   and will not sit with the wicked.

⁶I wash my hands in innocence,
   and go around your altar, O LORD,
⁷singing aloud a song of thanksgiving,
   and telling all your wondrous deeds.

⁸O LORD, I love the house in which you dwell,
   and the place where your glory abides.

Psalm 105:1–6, 23–26, 45b

¹O give thanks to the LORD, call on his name,
   make known his deeds among the peoples.
²Sing to him, sing praises to him;
   tell of all his wonderful works.
³Glory in his holy name;
   let the hearts of those who seek the LORD rejoice.
⁴Seek the Lord and his strength;
   seek his presence continually.
⁵Remember the wonderful works he has done,
   his miracles, and the judgements he has uttered,
⁶O offspring of his servant Abraham,
   children of Jacob, his chosen ones.
. . . .
²³Then Israel came to Egypt;
   Jacob lived as an alien in the land of Ham.
²⁴And the LORD made his people very fruitful,
   and made them stronger than their foes,
²⁵whose hearts he then turned to hate his people,
   to deal craftily with his servants.
²⁶He sent his servant Moses,
   and Aaron whom he had chosen.
. . . .
⁴⁵ᵇPraise the LORD!

Connecting the Psalm with Scripture and Worship

Psalm 26:1–8. It takes courage to invite divine scrutiny the way the psalmist does: "Prove me, O Lord, and try me; test my heart and mind" (Ps. 26:2). It takes confidence in one's own integrity to declare: "I do not consort with hypocrites [v. 4] . . . [or] sit with the wicked [v. 5]. . . . I wash my hands in innocence" (v. 6). This is more than most of us can manage most days. Nevertheless, if we are honest, there are occasions when we do feel unfairly accused, or satisfied in our avoidance of evil, or eager for God to declare us righteous. On those days, the preacher recognizes that this psalm speaks to us and for us, even as it speaks on behalf of Jeremiah.

The first reading, from Jeremiah, and Psalm 26 start in the same place, sounding notes of self-justification, pleading for God's decisive action. One might even imagine Psalm 26 as a bold expansion of the prayer Jeremiah offers in 15:15: *Lord, you know me; I have been good. Come on! Deliver me!* Jeremiah's prayer—and the psalmist's—are not predicated on self-declared righteousness. The psalmist's key virtue is *trust* in God (Ps. 26:1). That trust focuses her eyes on God's steadfast love (*hesed*); it sets his feet in God's faithfulness (v. 3).[1] The God deserving of that trust provides the strength to avoid evil and evildoers and to endure persecution and hardship.

One might be tempted to recognize a parallel between the two texts as they both speak of not "sitting with" certain types of people, but the psalmist's "worthless" and "wicked" are not to be equated with Jeremiah's "merrymakers" (Jer. 15:17). Jeremiah's choice of company has less to do with sin, and more to do with sorrow. The Word of the Lord is his delight, but its weight is heavy; he cannot rejoice in what he has been given to say. While the psalmist trusts "without wavering," Jeremiah wavers.

Yet even in his despair, Jeremiah hears the promise of the Lord, a promise of deliverance and redemption. God's rich history of promise and redemption is what prompts the psalmist to testify to God's wondrous deeds, singing "a song of thanksgiving" while processing around the altar (vv. 6, 7). The company both the prophet and the psalmist choose to keep is the one whose identity transforms theirs in sacramental suggestion, Jeremiah by the eating of the Word and the psalmist by waters of purification.

Because some scholars suggest that this psalm originates in and finds subsequent use in a rite of purification, it may be tempting to use the psalm to help shape a penitential rite, such as a prayer of confession and a responding declaration of God's pardon. Yet the text has no explicit admission of guilt, no penitence. This psalm could, however, be used as a *response* to the declaration, an antiphonal, aspirational, and baptismal reminder of our identity as the "great congregation" (Ps. 26:12).

Another liturgical use could be to deploy the psalm to shape the prayers of the people—not just us, but the *whole* church. In this case, a pastor might divide the prayer into two sections: intercession and thanksgiving. The intercessory section might take note of those in the world who are in a position of distress, of persecution, not unlike Jeremiah and the psalmist. Such an approach would make prominent use of the verbs of these texts: "With those who suffer illness we pray . . . (silence) . . . /remember and visit me. With those who endure the dehumanizing effects of racism we pray . . . (silence) . . . /vindicate me, O Lord." The thanksgiving section would also focus on the psalmist's verbs: we look, we walk, we sit, we consort, we love, we hate.

In any case, the psalm, if simply read or sung as one of the lections, should be framed so that the congregation recognizes it both as the prayer they offer, and the prayer they offer on behalf of others.

Psalm 105:1–6, 23–26, 45b. The reading from Exodus is one of the most significant in the entire Pentateuch. It tells the story of the burning bush and God's compelling holiness; it relates how God called a reluctant Moses to

---

1. There is a delightful ambiguity in the last half of the third verse, one reading of which might emphasize *God's* faithfulness rather than the psalmist's: "I walk in your faithfulness" rather than "I walk in faithfulness to you."

Prefer Nothing to Christ

Let us open our eyes to the light that comes from God, and our ears to the voice from heaven that every day calls out this charge: If you hear his voice today, do not harden your hearts. And again, You that have ears to hear, listen to what the Spirit says to the churches. And what does he say? Come and listen to me, sons; I will teach you the fear of the Lord. Run while you have the light of life, that the darkness of death may not overtake you. . . . Clothed then with faith and the performance of good works, let us set out on this way, with the Gospel for our guide, that we may deserve to see him who has called us to his kingdom. . . . Just as there is a wicked zeal of bitterness which separates from God and leads to hell, so there is a good zeal which separates from evil and leads to God and everlasting life. This, then, is the good zeal which monks must foster with fervent love: They should each try to be the first to show respect to the other, supporting with the greatest patience one another's weakness of body or behavior, and earnestly competing in obedience to one another. No one is to pursue what he judges better for himself, but instead, what he judges better for someone else. . . . Let them prefer nothing whatever to Christ, and may he bring us all together to everlasting life.

Benedict, *The Rule of Saint Benedict*, ed. Timothy Fry, OSB, Vintage Spiritual Classics series (Collegeville, MN: Order of Saint Benedict, 1998), 3, 69.

---

ministry; and it narrates the revelation of God's enigmatic name. This text is paired with an excerpt from one of the great salvation songs of the Psalter, Psalm 105, which tells the story of God's faithfulness to Israel. It sounds these themes through the use of three signal verbs: remember, seek, and sing.

We hear these verbs especially in the first six verses of the psalm. The first two verses invite the people to *testify in song* ("Give thanks to the Lord, call on his name. . . . Sing praises") to the glory of God's name, a holy and mysterious name disclosed in Exodus 3:14–15. The next two verses of the psalm emphasize *seeking* the presence and will of God, as Moses did when he turned aside to see the bush and what it meant. God's holiness prompts not just fear, but awe and attraction. Finally, verses 5–6 summon the people to "*remember* [God's] wonderful works"—not merely in the sense of bringing them to mind, but in the deep anamnetic sense of invoking the power of God's past action to shape our here and now.

Then verses 23–26 provide an immediate context and tone for the first reading. We are about to hear about Moses; the psalm tells us that Israel in Egypt was fruitful and strong—and hated—but God was listening, and God sent Moses.

The relationship between the psalm and the first reading suggests two complementary uses of the psalm. The first is as a prelude to the first reading. This functions as an abbreviated reminder of what God has already done, like the ninety-second recaps that air before the latest episode of a serialized television show: "Previously, on *God's Saving Wonders* . . ."

Reading the psalm in three voices would be a way to highlight these three themes of testifying in song (voice 1), seeking God's presence and will (voice 2), and remembering the power of God's past actions to shape our present-day life (voice 3). In this approach, each voice speaks the words that underscore a particular theme:

Reader 1: O give thanks to the Lord,
Reader 2: call on his name,
Reader 3: make known his deeds among the peoples.
Reader 1: Sing to him, sing praises to him; tell of all his wonderful works. Glory in his holy name;
Reader 2: let the hearts of those who seek the Lord rejoice. Seek the Lord and his strength; seek his presence continually.
Reader 3: Remember the wonderful works he has done, his miracles, and the judgments he uttered, O offspring of his

servant Abraham, children of Jacob, his chosen ones. Then Israel came to Egypt; Jacob lived as an alien in the land of Ham. And the Lord made his people very fruitful, and made them stronger than their foes, whose hearts he then turned to hate his people, to deal craftily with his servants. He sent his servant Moses, and Aaron whom he had chosen.

All: Praise the Lord!

RON RIENSTRA

Proper 17 (Sunday between August 28 and September 3 inclusive)

Romans 12:9–21

> [9]Let love be genuine; hate what is evil, hold fast to what is good; [10]love one another with mutual affection; outdo one another in showing honor. [11]Do not lag in zeal, be ardent in spirit, serve the Lord. [12]Rejoice in hope, be patient in suffering, persevere in prayer. [13]Contribute to the needs of the saints; extend hospitality to strangers.
> [14]Bless those who persecute you; bless and do not curse them. [15]Rejoice with those who rejoice, weep with those who weep. [16]Live in harmony with one another; do not be haughty, but associate with the lowly; do not claim to be wiser than you are. [17]Do not repay anyone evil for evil, but take thought for what is noble in the sight of all. [18]If it is possible, so far as it depends on you, live peaceably with all. [19]Beloved, never avenge yourselves, but leave room for the wrath of God; for it is written, "Vengeance is mine, I will repay, says the Lord." [20]No, "if your enemies are hungry, feed them; if they are thirsty, give them something to drink; for by doing this you will heap burning coals on their heads." [21]Do not be overcome by evil, but overcome evil with good.

Commentary 1: Connecting the Reading with Scripture

At the close of Romans 11, Paul has completed part 1 of his radical theological reimagination of God's reconciled and reconciling human community. Paul has explained the reconciling work of God by which this new community has been forged. The reconciliation between Jew and Gentile comes about not by means of law, whether the ancient law of the Jews or the natural law revealed to the Gentiles (Rom. 1:19–20), but by the radical, self-giving grace of God in Jesus Christ. An excursus in which Paul argues passionately for the continuing validity of God's promises to Israel closes with an extended doxology (11:33–36). At chapter 12, Paul does not "apply" his theological argument, but extends it: he shows that the effective, reconciling work of God continues, coming to expression before the world in communities forged by God's radical grace and animated by the Spirit.

Our lection, 12:9–21, cannot be understood without keeping verses 1–8 in view, since the organic connection of the self-giving God with a self-given community is the presupposition that enables each activity described beginning at verse 9. The chapter's opening motif is gift exchange—God's mercy motivates believers' self-giving to God (vv. 1–2). In turn, the Spirit pours out gifts into the community, a body organically one with Christ, its head (vv. 3–8).

At verse 9, Paul turns from the mutual self-giving of God and the believer, and begins to sketch what such self-giving looks like in relation to one another and the wider world. In every respect, it will be anchored in love. The opening words of verse 9, "Let love be genuine," could just as easily be translated, "Genuine love is . . . ,"[1] with subsequent phrases—some of them participial in form, others infinitive, and still others imperative—showing the many embodiments of such love. Some interpreters note that the phrasing almost suggests underlying liturgical material, perhaps a familiar hymn about the deep solidarity and border-crossing practices of God's new, radically inclusive community, where, at one table, Jesus' followers defy customary social divides between classes and ethnic groups.

---

1. Christopher Hutson, "Romans 12:9–21, Exegetical Perspective," *Feasting on the Word, Year A, Volume 4* (Louisville, KY: Westminster John Knox, 2011), 17.

The reality of church life in Rome may have fallen well short of this ideal. While Christians of both Hellenistic and Jewish cultural heritage had undoubtedly been represented in Roman house churches since the beginnings of the Christian movement there, Jews had been expelled from the city in 49 CE by the emperor, Claudius. When the ban was lifted in 54 CE and they began to return, it could well be that a more decisively Hellenistic church culture had developed, creating tension.

The apostle's rhetoric in these verses bears close attention. In format and themes, this paraenetic essay would be readily recognizable to Roman readers, since in both respects it parallels similar passages in the literature of many Mediterranean cultures. Yet the apostle fills this basic paraenetic structure with phrasing that echoes specifically *Jewish* sources. The result is a portrait of ethical life in God's new community that is as Jewish as it is Hellenistic. Paul has designed this community portrait to recruit both Gentile and Jewish Christians to become a "living argument" for the dynamic of reconciliation God has set in motion in Jesus Christ.

Any preacher willing to spend time checking cross-references to both canonical and intertestamental (Jewish) literature will be richly rewarded. Even a brief listing includes Amos 5:15, 21–24 (Rom. 12:9); Matthew 5:43–48; Luke 6:27–36 (Rom. 12:14ff.); Sirach 7:34 (Rom. 12:15), Proverbs 3:17 (Rom. 12:16), Matthew 7:12; Tobit 4:15; Proverbs 17:13, 20–22 (Rom. 12:17), Deuteronomy 32:35 (Rom. 12:19), Proverbs 25:21–22 (Rom. 12:20), and multiple allusions to the *Testament of the Twelve Patriarchs* (Rom. 12:21).[2]

What distinguishes Paul's sketch of the life of the reconciled and reconciling community is not novelty, but the motivating event that animates it: the self-giving love of God expressed in the self-sacrifice of Jesus. The practice of self-outpouring by which the community has been constituted becomes the signature practice of the community as it commends its message of divine reconciliation that overcomes deadly enmity in the wider world. The effect of embodying this radically self-giving love—self-giving to the point of practicing gift-giving to the enemy—is to signify the transformation God's Spirit is effecting in the world.

Because Paul's paraenesis is uniquely crafted to resonate with Jewish Wisdom sources, setting these verses into dialogue with Psalm 105 can be illuminating. The psalm celebrates the gracious interventions of God that resulted in the deliverance of God's beloved people from slavery in Egypt into an open future. As they became a new community through the gracious deliverance of God, so do we. As the ancient Israelites were delivered from bondage to slavery, we are delivered in our communities of faith from bondage to legalism, into the creative liberty of love. Our life continues to be an experience of the mighty acts of God.

In the Gospel reading from Matthew 16, the practice of self-giving, sacrificial love that Romans 12 describes takes flesh as Jesus hands himself over as a "living sacrifice" for our deliverance. In a sense, the Gospel text "exegetes" the epistle. Jesus demonstrates what it may look like, ultimately, to prefer the other above oneself, and gives concrete expression to boundary-crossing love toward one's declared adversary. Reading side by side the portrait of Jesus as he turns toward the cross, and the portrait of reconciling community that Paul paints, may create a rich homiletical weave.

An interesting variant on the translation of verse 11c may also be worthy of a preacher's attention. Some translators (Karl Barth and Ernst Käsemann among them) defend choosing the more arresting, albeit more weakly attested, alternative reading here. Instead of rendering verse 11, "Do not lag in zeal, be ardent in spirit, serve the Lord," Barth, Käsemann, and others translate, "*. . . serve the time.*" (Barth goes so far as to deem "serve the Lord" an "insipid" translation!) Choosing *kairō* over *kyriō* comports with Paul's concern with the momentous, decisive "time" of God's renewal of all things; the word *kairos* in some form occurs seven times in Romans alone, excluding this occurrence, as well as fourteen times in other Pauline letters, excluding the contested letters.

Such a reading heightens the emphasis and urgency of this entire section of the epistle,

---

2. Roy A. Harrisville, "Do not repay evil with evil: Preaching Romans 12:9–21," *Word & World* 28, no. 1 (Winter, 2008): 89.

underscoring its function as an extension into the world of relationship and action of Paul's argument. It is as if, for Paul, it has become critically important that the reconciled community God has established live up to its calling to exhibit a bold alternative in a world deeply divided ethnically, economically, and religiously.

It is not difficult to sense the parallels between the world in which Paul wrote and the globalized world of the twenty-first century, shot through with the rival claims and mutual distortions of groups that mistrust and demonize one another on many levels. Reframed in the urgent imperative, "Serve the time!" the plea that we turn toward one another in mutual regard, mutual honor, and mutual respect becomes a critical matter, not just a shallow gesture.

"Genuine love is . . ." —radical. Maybe the weary, frightened, undocumented stranger that we shelter is none other than Christ among us in our time. As Paul indicates, God's work of creating unthinkably reconciling, self-sacrificing communities is open-ended.

SALLY A. BROWN

Commentary 2: Connecting the Reading with the World

In this text Paul addresses several principles for Christian life in church and society. He begins with love. He emphasizes "authentic love" in verse 9. Authentic love is concrete practice, not abstract words. In verse 10 Paul highlights love as a form of affection siblings ought to have for one another, suggesting that Christians treat one another like family or kinfolk. Verse 11 encourages steadfastness, an earnest practice of Christian principles through the Spirit. Verse 12 emphasizes rejoicing, hope, perseverance, patience in suffering, and prayer without ceasing. Through verses 9–12, we see Paul teaching practical, transformative Christian principles for everyday living.

In verses 13–21, Paul focuses on the church's responsibility for meeting one another's concrete needs. We are to rejoice with humanity in situations of happiness and mourn with people in times of sorrow. Paul is also aware of division in the church and the world, a problem humankind struggles with today. One might consider framing Paul's concerns for freedom and authentic love in response to thirst and hunger with reference to present social contexts. For example, the problems of racism, sexism, classism, heterosexism, the prison industrial complex, the school-to-prison pipeline, misogyny, sexual assault, and other forms of violence are local and global problems. They are causes of great spiritual, mental, and physical suffering.

Focusing on the school-to-prison pipeline, one might examine the criminalization of black girls and boys in school. Statistically schools exact harsher disciplinary procedures against black girls and boys than they give to their white peers. Schools report a disproportionate number of black children as disciplinary problems to legal authorities. Simply because black children articulate thirst and hunger for learning in a manner that is culturally different or because of bias to the color of their skin, teachers and administration often treat black children as strangers instead of as family.

This racial and cultural bias may be conscious or unconscious, but the effects of it are damaging. Black children are vulnerable to the criminal justice system and the prison industrial complex when their tone, appearance, or manner is perceived as offensive. Rather than receiving affirmation for their intelligence, the children receive punishment. This is violence and a form of hatred. It is racial and cultural hatred. It is not love. Paul believed we should treat people who are different like beloved members of our family. That is love. Paul is aware of cultural biases, differences, and divisions. He is similarly aware of religious tensions.

Finally, in verses 19–21 Paul quotes Deuteronomy 32:35 and Proverbs 25:21, 22, counseling the church that vengeance belongs to God. Rather than seek vengeance, Christians are to feed their enemies when they are hungry and to give them drink when they are thirsty. In verse 17 Paul counsels Christians to do what is right when they are ill-treated and not to repay evil with evil. He restates this in verse 21 to give emphasis to his mandate not to seek revenge. Paul encourages Christians to act in the love that they profess. He cautions the church not to give up when persecuted. In counseling love and kindness toward perceived and real enemies, Paul is preaching Jesus' own message to love all humankind. To feed and give drink to one's enemies here entails sharing material resources with all and sharing Christian spiritual life with all.

One might read Paul here as warning us that "othering" those who "other" us perpetuates cycles of hatred and violence, the opposite of authentic love in verses 9–10. People try to build walls of many kinds to separate "us" from "them." For example, rejecting refugees and separating them from their children treats refugees as strangers and enemies. It reflects a worldview in which people from other countries seeking peace are not kin. For Paul, however, all of us human beings are family.

Offering material sustenance to everyone is a basic act of love in the presence of enmity. In communities where disinherited young people join gangs for a sense of family, survival, and protection, today some congregations choose to discourage youth who dress differently from entering the church. Some congregations, however, choose to offer an alternative Christian family that feeds, protects, and nurtures all people. The latter act offers an alternative sense of family that can be transformative. It is in keeping with Paul's counsel for an ethic of care. This ethic of care is prescriptive for personal and community relationships in church and society. How we treat one another is the heart of the Christian witness and mission of the church.

Is feeding one's enemies a denial of unhealthy, harmful relationships? Paul is not suggesting that people are not accountable for their actions. He does not condone persecution, bullying, or domestic violence. He is very clear that Christians should resist injustice, because he strongly speaks against evil. Verse 9 exhorts the reader to hate what is evil by turning away from it and to "hold fast to what is good." To hate in the biblical sense is to be repulsed. The point is to be so strongly repulsed that one "turns to the good."

In turning to the good, vengeance is not the tool for resisting evil, because vengeance comes from hatred. Hate is not love. The tool for resisting evil in all its forms is love. Paul is negotiating difficult real-life arguments in the early churches and the painful Roman imperial authority exacted against Jews, Christians, and Jewish Christians. Paul was writing to churches in late first-century Rome. According to Elisabeth Schüssler Fiorenza, Paul is part of a Jewish renewal movement. He is a missionary proselytizing the message of Jesus Christ and helping women and men found churches,[3] regardless of Rome's mandate that Caesar is god. He is a rebel who resists imperial claims to divinity with the love of Jesus Christ.

Overall Paul offers a new way of living for everyone. Experiencing God's love through the many gifts of Christian practitioners is powerful enough to turn anyone to the good news and practice of Jesus Christ. Paul suggests a model of interdependence or what black feminist theorist Kimberlee Crenshaw calls "intersectionality."[4] In this model, the good that affects one affects all, and the evil that affects one affects all. Realizing the kingdom of God, realm of God, or the "kin-dom" of God, to use the language of María Isasi-Díaz,[5] entails living out God's goodness in everyday life with constant prayer and earnestness. Communion with God and one another is at the heart of Christian life. To offer food and drink to all is related to the liturgy of Eucharist, the great thanksgiving, or Holy Communion.

KAREN BAKER-FLETCHER

---

3. Elisabeth Schüssler Fiorenza, *In Memory of Her: A Feminist Theological Reconstruction of Feminist Origins* (New York: Crossroad, 2000 [1994; 1983]), 169–99.

4. For a fuller discussion of "intersectionality" and Kimberlee Crenshaw's coining of this term that, in part, describes the historical and contemporary black feminist and womanist praxis described in earlier language of "overlapping systems of oppression" by the Combahee River Collective (CRC) in the 1970s, please see Patricia Hill Collins and Sirma Bilge, *Intersectionality* (Malden, MA: Polity Press, 2016), 64, 81–85. Intersectionality respects humankind in its multiplicity of forms in creation with attention to freedom from harm from social injustices such as racism, economic oppression, and class, gender, sexual orientation, ableism, ageism, nationalism, etc. It may also give attention to ecological justice.

5. Ada María Isasi-Díaz, *Mujerista Theology* (Maryknoll, NY: Orbis Books, 1996), 89.

Proper 17 (Sunday between August 28 and September 3 inclusive)

Matthew 16:21–28

²¹From that time on, Jesus began to show his disciples that he must go to Jerusalem and undergo great suffering at the hands of the elders and chief priests and scribes, and be killed, and on the third day be raised. ²²And Peter took him aside and began to rebuke him, saying, "God forbid it, Lord! This must never happen to you." ²³But he turned and said to Peter, "Get behind me, Satan! You are a stumbling block to me; for you are setting your mind not on divine things but on human things."

²⁴Then Jesus told his disciples, "If any want to become my followers, let them deny themselves and take up their cross and follow me. ²⁵For those who want to save their life will lose it, and those who lose their life for my sake will find it. ²⁶For what will it profit them if they gain the whole world but forfeit their life? Or what will they give in return for their life?

²⁷"For the Son of Man is to come with his angels in the glory of his Father, and then he will repay everyone for what has been done. ²⁸Truly I tell you, there are some standing here who will not taste death before they see the Son of Man coming in his kingdom."

Commentary 1: Connecting the Reading with Scripture

In Matthew's telling, Peter goes from being blessed for divinely granted insight (Matt. 16:17) to being berated as Satan (v. 23); from being designated as a *foundation* stone (vv. 18–19) to being depicted as a *stumbling* stone (v. 23). Jesus seems to take him on a hairpin turn at breakneck speed. Peter might be pardoned for saying: "I never saw this coming!"

Except, of course, in retrospect, he could have seen. Maybe not at his initial encounter with Jesus, one similarly abrupt, but less overtly threatening: "Follow me, and I will make you fish for people" (4:18–20). However, the trajectory of meaning that arcs from the initial encounter to the present one commences hard on the summons for Peter to redirect his fishing focus. The Beatitudes—the introduction of Matthew's Jesus to his first Discipleship Training Session—conclude with a blessing for followers who are persecuted (5:11). Shortly thereafter, in the same sermon, comes a series of injunctions to behavior significantly "self-denying" (e.g., 5:38–48)—behavior oriented toward rewards eschatological, not immediate (6:19–21 prefigures 16:27).

Not much later comes a warning that the way ahead for Jesus' followers will be very demanding (8:19–22). Then, in his second Discipleship Training Session, before the preaching, teaching, exorcising mission on which he sends his twelve disciples, Jesus makes it clear, in stark detail, that suffering lies ahead; and that rewards disciples will receive for serving him will come only at the end of time (10:16–42). In the setting of this mission charge, references to "taking up the cross," and "finding life only in losing it" are articulated clearly and explicitly (10:38–39).

Thus Peter cannot plausibly claim that he has never heard the likes of this before! If, in response to "Get behind me, Satan!" Peter had protested, "I had no idea!" Matthew's Jesus could well have responded, "You *heard* it, but you did not *get* it." Jesus would have had evidence ready-to-hand for another similar failure in disciple understanding.

Just prior to this interchange, the disciples, regardless of having recently distributed abundant bread for two large crowds, worry that Jesus is faulting them for failing to have bread on hand; when he has instead been trying to warn them about the "yeast of the Pharisees" (16:5–12). Critically important teachings clearly are *not* getting assimilated; so, going forward, Jesus is even more overt and frequent in his declarations. He issues a reminder about his own suffering right after the transfiguration (the recorded event immediately following, 17:12). At a gathering in Galilee (17:22–23) he reiterates, to the "great distress" of his disciples, his coming fate. He repeats the prediction again, taking the disciples aside, as he approaches Jerusalem (20:17–19). He also warns them, in graphic terms, of the persecutions they will have to face for following him (24:9–14).

The sharpness of the rebuke he issues to Peter resonates with his forceful repudiation, at the outset of his ministry, of the devil's final temptation of all the world's kingdoms in exchange for an act of worship (4:8–10). This face-off with Peter is more pronounced in Matthew than in either Mark or Luke. In both those Gospels, Peter does name Jesus as the Messiah. In Mark, Jesus names Peter as Satan for his distracting protest, but does not previously bless him for his authentic recognition (Mark 8:27–38). In Luke, neither the protest by Peter, nor the rebuke of Peter is recounted (Luke 9:18–27). Against the background of Matthew's widely deployed and intensely developed theme regarding "the cost of discipleship," this more protracted and tense interchange between the two is worth a preacher's noting. Related to, but distinguishable from this theme are two other connections, each particularly associated with one of the other two readings appointed for this day.

Exodus 3:1–15 is a classic example of a call narrative, where God calls an unsuspecting, unlikely, and seemingly ill-qualified individual to undertake a critically significant role in the history of salvation. The presence and power of God are promised, but the work is delegated to the person called. Moses meets God in a bush that burns but is not consumed. Abram and Joseph are prior call recipients. Gideon and David, Isaiah and Jeremiah subsequently receive such calls. Mary is confronted with an angel visitation. The list goes on. While these characters and others encounter challenges and obstacles, the "call" itself in many instances is portrayed in the biblical story as if it comes essentially "once—upon a time."

This can convey an impression that similar one-off encounters are normative for the people of God, that the "chosen few" are called in personal permutations of "burning bush" experiences (and if no bush has burned for you, you are not called—at least not yet). Matthew's Gospel briefly recounts what sound like such "immediate" encounters for Peter, Andrew, James, John, and Matthew, all of whom, in response to the call of Jesus, up and follow forthwith (Matt. 4:18–22; 9:9).

In contrast, consider today's account of the interaction of Jesus and Peter, followed by the admonition of Jesus to his disciples to "deny themselves, take up their cross, and follow"—to lose their lives in order to save them—coupled with the warning that one can gain the whole world and lose one's own life. In the setting of Matthew's story line, this account suggests that there is no single "moment of truth" but a series of them, that there are many decision points, instead of one (as the James Russell Lowell poem has it, "once to every man and nation").

Rather, God's call to self-sacrificing service is episodically unfolding, even if unidirectional. Our responses are more in accord with the line from the Shaker hymn "The Gift to Be Simple": that "by turning and turning we come round right." This, in turn, enables us to return to various call narratives in biblical stories, engaging them as more progressively unfolding, evolving faith journeys with illuminating analogues to our own. The faith story of Moses, his saga of self denying, life losing, and life gaining (along with that of others like Abraham and Joseph), is an ongoing story of "call and response."

The question can be raised, however, What does a life of cross-carrying self-denial—one realistic, responsive, and responsible—look like on the ground? Paul's counsel to the Romans is of considerable help in this regard. It is well to remember how Romans 12 begins: "I appeal to you, therefore, brothers and sisters, by the mercies of God [since *from, through*, and *to* God are 'all things'] that you present your bodies as a living sacrifice." In what does such a sacrifice, such self-denial, consist? Paul just happens to have a suggestive list, at once more challenging than we can easily achieve, yet fully engageable as a series of manageable steps taken in response to the call of God at any given moment: genuine love, tenacious goodness, mutual affection, competition not to *gain* honor, but to *give* it. The list goes on and on, prominently featuring such practices as suffering patiently, blessing those who persecute, refusing to repay evil in kind, and renouncing retribution—all clearly counterintuitive to a project of self-advancement, let alone self-survival (Rom. 12:9–21).

Yet no such activities should be construed as self-immolation, or suicide stands on the wrong hills. Situational discernment is required, and Matthew's Jesus, in his Third Discipleship Training Session (13:24–53 most notably) speaks of the necessity for those committed to the commonwealth of God to search long and hard for the pearl of great price, to sort good fish from bad, to draw from treasures old and new, and to do so while patiently awaiting the growth of seeds sown, of yeast worked into dough—expecting weed/wheat distinctions to be manifest only in the end.

DAVID J. SCHLAFER

Commentary 2: Connecting the Reading with the World

Even though one may not know these verses verbatim, key phrases and themes mentioned here permeate many Christians' and non-Christians' understanding of what it means to follow Jesus. Those inside and outside of the Christian faith are often aware of Jesus' suffering and death and the language of "carrying one's cross" and "denying oneself."

Suffering, death, cross carrying, and self-denial are not exciting topics. Anxiety producing may be a more apt description, because this passage unfolds in such a way that the challenging nature of discipleship is laid bare. If we, as followers of Jesus, were to be completely honest and did not have the benefit of knowing the end of the story, we might find ourselves to be more like Peter than we are comfortable with. Instead of falling in, rank and file, behind Jesus, we too may object to the passion he predicts and refuse to accept what many commentators call "the way of the cross." Surely, there must be a better way!

Perhaps the story has become too sanitized. We are now so comfortable with the end of the story, so confident in Jesus' resurrection, that his crucifixion no longer looms large. Jesus is no longer a threat to established religion or the sociopolitical system many religious groups lobby to uphold. The teachings of Jesus no longer confront but instead endorse the way things are. The result is that for many professing followers of Jesus, Jesus and the religious rulers are of one accord, backed by the government while simultaneously backing the government. Two thousand years have passed, and the scandalous, deadly language of the cross sounds almost hyperbolic amid the myriad of crosses decorating our paraments, houses of worship, clothing, knickknacks, and skin. Crosses are easily borne as ornaments disconnected from discipleship.

Indeed, this passage presents issues for us to consider if we are serious about following Jesus. It raises critical questions for us to ask and wrestle with to help shape our attitudes and behaviors as followers of Jesus Christ. Thankfully, there are connections that we can make to help us better understand discipleship in this day and age. I suggest that a helpful way of making these connections and exploring contemporary discipleship is to explore three main characters in Matthew's account: Jesus, Peter, and the disciples.

Our first connection is with *Jesus*. According to Matthew, Jesus' suffering and death are in some way "necessary." He uses the word *dei*, which can connote divine necessity and/or inevitability. On the one hand, we could interpret Jesus' suffering and death as God-willed. In other words, God sent Jesus for the express purpose of suffering and dying. By so doing, Jesus proves himself faithful to the will of God. On the other hand, we could interpret Jesus' suffering and death as an inevitable result of his ministry. That is to say, he suffers and dies because he refuses to appease the status quo and decides to continue the God-ordained ministry, even at the cost of his life. By so doing, he proves himself faithful to the will of God.

The former reading produces a suffering savior, a savior who is called to and characterized by his suffering. Suffering is a necessary and identifying characteristic of who he is. The latter yields a savior who suffers, a savior whose identity can be opened up to the fullness of his life and ministry. Suffering then becomes a consequence rather than a prerequisite of his divine work. This distinction, which may appear so slight on the surface, has profound implications for discipleship, because discipleship is about following Jesus, who is our ultimate example. Moreover, this distinction can have grave implications for people whose lives are marked by suffering.

If we are called to "make disciples" (Matt. 28:19), then this passage forces us to consider what kind of disciples we are making. Encouraging people to follow a suffering savior, who is primarily identified by his suffering, easily yields suffering followers who measure their discipleship by how much they suffer. It risks equating suffering with righteousness and making suffering people complacent and complicit in their own suffering. Rather than naming and fighting against death-dealing people, systems, and forces of life, suffering followers merely accept them as their crosses to bear or as proof of their self-denying ways. Their only comfort becomes the confidence in believing that they are suffering like Jesus.

However, disciples following a Jesus who suffers may become followers who suffer. "Follower" becomes the primary identifying factor, and suffering becomes a consequence that they are willing to endure for continuing the ministry of the one who lived, suffered, died, and was vindicated by resurrection. In other words, the suffering is never the goal or measuring stick of their discipleship. This enables them to see that all sorrow, pain, injustice, oppression, or torment inflicted by life or others is not the will of God for their lives and can be fought against rather than passively accepted. This understanding rails against sacralizing one's suffering. It willingly sacrifices for the cause of Christ but opposes sacrificing one's self for the greed of others. It prevents one from identifying every negative aspect of life as a cross, giving them the ability to discern if the so-called cross is something for them to bear.

The second connection is with *Peter*. This passage begs the church and individual Christians to assess how much we have become like Peter in this passage. Peter's problem, according to Jesus, is that his focus is on "human things" rather than "divine things" (16:23). In short, Peter still thinks according to the way the world thinks. There is a selfishness that pervades his understanding of how things should go. There is an assumption that Jesus, and therefore his followers, should be beneficiaries of the system, not enemies of or casualties to the system. Suffering is not a consequence of following Jesus. It should be avoided. However, the cost of avoiding suffering could be the loss of one's soul (vv. 25–26), if avoidance is achieved by forsaking Jesus.

Peter's reaction to Jesus' passion prediction has made him an adversary (*satanas*) and stumbling block (*skandalon*) to Jesus. Whereas Peter reacts to Jesus' prediction as if the prediction were scandalous, Jesus' response to Peter shows Peter's words to be the real scandal. As followers of Jesus, we too must ask ourselves, How scandalous have we become? Have we or how have we become caught up in the world's way of thinking to the point that we will not oppose current religious and political leaders for the cause of Christ if it means possible rejection, suffering, and death, whether these consequences be physical or social?

Our final connection is with the *other disciples*. Jesus invites anyone (*tis*) who desires to follow him (v. 24). We live in a world that uses exclusivity to increase the value of things and people. Colleges, organizations, institutions, and neighborhoods are seen as better when they let in fewer people. Items that few people can afford are deemed precious. This worldly mind-set can tempt us to limit our understanding of and openness to "anyone." It can deceive us into valuing people, places, and things in the same way.

As we approach a national recognition of Labor Day, this passage invites us to reflect upon God's divine plan and its significance for all of creation (Isa. 52–53). While there are numerous references to judgment according to one's actions (Matt. 5:17–20; 7:15–20; Rom. 2:6), Matthew also invites us to avoid a tendency to construe one's vocation as synonymous with one's humanity as we consider what a relationship with Jesus requires of us.

RAQUEL ST. CLAIR LETTSOME

Proper 18 (Sunday between September 4 and September 10 inclusive)

Ezekiel 33:7–11 and Exodus 12:1–14 Romans 13:8–14
Psalm 119:33–40 and Psalm 149 Matthew 18:15–20

Ezekiel 33:7–11

⁷So you, mortal, I have made a sentinel for the house of Israel; whenever you hear a word from my mouth, you shall give them warning from me. ⁸If I say to the wicked, "O wicked ones, you shall surely die," and you do not speak to warn the wicked to turn from their ways, the wicked shall die in their iniquity, but their blood I will require at your hand. ⁹But if you warn the wicked to turn from their ways, and they do not turn from their ways, the wicked shall die in their iniquity, but you will have saved your life.

¹⁰Now you, mortal, say to the house of Israel, Thus you have said: "Our transgressions and our sins weigh upon us, and we waste away because of them; how then can we live?" ¹¹Say to them, As I live, says the Lord GOD, I have no pleasure in the death of the wicked, but that the wicked turn from their ways and live; turn back, turn back from your evil ways; for why will you die, O house of Israel?

Exodus 12:1–14

¹The LORD said to Moses and Aaron in the land of Egypt: ²This month shall mark for you the beginning of months; it shall be the first month of the year for you. ³Tell the whole congregation of Israel that on the tenth of this month they are to take a lamb for each family, a lamb for each household. ⁴If a household is too small for a whole lamb, it shall join its closest neighbor in obtaining one; the lamb shall be divided in proportion to the number of people who eat of it. ⁵Your lamb shall be without blemish, a year-old male; you may take it from the sheep or from the goats. ⁶You shall keep it until the fourteenth day of this month; then the whole assembled congregation of Israel shall slaughter it at twilight. ⁷They shall take some of the blood and put it on the two doorposts and the lintel of the houses in which they eat it. ⁸They shall eat the lamb that same night; they shall eat it roasted over the fire with unleavened bread and bitter herbs. ⁹Do not eat any of it raw or boiled in water, but roasted over the fire, with its head, legs, and inner organs. ¹⁰You shall let none of it remain until the morning; anything that remains until the morning you shall burn. ¹¹This is how you shall eat it: your loins girded, your sandals on your feet, and your staff in your hand; and you shall eat it hurriedly. It is the passover of the LORD. ¹²For I will pass through the land of Egypt that night, and I will strike down every firstborn in the land of Egypt, both human beings and animals; on all the gods of Egypt I will execute judgments: I am the LORD. ¹³The blood shall be a sign for you on the houses where you live: when I see the blood, I will pass over you, and no plague shall destroy you when I strike the land of Egypt.

¹⁴This day shall be a day of remembrance for you. You shall celebrate it as a festival to the LORD; throughout your generations you shall observe it as a perpetual ordinance.

Commentary 1: Connecting the Reading with Scripture

After the congregation prays the Lord's Prayer in the eucharistic rite, the celebrant may invite the congregation to participate in the body and blood of Jesus Christ with the words, "Christ our Passover is sacrificed for us" (see 1 Cor. 5:7). These words find echoes in words of the two Old Testament readings for Proper 18. Christ our Passover, the lamb that was slain before the foundation of the world, does not annul the Passover commanded by Moses. In him the literal sense of the Scriptures receives a spiritual meaning without annulling its literal sense.

The Scriptures radiate out from Exodus 12:1–14 in preserving the "children of Israel" from slavery unto death into a life lived toward the fullness of the divine promise. As Christ, the Son of Man, fulfills the sentinel mentioned in Ezekiel 33:7–11, this sentinel simultaneously calls the people to remember, not their sin, but God's desire for their life. The biblical exhortation to remember well, emphasized in both passages, culminates in the remembrance and participation in the life, death, and resurrection of Jesus Christ in the Eucharist.

Exodus 12:1–14 occurs within the series of confrontations between God and Pharaoh. Scholars commonly call it the plague narrative. The Passover takes place immediately before the last plague, the death of the firstborn in Egypt. The earlier key verse, "God remembered [God's] covenant with Abraham, Isaac, and Jacob" (Exod. 2:24), ties the whole plague narrative with God's fulfillment of God's promises to the ancestors. Exodus 12:1–14 gives the second divine commandment before the giving of the Torah at Sinai. The first was God's command to Abraham to circumcise all male descendants as a sign of the participation of males in the divine promise. The divine commands before the gift of the law mark Israel's election and life.

The divine word in Exodus 12:1–14 commands a feast for the people of Israel. The text centers on the selection of the lamb for the feast's entrée (12:3–5). The congregation of Israel must select the lamb four days before its butchering. All from the congregation of Israel, rich and poor, must share in the feast. The people select a one-year male, a sheep or goat, so that the feast does not diminish the economic future of the flock. Males are more dispensable than females in animal husbandry. The people should not eat meat from defective or wounded or diseased (i.e., blemished) animals. The Passover prepares the congregation of Israel for their journey out of slavery toward the fullness of the divine promise.

The lamb gives life to Israel. Israel should eat the lamb to prepare them for their journey out of slavery. Verses 8–11 emphasize the importance of selection, slaughter, cooking, and meal. Roasted lamb with a flat (unleavened) bread: the Passover meal serves gyros without tzatziki sauce. The meal requires no cleanup and allows no leftovers. It serves as the last meal Israel will have time to eat before they head into the wilderness. The command requires the people to consume the meat, while they are dressed and ready to leave. The lamb's body is real food.

In obedience to the Noahic commandments, Israel does not consume the blood of the lamb. God instructs Moses and Aaron to command Israel to place the blood of the lamb around the gates/doorways into the residences where they consume the meal (v. 7). A summary statement and/or an announcement ends the command: "It is the passover of the Lord" (v. 11b). The brief sentence looks backward to the command and forward to its explanation, the reason for the command (vv. 12–13).

Verses 12–13 return to verse 7 to explain the reason for the command to place the blood of the lamb on the door lintels. A simple ring structure exists: the blood on the lintels surrounds the instructions to cook and eat the lamb. The blood of the lamb protects the firstborn inhabitants from death. It grants them life. The blood is a "sign," not for the angel of death, but for the congregation of Israel (v. 13). The blood of the slaughtered lamb signs God's preservation of Israel from the plague of death. The body and the blood of the lamb preserve Israel from death and strengthen Israel for their journey out of slavery.

A final command emphasizes the importance of the feast. The command celebrates the day as a "festival to the Lord" (v. 14). The second person plural pronoun suddenly becomes transhistorical. God gives the command to Moses and Aaron. They constitute the most immediate "you." The "you" in verses 3–13 includes Moses and Aaron and the congregation of Israel. Verses 2 and 14, however, enfold future generations into its reference. "You" includes all who find themselves within the future "congregation of Israel." "You" leaves linear time behind. In the act of "remembrance," "you" enfolds the text's present characters and the people's future. The act of remembrance and participation in the blood and body of the lamb form the future generations of the "congregation of Israel." The image of the Passover lamb becomes a powerful type for the life, death, and resurrection of Jesus.

If the lamb ties Christ our Passover to the Exodus reading, the language of "the Son of Man" (NRSV "mortal") connects the Ezekiel passage figuratively to Jesus. Ezekiel 33:7–11 exhorts Israel to remember correctly as well. The divine word speaks to the prophet as "the Son of Man." The language, of course, resonates with Jesus' own sayings about himself. Life and death form the issue in Ezekiel 33, as it does in Exodus 12. The divine word speaks to the "sentinel" to warn the house of Israel. The sentinel has a singular purpose: to call Israel to turn from their wickedness. The sentinel may preserve his life through warning Israel to repent (Ezek. 33:7–9). In the sentinel's obedience, the threat of death moves from the Son of Man to the house of Israel.

Israel, however, can remember only their sin (v. 10). Their inability to remember God's mercy cuts them off from repentance. Remembering only their sin enfolds them in judgment of their own making. They cannot see life beyond their own sin. The sentinel, told to warn them of judgment, instead reminds them that God is life and desires their life. The past does not determine the future. God does not desire the death of any. As God lives (v. 11), God desires life. Israel needs to repent from death and turn toward life (God). The house of Israel, as in Exodus 12, does not need to die (v. 11). Israel needs to remember God's mercy and desire for their life.

Moses and Aaron function as the sentinel in Ezekiel 33, even as the Son of Man in the Gospels calls to life. God's commitment to life over death of Israel stands central to both passages. To fail to observe Passover is to fail to remember God's faithfulness to Israel for the sake of the world. To fail to remember, to not participate in the body and blood of the slain lamb, leads to death. The sentinel asks Israel to remember not its sin, but God's desire for repentance and life. In a very real sense, it reminds Israel of the Passover of the Lord. Turn from your evil ways! Place the blood of the lamb on the lintels of your door. Why will you die, people of Israel? God has provided life to free Israel from slavery and lead them into the fullness of God's promise, a land flowing with milk and honey.

Christ our Passover is sacrificed for us.

JOHN W. WRIGHT

Commentary 2: Connecting the Reading with the World

In today's reading from Ezekiel, we are presented with the intriguing image of the sentinel, a person of exceptional skills. The sentinel is a skilled musician whose music, with its mix of loud short blasts and prolonged and sustained notes, must capture the hearer's attention with its insistence and urgency. The sentinel's task is not to lull people into relaxation and sleep, but rather to signal impending danger, and to call forth vigilance and immediate action.

Sentinels represent profiles in courage in roles that require great personal risk and vulnerability in the likelihood of an attack. The work requires mental alacrity and physical fitness. Whether the sentinel climbs up to a high point or runs through the streets, physical stamina is required to blow the trumpet with clarity. Even in times of relative peace, it is the sentinel's responsibility to be constantly alert and perceptive, even in the quiet but stressful hours of the dark. Along with courage, sentinels also embody a great sense of responsibility and obligation to their community.

The image of the sentinel can be helpful to faith communities today. Today, as in the Ezekiel text, the primary mission of the sentinel is to enhance and witness to human life and flourishing. The sentinel works on behalf of the Lord and giver of life to value, save, and promote life. For the faith community, the image of the sentinel is a reminder of our responsibility to all life forms in God's creation, our stewardship of the environment, our need for health care, our need for peaceful resolutions of our conflicts that do not lead to military engagement, destructive warfare, or nuclear annihilation.

The metaphor of sentinel can be applied to particular individuals or to the faith community as a whole. We respond individually or collectively to the divine imperative to focus on human life and to work toward human flourishing. We also become aware that the work of the sentinel is vital and indispensable, since the consequences are a matter of life and death. The sentinel's mission is to deliver a word from God's mouth to the wicked so that they do not die in their iniquity.

There are certain identifiable skills or gifts needed for those who are set apart for this work. The sentinel must hear both the music of heaven and the songs or laments of earth. The sentinel responds not only to the divine imperative, but also to the fears, cries, and concerns of the community. The sentinel hears the cry of the people: How then can we live? (v. 10). Through its worship and mission, the faith community can intentionally recognize those transgressions and sins that cause individuals and communities to waste away.

Sentinels are set apart for the work because they demonstrate the ability or gifts to hear a word from God's mouth. People of faith are called to be sentinels and to live a life of righteousness, but who are the wicked? Are they members of the faith community who falter? Strangers or people of other religious persuasions? Outsiders who live in total disregard of the basic rules of decency and civility? How does a twenty-first-century sentinel play the trumpet so that the wicked will hear?

One cannot miss the fact that sentinels do this work at great risk to their lives. Speaking to the wicked or to the iniquity in people and systems may pose a threat to one's safety and livelihood. We think also of those who work in local or global arenas to procure safety for the nation, to safeguard human rights and dignity across the world, and to provide for our defense against aggressors. How does the faith community understand its relationship to persons who serve as police officers or military personnel as sentinels for the nation?

Communities may experience conflict and trauma or gratitude and a sense of security. The sentinel must understand the cost as it relates to the city or to the community. The faith community must understand that in issues large and small the cost is eternal vigilance. These are issues of faithfulness to the life of righteousness, justice, truth, peace, love, mercy, compassion, and hospitality.

In Exodus 12:1–14, the Lord addresses Moses and Aaron in the land of Egypt. We are mindful that Moses' activities are contextual. The mention of the location may inform or remind us that our work, preaching, teaching, and engaging in theological reflection are contextual tasks. The naming of a particular place becomes an invitation to us to be attentive to the context of Moses' words and actions.

Egypt is a powerful nation that has enslaved the Israelite people (Exod. 1:8–14). In one context, Moses is charged with speaking truth to power, in the person of Pharaoh accompanied by his officials and magicians. He understands that he needs to be a faithful and obedient emissary from God to the court of Pharaoh (11:3b). In another context, Moses is called to be a credible messenger from God to the people of Israel. He receives instructions and messages from God, and he speaks and acts on God's behalf in his multiple roles as a leader, community organizer, prophetic voice, and priestly go-between who interprets God to others and petitions God on behalf of the people.

Moses is uniquely equipped for this role because of the circumstances of his birth, his formative years, and his experience. Our roles of leadership or service are not conducted in a vacuum but, rather, are informed and shaped by our contexts that may reflect our relationship to the land, institutions of power, different groups of people, and status derived from family or country of origin, socioeconomic status, education, personal gifts, and skills. In the same way, contexts are significant when sharing our call stories, observing holy days, or performing certain rituals. So we are intentional to recall or focus our attention on location, times, and circumstances.

In this text, Passover is instituted with attention to context, location, detailed instructions of the day and time of year, manner of preparation, and the significance of the festival. In terms of time, it speaks to the present, the past, and the future. The directions are given so that they may be meticulously executed with a sense of urgency, with a focus on the present, and with hospitality extended to each member of the household, and to the neighbor. Faith communities can help design rituals for households that invite participation of young and old. Most importantly, rituals that are designed for the twenty-first-century household must invite participants to look beyond the household and be mindful of the neighbor, the poor, and the marginalized.

It is also a ritual that points to the future when liberation is achieved among generations yet unborn, so that they may remember and commemorate the past. The rituals, locations, and monuments that we have built will certainly have historical significance for individuals and communities, and provide continuity, a sense of belonging and identity across generations. However, they are more meaningful when they help to make sense of the present and invite us into the future. The contextual imperative of our work necessitates new words, visions, and ways of being in community with each other. In addition, the community must be able to envision a new reality and celebrate new vocation.

LINCOLN E. GALLOWAY

Proper 18 (Sunday between September 4 and September 10 inclusive)

Psalm 119:33–40

³³Teach me, O LORD, the way of your statutes,
   and I will observe it to the end.
³⁴Give me understanding, that I may keep your law
   and observe it with my whole heart.
³⁵Lead me in the path of your commandments,
   for I delight in it.
³⁶Turn my heart to your decrees,
   and not to selfish gain.
³⁷Turn my eyes from looking at vanities;
   give me life in your ways.
³⁸Confirm to your servant your promise,
   which is for those who fear you.
³⁹Turn away the disgrace that I dread,
   for your ordinances are good.
⁴⁰See, I have longed for your precepts;
   in your righteousness give me life.

Psalm 149

¹Praise the LORD!
   Sing to the LORD a new song,
   his praise in the assembly of the faithful.
²Let Israel be glad in its Maker;
   let the children of Zion rejoice in their King.
³Let them praise his name with dancing,
   making melody to him with tambourine and lyre.
⁴For the LORD takes pleasure in his people;
   he adorns the humble with victory.
⁵Let the faithful exult in glory;
   let them sing for joy on their couches.
⁶Let the high praises of God be in their throats
   and two-edged swords in their hands,
⁷to execute vengeance on the nations
   and punishment on the peoples,
⁸to bind their kings with fetters
   and their nobles with chains of iron,
⁹to execute on them the judgment decreed.
   This is glory for all his faithful ones.
Praise the LORD!

Connecting the Psalm with Scripture and Worship

Psalm 119:33–40. Psalm 119, an extended ode to the glory of God's law, offers a thought-provoking counterpoint to the first reading from Ezekiel 33. In that text, we are reminded of Ezekiel's call to be a "sentinel" for the people of God. Like a watchman sounding the alarm at the sight of danger, he is to receive God's word and give the people warning of God's judgment. This call comes with additional responsibility, for the sentinel is liable for judgment if he does *not* warn the people to turn from their "wicked ways" (Ezek. 33:9).

It may be easy for a preacher to imagine herself as a sentinel, charged with speaking a hard "prophetic" word. There are, after all, plenty of people in the world who need a hard word spoken against them, though Christians might disagree about exactly who those people are. That fact alone is caution enough against too easily putting on the sentinel cap and stepping up on a soapbox to declare judgment.

The text offers two additional cautions here. First, the Ezekiel passage is about calling *God's people* to account. It is not about outsiders, but about the wicked in our own gospel communities, the people who sit with us trying to understand God's word, the people who make promises at baptism, the people with whom we break bread. Second, generations of interpreters have recognized that Ezekiel's calling belongs to *all* God's people, not just to clergy or self-appointed finger-waggers. In fact, the lectionary highlights this by pairing these texts with a Gospel lesson from Matthew 18 about church discipline and an epistle lesson from Romans 13 establishing that love is the fulfillment of the law.

The psalm, then, functions as a crucial preparatory prayer for those called to be sentinels to one another. It expresses the eager, passionate desire of God's people for God, for God's ways, and for God's Word. Like most of the rest of Psalm 119, it uses a host of synonyms for the Law (decree, precept, statute, commandment, ordinance, word, and promise) as a way to cast a wide net for all that God might speak. Before we can be warning speakers, we have to be God-seekers. We need to pray continuously for discernment, for understanding (Ps. 119:34); we need to long to know what is right and delight in the path of God's commandments (v. 35). This is a constant discipline. We cannot call the church to account without this relentless listening for the Word of the Lord. The psalm is what the Israelites should be praying, what the church should be praying.

If we do pray in this way, we find a God not just of warning and judgment, but of grace. The key connection point between the psalm and the Ezekiel text is the verb "turn," repentance. In Ezekiel, the people speak of God's judgment with despair: "Our transgressions and our sins weigh upon us; . . . how then can we live?" (Ezek. 33:10). However, God responds with another question: "Why will you die?" (v. 11). What God wants is repentance: "I have no pleasure in the death of the wicked, but that the wicked turn from their ways and live" (v. 11). This is the "promise" of the psalmist from verses 38 and 39: "Confirm to your servant your promise, which is for those who fear you. Turn away the disgrace that I dread."

The obvious liturgical use for this psalm, given its theme and its relationship to the other texts, is as a prayer for illumination. One might invite the congregation to speak it antiphonally, with one half speaking the plea in each verse ("Teach me, O Lord . . . , Give me understanding . . . , Lead me in the path . . .") and the other half responding with the second half of the verse ("and I will observe it . . . that I may keep your law . . . for I delight in it"). Another approach would be to compose a more contemporary prayer for illumination by using the key verbs that begin each verse of this excerpt in the psalm: teach, give, lead, turn, confirm. Note that there are both positive and negative longings in the psalm: longings for God's wisdom, and pleas to be protected from vanities, selfish gain, and the like.

Psalm 149. Psalm 149 is one of five great praise songs that close out the Psalter in a grand "Hallelujah!" Yet it takes an odd and unsettling turn in verse 6, moving from praise to vengeance, from a song in the throat to a sword in the hand. This is precisely the connecting point between this psalm and the semicontinuous first reading from Exodus 12, which details the instructions for celebrating the Passover. After all the specifics about the timing of the celebration and size of the lamb and the manner of its cooking and what to do with the blood and so on, we are reminded that all of this is because the Lord is executing judgment on the "gods of Egypt" (Exod. 12:12).

In places where the church has long enjoyed cultural privilege, it is hard to imagine praise connected to violence. It seems harsh, militaristic, triumphal, punitive. Yet it falls differently on our ears if we imagine the praise of the ancient Israelites, a small kingdom knocked around and enslaved by their more powerful neighbors, or if we can imagine the praise of Christians in other times and places, including today, who are suffering persecution, chaotic violence, and martyrdom.

In these contexts, the decree of God's judgment to bind kings and nobles with chains (Ps. 149:8–9) seems more fitting. It is like the satisfaction when the humble are adorned with victory (v. 4), when a successful slave uprising brings down the masters and enslavers. It may be helpful to think of this dynamic through the lens of the eschatological "already-and-not-yet." God has acted powerfully to save. There is a "new song" to be sung (v. 1), a new beginning for the marking of time (Exod. 12:2). Yet there are still dangers and threats to God's people, powers and principalities that fight against the reign of God and of his Christ.

Because Exodus 12 offers such strict liturgical instructions for the celebration of Passover and because Psalm 149 explicitly commends the use of dancing, melody, tambourine, and lyre as means for giving praise to the Lord, it may make sense for a congregation to sing a setting of Psalm 149 that affords the use of percussion and strings and, yes, even dancing. The Lord takes pleasure in such celebrations.

I am not familiar with a setting of this psalm that makes an appropriate musical "turn" at the pivotal verse 6. There is, however, a long tradition of reading that verse with the understanding that it is describing the same thing in two ways. That is to say, the "high praises of God" in the throats of the faithful *are* the "two-edged sword" in their hands. With the praise of God, the people declare God's judgments and give God glory. Their song is both the "already" and the "not yet." An excellent recent setting by Greg Scheer[1] puts it this way:

> Songs of worship in their throats, the sword of justice is at hand.
> Kingdoms of this world will tremble, bow before the king of kings.
> Righteousness will rule the nations, let God's people join to sing.

RON RIENSTRA

---

1. "Let God's People Sing a New Song: Psalm 149," words and music by Greg Scheer, © 2014 and used by permission. Available at www.gregscheer.com.

Proper 18 (Sunday between September 4 and September 10 inclusive)

Romans 13:8–14

⁸Owe no one anything, except to love one another; for the one who loves another has fulfilled the law. ⁹The commandments, "You shall not commit adultery; You shall not murder; You shall not steal; You shall not covet"; and any other commandment, are summed up in this word, "Love your neighbor as yourself." ¹⁰Love does no wrong to a neighbor; therefore, love is the fulfilling of the law.

¹¹Besides this, you know what time it is, how it is now the moment for you to wake from sleep. For salvation is nearer to us now than when we became believers; ¹²the night is far gone, the day is near. Let us then lay aside the works of darkness and put on the armor of light; ¹³let us live honorably as in the day, not in reveling and drunkenness, not in debauchery and licentiousness, not in quarreling and jealousy. ¹⁴Instead, put on the Lord Jesus Christ, and make no provision for the flesh, to gratify its desires.

Commentary 1: Connecting the Reading with Scripture

This week's lection from Romans is unusual in that it appears twice in Year A, here and on the First Sunday of Advent. There, it appears in the company of apocalyptic texts that draw our attention to verse 11 ("Besides this, you know what time it is, how it is now the moment for you to wake from sleep"). However, when it is read and interpreted in company with today's readings, the stress falls naturally on its opening line: "Don't be in debt to anyone, except for the obligation to love each other" (13:8, CEB).

In different ways, each of the day's lections deals with obligation. The Gospel lesson, Matthew 18:15–20, stipulates step-by-step procedures for dealing with egregious wrongdoing in the community of faith. One can choose between Old Testament readings—the story of God's inauguration of the Passover rite, and the divine commission to Ezekiel to speak prophetic warnings as commanded or bear the blame when, oblivious, the people are destroyed. The Psalter choices are Psalm 149, which welcomes the duty to take up the "two-edged sword" that wreaks vengeance on the nations who oppress Israel, and the more irenic Psalm 119:33–40, an individual's plea to be instructed in the obligations of righteousness.

Then come the opening sentences of the Romans text, piercing the heavy atmosphere like the voice of a single oboe: "Owe no one anything, except to love one another; for the one who loves another has fulfilled the law" (Rom. 13:8). If we are in any doubt as to the legitimacy of this "reframing" hermeneutic, Paul himself proceeds in verse 9 to list four representative commandments from the second table of the Decalogue, declaring that love is the "fulfilling" of all of them.

Tempting as it may be to wrest these opening lines from their context and head for the pulpit, these lines deliver their depth and richness only when we let them function within their literary context. This means reading them in connection with the immediate context of the lection itself (vv. 8–14); the context of the chapter, which means taking into account the chapter's difficult opening verses (vv. 1–7); and the context of the book of Romans as a whole.

Attending first to the lection itself, verses 11–14 form the closing "bookend" for the entire section that began at 12:1–2. There, and at the close of today's epistle reading, believers are summoned to give themselves over to the purposes of God. In 12:2, such self-relinquishment results in being transformed "by the renewing of your mind." In 13:11–14, God's new day is breaking, and the only fitting response is to "wake up" (v. 11), put down preoccupations that belong to darkness (v. 12a), be outfitted with "the armor of light" (v. 12b), "put on" the identity and comportment of Jesus Christ, and resist the magnetic pull of the world's claims (a mirror of 12:1a).

Interpreters remind us that the motif of self-dispossession in both 12:1–2 and 13:12–14 echoes the sacrificial self-giving of Jesus on our behalf. Keeping alert to this costly, self-giving element is a check against reducing our text's memorable opening line to Hallmark-card simplism, a bland "niceness" that simply goes along and gets along with everyone. The love the apostle has in mind is potentially as costly as Jesus' own.

Although the lectionary planners have chosen to set aside 13:1–7 altogether, we need to consider these verses in order to appreciate the impact of 13:8–14. A few observations may help. First, Paul is not laying down a doctrine of the power of the state. He is writing to help those who must deal with its demands; he is not sacralizing the state.

Second, the idea that the "authorities" are ordained by God for "good" purposes is best understood in relation to Paul's characterization of the power of Pharaoh in 9:17. Pharaoh has no intrinsic goodness or authority whatsoever; he is a divine instrument in God's drama of liberation for Israel; he serves at God's pleasure.[1] The same goes for the "God-ordained" authorities of Rome; they are not ultimate. It is only by divine permission that their "bearing" of "the sword" is not in vain (13:4b)!

Third, it has been suggested that Paul's short treatise on relating to state authorities may "idealize" the state's function with ironic intent, in much the same way that Seneca idealizes the role of the emperor Nero in *De Clementia* (55–56 CE). Seneca sketches an idealized portrait of the emperor, not because Nero himself was exemplary, for he was certainly not, but as a rhetorical strategy intended to hold up a mirror and prompt some self-evaluation on the emperor's part.[2]

Our unmistakable clue that Paul intends us to read 13:8–14 in light of 13:1–7 is their close linguistic relationship. Verse 7 repeats the Greek word *opheilō* ("that which is owed" or "that which is due") four times in verse 7: in relation to taxes, revenue, respect, and honor. Then the very *same* Greek root, *opheilō*, stands at the beginning of our lectionary text: "*Owe nothing* . . . except to love." After having spoken of "owing" nearly everything (taxes, revenue, respect, honor), Paul speaks of "owing" *nothing* . . . except to love. Paul certainly brings into view, whether intentionally or not, the possibility that the demanding dynamic of love reframes and limits even what is due to the state. History teaches us that there are times that obligation to the state's demands is interrupted by love, particularly in cases where the state (or its representative) presumes to claim ultimate, "god-like" authority. True authority is the authority of Jesus: self-giving love.

Verse 8 goes on to declare that "the one who loves has fulfilled the law." Here Paul evokes in a single phrase whole chapters of earlier argumentation in Romans (chaps. 1–5). There he has shown how Christ's self-offering death, expressive of God's love for us (5:8), fulfills the demands of every law—whether the law in question is Jewish law, the "law" inscribed in nature for Gentiles (1:19–21), or the laws of Rome. Thus one lives, if you will, "bifocally," respecting the "law" of the land, yet accountable to a higher law, the overarching obligation to love. This law of love, exemplified in the sacrificial self-giving, other-directed love of Christ, will keep us from blind obedience to the state, or to any other claim, that would interfere with our first and last obligation to be given over to love.

Romans 13:8–14 is rich in and of itself, and becomes more so when we recognize the many threads that connect it to layers of context: 13:1–7; the section in which it stands; the book of Romans as a whole; and other lections of the day. We need to preach and hear, again and again, the message that the obligation to love both binds and liberates us, restructuring every allegiance. The eschatological summons to

---

1. Beverly Roberts Gaventa, "Reading Romans with Simone Weil: Toward a More Generous Hermeneutic," *Journal of Biblical Literature* 136, no. 1 (2017): 14–17.
2. Troels Engberg-Pedersen, "Paul's Stoicizing Politics in Romans 12–13: The Role of 13:1–10 in the Argument," *Journal for the Study of the New Testament* 29, no. 2 (2006): 167–69.

Let the Last Act of Life Be Love

O infinite amiableness! When shall I love Thee without bounds? Without coldness or interruption, which alas! So often seize me here below? Let me never suffer any creature to be Thy rival, or to share my heart with Thee; let me have no other God, no other love, but only Thee.

Whoever loves, desires to please the beloved object; and according to the degree of love is the greatness of desire; make me, O God! Diligent and earnest in pleasing Thee; let me cheerfully discharge the most painful and costly duties; and forsake friends, riches, ease and life itself, rather than disobey Thee.

Whoever loves, desires the welfare and happiness of the beloved object; but Thou, O dear Jesus, can'st receive no addition from my imperfect services; what shall I do to express my affection toward Thee? I will relieve the necessities of my poor brethren, who are members of Thy body; for he that loveth not his brother whom he hath seen, how can he love God whom he hath not seen?

O, crucified Jesus! In whom I live, and without whom I die; mortify in me all sensual desires; inflame my heart with Thy holy love, that I may no longer esteem the vanities of this world, but place my affections entirely on Thee.

Let my last breath, when my soul shall leave my body, breathe forth love to Thee, my God; I entered into life without acknowledging Thee, let me therefore finish it in loving Thee; O let the last act of life be love, remembering that God is love.

Richard Allen, "Acts of Love," in *The Life, Experience, and Gospel Labors of the Rt. Rev. Richard Allen* (Philadelphia: F. Ford and M. A. Riply, 1880), 32.

"wake up" and "be clothed" for our God-given future, despite the mesmerizing, consumerist messages of our culture, can free and empower. It is the work of a lifetime to comprehend what it means to "owe no one anything but to love." We preachers can hope, at best, to set out a few flares.

SALLY A. BROWN

Commentary 2: Connecting the Reading with the World

The heart of the Christian message is love of God and neighbor. In the Epistle to the Romans, the apostle Paul is writing to a specific audience of believers in Jesus Christ in first-century Rome. Like many of the founders of these early Roman churches, Paul was Jewish. The earliest Christians were predominantly Jewish. As Gentiles converted to the Christian faith, tensions between Jewish cultural practices and Gentile cultural practices emerged. It was difficult for early Christians to make distinctions between culture and religion, between ritual form and what is necessary for salvation. Paul centers his message in the Letter to the Romans in an interpretation of the commandments found in Exodus and Deuteronomy. To love our neighbors as ourselves, Paul emphasizes, fulfills the law.

In the world across the centuries humankind has many debts to pay one another involving money, property, favors, and all manner of things. In verse 8 Paul cautions his audience that Christians ought to "owe no one anything, except to love one another; for the one who loves another has fulfilled the law." The general principles of love include not committing adultery, which causes harm to partners in marital relationships; not stealing, which produces mistrust in communities; and not doing anything that injures relationships. For Paul, the commandments can be summed up in verse 9 as "Love your neighbor as yourself," as he puts it in verse 10, "Love does no wrong to a neighbor." In other words, love does no harm. Love entails esteeming one another or, as Paul writes in verse 13, "let us live honorably as in the day." In verses 11–13 Paul emphasizes the nearness of salvation. He cautions readers to "wake up," because night has gone and the day of salvation is near. Here Paul is communicating a sense of urgency to start living in love immediately, now, today, in the present moment and in each coming moment.

Paul offers examples of what living honorably does not condone. "Reveling" refers to wild behavior that is destructive of self, neighbors, and property. "Drunkenness" refers specifically to alcohol abuse; it can also include any addictive substances and activities that cause harm to self, neighbors, family, community, and the larger society. "Debauchery" is a referent to wild partying that involves loss of self-containment or self-control, including sexual exploitation and substance abuse. Note that Elisabeth Schüssler Fiorenza finds that one of Paul's concerns in a different letter, 1 Corinthians 11:2–16, was to protect and keep the Jesus movement distinct from secret cults that practiced orgiastic rituals.[3] She observes that Pauline writings are ambiguous about freedom in Christ from patriarchal cultural gender norms surrounding human sexuality.

A question one might ask of the text is, "Where do the women and girls who are being debauched come from?" Often clergy have used this passage to sensationalize women's sexuality. The text itself contains no such language. Katie Cannon's essay "Womanist Interpretation and Preaching in the Black Church" is helpful for avoiding eisegesis of texts like this.[4] To correct misinterpretation and misuses of the text, one might consider this Pauline text from the perspective of neighbors who have been debauched historically and today.

One example is the commercial sex trade or, more precisely, the human trafficking trade. This trade is a concrete example of structural and systemic social debauchery. It is one specific example of sin that the church can address in its mission to transform the world. The human trafficking trade harms women and children in contemporary church and society. A helpful resource that listens to the voices of women and girls who have been exploited and marginalized by human trafficking is Irie Lynne Session's *Murdered Souls, Resurrected Lives: Postmodern Womanist Thought in Ministry with Women Prostituted and Marginalized by Commercial Sexual Exploitation.*[5] Session has served as a professional pastoral counselor for women of all ages who have been forced into the commercial sex trade and who seek freedom from slavery. Such exploitation of women and girls is contrary to the Christian ethic of love Paul espouses here.

One might note that licentiousness is a lack of moral and legal restraint. Commercial entities profit economically from immorality. Slave owners use grooming, drugging, terror, and violence to break the spirits of enslaved persons. The illegal drug trade and human trafficking trade work in tandem to make high profits for owners, murdering souls, as Session puts it, for the economic benefit of a few. In looking at the text in this way, one does not blame the neighbors whom debauchery exploits, but places the call to moral transformation on debauchers and consumers of commercial prostitution. It holds slave buyers, owners, and consumers of enslaved women accountable for licentiousness, morally and legally.

Paul emphasizes that God's laws are more than abstract legal codes. The commandments, which followers of Jesus Christ can "put on" when we "wake up," are practical ethical principles meant to protect self and others from intimate and social violence. They are a way of life that Jesus Christ most clearly summarized as God's ongoing call to "love your neighbor as yourself" with love as "the fulfillment of law." Love is a way of being and acting. In verse 14, "put[ting] on the Lord Jesus Christ" or clothing ourselves in Jesus Christ is an exhortation to embody Jesus Christ in everyday

---

3. Elisabeth Schüssler-Fiorenza, *In Memory of Her: A Feminist Theological Reconstruction of Christian Origins* (New York: Crossroad Publishing, 1994 [1983]), 228–30, 236.
4. Katie Geneva Cannon, "Womanist Interpretation and Preaching in the Black Church," in Mitzi J. Smith, ed., *I Found God in Me: A Womanist Biblical Hermeneutics Reader* (Eugene, OR: Wipf & Stock, 2015).
5. Irie Lynne Session, *Murdered Souls, Resurrected Lives: Postmodern Womanist Thought in Ministry with Women Prostituted and Marginalized by Commercial Sexual Exploitation* (Charleston, SC: CreateSpace Independent Publishing Platform, 2015).

personal, interpersonal, communal, and social interactions.

A question to ponder is, What does it mean for salvation to be near? If our salvation is in Jesus Christ and we "put on Jesus Christ," we can conclude that God is right here. It means that we need only stop doing the many things that take our attention away from God to experience God's presence and to live fully in God's presence. "Putting on Jesus Christ" is Paul's antidote to harmful, exploiting, and violent behavior. Since verse 8 directs Christians to owe one another nothing except the "debt of love," then one might say that putting on Jesus Christ is clothing oneself and the Christian community in the "debt of love."

To treat one another with love is to wear Jesus Christ like a garment that we "put on." The act of putting on Jesus Christ like a garment—along with the text's references to waking up, light, day, and the description of salvation as near—is language that audiences are familiar with in everyday life. When night is over, people wake up to the light of day and put on their clothing. Paul writes about shedding all egotistical, destructive habits and living in the light, another way of talking about God's love found in Jesus Christ. He uses the words "we" and "us" as well as "you" and "yourselves." The inclusive "we" suggests that the church has a corporate responsibility to end self-harm and the exploitation of others in church and society. Paul's letter to the church in Rome is a timely reminder in the twenty-first century that a Christian ethic of love "does no wrong to a neighbor."

KAREN BAKER-FLETCHER

Proper 18 (Sunday between September 4 and September 10 inclusive)

Matthew 18:15–20

[15]"If another member of the church sins against you, go and point out the fault when the two of you are alone. If the member listens to you, you have regained that one. [16]But if you are not listened to, take one or two others along with you, so that every word may be confirmed by the evidence of two or three witnesses. [17]If the member refuses to listen to them, tell it to the church; and if the offender refuses to listen even to the church, let such a one be to you as a Gentile and a tax collector. [18]Truly I tell you, whatever you bind on earth will be bound in heaven, and whatever you loose on earth will be loosed in heaven. [19]Again, truly I tell you, if two of you agree on earth about anything you ask, it will be done for you by my Father in heaven. [20]For where two or three are gathered in my name, I am there among them."

Commentary 1: Connecting the Reading with Scripture

Between the Gospel for last Sunday and the one for today, there seems to be a clear, decisive shift in focus and in tone—from what is urgent and immediate ("Pick up your cross and follow!" "Saving life means losing it!"), to what sounds far more mundane, even mechanical ("Take these steps—in sequence—when attempting to work toward conflict resolution"). The lectionary leapfrogs over Matthew's treatments (chap. 17) of the transfiguration, the healing of a demon-possessed boy, a second prediction of the passion, and a curious anecdote about using the coin found in the mouth of a fresh-caught fish to pay a temple tax.

In Matthew 18, our attention is redirected to a set of five strategies, all of which are essential if Christian communities are to sustain vital spiritual and social cohesion: (1) cultivate childlike humility, and welcome "children" intentionally (Matt. 18:1–5); (2) take utmost caution (extreme measures, if necessary) to avoid placing "stumbling blocks" in front of "little ones" (vv. 6–9); (3) treat every straying "little one" with the compassionate care a shepherd would expend in leaving ninety-nine safely folded sheep to search for only one (vv. 10–14);[1] (4) make systematic and sustained attempts to resolve church community conflicts in a manner that is redemptive and restorative (vv. 15–20, the focus of *today's* lesson); and (5) understand and offer forgiveness as *relational* rather than *transactional* (vv. 21–35, the focus for *next* week).

This list of practices for maintaining spiritual harmony in Christian community can fairly be described as seriously costly to those who undertake them, even (if not literally, still metaphorically) as *cross bearing*, and *life losing*; that is, these practices require radical renunciation of individual self-interest and self-preservation. They are, in fact, directly in line with what Jesus has been about in his words and deeds, the result of which (as he has now twice explicitly announced) *will* be—for him—a literal cross-carrying and life-losing practice. So perhaps the "shift in focus and tone" from the Gospel lesson *last* week to the one for *this* week is not as divergent as it might seem on first appearance.

It can be helpful to relate the instructions in this fourth Discipleship Training Session (Matt. 18), particularly those dealing with community

---

1. Note the significant difference in Matthew's treatment of "the lost sheep" from that in the parable trilogy found in Luke 15. Luke's treatmnt is part of a response to the indignant "grumble" of Pharisees that Jesus "welcomes sinners and eats with them." Here in Matthew the parable is part of an exhortation to do internally whatever it may cost to preserve the full integrity of a spiritual community. Indeed, this rendering of the story goes so far as to baldly state the "point," both before and after the telling (vv. 10–11, 14), declaring, in effect, "God is *intent* on losing *none*."

disruptions (the focus today), to the Sermon on the Mount (esp. 5:21–26), and the parables of the kingdom (esp. 13:24–30, 45–53), the first and third of the Discipleship Training Sessions Jesus offers in Matthew's Gospel.[2]

Anger is often an exacerbating factor in conflicts between community members; particularly in cases where "sin" may be overt in the behavior of one party (or all). Participants on all sides of a divisive issue are well advised to bring the injunctions of Jesus regarding anger from Matthew 5 to his instructions for engaging conflict in Matthew 18. On the other hand, few issues of conflict can be unequivocally characterized as "sin," pure and simple. Most moral issues of any substance entail layers of complex, interwoven factors. Few cases can be described accurately (or dispensed expeditiously) with a summary fiat: "*Here* is the sin; *you* are the sinner! Repent, or I will confront you with my two or three witnesses!"

Either/Or ultimatums sometimes work for energizing political bases; but they are a shortsighted strategy when dealing with the social-moral-spiritual fabric of life in a faith community. Hence, when approaching situations requiring confrontation, there is considerable value in bringing along the images unfolded across the sweep of parables in Matthew 13, images that imply the need for careful discrimination and nuanced discernment. Weeds intermingled with wheat (hard to distinguish from each other); a priceless pearl that takes an extensive investment of time and resources to find; good fish to be sorted out, one at a time, from a net wherein they are mixed with bad; and treasures that cannot be differentiated from trash simply because they are old or new: all these images evoke an almost visceral awareness of the fact that, however difficult to employ, patience, persistence, and discernment are essential in resolving moral issues. Conflicted issues and conflicting interpretations almost always underlie altercations wherein some or all parties to the conflict strongly (and reasonably) begin with a strong conviction that they have been in some way "deeply wronged."

In his letter, James takes a decidedly more "no nonsense/tough love" approach to the conflicts of which he hears in the community to which he writes (Jas. 4:1–12). If we place ourselves in the position of an embattled participant in the conflict he addresses, however, it is hard to imagine being motivated toward the kind of resolution that leads to restoration solely by the finger-wagging tone of his blunt speech. Perhaps, under some circumstances, such a move might be required as an initial intervention, followed with the more measured, mediational process of the Jesus who speaks through Matthew.

It is striking, however, that where James and Matthew hope a confrontation *ends* is essentially *identical*. The goal, for both, is "regaining" the offending member (Matt. 18:21). James (perhaps surprisingly after his earlier verbal fireworks display) even waxes eloquent: "whoever brings back a sinner from wandering will save the sinner's soul from death and will cover a multitude of sins" (Jas. 5:20).

Paul labors long and hard to bring contending Corinthians into an awareness of their need for the resolution of conflict and restoration of community wherein mutual dependence generates spiritual health and vitality. His widely cited "many members/one body" metaphor (1 Cor. 12) and his immediately ensuing attempt to sing them back into loving relationship (chap. 13) are in deep resonance with the theme addressed in the lesson for today from Matthew.

It is interesting that the "two or three witnesses" required as a stage in attempted conflict resolution (Matt. 18:16) is the same as the "two or three" who, when gathered in his name, ensure the presence of Jesus among then (v. 20). Individuals alone, be they sinner or accuser, by their very standing apart, dis-integrate the community, the body of Christ. Conversely, when resolution leads to reconciliation, and reconciliation to fully restored relationship—well, "anything is possible" (which might be one way of reading v. 19).

It is interesting also that the "last resort" in a failed reconciliation process is to declare the unrepenting community member "a Gentile

---

2. But note a potential tension with material in the second Training Session (10:34–39), where "taking up the cross" can entail setting family and household members *against* each other.

and a tax collector" (v. 17), which, of course, entails not a *repudiation* of relationship, but a deliberate refocus and redirection of community efforts to *reestablish* a relationship. Efforts that involve, for the Christian community, the kind of cross-carrying and life-losing way of its saving Lord. One more possible (albeit tongue-in-cheek) connection: Jesus, on his way to the cross, is selective regarding his choice of "which hill to die on." To pay, or not to pay, a temple tax is *not* a conflict worth confronting his own community of spiritual origin. So—he sends Peter fishing!

DAVID J. SCHLAFER

Commentary 2: Connecting the Reading with the World

We live in hostile, divisive times. To be sure, we are not the first people to live through such conflictual times. This is not anything new, perhaps just new to a younger segment of the current population. Heightened emotions, extreme polarities, intense levels of conviction, and deep personal attachments to issues we now face are the makings of a perfect storm that many feel ill-equipped to navigate. However, conflict is not new. It is not new to the world at large, and it is not new to the church, individual congregations, or church members. In fact, if there is anything that we can count on, it is the fact that conflict will arise. However, conflict arises in different forms, shaped by the realities of persons and groups involved.

One of the primary realities influencing how we handle current conflicts is social media. Many of us have witnessed firsthand the loss of friendships and breaks in relationships via social media postings. The lack of physical proximity, combined with the number of "friends" or "followers" one has, emboldens people to say things that they might not say in close quarters. Our social media feeds enable us to develop silos that insulate us from the ramifications of that which we post publicly. We can readily, sometimes instantly, receive feedback from people who agree with us, thereby making us deaf to dissenting voices and more intractable in our opinions. One's viewpoint need not be morally or factually right, only "liked." That is a goal of this emerging "postmodern fame-shame culture," in which fame becomes the "currency of power."[3]

What is clearly evident is that no matter who we are or what we believe, we are not immune to conflict. Conflict is not an ugly matter that only non-Christians must deal with; it is an issue threatening the bonds of fellowship among all of us, individually and collectively, who profess Jesus as Lord. Political affiliations, support of certain candidates, and individual, congregational, and denominational stances on certain issues have caused many Christians to question the fidelity to and membership of persons confessing the same Christian faith. Moreover, we too have seen how social media can exacerbate or mitigate these clashes.

Matthew 18:15–20 reminds us that conflict was just as real in the early church as it is today. Within these verses are guidelines on how to handle disputes that arise among church members. First, the offended party is to point out the "fault" to the offender and try to settle the conflict between the two of them (Matt. 18:15). If the offender will not listen to the offended person, then the offended person is to bring "two or three witnesses" and point out the wrong in the presence of the witnesses and the offender (v. 16). If the offender still will not listen, then the offended person is to tell it to the church. If the offender will not listen "even to the church," then they are to be treated as an outsider (v. 17).

This passage invites preachers to explore ways that can help congregants navigate a social climate that is fraught with hostility and division. The preacher can connect the passage to congregants on a personal level by inviting them to reflect upon how they handle conflict. After explaining the process of reconciliation outlined in Matthew 18:15–17, the preacher can remind congregants to ask themselves if they have

---

3. Andy Crouch, "The Return of Shame," *Christianity Today* 59/2 (March 2015): 38.

allowed a fame-shame culture to cause them to circumvent the process.

While the current social environment tends to make everything public first, this passage emphasizes the relationship between "kinship" and rules that govern communal life (see Lev. 19:15–18). Deviating from the form of accountability outlined in verses 15–17, the court of public opinion is called upon to adjudicate disagreements, oftentimes before the parties involved have a chance to iron things out privately. The preacher can ask, How do we exemplify Christian ideals of reconciliation and community when a fame-shame environment reduces us to silos of like-minded people? If we do not break the fame-shame cycle, how then do we extend the gospel to people who think differently than we do? How do we implement Matthew 18's version of conflict management to handle difference and disagreement without it becoming divisive?

This passage also invites preachers to look at ecclesial contexts to more deeply understand what it means to be the people of God. The preacher can probe questions like this: What is the resolution that we desire? Matthew 18:15 shows us what it should be for church members: "If the member listens to you, you have regained that [member]." The whole purpose of approaching the person one-on-one is to see if the matter can end in reconciliation, if we can "regain" a brother or sister. Rather than seeking the affirmation of the court of public opinion, the member is to seek the restoration of relationship.

It is interesting to note that many commentators read this passage as steps to excommunication, citing verse 17 as justification for cutting off a person who "refuses to listen" by treating them like a "Gentile and a tax collector." However, Warren Carter presents an alternative reading. He sees the Gentile and tax collector not as outcasts of the community, but as "objects of restorative action."[4] How do we use our individual and public platforms to promote reconciliation? What kinds of community could we create if, even at the height of disagreement, we viewed others not as enemies but as "objects of restorative action"?

Unlike traditional honor-shame societies, which use values of purity, wealth, power, and authority to amass honor, our fame-shame culture makes notoriety honorable. Being known, whether positively or negatively, is the objective. This in no way leads to reconciliation or community. Andy Crouch puts it succinctly: "The remedy for shame is not becoming famous. It is not even being affirmed. It is being incorporated into a community with new, different, and better standards for honor."[5] If reconciliation is our aim, what new standards of honor must we enact and embrace? How do we demonstrate these values in both public and private settings?

This brings us to another connection: social and ethical context. Here the preacher can reenvision the limits of honor. In traditional honor-shame societies, like the ones that loom in the background of this passage, honor is a limited resource. The pie analogy aptly demonstrates its nature. Once someone removes a slice, there is less pie left for everyone else. In similar fashion, there is only so much honor to be had. The accumulation of honor by one necessitates the loss of honor by another. Consequently, one must always strive to triumph over another in order to maintain or attain honor.

In similar fashion, the fame-shame model pits individuals and groups against each other. There are a limited number of "votes" to cast for approval. One must gain the most votes to triumph. The goal is not truth, fact, morality, or community but popularity, affirmation, and assent. Thus the system needs to be circumvented for community to prevail. Therefore, the preacher can explore ways in which we make community, fellowship, and reconciliation the standards by which we measure honor. The preacher can demonstrate ways in which congregants can promote and exemplify these values in our interactions with others. Finally, the preacher can posit ways that congregants can demand reorientation of those who stand in leadership positions inside and outside of the church.

RAQUEL ST. CLAIR LETTSOME

---

4. Warren Carter, *Matthew and the Margins* (London: T. & T. Clark, 2000), 368.
5. Crouch, "The Return of Shame," 40.

Proper 19 (Sunday between September 11 and September 17 inclusive)

Genesis 50:15–21 and
   Exodus 14:19–31
Psalm 103:(1–7) 8–13 and Psalm 114 or
   Exodus 15:1b–11, 20–21

Romans 14:1–12
Matthew 18:21–35

Genesis 50:15–21

15Realizing that their father was dead, Joseph's brothers said, "What if Joseph still bears a grudge against us and pays us back in full for all the wrong that we did to him?" 16So they approached Joseph, saying, "Your father gave this instruction before he died, 17Say to Joseph: I beg you, forgive the crime of your brothers and the wrong they did in harming you.' Now therefore please forgive the crime of the servants of the God of your father." Joseph wept when they spoke to him. 18Then his brothers also wept, fell down before him, and said, "We are here as your slaves." 19But Joseph said to them, "Do not be afraid! Am I in the place of God? 20Even though you intended to do harm to me, God intended it for good, in order to preserve a numerous people, as he is doing today. 21So have no fear; I myself will provide for you and your little ones." In this way he reassured them, speaking kindly to them.

Exodus 14:19–31

19The angel of God who was going before the Israelite army moved and went behind them; and the pillar of cloud moved from in front of them and took its place behind them. 20It came between the army of Egypt and the army of Israel. And so the cloud was there with the darkness, and it lit up the night; one did not come near the other all night.
   21Then Moses stretched out his hand over the sea. The LORD drove the sea back by a strong east wind all night, and turned the sea into dry land; and the waters were divided. 22The Israelites went into the sea on dry ground, the waters forming a wall for them on their right and on their left. 23The Egyptians pursued, and went into the sea after them, all of Pharaoh's horses, chariots, and chariot drivers. 24At the morning watch the LORD in the pillar of fire and cloud looked down upon the Egyptian army, and threw the Egyptian army into panic. 25He clogged their chariot wheels so that they turned with difficulty. The Egyptians said, "Let us flee from the Israelites, for the LORD is fighting for them against Egypt."
   26Then the LORD said to Moses, "Stretch out your hand over the sea, so that the water may come back upon the Egyptians, upon their chariots and chariot drivers." 27So Moses stretched out his hand over the sea, and at dawn the sea returned to its normal depth. As the Egyptians fled before it, the LORD tossed the Egyptians into the sea. 28The waters returned and covered the chariots and the chariot drivers, the entire army of Pharaoh that had followed them into the sea; not one of them remained. 29But the Israelites walked on dry ground through the sea, the waters forming a wall for them on their right and on their left.

³⁰Thus the LORD saved Israel that day from the Egyptians; and Israel saw the Egyptians dead on the seashore. ³¹Israel saw the great work that the LORD did against the Egyptians. So the people feared the LORD and believed in the LORD and in his servant Moses.

Commentary 1: Connecting the Reading with Scripture

One of the Old Testament readings for Proper 19 continues the narrative path through Exodus. The lectionary, however, backfills that narrative through another reading from the final chapter of Genesis. Exodus 14 continues the story of Genesis 50. The passage from Genesis 50 reaches toward Exodus 14. Both structure the biblical narrative in important ways that speak past our own human strivings to God's faithfulness seen in Jesus Christ.

Exodus 14:19–31 narrates perhaps the most famous scene from the Old Testament in the modern world. Some scholars call the exodus the most important event in the Old Testament. The passage echoes through other Old Testament passages as it becomes a type that later passages reuse. The literary trope echoes throughout the New Testament as well.

Early Christians, such as Origen, however, received the text as preparatory to Israel's crossing of the Jordan River into the promised land (Josh. 3). Israel's escape through the Red Sea foreshadowed Israel's entrance into the land God had promised. In the *Apostolic Tradition* of Hippolytus, the newly baptized, those who had passed through the Jordan River, received milk and honey with their first Eucharist. Such an understanding read both Exodus 14 and Joshua 3 within the plot of the whole narrative. Exodus 14 does not per se link to God's promise to the ancestors; Joshua 3 does. Exodus 14 tells the story of Israel as God's deliverance *from*; it speaks of a negative freedom. Joshua 3 tells its story as God's freedom *for*; it calls its readers to a positive freedom. Positive freedom presupposes negative freedom. But negative freedom, as the narrative suggests, finds no true end outside positive freedom. God delivers Israel in Exodus 14 from slavery to Pharaoh. As the Israelites complained, such deliverance means only that death replaces slavery without God leading Israel into the fullness of the promise.

Exodus 14:19–31 presents the reader with a terse narrative. Only two characters speak: the collective Egyptians, seemingly to themselves (Exod. 14:25), and the Lord, who commands Moses to stretch his hand back over the sea (v. 26). The passage briefly summarizes the story's movements: (1) the "angel of God" and the cloud move to separate the Egyptian army and the Israelites (vv. 19–21); (2) Moses stretches his hand over the sea (v. 21a); (3) the Lord divides the waters by an easterly wind (v. 21b); (4) the Israelites cross on dry ground (v. 22); (5) the Egyptians follow the Israelites (v. 23); (6) the Lord confuses the Egyptians (vv. 24–25); (7) Moses stretches his hand over the sea (vv. 26–27a); (8) the sea inundates the Egyptians (vv. 27b–28); and (9) the Israelites cross successfully (v. 29). Verses 30–31 summarize the point of the episode: Israel feared the Lord and trusted the Lord and Moses.

The narrative bifurcates the Israelites' and the Egyptians' army. No battle occurs. The sea ambushes the Egyptians. The summary does not emphasize the Egyptian defeat or Israelite deliverance. Before the episode, the Israelites fear Pharaoh and his army (v. 10) and blame Moses. After the successful crossing, the congregation of Israel "feared" the Lord and believed in the Lord and Moses (v. 31). God had already delivered Israel from Pharaoh before Exodus 14:19–31. The crossing of the Red Sea preserves Israel from Pharaoh's attempt to reclaim ownership of the Israelites.

God separates Pharaoh and the Egyptian army from the Israelites at the beginning of Exodus 14:19–31. The separation becomes permanent. Pharaoh and his army are "dead on the seashore" (v. 30). Exodus 14 does not play as important role in the plot of the narrative as does Exodus 12. Passover, not the deliverance at the sea, begins the new year and required annual celebration and memory.

Some early Christians like Origen read the separation of the Israelites from the Egyptians in Exodus 14 as a type for the entry of the new believer into the catechumenate. Delivered from "the fleshpots" of Egypt, the new believers awaited their baptismal entrances into the promised land. God separates the Israelites from the Egyptians to free them from slavery; yet the journey has just begun. Exodus 14:19–31 only opens Israel to a new and greater foe: themselves (Exod. 16–18). Israel's belief in the Lord and Moses his servant falters. The people desire to go back to Egypt. The narrative of Exodus 14:19–31 has divided Israel from the Egyptians. The Egyptians no longer have any coercive power over them. The gift of the Torah awaits, the worship of God on the mountain where God called Moses (see Exod. 3).

Exodus 14:19–31 does not indicate what awaits Israel. God has divided Israel from the Egyptians in the crossing of the sea. The event witnesses to God's faithfulness to God's promise to the ancestors, not to Israel's freedom from slavery per se. Exodus 14:19–31 prepares for the more important trip through a river on the dry ground, Israel's entry into the land of Canaan. The passage marks the end of the beginning. The rest is yet to come.

The second Old Testament reading depicts the end of the Joseph novella, Israel's establishment in Egypt, and Israel's assimilation into Egypt. Genesis 50 answers how the sons of Israel remained safe in Egypt rather than return immediately to the land that God had promised them.

Do not fall for the sentimentality of the tale. The eleven's story deceives commentators today, as it did Joseph within the text. The eleven sons of Israel lie in their apology to Joseph. In fear for their well-being, they create a fictitious account of their father's petition to Joseph. They manipulate Joseph so that he might not retaliate against his earlier mistreatment. Israel becomes Joseph's father (Gen. 50:16b), not theirs. They name themselves, not as Joseph's kin, but as "attendants of the God of your father" (v. 17). The lie works, as Joseph breaks down in tears.

The famous saying in verse 20 serves as a moral for the whole Joseph story: "though you intended to do harm to me, God intended it for good, in order to preserve a numerous people, as [God] is doing today" (v. 20). Irony fills this statement: the sons of Israel are not "a great people." Yet the story speaks truthfully: underneath the guiles and sin of God's people, God remains faithful to God's promises to Abraham and Sarah and the ancestors, a faithfulness ultimately seen in Jesus Christ.

The Scriptures tell two different narratives in both of these passages. One narrates the story of Israel. This sense speaks literally of the sins of the fathers and mothers. The irony is that the place of refuge becomes the place of slavery. The very increase of the people of which Genesis 50 speaks becomes the rationale for the later Pharaoh's enslavement of the very people preserved. If Scripture tells only the story of Israel, it does not speak hopefully.

The second story speaks of God's faithfulness to God's own promise. God preserves the people of Israel for God's promise. God delivers God's people from slavery to witness to God's faithfulness. Ultimately both stories find their fulfillment in Jesus Christ, the faithful one, in whom we see that God is faithful, even amid a world of slavery and lies. As God calls people to believe in God's faithfulness in Jesus, God moves us all imperceptively to participate in God's faithfulness through Jesus, as God moves us, sometimes against ourselves, from slavery toward our baptism and in our baptism into God's promise of life everlasting, the resurrection of Christ.

JOHN W. WRIGHT

Commentary 2: Connecting the Reading with the World

In today's reading from Genesis, the children of Jacob gather with the death of their father behind them and their future as a family before them. This is a familiar ritual for families who have lost a loved one. However, faith communities should continue to engage other research disciplines to understand end-of-life issues. Families may need to explore what if any ethical responsibilities children bear to their parents even in death. Families may need help to deal with grief, or depression, or to share both the positive and negative experiences and relationships with the deceased. Faith communities are challenged to consider what rituals of grieving, healing, remembrance, and forgiveness can lead from the brokenness of loss to wholeness and renewal.

Joseph is a positive example, and his actions reflect deep devotion to his father in private sorrow (Gen. 50:1), ensuring embalmment (50:2), providing days of public weeping and lamentation (vv. 3, 10), and finally, burial (vv. 7, 14). Joseph memorializes his father's name and memory. Joseph's brothers, whatever their motives, are focused on their future as a family. They have lived with the memory of their crimes against Joseph, having first conspired to kill him (37:18ff.), but eventually selling him for twenty pieces of silver (v. 28). Now after their father's death, the brothers invoke their father's name in their quest to have a positive relationship with Joseph (50:15–17).

When we transpose this narrative to large gatherings of tribes, communities, or nations, we may recognize the need for liturgies that actually name wrongdoing, abuse, or hurtful behavior that impact us individually as well as communally. We may remind ourselves of the Truth and Reconciliation work in South Africa that dealt with the crimes committed against humanity during the historical scourge of apartheid. In the United States there are the historical realities of genocide, slavery, lynching, and segregation. In homes, houses of worship, and the public square there is a need for rituals that narrate the truth of these events. Faith communities can lead public conversations that move toward forgiveness and reconciliation by speaking truthfully about matters that assail us, such as racism, sexism, human trafficking, hate crimes, terrorism, and warfare.

In the public square, we may learn from other fields and disciplines about mental or psychological anguish experienced by those who have lived through traumatic events. We may also find ways to give new language to theological ideas such as grace, salvation, and love. For example, what does forgiveness mean in our conversations that include horrendous crimes against others? It is not surprising that forgiveness is the popular language of faith communities, even when a person armed with a gun enters a sacred space and kills those who are kneeling in prayer. In our public discourse, we may reflect on the meaning or power of forgiveness, even as one navigates the judicial system that works to bring justice, hold individuals accountable for their actions, and provide penalties that may include life behind bars or death.

Even as we confront evil in the world, it is very common to hear the claim affirmed among faith leaders that everything happens for a reason. This may be an extrapolation from Joseph's well-known declaration that his brothers intended to harm him, but God intended it for good for the preservation of a numerous people (v. 20). This has led to a rather pervasive belief that God orchestrates every event in history, even the most disastrous, including slavery, apartheid, mass shootings, and the Holocaust. Our preaching, teaching, rituals, prayers, and litanies should be designed to confront and correct these theological ideas.

In our reading from Exodus, we have the stuff of which movies are made. The visuals in each frame require computer-generated images because the subject matter is supernatural and outside of our everyday experience. Only through special effects could one portray a divine messenger or presence (Exod. 14:24) residing in pillars of cloud that provide darkness and light (v. 20), or a strong wind that turns the sea into dry land (v. 21). Although natural phenomena such as hurricanes, tornadoes, forest fires, volcanoes, tsunamis, and earthquakes have been designated acts of God in certain legal documents, we do not think of natural disasters as divinely directed, certainly not in service to any particular group of people.

In the Exodus narrative, the divine works supernaturally in cloud, wind, fire, and water to deliver enslaved people from bondage. One of the most enduring and foundational dimensions of theologies of liberation is built on this conviction that God comes to the aid and works on behalf of those who are oppressed, the poor, the outcast, and marginalized. From Hannah's prayer (1 Sam. 2:1–10) to Mary's Magnificat

(Luke 1:46–55), there are biblical narratives that display confidence in divine intervention to reverse the fortunes of the powerful pharaohs and the oppressed of this world, to bring low, and to exalt. With such stories of divine deliverance, it is tempting to ask why terrible disasters happen to good people.

This narrative presents us with a scene of warfare during which the Egyptian army recognizes that the Israelites are receiving supernatural help (Exod. 14:25). It is common to understand God in military terms as a mighty warrior who protects and defends or as one who deploys a great army to surround and protect us from our enemies. Is our mighty warrior also creative Spirit, love, light, *shalom*, and healing presence? The diverse biblical metaphors that we employ in liturgical contexts may be at odds with each other and with our own understandings of God, and may be difficult to reconcile.

First, we are challenged to look to the Holy One who loved the world into being in creation, and continues to love the world in redemption and re-creation. We acknowledge God as creator and ourselves as made in the image of God and a part of the family of God. If God does not denigrate or repudiate God's wonderful creation, then neither should we on the grounds of difference in nationality, gender, sexual orientation, race, or socioeconomic status.

Second, we are challenged to examine the perspectives of our faith communities to recognize the Holy One, who is not just for our group but is for every tribe, language, religion, race, and ethnicity. From this context, how do we answer the question, "Who are our enemies?" The answer will shape our communities' prayers, teaching, and service.

Third, this conversation is not limited to our faith communities. Our understandings and metaphors for God influence our ethical and theological postulations in the wider culture. We all participate in the political discourse on war and peace. Our theological perspectives will certainly lead to difficult conversations as we individually and collectively articulate a position regarding community policing, gun violence, national security, military service, procurement, and use of weaponry, including nuclear armaments.

Finally, in this story the camp of Israel experiences divine deliverance and crosses over on dry ground. However, the camp of Egypt is thwarted and eventually destroyed in the sea. Both in our faith communities and also our national conversations, we are invited to reflect on our response when hardship, suffering, adversity, or calamity befalls those who threaten our welfare or seek to do us harm. Is our prayer for divine intervention to wipe our foes off the face of the earth, or are we concerned about their welfare? Do we celebrate their demise, or do we recognize their humanity?

LINCOLN E. GALLOWAY

Proper 19 (Sunday between September 11 and September 17 inclusive)

Psalm 103:(1–7) 8–13

¹Bless the LORD, O my soul,
   and all that is within me,
   bless his holy name.
²Bless the LORD, O my soul,
   and do not forget all his benefits—
³who forgives all your iniquity,
   who heals all your diseases,
⁴who redeems your life from the Pit,
   who crowns you with steadfast love and mercy,
⁵who satisfies you with good as long as you live
   so that your youth is renewed like the eagle's.

⁶The LORD works vindication
   and justice for all who are oppressed.
⁷He made known his ways to Moses,
   his acts to the people of Israel.
⁸The LORD is merciful and gracious,
   slow to anger and abounding in steadfast love.
⁹He will not always accuse,
   nor will he keep his anger forever.
¹⁰He does not deal with us according to our sins,
   nor repay us according to our iniquities.
¹¹For as the heavens are high above the earth,
   so great is his steadfast love toward those who fear him;
¹²as far as the east is from the west,
   so far he removes our transgressions from us.
¹³As a father has compassion for his children,
   so the LORD has compassion for those who fear him.

Psalm 114

¹When Israel went out from Egypt,
   the house of Jacob from a people of strange language,
²Judah became God's sanctuary,
   Israel his dominion.

³The sea looked and fled;
   Jordan turned back.
⁴The mountains skipped like rams,
   the hills like lambs.

⁵Why is it, O sea, that you flee?
   O Jordan, that you turn back?
⁶O mountains, that you skip like rams?
   O hills, like lambs?

⁷Tremble, O earth, at the presence of the LORD,
  at the presence of the God of Jacob,
⁸who turns the rock into a pool of water,
  the flint into a spring of water.

Exodus 15:1b–11, 20–21

¹ᵇ"I will sing to the LORD, for he has triumphed gloriously;
  horse and rider he has thrown into the sea.
²The LORD is my strength and my might,
  and he has become my salvation;
this is my God, and I will praise him,
  my father's God, and I will exalt him.
³The LORD is a warrior;
  the LORD is his name.

⁴"Pharaoh's chariots and his army he cast into the sea;
  his picked officers were sunk in the Red Sea.
⁵The floods covered them;
  they went down into the depths like a stone.
⁶Your right hand, O LORD, glorious in power—
  your right hand, O LORD, shattered the enemy.
⁷In the greatness of your majesty you overthrew your adversaries;
  you sent out your fury, it consumed them like stubble.
⁸At the blast of your nostrils the waters piled up,
  the floods stood up in a heap;
  the deeps congealed in the heart of the sea.
⁹The enemy said, 'I will pursue, I will overtake,
  I will divide the spoil, my desire shall have its fill of them.
  I will draw my sword, my hand shall destroy them.'
¹⁰You blew with your wind, the sea covered them;
  they sank like lead in the mighty waters.

¹¹"Who is like you, O LORD, among the gods?
  Who is like you, majestic in holiness,
  awesome in splendor, doing wonders?
. . . .
²⁰Then the prophet Miriam, Aaron's sister, took a tambourine in her hand; and all the women went out after her with tambourines and with dancing. ²¹And Miriam sang to them:

  "Sing to the LORD, for he has triumphed gloriously;
    horse and rider he has thrown into the sea."

Connecting the Psalm with Scripture and Worship

Psalm 103:(1–7) 8–13. One of the best ways to engage scriptural narratives is to find ourselves in the story. With which character, we ask, do we most closely identify? In some circumstances this is easy: For example, Jesus heals a man born blind (John 9), and we may see ourselves as the blind man in need of healing, or perhaps as the questioning disciples, or as the skeptical Pharisees, or even as a member of the crowd.

Typically, we do not identify with Jesus. No. Jesus is God incarnate, and it is presumptuous, perhaps even dangerous, to imagine that among the characters in a Bible story, we are most like *God*. Yet the pairing of Genesis 50 and Psalm 103 invites precisely this comparison. The psalm offers a rich character description of God, including these salient features: God is slow to anger and abounding in steadfast love. Then, in the narrative from Genesis 50, Joseph does what God does.

Joseph's brothers have wronged him grievously. He seems to have forgiven them already, but Jacob's recent death has made their situation precarious. Like Fredo in the second *Godfather* movie, they fear that they may be repaid for the betrayal of their brother, now that the beloved parent is gone. Joseph, however, is not angry with them; he does not accuse them perpetually, he does not deal with them according to their sins. He has compassion on them. He weeps when they come to him, repentant, and promises to provide for them generously. In verse 19 he wonders aloud whether it is his place to mete out punishment: "Am I in the place of God?" We answer: Well, as a matter of fact, Joseph, yes. Yes, you are.

Could this be an invitation to us too? Could this implicit call to forgive others draw us into the grace and compassion and providence of a God who intends that even actions undertaken for evil be turned to the good?

The clear repentance/forgiveness dynamic here invites the use of the psalm within a penitential parabola, one that moves down and then up, that is, a moment of weeping and begging for forgiveness from God, followed by an assurance of God's character ("slow to anger, and abounding in steadfast love," Ps. 103:8) and the forgiveness that flows from it ("so far [God] removes our transgressions from us," v. 12). The use of verse 12 in expressing the mercy of God has long attestation in the Christian tradition.

Singing is perhaps the best way to follow the psalmist's instruction to "bless the LORD" not just with lips and tongue, but with "all that is within me" (v. 1). Thus, a musical setting of Psalm 103 is strongly suggested. One might include a fully sung setting of the psalm, or one might use a shorter refrain from the psalm to punctuate the aforementioned penitential parabola. A setting of the psalm could also be sung as a congregational response to a sermon about God's grace and providential *hesed*.

Settings of Psalm 103 can be found in nearly every musical tradition. A few favorites include the hymns "Praise, My Soul, the King of Heaven" (text by Lyte; tune: LAUDA ANIMA) and "O Come, My Soul" (text by Walch; tune: TIDINGS). The classic "There's a Wideness in God's Mercy" articulates the heart of this section of Psalm 103 in two stunning verses. I can imagine framing a spoken reading of the psalm itself with it, though I admit partiality to a contemporary tune by Gregg DeMey over some of the older tunes with which the text has been paired. Matt Redman's popular "10,000 Reasons" emphasizes in its chorus the call to bless the Lord, with a middle verse that cribs directly from today's psalm. Graham Ord has contributed a bluesy setting of verses 1, 8, 11, and 12, focusing on God's forgiving heart. Other favorites include André Crouch's gospel-infused "Bless the Lord" for a celebration of God's *hesed*, and Brother Roger's "Bless the Lord, My Soul" from the ecumenical community of Taizé, for a more meditative treatment.

Psalm 114 or Exodus 15:1b–11, 20–21. The semicontinuous first reading from Exodus 14 is arguably the climax of the Old Testament: the story of the deliverance of God's people from slavery through the Red Sea. It is paired in the lectionary with two possible responding texts, Psalm 114 or the songs of Moses and Miriam from Exodus 15. Here is the key difference: Exodus 14 is narrative prose, and the psalm and the canticles are poetry. The first reading is epic, the responses are lyric. Yet all three texts tell the same tale; all three texts sound the same themes: God's power to command the mighty forces of nature, God's salvation given in grace to people in need, and God's fashioning of a people through trial and triumph. God's power, God's agency, our identity: a preacher could do worse than to select one of these three themes as a homiletical guidepost.

The songs of Moses and Miriam in Exodus 15 tell the story of deliverance in the stylized reporting of the bard. A preacher might want to occasionally borrow some of the bard's tools, anthropomorphizing nature: "At the blast of your nostrils the waters piled up" (Exod. 15:8), or making generous use of similes: "like a stone," "like stubble," "like lead." The baptismal theme is hard to avoid, as God's people are called to go through the waters of chaos and danger in order to emerge on the other side praising God, their salvation (v. 2). The exuberant character of the psalm is emphasized with words like "exalt" and the note that tambourines and dancing accompanied Miriam's song (v. 21).

In contrast, Psalm 114 sounds notes of awe and fear while following the same three-theme song. The key verse is 7, where the name of God is first articulated: "Tremble, O earth, at the presence of the LORD." It is a presence that causes the earth to shake and a people to bow down in worship.

Given the contrasting tones of the two responses, a worship leader may consider whether the services will emphasize celebration or awe. Celebration may suggest an energetic song, or a litany that uses verses 1 and 21 as a refrain. Since "horse and rider" represent the tools of war and oppression, one might consider composing additional lines that celebrate God's victory over other tools of war and oppression. Use of tambourine is optional, but strongly encouraged.

Alternatively, Psalm 114 suggests a response of awe and wonder. Greg Scheer's "Tremble before the Lord" conveys just the right sense of fear and love in the face of God's grace and power.

Finally, a word about the use of these texts in an era of politically driven enmity between Christians and Muslims. The verses the lectionary omits from Exodus 15 in particular (Exod. 15:12–19) have to do with God's leading and guiding the people of Israel to the promised land, and the dread that overcame Israel's enemies: Philistines, Edomites, Moabites, Canaanites. This is to say nothing of the verses the lectionary includes that revel in a violent victory over Egyptians. It is hard for Christians who follow the one who said, "Love your enemies," to wholeheartedly embrace these sentiments, especially when this lection falls close to the anniversary of 9/11. Yet preachers should not shy away from the challenge to boldly speak a word of victory, actual or aspirational, over God's enemies, without equating those enemies with those who trace their ancestry to Middle Eastern lands.

RON RIENSTRA

Proper 19 (Sunday between September 11 and September 17 inclusive)

Romans 14:1–12

¹Welcome those who are weak in faith, but not for the purpose of quarreling over opinions. ²Some believe in eating anything, while the weak eat only vegetables. ³Those who eat must not despise those who abstain, and those who abstain must not pass judgment on those who eat; for God has welcomed them. ⁴Who are you to pass judgment on servants of another? It is before their own lord that they stand or fall. And they will be upheld, for the Lord is able to make them stand.

⁵Some judge one day to be better than another, while others judge all days to be alike. Let all be fully convinced in their own minds. ⁶Those who observe the day, observe it in honor of the Lord. Also those who eat, eat in honor of the Lord, since they give thanks to God; while those who abstain, abstain in honor of the Lord and give thanks to God.

⁷We do not live to ourselves, and we do not die to ourselves. ⁸If we live, we live to the Lord, and if we die, we die to the Lord; so then, whether we live or whether we die, we are the Lord's. ⁹For to this end Christ died and lived again, so that he might be Lord of both the dead and the living.

¹⁰Why do you pass judgment on your brother or sister? Or you, why do you despise your brother or sister? For we will all stand before the judgment seat of God. ¹¹For it is written,

"As I live, says the Lord, every knee shall bow to me,
and every tongue shall give praise to God."

¹²So then, each of us will be accountable to God.

Commentary 1: Connecting the Reading with Scripture

The tone of Romans shifts at the beginning of chapter 14, from broad, theologically grounded revisioning of the way of life befitting the ethnically mixed Christian communities in Rome, to a focused discussion around a specific troublesome issue.

Interpreters continue to debate whether Paul is responding in this text to an *actual* conflict in the Roman churches, known to him secondhand (since he has never visited these churches), or he is simply choosing to take up a tension that characteristically arises in churches of mixed ethnicity across the empire. What is clear is that Paul takes up the situation to accomplish two things. First, he indicates that matters such as this are *adiaphora*, "matters of indifference," *not* fundamentally definitive of Christian identity. Second, and most importantly, Paul suggests the situation requires that the less constrained in matters of food and sacred days need to exercise nonjudgmental self-restraint, protecting the faith of believers more scrupulous in "indifferent" matters such as these, out of love.

Paul advances three reasons, all theological, why the "strong" need to refrain from judgment and defer to the sensitivities of the "weak." First, what the weak do with regard to food choices or observing special days is done in honor of the Lord (Rom. 14:6). Second, we all belong to *one* Lord; and it is this, not agreement on peripheral matters, that establishes our unity (vv. 7–9). Third, God is the only judge; the "weak" are accountable to God, as we all are (vv. 10–12).

A challenge in this text is Paul's identification of "weakness" (or "the weak") with scruples about food and holy days, and "strength" (the "strong") with an attitude of freedom with respect to these things.[1] Moreover, it is not the positions, but the persons who hold them, that Paul designates weak or strong. He will make clear his own position of freedom with regard to food in verse 14 (beyond the limits of our text), thus implicitly identifying himself as strong. On first blush, it appears that Paul is passing precisely the sort of judgment he maintains *no* Christian has a right to pass on another (see vv. 3, 4, 5, and 10)!

Exactly who are these strong and weak that Paul has in mind? Origen, along with other early interpreters of Paul, assumed that the weak were Jewish Christians who clung to long-held scruples about eating "unlawful" foods and distinguishing holy days. Paul alludes later in the chapter (v. 14, beyond the bounds of our lection) to the "clean"/"unclean" food distinction; but he does not directly connect this with the weak/strong binary.

Alternatively, a first-century-BCE Greek document suggests another possible source for Paul's strong/weak distinction. In this source, one Roman declines to enter into debate with another Roman. His reason? His regard for "the day," which happens to be a Jewish Sabbath (although he himself is not a Jew). He describes himself as "a somewhat weaker brother" for refusing to take up debate with his neighbor on such grounds.[2] It may be that Paul was simply appropriating in Romans 14 a common social trope of his time, in which strong referred to the socially, economically, or politically powerful, and weak to the less powerful.

If this was the reigning social hierarchy, Jewish Christians returning to Rome from exile after 54 CE, when Claudius's earlier edict banning them from the city had been lifted, could have been regarded as the socially, economically, or religiously weak within Rome's Christian congregations, which in the interim had taken on a distinctly Hellenistic character. The point in Romans 14, in any case, is that Paul insists (with characteristic irony) that true strength means refraining from judging or offending those with more sensitive consciences over debatable matters.

A closely related Pauline text is 1 Corinthians 8:1–11:1. Here Paul discusses different aspects of Christians' association with those who either revere idols or have recently abandoned idol worship to profess Christ. In this context, it is clear that specific questions have come up in Corinth about eating food used in idol worship. Paul lays down guidelines to sort out what constitutes idolatrous behavior and what does not, and how to proceed at a meal that may include food that has been offered to idols.[3] Later (1 Cor. 10:23–11:1), the apostle lays down approximately the same fundamental principle that we find in Romans: care for the conscience of the other is paramount.

Passages from Galatians also bear on the issue, albeit a little less directly. Writing in a state of urgent concern for the Galatian churches, Paul reports how he broke with the apostle Peter over his refusal to share a Gentile table (Gal. 2:11–14). He rails against the Galatians' observance of special "days . . . months . . . seasons, and years" as a symptom of a "turn back again to the weak and beggarly elemental spirits" (4:9–10). Why the tone of tolerance then in Rome? It is important to pay attention to the background situation in Galatia. There, heretical teachers were *imposing* rules about food and special days, along with circumcision, as *necessary* to justification before God. In other words, they made Christian identity into a matter of religious regulations (over which they themselves presided), not the free gift of God. By contrast, in Romans Paul is concerned about cases where tensions over "indifferent" matters threaten to rend table fellowship in that new, undivided humanity that God has forged through Christ's self-sacrificial death.

Allowing the Romans text to resonate with the day's other lections suggests different sermon paths. Exodus 14–15, the dramatic scene at the Red Sea, where God delivers Israel but judges the oppressor, underscores that judgment belongs to God, who upholds the weak. The

---

1. The opening line might be translated, "Welcome those who are weak—in *faith*, not in order to quarrel over different opinions." See Rom. 15:1; 1 Thess. 5:14.
2. Mark Reasoner, *The Strong and the Weak: Romans 14:1–15:3 in Context* (New York: Cambridge University Press, 1999), 54.
3. Peter J. Tomson, "Jewish Food Laws in Early Christian Community Discourse," *Semeia* 86 (1999): 203–4.

alternate Old Testament reading from Genesis 50, in which Joseph's brothers seek his forgiveness, foregrounds acting with mercy toward the vulnerable, especially when we find ourselves in a position of power. Matthew 18:21–35 has Peter asking Jesus how often he must forgive. Jesus' memorable "seventy times seven times" flows into the parable of the Unforgiving Servant, who, after experiencing mercy, turns around to someone over whom he has power, and acts without mercy. The parable powerfully illuminates Paul's point that we are all servants of the same (merciful) Lord.

Although the first suggested Psalter reading, Psalm 114, points directly to the Exodus story, Psalm 103 pairs well with Romans 14. Here a worshiper remembers the many-sided mercies of the Lord, alluding to the deliverance from Egypt (resonating with one of the Old Testament readings) and quoting the Deuteronomic creedal formula, "The LORD is merciful and gracious, slow to anger and abounding in steadfast love" (Ps. 103:8). Most tellingly, we are reminded in this psalm how God sees us: The Lord "remembers that we are dust. . . . [Our] days are like grass, [we] flourish like a flower of the field, for the wind passes over it, and it is gone" (vv. 14b–16). Can we do less, then, than to refrain from judgment, to bend and to accommodate, to protect with care the fragility of another's faith? For is this not what God, in infinite mercy—day in, day out—does for each of us?

SALLY A. BROWN

Commentary 2: Connecting the Reading with the World

Paul asks that we "welcome those who are weak in faith." When Paul wrote this letter to late-first-century Roman churches, the churches were small assemblies that often met in houses. Christians were a persecuted minority religion with internal cultural tensions. Many of the earliest Christians were Jewish converts to Christianity. Paul, like the majority of the earliest Christians, was a Jewish convert to the Christian movement. This movement was still very new. Not until the fourth century would Christianity become the official religion of the Roman Empire.

Paul was familiar with what it is like to be a new follower of Jesus Christ in a context in which Christians were a controversial minority religion. As a leader in Christian mission who planted and oversaw churches in Rome and South Asia, Paul was familiar with people's tendency to argue about what to eat, how, and when, as Jews and Gentiles gathered to worship the God of Jesus Christ. Jews from various backgrounds and Gentiles from various cultures also had different opinions about days to set aside to honor God. Bringing together people from distinct worldviews, economic classes, ethnicities, genders, and cultural practices was not an easy task. Apparently Roman churches were arguing about dietary laws, rules, and regulations. Paul offers a pastoral response, emphasizing that this is a matter of conscience and opinion. Each must act according to his or her own conscience.

Given arguments about dietary laws, in verses 1–3 Paul counsels Christians, "Welcome those who are weak in faith, but not for the purpose of quarreling over opinions. Some believe in eating anything, while the weak eat only vegetables. Those who eat must not despise those who abstain, and those who abstain must not pass judgment on those who eat; for God has welcomed them." God's welcome or acceptance of all believers is what matters. In verses 5–6 Paul responds to disagreements and opinions about which days of the week are set apart to honor God. Observing that "some judge one day to be better than another, while others judge all days to be alike," Paul's counsel is to leave people to their convictions, to be "convinced in their own minds." As long as people are setting aside time to honor God, the thanks they are giving to God on that day is more important than which particular day or days they do this.

Members of the churches in Rome were converts from multiple religions, philosophies, worldviews, and cultural traditions. Christianity was a new, emerging religion. Some Jewish Christians ate vegetables out of concern that meat purchased in Gentile markets may have been sacrificed to Gentile gods. They were concerned about how the food was prepared and to whom it was sacrificed. The text indicates that Paul's opinion is that those who worry about this are of "weaker faith." This indicates that Paul has his own opinion. It is also a rhetorical device. Paul's personal opinion matters no more than anyone else's in relation to God's acceptance of believers from all cultures. The matter of living and dying in a way that honors Jesus Christ is ultimately important. God's welcoming of all, regardless of what we eat and how we prepare food, is what matters most.

In Paul's era, as in our own, Christians have argued about the form of liturgical practices and the theological opinions that support them. We see such division in institutional churches today. Churches now exist in regions that were unavailable to Paul. North America, Central America, and South America were outside Paul's scope of knowledge. Paul's world was similar to ours in cultural multiplicity. Asian, Roman, Greek, and Jewish cultures were interacting with, influencing, and living in tension with one another. For Paul, whether we eat or abstain from certain foods in honor of God, whether we claim a particular day or every day holy in honor of God, we do all these things out of reverence for the Divine.

What is most important is that we make time, space, and ways to honor God from the heart. If our heart is in it, then we are in mutual relationship with God. When our heart is in it, then we live in full awareness that our very being is inseparable from God. We realize that we can neither breathe nor die without God. God's presence is the source of who we are in our living and the one to whom we return when we take our last breath. It is a waste of breath to judge one another, because our one and only judge is God. Thus, "whether we live or whether we die, we are the Lord's" (Rom. 14:8). Therefore, we need neither fear nor judge another, for ultimately God is the chief arbiter.

Paul reminds us that because we belong "to the Lord," our relationship with Christ should inform that which is of importance to us. As we shift our focus from inconsequential matters, we are invited to consider what a focus on life and death might entail with some awareness that our existence matters to God. This pericope asks us, with knowledge that "we will all stand before the judgment seat of God," to examine our personal motives and intents relative to our interaction with others and with the Divine.

Paul shifts from instruction on judgment to a focus on worship and adoration, which can function as both a personal and a communal system of accountability. Participating in such praise is more important than cultural forms of liturgy. When we distract ourselves with disagreements about cultural practices, we tend to lose focus on the larger picture, the welcoming way of Jesus Christ. The mission of the church in the world is not to judge rituals, liturgies, holy days, and dietary customs in various cultures. The text respects cultural sensitivities while also relativizing them in relation to Jesus Christ's goal of overcoming death, asking us to remember that what we consume and the days we designate as ritually holy are not an ultimate measure of our faith.

In contemporary church and society, as in Paul's late-first-century world, people often miss the goal of Jesus Christ's life and death. For instance, we sometimes fail to take into account prejudices or prejudgments we hold about one another in local churches, communities, and the wider world today and how this impacts our ability to reflect God's welcome to all in church and society. One might note concrete examples of the problem of judging some lives less valuable than others, the for-profit prison industrial complex, economic inequalities, misogyny, the dispensability of black and brown bodies, and the normalization of violence. Jesus Christ has freed us from the power of death and freed us to praise God. Jesus Christ did not die to give human beings power to condemn one another. Instead, Jesus Christ has freed us to love and honor God and to love one another.

Paul focuses on how we are to treat one another now. He counsels that this affects our future. Only when we really experience God's merciful love for us, can we share such merciful love with one another. The judgment we hope for is near us through Jesus Christ, the fullness of God's ever-present grace and love.

KAREN BAKER-FLETCHER

Proper 19 (Sunday between September 11 and September 17 inclusive)

Matthew 18:21–35

²¹Then Peter came and said to him, "Lord, if another member of the church sins against me, how often should I forgive? As many as seven times?" ²²Jesus said to him, "Not seven times, but, I tell you, seventy-seven times.

²³"For this reason the kingdom of heaven may be compared to a king who wished to settle accounts with his slaves. ²⁴When he began the reckoning, one who owed him ten thousand talents was brought to him; ²⁵and, as he could not pay, his lord ordered him to be sold, together with his wife and children and all his possessions, and payment to be made. ²⁶So the slave fell on his knees before him, saying, 'Have patience with me, and I will pay you everything.' ²⁷And out of pity for him, the lord of that slave released him and forgave him the debt. ²⁸But that same slave, as he went out, came upon one of his fellow slaves who owed him a hundred denarii; and seizing him by the throat, he said, 'Pay what you owe.' ²⁹Then his fellow slave fell down and pleaded with him, 'Have patience with me, and I will pay you.' ³⁰But he refused; then he went and threw him into prison until he would pay the debt. ³¹When his fellow slaves saw what had happened, they were greatly distressed, and they went and reported to their lord all that had taken place. ³²Then his lord summoned him and said to him, 'You wicked slave! I forgave you all that debt because you pleaded with me. ³³Should you not have had mercy on your fellow slave, as I had mercy on you?' ³⁴And in anger his lord handed him over to be tortured until he would pay his entire debt. ³⁵So my heavenly Father will also do to every one of you, if you do not forgive your brother or sister from your heart."

Commentary 1: Connecting the Reading with Scripture

"Forgive us our debts as we forgive our debtors." The words, nestled in this most widely recited of prayers, can trip off the tongue almost reflexively. In Christian worship, the formal confession of such "debts" is generally followed by a pronouncement of blanket absolution. Forgiveness follows confession, seemingly as a matter of course—akin to politely murmured exchanges of "Oh, excuse *me*!" In the Sermon on the Mount, however, the setting of the Lord's Prayer, divine forgiveness is bluntly depicted as clearly conditional: what we do not *give* to others, we do not *get* from God (Matt. 6:14–15).

This same stark warning resurfaces at the end of today's Gospel lesson (18:35), the narration of an exchange between Peter and Jesus about "how many times" forgiveness must be extended. The bottom line is as clear here as it was above: what is extended without limit must be extended without limit—or else. The point is underscored in graphic images of a servant, who—forgiven much but in turn forgiving little—has his own forgiveness decisively and violently rescinded. (If gratitude does not motivate, perhaps threat of torture will!)

Attention quickly focuses on this unsettling parable. Where is the gentle storyteller Jesus of Luke 15, wherein a father—perhaps foolishly, yet unconditionally—lavishes forgiveness on a younger son, one who might easily respond not with gratitude, but further greed (and perhaps refusal to follow his father in forgiving moral arrogance in his older brother)?

Serious reflections on what forgiveness entails under different circumstances is appropriately raised by the two parables, individually and in comparison. In the setting of Matthew, however, it is important to remember that this treatment of forgiveness comes as the last in a series of five explicit instructions that Jesus gives to his disciples regarding what is required in the faith logistics of a community committed to following him in the way of the cross, the way of self-denial, in which life is gained only by losing it. (See the essay for last Sunday's Gospel.) What those instructions "come down to" for the church is radical forgiveness, the kind that Jesus himself offers from the cross (Luke 23:34). Here Jesus tells Peter in effect, "if you have to count how many times you are forgiving, you do not understand the kind of relationship in which you are engaging."

By countering the seemingly generous "seven times" that Peter proposes with "seventy-seven," Matthew's Jesus may well be indirectly referencing, and directly reversing, the revenge cycle briefly described in Genesis 4:23–24. There a man named Lamech sings a song of boasting to his two wives, in which he gloats over "repaying" assault with murder; saying, in effect, "If someone wrongs me, I will repay them, not just in kind, but seventy-seven times over." Forgiveness, as Jesus presents it here, can be understood as the radical, self-sacrificing opposite of—and necessary alternative to—revenge. In the face of retaliation run amok, the only way to prevent an ever-exacerbating death spiral is by denying natural instincts toward self-defense, through unconditional forgiveness.

An extended biblical illustration is provided by the story of Joseph. An Old Testament lectionary alternative for this day is the very end of a story that is fraught with injustices visited on Joseph, including but not restricted to those committed by his own brothers. The full saga of the Joseph cycle (Gen. 37, 39–50) should be revisited to recover a sense of how long can be the process, how high can be the price, and how morally complex can be the motives involved in renouncing revenge and embracing the step-by-step process of forgiveness that leads to reconciliation and redemption.

The "harsh" initial responses of Joseph to his brothers, including his threats and deceptions when they come to Egypt in search of food (chaps. 42–44)—are they Joseph's own wrestling with his natural instincts toward revenge as he works his way toward the forgiveness that leads to reconciliation? Are those efforts, instead, part of the "tough love" that is needed to help his brothers come to realize how much, and in what ways, they need his forgiveness? Are those harsh, deceptive measures on Joseph's part perhaps a bit of both?

A much shorter reference to the cost for all members of a community (including the exponential spread of hurt and misunderstanding) is noted by Paul in his Corinthian correspondence (2 Cor. 2:4–11, which concludes with an astute observation regarding the divisive effects of the "designs of Satan"). It is clear that Paul has first recommended severe treatment for the offender; and clear as well that he is now saying, "Enough is enough." If the community has forgiven the offender, so has he. Paul unfolds what appropriating God's forgiving grace entails in his own efforts to "make up" with the fractious Corinthian church. What it means to be a forgiving follower of Jesus, walking in the way of the cross, is eloquently articulated in 2 Corinthians 5:16–6:13.

Perhaps some of the sharpness in the parable of the Unforgiving Servant arises from the fact that most of us can, sooner or later, recognize our need of forgiveness in specific instances, and, when we sense we have received it, offer God great thanks. Today's psalm (Ps. 103) is a classic instance: "Bless the LORD . . . do not forget all his benefits—who forgives all your iniquity" (vv. 2–3). God is "merciful and gracious . . . he does not deal with us according to our sins" (vv. 8, 10). He removes our transgressions from us "as far as the east is from the west" (v. 12). The Second Servant Song of Isaiah not only echoes the theme but extends it further (Isa. 55:6–11): God's thoughts are higher than human thoughts, specifically regarding compassion and forgiveness. God's forgiving work will accomplish its purpose as the fall of rain and snow accomplish theirs.

So far, so good. However, those who plead for divine forgiveness (e.g., Ps. 51) and praise God for it can be, well, rather less "forgiving" when it comes to dealing with the sins of the enemy "other." A quick survey of Psalms 5, 7, 35, 55, 58, 59, 69, 94, and especially 109 reveals a very Lamech-like orientation. Some psalms sing, "Please forgive us!" and "Thank you very much!" Others, in effect, cry, "Stick it to them! Do not let them off the hook!"

This Work of Justice

As solemnly as we are called to punish deliberate transgressors, are we called upon to shelter and protect the ignorant transgressor. It is ours as a nation to bid these dry bones live, to build up these waste places, to purge corrupted institutions, to upheave the roots of bitterness and sow upon the track of desolation the seeds of liberty and Christian love. And this also will we do, if God assist us by His grace, until ere long brighter harvests shall be waving on that sunny soil than ever yet were planted there; until a nationality is builded there which is bone of our bone and flesh of our flesh; with one temple for the people, consecrated to law and justice and true religion; with one loyal and fraternal impulse ruling the hearts of all who have come forth from this great tribulation, and who will stand before the world in brighter years to come, to proclaim the honors and to defend the rights of constitutional freedom in America.

This work of justice toward the people, which the providence of God now lays upon us, is brought the more impressively before us now as we stand on the threshold of that civic pageant which is to honor the memory of that great and good man whose life was consecrated to the union of these States, and whose death has sealed his glorious record.

It will be ours, as a community, to receive tomorrow the sacred dust, which comes to touch our hearts once more with pity, and to speak to us, through those sealed lips, more solemnly than any voice of eloquence or power could speak.

Robert Russell Booth, *Personal Forgiveness and Public Justice: A Sermon Preached in the Mercer Street Presbyterian Church*, New York, April 23, 1865 (New York: Anson D. F. Randolph, 1865), 21–22. This sermon was preached in response to the death of Abraham Lincoln.

"Remember not the sins of my youth," pleads Psalm 25:7. "Repay them according to their deeds," implores Psalm 28:4. In Psalms 34, 79, 81, 139, and 141 one can find evidence of both sentiments within the same psalm!

All this is to say that the parable of the Unforgiving Servant, conjoined with a direct command to "quit counting" when it comes to forgiving the sins of others, may be a way of highlighting the fact that we tend to bring to the issue of forgiveness some seriously selective perception. This violent story may be an attention getter precisely because, while in the abstract "forgiveness for all without limit" may sound not just reasonable but emotionally engaging, when we find ourselves in situations when we have been deeply wounded or continually inconvenienced by others, we "just do not get it." According to the story, *if* we do not get it—we do not *get* it. Forgiveness does not flow *to* us if it does not flow *through* us. When we find ourselves in a place like that, the "love your enemies" section of the Sermon on the Mount (Matt. 5:43–48) may be where today's parable can bring us.

DAVID J. SCHLAFER

Commentary 2: Connecting the Reading with the World

In the movie *Seabiscuit*, there is a scene that is particularly helpful in illuminating this passage. It occurs during one of the earlier races of the horse's career. When the race begins, Red, the jockey, and Seabiscuit are trailing the pack. It is initially of no concern, because Seabiscuit had been trained by his previous owners to lose. They would race Seabiscuit against bigger and supposedly faster horses to build those horses' confidence. The new approach was to let him see the horses in the lead, bring him neck to neck with one, then let Seabiscuit loose to run as fast as he could. As Red looks for an opening to break through and execute the plan, another jockey passes them by aggressively pushing them aside. Red becomes so consumed with retaliating against the jockey who fouled him that he forces Seabiscuit to catch up to the jockey so that he can push the jockey against the rails. He loses sight of the race and abandons their strategy. His only concern is getting back at the jockey, and he loses the race, with only the offending jockey finishing behind him.

When the race is over, Seabiscuit's owner and trainer question the jockey. They all know that Red could have ridden Seabiscuit to victory. They want to know why he did not follow the plan. His repeated response was that the guy fouled him.

"Am I supposed to let him get away with that?!" Red yells.

"Well, yeah, when he's 40 to 1," says the trainer, clearly exasperated.

"But he fouled me!" exclaims Red, as if they are ones who do not get it.

This scene *in Seabiscuit* helps illumine the theme of connectedness or mutuality found in Matthew 18:21–35.

The larger context of our passage, which includes all of chapter 18, deals with community and the quality of relationships that promote a healthy one. The foundation of Matthew's understanding is that we are all connected. These connections can be positive or negative, life-giving and affirming, or toxic and oppressive. In order to create and maintain communal bonds that are positive, individuals and communities must be able to deal with sin or, to put it in terms of the movie, they must be able to handle being fouled. Why? Because relationships, and therefore community, are impacted by our ability or inability to forgive.

As a community composed of people of God who have been "called out" (*ekklēsia*), our relationships should promote and affirm human life and dignity. Recognizing that people do not always behave in ways that foster this type of community, Matthew addresses how we handle being wronged. Perhaps this is one of the most important ways the people of God witness to the world. We model before others not only how to treat others, but how we handle the mistreatment of others. We model forgiveness, because like Red, we have all been fouled.

In Red's case, his actions did not affect only him. Red, Seabiscuit, the owner, the trainer, and the spectators who put their money on Seabiscuit lost. The race connected them. Red's inability to handle the foul in a way that allowed him to execute the race-day plan cost them all. Sure, he beat the person who fouled him, but he lost the race.

This movie allows the preacher to use popular culture to ask questions with which congregants and communities must wrestle in light of this passage. For example, a preacher may ask, To what are we choosing to connect ourselves? In other words, are we connecting to the foul, or to values and actions that identify us as God's people? The preacher might acknowledge that we may need to recognize how easy it is to become like Red or the unforgiving slave and lose focus of our identity as God's people, as well as the purpose(s) for which God has called us out. It is easy to resort to vengeful and retaliatory tactics to handle fouls. Moreover, the preacher can remind congregants that we must ask ourselves if a particular course of action will clarify or obfuscate our identity. Will it bring us closer to fulfilling our purpose(s) or lead us away from it?

Indeed, handling fouls is hard, and this scene in *Seabiscuit* allows the preacher to highlight this fact using cinematic details rather than personal events that may ring a bit too close to a listener's real-life experience. The movie enables the preacher to let Red's experience parallel that of a congregant. Indeed, many are like Red and the forgiven but unforgiving slave and feel as if forgiveness means letting someone get away with what they have done to them. It means letting them or anyone think that their treatment of them was acceptable. Like Red, they feel that they are owed something. Red views the offending jockey as having taken something from him that must be repaid. Red must even the score. The only currency he seems to know or have is retaliation. Therefore, Red must make him suffer or feel as he feels. That is how he gets paid back.

The preacher can also explore the perspective of the owner and the trainer. They saw letting the other jockey "get away with it" not as failure but as a way for Red to preserve his identity as a jockey. It meant not losing sight of the larger purpose: winning the race. This would require Red to handle his foul with a different currency.

Here the preacher can consider why Jesus uses a parable about debt to explain forgiveness. Debt connects the borrower and the lender until the debt is repaid. It binds both parties until the obligation of the debt is fulfilled. In the parable, the king chooses the currency of forgiveness to erase the debt. Yet the forgiven debtor chooses retaliation. He will make the one indebted to him feel as afraid and hopeless as he once did. He remains connected to the one indebted rather than freed from him. This connection causes him to share the fate (Matt. 18:34). Like Red and the competing jockey, both slaves lose, and their losses will ripple through the lives of those to whom they are connected.

It seems that one's perspective greatly affects one's willingness to forgive. As individuals and communities of believers, it is important for us to examine ourselves, not just the offender, when we are fouled. Perhaps, like Peter, the issue for us is not whether or not we should forgive, but the limits to our forgiveness. In short, we want to know under what circumstances we can withhold forgiveness. Jesus' telling of this parable is prompted by Peter's desire to know how many times he should forgive (v. 21). Jesus puts how much we forgive others in relation to how much we have been forgiven. We respond to fouls from a bank that deals in a different currency. We pay back out of the bank of God's mercy, compassion, and forgiveness to us. We refuse to withdraw from the branches of foul behavior we have experienced.

Finally, Peter's question provides an opportunity for personal reflection. It causes us to consider what limits we put on whom and how often we forgive. Is it the number of fouls they commit? The type of foul? Who they are? Whom they have fouled?

In similar fashion, the fate of the unforgiving slave provides an additional opportunity. It causes us to consider limits we want placed on receiving forgiveness ourselves. Is it the number of fouls we commit? The type of foul? Who we are? Whom we have fouled?

RAQUEL ST. CLAIR LETTSOME

Proper 20 (Sunday between September 18 and September 24 inclusive)

Jonah 3:10–4:11 and Exodus 16:2–15
Psalm 145:1–8 and Psalm 105:1–6, 37–45

Philippians 1:21–30
Matthew 20:1–16

Jonah 3:10–4:11

³:¹⁰When God saw what they did, how they turned from their evil ways, God changed his mind about the calamity that he had said he would bring upon them; and he did not do it.

⁴:¹But this was very displeasing to Jonah, and he became angry. ²He prayed to the LORD and said, "O LORD! Is not this what I said while I was still in my own country? That is why I fled to Tarshish at the beginning; for I knew that you are a gracious God and merciful, slow to anger, and abounding in steadfast love, and ready to relent from punishing. ³And now, O LORD, please take my life from me, for it is better for me to die than to live." ⁴And the LORD said, "Is it right for you to be angry?" ⁵Then Jonah went out of the city and sat down east of the city, and made a booth for himself there. He sat under it in the shade, waiting to see what would become of the city.

⁶The LORD God appointed a bush, and made it come up over Jonah, to give shade over his head, to save him from his discomfort; so Jonah was very happy about the bush. ⁷But when dawn came up the next day, God appointed a worm that attacked the bush, so that it withered. ⁸When the sun rose, God prepared a sultry east wind, and the sun beat down on the head of Jonah so that he was faint and asked that he might die. He said, "It is better for me to die than to live."

⁹But God said to Jonah, "Is it right for you to be angry about the bush?" And he said, "Yes, angry enough to die." ¹⁰Then the LORD said, "You are concerned about the bush, for which you did not labor and which you did not grow; it came into being in a night and perished in a night. ¹¹And should I not be concerned about Nineveh, that great city, in which there are more than a hundred and twenty thousand persons who do not know their right hand from their left, and also many animals?"

Exodus 16:2–15

²The whole congregation of the Israelites complained against Moses and Aaron in the wilderness. ³The Israelites said to them, "If only we had died by the hand of the LORD in the land of Egypt, when we sat by the fleshpots and ate our fill of bread; for you have brought us out into this wilderness to kill this whole assembly with hunger."

⁴Then the LORD said to Moses, "I am going to rain bread from heaven for you, and each day the people shall go out and gather enough for that day. In that way I will test them, whether they will follow my instruction or not. ⁵On the sixth day, when they prepare what they bring in, it will be twice as much as they gather on other days." ⁶So Moses and Aaron said to all the Israelites, "In the evening you

shall know that it was the LORD who brought you out of the land of Egypt, ⁷and in the morning you shall see the glory of the LORD, because he has heard your complaining against the LORD. For what are we, that you complain against us?" ⁸And Moses said, "When the LORD gives you meat to eat in the evening and your fill of bread in the morning, because the LORD has heard the complaining that you utter against him—what are we? Your complaining is not against us but against the LORD."

⁹Then Moses said to Aaron, "Say to the whole congregation of the Israelites, 'Draw near to the LORD, for he has heard your complaining.'" ¹⁰And as Aaron spoke to the whole congregation of the Israelites, they looked toward the wilderness, and the glory of the LORD appeared in the cloud. ¹¹The LORD spoke to Moses and said, ¹²"I have heard the complaining of the Israelites; say to them, 'At twilight you shall eat meat, and in the morning you shall have your fill of bread; then you shall know that I am the LORD your God.'"

¹³In the evening quails came up and covered the camp; and in the morning there was a layer of dew around the camp. ¹⁴When the layer of dew lifted, there on the surface of the wilderness was a fine flaky substance, as fine as frost on the ground. ¹⁵When the Israelites saw it, they said to one another, "What is it?" For they did not know what it was. Moses said to them, "It is the bread that the LORD has given you to eat."

Commentary 1: Connecting the Reading with Scripture

Jonah 3:10—4:11. Readers might be puzzled, put off, or even amused by Jonah's anger (Jonah 4:1, 4, 9), a feeling so intense he would rather die than continue to feel it (4:3, 8, 9). We are often fed a caricature of Jonah as a petty, xenophobic prophet who cannot stomach God's mercy on a foreign people. If Jonah had been called to a different city, perhaps in Syria or Phoenicia, this characterization might hold water, but Nineveh, capital city of the Neo-Assyrian Empire, was not just any "great city" (1:2; 3:2; 4:11). Canonical context helps us to view Jonah's anger through a wider geopolitical and historical lens.

Jonah son of Amittai is first introduced in 2 Kings 14:25. He is active during the reign of Jeroboam II (2 Kgs. 14:27), making his prophetic ministry roughly contemporary with that of the eighth-century-BCE prophets Amos and Hosea (also active in the northern kingdom, Israel) and just prior to that of Isaiah of Jerusalem and Micah (active in the southern kingdom, Judah). He hails from Gath-hepher, a small village in the northern kingdom of Israel, not far from Lake Kinneret, also known as the Sea of Galilee. From a later perspective, we would be interested to know that Gath-hepher was within jogging distance of Nazareth (5 km, to be precise). In Jonah's era, the more relevant datum is that Gath-hepher was a border town, and its residents would have known they were vulnerable to the lurking threat of Assyrian imperial aggression.

Vitriol at Nineveh's violence is not limited to Jonah; the book of Nahum calls Nineveh a "city of bloodshed" filled with plunder from the nations it has conquered (Nah. 3:1) and foretells God's vengeance against it (Nah. 3:2–7; cf. Zeph. 2:13; Tob. 14:4). Historian Richard Gabriel offers context: "Assyria emerged as the most powerful . . . military empire that the world had seen, . . . built on military force and policy terror. . . . Between 890 and 640 [BCE] . . . the Assyrians fought 108 major and minor wars, punitive expeditions, and other significant military operations against neighboring states."[1] Assyria's reputation for bloodshed was well-deserved, by admission of its own kings: "With their blood I dyed the mountain like crimson wool," declared Ashurnasirpal II; "I made a pile

---

1. Richard A. Gabriel, *The Culture of War: Invention and Early Development* (New York: Greenwood Press, 1990), 57.

of heads ... and the living I impaled."[2] In the historical narrative of 2 Kings, not three chapters after Jonah is introduced and a few decades after his prophetic ministry has ended, Assyria's armies invade the kingdom of Israel and take its people into captivity (2 Kgs. 17:6, 23). The historian identifies one cause for the destruction of Jonah's people: Israel had sinned (2 Kgs. 17:7).

Seen against the backdrop of other prophetic texts, biblical historical narrative, and Assyrian imperial propaganda, the reason for Jonah's anger becomes clearer. Jonah knows God will choose mercy toward Nineveh: "I knew that you are a gracious God and merciful" (Jonah 4:2, quoting God's self-revelation in Exod. 34:6–7; cf. Num. 14:17–19; Ps. 86:5,15; 145:8–9; contrast with Nah. 1:3).[3] While repentance has elicited God's forgiveness, it will not forever curtail Nineveh's violence. Nor will God forever show the same mercy to Israel: Jonah may already suspect that Nineveh will one day be the tool of God's justice toward Jonah's own, sinful people. Jonah's honest anger may help us confront the limits of our own capacity to forgive, even as we are schooled in God's outrageous mercy.

Exodus 16:2–15. God's gift of "bread from heaven" (Exod. 16:4) forms a core part of Israel's testimony, appearing many places throughout the Old Testament, including Numbers (11:6–9), Deuteronomy (8:3, 16), Joshua (5:12), Nehemiah (9:15, 20), Psalms (78:24), and Wisdom of Solomon (16:20), as well as several places in the New Testament (John 6:31–32, 49; Heb. 9:4; Rev. 2:17). Canonically speaking, Exodus 16 marks the tradition's first occurrence.

The setting is vital to understanding the significance of this testimony. Only six weeks previously, the Israelites had been freed from slavery in Egypt (Exod. 16:1). They celebrated God's victory over Pharaoh's army with song and dance (15:1–21), yet the mood shifted dramatically in the span of a few days and a single verse (v. 22). The path from the Reed Sea to a land they might call home led through wilderness and dry desert. Though they found an oasis at Elim (v. 27), its water and fruit provided only temporary provision. As their journey continued and rations dwindled, their joy and wonder at God's saving power was overtaken by thirst, hunger, fear, and anger. Victory song was replaced by grumbling (16:2).

The memory of "grumbling" or "complaining" is perhaps as central to Israel's testimony as the gift of bread that follows (15:24; 16:2, 7–9, 12; 17:2–7; Num. 11:1, 4; cf. Num. 14; 16:11, 41; 17:5, 10; Deut. 1:27; Ps. 106:25). Later in their journey, complaint will be met with the threat of death (e.g., Num. 14:27–29; 17:5, 10), but here it is not judged negatively. God's people barely know who this God is or where God has led them (cf. Exod. 16:6). Their hunger is real. When they voice it, God *hears* their complaint, a detail so important it is repeated four times (16:7–9, 12). Instead of responding with rebuke or anger, God responds by meeting the need they have voiced. God also responds by showing up: because God has heard their complaint, the people will see God's glory (vv. 7, 10).

God's visible presence at the passage's heart almost gets lost between the sound of complaint and the smell of food upon the ground. Yet, canonically speaking, this passage contains the first references within the Old Testament to God's "glory" (*kabod*, 16:7, 10), a term that denotes the awesome, visible manifestation of divine presence. Following its first occurrences in Exodus 16, the term recurs in the Sinai theophany (24:16–17), in the story of God's self-revelation to Moses (33:18, 22), and at the moment when God's presence fills the completed tabernacle (40:35).

Repeatedly, God makes divine glory visible in order to reveal aspects of God's nature and to demonstrate God's commitment to the people of Israel. This first revelation of God's glory offers the congregation of Israel deeper and surer knowledge of the God who journeys with them. The food they will eat provides sustenance, but also a daily reminder: "you shall have your fill

---

2. E. A. Wallis Budge and L. W. King, eds., *Annals of the Kings of Assyria, The Cuneiform Texts with Translations, Transliterations, etc., from the Original Documents in the British Museum*, vol. 1 (London: The British Museum, 1902), 272, 379. Such phrases were frequently used in propaganda (see, e.g., pp. 61, 234, 236, 336, 339).

3. For thoughtful and accessible analysis of this tradition, see Walter Brueggemann, *Theology of the Old Testament: Testimony, Dispute, Advocacy* (Minneapolis: Augsburg Fortress, 1997), 213–28.

of bread; then you shall know that I am the LORD your God" (16:12). God thus begins to reveal to them God's nature as a deity who is present in their midst, even in the heart of a barren wilderness, who saves them from oppression and sustains them in their direst need (vv. 10–12).

The obvious link between Exodus 16:2–15 and Matthew 20:1–16 is the theme of "grumbling": the Greek verb translated "grumbled" (*egongyzon*) in Matthew 20:11 echoes the intensive compound form translated "complained" (*diegongyzen* LXX; cf. use of the same compound in Luke 15:2 and 19:7) in Exodus 16:2. The comparison may help us to hear the grumbling as God hears it in these texts: an invitation to God to continue to reveal Godself to us, confounding our expectations while meeting our deepest needs.

ANATHEA E. PORTIER-YOUNG

The Beginning and End of Christ's Work

For it is actually the role of the Holy Spirit, as Christ himself taught, to lead believers into all truth and obedience and to glorify Christ. "He will bring glory to me by taking what is mine and making it known to you" (John 16:14). This glorifying or praising of Christ through the Holy Spirit actually takes place in his followers who accept and keep his word in true faith. As he said himself, "And glory has come to me through them (that is, his disciples)" (John 17:10). Christ is glorified in his followers just as the Father is glorified in Christ. The Father was glorified in Christ in that Christ revealed the name of the Father to his disciples, he spoke his Father's word, did his Father's will and fulfilled his Father's work. As he said himself, "I have brought you glory on earth by completing the work you gave me to do" (John 17:4).

Therefore, all followers of Christ must keep his teachings, do his will and fulfill his work. It is in this way that Christ will be glorified. And it is the beginning and end of Christ's work that we truly reform our lives, believe the gospel and be baptized on our faith in the name of the holy Trinity—the Father, Son and Holy Spirit. And then, through the Lord's grace, we must strive to hold all that Christ commanded us.

Dirk Philips, "Concerning the New Birth and the New Creature: Brief Admonition and Teaching from the Holy Bible," in *Early Anabaptist Spirituality*, The Classics of Western Spirituality, trans. and ed. Daniel Liechty (Mahwah, NJ: Paulist, 1994), 210.

Commentary 2: Connecting the Reading with the World

Jonah learns by experiences. The storm teaches him that he cannot flee from God. The fish teaches him God's mercy, as does the plant. Seeing the Ninevites and their flocks and herds put on sackcloth and ashes convinces him that they have repented. The worm eating the plant, the hot sun, and the east wind put him in a state of despair, ready to hear God's question. For readers and hearers who are moved by narrative more than by exhortation, Jonah is an absorbing account. Jonah is a man of dramatic actions and roller-coaster emotions. Instead of arguing with God about his initial commission to Nineveh, capital of the vicious Assyrian Empire, he takes off in the opposite direction, to the other end of the earth. He does this in spite of confessing belief in Yahweh, the creator of the sea and the dry land. He knows that God is merciful, but he does not like it.

Recent scholarly treatments of Jonah have pointed out the humor of the book, long recognized in versions of the story for children. Irony or satire seems to be at work; yet the book is not simply entertainment. It uses this story to teach the merciful justice of God, spelled out casuistically in Jeremiah 18:5–10, and to delve into the responses of God's people. God promises that the nations will turn to the Lord (e.g., Isa. 2:2–4). How will God's people feel when the wicked, tyrannical foreign king actually does this? Matthew 12:38–42 and Luke 11:29–32 compare Jesus' audience unfavorably to the repentant Ninevites. Jonah is an Israelite Everyman whose responses to God's mercy indicate a too-narrow view of what it means to be the chosen people of God.

The book of Jonah also demonstrates that even unconditional announcements of judgment are still invitations to repentance, thus providing a hermeneutical key to the ongoing applicability of old judgment prophecies. Jonah's short message prompted the outcome in Nineveh that God sent the prophets to achieve; it "turned them from their evil way, and from the evil of their doings" (Jer. 23:22).

There are many gaps in the narrative of Jonah, perhaps especially in this week's passage, 3:10–4:11. For example, why was he angry? Was he concerned about his own reputation, about God's glory, or did he just fear and hate Assyrians? These gaps have left space for many analyses of Jonah that find in him a kindred spirit or a cautionary example. Is he a survivor of attempted suicide (1:12), who still struggles with his desire for death? Is he an advocate of genocide against Israel's potential conquerors, or merely an all-too-human example how hard it is to forgive and welcome former enemies into one's own safe circle? Is he a realistic model of pastoral leadership or an arrogant fool who cannot integrate his theology and practice, what he believes and his emotional responses? The story of the person named Jonah has been used in these and other ways.

Jonah and the plant seldom appear in Christian art. Jonah and the big fish, however, are favorite subjects. The saying of Jesus in Matthew 12:38–40 identifies Jonah's three days in the fish as a sign of Jesus' days in the grave. Early Christian funerary art includes Jonah and the fish as representations of their belief in Christ's resurrection and their own.[4] In retellings of Jonah for children, the big fish or whale is the focus of the story too, but not as a type for the grave. These versions of the story teach lessons of obedience and responsibility, and assure children that God saves and forgives. Sometimes the author includes the plant and the worm to encourage children to love others.

The painting of Jonah by Michelangelo in the Sistine Chapel differs from these representations.[5] Fish and plant are depicted, but they appear to be too small to rescue him from sea or sun. Seated, Jonah's torso twists to his right while his face turns left and upward toward God and the sun in the creation panels. In the corner to Jonah's left, Moses raises the bronze serpent on a pole, another Old Testament type of Christ (John 3:14–15; Num. 21:4–9). Jonah's body is turned toward the other corner, where the execution of Haman appears (Esth. 7:9–10). The altar is below Jonah, and the wall behind it holds the fresco of the Last Judgment. Perhaps Michelangelo's Jonah is the person in chapter 4, twisting toward and away from the Creator, caught between God's mercy toward repentant ones and judgment on their unrepentant enemies. The fourth chapter of Jonah is an uncomfortable conclusion to the story. Jonah does not answer God's query, "Should I not be concerned about Nineveh, that great city?" In the Sistine Chapel, the crucified and risen Christ is just below Jonah, a reminder of God's ultimate solution to this dilemma.

The details of the Jonah story remind one of the Creator's rule and control. God appoints a fish and a worm, and causes a plant to grow up overnight. God throws a great wind at the sea and sends a hot east wind on the land outside of Nineveh. Exodus 16 shows the God of heaven, who made the sea and dry land, raining bread from heaven in the wilderness to feed the Israelites. The creation theme is underscored in Jonah by his desire to see the temple (Jonah 2:4) and by the appearance of the glory of God to the Israelites in Exodus 16:10. Jonah was in his own wilderness, where he built a shelter (*sukkah*) for himself, as Leviticus 23:42 instructs for the Feast of Booths, "so that your generations may know that I made the people of Israel live in booths (*sukkot,* plural) when I brought them out of the land of Egypt: I am the Lord your God."

---

4. E.g., a painting in the catacombs of Sts. Marcellinus and Peter shows Jonah being vomited out. http://www.vatican.va/roman_curia/pontifical_commissions/archeo/inglese/documents/rc_com_archeo_doc_20011010_cataccrist_en.html#Arte.

5. https://www.michelangelo.org/sistine-chapel-ceiling.jsp

Survival on a wilderness trek requires careful planning, following a course with water sources at regular intervals, and carrying adequate food for everyone in the party. A month after leaving Egypt, the Israelites face the wilderness fearing for their lives. Their need for food was legitimate. Dying by the Lord's hand in Egypt looks better to them than a lingering death by starvation. They desire to undo their salvation.

Numerous organizations calculate that the world produces enough food for everyone, but nearly a billion people are undernourished, especially women, children, and minority groups.[6] Some of the factors that contribute to food wastage are lack of safe storage, distribution, and taste. God's provision of manna and quail deals with each of these issues. The manna tasted like coriander or honey-flavored wafers (Exod. 16:31), and the birds provided the desired flesh. Everyone had access to this food daily, and all ate their fill. God's provision of this food is reflected in the familiar petition, "Give us this day our daily bread."

Bread from heaven "gives life to the world" (John 6:31–34). Christians use manna as a metaphor for Christ, the word of God, or the Holy Spirit. It is especially important as an image for the bread of the Lord's Supper. Like the Israelites, Christians obediently share God-given sustenance and are formed as a community who acknowledge and follow the Lord. Christians, by taking the bread of Christ, become bread for the world.

PAMELA J. SCALISE

---

6. https://www.oxfam.ca/there-enough-food-feed-world.

Proper 20 (Sunday between September 18 and September 24 inclusive)

Psalm 145:1–8

¹I will extol you, my God and King,
    and bless your name forever and ever.
²Every day I will bless you,
    and praise your name forever and ever.
³Great is the Lord, and greatly to be praised;
    his greatness is unsearchable.

⁴One generation shall laud your works to another,
    and shall declare your mighty acts.
⁵On the glorious splendor of your majesty,
    and on your wondrous works, I will meditate.
⁶The might of your awesome deeds shall be proclaimed,
    and I will declare your greatness.
⁷They shall celebrate the fame of your abundant goodness,
    and shall sing aloud of your righteousness.

⁸The Lord is gracious and merciful,
    slow to anger and abounding in steadfast love.

Psalm 105:1–6, 37–45

¹O give thanks to the Lord, call on his name,
    make known his deeds among the peoples.
²Sing to him, sing praises to him;
    tell of all his wonderful works.
³Glory in his holy name;
    let the hearts of those who seek the Lord rejoice.
⁴Seek the Lord and his strength;
    seek his presence continually.
⁵Remember the wonderful works he has done,
    his miracles, and the judgments he has uttered,
⁶O offspring of his servant Abraham,
    children of Jacob, his chosen ones.
. . . .
³⁷Then he brought Israel out with silver and gold,
    and there was no one among their tribes who stumbled.
³⁸Egypt was glad when they departed,
    for dread of them had fallen upon it.
³⁹He spread a cloud for a covering,
    and fire to give light by night.
⁴⁰They asked, and he brought quails,
    and gave them food from heaven in abundance.
⁴¹He opened the rock, and water gushed out;
    it flowed through the desert like a river.

⁴²For he remembered his holy promise,
   and Abraham, his servant.

⁴³So he brought his people out with joy,
   his chosen ones with singing.
⁴⁴He gave them the lands of the nations,
   and they took possession of the wealth of the peoples,
⁴⁵that they might keep his statutes
   and observe his laws.
Praise the LORD!

Connecting the Psalm with Scripture and Worship

Psalm 145. This is the only psalm that bears the title "a psalm of praise."[1] It is a declaration of praise: "Every day I will bless you, and praise your name forever and ever" (Ps. 145:2). This praise is offered in a variety of expressions: "extol, bless" (v. 1), "laud, declare" (v. 4), "meditate" (v. 5), "proclaim, declare" (v. 6), "celebrate, sing" (v. 7). Gratitude is given because of the nature of God: "The LORD is gracious and merciful, slow to anger and abounding in steadfast love" (v. 8). Beyond the pericope is found an essential truth, that God's reign on earth is expansive in scope: "The LORD is good to all, and God's compassion is over all that he has made" (v. 9). As a litany of divine attributes, the psalm invites a response of thanksgiving and praise from everyone.

The theme of praise comes from the lips of Jonah, who ran away from God and was thrown into the sea. Swallowed up by a large fish, Jonah prayed to God; his prayer was answered as he was delivered to dry ground. When God again called Jonah to go to Nineveh, Jonah obeyed and there proclaimed God's message to repent. Because of Jonah's witness, the people turned from the ways of sin; therefore, God did not destroy the city. Jonah should have rejoiced with the people, but, instead, "this was very displeasing to Jonah, and he became angry." He prayed, "O LORD! . . . That is why I fled to Tarshish at the beginning; for I knew that you are a gracious God and merciful, slow to anger, and abounding in steadfast love, and ready to relent from punishing" (Jonah 4:2). Jonah spoke words of thanks for God when he was saved by God. When the Ninevites were saved by God, Jonah spoke words of anger.

Although Jonah knows that it is God's nature to be gracious and merciful (Ps. 145:8) and good to all (v. 9), he wants the mercy for himself but punishment for others. This is a rich tension to explore in preaching, wondering: Why do we get so angry when others are blessed by God? Do we expect to earn our blessings by being better than others? Do we think we can take the blessings for ourselves, even out of the hands of others? Do we fear that if others receive blessings, then there will be none left for us? The Gospel text that compares the kingdom of heaven to a vineyard owner further illuminates this abundant mercy of God that confounds us: "Am I not allowed to do what I choose with what belongs to me? Or are you envious because I am generous?" (Matt. 20:15).

Psalm 145 has numerous liturgical uses. As a call to worship, the psalm can be a litany, repeating the refrain, "Great is the Lord, and greatly to be praised" (v. 3). As an assurance of pardon, the psalm declares that God's mercy covers all of our sins: "The LORD is gracious and merciful, slow to anger and abiding in steadfast love" (v. 8). As a prayer of thanksgiving, the psalm invites words of praise from the congregation, with a responsive refrain: "Every day I will bless you, and praise your name forever and ever" (v. 2). Hymns such as "Sing Praise to God Who Reigns Above," "God of the Sparrow," and "Praise Ye the Lord" would be fitting choices.

---

1. J. Clinton McCann Jr., "The Book of Psalms," in *The New Interpreter's Bible* (Nashville: Abingdon, 1996), 7:1258.

This psalm allows us to praise a God who is bigger than our selfishness, bigger than our anger, bigger than any divisions between people, big enough for all that God has made. The psalm ends with a glorious declaration that calls for universal praise: "My mouth will speak the praise of the LORD. Let every creature praise his holy name for ever and ever" (v. 21, NIV).

Psalm 105:1–6, 37–45. Psalm 105 is usually classified as historical, although it is primarily a retelling of Israel's story that inspires the ongoing faithfulness of God's people. By "remembering the wonderful works God has done" (Ps. 105:5), explains Walter Brueggemann, historical psalms "seek to make available to subsequent generations the experience and power of the initial astonishment which abides with compelling authority."[2] By re-creating a sense of awe, the psalm calls hearers to renewed gratitude, praise, and obedience. The first six verses are an invitation to praise the Lord in the present with various expressions, including "give thanks and make known his deeds" (v. 1), "sing praises, tell" (v. 2), "glory in his holy name, rejoice" (v. 3), "seek the LORD" (v. 4). The psalmist calls the people to "remember the wonderful works and miracles" (v. 5) by naming particular works God has done, including "spread a cloud and fire" (v. 39), "brought quails and gave them food from heaven in abundance" (v. 40), and "opened the rock, and water gushed out" (v. 41). The hope is that the people will experience anew the astonishment at the great lengths God goes to demonstrate love for and fidelity to God's people.

The psalm's reference of the "quails and food from heaven" (v. 40) is recounted in the Exodus passage. The people in the wilderness were hungry, doubtful, and disobedient, yet God provided for them in abundance. This passage comes before the establishment of the covenant with the Ten Commandments (Exod. 20). The order is theologically significant: God's grace and blessings go first; then God's people respond with gratitude and obedience. This holy order is reflected in the final verses of the psalm: "He gave them lands" (Ps. 105:44) "that they might keep his statutes and observe his laws" (v. 45). God's grace provides; God's people respond in kind with thanksgiving: "Praise the LORD!"

This historical psalm tells the history of God's actions on behalf of God's chosen people, even as it anticipates a future call to faithfulness. God's promise and provision could be explored in a sermon with attention to both the initial covenant with Abraham (v. 9) and the incarnation of the covenant with Jesus. Another homiletical approach might explore how the call to obedience to "keep [God's] statutes and observe [God's] laws" (v. 45) relates to the call to faithfulness to "live your life in a manner worthy of the gospel of Christ" (Phil. 1:27).

Liturgically, this psalm can evoke "abiding astonishment" with God's past wonders and inspire anticipation for God at work in the world today. As a call to worship or reading, some verses of the psalm can be printed or projected, allowing people to remember the story, even as they are called to celebrate it, with a response of "O give thanks to the Lord" or "Praise the Lord!" Hymns that reflect the themes of the day include "Great Is Thy Faithfulness," "Guide Me, O Thou Great Jehovah," "Glorious Things of Thee Are Spoken," and "Amazing Grace."

History comes alive in this psalm, recovering a communal memory in order to cultivate a covenant renewal, calling us first to astonishment and appreciation of the abiding promises of God and then to obedience, and finally, always, to praise.

DONNA GIVER-JOHNSTON

---

2. Walter Brueggemann, *Abiding Astonishment: Psalms, Modernity, and the Making of History* (Louisville, KY: Westminster John Knox, 1991), 34.

Proper 20 (Sunday between September 18 and September 24 inclusive)

Philippians 1:21–30

²¹For to me, living is Christ and dying is gain. ²²If I am to live in the flesh, that means fruitful labor for me; and I do not know which I prefer. ²³I am hard pressed between the two: my desire is to depart and be with Christ, for that is far better; ²⁴but to remain in the flesh is more necessary for you. ²⁵Since I am convinced of this, I know that I will remain and continue with all of you for your progress and joy in faith, ²⁶so that I may share abundantly in your boasting in Christ Jesus when I come to you again.

²⁷Only, live your life in a manner worthy of the gospel of Christ, so that, whether I come and see you or am absent and hear about you, I will know that you are standing firm in one spirit, striving side by side with one mind for the faith of the gospel, ²⁸and are in no way intimidated by your opponents. For them this is evidence of their destruction, but of your salvation. And this is God's doing. ²⁹For he has graciously granted you the privilege not only of believing in Christ, but of suffering for him as well— ³⁰since you are having the same struggle that you saw I had and now hear that I still have.

Commentary 1: Connecting the Reading with Scripture

"Come over to Macedonia and help us." These were the words Paul heard one night in a vision while he was staying in Troas. The next morning, Paul and Silas set sail and eventually made their way to a place of prayer by the river in a leading Macedonian city named Philippi. Baptism forms a parenthesis around the story of Paul's days in the city. Lydia and her household are the first to be baptized and the household of Paul's jailer the last. What happened in between brought Paul into conflict with merchants and magistrates (Acts 16:11–40), but it also brought the baptized into a lasting relationship of love and affection with Paul.

In his letter to them from prison, Paul begins by remembering them with joy "because of [their] sharing in the gospel from the first day until now" (Phil. 1:5) and his longing for them "with the compassion of Christ Jesus" (v. 8). Why this tone of intimate affection? Returning to Paul's beginning with the Philippian church before turning to the substance of his letter invites both the preacher and the congregation to reflect on their own sharing in the gospel from the first day until now. How can the current struggles or anxieties of any congregation be experienced as useful for the spread of the gospel? In the midst of setbacks or uncertainties, what difference might it make to be reminded that God, who began a good work among them, "will bring it to completion by the day of Jesus Christ" (v. 6)? Beginning where Paul begins with the Philippians is one way to set the context for considering the substance of this epistle.

Another place to begin is with the almost forgotten experience of writing and receiving a letter. Clicking on an email is vastly different from finding a handwritten letter in the mailbox, composed by a friend or a mentor whose whereabouts and personal circumstances have been cause for worry. Unlike face-to-face conversation, the letter is often a well-considered sort of communication, each word and sentence chosen with the writer imagining its effect on the reader. Then there is the expanse of time and distance that paradoxically invites the sort of self-disclosure and intimacy often lost in the rush of close encounters.

That same time and distance is significant in a wholly different way when multiplied by two millennia. Like studying other found correspondence between relatives who lived a generation ago, reading a letter not meant for another's eyes can fill in the blanks of one's own self-understanding. A grandfather's doubts, a grandmother's assurances, the love between them can make sense of the disparate pieces of life today from the perspective of another who has gone before us. This letter just may be the means of grace God is using now to pick up the pieces of Christ's church as God brings to completion the good work God has begun among God's people.

With no postmark on Paul's letter, scholars continue to speculate on his whereabouts. Caesarea? Ephesus? Rome? Just as Paul's imprisonment at Philippi figured into the Philippians' first encounter with him and led to the baptism of his jailer's household, now Paul offers his present imprisonment as an impetus for these partners in the gospel to "dare to speak the word with greater boldness and without fear" (v. 14). Here Paul is surely naming and so identifying with the Philippians' state of mind. They are fearful for Paul, but they also are fearful for themselves as they navigate life as Christians in the midst of an increasingly hostile empire. The state of mind shared by writer and readers, the readers being both the Philippians then and the gathered congregation now, is another way to hear God's living word in the words of this particular text. What are the fears that keep those reading Paul's letter today from speaking the word with boldness? When, in recent memory, has the church been intimidated by opponents (v. 28)?

After Paul cites his own bold speech in prison as the means by which Christ is exalted "whether by life or by death" (v. 20), his boldness takes an intimate turn. He writes to these partners in the gospel of his own life-and-death struggle, a struggle that is not in the hands of his jailers or the Roman authorities but in the hands of God. His "desire to depart and be with Christ" (v. 23) can be understood in contrast to the death wishes expressed in the choice of OT lections for this Sunday. The whole congregation of the Israelites complains, "If only we had died by the hand of the Lord in the land of Egypt," rather than dying of hunger in the wilderness (Exod. 16:3). Their wish is to be spared the difficulties of life as God's people. In the second OT lection, Jonah's death wish is expressed in response to God's changed mind toward the Ninevites: "And now, O Lord, please take my life from me, for it is better for me to die than to live" (Jonah 4:3). Again, in response to the punishing wind and sun, he says, "It is better for me to die than to live" (v. 8). The impetus for his request is his anger at God's graciousness.

Unlike the Israelites, Paul's desire to depart this life is not to avoid the difficulties of life with God. Unlike Jonah, he is not asking to die because God has been gracious toward sinners. Paul longs to dwell in the place Christ has prepared for him, which is in the love that God is. Moreover, because he has died in baptism to death's power over him, because life without Christ is behind him, "living is Christ and dying is gain" (Phil. 1:21). After a few sentences that must have had the church holding its collective breath, Paul assures them that he will come to them again (v. 26). How does Paul's own struggle with living and dying inform our own as individuals and as a church? How is Paul's desire to die and be with God different from Jesus' teaching that those who lose their lives will find them (Matt. 10:39; Mark 8:35; Luke 17:33; John 12:25)?

Since the Philippian community is "having the same struggle" that they saw Paul had and now hear he is still having (Phil. 1:30), how are they to live? Paul's advice can be summarized in one word: unity. For Paul, the unity of the body is the "manner [of life] worthy of the gospel" (v. 27). Given that so many of Paul's letters deal with disunity, a preacher or teacher could create a series of sermons or classes that compare or contrast disputes in the early church with disputes in various denominations. Three letters come immediately to mind: Paul's Letter to the Romans (disunity between Christian Gentiles and Christian Jews), his Letters to the Corinthians (disunity among factions), his Letter to the Galatians (disunity caused by rival missionaries concerning the admission of Gentiles). How does Paul try to move these congregations from disunity to unity and how could his strategies inform our own?

Looking forward, September marks a new beginning in the church's program year, a season when the community of faith has been granted, yet again, "the privilege not only of believing in Christ, but of suffering for him" (v. 29). In a nation divided, the preacher might imagine the bold, joyful, countercultural witness of a church that, in no way intimidated by its opponents, stands "firm in one spirit, striving side by side with one mind for the faith of the gospel" (v. 27).

CYNTHIA A. JARVIS

Commentary 2: Connecting the Reading with the World

In Philippians 1, Paul struggles with his choice, "Yet what shall I choose? I do not know! I am torn between the two" (Phil. 1:22–23 NIV). He could choose death, he explains, "I desire to depart and be with Christ, which is better by far" (v. 23 NIV), pointing to the wonderful eschatological reality of being at home with Christ in the kingdom of God. Yet he instead chooses "to remain in the flesh" (v. 24 NRSV), in the ongoing realities of this world with all of its pain, suffering, and evil. Like the incarnate Christ, Paul is driven by love and compassion, the desire to be with humans in the midst of suffering. He chooses to "continue with all of you" (v. 25), to be in messy solidarity with others.

The rhetorical framework of the text suggests that what Paul talks about is not quite free choice as we now understand it. For Paul, following Christ is grounded in the *koinōnia*, the gathering of disciples, working out new ways of living. This community, he believed, lived as part of the body of Christ being realized in the world where "if one member suffers, all suffer together with it; if one member is honored, all rejoice together with it" (1 Cor. 12:26). It is the place where followers are formed and where they support each other. Throughout his letters, Paul lays out aspects of what he calls here "standing firm in one spirit, striving side by side with one mind for the faith of the gospel" (Phil. 1:27). The new Christian way pulls disciples ineluctably toward each other as part of living out the gospel message.

Paul's understanding of the nature of Christian community has been foundational across centuries and cultures for forming strong ecclesial identities. When John Wesley preached on Ephesians 4:1–6, he remarked that "forbearing in love" for the church community means "the bearing of one another's burdens; yea, and lessening them by every means in our power. It implies the sympathizing with them in their sorrows, afflictions, and infirmities; the bearing them up when, without our help, they would be liable to sink under their burdens; the endeavouring to lift their sinking heads, and to strengthen their feeble knees."[1] Such mutual support was always particularly important for marginalized persons. For example, the black church in the United States has historically been a place where Christian discipleship supported the wholeness and worth of black humanity, "striving for one spirit" in the face of white oppression. Historically, the African American church functioned as an alternative *koinōnia* where those enduring slavery or, later, segregation, could live as the fully redeemed, fully persons they knew themselves to be.

Yet this collective identity grounded in love and compassion can face challenges when it moves beyond the immediate Christian community to those in the world who live outside its boundaries. Starting with the teachings of Jesus and the letters of Paul, it has been evident that love and compassion and solidarity should be shown not just within the Christian community but within the entire world. The scope of this calling might not have been so evident in Paul's time, as the Christian community was building its new identity in a hostile world, where the boundaries would necessarily be strongly drawn and the need was for support of their own. Nor

---

1. John Wesley, "Of the Church," Sermon 74, http://Wesley.nnu.edu/john-wesley/the-sermons-of-john-wesley-1872-edition/sermon-74-of-the-church/.

is it so visible when the Christian community *is* the world, as is true in any Christian state, so that the mandates for caring for the poor and marginalized can be understood simply as outreach to Christian outcasts in a Christian society.

We live now, however, in a society where we find ourselves one among many faiths, including many persons with no faith. How do we understand what it means to "remain in the flesh," loving those around us? Martin Luther King Jr. saw love for all humanity as the central practice for Christians. "*Agape*," he wrote, "is understanding, creative, redemptive good will toward all men [sic]."[2] Transformative Christian practices of solidarity, rooted in love for humans and, increasingly, other created entities, embrace others in the concreteness of their flawed magnificence. Love is particular, not general. As Bonhoeffer said in *Life Together*, "The person who loves their dream of community will destroy community, but the person who loves those around them will create community."[3]

As we seek to "remain in the flesh," I suggest two lenses to shape our actions: seeing love's range and seeing love's ordinariness.

Seeing Love's Range. Many US churches have long had special relationships with immigrants and refugees. For example, the United Nations High Commissioner for Refugees, the UN refugee agency, lists nine refugee resettlement agencies in the United States, of which five are Christian based. Each of these organizations shows a very particular love that spans a wide range of levels and types. Love can be shown through the time-consuming and challenging paperwork, fundraising, and organizing required for hosting those arriving from overseas. It can be shown in lobbying and advocating for laws supporting the lives of refugees and immigrants—or resisting laws and policies that harm those lives. It can be shown through the funds or love offerings that congregations, groups, and individuals send. It can be shown through the education programs on refugees presented in communities and congregations. And it can be shown in the concrete day-to-day work of staff and volunteers who prepare and furnish new homes, greet and settle families when they arrive, serve as mentors or after-school tutors.

Seeing Love's Ordinariness. Those of us who have spent time working in prisons know the powerful impact of the smallest gestures of love. By law, prisoners can have very few personal possessions, and what they can have is carefully regulated, by rules that vary widely from state to state, and even prison to prison. Often their allowances are as minimal as two pairs of shoes and a pair of slippers, one watch, one radio, perhaps twenty-five photographs, and a few books. There is no right to personal property in prison, so prisoners' possessions can be confiscated at any moment or strewn across the floor in the regular searches of prison living quarters for contraband, which includes everything from sharp blades or cell phones to an extra book or notebook.

In this atmosphere, expressions of love are important reminders of dignity, worth, and humanity. Love is shown by the care volunteers may spend in choosing books and supplies for groups or classes, by the smiles and greetings offered (touch is generally banned), and by the regularity of simple presence. Love happens when an incarcerated woman does not choose the one remaining purple notebook in class because she knows that is the favorite color of the woman across the room; when an incarcerated man hands another man a stamp, knowing that he has no family or friends to send money for the prison account enabling any purchases.

By practicing such love within and beyond the church, we come close to Paul's ideal, to "live [our] life in a manner worthy of the gospel of Christ" (v. 27).

ELIZABETH M. BOUNDS

---

2. Martin Luther King Jr., "A Christmas Sermon on Peace (1967)," in *A Testament of Hope: The Essential Writings and Speeches*, ed. James L. Washington (New York: HarperCollins, 1986), 256.
3. Dietrich Bonhoeffer, *Life Together* (New York: Harper & Row, 1954), 327.

Proper 20 (Sunday between September 18 and September 24 inclusive)

Matthew 20:1–16

¹"For the kingdom of heaven is like a landowner who went out early in the morning to hire laborers for his vineyard. ²After agreeing with the laborers for the usual daily wage, he sent them into his vineyard. ³When he went out about nine o'clock, he saw others standing idle in the marketplace; ⁴and he said to them, 'You also go into the vineyard, and I will pay you whatever is right.' So they went. ⁵When he went out again about noon and about three o'clock, he did the same. ⁶And about five o'clock he went out and found others standing around; and he said to them, 'Why are you standing here idle all day?' ⁷They said to him, 'Because no one has hired us.' He said to them, 'You also go into the vineyard.' ⁸When evening came, the owner of the vineyard said to his manager, 'Call the laborers and give them their pay, beginning with the last and then going to the first.' ⁹When those hired about five o'clock came, each of them received the usual daily wage. ¹⁰Now when the first came, they thought they would receive more; but each of them also received the usual daily wage. ¹¹And when they received it, they grumbled against the landowner, ¹²saying, 'These last worked only one hour, and you have made them equal to us who have borne the burden of the day and the scorching heat.' ¹³But he replied to one of them, 'Friend, I am doing you no wrong; did you not agree with me for the usual daily wage? ¹⁴Take what belongs to you and go; I choose to give to this last the same as I give to you. ¹⁵Am I not allowed to do what I choose with what belongs to me? Or are you envious because I am generous?' ¹⁶So the last will be first, and the first will be last."

Commentary 1: Connecting the Reading with Scripture

The logion at the end of the lection, "So the last will be first, and the first will be last," is a repetition (though in reverse order) of 19:30 and frames the parable. We expect then that the parable will focus on this reversal of status. We are in for a surprise.

The common premise is that the landowner represents God, the vineyard is Israel, and the laborers are the people of Israel. Jews in the time of Jesus would recognize this image, but the reader should first pay attention to the dynamics of the story itself.

The common title is something like the parable of the Laborers in the Vineyard, but the story would be better titled the parable of the Generous Householder.

The bulk of the parable does not address the specific issue of the first and last. Only the payment scene actually produces the reversal. The parable focuses first on the sequential hiring of laborers through the day, then on the payment schema, and finally on the discussion with the first workers. The objection of the first hired is not to the *order* of payment, but rather the *fairness* of equal payment for unequal work.

As is common with Matthew, the narrative is long on detail and short on explanation. Questions abound: Why did the householder make several trips to the market? Why did he give the same wages to all? What does "whatever is right" mean? Why did he not make wage arrangements with the last group of workers? What were they doing all day? The lack of answers to these and many other questions leads interpreters to inventive explanations. One should take care not to impose too ambitiously on the narrative.

In the history of interpretation, this parable has sometimes been given a supersessionist construal: the grumbling Jews object to the equal inclusion of Gentiles, or the legalistic Pharisees object to the works-free bestowal of grace, or Jewish Christians resent Gentile Christians. These interpretations do not reflect Matthew's theology. However hostile he is to the Pharisees and elders of Israel, Matthew is not hostile to Jews and the Jewish tradition, as is clear in Matthew 5:17–20. His increasingly heated debates with the Pharisees, as in the lection for the following week, were a normal part of rabbinical debate over the interpretation of the law, not the legitimacy of it.

Some modern interpretations tilt toward agonistic economics, the last workers being the dispossessed, or to ethnic meanings, the original workers being the dominant class and the later workers being minorities of some sort. All of these are avenues of interpretation, but none is clearly supported by the skeletal narrative itself.

These angles can lead to homilies highly relevant to current social issues, but at the risk of significant eisegesis. For instance, the narrative does not indicate that last group of workers are lazy, or otherwise different from those hired earlier, except for the time of their discovery by the householder. It is possible that they will return the next day for the full stretch.

Matthew is commonly divided into five blocks, parallel to the Pentateuch or Wisdom literature, of which the fourth goes from 16:21 to 25:46.

The block begins with Jesus' first prediction of his death. This continues to be a theme throughout the section, and indeed frames the section, 16:27–28 paralleling 25:30–31. The focus is on the disciples, rather than the crowds or the Jewish leaders. The third section ends with the declaration of Peter that Jesus is the Messiah, and Jesus' response that Peter will be the foundation of the church. The Twelve have difficulty comprehending both the reality of Jesus' impending crucifixion and the implications for their subsequent responsibilities. Jesus regularly provides parabolic analogies for the dynamic of kingdom of heaven/God, but the disciples struggle to grasp the concept. Would that he would be clear!

The issue of status, encapsulated by the logion framing our lection, is one theme, seen in the elevation of children and the response to the mother of James and John concerning seating arrangements in heaven. Another theme is the responsibility of the powerful: the householder, the rich young man, and the unforgiving servant. This latter motif is too often overlooked.

The declaration in 16:18 that Peter will be the foundation of the church raises the fundamental concern of the section: what kind of church, and what kind of leaders, will reveal the kingdom of heaven? In contrast to the rich young man, the disciples have left everything. They will be rewarded. They will also be tried and convicted by an unappreciative society.

The association with the other lectionary texts provides interesting contrasts and similarities on the themes of suffering and gratitude. The two psalms, 105 and 145, give strong expressions of gratitude. The last verse in the Psalm 145 lection is quoted by Jonah in 4:2. Psalm 105 rehearses God's protection of Israel from the covenanting with Abraham to the entry into Canaan, including the gift of manna that is the focus of the Exodus lection.

The manna story in Exodus records the suffering, or putative suffering, of Israel in the wilderness. They compare their hunger with their memory of "fleshpots" in Egypt. They complain to Moses, who defers to God, who provides manna and quail. There is no mention as to whether they are grateful for this generous response. Each is provided "enough" (Exod. 16:4), no matter how much they have gathered (v. 18), just as the workers of the vineyard are all given enough, no matter how much they had worked.

The Jonah passage provides a different angle. Jonah's suffering, while real—baking in the scorching sun—is largely self-imposed, or at least earned. While Israel complains to Moses in the desert, Jonah goes further, being angry directly with God (having no one else to blame). While his prayer from the belly of the fish, when he was really in danger, was formal and contrite, his prayer at the loss of shade is bitter and despairing. As with Israel, we do not know how he responded to God's logic of generosity at the end of the story.

Finally, in Philippians, Paul suffers in jail, but rejects despair (unlike the Israelites and Jonah) in favor of dutiful commitment, in contrast to

Jonah's grudging preaching to the Ninevites (he did it, but with the expectation, even hope, of failure). Paul recognizes that the church in Philippi has "the same struggle" (Phil. 1:30) in the face of opponents. He is nevertheless persistently grateful to God and expects the church to be so also.

The four stories (Israel with the manna, Jonah with the bush and the Ninevites, Paul with jail and the church at Philippi, and the workers in the vineyard) share a concern for suffering, despair, and gratitude, but each conceives the relationship among the three differently, according to context, but even more according to the actions and reflections of the actors.

Relative rank and the reversal or upsetting of perceived order is a major theme in Scripture. Younger sons become more prominent than older sons (Isaac, Jacob, David). In the New Testament this reversal is more associated with Luke than with Matthew (Luke 1:52 in the Magnificat, the Nazareth manifesto in chap. 4, and Lazarus and the rich man in chap. 16), but Matthew also makes this point.

The parable of the Generous Householder not only creates a reversal of status, but also indicates the generosity of God regardless of status. The first shall be last and the last shall be first, but everyone has to show up.

WHITNEY BODMAN

Commentary 2: Connecting the Reading with the World

At the heart of this parable lies a deadly sin: envy. The laborers who have done a full day's work are angry because they are receiving the same wage as laborers who have toiled less than an hour. The landowner chides the disgruntled workers, asking rhetorically, "Am I not allowed to do what I choose with what belongs to me? Or are you envious because I am generous?' (Matt. 20:15). In Greek, this last question reads, "Is your eye evil because I am good?" Given what scientists have discovered about envy, it is not just the eye that is evil.

Researchers have long known that human beings are hardwired to compare themselves to other members of their group or tribe. Noting the success, or failure, of peers is how individuals determine their place in a hierarchy. Such comparisons can give rise to positive feelings like ambition and empathy, or negative feelings like malice and envy. Even primates are sensitive to comparisons or perceived injustice. Psychologist and primatologist Frans de Waal conducted a study with monkeys in which all the monkeys did the same task, but when the rewards were handed out, one group received a better reward for their work.[1] When the monkeys were asked to perform the task again, the group who had received the lesser reward refused to work. Whether the reward is a denarius or bananas, everyone wants to be treated fairly.

Scientists suggest that envy is a useful tool for keeping a community in balance. Hierarchies exist in every society, but in the strongest communities, there is not much distance between the top and the bottom. When there is growing inequality in a society, envy signals that there is a problem, allowing the community to address it.

Yet envy can also cause real problems. Recent studies have found that people who regularly use apps like Facebook or Twitter are more likely to suffer from depression and other mental health problems than people who do not use social media. Remember, the central conflict in the parable arises when the first workers *see* that the workers they deem less worthy have received the same reward. This undermines their own sense of worth. In the same way, the rise of social media has created a culture where people constantly compare themselves to others, only to find themselves lacking. Facebook, Twitter, and Instagram are designed to generate dangerous amounts of envy.

If envy is a sin, research proves it is one that we come by honestly. One way to address this in

---

1. Frans de Waal, "Do Animals Have Morals?," *TED Radio Hour*, podcast audio, September 5, 2014; https://www.npr.org/2014/08/15/338936897/do-animals-have-morals.

a sermon is to differentiate between this world and the kingdom of God. Evolution has bred into us the ability to make comparisons and the desire to attain more. God's realm, on the other hand, is a place of plenty and wholeness, where the human hierarchies disappear and every person, regardless of rank or resource, has a place at the table. How does this text speak to us, if envy is human but sharing is divine?

Another way to connect to this text is to consider the ethical implications of the parable. In the story, God is the landowner who decides what is fair and what is right. The workers who began work early in the morning are angry when those who arrived later are given the same reward. Yet the text does not say those first workers were more capable or more talented; it notes only the time they arrived at the vineyard. They arrived first.

The current debate about immigration policies also centers around time of arrival. Some people argue that the United States should restrict immigration, because they believe immigrants are undesirable. Anti-immigration politicians and pundits have called immigrants "criminals" and "deviants," suggesting that immigrants are ruining this country. "Go back to where you came from" is their cri de coeur. What is ironic about this attitude is that the United States is a nation of immigrants. Some people just arrived earlier than others.

Jennifer Mendelsohn has taken it upon herself to remind politicians and pundits of their immigrant roots.[2] Using the internet and genealogy sites, Mendelsohn traces the ancestry of immigration critics and tweets the results. One prominent pundit who said the United States should welcome only English speakers had a great-grandmother who spoke only Yiddish. A commentator who called for harsher punishments for immigrants who break the law had a Russian great-great-grandfather who was indicted on charges of forging his immigration papers. Mendelsohn knows that most Americans came from someplace else; some of us just got here earlier than others. Despite what we tell ourselves, arriving early is a matter of luck, not personal virtue or merit.

When a preacher addresses the plight of immigrants, it is important to remember that God does not reward us based on what we deserve. We all fall short of the glory of God, which suggests we are all late-day laborers. Yet God still gives us what we need. This text raises the question, If Jesus means what he says, that "the last will be first, and the first will be last," then what are the ethical implications for the way we think about immigration in the United States?

For preachers who are searching for a contemporary connection to this parable, one need look no further than the story of Dan Price, the CEO of Gravity Payments in Seattle.[3] In 2015, Price announced that he was slashing his own million-dollar salary in order to raise the base salary for workers at his company to $70,000. Price, who was raised in a conservative Christian home, determined that $70,000 was the minimum amount a person needed in order to live in the Seattle area. His business advisors thought he was crazy, but since Price was willing to bear the cost of the increase himself, they let him do it.

At first, Price was celebrated as a champion of a true living wage, someone who was addressing the problem of growing income inequality in the United States. He was hailed as a hero of the working class, and analysts predicted that other businesses would follow his example.

Unfortunately, not everyone was happy about Price's decision. Gravity Payments lost some clients who feared that their fees would increase in order to pay for this social experiment. Price was accused of driving wages up in the Seattle area, which critics said would lead to unemployment. More importantly, Price lost some talented employees who left because they felt slighted. They grumbled against the CEO, saying it did not seem fair to double the pay of new hires while long-time employees got only a modest raise.

---

2. Jennifer Mendelsohn; www.resistancegenealogy.com.
3. Patricia Cohen, "One Company's New Minimum Wage: $70,000 a Year," *New York Times*, April 14, 2015; https://www.nytimes.com/2015/04/14/business/owner-of-gravity-payments-a-credit-card-processor-is-setting-a-new-minimum-wage-70000-a-year.html.

Despite this criticism, Dan Price has held firm, and it seems to be paying off. Gravity Payments has gained dozens of new clients, and the productivity and morale of its employees have improved remarkably. Wages in the Seattle area have not skyrocketed, though some business owners, inspired by Price's bold move, have raised entry-level pay. For Dan Price, paying people a fair wage has brought out the best in many workers. So often, sermons focus on the outrage of the full-day workers. This modern retelling of the parable lifts up the perspective of the short-day workers. What is the kingdom of God like for them? Why do so many of us think we are the first ones hired? A change of perspective may reveal new insights.

SHAWNTHEA MONROE

Proper 21 (Sunday between September 25 and October 1 inclusive)

Ezekiel 18:1–4, 25–32 and
   Exodus 17:1–7
Psalm 25:1–9 and Psalm 78:1–4, 12–16

Philippians 2:1–13
Matthew 21:23–32

Ezekiel 18:1–4, 25–32

¹The word of the LORD came to me: ²What do you mean by repeating this proverb concerning the land of Israel, "The parents have eaten sour grapes, and the children's teeth are set on edge"? ³As I live, says the Lord GOD, this proverb shall no more be used by you in Israel. ⁴Know that all lives are mine; the life of the parent as well as the life of the child is mine: it is only the person who sins that shall die. . . .

²⁵Yet you say, "The way of the Lord is unfair." Hear now, O house of Israel: Is my way unfair? Is it not your ways that are unfair? ²⁶When the righteous turn away from their righteousness and commit iniquity, they shall die for it; for the iniquity that they have committed they shall die. ²⁷Again, when the wicked turn away from the wickedness they have committed and do what is lawful and right, they shall save their life. ²⁸Because they considered and turned away from all the transgressions that they had committed, they shall surely live; they shall not die. ²⁹Yet the house of Israel says, "The way of the Lord is unfair." O house of Israel, are my ways unfair? Is it not your ways that are unfair?

³⁰Therefore I will judge you, O house of Israel, all of you according to your ways, says the Lord GOD. Repent and turn from all your transgressions; otherwise iniquity will be your ruin. ³¹Cast away from you all the transgressions that you have committed against me, and get yourselves a new heart and a new spirit! Why will you die, O house of Israel? ³²For I have no pleasure in the death of anyone, says the Lord GOD. Turn, then, and live.

Exodus 17:1–7

¹From the wilderness of Sin the whole congregation of the Israelites journeyed by stages, as the LORD commanded. They camped at Rephidim, but there was no water for the people to drink. ²The people quarreled with Moses, and said, "Give us water to drink." Moses said to them, "Why do you quarrel with me? Why do you test the LORD?" ³But the people thirsted there for water; and the people complained against Moses and said, "Why did you bring us out of Egypt, to kill us and our children and livestock with thirst?" ⁴So Moses cried out to the LORD, "What shall I do with this people? They are almost ready to stone me." ⁵The LORD said to Moses, "Go on ahead of the people, and take some of the elders of Israel with you; take in your hand the staff with which you struck the Nile, and go. ⁶I will be standing there in front of you on the rock at Horeb. Strike the rock, and water will come out of it, so that the people may drink." Moses did so, in the sight of the elders of Israel. ⁷He called the place Massah and Meribah, because the Israelites quarreled and tested the LORD, saying, "Is the LORD among us or not?"

Commentary 1: Connecting the Reading with Scripture

Ezekiel 18:1–4, 25–32. On its surface, the meaning of Ezekiel 18 is straightforward: past sin and virtue may shape present circumstances, but they do not determine one's choice in this moment, nor do they determine one's fate. *This moment can be a turning point, for good or ill.* Individuals may turn from their own past and make new choices (Ezek. 18:26–28, 30–31). A new generation may turn from the course set by their forebears (vv. 2–3). The command, "get yourselves a new heart and a new spirit!" (v. 31) emphasizes both a capacity for change and the efficacy of human initiative.

To appreciate how this moral anthropology fits within that of the book of Ezekiel as a whole, biblical scholar Jacqueline Lapsley examines Ezekiel 18 in the context of the book's broader presentation and construction of "moral selfhood." Lapsley argues that in Ezekiel 1–33, a productive but seemingly irresolvable tension emerges between two divergent moral models: a "traditional" model (the one described above, particularly evident in chaps. 3, 18, and 33), in which human beings have moral choice and agency; and a deterministic model (evident in chaps. 16, 20, and 23), in which human beings are "incapable of moral action." A third possibility emerges in chapters 36–37, wherein the focus is shifted from action to knowledge (of God and self) and from humanity to God.[1]

Recognizing the complexity of the overall portrayal of moral agency and capacity in Ezekiel makes it possible to engage this passage out of the complexity of our own experience as individuals and communities, and to resist simplistic moralizing or reductive dichotomies. For example, researchers across a broad range of sciences and social sciences continue to uncover ways in which the old dichotomy, nature vs. nurture, must be replaced by a complex interactive model that recognizes a range of influences from family systems and genetic inheritance to environmental conditions, neuroplasticity, and more.[2]

Ezekiel prophesies to a people in exile, confronting the failures of their leadership (chaps. 17 and 19) and a new generation's grim refusal of responsibility for charting a course beyond disaster. In the midst of sick systems, traumatic histories, and destructive patterns Ezekiel adumbrates a startling capacity for newness (18:31) that responds and testifies to God's claim over all human life (vv. 3–4).

This week, each lectionary text accentuates and expounds this moral complexity and capacity for newness in a distinctive way. In a petition that resonates with Ezekiel 18:27, the psalmist asks God to forget the transgressions of their youth (Ps. 25:7) and instead to show mercy. Repeatedly, the psalm locates the key to salvation in knowledge of God and God's ways (vv. 4–5, 8–9); divine instruction will enable the sinner to do what is right. The christological hymn in Philippians 2 is followed by a daunting instruction: "work out your own salvation with fear and trembling" (Phil. 2:12). Yet, like Ezekiel's text, what may seem morally simplistic on the surface is revealed on closer inspection to be more complex: a person does not work it out on their own, but has God at work within them, "enabling [him or her] both to will and to work for [God's] good pleasure" (v. 13). Finally, the lively dialogue in Matthew 21:23–32 explores the persistence of God's teaching and grace in the face of human resistance and openness, unbelief and belief, vacillation and repentance. Together these passages both complicate our understanding of the relationship between God and humans (e.g., Phil. 2:6–7; Matt. 21:25–26) and locate this relationship at the center of our moral life.

Exodus 17:1–7. In the NRSV, this brief passage contains no fewer than five questions (Exod. 17:2[x2], 3, 4, 7). Physical thirst, fear of death, and confusion regarding the future finally crystallize into one question that displaces the others: "Is the LORD among us or not?" (v. 7). The story

---

1. Jacqueline E. Lapsley, *Can These Bones Live? The Problem of the Moral Self in the Book of Ezekiel* (Berlin: Walter de Gruyter, 2000), 78, 183, and passim.
2. See, e.g., Tabitha M. Powledge, "Behavioral Epigenetics: How Nurture Shapes Nature," *Bioscience* 61, no. 8 (August 2011): 588–92.

in Exodus 17:1–7 closely parallels a similar story in Numbers 20:1–13. Yet the story in Numbers, also associated with the place name Meribah, has by contrast only three questions, and none of them is directly about God. The final question in the present passage thus helps us to focus in on the driving theme at its heart. For the Exodus writer, the tradition of miraculous provision of water from a rock was not simply about geology or atoms of hydrogen and oxygen, nor was it only about what human beings need to survive. It was about a people desperate to know, Where is God in relation to us?

God's reply to Moses includes instructions for striking the rock and a promise that water will flow from it for the people to drink. It also includes an unexpected guarantee of physical presence: "I will be standing there in front of you on the rock at Horeb" (v. 6). Horeb is named only three times in Exodus: firstly, as the "mountain of God" from which the Lord summons Moses (3:1); secondly, in the present passage; and thirdly, following the episode of the golden calf, as the Lord struggles to decide whether the Lord will continue to journey with the Israelites (33:5–6). In each case the parties voice arguments and questions with touchiness and raw honesty. History matters, futures are mapped. While the name "Sinai" is better known as the mountain of theophany and site of the giving of the law, the alternate place name "Horeb" accents the deeply personal struggles between God, Moses, and the people. It marks the place of contention, as the names "Massah" and "Meribah" doubly assert, but also the place where God and Moses convinced and taught one another to stand up for the people God had chosen.[3]

Locating the story of water from the rock within this broader nexus of Horeb traditions in Exodus suggests another dimension to the question, "Is the LORD among us or not?" The Hebrew expression translated "among us" (*beqirbenu*, v. 7) means literally "in our inner organ(s)," and so perhaps also something like "in our (parched) throats," "in our (cramping) muscles," "in our (racing) hearts." Yes, they wish to know if God is present in their midst, and if this presence is more than a notion or metaphor. They seem also to ask, When we are suffering, does God know it? When we are faint and close to death, can God feel it the way we feel it?

God's first appearance to Moses at Horeb, from within the burning bush, signaled both God's attention to the people's suffering and God's choice to be in the fiery midst of it. God's standing before Moses upon the rock was a bodily testament to God's presence in the place of contention and thirst. What finally motivates God to commit once again to journey with the people is the intimacy between God and Moses: "I know you by name" (33:17). This place where God and Moses taught one another to stand up for their people was thus also the place where God came to know their suffering, need, and weakness. God's choice in each moment, to deliver, provide, and journey with them, was born not of distant concern, but of intimate knowing.

ANATHEA E. PORTIER-YOUNG

Commentary 2: Connecting the Reading with the World

Israel's troubles in the wilderness continue in this week's reading—including thirst, hunger, and now thirst again, followed by a military attack. Having obediently traveled from the wilderness of Sin to Rephidim, they expect to find the water they need, but there is none. Doubt, fear, and genuine need make them charge Moses with bringing them out of Egypt to let them die of thirst. Moses cries out to God in fear of his life. God answers his prayer and the people's need with one stroke of Moses' rod.

Waterless deserts are indeed deadly. In June 2017, migrants from Nigeria and Ghana were crossing the Sahara, trying to reach Europe for

---

3. Within Exodus, the word "standing" (*'omed*) recurs with God as subject only at 33:10, where it recalls God's past presence with the people and foreshadows God's final decision to journey forward with them.

a better life, when their transport broke down. Forty-four people died, including infants and children.[4] Advice for recreational hikes and military maneuvers in the desert includes charts of the drinking water required for various levels of activity and temperature. One source has estimated that each person required six liters per day when crossing the Sinai.[5]

In Exodus 16, God tests Israel with the discipline of manna collection. At Rephidim, water becomes their test of God's presence with them. Several Old Testament passages characterize putting God to the test as rebellion (e.g., Ps. 95:8–9; cf. Luke 4:12), but in our passage the need for water is genuine. God provides it and does not punish them. God supplies the people's need and answers Moses' cry for help by appointing Moses' rod as the instrument for bringing water from the rock.

The positive tone of this narrative makes it available as a metaphor for God's bounty in believers' lives. Fanny Crosby commemorated an answer to her prayer in time of need with the song "All the Way My Savior Leads Me." The end of the second verse says, "Though my weary steps may falter, and my soul athirst may be, Gushing from the rock before me, Lo! A spring of joy I see." God invites Moses and the elders of Israel to the rock at Horeb. This appears to be another name for Sinai, the next stop on the Israelites' journey (Exod. 19:1–2). Horeb, the mountain of God, was the location of Moses' call (Exod. 3:1) and the place where Moses and the elders of Israel would accept the covenant, see God, eat, and drink (24:10–11). As water gushes from the rock at Horeb, so the presence of the Lord is associated with abundant water in Psalm 46:4; Isaiah 33:21; Ezekiel 47; and John 4:1–15.

Like the thirsty Israelites in the wilderness, Ezekiel's audience also thought that God had not lived up to their expectations. God's actions should measure up, they should be correct. (The Hebrew word *tkn*, translated "fair" by the NRSV, has this sense.) The proverb they use describes the problem well: as victims of conquest and exile, they experience the consequences of their parents' and ancestors' sinful actions. Yet their generation uses this proverb to dispute that their suffering is commensurate with their guilt. Children do not literally taste the bitterness of the sour grapes their parents eat.

God's answer first affirms their sense of fair play, but then asks, "Is it not your ways that do not measure up?" Although their own past sins and those of their ancestors do not stand in the way of repentance and amendment of life, their present transgressions are death dealing to others and to themselves. Ezekiel 18 is not about the Last Judgment, as in Matthew 25:31–46. It is about the way we live this life, when being separated from God is an experience of death, but intimacy with God, faithfully praising and serving, gives abundant life. "All lives are mine," God says. "I have no pleasure in the death of anyone" (Ezek. 18:4, 32).

Repentance is a basic aspect of Christian life. In periods of revival, in the liturgies of many Christian denominations, in the regular confessions made before pastors or in small groups, and in the practices of private prayer, confession of sin and assurance of God's merciful pardon precede commitment to do better, to turn one's life around.

This pattern of repentance and amendment is expected even in public life. When investigations reveal their deviation from law or generally accepted ethical standards, public figures, government agencies, corporations, and other institutions are expected to confess their mistakes, ask for forgiveness, and reveal plans to make restitution and/or change their practices. They take these steps in order to survive, and they often do. It is easy, however, to be cynical about their sincerity and how thorough and stable the amended practices will be.

God's commands in Ezekiel 18:30–31 call forth the commitments and practices required for a person to turn away from sins and failings toward God. (Ezek. 18:5–9 gives a short list of transgressions to avoid.) The command to "get yourselves a new heart and a new spirit" (18:31) balances God's promise to give you "a new heart" and "a new spirit" (36:26), and provides

---

4. http://www.bbc.com/news/world-africa-40118370.
5. Israel Eph'al, *The Ancient Arabs: Nomads on the Borders of the Fertile Crescent, 9th–5th Century B.C.* (Leiden: Brill, 1982), 140.

Share in Christ's Rest

Many of the weaker sort of men give up the effort of faith, and do not endure the deferring of their hope. They seek things present, and form from these their judgment of the future. When therefore their lot here was death, torments, and chains, and yet he says, they shall come to eternal life, they would not have believed, but would have said, "What sayest thou? When I live, I die; and when I die, I live? Thou promisest nothing on earth, and dost thou give it in heaven? Little things thou dost not bestow; and dost thou offer great things?" That none therefore may argue thus, he places beyond doubt the proof of these things, laying it down beforehand already, and giving certain signs. For, "remember," he says, "that Jesus Christ was raised from the dead"; that is, rose again after death. And now showing the same thing he says, "It is a faithful saying," that he who has attained a heavenly life, will attain eternal life also. Whence is it "faithful"? Because, he says, "If we be dead with Him, we shall also live with Him." For say, shall we partake with Him in things laborious and painful; and shall we not in things beneficial? But not even a man would act thus, nor, if one had chosen to suffer affliction and death with him, would he refuse to him a share in his rest, if he had attained it. But how are we "dead with Him"? This death he means both of that in the Laver, and that in sufferings. For he says, "Bearing about in the body the dying of the Lord Jesus"; and, "We are buried with Him by baptism into death"; and, "Our old man is crucified with Him"; and, "We have been planted together in the likeness of His death." But he also speaks here of death by trials: and that more especially, for he was also suffering trials when he wrote it. And this is what he says, "If we have suffered death on His account, shall we not live on His account? This is not to be doubted. 'If we suffer, we shall also reign with Him,'" not absolutely, we shall reign, but "if we suffer," showing that it is not enough to die once, (the blessed man himself died daily,) but there was need of much patient endurance.

John Chrysostom, "Homily 5," in *Homilies on Galatians, Ephesians, Philippians, Colossians, Thessalonians, Timothy, Titus, and Philemon*, trans. Gross Alexander, in *Nicene and Post-Nicene Fathers*, series 1, ed. Philip Schaff (Edinburgh: T. & T. Clark, 1888), 6:492.

---

a realistic view of what it takes to turn one's life around. Christians can claim God's help to effect personal transformation, but gaining freedom from hurtful and sinful urges and habits is seldom instantaneous.

Christian practices that cultivate a daily sense of sinfulness and need for God's mercy help one to remain open to the transforming work of the Holy Spirit. The Ignatian prayer of *examen* is one example. Asceticism, ranging from abstaining from sweets during Lent to flagellation, disciplines the self and focuses attention on following Christ. Western law and culture define some traditional Christian practices of mortification as illegal, unethical, and psychologically unbalanced. We must not flog others or harm ourselves. Such practices linger in our speech, however, when we advise our friends not to "beat themselves up" over a mistake. Christians seek to obey God's command with promise, "Turn . . . and live" (18:32).

Wisdom and therapy from the social science professions and spiritual directors are culturally acceptable resources that can help Christians to modify their destructive, transgressive behavior.

The self-help implied by God's commands in Ezekiel 18:31–32 to "cast away your transgressions" and to "get yourselves a new heart and a new spirit" appears at first to be consistent with the therapeutic view of individual development identified by Robert Bellah and colleagues.[6] Individual value and responsibility can be expressed by monitoring, managing, and acting upon one's inner feelings, in order to build a life that "works for me." The commands in Ezekiel, however, are plural. Contemporary science such as family systems theory, credited to Murray Bowen, teaches that individuals are not

---

6. Robert Bellah, Richard Madsen, William Sullivan, Ann Swindler, and Steven M. Tipton, *Habits of the Heart: Individualism and Commitment in American Life* (Berkeley: University of California Press, 1985).

independent of others. The proverb in Ezekiel 18:2 proves true.

Even in a person's curated collection of voluntary associations, each member's failings become part of a common web of responsibility. The Bible does not address Christians as a loose collection of individuals. Rather, individual responsibility before God is to be exercised in community for the good of God's creation. The familiar images of the church as a body, a flock, a family, and a pilgrim people all remind us of our obligations to one another in Christ. Prayers of protest and repentance both have their place in Christian life.

PAMELA J. SCALISE

Proper 21 (Sunday between September 25 and October 1 inclusive)

Psalm 25:1–9

¹To you, O LORD, I lift up my soul.
²O my God, in you I trust;
   do not let me be put to shame;
   do not let my enemies exult over me.
³Do not let those who wait for you be put to shame;
   let them be ashamed who are wantonly treacherous.

⁴Make me to know your ways, O LORD;
   teach me your paths.
⁵Lead me in your truth, and teach me,
   for you are the God of my salvation;
   for you I wait all day long.

⁶Be mindful of your mercy, O LORD, and of your steadfast love,
   for they have been from of old.
⁷Do not remember the sins of my youth or my transgressions;
   according to your steadfast love remember me,
   for your goodness' sake, O LORD!

⁸Good and upright is the LORD;
   therefore he instructs sinners in the way.
⁹He leads the humble in what is right,
   and teaches the humble his way.

Psalm 78:1–4, 12–16

¹Give ear, O my people, to my teaching;
   incline your ears to the words of my mouth.
²I will open my mouth in a parable;
   I will utter dark sayings from of old,
³things that we have heard and known,
   that our ancestors have told us.
⁴We will not hide them from their children;
   we will tell to the coming generation
the glorious deeds of the LORD, and his might,
   and the wonders that he has done.
   . . . .
¹²In the sight of their ancestors he worked marvels
   in the land of Egypt, in the fields of Zoan.
¹³He divided the sea and let them pass through it,
   and made the waters stand like a heap.
¹⁴In the daytime he led them with a cloud,
   and all night long with a fiery light.
¹⁵He split rocks open in the wilderness,
   and gave them drink abundantly as from the deep.
¹⁶He made streams come out of the rock,
   and caused waters to flow down like rivers.

Connecting the Psalm with Scripture and Worship

Psalm 25:1–9. Psalm 25 is a prayer of petition. The psalmist begins with a humble address and an affirmation of trust: "To you, O Lord, I lift up my soul. O my God, in you I trust" (Ps. 25:1–2a). With sure confidence in God, the psalmist can now make petitions: "do not let me be put to shame; do not let my enemies exult over me" (v. 2b); "make me to know your ways, . . . teach me your paths" (v. 4). The psalmist believes that prayers will be answered "for those who keep his covenant and his decrees" (v. 10), because the Lord's "mercy and steadfast love have been from of old" (v. 6). Psalm 25 is an individual's prayer directed to God and a testimony to others about the merciful character of God.

Sometimes the character of God is expressed in judgment, as is evidenced in the Ezekiel text, with the Lord laying down the law: "Therefore I will judge you, O house of Israel. . . . Repent and turn away from all your transgressions . . . that you have committed against me, and get yourselves a new heart and a new spirit!" (Ezek. 18:30–31). The psalmist provides a way for the people of Israel to "get a new heart and spirit" through prayer that first praises and then petitions God: "You are the God of my salvation" (Ps. 25:5). "Do not remember the sins of my youth or my transgressions; according to your steadfast love remember me" (v. 7). With sure and certain hope, the psalmist instructs readers, "All the paths of the Lord are steadfast love and faithfulness, for those who keep his covenant and his decrees" (v. 10). God's true character of love and mercy is revealed to those who are faithful to the covenant.

The psalm's rich themes of transgression and mercy, sin and salvation, shame and steadfast love, can be explored in the sermon. Alternatively, a sermon could focus on exploring the spirit of prayerful petition that is countercultural. "Instead of living for self, the psalmist offers his or her life to God; instead of depending on oneself, the psalmist depends on God in trust; instead of seeking instant gratification, the psalmist is content to wait for God."[1] Homiletical wisdom can illumine the tension between seeing prayer as a way to get what we want and seeing it as a way to seek God's path and be led in the truth. In the end, prayer is less petition for self and more sacrificial offering of self.

In the liturgy, this psalm can be used as a confession of sin and an assurance of pardon. The prayers of the people can invite the congregation to share their own petitions of prayer, ending with the refrain "To you, O Lord, I lift up my soul" (v. 1). If the sermon proclaims prayer as an offering and openness to God's way, appropriate hymns would be "There Is a Place of Quiet Rest" and "Lord, to You My Soul is Lifted." Singing the hymn "In an Age of Twisted Values" could reinforce the homiletical theme of the countercultural power of the psalm.

Psalm 25 sounds like a penitential prayer asking a merciful God to change an individual soul. Closer reading detects a deeper purpose: a communal call to change the worldly culture to that of a godly culture focused on the transformative power of offering, trust, and waiting on a powerful and trustworthy God.

Psalm 78:1–4, 12–16. The superscription of Psalm 78, "A Maskil of Asaph," indicates the psalmist's purpose. The Hebrew root of "maskil" is *sakal*, meaning "to have insight, to teach." Whether a musician or an officer of the court, Asaph would have served in the temple during the reigns of King David and Solomon, witnessing both faithfulness and corruption. This teaching song begins with the plea: "Give ear, O my people, to my teaching" (Ps. 78:1), "I will open my mouth in a parable; I will utter dark sayings from of old" (v. 2).

Once the psalmist has the people's attention, he continues with the purpose of the teachings: "We will tell to the coming generation the glorious deeds of the Lord, and his might, and the wonders that he has done" (v. 4). Throughout the remainder of the psalm, the wonders of the Lord throughout Israel's history are described as "glorious deeds and wonders" (v. 4), as "marvels" (v. 12). They are recounted in great detail:

---

1. J. Clinton McCann Jr., "The Book of Psalms," in *The New Interpreter's Bible* (Nashville: Abingdon, 1996), 7:779.

"He divided the sea and let them pass through it" (v. 13), "He split rocks open in the wilderness, and gave them drink" (v. 15). The objective is not just to inculcate an objective history of names and dates. Psalm 78 has a "didactic interest: history is recounted in order to teach the people the meaning of their history."[2] Told as a creative and compelling recollection of a shared history, this "storytelling psalm" seeks to teach the people how to live in the present and to inspire faithfulness in future generations.

The shape of Psalm 78 is a pattern: "the gracious acts of God are followed by human disobedience, which in turn creates destructive consequences and necessitates God's gracious forgiveness and restoration if the story of God's people is to continue."[3] Throughout the biblical story, God's people can choose to obey God's way or follow the path that leads to destruction.

This choice is evident in the other Scripture lessons for today. In Exodus, Moses obeys God's command to strike the rock, thus miraculously producing water for people to drink. Despite God's provisions throughout the wilderness and the promise of freedom, still the people doubt: "Is the LORD among us or not?" (Exod. 17:7). Despite Moses' affirmation, the people must answer the question for themselves.

In the Gospel lesson, Jesus says the choice to believe has eternal significance: "Truly I tell you, the tax collectors and the prostitutes are going into the kingdom of God ahead of you. For John came to you in the way of righteousness and you did not believe him, but the tax collectors and the prostitutes believed him" (Matt. 21:31–32). Likewise, Paul writes to the church of Philippi, "Therefore, my beloved, just as you have always obeyed me, . . . work out your own salvation with fear and trembling; for it is God who is at work in you" (Phil. 2:12–13). Preaching about the choice between doubting God's presence and trusting God's promise throughout the journey of faith would be a fruitful offering.

The theme of choosing to follow God's way can be reflected throughout the liturgy: in the call to worship, the prayer of confession and assurance of pardon, the readings, and the music. An altar call or a reaffirmation of faith using the water of the font would powerfully reinforce the biblical theme. Hymns that focus on the history of God's faithfulness and the call to the people's faithfulness include "People of the Lord," "Guide Me, O Thou Great Jehovah," "Will You Come and Follow Me," and "God of Our Life."

Although knowledge of God's mighty acts in the past does not guarantee faithfulness in the present, Psalm 78, along with the day's three readings, teaches with the hope of calling forth a faithful response from God's people.

DONNA GIVER-JOHNSTON

---

2. Bernhard W. Anderson, *Out of the Depths: The Psalms Speak for Us Today* (Philadelphia: Westminster, 1983), 54.
3. McCann, "The Book of Psalms," 993.

Proper 21 (Sunday between September 25 and October 1 inclusive)

Philippians 2:1–13

¹If then there is any encouragement in Christ, any consolation from love, any sharing in the Spirit, any compassion and sympathy, ²make my joy complete: be of the same mind, having the same love, being in full accord and of one mind. ³Do nothing from selfish ambition or conceit, but in humility regard others as better than yourselves. ⁴Let each of you look not to your own interests, but to the interests of others. ⁵Let the same mind be in you that was in Christ Jesus,

    ⁶who, though he was in the form of God,
        did not regard equality with God
        as something to be exploited,
    ⁷ᵇbut emptied himself,
        taking the form of a slave,
        being born in human likeness.
    And being found in human form,
        ⁸he humbled himself
        and became obedient to the point of death—
        even death on a cross.

    ⁹Therefore God also highly exalted him
        and gave him the name
        that is above every name,
    ¹⁰so that at the name of Jesus
        every knee should bend,
        in heaven and on earth and under the earth,
    ¹¹and every tongue should confess
        that Jesus Christ is Lord,
        to the glory of God the Father.

¹²Therefore, my beloved, just as you have always obeyed me, not only in my presence, but much more now in my absence, work out your own salvation with fear and trembling; ¹³for it is God who is at work in you, enabling you both to will and to work for his good pleasure.

Commentary 1: Connecting the Reading with Scripture

The Philippians have just heard that Paul expects them to live their lives in a manner worthy of the gospel of Christ, "standing firm in one spirit, striving side by side with one mind for the faith of the gospel" (Phil. 1:27). What sort of behavior in their life together would lead Paul to conclude they were living in a worthy manner?

Philippi was a center for the imperial cult, a retirement community for veterans of the Roman army, and a city saturated in social hierarchies. According to Joseph Hellerman, persons displayed worthiness by what they wore, where they were seated, the offices held, property and possessions acquired, and names chiseled on buildings or plaques. If Roman society in general had become the "most status-symbol-conscious culture of the ancient world, . . . no region east of Rome was more quintessentially Roman in this regard than the colony of

Philippi."[1] Paul longed to hear that the members of the Philippian church were behaving in ways that were in accord with Christ and therefore completely contrary to the social and political behavior expected of Roman citizens.

Paul's encounter with a slave girl during his first visit to Philippi confirms Hellerman's observation about the city's culture. When Paul orders the spirit of divination to come out of the girl, her owners are furious because their financial status is threatened (Acts 16:19). Paul and Silas are brought before magistrates, men of political and social status. They are accused of "advocating customs that are not lawful for us as Romans to adopt or observe" (v. 21). As the congregation reads Paul's letter together, in light of Paul's initial arrest and his present incarceration by Roman authorities, surely these recently baptized Christians are beginning to ponder the consequences of leading a life worthy of the gospel.

Paul's imperatives for the worthy life once again emphasize unity: "be of the same mind, having the same love, being in full accord and of one mind" (Phil. 2:2). Then he gets specific, surrounding these imperatives with two litanies of communal behaviors that had to be anomalies in Philippian society. First, he positively assumes that there is, among members of the community, "encouragement in Christ . . . consolation from love . . . sharing in the Spirit . . . compassion and sympathy" (v. 1). These behaviors engender unity and lack hierarchy. Next, he calls out and forbids ambition, conceit, and self-interest, behaviors prized by Roman society. Finally, he commands their opposite: humility and regard for the interest of the other (vv. 3–4).

The leap is minimal from the behaviors considered worthy of a significant life in the Roman colony of Philippi to the behaviors presently prized in the social worlds of many North American Christians. Pride, arrogance, vanity, egotism are a few of the behaviors that emanate from self-important, so-called socially worthy lives as they are portrayed in the media. Depending on the community surrounding any congregation, social and economic hierarchies may include education, profession, lineage, political connections, or simply the block a family lives on. Naming some of these hierarchies will help a congregation hear the dissonance Paul is naming between Roman or American society and the Christian life.

Yet Paul is not aiming at behaviors that, when added up, make a person or a community Christian. Christian behaviors are made manifest in a community that has as its center "the same mind that was in Christ Jesus" (v. 5). That is why church leaders in various denominations are elected not to represent a constituency in the congregation. They are to "represent the mind of Christ" as they lead the people of God. This is daunting enough in the abstract, but Paul is about to increase the dissonance between the lives of the Philippians as Roman citizens and the manner of life that demonstrates the reign of God breaking into human history. What might a life worthy of the gospel look like if the leaders or the members of a congregation have the same mind that was in Christ Jesus?

Paul invokes a hymn to explicate or incarnate the mind of Christ for the Philippians. In the spirit of the first verse of "O Sacred Head, Now Wounded," Paul borrows the language of a hymn not his own, a hymn known as the kenosis hymn. Perhaps its words will help the Philippians understand the radically offensive witness they are to bear to the world, as they let the same mind be in them that was in Christ Jesus. In proper Roman society, in the hierarchy that ordered the common life, a slave was without honor, and a crucified slave embodied a humiliation and shame that was beneath being human. "That a crucified *kyrios* is identified in the ensuing verses as the one who is greatly honored by God . . . utterly redefines social relations as understood among persons in the ancient world, especially those who inhabited first-century Roman Philippi."[2]

There is a subtle distinction to be made here: Christ does not give up his equality with God but he lets go of it. "From now on, he is equal

---

1. Joseph Hellerman, "The Humiliation of Christ in the Social World of Roman Philippi, Part 1," *Bibliotheca Sacra* 160 (July–September 2003): 324.
2. Joseph Hellerman, "The Humiliation of Christ in the Social World of Roman Philippi, Part 2," *Bibliotheca Sacra* 160 (October–December 2003): 424.

with God *in the obscurity of the form of a servant*," Karl Barth writes. "The *humilitas carnis* [humility of the flesh] covers the *divina majestas* [divine majesty] like a curtain, says Calvin."[3] To have this same mind means that the Philippian Christian chooses to let go of any status in Roman society and to humble himself or herself, not as a moral achievement to be rewarded but by becoming who they are in Christ. To have the same mind that was in Christ Jesus means they will become, personally and socially, a community of crucified slaves.

The hymn ends with the one who humbled himself being the same one who was highly exalted by God. To repeat: this is not a reward but an identification. Who Christ is as the humiliated one is precisely the same one who is exalted. Likewise, let the mind of the humiliated one whom God exalted be in you. Notice that the actor in Christ's exaltation is God, a critical detail as we come to the end of this lection. In a phrase that some see as opening the door to works righteousness, Paul admonishes the Philippians at the end of the hymn to "work out your own salvation with fear and trembling" (v. 12).

The emphasis should be on the fear and trembling. Paul speaks of fear and trembling in 1 Corinthians 2:3; 2 Corinthians 7:15; and Ephesians 6:5. Again, Paul is speaking of humility in the presence of God and in relation to all others who are to be accounted better than yourself. To work out salvation *in humility* is to labor "side by side with one mind for the faith of the gospel" (1:27) in the presence of the "God who is at work in you" (2:13) so that your works are in accord with God's will.

This reading may be paired with Exodus 17, where the Israelites complain against the Lord for lack of water, or with Matthew 21, where the religious authorities arrogantly reject Jesus' authority. By grace, the work God has done for us, the mind God has given us in Christ Jesus is the mind of him who humbled himself and became obedient to the point of death, even the death of a slave on a cross.

CYNTHIA A. JARVIS

Commentary 2: Connecting the Reading with the World

Humility or humbleness is a foxy virtue. When these lines were first heard by early Christians, "Do nothing from selfish ambition or conceit, but in humility regard others as better than yourselves. Let each of you look not to your own interests, but to the interests of others" (Phil. 2:3–4), they must have been shocked. Humility would *not* have been seen as a virtue in the Greco-Roman culture of the time. Aristotle certainly had no time for humility, naming it as a deficiency of appropriate pride. In societies organized by fixed structures of status, those with power could and should have pride, while those without power had to settle for humility. Paul's championing of humility, his insistence on "regard[ing] others as better than yourselves" was a countercultural move, echoing Jesus' words that "the last will be first, and the first will be last" (Matt. 20:16).

What starts out as countercultural can easily become the status quo. The marginalized Christian communities grew larger and more powerful and eventually became the religion of the empire. It is difficult to be countercultural when, as John Howard Yoder put it, "state, economy, art, rhetoric, superstition, and war have all been baptized."[4] Thus Thomas Aquinas could describe the virtue of humility as "keeping oneself within one's own bounds, not reaching out to things above one, but submitting to one's superior," where Christian obedience seems indistinguishable from social and political deference. While for Paul submission was to Christ and Christ alone, submission to Christ easily slid over in later Christianity to become submission to whoever was socially superior.

With modernity has come a new emphasis on the human individual, considered as detached

---

3. Karl Barth, *Epistle to the Philippians* (Louisville, KY: Westminster John Knox, 2002), 62–63.
4. John Howard Yoder, *The Royal Priesthood*, ed. M. Cartwright (Grand Rapids: Eerdmans, 1994), 57.

from community, with potentially unlimited capacity. In a world where science and technology can be used to create wealth and power, virtue may be seen as resting in the power to control, far more than the capacity to serve humbly. As Reinhold Niebuhr put it, "there is a pride of power in which the human ego assumes its self-sufficiency and self-mastery... [M]odern technology has tempted contemporary man to overestimate the possibility and value of eliminating his insecurity in nature."[5] No wonder the word "humility," while no longer assigned to a particular social class, carries for us negative connotations of low self-worth. In a society driven by fame, there is little reward for hiding your light under a bushel!

Yet Christian tradition, following Paul's counterctultural understanding, has always contained traces of other ways of understanding humility. For example, those writing guides for monastic life talked a great deal about humility, recognizing the temptation for monks and nuns to turn humility into pride and compete to be the most humble in their following of Christ, creating only-too-human competitions and hierarchies. While abbot of a new Benedictine abbey, Bernard of Clairvaux wrote a treatise, *The Twelve Degrees of Humility and Pride*, to help the monks understand the practice of humility. "Good also is the path of humility, for by it truth is sought, love is reached, and a share of the fruits of wisdom is obtained." He traced steps away from pride and toward humility, walking in God's love toward "Truth," that is, the clearest possible understanding of self, others, world, and God, with "that direct vision which belongs to the pure in heart."[6]

Following Bernard, Christian humility does not require low self-esteem or a rigorous program of self-diminishment. The challenge is not to reduce the self but to reorient it, that is, to "let the same mind be in you that was in Christ Jesus" (v. 5). To have this mind is to walk toward the fullest possible understanding of ourselves and what surrounds us, including God. To have this mind is to live toward the perfect love, described in the First Epistle of John, that "casts out fear; for fear has to do with punishment" (1 John 4:18).

What might this humility look like in today's world? Here are two possibilities.

1. Finding time for meditation, prayer, and reflection to strengthen a self who can live fully and truly in the midst of difficulties, suffering, and joy. As a vast number of books and blogs attest, this is no easy work, as we navigate among multiple needs and demands in a world that is online 24/7.

The challenge is to be present in the "mind ... that was in Christ Jesus," which takes practice. To develop this mind, be alert to your reactions to your daily experiences, attending to feelings of aversion, anger, gratitude, joy, and the other emotions of daily life. Then find some moments of quiet (even lying in bed or driving the car!) to bring these emotions before yourself and God. Do not worry about missed moments, but "lift your drooping hands and strengthen your weak knees, and make straight paths for your feet" (Heb. 12:12–13).

2. Opening the self to see different interests, motivations, concerns, and suffering in any given situation, particularly where there is conflict. For example, we are struggling now with the presence of immigrants in the United States, an issue made even more complex because we in the United States take pride in being a nation of immigrants. Spend time learning about the history of immigration, recent policies, statistics. At the same time keep looking at the current immigration crisis from the perspectives of refugees and immigrants, US citizens with jobs and those without, political leaders and business managers, ICE officers and local police. Listen well to each perspective with humility, that is, with a suspension of judgment while you gather information and views. While you are listening or viewing or reading, pay attention to any thoughts, images, and ideas that occur to you. Be particularly aware if any biblical texts or spiritual writings become present.

Then spend time in prayer and reflection, by yourself or with others. Consider this text from Philippians, along with other images or texts

---

5. Reinhold Niebuhr, *The Nature and Destiny of Man* (New York: Charles Scribner's Sons, 1941), 1:188, 191.
6. Bernard de Clairvaux, *The Twelve Degrees of Humility and Pride*, downloaded from http://www.saintsworks.net/#Main.

that have emerged either in your time of listening or your time of reflection. In relation to immigration, what does "having the same love, being in full accord and of one mind" look like? How do we let the same mind be in us that was in Christ Jesus? Where do we see God "at work in [us], enabling [us] both to will and to work for [God's] good pleasure"? We may first find ourselves talking and thinking in a very abstract or general way, considering an overall Christian perspective.

It is true of course that immigration is too complicated an issue for any simple set of actions by one group of people. Yet it is important to press ourselves to be as concrete as possible, remembering how concrete were Jesus' words and actions, and how limited they might have seemed to those in his own time. Nevertheless the small concrete actions undertaken by him and those around him grew, like the mustard seed. Imagine yourself finding the particular mustard seed you can plant with others, and the work that goes on, including understanding the nature and needs of the growing plant, to ensure its flourishing.

ELIZABETH M. BOUNDS

Proper 21 (Sunday between September 25 and October 1 inclusive)

Matthew 21:23–32

²³When he entered the temple, the chief priests and the elders of the people came to him as he was teaching, and said, "By what authority are you doing these things, and who gave you this authority?" ²⁴Jesus said to them, "I will also ask you one question; if you tell me the answer, then I will also tell you by what authority I do these things. ²⁵Did the baptism of John come from heaven, or was it of human origin?" And they argued with one another, "If we say, 'From heaven,' he will say to us, 'Why then did you not believe him?' ²⁶But if we say, 'Of human origin,' we are afraid of the crowd; for all regard John as a prophet." ²⁷So they answered Jesus, "We do not know." And he said to them, "Neither will I tell you by what authority I am doing these things.

²⁸"What do you think? A man had two sons; he went to the first and said, 'Son, go and work in the vineyard today.' ²⁹He answered, 'I will not'; but later he changed his mind and went. ³⁰The father went to the second and said the same; and he answered, 'I go, sir'; but he did not go. ³¹Which of the two did the will of his father?" They said, "The first." Jesus said to them, "Truly I tell you, the tax collectors and the prostitutes are going into the kingdom of God ahead of you. ³²For John came to you in the way of righteousness and you did not believe him, but the tax collectors and the prostitutes believed him; and even after you saw it, you did not change your minds and believe him."

Commentary 1: Connecting the Reading with Scripture

Chapters 21 and 22 of Matthew contain a sequence of symbolic acts in and around Jerusalem, starting with Jesus' entry into Jerusalem and then into the temple, followed by five controversy stories and three parables that attack the leadership of Jerusalem. Jesus is justified as the legitimate ruler who will restore Israel to righteousness through humility. There is little narrative, and little focus on the disciples. Here Jesus claims his authoritative role.

In Matthew 21:23–32, we find one of the controversies with Jerusalem authorities, religious in the case of the chief priests, and communal/political in the case of the elders. These are different from the Pharisees and scribes, who are influential throughout Israel but have no official responsibility. The Pharisees inexplicably appear in the story at the end, in 21:45.

Why Jesus is allowed back in the temple to teach after his disruption the day before is not explained. Perhaps this is a measure of his popularity with the crowd, his command of the situation such that the authorities dare not intervene.

The issue of authority, paired with the hypocrisy of the traditional authorities, is the focus of this whole section, from the entry into Jerusalem to the Last Supper. The key to the entire section is 21:23, addressed to Jesus: "By what authority are you doing these things?"

The lection consists of two parts that do not fit easily together. In the first part, a crowd is listening to Jesus teaching in the temple. The chief priests and elders approach him with a question. The question is not about his teaching but, rather, about the source of his authority. Given the context, this is not only his authority to teach, but also his authority to heal and disrupt the temple grounds, perhaps even to make a demonstrative entry, laden with symbolism, into Jerusalem the day before.

Jesus' challenge to the authorities puts them on the spot. We do not know what they felt about the authority of John the Baptist, but we know, and they knew, what the surrounding, restless crowd thought of John the Baptist. Clearly the authority of the Jewish leaders was dependent on crowd affirmation, not truth.

Jesus follows this challenge with a parable about two sons, one of which refused to be obedient, but then changed his mind. The second, like Jesus' opponents, agreed with his father, that is, the tradition of Israel, but did not act in accordance with that assent.

There is a fourfold dynamic, a tension between the authority of the Jewish leaders, that of John the Baptist, the sway of the crowd, and Jesus. Taking them in order, the Jewish leaders have clear authority, and Jesus recognizes this (Matt. 23:1–3). It is not their authority that is in question, but rather the hypocrisy and corruption of their performance (vv. 3–7). In the parable the disobedient son is a legitimate son, but is not trustworthy. The parable of the Wicked Tenants in next week's Gospel lection also illustrates the relationship. It does not question the standing of the tenants; it convicts their actions.

This underlines the important point that the status of Israel is not displaced by the Jesus movement, Christians, or Christianity. It is Israel's leaders who are called to task for their failures of faith and righteousness. The Jewish crowd, the people, are more receptive.

John the Baptist is recognized as a prophet independent of Jesus, even at the time of Matthew's writing. He is a martyr, a contemporary of Jesus, showing that prophecy continues from ancient times. He is rejected by the authorities but admired by the crowd. He is "more than a prophet," which most of the crowd does not understand. He is the forerunner, the announcer, of one greater than himself. If the chief priests and elders do not accept John, they certainly will not accept Jesus.

The crowd is a common participant in the Matthean narrative. They are the counterpoint to the various authorities. Through much of Matthew they are a constant, positively disposed toward Jesus, though often perplexed (who isn't?). The authorities do not have the loyalty of the people. John and Jesus can claim this, though the crowds, or some of them, turn against Jesus at the trial and crucifixion. They can be fickle.

Jesus is the constant. He will not claim his authority here. Others must come to their own conclusions. We must come to our conclusions. The elders and priests recognize the influence of Jesus, but seek to limit it, to undermine it. Do not we do the same? In what ways, the preacher might ask? The crowd recognizes authority *in* Jesus, but do they affirm the authority *of* Jesus? They are followers as long as they are being fed with knowledge and astonished at the healing miracles. Are we able to be astonished?

If this is not rich enough, enter the tax collectors and the prostitutes. The tax collectors are the political underside (contra the elders), and the prostitutes are the ethical underside (contra the chief priests). They enter the kingdom first, being like the first son, rejecters (because of their sin) but invited (because of their repentance). The authorities, rejecters still, are delayed but not denied entrance . . . yet. For none of us is the final judgment written (7:1–5).

The other passages of the lectionary elaborate on several themes. Psalm 25 is a cry to God for guidance and instruction, "teach me your paths" (Ps. 25:4), which requires humility and a trust in the authority of the teacher, who "leads the humble in what is right" (v. 9). Ezekiel transfers responsibility for this move: "get yourselves a new heart and a new spirit" (Ezek. 18:31). This is addressed collectively to all of Israel. God's judgment assumes that the people have the ability to repent and "turn from all your transgressions" (v. 30).

This is precisely the responsibility that the Israelites refuse to take in the desert. In Exodus 17 they blame the lack of water—certainly a very real issue in the desert—squarely on Moses. It is only God who can relieve their thirst. God does so by instructing Moses to strike a rock, which then produces water. The elders are witness to this, but it takes Jethro, his father-in-law, to tell Moses to share authority and responsibility with other able people in the next chapter. The quarrelsome Israelites who, as Ezekiel describes it, have eaten sour grapes, constantly complaining of the unfairness of God and the incompetence of Moses, are given the responsibility to tend to their own heart and spirit and repent.

In Matthew's parable of the Two Sons, the first son professes obedience but acts in disobedience. The second son rejects obedience but then has a change of heart. He is open to the instruction of God, the counsel of his conscience, which requires the humility to recognize that he has transgressed.

There is no greater hymn to humility than that of Philippians 2. Paul starts by encouraging the community at Philippi to be of one mind, in full accord with one another. The model is the self-emptying of Christ. It is through such humility that Christ is given authority. The irony is that the relinquishing of power, the power of entitlement such as would be due to the Son of God, yields authority and the worthiness of worship. Hence Jesus rebukes the chief priests and elders: "you did not change your minds and believe [John]" (Matt. 21:32).

The question of authority bedevils the entire Bible. Kings and prophets are both anointed and commissioned by God, yet their portfolios are usually opposed to each other. Checks and balances? If so, how is Jesus both prophet and king?

WHITNEY BODMAN

Commentary 2: Connecting the Reading with the World

By the time the elders and the chief priests confront Jesus in the temple, conflict seems inevitable. Jesus is not just challenging their position as religious leaders; he is disrupting their understanding of the way God works and who God is. Rather than enter into a debate with Jesus about the nature of the kingdom of God, they question his authority: "By what authority are you doing these things, and who gave you this authority?" (Matt. 21:23b).

A cognitive neuroscientist might say the chief priests suffer from confirmation bias.[1] Confirmation bias is the tendency to take in only data that confirms a prior conviction and to discount information that does not conform to what we already believe. Confirmation bias is the reason Galileo was condemned by the Inquisition. It is also why politicians continue to debate global warming and pediatricians still have to explain vaccine safety to skeptical parents.

When a person receives new information that contradicts a long-held belief, the individual will make every effort to reject the information. He or she will try to discredit the information by disparaging the source ("Can anything good come out of Nazareth?" John 1:46) or by questioning the authority of the source (Matt. 21:23b). The further away the new piece of data is from one's current point of view, the less likely one is to accept it. In addition, studies have found that if a belief is strongly held, even overwhelming evidence is unlikely to bring about a change of mind. As Jesus says to his challengers, "Even after you *saw* it, you did not change your minds and believe [John the Baptist]" (Matt. 21:32b).

Although studies show evidence alone cannot change minds, it turns out change is possible if emotions come into play. When we make a positive emotional connection with another person, we judge him or her to be a credible source of information. This might explain why tax collectors and prostitutes were willing to follow Jesus; he showed them compassion and cared about them.

This connection to science offers possibilities for preaching, because it helps us understand why it was so hard for the chief priests and elders to accept what Jesus was teaching. It was not simply that they did not want to lose power or position; it may have been that the new information was simply too far away from their strongly held beliefs. It also gives the preacher a new lens through which to examine the differences between those who believed in Jesus and those who doubted.

The parable of the Man with Two Sons takes up only four verses in Matthew's Gospel, but what a punch it packs! The contrast is simple: one son *says* the wrong thing but *does* the

---

1. Tali Sharot, "I'm Right, You're Wrong," *The Hidden Brain*, podcast audio, March 13, 2017; https://www.npr.org/2017/12/25/572162132/.

right thing, the other says the *right* thing and does the *wrong* thing. Which son did the will of the Father?

History is littered with examples of people whose actions do not match their words, in good ways and in bad ways. The starkest contrast comes from the time of the Crusades. As described in John Mann's *Saladin: The Sultan Who Vanquished the Crusaders and Built an Islamic Empire* (Boston: Da Capo Press, 2017), during the First Crusade (1095–1099), the Christian knights who sought to free the Holy Land from the infidels did not act particularly Christlike. On July 15, 1099, the months-long siege of Jerusalem ended when the Crusaders, led by Godfrey of Bouillon, breached the defenses. Once they were in the city, the men who bore the sign of Christ on their breasts mercilessly slaughtered all the inhabitants: men, women, and children, Muslims and Jews. Eyewitness accounts tell of streets running with the blood of the dead. Even at a time of brutal warfare, the atrocities committed by the Crusaders drew criticism.

Fast forward ninety years. Saladin, the great Fatimid general, defeated the Crusaders in the Battle of Hattin (1187). Saladin then moved on to take Jerusalem and, after a short siege, entered the city. The Christian inhabitants of Jerusalem were terrified; they recalled what the Crusaders had done in 1099 and thought that Saladin would take his revenge.

However, Saladin was merciful. He granted amnesty to the Christians and set a low ransom price, which enabled the residents to leave the city. For those who were too poor to pay, Saladin forgave the ransom or paid it himself, much to his advisors' chagrin. The Jews, who had been banished by the Christians, were invited to return to Jerusalem. Saladin did not even destroy the Crusader churches; instead, he repurposed them. Anyone who has stood under the medieval arches of the Church of St. Anne in Jerusalem has witnessed the work of Saladin. Though largely forgotten in the Muslim world until the twentieth century, Saladin was hailed as the epitome of chivalry in medieval Europe and celebrated for his bravery, his wisdom, and his generosity.

Which son did the will of the Father? Godfrey of Bouillon or Saladin? The Christian faith is more than a set of words or ideas; it is a way of acting in the world. What is more important, getting the words right or the work right? That is what the preacher is invited to explore.

At a personal level, the parable of the Two Sons fills me with hope. My congregation includes many older adults whose children do not attend church. This "lack of faith" is cause for much concern among a generation raised to believe that church attendance is a requirement for salvation. These children are good people who donate to charities, volunteer at homeless shelters, and work at the food pantry, but rarely attend church. I often use this parable as a way to reassure parents that people who do good work are still doing God's will, even if they will not enter God's house.

There is a similar ecclesial anxiety among clergy when we note the rapidly rising percentage of young adults who identify their faith as "none."[2] Much ink and energy is devoted to figuring out how to lure these folks into church. This makes sense if our concern is for the future of the church, but our concern may be misplaced if we are worrying about the salvation of these young people. There is a growing body of evidence that millennials are generous with their time and their money.[3] They seek out ways to connect to those in need and have a desire to live out their values, not just write a check or make a pledge. In many ways, they are the first son: they say they will not do "the will of the Father," but at the end of the day, they do the work. Moreover, this generation that insists on putting their values into action may have something to teach those who sit in the pews on Sunday.

Jesus is trying to open the eyes of religious leaders to an expanded understanding of God's

---

2. Daniel Burke, "Millennials leaving church in droves, study finds," *CNN*, May 14, 2015; https://www.cnn.com/2015/05/12/living/pew-religion-study/index.html.
3. Nicholas Fandos, "Connections to a Cause: The Millennial Way of Charity," *New York Times*, November 3, 2016; https://www.nytimes.com/2016/11/06/giving/connections-to-a-cause-the-millennial-way-of-charity.html.

kingdom work. Thus an attentive preacher might see this short parable as an opportunity to redefine the boundaries of God's vineyard or even enrich our understanding of what it means to be faithful. Ask yourself, what is the work we are asked to do? Are there people who are not in the church who are still doing the will of the Father? What motivates their good work and how might that be a point of connection with the Christian community?

SHAWNTHEA MONROE

Proper 22 (Sunday between October 2 and October 8 inclusive)

Isaiah 5:1–7 and Exodus 20:1–4, 7–9, 12–20
Psalm 80:7–15 and Psalm 19

Philippians 3:4b–14
Matthew 21:33–46

Isaiah 5:1–7

¹Let me sing for my beloved
  my love-song concerning his vineyard:
My beloved had a vineyard
  on a very fertile hill.
²He dug it and cleared it of stones,
  and planted it with choice vines;
he built a watchtower in the midst of it,
  and hewed out a wine vat in it;
he expected it to yield grapes,
  but it yielded wild grapes.

³And now, inhabitants of Jerusalem
  and people of Judah,
judge between me
  and my vineyard.
⁴What more was there to do for my vineyard
  that I have not done in it?
When I expected it to yield grapes,
  why did it yield wild grapes?

⁵And now I will tell you
  what I will do to my vineyard.
I will remove its hedge,
  and it shall be devoured;
I will break down its wall,
  and it shall be trampled down.
⁶I will make it a waste;
  it shall not be pruned or hoed,
  and it shall be overgrown with briers and thorns;
I will also command the clouds
  that they rain no rain upon it.

⁷For the vineyard of the LORD of hosts
  is the house of Israel,
and the people of Judah
  are his pleasant planting;
he expected justice,
  but saw bloodshed;
righteousness,
  but heard a cry!

Exodus 20:1–4, 7–9, 12–20

¹Then God spoke all these words:
²I am the LORD your God, who brought you out of the land of Egypt, out of the house of slavery; ³you shall have no other gods before me.
⁴You shall not make for yourself an idol, whether in the form of anything that is in heaven above, or that is on the earth beneath, or that is in the water under the earth. . . .
⁷You shall not make wrongful use of the name of the LORD your God, for the LORD will not acquit anyone who misuses his name.
⁸Remember the sabbath day, and keep it holy. ⁹Six days you shall labor and do all your work. . . .
¹²Honor your father and your mother, so that your days may be long in the land that the LORD your God is giving you.
¹³You shall not murder.
¹⁴You shall not commit adultery.
¹⁵You shall not steal.
¹⁶You shall not bear false witness against your neighbor.
¹⁷You shall not covet your neighbor's house; you shall not covet your neighbor's wife, or male or female slave, or ox, or donkey, or anything that belongs to your neighbor.
¹⁸When all the people witnessed the thunder and lightning, the sound of the trumpet, and the mountain smoking, they were afraid and trembled and stood at a distance, ¹⁹and said to Moses, "You speak to us, and we will listen; but do not let God speak to us, or we will die." ²⁰Moses said to the people, "Do not be afraid; for God has come only to test you and to put the fear of him upon you so that you do not sin."

Commentary 1: Connecting the Reading with Scriptures

Isaiah 5:1–7. Isaiah's vineyard song precedes his call narrative, and so we might imagine that he is not yet an officially recognized prophet or well-known public figure.[1] For a moment, he is able to be sly, to play on expectations of genre, culture, and sentiment, in order to surprise his audience with a scathing turn that trades longing for loathing and tenderness for wrath.

The prophet performs his song for an audience whose taste in music he has studied well (a few verses later he will note how they love to dine together with "lyre and harp, tambourine and flute and wine," Isa. 5:12) and whose love of wine motivates their mornings and sweetens their evenings (v. 11). That is, Isaiah chooses a medium and a metaphor that will resonate with the audience, lulling them into complacency and sympathy with the song's protagonist. Beyond the motifs of music and wine, the song's agrarian allegory is close to home for most of Isaiah's audience. Even among the city dwellers of Jerusalem, farm life was the driving engine of Israel's and Judah's economies and the fertile seedbed of its people's imaginations.

Finally, Isaiah hooks his listeners, and readers, with the promise of a love song. A love song might be sweet or playful, charmingly humble or foolishly optimistic, but more often than not, a love song promises to break open your heart and rake it. It promises to hit us in a sweet spot of desire, vulnerability, hope, and frustration. It is where we give it all away,

---

1. Christopher Seitz, *Isaiah 1–39*, Interpretation (Louisville, KY: Westminster John Knox, 1993), 49.

full knowing we may get less than nothing in return.

The lectionary pairing with Psalm 80:7–15 echoes Isaiah's testimony to the strenuous labor by which God planted the vine and the devastation that would be wreaked when God chose to break down its walls. The psalmist asks, "Why?" (Ps. 80:12). Isaiah offers an answer.

Isaiah's performative gambit draws the audience in to experience God's desire, vulnerability, hope, and frustration, then arrests them in a startling indictment that expresses God's fury to the fullest. A famous wordplay reveals the prophet's verbal art, while simultaneously reminding us how easy it is to peddle our crimes as virtues. God hoped for justice (*mishpat*) from God's people, but saw instead bloodshed (*mispah*). Instead of righteousness (*tsdaqa*), God heard an outcry (*tsa'aqa*) (Isa. 5:7). To better grasp the wordplay, change a letter and notice that "vine" becomes "vice," "village" becomes "pillage." This was not how the love song was supposed to end. Isaiah's song provides important background for the parable in Matthew 21:33–46, suggesting that the "fruits of the kingdom" (Matt. 21:43) must include justice and righteousness.

Within the broader context of Isaiah's book, Isaiah's first vineyard song finds a counterpoint in a second one (Isa. 27:2–6). The later song does not lack the dark note of judgment found in the first song: "If it gives me thorns and briers, I will march to battle against it. I will burn it up" (Isa. 27:4b–d). Yet framing this threat is a repeated emphasis on divine protection (vv. 3, 5a), followed by a twofold injunction for the vineyard to make peace with its protector and keeper (v. 5bc). The vineyard that chooses peace will "take root, . . . blossom and put forth shoots, and fill the whole world with fruit" (v. 6). This image of Israel's replanting, new growth, and abundant fruit of justice signals a possibility for the future that could hardly be imagined after the promised devastation of Isaiah 5:5–6. It reminds us that Israel remains God's beloved, never losing hope in God's promise of renewal and abundance.

Exodus 20:1–4, 7–9, 12–20. This lectionary passage contains a condensed and simplified presentation of the Ten Words (the meaning of "Decalogue") or Ten Commandments that are the first of the laws revealed to Israel through Moses at Sinai. They provide summary, structure, and rationale for much of the legal material that follows in Exodus 20:22–35:3. With an eye on future, settled life in agrarian villages, these laws aim to shape and guide Israel's life in community with one another and with God. A second iteration of the "ten words," containing subtle but important variations, occurs in Deuteronomy 5 and similarly grounds and precedes this later compendium of laws, with a view toward shifting historical realities that included centralized religious and political leadership.

Two commandments are substantially shortened in the lectionary passage, perhaps for ease of recitation. The shortened commandments are the prohibition of making idols (Exod. 20:5–6 is omitted) and the instruction regarding the Sabbath day (vv. 10–11 are omitted). Each contains important theological rationale and explanation regarding how the commandment relates to God's own nature and action.

The longer prohibition of idolatry (vv. 4–6) presents a challenging theology: God is "jealous," holding children accountable for the sins of their parents, up to four generations. Yet stronger than God's impulse to punish is God's covenant love, extending to the thousandth generation. This hard saying raises questions about the relationship between divine justice and mercy, and does not allow easy answers.

In a modern context it can remind us that our own idolatries are not free of consequences for our children and children's children. The world we leave to them has been stripped of its natural resources and polluted by our greed. Meanwhile, children around the world labor as slaves to provide cheap goods for our continued consumption. Yet our sins cannot erase God's covenant love or the hope it holds for the future. This law finds a complement in the Sabbath law. The mandate to rest from labor is grounded in God's work and rest in creation, anchoring the Decalogue within a broader, cosmic story. It further guides us to value and protect the sacred freedoms of all humans, as well of the animals whose life and labor we benefit from (vv. 8–11).

Within the structure of Exodus, the giving of the law occupies the book's middle portion.

It is preceded by the familiar narrative of liberation from slavery and followed by the (often less familiar!) plan and building of the tabernacle according to God's instruction. Understanding the vital interrelationship between liberation, law, and worship is a key to interpreting the book as a whole and the place of these commandments within it.

From this viewpoint, God's ongoing and enduring commitment to God's chosen people precedes and makes possible their freedom. This freedom in turn is a precondition for assenting to God's law and is the enduring gift the law prizes and makes possible. The mobile tabernacle testifies that the liberator is also the creator and sustainer, and it becomes the site for God's enduring presence in the people's midst, leading them forward to a place of promise. Seen within this framework, the Ten Words take on further meaning. They are the foundation for a future of freedom and promise and are of one piece with God's plan for and good governance of all creation.

These connections illuminate the unity of Psalm 19, which moves from cosmic liturgy to a moving meditation on the precepts of God. The psalm portrays the law and its teachings as a gift that brings life, wisdom, and clear sight to God's servants (Ps. 19:7–8, 11). Far from viewing the law as a burden, the psalm describes a joy that culminates in praise and is shared with the celestial bodies (vv. 5, 8). The people's fear in Exodus 20:18–20 is a response to the thundering theophany they have observed, rather than a response to a life guided by God's words. The psalmist answers their fear with humility and delight.

ANATHEA E. PORTIER-YOUNG

Commentary 2: Connecting the Reading with the World

In November 2018 Alabama voted on an amendment to the state constitution that would protect displays of the Ten Commandments on public property. Dean Young, the head of the Ten Commandments political action committee, asserted that a vote for this amendment would affirm that the United States is a nation founded on the Christian God.[2] Historians dispute this claim, however, suggesting instead that the founding fathers reflect the overwhelming influence of Deism, Enlightenment, Whig, and other classical republican theories, in addition to Christianity. The founding leaders did not, it seems, create a specifically Christian state. The First Amendment to the Constitution of the United States explicitly prohibits the government from establishing a religion and from inhibiting its citizens from exercising their multiple faiths.

Are the Ten Commandments a Christian identifier, as Mr. Young claims? They certainly are. Although they do not appear in the New Testament in their entirety, various passages discuss one or more of them. A catechism for teaching early Christians, the *Didache* (alternately known as *The Teaching of the Twelve Apostles*), is a brief anonymous Christian treatise, dated by most modern scholars to the first century, which lists several of the commandments among other teachings on "The Way of Life." The Heidelberg Catechism, the *Catechism of the Catholic Church*, and Luther's Large and Small Catechisms all include the complete list from Exodus or Deuteronomy. Even the Anabaptist catechism by Balthasar Hubmaier includes, like the others, the Ten Commandments, the Lord's Prayer, and the Apostles' Creed. Theologians of the early, medieval, and modern eras, including, for example, Thomas Aquinas, Martin Luther, John Calvin, John Wesley, and Karl Barth, composed sermons and treatises on the Ten Commandments.

The Ten Words from God to Israel at Sinai have long been embraced as an essential component of Christian discipleship. There is no space in this short essay to pursue the various ways that Christian theologians have variously described the relationship of the Ten

---

2. http://whnt.com/2018/04/27/abortion-ten-commandments-on-alabamas-ballot-in-november/.

Commandments to Christian faith and life. It is worth our time, however, to notice some ways that these commandments benefit Christians and the church. Specifically, they prompt an awareness of sin, but they also uphold community. According to Aquinas, the law is about community under God, for which "there are two requirements: the first is that each member should behave rightly towards its head, the second, that he [sic] should behave rightly to the rest of his fellows and partners in the community" (*Summa Theologica* 1a2ae, Article 5). Luther compared the Ten Commandments to the laws governing a town where one wants to live, and the rules and customs of a skilled trade (Small Catechism, "Preface"; Large Catechism, "Preface," 2). A Christian, he said, should know the basic contents of the faith before enjoying its benefits, that is, the sacraments. The Heidelberg Catechism teaches that good works, in conformity with God's law, build community: "so that by our godly living our neighbors may be won over to Christ" ("Gratitude," Q & A 86). The *Catechism of the Catholic Church* cites Irenaeus: "Thus, through the Decalogue, God prepared man to become his friend and to live in harmony with his neighbor" (*Adv. Haeres.*, 4, 16, 3–4; PG 7/1, 1017–1018.)

Some descriptions of the Ten Commandments as teaching that advances the common good are based on an edited version, stripped of the contextual and cultural particulars. The lectionary text omits the description of Yahweh as a jealous yet merciful God (Exod. 20:5–6) as well as details of the Sabbath command that reflect a particular kind of household and the motivation based on Genesis 1:1–2:3 (Exod. 20:10–11). The Heidelberg Catechism includes the full text of Exodus 20:1–17, but Luther and the Catholic Catechism use short forms of the commands (e.g., "thou shalt sanctify the holy day," in the Small Catechism, and only Exod. 20:8–9 in the Catholic document). The short form lists resemble the way that the commandments appear on most public displays, including the charm bracelet I had as a child. This editing helps to support the claim that the Ten Commandments are universalizable ethical and moral principles of value to Christians in all eras, and also to all human communities.

A poll conducted by *Deseret News* in March 2018 showed that the "First Table" commands, from Exodus 20:1–11, are not considered relevant by the majority of "unaffiliated" respondents in the US and the UK.[3] Perhaps surprisingly, among some Christian groups only 50 to 75 percent said that these four commands are "important to live by today." There was wide agreement (more than 90 percent) however, that "you shall not commit murder" and "you shall not steal" are relevant.

The themes made explicit in the Ten Words can be found woven throughout Scripture, particularly in the Old Testament. Behaving rightly toward God and neighbor are also themes of Isaiah 5:1–7. The prophet introduces this poem as a song for his beloved, about his vineyard. One expects a love song, like the poetry in the Song of Solomon. Unlike the Song, however, loving care is met by betrayal. Instead of choice grapes, the well-tended vines bear putrid ones. The conclusion of the passage shows that this is not a love song after all. The vineyard story is a parable, told to justify God's threat of judgment against Judah and Jerusalem. As Nathan led David to pronounce judgment on himself by means of a touching story (2 Sam. 12:1–14), so this prophet uses a sung parable of betrayal to lead audiences to acknowledge their willful failure to flourish in the place and for the purpose that God had given them.

In American history, the Ten Words have sometimes been evoked for social purposes. Outcry and bloodshed were heard and seen in the fields of eighteenth- and nineteenth-century America also. According to scholars Emerson B. Powery and Rodney S. Sadler, some enslaved people were granted a Sabbath day of rest during which there were opportunities for their own distinctive worship services, learning to read, and even escape. Women and men who gained their freedom argued the case for abolition by calling attention to the hypocrisy of slaveholders who broke the Sabbath command

---

3. https://www.deseretnews.com/article/900014033/poll-are-the-ten-commandments-still-relevant-today-americans-and-brits-differ-and-millennials-stand-out.html. This survey used the Reformed numbering, and short forms of the individual commands.

by requiring work on Sunday. For the enslaved, this commandment was evidence of the just and righteous God in whom they believed.

The Talmud states, "Beloved are the Israelites, for God has encompassed them with commandments" (*Babylonian Talmud*, Men. 43b).[4] This line from the Talmud points out a connection between the cultivation of the vineyard in Isaiah 5:1–7 and the Ten Commandments. The people had rejected God's instructions and commands that had been given to them in order to create a community of *shalom*, characterized at all levels by justice (*mishpat*) and righteousness (*tsdaqa*). God hears a "cry" (*tsaʿaq*) from the vineyard (Isa. 5:7) that echoes Israel's crying out (*tsʾq*) in the throes of slavery in Egypt (Exod. 2:23). "Bloodshed" (*mispah*; Isa. 5:7) should not be found in a nation that follows God's way. In Isaiah, justice and righteousness epitomize God's purpose for Israel and the world (Isa. 1:17, 27; 5:16; 9:7; 16:3, 5; 28:6, 17; 30:18; 32:16; 33:5; 40:14; 42:1, 3, 4; 51:4; 56:1; 61:8).

PAMELA J. SCALISE

---

4. Cited in Marty Stevens, "The Obedience of Trust: Recovering the Law as Gift," in *The Ten Commandments, the Reciprocity of Faithfulness*, ed. William P. Brown (Louisville, KY: Westminster John Knox, 2004), 19–29.

Proper 22 (Sunday between October 2 and October 8 inclusive)

Psalm 80:7–15

⁷Restore us, O God of hosts;
  let your face shine, that we may be saved.

⁸You brought a vine out of Egypt;
  you drove out the nations and planted it.
⁹You cleared the ground for it;
  it took deep root and filled the land.
¹⁰The mountains were covered with its shade,
  the mighty cedars with its branches;
¹¹it sent out its branches to the sea,
  and its shoots to the River.
¹²Why then have you broken down its walls,
  so that all who pass along the way pluck its fruit?
¹³The boar from the forest ravages it,
  and all that move in the field feed on it.

¹⁴Turn again, O God of hosts;
  look down from heaven, and see;
have regard for this vine,
  ¹⁵the stock that your right hand planted.

Psalm 19

¹The heavens are telling the glory of God;
  and the firmament proclaims his handiwork.
²Day to day pours forth speech,
  and night to night declares knowledge.
³There is no speech, nor are there words;
  their voice is not heard;
⁴yet their voice goes out through all the earth,
  and their words to the end of the world.

In the heavens he has set a tent for the sun,
⁵which comes out like a bridegroom from his wedding canopy,
  and like a strong man runs its course with joy.
⁶Its rising is from the end of the heavens,
  and its circuit to the end of them;
  and nothing is hid from its heat.

⁷The law of the LORD is perfect,
  reviving the soul;
the decrees of the LORD are sure,
  making wise the simple;
⁸the precepts of the LORD are right,
  rejoicing the heart;
the commandment of the LORD is clear,
  enlightening the eyes;

⁹the fear of the LORD is pure,
 enduring forever;
the ordinances of the LORD are true
 and righteous altogether.
¹⁰More to be desired are they than gold,
 even much fine gold;
sweeter also than honey,
 and drippings of the honeycomb.

¹¹Moreover by them is your servant warned;
 in keeping them there is great reward.
¹²But who can detect their errors?
 Clear me from hidden faults.
¹³Keep back your servant also from the insolent;
 do not let them have dominion over me.
Then I shall be blameless,
 and innocent of great transgression.
¹⁴Let the words of my mouth and the meditation of my heart
 be acceptable to you,
 O LORD, my rock and my redeemer.

Connecting the Psalm with Scripture and Worship

Psalm 80:7–15. John Calvin introduced Psalm 80 with these words: "This is a sorrowful prayer, in which the faithful beseech God that he would be graciously pleased to succor his afflicted Church."[1] Psalm 80 is sorrowful, but between the lines of despair are signs of faith and hope. The reading begins, "Restore us, O God of hosts; let your face shine, that we may be saved" (Ps. 80:7). As the psalmist laments the current condition of destruction and despair, he also confesses confidence that God can restore and save, as demonstrated by God's past faithfulness: "You brought a vine out of Egypt; you drove out the nations. . . . You cleared the ground for it" (vv. 8–9).

Only from a place of steadfast faith can such a pointed question be asked of God: "Why then have you broken down its walls, so that all who pass along the way pluck its fruit?" (v. 12). The sorrow of despair, "the boar from the forest ravages it" (v. 13), turns to an earnest plea: "Turn again, O God of hosts; look down from heaven, and see; have regard for this vine" (v. 14). The psalmist ends with a hopeful chord, plucking the heartstrings of the Lord, by renaming God's rebellious people as God's own people, "the stock that your right hand planted" (v. 15). Throughout the psalm, sorrow and confidence are interwoven to create a hopeful song.

The braided stems of sorrow, faith, and hope are evident in Isaiah: "For the vineyard of the LORD of hosts is the house of Israel, and the people of Judah are his pleasant planting; he expected justice, but saw bloodshed; righteousness, but heard a cry!" (Isa. 5:7). We see that the people are sorrowful, but so too is God, singing a song that bemoans the fact that the people were not faithful, all the while wondering, "What more was there to do for my vineyard that I have not done in it?" (v. 4).

Mixed themes of sorrow, faith, and hope are also reflected in the Gospel lesson; Jesus tells the parable of the Vineyard Owner, in which the tenants beat and kill the owner's slaves and, to his great sorrow, even kill his son. The expected response is that the owner will "put those wretches to a miserable death" (Matt. 21:41). Jesus said to them, "Have you never read in the scriptures: 'The stone that the builders rejected has become the cornerstone; this was the Lord's

---

1. John Calvin, *Commentary on the Book of Psalms*, vol. 3, Calvin Translation Society (Grand Rapids: Baker, 1981), 295.

doing, and it is amazing in our eyes'?" (v. 42). This is the good news to preach: while we deserve condemnation and death, God, through Jesus the Son, gives us forgiveness and new life.

Liturgically, the psalm highlights sorrow and shame, along with the assurance of God's pardon. In a litany of confession or lament, use the repeated refrain: "Restore us, O God of hosts; let your face shine, that we may be saved" (Ps. 80:3, 7, 19). The hymn "O Hear Our Cry, O Lord" can be sung to express deep sorrow for sin; "Just as I Am, without One Plea" as an offering of oneself; "Amazing Grace" to remind us that we are saved only by grace; and "God of the Sparrow" to enable us to grope for the words to stand before an all-forgiving God and express our deep gratitude.

The sorrow, faith, and hope in Psalm 80 reflect the mixture of feelings of God's people seeking to live faithfully, but never quite able to do it, but for the grace of God.

Psalm 19. Within a series of royal psalms (Pss. 18–21), Psalm 19 "describes the orientation to life that faithful kings were supposed to embody and model for the people."[2] The psalmist points to the law of the Lord as "perfect" (Ps. 19:7), "right" (v. 8), "pure and true" (v. 9), and able to keep mere mortals "blameless, and innocent of great transgression" (v. 13). The benefits of obeying the law are plentiful: "reviving the soul, making wise the simple" (v. 7), "rejoicing the heart, enlightening the eyes" (v. 8), "in keeping them there is great reward" (v. 11). The psalmist, confident that hearers will heed his words and God's law, ends the psalm with a communal prayer: "Let the words of my mouth and the meditation of my heart be acceptable to you, O Lord, my rock and my redeemer" (v. 14).

The psalmist refers to the law given to Moses on Mount Sinai in the form of the Ten Commandments, found in the Exodus text. The law begins: "Then God spoke all these words: I am the Lord your God, who brought you out of the land of Egypt, out of the house of slavery" (Exod. 20:1–2). Before the law is given, it is put in the context of a God who made a promise to provide and protect. In essence, the covenant is one of promise ("I will be your God") and responsibility ("and you will be my people"), calling the people of Israel to be the people of God. Just as the introduction to the law is important, so too is the ending. "Moses said to the people, 'Do not be afraid; for God has come only to test you and to put the fear of him upon you so that you do not sin'" (v. 20). Moses declares that God's law is difficult to keep but made possible with a reminder that it comes from a God who has already shown steadfast love and faithfulness, and tests only so that people will stay away from sin and stay close to God.

For the Christian sermon, the preacher can turn to Philippians to bridge law and grace, with Paul humbly confessing and firmly exhorting the church: "Not that I have already obtained this or have already reached the goal; but I press on to make it my own, because Christ Jesus has made me his own. . . . I press on toward the goal for the prize of the heavenly call of God in Christ Jesus" (Phil. 3:12–14). Paul admits that on his own, he cannot keep the law, but by the grace of God and with the call of Christ, he can press on, trusting that ultimately God is not the cosmic enforcer of the law, but the merciful giver of grace. The preacher can use the law of Exodus and the grace of Philippians to call the church to a place of humble prayer: "Let the words of my mouth and the meditation of my heart be acceptable to you, O Lord."

C. S. Lewis considered Psalm 19 to be "the greatest poem in the Psalter and one of the greatest lyrics in the world."[3] Worship leaders can craft the liturgy to reflect the poetry and to resound the lyrics. Psalm 19 can be sung using "Let's Sing unto the Lord," "God's Glory Fills the Heavens," or "O For a Thousand Tongues to Sing." In addition to giving God the glory, people can be empowered by God's grace to keep pressing on toward righteousness, singing "Fight the Good Fight" or "Guide My Feet."

Psalm 19 calls people to faithfulness, keeping the law in response to the grace God has graciously and powerfully poured out upon God's people.

DONNA GIVER-JOHNSTON

---

2. J. Clinton McCann Jr., "The Book of Psalms," in *The New Interpreter's Bible* (Nashville: Abingdon, 1996), 7:751.
3. C. S. Lewis, *Reflections on the Psalms* (New York: Harcourt, Brace, 1986), 63.

Proper 22 (Sunday between October 2 and October 8 inclusive)

Philippians 3:4b–14

⁴ᵇIf anyone else has reason to be confident in the flesh, I have more: ⁵circumcised on the eighth day, a member of the people of Israel, of the tribe of Benjamin, a Hebrew born of Hebrews; as to the law, a Pharisee; ⁶as to zeal, a persecutor of the church; as to righteousness under the law, blameless.

⁷Yet whatever gains I had, these I have come to regard as loss because of Christ. ⁸More than that, I regard everything as loss because of the surpassing value of knowing Christ Jesus my Lord. For his sake I have suffered the loss of all things, and I regard them as rubbish, in order that I may gain Christ ⁹and be found in him, not having a righteousness of my own that comes from the law, but one that comes through faith in Christ, the righteousness from God based on faith. ¹⁰I want to know Christ and the power of his resurrection and the sharing of his sufferings by becoming like him in his death, ¹¹if somehow I may attain the resurrection from the dead.

¹²Not that I have already obtained this or have already reached the goal; but I press on to make it my own, because Christ Jesus has made me his own. ¹³Beloved, I do not consider that I have made it my own; but this one thing I do: forgetting what lies behind and straining forward to what lies ahead, ¹⁴I press on toward the goal for the prize of the heavenly call of God in Christ Jesus.

Connections 1: Connecting the Reading with Scripture

Even though the lectionary passes over Paul's unpleasantries at the beginning of this section of his letter, the substance of the aside that follows cannot be understood without attention to Philippians 3:1b–3. Paul's passionate rebuke of "dogs . . . evil workers . . . those who mutilate flesh" (Phil. 3:2) before our lection and Paul's boasting of his Jewish credentials at the beginning of our lection (v. 4b–6) are equally in need of the historical context given in Acts 15:1–35 and the theological context found in Galatians 2:15–21.

Most congregations may be kept from an anti-Semitic mishearing of the beginning of this chapter if they are reminded that the first Christians were Jews who believed Jesus had been raised by God from the dead and so were baptized. They continued to circumcise male offspring or converts, follow dietary laws, and live in obedience to Torah, even as they confessed Jesus as Lord, celebrated Christ's resurrection on the first day of the week, and recognized his living presence in the breaking of bread.

The so-called "circumcised believers" (Acts 10:45) could have continued as a Christian sect of Jews—except for the fact that God's Spirit inexplicably began falling upon Gentiles (Acts 10:1–11:18). Once the mission to Gentiles was seen as the work of the Holy Spirit (11:17–18), the church was faced with an inherently divisive decision: What of Jewish identity had to be assumed in order for a Gentile to be saved? Circumcision? Dietary laws? Obedience to Torah? Twenty centuries later, a sermon could begin by acknowledging the irony of first-century Jewish Christians arguing about how Gentiles will be saved in relation to twenty-first-century Gentile Christians arguing over the need to save Jews.

By the time Paul writes to the Philippians, not only Paul but also the apostles and elders in Jerusalem were on record as opposing the circumcision of Gentile believers in Christ (see again Acts 15:1–35 and Gal. 5:2–12). Nevertheless, Paul's words imply that the "circumcision faction" (Gal. 2:12), who had caused him no end of grief in Galatia, were now threatening to turn the church in Philippi against the gospel Paul had proclaimed to them. How could the Philippians be convinced that there was no need, in particular, to "mutilate the flesh" (Phil. 3:2b, a wordplay on circumcision) in order to be Christians?

Paul's rhetorical strategy often involves a boasting that is sometimes counterintuitive. Who better to oppose the campaign of "circumcised believers" than one who could outdo them in every aspect of Jewish identity? Paul uses a similar strategy when he boasts of outdoing the false apostles in his suffering in order to validate his own ministry (2 Cor. 11:12–29). Throughout Scripture and the church's history, the changed minds and lives of outspoken proponents of the way things are and have always been—those who once favored segregation or who opposed women's ordination or who stood against same-sex marriage—have often been used by God's Spirit to lead the whole church toward the new thing God is doing.

The turn for Paul from his life as a circumcised member of God's people to his life in Christ was radical. Everything about which he used to boast is now considered loss, even rubbish (Phil. 3:7–8). Unfortunately, when paired with the parable of the Wicked Tenants (Matt. 21:33–46) in the lectionary readings for Proper 22, Paul's utter rejection of his own righteousness under the law in favor of the righteousness that comes through faith in Christ (Phil. 3:9) could lead the unmindful exegete to find warrant in Paul's words for supersessionism. The sure antidote for such a reading is the rereading of Romans 9–11. Remembering that Paul is arguing against Jewish Christians, a more helpful parallel to the conflict threatening Philippi might be the continuing debate between those who are accused of works righteousness and those who are seen as skirting the literal demands of Scripture. Again, this was the first internecine debate among Christians!

Once Paul has done his best to discredit his opponents, he then does his best to communicate his life-changing experience of knowing Christ Jesus as his Lord. The loss of his former identity as gain is powerfully described by Karl Barth in his commentary on Philippians 3:8a:

Because Jesus Christ is the Reality, the Real Factor, the Agent, in whom the lofty is humbled, the solid shattered, assurance dispelled, man [sic] in his self-made goodness exposed . . . because this Jesus Christ is *my Lord,* so that in effecting all this he is absolutely authoritative for me, and because he has given me to *know* that he is my Lord—*therefore* I consider the whole thing loss . . . dung, in order to gain Christ and be found in him.[1]

To capture the before and after experience of coming to know Christ in a congregation of people who often think of themselves as "cradle Christians" is a challenge. Some may have had a conversion experience like Paul's. The things that may have mattered to them before Christ—the things that conferred status and identity within a particular social class, such as an academic degree, a promotion in the company, recognition for their generosity or service in the community, even holding office in the church, all good things—no longer matter. What is it that makes a person realize that even their highest achievements are rubbish when compared to a life lived in relationship to the love revealed in Christ? The "before and after" life of just about any character in Scripture (Abraham, Moses, Hannah, Isaiah, Jeremiah, Mary, Mary Magdalene, Peter) could be used to illustrate how the gain of knowing God and obeying God's call makes all past deeds and previous lives inconsequential.

Yet even the dramatic story of conversion Paul can tell is tempered by his acknowledgment that "becoming like Christ in his death" (v. 10) is more like the life of a long-distance runner than the victory of a sprinter. Most cradle Christians in the congregation certainly could testify to their slow and seldom steady growth in faith since they were presented for baptism as infants. In baptism, God made them God's own as they died to life without God and entered the community in whose hold, at its best, God's love would be taught and embodied. Paul's words about the gradual nature of faith's claim of a person also is a word to the community of faith. Together the church presses on

---

1. Karl Barth, *Epistle to the Philippians, 40th Anniversary Edition* (Louisville, KY: Westminster John Knox, 2002), 98.

Following the Will of God in All Things

The advantage of entering is so great, that it is well that none should despair of doing so because God does not give them the supernatural gifts described above. With the help of divine grace true union can always be attained by forcing ourselves to renounce our own will and by following the will of God in all things.

Oh, how many of us affirm that we do this, and believe we seek nothing else—indeed we would die for the truth of what we say! If this be the case I can only declare, as I fancy I did before, and I shall again and again, that we have already obtained this grace from God. Therefore we need not wish for that other delightful union described above, for its chief value lies in the resignation of our will to that of God without which it could not be reached. Oh, how desirable is this union! The happy soul which has attained it will live in this world and in the next without care of any sort. No earthly events can trouble it, unless it should see itself in danger of losing God or should witness any offence offered Him. Neither sickness, poverty, nor the loss of any one by death affect it, except that of persons useful to the Church of God, for the soul realizes thoroughly that God's disposal is wiser than its own desires.

Teresa of Avila, *Interior Castle*, 3rd ed., trans. the Benedictines of Stanbook (London: Thomas Baker, 1921), 140.

Finally, to live "forgetting what lies behind and straining forward to what lies ahead" (v. 13) is to live in response to God's promise in Jesus Christ. "A promise goes: 'Because I will do such-and-such, you may await such-and-such.' The pattern is 'because ... therefore ...,' the exact opposite of 'if ... then ...' Here a future is opened independent of any prior condition, independent of what the addressee of the promise may do or be beforehand."[2] Not "if" the Philippians are circumcised, "then" they will be true Christians, but "because" Christ Jesus has made the Philippians God's own, "therefore" they may live as a people who "rejoice in the Lord always" (4:4a). They may enter God's future as a community that does not "worry about anything, but in everything by prayer and supplication with thanksgiving lets [their] requests be made known to God" (v. 6).

toward the goal of life in Christ, but always the goal is ahead, just out of reach.

CYNTHIA A. JARVIS

Commentary 2: Connecting the Reading with the World

"*For his sake I have suffered the loss of all things, and I regard them as rubbish, in order that I may gain Christ*" (Phil. 3:8b). Throughout Philippians, Paul is stressing the worthlessness of what he terms "the flesh" in light of the reality of Christ. By living in that reality, Paul says he can live as "righteous," not on his own merits, by "having a righteousness of my own that comes from the law," but because of what is possible "through faith in Christ, the righteousness from God based on faith." (v. 9).

The two vectors of Paul's argument rest upon the opposite poles of "flesh" (*sarkos*, the reference in this passage for "all things") and "justified" (*dikaios*). A justified life conformed to Christ requires turning away from the one and toward the other. Clearly the core of a disciple's identity, in Paul's view, is to be *dikaios*. For him that means living according to God's will and way, as exemplified by Jesus Christ. It is a word that can be understood only relationally, suggesting action appropriate to one's location (e.g., the *dikaios* of a judge is the capacity to embody the laws and nature of justice appropriate to the role of a judge). For Paul, as justified people, we have the possibility

2. Robert Jenson, *Story and Promise* (Ramsey, NJ: Sigler Press, 1989), 8.

of enacting the laws and nature, the *dikaios*, appropriate to God.

Virtually all English texts translate *dikaios* as "righteous." Until the early nineteenth century that was accurate, in that it suggested behavior according to one's status, in line with Paul's usage. Of course, the implied link to status or order meant that the God-orientation of the new *dikaios* could only too easily get coopted by the dominant powers. However, the more radical God-orientation was often rediscovered by those in marginalized situations. For example, African American slaves understood that living in Christ negated the inferior status of slavery or, as Frederick Douglass put it, "God is the Father of us all."

As Western society became more democratic, a new connotation of "righteous" emerged. It blended with what has become our use of "self-righteous," which implies a sense of moral superiority in relation to others, whether from a "pure" lifestyle or a law-abiding character. A cultural dislike of self-righteousness has developed, perhaps best embodied in fictional characters ranging from the stock Goody Two-shoes to Harry Potter's Dolores Umbridge. With this sense of "righteous," Paul quickly becomes an unattractive guide, apparently calling for renunciation of the joy of living in favor of a life of ascetic self-denial. Such a reading does not honor Paul—or Christianity! The Jesus of the Gospels clearly loved the wonders of everyday life, reflecting a God whose loving attention ensured that "even the hairs of your head are all counted" (Matt. 10:30) The death of Jesus on the cross was a death in service of love and life, enabling the new life signaled by the resurrection.

What Paul saw Jesus inaugurating in his death and resurrection was a new earth and new heaven that inverted the old values and beliefs. As Mary put it in the annunciation, this is a world where God "has brought down the powerful from their thrones, and lifted up the lowly" (Luke 1:52). In Paul's words, "God chose what is low and despised in the world, things that are not, to reduce to nothing things that are" (1 Cor. 1:28). That which was nothing is now something; "everything has become new" (2 Cor. 5:17). The nothing that swallowed him swallows us all: "hardship . . . distress . . . persecution . . . famine . . . nakedness . . . peril . . . sword . . . we are being killed all day long; we are accounted as sheep to be slaughtered" (Rom. 8:35, 36).

Living as a participant in the new age entails adopting a new epistemology, an epistemology decisively shaped by the cross. Thus the baptismal liturgy of Galatians 3:26–28 rejects sex, ethnicity, and social class as indicators of status within the church. This oneness of all gives expression to the eschatological system of values that governs the community that submits to the reign of God. The old markers of race, tribe, circumcision, and so forth are set aside in light of Christ's faithful death and resurrection and the righteousness that comes on the basis of the community's trust.

In his book *Beyond Retribution* New Testament scholar Christopher Marshall argues that we have mistranslated *dikaios*, because we have broken into two pieces, private and public, a concept meant to be enacted seamlessly in the world. By using "righteousness" as the translation, we think Paul is calling us to a privatized ethical purity and piety. However, the world Paul considers also includes the public and political. For Paul, Marshall says, *diakaiosynē* meant "comprehensive well-being, wholeness, and peace."[3] A righteous person, a follower of Christ, seeks the wholeness of the community, aware, as Paul says elsewhere, that "the members . . . have the same care for one another. If one member suffers, all suffer together with it; if one member is honored, all rejoice together with it" (1 Cor. 12:25b–26). To be righteous is to orient oneself and one's community to enacting God's justice in the world. Jesus, the embodiment of God's purposes, focused on relationships and community, because those living relationships, which included ensuring basic material well-being for all, were what God's justice looks like in the world.

So what might righteousness look like today? I offer two possible connections.

Our Prison System. Currently there are about 2.1 million persons incarcerated in prisons or jails through the United States. Roughly

---

3. Christopher Marshall, *Beyond Retribution* (Grand Rapids: Eerdmans, 2001), 36.

one-fifth of all persons incarcerated around the world, this number represents a rate of imprisonment higher than all other countries in the world (except the Seychelles!) and is at least six times higher than the countries we consider our counterparts (e.g., Europe, Japan). Poor, less-educated, darker-skinned, and mentally ill persons make up the vast majority of those inside. Sentencing lengths by crime vary widely across states, but all have increased sharply over the past years. One in nine are serving a life sentence, sometimes not for a violent crime.

Although imprisonment is supposed to represent justice, it is hard to see *dikaios* present in this system, which runs on isolation and humiliation. Although there are often claims for rehabilitation, in reality life in prison is an experience of isolation and rejection. Prisoners are well aware that society has both condemned and forgotten them. As one inmate writes, "No one measures the justice and fairness of our system and the cracks we've fallen through are wide and deep."[4] Called by Paul to follow the patterns set by Christ, Christians should be entering into our prisons and questioning the system behind them.

Immigration. Even though the United States is a nation of immigrants (apart from indigenous persons), there has often been bitter struggle over which immigrants and how many should be able to cross our borders. While no nation has completely open borders, Christians should bring to immigration debates perspectives shaped by the radical understandings of *dikaios* and *koinōnia* given by our tradition. What kinds of immigration policies would enact these norms for both those already inside and those who seek to enter? Policymaking is, of course, a complex enterprise, but a conversation with these starting points could point toward new possibilities.

ELIZABETH M. BOUNDS

---

4. E. George, *A Woman Doing Life* (New York: Oxford University Press, 2010), 148.

Proper 22 (Sunday between October 2 and October 8 inclusive)

Matthew 21:33–46

33"Listen to another parable. There was a landowner who planted a vineyard, put a fence around it, dug a wine press in it, and built a watchtower. Then he leased it to tenants and went to another country. 34When the harvest time had come, he sent his slaves to the tenants to collect his produce. 35But the tenants seized his slaves and beat one, killed another, and stoned another. 36Again he sent other slaves, more than the first; and they treated them in the same way. 37Finally he sent his son to them, saying, 'They will respect my son.' 38But when the tenants saw the son, they said to themselves, 'This is the heir; come, let us kill him and get his inheritance.' 39So they seized him, threw him out of the vineyard, and killed him. 40Now when the owner of the vineyard comes, what will he do to those tenants?" 41They said to him, "He will put those wretches to a miserable death, and lease the vineyard to other tenants who will give him the produce at the harvest time."

42Jesus said to them, "Have you never read in the scriptures:

'The stone that the builders rejected
 has become the cornerstone;
this was the Lord's doing,
 and it is amazing in our eyes'?

43Therefore I tell you, the kingdom of God will be taken away from you and given to a people that produces the fruits of the kingdom. 44The one who falls on this stone will be broken to pieces; and it will crush anyone on whom it falls."

45When the chief priests and the Pharisees heard his parables, they realized that he was speaking about them. 46They wanted to arrest him, but they feared the crowds, because they regarded him as a prophet.

Commentary 1: Connecting the Reading with Scripture

While the parable of the Wicked Tenants continues the setting of the vineyard from the previous pericope, it takes a dark, almost gruesome turn. The brutality of the tenants is shocking. The detailed account of their ruthlessness shows that this is intended. Elements of the parable follow Isaiah 5, but the narrative is entirely different. In Isaiah the vineyard is the focus, representing the house of Israel. Here the focus is on the tenants and the landowner.

Though it has been common in Christian interpretation to assign allegorical equivalencies to each feature—the fence is the law, the winepress is the altar, the tower is the temple, and so forth—the point may rather be that the landowner, though absentee, nevertheless takes care of his property.

The suggestion that the tenants might expect to inherit the vineyard if the heir is killed is narratively strange, but it conveys the expectation of the Jewish leadership that if Jesus, the Messiah, is killed, they retain authority. The response of the landowner to the brutality of the tenants is unknown. In answer to Jesus' question, the elders and chief priests describe what the landowner should have done or might be expected to have done, but this is speculation. Like the landowner, God has the right and justification for putting the "miserable wretches" to death, but Jesus does not verbally endorse this response (nor does he reject it).

Instead, he quotes from Psalm 118:22–23. Here it is not Matthew making the scriptural reference but Jesus himself, another assertion of authority. Though the relationship with the parable is loose—the son does not become a cornerstone—the larger message is clear. The son of David will be killed, and God will take away the authority of the current leadership and give it to others.

Though in history this has been seen as replacement theology, it is not the vineyard that is replaced, only the tenants. If we follow the allegorical interpretations of the wall, winepress, and tower, they all remain intact.

The violence of the response, those "broken to pieces" and "crushed," is discomforting. Is this the recommended way, the way of God or human authorities, to respond to brutality? Homiletically, the passage begs for consideration of the nature and deployment of violence in God's plan.

Though this parable, and others in this sequence, have commonly been interpreted as a rejection of Israel, in fact it is a rejection of transgressive authority, equally applicable to the political sphere, then and now, and to the church, then and now. Wherever those given responsibility by God do not return fruits to God, their station is in peril.

Once again, as in the controversy over the authority of John the Baptist, we see the crowds acting as a brake on the actions of Jewish leadership.

The Ten Commandments are an interesting inclusion in the lectionary. Christians have an awkward relationship with the Ten Commandments, trying to avoid legalism while accepting them as a foundation for Christian morality. For Jews the Ten Commandments or Ten Words are not set apart from the rest of the law.

It is notable that the lection skips over Exodus 20:5–6. Is this to counterbalance the violence of the Gospel passage or to avoid it? The multigenerational condemnation is modified by Ezekiel 18:2–4, but this does not remove the observation that children suffer from the actions of their parents. Certainly the son suffered from the actions of the landowner, who might have suspected that the tenants would not respect the higher station of the son after they had brutalized two missions of servants.

After the Ten Commandments are delivered, God puts on a display of power, both natural (thunder and lightning) and supernatural (the trumpet). The people are afraid, understandably, but Moses wishes to transform their fear into awe. This gives us another angle on violence.

The other lectionary passages focus heavily on the vineyard as the people of Israel. The vineyard is planted, tended, made lush and fruitful, but because of unrighteousness it is exposed to danger, trampled, destroyed.

The cornerstone image introduces a number of ideas. A cornerstone reports fundamental information about the entire structure (names, dates, and dedications), and its position sets the orientation of the building, the reference point for all other stones. It signals the beginning of a new project, and its establishment is witnessed by many who are in some way important to the building project. Often offerings and sacrifices accompany the laying of the cornerstone, perhaps a version of ancient dedications; more recently, time capsules, evidence of the present preserved for the future, are included. Being a foundation stone, one stone of many, is not its most significant property. One might explore in what sense or senses the Ten Commandments are a cornerstone of Judaism or Christianity. Are they an orientation or initiation? A time capsule? How does Jesus set out the plan, the architecture of what is built upon him?

Matthew 21:44 continues with the stone imagery but with a quite different meaning. Here the stone appears to sit apart, still unique but unrelated to a building. It is a wrecking ball and an anvil, extreme language in which Jesus is both the active destroyer, the stone that crushes, and the immovable rock upon which all other besetting objects will be shattered. How do we preach such a Jesus? Whereas the cornerstone image is passive, here the imagery is decidedly dynamic and aggressive.

Between the two stone images is Jesus' pronouncement that the kingdom of God will be removed from the Jewish leadership.

It is a challenge to interpret Paul's relationship with the law. In the passage in Philippians he sees the value of knowing Christ as his Lord to be of surpassing value. What does he reject or regard as of little value? It is not the law; it is the reliance on keeping the statutory law as a complete fulfillment of God's desire, the reckoning that being a Pharisee, being bound in the covenant of Israel, is enough. Now he knows that it is not enough. He must "press on." Like the tenants in the vineyard, he must produce fruit, not just for himself but for God, for the landowner.

Here Paul, as with the servants, is subjected to violence. At first he is himself the perpetrator of violence, the persecutor of the church, like the tenants slaughtering the landowner's emissaries. Then he realizes, or is forced on the Damascus road to recognize, the authority of the landowner and in that realization accepts the responsibility to be fruitful, not for his own sake but for the sake of the landowner. He replaces himself.

The parable leads to a prediction of fact. The kingdom of God will be taken away from them and given to fruitful people. Jesus' condemnation of the Jewish leadership—variably identified as Sadducees, elders, chief priests, Pharisees, and scribes—escalates to the catalog of "woes" in 23:13–36.

The central charge is hypocrisy. They assume the air of righteousness but are rotten to the core. The crowd is the jury, the silent witness of all that has come to pass. The leadership is constantly afraid of the crowds. Are not many preachers wary of the responses of our congregations? Does that make us hypocrites? How do we preach on hypocrisy? Who are the accused, and who is the jury for these accusations? This is perilous territory for the preacher and for the congregation, but all the more important for that.

WHITNEY BODMAN

Commentary 2: Connecting the Reading with the World

Jerome once wrote, "The scars of others should teach us caution." Thus, before I attempt to make any preaching connections with this passage, I feel compelled to begin with a word of caution. In 2004, when Mel Gibson released his gory gospel movie *The Passion of the Christ*, he was roundly criticized for the film's thinly veiled anti-Semitism. More than one detractor blamed Gibson's heavy reliance on Matthew's Gospel for the anti-Jewish imagery and dialogue. One particularly offensive scene (I am thankful it was cut from the final version of the film) had a crowd of Jews baying for blood before a calm and merciful Pilate. The climax of the scene featured Pilate washing his hands while the crowd cried out the words of Matthew 27:25: "His blood be on us, and on our children!"

Taken out of context, this verse from Matthew's Gospel has been the source of all sorts of anti-Semitic rhetoric and action over the last two millennia. It is why Jews were labeled Christ-killers. It caused great Christian thinkers like Augustine and Martin Luther to make outrageously anti-Semitic statements that were later used as the theological foundation for pogroms and even the Holocaust.

Though not as disturbing as Matthew 27:25, the parable of the Wicked Tenants casts the chief priests and elders as the bad guys. They are the evil tenants who abuse the servants and kill the son. Read without nuance or context, the passage clearly makes the case that the Jews, once a chosen people, are being replaced by Christians. This parable appears in all three Synoptic Gospels, but only in Matthew's version does Jesus explicitly say, "Therefore I tell you, the kingdom of God will be taken away from you and given to a people that produces the fruits of the kingdom" (Matt. 21:43). How does a faithful preacher proceed without risking sounding anti-Semitic?

The key is to remind listeners of Matthew's larger context. Scholars believe that Matthew's Gospel was written by a Jew for a Jewish Christian audience sometime after the fall of Jerusalem in 70 CE. Christianity began as an offshoot of Judaism, and in the first century the two traditions were not yet distinct, that is, it was not Jews vs. Christians, it was Jews vs. Jews. For Matthew, the fight with the Jewish authorities was a family feud; it was personal and it got ugly. Any sermon on this text should be careful not to demonize the Jewish authorities. Given the recent rise in anti-Semitism in the United States, using this passage to address the misuse and misunderstanding of the Gospel of Matthew might be a powerful sermon on its own.[1]

What other connections can be made? Since this reading usually appears at the beginning of October, many congregations will be conducting their annual stewardship campaigns. Parishioners will be thinking about how much money to give in support of the church, church leaders will be making budget decisions, and preachers will be fretting over the "Sermon on the Amount." As some churches slowly decline in size, the stewardship season may be a time of great anxiety and worry. How might this text provide encouragement and hope?

For a stewardship sermon, it is helpful to focus on the first verse of this passage. It tells of a landowner who creates a whole enterprise and then puts it into the hands of tenants. The tenants do not own the land, and anything their work produces will be credited to the landowner. We are not told that the tenants are wicked to begin with, just that at some point they forget for whom they are working.

Christians can fall into the same trap. God has given us wonderful gifts and entrusted us to make the most of them. Sometimes we get so caught up in our own success and accomplishments that we forget for whom we are working. One approach to preaching this text is to explore what it means to allow the landowner (God) to collect his or her share. What do we owe to God when everything we have is on loan? What "rent" do we pay to a creator who has endowed us with talent, ambition, and faith?

This parable offers a similar lesson for churches facing financial challenges. When money is tight, a congregation can be tempted to turn inward, focusing attention on things like upkeep of the building or retaining staff. Often benevolence giving and mission funds are cut in order to balance the budget. Is this a form of keeping the produce for ourselves? If we define the "vineyard" of the parable as the body of Christ, something built by God, and we are merely tenants doing the work, does it change the way we understand what is produced? Jesus tells us what our mission is: we are called to be "a people that produces the fruits of the kingdom" (21:43b). In times of diminishing financial resources, it is essential for a congregation to figure out what fruits they are supposed to be producing.

There is a fine French restaurant in Cleveland, Ohio, called EDWINS. The place is known for its duck confit and rabbit pie, but it is not just the food that is extraordinary. Brandon Chrostowski is the owner and head chef; he is also a convicted drug dealer. Chrostowski discovered for himself how difficult it is to get a job when you have a criminal conviction. Many employers simply reject any applicant with a record. So Chrostowski decided to open a restaurant with a mission: to give formerly incarcerated adults a foundation in the culinary and hospitality industry, while providing a support network necessary for their long-term success. Thus, EDWINS Leadership & Restaurant Institute was born.

Chrostowski struggled to get financial support for his venture. Many foundations thought his business model was too risky; turning convicted criminals into chefs and waiters seemed like a recipe for disaster. After years of rejection, Chrostowski finally cobbled together enough money to launch the Institute, and it has been a wild success. Since 2013, hundreds of people have graduated from the EDWINS program. They have a 97 percent employment rate and a 1 percent recidivism rate. The Institute has won dozens of awards and is hailed as a new model for social entrepreneurship, but the statistics and awards do not tell the whole story.

The story of EDWINS was turned into the short documentary *Knife Skills*, which was nominated for an Academy Award in 2017.[2] The film follows a group of students from the first day of class to graduation. At first, the students tell depressing tales of poverty, incarceration, and rejection, but by the end of the course, there is a sense of accomplishment, pride, and

---

1. The Associated Press, "American Jews Alarmed by Surge in Anti-Semitism," *Fortune*, November 17, 2016; http://fortune.com/2016/11/17/anti-semitism-donald-trump-jews/.
2. For the full story, see the movie at https://www.knifeskillsthemovie.com/.

hope. The final scene is the graduation ceremony, and one man leans in to Chrostowski and says, "Thank you for believing in us."

No one wanted to invest in EDWINS, and now it is hard to get a table on a Friday night. Chrostowski does not claim to be Christian, and yet the work he does looks like the fruits of the kingdom. He often says, "Everyone has a past, and everyone deserves a future," which is as good a summary of the doctrine of redemption as you can find. Reflecting on the EDWINS story, one hears echoes of Christ's words from Matthew 21:42: "The stone that the builders rejected has become the cornerstone; this was the Lord's doing, and it is amazing in our eyes." It is also a reminder to be careful about what—and whom—we reject.

SHAWNTHEA MONROE

Proper 23 (Sunday between October 9 and October 15 inclusive)

Isaiah 25:1–9 and Exodus 32:1–14
Psalm 23 and Psalm 106:1–6, 19–23
Philippians 4:1–9
Matthew 22:1–14

Isaiah 25:1–9

¹O LORD, you are my God;
   I will exalt you, I will praise your name;
for you have done wonderful things,
   plans formed of old, faithful and sure.
²For you have made the city a heap,
   the fortified city a ruin;
the palace of aliens is a city no more,
   it will never be rebuilt.
³Therefore strong peoples will glorify you;
   cities of ruthless nations will fear you.
⁴For you have been a refuge to the poor,
   a refuge to the needy in their distress,
   a shelter from the rainstorm and a shade from the heat.
When the blast of the ruthless was like a winter rainstorm,
   ⁵the noise of aliens like heat in a dry place,
you subdued the heat with the shade of clouds;
   the song of the ruthless was stilled.

⁶On this mountain the LORD of hosts will make for all peoples
   a feast of rich food, a feast of well-aged wines,
   of rich food filled with marrow, of well-aged wines strained clear.
⁷And he will destroy on this mountain
   the shroud that is cast over all peoples,
   the sheet that is spread over all nations;
   ⁸he will swallow up death forever.
Then the Lord GOD will wipe away the tears from all faces,
   and the disgrace of his people he will take away from all the earth,
   for the LORD has spoken.
⁹It will be said on that day,
   Lo, this is our God; we have waited for him, so that he might save us.
   This is the LORD for whom we have waited;
   let us be glad and rejoice in his salvation.

Exodus 32:1–14

¹When the people saw that Moses delayed to come down from the mountain, the people gathered around Aaron, and said to him, "Come, make gods for us, who shall go before us; as for this Moses, the man who brought us up out of the land of Egypt, we do not know what has become of him." ²Aaron said to them, "Take off the gold rings that are on the ears of your wives, your sons, and your

daughters, and bring them to me." ³So all the people took off the gold rings from their ears, and brought them to Aaron. ⁴He took the gold from them, formed it in a mold, and cast an image of a calf; and they said, "These are your gods, O Israel, who brought you up out of the land of Egypt!" ⁵When Aaron saw this, he built an altar before it; and Aaron made proclamation and said, "Tomorrow shall be a festival to the LORD." ⁶They rose early the next day, and offered burnt offerings and brought sacrifices of well-being; and the people sat down to eat and drink, and rose up to revel.

⁷The LORD said to Moses, "Go down at once! Your people, whom you brought up out of the land of Egypt, have acted perversely; ⁸they have been quick to turn aside from the way that I commanded them; they have cast for themselves an image of a calf, and have worshiped it and sacrificed to it, and said, 'These are your gods, O Israel, who brought you up out of the land of Egypt!'" ⁹The LORD said to Moses, "I have seen this people, how stiff-necked they are. ¹⁰Now let me alone, so that my wrath may burn hot against them and I may consume them; and of you I will make a great nation."

¹¹But Moses implored the LORD his God, and said, "O LORD, why does your wrath burn hot against your people, whom you brought out of the land of Egypt with great power and with a mighty hand? ¹²Why should the Egyptians say, 'It was with evil intent that he brought them out to kill them in the mountains, and to consume them from the face of the earth'? Turn from your fierce wrath; change your mind and do not bring disaster on your people. ¹³Remember Abraham, Isaac, and Israel, your servants, how you swore to them by your own self, saying to them, 'I will multiply your descendants like the stars of heaven, and all this land that I have promised I will give to your descendants, and they shall inherit it forever.'" ¹⁴And the LORD changed his mind about the disaster that he planned to bring on his people.

Commentary 1: Connecting the Reading with Scripture

The problem with a chosen people, all too often, is their sense of exceptionalism. Exceptionalism is often used as moral justification when empires claim that normative global ethical rules do not apply to those who are called. Although claims by dispossessed Israelites of being a chosen people may not have had a global impact in the ancient world, today such claims by self-professing Christians within the United States, who see themselves as a New Israel, are disproportionately responsible for so much of the terror globally experienced, a terrorism masked by American exceptionalism that claims to be ordained by the Almighty. In reality, church and state are bending their knees to golden idols.

The biblical text bears witness to people who were chosen to emulate their God. What does it mean for the church today to be composed of the so-called chosen? Chosenness has nothing to do with American exceptionalism. To be chosen by the Almighty ceases to be signified by some ritual cut conducted upon the male body. Those who seek to build a new social order of peace, justice, and compassion are the chosen, regardless of religious affiliation or beliefs. Those chosen struggle for justice; this defines our very faith and, more importantly, our very humanity—or lack thereof.

How does one imitate the Almighty in the struggle for justice? What is the praxis God's chosen are called to emulate? The prophet Isaiah provides a clue: "For you have been a refuge to the poor, a refuge to the needy in their distress, a shelter from the rainstorm and a shade from the heat" (Isa. 25:4). The church is called to seek justice for the marginalized, an outward sign of our conversion. The prophet may pray: "O LORD, you are my God; I will exalt you, I will praise your name; for you have done wonderful things" (v. 1); but we use the Lord's name in vain if our ornate words are void of praxis and fail to commit to do the things God has promised to do.

If our God is a refuge to the poor, then the hymns of praise we sing on Sunday are vain if we ignore the poor, if we insist on building walls to keep them out. If our God is a refuge to the needy in distress, then our prayers are hollow if we support cutting social services to bless the überwealthy with larger tax cuts. If our God is a shelter from the rainstorm and a shade from the heat, then we proclaim our lack of faith by ignoring the *imago Dei* of the homeless. The church ignores the cry of the poor at the peril of ceasing to be chosen.

The psalmist sings, "Happy are those who observe justice, who do righteousness at all times" (Ps. 106:3). We are chosen to do justice, not embrace the exceptionalism rhetoric popular within American political circles. All who do justice, regardless of faith tradition or lack thereof, are chosen. Like the king in the parable, who invites everyone to the wedding banquet but who exercises discipline on those without proper wedding garments, "many are called, but few are chosen" (Matt. 22:14). Those who show up wearing the wedding robe of righteousness and do not ignore the invitation to observe justice are chosen to sit at the banquet table of the wedding feast.

When chosenness or exceptionalism are claimed, so as to increase the power and privilege of a people, ethical and moral imperatives are suspended. An arrogance is reinforced that prevents constructive dialogue in forming a more just global order where, as Isaiah reminds us, "the Lord God will wipe away the tears from all faces" (Isa. 25:8). When exceptionality becomes jingoism, those who claim it relegate all who are racially or ethnically different to the margins of society by normalizing, spiritualizing, and legitimizing atrocities committed against those they perceive as their inferiors. The church is called to preach against this form of idolatry.

Whether it be the Hebrews of old or those who claim to be the new Jerusalem today, exceptionalism leads to creating gods in one's own image. Those who claim to be clergy are called to hold the people and their leaders accountable to the concepts of justice and righteousness, not coronate them as God's chosen. If this is true, then we must ask whether those who use, misuse, and abuse the disenfranchised, even when elected to lead the people, are following the Golden Rule or the golden calf. While pointing to political agendas and the cockalorum required to impose theocratic rules, the Aarons of today shout, "These are your gods, O Israel, who brought you up out of the land of Egypt!" (Exod. 32:4). The unsophisticated pronouncements of clergy chosen by politicians rather than by God dismiss justice for faith in golden images. Such a move condemns God to the realm of hackneyed superstitious platitudes.

Those who bow their knees to the golden calf of placing their nation first, of making their nation great again, are the spiritual descendants of the Hebrews who ate, drank, and reveled before the false idol. True worship has less to do with what occurs in a building we declare sacred, and more to do with what we do in secular spaces, demanding justice rain down like living water. The danger of chosenness is the development of pseudoreligious exceptional ideology, as was developed by displaced Hebrews in the desert and dispossessed Christians escaping European persecution over a century before the founding of their new republic. Euroamericans become sojourners to the new Israel, "a shining city upon a hill," as first vocalized by Puritan John Winthrop in a 1630 sermon that urged listeners to invade and conquer in Christ's name.

Since the foundation of nation building, chosenness and exceptionalism have reigned supreme, justifying invasion, genocide, and enslavement of indigenous people with names like Canaanites, Hittites, Amorites, or Cherokees, Hopi, Apache. US greatness was possible only because of Pilgrims' divine right to steal the winter provisions of indigenous people while thanking God for *his* merciful bounty. Only by stealing the labor of others, justifying slavery as God's call to bring civilization and Christianity to lost primitive peoples, whose only hope is to be servants to whites in this world and the next, could America ever have become great. Only by stealing the sovereignty of others, justifying a manifest destiny as God's call to physically invade another nation to steal their land, their resources, and their cheap labor by economically expanding through gunboat diplomacy, could America ever have become great. We still see today's exceptionalism in its latest neoliberal manifestation, which ensures the vast majority of the world's resources flow to support less than 5 percent of the global population.

Here is the question the people of God must answer if they are to claim chosenness: is our church standing with the oppressed, or justifying the actions of the oppressors? "Let your gentleness be known to everyone. The Lord is near," Paul writes to the Philippians (4:5). There is no gentleness in how we have treated the other within our midst, or those from the nations that contribute to our wealth. Our quest for the golden idols of power and privilege has made all who think they are chosen for riches enemies of God. As the psalmist reminds us, "They exchanged the glory of God for the image of an ox that eats grass" (Ps. 106:20). We are a stiff-necked people whose faith arrived to these shores stillborn.

MIGUEL A. DE LA TORRE

Commentary 2: Connecting the Reading with the World

Isaiah 25:1–9 casts an audacious portrait of security and future abundance for God's people and all nations. Its optimism and hope are set within a context of God's judgment (Isa. 24). It serves as a response of thanksgiving to the Lord for God's "wonderful" actions of salvation (25:1).

Isaiah 25:1–9 is a hymn of praise and thanksgiving. It reminds God's people that worship is central to identity. The Lord alone is worthy of praise because of the salvation that God enacts for God's people and the world. Praise reminds God's people of the greatness of the Lord. Our world revels in cheap grace and cheap praise. Today media elevate persons simply because they are famous for being famous or based on cults of beauty, myths of success, or temporary athletic prowess. Verse 1 challenges readers to imagine anew what it means to praise the Lord for God's acts of salvation on behalf of persons desperate for what only a god as great as the Lord could have accomplished.

In particular, the basis for the praise is the grand reversal of circumstances envisioned in verses 4–5. The Lord does not enrich the wealthy and fight for the powerful. This text is good news for the downtrodden, the forgotten, and the marginalized. God is an anchor, a refuge, and a shelter. Isaiah challenges both the church and world to reevaluate the metrics used for success and failure. It calls for a critique of any use of power that merely blesses the current winners. It reminds the church of God's work of liberating the marginalized from any status-quo system that suffocates the poor while appearing rigged for those already in power.

Isaiah 25:1–9 pairs particularly well with the vision of Jesus' parable of the Wedding Banquet (Matt. 22:1–14). Both texts remind God's people of the inclusive nature of God's kingdom. Isaiah and Matthew provide a critical statement that God is not for God's people *against* the nations, but for God's people for the sake of the nations. In other words, God may execute judgment against the powerful for the sake of the downtrodden, but God's goal is the salvation of all. Verses 2 and 3 testify to this. Yet the praise of God's people revels not in the mere destruction of the wicked but in God's salvation of the poor and marginalized (Isa. 25:4–5). Isaiah's word reaches its climax in its vision of a feast for "all peoples" (v. 6). So this text is an invitation to outsiders to come to the banquet that the Lord has prepared. It challenges God's people to ask, How do we need to change in our stance toward those outside of our community in order to embody the good news for the world? What does it mean to live in a land of plenty when much of the world does not?

If Isaiah 24 explored the darkness of judgment, Isaiah 25:1–9 represents the dawn of new creation. This text invites readers to live with courage and perseverance in light of a guaranteed future. This provides a vision of hope for the present. When God's people reflect on the eschatological vision of the future, they gain courage to live holy and faithful lives now. Revelation 21:1–4 echoes the language of verses 6–8. The imagery of a final consummation of God's mission centers on Zion/Jerusalem as the symbol of God's reign. Verse 9 roots ultimate security in a trust that manifests itself through waiting for the Lord to act. For persons facing difficulties and pain in the present, Isaiah's words instill a hope to carry on in a patient longing for God's final victory.

The theme of waiting as the response of trust recurs throughout Isaiah (8:17; 26:8; 33:2; 40:31; 49:23; 51:5; 59:9; 60:9). This is not a passive waiting. Verse 2 adds a critical dimension to the theme of waiting. It is a deep trust that God acts according to God's plans and purposes. These may not be discernible to God's people in the moment, but they do manifest at the right time. In our day, many churches are in decline, and congregations lose hope. Isaiah's bold vision calls us to remain faithful and continue to proclaim the word, offer the sacraments, and practice justice for our neighbors.

Exodus 32:1–14 stands as a warning of the danger of idolatry and the stakes of living as God's missional people for the world. Idolatry is the opposite of the Torah's command to love the Lord. The placement of Exodus 32–34 within the tabernacle account (Exod. 25–31 and 35–40) highlights the irony and sin of idolatry. The tabernacle texts model faithfulness to God's instructions. The golden calf narratives (Exod. 32–34) serve as a warning about the grave danger of disobedience. The book of Exodus will reach its climax in the completion of the tabernacle in precise accordance with the Lord's instructions to Moses. At that moment, the glory of the Lord fills the tabernacle, and God's people live with the holy God at their center when camped and as their vanguard when moving forward to the promised land. This climax is possible only when God's people practice faithfulness rather than chase false gods.

Israel's grave sin of turning away from the demand of exclusive worship and commitment (20:2–7) by molding a calf idol is a powerful metaphor. It serves to illustrate the lessons of its cotexts in the lectionary. Psalm 106 explores ways for God's people to move forward postexile through an earnest confession of past sins. The psalmist ends with a plea for deliverance and liberation (Ps. 106:47). Matthew 22:1–14 warns God's people of the danger of privilege apart from faithfulness. Being God's people is not a status to be exploited or to be embraced only when convenient. Instead, God's people must live out their faith with integrity for the sake of the world that God desires to bless. Philippians 4:1–9 grounds faithfulness in the habits of godliness: rejoicing, gratitude, prayer, nourishment of the soul with the good, and following the examples of the godly.

The image of the golden calf serves as an invitation to explore idolatrous cultural images that God's people today have appropriated. What images/metaphors do moderns use for God within the community of faith? Are they faithful to the biblical narrative, or do they subvert the gospel by associating the Lord with a false god rooted in a human ideology or any part of creation itself?

This text also offers distinct portraits of spiritual leadership for consideration. Aaron models a malleable character and people-pleasing tendencies. In the absence of Moses he allows God's people to set the primary agenda. Aaron compounds the error by associating the gold calf with the Lord. God's people failed, but Moses interceded, and the Lord promised to make Moses' name great (a clear allusion to God's promises to Abraham in Gen. 12:2). The sin of God's people has devastating effects on the efficacy of their witness to the world. It is an affront to God's holy love and is a grave threat to God's mission in the world.

Exodus 32:1–14 is a testimony that God's mercy triumphs over wrath and judgment. Israel's sin was grave, but the Lord's love was greater. God's internal character will be fully revealed in Exodus 34:6–7a, where the Lord reveals his internal character as loving-kindness. God's capacity to relent from judgment serves as a dual invitation for God's people to worship the Lord for God's loving nature, while simultaneously turning away from the sins of idolatry.

BRIAN D. RUSSELL

Proper 23 (Sunday between October 9 and October 15 inclusive)

Psalm 23

¹The LORD is my shepherd, I shall not want.
　²He makes me lie down in green pastures;
he leads me beside still waters;
　³he restores my soul.
He leads me in right paths
　for his name's sake.

⁴Even though I walk through the darkest valley,
　I fear no evil;
for you are with me;
　your rod and your staff—
　they comfort me.

⁵You prepare a table before me
　in the presence of my enemies;
you anoint my head with oil;
　my cup overflows.
⁶Surely goodness and mercy shall follow me
　all the days of my life,
and I shall dwell in the house of the LORD
　my whole life long.

Psalm 106:1–6, 19–23

¹Praise the LORD!
　O give thanks to the LORD, for he is good;
　for his steadfast love endures forever.
²Who can utter the mighty doings of the LORD,
　or declare all his praise?
³Happy are those who observe justice,
　who do righteousness at all times.

⁴Remember me, O LORD, when you show favor to your people;
　help me when you deliver them;
⁵that I may see the prosperity of your chosen ones,
　that I may rejoice in the gladness of your nation,
　that I may glory in your heritage.

⁶Both we and our ancestors have sinned;
　we have committed iniquity, have done wickedly.
. . . .
¹⁹They made a calf at Horeb
　and worshiped a cast image.
²⁰They exchanged the glory of God
　for the image of an ox that eats grass.

> ²¹They forgot God, their Savior,
>   who had done great things in Egypt,
> ²²wondrous works in the land of Ham,
>   and awesome deeds by the Red Sea.
> ²³Therefore he said he would destroy them—
>   had not Moses, his chosen one,
> stood in the breach before him,
>   to turn away his wrath from destroying them.

Connecting the Psalm with Scripture and Worship

Psalm 23. Psalm 23 may evoke more memories than any other biblical passage. Indeed, it is limited by overexposure, especially since so much of its familiarity comes from its use in times of grief. Without diminishing its power to comfort the bereaved, today's lections let you expand your congregation's associations with this text by exploring it as a response to Isaiah 25:1–9. Reciprocally, the psalm's imagery expands the picture of God that Isaiah presents.

The psalm opens with a famous metaphor for God; "shepherd" instantly transports us to a bucolic setting of "green pastures . . . still waters" (Ps. 23:2). The metaphor also gives the reader a role: if God is "my shepherd," then I must be a sheep. Though the relationship between shepherd and sheep is emphasized—God "makes [the psalmist] lie down" (v. 2a); God "leads [the psalmist] in right paths" (v. 3b); God's "rod and . . . staff" comfort the psalmist (v. 4b)—another vital relationship is also expressed here: God is the provider who relieves all want (v. 1b), even to the point of restoring the soul (v. 3a).

The mention of "paths" (v. 3b) facilitates a shift in setting and tone. No longer resting in pleasant pastures, the psalmist now "walk[s] through the darkest valley" where evil lurks, though God's companionship eliminates its fearsomeness (v. 4).

Finally, the metaphor changes from the opening verses' accompanying shepherd to the closing verses' gracious host. Not merely a sheep, the psalmist is protected as a guest, honored with a banquet, and anointed with oil (v. 5). The sufficiency of "I shall not want" (v. 1) becomes the superabundance of "my cup overflows" (v. 5). No wonder the psalmist concludes that "goodness and mercy" will never depart as our divine Host welcomes us into God's own abode (v. 6).

The God who kept evil at bay (v. 4) and neutralized the psalmist's enemies (v. 5) also strides awe-inspiringly through the Isaiah pericope. While the entire book of Isaiah presents a nuanced portrait of YHWH, God's sovereignty is always the dominant note, and God's power is certainly on display here: God "has done wonderful things" (Isa. 25:1); God has "made . . . the fortified city a ruin" (v. 2); God "subdued the heat" (v. 5); God "will swallow up death forever" (v. 8).

To preach this text, you must proclaim a truly mighty God, and Psalm 23 rounds out the prophet's picture of God. A sermon could consider how our almighty God is also our Comforter. Comfort is a theme of both texts. Isaiah depicts God wiping away tears (v. 8), but presents God relating only to people en masse. Beyond the first verse's singular pronouns, every reference to humanity is plural: "cities," "nations," "peoples," "aliens," "the poor," "the needy," "the ruthless," "all faces," "all the earth," as well as plural pronouns (vv. 2–9).

How different is the personal touch of Psalm 23! Further, the psalm's green pastures and still waters (Ps. 23:2) offer soothing contrast to images of fortified cities (Isa. 25:2) and "the noise of aliens" (v. 5), and while the "palace of aliens . . . will never be rebuilt" (v. 2), God restores the psalmist's soul (Ps. 23:3).

A sermon might also explore how these passages present God's provision for our lives alongside God's defeat of death: the psalmist dines alone in the face of "enemies" (v. 5); Isaiah depicts a lavish feast for "all peoples" (Isa. 25:6) on the mountain where death will die (v. 7). This sermon could utilize Psalm 23's associations with bereavement, especially since "GOD will wipe away the tears from all faces" (Isa. 25:8) is echoed in New Testament texts favored for funerals (e.g., 1 Cor. 15:54; Rev. 7:17; 21:4).

Psalm 23 offers a prime opportunity for congregational participation. Invite parishioners to use the translation closest to their hearts or provide your preferred version, whether spoken or sung. Regardless, let your flock feel these words in their mouth as well as in their heart.

Psalm 106:1–6, 19–23. Exodus 32:1–14 is this week's episode from the Israelites' great wilderness saga, and these selected verses from Psalm 106 provide a direct response to the events of that story. This entire psalm considers the many sins of the Israelites, and these verses focus particularly on the foundational sin of idolatry, specifically citing the events recounted in the Exodus epic.

The psalm opens by praising and thanking God, lifting up God's everlasting *hesed* (Ps. 106:1). The fact that this is the psalmist's starting point could provide an interesting sermon angle for this Exodus pericope: begin at the end of the story, giving glory to God for not wiping out the Israelites (or us) despite human sinfulness.

Immediately, the psalmist questions who is qualified to "utter the mighty doings of the LORD" (v. 2) or to offer the sort of praise offered in the preceding verse. The answer is found in a beatitude: "those who observe justice, who do righteousness at all times" (v. 3). A second homiletical approach is suggested by the reality that, due to the relentless grip of sin, "do[ing] righteousness at all times" seems sadly aspirational. Just as the Israelites were so sinful as to "turn aside from the way that [God] commanded them" (Exod. 32:8), we too fall short and must therefore rely on God's mercy. The psalmist's plea to God to "remember" and to "help" (Ps. 106:4) continues in this vein.

The psalm's opening five verses are preparation for a broad confession of corporate sin in which the psalmist asserts that the Israelites, both past and present, "have committed iniquity, have done wickedly" (v. 6). While the rest of the psalm identifies Israel's historic transgressions—from before they left Egypt until after they arrived in the promised land—this passage zeroes in on sin committed in the wilderness at Horeb (v. 19).

The psalmist's dissection of this ancient sin could lead to a sermon. Your hearers may assume they know the nature of the sin that goes by the shorthand "the golden calf." The psalmist identifies three distinct angles to this multifaceted transgression. First, "they made a calf . . . and worshiped a cast image" (v. 19). This, of course, is no small matter: it is a violation of the Ten Commandments! Wait, there is more: "they exchanged the glory of God for the image of an ox" (v. 20). Finally, more appalling still, "they forgot God, their Savior, who had done great things in Egypt . . . and awesome deeds by the Red Sea" (vv. 21–22). A sermon could use these painstakingly distinct insights from the psalmist to help a listeners recognize the complexity of our own sinful thoughts, words, and deeds.

While the psalm is overwhelmingly a recitation of human sins, it concludes with a startling portrait of God. Unlike the powerful God reflected in the opening verses, this God is seemingly held in check by Moses (Exod. 32:14). Moses' gutsy opposition to God's wrathful intent to "consume" (v. 10) the "stiff-necked" (v. 9) Israelites is such an uncommon image of the human-divine relationship that a preacher may find it fruitful. The psalmist's concise take on Moses as God's "chosen one [who stands] in the breach" before God to deflect God's anger (Ps. 106:23) will be a provocative, pre-Christian phrase.

Liturgically, the psalm's first verse is a ready-made call to worship. Apt hymns include "Great Is Thy Faithfulness," Taizé's "Confitemini Domino," and any others that emphasize our merciful God as being the only one worthy of worship.

LEIGH CAMPBELL-TAYLOR

Proper 23 (Sunday between October 9 and October 15 inclusive)

Philippians 4:1–9

¹Therefore, my brothers and sisters, whom I love and long for, my joy and crown, stand firm in the Lord in this way, my beloved.
²I urge Euodia and I urge Syntyche to be of the same mind in the Lord. ³Yes, and I ask you also, my loyal companion, help these women, for they have struggled beside me in the work of the gospel, together with Clement and the rest of my co-workers, whose names are in the book of life.
⁴Rejoice in the Lord always; again I will say, Rejoice. ⁵Let your gentleness be known to everyone. The Lord is near. ⁶Do not worry about anything, but in everything by prayer and supplication with thanksgiving let your requests be made known to God. ⁷And the peace of God, which surpasses all understanding, will guard your hearts and your minds in Christ Jesus.
⁸Finally, beloved, whatever is true, whatever is honorable, whatever is just, whatever is pure, whatever is pleasing, whatever is commendable, if there is any excellence and if there is anything worthy of praise, think about these things. ⁹Keep on doing the things that you have learned and received and heard and seen in me, and the God of peace will be with you.

Commentary 1: Connecting the Reading with Scripture

As those in ecclesiastical ministry know all too well, many are the problems that can befall a body of believers. Paul was quite accustomed to this reality. With the joy of leading others in the way of Christ, as the church, comes the need to anticipate and respond to lingering selfishness that can flare up like wildfire. It is easy to forget that Paul's letters did not emerge out of situations of peace, harmony, and tranquility. Quite the opposite. The impetus behind the writing of most of his letters is the reception of oral or written reports of problems in the local churches.

Paul has vied for the gospel in a city and begun to gather converts there. After Paul followed God's leading elsewhere, problems and issues inevitably arose. Paul could not pass on that responsibility to another minister or church as he left a city. While he did have coworkers, and some native converts developed into leaders in their cities, his breadth of responsibility and continued oversight expanded with each additional geographical location God sent him to. Paul remained a father figure in the faith for most of the places where he pioneered the gospel, which required having a continued eye on unity and disunity in those places.

The Letter to the Philippians is no exception to this hovering reality. Even in a letter that has "joy" as a central theme, and where the body of believers are lauded as being generous and mature, the need for unity and call to unity are not absent. Philippians 4:1–9 bridges the body and exhortation section and the closing section of the letter. Some see 4:1–3 capping Paul's warning and appeal to the Philippians (Phil. 3:1–4:3), and then 4:4–9 as the first part of the closing of the letter. Others take all of 4:1–9 as the beginning of the letter's closing section.

Wherever the interpreter lands on this structural question, two things are clear. First, Paul sees the need to stress unity among the Philippians as he nears the end of the letter. Second, though closing sections of Paul's letters often are collections of seemingly disparate items (e.g., individual greetings, well wishes, benedictions, travel notes), the closing items in 4:4–9 can be seen as thematically and practically significant in his call to unity.

In the myriad of problems visible within the church, now and then, it is easy to overlook the reality that disunity is not a resulting symptom from other problems but the root problem itself. For Paul, unity is not a hoped-for state that occurs when strife, turmoil, and competing interests are not present. It is rather the opposite. Unity is something to be sought after, worked for, and continually practiced in the church when differences are in full view. Unity is also not some content-less state of agreement that masks real issues and problems for the sake of outward harmony. Unity has a content, a practice, and calls for humility and sacrifice within the body of Christ.

In our passage, we see a fractured relationship between two women, Euodia and Syntyche, about whom we know little. The fallout from it is significant enough for Paul to note it in his letter and call the Philippians to action. These women seem not to be your typical malcontents or regular troublemakers. They "have struggled beside me [Paul] in the work of the gospel" (4:3), indicating two within the ministry leadership of the body. Paul's love (v. 1) for them, and all of the Philippians, motivates his urging to unity. Though there is some debate about to whom "my loyal companion" (v. 3) refers, the lack of a specific name, along with the fact that the letter is to be read to each house church upon its arrival, intimates that the whole Philippian body are the ones called to lead these two women to unity.

Even a cursory reading of Paul's letters highlights his focus on unity as a calling to believers. Earlier in Philippians, he makes no less than five calls to unity in the span of only four verses: to be like-minded; have the same love and spirit; reject selfishness and vanity; practice humility; and serve others (2:1–4). This is the lead-in to the famous Christ Hymn of Philippians 2:5–11, which offers Jesus' consistent and constant descent, from preexistence to incarnation to death on a cross, as the only basis for the mindset that can produce a real, living unity.

Outside of Philippians, two other instances are of particular note for rounding out Paul's conception of and call to unity. In Ephesians, right after calling the believers to bear "with one another in love" (Eph. 4:2), Paul stresses three other details about Christian unity (v. 3): (1) it is maintained or kept, rather than attained; (2) the source of unity is the Holy Spirit, and not any humanly contrived basis for remaining together; (3) it is kept through the practices of peace. This verse may be the most programmatic teaching Paul has on unity, thus informing each instance he stresses it in a letter.

In Corinth, disunity was particularly acute. The believers there were not only consciously dividing themselves along charismatic personalities (1 Cor. 1:12). Their behavior and practices were thoroughly infused with arrogance, self-centeredness, and a wisdom that tilted freedom and rights toward selfish ambition. Therefore, their arrogance in tolerating an incestuous relationship within the body (5:1–8), the lawsuits among believers (6:1–11), the drunkenness and gluttony at the Lord's Supper at the expense of the poor believers (11:17–34), and the lack of willingness to rein in freedoms for the sake of order and clarity in worship (11:2–16; 12–14) are not just separate issues to be addressed and corrected. They all exemplify the larger, even more cancerous, problem of disunity within the body of Christ, which threatens the very witness of the churches in Corinth. The rampant disunity standing behind these issues, if unaddressed, may sink the validity of the church in that place. This caution and warning are not limited to Corinth or the first century CE.

In canonical perspective, the NT epistolary literature is where the topic of unity and disunity is most often found. The context for why letters were written—that is, the addressing and often resolving of issues within a *body* of believers—clarifies why the topic predominates in this genre. Outside of Paul there are sightings of teaching on unity in a number of other letters, including 1 Peter (3:8), James (3:13–18), and 1 John (3:11–22). Though there are plenty of places in the OT and NT where lack of agreement can be noted, many of them are between two individuals, within an individual (e.g., hypocrisy), or between believers and those outside the body. We are reminded from this that the call to unity is a call to persons, plural, within the church.

Returning to Philippians 4:4–8, the seemingly disconnected final admonitions—to rejoice always, to be gentle, to not worry, to remain in prayer, and to keep one's mind on praiseworthy things—when read within the preceding call to unity, come to life as the very "bonds of peace" (Eph. 4:3) that can maintain unity. By extension, when disunity is reigning and a body desperately seeks the unity of the Holy Spirit, these too are the practices for reviving unity. Paul's words in the final verse of the passage teach it to be so: "Keep on doing the things that you have learned and received and heard and seen in me, and the God of peace [and therefore unity] will be with you" (Phil. 4:9).

TROY A. MILLER

Commentary 2: Connecting the Reading with the World

What a wonderful, encouraging, and inspiring letter Paul writes to the community of believers at Philippi, while at the same time trying to deal with a dispute among two women, Euodia and Syntyche. Paul encourages the community to stand firm in Christ (Phil. 4:1). He asks one of his unnamed loyal companions to serve as a mediator between the two women who seem to have an unresolved dispute between them (vv. 2–3). He then returns to a more joyous tone and exhorts the community to rejoice in God always, to let gentleness be their characteristic for all to see, to worry about nothing, and to be a people of prayer (vv. 4–7). In his closing words to this part of the letter, Paul encourages the believers to live a virtuous life, one that resembles his own virtuous life.

Hearing the letter in social, ethical, and ecclesiastical contexts today, the church learns how to be a people of God, which involves settling disputes and employing facilitators if necessary; finding joy in one's relationship with God; avoiding unnecessary worry, which implies having trust in God's goodness and care; being engaged in active prayer, whereby one's needs are made known to God; and living a life of virtue that has gentleness as its cornerstone. The reward for living this type of life is the peace of God.

From a social and ethical perspective, the preacher could offer reflections on the various methods for settling disputes, especially when they arise among members of one's own community, as in the case of Euodia and Syntyche at Philippi. One step is *negotiation*. This step is the most basic one for settling disputes, and it involves a back-and-forth communication between the parties of conflict with the goal of settling a dispute.

Mediation is often the next step if negotiation proves unsuccessful. This is a voluntary process in which an impartial person (the mediator), like Paul's unnamed companion in verse 3, helps with communication and promotes reconciliation between the parties that will allow them to reach a mutually acceptable agreement.

A third method is *arbitration*. This step involves the submission of a disputed matter to an impartial person (the arbitrator) for decision. People's personal needs and the nature of the dispute need to be considered when selecting a method to resolve a dispute. These are three of many methods that the preacher can bring to the attention of the community members so that a community's unity can be preserved. The preacher can also make the point that these three methods are ways to resolve disputes in everyday life and in the workplace.

From an ecclesial perspective, grounding one's relationship in God is essential to the physical, psychological, and spiritual health of a community's individual members and the community as a whole. The preacher could suggest ways in which a joyous relationship with God can be nurtured and sustained, like making time to simply "be" with the sacred presence that permeates all of life. Embracing times of silence and solitude and taking walks in the natural world can rejuvenate one's mind and spirit. Spending quality time with loved ones, friends, family, and colleagues, and learning to discover the wonder and mystery of the Divine in each person, as well as in all of the created world, cultivate a joyous relationship with God.

Seeing the cup of life as being half full and not half empty, and choosing to live a life of gratitude can also help to foster a joyous relationship with God. The preacher could reflect on these possibilities as well as countless others while reminding the community members that we are postresurrection, post-Pentecost people imbued with and empowered by the Spirit of God, whose gift and fruit is peace.

Paul encourages the Philippians not to worry about anything. The preacher could also reflect on how to deal with stress and anxiety to help community members navigate in a chaotic world yearning for peace and alternative solutions to global problems that cause divisions among nations, neighbors, communities, and families, not to mention the reality of climate change, which has the entire planet in crisis. Evidence from the Mayo Health Clinic indicates that worry is the main contributor to depression, nervous breakdowns, high blood pressure, heart attacks, and early death. Essentially, stress kills. The preacher can reflect with the community on the drawbacks of worry and the need to be deeply rooted in prayer.

Prayer has many benefits: it can help people cultivate a sense of gratitude, offer a moderate sense of optimism and a healthy dose of hope, and allow people time to be able to see things from a broader perspective. That by itself can help with obsessive acts and compulsive thought or limited thinking. The preacher can help people explore the many benefits of prayer.

With respect to Paul's teaching that believers should make their needs known to God, the preacher can comment on a deep theological reality, namely, that God is both transcendent and incarnational. The presence of God, although transcendent, also rests in the midst of the community as a whole and its members individually. The preacher can comment on prayer as a dynamic experience wedded to everyday life. Wherever people are gathered, God is present. Thus the preacher can help believers understand that by making one's needs known to the community, one is making one's needs known to God, whose love and care become incarnational through the community and its members. The preacher can offer believers a deep understanding of God, who is both transcendent and incarnational.

Paul's exhortation to the believers at Philippi to live a life of virtue opens up many possibilities for the preacher from an ethical perspective. Paul points to a set of virtues that must be in place in order for justice to be established. These virtues are key to a peaceful communal life. The preacher can reflect on the issue of discrimination involving race, gender, culture, and sexual orientation that often divides a community locally, nationally, and globally. Such discrimination demands a just response. Related to discrimination is immigration. The preacher can comment on the restrictive immigration policies globally, and especially on discrimination within immigration policies.

Related to immigration is forced migration of human and nonhuman communities of life as a result of climate change. The preacher can draw attention to the United Nations High Commissioner for Refugees (UNHCR), which estimates

---

Safety in the Fires

Fiery trials are not strange things to the Lord's anointed. The rejoicing in them is born only of the Holy Spirit. Oh, praise his holy name for a circumcised heart, teaching us that each trial of our faith hath its commission from the Father of spirits. Each wave of trial bears the Galilean Pilot on its crest. Listen: his voice is in the storm, and winds and waves obey that voice: "It is I; be not afraid." He has promised us help and safety in the fires, and not escape from them.

"And hereby we know that he abideth in us by the Spirit which he hath given us." Glory to the Lamb for the witness of the Holy Spirit! He knoweth that every step I have taken has been for the glory of God and the good of souls. However much I may have erred in judgment, it has been the fault of my head and not of my heart. I sleep, but my heart waketh; bless the Lord.

Julia A. J. Foote, *A Brand Plucked from the Fire: An Autobiographical Sketch* (New York: G. Hughes, 1879), 81–82.

that every year since 2008, an average of 21.5 million people have been forcibly displaced by climate change. Conservative projections are that by 2050, up to 250 million people will be displaced as a result of extreme weather conditions. The preacher can point to the further injustice of forced migration by exploring the fact that climate migrants are not protected by international law. Forced migration is also the result of war and persecution. The preacher can explore the Global Trends report, also produced by the UNHCR, to bring to light the 65.6 million people displaced since 2016, mainly due to conflicts, violence, and war in Middle Eastern countries such as Syria, Iraq, and Yemen, as well as sub-Saharan Africa, including Central African Republic, Burundi, the Democratic Republic of the Congo, South Sudan, and Sudan. In order for peace to exist on the planet, the work of justice must be done and take root among all peoples.

Thus, Paul's Letter to the Philippians offers the preacher many preaching opportunities to bring the biblical text into the contemporary world.

CAROL J. DEMPSEY, OP

Proper 23 (Sunday between October 9 and October 15 inclusive)

Matthew 22:1–14

¹Once more Jesus spoke to them in parables, saying: ²"The kingdom of heaven may be compared to a king who gave a wedding banquet for his son. ³He sent his slaves to call those who had been invited to the wedding banquet, but they would not come. ⁴Again he sent other slaves, saying, 'Tell those who have been invited: Look, I have prepared my dinner, my oxen and my fat calves have been slaughtered, and everything is ready; come to the wedding banquet.' ⁵But they made light of it and went away, one to his farm, another to his business, ⁶while the rest seized his slaves, mistreated them, and killed them. ⁷The king was enraged. He sent his troops, destroyed those murderers, and burned their city. ⁸Then he said to his slaves, 'The wedding is ready, but those invited were not worthy. ⁹Go therefore into the main streets, and invite everyone you find to the wedding banquet.' ¹⁰Those slaves went out into the streets and gathered all whom they found, both good and bad; so the wedding hall was filled with guests.

¹¹"But when the king came in to see the guests, he noticed a man there who was not wearing a wedding robe, ¹²and he said to him, 'Friend, how did you get in here without a wedding robe?' And he was speechless. ¹³Then the king said to the attendants, 'Bind him hand and foot, and throw him into the outer darkness, where there will be weeping and gnashing of teeth.' ¹⁴For many are called, but few are chosen."

Commentary 1: Connecting the Reading with Scripture

The material in Matthew 22 is filled with a tension, a tension that makes many readers uncomfortable and must be understood very carefully. In the narrative arc of Matthew's Gospel, Jesus has made his descent from the region of Galilee to Judea and the fateful events in Jerusalem that will culminate in his crucifixion. This chapter portrays Jesus' conflicts with the religious authorities in dramatic terms, and Jesus' rhetoric is often difficult for the modern ear to hear. Yet, understood properly, this passage speaks to important themes in Christian discipleship.

The context for this parable in Matthew is that Jesus has entered Jerusalem (Matt. 21:10) and is engaged in several disputes with those identified as "chief priests and scribes" (v. 15), "chief priests and elders" (v. 23), and "chief priests and Pharisees" (v. 45). While these disputes sometimes take the form of direct argumentation, such as the back-and-forth dialogue over Jesus' authority (vv. 23–27), they also appear in various parables that make a stern judgment on these religious authorities. In sum, they are not worthy of God's reign, about which Jesus preaches.

The parable of the Wedding Feast (22:1–14) is the third in a series of parables. It follows the parable of the Two Sons (21:28–32) and that of the Wicked Tenants (21:33–46); its tale about a wedding feast and those that are invited shares elements with these two preceding parables. Most prominently, each parable involves divided groups, one that is deemed worthy of the reign of God, and another that is not.

The passage begins by noting the addressees of this parable. Jesus is not speaking to his disciples. Rather, the "them" in 22:1 refers to the chief priests and the Pharisees mentioned two verses earlier. It is a parable of the reign or kingdom (in Greek, *basileia*), a reign that the Gospel of Matthew frequently appends with the phrase "of heaven." It is this reign of heaven that is compared to a wedding banquet.

The image of a great banquet is common in ancient Jewish and Christian literature. We see the imagery in Isaiah 25's vision of the feast on the mountain of the Lord with its rich food and well-aged wine. Many scholars also note the echoes of Lady Wisdom's feast in Proverbs 9 and its contrast to Lady Folly's banquet. In Matthew, the meal motif appears several times, so that this parable connects to Jesus' table fellowship with social outcasts, an important part of his ministry, and of course, his Last Supper with his disciples. Because the end we hope for directs the way to it, the notion of paradise as a banquet in which all are invited says much about values like hospitality and generosity in our community.

In this parable, a king plans a wedding feast for his son, sends out servants to invite the guests, and as in Luke 14:16–20, the invitation is rejected by the invitees. Yet, while Luke has the invitees simply offer excuses, the Matthean text takes on a much different flavor. In Matthew, the first invitation is refused without explanation: "They would not come." Yet the king will not be dissuaded. God does not give up so easily. Therefore, the king issues a second invitation, and while some of the invitees offer excuses as in Luke, Matthew has some of the invitees take the servants who offered the invitation and kill them (v. 6). In response, the king destroys the murderers and burns their city (v. 7).

The dramatic events in the story echo the earlier parable of the wicked tenants in which the servants, and eventually the son himself, are killed. In each parable, the angry master has the murderous groups killed and selects others to take their place. Most scholars understand the language in verse 7 of invasion, destruction, and burning of the city as a link to the events that occurred in the Roman devastation of Jerusalem in 70 CE. So this is an attempt by the author of Matthew's Gospel to understand those traumatic events and to interpret them for the nascent Jewish Christian community. Though Matthew seems to portray God in a harsh light, it is the situation that is harsh, and the author is trying to interpret it.

Because the addressees of this parable are the chief priests and Pharisees, there is no escaping the fact that Jesus appears to condemn the Jewish religious authorities in this parable. Moreover, Matthew clearly is addressing the mixed reception of the gospel within Israel and tying the response to God's judgment. After the destruction of the Second Temple in Jerusalem, all Jews had to take stock of their identity and move forward into an unknown future. The rabbis tied to the Pharisee movement, the separatist Essenes, and yes, those Jews who embraced belief in Jesus Christ were all forging their paths and were even rivals for converts. This Gospel, then, reflects those tensions. Matthew's identifying the rejected guests to the wedding feast speaks to those conflicts.

After declaring the unworthiness of the first invitees, the king sends servants out again to the thoroughfares (*diexodous*, a term that indicates where a street would cross through a city boundary and go out into the country) with a second invitation.

In some sense, the parable could end with the wedding hall being filled with the new guests. It would reinforce the message of the two previous parables regarding those who are worthy of God's reign and those who are not. Moreover, it picks up the important parallel with Luke 14, that the second group consists of those who were on the margins of society, those with whom Jesus shared table fellowship. Verse 10 notes that the servants gathered whomever they could find "both good and bad," and it might be signaling this propensity of Jesus to include those who were seen socially as '"bad."

However, the parable ends with a striking image that suggests a different set of connections in this Gospel. The king sees a guest without a wedding garment. When the guest offers no explanation for this lack, the king instructs the attendants to bind the guest "hand and foot" and cast him into the "outer darkness."

The description of this second group, which is rejected and cast into darkness with weeping and teeth gnashing, vividly connects the parable of the Wedding Feast with the eschatological parables of chapter 24 and 25 that also portray mixed groups, such as the good and wicked servant (24:45–51), the ten virgins (25:1–13), those given talents (25:14–30), and the nations separated as sheep and goats (25:31–46).

Those parables serve as a warning to believers to stay watchful. They are discipleship parables that warn believers to live in such a way that they are always ready to respond to God's invitation. They must be watchful, for they know not the time or place. They must use all that has been given them. They must care for the "least of these."

Thus, while the parable of the Wedding Feast portrays the immediate conflict between Jesus and religious authorities, and comes out of that conflict between Matthew's Jewish Christian community and other Jewish communities, the parable cannot be read as an insider's tale that rejects outsiders. No, ultimately this parable connects to broader themes in Matthew about the nature of true discipleship and how any who wish to partake of God's banquet must respond to the invitation with a yes borne out in their lives.

MICHAEL E. LEE

Commentary 2: Connecting the Reading with the World

In this particular week of Ordinary Time, the church is led to a parabolic picture of what the Christian faith looks like when we get it right. So often, of course, we get it wrong—when the faith appears hypocritical, or judgmental, or too eager to be aligned with the powers that be—but so many in our time yearn for a community of faith that gets it right.

There was a cartoon a while back, probably in *The New Yorker*, that showed a man walking down a city sidewalk who had just passed someone holding a sign that said, "Prepare to Meet Thy God!" The man's reaction to that sign was to stop in front of the next plate-glass window, look at his reflection, slick down his hair, and straighten his tie. Clearly, for him there was no fooling around with the realm of God. He is a sort of meme for a lot of Christians. For him, and maybe for us much of the time, the realm of God is serious business—something requiring a load of gravitas on our part—but there is still that yearning for a community that gets it right.

I once served a church in which a preschool program rented our educational space during the week. They were there, these preschoolers, every weekday morning. After recess, day after day, their leader would line up all the children—right outside my study window—and would give them the same stern lecture before leading them back into the building. It was a lecture, from the leader's perspective, on how to behave in church. "Boys and girls," said the leader, "I know you have heard me say this many times, but you cannot be reminded often enough how to behave in God's house. Now when you go inside these doors, there is to be no talking, no laughing, no giggling, no playing, no running, no tickling . . ." She really said tickling! She thought of every conceivable behavior that might be upsetting to God. "No chasing, no breaking in line, no fighting, no slapping, no kissing . . ." It was a long list of things that could not be done in God's house, and every day I heard that list, I got more and more depressed. One day, I happened to walk out of the office into the hallway. One of the children happened to be in the hall drinking from the water fountain, and at the sight of me she gasped and shrank away and blurted out, "I'm sorry!"

She was learning that the realm of God is serious business—but does it have to be?

In this text from Matthew, there is the refreshing suggestion that the realm of God is like a party. This suggestion is also at the root of so many other biblical texts. The psalmist, for example, thought of life lived in the presence of God and immortalized that thought with words that often call us to worship: "This is the day that the LORD has made; let us rejoice and be glad in it" (Ps. 118:24). Elsewhere in Scripture, the Israelites are delivered by God from Pharaoh's armies at the Red Sea, and they set their grateful joy to music: "Sing to the LORD, for he has triumphed gloriously; horse and rider he has thrown into the sea" (Exod. 15:21). There is singing and dancing throughout Scripture, celebrating the victory of life over death. Such joy, thank God, is at the root of our faith.

Elie Wiesel once wrote that the celebration of life is more important than mourning for the dead. "When a wedding procession encounters a funeral procession in the street," he said, "the mourners must halt so as to allow the wedding party to proceed. Surely you know what respect we show our dead," Wiesel continued, "but a wedding—symbol of life and renewal, symbol of promise, too—takes precedence."[1]

The great symbols of God's realm are celebratory symbols—wedding receptions and banquets, feasts and festivals, the bread of life and the wine of gladness. God is forever inviting us to a party, and not just a party of people who look and think just like we do. God invites us to see what is miraculous about a party with the oddest sort of invitation list that you can imagine.

In this text, a peculiarly touchy king throws a wedding banquet for his son. He invites all the proper folks—precisely the folks you would expect to be invited to such a party—but, for a variety of reasons, everyone declines. Some ignore the invitation, others think up disingenuous excuses, and still others even kill the king's servants who were simply delivering the invitations. The enraged king returns the favor, killing the murderers, burning down their city, declaring the original invitation list to be a collection of the unworthy, and sending other servants out into the streets—this time with no particular guest list and simply an instruction to invite whomever they encounter. The banquet hall ends up being filled to capacity with all sorts of guests—"both good and bad" (Matt. 22:10). They are all there, and presumably all distinctions cease to matter, all barriers cease to divide. At first, the king's message seems to be, "Come to my party, regardless!"

If Matthew's text ended here with verse 10, the sermon could practically write itself—but there's another move here. In verses 11 through 14, the king has an issue with one guest's attire. A man is not wearing a proper wedding garment, so the king has him hog-tied and thrown into the outer darkness, "'where there will be weeping and gnashing of teeth.' For many are called, but few are chosen" (vv. 13–14).

Perhaps, even when the realm of God is like a party, there is a distinction between being invited into the party, and being ready for the party. The late Fred Craddock once put it this way: "Matthew knew how easily grace can melt into permissiveness; he knew that for those who presume upon grace, forgiveness does not fulfill righteousness but negates it. Matthew apparently is addressing a church that has lost the distinction between accepting all persons and condoning all behavior."[2]

So it may just be that when we decide to enter into God's ongoing party, we need to be ready to put on the garments of gladness and the cloak of thanksgiving.

Come to the banquet table of my realm, says God. Some do. Some do not. Some procrastinate. Some loiter. Some get distracted and wander down the wrong streets and miss the party. Some lose the invitation, or do not have the address, or just never make it. Some say, "I will put on my own party," and set out to do just that.

The good news of the gospel is that God keeps issuing the invitation. In our churches, the eucharistic feast is regularly made ready, the table is gratefully prepared, the community gathers round with ample reason to be joyful and thankful and eager to welcome all. Come, all of you, and be my guests, says God; and at our best, we do the same in God's name.

For God has left us with challenging questions: Having caught a glimpse of my banquet, what are you going to do now? Are you going to fall back upon some notion of my realm as joyless and restrictive and not for you? Or will you also come to my party?

THEODORE J. WARDLAW

---

1. Elie Wiesel, *A Jew Today* (New York: Vintage Books, 1978), 193.
2. Fred Craddock, *Preaching the New Common Lectionary* (Nashville: Abingdon, 1987), 230.

Proper 24 (Sunday between October 16 and October 22 inclusive)

Isaiah 45:1–7 and Exodus 33:12–23
Psalm 96:1–9 (10–13) and Psalm 99

1 Thessalonians 1:1–10
Matthew 22:15–22

Isaiah 45:1–7

> ¹Thus says the LORD to his anointed, to Cyrus,
>   whose right hand I have grasped
> to subdue nations before him
>   and strip kings of their robes,
> to open doors before him—
>   and the gates shall not be closed:
> ²I will go before you
>   and level the mountains,
> I will break in pieces the doors of bronze
>   and cut through the bars of iron,
> ³I will give you the treasures of darkness
>   and riches hidden in secret places,
> so that you may know that it is I, the LORD,
>   the God of Israel, who call you by your name.
> ⁴For the sake of my servant Jacob,
>   and Israel my chosen,
> I call you by your name,
>   I surname you, though you do not know me.
> ⁵I am the LORD, and there is no other;
>   besides me there is no god.
>   I arm you, though you do not know me,
> ⁶so that they may know, from the rising of the sun
>   and from the west, that there is no one besides me;
>   I am the LORD, and there is no other.
> ⁷I form light and create darkness,
>   I make weal and create woe;
>   I the LORD do all these things.

Exodus 33:12–23

> ¹²Moses said to the LORD, "See, you have said to me, 'Bring up this people'; but you have not let me know whom you will send with me. Yet you have said, 'I know you by name, and you have also found favor in my sight.' ¹³Now if I have found favor in your sight, show me your ways, so that I may know you and find favor in your sight. Consider too that this nation is your people." ¹⁴He said, "My presence will go with you, and I will give you rest." ¹⁵And he said to him, "If your presence will not go, do not carry us up from here. ¹⁶For how shall it be known that I have found favor in your sight, I and your people, unless you go with us? In this way, we shall be distinct, I and your people, from every people on the face of the earth."

¹⁷The Lord said to Moses, "I will do the very thing that you have asked; for you have found favor in my sight, and I know you by name." ¹⁸Moses said, "Show me your glory, I pray." ¹⁹And he said, "I will make all my goodness pass before you, and will proclaim before you the name, 'The Lord'; and I will be gracious to whom I will be gracious, and will show mercy on whom I will show mercy. ²⁰But," he said, "you cannot see my face; for no one shall see me and live." ²¹And the Lord continued, "See, there is a place by me where you shall stand on the rock; ²²and while my glory passes by I will put you in a cleft of the rock, and I will cover you with my hand until I have passed by; ²³then I will take away my hand, and you shall see my back; but my face shall not be seen."

Commentary 1: Connecting the Reading with Scripture

"The Lord is king" [*sic*] of all the earth, which, according to the psalmist, "quakes" in God's presence (Ps. 99:1). God is a "lover of justice," who "established equity" (v. 4). The psalmist continues by proclaiming that our Lord is revered above everyone else's gods (96:4). All, whether they believe in our God or the gods of their own culture, will stand trial before ours, who "is coming to judge the earth. He [*sic*] will judge the world with righteousness, and the peoples with his [*sic*] truth" (v. 13). We are presented with a "he" who reigns as an emperor. Such a God is hierarchical, providing a pattern for earthly kingdoms and the eventual colonial conquest. Such imagery has proved problematic for the world's wretched, who have suffered disenfranchisement before invaders who justify land theft and genocide and believe they are called by God. Can this "lover of justice" truly be just while those claiming to be disciples justify all manner of conquest in the name of this God?

Moses is called and chosen by God because he has found favor in God's sight (Exod. 33:12). He is called to lead God's chosen people, God's nation (v. 13) from the slavery of Egypt to a new promised land. This has always been a liberative image for the enslaved, who sang songs to Moses the liberator. There is something powerful about a motif where God's servant leads God's people away from slavery and oppression toward liberation. Because Moses is God's chosen, and the people constitute God's nation, we are comforted by a God who goes before them and us toward a promised land that flows with milk and honey. Unfortunately, the dream of liberation for the oppressed Hebrew slaves is also the nightmare for the native people of Canaan who must first succumb to genocide before God's blessings can be showered upon those whom God has elected as God's own. Yes, the psalmist is right: "let the peoples tremble" especially the Canaanites, because "the Lord is great in Zion; he [*sic*] is exalted over all the people" (Ps. 99:1–2). The people tremble for what was about to befall them before God's chosen of ancient times; even as the new Israelites who were Pilgrims from the Protestant North or Crusaders in the Catholic South, massacred the indigenous people of the Western Hemisphere.

Can God's people do wrong? If so, is it God's fault for making the wrong choice? God chose Moses, and the people whom God called him to lead, even though they participated in what we today would call crimes against humanity. Not only does a certain danger exist for those relegated to the underside of history by those whom God anointed. A danger exists for all, especially the chosen, when alliances are made with those who do not know God, who live lives contrary to the equity which the Lover of Justice wishes to establish. Take the example of the pagan King Cyrus. In 539 BCE, God chose and used the nonbelieving Persian king to bring forth God's political purposes. "Thus says the Lord to his anointed, to Cyrus, whose right hand I have grasped to subdue nations before him and strip kings of their robes, to open doors before him—and the

He Rules by Serving

The lordship of Christ is no royal, kingly lordship but the lordship of the obedient servant of God, the Lamb of God! Nor is the lordship of Christ a "religious rule," separated from the kingdom of the world; it is rather the rule of the real bodily crucified one. . . . He rules by serving. He redeems through suffering. He liberates through his sacrifice. The unity of the risen and the crucified one is grasped by neither a two kingdoms doctrine nor by the doctrine of the kingly lordship of Christ, but only by an eschatological Christology. . . .

Christian messianic ethics celebrates and anticipates the presence of God in history. It wants to practice the unconditioned within the conditioned and the last things in the next to last. In the economic dimension, God is present in bread; in healing, as health. In the political dimension God is present as the dignity of the human being; in the cultural dimension, as solidarity. In the ecological area, God is present as peace with nature; in the personal area, in the certainty of the heart. Every form of his presence is veiled and sacramental; it is not yet a presence face-to-face. God's presence encounters human persons in the concrete messianic form of his liberation from hunger, oppression, alienation, enmity, and despair. These messianic forms of his presence point at the same time, however, beyond themselves to a greater presence, and finally to that present in which "God will be all in all."

Jürgen Moltmann, "Political Theology and Political Hermeneutics," in *The Politics of Discipleship and Discipleship in Politics*, ed. Williard M. Swartley (Eugene, OR: Cascade Books, 2006), 41, 48.

---

gates shall not be closed . . . For the sake of my servant Jacob, and Israel my chosen, I call you by your name, I surname you, though you do not know me" (Isa. 45:1, 4).

Like Moses, Cyrus is chosen by name. It matters little if Cyrus knows God; it matters less if Cyrus is righteous or not. All that matters is that the ends justifies the means. How God's rule is established is of little importance, only that the reign be established—by whatever means necessary. Such a political theology appears contrary to the God who chooses those who, according to Paul, remain within a "work of faith and labor of love and steadfastness of hope in our Lord Jesus Christ," the faithful who are remembered before God in thanksgiving and offered prayers (1 Thess. 1:3). They are recognized as chosen because they have become "imitators . . . of the Lord, for in spite of persecution [they] received the word with joy inspired by the Holy Spirit" (v. 6).

However, different from Paul's description of the chosen, Christians have embraced many modern-day Cyruses whose actions seem contrary to the gospel message. It matters little if the person elected is a sexual predator who brags about his conquests or a person considered as "one of their own" by racist groups; support continues by a majority. If God can use the pagan Cyrus to bring about God's will, then why not today's politicians? Rather than modern-day "imitators of the Lord" (v. 6) who become the salt of the earth, many take the role of serving as a shield against those who question certain politicians' immorality, due to a concocted exegesis claiming God is using a flawed human in order to establish God's reign in the new promised land.

Does the church commit apostasy when laying holy hands upon the incarnation of the very vices Jesus condemned to advance a political agenda that trumps a biblical call to truth, mercy, and justice? When political leaders like Cyrus, whose lives are antithetical to the gospel message, are defended because they advance the special interests of those who think they are chosen, are we prostituting the gospel for the cheap coins of partisan politics?

How then does the church read biblical passages that celebrate invading the land occupied by indigenous people and call for their genocide to purify the land for those people called by God's name? What do we do when those who supposedly are God's chosen revive a biblical interpretation to justify politically supporting and propelling to power one who is antithetical to the gospel? In short, what do we do when

Scripture passages like these are used to justify political actions that are contrary to the one we call "lover of justice"? Simple explanations can never be the sermon's topic.

Churches who fail to wrestle with the text and instead dismiss the injustices with rhetorical simplistic answers like the mystery of God, or that God can work though evil situations, commit a great disservice. The text is problematic, and the faithful, like Jacob, are called to wrestle with the text. What does it mean that God calls for genocide, or appoints emperors? What does it mean that God sends evil spirits (1 Sam. 16:14) or brings evil unto the city (Amos 3:6)? The church is not called to save God from God, nor to provide answers for problematic texts such as these; but to wrestle with them, even if there is no clear resolution.

Jesus said, "Give therefore to the emperor the things that are the emperor's, and to God the things that are God's" (Matt. 22:21). The so-called chosen have become adept at giving to the God the things that are the emperor's: specifically conquest and a genocide that kills figuratively and literally the disposed and disenfranchised. Unless the things that are of God—to act justly, to love mercy, and to walk humbly—are demonstrated by those who say they are chosen, or by those whom they proclaim to be modern-day Cyrus, they do not know God—regardless as to how much the political interests of the empire are advanced.

MIGUEL A. DE LA TORRE

Commentary 2: Connecting the Reading with the World

Isaiah 45:1–7. This text is disturbing and hopeful. The tensions present offer the interpreter multiple angles for proclaiming the gospel.

The disturbing elements of Isaiah 45:1–7 are twofold: (1) the Lord claims Cyrus, a ruthless totalitarian king, as God's anointed (v. 1); (2) the Lord uses this *unbelieving* non-Israelite ruler as an agent in God's mission to bless the nations. Both of these present challenges to God's people to hear the word.

The hopeful truths that emerge from Isaiah are the assurances that the Lord, Israel's God, is indeed creator, Lord of all nations, and uniquely God. Isaiah has a grand view of history and sees it unfolding in ways that make the Lord known to all peoples everywhere. This is a vision of abundance in which there is enough for all.

The cotexts from the lectionary (Ps. 99; Matt. 22:15–22; and 1 Thess. 1:1–10) offer liturgical pathways for reflecting on both disturbing elements and hopeful ones. Psalm 99 is part of the enthronement psalms (Pss. 93–99), which anchor security and hope in the truth that God is the true king. God is exalted over all people and reigns with justice and righteousness (Ps. 99:2–4). Matthew 22:15–22 offers Jesus' answer to the question of paying taxes to an oppressive overlord like the Roman emperor. Jesus separates paying taxes from allegiance to the power of the empire. First Thessalonians 1:1–10 celebrates the spread of the gospel through persons who once worshiped idols. The preacher will want to reflect deeply on the tensions of living as God's people under political systems run by those who may not yet know the Lord. Isaiah 45 stresses the commitment of the Lord to God's people in the mission to make the Lord known to all nations.

The danger for the reader is the temptation to withdraw from the wider political world. Isaiah 45 is proclaiming God's hand in guiding history, a declaration to an Israel that is powerless, exiled, and seemingly at the mercy of its totalitarian overlords. It is a misreading if persons in power use it to suppress others by appealing to God's appointment of rulers. Cyrus was the Persian king who defeated the Babylonians and permitted Jewish persons in exile to return to their homeland and rebuild the temple. This text is not a blanket blessing of rulers who act wickedly and unjustly. It does not advocate for God's people to silence their prophetic witness for justice and for the blessing of the world through the gospel.

Isaiah 45:1–7 is missional in its outlook. The goal of the Lord's actions is for Cyrus to recognize the Lord's hand and ultimately for all the earth to know that the Lord is God alone over all pretenders. Ezra 1:2–4 records Cyrus's acknowledgment of the Lord. This is a reminder of the missional center of the Old Testament (Gen. 12:3b; Exod. 19:6; Isa. 42:6; 49:6). Israel is the conduit of God's blessing to the world. By calling Cyrus, God furthers this mission by delivering Israel. This is part of the long story that reaches its climax in the life, death, and resurrection of Jesus. Jesus becomes the one to whom all bow (Phil. 2:9–10; cf. Isa. 45:22–23). God's action in saving Israel through Cyrus for the sake of all nations demonstrates the Lord's incomparability with any other god.

Exodus 33:12–23. Exodus 33:12–23 is the third intercession that Moses makes on behalf of God's people after their calamitous forging of a golden calf idol. Moses had previously interceded for their forgiveness. Now Moses pleads for God's presence to accompany them to the promised land.

Worshipers will recall the hymn "Rock of Ages, Cleft for Me." Exodus 33:12–23 serves as the inspiration for this classic hymn. The imagery of the hymn connects Moses' experience with God on Sinai with the cross of Christ as the ultimate refuge.

The lectionary coreadings provide a framework for thinking about the dynamic interplay between God's people and God's presence in the mission of the gospel. Psalm 99 declares the universal kingship of the Lord. Matthew 22:15–22 recognizes that God's people live in a reality where the kingdom of God and the kingdom of the world stand in dynamic tension. First Thessalonians 1:1–10 reminds the Christians in Thessalonica of Paul's ministry and in particular emphasizes the presence of the Holy Spirit in the spread of the good news.

At Sinai, God's people received the commission to serve as a "kingdom of priests and a holy nation" (Exod. 19:6) for the world. This missional calling assumed that Israel was God's "treasured possession" (v. 5). This identity and calling is at stake in 33:12–23. Yes, the Lord forgave God's people and fully supports the leadership of Moses, but God's mission is in vain apart from God's presence with God's people. This text articulates two needs. Human leadership must recognize its inadequacy apart from God's powerful indwelling presence. Postresurrection, God's real presence becomes personified in the work of the Holy Spirit. God's people (in particular Exod. 33:12–23 speaks of religious leaders) must commit to prayer for the abiding presence of God in their work. The temptation is reliance on human strength, planning, and talent. Moses eschews this and intercedes for God's accompaniment of the people to Canaan.

Spiritual growth is not merely about receiving affirmation and acceptance from God. The Lord responds positively (v. 17) to Moses' requests for God's presence with the people, but Moses is not content at this point to bask in God's approval. Receiving affirmation and blessing moves Moses to want to know God more profoundly. What does it look like for God's people today to desire a deeper relationship beyond one in which God grants our prayers? Moses' response points a way forward. Moses asks to experience God in God's fullness (v. 18).

Thus Exodus 33:12–23 is about the deeper revelation of God's character. This is critical for thinking about God in our day. Who is God? What is God really like? This text begins to tease out the life-affirming good news about the God of Scripture. The book of Exodus contains frightening elements: the ecological disasters, plagues, and the Passover were good news for God's enslaved people, but bad news for the Egyptians, who experienced God's wrath. Now, in Exodus 32–34, God's people have angered the Lord through idolatry. Will God treat Israel as God treated the Egyptians? The answer is no, and it is not because Moses was an effective intercessor (cf. 32:11–14; 32:31–33:4). God forgives and shows mercy to Israel because grace and mercy are central to God's character.

What Exodus 33:19 hints at is fully revealed in 34:6–7. The Lord's love is infinite; the Lord's judgment is finite. One may object that God did not demonstrate infinite love to Egypt. The truth of Scripture is this God is for God's people for the sake of the nations (including Egypt). However, in Scripture, when nations/individuals (including God's people themselves, e.g., Ps. 89) acted in ways that seek to thwart God's mission of bring salvation to the world, God brought *temporary* times of judgment.

The truth of the Lord's infinite love reaches its climactic form in the life, death, and resurrection of Jesus the Messiah. The biblical story demonstrates that God's love will be the final verdict in this world and grounds our hope and our ethic in this reality. See Revelation 21:1–6.

BRIAN D. RUSSELL

Proper 24 (Sunday between October 16 and October 22 inclusive)

Psalm 96:1–9 (10–13)

¹O sing to the LORD a new song;
    sing to the LORD, all the earth.
²Sing to the LORD, bless his name;
    tell of his salvation from day to day.
³Declare his glory among the nations,
    his marvelous works among all the peoples.
⁴For great is the LORD, and greatly to be praised;
    he is to be revered above all gods.
⁵For all the gods of the peoples are idols,
    but the LORD made the heavens.
⁶Honor and majesty are before him;
    strength and beauty are in his sanctuary.

⁷Ascribe to the LORD, O families of the peoples,
    ascribe to the LORD glory and strength.
⁸Ascribe to the LORD the glory due his name;
    bring an offering, and come into his courts.
⁹Worship the LORD in holy splendor;
    tremble before him, all the earth.

¹⁰Say among the nations, "The LORD is king!
    The world is firmly established; it shall never be moved.
    He will judge the peoples with equity."
¹¹Let the heavens be glad, and let the earth rejoice;
    let the sea roar, and all that fills it;
        ¹²let the field exult, and everything in it.
Then shall all the trees of the forest sing for joy
        ¹³before the LORD; for he is coming,
    for he is coming to judge the earth.
He will judge the world with righteousness,
    and the peoples with his truth.

Psalm 99

¹The LORD is king; let the peoples tremble!
    He sits enthroned upon the cherubim; let the earth quake!
²The LORD is great in Zion;
    he is exalted over all the peoples.
³Let them praise your great and awesome name.
    Holy is he!
⁴Mighty King, lover of justice,
    you have established equity;
you have executed justice
    and righteousness in Jacob.

⁵Extol the LORD our God;
    worship at his footstool.
    Holy is he!

⁶Moses and Aaron were among his priests,
    Samuel also was among those who called on his name.
    They cried to the LORD, and he answered them.
⁷He spoke to them in the pillar of cloud;
    they kept his decrees,
    and the statutes that he gave them.

⁸O LORD our God, you answered them;
    you were a forgiving God to them,
    but an avenger of their wrongdoings.
⁹Extol the LORD our God,
    and worship at his holy mountain;
    for the LORD our God is holy.

Connecting the Psalm with Scripture and Worship

Psalm 96:1–9 (10–13). Both of today's psalms are enthronement psalms, praising God as ruler of all. While Psalm 99 opens with the classic enthronement proclamation, "YHWH reigns" (NRSV "The LORD is king"), Psalm 96 sets this phrase more than halfway through the text. Regardless of placement, this emphasis on God's enthronement provides the broadest connection with today's Isaiah pericope: Psalm 96 is liturgical reinforcement for the prophet's insistence that Cyrus is powerful purely because YHWH chooses to be *the* power behind this emperor's throne.

The Isaiah text begins by cataloging the great works that God will do through Cyrus: God will "subdue nations . . . strip kings of their robes" (Isa. 45:1), "level mountains . . . break . . . doors of bronze and cut through the bars of iron" (v. 2), provide "treasures of darkness and riches hidden in secret" (v. 3). Such is the work of God. Meanwhile, the work of God's people is laid out in Psalm 96.

Leading up to the enthronement proclamation are impassioned instructions regarding how and why we must worship the sovereign God. Listen to these fervent verbs! We are to "sing to the LORD . . . bless [God's] name; tell of [God's] salvation . . , declare [God's] glory" (Ps. 96:1–3). Why? Because "great is the LORD . . . the LORD made the heavens" (vv. 4–5). Then, we are to "ascribe to the LORD glory and strength . . . bring an offering, and come into [God's] courts . . . worship the LORD . . . tremble before [God]" (vv. 7–9). Why? Because "[YHWH] is coming to judge the earth . . . with righteousness" (v. 13). It is all about God, underscoring that Cyrus—or anyone else—can be nothing greater than a tool of YHWH.

Both texts focus on God's "marvelous works among all the peoples" (96:3), and it is hard to imagine a more comprehensive call to praise than Psalm 96. In addition to "the peoples" (vv. 3, 7, 10, 13), the psalmist calls forth adoration from "the heavens . . . the earth . . . the sea . . . all that fills it . . . the field . . . everything in it . . . all the trees of the forest" (vv. 11–12).

No part of creation is exempt from praising YHWH, and no other gods are to be praised: "all the gods of the peoples are idols" (v. 5). Isaiah sounds a similar note with "I am the LORD, and there is no other" (Isa. 45:6), which could lead to a sermon on humankind's ageless tendency toward idolatry. By emphasizing YHWH's initiative, Isaiah warns against idolizing Cyrus, just one example of earthly powers we must not worship, because YHWH "is to be revered above all gods" (Ps. 96:4)—and above all emperors too.

Alternatively, a sermon might grow from the repeated statement that Cyrus does not "know" YHWH (Isa. 45:4, 5), despite the need for YHWH to be known by one and all (vv. 3, 6). Use Psalm 96 as Cyrus's tutor! Or base your sermon around the psalm's opening directive to "sing to the LORD a new song." Consider how Cyrus led Persia to sing a new song in its treatment of captive Israel.

Psalm 96 is structured as two calls to worship (Ps. 96:1–3, 7–12). Such an arrangement might call worshipers to praise as they feel the text's poetic surging:

> Reader 1: O sing to the Lord a new song;
> Reader 2: sing to the Lord, all the earth.
> All: Sing to the Lord, bless God's name; tell of God's salvation from day to day.
> Reader 1: Ascribe to the Lord, O families of the peoples,
> Reader 2: ascribe to the Lord glory and strength.
> All: Ascribe to the Lord the glory due God's name; bring an offering, and come into God's courts.
> Reader 1: Let the heavens be glad, and let the earth rejoice;
> Reader 2: let the sea roar, and all that fills it;
> All: let the field exult and everything in it. Worship the Lord in holy splendor. (Ps. 96:1–2, 7–9)

Psalm 99. The Exodus reading prescribed for this day depicts two aspects of God: God who would "speak to Moses face to face, as one speaks to a friend" (Exod. 33:11), and God who explains, "No one shall see me and live" (v. 20). Psalm 99 is useful to a preacher exploring either characteristic, or both.

As we listen in on his unexpectedly personal conversation with YHWH, Moses boldly reminds God of God's declaration, "I know you by name, and you have found favor in my sight" (vv. 12, 13, 16). Moses also presses God to reinforce Israel's standing as God's chosen people (vv. 13, 16) by accompanying the Israelites on their journey. Instead of rebuking Moses' brazenness, God consents to his request but imposes limitations. For all their face-to-face friendliness, this is not a relationship between equals. God must shield Moses from the full brunt of divine glory, and thus their conversational intimacy leads to God carefully protecting the mortal man.

Psalm 99, by contrast, includes no intimacy. In fact, the psalmist barely ventures to address God directly, preferring to talk *about* God (Ps. 99:1–3, 5–7, 9) rather than *to* God (vv. 3a, 4, 8). The psalm's purpose is to praise God by emphasizing God's sovereignty (vv. 1, 4) and holiness (vv. 3, 5, 9). While the image of God as king is prominent throughout the Psalter, this psalm definitely underscores the majesty of God emphasized in the latter part of today's Exodus text.

After beginning with the proclamation that "YHWH reigns" (NRSV "The LORD is king"), the psalmist proceeds to depict God as "enthroned upon the cherubim," so great that "the peoples tremble" and "the earth quake(s)" (v. 1). God is "exalted over all the peoples" (v. 2), and we are called to praise God's "great and awesome name" (v. 3). Sermons focused on God's glory will find these images helpful.

The psalm's second section describes how God conducts God's rule: addressed as "lover of justice," God is extolled as the king who "established equity . . . [and] executed justice and righteousness in Jacob" (v. 4). These images could be effective in a sermon focused on Moses' insistence that God "consider too that this nation [aka Jacob] is [God's] people" (Exod. 33:13), and his eagerness for God to "go with" the people so that they "shall be distinct . . . from every people on the face of the earth" (v. 16).

The psalm's final section actually names Moses, though not in terms of the one-on-one relationship glimpsed in Exodus 33. Instead, Moses is identified as "among those who called on [God's] name" (Ps. 99:6) and "kept [God's] decrees and the statutes that [God] gave them" (v. 7b). The psalmist thereby highlights two other attributes of God's sovereignty: God is responsive to our cries, and God provides rules of conduct for us. These two aspects coalesce in a final example of how God rules God's people: God is "a forgiving God to them, but an avenger of their wrongdoings" (v. 8b). A sermon that considers how this cosmic ruler is also the caring companion of Moses could make use of this section.

The psalm closes with a final call to "extol" and "worship" God because "the LORD our God is holy" (v. 9). Sermons emphasizing the unseeable holiness of God (Exod. 33:19–23) can make use of this entire psalm.

In that vein, a responsive reading of Psalm 99 would be liturgically effective. Have an expressive lector read all the verses and invite the congregation to join in on the three declarations of God's holiness, crying "Holy is he!" or "Holy is God!" (Ps. 99:3b, 5b, 9b). The shouts of praise in the psalm suggest a singing of "Holy, Holy, Holy! Lord God Almighty!"

LEIGH CAMPBELL-TAYLOR

Proper 24 (Sunday between October 16 and October 22 inclusive)

1 Thessalonians 1:1–10

¹Paul, Silvanus, and Timothy,
To the church of the Thessalonians in God the Father and the Lord Jesus Christ:
Grace to you and peace.
²We always give thanks to God for all of you and mention you in our prayers, constantly ³remembering before our God and Father your work of faith and labor of love and steadfastness of hope in our Lord Jesus Christ. ⁴For we know, brothers and sisters beloved by God, that he has chosen you, ⁵because our message of the gospel came to you not in word only, but also in power and in the Holy Spirit and with full conviction; just as you know what kind of persons we proved to be among you for your sake. ⁶And you became imitators of us and of the Lord, for in spite of persecution you received the word with joy inspired by the Holy Spirit, ⁷so that you became an example to all the believers in Macedonia and in Achaia. ⁸For the word of the Lord has sounded forth from you not only in Macedonia and Achaia, but in every place your faith in God has become known, so that we have no need to speak about it. ⁹For the people of those regions report about us what kind of welcome we had among you, and how you turned to God from idols, to serve a living and true God, ¹⁰and to wait for his Son from heaven, whom he raised from the dead—Jesus, who rescues us from the wrath that is coming.

Commentary 1: Connecting the Reading with Scripture

An interesting structural feature to Paul's letters is the thanksgiving section, which comes directly after a letter's salutation. This section allows Paul to reconnect with the recipients of his letters, reminding them of their faith, the faithfulness of God, and/or their time together in the sharing of the gospel. Paul, now no longer physically present in that geographical location, desires to close the gap of time and distance with the writing of a letter. The thanksgiving section plays a key role in that. It calls to mind that which they have in common, ripening them to hear what he has to say in the letter. While some would be predisposed to hear and follow Paul's instruction, others may need further convincing. Therefore, one function for the thanksgiving is for Paul to reearn a hearing for the letter. Thanking God for others is not only an encouragement but also a persuasive rhetorical act.

Some features are common to the thanksgiving sections of Paul's letters, but other aspects are unique to the circumstances and main teaching of the individual letter. This is true of 1 Thessalonians. With the exception of the very first verse, which is a brief salutation, the passage for this week is a thanksgiving section that makes clear connections to the setting of the letter. Key to the background of the letter is the good deal of success that resulted from Paul's gospel work in Thessalonica. Many responded, and the news of their conversions spread even to surrounding cities (1 Thess. 1:7–8; Acts 17:4).

However, Paul's time there came to a rather abrupt ending. Other Jews, who stood in opposition to Paul and Silas's proclamation of the gospel, led a contingent asking for their arrest. Unable to find Paul and Silas, they nabbed Jason instead (Acts 17:5–9). With the looming threat of their arrest, Paul and Silas were covertly sent out of the city to Berea (v. 10). The rather sudden exit and ensuing inability to return, due to the persistence of the persecution, likely would have cut short any plans Paul had for further discipleship and instruction for the Thessalonians.

Still at a distance, Paul's pastoral heart would have yearned to affirm that the believers were not abandoned, and that they could persist in the faith, even in the midst of the persecution. Though Paul himself could not communicate this in a personal visit, he was able to do the next best thing. He sent Timothy, a young coworker in the faith who seemingly would not be in personal danger, because of his lack of recognition in that locale. Timothy, upon his return to Paul and Silas (now in Corinth), reports that the Thessalonians persist in the faith though still surrounded by ongoing persecution (1 Thess. 3:6–8). However, the report also indicates areas of lack in their understanding and practice of their new faith. Thanksgiving was certainly of need for these believers.

In light of this context, three aspects of the thanksgiving section in 1 Thessalonians stand out. First, Paul reminds them of the Holy Spirit's role in securing their salvation (1:5–6). Paul's mention of the Holy Spirit is a reminder that God, not Paul, is the source of their salvation. Paul's present absence does not diminish the reality of their conversion, nor does it influence their ability to persist in the faith. The joy of their salvation is in and from the Holy Spirit (v. 6).

Joy and the presence of the Holy Spirit are connected in a number of passages in Scripture. We see it in Elizabeth when the baby leaps in her womb (Luke 1:41–45), in Jesus as he talks with the disciples (Luke 10:21), and in some disciples of Paul and Barnabas following their proclamation of the gospel (Acts 13:52). The lack of surety in the Thessalonians' current circumstances is overmatched by the surety of the salvific work of the Holy Spirit in their lives. The former is temporal, but the latter is not. Therefore be encouraged.

A second aspect of note here is the Thessalonians' coming to the faith in the midst of persecution. This resistance to the gospel was stiff enough to force Paul and Silas out of town. While bringing up their persecution may initially seem to run counter to the encouragement desired in a thanksgiving section, it actually serves as a testimony to the durability of the gospel and the Thessalonians' faith. Anything weak would have been thwarted or destroyed by this opposition. However, their faith took root and persisted in the face of it. What can explain that, other than it being truly of God?

Looking more widely in the NT, we see this theme in many places. In the Beatitudes, those who are persecuted for the sake of righteousness are said to be "blessed" (Matt. 5:10; cf. Luke 6:22). Believers are told to rejoice when "fiery" ordeals come their way, in that they have an opportunity to "participate in the sufferings of Christ" (1 Pet. 4:12–16, NIV). Paul, more boldly and broadly, states: "All who want to live a godly life in Christ Jesus will be persecuted" (2 Tim. 3:12). The presence of persecution is an indicator of the existence of faith, rather than a hallmark of its absence or weakness. One likely reason that the Thessalonians' faith spilled over into Macedonia and Achaia, and that they became "an example" to all the believers there (1 Thess. 1:7), is that it was flourishing in the midst of testing. Others could not help but take notice, which is itself an encouragement to stand.

A third key feature of the thanksgiving section is the Thessalonians' conversion noted as a turning away from idolatry and a waiting for Christ's return (vv. 9–10). Turning away from idols in the Greco-Roman world was a subversive act, as religion in that culture was not simply one separate facet of life (as in the modern-day Western world) but something infused in every aspect of it. The various gods had authority over one's job, health, home, family, travel, crops, and almost any other area of life one can imagine. The quick spreading news of the Thessalonians' faith also was likely due to this rejection of the whole system of gods and idols. In its stead came a faith placed in one all-powerful God.

Replacing offerings to the gods was the Thessalonians' trust and waiting for the return of Jesus, the Lord ruling over all things. The Scriptures contain a constant condemnation of idols. Believers are to "flee" idolatry (1 Cor. 10:14), "keep yourselves from idols" (1 John 5:21), and "put to death" the earthly nature, as it is idolatry (Col. 3:5). In the OT, we see that "those who worship vain idols forsake their true loyalty" to God (Jonah 2:8), and the Israelites are not to turn to or make idols for themselves because of the Lord being their God (Lev. 19:4). Those who construct idols and trust in them "shall become like them" (Ps. 135:18).

The list of references and emphasis on idols as a departure from God goes even deeper in both the OT and NT. The Thessalonians' turning away from idols was just the opposite; it was a turning to God as they awaited Jesus' return for the full establishing of the kingdom of God. Though some had seemed to grow weary at the loss of loved ones in the community of faith (1 Thess. 4:13–18), the focus on the return of Jesus, the one true Lord, is an encouragement that their faith is rightly placed (cf. Jas. 5:7; Phil. 3:20; Titus 2:13). This is the basis for their persistence in the faith.

TROY A. MILLER

Commentary 2: Connecting the Reading with the World

Paul addresses his letter to the community of believers at Thessalonica. In the company of his companions, Silvanus and Timothy, Paul praises the Thessalonians for their virtue, labors, and commitment to the gospel.

Hearing Paul's letter in a social and ethical context today, we receive insights into what constitutes good leadership style. In some of Paul's other writings, we see a somewhat authoritarian leadership style—for example, when he called for women to be silent, in conflict with other apostles. In this letter, however, Paul gives thanks for this community at Thessalonica. He remembers their work of faith, their labor of love, their steadfast hope (1 Thess. 1:3). He praises them and offers them even greater words of affirmation when he says that the believers in Thessalonica have become an example to all the believers in Macedonia and Achaia (v. 8).

In many corporations today and in some churches, an autocratic style of leadership is in place. With this model, the leader exercises a hierarchical position over workers or believers, is rarely seen or heard interacting with them, and requires unquestioned submission, obedience, and loyalty. This style of leadership appears in governments across the globe as well.

The objective of this leadership style is to assert power over others, to control others, and to be sure that no one under the leader rises up to undermine the power of the one in charge. One only has to look at the place of the laity in some clerical ecclesiastical structures, who remain impotent when church leadership is from the top down. The gospel message becomes stunted when delivered by only one voice, and dialogue and negotiation, the primary forces behind inclusivity and theological vitality, become nonexistent. Creative ideas stop flowing among people, resulting in a lack of personal, social, professional, and spiritual growth. Finally, a general malaise soon replaces confidence and joy. Thus the system of hierarchy, embodied by an autocratic leader, causes tremendous suffering within an organization, and life is essentially squelched.

The preacher can help hearers of the text to understand how a hierarchical style of leadership that exercises inordinate power over others does not foster individual or communal growth. Another model of leadership is possible, as in the example of Paul, who as a leader—in this case, a church leader—affirms the church at Thessalonica and acknowledges the presence of the Holy Spirit among the believers. By acknowledging the work of the Holy Spirit, Paul recognizes that the believers are already empowered, and he celebrates that reality. Paul does not view the believers as people who are less than himself in stature; instead, he sees them as beloved by God. As a leader, Paul honors the community. Such a leadership style affirms and supports the gifts, talents, and life of a community and affirms the real strength of a leader whose power is best when shared.

Paul's statement that the community of believers at Thessalonica became imitators of him, Silvanus, Timothy, and the Lord raises eyebrows. Since when is "imitation" good, as it implies following someone else? Again, from a social and ethical context, the preacher can help hearers of the text to understand that Paul is not rejoicing over the fact that the community members are following exactly in his footsteps. Rather, they are enduring what he has endured, namely, distress and persecution for the sake of the gospel.

The idea of enduring persecution is an important one. From an ecclesial perspective, the preacher can draw out the point that receiving and living out the gospel will, at times, cost believers not less than everything. Paul is not descriptive with respect to the type of persecution to be endured. It could be physical persecution, emotional persecution, or even psychological persecution. The preacher might name and reflect upon the lives of the eleven US missionaries murdered in Central America; of the four US church women, specifically, Ita Ford, MM; Dorothy Kazel, OSU; Maura Clarke, MM; and Jean Donovan, who were murdered in El Salvador while trying to free people from injustices caused by the Salvadoran government.

The preacher could recall and discuss the socialist education movement in China (1962–65) that put tremendous pressures on local church leaders. If church leaders belonged to landholding merchant families, they were labeled as landlords and capitalists, resulting in an uncertain future for them and their children. Despite the state's persecution, Christian families kept faith alive.

The preacher might also reflect on the community of believers in Syria today. Scores of Christians are being put to death because of their Christian faith. Thousands have been forced from their homes by the threat from hardline Islamist rebels and jihadist militants. In areas seized by the jihadist group Islamic State, Christians have been ordered to convert to Islam, pay jizya, which is a religious levy, or face death. Furthermore, senior Christian clerics have also been kidnapped by unknown gunmen.

Paul also commends the Thessalonians for having turned away from idols to serve a living and true God. Paul reminds the Thessalonians that turning away from mainstream Greco-Roman culture calls for new cultural, social, and religious relationships. In Paul's day, the idols would have ranged across a wide spectrum of deities related to the Greek pantheon, as well as various Egyptian and Roman gods and Roman emperor worship. Here the preacher could reflect on the text in a personal context. What are some of the idols that believers hold onto today that keep us from having both a deeply personal relationship with God and an ethical praxis as part of that relationship? Status, power, wealth, comfort zones, self-interest, reputation, peace at any price, insular nationalism are some of the idols we worship today, at the expense of taking a stand on and working for global justice that includes the social and environmental crises that are engulfing and strangling all the planet's communities of life today.

Finally, Paul's First Letter to the Thessalonians reminds the community that God has raised Christ from the dead. From a personal context, the preacher might reflect on how today's believers are embodying the reality of the resurrected Christ in their lives. Is today's faith community a joyous people, filled with the Spirit, committed to justice at all costs, in communion with Christ, and in union with the living God? If so, then what are the fruits? If community members are not joyous, Spirit-filled, committed to justice, in communion with Christ and union with God, then what must change personally?

Furthermore, as for being rescued from the wrath that is coming, the preacher could note that the wrath coming is not from God, as a Christian fundamentalist perspective would suggest. Rather, the wrath that is coming, and is already in our midst, is the inordinate continued and calculated misuse and abuse of power on the part of many world leaders that will eventually leave the planet in an ash heap of ruins. The work of the resurrected Christ, the "Savior of the world," is to liberate the world from the social, political, economic, religious, and environmental forces of evil at work. The human community needs to act in radical, new ways. The preacher could emphasize that profession of belief can no longer be a privatized, personal matter. If what believers profess does not have a local, national, and global perspective and ethical praxis, then the profession of belief is nothing more than a self-serving faith and self-serving commitment to faith.

CAROL J. DEMPSEY, OP

Proper 24 (Sunday between October 16 and October 22 inclusive)

Matthew 22:15–22

[15] Then the Pharisees went and plotted to entrap him in what he said. [16] So they sent their disciples to him, along with the Herodians, saying, "Teacher, we know that you are sincere, and teach the way of God in accordance with truth, and show deference to no one; for you do not regard people with partiality. [17] Tell us, then, what you think. Is it lawful to pay taxes to the emperor, or not?" [18] But Jesus, aware of their malice, said, "Why are you putting me to the test, you hypocrites? [19] Show me the coin used for the tax." And they brought him a denarius. [20] Then he said to them, "Whose head is this, and whose title?" [21] They answered, "The emperor's." Then he said to them, "Give therefore to the emperor the things that are the emperor's, and to God the things that are God's." [22] When they heard this, they were amazed; and they left him and went away.

Commentary 1: Connecting the Reading with Scripture

It is often said that one should not mix politics and religion, yet this Gospel passage is filled with both. Whether political or religious, the exchange about Caesar's coin raises questions about obedience, loyalty, and authority that demonstrate how faith has an inescapable political dimension, but not a partisan one.

Just as it might be uncomfortable for modern hearers of this gospel to talk about religion and politics, the immediate context of this passage makes clear that Jesus is in a difficult situation as well. The taxes paid to Caesar were poll or "head" taxes that all subjects of the empire had to pay, whether men, women, or slaves. (The Latin word for this tax is "census.") It also had to be paid in Roman currency. When verse 19 mentions that they brought Jesus a coin, the term used is "denarius." In Jesus' time, the most common denarius was stamped with the image of the emperor Tiberius, and its inscription read, "Tiberius Caesar, son of the divine Augustus, high priest."

That inscription points to why this tax caused controversy in Jesus' time. No taxes, whether in the first century or today, are popular, even less so when they have to be paid to a foreign occupying force. To ardent nationalists, payment of the tax meant the humiliation of Israel at the hands of Rome. Moreover, for Jews, the very currency to be used was a problem. A coin that proclaims the divinity of Caesar and has his graven image is blasphemous. So there was a great deal of religious as well as political controversy regarding this tax.

From the start of this encounter, we are made aware that Jesus' questioners are trying to set a trap for him. Matthew describes the group questioning Jesus as the disciples of the Pharisees and the Herodians. This pairing is strange, because they would probably have been on opposite sides of the tax question. The Herodians were supporters of Herod the Great and, in Jesus' time, Herod Antipas. They would have been supportive of paying the tax because the Herods derived their power from Roman support. On the other hand, the Pharisees would more likely have been resentful of the tax. When the passage portrays them as uniting forces against Jesus, it sets the stage for a situation many readers can identify with. Clearly, Jesus is being put in a no-win situation. However he answers, he will face opposition that discredits him.

Jesus does not fall into the trap. When he asks to be shown the coin, it is his opponents who have to handle the blasphemous currency. When he turns the question on them, they are silenced. Yet we are left wondering what the rendering to Caesar might mean. Does it mean pay nothing to Caesar because everything belongs to God? Pay the tax because earthly authority is different than heavenly authority? Are we left without a definitive answer because payment is actually secondary to something else going on here?

The debate over Caesar's tax is part of Matthew's wider portrayal of a conflict between Jesus and the Jewish religious leaders over authority. One of the primary ways that Jews, both in Jesus' time and in the time of Matthew's Jewish Christian community, would frame authority and obedience is in relation to the law. The question the Pharisees ask Jesus about whether it is lawful to pay the tax (Matt. 22:17) has several precedents. In Matthew 12:2, the Pharisees criticize Jesus and his disciples for doing what is not lawful, plucking grain on the Sabbath to feed themselves. Right after that episode, the Pharisees question Jesus about healing on the Sabbath (12:10). Using the very same words as with the coin, they ask, Is it lawful?

Plucking grain and healing illnesses bring out an important dimension underlying the coin episode regarding obedience. Obedience to the law should not devolve into legalism, where the letter of the law stands in the way of carrying out God's will. Satisfying hunger and healing infirmity are just two examples of this principle throughout Matthew. The law should not be an obstacle to serving, nor an excuse for avoiding, the higher purpose of God's merciful desire that all people should flourish.

Of course, this principle does not mean rejecting obedience to the law. Indeed, in other passages of Matthew, obedience to the law is a minimum, but necessary, requirement on the way to perfection. Matthew 19:3 illustrates this perfection in a dispute similar to that of Caesar's coin. The Pharisees, once again, test Jesus by asking him whether it is lawful to divorce. Jesus responds by demanding behavior that includes and supersedes that which is lawful. Obedience to God, in this case, is a challenge to live up to the highest standards possible, even beyond a legal minimum.

Finally, the other mention of an unlawful act in Matthew is Herod Antipas's marriage to Herodias. John the Baptist denounces it as unlawful. In doing so, he demonstrates a remarkable courage that does not fear the consequences of speaking the truth. As we see, John the Baptist's obedience to the law leads to his death at the hands of those whom he denounces. Thus the question of Caesar's coin touches upon several different dimensions of obedience. Discerning how to render to God what is God's can range from mercifully relativizing the letter of the law, to going beyond the law's demands, and even to enduring persecution to uphold the law. In each case, obedience to the law means seeking God's will.

The other lectionary selections for the day provide more ideas about what obedience to God's authority in troubled times might look like. The reading from Paul's letter praises the Thessalonians for their reception of the gospel in the face of persecution. The ominous mention of a coming wrath indicates the intensity of Paul's context. The Thessalonians are commended for being imitators of Paul and of Jesus himself in their living out of the gospel's call despite persecution.

At the heart of the Old Testament is the assertion of God's authority over all of the earth and the mysterious way in which God's greatness is revealed. In Isaiah 45, Cyrus is described as the Lord's "anointed" or messiah. As king of the Persians, Cyrus conquered the Babylonians and permitted the Israelite exiles to return and reestablish their homeland. For this, he is the only non-Jew in the OT given this lofty title. Key to this attribution is the reckoning that whatever great deeds Cyrus may achieve, they are nothing compared to God's. Cyrus is merely an instrument.

It is not that God blesses secular rulers in some special way. This is the danger of idolatry that always lurks with the interaction between religion and politics. Rendering unto Caesar does not of necessity mean believing that Caesar is performing the will of God. Paul's First Letter to the Thessalonians and the book of Revelation cast a suspicious eye on the terrible ways that empires treat people.

Whichever "Caesar" we may confront, at the heart of Jesus' injunction for us is the constant challenge to render unto God what is God's. Jesus' message is not escapist. It means living in a world with various commitments and societal obligations. Yet ultimately the criteria of the gospel must guide believers' choices. To live out the gospel, one cannot avoid political commitments, but that does not mean claiming partisan politics or ideologies as God's will. Rather, it is that constant challenge to seek God's merciful will and to imitate Jesus' example in order to render all things to God.

MICHAEL E. LEE

Commentary 2: Connecting the Reading with the World

Matthew's church was a "new church development." Such new churches are often sprouting in the midst of suburban communities being planted on the edges of growing cities, or in redeveloping neighborhoods where exhausted old buildings are repurposed to host new faith communities expressing themselves in fresh paradigms. A surprising struggle that often emerges in such settings is a tension between that which is genuinely new and different and that which hearkens back to the memories that parishioners hold of the way things used to be in some other church.

In Matthew's Gospel, we read often of these natural tensions, for Matthew's congregation is made up of Jews who have become Christians. While some scholars suggest that they practiced a kind of "dual membership," most scholars believe that in Matthew's church a split has already occurred, and that there is in the air a vigorously antagonistic relationship with the synagogue. The rhetoric is often angrily directed against the Jewish authorities and "their synagogues." It would therefore be tempting for the preacher to overinterpret these themes, to read them, for example, against the modern conflict between Christians and Jews, thus rendering much of this rhetoric "anti-Semitic."

A more appropriate connection would be to understand that, at root, much of the vitriol in Matthew reflects the essential family dispute between two groups of loyal and devout Jews: those who hold that Jesus of Nazareth is the Messiah, and those who do not. This approach could lead the preacher to explore the inherent conflicts between the values of tradition and the fresh winds always blowing through any congregation.

Thomas G. Long, a noted homiletician, gives credence to this connection. "Because the members of Matthew's church had a Jewish heritage," Long writes,

> their scriptures were what is now called the Old Testament, and their traditions of worship and devotion were firmly shaped in the cradle of the synagogue. Thus, now that they had ventured into the uncharted waters of Christianity, the major question facing them was the relationship between the old and the new, between the cherished traditions and commandments of their Jewish legacy and the new demands of Christian discipleship.[1]

In this new church development, Long suggests that this question eventually drove them to retain what was lively and still relevant with respect to their roots, but also "to develop the theological position that Jesus Christ fulfills rather than abolishes the Law and the Prophets."[2] In such ways as this, reckoning with tradition in any age, and certainly in ours, requires a sustained conversation with the past in order to take from the altars of yesterday the flame and not the ashes.

Another connection between this text and our context is the way this text invites us to ponder the church's ongoing relationship with civil authorities. If we read it superficially, it becomes contorted into the Bible's ultimate endorsement of a blind patriotism: "Give therefore to the emperor the things that are the emperor's, and to God the things that are God's" (Matt. 22:21).

To read the text carefully is to see beyond a binary choice between two equal-sized options. The Pharisees and Herodians soak Jesus in

---

1. Thomas G. Long, *Matthew* (Louisville, KY: Westminster John Knox, 1997), 248.
2. Long, *Matthew*, 248.

flattery and then ask a trick question: "Is it lawful to pay taxes to the emperor, or not?" (v. 17). If Jesus says, "Do not pay taxes to the emperor," the Romans will get him for treason. If he says, "Yes, we should pay taxes to the emperor," his own followers there in that occupied country will call him a traitor. Nonetheless, his answer regarding "the things that are the emperor's" and "the things that are God's" is a profound testimony to the heart of our faith: we belong not to Caesar but to God.

We belong not to our possessions, but to God. We belong not to the partisan political claims we make in election seasons, but to God. We belong not to the demands of our vocations, but to God. We belong not to the charms of our secular world, but to God. Christians may have to pay the emperor the tax, but that does not mean a neat division of loyalties that ends up giving Caesar far more than his due. Instead, our greatest loyalty is to the one who made us and to whom, in body and soul, we ultimately belong. To give to God the things that are God's is, first, to testify that all of creation belongs to God, and, second, to place in a subordinate context that which really belongs to the numerous "emperors" we wrongly crown in our lives.

It takes most of us a lifetime to discern the difference between what we think we own, and who finally owns us. Here we are encouraged in that discernment by the challenge that we not give to the emperor more than the emperor is due. Do not give the emperor your faith, do not give the emperor your ultimate allegiance, do not forge a relationship with the emperor that forces you to figure out how God can rightly fit into the emperor's pocket. Do not give to the emperor what belongs to God! For what belongs to God is vastly larger than what belongs to the emperor. This is perhaps the grandest faith statement we can ever make:

> Finally, it is all God's!

A number of years ago, my family and I spent a three-month sabbatical in Cambridge, England. One day, we drove to Coventry. There was not much about that industrial city that drew us there—except for its cathedral. In World War II, the city had been bombed to smithereens during a punishing air raid, and its medieval cathedral had been destroyed. However, in just a few years, the intrepid people of Coventry built a new cathedral, angular and airy and representing the best of mid-twentieth-century modern architecture. Their mission was to build a church not to glorify the majesty of God, as the old cathedral had, but instead to recall the suffering of God as a newly rediscovered insight after the brutality of that horrendous war.

When we went through that modern church, we saw—in steel and glass and stone—vivid testimony to the Christ who suffers with us in our suffering. We saw dominant motifs: the crown of thorns, a giant mosaic of Jesus in Gethsemane praying for the cup to pass from him, the vast tapestry behind the high altar pulling one's attention not to the face of Jesus but to his bloody, nail-scarred feet.

Finally, on a remote wall to the right of the altar, we saw the sculpture of a city with its tall buildings and towers and steeples. It was Coventry itself. Hanging above its skyline was what at first looked like a bomb falling from the sky. Further scrutiny revealed that that bomb was actually a plumb line, what a builder uses to judge whether a wall is straight or crooked.

God found, through Jesus, the ultimate plumb line, one who, because he has suffered with us, takes measure not just of God's standard for the world, but also of God's hope for the world. However flawed, we are more than that, because we believe in a God who sees in us not just what is crooked, but also what is possible. We are beloved children, able partners in the ongoing work of creation, people who are living daily into their baptismal identity by giving God what is God's: our lives, ourselves, our energy, our everything, until we become living sacraments, and our world becomes a place of meeting.

THEODORE J. WARDLAW

Proper 25 (Sunday between October 23 and October 29 inclusive)

Leviticus 19:1–2, 15–18 and
  Deuteronomy 34:1–12
Psalm 1 and Psalm 90:1–6, 13–17

1 Thessalonians 2:1–8
Matthew 22:34–46

Leviticus 19:1–2, 15–18

¹The LORD spoke to Moses, saying: ²Speak to all the congregation of the people of Israel and say to them: You shall be holy, for I the LORD your God am holy. . . .
¹⁵You shall not render an unjust judgment; you shall not be partial to the poor or defer to the great: with justice you shall judge your neighbor. ¹⁶You shall not go around as a slanderer among your people, and you shall not profit by the blood of your neighbor: I am the LORD.
¹⁷You shall not hate in your heart anyone of your kin; you shall reprove your neighbor, or you will incur guilt yourself. ¹⁸You shall not take vengeance or bear a grudge against any of your people, but you shall love your neighbor as yourself: I am the LORD.

Deuteronomy 34:1–12

¹Then Moses went up from the plains of Moab to Mount Nebo, to the top of Pisgah, which is opposite Jericho, and the LORD showed him the whole land: Gilead as far as Dan, ²all Naphtali, the land of Ephraim and Manasseh, all the land of Judah as far as the Western Sea, ³the Negeb, and the Plain—that is, the valley of Jericho, the city of palm trees—as far as Zoar. ⁴The LORD said to him, "This is the land of which I swore to Abraham, to Isaac, and to Jacob, saying, 'I will give it to your descendants'; I have let you see it with your eyes, but you shall not cross over there." ⁵Then Moses, the servant of the LORD, died there in the land of Moab, at the LORD's command. ⁶He was buried in a valley in the land of Moab, opposite Beth-peor, but no one knows his burial place to this day. ⁷Moses was one hundred twenty years old when he died; his sight was unimpaired and his vigor had not abated. ⁸The Israelites wept for Moses in the plains of Moab thirty days; then the period of mourning for Moses was ended.
⁹Joshua son of Nun was full of the spirit of wisdom, because Moses had laid his hands on him; and the Israelites obeyed him, doing as the LORD had commanded Moses.
¹⁰Never since has there arisen a prophet in Israel like Moses, whom the LORD knew face to face. ¹¹He was unequaled for all the signs and wonders that the LORD sent him to perform in the land of Egypt, against Pharaoh and all his servants and his entire land, ¹²and for all the mighty deeds and all the terrifying displays of power that Moses performed in the sight of all Israel.

Commentary 1: Connecting the Reading with Scripture

The call seems simple enough. "You shall be holy, for I the Lord your God am holy" (Lev. 19:2). What does it mean to be holy? Unfortunately, the word "holy" in English has come to mean "sacred, consecrated, or hallowed." When referred to people, it connotes saintly, godly, or pious—hence undergirding the importance for personal piety. To be holy has come to mean more an individual personal behavior, a way of being that reinforces a pious façade, rather than actions taken toward others. The focus is on the individual who is called to be holy. This should not be surprising when we consider how Eurocentric hyperindividualism undergirds the dominant worldview.

When the text is read in English, the call to be holy is often confused with individual acts of behavior based on denial of self. We consider churchgoing folk who do not drink, lie, dance, swear, or engage in sex to be holy. Many sermons look inward, toward individual well-being. Yet this was not the passage's intent. Probably a better way of understanding the Hebrew word used in the passage that has come to signify our English word "holy" is "being separate" or "set apart." The verse would thus better read: "You shall be set apart, for I the Lord your God am separate."

Separate from what? Because God is separate from other gods, then God's people must be separate from other people. In a world where greed and self-interest are the norm, what does it mean to separate oneself from this world? To be separate from how the world normatively acts toward each other? According to the psalmist, those who are set apart and delight in the Lord's way "are like trees planted by streams of water, which yield their fruit in its season, and their leaves do not wither. . . . The wicked are not so, but are like chaff that the wind drives away" (Ps. 1:3–4). To be set apart produces fruit, but to follow the norms of the world leads to a withered existence, to be tossed aside.

How do we know if we are separate, set aside, holy? Many Euroamericans, heavily influenced by the individualism of the so-called Enlightenment, focus on personal piety and individual virtues. For many of us who instead read the biblical text in Spanish and from a different geographical perspective, our focus is on the praxis called for to bring about justice. When we read Leviticus, we clearly see that this holiness has less to do with personal piety, than with the actions undertaken toward others within community. To be holy is a communal act based on our interaction with others, not only an individual behavior.

For the faith community to be separate means we are not to participate in the unjust treatment of our neighbor. Rather, we are to judge justly, regardless of status, thus to be communal (Lev. 19:15). To be separate means we are not to slander our neighbor or profit from spilling their blood, thus to be communal (v. 16). To be separate means we are not to hold hate in our heart for others, thus to be communal (v. 17). To be separate means we are not to take vengeance or bear grudges but instead to love others as ourselves, thus to be communal (v. 18).

In fact, Jesus calls us to this level of holiness. He raises this latter communal action to the second greatest commandment of all. After loving God with all our heart, and all our soul, and all our mind: "You shall love your neighbor as yourself" (Matt. 22:39). While the biblical text makes holiness possible only if there exists a neighbor to whom the acts of holiness are geared, Eurocentric eyes have reduced holiness to the individual, separate from others. "Holy" has been defined so that one can be holy on a deserted island, but the holiness God calls us to requires a community with whom to be holy. Holy is not a solitary act.

Faith, rooted in subjective personal piety and self-serving virtues, is incongruent with the holiness, the separateness, God is calling us toward. "Happy," the psalmist cries out, "are those who do not follow the advice of the wicked, or take the path that sinners tread, or sit in the seat of scoffers" (Ps. 1:1). To be a holy people is a communal praxis, a communal act geared toward others, separating us from others. Why then should we be holy? We seek holiness not for personal gain, nor for heavenly reward.

Take Moses as our example. Moses, who murdered an Egyptian and tried to hide the deed, lacked the personal piety used by many today to describe holiness. Yet we are told, "Never since has there arisen a prophet in Israel like Moses, whom the Lord knew face to face" (Deut. 34:10). Moses labored intensively to lead his people toward their reward. From the top of Pisgah he was able to cast his eyes upon the land promised by God, a land he was forbidden to enter (Deut. 34:4). Holiness often does not lead to the outcome hoped for. In fact, more often than not it leads to forsakenness. All too often, as Paul experienced, seeking God's holiness and justice means suffering and shameful mistreatment (1 Thess. 2:2).

Why bother being holy if we are denied what we worked our whole life to visualize, as was Moses, or if we face abuse at each turn, as did Paul? Do we seek holiness even if we never get to enter into our reward, our own promised land? What if this temporal life is all there is? What if, as the psalmist sings, "You turn us back to dust, and say, 'Turn back, you mortals'" (Ps. 90:3)? If there is no heaven, do we still seek to be holy, just because our God is holy? If the future is but dust, then what is in it for me? We must ask ourselves, Is our holiness based on a faith in God, or on what we get out of the transaction?

To embrace holiness can be hopeless where the future is not assured, where we may never get to set foot in the promised land that we spent a lifetime walking toward. To be holy can mark us for a life full of suffering and shameful mistreatment. To be holy may very well be the worst transaction in which we can ever engage. Regardless of the love we show our neighbors, our lives may still come to an end on top of a mountain looking toward a reward we will never experience. So again, why bother?

We, as a collection of believers, struggle to be holy, we struggle to love the neighbor who may not deserve our love, we struggle for justice not because of some eschatological reward. We struggle to be holy, loving, and just because it is what defines our very humanity. We struggle, regardless of outcome, because we have no other choice. To do nothing is to be driven away by the wind like chaff. If we think being holy will existentially yield the fruit in its season and prevent our leaves from withering for all to see, then we are sadly mistaken. One's holiness, one's chosenness, can never be measured proportionately to our external riches. The fruit yielded and the unwithered leaves are the faith that is defined by our very struggle to be holy, to love unconditionally, to be just.

MIGUEL A. DE LA TORRE

Commentary 2: Connecting the Reading with the World

Leviticus 19:1–2, 15–18. This text is critical to the ethos of God's people. It contains two central claims that shape the relationship between God and God's people and form their witness to the world. Leviticus 19 reminds God's people that its covenantal relationship finds its roots in the holiness of the Lord, expressed in life as love for God and neighbor. The call to holiness is central to Leviticus (Lev. 11:44–45).

The lectionary texts provide rich connections to the life of faith. Psalm 90 serves as a signpost in the Psalter of the Mosaic roots of the faith. It is the only psalm with a title connected to Moses. In Moses' voice, it serves as a plea for God's favor to return after a season of unfaithfulness. Implicit is an intention by God's people to rediscover Torah's call to faithfulness. Matthew 22:34–46 articulates the core Torah commitments of love for God and neighbor. First Thessalonians 2:1–8 describes Paul's motives and actions in his ministry among the Thessalonian believers. Paul stresses his desire to act in ways pleasing to God and the care that he showed for the faithful.

Leviticus 19:1–2, 15–18 roots holiness in the Lord. There are two temptations for preachers regarding holiness. One is to define holiness purely in ways that mute its moral demand and merely emphasize God's otherness. The second is to moralize holiness so that holy living becomes equated with avoiding certain moral peccadilloes. Biblical holiness is a calling to reflect God's character in deep relationship with God (loving God) and in relationship with the covenantal community, the nations, and all creation (loving neighbor). We love God in some respects by loving our neighbor. Moreover, we love our neighbor by learning to love ourselves as God loves us.

Leviticus 19:15–18 reminds God's people that a commitment to holy love is more than a slogan. God's people must have "skin in the game." Verses 15–18 lay out detailed and specific applications of the law of love to everyday situations where the possibilities for abuse and injustice are present. Readers need to observe carefully these injunctions. God's holy character calls for impartiality. Justice is for all persons, regardless of status (see Rom. 12:3–13; Gal. 3:27–29). This text invites readers to imagine what a community that chose to live out this ethic would look like. Leviticus 19 is a communal call to holiness. Modern congregations will want to ask, How does this community of faith need to change in order to be known as a community of holy love for the neighborhood?

For individual believers, Leviticus 19:1–2 asks, What kind of person do I need to become to live out a life of holy love for God and neighbor? Verses 15–18 invite individual applications of the law of love in daily life. What are specific areas in today's culture where individuals are mistreated? What concrete daily practices can serve "neighbors" tangibly? Who is my mission? To whom do I need to extend loving service today?

The ethic of love for neighbor runs counter to human tendencies to love merely those who love us first, but it is central to the gospel (Matt. 5:43–48). Leviticus 19:18 offers the law of love as a contrast to typical human actions. Verse 18a warns against vengeance or grudge holding. Yet in response, the Torah calls for a proactive, life-affirming response of love for neighbor. In other words, this text subverts retaliation by elevating an offender to the position of neighbor. In our divided political climate, the practice of expanding our definition of neighbor is critical for working for a loving picture of justice and mercy for all. Rather than following the culture by demonizing and disenfranchising the political "other," Christ's followers must elevate all sides to the status of *neighbor*.

Deuteronomy 34:1–12. Deuteronomy 34:1–12 concludes the book of Deuteronomy and the Torah as a whole by reporting Moses' death and legacy. It provides an apt testimony of Moses' pivotal role in God's mission to liberate and sanctify God's people for mission in the world.

Deuteronomy 34:1–12 focuses on Moses' legacy. Verses 10–12 emphasize the unique role of Moses as greater than subsequent prophets. These verses stress his actions as God's human agent in the deliverance from Egypt. In verses 1–4, the Lord had shown Moses the entire promised land. Moses had served as the leader who guided Israel from bondage in Egypt to the border of their future home. Yet Moses' legacy and model lived on. First, Moses laid hands on Joshua (Deut. 34:9). Second, the cotexts in the lectionary explicitly reflect the influence of Moses' exemplary life. Psalm 90 continues the teaching legacy of Moses. The words attributed to him in Psalm 90 affirm the finiteness of human life and call God's people to turn to the Lord for salvation. In Matthew 22:34–46, Jesus reaffirms the love for God and neighbor as the essence of the Mosaic Torah. The Matthean cotext implicitly declares Jesus as greater than Moses, greater than even David. First Thessalonians 2:1–8 shows Paul modeling ministry through his relational actions with the church in Thessalonica.

Deuteronomy 34:1–4 stresses God's faithfulness in leading God's people to the promised land through the leadership of Moses. These verses describe in detail the totality of the land God's people will inherit in the book of Joshua. This moment is the fulfillment of the promises that God had made repeatedly to Israel's ancestors (Abraham, Isaac, Jacob, and their families) in Genesis 12–50. Verse 4b reminds Moses that he will see but not experience this land. The Torah is the story of the Lord calling a people to serve as agents of blessing to the nations. This story began with Abram/Sarah in Genesis 12, centered geographically on the land of Canaan. The Torah tells the story of God's relationship with Israel in preparing them living as God's missional people in the land. In the Torah, God's people continually struggle with faithfulness. The one clear reality is that Israel's loving and merciful God remains steadfast and faithful.

Deuteronomy 34:1–12 serves as a warning for God's people (corporately and individually) regarding the danger of disobedience. Moses did great deeds (Deut. 34:10–12), but due to his momentary lapse at the waters of Meribah (Deut. 32:48–52; cf. Num. 20:1–13), he forfeited the right to lead God's people all the way into Canaan. Joshua will serve this role (Deut. 34:9).

Moses' failure reminds individuals and communities that God's mission is bigger than any one person (no matter how significant that person may seem in the moment). This text critiques any cult of personality within the Christ-following movement. The gospel is about God's glory. God has a mission. The mission has a church. The church has leaders, but it is always to the glory of God and not to the glory of a particular woman or man.

Moses does not dispute God's judgment here (vv. 5–8). He faithfully accepts this ending for his life. Moses remains a witness to God's people of faithfulness (mixed with warning) and, according to tradition, Moses' enduring contribution is the Scripture ("book of the law," Deut. 31:26) that continues to shape God's people for mission by articulating a holy love for God and neighbor.

BRIAN D. RUSSELL

Proper 25 (Sunday between October 23 and October 29 inclusive)

Psalm 1

¹Happy are those
   who do not follow the advice of the wicked,
or take the path that sinners tread,
   or sit in the seat of scoffers;
²but their delight is in the law of the LORD,
   and on his law they meditate day and night.
³They are like trees
   planted by streams of water,
which yield their fruit in its season,
   and their leaves do not wither.
In all that they do, they prosper.

⁴The wicked are not so,
   but are like chaff that the wind drives away.
⁵Therefore the wicked will not stand in the judgment,
   nor sinners in the congregation of the righteous;
⁶for the LORD watches over the way of the righteous,
   but the way of the wicked will perish.

Psalm 90:1–6, 13–17

¹Lord, you have been our dwelling place
   in all generations.
²Before the mountains were brought forth,
   or ever you had formed the earth and the world,
   from everlasting to everlasting you are God.

³You turn us back to dust,
   and say, "Turn back, you mortals."
⁴For a thousand years in your sight
   are like yesterday when it is past,
   or like a watch in the night.

⁵You sweep them away; they are like a dream,
   like grass that is renewed in the morning;
⁶in the morning it flourishes and is renewed;
   in the evening it fades and withers.
. . . .
¹³Turn, O LORD! How long?
   Have compassion on your servants!
¹⁴Satisfy us in the morning with your steadfast love,
   so that we may rejoice and be glad all our days.
¹⁵Make us glad as many days as you have afflicted us,
   and as many years as we have seen evil.
¹⁶Let your work be manifest to your servants,
   and your glorious power to their children.

¹⁷Let the favor of the Lord our God be upon us,
    and prosper for us the work of our hands—
    O prosper the work of our hands!

Connecting the Psalm with Scripture and Worship

Psalm 1. The reading from Leviticus to which Psalm 1 responds is a key excerpt from a chapters-long transmission of God's decrees to Moses. Scholars refer to this text's source as the Holiness Code, and this passage reflects that source, with these particular statutes prefaced by God's overall expectation of the people: "You shall be holy, for I the Lord your God am holy." Psalm 1 helps us grasp what such holiness—as well as its antithesis—can be like.

The psalm opens with the formulaic phrasing of a beatitude, "Happy are those . . . " (Ps. 1:1), and then spends its six verses considering the experience of these happy ones as opposed to the experience of "the wicked" (vv. 1, 4–6). The psalmist is unflinchingly dualistic, laying out exactly two paths: the way of those who are "happy" (v. 1) and "righteous" (vv. 5, 6) is contrasted with the way of those who are "wicked" (vv. 4–6). It is worth noting that there is human agency in choosing which path to follow; we are not hapless victims of fate.

The bulk of the psalm focuses on those who make the choices that lead to happiness. These happy ones avoid "the advice of the wicked, . . . the path that sinners tread, . . . [and] the seat of scoffers" (v. 1), choosing instead "the law of the Lord," on which "they meditate day and night" (v. 2). As a result, they are "like trees planted by streams of water" (v. 3), fruitful and eternally green. In fact, "in all that they do, they prosper" (v. 3).

Compared to the happy ones, the wicked ones are accorded minimal textual real estate. Their amount-to-nothing outcome, to be "like chaff that the wind drives away" (v. 4), is reflected in the psalmist's impassive dismissal of them: they "will not stand in the judgment" (v. 5), their way "will perish" (v. 6).

The psalm's prescription for avoiding this fate is straightforward: make choices that center your life on "the law of the Lord" (v. 2). While a reader of the psalm might turn to Leviticus for some specifics (lots of specifics, actually!), a preacher of Leviticus might turn to the psalm for some motivation and some poetry.

To a sermon on the profound theological claim that, thanks to God's holiness, we too are capable of holiness (Lev. 19:2), today's psalm could add an element utterly lacking in Leviticus: the promise of being "happy" (Ps. 1:1) and experiencing "delight" (v. 2). What a welcome complement to the "shalls" and "shall nots" of Leviticus.

Another homiletical approach would be to consider God's unembellished self-identification, "I am the Lord" (Lev. 19:2, 16, 18), which appears a total of twenty-four times in Leviticus 18–20. Psalm 1's depiction of obedient people as well-watered trees (Ps. 1:3) could provide thought-provoking counterpoint.

Given their shared focus on how we are to live life in the presence of our holy God, one might draw on both pericopes to shape a prayer of confession, such as this:

> Holy God, You are the Lord.
> You call us to follow you in holiness, but we often do not.
> Instead, we follow the advice of the wicked,
> and take the path that sinners tread,
> and sit in the seat of scoffers.
> We ignore your law, failing to love our neighbors as ourselves.
> We are like useless chaff blown by the wind,
> instead of fruitful trees planted by the water.
> Forgive us. Correct us. Watch over us.
> By your grace, help us to stand in the congregation of the righteous.
> By your holiness, help us to be holy.

Psalm 90:1–6, 13–17. Today's Hebrew Bible lections let us glimpse the relationship between YHWH and Moses and the Israelites. Each lection touches upon the theme of faithful obedience. Each is accompanied by a psalm that

Everything Is Dark That God Does Not Enlighten

If religion commands a universal charity, to love our neighbor as ourselves, to forgive and pray for all our enemies without any reserve, it is because all degrees of love are degrees of happiness that strengthen and support the divine life of the soul, and are as necessary to its health and happiness as proper food is necessary to the health and happiness of the body.

If religion has laws against laying up treasures upon earth, and commands us to be content with food and raiment, it is because every other use of the world is abusing it to our own vexation, and turning all its conveniences into snares and traps to destroy us. It is because this plainness and simplicity of life secures us from the cares and pains of restless pride and envy, and makes it easier to keep that straight road that will carry us to eternal life. If religion saith, "Sell that thou hast, and give to the poor," it is because there is no other natural or reasonable use of our riches, no other way of making ourselves happier for them; it is because it is as strictly right to give others that which we do not want ourselves as it is right to use so much as our own wants require.

If religion calleth us to a life of watching and prayer, it is because we live amongst a crowd of enemies, and are always in need of the assistance of God. If we are to confess and bewail our sins, it is because such confessions relieve the mind and restore it to ease, as burdens and weights taken off the shoulders relieve the body, and make it easier to itself. If we are to be frequent and fervent in holy petitions, it is to keep us steady in the sight of our true good, and that we may never want the happiness of a lively faith, a joyful hope, and well-grounded trust in God. If we are to pray often, it is that we may be often happy in such secret joys as only prayer can give, in such communications of the divine presence as will fill our minds with all the happiness that beings not in heaven are capable of. Was there anything in the world more worth our care, was there any exercise of the mind or any conversation with men that turned more to our advantage than this intercourse with God, we should not be called to such a continuance in prayer. . . .

If religion commands us to live wholly unto God and to do all to His glory, it is because every other way is living wholly against ourselves, and will end in our own shame and confusion of face. As everything is dark that God does not enlighten; as everything is senseless that has not its share of knowledge from Him; as nothing lives but by partaking of life from Him; as nothing exists but because He commands it to be; so there is no glory or greatness but what is of the glory or greatness of God. We indeed may talk of human glory as we may talk of human life or human knowledge; but as we are sure that human life implies nothing of our own but a dependent living in God, or enjoying so much life in God, so human glory, whenever we find it, must be only so much glory as we enjoy in the glory of God.

William Law, *A Serious Call to a Devout and Holy Life* (New York: Macmillan and Co., 1898), 111–13.

---

conjures an emotional context for that particular passage of the Torah.

Consider the superscription to Psalm 90. This is the only psalm traditionally attributed to Moses, a connection likely rooted in Moses' plea to God in the wake of Israel's golden-calf idolatry, "Turn from your fierce wrath; change your mind and do not bring disaster on your people" (Exod. 32:12b), which is now echoed in "Turn, O LORD! . . . Have compassion on your servants" (Ps. 90:13). We often ignore superscriptions, but given the reading from Deuteronomy, this one may be enlightening.

The entire psalm can be read in light of what Marilyn McCord Adams has termed "the metaphysical size gap":[1] the complete power disparity that characterizes the divine-human relationship. From the psalm's opening verse, God is portrayed as so far beyond us in scope and scale that God is able to contain us and

---

1. Marilyn McCord Adams, "The Metaphysical Size Gap," *Sewanee Theological Review* 47, no. 2 (2004): 129–44.

has "been our dwelling place in all generations" (v. 1). The psalmist proceeds to juxtapose God's immortality with our own mortality: not only does God preexist all creation, but at God's command that creation, including us, may cease to exist (vv. 2–6).

Since the psalm's central section is omitted, the reading resumes with the psalmist's cry for mercy (v. 13), which is reminiscent of the Exodus account. The final section then continues the exploration of the divine-human power disparity but does so from a new angle. Instead of God being able to "sweep [us] away" (v. 5), God's unmatchable power now takes the form of love and joy (vv. 14–15), glory and favor (vv. 16–17), which, in a series of prayer requests, God is asked to bestow upon us (vv. 14–17).

All of this—the unique connection with Moses; the "metaphysical size gap" between God and humanity; the array of circumstances that this disparity creates, from "turn[ing] us back to dust" (v. 3) to "prosper[ing] the work of our hands" (v. 17)—could be helpful when preaching on Deuteronomy 34.

The first reading from the semicontinuous track consists of the entire concluding chapter of the book of Deuteronomy, which means that these are the final words of the Torah: here are the conclusion of the story of Israel's formation and the conclusion of Moses' life.

In preaching this poignant text, take the psalm's superscription, "A Prayer of Moses, the man of God" (Ps. 90:1a), at its word and imagine Moses praying Psalm 90 there at "the top of Pisgah" (Deut. 34:1). You and your congregation are thereby enabled to witness Moses facing his mortality within the context of God's protection; "dwelling place" (Ps. 90:1) can also be translated "refuge" and God's "steadfast love" (v. 14).

Alternatively, a sermon focused on the Israelites as they grieve for Moses (Deut. 34:8) and then move on under new leadership (v. 9) could imagine the people praying Psalm 90 during their thirty days of mourning (v. 8). The text's plural pronouns (vv. 1, 3, 13–17) readily link the people of Israel with the people in your pews. Such a sermon might be especially potent for a church in any type of leadership transition.

Psalm 90 could also facilitate a sermon that uses the Deuteronomy text to review the complex relationship between God, Moses, and Israel. After all, in the midst of this prayer that begins and ends with deeply faithful sentiments, the psalmist acknowledges the undeniable afflictions visited upon the Israelites (Ps. 90:15).

"Our God, Our Help in Ages Past" is Isaac Watts's paraphrase of this psalm and would be an excellent choice for a closing hymn or a sung psalm setting. Another hymn option is "Immortal, Invisible, God Only Wise."

LEIGH CAMPBELL-TAYLOR

Proper 25 (Sunday between October 23 and October 29 inclusive)

1 Thessalonians 2:1–8

> ¹You yourselves know, brothers and sisters, that our coming to you was not in vain, ²but though we had already suffered and been shamefully mistreated at Philippi, as you know, we had courage in our God to declare to you the gospel of God in spite of great opposition. ³For our appeal does not spring from deceit or impure motives or trickery, ⁴but just as we have been approved by God to be entrusted with the message of the gospel, even so we speak, not to please mortals, but to please God who tests our hearts. ⁵As you know and as God is our witness, we never came with words of flattery or with a pretext for greed; ⁶nor did we seek praise from mortals, whether from you or from others, ⁷though we might have made demands as apostles of Christ. But we were gentle among you, like a nurse tenderly caring for her own children. ⁸So deeply do we care for you that we are determined to share with you not only the gospel of God but also our own selves, because you have become very dear to us.

Commentary 1: Connecting the Reading with Scripture

Reminders play a vital role in life. Just in the past week, several key reminders have aided me. A colleague saved me with a text about a "Dialogue with the Deans" student event that had escaped me. I am admittedly dependent on the regular reminders that pop up on my cell phone so that I do not forget an appointment, meeting, or deadline.

At church this past Sunday, during a marriage study, I was reminded of how vital forgiveness is for a Christian marriage. I had not literally forgotten about forgiveness, nor had a recent incident come up where lack of forgiveness was a problem. Still, even in my knowing, I needed this timely reminder. The force of the reminder was so palpable that we (my wife and I) were persuaded to be even more intentional about our commitment to the regular practice of forgiveness to each other. In all, some reminders help us when things have been entirely forgotten. Other reminders buttress what we already know, expanding our surety of understanding. This latter type of reminder mirrors what is seen in the passage for this week (1 Thess. 2:1–8).

In the first two verses of 1 Thessalonians 2, there are two instances where Paul reminds the Thessalonians of something that they "know." They know that Paul, Silas, and Timothy's original travel to Thessalonica for the sake of the gospel was not "in vain" (v. 1), even though the present persecution may seem to argue otherwise. The Thessalonians likely do not actually believe that all of the work of these men is completely without value. However, Paul deems them to be in need of a reminder concerning what he and the others did among them, including the source from which it came.

Why might that be the case? Persecution and suffering can revise one's understanding of the past. It did not challenge the fact of the actual coming of Paul, Silas, and Timothy, but it likely did bring into question the efficacy and purpose of it. While some instances of suffering and persecution harden the past narrative for a people, galvanizing them, it also can weaken and/or challenge it. The latter option seems to be Paul's read of the Thessalonians' current state amid the circumstances of persecution.[1]

The second reminder of what the Thessalonians "know" concerns the experience of suffering and mistreatment of Paul and his coworkers in Philippi prior to their coming to

---

1. See the essay from last week, on 1 Thess. 1:1–10, for a fuller description of the circumstances and occasion for the letter.

Thessalonica, and the fact that they still came (v. 2). The "great opposition" (v. 2) did not cause them to freeze in fear in Philippi. Rather, they had courage in God to persist. These reminders convey a strong rhetorical push. If Paul and the others did not give in to the persecution against them and the gospel, and the result was the salvation of the Thessalonians through God's power, the persistence of the Thessalonians in this current round of persecution will likewise result in goodness, as God also guides it. Paul calls them to remember those things, that narrative, so as to look to the future in faith for what God will do.

Reminding language is a motif that runs through much of Scripture. The festivals that Israel is called to observe are grounded in remembrance. Passover is a remembrance of God's liberation from slavery in Egypt (Exod. 12:1–27). Pentecost is a remembrance of the giving of the Law at Mount Sinai. Tabernacles or Booths draws Israel back to the wilderness (Lev. 23:33–43). The remembrance is so that Israel does not forget who God is and how God acted, which in turn serves as a present and future encouragement. Israel knows, but the annual festival is a needed reminder.

Jesus explains part of the function of the Holy Spirit to be that of remembrance. When instructing and consoling the disciples about what will occur after he leaves the earth, Jesus notes that the Holy Spirit will teach them in all things and "remind you of all that I have said to you" (John 14:26). Included in this remembrance is the keeping of the commandments of Jesus, which demonstrates love for him (vv. 15–24). There are some interesting parallels in the call to remembrance evident in the festivals and in the coming (and activity) of the Holy Spirit.

Paul's remembrance emphasis goes beyond 1 Thessalonians. In Romans Paul tells the believers of his great confidence in them, but says "nevertheless on some points I have written to you rather boldly by way of reminder" (Rom. 15:14–15). They are not lacking the foundational teaching, though Paul still deems them to be in need of key reminders to reset their understanding. In 1 Corinthians he reminds the believers of his teaching on the resurrection of Christ (1 Cor. 15:1) so that they do not fall into heresy, unbelief, or despair. Later, he calls Timothy to remember the faith that lived in his grandmother Lois and mother Eunice, so as to emphasize the living reality of his own faith and faithfulness (2 Tim. 1:5). These calls to remembrance by Paul are to bring courage for today and the future, since God "did not give us a spirit of cowardice, but rather a spirit of power and of love and of self-discipline" (2 Tim. 1:7). Remembrance is powerful and needed.[2]

As a further reminder to the Thessalonians, Paul then stresses *how* they presented the gospel among them (1 Thess. 2:3–8). They did not come with "deceit or impure motives or trickery" (v. 3), nor with "words of flattery or with a pretext of greed" (v. 5). They did not come seeking the commendation or praise from the Thessalonians or other "mortals" (v. 6). Instead, they arrived as ones "approved by God" (v. 4) and desiring to "please God" (v. 4), caring for them as a nurse does for her own children (v. 7). Their love for the Thessalonians ran so deep that they shared "not only the gospel of God but also our own selves" (v. 8). Paul desires for them to remember not only the dire circumstances under which they came, but also the love that compelled them to remain in Thessalonica. Both were motivated and secured by God, who will do likewise for the Thessalonians in their current circumstances.

There are two lections that present at least a thin connection to the theme of remembrance. The command to not render unjust treatment, show partiality, slander, hate your neighbor, or take vengeance (Lev. 19:15–18) is grounded in the twice-rendered statement in that passage: "I am the LORD." Proper motive and action within the community of faith stem from seeing one's own (and others') identity within God's identity. Paul's motive and actions among the Thessalonians came from this same place. When this is rightly understood and lived out, a result is evident in Psalm 1: those who walk in these ways are "happy" (Ps. 1:1),

---

2. The theme and focus on remembrance in NT letters outside of Paul are found in 2 Pet. 1:12 regarding God's provision of all that the believers need; 2 Pet. 3:1 on the second coming of Jesus; and Jude 5 on God's sure ability to deal with—bring judgment on—false teachers.

and I would add grounded and nourished. The opposite is true for those who tread in the ways of the wicked (vv. 4–6). It would be too much to claim that Paul was thinking of the words of Psalm 1 in communicating with the Thessalonians, but we do well to hear them in connection for us today.

TROY A. MILLER

Commentary 2: Connecting the Reading with the World

Warmth, sincerity, gentleness, great love, and intimacy characterize 1 Thessalonians 2:1–8. Paul, Silvanus, and Timothy have come to Thessalonica by way of Philippi, where they encountered opposition (1 Thess. 2:2). Such opposition, however, did not curtail their declaring the gospel of God to the believers at Thessalonica. Paul reminds the community of believers that their appeal—their conduct among the believers—did not involve deception, pleasing people, flattery, greed, or becoming a financial burden (vv. 5–9). The apostles' attitude toward the Thessalonians is one of deep care and a willingness to share not only the gospel but also their own lives. The trust of Paul and his companions is deep.

When Paul's words are heard in an ecclesial context today, the church becomes confronted by a preacher and leader par excellence whose focus is not on money or flattery and whose mission is rooted in God and the preaching of the gospel, no matter the cost. Paul's life as a preacher influenced Dominic de Guzman, a Spaniard from Caleruega, Spain, who founded the Dominican order in 1215, whose mission was and is to preach. Among famous Dominican preachers are Thomas Aquinas, Catherine of Siena, Albert the Great, and, in present times, Timothy Radcliffe, an internationally known preacher and writer known for pushing the boundaries of Catholic orthodoxy (in some places, Timothy has been uninvited to preach).

Like Paul and Dominic, another famous preacher was Dietrich Bonhoeffer, also a German pastor, theologian, and anti-Nazi dissident. He suffered on account of his political stance against Hitler and for his sermons and other writings that chronicle his views. Bonhoeffer insisted that the church, like Christians, had to share in God's sufferings if it were to be a true church of Christ. Bonhoeffer lived as he preached, and his execution because of his opposition to Nazism became inspirational for Christians across many denominations and ideologies. One person deeply influenced by Bonhoeffer was another preacher, Martin Luther King Jr.

Martin Luther King Jr. was an American Baptist minister and preacher who became the most visible spokesperson and leader in the civil rights movement from 1954 until his assassination in 1968. He helped organize the 1963 March on Washington, where he preached his famous "I Have a Dream" speech. The preacher could also reflect on not only Martin Luther King Jr., but also those African American women preachers today such as Renita Weems, Suzan Johnson Cook, and Ann Farrar Lightner-Fuller, whose compassion and prophetic spirit and preaching have had profound effects on their congregations.

Like Paul, many of these preachers endured hardship because of the mission. None of these preachers sought the flattery of others, and all were filled with courage to preach what needed to be preached in the face of opposition, and for some, in the face of persecution that eventually led to death. The preacher can recall these great preachers and others who are not afraid to preach the gospel, not only with their words but also with their actions and lives. The preacher could also reflect on this important question: Are the preachers in today's churches ready to lay down their lives for the gospel message—a message that speaks of justice and liberation for all creation?

Paul's use of metaphor offers the preacher much room for comment in a social and ethical context. In verse 7, Paul reflects upon his approach to the newly converted believers at Thessalonica. He writes that he and his two companions were gentle among them, like a nurse caring for her own children. In a patriarchal, hierarchal Greco-Roman world of Paul's day, this feminine image and metaphor can be refreshing and also challenging to the status quo. By using this metaphor, Paul celebrates the so-designated maternal and feminine qualities that are possible and active within him and his male companions. For those who tend to read Paul as someone who is prone to autocratic and androcentric language, who is often harsh and offensive to women in his letters, this metaphor comes as a surprise.

True to the culture of his day and its influences upon him, Paul could have used metaphors that reflected military life, politics, or patronage. Instead, he uses a domestic image. Whether the nurse is a wet nurse or a feeding nurse is unclear. A wet nurse would be of a lower social class than the father image and metaphor that Paul puts forth later on in verse 11 of the letter. If a wet nurse is implied, then we have Paul and his companions not asserting a position of "power over" but, instead, assuming a role of deep care and thus affirming the work and place of the wet nurse in his society.

If the metaphor implies a feeding nurse, then the idea conveyed is that Paul and his companions are more like a mother toward the Thessalonians, feeding them with great care while being a source of comfort and security for them. This understanding opens up the possibility that Paul is teaching the Thessalonians that their true food is the gospel that he and his companions are offering this believing community (cf. 1 Cor. 3:2). The preacher can point out the effectiveness of Paul's feminine metaphor that communicates a powerful message while validating the presence and role of women in the society and culture of the day.

By using a feminine metaphor when speaking about himself and his companions, Paul also validates the qualities of the feminine that males are capable of embodying if males are willing to be in touch with their true androgynous inner selves. The preacher can comment on how Paul's metaphor has rich social and ethical implications not only for the Thessalonian community but also for the males of Paul's day. Additionally, the preacher can reflect on how gender-inclusive metaphors need to be a part of today's sermons and homilies and the need for male pastors not only to include such metaphors in their preaching, but also to allow their lives to embody such metaphors so that the gospel serves to nurture and nourish communities and not cast judgment upon them or cause unnecessary divisions among them.

Paul's point about suffering and being mistreated has personal implications for believers today. For those who preach the gospel—the liberating word of God's compassionate love for all creation—and for those who choose to live their lives accordingly to the gospel message, suffering will always be a part of their experience, especially for women. Throughout the world, Christian women, especially those who have converted to Christianity, suffer from all kinds of injustices. In some Middle Eastern countries, Christian women, as well as other women, are systematically deprived of their freedom, and oftentimes they are denied the basic human necessities for life, which would include nutrition, education, and health care. The preacher can reflect on the global situation of Christian women, and women in general, and note how many of these women are being persecuted for their faith.

Thus Paul's letter provides a wonderful vision for all people of what an effective preacher looks like. His letter invites Christians everywhere to embrace the lived experience of the gospel, which involves ethical praxis and joy but also suffering.

CAROL J. DEMPSEY, OP

Proper 25 (Sunday between October 23 and October 29 inclusive)

Matthew 22:34–46

³⁴When the Pharisees heard that he had silenced the Sadducees, they gathered together, ³⁵and one of them, a lawyer, asked him a question to test him. ³⁶"Teacher, which commandment in the law is the greatest?" ³⁷He said to him, "'You shall love the Lord your God with all your heart, and with all your soul, and with all your mind.' ³⁸This is the greatest and first commandment. ³⁹And a second is like it: 'You shall love your neighbor as yourself.' ⁴⁰On these two commandments hang all the law and the prophets."

⁴¹Now while the Pharisees were gathered together, Jesus asked them this question: ⁴²"What do you think of the Messiah? Whose son is he?" They said to him, "The son of David." ⁴³He said to them, "How is it then that David by the Spirit calls him Lord, saying,

⁴⁴'The Lord said to my Lord,

"Sit at my right hand,
   until I put your enemies under your feet"'?

⁴⁵If David thus calls him Lord, how can he be his son?" ⁴⁶No one was able to give him an answer, nor from that day did anyone dare to ask him any more questions.

Commentary 1: Connecting the Reading with Scripture

In this passage, Matthew portrays Jesus as participating in activity that was common for rabbis. Considering that the Torah contained 613 commandments, rabbis sought ways to empower believers' attempts at following the law. Some would prioritize laws by distinguishing more important commandments from lesser ones. It is not that the lesser ones were to be ignored, but rather that certain laws (say, like the Ten Commandments) would direct behavior that is implied in the Torah as a whole. One might think of the way that the Bill of Rights is used to identify the central tenets of the US Constitution. So the question about the greatest commandment is not so much a ranking, but a way for teachers to communicate what they believe to be the central calling of the law. Reflecting on the greatest commandment invites all believers to examine what they think is at the heart of their faith and directs the way they live their lives.

Having debated (and silenced) the Sadducees in the previous passage, Jesus is asked by one of the Pharisees about the greatest commandment. The answer that Jesus gives combines two important passages from the Old Testament. The first comes from Deuteronomy 6, which is the basis for the Shema, a prayer recited daily by observant Jews. While it is important to remember that ancient ways of thinking about the human body are different than modern ones, the terms "heart," "soul," and "mind" provide us interesting opportunities to think about how we might talk about giving oneself completely to God.

In the Hebrew thinking that gets translated into Greek, the heart (*kardia*) was where emotions, thought, and choice were centered. ("For where your treasure is, there your heart will be also" Matt. 6:21). The soul (*psychē*) had to do with the life breath, the force that animates a body, feelings, and consciousness. Finally, the mentioning of mind is interesting because it is a departure from the Deuteronomy text. In the Septuagint, the Greek translation of the Hebrew Bible, the term "power/strength" (*dynamis*) is used. Matthew uses the term "mind" (*dianoia*), which emphasizes thinking or understanding.

As interesting and thought provoking as Jesus' answer is, it really is a rather mainstream response that would be perfectly acceptable among rabbis of his day. More distinctive than Jesus' invocation of the Shema and the command to love God with one's entire self is the way that he links that with love of neighbor. By describing this command of Leviticus 19:18 as "like" the Shema, Jesus is placing the love of God and love of neighbor on equal footing. Both are the key, the hooks upon which all of the law hangs. So it is important to understand multiple layers of this call to love God and neighbor.

"Loving neighbor as self" echoes the "golden rule" of Matthew 7:12, in which Jesus declares, "In everything do to others as you would have them do to you; for this is the law and the prophets." Indeed, one can think of instances throughout the New Testament (1 John 4; Jas. 2) in which the love of God and neighbor are intimately connected such that one cannot speak of loving or having faith in God unless one is in fact loving one's neighbor or expressing that faith in love.

Yet, as much as the love commandment is a cornerstone of Christian teaching, it should not be thought of in contrast to Jewish observation of the law. The entire episode of the greatest commandment revolves around Jesus' interpretation of the Hebrew Torah. Considering that the first-century Rabbi Hillel declared, "What is hateful to you do not do to your neighbor,"[1] we can affirm that the love command is a Jewish inheritance.

Indeed, our understanding of the neighbor love that Jesus mentions deepens when we explore the connection to Leviticus 19. In that section of Leviticus, the command to love one's neighbor is given after a series of directives that govern behavior to the weakest members of society. For example, among the commands are leaving the edges of one's field, stray ears of corn, and fallen grapes for the poor or aliens (Lev. 19:9–10); not withholding wages from day laborers and not discriminating against the blind or deaf (vv. 13–14); showing no partiality, not acting dishonestly, and not standing by when another's life is at stake (vv. 15–16).

These commands demonstrate how love of neighbor was intrinsic to the proper obedience of the law and how Israel's covenant with God called them to prioritize those who were most vulnerable. While "neighbor" is a term that we might use for those near us or just like us, this passage calls us to think of those most poor and marginalized as that neighbor needing love.

The communal dimension of neighbor love in the covenant teaches us something important about self-love. Modern psychology has something to say about the necessity of self-love as crucial to the ability to love others. Yet, while modern ideas about self-love would not necessarily be rejected by Matthew, it is anachronistic to separate love of self and love of neighbor. Jesus' response calls into question any ideas of the self that are so individualistic that they do not recognize our interpersonal natures. Jesus is carrying on the Levitical understanding that Israel is one people. The fact that personal identity is intertwined in a larger communal one takes on a greater significance in our interconnected, global context.

The debate over David's son seems quite divorced from the discussion about the greatest commandment, but seen with the Great Commandment, it provides Matthew an opportunity to make a statement about Jesus' identity and authority.

In the context of Matthew's Gospel, the question about David's son concludes the activity and interactions that Jesus has after his entry into Jerusalem (Matt. 21:1). Whether in arguments or parables, the conflict with the religious authorities has been at the forefront, and the issue of Jesus' authority is paramount. The question about David's son is the third of three consecutive debates that focus on the interpretation of Scripture. The Sadducees' question about the resurrection (22:23–33) and the Pharisees' question about the greatest commandment are now concluded with Jesus himself prompting the question about David's son. His interpretation of Psalm 110 suggests that the Christ (Messiah) must be someone greater than simply a son of David. His opponents cannot say a word—Jesus is the authoritative interpreter of Scripture—but what does that interpretation mean?

---

1. b. *Sabb.* 31a.

The invocation of various titles for Jesus is an important part of Matthew's Gospel. From the beginning of his ministry, when, at his baptism, the voice from heaven says, "This is my Son" (3:17), to the confession of the centurion at Jesus' death, "Truly this man was God's Son" (27:54), Jesus' identity as Son of God is the most important confession. That title is often combined with others. Peter's confession at Caesarea Philippi makes the messianic connection, "You are the Christ, the Son of the living God" (16:16). In this passage, it is interesting to note that while the crowds called Jesus the "Son of David" (21:9), the Pharisee who asks Jesus about the greatest commandment addresses him simply as teacher. Matthew is clearly indicating that Jesus is a teacher, but more. He is a Son of David, but more. He is the Messiah, but more.

The combination of these two stories leads us to reflect on how the confession of Jesus as Son of David, as Messiah, or as Son of God is done most faithfully when rooted in a faith that loves God and our neighbors, particularly those most vulnerable, with everything we have.

MICHAEL E. LEE

Commentary 2: Connecting the Reading with the World

". . . and one of them, a lawyer, asked him a question to test him" (Matt 22:35).

This text is likely to set you on edge, as you begin to prepare how to preach from it. It is also likely, if they are listening carefully, to set at least some portion of your hearers on edge when it is read in worship. It starts with a challenging question in public, and who of us enjoys that? Moreover, attentive listeners are likely to sense at this point in Matthew's Gospel the increasingly menacing presence of conflict and controversy between Jesus and his enemies. In the verses immediately ahead of this text, the conflict is with the Sadducees. Now, it is the Pharisees who are closing in on Jesus; and all of this is happening against the emerging backdrop of Jerusalem in the last chapter of Jesus' life. The tension just hangs in the air like a drumbeat that gets louder and louder. The lawyer here is not like the attorneys likely to populate so many churches; he is instead what we might call in our context a canon lawyer, an expert on the polity, the "canon laws" of the church. In this case, the lawyer is a Pharisee deeply versed in Jewish law.

Whether or not there are lawyers in your church, your parishioners know what it means to be set on edge by test questions, whoever is posing them. So an immediate connection here turns around how the gospel speaks to those parts of any faith tradition that have become ossified and have hardened into a list of rules that fail to capture the rich expansiveness of faith.

When I was examined for ordination by a regional judicatory from my denomination, the examining committee had asked numerous questions of me and several other seminary graduates presenting ourselves that day, and it was finally time for the dreaded questions from the floor. A hand shot up from the audience. The questioner asked me, "Where did Cain and Abel find their wives?" I could see his sneer. It was a trick question, designed to tease out my position on biblical authority. To take the question literally would be to acknowledge that Adam and Eve were literally the first man and woman, and that Cain and Abel were literally the first children. However, to approach the Bible seriously even if not literally, would be to discuss the creation story as a magnificent and holy saga in which we ponder more the whys of creation than the hows. That is what I did with that question; and I finished by saying triumphantly that, when it comes to where Cain and Abel found their wives, my answer was that I do not know and that, ultimately, it does not matter. Unfortunately, it mattered a great deal to my questioner, and I spent another half hour being grilled by the man with the trick question.

I imagine that the man standing there in the face of Jesus was a lot like him. He knew that there were 613 laws in his tradition, and he was sure that Jesus would be tongue-tied by the task of discerning, on the spot, which of those laws was the greatest. He had probably proof-texted his way up a huge heap of religious esoterica, at the top of which he now just luxuriated in his own irrelevant self-satisfaction, oblivious to the fact that, buried deeply beneath such a heap, something called gospel was struggling to be free. From that place of self-satisfaction, he would enjoy watching Jesus squirm when he asked his sneering question: "Teacher, which commandment in the law is the greatest?"

What may set us on edge about that man is that, at our best, we can remember when we have asked that question with quivering lips and a frog in the throat. When we have seen news footage of a child sitting in an ambulance in shock, having been removed from the rubble of his bombed-out home after an air strike in Aleppo, Syria. Or closer to home, when addiction or disease or a hurricane has drawn near, upending everything and turning our whole neatly packaged life on its side. In such moments we have asked this lawyer's question, or one very much like it: "What is the most important thing?" "When everything in our lives is falling from its foundation, what will endure?"

If only he had asked Jesus that question with tears in his eyes, rather than a smirk on his face. There would have been a lot to lose if he had really taken his own question seriously. He would have had to watch the framework of his life, all of those rules and regulations that the rabbis referred to as "the fence around the Torah," come crashing down like a house of cards. He would have had to watch all of those laws—the "great" ones or the "heavy" ones, as well as the "light" ones or the "small" ones—get pulled out of the framework, like a load-bearing wall, until it all came falling down. He would have had too much to lose if his world had toppled over on its side, so he did not take his own question seriously.

Nevertheless Jesus did. "He said to him, 'You shall love the Lord your God with all your heart, and with all your soul, and with all your mind.' This is the greatest and first commandment. And a second is like it: 'You shall love your neighbor as yourself.' On these two commandments hang all the law and the prophets" (Matt. 22:37–40). Jesus' answer reveals that, when all 613 laws are boiled down to their essence, the remainder at the root of all of it is love, love of God and love of neighbor.

We do not hear another word from the master of the trick question.

Another connection here turns around the struggle between the boundaries we are often prone to draw around God and the expansiveness of the gospel. Matthew is pushing beyond prevailing Jewish expectations toward what Jesus represents as faith in a big God, a God who refuses to be subjected to human agendas, a God big enough to live within a text as well as within a temple. No matter how we attempt to pigeonhole such a God, this God will continue to break loose from the boundaries we attempt to build. This God, after all, redefines Jesus not as "David's son" but as "David's lord." Jesus' own sense of his messianism is not just to fulfill the law but to go beyond it. Far more important than the lineage of David, therefore, is the call to follow God to a new kingdom, a new creation. "We reject the false doctrine," as the Theological Declaration of Barmen puts it, "as though the church in human arrogance could place the Word and work of the Lord in the service of any arbitrarily chosen desires, purposes, and plans."[2]

A final connection, a liturgical one, is this prayer from Ulrich Zwingli:

> Living God, by the power of your Spirit,
> help us so to hear your holy word
> that we may truly understand;
> that, understanding, we may believe;
> and believing, we may follow
> in faithfulness and obedience,
> seeking your honor and glory in all that we do;
> through Jesus Christ our Lord. Amen.[3]

THEODORE J. WARDLAW

---

2. *The Book of Confessions* (Louisville, KY: The Office of the General Assembly, 1999), 250.
3. *Book of Common Worship* (Louisville, KY: Westminster John Knox, 2018), 1111.

All Saints

Revelation 7:9–17
Psalm 34:1–10, 22

1 John 3:1–3
Matthew 5:1–12

Revelation 7:9–17

⁹After this I looked, and there was a great multitude that no one could count, from every nation, from all tribes and peoples and languages, standing before the throne and before the Lamb, robed in white, with palm branches in their hands. ¹⁰They cried out in a loud voice, saying,

> "Salvation belongs to our God who is seated on the throne, and to the Lamb!"

¹¹And all the angels stood around the throne and around the elders and the four living creatures, and they fell on their faces before the throne and worshiped God, ¹²singing,

> "Amen! Blessing and glory and wisdom
> and thanksgiving and honor
> and power and might
> be to our God forever and ever! Amen."

¹³Then one of the elders addressed me, saying, "Who are these, robed in white, and where have they come from?" ¹⁴I said to him, "Sir, you are the one that knows." Then he said to me, "These are they who have come out of the great ordeal; they have washed their robes and made them white in the blood of the Lamb.

> ¹⁵For this reason they are before the throne of God,
>   and worship him day and night within his temple,
>   and the one who is seated on the throne will shelter them.
> ¹⁶They will hunger no more, and thirst no more;
>   the sun will not strike them,
>   nor any scorching heat;
> ¹⁷for the Lamb at the center of the throne will be their shepherd,
>   and he will guide them to springs of the water of life,
> and God will wipe away every tear from their eyes."

Commentary 1: Connecting the Reading with Scripture

As this biblical text is read aloud in our congregations for All Saints' Day, the glorious image of a beautiful diversity of people from every nation joining the angels to gather around God's throne brings comfort to those mourning the deaths of loved ones. Some churches publicly acknowledge members who have died over the past year in their bulletins and commemorate them during worship services with the lighting of a candle or tolling of a bell. One obvious connection between the text and today is the participation of the recently deceased in this majestic and joyous heavenly celebration. The congregation imagines their presence among the multitude singing praises in Revelation 7:12.

Despite this compelling message of hope in 7:9–17, the larger context of the entire book of Revelation, with its apocalyptic visions of desolation and destruction emerging from scrolls and seals, confounds some Christians today. One interpretative strategy is for preachers to utilize passages like this one—with promises of eternal "springs of the water of life" and the God who removes "every tear" (Rev. 7:16)—and ignore the many parts about judgment and suffering. Revelation was written to be read aloud and all at once in churches (1:3). The earliest worshipers heard Revelation in its entirety and would have recognized the repetition of certain themes, such as the juxtaposition of divine deliverance and wrath, across a sweeping story of battle, struggle, and triumph. The original audience would have understood Revelation as a coherent narrative about God's attributes and actions spurring them toward faithful devotion and courageous witness.

In Revelation 4:1 and 7:9, the author employs the phrase "After this I looked" (*meta tauta eidon*) to indicate a transition from one vision to the next. The structure of Revelation is not chronological; the visions do not depict actual future events one after the next. The author employs literary transitions to connect themes. In both these transitions, the scene shifts to the heavenly throne room. The chapters preceding chapter 4 address seven specific churches under imperial Roman rule in Asia. Christ commends some churches for persevering through affliction and rebukes other churches for lukewarm commitment. A few of the churches, like the church in Ephesus, are simultaneously celebrated and criticized with precise observations and instructions. The chapters preceding Revelation 7:9 entail vivid yet chaotic visions of different colored horses and riders carrying an assortment of weapons to bring eschatological justice and judgment.

Just as the activity in the throne room in Revelation 4:1–11 is connected to the first three chapters, the victorious celebration in 7:9–17 is connected to the preceding visions of justice and judgment in 5:1–7:8. Because these chapters are not included within the lectionary reading, and often overlooked in our overall Christian education curriculum, preachers and listeners today can miss two significant connections. The first is eschatological and the second is practical. Revelation 6 ends with a cliffhanger after an apocalyptic catastrophe of cosmic proportions ravages the earth. Who can withstand God's wrath? The vision in 7:1–8 provides the immediate answer: a marked remnant of 144,000 persons divided evenly across twelve tribes of Israel. The number 144,000 is meant to be interpreted symbolically, not literally. The list of tribes in 7:5–8 differs from lists in the Old Testament in several ways. This list begins with Judah instead of Reuben, whose name is at the head of most Old Testament registers, because Christ was understood to have belonged to the tribe of Judah (Heb. 7:14). More striking is the omission of Dan and Ephraim in 7:5–8. One explanation suggests their connections to the sin of idolatry resulted in the inclusion of Joseph and Levi in their place (Judg. 18:14–31; Hos. 4:17–5:9).

Ultimately, the author employs mathematical imagery, multiplying 12 by 12,000. This is consistent with the larger context of the Scriptures, such as the twelve tribes of Israel in the Old Testament and the twelve disciples of Jesus in the New Testament, and signifies wholeness and completion.[1] The vision in Revelation 7:9–17 provides the ultimate answer when it is all said and done: The "great multitude" of people described in 7:9 far exceeds the remnant of 144,000, so vast that it cannot be counted, and comprises people from every nation. Just as the original readers and hearers of Revelation would have experienced assurance through two nuanced layers of eschatological hope—from the promise of a saved remnant in 7:1–8 to that of a great multitude in 7:9–17—Christians today may more fully grasp the glorious and joyous hope of God's salvation when it is presented in proclamation alongside admonitions of divine judgment and instructions for faithful discipleship.

One of the practical messages in Revelation 6 and 7 is the direct connection between heaven and earth. The opening of the seals in heaven produces dramatic results on earth in chapter 6. Lands are devastated. Families are uprooted. Nations rage against one another. Weather patterns are unpredictable and destructive. The

---

1. Brian K. Blount, *Revelation: A Commentary* (Louisville, KY: Westminster John Knox, 2009), 146.

promise of salvation in 7:9–17 should elicit anticipation—hope for what has been promised—and faithfulness. The seven Asian churches from Revelation 2 and 3 are called to trust in God's future deliverance and enact God's mercy in the present (Rev. 2:9–11 and 3:10–12). In the throne room (4:1–11 and 7:9–17) God's mighty power stands above human empires (4:9–11), and God's radically inclusive plan welcomes people of every racial, ethnic, political, and cultural background (7:9). This vision of a powerful, faithful, and inclusive God encourages the persecuted churches in Revelation to resist oppressive Roman imperial structures and attend to one another's needs and afflictions.

The themes of perpetual worship and social justice in 7:15–16 integrate this dynamic of simultaneous anticipation and application. With the ultimate victory of good over evil and life over death, the author of Revelation writes that the diverse assembly is engaged in worship "day and night" under God's everlasting protection. Christians are therefore inspired to continuously praise God together and take refuge in God's salvation (Ps. 34:1–10, 22). In the following verse, we read that none hunger or thirst and all have shelter from fierce weather conditions like the "scorching heat." The language of "hunger no more," "thirst no more," and "sun will not strike them" evokes prophecy in Isaiah 49:10 and represents eschatological fulfillment. The same phrases from Revelation 7:16 also remind readers and hearers of Christ's challenge in Matthew 25:31–46 to feed the hungry, clothe the naked, care for the sick, welcome the stranger, and visit the imprisoned. Perpetual worship includes participation in faithful efforts to end world hunger, eradicate global poverty, and combat climate change.

Revelation 7:9–17 is located between the sixth and seventh seals of judgment and precedes the calamities that accompany the blaring trumpets and vicious woes in Revelation 8 and 9. Yet its images of eschatological completion and ultimate deliverance most closely align with the book's last two chapters, 21 and 22. The author of Revelation interrupts the unfolding plot of the grand narrative with this strategic interlude.[2] If the genre of the text were fantasy or science fiction, a literary critic might deem the author's decision to reveal (or spoil) the ending in the first third of the book as peculiar or unwise. However, in Revelation, this spoiler serves a holy purpose. Knowing how the story ends instructs and inspires Christians to continue making the earth more like heaven in the here and now.

WILLIAM YOO

Commentary 2: Connecting the Reading with the World

The feast of All Saints can be a confusing celebration for worshipers. Who and what are we celebrating? What makes a saint? This Revelation reading can open up the meaning of All Saints for participants. The opening verse, with "a great multitude that no one could count," reminds the congregation that the feast of All Saints celebrates *all* the saints. This includes famous saints of the church: biblical figures, as well as heroes and heroines of the early church who have a capital-S "Saint" in front of their names, such as Saint Francis, fresh in the minds of congregants who took their pets to a blessing of the animals a month before. Those are not the only saints honored on this day. Our loved ones who have died in the faith *and* disciples who are hard at work in the church today are also the saints who comprise the church.

While All Souls' Day, with its historical emphasis on Purgatory, was removed from most Protestant calendars during the Reformation, some believers yearn for a dedicated day to remember loved ones who have died. If churches do not observe a separate commemoration for the departed, such an observance will likely be absorbed into All Saints' Day.

---

2. Robert H. Mounce, *The Book of Revelation*, rev. ed., New International Commentary on the New Testament (Grand Rapids: Eerdmans, 1998), 154.

The last two verses of this Revelation reading are common at funerals, especially the comforting image of God wiping away every tear from mourners' eyes, so discussion of death in an All Saints sermon may be appropriate.

Preachers need to be aware that choosing Revelation as this week's text could feed into an unrealistic cultural understanding of death. Revelation gets less attention than other New Testament works in the Revised Common Lectionary, so some listeners may tune out this reading. Others may pay closer attention, excited to see a lection from a fantastical book they may have trouble understanding. Many in contemporary culture, including Christians in our pews, may have a disembodied understanding of death. Halloween, a cultural celebration just over when All Saints arrives, can contribute to a cultural distancing from death. While Halloween offers an opportunity to focus on macabre costumes of zombies, such depictions are typically anonymous. Skeletons and ghosts on Halloween rarely represent someone specific. Contrast this with the Mexican Day of the Dead, celebrated on All Souls' Day, November 2, and its focus on remembering and communing with loved ones. Celebrations of All Saints should help hearers learn about and better integrate into their worldviews a mature theological understanding of death and the communion of the saints.

The animated movie *Coco,* in which a boy is accidentally transported into the land of the dead, may provide an avenue through which preachers can open a conversation about how different cultures grapple with death, some more effectively than the dominant culture of the United States. In the movie, the dead long to be remembered by a picture on an *ofrenda* (offering) altar, which those who observe the Day of the Dead set up for their deceased loved ones. Participants personalize such *ofrendas* with photos and favorite foods, and they engage the senses with marigolds and incense. Encouraging sensory remembrances of our particular loved ones, such as bringing their photos to church and even lighting candles for them on this day, coheres with an All Saints observance, versus anonymous, smiling skeletons and friendly ghosts on Halloween.

The movie *Coco* features music as a prominent theme. This can be an opening to explore music used in the All Saints service. The words "one was a soldier, and one was a priest" in the hymn "I Sing a Song of the Saints of God" can help expand the understanding of saints as ordinary disciples rather than as perfect examples of virtue. Unfortunately, the lyrics of this hymn can also create distance with lines like "one was slain by a fierce wild beast," which sounds mythic, or "one was a shepherdess on the green," which sounds dated. Acknowledging these lyrics from the pulpit and digging into the theology of "saints" referring to all the baptized can yield fruit, especially if hymns such as "For All the Saints" and "Hark! the Sound of Holy Voices" are also sung on this day, as such hymns sound as though we are celebrating only capital-S saints.

Towering figures from Christian tradition, such as Saint Peter, who was a cornerstone of the early church, can be held up as examples on All Saints. A more recent example of a saint, someone who achieved more than we can imagine but to whom we can still relate, is Mother Teresa of Calcutta (1910–1997). Her compassion in working with the poor and outcast in India is legendary, yet, as she recounted in her journal, Teresa struggled for many years with depression and suffered greatly from what she experienced as God's absence.[3] Knowing that such a stellar example of sainthood sometimes struggled like the rest of us can counter any hymns or liturgy that appear to celebrate only the greats, as well as encourage ordinary saints in the church to try combating big problems in small ways. Saints who struggle to feel God's presence in church, for example, could stay home from church, but the preacher can encourage them instead to try emulating a saint like Mother Teresa by finding people in need to serve.

Discussion of hymns can lead into an exploration of other music prevalent in contemporary culture that relates to the themes of All Saints. One country music song, "Live Like You Are Dying," can help preachers tie All Saints

---

3. See Mother Teresa, *Come Be My Light: The Private Writings of the Saint of Calcutta* (New York: Doubleday, 2007).

celebrations to ethical living. The song portrays a man who in his forties receives a dire diagnosis but comes to see it as a gift, because he begins to acknowledge that his time on earth is limited and to act in ways he had not before. Some examples in this song's lyrics may not be especially helpful as guides to ethical living, such as "skydiving and rocky mountain climbing"; but others are, including "I gave forgiveness I'd been denying" and "I finally read the Good Book." When we acknowledge that all of us are mortal, we have an opportunity to explore injustice in our world and to act to change, as well as focusing on smaller things in our lives that are worth changing.

The mention of angels in Revelation 7:11 can contribute to the confusion some Christians have about the distinction between saints and angels. Many Christians think of angels not as separately created beings, as they are portrayed in the Bible, but as something into which humans are transformed after death. Peter at the pearly gates is often portrayed with a halo, which is associated with angels. A halo was also used in early depictions of saints, and in pre-Christian times, halos were used in images of emperors to show their semidivine status.

Our Revelation reading, with the angels and the robed living creatures, provides an opportunity for the preacher to explore the biblical portrayal of angels over against saccharine images of angels in our culture. As soon as Halloween is over, Christmas décor begins to creep into the culture, and angels in Christmas decorations appear tamer than the angels who lead battles in the Bible. This Revelation reading can open up a biblical discussion of angels, who are frightening enough in the Bible that they consistently need to tell the humans they encounter not to be afraid. The preacher can go on to contrast angels with saints. We are saints and can become saints. Angels, however, are differently created beings. Together, saints and angels serve and worship God.

ELIZABETH FELICETTI

All Saints

Psalm 34:1–10, 22

¹I will bless the LORD at all times;
   his praise shall continually be in my mouth.
²My soul makes its boast in the LORD;
   let the humble hear and be glad.
³O magnify the LORD with me,
   and let us exalt his name together.

⁴I sought the LORD, and he answered me,
   and delivered me from all my fears.
⁵Look to him, and be radiant;
   so your faces shall never be ashamed.
⁶This poor soul cried, and was heard by the LORD,
   and was saved from every trouble.
⁷The angel of the LORD encamps
   around those who fear him, and delivers them.
⁸O taste and see that the LORD is good;
   happy are those who take refuge in him.
⁹O fear the LORD, you his holy ones,
   for those who fear him have no want.
¹⁰The young lions suffer want and hunger,
   but those who seek the LORD lack no good thing.
. . . .
²²The LORD redeems the life of his servants;
   none of those who take refuge in him will be condemned.

Connecting the Psalm with Scripture and Worship

All Saints' Day is a unique moment in the liturgical year. On this day, we proclaim a distinct expression of God's great good news: When all is ended, an uncountable throng of absolute diversity (Rev. 7:9) will worship together in the presence of the God who wipes away every tear (v. 17). It is a breathtaking vision.

It is also a challenge, because All Saints injects into our secular society's queasiness about mortality a startling focus on our dead. Additionally, this feast day brushes up against traditions—from concepts of sainthood to celebrations of Dia de los Muertos—that may be unfamiliar to some congregants. If that were not enough, in most years (including this year), All Saints dips into the mind-blowing book of Revelation. As you lead your parishioners into these deep waters, Psalm 34 can be a helpful companion.

In contrast to the cosmic scale of Revelation, Psalm 34 is a personal text. Written in the first-person singular, it carries the force of personal witness. Testifying to God's goodness, the psalmist recalls a difficult time when "I sought the LORD, and God answered me, and delivered me from all my fears" (Ps. 34:4). Further, the writer remembers an experience of unspecified struggle when "this poor soul cried, and was heard by the LORD, and was saved from every trouble" (v. 6). Consider making use of these ancient phrases as you enter the enormous vision written by John of Patmos, because, whether or not the people in your pews are able to relate to "com[ing] out of the great ordeal" (Rev. 7:14), they have surely sought the Lord or cried out to God and felt—or waited for—God's response.

This two-part tale of the psalmist asking for God's help (Ps. 34:4, 6) and offering praise for God's help (vv. 1, 8, 22) is written very large in today's Revelation pericope. After all, that innumerable multitude of no-exceptions inclusivity standing before God (Rev. 7:9) must surely have cried out for God's help as they went through "the great ordeal" (v. 14), and now they offer thanks and praise to God (vv. 10, 15). A sermon that ponders seeking and receiving and giving thanks for God's saving help is relevant to everyone and might offer assurance to those for whom All Saints is a difficult day.

For the church, the purpose of personal testimony is not simply to tell one's story but to glorify God and bring others to faith. Thus, we see the psalmist deploying personal testimony evangelically, using lived experience to exhort others to faithfulness: "O magnify the Lord with me" (Ps. 34:3). An All Saints sermon on that theme might focus on the power of sharing our faith with others. You could explore the psalmist's choice to write of personal faith, as well as John of Patmos's choice to share the vision we know as the book of Revelation, and connect those texts with saints in your church making the choice to share their faith.

In all of Psalm 34, surely the most well-known words are "O taste and see that the Lord is good" (v. 8). A preacher could link this sensory-rich phrase to the assurance that "the one who is seated on the throne will shelter them. They will hunger no more" (Rev. 7:15b–16a). A sermon using this textual connection could be designed to comfort those who are grieving a death and to reassure those who are fearing death. Alternatively, a preacher might use the "taste and see" image to launch an exploration of the sensory overload that is the book of Revelation, as it attempts to communicate the inexpressible glory of God and God's coming reign.

In case there is any question, this is definitely a day to celebrate the Eucharist! Help your congregation glimpse the communion of saints and recognize their own place in that faithful throng. Speak of your Communion table as stretching all the way back to Jesus and all the way forward to the eschatological banquet when all will be united "before the throne and before the Lamb" (v. 9). Although Psalm 34 is a pre-Christian text, all of our saints and all of us are like the psalmist: each is an individual seeking God.

An obvious choice for this day's Communion music is the James E. Moore Jr. setting of "Taste and See," a powerful paraphrase of Psalm 34. Allowing your congregation to sing at least the refrain would be in keeping with the vision of countless voices lifted together in praise of God (vv. 10–12).

Phrases from the psalm lend themselves to use as a call to worship. To emphasize the sense of a feast-day celebration, consider stationing multiple readers around the sanctuary—think of the four angels posted at Earth's "four corners" (v. 1)—to convey something of the magnificence of the Revelation text. For example:

Reader 1: I will bless the Lord at all times.
Reader 2: God's praise shall continually be in my mouth.
Reader 3: My soul makes its boast in the Lord.
Reader 4: Let us exalt God's name together.
All: The Lord redeems the life of God's servants. Happy are those who take refuge in God. (Psalm 34:1–3, 8, 22)

Notice that "Happy are those who take refuge in God" (v. 8) is a beatitude; it echoes those found in the day's Gospel reading. Psalm 34 offers a liturgical link between "Rejoice and be glad, for your reward is great in heaven" (Matt. 5:12) and Revelation's vision of that heavenly reward.

Marking the unique moment of All Saints in the liturgical year, you are empowered to proclaim that saints above and saints below are all called to "worship God day and night" (Rev. 7:15). You, earthly and broken saint that you are, are blessed to invite your throng to "bless the Lord at all times" (Ps. 34:1).

LEIGH CAMPBELL-TAYLOR

All Saints

1 John 3:1–3

¹See what love the Father has given us, that we should be called children of God; and that is what we are. The reason the world does not know us is that it did not know him. ²Beloved, we are God's children now; what we will be has not yet been revealed. What we do know is this: when he is revealed, we will be like him, for we will see him as he is. ³And all who have this hope in him purify themselves, just as he is pure.

Commentary 1: Connecting the Reading with Scripture

Although traditionally categorized as an epistle, 1 John is not really a letter. It does not have names of any authors or recipients; there is no epistolary opening or closing; and its organization, if it exists, is very loose.[1] However, like a letter, the document is written by a particular author to a particular group of people and contains important messages for them. From the earliest centuries of the Common Era, church leaders and scholars have noted similarities in language, imagery, and ideas between the Fourth Gospel and the epistles of John. This led to a claim that the apostle John authored all these biblical books. However, significant differences between the Gospel and the epistles of John throw that claim into doubt. The work probably dates from the end of the first century CE.

First John 3:1–3, like any other portion of the work, needs to be read with the whole document in mind. Common themes and assertions run throughout this "epistle," in effect, a long and loving exhortation in Johannine style to a Christian community dealing with schism. There is a group that has split off and left it, most likely due to differences in opinion regarding Christology. The author therefore urges his readers to cleave to a right understanding of Christ's person and work and to support each other in the love that comes from God, who is love. As in the Gospel of John, there is a tendency to think in dualistic terms: God vs. Satan, Christians vs. the world. Unlike John's Gospel, there is no mention of Jews in the epistle; instead, the opponents are called antichrists (1 John 2:18–26).

The text for the day, 1 John 3:1–3, is short but packed full of ideas. (1) God is the origin, the Father of the Christian community (2) who deeply loves this community and (3) gives its members the privilege of being called the children of God. (4) Outsiders who do not recognize these Christians as God's children do not know God. (5) However, being children of God now does not mean Christians have fulfilled their destiny, because (6) Christ will be fully revealed only at his coming. (7) Then they shall be changed to be in conformity with Christ, (8) whom they shall see in his fullness only at his coming. (9) Those who live in this hope of being like Christ, like God, lead ethical, loving lives, since (10) Jesus is pure. This short, compact passage makes clear that for 1 John, "true eschatology, true Christology, and true ethics all go hand in hand."[2]

All Saints' Day is one of those celebrations in the liturgical year that can be so important, so laden with intellectual and emotional content, that it functions as a text in its own right. First John intervenes in this celebration in at least two helpful ways. The term "saint" can be

---

1. Information for this essay has come from David Rensberger, *1 John, 2 John, 3 John*, Abingdon New Testament Commentaries (Nashville: Abingdon, 1997); D. Moody Smith, *First, Second, and Third John*, Interpretation (Louisville, KY: John Knox, 1991); and Georg Strecker, *The Johannine Letters*, trans. Linda M. Maloney (Minneapolis: Fortress, 1996).
2. Rensberger, *1 John, 2 John, 3 John*, 94.

confusing, especially in Protestant traditions. Pauline, Roman Catholic, and secular understandings collude and collide with each other in the minds of many. First John 3:1 provides a good working definition of "saints": those who are "children of God."

Second, many congregations spend a few minutes, at least, remembering those who have died. Such remembrance is highly appropriate. However, 1 John 3 pushes the congregation also to consider the sainthood of those who are still living. What does it mean to be the children of God? This designation is not our own achievement, but a gift of love from God. It describes our state, who we are; but it also provides us with a future goal, who we are to become. It names our origins in God, but also compels us to "purify" ourselves so we may be like Christ, who is pure (1 Cor. 13:12).

The other biblical texts for All Saints' Day are Revelation 7:9–17 (the eschatological gathering of nations), Psalm 34:1–10, 22 (a psalm of praise for deliverance from trouble), and Matthew 5:1–12 (the beginning of the Sermon on the Mount). In many ways, Revelation 7 describes an iteration, immeasurably amplified, of Psalm 34. The four readings can be arranged so that they present us with expanding visions of the saints, of "the children of God." Psalm 34 involves primarily a single person, albeit in the context of a worshiping congregation. First John 3 focuses on a particular community. Matthew 5 enlarges our vision of the children of God to include various classes of people in society: the poor in spirit, those who mourn, the meek, and so on. Finally, Revelation 7 describes countless multitudes, from every nation and people, praising God and the Lamb.

The lectionary texts, like the biblical witness as a whole, give us a certain freedom in deciding how we are going to talk about the saints in our particular context, on one particular day. At the same time, the texts remind us that as necessary as it is to focus on certain people—individuals, communities, societies, nations—in our own marking of All Saints' Day, there are others in the background of whom we should be aware, even if we do not mention them. If we are meditating on one particular saint today, what does it mean that there is a countless multitude of saints as well?

Finally, 1 John 3:1–3 stands in some tension with Matthew 5:1–12. Whereas for the author of 1 John the "children of God" are those who believe correctly about Jesus and his return, the passage from the Sermon on the Mount ignores any criterion that has to do with correct understanding of doctrine. Instead, the blessed are certain classes of people: those who are weak, in distress, vulnerable, and righteous, as well as Jesus' followers who are reviled, maligned, and persecuted for being his followers.

Of course, the audiences of 1 John and of Matthew 5 are very different: in the former, the author is trying to strengthen a community weakened by controversy and defections, whereas in Matthew's Gospel, Jesus is teaching about God's vision of righteousness. Yet the clash in understandings of who are "blessed" and who are "children of God" is inescapable. Such ambiguity arising out of the lectionary readings, if treated with wisdom and insight, is salutary for the church.

Too often in our history we have been too quick to pronounce who is a saint and who is a sinner, who is orthodox and who a heretic, who is included among the people of God and who is not. On the other hand, such discernment is absolutely vital for the life of faith, indeed for the existence of the religion. While such judgments are necessary, they are provisional, made with incomplete knowledge. As important as it is to decide who is of "the world" and who is of God, our decisions are fallible, for "what we will be has not yet been revealed" (1 John 3:1–2). The Bible, by consistently preserving conflicting voices, keeps warning us that at the end, it is God alone who will decide who is among the numberless multitudes surrounding the throne. In the meantime, we remember our saints and our sainthood, conscious all the while that there are others whom God has called, but whom we do not yet recognize.

ARUN W. JONES

Commentary 2: Connecting the Reading with the World

Tucked away in a corner of the liturgical calendar is All Saints' Day, practically masked by the consumerism promoted by Halloween. The remembrance of Christian luminaries, such as Monica of Hippo (Augustine's mother, d. 387), Augustine (d. 430), Francis of Assisi (d. 1226), and others on All Saints' Day accentuates their faithfulness and their singular contributions to the advancement of the kingdom of God. We are blessed and encouraged by the lives and the ministries of these saints. However, such a focus can have a spiritual and theological downside: it can create the impression of a tiered spirituality hinging on whether or not we can measure up to these saints, and it can confound understanding about the status we all share as children of God (1 John 3:1).

It is not unusual for believers to feel so "unsaintly" that the strong affirmation of Christian identity in 1 John 3:1, "See what love the Father has given us, that we should be called children of God," may read more like a misplaced wish list rather than a promise from God. The call to "see" embodies an element of surprise and an invitation to experience wonder. We are called to behold "*what* love," to ponder its depth and width. To behold this is to grasp who we really are and points to Christ's advocacy on behalf of the church, despite our propensity to sin (1 John 2:1–2).

The liturgy for this day should affirm that the believers of today are to be counted in the same company as those who have come before, for they too shall gather with them before the throne of the Lamb and worship! Focusing on the blessing of being a child of God and our own particular calling as God's vessels in this world, might help avoid any tendency to compare one's worth with that of the saints before them. This is an excellent opportunity to emphasize the belief that the gathered are included among the great cloud of witnesses (Heb. 12:1–2) who bring the good news of the reality of God's kingdom, even in a hostile world.

The ecclesial context can point us in other directions as well. The celebration of *All* Saints' Day may be a grand time to emphasize the universal scope of God's people—believers from every corner of the globe, from every language and culture, and from all walks of life—all at different way stations in the heavenward journey of the life of faith. The challenges faced by Western Christianity can be balanced and put into perspective by proclaiming the global nature of the church and bringing to the forefront today's saints from places like Sri Lanka, Burundi, Uzbekistan, the Gaza Strip, and so on. Verse 1c reminds us that the world is ignorant of the reality of the saints living among them. Sadly, as Western Christians, we seem to be unaware of those who bravely proclaim the gospel of Jesus Christ at the cost of earthly comforts, often resulting in martyrdom. The text transcends and overcomes the barriers of time and space connecting believers to all the saints from the distant past as well as the distant future.

Lest preachers delegate this promised "sainthood" to distant lands and remote contexts only, this is a good day also to highlight the bonds of faith that we share with the marginalized and disenfranchised in our own country, even our very neighborhoods. Some persons are demonized because they seem to be "less" than what we deem worthy. Those experiencing homelessness, those struggling with addiction, gender-nonconforming persons, and others are all too often shamed or ignored by communities of faith. There are saints to be celebrated all around us and, more likely than not, they are to be found in places we do not esteem. Indeed, many in our churches run the risk of not recognizing the saints that dwell even in our own backyard. Enamored with the idea of sainthood, the church promotes the ancient practice of pilgrimage (El Camino de Santiago de Compostela comes to mind), a voluntary setting aside of routine for the sake of a spiritual objective. Yet often we dismiss those whose pilgrimage is not optional, trekking for days, weeks, and months across geographical borders in pursuit of a better life.

Later in this chapter, John declares that "no one who abides in him sins" (1 John 3:6), a bold statement given the reality that, as "saints in waiting," believers face the reality of sin every single day. Reflection on the daily, routine interactions of those who populate our churches often highlights Christians' failure to live into the admonition not to abide in sin. This can drive them into despair that is diametrically opposed to the hope we have in Christ. Mired in this despair, many may feel that no change is possible.

This text allows the preacher to confront this sense of hopelessness in the face of sin with the good news of the gospel. The opening statement of wonderment ("that we should be called children of God") is followed by an even stronger affirmation: "and that is what we are." Far too often the preaching focuses on our collective and individual shortcomings: the ways in which we fail to live into the reality of our identity in Christ. The lectionary reading provides a reprieve, a time for our congregations to hear and, we hope, understand who they truly are in Christ. We are believers who, loved by God in Christ, are now called children of God. Although the fullness of this reality is yet to be revealed (v. 2), the text intentionally moves the readers from the principle, "we should be called children of God," to the reality, that "that is what we are" (v. 1).

What we are is not fully manifested in the present, however. In 2:18 and following, John tells his audience to consider the harsh reality of the present, the last days, and the presence of evil that opposes God's church. Believers are to live this interim life in, and through, our hope in him (3:3) who loves us. This hope in the God whose love we are to "see" compels us to believe even though we are unable to comprehend fully. When the Lord is revealed in the fullness of his glory, the world will indeed acknowledge who he really is, and believers will be just like him.

Living in the hope that the fullness of Christ's glory will be revealed to the world is an acknowledgment that at present the world does not know us (followers of Christ) because it does not know him. It might be worthwhile for the preacher to explore this concept at length. Basic information about the life of Christ, or even basic Christian doctrine, is not what John has in mind when he states that the world "did not know him." John has in mind the experiential knowledge of walking with him as he walks, for example, toward Jerusalem, living out the tenets of the gospel as he pours out love and compassion on those he encounters along the way (Luke 9:51–19:44).

The expectant hope that all saints will be revealed as they truly are in Christ calls all Christians to be focused on becoming what they truly are; thus, we see the demand for purification in verse 3. Since all shall be like him, why not strive for that reality even now?

ALVIN PADILLA

All Saints

Matthew 5:1–12

¹When Jesus saw the crowds, he went up the mountain; and after he sat down, his disciples came to him. ²Then he began to speak, and taught them, saying:
³"Blessed are the poor in spirit, for theirs is the kingdom of heaven.
⁴"Blessed are those who mourn, for they will be comforted.
⁵"Blessed are the meek, for they will inherit the earth.
⁶"Blessed are those who hunger and thirst for righteousness, for they will be filled.
⁷"Blessed are the merciful, for they will receive mercy.
⁸"Blessed are the pure in heart, for they will see God.
⁹"Blessed are the peacemakers, for they will be called children of God.
¹⁰"Blessed are those who are persecuted for righteousness' sake, for theirs is the kingdom of heaven.
¹¹"Blessed are you when people revile you and persecute you and utter all kinds of evil against you falsely on my account. ¹²Rejoice and be glad, for your reward is great in heaven, for in the same way they persecuted the prophets who were before you."

Commentary 1: Connecting the Reading with Scripture

The Beatitudes in Matthew introduce Jesus' Sermon on the Mount in a fitting manner. The sermon, as a whole, serves to encapsulate the ethics of the kingdom of heaven in contrast to the ethics of this world. Whereas the values of the Roman world in Jesus' day placed position, power, and possessions as elements essential to the good life, the values of the kingdom of God are shaped by an otherworldly mind-set that, paradoxically, includes poverty, peacemaking, and persecution. In short, the Beatitudes announce a reversal of values by providing a glimpse of the kingdom of heaven in comparison to the upside-down ethics of this present world.

Had an ancient thinker written a manual for achieving the good life, no doubt the one most likely to attain it would have been a wealthy, married man with power and at least one male child. Central to Jesus' message to his followers are new ethical principles for the blessed life that run contrary to the values of the rich and powerful. Instead of privileging the privileged, the kingdom of God favors the dispossessed. The crowds that followed Jesus were certainly not the upper echelon of Roman society, and not even those of the ruling wealthy Jewish aristocracy. The 'am ha'aretz, the so-called "people of the land," listening to Jesus on the side of the mountain, were the poor of the land: some may have had nothing to eat, and others may have had nowhere to live. Jesus' Sermon on the Mount outlining a new ethics based on the kingdom of God captivated them.

How oddly refreshing it must have been for the poor and disinherited to hear Jesus' words! Jesus' verbal reversal of values was both shocking and uplifting. In a world where happiness was measured by the prestige one could possess on account of who they were and what they had, Jesus identifies the blessed ones (*makarioi*) differently. "Happy are the poor [in spirit]" would have been heard with confused amazement at the oxymoronic juxtaposition of two seemingly opposing living conditions (Matt. 5:3). Significantly, it is important to acknowledge the Matthean embellishment that adds "in spirit" to the more probable early rendition in Luke 6:20 that omits it. Still, we cannot overlook the real material poverty experienced by the first-century audience. Indeed, although wealth may be accounted an ephemeral sign of happiness, yesterday and today, true blessedness is found in a life that adopts the ethics of the eschatological kingdom of heaven, the eternal inheritance of the disinherited.

The rest of the Beatitudes continue to describe the blessed life by providing otherworldly ethical mind-sets and behaviors contrasting the typical earthly insatiable thirst for power, wealth, and dominion. The downtrodden can certainly identify with these core values because they have been on the receiving end of the oppressive arm of the powerful. They are called blessed because they have experienced great loss and will continue to mourn until the coming of the Messiah when, as in the eschatological vision of Revelation 7:9–17, they will be comforted once and for all (v. 4). Moreover, the eschatological kingdom of God envisions the ultimate destruction of the dragon and its followers who will be overcome by the power of the Lamb (Rev. 20–22). Indeed, the contrast between the kingdoms of this world and the coming kingdom of God is a powerful visual for illustrating the aim of the Beatitudes; the values of this age are not the values of God's kingdom.

The next set of Beatitudes continues to juxtapose present-day values with a heavenly mind-set and its reward. This is not a life of submissive passivity, as the English word "meek" might imply in Matthew 5:5. Meekness here is more accurately defined by Donald Hagner, who comments that "those who are humble in the sense of being oppressed," are, in other words, those who "have been humbled" and are "bent over by the injustice of the ungodly."[1] More poignantly, the meek are those who have learned to live in the oppressive conditions created by the powerful and who rest their hope solely in the Lord. With the psalmist, they extol God in spite of their present circumstance: "I will bless the Lord at all times; his praise shall continually be in my mouth" (Ps. 34:1). Furthermore, they are blessed because of their continual desire to seek justice, even though that justice may not be experienced until the eschaton (Matt. 5:6).

Not only do the Beatitudes provide the right ethical mind-set to confront an unjust world; the blessed ones are also exemplary in the behavior they model in the midst of a cruel society. Not having received mercy at the hands of their oppressors, they show mercy, nonetheless (v. 7). As the ancient sages declared, the blessed are those who are "kind to the poor" (Prov. 14:21). Moreover, even in their thoughts and intentions they are "pure in heart" (Matt. 5:8) and seek the way of peace in all relationships (v. 9). Lastly, because of their righteous actions they are wrongly persecuted, but have become heirs of the kingdom on account of their unjust suffering (vv. 10–12).

As we look around at modern society, not much has changed with regard to how most people measure happiness and prosperity; people still value power over weakness, possessions over poverty, and even war over peace. The way of the blessed is different! What truly brings blessing to life, in the present upside-down world, is to live out the values and justice of God's eschatological future reign. A powerful list of virtues introducing the Sermon on the Mount, Jesus' Beatitudes contrast the way of the Lamb with the way of the dragon. The eschatological showdown envisioned in the book of Revelation (Rev. 17:13–14; 19:19–20) depicts the end-time hope the Beatitudes announce. Comfort, justice, and mercy will finally be attained by those who live and walk in accordance to the values of the kingdom of heaven.

As we remember all the saints who have lived before us and stand before the Lord, we should be mindful of the life they modeled for us to live through their patience and hope for a better tomorrow. As the cloud of witnesses whose faith is vividly portrayed in Hebrews 11, they have gone before us, awaiting the coming kingdom of God with joyful expectation and a relentless pursuit of justice. Such is the challenge of the Beatitudes: to live a life worthy of the coming kingdom of God, regardless of any earthly rewards. This too is the challenge posed to us by the testimony of many past and present heroes of the faith who did not experience such rewards (Heb. 11:39).

More than a simple "to do" list for heavenly rewards, the Beatitudes contain principles to govern how we should live our lives, even

---

1. Donald A. Hagner, *Matthew 1–13* (Dallas: Word, 1993), 1:92.

That Delightful City

Let us not hesitate then one single moment, Dear Christians, to resolving to sacrifice all, to obtain so great a happiness. The example of all the Saints whose memory the Church celebrates on this great Day strongly invites us thereunto. These are not proposed to us as models, those heroes of religion, those famous Penitents, whose lives were a series of such great and extraordinary mortifications, that one cannot hear spoken of without fear; and especially of the martyrs of Jesus Christ who have suffered such horrible torments, who have shed their blood and sacrificed their life for their faith, but these are proposed to us the Saints of our own state, age, and condition, of our own country; there are no doubt some amongst them, with whom, we, have loved and conversed, of our relations friends, and acquaintance[s], whose lives have manifested nothing extraordinary, and whom we may easily imitate if we will. They have been subject to the same infirmities, the same temptations, and the same trials as we; and we have the same helps, the same graces, the same sacraments, and the same means as they had. . . .

Courage then, Christian [Auditors]. Let us animate ourselves to the conquest of this Kingdom, and cost what it will [to] gain the victory, that we may obtain an immortal crown. Every one may aspire to this great happiness; the rich the poor, the King and the subject. It depends on you to be Kings and Queens in heaven, to shine like the Sun throughout all ages, seated on thrones with crowns on your heads. Then you will be more rich than all the Emperors and Kings in the world, more honoured than were ever the greatest men on earth, you will be among the Angels and the princes of the Celestial Court. The poor beggar may change if he pleases his rags for the robe of immortality. Sick & infirm, in a few days you may be citizens of that delightful City where there is neither weakness, pains, nor sickness. All you who are present hearken unto what I say, you may participate of the same happiness . . . you have only to begin to do what the Saints do in heaven, that is to love the Lord your God with your whole heart, and your neighbours as yourselves.

James Archer, "Sermon for the Feast of all Saints," manuscript sermon, Pitts Theology Library MSS 006. https://s3-us-west-2.amazonaws.com/pittsarchives/mss006/pdf/mss006_01_trans.pdf.

---

despite the possible negative consequences for following Jesus' ethical demands. As the rich get richer and the poor get poorer, as wealth continues to overpower justice, Christians around the world are called to return to a life of simple faith by following Jesus' ethical guidelines. More than ever, we need to honor the message of the gospel by denouncing injustice and standing up for the poor and oppressed. Jesus' words must lead us to "hate evil and love good, and establish justice in the gate" (Amos 5:15).

SAMMY G. ALFARO

Commentary 2: Connecting the Reading with the World

In a world of "Top ten exercises to stay young" and "Five ways to jump-start your best life now," the Beatitudes can feel like a Christian to-do list for those hoping to find their way into God's reign. When coupled with All Saints' Day, these opening verses of Matthew's Sermon on the Mount read like a litany of holy behavior, the be-saintly attitudes that Jesus proclaimed and that the church has, sometimes literally, sanctified. Sermons on the Beatitudes, especially on All Saints' Day, tend to exalt modern-day saints, exemplifying Martin Luther King Jr. and Mother Teresa but leaving most of us embarrassed about our lack of time or chutzpah to follow their seemingly impossible lead.

The Beatitudes are not a sacred checklist to organize and download into a Google calendar. The Beatitudes reflect who is honored and exalted in God's eyes. It is not that being poor in spirit earns the kingdom of heaven or being merciful means mercy lands on your doorstep. God's purposes are to lift up those who are burdened and broken, shoved to the margins, left at the bottom of the heap. If that is where you are, you are even more likely to be aware of your need for God's loving presence and life-giving hope. This can be a challenging word for more affluent and comfortable congregations whose members may have difficulty finding themselves among those honored by God in this text.

Some might find consolation in "Blessed are those who mourn," because everyone experiences sorrow; as musician Buddy Guy says, "If you don't think you've got the blues, just keep living." Meanwhile, some Christians have sought to read themselves *into* Beatitudes by equating being offended or not getting their way with being "persecuted." This kind of "persecution" recurs annually in the so-called "War on Christmas," wherein some US Christians see civic inclusion of other religious holidays as a sign of the persecution of Christians, despite Christmas being a national holiday and Christianity continuing to be the religious majority.

It is natural for Christians to want to see themselves among these groups of people Jesus calls blessed, but the Beatitudes are not about trying to "get on the list." The Beatitudes reflect what God values, not how to curry God's favor. These are not tasks that result in rewards. Rather, when we align our aims with God's, we are formed and shaped toward God's purposes. Theologians Dorothy Bass and Craig Dykstra suggest that participating in Christian practices such as compassion, hospitality, and acts that enhance the well-being of creation changes the being and knowing of the participants over time. We begin to value what God values. We come to honor what God honors. Not only do we comprehend the needs of those around us more fully; Bass and Dykstra write that "insofar as a Christian practice is truly attuned to the active presence of God for the life of the world, participating in it increases our knowledge of the Triune God."[2] Faithfulness to God's values shapes the way we understand God's work in the world, and ways of living *beatitudinally* flow naturally out of faithfulness to God's purposes.

As was true at the time of the first hearers of Jesus' words in Matthew 5, God's purposes often seem at odds with the world's values. "Meek," "merciful," "pure in heart," "peacemaker": these words are not often spoken in the public sphere today—at least not as virtues. In the abstract, they sound passive, submissive, even weak in a social calculus in which there are only winners or losers, victory or capitulation. However, enacted in real life, they are dynamic and unexpectedly potent.

Toward the end of World War II, the University of Michigan conducted a study on hunger and starvation in which American volunteers were put on a starvation diet in order to test ways to aid emaciated war victims. One of the findings of the study was that, when the volunteers were denied the food they needed, they experienced a kind of "tunnel vision" in which they become fixated on food. Participants in the study did not want just to eat; they memorized recipes, talked about opening restaurants, and compared food prices in the newspaper.[3] The researchers found that scarcity made the brain focus almost entirely on the thing that was lacking, in this case, food, to the exclusion of almost everything else.

The Greek word often translated "righteousness" can also be translated "justice"; put that alongside the starvation study explained above. What if verse 6 read, "Blessed is the one who has tunnel vision for making things right"? Perhaps this blessing now includes the wrongly convicted death-row inmate, or the lawyer arguing a toxic waste case before the Supreme Court. *Blessed is the Black Lives Matter activist who has lost too many neighbors and friends to gun violence. Blessed is the Syrian refugee trying to gain asylum in a country that did nothing to prevent the war from escalating.* Suddenly the frescoed saints of cathedral ceilings become more multidimensional.

---

2. Craig Dykstra and Dorothy C. Bass, "A Theological Understanding of Christian Practices," in *Practicing Theology: Beliefs and Practices in Christian Life*, ed. Miroslav Volf and Dorothy C. Bass (Grand Rapids: Eerdmans, 2001), 25.

3. Shankar Vedantam, "Tunnel Vision," *Hidden Brain*, National Public Radio podcast audio, March 2017; https://www.npr.org/search?query=Tunnel%20vision&page=1.

The Beatitudes also come to life in conversation with each other. A beatitude in isolation is a beatitude out of balance. A hunger for justice is the partner of peacemaking and reconciliation. Mercy cannot be discarded in the pursuit of righteousness, and justice cannot be sacrificed on the road to peace. Those who mourn are also those who are merciful. Those who are poor in spirit, humbly aware of their need for God, stand with those who are persecuted when they show mercy, or seek what is right, or commit to peacemaking.

International conflict expert John Paul Lederach, a Mennonite, tells of working with peacemakers in Nicaragua in the 1980s. Using a translation of Psalm 85:10, "Truth and mercy have met together, justice and peace have kissed," he imagines the four elements—truth, mercy, justice, and peace—as people in conversation, each seeking what they need in the resolution of conflict. He then has participants in his peacemaking workshops take on these characters and act out dialogue together, improvising together toward reconciliation.[4] "Truth," he might ask, "what do you need for this conflict to be resolved? Justice, what is most difficult for you in getting to reconciliation?" No one would argue that true reconciliation would be possible if truth, mercy, justice, or peace was omitted. By putting these seemingly disparate, but ultimately crucial elements for human flourishing into dialogue with each other, a fuller picture of the final reconciliation becomes clearer. The Beatitudes can similarly be considered dialogue partners. The reign of God is not complete if any of these honored ones is omitted; they shape, temper, and strengthen one another.

Finally, the Beatitudes convey poignant longing: that what was wrong will be made right, that those who have suffered will be uplifted, that mercy and peacemaking truly will cure the warring madness of God's children, and that all will find themselves in the reign of God. As we desire to be among those God honors, to be part of God's reign, and to see justice and peace flourish, we are assured that the promises of God will be fulfilled. Our passion for that fulfillment demonstrates God already at work among us, prodding and encouraging us toward gracious divine love.

AIMEE MOISO

---

4. John Paul Lederach, *Reconcile: Conflict Transformation for Ordinary Christians* (Harrisonburg, VA: Herald, 2014), 84–85.

Proper 26 (Sunday between October 30 and November 5 inclusive)

Micah 3:5–12 and Joshua 3:7–17 1 Thessalonians 2:9–13
Psalm 43 and Psalm 107:1–7, 33–37 Matthew 23:1–12

Micah 3:5–12

⁵Thus says the LORD concerning the prophets
   who lead my people astray,
who cry "Peace"
   when they have something to eat,
but declare war against those
   who put nothing into their mouths.
⁶Therefore it shall be night to you, without vision,
   and darkness to you, without revelation.
The sun shall go down upon the prophets,
   and the day shall be black over them;
⁷the seers shall be disgraced,
   and the diviners put to shame;
they shall all cover their lips,
   for there is no answer from God.
⁸But as for me, I am filled with power,
   with the spirit of the LORD,
   and with justice and might,
to declare to Jacob his transgression
   and to Israel his sin.

⁹Hear this, you rulers of the house of Jacob
   and chiefs of the house of Israel,
who abhor justice
   and pervert all equity,
¹⁰who build Zion with blood
   and Jerusalem with wrong!
¹¹Its rulers give judgment for a bribe,
   its priests teach for a price,
   its prophets give oracles for money;
yet they lean upon the LORD and say,
   "Surely the LORD is with us!
   No harm shall come upon us."
¹²Therefore because of you
   Zion shall be plowed as a field;
Jerusalem shall become a heap of ruins,
   and the mountain of the house a wooded height.

Joshua 3:7–17

⁷The LORD said to Joshua, "This day I will begin to exalt you in the sight of all Israel, so that they may know that I will be with you as I was with Moses. ⁸You are the one who shall command the priests who bear the ark of the covenant, 'When you come to the edge of the waters of the Jordan, you shall stand still in the Jordan.'" ⁹Joshua then said to the Israelites, "Draw near and hear the words of the LORD your God." ¹⁰Joshua said, "By this you shall know that among you is the living God who without fail will drive out from before you the Canaanites, Hittites, Hivites, Perizzites, Girgashites, Amorites, and Jebusites: ¹¹the ark of the covenant of the Lord of all the earth is going to pass before you into the Jordan. ¹²So now select twelve men from the tribes of Israel, one from each tribe. ¹³When the soles of the feet of the priests who bear the ark of the LORD, the Lord of all the earth, rest in the waters of the Jordan, the waters of the Jordan flowing from above shall be cut off; they shall stand in a single heap."

¹⁴When the people set out from their tents to cross over the Jordan, the priests bearing the ark of the covenant were in front of the people. ¹⁵Now the Jordan overflows all its banks throughout the time of harvest. So when those who bore the ark had come to the Jordan, and the feet of the priests bearing the ark were dipped in the edge of the water, ¹⁶the waters flowing from above stood still, rising up in a single heap far off at Adam, the city that is beside Zarethan, while those flowing toward the sea of the Arabah, the Dead Sea, were wholly cut off. Then the people crossed over opposite Jericho. ¹⁷While all Israel were crossing over on dry ground, the priests who bore the ark of the covenant of the LORD stood on dry ground in the middle of the Jordan, until the entire nation finished crossing over the Jordan.

Commentary 1: Connecting the Reading with Scripture

In 1912, German Protestant theologian Ernst Troeltsch surmised that "the understanding of the present is always the final goal of history."[1] Troeltsch explained that students of history endeavored to learn about what happened in the past to make more sense of their lives in the present. The book of Joshua recounts the history of the Israelites when they conquered and settled in the land of Canaan. Writing during the exilic or early postexilic period, the authors looked back to an era of divine favor and human courage to construct stories of military victory, land distribution, and liturgical ceremonies that would remind their contemporaries of God's faithfulness and their ancestors' obedience. Some of the original audience may have felt hope and resolve as they read about Joshua leading the Israelites across the Jordan River with the ark of the covenant (Josh. 3:7–17). Others may have felt a wave of sorrow or a surge of anger as they compared the fragility of their present existence with a glorious past.

Narratives like Joshua 3:7–17 have historical purposes but are not meant to be interpreted as historical facts. Some of the geographical markers and boundaries in Joshua are accurate, but accounts of a successful large-scale invasion of Canaan do not correspond with archaeological evidence. The direct parallels between the crossing of the Jordan River in Joshua 3:7–17 and the parting of the Red Sea in Exodus 14 and 15 are intended to help readers make connections

---

1. Ernst Troeltsch, *Protestantism and Progress: A Historical Study of the Relation of Protestantism to the Modern World*, trans. W. Montgomery (New York: G. P. Putnam's Sons, 1912), 3.

about God's attributes and plans for Israel. Our reading draws on a specific moment in history but shapes the narrative as a liturgical re-creation of the Red Sea crossing.

Although the scene has shifted from the Red Sea to the Jordan River with a transition in leadership from Moses to Joshua, the same God is in control. As the Israelites come to the overflowing banks of the Jordan River, they place their trust in the God who delivered them from Egypt, and the rushing waters miraculously stand still in a "single heap" in order for them to cross over to "dry ground" (vv. 14–17). Rarely employed, the Hebrew word for "single heap" (*ned*) in 3:16 also occurs in Exodus 15:8. Similarly, the Hebrew word for "dry ground" (*charabah*) in Joshua 3:17 is an uncommon phrase also found in Exodus 14:21.[2]

This account denotes the beginning of Joshua's rise as a divinely anointed leader. In chapter 1, God commands Joshua to be "strong and courageous" (1:6–9) as he prepares to enter a hostile land. The first sign of God's protection unfolds in Jericho as two Israelite spies receive the surprising support of a local woman, Rahab (2:1–21), to evade capture. The second sign of God's favor includes the entire people of Israel crossing the Jordan River. Before they cross, God again speaks to Joshua and identifies "this day" as the inauguration of Joshua's rule "in the sight of all Israel" (3:7). After hearing from God, Joshua powerfully addresses the Israelites with a legacy of the past before instruction for the present. However, before telling them what to do, he reminds them of whom they serve, the "living God" (v. 10). Joshua repeats this pattern of connecting legacy with instruction at the end of his life at the ritual ceremony of covenant renewal in Shechem. He first recounts God's faithfulness to Israel, from the time of Abraham to their present moment (24:2–13), and then issues a clarion call for the people to recommit themselves with uncompromising devotion to God (vv. 14–15).

The lectionary's juxtaposition between Joshua 3:7–17 and Micah 3:5–12 is jarring. Like the book of Joshua, the book of Micah was written in the exilic or early postexilic period. Whereas the authors of Joshua examine the past to better understand their present, the authors of Micah are more directly assessing their contemporary context. The characters of Micah and Joshua share little apart from a spiritual calling to proclaim God's word. They possess different perspectives and inhabit different social locations. Joshua occupies the political center, and the narratives are therefore told "from above," as the readers follow Israel's journey from the viewpoint of Joshua's exalted leadership. Micah's perspective is "from below," as a resident of the agricultural village of Moresheth, twenty miles away from Jerusalem. From these rural outskirts, Micah does not hesitate to criticize incisively the immorality of military imperialism and wealthy elitism.

Micah 3:5–12 continues the message of divine judgment from the beginning of the chapter. The chapter is divided into three parts with specific accusations against heads of households (Mic. 3:1–4), false prophets (vv. 5–8), and rulers (vv. 9–12). The imperative for the Hebrew verb, "to hear" (*shama*), appears five times in Micah: 1:2; 3:1; 3:9; 6:1; and 6:9. On each occasion, it startles and causes the reader to pay closer attention to what comes next. In both Micah 3:1 and 3:9, God condemns political and religious leaders for ignoring "justice" (*mishpat*) and failing to care for the lowly and poor. In Micah 3:11, the corrupt leaders are derisively mocked for "lean[ing] upon the Lord" without the faintest hints of remorse, repentance, or reform.

The Israelites are encouraged to rely on God's saving power and promises (Josh. 3:7–17). The visible manifestation of their faith in God is the rushing waters of the Jordan River forming into a "single heap" for safe and easy travel (v. 16). In Micah 3:12, the images that accompany the leaders' errant and misguided trust in God are annihilated fields, broken cities, and crumbling mountains. Although the Hebrew word for "heap of ruins" (*iy*) in 3:12 differs from "single heap" (*ned*) in Joshua 3:16, the repetition in English translations provides an ironic connection and sharp contrast between the two lectionary passages.

Despite their differing themes, Joshua 3:7–17 and Micah 3:5–12 share the following

---

2. Jerome F. D. Creach, *Joshua*, Interpretation (Louisville, KY: Westminster John Knox, 2003), 45.

connection: both passages can be interpreted as vistas into the historical context of the exilic and postexilic periods as the Israelites wrestled with complex questions concerning their group identity, economic inequality, cultural conflict, political strife, migration, and theodicy. As they grappled with displacement, some repented of their sins and turned their attention to loving God and loving their neighbors. Others doubted God's justice and struggled to put their hope in God, because they could not reconcile the promise of divine goodness with the prevalence of existing evils. The former text recalls a transformative moment in the history of Israel from desert vagabonds to a mighty nation. The latter text reminds an exiled people to remain steadfast in their faith and in their search for justice in their daily living.

Similarly, the call for priests and prophets to lead by example is a theme prevalent in the lectionary readings in Micah and Joshua and is especially emphasized in the New Testament readings that accompany them. First Thessalonians 2:9–12, for instance, names those qualities of ministry that encourage others to lead lives worthy of God, while Matthew 23:1–12 chides those who do not practice what they teach.

Although many Christians today find themselves in vastly different conditions from the ancient Near Eastern context of these passages, complex questions concerning group identity, economic inequality, cultural conflict, political strife, immigration, and theodicy still abound. The crucial challenges of pursuing right worship, practicing effective witness, and persevering under trials in a divisive age are not at all dissimilar.

WILLIAM YOO

Commentary 2: Connecting the Reading with the World

Preaching on the Micah passage can speak to an ecclesial context. What is the role of clergy in the life and mission of the church? Preachers might approach this text with trepidation, given its language about "seers . . . disgraced, and . . . diviners put to shame" (Mic. 3:7). Secular leadership is corrupt: rulers succumb to bribes; and religion is complicit, with "priests [teaching] for a price" (v. 11). This lesson is in the thematic track in the lectionary, so preachers can appropriately tie this to the Matthew reading about the scribes and Pharisees loving the places of honor at banquets and best seats in the synagogue (Matt. 23:1–12). The Bible has high standards for leaders, secular and ordained. How does ordained leadership in the preacher's church and judicatory measure up against these high standards?

The issues raised in Micah present an ethical opportunity to explore the prosperity gospel, a theology that asserts one can not only become wealthy through faith but also triumph over any trauma or sobering diagnosis. Like the rulers and priests of Israel, prosperity preachers believe that God is with them, so no harm shall come upon them (Mic. 3:5). The oppressed, however, clearly experience harm. Prosperity theology maintains God will give us what we claim for ourselves. While we recognize this as a perversion of Scripture, we must acknowledge that some texts can be interpreted to give credence to the prosperity gospel. Micah addresses such faulty exegesis, proclaiming woe to prophets who advocate for peace while they have enough to eat, but declare war on those who hunger. The people of God must practice justice. This reading invites preachers to examine ways in which our current society lacks justice.

Drawing a cultural connection to the Micah reading could be possible through the 2006 movie *Marie Antoinette*. Though a flawed film, it succeeds in making Marie a somewhat sympathetic character, while exposing the corruption inherent in a system such as the one against which Micah railed. In the movie, the royals lead a lavish lifestyle that includes opulent parties thrown by the young queen; meanwhile, France faces critical food shortages. The film ends with the fall of Versailles, home of the royal family, and a haunting final image of Marie Antoinette's bedroom in ruins following riots. These dramatic images can help hearers connect the film to Micah's dire warning about Zion being plowed as a field and Jerusalem becoming a heap of ruins (v. 12).

The Joshua reading is part of the sequential track of the Revised Common Lectionary, intended to help churchgoers hear Old Testament stories in their integrity on Sundays, rather than being paired thematically with the Gospel. Only two lections from Joshua appear in Year A of the RCL, so preachers may want to fill in some gaps when preaching on Joshua, in particular addressing the violent ideology of the book of Joshua, as the two Joshua lessons in the sequential track are not as violent as much of the rest of the book.

If the only Scripture the congregation hears is what is read aloud on Sunday mornings, gaps remain, which could leave the congregation with the impression that after the Israelites wandered in the wilderness for forty years, they simply took the ark across the Jordan and vowed to serve the Lord. The lectionary sequence omits all narratives about Israel's militarized colonization of Canaan. In our lesson, the only reference to the force required to "settle" in the promised land comes in Joshua 3:10: "By this you shall know that among you is the living God who without fail will drive out from before you the Canaanites, Hittites, Hivites, Perizzites, Girgashites, Amorites, and Jebusites." The lectionary does not address violent incidents such as Rahab assisting the invaders at Jericho (Josh. 2; 6:21–25), the ambush at Ai (8:1–24), or the victory at Gibeon (chap. 10). Violence is all around us in our wider culture. Does this reticence in the lectionary reflect discomfort with violent parts of the Bible?

Preachers who choose the Old Testament sequential track may find it important to discuss what the text does not say. The people of God were violent in the time of Joshua, and the people of God are violent today. What does God think of the violence we perpetrate against one another? Does silence about such violence in church perpetuate the problem? Do people come to church to get away from the ills of our culture, such as violence? If so, should that dictate the way preachers use Holy Writ to address the pressing problems of our time?

In an ecclesial context, the place of the priests in the Joshua reading might be a helpful connection to explore in a sermon. Explaining the role of priests in ancient Jewish practice can help believers make a connection to how priests and pastors in churches function today. Preachers who wear robes and stoles can appear more "important" than laity. When the clergy and ministers process in to an opening hymn, people may associate standing up with honoring the clergy, rather than with singing to God or reverencing the cross.

This text provides an opportunity to correct misunderstandings about clerical authority. The twelve chosen priests in the reading do not go in front of the people because they are more important but because they carry the holy ark, acknowledging that the mighty God of Israel goes before the people. The waters of the Jordan are parted only by the power of God (3:13); the priests do not have that power on their own, just as ordained clergy today do not have power on their own. Being set apart to preach and preside over sacraments does not endow one with special holiness; it offers an opportunity to serve others. Clergy serve as trail guides on the path, not as gurus with all of the answers.

The dramatic imagery of the Jordan River in Joshua 3 presents an opportunity to explore our knowledge about water and how it connects to the world of the text. Water was an urgent concern of the Israelites as they migrated for forty years through the desert (see Exod. 17:1–7; Num. 20:1–13). A mysterious entity, water was necessary for life but could be unpredictable and dangerous (see Exod. 14:26–29).

In our own time, we still do not have control over water. Rising sea levels threaten to inundate coastlines, putting millions of people and other living creatures at risk. Droughts plague many regions, making life brutally hard for farmers dependent on rain for their crops. Water is a concern for those who live in arid terrain. Dams and other technologies have allowed people to live in regions in which they could not have thrived in ancient times. Rather than conserving water, however, some communities in these areas with little water build golf courses that need water to keep the grass green and the water traps filled. Meanwhile, in many parts of the Middle East and Africa, access to water is contested, and deadly conflicts flare as groups struggle over control of water sources. The preacher working with Joshua 3 may wish to explore interconnections among three foci: water as the site of divine miracles in Scripture, water as vital for Earth's ecosystems, and water as a precious resource in communities under threat.

The preacher might reflect on metaphorical and spiritual meanings of the Joshua lesson as well. What waters need to be "crossed" for our own communities to arrive at a fuller experience of God's blessing? The preacher might consider racism, sexism, xenophobia, homophobia, classism, or other obstacles to human flourishing. How might our gracious God be "parting the waters" today?

ELIZABETH FELICETTI

Proper 26 (Sunday between October 30 and November 5 inclusive)

Psalm 43

¹Vindicate me, O God, and defend my cause
   against an ungodly people;
from those who are deceitful and unjust
   deliver me!
²For you are the God in whom I take refuge;
   why have you cast me off?
Why must I walk about mournfully
   because of the oppression of the enemy?

³O send out your light and your truth;
   let them lead me;
let them bring me to your holy hill
   and to your dwelling.
⁴Then I will go to the altar of God,
   to God my exceeding joy;
and I will praise you with the harp,
   O God, my God.

⁵Why are you cast down, O my soul,
   and why are you disquieted within me?
Hope in God; for I shall again praise him,
   my help and my God.

Psalm 107:1–7, 33–37

¹O give thanks to the LORD, for he is good;
   for his steadfast love endures forever.
²Let the redeemed of the LORD say so,
   those he redeemed from trouble
³and gathered in from the lands,
   from the east and from the west,
   from the north and from the south.

⁴Some wandered in desert wastes,
   finding no way to an inhabited town;
⁵hungry and thirsty,
   their soul fainted within them.
⁶Then they cried to the LORD in their trouble,
   and he delivered them from their distress;
⁷he led them by a straight way,
   until they reached an inhabited town.
. . . .
³³He turns rivers into a desert,
   springs of water into thirsty ground,
³⁴a fruitful land into a salty waste,
   because of the wickedness of its inhabitants.

> ³⁵He turns a desert into pools of water,
>   a parched land into springs of water.
> ³⁶And there he lets the hungry live,
>   and they establish a town to live in;
> ³⁷they sow fields, and plant vineyards,
>   and get a fruitful yield.

Connecting the Psalm with Scripture and Worship

Psalm 43. This psalm concludes a prayer that began in Psalm 42. Together, Psalms 42 and 43 represent an expression of the psalmist's deep yearning for God and a plea for vindication against Israel's enemies. Some scholars assert these psalms were written during exile, when the people of Israel were forced to live among their oppressors. Others are less sure of the setting or the identity of the enemies, though it is clear that the psalmist is taunted by those who continually ask, "Where is your God?" The psalmist experiences a keen sense of separation from God, particularly as she is kept from encountering God in the temple, the place of worship.

Psalms 42 and 43 were apparently written for liturgical use. In this song of preparation for journeying to the temple in Jerusalem, a refrain that sounds the psalmist's ultimate confidence in God occurs three times throughout the two psalms: "Hope in God; for I shall again praise him, my help and my God" (Ps. 42:5b, 11b; 43:5b).

Psalm 43 is, then, a fitting response to the first reading, Micah 3:5–12. The prophet Micah minces no words: no one in power is righteous, not the religious or political authorities, not the business leaders or those with the most influence in society. Not even other prophets are to be trusted. Everyone who is anyone is corrupt; all of them have failed the very people for whom they are responsible. Micah declares that the whole rotten system is about to come crashing down, predicting the complete devastation of Jerusalem.

Contemporary worshipers might cheer along with Micah and pray for the hastening of justice. There is plenty of evidence that the leaders of our own society ensure their own prosperity and comfort while habitually ignoring, and even oppressing, those with little standing. Yet when we consider our own complicity in the systems that keep the poor in poverty, turn away refugees, deny equal rights for women, and discriminate against those with the wrong gender identity or racial profile, our cheering may subside. To what extent do we participate in these systems, or fail to work against them?

Psalm 43, then, may serve as a guide for those who preach or plan worship for this day. Just as the psalmist bemoans his separation from God and complains that people all around him sneer, "Where is your God?" (Ps. 42:3, 10), we may also ask why it seems that God allows such injustice to persist in our own time. Even while we continue to sing and pray faithfully, evil seems to prevail, while those outside the church wonder why in the world we bother. With the psalmist, we may also pray, "O send out your light and your truth; let them lead me" (43:3a), as we anticipate praising God for bringing about justice. "Hope in God," we encourage one another, along with the psalmist, "for I shall again praise him, my help and my God" (43:5b). Even if a preacher does not mention the psalm in the sermon, its structure might well guide the shape of a sermon that moves from complaint to lament to confident hope.

As Rolf Jacobson points out, the prayer that is Psalm 42–43 features the poetic motif of water.[1] The psalmist's weeping, the pouring out of his soul, and his sense of being drowned in a sea of sorrow reflect his yearning; "like one dying of thirst who is tortured by memories of

---

1. Rolf Jacobson, "Psalm 42/43," in *The New Interpreter's Bible One-Volume Commentary*, ed. Beverly Roberts Gaventa and David Petersen (Nashville: Abingdon, 2010), 321.

water, the psalmist's very memories of joyful singing in God's presence torture him in exile from the Temple."[2] Nevertheless he does not allow the taunts of his enemies to drown out the confidence he has in the faithfulness of his God.

Worship planners will find a wide array of musical settings in a range of styles for Psalm 42/43 in *Psalms for All Seasons*.[3] Singing "Como el ciervo/Like a Deer" (in Spanish and English) or "Chuyŏ sasŭmi/O Lord, As a Deer" (in Korean and English) before the reading of Psalm 43 would allow a congregation to sing of the longing for God expressed in Psalm 42. "As the Deer Pants for the Water" paraphrases portions of both psalms, expressing yearning, asking for light and truth, and, in each refrain, reaffirming the psalmist's hope.

Psalm 107:1–7, 33–37. Psalm 107 is clearly a psalm of thanksgiving for all the ways God has come to the aid of the people of Israel. This too is a psalm written for liturgical use; a refrain urges the people to "thank the Lord for his steadfast love, for his wonderful works to humankind" four times during the course of the psalm (although this refrain does not appear in the lection as it is assigned). The psalm is both a litany of Israel's troubles and a listing of the ways God rescued the people. As in the Gospel reading, the humble are exalted: the hungry are fed, the thirsty are satisfied, and the wandering homeless are given a place to dwell, while those who had lived in prosperous wickedness are sent away with nothing.

Psalm 107 is a logical response to the Joshua narrative (Josh. 3:7–17), which recounts the story of the Hebrew people crossing into the promised land. The account echoes that of the exodus, except that this time the Hebrew people are not fleeing from a country but entering into one. The current inhabitants are, according to Joshua, those whom God will drive out, so that God's own people, who have been wandering in the wilderness for forty years, might finally have a home. While this may sound to contemporary ears like a hostile takeover of the original inhabitants of the land—similar to what happened to those people we now call Native Americans or First Nations—in the context of the Old Testament world, the land represents a gift from God, and those who dwell in it are bound to be faithful to that God if they wish to stay.

The first verse of the psalm serves as a summons to give thanks to God, who is good, whose "steadfast love endures forever," and would serve well as opening sentences or the basis of a newly written call to worship. The entire psalm is a song of praise for the faithfulness of God. Ruth Duck's hymn "Give Thanks to God Who Hears Our Cries" adapts the language of the psalm so that it not only remembers God's past deliverance, but assures present-day singers that God will save them too. It could be sung as a psalm paraphrase, or after the reading of the lection as a contemporary response. This tone of thanksgiving may imbue the entire service, or suggest to worship planners that one or more hymns or songs of thanksgiving be included in the day's liturgy.

The readings for this Sunday signal a turn that is soon to come. As we drawer nearer to the end of the liturgical year, culminating in Reign of Christ/Christ the King Sunday, we begin to hear texts that alert us to the coming reign of God. Here at the close of the Christian year we anticipate what will begin again at Advent, the watching and waiting for God's reign of justice.

KIMBERLY BRACKEN LONG

---

2. Jacobson, "Psalm 42/43," 321.
3. *Psalms for All Seasons: A Complete Psalter for Worship*, ed. Martin Tel, Joyce Borger, and John Witvliet (Ada, MI: Brazos Press, 2010).

Proper 26 (Sunday between October 30 and November 5 inclusive)

1 Thessalonians 2:9–13

> [9]You remember our labor and toil, brothers and sisters; we worked night and day, so that we might not burden any of you while we proclaimed to you the gospel of God. [10]You are witnesses, and God also, how pure, upright, and blameless our conduct was toward you believers. [11]As you know, we dealt with each one of you like a father with his children, [12]urging and encouraging you and pleading that you lead a life worthy of God, who calls you into his own kingdom and glory.
>
> [13]We also constantly give thanks to God for this, that when you received the word of God that you heard from us, you accepted it not as a human word but as what it really is, God's word, which is also at work in you believers.

Commentary 1: Connecting the Reading with Scripture

Paul's first letter to the church at Thessalonica is, by the reckoning of most scholars, the earliest piece of Christian writing in the Bible.[1] According to Abraham Malherbe, who specialized in the study of Paul's Thessalonian correspondence, this first letter was written around 50 CE, about six to eight months after the apostle had founded the Christian community in Thessalonica, and about four months after he had been forcibly removed from the city. Situated on the Aegean Sea with an excellent harbor, Thessalonica was the largest city in Macedonia, a province of the Roman Empire, and an important center for trade. In the first century, the city's population was large and varied, consisting of about 100,000 people from all walks of life. The letter tells us that Paul had lived in Thessalonica as a manual laborer, working long hours in order to support himself as he introduced the gospel in the city and gathered and formed an exemplary Christian community drawn primarily, if not exclusively, from the Gentile (rather than the Jewish) population (1 Thess. 1:6–9).

The purpose of 1 Thessalonians becomes clear as one reads the letter. Paul wants to keep in touch with this fledgling congregation, offering the Christians encouragement and support as they seek to live out a new way of life without him, the founder and acknowledged leader of the community. He had earlier sent Timothy to check on them (3:2), and has been greatly encouraged by the news that Timothy brought back, namely, that the Thessalonian Christians remember Paul with deep love and affection and are following his example and teaching in living out their new faith. The style of the letter is paraenesis, which can be loosely translated as moral exhortation. However, Paul gives more than a moral lecture to the Thessalonians. He reinforces his relationship to them and encourages them in difficulty, praying that the Lord will make them "abound in love for one another and for all" and "strengthen [their] hearts in holiness" (3:12–13). In 1 Thessalonians, Paul is offering pastoral care to a congregation that is in some distress and that looks up to him for exemplary leadership and guidance.

The passage for today may seem a bit odd, even off-putting, in our own context. For here Paul proudly points to himself as a morally upright person—something a contemporary preacher may hesitate to do from the pulpit, lest the congregation think she is inappropriately boastful or perhaps is covering up some serious misdeeds. Paul's milieu was different from ours in this respect. In his day, it was standard

---

1. The information in this essay comes primarily from two commentaries: Beverly Roberts Gaventa, *First and Second Thessalonians*, Interpretation (Louisville, KY: John Knox, 1998), and Abraham J. Malherbe, *The Letters to the Thessalonians*, Anchor Bible 32B (New York: Doubleday, 2000).

The Comprehension of Sacred Truth

I know, O Lord God Almighty, that I owe Thee, as the chief duty of my life, the devotion of all my words and thoughts to Thyself. The gift of speech which Thou hast bestowed can bring me no higher reward than the opportunity of service in preaching Thee and displaying Thee as Thou art, as Father and Father of God the Only-begotten, to the world in its blindness and the heretic in his rebellion. But this is the mere expression of my own desire; I must pray also for the gift of Thy help and compassion, that the breath of Thy Spirit may fill the sails of faith and confession which I have spread, and a favouring wind be sent to forward me on my voyage of instruction. We can trust the promise of Him Who said, *Ask, and it shall be given you, seek, and ye shall find, knock, and it shall be opened unto you*; and we in our want shall pray for the things we need. We shall bring an untiring energy to the study of Thy Prophets and Apostles, and we shall knock for entrance at every gate of hidden knowledge, but it is Thine to answer the prayer, to grant the thing we seek, to open the door on which we beat. Our minds are born with dull and clouded vision, our feeble intellect is penned within the barriers of an impassable ignorance concerning things Divine; but the study of Thy revelation elevates our soul to the comprehension of sacred truth, and submission to the faith is the path to a certainty beyond the reach of unassisted reason.

Hilary of Poitiers, "On the Trinity," in *St. Hilary of Poitiers, John of Damascus*, trans. E. W. Watson, in *Nicene and Post Nicene Fathers*, series 2 (Oxford: James Parker and Co., 1899), 9:50.

---

practice for philosophers to talk and write this way in order to differentiate themselves from dishonorable figures who presented themselves to the public as moral teachers.

Paul then is following convention when he writes that his conduct was "pure, upright, and blameless" (2:10). He also reminds his readers how tenderly he dealt with them, "like a father with his children" (v. 11), working "night and day" so that he would not be a financial burden on them (v. 9). Although our lectionary reading does not include verse 7 from this chapter, it might be good to note that Paul also speaks of himself as "a nurse tenderly caring for her own children." Wet nurses were common in the Greco-Roman world, and Paul emphasizes his love for the Christians using the image of a nurse caring for her very own children.

What is Paul's reason for stressing his deep love and care for the Thessalonian Christians? He wants to reinforce his position as their leader, so that they will continue to "lead a life worthy of God" (v. 12). He had been separated from them after a brief period of ministry, two to four months. Moreover, they are being persecuted for their faith by their compatriots (v. 14). He wants them to hold fast to his instructions, his word, which they had accepted "not as a human word but as what it really is, God's word" (v. 13). Paul is not setting himself up as a "servant leader," a phrase more appropriate to the Gospel lesson of the day. Rather, Paul underscores on the one hand his equality with his congregation—he lived as a manual laborer among manual laborers (4:11)—and urges them to imitate him (1:6). On the other hand, he presents himself in parental terms as a deeply loving provider, guide, and role model.

Paul's leadership style stands in stark contrast to that of the scribes and Pharisees whom Jesus castigates in Matthew 23:1–12. Paul conducts himself in a righteous and blameless manner so that the Thessalonians may imitate him in order to live faithfully as Christ's followers; the scribes and Pharisees behave in a manner that Jesus says should never be imitated (Matt. 23:3). Paul works night and day as a manual laborer so as not to be a burden to others; the scribes and Pharisees "tie up heavy burdens, hard to bear, and lay them on the shoulders of others; but they themselves are unwilling to lift a finger to move them" (v. 4). Paul cares for the Thessalonians as a loving parent with her or his children; the scribes and Pharisees "love to have the place of honor at banquets and the best seats in the synagogues, and to be greeted with respect in the marketplaces, and to have people call them rabbi" (vv. 6–7). Indeed, Jesus paints the scribes and the Pharisees as the very antithesis of moral community leaders. The reading from Micah 3:5–12 reminds us that Jesus was not unique in his trenchant criticism of Israel's leaders. He was engaging a long prophetic tradition of Israel that called both religious and secular leaders to account for the abuses they heaped on their people.

The purpose of Jesus' rebukes is not, according to Matthew, to reform the religious leadership in his day. Rather, Jesus wishes to instill in his disciples a very different kind of leadership: "you are not to be called rabbi, for you have one teacher . . . and call no one your father on earth, for you have one Father . . . nor are you to be called instructors, for you have one instructor, the Messiah. The greatest among you will be your servant. All who exalt themselves will be humbled, and all who humble themselves will be exalted" (Matt. 23:8–12). In other words, the leaders of the church are to follow God the Father and their Lord Jesus Christ, not behave like the deeply flawed religious leaders of their day. In Joshua 3:7–17, for all his differences from Jesus and Paul, Joshua is presented as the kind of leader that Jesus and Paul are trying to cultivate: those who follow God as well as their godly teacher, who in the case of Joshua was Moses.

What Paul does in 1 Thessalonians 2:9–13 is describe how he has taken Jesus' instructions about Christian leadership to heart. He has sacrificed himself for the good of the community so that the Thessalonian Christians may know how to follow Jesus Christ, the Son of God (1 Thess. 1:6). Yet Paul does not follow Jesus' instructions in Matthew 23 in a wooden or simplistic manner. Rather, he translates and adapts Jesus' words so that they could be made effective in Paul's Greco-Roman setting. The challenge for us is to do the same in our own contexts.

ARUN W. JONES

Commentary 2: Connecting the Reading to the World

The "ordinariness" or routine of daily living came to mind when, as a teenager, I pondered the readings for an "ordinary" Sunday—a reading such as this one. The festal days of Easter and Pentecost are now a distant memory and we settle down to deal with the routine of life, anticipating the coming seasons of Advent and Christmas. First Thessalonians 2:9–13 elicits such memories as we read about labor, toil, and living a life worthy of God.

Many who hear this passage live lives marked more by routine than by innovation or risk-taking. These lives seem ordinary, but one of the great mysteries of the marvelous gospel message that I always treasure is that such a wondrous proclamation—the Son of God became a human being that humans might become children of God—is to be lived out in the day-to-day affairs of ordinary human beings. Sitting expectantly in the pews, they wait to hear God speak to them, even in their ordinariness; they wait to see what God's Word says to and about their lives in the marketplace and in the day-to-day spaces in which they find themselves.

Today's reading points the preacher toward the importance of infusing those seemingly mundane places and everyday hustle and bustle with the glorious gospel message. What is proclaimed from the pulpit on this Sunday ought to link with Monday-morning work. A biblical and theological reflection on labor and toil as the backbone of all human flourishing might very well elevate us from the daily, and often insipid, routines of life, to the extraordinary mission of the kingdom of God.

Another angle that we might want to pursue as we proclaim this text could be to address the course of action most beneficial in promoting the work of the kingdom and the glory of God. How do the stated vision and mission of the local community incorporate the gifts, talents, and personhood of all who gather to worship and serve? The priesthood of all believers (1 Pet. 2:9) informs us how we are to see the contributions of each person in the advancement of the kingdom of God. Paul's recollection of how he led the flock in Thessalonica, however brief that might have been, provides yet another opportunity to the preacher to exhort and encourage the men and women who lead the church today, be it as church staff or as volunteers.

This text offers an opportunity to bring to light the dignity of this human endeavor called work, which may vary from culture to culture. Far too many persons in capitalist economic systems think of work as merely a conduit through which money flows from employer to employee, from investor (venture capitalist) to the "common laborer"—with the former given more dignity than the latter. This lower perception and valuation of the common laborer is not new to our times or to our society. Even in the century before Christ, we find this view espoused in the famous writings of first-century-BCE Roman statesman Cicero, who did not place high value on manual labor.[2] Yet this particular treatise on moral values was highly esteemed and recommended by church fathers from Ambrose to Augustine and beyond, thereby, intentionally or not, disseminating such valuations among the faithful.

The people who perform so-called menial tasks in our society, however, provide services that promote the social and economic well-being of the community. The words of Martin Luther King Jr. are apropos for reminding everyone of the dignity of all kinds of work: "If it falls your lot to be a street sweeper, sweep streets like Michelangelo painted pictures, sweep streets like Beethoven composed music, sweep streets like Leontyne Price sings before the Metropolitan Opera. Sweep streets like Shakespeare wrote poetry. Sweep streets so well that all the hosts of heaven and earth will have to pause and say: Here lived a great street sweeper who swept his job well."[3] There is no work that is, to quote Cicero, "unbecoming" when done unto the glory of God. Working night (proclaiming the Word of God) and day (as a tentmaker) was, for Paul, a way to honor and serve the women and men of Thessalonica while being faithful to his calling.

The manifold and difficult tasks of managing human relationships in the marketplace, and even in the church, can be emotionally draining. Flawed human beings are thrust into positions of leadership and power often without an unequivocal commitment to the institutional vision and mission. The preacher seeking to untangle these emotional knots can benefit from principles mined from this text. We are to work tirelessly for the sake of others, and we are to do so through conduct that is pure, upright, and blameless, that is, without ulterior motives. The one motive that matters is the faithful proclamation and modeling of the gospel. This adds holy and divine purpose and meaning to all that we do.

Networking is pervasive in today's marketplace. This is made more prevalent and easier by the advent of social media. No one is able to function effectively without adequate networking. In its most basic form, networking is the interplay of human relationships that permits human beings to have access to multiple spheres of influence. However, the sole focus of our networking should not be our own personal advancement in the system. We are not to use others to move ahead in life. Such conduct is contrary to the gospel and is unbecoming of a person who follows Christ. Paul's network of interrelationships was evident to all; "you remember" (1 Thess. 2:9a) is an example of how, as followers of Christ, we should endeavor to be channels (network agents) through which others can enjoy a life of abundance in the gospel.

The apostle points to the parent-children relationship (v. 11) as the primary principle that informs networking circles. A possible way to expound this text could be along that very trajectory: Are we approaching our relationships in the marketplace, in the church, and at home as a parent, as one whose ultimate pleasure is to channel, and thus witness, a child's development into a faithful and productive member of society? What is our ultimate goal in making friends and acquaintances?

The world's purpose for networking is upward mobility. For people of faith, the trajectory might well be upward, but only in the sense of how we might help those around us

---

2. See Cicero, *De Officiis I. xlii*, in http://penelope.uchicago.edu/Thayer/E/Roman/Texts/Cicero/de_Officiis/home.html.
3. Martin Luther King, "What Is Your Life's Blueprint?" a speech delivered at Barratt Junior High School in Philadelphia on October 26, 1967, *Scholastic Scope* 51, no. 1 (January 10, 2003), 16, https://1ccaxf2hhhbh1jcwiktlicz7-wpengine.netdna-ssl.com/wp-content/uploads/2017/01/MLK-Lifes-Blueprint.pdf.

upward into a right relationship with God in Christ and with each other. This may include helping them in their own personal and professional development. Again, this is contrary to a culture of success where achievement may entail climbing over others, or destroying their careers and chances as we make our way to the top. As Christian disciples, our objective for dwelling and moving in our particular circles should be the flourishing of those around us. Rather than seeking out people because of what they can offer us, we should always be mindful of what we can offer them. Sadly, far too often we succumb to a self-centered understanding of networking, to our own detriment. For in seeking human flourishing around us, we expand our own capacity to flourish. Our flourishing, however, is never at the expense of another; rather, only as we live out the gospel in our communities of faith—enabling the *other* to flourish—can we live lives truly worthy of our calling.

ALVIN PADILLA

Proper 26 (Sunday between October 30 and November 5 inclusive)

Matthew 23:1–12

¹Then Jesus said to the crowds and to his disciples, ²"The scribes and the Pharisees sit on Moses' seat; ³therefore, do whatever they teach you and follow it; but do not do as they do, for they do not practice what they teach. ⁴They tie up heavy burdens, hard to bear, and lay them on the shoulders of others; but they themselves are unwilling to lift a finger to move them. ⁵They do all their deeds to be seen by others; for they make their phylacteries broad and their fringes long. ⁶They love to have the place of honor at banquets and the best seats in the synagogues, ⁷and to be greeted with respect in the marketplaces, and to have people call them rabbi. ⁸But you are not to be called rabbi, for you have one teacher, and you are all students. ⁹And call no one your father on earth, for you have one Father—the one in heaven. ¹⁰Nor are you to be called instructors, for you have one instructor, the Messiah. ¹¹The greatest among you will be your servant. ¹²All who exalt themselves will be humbled, and all who humble themselves will be exalted."

Commentary 1: Connecting the Reading with Scripture

The theme of leadership looms large in the lectionary readings for this Sunday. Whole nations may rise or fall as a consequence of true or poor leadership. Moreover, society is in need of effective leaders in every arena: family, work, politics, and faith communities. How we lead in these spheres is important, but more significant is who we are as leaders. Indeed, Jesus' words to his disciples in Matthew 23:1–12 remind us of this powerful truth: excellence in character will always be a far greater indicator of true leadership than charisma or competency alone.

Jesus' castigation of the Pharisees and scribes surprisingly begins with a positive affirmation of their position and authority. Verse 2 establishes their religious status in the community: "they sit on Moses' seat." Thus, on the basis of their office, their teaching is to be respected and obeyed (Matt. 23:3). That is where the niceties end, for Jesus will use them as negative examples in leadership, with the purpose of teaching his followers how to lead with character and service.

Jesus forcefully exhorts his followers, "Do not do as they do, for they do not practice what they teach" (v. 3b). In the following sentences, Jesus will unpack what he means, by laying down a heavy indictment on the scribes and Pharisees.

This denunciation is reminiscent of the prophet Micah's condemnation of Israel's wayward leadership; they led God's people astray, neglected to uphold justice, and took bribes (Mic. 3:5–12). Akin to the denunciation of the hypocrisy of the leadership in that Old Testament passage, Jesus' own accusations of the scribes and Pharisees place him in the tradition of the prophets who were sent by God to correct Israel's leadership.

In addition, Jesus' criticism ultimately grounds the credibility of his ministry and teachings in his own character. It is not about his ability to "own the stage" or his capacity to perform for the audience. If his followers are to take him seriously as a prophet sent by God, his own life and actions must go hand in hand with the message he proclaims. As the modern adage goes, preachers must practice what they preach. Jesus certainly could have said, like the apostle Paul in 1 Thessalonians 2:10, "You are witnesses, and God also, how pure, upright, and blameless our conduct was toward you believers."

Contrary to Paul's exemplary standard, the scribes and Pharisees were weighed and found wanting. Whereas Paul could boldly instruct his readers to imitate his conduct (1 Cor. 4:16) in light of his imitation of Christ (11:1), the actions of the scribes and Pharisees did not match their words. Their teachings placed heavy burdens on their followers, and despite knowing this, they did nothing to lighten the load (Matt. 23:4). Furthermore, their practice of righteousness was merely external and not the fruit of their interior spirituality. Instead, the true motive of their "righteous" actions stemmed from their desire to be seen and loved by others (v. 5). For this purpose, they wore their phylacteries (small leather boxes containing written Scripture texts) and tied them down with long visible ribbons. This of course was merely a hypocritical observance of the Mosaic commandment in Numbers 15:37–39 and Deuteronomy 22:12. Jesus saw these as fake badges of piety designed to bring glory to the wearers and increase their spiritual prominence within the community—hypocrisy at its worst.

Two additional signs of false humility were their involvement in community events and encounters in the marketplace, where they loved to have the place of honor and be hailed by their titles (vv. 6–7). What a strange way to live out your calling to be a servant of God! How strong are the temptations to be lured into pride when on a daily basis the people of God look to ministry leaders for counsel and guidance! Certainly, this habitual arrogance was not what originally had drawn them to become teachers of the Torah. More than likely, the scribes and Pharisees began their careers with a genuine love for God and people, but their pride grew with every party invitation, synagogue service, and use of their title (vv. 6–7).

In Luke 14:7–8, Jesus likewise warns his disciples not to look for the best seat in the house when invited to a banquet. Perhaps after kindly refusing the seat of honor multiple times, some ancient scribes decided that the idea of merit inherent in their position should lead them humbly to accept it. Possibly, after being urged, time after time, to take the seat of honor in the synagogue, they grudgingly assented to partake in the adoring practices of the community who admired them. Whatever their road to pride, one thing was clear: their growing love of honor and fame led them to relinquish their call to be servants. They longed to be served, rather than to serve. With every use of their title, their heads swelled with pride to such a degree that they eventually forgot the purpose of their vocation.

The accompanying Old Testament narrative for this Sunday, Joshua 3:7–17, relates the crossing of the Jordan River by the Israelite community and provides a fine contrast to the attitude of the scribes and the Pharisees. In this passage, the leaders of Israel display an exemplary attitude of service for their people. Not only were they the first to exercise their faith in an act of obedience by entering the river prior to its parting (Josh. 3:13), they also stood in the middle of the river as each and every member of the community of Israel passed by on dry ground (v. 17). What an extraordinary demonstration of love and service to their people! Any fears or doubt the people may have entertained would have dissipated upon seeing the reassuring eyes of their priests. Inversely, the scribes and Pharisees Jesus spoke about sought only their own glory.

Finally, Jesus reveals the main lesson his disciples needed to learn from the negative example set forth by the scribes and Pharisees: "The greatest among you will be your servant" (Matt. 23:11). Unlike the haughty attitude of the religious leadership within the Judaism of his time, Jesus expected his followers to model servant leadership. Instead of seeking titles and position (vv. 8–10), leaders in the community of believers needed to serve with humility (vv. 11–12), the hallmark of leadership among Jesus' disciples. The way toward true authority in the beloved community is found in humble service to others.

What a refreshing reminder for the church of today! What a powerful challenge for anyone who, out of a sense of Christian calling, leads in any capacity in or outside the church! As Christian parents, we are called to model servant leadership instruction and discipline to children in our care (Eph. 6:4). We are expected humbly to practice true *diakonia* (service) for everyone in the community of believers. In the workplace and community structures we lead, we are challenged to avoid the exercise of authority from a standpoint of power, and instead must have a genuine desire to serve, not those who are "under us," but, rather, those who are next to us. How different might our world be if so-called Christian leaders and politicians actually took Jesus' words to heart and decided to use their position of influence and power to serve with humility the communities they represent? May God help us to follow Jesus' example of servant leadership in word and in deed, for the world desperately needs it.

SAMMY G. ALFARO

Commentary 2: Connecting the Reading with the World

Matthew 23 begins with a judgment discourse, a set of teachings and speeches that includes warnings and "woes" (counterpoints to the Beatitudes of Matt. 5) that in Matthew 24 and 25 builds to an eschatological vision of coming judgment. The writer of the Gospel of Matthew has a clear purpose: to draw stark contrasts between those who follow Jesus and those who do not, between those who see Jesus as the sign of God's coming kingdom and those who do not.

While Matthew's purpose may be clear, interpretation of the text raises significant challenges for today's preacher. The straw-man depiction of scribes and Pharisees as self-serving hypocrites has, over centuries of interpretation, fostered erroneous and ignorant understandings of Judaism and has been used most egregiously to justify horrific anti-Semitism. While Jesus critiqued aspects of the behavior and practices of some Jewish leaders, he also ate in their homes, talked with them about their teachings and his, and honored Jewish traditions and the authority of the Torah. Any interpretation of this text requires a broad and comprehensive understanding of Jewish traditions and leaders and a vigilant awareness of slanderous uses of these texts for anti-Semitic purposes throughout Christian history. Moreover, Matthew's Jesus cannot be referring to *all* scribes and Pharisees because at the time the Gospel was written there was no monolithic Judaism. Rather, Judaism was made up of various sects and movements within the tradition—of which Matthew's group of Jesus-followers was one.

In fact, it is likely that disputes between Jewish and emerging Christian factions, such as Matthew's in the late first century CE, were the catalyst for this scene in Matthew. Jesus has been responding to opposition from rival groups, and now he makes polemic charges against those rivals. The type of polemic attack Jesus uses—accusations of hypocrisy, pride, haughtiness, and falseness—was familiar and standard practice across the Hellenistic world at the time.[1] Charges were intended to be undeniable; after all, can anyone claim to have *never* acted hypocritically or out of pride or self-interest?

It may be jarring, from within our contemporary experience of coarse, damaging, and deceitful political rhetoric, to realize that Jesus used harsh polemical hyperbole to make his point or to best an opponent. However, Jesus is operating within the oratorical norms of his cultural context and, in so doing, is meeting his hearers' expectations of a leader. Moreover, scribes and Pharisees are not the audience; Jesus is speaking to the disciples and the crowds. His words are designed to strengthen the identity and convictions of those who are already on board as they prepare to face opposition. This is speech akin to a political convention or a pep rally before the big game.

Jesus may have been behaving perfectly respectably within his own context, but his actions are complicated in our context. We might wish to soften or skip over Jesus' denunciations or to argue that their origin comes more from Matthew's pen than Jesus' mouth. Many of us would prefer a Jesus who behaves in accordance with our norms of above-board conduct and whose behavior is easily translatable to our context. Instead, we get a hyperbolic Jesus and insulting caricatures of scribes and Pharisees. Does Jesus' use of hyperbolic insult warrant our own? Are we to emulate his rhetorical strategy alongside his other teachings? How does slandering scribes and Pharisees square with loving neighbors or being peacemakers? How are we to

---

1. See Luke Timothy Johnson, "The New Testament's Anti-Jewish Slander and the Conventions of Ancient Polemic," *Journal of Biblical Literature* 108 (1989): 419–41.

distinguish between Jesus' tactics and his message? These verses, and many others, remain uncomfortable and difficult to interpret cleanly. One tactic for deeply engaging such a text is to admit the ways in which it decenters us as readers and forces us to examine it on its own terms. When Scripture texts refuse to answer the questions we bring to them, it can be helpful to step back and ask instead, If this text is an answer, what was the question?

For Matthew, this text could answer a question like "How do followers of Jesus understand what they are called to be, *in contrast* to what they see around them?" When Jesus points out leaders who do not practice what they preach and who act for the wrong reasons, he contrasts them with a vision of mutual servanthood and humility. Likewise, honorific titles are not appropriate in Jesus' fellowship because all are equal, valued siblings who, together, are the children of God. Jesus uses these contrasts not so much to tear down scribes and Pharisees as to lift up the kind of community he is building. There is little room for gloating in a community that esteems humility; any disciple who intends to use Jesus' words to lord over others will have sorely missed the point. Preachers might consider how sermon illustrations that seek to contrast Christians with other groups could express this same humility.

This text also brings up questions about how words and actions are related to authority. Does authority depend on the behavior of the person in the office? Is the authority of the office immune from any particular individual's actions? In the United States, what is considered acceptable behavior for elected leaders has morphed and shifted dramatically. Some behaviors, such as being divorced or adhering to a nonmajority religious faith, are more accepted than they once were, while others, such as the use of anti-Semitic, sexist, or anti-gay language, became taboo.

In the church, abuses of power by priests and ministers that had been ignored or covered up for generations are now front-page news. In April 2018, Pope Francis went so far as to say that he had made serious mistakes in his handling of sexual-abuse allegations against Catholic church leaders in Chile and asked explicitly for forgiveness from those he had wronged. A confession of sin and wrongdoing, though central to Christian teaching, seemed shocking from the papal office, not least because church leaders have a mixed record of owning up to transgressions or even admitting capacity for error. Some in the church might believe that by virtue of office, the pope is incapable of sin, while others argue that sin taints the man but not the office.

When Jesus points at scribes and Pharisees and tells his followers to follow their words but not their deeds, because they "sit in Moses' seat," he is suggesting that their teaching authority could be uncorrupted by their actions. Hearers of this text today might consider their own viewpoints: for some, the behavior of the officeholder is what determines authority, and thus behavior can tarnish or even destroy the office itself. For others, honoring authority requires publicly objecting to problematic behaviors of the officeholder. For still others, the authority of the office means behaviors of the officeholder can or should be ignored or dealt with privately.

Perhaps most confounding in interpreting this passage is that neither the religious leaders nor the disciples live up to the one-dimensional picture painted of them. Leaders are hypocritical and self-serving sometimes, but not others; disciples are humble and self-giving sometimes, but not others. For myriad reasons, the historical church itself chose not to eschew titles and hierarchy, and in some cases deliberately adopted titles such as "father" and "teacher" for its leadership. In the end, all of us are implicated by Jesus' words, which should be cause for corporate humility.

AIMEE MOISO

Proper 27 (Sunday between November 6 and November 12 inclusive)

Joshua 24:1–3a, 14–25 and
   Amos 5:18–24
Psalm 78:1–7 and Psalm 70

1 Thessalonians 4:13–18
Matthew 25:1–13

Joshua 24:1–3a, 14–25

¹Then Joshua gathered all the tribes of Israel to Shechem, and summoned the elders, the heads, the judges, and the officers of Israel; and they presented themselves before God. ²And Joshua said to all the people, "Thus says the Lord, the God of Israel: Long ago your ancestors—Terah and his sons Abraham and Nahor—lived beyond the Euphrates and served other gods. ³Then I took your father Abraham from beyond the River and led him through all the land of Canaan and made his offspring many. . . ,

¹⁴"Now therefore revere the Lord, and serve him in sincerity and in faithfulness; put away the gods that your ancestors served beyond the River and in Egypt, and serve the Lord. ¹⁵Now if you are unwilling to serve the Lord, choose this day whom you will serve, whether the gods your ancestors served in the region beyond the River or the gods of the Amorites in whose land you are living; but as for me and my household, we will serve the Lord."

¹⁶Then the people answered, "Far be it from us that we should forsake the Lord to serve other gods; ¹⁷for it is the Lord our God who brought us and our ancestors up from the land of Egypt, out of the house of slavery, and who did those great signs in our sight. He protected us along all the way that we went, and among all the peoples through whom we passed; ¹⁸and the Lord drove out before us all the peoples, the Amorites who lived in the land. Therefore we also will serve the Lord, for he is our God."

¹⁹But Joshua said to the people, "You cannot serve the Lord, for he is a holy God. He is a jealous God; he will not forgive your transgressions or your sins. ²⁰If you forsake the Lord and serve foreign gods, then he will turn and do you harm, and consume you, after having done you good." ²¹And the people said to Joshua, "No, we will serve the Lord!" ²²Then Joshua said to the people, "You are witnesses against yourselves that you have chosen the Lord, to serve him." And they said, "We are witnesses." ²³He said, "Then put away the foreign gods that are among you, and incline your hearts to the Lord, the God of Israel." ²⁴The people said to Joshua, "The Lord our God we will serve, and him we will obey." ²⁵So Joshua made a covenant with the people that day, and made statutes and ordinances for them at Shechem.

Amos 5:18–24

¹⁸Alas for you who desire the day of the Lord!
   Why do you want the day of the Lord?
It is darkness, not light;
   ¹⁹as if someone fled from a lion,
   and was met by a bear;

or went into the house and rested a hand against the wall,
   and was bitten by a snake.
²⁰Is not the day of the LORD darkness, not light,
   and gloom with no brightness in it?

²¹I hate, I despise your festivals,
   and I take no delight in your solemn assemblies.
²²Even though you offer me your burnt offerings and grain offerings,
   I will not accept them;
and the offerings of well-being of your fatted animals
   I will not look upon.
²³Take away from me the noise of your songs;
   I will not listen to the melody of your harps.
²⁴But let justice roll down like waters,
   and righteousness like an ever-flowing stream.

Commentary 1: Connecting the Reading with Scripture

In 1963, the Rev. Dr. Martin Luther King Jr. invoked Amos 5:24 in his address to more than 200,000 people during the March on Washington for Jobs and Freedom. As he stood in front of the Lincoln Memorial, King challenged all Americans to remember the promises of equality and freedom that President Abraham Lincoln ushered in with the Emancipation Proclamation in 1863. One hundred years had passed, and African Americans remained "crippled by the manacles of segregation and the chains of discrimination." King implored his fellow citizens to acknowledge these injustices and to enact changes to end them. Critics often asked King what it would take for him and the civil rights movement to be satisfied. King responded that they would not relent until African Americans had equal access to voting, employment, and public facilities and were no longer subject to "the unspeakable horrors of police brutality." King concluded, "No, we are not satisfied, and we will not be satisfied until justice rolls down like waters and righteousness like a mighty stream."[1]

Just as King's speech was aimed at two audiences—the marchers with him in Washington, DC, and the larger American public—the message of Amos 5:18–24 was meant for both its immediate hearers, likely worshiping in a temple in Bethel, and the wider inhabitants across the northern kingdom in the eighth century BCE. A shepherd from Tekoa, Amos ministered from 783 to 742 BCE, during "the days of King Uzziah of Judah and . . . King Jeroboam son of Joash of Israel" (Amos 1:1). The reigns of Uzziah and Jeroboam marked an era of flourishing, prosperity, and security. Israelites lived in a milieu of robust public worship with elaborate rituals and extravagant festivals. They anticipated and celebrated the "day of the LORD" (5:18) as the ultimate moment, when God would grant them victory over all their enemies. The phrase "day of the LORD" occurs only in prophetic texts and its appearance in Amos is likely the earliest reference.[2] Amos 5:18–20 is, therefore, an utterly staggering message that catches its immediate audience off guard. Amos reverses expectations and warns that the "day of the LORD" will be a calamitous reckoning, because these worshipers will have to account for their sins of economic exploitation of small farmers (v. 11) and callous disregard of the poor (v. 12).

The wider audience across Israel must also grapple with God's searing indictments (vv. 18–24). Amos observes that too many

---

1. Martin Luther King Jr., "I Have a Dream," in *A Call to Conscience: The Landmark Speeches of Dr. Martin Luther King, Jr.*, ed. Clayborne Carson and Kris Shepard (New York: Warner Books, 2001), 81–84.
2. Bruce C. Birch, *Hosea, Joel, and Amos* (Louisville, KY: Westminster John Knox, 1997), 217.

Israelites are practicing insincere and incomplete religion that disconnects civic morality from public worship. In 5:21, the use of two different verbs, "to hate [*sane*]" and "to despise [*maas*]," underscores God's fierce displeasure with hollow outward piety. God rejects seven aspects of public worship—from material offerings to melodious songs (vv. 21–23). The use of the number seven, employed in Scripture to symbolize completion (Gen. 2:2; Lev. 25:4; Rev. 8:1–2), signifies the totality of God's denunciation of Israel's failure to connect their public worship to their daily ethics.

Amos 5:18–24 need not be interpreted as a once-for-all condemnation of public piety in its immediate or larger context. One common theme across the prophetic literature is God's delight in those who integrate their passion for steadfast worship with compassion for other people (Isa. 1:10–17; Hos. 6:6; Mic. 6:6–8). In Amos 5:24, justice and righteousness are not presented as alternatives to replace festivals and solemn assemblies. Instead, God is calling for increased and sustained attention to societal inequities. The combination of justice (*mishpat*) and righteousness (*tsedaqah*) also occurs in 5:7 and 6:12. The former is a legal concept to signify the establishment of equal rights; the latter is a relational term to denote how persons should engage with one another.

Micah 5:24 employs vivid yet familiar agrarian imagery, rushing rivers and surging streams, to capture the vitality and necessity of justice and righteousness. These images of water are simultaneously breathtaking and life-giving for farmers responsible for tending fields and growing crops. Seeking justice and righteousness are not limited to isolated or occasional actions, such as visiting a homeless shelter or donating to a food pantry, but rather meant to encompass a lifestyle of daily attentiveness and constant care for others, especially the poor, the vulnerable, and the marginalized.

King's "I Have a Dream" speech in 1963 and Joshua 24 both illustrate leaders offering inspiration and instruction before an assembly of people united in purpose and cause, but there are several differences between the two. King's address comes in the middle of a growing movement for justice. Joshua is delivering his final public words in Shechem for a ceremony to renew Israel's covenant with God. Joshua 24:2–3a marks the fulfillment of God's promise to Abraham. The ancestors of Abraham now inhabit the land of Canaan. King criticized the use of violence in his campaign, whereas Joshua celebrates imperial invasion and military conquest. The tenor of Joshua 24 also differs from King's address, which highlights the struggle for racial equality in the United States, and Amos 5:18–24, which rebukes the moral failings of Israel. Reading the lectionary passages in Joshua and Amos together presents an opportunity for preachers honestly to engage questions of violence and oppression in the Scriptures, alongside divine blueprints for communities marked by justice and righteousness.

One way to address these tensions is to highlight the larger context of Joshua. The book of Joshua was written in the exilic or early postexilic period. The original audience comprised a diasporic people living away from Israel in polytheistic contexts. An overarching theme in Joshua 24 emphasizes God as the main actor of Israel's journey. There are eighteen occurrences of God in the first person singular (e.g., "I gave," "I sent," "I brought") across the first thirteen verses in this chapter. The repetitive use of the divine "I" as well as the inclusion of Abraham's family having once "served other gods" in Joshua 24:2 contrast the exclusivity of monotheistic allegiance in Israel with the porous religious boundaries and fluid multireligious identities of surrounding communities.

It is no small challenge for preachers to illustrate how the bellicose language in some passages of the Old Testament, including several in the book of Joshua, is primarily meant to accentuate the incomparable glory of the God of Israel and admonish the folly of an unfaithful people who have betrayed their commitments. Our task as preachers is to make connections that neither minimize nor rationalize the brutal depictions of violence and oppression in the Scriptures. Our explanations must utilize the breadth and depth of biblical and historical scholarship to help congregations understand scriptural passages in relation to the entire Bible as well as the contexts in which they were written.

The Assurance of Faith

We believe that by faith the forgiveness of sins is most assuredly granted to us when we pray to God through Christ. For if Christ told Peter that we are to forgive unto seventy times seven, that is, without limit, necessarily he himself will always pardon our offences. But we said that it is by faith that sins are forgiven. By this we simply meant to affirm that it is faith alone which can give the assurance of forgiveness. . . . For as it is only the Holy Ghost that can give faith, so it is only the Holy Ghost that can give the forgiveness of sins.

Before God restitution, satisfaction, and atonement for sin have been obtained once and for all by Christ who suffered for us. He himself is the propitiation for our sins, and not for ours only, but for the sins of the whole world. . . . Therefore if he has made satisfaction for sin, I ask who are the partakers of that satisfaction and reconciliation. Let us hear what he himself says. "He that believeth on me, that is, trusteth in me or relieth on me, hath everlasting life." But none can attain to everlasting life except he whose sins are remitted. I therefore it follows that those who trust in Christ have the remission of sin. Now since none of us knows who believes, none of us knows whose sins are remitted except the one who by the illumination and power of grace enjoys the assurance of faith, knowing that through Christ God has forgiven him and having therefore the assurance of forgiveness. For he knows that God cannot deceive or lie and therefore he cannot doubt his grace to the sinner.

Ulrich Zwingli, "An Exposition of the Faith," in *Zwingli and Bullinger*, ed. G. W. Bromiley, The Library of Christian Classics (Philadelphia: Westminster, 1953), 268–69.

Like Amos 5:18–24, Joshua 24:14–25 issues a stern challenge to Israel. Joshua demands the people either "serve the LORD" or serve "the gods your ancestors served in the region beyond the River or the gods of the Amorites" (Josh. 24:15). After the assembly responds with an unequivocal commitment to the Lord, Joshua immediately retorts that they are unable to serve such a "holy" and "jealous" God (v. 19). The assembly is forced again to declare their wholehearted devotion to God before Joshua completes the covenant ceremony (vv. 21–25). These two lectionary passages, along with Matthew 25:1–13, remind congregations today constantly to examine and reexamine their commitment to connecting public worship and social witness.

WILLIAM YOO

Commentary 2: Connecting the Reading with the World

As the church year draws to a close and Advent approaches, the Sunday readings get wilder. Sitting in church and hearing "I hate, I despise your festivals" (Amos 5:21) perplexes those who have given up a Sunday morning lingering in bed to attend services; and "I take no delight in your solemn assemblies" can startle listeners to the extent that they will not hear "let justice roll down like waters" (v. 24) at the end of the passage.

This is a shame, because the life and mission of the church extend beyond the Sunday liturgy. Are the people to whom you are preaching acting as the church after they leave the building on Sunday morning? Are their offerings limited to putting something in the plate as it passes them in their pews? This reading offers a perfect way to explore such questions. The best worship needs to lead to action, according to the prophet Amos. "Take away from me the noise of your songs" (v. 23) convicts those who come to worship solely as an escape. Music in church is not a concert: it is an offering to God. Beautiful worship without justice can be meaningless. This reading may challenge church leaders to attend more carefully to hymn choices for the service, inspiring exploration of wider liturgical and ecclesial themes and how they tie together. Are the songs the congregation sings today stirring them to act as Christians after they leave?

Moving from the ecclesial to the ethical works well with Amos. Preachers can offer congregations opportunity to scour the news of the week and ask parishioners to seek justice outside of the church walls. One can easily draw connections between the world in the time of this prophet and our own time, when the gap between the wealthy and the oppressed grows. What are the implications for Christians? Do we as churches throw money at societal problems, or do we become personally involved? Are the ways we become personally involved actually helpful, or are we offering boxes of ball gowns to flood victims who need toiletries? While nonprofits and charities that work for justice or in times of emergency desperately need gifts of money, limiting action to sending money allows churchgoers to maintain some distance from social problems. How does the parish serve as the hands and feet of Christ, as opposed to merely holding the purse that funds the ministry? Where can the church find the darkness in its neighborhood, and how can the church shine a light upon it?

Amos asserts about the day of the Lord, "It is darkness, not light (5:18)." Daylight Saving Time has ended when this proper appears, and any short-lived benefit from an extra hour of sleep has been forgotten. Seasonal depression sets in for some, as each day darkness creeps in earlier. The wider culture has started to celebrate Christmas, even though Thanksgiving and Advent have not yet arrived in the church calendar. The premature celebrations will delight some but depress others.

Connect images of darkness and light to the culture by illustrating ways we bring light into this dark time of year. Your community may have some sort of light show, for example, at a boardwalk or botanical garden. Neighborhoods will begin to decorate with lights as well. Many people declare their favorite part of Christmas Eve services to be singing "Silent Night" by candlelight. The shadowy origins of yule logs can prove promising. Finally, recognizing that depression rises in dark times and is a medical condition, not simply something to pray our way out of, can bring light to some who desperately need it and who can feel guilty about their inability to use their faith to cheer up this time of year.

This may be the only time congregants hear the book of Joshua read in church, as it shows up only two times in the Revised Common Lectionary, and the reading the week before may have been superseded by the All Saints lections. In the ten and a half verses that are not skipped in this selection, God recounts all that God did for Israel, including some incidents that do not show up in the lectionary, such as Balaam blessing instead of cursing the people, thanks to God's interference. God further explains, in the missing verses, that God gave to the Israelites land on which towns had already been built, as well as vineyards and olive groves that the people did not have to plant.

The limited readings from Joshua can leave people who do not have extensive biblical knowledge with the impression that there were not people already living in the promised land when God finally "gave" it to the Israelites. Not reading these sections on Sundays dodges ethical issues that are worth exploring. How do we benefit from the toil of others, for example, as the Israelites benefited from those who planted the vineyards and olive groves, and who built the towns? How are we privileged, and is the church ever silent about such privilege, as the lectionary can be silent when skipping problematic verses and themes?

"As for me and my household, we will serve the Lord" (Josh. 24:15) can be found on refrigerator magnets, bookmarks, and framed calligraphed plaques in homes. Setting this sound bite in its biblical context enables worshipers to see beyond the snappy verse into the demands being made upon the people of God. Some of these demands will be too easy for them to tune out, because they have trouble seeing themselves in the gods the Israelites' ancestors served. This presents a ripe opportunity to explore current idols in their personal context.

Many worship their phones, wanting immediate access to social media updates at all times. Some may sneak peeks at their phones while you preach. Speak about the idols that distract us in this age of instant communication. Not only do we have twenty-four access to social media, but we no longer wait for television programs to come on: they are instantly available through streaming services. When people do not worship in church on Sunday mornings, where are they? Are they serving idols? Another way to help discern idols in our lives is to examine our spending habits. Break out credit card receipts. Where does our money go? Examining these questions can help identify what we value, and at a time of year when stewardship campaigns are wrapping up, such examinations are well-timed. What gets in the way of our relationship with God, with the church, and with each other? We may not carry wooden idols of other gods in our pockets, but we probably have more than one screen to distract us at any given time.

In the second part of the Joshua reading (vv. 14–25), Joshua calls on the people to be witnesses against themselves, and they comply. Preachers can tie this into the culture by a multitude of references to trials. New legal dramas premiere regularly, and some run for decades, proving the popularity of courtroom spectacles. Connecting such shows to Joshua asking the people to serve as witnesses can help listeners place themselves in the story. Similarly, novels by the likes of John Grisham and Michael Connelly, or a variety of books in the true crime genre, can illuminate this reading, as can movies like *To Kill a Mockingbird* or *12 Angry Men*. Earnest, idealistic Joshua can be linked to a number of fictional prosecutors. Where does this place worshipers in the courtroom? Are they observers or jurors? Are we all on trial?

ELIZABETH FELICETTI

Proper 27 (Sunday between November 6 and November 12 inclusive)

Psalm 78:1–7

¹Give ear, O my people, to my teaching;
    incline your ears to the words of my mouth.
²I will open my mouth in a parable;
    I will utter dark sayings from of old,
³things that we have heard and known,
    that our ancestors have told us.
⁴We will not hide them from their children;
    we will tell to the coming generation
the glorious deeds of the LORD, and his might,
    and the wonders that he has done.

⁵He established a decree in Jacob,
    and appointed a law in Israel,
which he commanded our ancestors
    to teach to their children;
⁶that the next generation might know them,
    the children yet unborn,
and rise up and tell them to their children,
⁷so that they should set their hope in God,
and not forget the works of God,
    but keep his commandments.

Psalm 70

¹Be pleased, O God, to deliver me.
    O LORD, make haste to help me!
²Let those be put to shame and confusion
    who seek my life.
Let those be turned back and brought to dishonor
    who desire to hurt me.
³Let those who say, "Aha, Aha!"
    turn back because of their shame.

⁴Let all who seek you
    rejoice and be glad in you.
Let those who love your salvation
    say evermore, "God is great!"
⁵But I am poor and needy;
    hasten to me, O God!
You are my help and my deliverer;
    O LORD, do not delay!

Connecting the Psalm with Scripture and Worship

Psalm 70. Psalm 70 is nearly identical to Psalm 40:13–17. Scholars posit various theories on its place within the Psalter. Some think Psalm 70 was written first and borrowed to form the conclusion of Psalm 40. Others think the verses from Psalm 40 were lifted and adapted to form Psalm 70. Still others believe it is meant to be read in conjunction with Psalm 71, which is an extended plea for deliverance. The psalmist first prays that God will punish all those who seek to harm him (Ps. 70:1–2), then asks that all who seek God be rewarded with joy and salvation (v. 4). The psalm concludes with an expression of dependence upon the Almighty, as the psalmist acknowledges her utter need for God's deliverance with intensity and urgency.

This prayer is heard in response to the first reading, Amos 5:18–24, which includes the oft-quoted injunction, "Let justice roll down like waters, and righteousness like an ever-flowing stream" (Amos 5:24). What is quoted less often perhaps is verse 21: "I hate, I despise your festivals, and I take no delight in your solemn assemblies." These words are cringe-worthy for anyone who plans or leads worship, and they have been interpreted as a critique against liturgical forms in favor of a purer, more spiritual worship. Amos is not criticizing worship styles; he is condemning those who worship God but do not otherwise concern themselves with bringing about God's justice.[1]

As a response to the prophet's words, Psalm 70 serves as a kind of confession of sin. Along with Amos, we pray for justice, yet acknowledge that we will be caught up in the upheaval that will come when God rights every wrong. Like bathers in the sea who anticipate with joy the coming waves, then find themselves tumbling in the foam and grit, we both seek and fear the coming of justice, for we know we will be implicated. The psalmist's prayer, then, enables us to acknowledge our own need for salvation, even as we offer our praise.

When Psalm 70 is sung after the first reading, worshipers are invited into this dynamic. Bert Polman's setting to a minor tune from *Southern Harmony*, "Come Quickly, Lord, to Rescue Me" captures the mournful urgency of the psalm. A sung refrain using the words "God make speed to save me, Lord, make haste to help me" could be used to punctuate the reading of the psalm's verses or the sentences of a prayer of confession.[2]

Verses 1 and 5 of the psalm may also serve as the basis for a prayer of confession for this day. After a call to confession is spoken, in which worshipers are assured of the promised grace of God, a prayer of confession might include paraphrased verses from the psalm followed by periods of silent prayer:

> Be pleased, O God, to deliver me.
> O Lord, make haste to help me!
> I am in need of grace, O God.
> Listen to my prayer:
> (silent confession)
> You are my help and my deliverer,
> O Lord, in you I trust.

A declaration of forgiveness would follow.

Psalm 78:1–7. Psalm 78 is considered one of the historical psalms, as it recounts the ways God has delivered, provided for, sustained, and blessed the people of Israel. Teach your children well, the psalmist instructs, so that they will never forget all of the marvelous things God has done. The entire psalm—seventy-two verses in all—comprises the second longest in the Psalter. Its poetic form enables it to be used as a chant or recitation in worship. Only seven verses are chosen for this Sunday, however; they serve as an introduction to the psalm, a general statement regarding the content of the psalm and why it is important. The verses that follow add a new wrinkle, however; not only is Israel to remember its history so that the children will carry on the faith, but it is never to forget its mistakes, so that they will not be repeated. Psalm 78

---

1. J. Clinton McCann Jr., "Psalms," in *The New Interpreter's Bible* (Nashville: Abingdon, 1996), 7:394.
2. "Come Quickly, Lord, to Rescue Me" is found in *Glory to God: The Presbyterian Hymnal* (Louisville, KY: Westminster John Knox, 2013), 780. The sung refrain by David Lee is found in *Psalms for All Seasons: A Complete Psalter for Worship*, ed. Martin Tel, Joyce Borger, and John Witvliet (Ada, MI: Brazos Presss, 2010), 70B.

recounts the number of ways that God's people have failed to be faithful.

As a response to Joshua 24:1–3a, 14–25, the first reading, Psalm 78:1–7 plays a cautionary role. As Joshua stands before all the tribes of Israel, preparing them to take a vow that would put them in a covenant relationship with God, he warns them that this is the moment of decision; if they do not follow the God of Israel, they must choose which god they will serve. The people reply that of course they will follow their God. Joshua then puts forth yet another caution: their God is a jealous God who will not put up with their philandering with other gods. The people of Israel must be sure they want to make this commitment. The scene is reminiscent of that moment in a wedding when the presider asks the couple to be wed, "Do you desire to enter into the covenant of marriage?" It is the point of no return; this is either the last chance to back out or the time to affirm your sincere intentions to make sacred vows. Israel says yes, and the covenant with God is formed.

Psalm 78:1–7, then, serves to remind Israel to remember its history—all the ways that God has been faithful, as well as the ways that Israel has been unfaithful—so that the people may choose fidelity to God as they move forward. In the same sense that Matthew's parable of the Ten Bridesmaids urges Jesus' followers to be alert to the coming of the bridegroom, so they do not miss the arrival of the Messiah, Psalm 78 exhorts the people to be attentive to their tendencies to turn away from the God who has come to save them.

Those planning worship for this day might consider using various musical settings of this portion of Psalm 78 to call the people to hear the Word of God proclaimed. (Churches who commonly pray a prayer for illumination before the reading of Scripture could include the singing of this psalm after that prayer and before the first reading.) "Open Your Ears, O Faithful People," sung to a traditional Hasidic tune, summons the people to attend carefully to God's Word. "We Will Tell Each Generation" would serve well in a service where the focus is on remembering past mistakes, claiming God's mercy, and seeking God's leading into the future.[3]

As the church moves another week closer to the end of the liturgical year, it is a time for taking stock of the road we have traveled since the year began on that First Sunday of Advent. We remember the ways we have failed to live up to God's calling on our lives, and also recall God's continued faithfulness. Together, we move toward the proclamation that whatever evil the world has conjured, and however we may have taken part in it, Christ is indeed coming to set things right. Justice will come, and with it, God's mercy.

KIMBERLY BRACKEN LONG

---

3. Both settings are found in *Psalms for All Seasons: A Complete Psalter for Worship* (Grand Rapids: Calvin Institute of Christian Worship, Faith Alive Christian Resources, and Brazos Press, 2012), 78C and 78E, respectively.

Proper 27 (Sunday between November 6 and November 12 inclusive)

1 Thessalonians 4:13–18

¹³But we do not want you to be uninformed, brothers and sisters, about those who have died, so that you may not grieve as others do who have no hope. ¹⁴For since we believe that Jesus died and rose again, even so, through Jesus, God will bring with him those who have died. ¹⁵For this we declare to you by the word of the Lord, that we who are alive, who are left until the coming of the Lord, will by no means precede those who have died. ¹⁶For the Lord himself, with a cry of command, with the archangel's call and with the sound of God's trumpet, will descend from heaven, and the dead in Christ will rise first. ¹⁷Then we who are alive, who are left, will be caught up in the clouds together with them to meet the Lord in the air; and so we will be with the Lord forever. ¹⁸Therefore encourage one another with these words.

Commentary 1: Connecting the Reading with Scripture

The background information regarding Paul's first letter to the Thessalonian Christian community has been provided in the previous week's commentary.[1] One of the difficulties of correctly interpreting 4:13–18 is that we do not know the exact questions or problems to which Paul was responding. We have to deduce these from Paul's words to the community, much as we deduce a full phone conversation by overhearing only one side of it. Clearly, the Thessalonian Christians are grieving for those who have died. Yet their grief is not simply for loved ones who are no longer present; it is a terrifying grief for those who died and will not join the living when Jesus returns to gather up his people on the day of the Lord. It is not completely clear what assumptions or beliefs the Thessalonians held regarding the return of Jesus. We can, with confidence, say that they expected Jesus to return soon—certainly within their lifetimes. They also expected that Jesus would return in the context of judgment and save those who follow him from God's anger. In 1:10, Paul commends the Thessalonians for waiting "for [God's] Son from heaven, whom he raised from the dead—Jesus, who rescues us from the wrath that is coming." Yet we do not know why they thought their dead companions would not be united with them, the living, at Jesus' return. Were they led to believe that Jesus would return before any of the Thessalonian Christians had died? Did they as Gentiles not properly grasp Jewish apocalyptic ideas and the concept of the Parousia?[2]

Whatever the reason for their fear-filled grief, Paul responds with consolation for the Thessalonians by reminding them of the Christian belief regarding death and resurrection: that just as "Jesus died and rose again, even so, through Jesus, God will bring with him those who have died" (1 Thess. 4:14). When the Lord descends from heaven with shouts and fanfare, "the dead in Christ will rise first" and then those who are alive "will be caught up in the clouds together with them to meet the Lord in the air"; and all those who belong to Jesus "will be with the Lord forever" (vv. 16–17). Thus the community should not grieve like those "who have no hope" (v. 13) in the resurrection, but rather be consoled that all members of the Christian community, whether living or dead, will be united with each other and with Jesus for eternity.

---

1. The information in these essays comes primarily from two commentaries: Beverly Roberts Gaventa, *First and Second Thessalonians*, Interpretation (Louisville, KY: John Knox, 1998), and Abraham J. Malherbe, *The Letters to the Thessalonians* (New York: Doubleday, 2000).
2. Gaventa, *First and Second Thessalonians*, 63; Malherbe, *The Letters to the Thessalonians*, 284.

The reading from 1 Thessalonians is one of three texts for the day that addresses "the day of the Lord," as Amos 5:18 puts it, the day when God (or God's representative) will personally come and confront God's people. The parable in Matthew 25:1–13 of the Ten Bridesmaids or Virgins, five foolish and five wise, is also a parable about the day of the Lord's return, as verse 13 makes clear. In fact, the reading from Joshua also assumes a confrontation with God: The Lord "is a holy God. He is a jealous God; he will not forgive your transgressions or your sins" (Josh. 24:19).

While the three texts that directly address the day of the Lord's coming understand that day in quite different ways, it is important to see what they hold in common.

First, belief in the day of the Lord is deeply rooted in Jewish tradition, as evidenced by the reading from Amos. In fact, some of the confusion about the day of the Lord among the Gentile believers in Thessalonica occurs because of its Jewish origins and provenance. Therefore, the belief in the return of Jesus is not a Christian innovation; rather, it carries forward basic Jewish convictions about God's ways of interacting with humanity.

Second, all three readings view the day of the Lord as one of judgment by God. Moreover, that judgment is harsh and terrifying (Amos 5:18–20; Matt. 25:12; 1 Thess. 1:10).

Third, the day of the Lord involves a division of God's people, whether that is Israel (Amos 5), the church (Matt. 25), or humanity in general (1 Thess. 1:10; 4:13).

Fourth, the basis of division is at least partly ethical: Amos calls for justice and righteousness (Amos 5:24), while Paul warns the Thessalonian Christians that God is an "avenger" when it comes to wrongdoing (1 Thess. 4:6; see 5:1–11). Since Matthew's Gospel is a call to right living (orthopraxis), it makes sense to see the "wise" women in Matthew 25 as those who have preserved their resources to keep the "light" of their "good works" shining (Matt. 5:14–16, and the rest of Matt. 25).

Taken together, these readings challenge a far too common contemporary theological assumption: that a focus on getting to heaven diverts our attention from working on salvation in the here and now. In fact, the readings make the opposite claim: that it is the belief in God's coming judgment and salvation that provides the fuel (Matt. 25:13) for our exertions for good in the world. Ethical apathy is not a result of eschatological excitement; rather, ethical apathy arises when we no longer believe that the holy and righteous God is going to confront us personally (Josh. 24:19–25).

Note that Paul is not simply concerned about proper understanding (orthodoxy) and behavior. He is also intent on inculcating what the late Methodist theologian Theodore Runyon termed orthopathy.[3] The Christian's affective life is just as important an arena for development and discipline as her mental understanding and practical comportment (1 Thess. 4:9–10, 13, 18). Correct understanding, ethical behavior, and appropriate affections combine to produce a fully Christian life.

Especially when read in conjunction with Matthew 25:1–13 and Amos 5:18–24, 1 Thessalonians 4:13–18 holds in tension two fundamental Christian affirmations about God's judgment. The first is that God will save the righteous and punish the wicked, no matter what their social and religious status or affiliation. The second is that those who are in Christ need not fear God's judgment because of Christ's death and resurrection (1 Thess. 5:9–10). For Paul, it is precisely this tension that keeps us living in peace and love with God and neighbor while, at the same time, continually striving to do good in our world. For him, belief that Jesus Christ is Lord compels us to live an ethical and godly, compassionate life (4:1–12), always confident of our salvation through Christ (vv. 13–18).

Historically, however, Christian communities and traditions have tended to emphasize either God's judgment or God's free gift of salvation. In the first case, we tend to become highly censorious of ourselves and our fellow human beings, whether within or outside the covenant community. In the second case, we tend to find ways to circumvent and even

---

3. Theodore Runyon, *The New Creation: John Wesley's Theology Today* (Nashville: Abingdon, 1998).

controvert fundamental ethical living (Amos 5:18–19). The task of the preacher is continually to restore the theological and practical tension between holy fear of God's judgment and holy peace regarding God's salvation for the Christian community, and for the world in which it lives. This is what Paul was trying to do in the Christian community at Thessalonica, whose ethics were highly commendable, but whose fear of the Lord was misplaced. Paul reminds us that our life in Christ gives us peace and impels us to live as "children of light and children of the day" (1 Thess. 5:5).

ARUN W. JONES

Commentary 2: Connecting the Reading with the World

A word of caution should guide the preaching of this text. Often it is said that the community at Thessalonica never imagined that some of their members would die before the Parousia. We should refrain from focusing on that, for it is a bit misleading. Believers in Christ had faced the specter of death since the times of Stephen (Acts 7) and James (Acts 12). We can well imagine that by this time in his apostolic ministry, twenty years or so after Jesus' resurrection, the apostle Paul similarly would have faced the possibility of death, whether his own or that of his fellow believers. Yet he always faced it with the hope of the resurrection, a hope that Paul would have been very familiar with, given his previous self-designation as a Pharisee (the Pharisees, unlike the Sadducees, believed there would be life after death). The apostle could endure the hardships and fears he enumerates in 2 Corinthians 4 because of the hope of the resurrection, a hope that must be understood more as assurance than wishful expectation.

So the concern in Thessalonica is not about the unexpected death of those who believed in eternal life. Rather, it was whether the dead in Christ would participate, that is, be present, at the vindication of Jesus as he triumphantly descends from heaven in power and glory. In other words, it seems that the anxiety and grief evident in the community emerged from the idea that physical death had somehow placed the departed ones in a disadvantageous position at the Parousia. With the statement "the dead in Christ will rise first" (1 Thess. 4:16), the apostle assures his readers that the dead in Christ will join the triumphant parade welcoming (and vindicating) the Lord.

The apocalyptic imagery of this passage and its popularity with "end of the world/left behind" preaching and teaching may easily distract us from the pastoral (ecclesial) context invoked by the words penned by the apostle. There is no denying that its doctrinal focus invites eschatological reflection. Opportunities for preaching may lend themselves to such use. However, we can easily miss the mark here by focusing on verses like 16 and 17, rather than invoking the joy of expectation and trust in God's faithfulness, not only to those who are alive, but to those who have died in him. The apocalyptic imagery invoked by the apostle Paul intends to serve an important pastoral task that every person called to proclaim the gospel must perform on a regular basis: confront the reality of death. Paul pens these words as a way of consoling and comforting those in the community of faith who have suffered the loss of a dear family member or friend.

The death of loved ones elicits different ways of coping with finality. All are informed in some capacity by culture and context. In response to death, some cultures are more expressive, while others are extremely stoic. Whatever the social context and modes of expressing grief, Paul admonishes Christians not to grieve as others do who have no hope (v. 13). This exhortation is grounded in a sound theological principle: "since we believe that Jesus died and rose again" (v. 14). The basis for comfort lies in the gospel itself, in the crucified and risen Christ. The story of Jesus Christ reaches beyond the limitations of present circumstances or sociocultural location. The hope of Christians is grounded in the reality of the resurrection of Christ from the dead (1 Cor. 15).

Earlier in 1 Thessalonians 4, Paul describes unbelieving Gentiles as those "who do not know God" (1 Thess. 4:5). In verse 13, however, they are described as those "who have no hope." The shift from ethical exhortation (paraenesis) to comfort in the face of death, or pastoral care, should prompt the interpreter to consider how the latter flows from the former. Those who do not live in step with the demands of the gospel (vv. 1–12) have beliefs that may give meaning to their present existence; nevertheless, those beliefs cannot give them the enduring hope that Christians have as a result of the relationship that God in Christ has wrought on their behalf. The Gospel lesson for today reminds us too that this relationship demands readiness (Matt. 25:10b). In the parable of the Ten Bridesmaids, only "those who were ready went with him into the wedding banquet." To hope in God is to be ready with anticipation.

Paul reminds the Thessalonians that they can trust what he says because he does so by "the word of the Lord," who is faithful (1 Thess. 4:15a). Because of God's faithfulness, we can, as the writer to the Hebrews also reminds us, "seize the hope set before us" (Heb. 6:18). Though pastoral care is, for the most part, a private affair normally carried out through one-on-one sessions, this text invites us to consider that all pastoral counseling is based on sound theological teaching and not merely on consolation. Well-defined theological foundations produce endurance amid life's trials, even death.

Our ecclesial contexts (note the basic creedal formula, "For since we believe that Jesus . . . ," 1 Thess. 4:14) also suggest to us that the subject of hope be addressed. Far too few in our communities truly understand the NT concept of hope as assurance, even certainty (Heb. 11:1). Instead, many choose to dwell in hope as "wishful thinking." Paul offers a corrective against the hopelessness that such groundless wishful thinking fosters. The creedal form lodges this affirmation as foundational to the Christian life; indeed, it is the "sure and steadfast anchor of the soul" (6:19–20). The death and resurrection of Jesus assures believers of their rising with Jesus into eternal life; he is the means by which God achieves their salvation. Hence our grieving, though real at present, is shrouded by the comforting blanket of Christian hope.

The admonition not to "grieve as others do who have no hope" acknowledges that grieving does take place. How that grieving is processed, however, is culturally bound. One culture may welcome expressive, public modes of grieving, while others may be more subdued to the point of being undetectable. One is not necessarily better than the other. Rather, the text bids us to be aware of the culture in which grieving is taking place and not to impose one cultural style on another, which could very well result in the opposite of the intended consolation. For the believer, this grieving should have in mind the hope of the resurrection.

Another angle into this passage is to consider focusing on the nature of the church as one. Although the church stretches across the span of time and space and is composed of different theological identities and denominational affiliations, *all* the dead in Christ will arise in unison and join the triumphant procession of the King of kings and Lord of lords. (This vision of the kingdom of God is painted for us in texts including Rev. 7:9.)

Notwithstanding my initial word of caution in the face of apocalyptic imagery, the text does indeed merit serious reflection on the doctrine of the last things (eschatology). Given what I consider the overabundance of teaching regarding the Parousia in popular circles, it is necessary that preaching from this text should lead to careful articulation of eschatological doctrines within historical orthodoxy. In this text, eschatological teaching does not foster fear and anxiety vis-à-vis the Parousia. That should be highlighted in our proclamation of the gospel.

ALVIN PADILLA

Proper 27 (Sunday between November 6 and November 12 inclusive)

Matthew 25:1–13

[1]"Then the kingdom of heaven will be like this. Ten bridesmaids took their lamps and went to meet the bridegroom. [2]Five of them were foolish, and five were wise. [3]When the foolish took their lamps, they took no oil with them; [4]but the wise took flasks of oil with their lamps. [5]As the bridegroom was delayed, all of them became drowsy and slept. [6]But at midnight there was a shout, 'Look! Here is the bridegroom! Come out to meet him.' [7]Then all those bridesmaids got up and trimmed their lamps. [8]The foolish said to the wise, 'Give us some of your oil, for our lamps are going out.' [9]But the wise replied, 'No! there will not be enough for you and for us; you had better go to the dealers and buy some for yourselves.' [10]And while they went to buy it, the bridegroom came, and those who were ready went with him into the wedding banquet; and the door was shut. [11]Later the other bridesmaids came also, saying, 'Lord, lord, open to us.' [12]But he replied, 'Truly I tell you, I do not know you.' [13] Keep awake therefore, for you know neither the day nor the hour."

Commentary 1: Connecting the Reading with Scripture

The role of wisdom in this Sunday's lectionary readings is a key theme to consider, especially because of its importance for teaching how one lives with eschatological hope. The significance of wisdom in Jewish literature from the Second Temple period is evident in the many popular writings preserved for posterity, such as the Wisdom of Solomon. What is especially significant in the Wisdom literature and Jesus' teachings is the relationship between wisdom and eschatological hope. As substantiated in the Gospel of Matthew, wisdom, or its absence, becomes a central motif in Jesus' sayings and parables. The story of the ten bridesmaids is one vivid and powerful example of those parables.

It could be argued that Matthew aims to portray Jesus as the new Moses who establishes a new ethical law for his people through the Sermon on the Mount (Matt. 5–7). In fact, the conclusion to the composite sermon illustrates the main point by contrasting the foolishness of a builder who uses sand as a foundation to the wisdom of another "who built his house on rock" (Matt. 7:24). Later, in Matthew 12:42, Jesus makes the startling claim that he is greater in wisdom than even Solomon himself. Clearly, Jesus understands his teachings to contain not just life-changing truths, but eschatological wisdom for the here and now and the age to come.

A similar motif is found in Wisdom of Solomon 6:17–20, where love of wisdom assures immortality (Wis. 6:18) and the "desire for wisdom leads to a kingdom" (v. 20). Despite the enigmatic nature of these sayings, one thing can be established with certainty: attaining wisdom "brings one near to God" (v. 19). Similarly, this is at the heart of Jesus' teachings and a key principle in the parable of the Ten Bridesmaids who wisely await the bridegroom despite his delay.

Significantly, just before this parable, Jesus makes reference to a wise and faithful servant who is found being very productive, even when the master is delayed in his return (Matt. 24:45–47). The literary links between the two parables is remarkable. The contrast between the wise and foolish servants/bridesmaids and the motif of delay are thematically linked. The delay of the master (24:48) and the delay of the bridegroom (25:5) both refer to what theologically has been labeled "the delay of the Parousia," or his second coming. This is the thematic key for interpreting both parables.

In short, the master and the bridegroom are both symbolic of Jesus, and their delay represents the present period lived between Jesus' first coming and his expected return. The parable begins like many of Jesus' illustrative stories, by announcing a comparison to the kingdom of heaven (13:24; 18:23; 22:2). The use of the future tense here indicates its eschatological orientation. Thus it is a story of how to live considering the imminent establishment of the kingdom. Whereas in other parables the kingdom of heaven is likened to a seed (13:31–32), a net (vv. 47–50), and other ordinary objects (vv. 33 and 44 to leaven and treasure), here it is compared to the actions of the ten virgins.

The parable envisions ten bridesmaids who are awaiting the bridegroom in order to attend the wedding banquet. The exact place and timing of the wedding party are somewhat inconsequential to the meaning of the parable. Instead, the story hinges on how the "foolish" and "wise" bridesmaids respond to the delay of the bridegroom's coming (25:5). The main point is the lack of preparedness of the foolish bridesmaids, who, imprudently, are caught off guard with insufficient oil for their lamps (v. 3) to allow them to see their way to meet the groom in the middle of the night. Conversely, the wise bridesmaids not only take their lamps filled with oil, but also take extra flasks of oil just in case they run out (v. 4). Their exemplary preparedness is the main lesson of the parable.

As in the previous parable, the juxtaposition of the foolish and the wise follows in the pattern of Jewish wisdom. This is a constant theme in Wisdom literature. Another related theme contrasts the way of the righteous with the way of the wicked (Ps. 1:1–6). An interesting parallel passage yields a valuable insight to the parable: "The light of the righteous rejoices, but the lamp of the wicked goes out" (Prov. 13:9). Another proverbial theme is laziness, which also seems to have connections to this parable (26:13–16). However, in this parable, the foolish virgins are not the only ones who succumb to weariness; all of them "became drowsy and slept" (Matt. 25:5). They all could have used the Pauline admonition to the Thessalonians: "So then let us not fall asleep as others do, but let us keep awake and be sober" (1 Thess. 5:6).

The unique and more serious flaw of the foolish bridesmaids, then, was not falling asleep. Instead, they are called foolish, in contrast to the wise bridesmaids, for not being fully prepared for the possible delay of the bridegroom. When the bridegroom finally arrived, it was midnight (Matt. 25:6). When they all got up to receive him, the foolish ones noticed their lamps were flickering due to the shortage of oil in their lamps (vv. 7–8). Hastily, and with much distress, the foolish unprepared bridesmaids saw one possible way out of their dilemma; they told the wise ones to give them some of their oil. The wise bridesmaids, however, did not fall prey to their plea. They had the wisdom not to give away their extra oil and sent the foolish bridesmaids to the store to buy more oil for themselves (v. 9). Caught unprepared, they missed out on the opportunity to attend the wedding banquet (v. 10).

Already in Matthew, the end times are portrayed as a wedding banquet prepared by a father for a son (22:2–9). Moreover, this same imagery will be used in the book of Revelation to announce the eschatological marriage supper of the Lamb (Rev. 19:9). The idea of Jesus being the bridegroom of the parable is easily established, since already in Matthew 9:15 Jesus himself alludes to it. Together, the theological connections in these texts point to a foreseeable delay of the Parousia for which believers are encouraged to be alert and prepared (Matt. 25:13).

The purpose of this parable, then, is to encourage vigilant preparation for the return of the Lord, who will "come like a thief in the night" (1 Thess. 5:2). Like a bride awaiting the coming of the bridegroom, believers are cautioned to live with expectancy, cognizant of the imminent second coming of Jesus. This is not a mere pie-in-the-sky existence simply awaiting the coming of Jesus, while doing nothing of earthly good in this world. Rather, this same eschatological hope should guide believers to serve others with their talents, as the next parable in the chapter envisions (Matt. 25:14–30).

The third parable in the chapter further advises that the expectation of the soon coming of Jesus should also lead believers to feed, clothe, and provide shelter for the less fortunate (vv. 31–46). As the wise bridesmaids of this parable, believers are called to maintain their lamps lit and live as children of the light in the midst of a dark world: "But you, beloved, are not in darkness, for that day to surprise you like a thief; for you are all children of light and children of the day; we are not of the night or of darkness" (1 Thess. 5:4–5).

SAMMY G. ALFARO

Commentary 2: Connecting the Reading with the World

Church budgets can be a battleground. Yes, committee leaders and other parishioners are sometimes territorial about protecting their favorite ministries or pet projects. Often, deeper questions about how churches allocate funds come down to taking care of immediate needs versus laying groundwork for the future. Should the church borrow money for a new heating and cooling system, or add more duct tape to the existing machinery? Do we really need a new sound system, or can we keep taking our chances with the old one? More heart-rending, can we still afford our donation to the city's homeless ministry, now that our church staff's health insurance premiums have gone up? Should we continue to support that program for at-risk kids when we really need to replace our leaky roof?

The parable of the Ten Bridesmaids is, at its heart, a parable about being prepared, being ready. The role of the bridesmaids was to await the groom and accompany him to the wedding, but when he was delayed, they forgot the task at hand, namely, to be ready for him. Some who had planned ahead had enough oil for their lamps and were ready when the groom arrived. Others were not ready and missed the wedding. Allegorically, the parable is generally understood to refer to the coming of Jesus, who, in Matthew's late-first-century-CE context, had been expected to return quickly but had not yet reappeared.

Two millennia later, staying ready at all times is not an easy task. The parable implies that some bridesmaids were foolish in their lack of preparation, and perhaps they should have known better. When it comes to the church, being ready could mean responding to someone unemployed and hungry knocking on the door, or budgeting years in advance to ensure the preschool classrooms are large enough and built to code. Jesus may have said, "Keep awake, therefore, for you know neither the day nor the hour" (Matt. 25:13), but few among us are interested in casting aside all long-term planning because Jesus might arrive tomorrow. Still, it is hard to know *how* to stay ready for an uncertain future and what to take care of right now. What is foolish or wise is rarely as simple as keeping enough oil on hand.

Part of what is difficult about interpreting this parable today is that it conjures up two dynamics that feel antithetical to the abundant life Jesus promises. First, the tale seems to be one of *scarcity*, in which there is not enough oil to share, and those with oil choose to take care of themselves instead of working for a common solution. The parable rubs against Christian inclinations to help one another, foolish or wise. *Certainly, there must have been other options,* we might want to protest. *Light cast by a flame is not a zero-sum resource; if the oil could not be shared, surely the light of the lamps could have been.* In any case, an interpretive pitfall is to hear the parable as a call to save ourselves at the expense of others. Acknowledging that the parable is about *being ready*, not about generosity or distribution of resources, can help mitigate interpretations that are self-serving or congratulatory about our own oil supplies.

Second, this text can also evoke *fear*: fear of *not* being ready, and therefore of being left out. Matthew's heavy emphasis on judgment in its concluding chapters does little to ease anxieties; for better or worse, Jesus uses fear to make his point: *be ready*.

Unsurprisingly, where contemporary life is oriented toward being ready, fear is often the motivating factor. We buy home and car insurance in preparation for an unforeseen accident. We take multivitamins and go to the gym to prevent health problems. A 2016 study on US gun ownership by researchers at Harvard and Northwestern Universities showed that fear of other people was the driving force behind record gun sales in recent decades, despite the fact that violent crime rates had plummeted.[1] Fear of an unknown future can help us make smart decisions and plan for contingencies, but it can also be debilitating and isolating if we become consumed by anxiety, afraid of all that could happen if we are caught unprepared. The fearful questions can be contagious: Are the choices we are making to support the local food pantry, or fix the organ, or install low-flow faucets the right ones, the ones that demonstrate wisdom and faithfulness? Which kind of bridesmaid are we, wise or foolish? *How can I personally, or we as a church, know if we are ready for Jesus?*

The judgment discourses in these chapters are counterparts to the Sermon on the Mount in Matthew 5 and culminate with the judgment of the nations in Matthew 25. Both the Beatitudes and the final judgment point the way. Being ready is a way of life more than a checklist of dos and don'ts; it is an orientation to the world that looks for Jesus in the stranger and is ready to respond to the neighbor in need. Jesus urges his hearers to "keep awake" and be ready for his appearance at any time, and then he immediately tells them he is present in each person who is hungry or thirsty, naked or in prison. Being ready means living a full life of humble service to others, of mercy and compassion, of peacemaking and justice.

A late or absent bride or groom is a common trope in sitcoms and romantic comedies. The groom stands at the front of the church awaiting a missing bride as the congregation titters and speculates. The bride in a fluffy gown paces nervously as the best man chases down the runaway groom. Did he get lost in Vegas? Is she caught in traffic? Did someone get cold feet? In his parable, Jesus does not tell us why the groom is delayed. Maybe the bridesmaids without enough oil found themselves unprepared because, once the groom was delayed, they had little faith he was coming at all. In our context, which seems rife with the "delay" of the reign of God, it can be hard to maintain hope that all wrong might one day be made right. In a world dominated by endemic injustice and suffering, problems can seem insurmountable and impossible to solve. As we dash about trying to address overwhelming needs all around us, we become exhausted and ineffective, instead of being prepared and faithful disciples.

Theologian Nancy E. Bedford suggests that our communities discern together how to make "little moves against destructiveness": imaginative and creative efforts, even if small, that follow God's leading.[2] Such discernment and response fosters new hope and can help transcend feelings of despair and defeat. The bridesmaids who brought flasks of oil also brought hope that though the groom might be delayed, he would still arrive. In the end, they were ready not only for the wedding, but for the wait.

AIMEE MOISO

---

1. Kate Masters, "Fear of Other People Is Now the Primary Motivation for American Gun Ownership, a Landmark Survey Finds," *The Trace*, September 19, 2016; https://www.thetrace.org/2016/09/harvard-gun-ownership-study-self-defense/.
2. Nancy E. Bedford, "Little Moves Against Destructiveness: Theology and the Practice of Discernment," in Miroslav Volf and Dorothy C. Bass, eds., *Practicing Theology: Beliefs and Practices in Christian Life* (Grand Rapids: Eerdmans, 2001), 157–81.

Proper 28 (Sunday between November 13 and November 19 inclusive)

Zephaniah 1:7, 12–18 and Judges 4:1–7
Psalm 90:1–8 (9–11), 12 and Psalm 123
1 Thessalonians 5:1–11
Matthew 25:14–30

Zephaniah 1:7, 12–18

[7]Be silent before the Lord GOD!
    For the day of the LORD is at hand;
the LORD has prepared a sacrifice,
    he has consecrated his guests.
. . . .
[12]At that time I will search Jerusalem with lamps,
    and I will punish the people
who rest complacently on their dregs,
    those who say in their hearts,
"The LORD will not do good,
    nor will he do harm."
[13]Their wealth shall be plundered,
    and their houses laid waste.
Though they build houses,
    they shall not inhabit them;
though they plant vineyards,
    they shall not drink wine from them.

[14]The great day of the LORD is near,
    near and hastening fast;
the sound of the day of the LORD is bitter,
    the warrior cries aloud there.
[15]That day will be a day of wrath,
    a day of distress and anguish,
a day of ruin and devastation,
    a day of darkness and gloom,
a day of clouds and thick darkness,
    [16]a day of trumpet blast and battle cry
against the fortified cities
    and against the lofty battlements.

[17]I will bring such distress upon people
    that they shall walk like the blind;
because they have sinned against the LORD,
their blood shall be poured out like dust,
    and their flesh like dung.
[18]Neither their silver nor their gold
    will be able to save them
    on the day of the LORD's wrath;
in the fire of his passion
    the whole earth shall be consumed;
for a full, a terrible end
    he will make of all the inhabitants of the earth.

Judges 4:1–7

¹The Israelites again did what was evil in the sight of the LORD, after Ehud died. ²So the LORD sold them into the hand of King Jabin of Canaan, who reigned in Hazor; the commander of his army was Sisera, who lived in Harosheth-ha-goiim. ³Then the Israelites cried out to the LORD for help; for he had nine hundred chariots of iron, and had oppressed the Israelites cruelly twenty years. ⁴At that time Deborah, a prophetess, wife of Lappidoth, was judging Israel. ⁵She used to sit under the palm of Deborah between Ramah and Bethel in the hill country of Ephraim; and the Israelites came up to her for judgment. ⁶She sent and summoned Barak son of Abinoam from Kedesh in Naphtali, and said to him, "The LORD, the God of Israel, commands you, 'Go, take position at Mount Tabor, bringing ten thousand from the tribe of Naphtali and the tribe of Zebulun. ⁷I will draw out Sisera, the general of Jabin's army, to meet you by the Wadi Kishon with his chariots and his troops; and I will give him into your hand.'"

Commentary 1: Connecting the Reading with Scripture

This Zephaniah passage falls within the prophet's proclamation of coming punishment against Judah and the world at large for their idolatry. The prophet summons the people of Jerusalem to be silent (Zeph. 1:7), providing narrative details about impending destruction (vv. 12–18). Zephaniah repeatedly employs the metaphor of "the day of the LORD" (vv. 7b, 15, 16) to describe a time of divine judgment on those who had become apathetic (v. 12) and sinful (v. 17). The focus of the text, however, is not the nature of sin but the nature of the day of judgment.

The superscription (v. 1) places the activities of the prophet in the reign of Josiah (640–609 BCE) and may reflect that king's religious reform against idolatry (2 Kgs. 22). Like many of the minor prophets, Zephaniah speaks a divine word of judgment and restoration, announcing who will be subjected to divine judgment, why, and when it will come. The narrative arc of the book moves from divine judgment in the form of exile on the "day of the LORD" (1:2–3, 7) to the promise of restoration from diaspora (3:16–20).

Zephaniah's description of the "day of the LORD" finds thematic and linguistic resonance with Joel 2:1–11. The "day of the LORD is near" (Zeph. 1:14; see Joel 2:1); it will be a great day (Zeph. 1:14; see Joel 2:11) of darkness and gloom, clouds and blackness (Zeph. 1:15; see Joel 2:2) and sounding trumpet (Zeph. 1:16; see Joel 2:1). This day will affect all inhabitants of the earth (Zeph. 1:18; see Joel 2:1).

The thematic resonances extend to the Deuteronomic tradition with its retributive theology. Zephaniah 1 shares these themes with Deuteronomy: to build houses but not dwell in them (Zeph. 1:13; see Deut. 28:30); to plant vineyards but not drink from them (Zeph. 1:13; see Deut. 28:39); a day of constraint and distress (Zeph. 1:15; see Deut. 28:53, 55, 57); a day of thick darkness and cloud (Zeph. 1:15; see Deut. 4:11); blind persons groping to find their way (Zeph. 1:17; see Deut. 28:29); divine jealousy portrayed as fire consuming the earth (Zeph. 1:18; see Deut. 32:21–22). These thematic and linguistic echoes indicate the impossibility of simply glossing over judgment en route to salvation. Prophetic work requires the courage to name and challenge practices and systems of oppression while guiding believers into the opportunities, methods, and processes for renewal and transformation.

Although the opening words are addressed to Judah (Zeph. 1:7), the judgment extends to "all the inhabitants of the earth" (v. 18), echoing the opening words of the book in 1:2. There is tension between the particularity of the message and its universality. The universality associated with the "day of the LORD" forecloses the privatization of faith and opens up the space for contemplating communal accountability. Like Isaiah (chap. 34) and Jeremiah (chap. 46), Zephaniah speaks of the "day of the LORD" as a day of sacrifice, presumably some kind of a fellowship offering (see Lev. 7:11–21). Unlike the other two prophets, Zephaniah does not specify the identity of the sacrificial victim. This leaves open the nature of vicarious faith and living.

Concerns about the coming "day of the LORD" find parallels in Isaiah 13 and 22, in Joel 2–3, in Amos 5, and Malachi 3:2. The "day of the LORD" could be present (Joel 1:15); it could be in the near future (Isa. 2:12–22; Jer. 46:10; Ezek. 13:5; Joel 2:1; Amos 5:18–20); it could be future-eschatological (Isa. 13:6; Ezek. 30:23); or it could be primarily eschatological (Joel 3:14–15 [Heb. Joel 4:14–15]; Zech. 14:1–21; 1 Thess. 5:1–11; 2 Pet. 3:10–13). Expectations grow out of the community's yearning for new beginnings and God's desire to create newness where life can flourish. Each generation of the faithful diagnoses the character of that eschatology, but that yearning itself becomes a vital part of their faith.

A familiar literary sequence in Judges structures Deborah's story: Israel did what was evil in the eyes of the Lord (Judg. 4:1); they were handed over to oppressors (v. 2); they cried out to the Lord (v. 3); Deborah is introduced, but there is no mention of the Lord raising a "savior" (vv. 4–7). The lack of detail about Deborah leaves open who the "savior" is, although the narrative uses "judge" in association with "savior" (2:11–19). Deborah's story holds a distinction between a judge and a military leader, and their roles in delivering the oppressed.

The larger literary context of Judges 1 through 1 Samuel 7 depicts life in Israel without a united monarchy, and most scholars date the book after the Babylonian exile. There is no clear sense of a "unified Israel," only of tribal and regional identities (see Judg. 1:3–15, 17–20, 22–26), including Canaanite cities (Judg. 1:21, 27–33). A repetitive cycle of sin, punishment, repentance, and restoration shapes the entire narrative. A slow decline in political and religious life defines the narratives of six judges in chapters 3–16.

Deborah's story is told in prose (chap. 4) and poetry (chap. 5), with some common facts: Israel faces oppression; Deborah prophesies and instigates the process of deliverance; Barak leads Israelite troops against Sisera; the battle takes place in the plains of Megiddo, where Sisera meets his fate at the hands of Jael; and a period of peace ensues. There are differences in the two accounts. In the prose, Israel's principal opponent is Jabin, for whom Sisera works. In the poetry, no mention is made of Jabin, and Sisera is portrayed as a kingly character. In the prose, fighters come from two tribes only (4:6 versus 5:14, 15, 18). In the prose, Deborah is described as "a prophetess" (4:4) instead of "mother in Israel" (5:7). Reading chapters 4 and 5 together highlights a move toward a unified Israelite identity.

The story is part of the overall deteriorating crisis in Israel, depicted in the Judges narratives: As Israel's evil moves from unspecified action (3:12; 4:1a) to specific charges of idolatry and worship of foreign gods (6:10; 8:24–27, 33–35; 10:6), the experience of oppression moves from brief (3:13; 4:2) to longer and more severe forms (6:1–6; 10:6–16), and God's response to Israel's cry also shifts from positive (3:15; 4:3) to rejection (10:10–14). The story culminates with Samson, where there is no cry at all (13:1).

Israel alternates between war and peace under various judges (3:8, 11, 14, 30; 4:3; 5:31; 6:1; 8:28). With Jephthah and Samson, there is no mention of peace (10:8; 12:7; 13:1; 16:31). Within that narrative structure, the story of Deborah constitutes part of the rich legacy of biblical leadership in times of crisis. It portrays a community hard at work on its survival, while being engaged with issues of justice in the face of social, political, and religious chaos.

Deborah's story thus gestures toward the story of all of Israel. Her story is the third of six judges narratives in the book. Her gender is doubly referenced as "prophetess" and "wife." But she is not the only woman in the book of Judges; Jael also appears in Judges 4, and the unnamed woman in Thebez (9:53–54). Deborah's prophetic words stand alongside Miriam's (Exod. 15:20) and Huldah's (2 Kgs. 22:14). In

Deborah's story, omens play a vital role, determining the shape and character of faith and faithful leadership.

These texts raise questions about divine judgment, human survival, and accountability. They also reflect on unified consciousness in religious communities. The question of "us vs. them" pervades both texts, even as divine judgment comes on both "us" and "them." We are invited to reflect on justice and restoration as a function of multiple heroes, not just one.

KENNETH N. NGWA

Commentary 2: Connecting the Reading with the World

Our Zephaniah text may initially give us pause. This must have been a difficult proclamation to make and to hear. The prophet heralds an announcement that the people will not like: a terrifying judgment is coming, and God is the one at the helm. Zephaniah informs the idolatrous people that the LORD has consecrated them—prepared them for sacrifice (Zeph. 1:7). The people of Israel have had several warnings calling them to repent and turn back to God. They have failed to do so, bowing down to false gods (v. 5) and failing to inquire of YHWH as to what their path should be (v. 6). Now the time has come for God's response; they must be silent and hear what God has to say.

When people invest their money in the stock market at the end of the business day, if there is a loss on the investment the stockbroker will announce a margin call to put more money in to cover the losses. There will be a penalty to pay if the investor is unable to cover the losses. The people of Judah have been losing for a long time, and now it is time to cover their losses. Zephaniah is the broker who makes a margin call; the people cannot pay up, and there will be a stiff penalty. God admonishes the people: be silent and watch what is going to happen. Often, we commit to actions without serious consideration as to what the consequences might be; sometimes we are forced to watch negative consequences unfold without being able to do anything about them. This is how the people of Judah must have felt.

Zephaniah's message for God's people is that God will search Jerusalem with lamps, relentlessly searching for the complacent, the careless, and the indifferent in order to punish them (v. 12). God will seek out those who did not consider God in their behavior, those who did not think anything would happen to them because of their decisions, and those who were not concerned with consequences. In the darkness that has become Jerusalem, God is going to look for those complacent people with a flashlight, and no matter how they try to stay out of the spotlight and slip away into the night, they will most certainly face the consequences.

It is impossible to escape the presence of God (Ps. 139:1–12; Amos 9:1–4). As children, we are told, "God is everywhere" (see Jer. 23:23–24). It may have seemed that someone was watching us when we were being less than saintly. Not being able to escape God's presence, however, goes deeper than that. God's presence speaks to our moral center; we can feel the pull of God to consider the decisions and choices we make. God is telling the people of Judah that they have continued to choose poorly, and God is seeking them out to get their attention. Everything they deem important will be taken from them. Houses will be demolished, wealth will be lost, and they will not benefit from all their hard work. They will put energy into activities that they will not enjoy. The loss and emptiness they experience will be terrible (Zeph. 1:10–11). The disastrous consequences of their sin will be vast. Zephaniah warns of destruction on a cosmic scale: "the whole earth shall be consumed" (v. 18).

We hear of the "great day of the LORD" (v. 14), when the agony of separation will take place. It will be a time when the toughest of individuals will struggle; even warriors will feel the weight of the Lord's day. The Lord declares that this sinful people will be so aimless and lost that they will be like those who cannot see (v. 17). Their possessions and silver and gold will not be able to stop what God is sending their way.

God Who Is Already Seeking Us

This is a not a God of wrath, not a God who is indifferent to the world, not a ghoul of a God who spies on us in hope of watching us fall from grace. Most of all, this is not a "gotcha God" who simply lies in wait to punish us when we do. On the contrary. In this light, God, the Doer of Magical Miracles outside the natural order, disappears. Instead, the God of Creation frees nature to take its course with us as we, too, test and taste and grow in wisdom, age, and grace. Having experienced life in all its glory, all its grief, we grow to the full height of our humanity. It is a slow process, yes, but in the end our choice for God is valid, is holy, because it is real, considered, not forced, not extorted. This God wants for creation the fullness of all the good that is in it.

Most of all, this caring God loves us and so refuses to interfere with our judgments or prevent our experiments with life. Instead, this God does us the respect of simply standing by, of being there to hold us up, of confirming our trust by leading us through the dim days and long nights. . . . No doubt about it: This God trusts humanity to work its own way to the fullness of its soulfulness. Then the real miracle of Life—this right to choose our own destiny as well as the way we get there—with all its learnings, all our lessons, welcomes us home to new life and fresh understandings of God's way with God's creatures.

This first step of humility . . . does not crush us in the dust. Instead it makes us vulnerable to God. We are now accessible to the call of God. We are ready to live in the presence of God. We are open to the will of God both for each of us and for the world. God and God's will now stand to make an imprint in our lives. Most important of all, this bald statement about the presence of God in our lives upends what the world knows as "merit theology." . . . The truth is that no one can merit God. We don't earn God a prayer, a legalistic hurdle, a devotion at a time. We don't need to earn God because the basic, life-giving truth is that we already have God. God is here. With us. Now. In this. Forever. What is important is for us to seek God—to come into touch with God—who is already seeking us. That is union with God. That is the marriage of two souls.

Joan Chittister, *Radical Spirit: 12 Ways to Live a Free and Authentic Life* (New York: Convergent, 2017), 28–30.

How tragic it is to get to a place in life where we have acquired and amassed much, but still find ourselves empty in spirit! This text reminds us that the success often applauded by the world does not guarantee a right relationship with the Divine. Our hope is that we would not gain the world but lose our souls (Matt. 16:26; Mark 8:36; Luke 9:25); we desire to walk faithfully with God on the journey. The alternative would be to discover that all that we have done is useless in the eyes of God.

Our comparative text, Judges 4:1–7, sheds light on what God expects from us when our situation seems bleak and hopeless. The opening of Judges establishes a pattern of apostasy and deliverance that serves as a framework for stories of individual judges (see Judg. 2:1–2, 11–15). As the scene opens in Judges 4, the covenant people Israel has once again fallen short of staying in right relationship with the Lord. Having done "what was evil in the sight of the Lord," the Israelites find themselves suffering under the oppression of the Canaanite king Jabin (vv. 1–2). The severity of Israel's plight is signaled by the narrative note that Jabin's general, Sisera, dominates Israel with overwhelming military force, "nine hundred chariots of iron" (v. 3). Having endured oppression for twenty years, the Israelites cry out to God. Deborah, a judge leading the people at the time, has a prophetic word for Israelite commander Barak: God will give the enemy into Barak's hand (v. 7). What an announcement this must have been! After twenty years of living under the boot of Sisera and his army, the Israelites will be saved. God is going to deliver their enemies into the hands of Barak and ten thousand Israelite soldiers.

Sometimes we can be dealing with challenges for so long that we can begin to see them as foregone conclusions. We tell ourselves, "I will never be able to change that," or "I will always have that issue." The armies we face in our minds have been there for a long time, and we may believe that our adversaries are invincible. We look at what we have and think it is insignificant. We have trouble believing that which other people tell us is possible. They can see certain things that we cannot; they can tell us about the possibilities with God on our side, but often we are too intimidated to try. In those moments, we can learn from Judges 4. Deborah teaches us that we need only to trust God. The power that would cause Barak to be victorious would not come from the ten thousand soldiers with him; Barak's victory would come from the divine Warrior who fights alongside the covenant people (see vv. 15, 23).

Sometimes we can let the oppression we have experienced and the obstacles in our path convince us that transformation is not possible. Twenty years is a long time to live in fear of Sisera's army, as it were. God's promise of victory can overcome our fear, empowering us to change our sinful ways. The preacher can emphasize that we are called to trust God's voice despite the obstacles that loom large in front of us. Here the community of faith can help, a message reinforced in 1 Thessalonians 5. Paul exhorts believers to live as "children of light" (1 Thess. 5:4–5), to keep awake spiritually (v. 6), and to "encourage one another" (v. 11). The Christian hope articulated in this passage is nothing less than the hope of grace, something to which believers can cling in times of challenge: "God has destined us not for wrath but for obtaining salvation through our Lord Jesus Christ" (v. 9).

WM. MARCUS SMALL

Proper 28 (Sunday between November 13 and November 19 inclusive)

Psalm 90:1–8 (9–11), 12

¹Lord, you have been our dwelling place
  in all generations.
²Before the mountains were brought forth,
   or ever you had formed the earth and the world,
   from everlasting to everlasting you are God.

³You turn us back to dust,
   and say, "Turn back, you mortals."
⁴For a thousand years in your sight
   are like yesterday when it is past,
   or like a watch in the night.

⁵You sweep them away; they are like a dream,
   like grass that is renewed in the morning;
⁶in the morning it flourishes and is renewed;
   in the evening it fades and withers.

⁷For we are consumed by your anger;
   by your wrath we are overwhelmed.
⁸You have set our iniquities before you,
   our secret sins in the light of your countenance.

⁹For all our days pass away under your wrath;
   our years come to an end like a sigh.
¹⁰The days of our life are seventy years,
   or perhaps eighty, if we are strong;
even then their span is only toil and trouble;
   they are soon gone, and we fly away.

¹¹Who considers the power of your anger?
   Your wrath is as great as the fear that is due you.
¹²So teach us to count our days
   that we may gain a wise heart.

Psalm 123

¹To you I lift up my eyes,
   O you who are enthroned in the heavens!
²As the eyes of servants
   look to the hand of their master,
as the eyes of a maid
   to the hand of her mistress,
so our eyes look to the LORD our God,
   until he has mercy upon us.

³Have mercy upon us, O Lord, have mercy upon us,
  for we have had more than enough of contempt.
⁴Our soul has had more than its fill
  of the scorn of those who are at ease,
  of the contempt of the proud.

Connecting the Psalm with Scripture and Worship

Psalm 90:1–8 (9–11), 12. Psalm 90 begins in praise to the one who created the cosmos; this is the same one who has claimed Israel as God's own and has accompanied the people throughout their entire history. With verse 3, however, the psalmist moves to acknowledge that human life is brief and that the same God who gives us life also takes it from us in the end. The psalmist attributes this fate to God's wrath, God's anger at the evil humans have wrought. It is a rather grim picture; even if we manage to live long lives, our years are characterized by "toil and trouble" (Ps. 90:10) before we are swept away.

It would seem that the psalmist has a bleak view of Israel's relationship with God. Yet, in the final verse of the reading, it is clear that the psalm is sung against the backdrop of God's enduring relationship with the people. "So teach us to count our days," the psalmist says, "that we may gain a wise heart" (v. 12). This is the prayer of one who believes that in spite of human sinfulness and the divine anger it arouses, God remains in relationship with God's people, ready to teach them a better way.

The architects of the lectionary place this psalm in response to Zephaniah 1:7, 12–18, which is part of the prophet's oracles announcing God's judgment of Judah. The mention of a sacrifice suggests that these words may have been spoken in the temple.[1] The implication is that God is the high priest who intends to sacrifice Judah in the presence of its enemies, who are God's invited guests.[2] Of what are the people of Judah guilty? Complacency. They are too comfortable, too wealthy, too secure, and too unconcerned with the needy and the weak. Zephaniah warns that "the great day of the Lord is near" when the people will experience "distress and anguish," "ruin and devastation," "darkness and gloom" (Zeph. 1:14–16). Even all their money will do them no good. They cannot be saved from God's punishment, for "the whole earth shall be consumed" (v. 18).

Here at the end of the liturgical year, Christians contemplate the ultimate reign of God, a reign of justice and peace marked by the return of Christ. This anticipation is the basis of our hope; God will make good on the divine promises to right all wrongs, end all suffering, and conquer death forever. Yet in order to do this, the world as we know it must pass away. All complacency and cowardice will be destroyed. The greedy and the comfortable will be pushed aside to make way for those who have long waited to be fed. Zephaniah's words ring out just as clearly in our own time; the day is coming when God's wrath will consume every evil.

So we sing with the psalmist. We are all too aware of the shortness of life and the reality of death, which is one reason why this psalm is often read at funerals. We cannot avoid the fact that we will lose people we love, some far too soon, and that we ourselves will die. Nor can we deny that even the most righteous among us live lives marked by sin, both overt and secret. We deserve God's wrath. Yet the psalmist, in asking God to teach us to count our days so that we might gain wisdom, reassures us that despite all of this, our relationship with God endures.

Christians understand this relationship to have been forged at the cross of Jesus. We confirm and seal this new covenant whenever we

---

1. Robert A. Bennett, "Zephaniah," in *The New Interpreter's Bible* (Nashville: Abingdon, 1996), 14:677.
2. Bennett, "Zephaniah," 678.

gather at the Lord's Table. To sing Psalm 90 is to acknowledge the truth about ourselves—about the whole human race—and to trust in God's mercy, even as we anticipate the ending of the world as we know it. On this penultimate Sunday of the Christian year, worshipers might sing "Our God, Our Help in Ages Past," Isaac Watts's classic paraphrase of Psalm 90. Even as we contemplate God's judgment, we affirm our trust in God's mercy as we watch and wait for the coming of the Lord. For we know that the remaking of this world that God will bring about will be far greater, and far more beautiful, that we can even imagine.

Psalm 123. Psalm 123 is one of fifteen Songs of Ascent (Pss. 120–134). These songs feature liturgical elements such as cues for the people to respond, professions of faith, and blessings. The songs may have been sung by pilgrims making their way to Jerusalem to take part in religious celebrations. Their liturgical features, along with their brevity, make them well suited for such a journey.[3] Psalm 123 is short, as are most of the Songs of Ascent, just four verses long. Furthermore, the message of the psalm is plain. The singers of the psalm look up to God as servants would to a master or mistress, seeking mercy from the only one who can give it. They are fed up with the scorn of the rich and the contempt of the proud, and they want release. The people have been in exile, and even after they have been freed, their suffering continues.

Psalm 123 is sung in response to the first reading, Judges 4:1–7. The seven verses appointed for the day summarize the gruesome war story that is to follow. In this narrative, a seemingly innocent female bystander, Jael, offers comfort to Sisera, the commander of the oppressor's army. She welcomes him into her tent, covers him with a blanket so he can rest, and gives him warm milk. The unsuspecting soldier drifts off to sleep. Then Jael creeps over to him and drives a tent peg clear through his temple, nailing him to the ground. When Barak, who had been sent by the judge Deborah to conquer Sisera, follows the trail of his enemy, he ends up at Jael's tent. There, she proudly leads him to the corpse.

One can see how the psalm might express the attitude of the people of Israel. They have returned from exile, and yet they are still experiencing injustice and persecution. They are sick of it, and they want freedom now. In a service where a sermon is based on the Judges text, worshipers might join their voices with those of the psalmist in a cry for justice, whether they are in positions of privilege or whether they endure the injustices of poverty, racism, or marginalization. As Emma Lazarus once said, and others have echoed, none of us is free until all of us are free.

Were we pilgrims on our way to Jerusalem, we might follow the singing of Psalm 123 with Psalm 124, which affirms that if God had not been on our side, we would not have survived. We know that the people of God *do* survive, for even in the worst of times, God is steadfastly faithful. On this last Sunday before Reign of Christ/Christ the King, we sing Psalm 123 along with our ancestors, beseeching God to grant relief to those who have suffered for so long. Even as we hear the warnings of Matthew's parable as we anticipate the judgment of God, we do not fear. For, as the writer of the epistle reminds us, "God has destined us not for wrath but for obtaining salvation through our Lord Jesus Christ" (1 Thess. 5:9).

KIMBERLY BRACKEN LONG

---

3. J. Clinton McCann Jr., "Psalms," in *The New Interpreter's Bible* (Nashville: Abingdon, 1996), 7:1176.

Proper 28 (Sunday between November 13 and November 19 inclusive)

1 Thessalonians 5:1–11

¹Now concerning the times and the seasons, brothers and sisters, you do not need to have anything written to you. ²For you yourselves know very well that the day of the Lord will come like a thief in the night. ³When they say, "There is peace and security," then sudden destruction will come upon them, as labor pains come upon a pregnant woman, and there will be no escape! ⁴But you, beloved, are not in darkness, for that day to surprise you like a thief; ⁵for you are all children of light and children of the day; we are not of the night or of darkness. ⁶So then let us not fall asleep as others do, but let us keep awake and be sober; ⁷for those who sleep sleep at night, and those who are drunk get drunk at night. ⁸But since we belong to the day, let us be sober, and put on the breastplate of faith and love, and for a helmet the hope of salvation. ⁹For God has destined us not for wrath but for obtaining salvation through our Lord Jesus Christ, ¹⁰who died for us, so that whether we are awake or asleep we may live with him. ¹¹Therefore encourage one another and build up each other, as indeed you are doing.

Commentary 1: Connecting the Reading with Scripture

As the young Christian movement went beyond the confines of its birthplace, its appeal drew many from outside the Jewish heritage. The conversion of those in Acts 2 would serve as a prelude for how the gospel would spread into lands beyond Jerusalem, holding out a hope and promise that would be for everyone (Acts 2:39). This rapid expansion brought with it challenges and questions from populations whose cultural and religious assumptions were not grounded in the Hebrew tradition. The first followers of Jesus were bound by their common observance of Mosaic law. This was not the case for the Thessalonians. In this cultural center and port city, some two hundred miles north of Athens, the new believers embraced the message of the gospel in a world of Greek and Roman cultures. It was a place open to the gospel, but it was also a place where gospel values would collide with the values of the world around them.

In what is believed to be the earliest of his letters, Paul's First Letter to the Thessalonians provides insights into questions that come from a new generation of believers, a people who did not have the firsthand experience of walking with Jesus. They are faithfully responding to the preaching of Paul, Timothy, and Silvanus (Silas).

A primary concern for these new believers is the question of the end times and when they might occur. Engaging the metaphor used by Jesus (Matt. 24:43–44; Luke 12:39), Paul reminds them that "the day" will happen when it is not expected, like a thief in the night (1 Thess. 5:2).

As portrayed in Zephaniah 1:12–18, the end times were believed to be a time of despair for nonbelievers. Throughout the Old Testament the end time is understood as a time of destruction for the world (Isa. 22:5; Amos 5:18; Joel 2:31; Jer. 30:7). Paul understood it as a time of great pain, like that of a woman in labor (1 Thess. 5:3). These historic Jewish teachings would need to be interpreted to a new people of faith. How do believers live between "the now and the not yet"? Paul pastorally navigates the foundational teachings of Jewish tradition with the concerns of these new believers. Paul remembers and celebrates the accomplishments of their faith (1:3, 8), while focusing on their new identity as children of light and of the day (5:4, 5). It is this identity—not the knowledge of what will happen on the day of the Lord—that shapes their witness in this life.

The desire to seek answers to the many questions of life is common among believers.

As Christianity spread, its distinctive teachings challenged the norms around them. Greek and Roman gods were worshiped in ancient Thessalonica. Temples and statues stood as visible reminders of their power. The new followers of Jesus were, however, claiming one true sovereign and invisible God. How would new believers navigate and solidify their identity in the midst of these contrasting images? How would they understand questions foundational to their new faith, such as the promised return of the Lord? Paul is keenly aware of these concerns in their daily lives. He is also aware of the political propaganda of the imperial Roman government, promising "peace and security" to residents of the empire, which could withstand any problem.[1] Countering the claims of such powers, Paul reaffirms that there is no power that can stand against the "breaking in" of God's kingdom, a teaching important across the centuries.

Understanding that the journey of faithfulness could feel like a battle at times, Paul reminds the Thessalonians that their "very identity" clothes them with what they need to find the strength to embody the values of Christ in a challenging world. He equips them by inviting them to put on the metaphorical armor—the breastplate of faith and love—and to don the hope of salvation as a helmet (5:8). He does not minimize the complexity of their journey. Instead, he affirms in them the traits he valued and experienced in their young community of faith (1:3). Their faith, love, and hope in salvation would uphold them against a world still in darkness.

In Isaiah 59:17, we are reminded that it is the Lord who puts on righteousness like a breastplate and a helmet of salvation on his head. If the armor belongs to God, then it is God who bestows it upon the faithful.[2] This gift from God would sustain them (1 Thess. 5:9). The presence of this truth in their lives—the claim of who they are because of whose they are—would motivate them to encourage and build one another up (v. 11).

These words of encouragement reflect the intended spirit of this letter to the saints in Thessalonica. By way of his letters, Paul defines his ministry by responding to the real challenges and hopes of young and growing worshiping communities. As Christianity spread among both Gentiles and Jews, Paul's pastoral heart understood the importance of engaging these communities from their particular cultural contexts.

As we consider challenges for the church in our context today, two connections come to mind. The first is a reminder that in certain respects, we exist in a context not unlike that of first-century Christianity. The assumptions and values we often bring into our worshiping communities are not the assumptions and values of the culture around us. Many coming through our doors are not familiar with traditions that have been foundational to our practices as communities of faith. Cherished hymns and prayers may seem foreign to many who have not grown up in the church. How will we bridge that gap in order to build up the body of Christ?

Religious institutions are also often viewed with suspicion by nonbelievers, who may see them as inward-looking communities of judgment and rejection, instead of outward-serving communities of grace and hope. As we consider our strategies for church growth and evangelism, we could learn much from the spirit Paul embodies in order to strengthen and offer encouragement to new followers. He meets them where they are, understanding that we can lead only a people we choose to engage and love. In a world of increased polarization, Paul's tone of grace and authentic concern is an important consideration for Christian leaders as we seek to reach and grow a new generation of believers.

A second connection to explore would be to consider the current idols and gods often pursued in order to feel some sense of security—especially when our lives seem frenetic or out of our control. The gods around us may not be chiseled in stone, but they are sculpted into the cultural values of wealth, success, sexuality, and addiction, to name a few. The church today is also wrestling with our own internal idols. Our buildings, doctrines, and traditions can make us risk-averse, recalling the parable of the Talents in Matthew 25:14–30. Because we fear

---

1. N. T. Wright, *Paul for Everyone: Galatians and Thessalonians* (Louisville, KY: Westminster John Knox, 2002), 128.
2. Beverly Roberts Gaventa, *First and Second Thessalonians*, Interpretation (Louisville, KY: Westminster John Knox, 1998), 72.

losing what we have, we embody a theology of scarcity that prevents us from recognizing the abundance around us. Idolatry is a strong temptation, offering us pseudosecurity while cheating us of the possibilities of the very faith we claim. It prevents us from living boldly as a people serving a broken world. It robs us from trusting in God's breastplate of faith and love and God's helmet of the hope of salvation that will sustain our Christ-centered witness, much needed in a time such as this.

RUTH FAITH SANTANA-GRACE

Commentary 2: Connecting the Reading with the World

With its abundance of metaphors—the thief in the night, the woman in labor, the sleepy drunkards—this passage from the First Letter to the Thessalonians offers a number of ways for the preacher to connect with the contemporary world. Even centuries after the original writing, we can imagine the shock and fear of someone breaking into our house in the middle of the night. We know that babies are rarely born on the schedule we have planned. We know the grogginess of sleep after a party that went on too long. We know then too the truth Paul conveys: we had better be ready for God to appear.

The lectionary positions this text at the end of the long period of Ordinary Time that stretches from Pentecost to the beginning of Advent. Preachers may find themselves out of gas by this time in the fall, tired out from stewardship campaigns and fall programs, eager for the beloved, and perhaps more easily preachable, gospel stories of Advent. Church members who have tended to the day in, day out work of the church throughout the year may now be wondering why their hard work has not paid off in fuller pews and offering plates and look forward to an uptick in attendance come December.

This text offers a good word to those preachers and faithful folks who have carried the church through the times between the high holy days. It is worth noting that the word "ordinary" in the liturgical calendar is confusing; we might think it means *boring*, a time when nothing much happens, but in fact it refers to the *ordered* nature of this season, a way of marking time together as the church. Paul's letter reminds us that the Christian life is one of active readiness. Church people, the sort who show up for church on ordinary Sundays when there is nothing particularly extraordinary going on, know that that is exactly when Christ shows up too. In the conversations at coffee hour after worship, in the hymns and prayers lifted high in the sanctuary, in the potluck dinners, in the church nursery, in the hospital visits, in the funeral receptions: this is where Christ appears. People in the pews on this Sunday will be able to recall a time when seemingly mundane church work became the catalyst for something divine. Sometimes when we least expect it, in the most ordinary of moments, we are moved by the extraordinary presence of God. The text ends with an exhortation to "keep up the good work," which perhaps is just what tired church folks—and tired preachers—need to hear.

One challenge of preaching this text is that congregations today may feel little connection with Paul's original readers at the church in Thessalonica, who were only a generation or so removed from the life of Jesus, and were still sorting out what it meant to be the church. This small group of Jesus-followers presented a threat to the status quo for the Thessalonians who were loyal to the emperor and whose city, an important regional trading center, had benefited greatly from Roman rule.[3] A movement that proclaimed a new kingdom would have drawn the attention of the empire and would have challenged the small church's very existence. Paul's words to them would have been a comfort and encouragement as they foraged their way into uncharted territory.

Today Christianity in the United States is no longer a fledgling movement but the dominant culture in which most of us live. Now the

---

3. Abraham Smith, "The First Letter to the Thessalonians," in *The New Interpreter's Bible* (Nashville: Abingdon, 2000), 11:177.

threats against the church look different: those who claim to be Christian but corrupt the gospel, those who champion religious freedom but present a narrow view of what religion is, those who see the practice of faith as a priority only as long as it does not conflict with weekend camping trips and T-ball games. There are times when it seems that our proclamation of the good news will be drowned out by the louder voices of the world around us. Even in a Christian-dominated culture, it turns out we are not such a far cry from the Thessalonian church. Could the followers of Jesus again become a countercultural movement speaking out against an empire of power and proclaiming that there is another way to live?

Paul points forward to something that will happen at some unknown time in the future—the second coming of Christ—but his encouragement to the Thessalonians is more about how they will live in the here and now. Will they fall asleep and live in a dark, drunken stupor until that day? Or will they live in the light, encouraging one another and building each other up in the present?

Paul cautions his readers not to be lulled into a false sense of "peace and security." Vulnerability, not safety, is the gospel of Jesus. One needs only to stand in line at an airport security checkpoint to be reminded of the lengths to which we will go to assure ourselves that we are safe. In a country with more guns per capita than any other nation, with the most powerful military in the world, are we secure? Is there peace? Of course, there is not. Guns and security checks will not make us safe; that is why Paul instead advocates for the armor of faithfulness, love, and hope. Such armor is seemingly useless against physical violence, but for Christians who long for a better world and yet live in the here and now, such armor is a means of grace.

Scripture passages with eschatological themes bring to mind the classic song by the North American rock band R.E.M., "It's the End of the World as We Know It."[4] However, it is not clear whether we are meant to "feel fine," as the song suggests, as Paul points us forward to a time when the whole world will be turned upside down. To really understand this passage in its fullness, we first need to consider the previous chapter. In 4:16, we see a dramatic depiction of what Paul thinks will happen when Christ comes again: there will be angels and trumpets, and the dead will rise. Back up a few verses further to 4:13, and we see that Paul clearly means his words to be a comfort to his readers: "so that you might not grieve as others do who have no hope."

Are we then to look forward to the end of the world? The prevalence of apocalyptic books and movies in our popular culture betrays our anxiety about everything crashing down around us. Bookstores and movie theaters are awash with stories that predict a dystopian future: *WALL-E*, *The Book of Eli*, *The Matrix*, *Ready Player One*, and *Ender's Game,* to name a few of many. As a society, we seem to have little hope life will get better. Particularly for those of us who live comfortably, the end of the world as we know it sounds more terrifying than reassuring.

Perhaps for those of us who are privileged enough to feel the present is just fine, this text, paired with one or more of these cultural artifacts, may prompt reflection on why we are so anxious about the future. Could it be that we are living, as Paul suggests, in darkness? What might we do differently now to live in the light and be more hopeful about what is to come?

LEE HULL MOSES

---

4. R.E.M., "It's the End of the World as We Know It (and I Feel Fine)"; https://www.youtube.com/watch?v=bfyNlISf_No.

Proper 28 (Sunday between November 13 and November 19 inclusive)

Matthew 25:14–30

[14]"For it is as if a man, going on a journey, summoned his slaves and entrusted his property to them; [15]to one he gave five talents, to another two, to another one, to each according to his ability. Then he went away. [16]The one who had received the five talents went off at once and traded with them, and made five more talents. [17]In the same way, the one who had the two talents made two more talents. [18]But the one who had received the one talent went off and dug a hole in the ground and hid his master's money. [19]After a long time the master of those slaves came and settled accounts with them. [20]Then the one who had received the five talents came forward, bringing five more talents, saying, 'Master, you handed over to me five talents; see, I have made five more talents.' [21]His master said to him, 'Well done, good and trustworthy slave; you have been trustworthy in a few things, I will put you in charge of many things; enter into the joy of your master.' [22]And the one with the two talents also came forward, saying, 'Master, you handed over to me two talents; see, I have made two more talents.' [23]His master said to him, 'Well done, good and trustworthy slave; you have been trustworthy in a few things, I will put you in charge of many things; enter into the joy of your master.' [24]Then the one who had received the one talent also came forward, saying, 'Master, I knew that you were a harsh man, reaping where you did not sow, and gathering where you did not scatter seed; [25]so I was afraid, and I went and hid your talent in the ground. Here you have what is yours.' [26]But his master replied, 'You wicked and lazy slave! You knew, did you, that I reap where I did not sow, and gather where I did not scatter? [27]Then you ought to have invested my money with the bankers, and on my return I would have received what was my own with interest. [28]So take the talent from him, and give it to the one with the ten talents. [29]For to all those who have, more will be given, and they will have an abundance; but from those who have nothing, even what they have will be taken away. [30]As for this worthless slave, throw him into the outer darkness, where there will be weeping and gnashing of teeth.'"

Commentary 1: Connecting the Reading with Scripture

The judgment-wary among us may wish to skip this passage or use it only during stewardship season. Either approach may miss the wealth of faith insights in the text and the opportunity to grapple with uncomfortable subjects, such as slavery in the ancient world, judgment, punishment, and economics.

This parable in Matthew about a man who leaves for a long time, entrusting his slaves with his property, is in a row of parables and exhortations focused on the coming of the Son of Man. Jesus says, "About that day and hour no one knows, neither the angels of heaven, nor the Son, but only the Father" (Matt. 24:36). It follows the parable of the Ten Bridesmaids, five wise and five foolish (25:1–13). The parable lifts up the impossibility of knowing when the bridegroom (Christ) will return. The parable before that is of the slave who works as though his master will come home at any time (24:45–51). The apocalyptic themes anticipating the coming of the kingdom also run through this passage. This time, it is about a master who will return at an unexpected time and hold his slaves accountable for their actions with the extremely large amount of money he gave them.

This parable of the Talents is placed in Matthew's narrative during the final week of Jesus' life and ministry in Jerusalem, on a rising wave of tension between Jesus and the Pharisees. The subsequent chapter focuses on Jesus' betrayal and arrest. Jesus is preoccupied with sharing about the end of the age and how the faithful are to await the day of the coming of the Son of Man. The sense of urgency is high at this point in the text.

The psalm and epistle readings for this Sunday play on themes of unknown timing and God's mercy. The reading from the psalm pleads for God's mercy: "As the eyes of servants look to the hand of their master . . . so our eyes look to the LORD our God, until he has mercy upon us" (Ps. 123:2). It is a stark contrast between the mercy for which a servant looks in a master and the harsh condemnation of the third slave by the master in Matthew, who calls him "wicked and lazy slave" (Matt. 25:26). Indeed, the Gospel passage portrays a master whose words and behavior seem far out of step with the God who freed the enslaved Israelites and the Jesus who healed two blind men on the side of the road out of compassion (20:29–34).

The sense of urgency and the unknown resonates with the epistle reading in 1 Thessalonians 5:1–11. It plays on the theme of being alert, keeping ready for "the day of the Lord" (v. 2). A sermon could consider this theme—the urgency of being ready even now for the imminent return of Jesus—in the lectionary readings of both Matthew and 1 Thessalonians. We would do well to remember, however, that Matthew was written toward the end of the first century CE and that the audience hearing the parables believed that Jesus' impending return was at hand. Instead of approaching this urgency out of fear of judgment, we might embrace it eagerly in anticipation of being in God's presence.

The master's responses to the first two slaves and the third slave are vastly different. The crux of the rhetoric focuses on the third slave, and the master and slave exchange strong words. To the contemporary hearer of the text, the theme of slavery is disturbing; this is something the preacher may need to address. While this is not the same manifestation of slavery as the chattel slavery with which we in North America are familiar, the ancient practice of slavery was dehumanizing in its own way, and the world of this text did see slavery as normative. This calls for more than a passing mention of slavery in antiquity; it provides the preacher with an opportunity to speak to the differences in mores and values between the contemporary world and the ancient world. Even in the midst of this difficulty, the first two slaves provide an example of using the resources one is given, wisely and faithfully, even in the face of an uncertain time line.

The third slave clearly states his fear, saying, "Master, I knew that you were a harsh man . . . so I was afraid, and I went and hid your talent in the ground." Burying the talent in the ground is indeed the most secure way to handle a large sum of money (25:24–25). The master declares that the third, "wicked and lazy" slave be thrown "into the outer darkness" (v. 30). This condemnation is the polar opposite of the blessings he bestowed upon the other two "good and trustworthy" slaves, inviting them to "enter into the joy of your master" (v. 21).

As in the prior two parables, we might assume the master is Jesus, due to his title, but the harsh behavior of the master toward the third slave makes this association somewhat dubious. Maybe the third slave is Jesus, exposing the reality of the system. If so, a sermon could address the question about which character in this story might represent Jesus and why. It could also explore what the answers to that question tell us about our faith and how we respond to questions of economic exploitation. After all, Jesus was known for addressing economic injustice, overturning tables, and tossing out the money changers in the temple (Matt. 21).

The third slave points out that the slaves were asked to do the master's work for him without the promise of any return. They were not told to expect any material reward, although we might speculate they were motivated by fear, obligation toward their master, or hope for a small share of the earnings. This underlines the inequality of the relationship. Perhaps "no one in this parable is truly free except the third servant. The first two servants made more money, but they were still part of an economic system based on fear, greed, and exploitation."[1]

Matthew refers frequently to the coming judgment. A sermon might explore the Matthean concepts of hell, judgment, and punishment, alongside the love and mercy also portrayed in the Gospel. It is difficult to sidestep the theme of judgment in Matthew, as the author refers seven times to a place called Gehenna (5:22, 29, 30; 10:28; 18:9; 23:15, 33) and six times to weeping and gnashing of teeth (8:12; 13:42, 50; 22:13; 24:51; 25:30). In the same discourse, there is reference to a master who returns to a wicked slave, to "cut him in pieces and put him with the hypocrites, where there will be weeping and gnashing of teeth" (24:51). Gehenna refers to fire and future judgment,[2] clearly a theme important to the author of Matthew.

The recurring theme provides a sharp distinction and clear choice between the consequences for different courses of action the author describes throughout the Gospel. This heightens the sense of urgency; the prospect of future judgment and punishment should be taken seriously. The actions of the hearers have significance and should be carefully considered. Rather than inspiring fear, however, we might explore the contrast this judgment provides to the coming kingdom of heaven.

LAURA MARIKO CHEIFETZ

Commentary 2: Connecting the Reading with the World

Explaining the English word "talent" as "aptitude" will help this parable speak to hearers of all ages. God, as the creator, gives people different skills and abilities. Some talents are deemed more valuable than others in a particular society and those come with greater responsibility to maximize. Wasting one's skills and abilities is a misuse of God's creation and, per this Matthew reading, is deserving of punishment. On individual and community levels, this reading is useful for reminding God's people that in Jesus' absence we are called to responsibility amid our differences. Yet reading talents as gifts and abilities elides other more difficult interpretations. What if the talents are only monetary? What if the talents are understood theologically as grace?

The parable of the Talents shares a basic format with the two parables that come before, Matthew 25:1–13 and 24:45–51. In all three parables, two groups are set against each other and judged on their actions in response to crisis. Matthew's Jesus foreshadows this crisis period as the delay of the Parousia, the return of Jesus.[3] Similar themes related to God's judgment emerge in the readings from Zephaniah 1:7, 12–18; Judges 4:1–7; and 1 Thessalonians 5:1–11. In the Thessalonians passage, believers are separated and destined for salvation based on their actions. If talents are understood as money or grace, judgment is based on productivity in the absence of the master. The implication eschatologically—in the here-and-not-yet of God's kingdom—encourages us to move past our fear of judgment and live in abundance, now.

The ecclesial placement of this text at the end of the Proper period after Pentecost and two weeks prior to Advent suggests both closure and anticipation. The liturgical moment is yet another chance to *get it right* according to God's plan, as Jesus, the newborn, is about to be welcomed again. The text falls right before the US celebration of Thanksgiving, a holiday with as complicated a past as the sociocultural implications of this parable. Both require a reckoning with material abundance and whom it benefits. At the first Thanksgiving, Native Americans gave from their abundance to provide life to the European settlers. On a communal level, colonization wreaked destruction, caused death, and appropriated Native lands. Were early Christian settlers

---

1. Michelle Hwang, *Which One?*, sermon given at Central Presbyterian Church in Atlanta, GA, November 2017.
2. Jonathan T. Pennington, *Heaven and Earth in the Gospel of Matthew* (Grand Rapids: Baker Academic, 2009), 207.
3. See Marie-Eloise Rosenblatt, "Got into the Party after All: Women's Issues and the Five Foolish Virgins," in *A Feminist Companion to Matthew*, ed. Amy-Jill Levine with Marianne Blickenstaff (Sheffield: Sheffield Academic Press, 2001), 171–95, esp. notes 3 and 4 (173).

returning their abundance to God for God's purposes, or were they claiming abundance in God's name and using it for their own benefit?

If God is the master, God can give something to everyone, though God does so in unequal measure. God, however, does not expect an equal measure in return, requiring the recipient to *make up the difference* (Matt. 25:27). Rather, the recipient is to contribute in any manner possible. The abundance or earning is for God; the recipients do not keep the earnings. Reinforcing the purpose of wealth, we hear in the Zephaniah passage that neither idleness (Zeph. 1:12) nor wealth accumulation will protect one from the wrath of God (v. 13). Yes, more comes to those who show a return on God's investment; they receive based on their initiative, not the amount they were given.

Reading the parable literally, with God as money collector and investment banker (Matt. 25:24), we might be drawn into a prosperity-gospel reading that justifies the monetary wealth of some as a result of their faithfulness and the poverty of others as evidence of unfaithfulness. We might be tempted by a reading that celebrates capitalist wealth production as divinely ordained. Such an interpretation requires an assessment of how personal acquisition of wealth is used for God. A similar line of thinking is used in stewardship calls—to whom much has been given, much is required—and we give out of our abundance to the mission of the church. Most churches' use of wealth disrupts an individual-prosperity or capitalist-accumulation model. Material poverty is not a de facto judgment on one's morality. Rather, God's people are to share their wealth for the benefit of others.

Perhaps the lending model in the parable of the Talents is more akin to gender-based microlending initiatives in the Global South or living-wage practices in the US. Women's microlending programs represent some of the most successful economic, political, and social investments on offer today. When women in specific contexts are given capital, sometimes in the form of animals, sewing machines, or ovens, the return is much like that reaped by the man with five talents. A full measure (of ten) is gained in the form of increased education for her children, employment for other women in her business, and greater political participation in service of sustainable practices and safety.

However, unlike the parable, women who receive these loans are required to establish a collective of women who come together to function as a community bank, which decenters the master in this narrative. Microfinancing of women spreads the benefit to a much greater number of people than does traditional lending to male stakeholders.[4] In 1 Thessalonians, we are reminded that God's chosen encourage and build up one another (1 Thess. 5:11). Similarly, living-wage practices in the US often uplift the well-being of a workforce, increasing community health, educational opportunities, and family security.[5] These models closely resemble a return on God's abundance.

Yet the interpretation of talents as microfinancing ignores the uncomfortable, even hyperbolic conclusion of the passage, where the master attempts a mathematical impossibility. In verse 28, the master is talking to a third party when saying, "Take the talent from him," then declaring, "From those who have nothing, even what they have will be taken away" (Matt. 25:29). How can you take something away from someone with nothing? If the passage focuses on concrete money, this is not a possibility. Perhaps this last line is a clue and signals a transition from the concrete description of money to a metaphorical and theological suggestion of it as grace: spiritual well-being and an afterlife in heaven can still be taken away from one with no monetary possessions (v. 30).

If the talents are God's grace, it is given to be multiplied. Paradoxically, sharing grace with those around us yields more. Grace multiplies to the recipient, for others, and with God's abundance. The burying of grace results in a diminution of it; concealing it results in rejection. Whether or not one's theology can be

---

4. See Lynn Horton, *Women and Microfinance in the Global South: Empowerment and Disempowerment Outcomes* (Cambridge: Cambridge University Press, 2017).

5. See *To Do Justice: A Guide for Progressive Christians*, ed. Rebecca Todd Peters and Elizabeth Hinson-Hasty (Louisville, KY: Westminster John Knox, 2008), esp. chaps. 1 and 7.

reconciled with various levels of distribution of God's grace, *all* receive something and are called to build on what they have. Fear and inaction will be met with harsh judgment, as we hear from the master in the passage.

Today, we continue to struggle with how to parse differences in levels of faithfulness, gains in material success, and distribution of God's abundance. Based on our own social and economic location, with whom we identify in the parable makes a significant difference for our reading, as does consideration of talents as aptitudes, money, or grace. As the one with five talents, a person could have significant earthly wealth and need to hear a good word about how to best direct their earnings for God's abundance. At the same time, an individual with significant earthly wealth could also be the person with one talent burying the grace God freely gives by ignoring God's purpose in their life. At the heart of the parable is a connection between abundance and accountability in Christian living that anticipates Jesus' return.

KATE OTT

Proper 29 (Reign of Christ)

Ezekiel 34:11–16, 20–24
Psalm 95:1–7a and Psalm 100

Ephesians 1:15–23
Matthew 25:31–46

Ezekiel 34:11–16, 20–24

¹¹For thus says the Lord GOD: I myself will search for my sheep, and will seek them out. ¹²As shepherds seek out their flocks when they are among their scattered sheep, so I will seek out my sheep. I will rescue them from all the places to which they have been scattered on a day of clouds and thick darkness. ¹³I will bring them out from the peoples and gather them from the countries, and will bring them into their own land; and I will feed them on the mountains of Israel, by the watercourses, and in all the inhabited parts of the land. ¹⁴I will feed them with good pasture, and the mountain heights of Israel shall be their pasture; there they shall lie down in good grazing land, and they shall feed on rich pasture on the mountains of Israel. ¹⁵I myself will be the shepherd of my sheep, and I will make them lie down, says the Lord GOD. ¹⁶I will seek the lost, and I will bring back the strayed, and I will bind up the injured, and I will strengthen the weak, but the fat and the strong I will destroy. I will feed them with justice. . . .

²⁰Therefore, thus says the Lord GOD to them: I myself will judge between the fat sheep and the lean sheep. ²¹Because you pushed with flank and shoulder, and butted at all the weak animals with your horns until you scattered them far and wide, ²²I will save my flock, and they shall no longer be ravaged; and I will judge between sheep and sheep.

²³I will set up over them one shepherd, my servant David, and he shall feed them: he shall feed them and be their shepherd. ²⁴And I, the LORD, will be their God, and my servant David shall be prince among them; I, the LORD, have spoken.

Commentary 1: Connecting the Reading with Scripture

Ezekiel's message in chapter 34 constitutes three themes: (a) the proclamation of deliverance (Ezek. 34:1–10); (b) the nature of deliverance (vv. 11–22), itself in two subunits: deliverance from external forces (vv. 11–16), deliverance from internal exploitation (vv. 17–22); and (c) the evidence and purpose of deliverance (vv. 23–31). The prophet's words in 34:11–16, 20–24 belong to the second and third themes. The preceding woe oracle (vv. 1–10) is reminiscent of the oracle against false prophets in chapter 13, and anticipates the oracle against Mount Seir/Edom that precedes the promise of restoration in 35:1–15. The passage is part of the larger narrative corpus of Ezekiel 34–48, which transitions from the largely judgment oracles in the preceding chapters to a message of hope and restoration for Israel. The message of hope is not completely separated from the ongoing message of communal accountability.

Two things define Ezekiel's proclamation. First, deliverance is a result of divine activity. This is signaled by the divine self-commission ("here I am," au. trans. here and throughout) that follows the traditional prophetic introductory formula, "thus says the LORD." The Deity embarked on delivering the people engages in several actions: *seeking* the welfare of the flock; *examining* them, *rescuing* them, *leading* them out, *gathering* them, and *bringing* them to their land. The language of shepherding merges with new exodus language (cf. 20:34–35, 41–42;

36:24; 37:12, 21). After the rescue and return, the flock is nurtured (34:13b–15). Again, the divine shepherd is active: tending the sheep in the mountains, valleys, and inhabited places (the repeated verb "to tend" emphasizes the urgency and enduring nature of the work), and letting the sheep lie down. The welfare of the sheep is ensured by their access to economic and spiritual nourishment and rest.

Second, deliverance itself—the work of seeking the lost, fetching the strayed, binding up the injured, and strengthening the sick—is premised on the divine virtue of justice that rectifies the imbalance between the well-to-do and the poor. Righteous and just shepherding (v. 16) is the virtue around which prophetic proclamation and leadership converge. Justice and righteousness manifest themselves as life in solidarity with the marginalized, rather than *right relationship* within the existing status quo. It requires more than sympathetic patronage to effect spiritual and social transformation.

The theme of justice evoked in verse 16 is repeated in verse 20. The divine shepherd is not just restoring the community from the trauma of exile. God is also creating a set of values and principles that will enhance the welfare of the community from within. The focus is on protecting weak sheep from powerful ones. Restoration is framed in covenantal language (vv. 23, 24) that brings together political/human and divine leadership around oneness: "I will appoint a single shepherd over them." The language of "one" shepherd echoes covenantal language, "the LORD is one" (Deut. 6:4). Although God's unconditional covenant with David is taken up in the promise and work of divine shepherding, that promise is linked to the ongoing relationship between the Divine and the people: "I will be their God." For Ezekiel, the community's relationship with God is unfolding and in need of tending.

Called to speak to God's people in exile, Ezekiel was one of the deportees taken to Babylon in 598/7 BCE (2 Kgs. 24:12–16). It is likely that his entire prophetic and priestly ministry was carried out in the Babylonian Diaspora, including the major Diaspora of 587 that saw the fall of the monarchy and the destruction of the Jerusalem temple. It is from this space of disaster and alienation that Ezekiel speaks to the people and depicts God acting to restore them.

Ezekiel 34 is defined by several features: (a) the prophetic formula, "thus says the LORD," in 34:2, 10, 11, 17, 20; (b) the divine self-commissioning "Here I am" and self-revelatory "I am the LORD" (vv. 11, 24); and (c) a covenantal divine oath, "As I live" (vv. 20, 24). These features reflect the character of the text as prophetic proclamation and as a form of divine self-commissioning. In this proclamation, Ezekiel is not imagining some kind of resurrection by the historical king, nor signaling a form of serial Davidic monarchy. Instead, the association of the ruler with the divine work of shepherding the flock signals that Ezekiel combines prophetic proclamation ("thus says the LORD") and priestly self-commissioning ("here I am") to effect durable sociopolitical and spiritual transformation. God is not just the proclaimer of restoration, but also the doer of restoration.

The passage is a salvation oracle that fits into ancient Near Eastern patterns of national restoration accounts, including (a) the gathering of dispersed people, (b) the renewal of covenantal relation between the people and their Deity, and (c) the installation of indigenous rulership. Conventional ancient Near East accounts follow a judgment-restoration pattern, and the biblical Deuteronomic tradition follows a pattern of sin-punishment-repentance-restoration. Ezekiel does not focus on the people's repentance as a prerequisite for restoration; rather, he focuses on effective leadership, hence the emphases on the shepherd. The choice of a leader is a divine prerogative, established through Moses (Deut. 17:14–20).

The focus on "one shepherd" contrasts Jeremiah's vision of multiple shepherds (Jer. 23:4) and addresses the divisions of the nation into northern and southern kingdoms after the collapse of the united monarchy (1 Kgs. 11–12). In his vision of restoration of the dry bones, Ezekiel repeatedly returns to this theme of oneness (Ezek. 37:15–24). The metaphor of shepherding recognizes the vulnerability of the sheep and establishes the relation between leaders and the people they were intended to serve and lead. The shepherd (David) is described as a servant of the Lord, in contrast to the self-assuming shepherds of 34:1–10; David is positioned in the category of God's servants in the Old Testament, characters who bear a special burden of bringing the divine word and blessing to the community.

This text has a strong connection to Ezekiel's contemporary and immediate predecessor, Jeremiah (Jer. 23:1–8). The similarities between the two texts are striking and suggest that Ezekiel may have used Jeremiah's prophecy or provided an extended commentary on his contemporary's words. However, Ezekiel's work extends beyond his immediate contemporary to include echoes of other biblical texts (Lev. 26). David's rise to political leadership is linked to a narrative tradition about his occupation as a shepherd (1 Sam. 16:11; 17:15, 34–37; Ps. 78:70–71). Moses is called to lead the people out of bondage in the context of his work as a shepherd (Exod. 3); Zipporah and her sisters are portrayed as taking care of their father's flock (Exod. 2:16–19); Rachel is also portrayed as a shepherd of her father's flock (Gen. 29:9). The shepherd was responsible not only for ensuring the protection of the sheep from danger (e.g., the lion, 1 Sam. 17:34–35). A hired shepherd was expected to account for the sheep (cf. Ezek. 20:37; Jer. 33:13; Lev. 27:32) by either paying for lost sheep or providing evidence that the sheep had been killed by a predator (Exod. 22:13; Amos 3:12).

By portraying the Divine as a self-accountable shepherd (cf. Ps. 23), Ezekiel continues a tradition that carries into the New Testament's portrayal of Jesus as the Good Shepherd, as distinct from a hired shepherd (John 10:11–16). Jesus and his ministry stand in a long tradition of theological insight and practical ethos that God's enduring relationship with the world is continuously defined and shaped as that of a concerned shepherd, seeking to bring the world to just and righteous living in community with God, with one another, and with creation.

KENNETH N. NGWA

Commentary 2: Connecting the Reading with the World

In Ezekiel 34, we deal with yet another prophecy from the Lord that reveals God's restorative nature. Ezekiel has warned the people of judgment against Judah, to no avail (Ezek. 33:23–33). Ezekiel has harsh words for the shepherds of his people who have been derelict in their responsibilities (34:1–3, 10), but he has a word of hope for those who are in dire need of some encouragement and healing (vv. 11–16). The shepherds have improved their lives at the expense of the people they were called to serve. The people suffered as a result. God is not pleased and has promised to deal with them in due time. For those suffering from a lack of effective shepherding, the good news is that YHWH will be their shepherd (v. 15). The shepherds having neglected their call to tend the sheep, God takes the "If you want something done right, you have to do it yourself" approach. Disdain for God's flock is something God takes personally.

There have been moments when we have been let down by people we thought were genuine in their desire to help us. As individuals, we have turned to different people in our lives—family members, spouses, clergy, close friends—only to be disappointed. This reading creates an opportunity to remind hearers that, despite this, God has declared that when others are unable or unwilling to help us, God is willing and able. As believers we have discovered over and over again that God has remained consistently faithful when others could not or would not.

Ezekiel proclaims that God is going to search for the sheep that have scattered because of incompetent shepherds (v. 11). God will find the sheep that have made their way to other countries to live in other "pastures," and God will make a place for them. God promises a good pasture, to restore them to a familiar land. The reference to "land" here does not necessarily have to mean a geographical location; it can be likened to a footing, a grip on things, or a solid base from which to begin anew.

Seeing it in this way will provide a springboard to the topic of feeling "lost" in the ups and downs of life. God promises to restore the people who are shoved to the margins of despair, to a place or experience of strength, love, and protection. God also informs them that justice will prevail; those who were tasked with their care, but have instead used and abused them for their own gain, will be brought to account (v. 10). Those who consume others with their mistreatment and injustice will themselves be consumed (v. 16). On the other hand, God will give rest to those who tend to the flock. The flock will graze because there will be plenty of resources (v. 14). God will find those who have strayed and bring them back, bind up their wounds, and help the weak regain their strength. All of this is not going to be done by proxy; God in the fullness of God's presence will see to this. Ezekiel declares that God will shepherd the people with justice (v. 16).

In the world in which we live, there are many who seek a new shepherd. Many people are looking for a new promise and new direction to follow. For whatever reason, people who once lived with hope have been scattered and frayed because of the circumstances of their lives. Economic issues have caused people to scatter and stray from God; family health issues, political disputes, racism, sexism, ageism, and other harms can cause people to lose hope and scatter. More people than we care to admit have strayed or have been nudged away from the flock.

God has promised to bring them back by seeking them out and finding them through Jesus Christ the Savior. Christ mirrors God's call in reaching out to all those who need a shepherd: the lost, the weary, and the brokenhearted (see Luke 4:14–19). Just as God seeks out all of those who are scattered, so that they may have the opportunity to find rest, so too Christ reaches out so that those who are on the fringes may find a sense of peace and a place to belong. In our economic and other life challenges, God wants to offer us peace. God, through Christ, seeks us out and reminds us that God wants to help us carry the load we bear in our lives.

Ezekiel's oracle about the Lord looking for the sheep is not simply about shepherds sleeping on the job. God also has something to say about how the sheep treat one another. God will judge between the fat and the lean sheep (Ezek. 34:20). How the sheep have treated each other will be a factor in the divine judgment. Sheep who have shoved and butted the weaker sheep have created a kind of separation between them (v. 21). This brings us to the Gospel reading in Matthew 25:31–46. The sheep, those who will inherit the blessings of God, are the ones who have fed the hungry, given the thirsty water to drink, clothed the naked, and taken in the stranger (Matt. 25:33–36).

Is it possible that the stranger in our midst whom we are called to take in is one of the scattered sheep to which God is wanting us to tend? Will our actions merit Jesus' words, "Truly I tell you, just as you did it to one of the least of these who are members of my family, you did it to me" (Matt. 25:40)? Or will we be those who are "accursed" (v. 41) like the shepherds and the sheep who took advantage of the weak (Ezek. 34:10, 20–22)?

When we look at the challenges that we face, many of our struggles come from poor direction. Without the proper guidance from a faithful shepherd, we do not know how to relate to people, respecting and treating them as children of God. In the in-your-face culture in which we live, people are constantly shoving and butting one another for position and placement, competing for status, resources, or the opportunity to be noticed.

God still speaks up—through you and me—on behalf of those who are pushed to the side. God has a place for those who seem to be left on the margins, forgotten, or just plain ignored. God has a plan for all of God's flock; no one is dispensable to God. For this reason, God calls and sends faithful shepherds—servants of God and, therefore, of God's people—for us to follow. For Israel, that servant shepherd would be a Davidic ruler who would lead the people and tend to their needs (v. 23). He would make it so that they could feel confident and have the resources for the necessities of life.

As believers, we know that David was the precursor for the coming of Jesus into the world. As far as examples go, David did the best he could. David was a man after God's own heart (1 Sam. 13:14; Acts 13:22), but Jesus had the heart of God, as he says, "The Father and I are one" (John 10:30). Thus Christian believers look to Jesus Christ as the best example of a shepherd for our journey, for he is the Good Shepherd (John 10:11). We see the love of God in the care and concern of Christ for us, and for others, and we walk in the belief that no matter where we are, as a part of the flock, Jesus is always looking out for all of us.

WM. MARCUS SMALL

Proper 29 (Reign of Christ)

Psalm 95:1–7a

¹O come, let us sing to the L<small>ORD</small>;
  let us make a joyful noise to the rock of our salvation!
²Let us come into his presence with thanksgiving;
  let us make a joyful noise to him with songs of praise!
³For the L<small>ORD</small> is a great God,
  and a great King above all gods.
⁴In his hand are the depths of the earth;
  the heights of the mountains are his also.
⁵The sea is his, for he made it,
  and the dry land, which his hands have formed.

⁶O come, let us worship and bow down,
  let us kneel before the L<small>ORD</small>, our Maker!
⁷For he is our God,
  and we are the people of his pasture,
  and the sheep of his hand.

Psalm 100

¹Make a joyful noise to the L<small>ORD</small>, all the earth.
  ²Worship the L<small>ORD</small> with gladness;
  come into his presence with singing.

³Know that the L<small>ORD</small> is God.
  It is he that made us, and we are his;
  we are his people, and the sheep of his pasture.

⁴Enter his gates with thanksgiving,
  and his courts with praise.
  Give thanks to him, bless his name.

⁵For the L<small>ORD</small> is good;
  his steadfast love endures forever,
  and his faithfulness to all generations.

Connecting the Psalm with Scripture and Worship

Both psalms appointed for this day are considered "kingship" psalms. Psalm 95 includes clear references to God as king; "the L<small>ORD</small> is a great God, and a great King above all gods" (Ps. 95:3). Although Psalm 100 does not use the language of kingship, it sounds similar notes to the previous group of kingship psalms.

Those worship planners who are particularly concerned with expansive language for God might consult the inclusive language version of the Psalter that appears in both *Evangelical*

Lutheran Worship, the worship book of the Evangelical Lutheran Church in America, and the *Book of Common Worship* of the Presbyterian Church (U.S.A.).[1] In this version, the word "ruler" is used instead of "king," and the language of Psalm 100 has been altered to remove masculine pronouns for God (e.g., "we are God's people and the sheep of God's pasture" in v. 3).

Both psalms are chosen to serve as responses to the same passage, Ezekiel 34:11–16, 20–24, which portrays God as a shepherd. Similarly, both psalms refer to God's people as the sheep of God's pasture. The Gospel narrative for the day, Matthew 25:31–46, features the Son of Man who comes in glory, seated on a throne like a king. When worshipers gather on this final Sunday of the Christian year, they proclaim that Jesus Christ is the ruler of all, who separates the just from the unjust and ushers in a realm of plenty and peace for all.

Psalm 95. This psalm is a call to worship, summoning God's people into the presence of their Creator so they may sing out their thanks and praise with joy (vv. 1–2). God is lauded as the greatest of all gods and likened to a king (v. 3). As if to prove her point, the psalmist describes why this ruler is so great. God holds the entire cosmos in divine hands: earth's lowest depths and its highest heights, both the dry land and the sea (vv. 4–5). God has made all of creation, including the people of the earth, and this is reason enough to worship. Yet the people do not worship a God who reigns from some lofty throne; rather, this God is like a shepherd to them, giving them shelter and care, and they are like God's sheep.

This psalm is a beautifully exuberant response to the first reading from Ezekiel, which is an extended metaphor portraying God as a good shepherd. This shepherd promises to go out after the sheep that have been scattered and rescue them from the farthest reaches. He will restore the refugees to their fold and bring home those who have been driven away by war and oppression. This shepherd will feed those who have been hungry and give rest to those who are weary. He will heal the wounded and restore them to strength. Yet this caring and nurturing shepherd will also ensure that those who have grown comfortable and powerful by trampling over others can never take advantage of anyone again. The greedy ones and the bullies will be sent away; God the good shepherd will "feed them with justice" (Ezek. 34:16).

This passage from Ezekiel carries echoes of Psalm 23; the shepherd feeds the sheep by streams of water, lets them graze in good pastures, and makes them lie down. It also resonates with the Gospel reading for the day, Matthew 25:31–46. In the Matthew text, the enthroned Son of Man separates the righteous sheep from the unrighteous goats, judging them by whether or not they treated others with mercy and compassion. Both Ezekiel and Matthew make it clear that righteousness is directly related to caring for those who need it most; there is no room in the realm of God for selfishness, greed, or exploitation.

To join in singing Psalm 95, then, is to praise God for being concerned with the welfare of all people and rooting out injustice. This is the God whom Israel worships. This is the God who watches over Israel and does not slumber or sleep (Ps. 121:4).

The entire psalm can be used as opening sentences (or call to worship), as it calls the people to give their thanks and praise. Metrical settings of this psalm would serve well as opening hymns of praise; "Come, Worship God" and "O Come and Sing unto the Lord" are two examples.[2] Verses 6 and 7 might be used before the first reading (and after the prayer for illumination, if one is used) to encourage attending to the reading of the Word. *Psalms for All Seasons: A Complete Psalter for Worship* includes still more metrical settings, along with several responsive settings (where the congregation sings a refrain) and one setting written in four parts that allows chanting by the assembly or by an ensemble.

---

1. *Evangelical Lutheran Worship* (Minneapolis: Augsburg Fortress, 2006); *Book of Common Worship* (Louisville, KY: Westminster John Knox, 2018).
2. "Come, Worship God," with text by Michael Perry and music based on seventeenth- and nineteenth-century French musical sources, can be found in *Glory to God: The Presbyterian Hymnal* (Louisville, KY: Westminster John Knox, 2013), 386. "O Come and Sing unto the Lord," also found in *Glory to God*, 638, features a metrical version of Psalm 95, written in 1909, and an anonymous tune.

Psalm 100. This psalm may be among the most well-known in the Psalter. It is the quintessential call to worship, beginning with verses 1 and 2:

> Make a joyful noise to the LORD, all the earth.
> Worship the LORD with gladness;
> come into his presence with singing.

The people are enjoined to worship God because the Lord is their creator. God is like their shephed; therefore they are like the sheep of God's pasture. This God is like the good shepherd portrayed in Ezekiel 34: good, known for love that is steadfast and eternal, faithful to every generation.

As a psalm of praise, Psalm 100 could be used in multiple places during a worship service. In addition to serving as a call to worship, this psalm could also be sung as a response to the declaration of forgiveness that follows confession. The myriad settings of this psalm make it available to be sung by congregations, cantors, and choirs; furthermore, the text of this psalm has been set in numerous musical styles.

Some of the church's most familiar hymns are based on Psalm 100, among them "All People That on Earth Do Dwell," "We Praise You, O God, Our Redeemer, Creator," "Praise Ye the Lord, the Almighty," "Let All Things Now Living," and "Now Thank We All Our God." Several shorter songs or choruses based on Psalm 100 would work well as introits or processionals, sung by choirs of either adults or children. Such refrains as "In the Lord I'll Be Ever Thankful" and "Raise a Song of Gladness/Jubilate Deo" from the Taizé community would also lend themselves to use around the time of the offering. "God, We Honor You" features a simple tune that lends itself well to children's voices and would also be fitting to use at the time of the offering.[3]

It is instructive that both psalms appointed for Reign of Christ are songs of uninhibited praise. As we contemplate the return of Christ and the transformation of the world as we know it, we need not fear, for what God intends for the whole world—a reign of justice and peace—is good news for us all.

KIMBERLY BRACKEN LONG

---

[3]. *Glory to God*, 654, 155, and 709.

Proper 29 (Reign of Christ)

Ephesians 1:15–23

[15] I have heard of your faith in the Lord Jesus and your love toward all the saints, and for this reason [16] I do not cease to give thanks for you as I remember you in my prayers. [17] I pray that the God of our Lord Jesus Christ, the Father of glory, may give you a spirit of wisdom and revelation as you come to know him, [18] so that, with the eyes of your heart enlightened, you may know what is the hope to which he has called you, what are the riches of his glorious inheritance among the saints, [19] and what is the immeasurable greatness of his power for us who believe, according to the working of his great power. [20] God put this power to work in Christ when he raised him from the dead and seated him at his right hand in the heavenly places, [21] far above all rule and authority and power and dominion, and above every name that is named, not only in this age but also in the age to come. [22] And he has put all things under his feet and has made him the head over all things for the church, [23] which is his body, the fullness of him who fills all in all.

Commentary 1: Connecting the Reading with Scripture

Gratitude and the celebration of Christian identity frame the opening chapter of Ephesians, offering encouragement to communities of faith as it addresses the unique role of the church in this world and its relationship to Christ. Tradition has it that this letter was written as one of the prison letters of Paul, as were the letters to the Colossians and Philemon. Notwithstanding divergent views about the authorship and intended recipients of this letter, its message is consistent with the apostle Paul's care and concern for discipling and equipping the rapidly growing communities of faith in Asia Minor (current Turkey). At its center is an affirmation of what God has accomplished through the raising up of Jesus Christ from the dead and the ramifications of that cosmic act for the world, a world in which God's power is demonstrated by caring for the vulnerable and "the least of these" as framed in Matthew 25:45.

In what could be a liturgical prayer of intercession for the church today, the author offers a series of petitions responding to the cultural challenges experienced by the faithful of that region and time. A center of social and civic influence, Ephesus was home to many beliefs, including Gnosticism (from the Greek term *gnōsis* or "knowledge"). Gnostics taught a duality between the divine and humanity, the material and the spiritual, thus "driving a wedge between God and creation."[1] The church is being encouraged to pursue a deeper spirit of "wisdom and revelation" beyond Greek and Roman practices that included the cultic worship of gods and goddesses, such as Artemis, the Greek goddess of the hunt, childbirth, and virginity, and protector of young girls. The writer offers an alternative response to questions concerning the fear of the unknown and the mysteries of life. This prayer for continued insight urges believers to remain steadfast before rival beliefs and teachings that could divert them from their faith in Christ (Eph. 4:14; 5:6).

While affirming the hope (mentioned again in 4:4) to which God has called this community of faith, this prayer also reminds them of their inheritance (introduced in 1:14), which will come when Christ returns and reigns above the whole of creation, making right all that is broken. This Christian hope is grounded in the cosmic act caused by God at the resurrection of Jesus, defying the powers of death and sin for

---

1. Ralph P. Martin, *Ephesians, Colossians, and Philemon*, Interpretation (Louisville, KY: Westminster John Knox, 1991), 2.

all creation. The resurrection, however, does not tell the whole story. In a world obsessed with power, this Pauline writer reminds believers that the crucified and resurrected Jesus was elevated to God's right hand, where he continues to be seated (Matt. 25:31). Foreshadowed in Psalm 110:1, this image reaffirms and establishes God's sovereign power over all creation, with Jesus at God's side (Eph. 1:20). It echoes across the centuries in the prophetic voice of Ezekiel, who speaks of God's ultimate victory as one of a shepherd who will protect and seek out the flock, destroying the strong while strengthening the weak (Ezek. 34:10–22). Such language stands in contrast to the images of power often framing human understanding.

In this case, the writer is addressing the political and imperial rulers, and cultic practices that sought to demonstrate their power by influencing people and events, while seeking to control the uncontrollable mysteries of life. Believers are reminded of God's cosmic victory over death in the resurrection of Jesus. They are reminded that "this same power, the power seen at Easter and now vested in Jesus, is available to them."[2] It is this resurrection power that will ultimately bring about the transformation of the world.

The question of how that transformation is worked out in the world leads to the final verses, which speak to the presence and role of the church (Eph. 1:22–23). Building on Paul's understanding of the church, this letter strengthens the relationship between Christ and the body by uniting the two, body and head (1:22–23; 4:15–16; 5:29–30). This metaphor reinforces the importance of the unity of the body known as the church, with Christ as its head. Through this reality, God's grace has birthed a new humanity (2:16) to which both Jews and Gentiles belong as one family, echoing familiar themes found in Paul's letters to the Galatians (Gal. 3:28–29) and the Corinthians (1 Cor. 12:12–13), in which barriers of race, culture, and social status are removed. It is this new humanity that will reflect the values of Christ on this earth. In a world that uses divisions to separate one from another, the church is to work to bring about unity wherever it is found, in the name of the one who has broken down those divisions with his life, death, and resurrection.

As we reflect on the words of this text, it is evident that the Pauline writer is anticipating and responding to real and contemporary challenges that, if left unaddressed, could tempt new believers to turn back to their previous non-Christian beliefs and practices. The writer is concerned with how those beliefs and practices could deceive new believers (Eph. 5:6), causing them to fall away from the centrality of their new faith. By keeping the readers aware of the world around them, the writer strengthens their understanding, preparing them for possible stumbling blocks along their faith journey.

It is apparent that we also live in a time when current cultural teachings perpetuate an understanding of power that often counters the values of our faith, including the upside-down order of the kingdom of God. These values can be summed up in Micah 6:8 in God's call to "do justice, and to love kindness, and to walk humbly with your God." They are reflected in the words of Jesus as he shares the two great commandments in Matthew 22:37–40 that call us to love God and one another.

As we consider the challenges for the faithful in our pews, it seems appropriate to ponder ways our culture has perpetuated the quest for an individualism that sacrifices the common good. What are these forces causing us to turn from God and one another, prompting division and indifference, even within our churches? What are the values of Christ that inform the work of the body when we are faced with hunger, homelessness, and injustice in a cultural climate where differences of race, class, and political views cause disunity and unrest?

The prayers offered in the Pauline letters offer a conviction that can move believers from their individual knees and petitions into incarnational actions reflecting the grace of Jesus Christ. The prayers of this letter call and compel believers beyond a moment of private reflection into a lifestyle that embodies the love of God and neighbor: the new humanity that the church is

---

2. N. T. Wright, *Paul for Everyone: The Prison Letters: Ephesians, Philippians, Colossians, and Philemon* (Louisville, KY: Westminster John Knox, 2004), 16.

A Communion That Can Endure

The most important thing for the man who is to submit himself to God is surely that he should be absolutely certain of the reality of God, and Jesus does establish in us, through the fact of His personal life, a certainty of God which is superior to every doubt. When once He has attracted us by the beauty of His Person, and made us bow before Him by its exalted character, then even amid our deepest doubts the Person of Jesus will remain present with us as a thing incomparable, the most precious fact in history, and the most precious fact our life contains. If we then yield to His attraction and come to feel with deep reverence how His strength and purity disclose to us the impurity and weakness of our souls, then His mighty claim comes home to us. We learn to share His invincible confidence that He can uplift and bless perfectly those who do not turn away from Him. In this confidence in the Person and cause of Jesus is implied the idea of a Power greater than all things, which will see to it that Jesus, who lost His life in this world, shall be none the less victorious over the world. The thought of such a Power lays hold of us as firmly as did the impression of the Person of Jesus by which we were overwhelmed. It is the beginning of the consciousness within us that there is a living God. This is the only real beginning of an inward submission to Him. . . . The man who has felt these simple experiences cannot possibly attribute them to any other source. The God in whom he now believes for Jesus' sake, is as real and living to him as the man Jesus is in His marvelous sublimity of character. The idea of a Power supreme over all things wins a marvelous vividness for us because we are obliged to pay to Jesus the homage of believing that He must certainly succeed, even if all the world besides be against Him. The Omnipotence of which we become conscious in this way must be wielded by that same purpose which produced the life-work of Jesus.

Thus God makes Himself known to us as the Power that is with Jesus in such a way that amid all our distractions and the mist of doubt He can never again entirely vanish from us. We are obliged, then, to confess that the existence of Jesus in this world of ours is the fact in which God so touches us as to come into a communion with us that can endure.

Wilhelm Hermann, *The Communion of the Christian with God*, ed. Robert T. Voelkel (Philadelphia: Fortress, 1971), 97–98.

---

called to be and nurture. Prayer is understood as the fuel for responding to the challenges around us, while also making the work of reconciliation possible. The liturgical sounds of this prayerful letter remind our hearts to sing of the glory and the power of which we are a part, affirming our identity as a people "blessed in Christ" (1:3). In a world where prayer is seen by many as passive and nonresponsive, it would be appropriate to consider how the prayers spoken in Sunday morning worship inspire and translate into concrete action on Monday morning, actions reflecting the transformative reign of Christ among us.

RUTH FAITH SANTANA-GRACE

Commentary 2: Connecting the Reading with the World

The fact that Ephesians was likely originally penned as an open letter, not to a particular church or in response to a particular local conflict, makes it somewhat easier to connect to a contemporary audience. The preacher need not explain the complexities of an ancient theological debate or identify a parallel situation in her own community. The passage very nearly stands on its own, a prayer of thanksgiving that could be offered for any group of faithful people in any time and place.

Beautiful turns of phrase grace almost every verse in this passage: "a spirit of wisdom and revelation," "with the eyes of your heart enlightened," "the immeasurable greatness of his power." The poetic nature of the letter captures—as poetry so often does—something that is not otherwise easily expressed. Such poetic language is necessary in proclaiming the gospel, asserts Old Testament scholar Walter Brueggemann, who calls for preaching that offers "poetry in a prose-flattened world."[3] The poetic language throughout the letter, but particularly in this passage, brings to mind the language of liturgies and hymns, or the lofty vocabulary of one recently in love. We might even think of Ephesians as a love letter to the body of Christ, flowing from gratitude to adoration to inspiration. Could the preacher take a cue from the lyrical tone of Ephesians and craft her own love letter to her congregation, or to the church at large?

The liturgical timing of this passage offers a number of connections that can enrich our reading of the text. As it is usually read on the Sunday before or after Thanksgiving, this love letter to the church can prompt reflection on our own practices of gratitude and prayer. Who are the saints we have loved? For what or whom do we give thanks without ceasing? How does our lived faithfulness express our gratitude for what we have been given?

Many congregations will read this passage on what they name Christ the King Sunday. While this designation conveys an important truth, that Christ's power and authority are higher than that of any of the powers and authorities on earth (more on this momentarily), one might be cautious of the patriarchal and gendered language involved in observing this as an ecclesial holiday. Some traditions have taken to using Reign of Christ to avoid the gendered language.

Whatever we call it, this Sunday is also the final Sunday of the church year and the Sunday before Advent begins. This provides an opportunity to remind congregations about the liturgical calendar and why it matters. Most casual churchgoers are likely oblivious to the liturgical timekeeping that goes on in front of them every week. In Godly Play, a worshipful way of teaching Bible stories to young children, the storyteller introduces the liturgical calendar as "how the church tells time." The story begins with time as a straight line; as the story proceeds, it becomes a circle as the two ends of the line meet. "Now the ending is the beginning and the beginning is the ending," the storyteller says.[4] Time, for the church, is not linear but cyclical. So, on the last Sunday of the church year, the end becomes the beginning again. Understanding the rhythm of the church year helps us live in the time between, in the "already and not yet," in this age as we look with hope to the age to come.

This passage ends with bold assertions: that Christ is "far above all rule and authority and power and dominion," and that the church is the body of Christ. Readers steeped in church language their whole lives may not notice just how bold and countercultural these claims are. If Christ transcends all powers on earth and the church is Christ's body, then it naturally follows that the church is no longer beholden to the authorities of this age. Of course, this does not mean we ought to skip out on parking tickets and avoid paying our taxes. How we live in this world as citizens of our own communities must, first and foremost, be determined by our loyalty to the way of God and our belonging in the body of Christ. "So what is the political meaning of the Kingdom of God?" asks theologian Marcus Borg. "In a sentence: it is what life would be like on earth if God were king and the rulers of this world were not."[5] The letter to the Ephesians challenges us to consider what earthly powers Christ stands against and above.

Reflecting on what it means to be the body of a Christ who transcends earthly powers, we might turn to the words often attributed to Teresa of Ávila: "Christ has no body on earth but yours. Yours are the feet with which he walks to do good; yours are the hands with which he blesses all the world." The lived reality of following Jesus takes on new and dramatic meaning. Yes, we use our hands and feet—the body of Christ—to feed the hungry and house the homeless and clothe the poor. Also, if we are to take Ephesians seriously, we must challenge the very powers that oppose the way of God.

---

3. Walter Brueggemann, *Finally Comes the Poet: Daring Speech for Proclamation* (Minneapolis: Augsburg Fortress, 1989), 1.
4. Sonja M. Stewart and Jerome W. Berryman, *Young Children and Worship* (Louisville, KY: Westminster John Knox, 1989), 126.
5. Marcus Borg, *The Heart of Christianity: Rediscovering a Life of Faith* (New York: HarperCollins, 2004), 132. Borg credits the point to a 2002 presentation by John Dominic Crossan at Trinity Episcopal Cathedral in Portland, OR.

Here the preacher could tell stories of those who have courageously defied the authority of earthly powers in favor of following the authority of the kingdom of God: Dietrich Bonhoeffer and Óscar Romero come to mind, as do Harriet Tubman and Martin Luther King Jr., along with so many others who championed the cause of civil rights. In our own time, William Barber's New Poor People's Campaign for a living wage, the Me Too movement against sexual harassment and assault, and the student-led March for Our Lives that calls for an end to gun violence are all examples of faithful efforts to push back against the rulers of our age by calling us to lives of freedom, justice, and peace.

Such examples are inspiring to be sure, and people in our pews may indeed be called to prophetic truth-telling, political action, and civil disobedience. It also behooves the preacher to suggest some ways to oppose the earthly ruling powers in subtler, less dramatic ways. What would it be like if we put our loyalty first to the way of Christ? How would that affect the way we vote, where we shop, or how we spend our time? In what ways are we acquiescing to earthly authorities without even realizing it? How do we determine which authorities are in line with the kingdom of God and which are not? Such questions will provide rich fodder for preaching and discussion.

Poised here on the brink of a new church year, when endings become beginnings, this poetic passage from Ephesians can stir us from our complacency and call us to new life as we witness to the one who is above all earthly powers, and who loves us in this age and in the age to come.

LEE HULL MOSES

Proper 29 (Reign of Christ)

Matthew 25:31–46

³¹"When the Son of Man comes in his glory, and all the angels with him, then he will sit on the throne of his glory. ³²All the nations will be gathered before him, and he will separate people one from another as a shepherd separates the sheep from the goats, ³³and he will put the sheep at his right hand and the goats at the left. ³⁴Then the king will say to those at his right hand, 'Come, you that are blessed by my Father, inherit the kingdom prepared for you from the foundation of the world; ³⁵for I was hungry and you gave me food, I was thirsty and you gave me something to drink, I was a stranger and you welcomed me, ³⁶I was naked and you gave me clothing, I was sick and you took care of me, I was in prison and you visited me.' ³⁷Then the righteous will answer him, 'Lord, when was it that we saw you hungry and gave you food, or thirsty and gave you something to drink? ³⁸And when was it that we saw you a stranger and welcomed you, or naked and gave you clothing? ³⁹And when was it that we saw you sick or in prison and visited you?' ⁴⁰And the king will answer them, 'Truly I tell you, just as you did it to one of the least of these who are members of my family, you did it to me.' ⁴¹Then he will say to those at his left hand, 'You that are accursed, depart from me into the eternal fire prepared for the devil and his angels; ⁴²for I was hungry and you gave me no food, I was thirsty and you gave me nothing to drink, ⁴³I was a stranger and you did not welcome me, naked and you did not give me clothing, sick and in prison and you did not visit me.' ⁴⁴Then they also will answer, 'Lord, when was it that we saw you hungry or thirsty or a stranger or naked or sick or in prison, and did not take care of you?' ⁴⁵Then he will answer them, 'Truly I tell you, just as you did not do it to one of the least of these, you did not do it to me.' ⁴⁶And these will go away into eternal punishment, but the righteous into eternal life."

Commentary 1: Connecting the Reading with Scripture

Finally, after three parables anticipating the coming of the Son of Man, the text turns to what happens when the Son of Man finally "comes in his glory, and all the angels with him" (Matt. 25:31). This final judgment scene is packed with metaphors and examples, with the separation of the nations as "a shepherd separates the sheep from the goats" (v. 32), and an illustration of who will inherit the kingdom. Matthew returns to the consequences of "the eternal fire prepared for the devil and his angels" (v. 41) and "eternal punishment" (v. 46) referenced in the prior passage (v. 30) and several other times in Matthew. There are real consequences for not giving food to the hungry or drink to the thirsty, not welcoming the stranger or clothing the naked.

This falls immediately before the passage in which we learn of the conspiracy to arrest and execute Jesus in the final week of his ministry. It is Jesus' last time to teach his followers. The parables preceding this emphasize being ready at any time for the return of the Son of Man (v. 13: "Keep awake therefore, for you know neither the day nor the hour"), and the judgment of the master on the trustworthy and untrustworthy, the wise and the wicked slave put in charge of supervising the household (24:45–51), the faithful and unfaithful given stewardship of talents (25:14–30). The judgment of the bridegroom means the foolish bridesmaids are shut out of the celebration (vv. 10–13), while the master's judgment bestows favor on "faithful and wise" or "trustworthy" slaves (24:46–47;

25:21, 23). The consequences are dire, if not terrifying; the wicked are condemned to "the outer darkness where there will be weeping and gnashing of teeth" (25:30), or they will be cut into pieces where, along with the hypocrites, they will experience "weeping and gnashing of teeth" (24:51).

While this seems so harsh in many contemporary Christian contexts where the predominant theme is God's love and grace, it fits perfectly into Matthew's frequent references to judgment (8:12; 13:42; 13:50; 22:13; 24:51; and 25:30). This passage is an opportunity for the preacher to dwell a bit on judgment, thereby complicating and deepening what we know of Jesus. A sermon could explore how and why Jesus could be portrayed as both merciful—open to sharing the good news with those beyond the Jewish community—and serious about the final judgment.

This final judgment of the Son of Man will be comprehensive, gathering "all the nations" 25:32). The inclusive theme flows throughout Matthew from beginning to end. The genealogy in Matthew 1, for instance, includes Gentile women who join the people of Israel (Rahab, Tamar, Ruth, and Bathsheba) and are considered ancestors of Jesus. Matthew concludes with a command to "go . . . and make disciples of all nations" (28:19). This is unique to Matthew. Matthew refers thirteen times to "the nations," meaning Gentiles.[1]

In the final judgment, the Son of Man will sort and separate people as a shepherd separates the sheep and goats. It was common in Palestine for goats and sheep to be kept together in flocks. Goats are willful, but useful. In contrast, sheep are extremely dependent, requiring a shepherd to bring them to graze, give them water, and protect them from other animals. Shepherds are their leaders, and sheep come to recognize the sound of their shepherd's voice. In the Old Testament reading for the week, Ezekiel 34:17, God is portrayed as the shepherd and the judge between sheep and rams. God protects the sheep (Ezek. 34:14), ensuring they are grazing on good pasture. Likewise, Psalm 100:3 assures the listeners that "we are [God's] people, and the sheep of [God's] pasture." This casting of the Son of Man as shepherd would have been a familiar analogy for the Jewish hearers of Matthew's Gospel.

This specific list of criteria for judgment of the nations may be a reference to those Gentiles who act with generosity toward those followers of Jesus who go out to teach about Jesus. However, there are clear implications for those hearing this list of behaviors by which the nations will be judged.

In Matthew 25:35–44, the list of actions the Son of Man cites as having done to him through caring for others is repeated in the positive three times, and in the negative once. Good works are judged, and the result is the expansion of the circle. Neither belief itself nor religious identity is the distinguishing mark of those who will go to eternal life.

The surprise expressed by the hearers in verse 37 ("Lord, when was it that we saw you?") indicates that the Son of Man perceived these acts of mercy and justice carried out with no expectation or promise of any reward. These actions take on a particular purity; rather than extending generosity and care for personal gain, these outsiders appear to be untainted by a desire to get something for giving. There is no quid pro quo. These self-giving actions do not emerge from a vacuum, however; they take precedence throughout the Scriptures.

Outsiders in Genesis are judged by how they treat Abraham and his descendants (Gen. 12:3). Deuteronomy 10:18 (as well as Deut. 14:29; 24:17; 26:12, and other passages) urges special care of the widow, the orphan, and the stranger, and 24:19–21 mandates enough grain, olives, and grapes be left behind at harvest so the widow, the orphan, and the stranger—the most vulnerable people—could glean enough to eat.

Taking care of the hungry is expected of Jesus' followers, and this was taken seriously in the early church. Acts 6:1 refers to the feeding of widows, for instance. Caring for those in prison was a life-and-death matter; prisoners subsisted on what was brought to them by visitors. The preacher might explore these particular acts of compassion and what they indicate about the

---

1. Daniel J. Harrington, SJ, *The Gospel of Matthew*, Sacra pagina 1 (Collegeville, MN: Liturgical, 2007), 356.

ongoing work of the church. How do these connect with the love and grace of God? How do these acts demonstrate that love and grace as a living witness?

Rather than emphasizing that those of us who are Gentiles can give a sigh of relief that eternal life is open to us, a sermon could raise the possibility that this passage tells us that it is those outside of our group who may receive eternal life based on their compassionate actions. What does this say about the boundaries of faith? Of salvation? Of judgment? Righteousness may not be judged by group membership, adherence to general group norms, or following the rules of group behavior, but by concrete acts of compassion toward all people. Even those who are not members of our congregation, our community, our religion, may be judged as performing acts of loving-kindness to the Son of Man himself.

A sermon could grapple with the unknown timing of the Son of Man and what we should be about while we await his return. While in the preceding chapter we learn that we do not know the hour or the day, we face no uncertainty about what we are to do in the meantime. The hearers receive a clear directive, something onto which we can hold in the midst of our questions about how we are to live as trustworthy, faithful servants until his return in glory . . . and in judgment.

LAURA MARIKO CHEIFETZ

Commentary 2: Connecting the Reading with the World

Ethical observation suggests that individuals are more likely to take action on behalf of someone they know well or are close to, in contrast to a stranger. This is called a proximity factor: the closer someone is, the closer the impact of the action, the more likely one is to act. Proximity is not always geographic; it can be based on relationship, years of knowledge, and so on. Family is often the primary reference point for this kind of proximity. The passage often referred to as the "Sheep and Goats" responds to this ethical issue by exponentially expanding and preferentially delineating the definition of family, while raising practical questions about charity.

The beginning of the passage situates Jesus in a familial relationship to God and humans. In this passage, after asserting Jesus' role as Son of Man in verse 31, Matthew's Jesus refers to God as Father in verse 34 and to inheritance rights. Matthew juxtaposes Jesus' use of "Father" for God with a rejection of earthly fathers in an effort to strengthen the family of believers; they have a new family origin and belonging. Those named as in need (the hungry, thirsty, stranger, naked, sick, prisoner) are also members of Jesus' family (Matt. 25:40). In this new family configuration, ethical action is based not on prior relationship or closeness but on need. Furthermore, doing something for the "least of these" is the equivalent of doing so for Jesus.

Similarly, in Ezekiel 34:11–16, God is imaged as a different kind of shepherd, in contradistinction to failed kings. God is one who seeks the lost, binds the injured, and strengthens the weak (Ezek. 34:16). The *mujerista* theologian Ada María Isasi-Díaz suggests a renaming of kingdom of God to kin-dom. While kingdom carries both male (king) and "hierarchical and elitist" meanings, Isasi-Díaz writes, "'Kin-dom' makes it clear that when the fullness of God becomes a day-to-day reality in the world at large, we will all be sisters and brothers [siblings]—kin to each other: we will indeed be the family of God."[2] This invites an eschatological—here and not yet—interpretation of the family of God. If one helps those whom Jesus already considers family, they too will be welcomed into the family.

For a newly forming Christian community awaiting the imminent return of Jesus—the Parousia—the passage is direct and clear. The God incarnate, Jesus, will be gone, but his presence will be experienced in a new way. Whenever we help a fellow human, we are helping Jesus.

---

2. Ada Maria Isasi-Díaz, *Mujerista Theology: A Theology for the Twenty-First Century* (Maryknoll, NY: Orbis, 1996), 103, n. 8.

This changes the popular adage "What would Jesus do?" to "Do I recognize Jesus in you?" Paul's prayer in Ephesians 1:15–23 praises the community for living this ethic in Jesus' absence. Paul also reminds them that Christ is now ruler over the church (Eph. 1:21–22) and that with the Parousia will come judgment. There are specific and significant actions one must take in response to specific individuals in order to show one's faithfulness for eternal life (Matt. 25:46).

Simple, right? Dorothy Day, the founder of the Catholic Worker movement, believed the instruction was simple, but living it out was difficult. The Catholic Worker movement is founded on the corporal works of mercy that come from this passage.[3] She and other Catholic Workers took the passage literally, dedicating their lives to these practices. This radical choice is not one many people are willing to make. Are the rest then bound for eternal punishment? Every day we make moral distinctions striving for an honest assessment of our responsibilities and potentialities. Only some are capable of saintly living like Dorothy Day.

The reading of this passage often comes on New Year's Day and, in Year A, on Reign of Christ, the Sunday prior to Advent. The timing may serve as a call to renew basic Christian commitments. Those commitments might comprise immediate responses, such as providing charity. In the "Neighborhood of Good" campaign launched by State Farm Insurance in 2017, an advertisement updates the message of Matthew 25:31–46 by having "the needy" follow around an ordinary man until he finally responds by volunteering at a youth center. He responds to a community need, rather than every need presenting itself. Perhaps the passage is a call to reorient ourselves to the radical ethical shift Jesus' birth brings about. Jesus is in fact a different kind of king, more often found with the least of these. His solidarity with the disenfranchised reconfigures the status quo for royalty and religious leaders.

For many, this passage establishes God's preferential option for the poor, a concept that gained popularity with the liberation theology movement. Because the naked, sick, hungry, prisoner, and so on are already part of God's family, we are not only to respond to their needs first; we are to place them at the center of theological and ethical inquiry. How would church council meetings operate differently if the central question was, Are we helping the poor? Yet being sick, hungry, prisoner, or stranger is not and should not be a permanent status. For example, one is not always a prisoner. Some are born with particular illnesses, and others become ill.

The passage, read literally, suggests the status of the least of these is permanent, as is their membership in Jesus' family. The response of charity by another does not change their status; it offers only temporary relief. Canadian musician Aubrey "Drake" Graham and his hit song and video "God's Plan" gained acclaim when he gave away the video's budget of $996,631.90 for scholarships, a women's shelter, an after-school youth program, and food, cars, and cash for those in need. Drake gives directly to those in need without judgment. Charity meets immediate needs, but it does not solve the root causes. Global poverty, entrenched homelessness, mass incarceration, and health disparities are linked to systemic causes.

The passage does not blame the individuals for suffering caused by systems of injustice; rather, Jesus calls others to respond. Is feeding the hungry, clothing the naked, and visiting the prisoner enough? Are we only to respond when we *see* the need? Many isolate themselves from ever seeing individuals affected by homelessness, poverty, incarceration, and health disparities. Are we to respond only with charity? Some may visit the prisoner; others may support the Campaign for Youth Justice, a nonprofit organization working to change the systemic impact of incarceration and crime for youth in the United States. Social change is a combination of individual and systemic change.[4] After all, systems of oppression are held in place by the collective impact of individual actions or inaction.

---

3. See "Works of Mercy," Catholic Worker Movement, https://www.catholicworker.org/works-of-mercy.html; and Elizabeth Hinson-Hasty, *Dorothy Day for Armchair Theologians* (Louisville, KY: Westminster John Knox, 2014), 36.

4. See *To Do Justice: A Guide for Progressive Christians*, ed. Rebecca Todd Peters and Elizabeth Hinson-Hasty (Louisville, KY: Westminster John Knox, 2008).

A church that shares communion at a table swelling with bags of donated groceries and invests in legislation and in organizations that promote food sustainability models one multifaceted example of a theologically rooted, charitable, and justice-based response. Faith communities and families make difficult decisions about resources of time, money, and care; Matthew's concept of God's family requires Christians to reorient in creative and concrete ways the bounds and priorities for deployment of these resources.

KATE OTT

Contributors

EFRAÍN AGOSTO, Vice President for Academic Affairs and Academic Dean, Professor of New Testament Studies, New York Theological Seminary, New York, NY

SAMMY G. ALFARO, Professor of Theology, Grand Canyon Theological Seminary, Phoenix, AZ

KAREN BAKER-FLETCHER, Professor of Systematic Theology, Perkins School of Theology, Southern Methodist University, Dallas, TX

WHITNEY BODMAN, Associate Professor of Comparative Religion, Austin Presbyterian Theological Seminary, Austin, TX

ELIZABETH M. BOUNDS, Associate Professor of Christian Ethics, Candler School of Theology, Emory University, Atlanta, GA

GENNIFER BENJAMIN BROOKS, Ernest and Bernice Styberg Professor of Preaching, Garrett-Evangelical Theological Seminary, Evanston, IL

SALLY A. BROWN, Elizabeth M. Engle Associate Professor of Preaching and Worship, Princeton Theological Seminary, Princeton, NJ

LEIGH CAMPBELL-TAYLOR, Interim Pastor, Morningside Presbyterian Church, Atlanta, GA

NICK CARTER, President Emeritus, Andover Newton Theological School at Yale Divinity School, New Haven, CT

LAURA MARIKO CHEIFETZ, Assistant Dean of Admissions, Vocation, and Stewardship, Vanderbilt Divinity School, Nashville, TN

JANA CHILDERS, Dean of the Seminary; Vice President for Academic Affairs, San Francisco Theological Seminary, San Anselmo, CA

ANDREW FOSTER CONNORS, Pastor and Head of Staff, Brown Memorial Park Avenue Presbyterian Church, Baltimore, MD

MIGUEL A. DE LA TORRE, Professor of Social Ethics and Latinx Studies, Iliff School of Theology, Denver, CO

CAROL J. DEMPSEY, OP, Professor of Theology: Biblical Studies, Department of Theology, University of Portland, Portland, OR

MINDY DOUGLAS, Pastor and Head of Staff, First Presbyterian Church, Durham, NC

SUSAN GROVE EASTMAN, Associate Research Professor of New Testament, Duke Divinity School, Durham, NC

WENDY FARLEY, Rice Family Chair of Spirituality, San Francisco Theological Seminary Graduate School of Theology, Redlands University, San Anselmo, CA

ELIZABETH FELICETTI, Rector, St. David's Episcopal Church, Richmond, VA

MARY F. FOSKETT, Wake Forest Kahle Professor of Religious Studies and Albritton Fellow, Department for the Study of Religions, Wake Forest University, Winston-Salem, NC

RENATA FURST, Associate Professor of Scripture and Spirituality, Oblate School of Theology, San Antonio, TX

LINCOLN E. GALLOWAY, K. Morgan Edwards Associate Professor of Homiletics, Claremont School of Theology, Claremont, CA

DONNA GIVER-JOHNSTON, Pastor, Community Presbyterian Church of Ben Avon, Pittsburgh, PA

W. SCOTT HALDEMAN, Associate Professor of Worship, Chicago Theological Seminary, Chicago, IL

ANGELA DIENHART HANCOCK, Associate Professor of Homiletics and Worship, Pittsburgh Theological Seminary, Pittsburgh, PA

SARAH S. HENRICH, Professor Emerita, Luther Seminary; Pastor, Atonement Lutheran Church, St. Paul, MN

ELIZABETH HINSON-HASTY, Professor of Theology, Bellarmine University, Louisville, KY

LYNN JAPINGA, Professor of Religion, Hope College, Holland, MI

CYNTHIA A. JARVIS, Minister and Head of Staff, The Presbyterian Church of Chestnut Hill, Philadelphia, PA

PATRICK W. T. JOHNSON, Pastor, First Presbyterian Church, Asheville, NC

ARUN W. JONES, Dan and Lillian Hankey Associate Professor of World Evangelism; Director of the Master of Theology Program, Candler School of Theology, Emory University, Atlanta, GA

JOHN KALTNER, Virginia Ballou McGehee Professor of Muslim-Christian Relations, Department of Religious Studies, Rhodes College, Memphis, TN

MIHEE KIM-KORT, PhD student in Religious Studies, Indiana University, Bloomington, IN

MICHAEL E. LEE, Associate Professor of Theology, Fordham University Theology Department, Bronx, NY

JOEL MARCUS LEMON, Associate Professor of Old Testament; Director of the Graduate Division of Religion, Candler School of Theology, Emory University, Atlanta, GA

RAQUEL ST. CLAIR LETTSOME, Associate Minister, Union African Methodist Episcopal Church, Warwick, NY

KIMBERLY BRACKEN LONG, Editor, *Call to Worship*, Presbyterian Church (U.S.A.), Louisville, KY

HUGO MAGALLANES, Associate Professor of Christianity and Cultures, Perkins School of Theology, Southern Methodist University, Dallas, TX

J. CLINTON MCCANN JR., Evangelical Professor of Biblical Interpretation, Eden Theological Seminary, St. Louis, MO

TROY A. MILLER, Vice President for Academic Affairs, Memphis Center for Urban and Theological Studies, Memphis, TN

AIMEE MOISO, PhD Candidate, Vanderbilt University, Nashville, TN

SHAWNTHEA MONROE, Senior Pastor, Plymouth Church (UCC) at Shaker Heights, Cleveland, OH

LEE HULL MOSES, Senior Minister, First Christian Church (Disciples of Christ), Greensboro, NC

D. CAMERON MURCHISON, Professor Emeritus, Columbia Theological Seminary, Decatur, GA

KENNETH N. NGWA, Associate Professor of Hebrew Bible, Drew University Theological School, Madison, NJ

PAUL T. NIMMO, King's Chair of Systematic Theology, University of Aberdeen, Aberdeen, Scotland

KATE OTT, Associate Professor of Christian Social Ethics, Drew University Theological School, Madison, NJ

ALVIN PADILLA, Academic Dean and Vice President of Academic Affairs, Western Theological Seminary, Holland, MI

LANCE PAPE, Granville and Erline Walker Associate Professor of Homiletics, Brite Divinity School, Texas Christian University, Fort Worth, TX

SONG-MI SUZIE PARK, Associate Professor of Old Testament, Austin Presbyterian Theological Seminary, Austin, TX

MICHAEL PASQUARELLO III, Beeson Professor of Methodist Divinity, Beeson Divinity School, Samford University, Birmingham, AL

ANATHEA E. PORTIER-YOUNG, Associate Professor of Old Testament, Duke Divinity School, Durham, NC

MARK RAMSEY, Executive Director, Macedonian Ministry, Atlanta, GA

ROBERT A. RATCLIFF, Editor-in-Chief, Westminster John Knox Press, Louisville, KY

STEPHEN BRECK REID, Professor of Christian Scriptures, George W. Truett Seminary, Baylor University, Waco, TX

WYNDY CORBIN REUSCHLING, Professor of Ethics and Theology, Ashland Theological Seminary, Ashland, OH

RON RIENSTRA, Professor of Preaching and Worship Arts, Western Theological Seminary, Holland, MI

BRIAN D. RUSSELL, Professor of Biblical Studies and Dean of the School of Urban Ministries, Asbury Theological Seminary, Orlando, FL

RUTH FAITH SANTANA-GRACE, Executive Presbyter, Presbytery of Philadelphia, Philadelphia, PA

PAMELA J. SCALISE, Senior Professor of Old Testament, Fuller Theological Seminary, Pasadena, CA

DAVID J. SCHLAFER, Independent Consultant in Preaching and Assisting Priest, The Episcopal Church of the Redeemer, Bethesda, MD

WM. MARCUS SMALL, Pastor, New Calvary Baptist Church, Norfolk, VA

F. SCOTT SPENCER, former Professor of Religion, Wingate University, Wingate, NC, and former Professor of New Testament and Biblical Interpretation, Baptist Theological Seminary at Richmond, Richmond, VA

NIBS STROUPE, Pastor, Retired, Oakhurst Presbyterian Church, Decatur, GA

DEAN K. THOMPSON, President and Professor of Ministry Emeritus, Louisville Presbyterian Theological Seminary, Pasadena, CA

DENISE THORPE, Minister of Word and Sacrament, Presbyterian Church (U.S.A.), Raleigh, NC

THEODORE J. WARDLAW, President and Professor of Homiletics, Austin Presbyterian Theological Seminary, Austin, TX

SONIA E. WATERS, Assistant Professor of Pastoral Theology, Princeton Theological Seminary, Princeton, NJ

KHALIA J. WILLIAMS, Assistant Dean of Worship and Music; Assistant Professor in the Practice of Worship, Candler School of Theology, Emory University, Atlanta, GA

JOHN W. WRIGHT, Independent scholar, San Diego, CA

OLIVER LARRY YARBROUGH, Tillinghast Professor of Religion, Middlebury College, Department of Religion, Middlebury, VT

WILLIAM YOO, Assistant Professor of American Religious and Cultural History, Columbia Theological Seminary, Decatur, GA

Author Index

Abbreviations

C1	Commentary 1	NT	New Testament
C2	Commentary 2	OT	Old Testament
E	Epistle	PS	Psalm
G	Gospel		

Contributors and entries

Efraín Agosto	Proper 5 E C1, Proper 6 E C1, Proper 7 E C1
Sammy G. Alfaro	All Saints G C1, Proper 26 G C1, Proper 27 G C1
Karen Baker-Fletcher	Proper 17 E C2, Proper 18 E C2, Proper 19 E C2
Whitney Bodman	Proper 20 G C1, Proper 21 G C1, Proper 22 G C1
Elizabeth M. Bounds	Proper 20 E C2, Proper 21 E C2, Proper 22 E C2
Gennifer Benjamin Brooks	Proper 14 G C1, Proper 15 G C1, Proper 16 G C1
Sally A. Brown	Proper 17 E C1, Proper 18 E C1, Proper 19 E C1
Leigh Campbell-Taylor	Proper 23 PS, Proper 24 PS, Proper 25 PS, All Saints PS
Nick Carter	Proper 11 E C1, Proper 12 E C1, Proper 13 E C1
Laura Mariko Cheifetz	Proper 28 G C1, Proper 29 G C1
Jana Childers	Proper 11 OT C2, Proper 12 OT C2, Proper 13 OT C2
Andrew Foster Connors	Trinity Sunday OT C2, Proper 3 OT C2, Proper 4 OT C2
Miguel A. De La Torre	Proper 23 OT C1, Proper 24 OT C1, Proper 25 OT C1
Carol J. Dempsey, OP	Proper 23 E C2, Proper 24 E C2, Proper 25 E C2
Mindy Douglas	Proper 14 E C2, Proper 15 E C2, Proper 16 E C2
Susan Grove Eastman	Proper 14 E C1, Proper 15 E C1, Proper 16 E C1
Wendy Farley	Proper 11 E C2, Proper 12 E C2, Proper 13 E C2
Elizabeth Felicetti	All Saints NT C2, Proper 26 OT C2, Proper 27 OT C2
Mary F. Foskett	Trinity Sunday G C2, Proper 3 G C2, Proper 4 G C2
Renata Furst	Proper 8 E C1, Proper 9 E C1, Proper 10 E C1
Lincoln E. Galloway	Proper 17 OT C2, Proper 18 OT C2, Proper 19 OT C2
Donna Giver-Johnston	Proper 20 PS, Proper 21 PS, Proper 22 PS
W. Scott Haldeman	Proper 5 PS, Proper 6 PS, Proper 7 PS
Angela Dienhart Hancock	Proper 11 PS, Proper 12 PS, Proper 13 PS
Sarah S. Henrich	Trinity Sunday E C2, Proper 3 E C2, Proper 4 E C2
Elizabeth Hinson-Hasty	Proper 11 OT C1, Proper 12 OT C1, Proper 13 OT C1
Lynn Japinga	Trinity Sunday OT C1, Proper 3 OT C1, Proper 4 OT C1
Cynthia A. Jarvis	Proper 20 E C1, Proper 21 E C1, Proper 22 E C1

Author Index

Patrick W. T. Johnson	Proper 9 E C2
Arun W. Jones	All Saints E C1, Proper 26 E C1, Proper 27 E C1
John Kaltner	Proper 14 OT C1, Proper 15 OT C1, Proper 16 OT C1
Mihee Kim-Kort	Proper 8 G C1, Proper 9 G C1, Proper 10 G C1
Michael E. Lee	Proper 23 G C1, Proper 24 G C1, Proper 25 G C1
Joel Marcus Lemon	Trinity Sunday PS, Proper 3 PS, Proper 4 PS
Raquel St. Clair Lettsome	Proper 17 G C2, Proper 18 G C2, Proper 19 G C2
Kimberly Bracken Long	Proper 26 PS, Proper 27 PS, Proper 28 PS, Proper 29 PS
Hugo Magallanes	Proper 14 OT C2, Proper 15 OT C2, Proper 16 OT C2
J. Clinton McCann Jr.	Proper 8 PS, Proper 9 PS, Proper 10 PS
Troy A. Miller	Proper 23 E C1, Proper 24 E C1, Proper 25 E C1
Aimee Moiso	All Saints G C2, Proper 26 G C2, Proper 27 G C2
Shawnthea Monroe	Proper 20 G C2, Proper 21 G C2, Proper 22 G C2
Lee Hull Moses	Proper 28 E C2, Proper 29 E C2
D. Cameron Murchison	Proper 10 E C2
Kenneth N. Ngwa	Proper 28 OT C1, Proper 29 OT C1
Paul T. Nimmo	Trinity Sunday E C1, Proper 3 E C1, Proper 4 E C1
Kate Ott	Proper 28 G C2, Proper 29 G C2
Alvin Padilla	All Saints E C2, Proper 26 E C2, Proper 27 E C2
Lance Pape	Proper 14 G C2, Proper 15 G C2, Proper 16 G C2
Song-Mi Suzie Park	Proper 5 OT C1, Proper 6 OT C1, Proper 7 OT C1
Michael Pasquarello III	Proper 11 G C2, Proper 12 G C2, Proper 13 G C2
Anathea E. Portier-Young	Proper 20 OT C1, Proper 21 OT C1, Proper 22 OT C1
Mark Ramsey	Proper 5 OT C2, Proper 6 OT C2, Proper 7 OT C2
Robert A. Ratcliff	Proper 8 OT C1, Proper 9 OT C1, Proper 10 OT C1
Stephen Breck Reid	Proper 8 OT C2, Proper 9 OT C2, Proper 10 OT C2
Wyndy Corbin Reuschling	Proper 5 E C2, Proper 6 E C2, Proper 7 E C2
Ron Rienstra	Proper 17 PS, Proper 18 PS, Proper 19 PS
Brian D. Russell	Proper 23 OT C2, Proper 24 OT C2, Proper 25 OT C2
Ruth Faith Santana-Grace	Proper 28 E C1, Proper 29 E C1
Pamela J. Scalise	Proper 20 OT C2, Proper 21 OT C2, Proper 22 OT C2
David J. Schlafer	Proper 17 G C1, Proper 18 G C1, Proper 19 G C1
Wm. Marcus Small	Proper 28 OT C2, Proper 29 OT C2
F. Scott Spencer	Proper 11 G C1, Proper 12 G C1, Proper 13 G C1
Nibs Stroupe	Proper 8 G C2, Proper 9 G C2, Proper 10 G C2
Dean K. Thompson	Proper 8 E C2
Denise Thorpe	Proper 5 G C2, Proper 6 G C2, Proper 7 G C2
Theodore J. Wardlaw	Proper 23 G C2, Proper 24 G C2, Proper 25 G C2
Sonia E. Waters	Proper 5 G C1, Proper 6 G C1, Proper 7 G C1
Khalia J. Williams	Proper 14 PS, Proper 15 PS, Proper 16 PS
John W. Wright	Proper 17 OT C1, Proper 18 OT C1, Proper 19 OT C1
Oliver Larry Yarbrough	Trinity Sunday G C1, Proper 3 G C1, Proper 4 G C1
William Yoo	All Saints NT C1, Proper 26 OT C1, Proper 27 OT C1

Scripture Index

OLD TESTAMENT

Genesis

Reference	Page
1–2	142
1–11	4
1:1–2:3	357
1:1–2:4a	**2–7**, 37
1:10–13	206
1:20–23	206
1:24–31	9
1:26	9
1:28–31	206
1:31	34
2	6
2–3	142, 247
2:1–4	206
2:2	460
2:2–3	4
2:4b–3:24	4
3:1	83
3:16	129
4:23	80
4:23–24	312
6–9	34, 36
6:6	34
6:9–22	4, **33–37**, 39
6:11	81
6:24	81
6:25–33	81
7:24	**33–37**, 39
8:1	34
8:14–19	**33–37**, 39
8:21	37
9	80
9:1–17	182
9:11	34
9:15	34
9:18–27	37
10	80
11:26–32	57
12	4, 57, 65, 69
12–23	104
12–50	51, 104, 122, 141, 174, 410
12:1–3	105–6, 247
12:1–4	110
12:1–8	158
12:1–9	**50–54**, 61
12:3	507
12:3b	393
12:5	57
12:10–20	104, 230
13:1–9	158
13:22	81
15:2	104
15:6	60, 76, 112
16	87
16:1–15	104
16:7–13	104
17:15–22	59
17:18–22	141
18	69, 70, 81
18–21	124
18:1–15	**68–72**, 74
18:19	141
19	69
19:20–22	81
20:1–18	104
20:3–7	104
21	69–70, 87, 96
21:1–3	61
21:1–7	**68–72**
21:8–21	**85–90**, 99
21:8–34	104
21:13	93
21:17–19	93
21:17–21	104
22	103, 124, 183
22:1–14	**102–7**, 109, 110, 112, 117
22:2	93
22:6	109
22:11–13	109
24	123–25, 128
24–35	104
24:14–16	174
24:34–38	**120–25**, 128
24:42–49	**120–25**, 128
24:58–67	**120–25**, 128
24:65	136
25	52, 123, 141, 153
25:9	87
25:19–34	**139–43**, 146
25:21	61
25:23	143
26:8	87
27	123, 158, 176
27:1–40	104
27:1–45	143
27:5–17	122
27:19	174
27:40–45	143
28	166
28:1	181
28:10	164
28:10–19	168
28:10–19a	**157–61**
28:10–22	104
28:17	164
28:20–22	158
29	180–81, 183
29:9	495
29:9–14	174
29:15–28	**173–77**
29:15–30	104
29:31	174
31	176
32	201
32:1–2	158
32:22–31	**192–96**, 198
32:30	199
33:1	193
33:1–5	229
33:1–17	193
35:1–15	159
37	229, 312
37–50	211–12, 247
37:1–4	**209–13**, 218
37:5–8	141
37:5–11	211–12
37:12–28	**209–13**, 218
37:12–36	104

Scripture Index

Genesis (*continued*)
37:18–36	301
37:19–24	106
39–50	312
39:1–6	211
39:20–23	211
40:5–19	212
41:1–36	212
41:14	211
41:37–45	211
41:42	211
42–44	229, 312
45:1–15	**227–32**, 237
46:5–27	229
48:8–9	230
49:10–11	122
50	299–300, 305
50:1–3	301
50:7	301
50:10	301
50:14	301
50:15–17	301
50:15–21	**298–302**
50:19	305
50:20	212, 218, 301

Exodus
	87–88, 291
1:8–14	284
1:8–2:10	**245–50**
2	248, 263
2:16–19	495
2:23	358
2:24	34, 282
3	300, 495
3:1	211, 336–37
3:1–15	**262–67**, 277
3:2	336
3:6	211
3:14–15	270
7–11	247
11:3b	284
12	211, 299
12–14	247
12:1–14	**281–85**, 288
12:1–27	417
12:8–20	188
13:3–10	188
14	299–300, 305
14–15	308–9, 441
14:10	299
14:19–31	**298–302**
14:21	442
14:26–29	444
15	305–6
15:1–22	318
15:1b–11	**303–6**
15:8	442
15:12–19	306
15:20	477
15:20–21	**303–6**
15:21	387
15:24	318
15:27	318
16	337
16–18	300
16:1–2	318
16:1–12	206
16:2–15	**316–21**
16:3	326
16:4	330
16:7–9	318
16:12	318
16:18	330
16:31	321
17	345, 349
17:1–7	**334–39**, 444
17:2	206
17:2–7	318
17:7	342
19	69
19:1–2	337
19:2–8a	**68–72**, 74
19:3	266
19:5–6	393
20	324, 368
20:1–2	361
20:1–4	**353–58**
20:1–11	357
20:1–17	357
20:2–7	376
20:5–6	355, 357, 368
20:7–9	**353–58**
20:8–9	357
20:8–11	355
20:10–11	355, 357
20:12–20	**353–58**
20:20	361
20:22–35:3	355
22:13	495
24:10–11	337
24:15	266
24:16–17	318
25:17	45
30:6	45
32–34	376, 393
32:1–14	**372–76**, 379
32:8	374
32:12b	414
33:5–6	336
33:10	336n3
33:11–13	397
33:12–23	**389–94**
33:16	397
33:17	336
33:17–23	211
33:18	318
33:19	254
33:19–23	398
33:20	397
34:6	128
34:6–7a	376
34:6–7	318, 393
35–40	376
40:35	318

Leviticus
7:11–21	477
9:14–16	421
11:44	266
11:44–45	409
18–20	413
18:5	219
19	410
19:1–2	**407–11**
19:2	413
19:9–10	421
19:15–18	296, **407–11**
19:16	413
19:18	413, 421
19:33–34	69
20:1–5	118
23:33–43	417
23:42	320
25:4	460
26	495
27:32	495

Numbers
6:24–26	234
11:1	318
11:4	318
11:6–9	318
14	318
14:17–19	318
14:22	206
14:27–29	318

Scripture Index **519**

15:37–39	455	6:21–25	444	12:7	477
15:38–41	64	8:1–24	444	13:1	477
16:11	318	10	444	16:13	477
16:41	318	18:25	175	18:14–31	425
17:5	318	21:17	175		
17:10	318	24	460	**1 Samuel**	
20:1–13	336, 411, 444	**24:1–3a**	**458–63**, 465	1:12–20	61
21:4–9	320	24:2–15	442	2:1–10	301
		24:14–25	**458–63**, 465	7	477
Deuteronomy	35, 291, 476	24:19	468	13:14	497
1:27	318	24:19–25	468	16:11	495
5:32–33	97			16:14	392
6	420	**Judges**		17:15	495
6:4	494	1:3–15	477	17:34–35	495
8:3	318	1:17–20	477	17:34–37	495
8:16	318	1:21	477		
8:17	219	1:22–26	477	**2 Samuel**	
9:4	219	1:27–33	477	7:1–17	109
10:18	507	2:1–2	479	11	175
10:18–19	69	2:11–15	479	11:3	175
11:18–21	**33–37**, 39–40	2:11–19	477	12:1–14	357
11:26–28	**33–37**, 39–40	3–16	477	20:8	175
14:29	507	3:8	477		
17:14–20	494	3:11	477	**1 Kings**	
17:20	176	3:12	477	1	175
18:21–22	109	3:13	477	3	174
22:12	455	3:14	477	3:1–4	180
24:17	507	3:15	477	**3:5–12**	**173–77**, 179, 182
24:19–21	507	3:30	477	3:13–14	180
25:1–3	82	4	477, 480	11–12	494
26:12	507	4–5	477	11:3–4	180
28:29–30	476	**4:1–7**	**475–80**, 483, 490	17–19	210
28:39	476	4:2	477	17:2	210
30:11–14	219–20	4:3	477	17:8	210
30:15	167	4:15	480	17:17–24	64
31:26	411	4:23	480	18	105
32:21–22	476	5:7	477	18:1	210
32:35	273–74	5:14–15	477	18:29	211
32:48–52	411	5:18	477	19	220
34	247, 414	5:31	477	**19:9–18**	**209–13**
34:1–12	**407–11**	6:1	477	21	210
34:4	409	6:1–6	477	21:17	210
34:10	409	6:10	477	21:28	210
		8:28	477		
Joshua	441–42, 445	8:33–35	477	**2 Kings**	
1:6–9	442	8:34–27	477	1–2	210
2	443	9:53–54	477	2	211
2:1–21	442	10:6	477	4:18–37	64
3	299	10:6–16	477	14:25	317
3:7–17	**440–45**, 448, 451, 455	10:8	477	14:27	317
		10:10–14	477	17:6–7	318
5:12	318	11:29–40	104	17:23	318

2 Kings (continued)

22	476
22:14	477
24:12–16	494

1 Chronicles

14:16	175

2 Chronicles

1:2–4	393
1:3	175

Nehemiah

9:15	318
9:20	318

Esther

7:9–10	320

Job

1–2	5
6:16	142
37:6	142

Psalms

1	**412–15**
1:1	408, 417–18
1:1–6	472
1:3–4	408
1:4–6	418
3:17	273
5	312
5:43–48	313
7	312
8	**2, 8–9**
8:1	10
12	**251–53**
13	**108–10**
17	201
17:1–7	**197–99**
17:8–9	199
17:13	199
17:15	**197–99**
18–21	361
19	356, **359–61**
19:1	9
22	392
23	**377–79**, 495, 499
25	341, 349
25:1–9	**340–42**
25:4	349
25:4–5	335
25:7	313, 335
25:8–9	335
25:9	349
25:10	341
26:1–8	**268–71**
26:12	269
28:4	313
31	39–41
31:1–5	**38–41**
31:6–8	39
31:6–18	40
31:9	39
31:14	39
31:15–18	39
31:19–24	**38–41**
33	57
33:1–12	**55–57**
33:16–23	56
34	313, 429, 430
34:1	436
34:1–10	426, **429–30**, 432
34:22	426, **429–30**, 432
35	312
40	465
40:13–17	465
42	447–48
43	**446–48**
45	128, 131
45:10–17	**126–29**
46	**38–41**
46:1	43
46:4	337
46:9–10	128
50	56
50:7–15	51, **55–57**
51	312
51:7	142
55	312
58	312
59	312
65	145, 149
65:1–13	**144–47**
67	233–35
67:3	146
67:5	146
69	92, 312
69:7–18	**91–93**
69:8–9	99
69:35	92
70	**464–66**
71	465
72	109, 128, 145
78	341–42, 465
78:1–4	**340–42**
78:1–7	**464–66**
78:12–16	**340–42**
78:24	318
78:70–71	495
79	313
80	361
80:1	212
80:3	361
80:7–15	355, **359–61**
81	313
82	109
85	216
85:8–13	**214–16**
85:10	439
86	93, 163
86:1–10	**91–93**
86:3	243
86:5	318
86:11–17	**162–64**
86:15	128, 318
86:16–17	**91–93**
86:14–17	99
89	109, 394
89:1–4	**108–10**, 128
89:15–18	**108–10**, 128
90	409–10, 414, 483
90:1–6	**412–15**
90:1–12	**481–83**
90:3	409
90:13–17	**412–15**
93–99	392
94	312
95	499
95:1–7a	**498–500**
95:8–9	337
96:1–13	**395–98**
96:7–9	146
96:11–13	146
96:13	99
98:7–9	146
99	393, **395–98**
99:1–2	390
99:4	390
99:13	390
100	**73–75, 498–500**
100:1	146
100:3	507
103	305, 309, 312
103:1–13	**303–6**
103:8	128, 309

103:14b–16	309	139:13–16	164	5	367
103:20–22	146	139:19–22	164	5–7	131
105	180, 215–16, 270, 273, 330	**139:23–24**	**162–64**	**5:1–7**	**353–58**
		141	313	5:4	360
105:1–6	**214–16, 268–71, 322–24**	145	126, **131**, 132, 198, 201, 330	5:7	360
				5:11	354
105:1–11	**178–81**	**145:1–8**	**322–24**	5:12	354
105:16–17	230	**145:8–9**	**197–99, 318**	5:16	358
105:16–22	212, **214–16**, 218	**145:8–14**	**126–29**, 146	6:11	131
		145:9	128	7	130
105:23	230	145:10–12	146	7:14	15
105:23–26	**268–71**	145:14	202	8:7	194
105:37–45	**322–24**	**145:14–21**	**197–99**	8:17	376
105:45a	181	145:21	324	8:39	134
105:45b	**178–81, 214–16, 268–71**	146:7	122	9:7	358
		148:1–10	146	10:32	19
106	376	148:8	142	11	142
106:1–6	**377–79**	148:11–13	146	13	477
106:3	374	**149**	**286–88**, 289	13:6	477
106:19–23	**377–79**	149:1	109	16:1	19
106:20	375	149:5	109	16:3	358
106:25	318	149:8–9	288	16:5	358
106:47	376	149:9	109	22	477
107:1–7	**446–48**	150:6	146	22:5	484
107:33–37	**446–48**			24	375
109	312	**Proverbs**		25	386
110	421	8	175	**25:1–9**	**372–76**, 378
110:1	502	9	386	25:4	373
114	**303–6**, 309	9:1–5	194	25:6–8	379
116	74, 93	9:10	137	26:8	376
116:1–2	**73–75**, 79	13:9	472	27:2–6	355
116:12–19	**73–75**	14:21	436	28:6	358
117:1	146	25:21–22	273–74	28:16	218–19
118:22–23	368			28:17	358
118:24	387	**Ecclesiastes**	35	30:18	358
119	147, 179–80, 287			32:16	358
119:33–40	**286–88**, 289	**Song of Solomon**	129, 131, 357	33:2	376
119:105–112	**144–47**			33:5	358
119:129–136	**178–81**	2	128	33:21	337
120–134	483	**2:8–13**	**126–29**	34	477
121:4	499	7:1–10	128	37:12	247
123	**481–83**			40	86, 140, 194, 247
123:2	489	**Isaiah**	130, 317	40–55	145, 159, 193
124	**251–53**, 255, 483	1:8	19	40:1	247
128	**178–81**	1:10–17	460	40:3	247
131	20, **23–24**	1:16–17	130–31	40:4	142
133	**233–35**, 237	1:17	358	40:6–8	247
135:18	401	1:27	358	40:14	358
138	**251–53**	2:2–4	128, 319	40:15–17	247
139	164, 167	2:12–22	477	40:28	145
139:1–12	**162–64, 478**	3:9–20	131	40:31	376
139:1–18	20	4:18–25	131	41–48	159

Scripture Index

Isaiah (*continued*)
41:14	145
41:21	145
42:1	358
42:1–4	15, 19
42:3–4	358
42:6	146, 393
42:7	122
42:9	15
42:18	246
43:14	145
43:15	145
44:1	246
44:3	160
44:6	145
44:6–8	**157–61**, 163, 168
44:26–28	159
44:28	160
45	404
45:1–3	396
45:1–7	**389–94**
45:3–6	397
45:6	396
45:22–23	393
46:3	246
46:12	246
48:1	246
49	19–21
49:1	246
49:1–6	19
49:6	19, 146, 393
49:8–16a	**18–22**
49:10	426
49:13	26
49:14–15	24
49:14–23	159
49:16	26
49:21	19
49:23	376
50:4–7	19
51	252
51:1–6	**245–50**
51:3	247
51:5	376
51:7	246–47
52–53	280
52:7	145
52:13–53:12	19
54	194
54:11	140
55	140–41, 143, 146, 149, 194
55:1	201
55:1–2	140, 145
55:1–3	207
55:1–5	**192–96**, 198
55:4–5	146
55:6–11	312
55:7–13	145
55:10	145
55:10–12	156
55:10–13	**139–43**, 145
55:11–13	146
56–66	228
56:1	**227–32**, 358
56:3–8	146
56:6–8	**227–32**
58:1	146
59:9	376
59:17	485
60:9	376
61:8	358
62:11	19
65:22	142

Jeremiah
1:4–5	87
1:8	87
1:14–15	122
3:8	19
6:14	103
13:15–21	269
15:15	269
15:15–21	**262–67**
15:17	269
18:5–10	319
20	92
20:4–5	121
20:7–13	**85–90**
20:7–18	105
21:5	122
23:1–8	495
23:4	494
23:22	320
23:23–24	478
24:4–7	121
27–28	103
27:14	105
28	109
28:1–4	103
28:5–9	**102–7**, 108
28:12–14	104
29:7	93
29:18	140
30:7	484
30:8	122
31:31–34	109
33:13	495
46	477
46:10	477

Ezekiel
1–33	335
3	335
5:15	140
13	493
13:5	477
13:8–10	103
16	335
16:49	69
17	335
18	335, 337
18:1–4	**334–39**
18:2–4	368
18:5–9	337
18:25–32	**334–39**
18:30	349
18:30–31	341
18:31	349
19	335
20	335
20:34–35	493
20:37	495
20:41–42	493
23	335
23:24	122
30:23	477
33	283, 335
33:7–11	**281–85**, 287, 298
33:10	287
33:11	287
33:23–33	495
34–48	493
34	81, 495, 500
34:1	499
34:1–3	495
34:1–10	493, 495
34:2	122, 494
34:10	494–96
34:10–22	502
34:11–16	**493–97**, 499, 508
34:14	507
34:16	81, 499, 508
34:17	494, 507
34:17–22	493
34:20–24	**493–97**, 499

34:23–31	493	2:4	320	**Malachi**	121		
34:27	122	2:8	400	3:2	477		
35:1–15	493	3:2	317				
36–37	335	**3:10–4:11**	**316–21**	**NEW TESTAMENT**			
36:24	494	4	228				
36:26	337	4:2	323, 330	**Matthew**	471		
37:12	494	4:3	326	1:1	109, 206		
37:15–24	494	4:8	323, 326	1:1–17	117		
37:21	494	4:9	323	1:3	206		
47	337			1:5–6	206		
		Micah	317, 442	1:8b–9a	241n1		
Hosea	317	1:2	442	1:16–17	135		
2	19	3:1–4	442	1:17	206		
4–6	52	**3:5–12**	**440–45**, 447,	1:20–23	15		
4:17–5:9	425		451, 454	1:21	64		
5:15–6:6	**50–54**	5:24	460	1:21–22	206		
6:6	64–65, 460	6:6–8	460	1:23	15, 17, 171, 208		
13:8	20	6:8	228, 502	2	135, 248		
		6:9	442	2:6	81		
Joel		7:4b–7	99	2:13–16	207		
1:15	477			2:13–23	206		
2–3	477	**Nahum**		2:16–18	17		
2:1	477	1:3	318	3:13–17	15, 94		
2:1–11	476	3:1	317	3:13–4:11	47n2		
2:31	484	3:2–7	317	3:17	259, 422		
2:32a	224			4	29, 29n1		
2:32	219	**Habakkuk**		4:1–4	206		
3:14–15	477	2:4	112	4:1–11	15, 106, 206		
				4:2–4	205		
Amos	317	**Zephaniah**		4:8–10	277		
1:1	459	1:1–3	476	4:17	147		
1:3–2:6	103	1:5–6	478	4:18–20	276		
2:6–8	228	**1:7**	**475–80**, 482,	4:18–21	63		
3:6	392		490	4:18–22	15, 189, 277		
3:12	495	1:10–11	478	5	224, 432, 438, 474		
5	468, 477	1:12–13	491	5–7	15, 48, 471		
5:7	460	**1:12–18**	**475–80**, 482,	5–9	81, 98		
5:15	212, 273, 437		484, 490	5:1–2	206		
5:18	468, 484	2:13	317	**5:1–12**	30–31, 242,		
5:18–19	469	3:14–15	122		**435–39**, 456		
5:18–20	468, 477	3:16–20	476	5:3	188		
5:18–24	**458–63**, 465			5:3–7:27	48		
5:21–24	273	**Zechariah**	121	5:9	135		
5:24	468	1:1–8	121	5:10	400		
6:6	212	9	123–24, 132	5:11–12	82		
6:12	460	9–14	122	5:12	430		
7:10–17	105	9:9–10	128	5:14–16	468		
9:1–4	478	**9:9–12**	**120–25**, 126,	5:17	147		
			128, 131, 146	5:17–20	189, 280		
Jonah	320, 323, 331	9:9–17	122	5:17–48	206		
1:2	317	9:10	128	5:19–48	47		
1:12	320	14:1–21	477				

Scripture Index

Matthew (*continued*)

Reference	Pages
5:20	48, 189
5:21–26	295
5:21–48	189
5:22	295, 490
5:29–30	490
5:34–39	295n2
5:38–48	276
5:43–47	64
5:43–48	188, 273, 410
5:44–45	171–72
6:1–18	47
6:7	48
6:7–15	222
6:9–13	48
6:10	47, 169, 188
6:11	206
6:14–15	311
6:19–21	31, 276
6:21	420
6:24–34	**29–32**
6:26	188
6:30	15
7:1–5	349
7:7–11	206
7:11	47
7:12	273, 421
7:13–20	48
7:14	138
7:15–20	280
7:21	43, 46n1
7:21–23	14
7:21–29	35, **46–49**
7:24	46n1, 471
7:26	46n1
8:1–4	241
8:12	490
8:14–17	206
8:19–22	63, 276
8:20	81, 206
8:21–28	260
8:23–27	223
8:26	15
8:26b	241n1
8:28–34	118, 241
8:29	259
9	63–64
9:2–8	46
9:3	189
9:9	277
9:9–13	51, **63–67**, 188
9:10–13	188
9:11	189
9:14	189
9:14–17	64–65
9:15	472
9:17	66
9:18–25	135
9:18–26	51, **63–67**, 206
9:20–22	241
9:27–28	206
9:35–38	15
9:35–10:8	69, 78
9:35–10:23	**80–84**
9:36	116
10	15, 47, 98, 116, 136
10:1	17
10:1–4	206
10:5–6	74
10:6	83
10:8	113
10:9–13	206
10:9–23	**80–84**
10:16	118
10:16–42	276
10:22	100
10:24–39	**98–101**
10:28	490
10:30	365
10:34	103
10:34–39	118
10:38–39	276
10:39	326
10:40–42	100, **112–19**
10:42	135
11	131–32, 138
11:1	136
11:2–6	137
11:4–5	81, 136
11:4–6	64
11:16–17	117
11:16–19	**135–38**
11:18–19	188
11:25–27	206
11:25–30	**135–38**
11:27	16
11:28	132
11:28–30	128
12	152
12:2	404
12:7	65
12:10	404
12:13	376
12:18–21	15
12:23	206
12:38–40	320
12:38–42	320
12:42	206, 471
12:46–50	206
12:49–50	47
12:50	167
13	15, 149, 152, 169, 295
13:1–9	141, 146, **152–56**, 169, 187
13:1–50	187
13:4	170, 188
13:18–23	141, 146, **152–56**, 169
13:19	170, 188
13:24–30	**169–72**, 187, 295, 472
13:24–43	167
13:24–53	278
13:25	188
13:31–32	472
13:31–33	171, **187–91**
13:33	205–6, 472
13:35	171
13:36–43	**169–72**
13:37–43	188
13:42	490
13:44	31, 472
13:44–52	**187–91**
13:45–46	31, 183
13:45–53	295
13:47–50	472
13:50	490
13:54–58	152–53
14	207, 220
14:1–12	205, 207
14:3–11	404
14:8–11	206
14:13	206, 222
14:13–21	**205–8**, 243
14:15	206
14:22–33	15, 218, **222–26**, 242
14:28–30	187
14:31	15
14:31b	241n1
15:10–28	**240–44**
15:21–28	135, 206, 237
15:22	206
15:23	242

Scripture Index

15:26	242	20:29–34	489	24:9–14	277
15:38	206	20:30–31	206	24:14	17
16:5–12	277	21	345, 489	24:36	488
16:13–20	**258–61**	21–22	348	24:36–44	170
16:16	422	21:1	421	24:43–44	484
16:17–19	276	21:5	122–23, 128	24:45–48	471
16:18	170, 330	21:9	206, 422	24:45–51	386, 488, 490, 506
16:21	205, 259	21:10	385		
16:21–22	187	21:15	385	24:46–47	506
16:21–23	258	21:23–27	46, 385	24:51	490, 507
16:21–28	273, **276–80**	**21:23–32**	335, **348–53**	25	31, 468, 474
16:21–25:46	330	21:25–26	335	25:1–12	386
16:26	479	21:28–32	46, 385	**25:1–13**	47, 170, 461, 468, **471–74**, 488, 490
16:26–27	330	21:31	64		
17	294	21:31–32	342		
17:1–8	211	21:32	350	25:6–13	206
17:4–6	187	**21:33–46**	355, 363, **367–71**, 385	25:10–13	506
17:5–6	259			25:10b	470
17:12	277	21:41	360	25:12	468
17:14–18	135	21:42	360–61	25:13	472, 506
17:19–20	241n1	21:45	348, 385	**25:14–30**	386, 472, 485, **488–92**, 506
17:20	15, 225	22	106–7		
17:22–23	205, 277	**22:1–14**	375–76, **385–88**	25:21	507
18	15, 294, 314	22:2	472	25:23	507
18:6	117	22:2–9	472	25:30	490, 506–7
18:9	490	22:8–10	188	25:30–32	330
18:10–14	117	22:35–40	36	25:31	502
18:14	47	22:13	490	25:31–40	100
18:15–20	287, 289, **294–97**	22:14	374	**25:31–46**	47, 99, 337, 386, 426, 472, 496, 499, **506–10**
		22:15–22	392–93, **403–6**		
18:17	170	22:21	392		
18:18–20	17	22:23–33	421	25:40–41	496
18:20	15	**22:34–46**	82, 409–10, **420–23**	25:43	69
18:21	295			25:45	501
18:21–35	309, **311–15**	22:37–40	502	26:1–2	205
18:23	472	22:39	408	26:13	17
19:3	404	23	451	26:13–16	472
19:13–15	135	23:1–3	349	26:26	206
19:14	117	**23:1–12**	443, 450, **454–57**	26:31–35	187
19:17–22	153			26:32	16–17
19:21	188	23:2–3	189	26:36–46	47, 170
19:27	206	23:3–7	349	26:47–27:50	98
19:27–28	99	23:8–12	451	27	141
19:28	206	23:13	189	27:19	206
19:30	141, 329	23:13–36	369	27:25	369
20:1–16	**329–33**	23:15	490	27:54	422
20:11	319	23:23–29	189	28:1–10	206
20:15	323, 331	23:33	490	28:7	16, 17
20:16	141, 345	23:37	206	28:9–10	17
20:17–19	205, 277	24	122	**28:16–20**	**2, 14–17**, 46
20:20–23	206	24–25	456	28:18	46
20:20–28	206	24:9	100	28:19	11, 279, 507

Mark

1:9–11	94
4:1–9	153
4:13–20	153
8:27–38	277
8:35	326
8:36	479
9:2–8	211
9:2–9	266
11:17a	229
12:28–34	36
12:35–37	109
14:36	166
15:18	236
15:26	236
15:32	236

Luke

1:5–24	61
1:36	136
1:41–45	400
1:46–55	140, 302
1:52	331, 365
2:14	128
3:1–22	94
3:10–11	137
4:1–13	106
4:12	337
4:14–19	496
4:16–21	331
4:18	122
6:20	435
6:22	400
6:27–36	273
6:49	318
9:18–27	277
9:25	479
9:29–36	211
9:51–19:44	434
10:21	400
10:25–28	36
10:25–42	48
11:29–32	320
12:39	484
13:25–27	46
14:7–8	455
14:15–35	140
14:16–20	386
15	294n1, 311
15:2	319
16:19–31	331
17:33	326
19:4	401
19:7	319
23:34	312

John

1:32–34	431
1:46	94
3:14–15	350
4:1–15	320
4:20–21	337
6:31–32	266
6:31–34	318
9	321
10:11	304
10:11–16	497
10:30	495
12:15	497
12:25	123
14:6	326
14:15–24	97
14:26	417
17:4	417
17:10	319

Acts

1:8	319
2	81
2:1–4	16
2:21	484
2:38	16
2:39	224
4:1–22	14
6:1	484
7	82
7:9–16	507
7:20–22	469
7:51–53	212, 230
8:16	248
8:26–40	87
9:1–2	14
9:36–41	166
10:1–11:18	82
10:45	64
10:48	362
12	362
13:22	14
13:52	469
15:1–35	497
16:9	400
16:11–40	362
	325
	325
16:19	344
16:21	344
17:4–10	399
20:34	81
22:24	82
24:16	200
25:8	200

Romans

	43, 165, 291
1–4	59
1–5	290
1–8	149, 200, 218
1:1	183
1:7	111
1:16	76, 219
1:16–17	**42–45**, 218
1:17	96, 112
1:18–32	76–77, 94
1:18–2:16	58
1:18–8:39	236
1:19–20	272
1:19–21	290
1:28	255
2–3	237
2:1	186
2:1–29	76
2:6	280
2:16	182
2:17–3:31	58
3	43
3:8	94
3:9–23	77
3:21–26	94
3:21–30	218
3:22	76
3:22b–28	**42–45**
3:23	76
3:23–24	218
3:28–30	218
4	166, 237
4:1–12	58–60
4:3	76
4:3–5	76
4:13–25	51, **58–62**, 65
4:15	76
4:16–17	61
4:18	57
4:21	57
4:23–25	76–77
5	78, 183
5–6	255

5:1–8	69, **76–79**, 82–83	9:1–13	217	14	308
5:1–11	60, 94	9:1–11:35	236	14:1	255
5:2–5	256	9:6–18	237	**14:1–12**	**307–10**
5:3–10	77	9:7	236	14:1–15:6	165
5:6–9	232	9:11–17	183	14:1–15:7	237
5:8	74, 290	9:15–18	254	14:4	255
5:9–11	77, 95	9:17	290	14:10	255
5:12–13	148, 150	9:23–24	254	14:13	255
5:12–21	94–95, 237, 255	9:24–25	217	14:14	308
5:17	255	9:30–33	217	14:15	255
5:18	236	9:30–10:13	218	15:1	308n1
5:21	255	9:33	218–19	15:5–6	237
6	95, 98	10:1	217	15:5–7	237
6:1	96	10:1–5	217	15:6	218
6:1–15	94	10:1–13	218	15:7	255
6:1b–11	**94–97**	10:1–15	218–19	15:7–13	236
6:4	255	**10:5–15**	**217–21**	15:13	237
6:4–5	93	10:8–10	218	15:14–15	417
6:12–19	255	10:11	218	15:25–28	166
6:12–23	**111–15**	10:12–13	218	16:18	111
6:16–19	45	10:17	218		
6:16–23	94	10:18–21	236	**1 Corinthians**	
6:18	117, 232	11	237	1:1	183
6:22	117	**11:1–2a**	**236–39**	1:10–17	14
7	95, 237	11:2–28	236	1:12	381
7:14	166	11:11–32	218	1:14–17	95
7:15–25a	**130–34**	11:15	237	1:27–28	141
7:18	166	11:28	202–3, 236	1:28	365
7:21–25	148	11:29	256	2:1	27
7:23	136	**11:29–32**	**236–39**	2:3	345
8	148, 150, 166, 168	11:32	202	2:7	27
8:1–11	**148–51**, 153	11:33	237	2:16	255
8:5–14	170	11:33–36	256, 272	3:2	419
8:12–25	**165–68**, 170	11:35	236	3:11	261
8:12–39	188	11:36	236	4:1	27
8:15	201	12–16	200	**4:1–5**	**25–28**
8:18	168n5	12:1	236, 277	4:5	182
8:18–39	150	12:1–2	289–90	4:16	454
8:19–21	149	**12:1–8**	252, **254–57**, 272	5:1–8	381
8:22	44	12:1–21	237	5:7	282
8:23	201	12:1–15:13	47, 218, 236	6:1–11	381
8:26–39	**182–86**	12:3–13	410	8:1–13	200
8:29	184n2	**12:9–21**	168, 255, **272–75**, 278	8:1–11:1	308
8:31–39	236			10:14	400
8:35–36	365	13	248	10:23–11:1	308
8:37–39	200	13:1–7	290	11:1	454
9	184	13:4b	290	11:2	28
9–11	200, 218, 236–37, 363	13:8–10	255	11:2–16	292, 381
		13:8–14	287, **289–93**	11:17	28
9:1–5	**200–204**, 236	13:9	48	11:17–34	381
				11:22–29	28

1 Corinthians (*continued*)

12	256
12–13	295
12–14	381
12:12–13	502
12:25b–26	365
12:26	327
13	12, 168
13:2	27
13:12	432
15	469
15:1	417
15:22	236
15:51–57	95
15:54	379

2 Corinthians

1:1	183
2:4–11	312
4	13, 469
4:1–2	12
5:16–6:13	312
5:17	95, 365
5:18–21	77
7:15	345
11:12–19	363
11:24–25	82
13	12
13:11–13	**10–13**, 14

Galatians

1:1	183
2:11–14	308
2:12	362
2:15–21	59, 111, 362
2:16	76
3:6–9	76
3:6–18	183
3:19	59, 76
3:24	59
3:26–28	365
3:27–29	95
3:28	242
3:28–29	502
4:5–7	166
4:9–10	308
5:2–12	362
5:16	95, 97
5:22–26	168
6:7–9	170

Ephesians

1:3	503
1:14	501
1:15–23	**501–5**, 509
2:16	502
4:1–6	327
4:2–3	381
4:3	382
4:4	501
4:14	501
4:15–16	502
5:6	501–2
5:29–30	502
6:4	455
6:5	345

Philippians

1	327
1:5	325
1:6	325
1:7	330
1:8	325
1:14	326
1:20	326
1:21–30	**325–28**
1:27	324, 343, 345
1:28	326
1:30	331
2	335, 350
2:1–4	381
2:1–5	168
2:1–13	**343–47**
2:5–8	77
2:5–11	381
2:6–7	335
2:7	25
2:9–10	393
2:12–13	335, 342
3:1–4:3	380
3:1b–3	362
3:2b	363
3:4b–14	**362–66**
3:12–14	361
3:20	401
3:21	255
4:1–9	376, **380–84**
4:4a	364
4:5	375
4:7	182

	503–4
	503
	501
	501–5, 509
	502
	327
	381
	382
	501
	501
	502
	501–2
	502
	455
	345

Colossians

3:5	400
3:27–29	410

1 Thessalonians 449, 484

1:1–10	392–93, **399–402**, 404
1:3	391, 484–85
1:6	391, 450–51
1:6–9	449
1:8	484
1:10	468
2:1–8	409–10, **416–19**
2:2	409
2:9	81, 417, 452
2:9–11	442
2:9–13	**449–53**
2:10	454
2:14	450
3:2	449
3:6–8	400
3:12–13	449
4:1–12	468, 470
4:5	470
4:6	468
4:9–10	468
4:11	450
4:13	487
4:13–18	401, **467–70**
5:1–11	468, 477, **484–87**, 489, 490
5:2	472
5:4–5	473
5:4–6	480
5:5	469
5:6	472
5:9	480, 483
5:9–10	468
5:11	480, 491
5:14	308n1
5:18–24	468

2 Thessalonians

3:8	81

2 Timothy

1:5	417
1:7	417
2:12	99
3:12	400

Titus		1 John	431–32	7:10–12	430
2:13	401	2:1–2	433	7:11	428
		2:18	434	7:14	429
Hebrews		2:18–26	431	7:14–15	430
5:11	276	3	432	7:15b–16a	430
6:18	470	**3:1–3**	**431–34**	7:17	379, 429
6:19–20	470	3:6	433	8–9	426
7:14	425	3:11–22	381	8:1–2	460
9:4	318	4	421	17:13–14	436
11	436	4:18	346	19:1–2	99
11:1	470	5:21	400	19:9	472
11:2	117			19:19–20	436
11:8	51	**2 John**	431	20–22	436
11:23–24	248			21–22	426
11:39	436	**3 John**	431	21:1–4	376
12:1–2	433			21:1–6	394
12:12–13	346	**Jude**		21:4	379
13:2	69	1:5	417n2		

James		**Revelation**	265
1:22–2:26	48	1:3	425
2	421	2–3	425–26
3:13–18	381	2:9–11	426
3:13–4:17	48	2:17	318
4:1–12	295	3:10–12	426
5:7	401	4:1	425
5:20	295	4:1–11	425–26
		5:1–7:8	425
1 Peter		6	425
2:9	451	6–7	425
3:8	381	7	432
4:12–16	400	7–15	430
		7:1	430
2 Peter		7:1–8	425
1:12	417n2	7:4	436
3:1	417n2	7:9	425, 429–30, 470
3:10–13	477	**7:9–17**	**424–28**, 432, 436

APOCRYPHAL/ DEUTERO- CANONICAL BOOKS

Ecclesiasticus/Sirach	
7:34	273
24:18–20	194

Tobit	
4:15	273
14:4	317

Wisdom of Solomon	471
6:17–20	471
6:18–20	471
12:13	168
12:16–19	168
16:20	318

Comprehensive Scripture Index for Year A

Scripture citations that appear in boldface represent the assigned readings from the Revised Common Lectionary.

ABBREVIATIONS
A1   Year A, Volume 1
A2   Year A, Volume 2
A3   Year A, Volume 3

OLD TESTAMENT

Genesis	41–42, 329 (A2)
1–2	112–13 (A1); 142 (A3)
1–3	174 (A1)
1–11	41 (A2); 4 (A3)
1:1	109 (A1)
1:1–2:3	357 (A3)
1:1–2:4a	**2–7**, 37 (A3)
1:2	85, 101, 142, 323, 329 (A2)
1:3	85 (A2)
1:5	188 (A2)
1:10–13	206 (A3)
1:20–23	206 (A3)
1:24–31	9 (A3)
1:26	9 (A3)
1:26–27	94 (A2)
1:26–28	266 (A1)
1:28	142 (A2)
1:28–31	206 (A3)
1:31	34 (A3)
2	6 (A3)
2–3	24–30, 41 (A2); 142, 247 (A3)
2:1–4	206 (A3)
2:2	460 (A3)
2:2–3	4 (A3)
2:4b–3:24	4 (A3)
2:7	94, 323, 329 (A2)
2:15	26 (A2)
2:15–17	**24–30**, 33 (A2)
2:16–17	27 (A2)
2:17	24 (A2)
3	24–26, 41 (A2)
3:1	27 (A2); 83 (A3)
3:1–7	**24–30**, 33, 37–38 (A2)
3:2–3	27 (A2)
3:3	25 (A2)
3:4–5	27 (A2)
3:5	27 (A2)
3:5–7	238 (A2)
3:6	30 (A2)
3:12	25 (A2)
3:13	25 (A2)
3:14–19	25 (A2)
3:16	25 (A2); 129 (A3)
3:17–19	26 (A2)
3:19	17 (A2)
3:22	24–25, 27–28 (A2)
3:22–24	28 (A2)
4	254 (A1)
4:2	253 (A2)
4:3	253 (A2)
4:8	67 (A1)
4:18–19	49 (A2)
4:23	80 (A3)
4:23–24	312 (A3)
5:1	174 (A1)
5:24	32 (A1)
6	280 (A2)
6–9	34, 36
6:6	34 (A3)
6:9–22	4, **33–37**, 39 (A3)
6:11	81 (A3)
6:24	81 (A3)
6:25–33	81 (A3)
7:11	292 (A2)
7:24	**33–37**, 39 (A3)
8	41 (A2)
8:1	34 (A3)
8:14–19	**33–37**, 39 (A3)
8:21	37 (A3)
9	80 (A3)
9:1–17	182 (A3)
9:11	34 (A3)
9:15	34 (A3)
9:18–27	37 (A3)
10	336 (A2); 80 (A3)
11	41, 185, 336 (A2)
11:1–9	334, 336 (A2)
11:9	41 (A2)
11:10–31	41 (A2)
11:26–32	57 (A3)
11:31	41 (A2)
12	41, 42 (A2); 4, 57, 65, 69 (A3)
12–23	104 (A3)
12–50	51, 104, 122, 141, 174, 410 (A3)
12:1	43, 45, 46 (A2)
12:1–3	69 (A2); 105–6, 247 (A3)
12:1–4	110 (A3)
12:1–4a	26, **41–46** (A2)
12:1–8	158 (A3)
12:1–9	**50–54**, 61 (A3)
12:2	48 (A2)
12:3	180, 274 (A1); 44 (A2); 507 (A3)
12:3b	393 (A3)
12:4	44 (A2)
12:4a	43 (A2)
12:5	57 (A3)
12:6–7	72 (A2)
12:10–20	104, 230 (A3)
13:1–9	158 (A3)
13:22	81 (A3)
14	166 (A2)
15:1–6	49 (A2)
15:2	104 (A3)
15:6	67, 217 (A2); 60, 76, 112 (A3)
16	87 (A3)
16:1–15	104 (A3)
16:7–13	104 (A3)

Genesis (continued)		25:9	87 (A3)	39–50	312 (A3)
17	83 (A1); 42 (A2)	**25:19–34**	**139–43**,	39:1–6	211 (A3)
17:2	42 (A2)		146 (A3)	39:2–3	50 (A1)
17:5	42 (A2)	25:21	61 (A3)	39:20–23	211 (A3)
17:8	42 (A2)	25:23	143 (A3)	39:21	50 (A1); 176 (A2)
17:15–22	59 (A3)	26:1–5	42 (A2)	39:23	50 (A1)
17:18	42 (A2)	26:8	87 (A3)	40:5–19	212 (A3)
17:18–22	141 (A3)	26:24	57 (A1)	41:1–36	212 (A3)
17:19	42 (A2)	27	123, 158, 176	41:14	211 (A3)
17:23	42 (A2)	27:1–40	104 (A3)	41:37–45	211 (A3)
17:23–27	67 (A2)	27:1–45	143 (A3)	41:42	211 (A3)
18	42 (A2); 69, 70, 81 (A3)	27:5–17	122 (A3)	42–44	229, 312 (A3)
		27:19	174 (A3)	42:32	49 (A1)
18–21	124 (A3)	27:40–45	143 (A3)	**45:1–15**	**227–32**, 237 (A3)
18:1–15	**68–72**, 74 (A3)	28	166 (A3)	46:5–27	229 (A3)
18:14	15 (A1)	28:1	181 (A3)	48:8–9	230 (A3)
18:17–48	42 (A2)	28:10	164 (A3)	49:10–11	122 (A3)
18:19	141 (A3)	28:10–19	168 (A3)	50	299–300, 305 (A3)
19	238 (A2); 69 (A3)	**28:10–19a**	**157–61** (A3)		
19:20–22	81 (A3)	28:10–22	289 (A2); 104 (A3)	50:1–3	301 (A3)
20	42 (A2)			50:7	301 (A3)
20:1–18	104 (A3)	28:13–15	42 (A2)	50:10	301 (A3)
20:3–7	104 (A3)	28:17	164 (A3)	50:15–17	301 (A3)
21	42 (A2); 69–70, 87, 96 (A3)	28:20–22	158 (A3)	**50:15–21**	**298–302** (A3)
		29	180–81, 183 (A3)	50:19	305 (A3)
21:1–3	61 (A3)	29:1–11	72 (A2)	50:20	212, 218, 301 (A3)
21:1–7	48 (A2); **68–72** (A3)	29:9	495 (A3)	50:20–21	159 (A2)
21:8–21	**85–90**, 99 (A3)	29:9–14	174 (A3)		
21:8–34	104 (A3)	**29:15–28**	**173–77** (A3)	**Exodus**	82 (A1); 142 (A2); 87–88, 291 (A3)
21:13	93 (A3)	29:15–30	104 (A3)		
21:17–19	93 (A3)	29:31	174 (A3)	**1:1–7**	**60–63** (A2)
21:17–21	104 (A3)	30:4	253 (A2)	1:7	142 (A2)
21:20	50 (A1)	30:8	193 (A1)	1:8–14	284 (A3)
22	218 (A2); 103, 124, 183 (A3)	31	176 (A3)	**1:8–2:10**	**245–50** (A3)
		32	83 (A1); 201 (A3)	1:22	142 (A2)
22:1–14	**102–7**, 109, 110, 112, 117 (A3)	32:1–2	158 (A3)	2	248, 263 (A3)
		32:22–31	**192–96**, 198 (A3)	2–4	66 (A1)
22:1–19	48 (A2)	33:1	193 (A3)	2:15–22	72 (A2)
22:2	93 (A3)	33:1–5	229 (A3)	2:16–19	495 (A3)
22:6	109 (A3)	33:1–17	193 (A3)	2:23	358 (A3)
22:11–13	109 (A3)	33:18–19	72 (A2)	2:24	34, 282 (A3)
22:16–18	42 (A2)	35:1–15	159 (A3)	3	56 (A2); 300, 495 (A3)
24	123–25, 128 (A3)	37	229, 312 (A3)		
24–35	104 (A3)	37–50	211–12, 247 (A3)	3–4	78 (A2)
24:10–27	72 (A2)	**37:1–4**	**209–13**, 218 (A3)	3:1	253 (A2); 211, 336–37 (A3)
24:14–16	174 (A3)	37:5–8	141 (A3)		
24:34–38	**120–25**, 128 (A3)	37:5–11	211–12 (A3)	**3:1–15**	**262–67**, 277 (A3)
24:42–49	**120–25**, 128 (A3)	**37:12–28**	**209–13**, 218 (A3)	3:2	336 (A3)
24:58–67	**120–25**, 128 (A3)	37:12–36	104 (A3)	3:6	211 (A3)
24:65	136 (A3)	37:18–36	301 (A3)	3:13–14	173 (A2)
25	52, 123, 141, 153 (A3)	37:19–24	106 (A3)	3:14–15	270 (A3)

4:22–23	142 (A2)	15:2	184 (A2)	20	259, 306 (A1);
5:1	227 (A1)	15:8	442 (A3)		324, 368 (A3)
6:7	131, 179 (A1)	15:12–19	306 (A3)	20–23	306 (A1)
6:18	31 (A1)	15:13	253 (A2)	20:1–2	361 (A3)
7–11	247 (A3)	15:17	253 (A2)	20:1–3	68 (A2)
8:2	176 (A2)	15:20	477 (A3)	**20:1–4**	**353–58** (A3)
10:7	141 (A2)	**15:20–21**	**303–6** (A3)	20:1–11	357 (A3)
10:21–23	142 (A2)	15:21	387 (A3)	20:1–17	253 (A1); 357 (A3)
10:21–29	85 (A2)	15:22–25a	61 (A2)	20:2–7	376 (A3)
11:1	144 (A2)	15:23–25a	60 (A2)	20:5	89 (A2)
11:1–10	143 (A2)	15:24	318 (A3)	20:5–6	355, 357, 368 (A3)
11:3b	284 (A3)	15:27	318 (A3)	**20:7–9**	**353–58** (A3)
12	141, 143–44,	16	144 (A2); 337 (A3)	20:8–9	357 (A3)
	147 (A2); 211,	16:10	307 (A1)	20:8–11	355 (A3)
	299 (A3)	16–18	300 (A3)	20:10–11	355, 357 (A3)
12–14	247 (A3)	16:1–2	318 (A3)	**20:12–20**	**353–58** (A3)
12:1	144 (A2)	16:1–12	206 (A3)	20:13	254 (A1)
12:1–4 (5–10)	**141–45**,	**16:2–15**	**316–21** (A3)	20:14	254 (A1)
	149 (A2)	16:3	326 (A3)	20:17	254 (A1); 100 (A2)
12:1–14	**281–85**,	16:4	330 (A3)	20:20	361 (A3)
	288 (A3)	16:7–9	318 (A3)	20:21	307 (A1)
12:1–27	417 (A3)	16:12	318 (A3)	20:22–35:3	355 (A3)
12:3–4	144 (A2)	16:13	60 (A2)	21:22–25	271 (A1)
12:4	144, 147 (A2)	16:14	60 (A2)	21:24	269 (A1); 248 (A2)
12:5–10	144 (A2)	16:18	330 (A3)	22:13	495 (A3)
12:8–9	144 (A2)	16:31	321 (A3)	22:21	282n2 (A2)
12:8–11	143 (A2)	16:35	274 (A1)	22:26–27	269 (A1); 4 (A2)
12:8–20	188 (A3)	17	319 (A2); 345,	24	304–6, 309–10
12:11	144 (A2)		349 (A3)		(A1); 56 (A2)
12:11–14	**141–45**,	17:1	65 (A2)	24:1	307 (A1)
	149 (A2)	17:1–3	64 (A2)	24:1–11	304 (A1)
12:13	144 (A2)	**17:1–7**	**60–63**, 68 (A2);	24:6	307 (A1)
12:14	142, 146 (A2)		**334–39**, 444 (A3)	24:8	307 (A1)
12:31–32	144 (A2)	17:2	206 (A3)	24:9	304 (A1)
13:3–10	188 (A3)	17:2–7	318 (A3)	24:10–11	337 (A3)
13:4	143 (A2)	17:3b	60 (A2)	24:11	304 (A1)
13:8	142 (A2)	17:6	274 (A1)	**24:12–18**	**304–7**, 312,
13:11–16	142 (A2)	17:7	66 (A2); 342 (A3)		315 (A1)
13:18	32 (A1)	17:8–13	319 (A2)	24:13	315 (A1)
13:21	307 (A1); 253 (A2)	18:13–26	319 (A2)	24:15	266 (A3)
14	299–300, 305 (A3)	19	221 (A1); 69 (A3)	24:16–17	318 (A3)
14–15	308–9, 441 (A3)	19:1–2	337 (A3)	25–26	178 (A2)
14:10	299 (A3)	**19:2–8a**	**68–72**, 74 (A3)	25–28	305 (A1)
14:19–31	**298–302** (A3)	19:3	266 (A3)	25–32	306 (A1)
14:21	442 (A3)	19:5–6	393 (A3)	25:8	142 (A1)
14:21–31	205 (A2)	19:6	263 (A2)	25:17	45 (A3)
14:26–29	444 (A3)	19:9	307 (A1)	30:6	45 (A3)
14:31	57 (A1)	19:11	307 (A1)	30:23–32	159 (A1)
15	305–6 (A3)	19:16	307 (A1)	30:34	159 (A1)
15:1–22	318 (A3)	19:20	306 (A1)	32	305 (A1)
15:1b–11	**303–6** (A3)	19:25	306 (A1)	32–34	376, 393 (A3)

Exodus (*continued*)
32:1–14	**372–76**, 379 (A3)
32:8	374 (A3)
32:12b	414 (A3)
33	115 (A1)
33:5–6	336 (A3)
33:9	142 (A1)
33:9–10	307 (A1)
33:10	336n3 (A3)
33:11–13	397 (A3)
33:12–23	**389–94** (A3)
33:16	397 (A3)
33:17	336 (A3)
33:17–23	211 (A3)
33:18	143 (A1); 316 (A2); 318 (A3)
33:19	254 (A3)
33:19–23	398 (A3)
33:20	143, 304 (A1); 397 (A3)
34	56 (A2)
34:5	307 (A1)
34:6	21 (A2); 128 (A3)
34:6–7a	376 (A3)
34:6–7	186 (A2); 318, 393 (A3)
34:29–35	312 (A1)
35–40	376 (A3)
40:34	142 (A1)
40:34–38	307 (A1)
40:35	318 (A3)

Leviticus 307 (A1)
2:1	159 (A1)
2:13	238 (A1)
7:11–21	477 (A3)
9:14–16	421 (A3)
11:44	85 (A2); 266 (A3)
11:44–45	409 (A3)
11:45	85 (A2)
12:8	144 (A2)
16	180 (A2)
16:1–34	179 (A2)
17–26	263 (A1)
18–20	413 (A3)
18:5	219 (A3)
19	258–60, 263 (A1); 410 (A3)
19:1–2	**258–62**, 269 (A1); **407–11** (A3)
19:2	266 (A1); 413 (A3)
19:8	24 (A1)
19:9–10	421 (A3)
19:9–18	**258–62, 269** (A1)
19:12	255 (A1)
19:15–18	296, **407–11** (A3)
19:16	413 (A3)
19:18	264, 266 (A1); 147, 326 (A2); 413, 421 (A3)
19:20–29	260 (A1)
19:33–34	282n2 (A2); 69 (A3)
19:34–36	259 (A1)
20:1–5	118 (A3)
23:33–43	417 (A3)
23:42	320 (A3)
24:7	159 (A1)
24:19–20	271 (A1)
24:20	269 (A1)
25:4	460 (A3)
26	495 (A3)
26:11–13	227 (A1)
26:12	131 (A1)
27:32	495 (A3)

Numbers
1–10	318 (A2)
6	126 (A1)
6:24–26	234 (A3)
11	321 (A2)
11–25	318 (A2)
11:1	318 (A2); 318 (A3)
11:1–10	321 (A2)
11:4	318 (A3)
11:5	60 (A2)
11:6–9	318 (A3)
11:11–15	321 (A2)
11:14	321 (A2)
11:16–17a	321 (A2)
11:17b	321 (A2)
11:24	319 (A2)
11:24–30	**318–21**, 329, 335, 339 (A2)
11:25	320, 321 (A2)
11:26	320 (A2)
11:29	320, 329 (A2)
11:31–35	321
14	21 (A2); 318 (A3)
14:13–16	21 (A2)
14:17–19	318 (A3)
14:18	89 (A2)
14:18–19	21 (A2)
14:22	206 (A3)
14:27–29	318 (A3)
15:37–39	455 (A3)
15:38–41	64 (A3)
16:11	318 (A3)
16:41	318 (A3)
17:5	318 (A3)
17:10	318 (A3)
20:1–13	336, 411, 444 (A3)
20:2–13	338 (A2)
20:12	64 (A2)
21:4–9	320 (A3)
21:19	61 (A2)
22	66, 212 (A1)
22–24	210 (A1)
24:17	158 (A1)
25:1–15	210 (A1)
26–36	318 (A2)
27:17	252 (A2)
28:7	147 (A2)
28:19	238 (A1)
31	66 (A1)

Deuteronomy 307 (A1); 318 (A2); 35, 291, 476 (A3)
1:19	32 (A1)
1:27	318 (A3)
2:7	176 (A2)
4:34	82 (A1)
4:37	243 (A1)
5:1–21	253 (A1)
5–6	288 (A1)
5:6–10	288 (A1)
5:15	82 (A1)
5:17	254 (A1)
5:18	254 (A1)
5:21	254 (A1); 100 (A2)
5:32–33	97 (A3)
6	420 (A3)
6:4	494 (A3)
6:4–5	288 (A1)
6:5	147, 326 (A2)
6:16	54, 66 (A1)
7:6	243 (A1)
7:6–7	243 (A1)
7:7–8	317 (A1)
7:7–11	68 (A2)
7:8	68 (A2)
7:19	82 (A1)

8:3	318 (A3)	30:2	21 (A2)	1:17–20	477 (A3)
8:16	318 (A3)	30:11–14	219–20 (A3)	1:19	50 (A1)
8:17	219 (A3)	30:15	167 (A3)	1:21	477 (A3)
9:4	219 (A3)	30:15–16	255 (A1)	1:22	50 (A1)
9:5	243 (A1)	**30:15–20**	**242–46**,	1:22–26	477 (A3)
9:19	32 (A1)		251 (A1)	1:27–33	477 (A3)
10–11	288 (A1)	30:17	255–56 (A1)	2:1–2	479 (A3)
10:12–11:32	288–89 (A1)	31:17–18	119 (A2)	2:11–15	479 (A3)
10:15	243 (A1)	30:19	300 (A1)	2:11–19	477 (A3)
10:16	289 (A1)	30:20	257 (A1)	2:18	50 (A1)
10:17–19	282n2 (A2)	31:26	411 (A3)	3–16	477 (A3)
10:18	507 (A3)	32	314 (A2)	3:8	477 (A3)
10:18–19	69 (A3)	32:2	119 (A2)	3:11	477 (A3)
11	293 (A1)	32:21–22	476 (A3)	3:12	477 (A3)
11:2	82 (A1)	32:35	273–74 (A3)	3:13	477 (A3)
11:18–21	**288–91** (A1);	32:43	25 (A1)	3:14	477 (A3)
	33–37, 39–40 (A3)	32:48–52	411 (A3)	3:15	477 (A3)
11:19–22	295 (A1)	33	314 (A2)	3:30	477 (A3)
11:22–25	290 (A1)	34	56 (A2); 247,	4	477, 480 (A3)
11:26	295 (A1)		414 (A3)	4–5	477 (A3)
11:26–28	**288–91**, 295,	34:1–4	221 (A1)	**4:1–7**	**475–80**, 483,
	300 (A1); **33–37**,	**34:1–12**	**407–11** (A3)		490 (A3)
	39–40 (A3)	34:4	409 (A3)	4:2	477 (A3)
11:29–32	290 (A1)	34:10	409 (A3)	4:3	477 (A3)
12–26	288 (A1)			4:15	480 (A3)
14:2	243 (A1)	**Joshua**	441–42, 445 (A3)	4:23	480 (A3)
14:29	507 (A3)	1:6–9	442 (A3)	5:4–5	130 (A2)
16:7	144 (A2)	2	443 (A3)	5:7	477 (A3)
17:14–20	494 (A3)	2:1–21	442 (A3)	5:14–15	477 (A3)
17:20	176 (A3)	3	299 (A3)	5:18	477 (A3)
18:21–22	109 (A3)	3:7	50 (A1)	5:31	477 (A3)
19:21	269, 271 (A1)	**3:7–17**	**440–45**, 448,	6–8	196 (A1)
20:19	244 (A1)		451, 455 (A3)	6:1	477 (A3)
22:12	455 (A3)	4:19–5:12	210 (A1)	6:1–6	477 (A3)
23	243 (A1)	5:12	318 (A3)	6:10	477 (A3)
24:1–4	254 (A1)	6:21–25	444 (A3)	6:11–17	78 (A2)
24:12–13	269 (A1)	6:27	50 (A1)	6:15	49 (A1)
24:17	507 (A3)	8:1–24	444 (A3)	6:16	66 (A1)
24:17–18	227 (A1)	10	444 (A3)	6:36	66 (A1)
24:19–21	507 (A3)	18:25	175 (A3)	6:39–40	66 (A1)
25:1–3	82 (A3)	21:17	175 (A3)	7:2–7	66 (A1)
26:8	82 (A1)	24	289 (A1); 460 (A3)	7:4–23	205 (A2)
26:12	507 (A3)	**24:1–3a**	**458–63**, 465 (A3)	8:24–35	67 (A1)
28	82 (A1)	24:2–15	442 (A3)	8:28	477 (A3)
28:3	185 (A2)	**24:14–25**	**458–63**, 465 (A3)	8:33–35	477 (A3)
28:20–25	20 (A2)	24:19	468 (A3)	8:34–27	477 (A3)
28:29	66 (A1)	24:19–25	468 (A3)	9	67 (A1)
28:29–30	476 (A3)	24:32	72 (A2)	9:53–54	477 (A3)
28:39	476 (A3)			10:6	477 (A3)
30:1	21 (A2)	**Judges**	307 (A1)	10:6–16	477 (A3)
30:1–10	20 (A2)	1:3–15	477 (A3)	10:8	477 (A3)

Judges (continued)		18:28	50 (A1)	2	211 (A3)
10:10–14	477 (A3)	19	79 (A2)	2:11	32 (A1); 56 (A2)
11:29–40	104 (A3)	25	79 (A2)	2:20–21	238 (A1)
12:7	477 (A3)	28	79 (A2)	4:18–37	106 (A2); 64 (A3)
13:1	477 (A3)			14:25	317 (A3)
13:5–7	126 (A1)	**2 Samuel**	289, 307 (A1)	14:27	317 (A3)
14–16	79 (A2)	5:2	158 (A1)	15:29	204 (A1)
16:13	477 (A3)	5:10	50 (A1)	16	54 (A1)
18:14–31	425 (A3)	7:1–17	109 (A3)	16:1–20	50 (A1)
		7:5	57 (A1)	16:7–9	50 (A1)
Ruth		7:8	57 (A1)	17:6–7	318 (A3)
1:16–17	176 (A2)	7:12–16	51 (A1)	17:23	318 (A3)
		7:16	31, 63 (A1)	17:24–41	72 (A2)
1 Samuel	289 (A1)	11	175 (A3)	18:7	51 (A1)
1:12–20	61 (A3)	11:3	175 (A3)	18:13	210 (A1)
2:1–10	161 (A2); 301 (A3)	12:1–14	357 (A3)	18:13–16	51, 67 (A1)
2:3	217 (A1)	20:8	175 (A3)	19:32–37	51 (A1)
2:10	31 (A1)	22:8	130 (A2)	20:1–11	66 (A1)
2:35	31 (A1)	22:47	61 (A2)	22	476 (A3)
3	77 (A2)	22:50	25 (A1)	22:14	477 (A3)
3:1	77 (A2)			24:12–16	494 (A3)
3:19	50 (A1)	**1 Kings**	289, 307 (A1)		
8	183 (A2)	1	175 (A3)	**1 Chronicles**	
7	477 (A3)	3	174 (A3)	11:9	50 (A1)
9	78 (A2)	3:1–4	180 (A3)	14:16	175 (A3)
9:2	73 (A2)	3:4	210 (A1)		
9:3–12	72 (A2)	**3:5–12**	**173–77**, 179,	**2 Chronicles**	307 (A1)
10:1	79 (A2)		182 (A3)	1:1	50 (A1)
10:6	79 (A2)	3:13–14	180 (A3)	1:2–4	393 (A3)
10:23	78 (A2)	11–12	494 (A3)	1:3	175 (A3)
12:3	31 (A1)	11:3–4	180 (A3)	13:5	238 (A1)
12:5	31 (A1)	17–19	210 (A3)	15:9	50 (A1)
13:6	83 (A2)	17:2	210 (A3)	17:3	50 (A1)
13:14	497 (A3)	17:8	210 (A3)	24:9	57 (A1)
16:1–13	**77–83**,	17:17–24	106 (A2); 64 (A3)	28	50, 54 (A1)
	85–86 (A2)	18	32 (A1); 105 (A3)	28:4–8	51 (A1)
16:7	73, 86 (A2)	18:1	210 (A3)	35:13	144 (A2)
16:7b	78–79 (A2)	18:29	211 (A3)		
16:11	78, 253 (A2);	19	56 (A2); 220 (A3)	**Nehemiah**	307 (A1)
	495 (A3)	**19:9–18**	**209–13** (A3)	9:15	318 (A3)
16:12	78 (A2)	19:11–12	130 (A2)	9:20	318 (A3)
16:13	73, 79, 95 (A2)	19:19–21	205 (A1)		
16:14	392 (A3)	21	210 (A3)	**Esther**	
17:15	495 (A3)	21:17	210 (A3)	5	176 (A2)
17:31–51	94 (A2)	21:28	210 (A3)	7	176 (A2)
17:34–35	495 (A3)	22	47 (A1)	7:9–10	320 (A3)
17:34–37	495 (A3)	22:17	252 (A2)	8:8	15 (A1)
17:40–54	205 (A2)				
17:45–46	94 (A2)	**2 Kings**	289 (A1)	**Job**	289, 307 (A1); 35 (A3)
18:12	50 (A1)	1	47 (A1)	1–2	5 (A3)
18:14	50 (A1)	1–2	210 (A3)	5:10–11	42 (A1)

5:14	66 (A1)	16:8	210 (A2)	23:2–3	82 (A2)
6:6	238 (A1)	16:9	214 (A2)	23:3a	252 (A2)
6:16	142 (A3)	16:10–11	101 (A2)	23:4	85, 165, 245 (A2)
9:6	130 (A2)	16:11	222 (A2)	23:4–5	82 (A2)
15:5	24 (A2)	17	119 (A2); 201 (A3)	23:5	82, 245 (A2)
19:25	146 (A1)	**17:1–7**	**197–99** (A3)	23:6	82, 165, 245, 246 (A2)
37:6	142 (A3)	17:8–9	199 (A3)	24:3	300n1 (A2)
38–42	94 (A2)	17:13	199 (A3)	**25**	**341, 349** (A3)
38:11	293 (A2)	**17:15**	**197–99** (A3)	25:1–9	340–42 (A3)
40:3–7	94 (A2)	18–21	361 (A3)	25:4	349 (A3)
		18:7	130 (A2)	25:4–5	335 (A3)
Psalms	82, 307 (A1); 105, 252, 261, 278, 298–99, 307, 315–16, 323, 336 (A2)	18:49	25 (A1)	25:7	313, 335 (A3)
		19	356, **359–61** (A3)	25:8–9	335 (A3)
		19:1	9 (A3)	25:9	349 (A3)
		19:24	61 (A2)	25:10	341 (A3)
1	**412–15** (A3)	21	110 (A2)	26	119 (A2)
1:1	408, 417–18 (A3)	21:42	110 (A2)	**26:1–8**	**268–71** (A3)
1:1–6	472 (A3)	**22**	131, 139, **162–65**, 167, 177, 214 (A2); 392 (A3)	26:12	269 (A3)
1:3–4	408 (A3)			27	197–99 (A1); 119 (A2)
1:4–6	418 (A3)	22:1	139, 160 (A2)		
2	63, 101, **304, 308–10**, 312, 315 (A1)	22:1–2	163, 164 (A2)	**27:1**	**193, 197–99** (A1); 85 (A2)
		22:3	164 (A2)		
2:6	31, 221 (A1)	22:3–5	163 (A2)	27:2–3	197 (A1)
2:7	173–74 (A1)	22:6	164 (A2)	**27:4–9**	**193, 197–99** (A1)
2:8–9	316 (A1)	22:6–7	164 (A2)	27:10–14	197 (A1)
3:4	221 (A1)	22:6–8	163 (A2)	28:4	313 (A3)
3:6	30 (A2)	22:7	164 (A2)	**29**	**162, 167–68** (A1)
3:17	273 (A3)	22:9	164 (A2)	31	301 (A1); 118, 121–22, 160, 260–61 (A2); 39–41 (A3)
5	119 (A2); 312 (A3)	22:9–10	163 (A2)		
5:7	68 (A2)	22:11–18	163 (A2)		
5:8	68 (A2)	22:12	164 (A2)	**31:1–5**	**288, 292–93** (A1); **260–61**, 264 (A2); **38–41** (A3)
5:43–48	313 (A3)	22:13	164 (A2)		
7	119 (A2); 312 (A3)	22:14	164 (A2)		
8	266 (A1); **2, 8–9** (A3)	22:15	164 (A2)	31:2a	261 (A2)
8:1	10 (A3)	22:16	164 (A2)	31:2b	261 (A2)
8:4	312 (A1)	22:18	164 (A2)	31:4	261 (A2)
8:5	313 (A1)	22:19–21	164 (A2)	31:5	295 (A1); 260 (A2)
9:14	83 (A1)	22:19–31	131, 139 (A2)	31:6–8	39 (A3)
12	**251–53** (A3)	22:22–26	164 (A2)	31:6–18	40 (A3)
13	105 (A2); 108–10 (A3)	22:22–31	164 (A2)	31:9	122 (A2); 39 (A3)
13–15	213 (A2)	22:25	164 (A2)	31:9–10	121 (A2)
15	**209, 214–15** (A1)	22:27–28	164 (A2)	31:9–13	118 (A2)
15:1	221 (A1)	22:29–31	164 (A2)	**31:9–16**	**121–22**, 137 (A2)
15:2–5	222 (A1)	22:31b	167 (A2)	31:11	121 (A2)
15:3–5	218 (A1)	**23**	96, 131, 274, 276 (A1); 82–83, 161, **245–46**, 252, 253 (A2); **377–79**, 495, 499 (A3)	31:13	121 (A2)
16	210–211, **213–15**, 217, 222, 230 (A2)			31:14	39 (A3)
				31:15	121, 160, 261 (A2)
16:1	214 (A2)			**31:15–16**	**260–61**, 264 (A2)
16:2	222 (A2)			31:15–18	39 (A3)
16:6	213 (A2)	23:1	245, 246, 248 (A2)	31:16	118 (A2)
16:7	214 (A2)	23:2	245 (A2)		

Psalms (*continued*)

31:19–24	**288, 292–93** (A1); 121 (A2); **38–41** (A3)
31:21	295 (A1)
31:23	290, 295 (A1)
32	25, 26, **29–31** (A2)
32:1	30, 31 (A2)
32:1–2	29, 30 (A2)
32:2b	30 (A2)
32:3a	31 (A2)
32:3–4	29, 30 (A2)
32:5	25, 30, 31 (A2)
32:5–9	29, 30 (A2)
32:6	31 (A2)
32:7	30 (A2)
32:7b	30 (A2)
32:10–11	29, 30 (A2)
32:10b	30 (A2)
32:12–14	33 (A2)
33	57 (A3)
33:1–12	**55–57** (A3)
33:6	141 (A1)
33:16–23	56 (A3)
34	222 (A1); 279 (A2); 313, 429, 430 (A3)
34:1	436 (A3)
34:1–10	426, **429–30**, 432 (A3)
34:8	262 (A2)
34:22	426, **429–30**, 432 (A3)
35	312 (A3)
37:11	224 (A1)
40	189 (A1); 465 (A3)
40:1–11	**177, 182–83**, 189 (A1)
40:12–17	183 (A1)
40:13–17	465 (A3)
42	447–48 (A3)
42:1–2	72 (A2)
43	**446–48** (A3)
44	114 (A1)
44:9–22	161 (A2)
44:11	252 (A2)
44:22	252 (A2)
45	128, 131 (A3)
45:6	166 (A2)
45:10–17	**126–29** (A3)
46	**38–41** (A3)
46:1	43 (A3)
46:4	337 (A3)
46:9–10	128 (A3)
46:10	305 (A1)
47	295 (A2)
50	56 (A3)
50:7–15	**55–57** (A3)
51	9–10, 21, 178 (A2); 312 (A3)
51:1	9 (A2)
51:1–6	9 (A2)
51:1–17	4, **8–10** (A2)
51:2	32 (A1); 9 (A2)
51:3	9 (A2)
51:4	9 (A2)
51:5	9 (A2)
51:5–8	9 (A2)
51:6	9 (A2)
	142 (A3)
51:7	9 (A2)
51:7–11	9 (A2)
51:8	9 (A2)
51:9	9 (A2)
51:10	250 (A1)
51:11	9 (A2)
51:12	9 (A2)
51:12–17	9 (A2)
51:13	9 (A2)
51:13–14	9 (A2)
51:14	9 (A2)
51:15–17	9 (A2)
51:17	4 (A2)
55	312 (A3)
55:22	310 (A2)
58	312 (A3)
59	312 (A3)
62:1–5	83 (A1)
62:2	61 (A2)
65	145, 149 (A3)
65:1–13	**144–47** (A3)
66	278 (A2)
66:8–20	**277–78** (A2)
66:18	278 (A2)
67	233–35 (A3)
67:3	146 (A3)
67:5	146 (A3)
68	307, 315 (A2)
68:1	307, 309, 315 (A2)
68:1–10	**306–8** (A2)
68:4	307, 315 (A2)
68:5	307, 315 (A2)
68:6	307, 315 (A2)
68:7	307 (A2)
68:7–8	130 (A2)
68:8	307, 315 (A2)
68:9	315 (A2)
68:18	300n1 (A2)
68:30	48 (A1)
68:32	307, 315 (A2)
68:32–35	**306–8** (A2)
68:34	307 (A2)
69	119 (A2); 92, 312 (A3)
69:7–18	**91–93** (A3)
69:8–9	99 (A3)
69:9	24 (A1)
69:35	92 (A3)
70	464–66 (A3)
71	465 (A3)
72	151, 157 (A1); 109, 128, 145 (A3)
72:1–7	**17, 22–23, 146, 150–51** (A1)
72:2	26 (A1)
72:4	26 (A1)
72:7	26 (A1)
72:10–14	**146, 150–51** (A1)
72:11	147 (A1)
72:18	19 (A1)
72:18–19	**17, 22–23**, 26 (A1)
74:2	56 (A2)
77:7–10	105 (A2)
78	341–42, 465 (A3)
78:1–4	**340–42** (A3)
78:1–7	**464–66** (A3)
78:12–16	**340–42** (A3)
78:24	318 (A3)
78:35	61 (A2)
78:70–71	495 (A3)
79	313 (A3)
80	51, 55 (A1); 361 (A3)
80:1	212 (A3)
80:1–7	**50, 54–55** (A1)
80:2–3	55 (A1)
80:3	361 (A3)
80:5	55 (A1)
80:7–15	**355, 359–61** (A3)
80:17–19	**50, 54–55** (A1)
81	313 (A3)
82	109 (A3)
82:5	313 (A1)
84	184 (A2)

85	216 (A3)	96:12–13	73 (A1)	106:25	318 (A3)
85:8–13	**214–16** (A3)	96:13	99 (A3)	106:47	376 (A3)
85:10	439 (A3)	**97**	**81, 86–88** (A1)	**107:1–7**	**446–48** (A3)
86	93, 163 (A3)	97:11	95 (A1)	107:4	32 (A1)
86:1–10	**91–93** (A3)	**98**	**98, 102–3** (A1)	**107:33–37**	**446–48** (A3)
86:3	243 (A3)	98:7–9	146 (A3)	109	312 (A3)
86:5	318 (A3)	**99**	**304**, 305, **308–10**,	109:13–14	89 (A2)
86:11–17	**162–64** (A3)		312 (A1); 393,	110	421 (A3)
86:14–17	99 (A3)		**395–98** (A3)	110:1	502 (A3)
86:15	128, 318 (A3)	99:1–2	390 (A3)	112	239–41 (A1)
86:16–17	**91–93** (A3)	99:4	390 (A3)	**112:1–10**	**225, 230–32** (A1)
88	105 (A2)	99:13	390 (A3)	112:5	237 (A1)
89	82 (A1); 109,	**100**	**73–75**,	112:9	237 (A1)
	394 (A3)		**498–500** (A3)	113–118	147, 188, 230 (A2)
89:1–4	**108–10, 128** (A3)	100:1	146 (A3)	113:5–9	165 (A1)
89:15–18	**108–10, 128** (A3)	100:3	252 (A2); 507 (A3)	**114**	188 (A2); **303–6**,
89:26	61 (A2)	103	305, 309, 312 (A3)		**309** (A3)
90	409–10, 414,	**103:1–13**	**303–6** (A3)	116	146–47, 188,
	483 (A3)	103:8	128, 309 (A3)		230–31, 238 (A2);
90:1–6	**412–15** (A3)	103:14b–16	309 (A3)		74, 93 (A3)
90:1–12	**481–83** (A3)	103:20–22	146 (A3)	116:1	146, 147, 230,
90:3	409 (A3)	104	323 (A2)		231 (A2)
90:13–17	**412–15** (A3)	104:3	325, 329,	**116:1–2**	**146–47** (A2);
93	**292–93, 295** (A2)		330 (A2)		**73–75**, 79 (A3)
93–99	392 (A3)	104:24–25	323 (A2)	**116:1–4**	**230–31** (A2)
93:2–4	293 (A2)	**104:24–34**	320, **322–23** (A2)	116:1–11	147 (A2)
93:6	293 (A2)	104:25–26	323 (A2)	116:2	230 (A2)
94	312 (A3)	104:26	323 (A2)	116:3	146, 147, 231 (A2)
95	**64–66**, 68 (A2);	104:27–28	323 (A2)	116:3–9	146 (A2)
	499 (A3)	104:29–30	323 (A2)	116:3–11	147 (A2)
95:1–2	65 (A2)	104:35	323 (A2)	116:4	231, 238 (A2)
95:1–7	65 (A2)	**104:35b**	320, **322–23** (A2)	116:8	146 (A2)
95:1–7a	64 (A2);	105	180, 215–16, 270,	116:9	146 (A2)
	498–500 (A3)		273, 330 (A3)	116:10–19	146 (A2)
95:3–5	65 (A2)	**105:1–6**	**214–16, 268–71,**	116:12	147 (A2)
95:6	65 (A2)		**322–24** (A3)	116:12–13	146 (A2)
95:6–8	65 (A2)	**105:1–11**	**178–81** (A3)	**116:12–19**	**146–47, 230–31**
95:7–11	65 (A2)	105:16–17	230 (A3)		(A2); **73–75** (A3)
95:7a	65, 252 (A2)	**105:16–22**	**212, 214–16,**	116:13	147, 231 (A2)
95:7b	65 (A2)		**218** (A3)	116:14–18	233 (A2)
95:8	65 (A2)	105:23	230 (A3)	116:15	231, 233, 238 (A2)
95:8–9	337 (A3)	**105:23–26**	**268–71** (A3)	116:16	147, 233 (A2)
95:8–11	65 (A2)	**105:37–45**	**322–24** (A3)	116:17	233 (A2)
95:9b	65 (A2)	105:45a	181 (A3)	116:18–19	231 (A2)
95:11	68 (A2)	**105:45b**	**178–81, 214–16,**	116:19	231 (A2)
96	**65, 70–71**, 87 (A1)		**268–71** (A3)	117:1	25 (A1); 146 (A3)
96–97	102 (A1)	106	376 (A3)	118	110, 187–89 (A2)
96:1–13	**395–98** (A3)	**106:1–6**	**377–79** (A3)	118:1	188 (A2)
96:7–9	146 (A3)	106:3	374 (A3)	**118:1–2**	**109–10, 187–89,**
96:10–13	68 (A1)	**106:19–23**	**377–79** (A3)		**201** (A2)
96:11–13	146 (A3)	106:20	375 (A3)	118:1–4	187 (A2)

Psalms (continued)

118:2	201 (A2)
118:3–18	109 (A2)
118:5–8	187 (A2)
118:5–18	187, 188 (A2)
118:14–24	**187–89** (A2)
118:15	188 (A2)
118:15–16	188 (A2)
118:17	188 (A2)
118:19	109, 188 (A2)
118:19–28	187, 188 (A2)
118:19–29	**109–10**, 146, 201 (A2)
118:21	110 (A2)
118:22	110, 188, 263 (A2)
118:22–23	368 (A3)
118:23	188 (A2)
118:23–24	110 (A2)
118:24	110, 187, 188, 201 (A2); 387 (A3)
118:25	110 (A2)
118:25a	188 (A2)
118:26	110, 188 (A2)
118:27b	110 (A2)
118:28	110 (A2)
118:29	110, 187, 188 (A2)
119	82, 247, 264 (A1); 147, 179–80, 287 (A3)
119:1–2	255, 257 (A1)
119:1–8	**242, 247–48** (A1)
119:2	251 (A1)
119:4	255 (A1)
119:7	255–56 (A1)
119:33–40	**258**, 259, 263–64, 270 (A1); 286–88, 289 (A3)
119:105–112	**144–47** (A3)
119:129–136	**178–81** (A3)
120	9 (A1)
120–134	9 (A1); 483 (A3)
121	9 (A1); **45–46** (A2)
121:1	46 (A2)
121:1a	45 (A2)
121:1b	45 (A2)
121:2	46 (A2)
121:2a	45 (A2)
121:2b	46 (A2)
121:3–8	45 (A2)
121:3a	46 (A2)
121:3b	46 (A2)
121:3b–4	46 (A2)
121:4	499 (A3)
121:5a	46 (A2)
121:6	45, 46 (A2)
121:7	46 (A2)
121:7a	46 (A2)
121:7b	46 (A2)
121:8	45, 46 (A2)
121:8b	46 (A2)
122	**2, 6–7, 7,** 9 (A1); 184 (A2)
123	**481–83** (A3)
123:2	489 (A3)
124	**251–53**, 255, 483 (A3)
128	**178–81** (A3)
130	**97–99**, 101 (A2)
130:1	97 (A2)
130:3–4	97 (A2)
130:5	97 (A2)
130:6	97 (A2)
130:7	97 (A2)
131	**273, 278–79**, 280, 284 (A1); 20, **23–24** (A3)
131:1	281 (A1)
131:3	275 (A1)
133	**233–35**, 237 (A3)
135:18	401 (A3)
137	180 (A1)
138	**251–53** (A3)
138:6	341 (A2)
139	164, 167 (A3)
139:1–12	**162–64**, 478 (A3)
139:1–18	20 (A3)
139:8	300n1 (A2)
139:13–16	164 (A3)
139:19–22	164 (A3)
139:23–24	**162–64** (A3)
140:3	32 (A1)
141	313 (A3)
142:1–2	105 (A2)
145	126, 131, 132, 198, 201, 330 (A3)
145:1–8	**322–24** (A3)
145:8–9	**197–99, 318** (A3)
145:8–14	**126–29**, 146 (A3)
145:9	281 (A1); 128 (A3)
145:10–12	146 (A3)
145:14	202 (A3)
145:14–21	**197–99** (A3)
145:21	324 (A3)
146:5–10	**34**, 36, **39–41** (A1)
146:7	90 (A2); 122 (A3)
147	136–37 (A1)
147:1–2	135 (A1)
147:12–20	**130, 135–36** (A1)
148	**114, 118–19**, 120, 125 (A1)
148:1–10	146 (A3)
148:6	15 (A1)
148:7–8	119 (A1)
148:8	142 (A3)
148:11–13	146 (A3)
149	**286–88**, 289 (A3)
149:1	109 (A3)
149:5	109 (A3)
149:8–9	288 (A3)
149:9	109 (A3)
150:6	146 (A3)

Proverbs
87, 286 (A1)

8	175 (A3)
8:22	217 (A1)
8:22–31	243 (A1)
9	386 (A3)
9:1–5	194 (A3)
9:10	137 (A3)
13:9	472 (A3)
14:21	436 (A3)
25:21–22	273–74 (A3)

Ecclesiastes
35 (A3)

9:2	245 (A1)

Song of Solomon
129, 131, 357 (A3)

2	128 (A3)
2:8–13	**126–29** (A3)
7:1–10	128 (A3)

Isaiah
57, 162–63, 194, 307 (A1); 130, 317 (A3)

1–39	98, 147 (A1)
1:1	2 (A1)
1:2	210 (A1)
1:4	195 (A1)
1:5	6 (A1)
1:8	83 (A1); 19 (A3)
1:10–17	460 (A3)

Comprehensive Scripture Index for Year A

1:16–17	130–31 (A3)	8:5–8	51 (A1)	25:6	100 (A1)
1:17	358 (A3)	8:7	194 (A3)	25:6–8	379 (A3)
1:23	226 (A1)	8:8	51, 66 (A1)	25:8	100 (A1)
1:27	358 (A3)	8:9–10	51 (A1)	26:8	376 (A3)
2	99 (A1)	8:10	51 (A1)	27:2–6	355 (A3)
2–3	6 (A1)	8:12–13	279 (A2)	28–33	35 (A1)
2:1	2 (A1)	8:14	263 (A2)	28:6	358 (A3)
2:1–5	3, **2–5**, 10 (A1)	8:16	117 (A2)	28:16	263 (A2); 218–19 (A3)
2:2	9 (A1)	8:17	376 (A3)		
2:2–3	147 (A1)	8:39	134 (A3)	28:17	358 (A3)
2:2–4	239 (A1); 128, 319 (A3)	9	55, 71, 197–99 (A1)	29:6	130 (A2)
		9:1	67 (A1)	29:14	216 (A1)
2:3	6 (A1)	9:1–2	195, 204 (A1)	29:18	66 (A1)
2:4	196 (A1); 12 (A2)	**9:1–4**	**193–96** (A1)	30:18	358 (A3)
2:5	9 (A1)	9:2	55, 78, 205 (A1)	32:16	358 (A3)
2:12	281 (A1)	**9:2–7**	**65–69**, 71 (A1)	33:2	376 (A3)
2:12–22	477 (A3)	9:5	196 (A1)	33:5	358 (A3)
3:9–20	131 (A3)	9:6–7	73, 205 (A1)	33:14	32 (A1)
3:13–15	195 (A1)	9:7	196 (A1); 358 (A3)	33:21	337 (A3)
3:15	226 (A1)	9:8–21	66 (A1)	34	477 (A3)
3:23	90 (A1)	9:8–10:4	65 (A1)	34–35	35 (A1)
4:18–25	131 (A3)	10	18 (A1)	35	36–38, 40 (A1)
5	367 (A3)	10:1	226 (A1)	35:1	43 (A1)
5–7	131 (A3)	10:1–5	66 (A1)	**35:1–10**	**17, 34–38** (A1)
5:1–7	195, 250 (A1); **353–58** (A3)	10:2	226 (A1)	35:4	38 (A1)
		10:21	66 (A1)	35:4–10	43 (A1)
5:4	360 (A3)	10:26	66 (A1)	35:7	43 (A1)
5:7	360 (A3)	10:32	19 (A3)	35:9	36 (A1)
5:8	226 (A1)	10:33–34	18 (A1)	37:12	247 (A3)
5:11	354 (A3)	11	142 (A3)	40	98 (A1); 86, 140, 194, 247 (A3)
5:12	354 (A3)	11–12	66 (A1)		
5:16	358 (A3)	11:1	23, 126 (A1)	40–53	273 (A1)
5:20	226 (A1)	**11:1–10**	**17–21** (A1)	40–55	98, 146–47, 164–65, 226 (A1); 3, 116–18 (A2); 145, 159, 193 (A3)
5:23	226 (A1)	11:4–9	26 (A1)		
6:1	68 (A1)	11:9	23 (A1)		
6:8	183 (A1)	11:10	25–26 (A1)		
6:9	147 (A1)	11:15–16	117 (A2)	40:1	99 (A1); 247 (A3)
6:11	131 (A3)	12:1–2	92 (A1)	40:3	30, 32, 82, 188 (A1); 247 (A3)
7	130 (A3)	12:3	338 (A2)		
7–8	50 (A1)	13	477 (A3)	40:4	274 (A1); 142 (A3)
7–9	205 (A1)	13:6	477 (A3)	40:6–8	141 (A1); 247 (A3)
7:3	51 (A1)	16:1	19 (A3)	40:7a	233 (A2)
7:7–9	50 (A1)	16:3	358 (A3)	40:8	233 (A2)
7:10–16	**50–53**, 57 (A1)	16:5	358 (A3)	40:14	358 (A3)
7:12	66 (A1)	22	477 (A3)	40:15–17	247 (A3)
7:13	63 (A1)	22:5	484 (A3)	40:28	145 (A3)
7:14	51, 55, 62, 66–67 (A1); 176 (A2); 15 (A3)	22:12–14	15 (A1)	40:31	48, 146 (A1); 376 (A3)
		24	375 (A3)	41–48	159 (A3)
		25	99 (A1); 386 (A3)	41:1	312 (A2)
7:20	51 (A1)	**25:1–9**	**372–76**, 378 (A3)	41:8–9	160–61 (A2)
7:23–25	51 (A1)	25:4	373 (A3)	41:10	51, 66 (A1)

Isaiah (*continued*)

41:14	145 (A3)
41:21	145 (A3)
42	180, 183 (A1)
42:1	100, 139, 173–74 (A1); 358 (A3)
42:1–4	116, 158, 160 (A2); 15, 19 (A3)
42:1–6	118, 158 (A2)
42:1–9	**162–66**, 168 (A1); 118 (A2)
42:3	19 (A1); 118 (A2)
42:3–4	358 (A3)
42:4–7	174 (A1)
42:6	31, 154, 174 (A1); 146, 393 (A3)
42:7	66 (A1); 122 (A3)
42:8	164 (A1)
42:9	15 (A3)
42:16	66 (A1)
42:18	246 (A3)
42:18–22	160–61 (A2)
43:2	174 (A1)
43:8–10	160–61 (A2)
43:14	145 (A3)
43:14–21	117 (A2)
43:15	145 (A3)
43:16–21	174 (A1)
43:20–21	263 (A2)
44	42 (A2)
44:1	246 (A3)
44:1–2	160–61 (A2)
44:3	42 (A2); 160 (A3)
44:6	145 (A3)
44:6–8	**157–61**, 163, 168 (A3)
44:9–20	195 (A1)
44:21	160–61 (A2)
44:26–28	159 (A3)
44:28	160 (A3)
45	404 (A3)
45:1	31 (A1)
45:1–3	396 (A3)
45:1–7	**389–94** (A3)
45:2	253 (A2)
45:3–6	397 (A3)
45:4	160–61 (A2)
45:6	396 (A3)
45:14	51, 66 (A1)
45:15	317 (A1)
45:22–23	393 (A3)
46:3	246 (A3)
46:6	160 (A2)
46:12	246 (A3)
48:1	246 (A3)
48:2	160–61 (A2)
48:10	226 (A1)
49	183, 274 (A1); 19–21 (A3)
49:1	246 (A3)
49:1–6	278 (A1); 116, 160 (A2); 19 (A3)
49:1–7	**177–81**, 189 (A1); 158 (A2)
49:3	117, 160–61 (A2)
49:6	100, 274 (A1); 19, 146, 393 (A3)
49:7	179 (A1)
49:8–15	278 (A1)
49:8–16	**273–77**, 281, 284 (A1)
49:8-16a	18–22 (A3)
49:10	426 (A3)
49:13	26 (A3)
49:14–15	24 (A3)
49:14–23	159 (A3)
49:15	285 (A1)
49:16	281 (A1); 26 (A3)
49:18	146 (A1)
49:21	19 (A3)
49:23	376 (A3)
50	117, 118, 119 (A2)
50:1	116 (A2)
50:4	117, 121–22 (A2)
50:4–7	19 (A3)
50:4–9	217 (A1); 158 (A2)
50:4–9a	**116–22**, 124 (A2)
50:4–11	118, 160 (A2)
50:4a	118 (A2)
50:4b	118 (A2)
50:5–6	118 (A2)
50:6	117, 122 (A2)
50:6b	119 (A2)
50:7–8	117 (A2)
50:7–9a	120 (A2)
50:7a	122 (A2)
50:8–9	117 (A2)
50:8b	122 (A2)
51	252 (A3)
51:1–2	42 (A2)
51:1–6	**245–50** (A3)
51:1–12	98 (A1)
51:3	247 (A3)
51:4–5	42 (A2)
51:5	376 (A3)
51:7	246–47 (A3)
52	102–3, 274 (A1)
52–53	57 (A1); 118 (A2); 280 (A3)
52:3	99 (A1)
52:7	57 (A1); 145 (A3)
52:7–10	**98–101**, 103 (A1)
52:11	274 (A1)
52:12	227 (A1)
52:13	158 (A2)
52:13–15	158, 161 (A2)
52:13–53:12	116, 117, 118, 137, **157–61**, 164, 177 (A2); 19 (A3)
52:15a	159 (A2)
53	218 (A1); 167 (A2)
53:1	164 (A2)
53:1–9	217 (A1)
53:3	164, 248 (A2)
53:4–6	161 (A2)
53:5	117 (A2)
53:6	276 (A1); 248 (A2)
53:6a	118 (A2)
53:7	118 (A2)
53:11	161 (A2)
53:11–12	158 (A2)
53:12	117, 164 (A2)
54	194 (A3)
54:11	140 (A3)
54:13	117 (A2)
54:17	161 (A2)
55	140–41, 143, 146, 149, 194 (A3)
55:1	201 (A3)
55:1–2	140, 145 (A3)
55:1–3	207 (A3)
55:1–5	**192–96**, 198 (A3)
55:2	179–80 (A2)
55:4–5	146 (A3)
55:6–11	312 (A3)
55:7–13	145 (A3)
55:8–9	78 (A2)
55:10	136 (A1); 145 (A3)
55:10–11	141 (A1)
55:10–12	156 (A3)

55:10–13	**139–43**,	60:9	376 (A3)	5:23	131 (A1)
	145 (A3)	60:14	146 (A1)	6:7	131 (A1)
55:11–13	146 (A3)	60:19	115, 147 (A1)	6:14	103 (A3)
56–66	115, 147 (A1);	60:22	147 (A1)	6:16	131 (A1)
	3 (A2); 228 (A3)	61	48 (A1)	6:23	83 (A1)
56:1	**227–32**, 358 (A3)	61:1	194 (A1)	7:3	131 (A1)
56:1–8	282n2 (A2)	61:8	358 (A3)	7:5–7	282 (A2)
56:3–8	146 (A3)	62	86, 88 (A1)	7:23	131 (A1)
56:6	161 (A2)	62:4	94, 115 (A1)	9:23–24	217 (A1)
56:6–8	**227–32** (A3)	**62:6–12**	**81–85**, 100 (A1)	11:4	131 (A1)
56:7	100, 147 (A1)	62:7–9	82 (A1)	13:15–21	269 (A3)
56:10	115 (A1)	62:8–9	93 (A1)	15:15	269 (A3)
57:13	115 (A1)	62:10–11	84 (A1)	**15:15–21**	**262–67** (A3)
57:19	115 (A1)	62:11	19 (A3)	15:17	269 (A3)
58	226, 235, 237 (A1);	62:12	94 (A1)	16:16	206 (A1)
	3–7 (A2)	63	125, 116–16 (A1)	16:19–21	206 (A1)
58–59	148 (A1)	63:7	120 (A1)	18:5–10	319 (A3)
58:1	6 (A2); 146 (A3)	**63:7–9**	**114–17**, 119 (A1)	20	92 (A3)
58:1–5	9 (A2)	63:7–64:12	114, 120 (A1)	20:4–5	121 (A3)
58:1–12	**225–29**, 239 (A1);	63:10	115 (A1)	**20:7–13**	**85–90** (A3)
	2–7, 9, 26 (A2)	63:10–19	115 (A1)	20:7–18	105 (A3)
58:3	3, 4, 6 (A2)	63:15	115 (A1)	21:5	122 (A3)
58:4	3 (A2)	63:17	161 (A2)	23	301 (A1)
58:4–5	4 (A2)	64:1	115 (A1)	23:1–8	495 (A3)
58:5	5 (A2)	64:7	115 (A1)	23:4	494 (A3)
58:5–7	6 (A2)	64:8	115 (A1)	23:22	320 (A3)
58:6	6 (A2)	64:12	114 (A1)	23:23–24	478 (A3)
58:6–7	5 (A2)	65:5	115 (A1)	24:4–7	121 (A3)
58:6–10	241 (A1)	65:8–16	161 (A2)	24:7	131 (A1)
58:7	4, 5, 6 (A2)	65:17–18	94 (A1)	26:13	131 (A1)
58:8	6 (A2)	65:22	142 (A3)	27–28	103 (A3)
58:8–12	6 (A2)	65:24	115 (A1)	27:5	82 (A1)
58:9	115 (A1); 6 (A2)	66:1	68 (A1)	27:14	105 (A3)
58:9–10	147 (A1)	66:3–4	115 (A1)	28	109 (A3)
58:10	241 (A1)	66:10–13	250 (A1)	28:1–4	103 (A3)
58:11	115 (A1); 6 (A2)	66:14	161 (A2)	**28:5–9**	**102–7, 108** (A3)
58:12	3, 4, 6 (A2)	66:24	147 (A1)	28:12–14	104 (A3)
58:14	227 (A1)			29:5–7	131 (A1)
59:1	115 (A1)	**Jeremiah**	82, 226 (A1)	29:7	93 (A3)
59:3	115 (A1)	1–29	184 (A2)	29:11	132 (A1)
59:9	376 (A3)	1:1	183, 184 (A2)	29:18	140 (A3)
59:10	115 (A1)	1:4	160 (A2)	30–31	132 (A1); 184 (A2)
59:17	485 (A3)	1:4–5	87 (A3)	30:7	484 (A3)
59:20	146 (A1)	1:4–19	78 (A2)	30:8	122 (A3)
60	146, 148–49 (A1)	1:8	87 (A3)	30:22	131 (A1)
60:1	150, 157 (A1)	1:14–15	122 (A3)	31	126, 131–32, 134
60:1–4	152 (A1)	3:8	19 (A3)		(A1); 182–84 (A2)
60:1–6	**146–49** (A1)	3:17	83 (A1)	31:1	184 (A2)
60:2	115 (A1)	4:30–31	185 (A2)	**31:1–6**	**182–86**, 188 (A2)
60:4	153 (A1)	4:31	83 (A1)	31:2	185 (A2)
60:6	158 (A1)	5:17	131 (A1)	31:3	183, 185 (A2)

Jeremiah (*continued*)

31:4	183, 185 (A2)
31:4a	185 (A2)
31:4b	185 (A2)
31:7	137 (A1)
31:7–14	**130–33**, 135, 143 (A1)
31:8	136 (A1)
31:10	136 (A1)
31:11	137 (A1)
31:12–14	136 (A1)
31:15	128, 134 (A1)
31:17	132 (A1)
31:29–30	89 (A2)
31:30–33	182 (A2)
31:31–34	178 (A2); 109 (A3)
31:33	131, 147 (A1)
31:38–40	132 (A1)
31:40	133 (A1)
32:17	82 (A1)
32:18	89 (A2)
33:5	119 (A2)
33:13	495 (A3)
40:1	126 (A1)
46	477 (A3)
46:10	477 (A3)

Lamentations

1–5	160 (A2)
2	83 (A1)

Ezekiel 226, 307 (A1)

1	93 (A2)
1–33	335 (A3)
3	335 (A3)
3:28	123 (A1)
5:15	140 (A3)
9:11–12	217 (A1)
10:18	221 (A1)
11:19	101 (A2)
11:23	221 (A1)
13	493 (A3)
13:5	477 (A3)
13:8–10	103 (A3)
14:11	131 (A1)
16	335 (A3)
16:49	69 (A3)
17	335 (A3)
18	89 (A2); 335, 337 (A3)
18:1–4	**334–39** (A3)
18:2–4	368 (A3)
18:5–9	337 (A3)
18:25–32	**334–39** (A3)
18:30	349 (A3)
18:30–31	341 (A3)
18:31	349 (A3)
19	335 (A3)
20	335 (A3)
20:34–35	493 (A3)
20:37	495 (A3)
20:41–42	493 (A3)
23	335 (A3)
23:24	122 (A3)
30:23	477 (A3)
33	283, 335 (A3)
33:7–11	**281–85**, 287, 289 (A3)
33:10	287 (A3)
33:11	287 (A3)
33:23–33	495 (A3)
34	161 (A2), 81, 495, 499–500 (A3)
34–48	493 (A3)
34:1	499 (A3)
34:1–3	495 (A3)
34:1–10	493, 495 (A3)
34:2	122, 494 (A3)
34:10	494–96 (A3)
34:10–22	502 (A3)
34:11–16	**493–97**, 499, 508 (A3)
34:14	507 (A3)
34:16	81, 499, 508 (A3)
34:17	494, 507 (A3)
34:17–22	493 (A3)
34:20–24	**493–97**, 499 (A3)
34:23–31	493 (A3)
34:27	122 (A3)
35:1–15	493 (A3)
36–37	335 (A3)
36:24	494 (A3)
36:26	101 (A2); 337 (A3)
36:27	101 (A2)
37	93, 98 (A2)
37:1	94, 97, 101, 329 (A2)
37:1–14	**93–96**, 101 (A2)
37:2	97 (A2)
37:3	97 (A2)
37:5	101, 329 (A2)
37:6	101, 329 (A2)
37:8	94 (A2)
37:9	94, 101, 329 (A2)
37:12	97 (A2); 494 (A3)
37:12–14	329 (A2)
37:14	94, 97 (A2)
37:15–24	494 (A3)
37:21	494 (A3)
37:27	142, 190 (A1)
38–42	94 (A2)
40:3–7	94 (A2)
43:24	238 (A1)
47	340 (A2); 337 (A3)
48:35	83 (A1)

Daniel 307 (A1)

2	235 (A1)
3	176 (A2)
4:8	51 (A1)
5:11	51 (A1)
6	176, 205 (A2)
6:12	15 (A1)
7	31, 317 (A1)
7:14	15 (A1)
11:35	15 (A1)
12	201 (A2)

Hosea 317 (A3)

2	19 (A3)
4–6	52 (A3)
4:17–5:9	425 (A3)
5:8	20 (A2)
5:15–6:6	**50–54** (A3)
6:6	64–65, 460 (A3)
11:1	119, 126 (A1)
13:8	20 (A3)

Joel

1	21 (A2)
1:2	21 (A2)
1:5	20 (A2)
1:7	21 (A2)
1:9	21 (A2)
1:10–12	21 (A2)
1:11	21 (A2)
1:14	21 (A2)
1:15	477 (A3)
1:17	21 (A2)
1:19	21 (A2)
2	5, 20, 22, 339 (A2)
2–3	477 (A3)
2:1	9, 21, 22, 130 (A2); 477 (A3)

2:1–2	4, **19–23** (A2)	6:6	212 (A3)	**Nahum**	
2:1–11	476 (A3)	6:12	460 (A3)	1:3	318 (A3)
2:2b	20 (A2)	7:10–17	105 (A3)	1:5	130 (A2)
2:3–11	20 (A2)	9:1–4	478 (A3)	3:1	317 (A3)
2:4–5	20 (A2)			3:2–7	317 (A3)
2:11	20 (A2)	**Jonah**	320, 323, 331 (A3)		
2:12	4, 9, 21 (A2)	1:2	317 (A3)	**Zephaniah**	
2:12–14	20, 22 (A2)	1:12	320 (A3)	1:1–3	476 (A3)
2:12–17	4, **19–23** (A2)	2:4	320 (A3)	1:5–6	478 (A3)
2:13	9, 21, 23 (A2)	2:8	400 (A3)	**1:7**	**475–80**, 482,
2:13–14	9, 21 (A2)	3:2	317 (A3)		490 (A3)
2:14	4, 9 (A2)	**3:10–4:11**	**316–21** (A3)	1:10–11	478 (A3)
2:14a	21 (A2)	4	228 (A3)	1:12–13	491 (A3)
2:15	21, 22 (A2)	4:2	323, 330 (A3)	**1:12–18**	**475–80**, 482,
2:15–17	21 (A2)	4:3	326 (A3)		484, 490 (A3)
2:16	21 (A2)	4:8	323, 326 (A3)	1:14–18	20 (A2)
2:16–17	22, 23 (A2)	4:9	323 (A3)	2:13	317 (A3)
2:16–18	335 (A2)			3:14–15	122 (A3)
2:17	21, 22 (A2)	**Micah**	317, 442 (A3)	3:16–20	476 (A3)
2:18	337 (A2)	1–3	210 (A1)		
2:18–27	339 (A2)	1:2	442 (A3)	**Haggai**	
2:28–32	281 (A1);	1:13	83 (A1)	2.6	130 (A2)
	334–35, 339 (A2)	3:1–4	442 (A3)	2.21	130 (A2)
2:31	484 (A3)	3:2–4	154 (A1)		
2:32	219 (A3)	3:5	15 (A1)	**Zechariah**	121 (A3)
2:32a	224 (A3)	**3:5–12**	**440–45**, 447,	1–6	31 (A1)
3:14–15	477 (A3)		451, 454 (A3)	1:1–8	121 (A3)
		3:6	66 (A1)	1:11	237 (A2)
Amos	317 (A3)	3:12	210 (A1)	2:10–11	142 (A1)
1:1	459 (A3)	4–5	210 (A1)	2:29–32	237 (A2)
1:3–2:6	103 (A3)	4:3	196 (A1)	8:8	131 (A1)
1:4	32 (A1)	5:2	158 (A1)	8:13	42 (A2)
1:7	32 (A1)	5:2–5	159 (A1)	9	123–24, 132 (A3)
1:12	32 (A1)	5:24	460 (A3)	9–11	112 (A2)
2:6–8	228 (A3)	6	218 (A1); 4 (A2)	9–14	122 (A3)
2:8	4 (A2)	**6:1–8**	**209–13** (A1)	9:9	111, 112, 114 (A2)
3:6	392 (A3)	6:6–8	165 (A1); 460 (A3)	9:9–10	128 (A3)
3:12	495 (A3)	6:7–8	4 (A2)	**9:9–12**	**120–25**, 126, 128,
5	468, 477 (A3)	6:8	21, 214, 217–18,		131, 146 (A3)
5:7	460 (A3)		222 (A1); 185 (A2);	9:9–17	122 (A3)
5:11	82 (A1)		228, 502 (A3)	9:10	128 (A3)
5:14–21	165 (A1)	6:9	442 (A3)	13:4	30 (A1)
5:15	212, 273, 437 (A3)	6:9–16	213 (A1)	14	340 (A2)
5:18	468, 484 (A3)	6:9–7:7	210 (A1)	14:1–21	477 (A3)
5:18–19	469 (A3)	6:15	82 (A1)	14:9	221–22 (A1)
5:18–20	281 (A1); 20 (A2);	7:4b–7	99 (A3)		
	468, 477 (A3)	7:7	48 (A1)	**Malachi**	121 (A3)
5:18–24	**458–63**,			3:2	477 (A3)
	465 (A3)	**Habakkuk**		3:10	66 (A1)
5:21–24	273 (A3)	2:4	112 (A3)	3:19	32 (A1)
5:24	21 (A1); 468 (A3)	3:7	66 (A1)	3:23–24	31 (A1)
6:4–6	15 (A1)	3:13	31 (A1)	4:4–5	318 (A1)

Comprehensive Scripture Index for Year A

NEW TESTAMENT

Matthew 159, 168, 194 (A1); xv, 15–16, 18, 37–40, 53, 56–58, 112–13, 129–30, 137–39, 304, 316 (A2); 471 (A3)

1	36–37 (A2)
1–2	64, 158 (A1)
1–4	16 (A2)
1:1	109, 206 (A3)
1:1–17	51, 51n2, 61 (A1); 117 (A3)
1:2–3	52 (A1)
1:3	147 (A1); 206 (A3)
1:5–6	206 (A3)
1:8b–9a	241n1 (A3)
1:16–17	135 (A3)
1:17	206 (A3)
1:18–25	**50**, 57, **61–64** (A1)
1:20	159 (A1)
1:20–21	61 (A1)
1:20–23	15 (A3)
1:21	64 (A3)
1:21–22	206 (A3)
1:22	62 (A1); 112 (A2)
1:23	222 (A1); 15, 17, 171, 208 (A3)
2	125–26 (A1); 37, 218 (A2); 135, 248 (A3)
2:1–12	**146**, 147, 152, **157–61**, 317 (A1)
2:6	112 (A2); 81 (A3)
2:12–13	61 (A1)
2:13	119, 159 (A1)
2:13–16	207 (A3)
2:13–23	**114**, 115, **125–29** (A1); 206 (A3)
2:15	112 (A2)
2:16	112 (A2)
2:16–18	17 (A3)
2:18	119 (A1)
2:19	61, 159 (A1)
2:19–30	126 (A1)
2:22	61, 159 (A1)
2:23	112 (A2)
2:26–27	226 (A2)
3	37 (A2)
3:1–2	173 (A1)
3:1–12	17, 19, **29–33** (A1)
3:2	43, 148, 205, 2 22 (A1)
3:3	26, 30, 83, 223 (A1)
3:5–6	173 (A1)
3:7–10	26 (A1)
3:11	47 (A1)
3:11–14	46 (A1)
3:13–17	**162**, 317, **173–76** (A1); 15, 94 (A3)
3:13–4:11	47n2 (A3)
3:17	63, 105, 315, 318 (A1); 259, 422 (A3)
4	36, 37, 39 (A2); 29, 29n1 (A3)
4:1–4	206 (A3)
4:1–11	174 (A1); 16, 25–26, **36–40**, 57 (A2); 15, 106, 206 (A3)
4:2	16, 252 (A2)
4:2–4	205 (A3)
4:4	285 (A1)
4:7	66 (A1)
4:8	221 (A1)
4:8–10	277 (A3)
4:12–23	**193, 204–8** (A1)
4:13–16	194 (A1)
4:16	66 (A1)
4:17	42, 173, 222–23 (A1); 147 (A3)
4:18–20	276 (A3)
4:18–21	63 (A3)
4:18–22	15, 189, 277 (A3)
4:18–25	221 (A1)
4:22	252 (A2)
4:23	223 (A1)
5	253 (A1); 224, 432, 438, 474 (A3)
5–7	223, 284, 295 (A1); 15, 48, 471 (A3)
5–9	81, 98 (A3)
5:1	284 (A1); 40, 279, 310 (A2)
5:1–2	206 (A3)
5:1–12	**209, 221–24** (A1); 30–31, 242, **435–39**, 456 (A3)
5:1–14	303 (A1)
5:2	16 (A2)
5:3	188 (A3)
5:3–9	241 (A1)
5:3–12	218 (A1)
5:3–7:27	48 (A3)
5:4	18 (A2)
5:6	253 (A1)
5:8–9	253 (A1)
5:9	135 (A3)
5:10	400 (A3)
5:11	239 (A1)
5:11–12	82 (A3)
5:12	430 (A3)
5:13	139 (A2)
5:13–14	257 (A1)
5:13–16	235, 270 (A1)
5:13–17	237 (A1)
5:13–20	**225, 238–41** (A1)
5:14	227, 266 (A1); 85 (A2)
5:14–16	468 (A3)
5:16	16 (A2)
5:17	253 (A1); 147 (A3)
5:17–18	255 (A1)
5:17–20	174, 300 (A1); 189, 280 (A3)
5:17–48	206 (A3)
5:19	248 (A1)
5:19–48	47 (A3)
5:20	222, 253, 270 (A1); 48, 189 (A3)
5:21	271 (A1)
5:21–22	18 (A2)
5:21–26	271 (A1); 295 (A3)
5:21–37	**242**, 248, **253–57** (A1)
5:21–48	239, 269, 286, 301, 303 (A1); 189 (A3)
5:22	295, 490 (A3)
5:27	271 (A1)
5:27–30	271 (A1)
5:28	18 (A2)
5:29–30	490 (A3)
5:31	271 (A1)
5:31–32	18 (A2)
5:33	271 (A1)
5:33–37	271 (A1)
5:34–39	295n2 (A3)
5:38–39	248 (A2)
5:38–48	**258**, 259, **269–72** (A1); 276 (A3)

5:39	254 (A1); 118 (A2)	7:14	138 (A3)	9:36	252 (A2); 116 (A3)
5:43–47	64 (A3)	7:15–20	301–2 (A1); 280 (A3)	9:36–38	206 (A1)
5:43–48	174, 205 (A1); 188, 273, 410 (A3)	7:17	250 (A1)	10	228 (A2); 15, 47, 98, 116, 136 (A3)
5:44	254, 266 (A1)	7:21	222, 295 (A1); 43, 46n1 (A3)	10:1	17 (A3)
5:44–45	171–72 (A3)	7:21–23	14 (A3)	10:1–4	206 (A3)
5:45	245 (A1)	**7:21–29**	**288**, 290, **300–303** (A1); 35, **46–49** (A3)	10:5–6	205 (A1); 74 (A3)
5:47–48	266 (A1)			10:6	83 (A3)
5:48	266n2 (A1)	7:24	295 (A1); 46n1, 471 (A3)	10:8	113 (A3)
6	278 (A1); 5, 16, 17, 18, 36 (A2)			**10:9–13**	**206** (A3)
		7:24–27	300 (A1)	10:9–23	80–84 (A3)
6:1–6	5, **15–18** (A2)	7:26	295 (A1); 46n1 (A3)	10:16	118 (A3)
6:1–18	301 (A1); 47 (A3)	7:28	48, 223, 295 (A1)	10:16–31	62 (A1)
6:1–34	303 (A1)	7:28–29	284 (A1); 118 (A2)	10:16–42	276 (A3)
6:2	239 (A1); 18 (A2)	7:29	240 (A1)	10:17	239 (A1)
6:3–4	5 (A2)	8:1	223 (A1)	10:19	239 (A1)
6:5	239 (A1)	8:1–4	241 (A3)	10:22	100 (A3)
6:6	18 (A2)	8:12	490 (A3)	**10:24–39**	**98–101** (A3)
6:7	48 (A3)	8:14–17	206 (A3)	10:28	490 (A3)
6:7–15	16 (A2); 222 (A3)	8:19–22	63, 276 (A3)	10:30	365 (A3)
6:9	145 (A2)	8:20	105 (A1); 81, 206 (A3)	10:34	103 (A3)
6:9–13	48 (A3)			10:34–39	118 (A3)
6:10	174 (A1); 47, 169, 188 (A3)	8:21–22	205 (A1)	10:38–39	276 (A3)
		8:21–28	260 (A3)	10:39	287 (A1); 326 (A3)
6:11	144 (A2); 206 (A3)	8:23–27	223 (A3)		
6:12	254 (A1)	8:26	15 (A3)	**10:40–42**	100, **112–19** (A3)
6:14–15	329 (A2); 311 (A3)	8:26b	241n1 (A3)	10:42	135 (A3)
6:16	239 (A1)	8:28–34	118, 241 (A3)	11	48 (A1); 131–32, 138 (A3)
6:16–18	21 (A2)	8:29	259 (A3)		
6:16–21	5, **15–18** (A2)	9	63–64 (A3)	11:1	48 (A1); 136 (A3)
6:17–18a	15 (A2)	9:2–8	46 (A3)	11:2–6	137 (A3)
6:19–21	286 (A1); 31, 276 (A3)	9:3	189 (A3)	**11:2–11**	**34**, 36, **46–49** (A1)
		9:8	239 (A1)	11:3	43 (A1)
6:19–7:12	284, 301 (A1)	9:9	205 (A1); 277 (A3)	11:4–5	81, 136 (A3)
6:21	420 (A3)	**9:9–13**	51, **63–67**, 188 (A3)	11:4–6	64 (A3)
6:22–23	284 (A1)			11:5	43 (A1)
6:22–34	16 (A2)	9:10–13	188 (A3)	11:10	40 (A1)
6:24–34	**273**, 275, **284–87** (A1); 29–32 (A3)	9:11	189 (A3)	11:11	43 (A1)
		9:14	189 (A3)	11:12–15	49 (A1)
6:25–34	310 (A2)	9:14–17	64–65 (A3)	11:16–17	117 (A3)
6:26	281 (A1); 188 (A3)	9:15	472 (A3)	**11:16–19**	**135–38** (A3)
6:30	15 (A3)	9:17	66 (A3)	11:18–19	15 (A1); 188 (A3)
6:30–31	281 (A1)	9:18–25	135 (A3)	11:25–27	206 (A3)
6:33	281 (A1)	**9:18–26**	51, **63–67**, 206 (A3)	**11:25–30**	**135–38** (A3)
7:1–5	349 (A3)			11:27	16 (A3)
7:1–14	303 (A1)	9:20–22	241 (A3)	11:28	132 (A3)
7:7–11	206 (A3)	9:27–28	206 (A3)	11:28–30	224 (A1); 118 (A2); 128 (A3)
7:11	47 (A3)	9:27–31	89 (A2)		
7:12	273, 421 (A3)	9:35–38	15 (A3)		
7:13–20	48 (A3)	9:35–10:8	69, 78 (A3)	11:29	194, 224 (A1)
7:13–27	300 (A1)	**9:35–10:23**	**80–84** (A3)	12	152 (A3)

Matthew (*continued*)

12:2	404 (A3)
12:7	65 (A3)
12:10	404 (A3)
12:13	376 (A3)
12:18–21	163, 174 (A1); 15 (A3)
12:22	224 (A1)
12:22–23	89 (A2)
12:23	206 (A3)
12:38–40	320 (A3)
12:38–42	320 (A3)
12:42	206, 471 (A3)
12:46–50	206 (A3)
12:49–50	47 (A3)
12:50	167 (A3)
13	15 (A1); 15, 149, 152, 169, 295 (A3)
13:1–9	141, 146, **152–56**, 169, 187 (A3)
13:1–50	187 (A3)
13:4	170, 188 (A3)
13:11	9 (A1)
13:14–16	204 (A2)
13:17	254 (A1)
13:18–23	141, 146, **152–56**, 169 (A3)
13:19	170, 188 (A3)
13:24	222 (A1)
13:24–30	**169–72**, 187, 295, 472 (A3)
13:24–43	167 (A3)
13:24–53	278 (A3)
13:25	188 (A3)
13:31	222 (A1)
13:31–32	472 (A3)
13:31–33	171, **187–91** (A3)
13:33	222 (A1); 205–6, 472 (A3)
13:35	111 (A2); 171 (A3)
13:36–43	**169–72** (A3)
13:37–43	188 (A3)
13:42	490 (A3)
13:44	31, 472 (A3)
13:44–45	222 (A1)
13:44–52	**187–91** (A3)
13:45–46	31, 183 (A3)
13:45–53	295 (A3)
13:47–50	472 (A3)
13:50	490 (A3)
13:52	222 (A1)
13:53	48 (A1)
13:54–58	152–53 (A3)
14	207, 220 (A3)
14:1–12	205, 207 (A3)
14:3–11	404 (A3)
14:3–17	31 (A1)
14:6–11	47 (A1)
14:8–11	206 (A3)
14:13	30 (A1); 206, 222 (A3)
14:13–14	47 (A1)
14:13–21	**205–8**, 243 (A3)
14:14–21	30 (A1)
14:15	206 (A3)
14:19	238 (A2)
14:22–33	15, 218, 222–26, 242 (A3)
14:23	221 (A1); 40 (A2)
14:28–30	187 (A3) (A3)
14:31	15 (A3)
14:31b	241n1 (A3)
15:7	112 (A2)
15:10–28	**240–44** (A3)
15:19	255 (A1)
15:21–28	135, 206, 237 (A3)
15:22	206 (A3)
15:23	242 (A3)
15:24	205 (A1)
15:26	242 (A3)
15:29	40 (A2)
15:31	239 (A1)
15:32–39	30 (A1)
15:36	238 (A2)
15:38	206 (A3)
16–19	317–18 (A1)
16:5–12	277 (A3)
16:13–20	**258–61** (A3)
16:16	315–16 (A1); 422 (A3)
16:17–19	276 (A3)
16:18	170, 330 (A3)
16:20–23	316 (A1)
16:21	173, 317 (A1); 57, 58, 204 (A2); 205, 259 (A3)
16:21–22	187 (A3)
16:21–23	258 (A3)
16:21–28	273, **276–80** (A3)
16:21–25:46	330 (A3)
16:23	314 (A2)
16:24–28	316 (A1)
16:25	287 (A1)
16:26	479 (A3)
16:26–27	330 (A3)
17	294 (A3)
17:1	221 (A1)
17:1–2	40 (A2)
17:1–8	137 (A2); 211 (A3)
17:1–9	304, **305–6, 315–19** (A1); **56–59** (A2)
17:1–13	313 (A1)
17:4–6	187 (A3)
17:4–8	312 (A1)
17:5	307 (A1)
17:5–6	259 (A3)
17:9	221 (A1); 56 (A2)
17:12	58 (A2); 277 (A3)
17:14–18	59 (A2); 135 (A3)
17:19–20	241n1 (A3)
17:20	15, 225 (A3)
17:22–23	173 (A1); 58, 204 (A2); 205, 277 (A3)
18	15, 294, 314 (A3)
18:1–14	205 (A1)
18:3	222 (A1)
18:6	117 (A3)
18:9	490 (A3)
18:10–14	117 (A3)
18:14	47 (A3)
18:15–20	254 (A1); 287, 289, **294–97** (A3)
18:17	170 (A3)
18:18–20	17 (A3)
18:20	15 (A3)
18:21	295 (A3)
18:21–22	254 (A1)
18:21–35	309, **311–15** (A3)
18:23	222 (A1); 472 (A3)
19:1	48 (A1)
19:3	404 (A3)
19:3–9	254 (A1)
19:6	254 (A1)
19:13–15	135 (A3)
19:14	117 (A3)
19:17–22	153 (A3)
19:21	188 (A3)
19:23	222 (A1)
19:26	274 (A1)
19:27	206 (A3)

19:27–28	99 (A3)	22	106–7 (A3)	24:45–48	471 (A3)
19:28	206 (A3)	**22:1–14**	375–76,	24:45–51	386, 488, 490,
19:29	224 (A1)		**385–88** (A3)		506 (A3)
19:30	141, 329 (A3)	22:2	222 (A1); 472 (A3)	24:46–47	506 (A3)
20:1	222 (A1)	22:2–9	472 (A3)	24:51	490, 507 (A3)
20:1–16	**329–33** (A3)	22:8–10	188 (A3)	25	181, 241 (A1); 16 (A2);
20:11	319 (A3)	22:13	490 (A3)		31, 468, 474 (A3)
20:15	323, 331 (A3)	22:14	374 (A3)	25:1	222 (A1)
20:16	156 (A2); 141,	**22:15–22**	392–93,	25:1–12	386 (A3)
	345 (A3)		**403–6** (A3)	**25:1–13**	47, 170, 461,
20:17–19	173 (A1);	22:21	392 (A3)		468, **471–74**,
	204 (A2); 205,	22:23–33	421 (A3)		488, 490 (A3)
	277 (A3)	22:34–40	326 (A2)	25:4	132 (A2)
20:20–23	173 (A1);	**22:34–46**	82, 409–10,	25:6–13	206 (A3)
	206 (A3)		**420–23** (A3)	25:10–13	506 (A3)
20:20–28	311 (A2);	22:35–40	36 (A3)	25:10b	470 (A3)
	206 (A3)	22:36	241 (A1)	25:12	468 (A3)
20:26	114 (A2)	22:37–39	283 (A2)	25:13	9 (A1); 472,
20:26–28	311 (A2)	22:37–40	502 (A3)		506 (A3)
20:28	130 (A2)	22:38–39	147 (A2)	**25:14–30**	386, 472, 485,
20:29–34	89 (A2);	22:39	270 (A1);		**488–92**, 506 (A3)
	489 (A3)		408 (A3)	25:21	507 (A3)
20:30–31	206 (A3)	22:39–40	241 (A1)	25:23	507 (A3)
21	345, 489 (A3)	23	224, 239 (A1);	25:30	490, 506–7 (A3)
21–22	348 (A3)		451 (A3)	25:30–32	330 (A3)
21:1	110, 115 (A2);	23:1–3	349 (A3)	25:31	502 (A3)
	421 (A3)	**23:1–12**	443, 450,	25:31–40	5 (A2); 100 (A3)
21:1–11	**111–15** (A2)		**454–57** (A3)	**25:31–46**	62, 62n2 (A1);
21:4–5	111 (A2)	23:2–3	189 (A3)		53 (A2); 47, 99,
21:5	224 (A1); 122–23,	23:3–7	349 (A3)		337, 386, 426,
	128 (A3)	23:8–12	451 (A3)		472, 496, 499,
21:6–7	112 (A2)	23:13	189 (A3)		**506–10** (A3)
21:8	112 (A2)	23:13–36	369 (A3)	25:40	222 (A1)
21:9	110, 112 (A2);	23:15	490 (A3)	25:40–41	496 (A3)
	206, 422 (A3)	23:23–29	189 (A3)	25:43	69 (A3)
21:10	385 (A3)	23:33	490 (A3)	25:45	222 (A1); 501 (A3)
21:10–11	112 (A2)	23:37	206 (A3)	26:1	48 (A1)
21:15	385 (A3)	24	3 (A1); 122 (A3)	26:1–2	205 (A3)
21:23–27	46, 385 (A3)	24–25	221, 301 (A1);	26:6–13	137 (A2)
21:23–32	335, **348–53** (A3)		456 (A3)	26:13	17 (A3)
21:25–26	335 (A3)	24:3	9 (A1); 40 (A2)	26:13–16	472 (A3)
21:28–32	47, 385 (A3)	24:8	130 (A2)	**26:14–27:66**	111, 129,
21:31	64 (A3)	24:9	239 (A1); 100 (A3)		**133–40** (A2)
21:31–32	342 (A3)	24:9–14	277 (A3)	26:21	122 (A2)
21:32	350 (A3)	24:14	17 (A3)	26:22	137 (A2)
21:33–46	355, 363,	24:22	6 (A1)	26:26	238 (A2); 206 (A3)
	367–71, 385 (A3)	24:36–44	170	26:26–28	140 (A2)
21:41	360 (A3)	24:36	488 (A3)	26:26–35	122 (A2)
21:42	360–61 (A3)	24:36–44	170 (A3)	26:28	130 (A2)
21:43	222 (A1)	24:43–44	484 (A3)	26:30	221 (A1)
21:45	348, 385 (A3)	24:45–47	14 (A1)	26:31–32	138 (A2)

Matthew (continued)		28	239 (A1)	9:5–6	312 (A1)
26:31–35	187 (A3)	28:1	204, 205,	9:7	307 (A1)
26:32	16–17 (A3)		206 (A2)	9:32	314 (A2)
26:36–46	137 (A2); 47,	**28:1–10**	188, 191, **204–8**	9:38–41	319 (A2)
	170 (A3)		(A2); 206 (A3)	10:2–9	254 (A1)
26:37	137 (A2)	28:2	130, 206, 312 (A2)	10:9	254 (A1)
26:38–39	138 (A2)	28:3–4	206 (A2)	10:29–30	224 (A1)
26:41	250 (A1)	28:4	205 (A2)	10:45	280 (A2)
26:47–52	271 (A1)	28:5–7	206 (A2)	10:46–52	89 (A2)
26:47–27:50	98 (A3)	28:6–7	204 (A2)	11:7	112 (A2)
26:56	138, 205 (A2)	28:7	205 (A2); 16, 17 (A3)	11:17a	229 (A3)
26:61	267 (A1)	28:8	206 (A2)	12:18–27	106 (A2)
26:63–64	112 (A2)	28:8–10	206 (A2)	12:28–34	251 (A1); 36 (A3)
26:67	119 (A2)	28:9	206 (A2)	12:31	24 (A1)
26:68	112 (A2)	28:9–10	204 (A2); 17 (A3)	12:35–37	109 (A3)
26:69–75	138, 205 (A2)	28:16	221 (A1)	13:32	15 (A1)
27	122 (A2); 141 (A3)	**28:16–20**	205 (A1); 40, 56,	13:33	144 (A2)
27:1–2	158 (A1)		204 (A2); **2,**	13:34–37	15 (A1)
27:1–10	138 (A2)		**14–17** (A3)	13:35	144 (A2)
27:3	119, 204 (A2)	28:17	204 (A2)	14:22	238 (A2)
27:11	112 (A2)	28:18	46 (A3)	14:36	176 (A2); 166 (A3)
27:11–54	111, **128–32**,	28:18–20	52, 62n2 (A1)	14:51	217 (A1)
	137 (A2)	28:19	62, 159, 221 (A1);	14:58	267 (A1)
27:14	122 (A2)		11, 279, 507 (A3)	15:18	236 (A3)
27:16	62 (A1)	28:19–20	180 (A1)	15:26	236 (A3)
27:17	112 (A2)	28:20	62 (A1)	15:27	174 (A2)
27:19	159 (A1); 206 (A3)			15:29	267 (A1)
27:20–23	204 (A2)	**Mark**	xv, 130, 137, 164,	15:32	236 (A3)
27:22	112 (A2)		204, 304, 319 (A2)	15:34	217 (A1); 164 (A2)
27:22–23	115 (A2)	1:2–3	83 (A1)	16:6–7	197 (A2)
27:25	369 (A3)	1:3	32 (A1)	16:9	299 (A2)
27:26	204 (A2)	1:9–11	152 (A1); 94 (A3)		
27:28	204 (A2)	1:11	105 (A1)	**Luke**	77, 170, 314 (A1);
27:28–29	112 (A2)	1:15	42 (A1)		xv, 16, 39, 72, 202,
27:29	158 (A1); 112,	2:28	105 (A1)		210–12, 222, 225,
	204 (A2)	3:1–6	90 (A2)		227, 233, 237, 239,
27:31	204 (A2)	4:1–9	153 (A3)		244, 287–89, 295,
27:32–60	204 (A2)	4:13–20	153 (A3)		298–305, 307, 316,
27:35	137 (A2)	6:31–33	30 (A1)		322, 329 (A2)
27:37	112 (A2)	6:34	252 (A2)	1	158 (A1); 277 (A2)
27:40	267 (A1)	6:41	238 (A2)	1–2	78, 76–77 (A1)
27:42	144 (A2)	6:52	314 (A2)	1:1–4	77 (A1)
27:46	131, 139, 160,	7:21	255 (A1)	1:2	303, 307 (A2)
	164 (A2)	8:6	238 (A2)	1:4	237 (A2)
27:51b–53	129 (A2)	8:22–26	89 (A2)	1:5	77 (A1)
27:52	130 (A2)	8:27–38	167 (A2); 277 (A3)	1:5–24	61 (A3)
27:54	139 (A2); 422 (A3)	8:35	326 (A3)	1:8	77 (A1)
27:55	204 (A2)	8:36	479 (A3)	1:11	237 (A2)
27:60–66	122 (A2)	9:2–8	313 (A1); 211 (A3)	1:14	78 (A1)
27:61	122, 204 (A2)	9:2–9	266 (A3)	1:28	43 (A1)
27:62–66	205 (A2)	9:5	139 (A2)	1:33	94 (A1)

1:36	136 (A3)	6:49	318 (A3)	15	294n1, 311 (A3)
1:38	218 (A2)	7:11-15	106 (A2)	15:2	319 (A3)
1:39	43 (A1)	7:25	49 (A1)	15:3–7	276 (A1)
1:41–45	400 (A3)	7:36–49	77 (A1)	15:8–10	237 (A2)
1:42	43 (A1)	8:1–3	237, 307 (A2)	16:9	237 (A2)
1:44	43, 78 (A1)	8:19–21	307 (A2)	16:19–31	331 (A3)
1:46–55	**34, 39–41**,	8:49-55	106 (A2)	16:21	77 (A1)
	84 (A1); 161 (A2);	9:1–6	155 (A1); 288 (A2)	17:1	165 (A2)
	140, 302 (A3)	9:18–27	277 (A3)	17:1–5	226 (A2)
1:48	43, 94 (A1)	9:23	258 (A2)	17:7	77 (A1)
1:52	290 (A2); 331,	9:25	479 (A3)	17:22	254 (A1)
	365 (A3)	9:28–36	313 (A1); 303 (A2)	17:28	15 (A1)
1:53	94 (A1)	9:29–36	211 (A3)	17:33	15 (A1); 326 (A3)
2	79, 95 (A1);	9:31	237 (A2)	18	167 (A2)
	277 (A2)	9:32	305 (A1)	18:1–12	153 (A2)
2:1–20	**65**, 66, 73,	9:34	305 (A1)	**18:1–19:42**	164, **170–77** (A2)
	76–80, 81,	9:34–35	307 (A1)	18:4	174, 252 (A2)
	93–97 (A1)	9:45	314 (A2)	18:5	73 (A2)
2:5	314 (A2)	9:51–56	72 (A2)	18:6	167 (A2)
2:6–7	79n3 (A1)	9:51–19:44	434 (A3)	18:8	173 (A2)
2:9	67 (A1)	10	78 (A1);	18:11	173 (A2)
2:12	66–67 (A1)		74–75 (A2)	18:15–27	252 (A2)
2:14	128 (A3)	10:1–2	319 (A2)	18:16–17	252 (A2)
2:24	144 (A2)	10:1–12	288 (A2)	18:17	173 (A2)
2:29–32	172 (A1); 237 (A2)	10:1–20	155 (A1)	18:22	173 (A2)
2:34–35	94 (A1)	10:2	74 (A2)	18:25	173 (A2)
2:36	337 (A2)	10:17–24	288 (A2)	18:27	173 (A2)
2:48	94 (A1)	10:21	400 (A3)	18:28–32	173 (A2)
3	228 (A2)	10:25–28	36 (A3)	18:29	224 (A1)
3:1–2	307 (A2)	10:25–37	282n2 (A2)	18:30	224 (A1)
3:1–22	94 (A3)	10:25–42	48 (A3)	18:32	119 (A2)
3:4	32, 83 (A1)	11:2	145 (A2)	18:33–38	173 (A2)
3:6	172 (A1)	11:3	144 (A2)	18:35–43	89 (A2)
3:10–11	137 (A3)	11:29–32	320 (A3)	18:37	252 (A2)
3:21	261 (A2)	11:37	77 (A1)	18:38	173 (A2)
3:22	105 (A1)	12:22–33	310 (A2)	18:38b–40	173 (A2)
4	48, 54 (A1)	12:39	484 (A3)	19:4	401 (A3)
4:1–13	57 (A2); 106 (A3)	12:48	155 (A2)	19:7	319 (A3)
4:12	66 (A1); 337 (A3)	13:1–5	89 (A2)	19:23–29	226 (A2)
4:14–19	496 (A3)	13:10–17	90 (A2)	19:28	253 (A2)
4:16–21	331 (A3)	13:25–27	46 (A3)	19:28–53	298 (A2)
4:16–30	260 (A2)	13:32	311 (A2)	19:40	84 (A1)
4:18	122 (A3)	13:42–45	226 (A2)	19:42	237 (A2)
4:21	147 (A1)	14	77 (A1)	21:1	143 (A2)
5:1–11	237 (A2)	14:1–2	226 (A2)	21:7	143 (A2)
5:29	77 (A1)	14:1–6	90 (A2)	21:8	143 (A2)
6:12–16	307 (A2)	14:7–8	455 (A3)	21:11	143 (A2)
6:20	435 (A3)	14:15–35	140 (A3)	21:12–16	257 (A2)
6:22	400 (A3)	14:16–20	386 (A3)	21:13	143 (A2)
6:27–36	273 (A3)	14:34	139 (A2)	21:15	143 (A2)
6:45	224 (A1)	14:35	240 (A1)	22	77 (A1)

Luke (*continued*)

22:1	143 (A2)
22:4	237 (A2)
22:6	237 (A2)
22:7	143 (A2)
22:8	143 (A2)
22:11	143 (A2)
22:13	143 (A2)
22:15	143, 237 (A2)
22:17–19	237 (A2)
22:19–20	238 (A2)
22:21–22	237 (A2)
22:23	237 (A2)
22:31–32	237 (A2)
22:37	159 (A2)
22:48	237 (A2)
22:64	237 (A2)
22:69	105 (A1)
23:21–33	237 (A2)
23:34	271 (A1); 180, 256, 261, 264n1 (A2); 312 (A3)
23:42–46	263 (A2)
23:46	295 (A1); 256, 261 (A2)
23:52	237 (A2)
23:55	237 (A2)
23:55–56	237 (A2)
24	287 (A2)
24:1–7	288n2 (A2)
24:1–10	237 (A2)
24:1–12	237 (A2)
24:2	237, 238 (A2)
24:3	238, 239 (A2)
24:4	78 (A1)
24:5	303 (A2); 287 (A2)
24:11	212 (A2)
24:13	237 (A2)
24:13–35	233, **236–40** (A2)
24:15	237 (A2)
24:16	236, 237 (A2)
24:18	236, 237, 238 (A2)
24:19	237 (A2)
24:19–24	237 (A2)
24:21	237, 239 (A2)
24:22–24	237 (A2)
24:23	238 (A2)
24:25	226, 233, 237 (A2)
24:25–27	211, 236, 240 (A2)
24:26	237, 238, 240 (A2)
24:27	201, 226, 239 (A2)
24:29	236 (A2)
24:30	77 (A1)
24:30–31	15 (A1)
24:31	236, 237, 240 (A2)
24:32	226, 233 (A2)
24:33	236 (A2)
24:34	237, 238, 240 (A2)
24:35	238, 240 (A2)
24:36	78 (A1); 299 (A2)
24:36–49	222 (A2)
24:37	299 (A2)
24:42–43	222 (A2)
24:44	201, 299 (A2)
24:44–53	**298–301** (A2)
24:45	299 (A2)
24:46–47	222 (A2)
24:47	295 (A2)
24:47–49	300, 336 (A2)
24:48	299 (A2)
24:48–49	299 (A2)
24:49	209, 288 (A2)
24:50–51	287 (A2)
24:50–53	292, 300, 303 (A2)
24:52	78 (A1); 299 (A2)
24:52–53	300 (A2)
26:11–12	190 (A1)

John 113 (A1); xv, 53–54, 72–75, 85, 89–90, 105–7, 113, 142–43, 164, 167, 173–74, 195–97, 220–23, 242, 251–52, 257, 268–69, 285, 302, 304, 314, 316, 320, 328–331, 338–339, 341 (A2); 431 (A3)

1–13	74, 90–91 (A2)
1:1–14	**98**, 104, **109–13**, 115 (A1)
1:1–18	**130, 141–45**, 188 (A1)
1:2–3	121 (A1)
1:3	105 (A2)
1:5	131, 196 (A1); 85, 196 (A2)
1:9	131, 190 (A1); 85, 196 (A2)
1:10–11	131 (A1)
1:11	252 (A2)
1:12–13	340 (A2)
1:12–16	221 (A2)
1:13	174 (A2)
1:14	196, 315, 316 (A2)
1:15	190 (A1)
1:16	131 (A1)
1:18	316 (A2)
1:18–34	143 (A1)
1:19–42	188 (A1)
1:26	221, 340 (A2)
1:27	111, 190 (A1)
1:29	144 (A2)
1:29–42	**177, 188–92** (A1)
1:30	111 (A1)
1:30–34	142 (A1)
1:32–33	221 (A2)
1:32–34	94 (A3)
1:33	329, 340 (A2)
1:34	141 (A1)
1:36	144 (A2)
1:37–43	252 (A2)
1:38	173, 197 (A2)
1:38–39	73 (A2)
1:39	142 (A1)
1:42–51	72 (A2)
1:43–51	289 (A2)
1:46	193 (A1); 73 (A2); 350 (A3)
1:48	73 (A2)
1:49	142 (A1); 73 (A2)
2:1–12	174 (A2)
2:4	153, 174 (A2)
2:6	340 (A2)
2:9	340 (A2)
2:11	143 (A1); 105, 221, 341 (A2)
2:12–14	340 (A2)
2:13–22	153 (A2)
2:18	222 (A2)
2:19	267 (A1)
3	94 (A2)
3:1–2	173 (A2)
3:1–17	**52–56** (A2)
3:1–21	72 (A2)
3:2	85, 196 (A2)
3:3–5	340 (A2)
3:5	94, 339 (A2)
3:6	94 (A2)
3:8	55, 94, 329 (A2)
3:11	221 (A2)
3:14–15	320 (A3)
3:15–16	252 (A2)

3:15–18	221 (A2)	6:16	221 (A2)	9:4	90 (A2)
3:16	54, 106, 160, 315 (A2)	6:27–29	74 (A2)	9:5	53, 73 (A2)
		6:31–32	318 (A3)	9:9	89 (A2)
3:16–17	221 (A2)	6:31–34	321 (A3)	9:11	90 (A2)
3:17	252 (A2)	6:35	53, 73, 252 (A2)	9:12	91 (A2)
3:18	142 (A1)	6:36	221 (A2)	9:14	90 (A2)
3:19	196 (A2)	6:39–40	106 (A2)	9:15	90 (A2)
3:29	221, 252 (A2)	6:41	53 (A2)	9:16	90, 221 (A2)
3:34	221, 329 (A2)	6:44	106 (A2)	9:17	90, 91 (A2)
3:36	106, 252 (A2)	6:46	221 (A2)	9:18	89 (A2)
4:1	72 (A2)	6:47	106, 252 (A2)	9:22	90 (A2)
4:1–15	337 (A3)	6:48	53, 73 (A2)	9:24	90 (A2)
4:5–42	68–69, **71–76** (A2)	6:51	53, 73 (A2)	9:25	92 (A2)
		6:53–54	252 (A2)	9:33	90 (A2)
4:7	174 (A2)	6:54	106 (A2)	9:34	91 (A2)
4:7–26	339 (A2)	6:63	329 (A2)	9:35	83 (A2)
4:9	72 (A2)	6:68	252 (A2)	9:35–41	85 (A2)
4:10–14	340 (A2)	7	54, 340 (A2)	9:38	83, 90 (A2)
4:10–15	339 (A2)	7:2	339 (A2)	10	242, 251, 252 (A2)
4:12–14	340 (A2)	7:4	338 (A2)	10:1	242 (A2)
4:14	74, 174, 340 (A2)	7:5	53 (A2)	10:1–2	251 (A2)
		7:28–29	338 (A2)	10:1–5	251, 252 (A2)
4:19	73 (A2)	7:33	288n1 (A2)	10:1–6	253, 314 (A2)
4:20–21	266 (A3)	7:37–38	338, 340 (A2)	**10:1–10**	248, **251–54** (A2)
4:22	74 (A2)	**7:37–39**	333, 335, **338–41** (A2)	10:2–4	252 (A2)
4:23	256 (A1)			10:3	106, 251 (A2)
4:25	73 (A2)	7:37b–38	338 (A2)	10:3–5	251 (A2)
4:26	73 (A2)	7:38	174, 340 (A2)	10:4	252, 253 (A2)
4:27	72 (A2)	7:39	221, 339, 340, 341 (A2)	10:4–5	242 (A2)
4:29	142 (A1)			10:5	52 (A1); 251 (A2)
4:37–38	72 (A2)	7:40–42	193 (A1)	10:6	251 (A2)
4:43–54	105 (A2)	7:41	338 (A2)	10:7	73, 251 (A2)
4:54	143 (A1); 221 (A2)	8:2	153 (A2)	10:7–10	242, 251, 252 (A2)
5–12	338 (A2)	8:11	185 (A2)		
5:1–9	340 (A2)	8:12	110, 241 (A1); 53, 73, 85, 252 (A2)	10:8	251, 254 (A2)
5:1–18	90 (A2)			10:8–34	90 (A2)
5:1–19	105 (A2)	8:24	73, 106 (A2)	10:9	73, 242, 246, 249, 251, 252, 253 (A2)
5:15	118 (A2)	8:27	314 (A2)		
5:16	222 (A2)	8:28	142 (A1); 73 (A2)	10:10	276 (A1); 249, 251, 252, 253 (A2)
5:19	118, 190 (A2)	8:38	221 (A2)		
5:24	106, 252 (A2)	8:44	340 (A2)	10:11	53, 73, 106, 251, 252, 253 (A2); 497 (A3)
5:25	252 (A2)	8:56	221 (A2)		
5:26	201, 252 (A2)	8:58	73, 106 (A2)		
5:28	252 (A2)	8:59	106 (A2)	10:11–16	495 (A3)
5:28–29	106 (A2)	9	78 (A2); 304 (A3)	10:12–15	252 (A2)
5:39–44	314 (A2)	9:1–7	340 (A2)	10:14	53, 73, 251, 252 (A2)
6	238 (A2)	**9:1–41**	83, 85, **88–92**, 105 (A2)		
6:2	73 (A2)			10:16	252 (A2)
6:4	252 (A2)	9:2	89, 91 (A2)	10:18	153, 173, 201 (A2)
6:4–14	153 (A2)	9:3	105 (A2)	10:21	90 (A2)
6:14	143 (A1); 221 (A2)	9:3–5	89 (A2)	10:22	251 (A2)

Comprehensive Scripture Index for Year A **553**

John (*continued*)

10:27	52 (A1)
10:27–29	252 (A2)
10:28	106 (A2)
10:30	497 (A3)
10:31	106 (A2)
10:35	313 (A1)
11	98, 106–7, 251 (A2)
11:1–45	101, **104–8** (A2)
11:3	107 (A2)
11:4	105, 341 (A2)
11:5	107 (A2)
11:16	221 (A2)
11:17	106 (A2)
11:21	105 (A2)
11:22	98 (A2)
11:23	106 (A2)
11:25	53, 73, 107, 252 (A2)
11:27	142 (A1); 106 (A2)
11:32	105 (A2)
11:33	107 (A2)
11:35	107 (A2)
11:36	107 (A2)
11:37	105 (A2)
11:38	107 (A2)
11:42	106 (A2)
11:43	98, 252 (A2)
11:43–44	106 (A2)
11:45	106 (A2)
11:50–53	280 (A2)
11:53	106 (A2)
11:55–12:8	153 (A2)
12	106 (A2)
12:1–8	106 (A2)
12:2	153 (A2)
12:6	252 (A2)
12:9	153 (A2)
12:15	123 (A3)
12:16	196, 314, 341 (A2)
12:17–18	221 (A2)
12:18	143 (A1)
12:19	153 (A2)
12:23–24	341 (A2)
12:25	326 (A3)
12:26	252 (A2)
12:32	217 (A1); 161, 172 (A2)
12:36	196 (A2)
13	155–56, 221, 267 (A2)
13–19	221 (A2)
13–21	314 (A2)
13:1	142, 153, 155, 252, 315 (A2)
13:1–11	314 (A2)
13:1–17	148, **152–56** (A2)
13:1a	315 (A2)
13:1b	153 (A2)
13:3	85, 153, 154, 196 (A2)
13:5–8	153 (A2)
13:8	155–56 (A2)
13:8–9	154 (A2)
13:8–11	154 (A2)
13:12	154 (A2)
13:12–17	315 (A2)
13:13	155 (A2)
13:17	252 (A2)
13:31–32	105 (A2)
13:31b–35	148n1, **152–56** (A2)
13:34	110 (A1); 146, 147, 152, 155, 235, 257, 285, 286, 315 (A2)
13:34–35	153, 285 (A2)
13:35	155–56 (A2)
13:36–14:1	285 (A2)
13:36–14:7	154 (A2)
14	267, 270, 283 (A2)
14–17	314 (A2)
14:1	267 (A2)
14:1–14	264, **267–70** (A2)
14:2	153, 197, 267, 268, 269 (A2)
14:2–3	252 (A2)
14:3	267 (A2)
14:4–5	221 (A2)
14:5	267, 314 (A2)
14:6	53, 73, 153, 221, 252, 268, 269, 270 (A2); 97 (A3)
14:8–9	221, 314 (A2)
14:9	268 (A2)
14:10	142 (A1)
14:12	252, 269, 270 (A2)
14:13	105, 269 (A2)
14:15	283, 286 (A2)
14:15–21	**283–86** (A2)
14:15–24	417 (A3)
14:16	252, 273, 284, 286 (A2)
14:16–17	221, 328 (A2)
14:17	272, 285, 286, 329 (A2)
14:18	284, 286 (A2)
14:18–19	198 (A2)
14:19	285, 286 (A2)
14:21	285, 286, 315 (A2)
14:25–27	328 (A2)
14:26	221, 286, 328, 341 (A2); 417 (A3)
14:27	221, 286, 329 (A2)
14:28	252 (A2)
15:1	53, 73, 252 (A2)
15:1–11	250 (A1)
15:5	53 (A2)
15:9	315 (A2)
15:15	118, 340 (A2)
15:26	221, 329, 341 (A2)
15:26–27	340 (A2)
16:5	221 (A2)
16:7–11	340 (A2)
16:13	221, 329, 340 (A2)
16:13–15	340 (A2)
16:14–15	340, 341 (A2)
16:18	314 (A2)
16:20–21	94 (A1)
16:20–22	221 (A2)
16:22	95 (A1)
16:27–28	197 (A2)
16:28	252 (A2)
16:30–31	314 (A2)
16:33	221, 329, 330 (A2)
17	221, 305, 316 (A2)
17:1	105, 167, 315 (A2)
17:1–11	302, **314–17** (A2)
17:2	106, 315 (A2)
17:2–3	221 (A2)
17:4	315 (A2); 319 (A3)
17:5	315 (A2)
17:6	315 (A2)
17:8	302 (A2)
17:9	315 (A2)
17:10	319 (A3)
17:11	28 (A1); 315, 317, 329 (A2)
17:18	221, 328, 329 (A2)
17:20–23	315 (A2)
17:21	28 (A1); 317 (A2)
17:21–23	329, 330 (A2)
17:22	317 (A2)
17:23	317 (A2)
17:24	315 (A2)

19:1–3	173 (A2)	20:24–28	195 (A2)	1:17	210 (A2)
19:2–5	341 (A2)	20:25	220, 221, 222 (A2)	1:21	210 (A2)
19:3	164, 341 (A2)	20:26	220 (A2)	1:21–23	253 (A2)
19:4–8	173 (A2)	20:27	220, 222, 223, 224 (A2)	1:22	210 (A2)
19:6	164 (A2)			1:23	253 (A2)
19:9–11	173 (A2)	20:28	222 (A2)	1:31	210 (A2)
19:12	173 (A2)	20:29	210, 221, 222 (A2)	2	211, 227, 229, 231, 241, 242, 243, 322, 334, 336, 337 (A2); 484 (A3)
19:12–16a	173 (A2)	20:29–31	195, 220 (A2)		
19:14	142 (A2)	20:30–31	222 (A2)		
19:14–15	174 (A2)	20:31	142 (A1); 105, 221, 222, 252 (A2)		
19:16–18	153 (A2)			2:1–4	335 (A2); 16 (A3)
19:19	341 (A2)	21	242 (A2)	2:1–13	229 (A2)
19:23–24	164 (A2)	21:12	304 (A1)	**2:1–21**	319, 325, **333–37**, 339 (A2)
19:26	174 (A2)	21:16–17	252 (A2)		
19:26–27	174 (A2)	21:19–21	252 (A2)	2:2–3	330 (A2)
19:28	164 (A2)			2:3	237 (A2)
19:31–34	175 (A2)	**Acts**	77, 168–70 (A1); 210, 212–13, 222, 225, 227, 230–31, 233, 237, 242–44, 246, 255–56, 272–73, 277, 289, 295, 300, 303–4, 320, 326, 329, 333–334, 339 (A2); 81 (A3)	2:4	226, 229, 231, 272 (A2)
19:34	221, 341 (A2)				
19:34–35	341 (A2)			2:4–18	336 (A2)
19:39	159 (A1); 53 (A2)			2:5	225, 272 (A2)
19:39–42	196 (A2)			2:5–13	336 (A2)
20	195 (A2)			2:8–11	325, 334 (A2)
20:1	195 (A2)			2:11	336 (A2)
20:1–10	195, 197 (A2)	1	287, 308, 315, 335 (A2)	2:12	335 (A2)
20:1–18	188, **195–99** (A2)			2:13	272 (A2)
20:2	220, 221, 222 (A2)			2:14–36	272 (A2)
20:2–10	220 (A2)	1–11	8 (A1)	**2:14a**	**209–12**, 217, 222, **225–29**, 233, 237 (A2)
20:3	222 (A2)	1:1	289 (A2)		
20:8	142 (A1); 196 (A2)	1:1–2	225 (A2)		
20:8–9	328 (A2)	1:1–5	304 (A2)	2:15	272 (A2)
20:9	196, 314 (A2)	**1:1–11**	**287–91** (A2)	2:16–18	335 (A2)
20:11	196 (A2)	1:1–14	292 (A2)	2:17	337 (A2)
20:11–18	195, 196, 198 (A2)	1:2	289 (A2)	2:17–18	336, 337 (A2)
20:12	196 (A2)	1:3	209, 289, 304 (A2)	2:18	337 (A2)
20:14	201 (A2)	1:4	209, 334 (A2)	2:21	172 (A1); 224 (A3)
20:14–15	190 (A1)	1:5	330, 334 (A2)	2:22	210, 222 (A2)
20:15	173, 197 (A2)	1:6	290, 310, 314, 315, 330 (A2)	**2:22–32**	**209–12**, 217, 222 (A2)
20:17	197, 220 (A2)				
20:18	220 (A2)	**1:6–14**	**302–5** (A2)	2:23	210, 214, 226 (A2)
20:19	220, 221, 222, 328 (A2)	1:7	290, 310 (A2)		
		1:8	154–55 (A1); 200, 212, 257, 288, 290, 295, 303, 310, 315, 330, 334, 336 (A2); 16 (A3)	2:23–24	226 (A2)
20:19–23	195, **328–32**, 335, 339 (A2)			2:24	210 (A2)
				2:25	210, 211 (A2)
20:19–31	210, 217, **220–24** (A2)			2:25–28	214 (A2)
				2:25–31	226 (A2)
20:20–25	328 (A2)	1:9	304 (A2)	2:26–41	237 (A2)
20:20b	328, 330 (A2)	1:11	287 (A2)	2:27	210, 222 (A2)
20:21	221, 331 (A2)	1:12	287 (A2)	2:29	210 (A2)
20:21–23	220 (A2)	1:14	289, 305 (A2)	2:31	222 (A2)
20:21b	330 (A2)	1:15	334 (A2)	2:32	210, 212, 222 (A2)
20:22	222, 335 (A2)	1:15–26	302 (A2)	2:33–35	211, 212 (A2)

Comprehensive Scripture Index for Year A

Acts (continued)		7:53	255 (A2)	14:1	225 (A2)
2:36	211, 212, 226, 227, 238 (A2)	7:55	256, 257, 261, 272 (A2)	14:1–2	226 (A2)
				14:15–17	272 (A2)
2:36–41	**225–29**, 233, 237, 246 (A2)	7:55–56	257, 261, 288 (A2)	15	242 (A2)
				15:1–5	294 (A2)
2:37	226, 227, 233, 238, 241 (A2)	**7:55–60**	**255–59**, 271, 274 (A2)	15:1–35	362 (A3)
				16:9	325 (A3)
2:38	226, 229 (A2); 14 (A3)	7:59	261 (A2)	16:11–40	325 (A3)
		7:59–60	256 (A2)	16:13–15	225, 237 (A2)
2:38–39	336 (A2)	7:60	261 (A2)	16:19	344 (A3)
2:39	226, 229, 231 (A2); 484 (A3)	8	256 (A2)	16:21	344 (A3)
		8:12	225 (A2)	16:25–31	176 (A2)
2:41	231, 242 (A2)	8:16	14 (A3)	16:31–33	225 (A2)
2:42	77 (A1); 241 (A2)	8:26–40	166 (A3)	17	234–35 (A1); 277 (A2)
2:42–47	**241–44** (A2)	8:31–37	272 (A2)		
2:44	241 (A2)	8:32–35	161 (A2)	17:1–5	226 (A2)
2:44–45	244, 336 (A2)	9:1–2	82 (A3)	17:4–10	399 (A3)
2:46	77 (A1); 244 (A2)	9:1–19	169 (A1)	17:16	274 (A2)
2:47	241, 244 (A2)	9:2	225 (A2)	**17:22–31**	**271–76** (A2)
3:1–4:4	256 (A2)	9:3–6	225 (A2)	17:23	274 (A2)
3:6	170 (A1)	9:19	237 (A2)	17:24	276 (A2)
4:1–3	241 (A2)	9:36-41	106 (A2); 64 (A3)	17:26	275 (A2)
4:1–22	82 (A3)	9:36–42	237 (A2)	17:27	274 (A2)
4:4	225, 242 (A2)	9:42	106 (A2)	17:30–31	275 (A2)
4:5–31	256 (A2)	9:46	238, 244 (A2)	17:32–34	272 (A2)
4:21–23	260 (A2)	10	202, 319 (A2)	18:8	225 (A2)
5:1–11	242 (A2)	10:1	172 (A1)	19:5–7	225 (A2)
5:12–42	256 (A2)	10:1–11:18	362 (A3)	19:6	335 (A2)
5:19	260 (A2)	10:4	201 (A2)	19:23–29	226 (A2)
6:1	507 (A3)	10:28	337 (A2)	20:7	222, 238 (A2)
6:1–4	242 (A2)	10:34	188 (A2)	20:7–12	272 (A2)
6:1–6	258 (A2)	10:34-35	200 (A2)	20:11	238 (A2)
6:1–7	256 (A2)	**10:34–43**	162, **169–72** (A1); 188, **200–203**, 272 (A2)	20:17–35	272 (A2)
6:3	256 (A2)			20:34	81 (A3)
6:5	256 (A2)			21–26	241–42 (A2)
6:8	256, 258 (A2)	10:36	201 (A2)	21:9–10	337 (A2)
6:11	257 (A2)	10:41	201 (A2)	21:17–29	242 (A2)
7	255, 263 (A2); 469 (A3)	10:45	362 (A3)	21:35	298 (A1)
		10:46	335 (A2)	22:1–21	272 (A2)
7:2–53	260 (A2)	10:47	337 (A2)	22:6–16	169 (A1)
7:2a	261 (A2)	10:48	225 (A2); 14 (A3)	22:24	82 (A3)
7:6	238 (A2)	11	203 (A2)	22:46	246 (A2)
7:9–16	212, 230 (A3)	11:1–18	172 (A1)	23:6–8	106 (A2)
7:15	261 (A2)	11:5–17	272 (A2)	24:10–21	272 (A2)
7:16	261 (A2)	12	469 (A3)	24:16	200 (A3)
7:16–21	271 (A2)	12:13	237 (A2)	24:21	106 (A2)
7:20–22	248 (A3)	13:22	497 (A3)	25:8	200 (A3)
7:29	238 (A2)	13:33	63 (A1)	26:12–18	169 (A1)
7:38–40	257 (A2)	13:42–45	226 (A2)	27:35	238 (A2)
7:51–52	257, 261 (A2)	13:48	225 (A2)	28:24	226 (A2)
7:51–53	87 (A3)	13:52	400 (A3)	28:25–28	226 (A2)

28:26–28	272 (A2)	3:22–31	288, 294–99,	5:11	67, 68 (A2)
28:28	303 (A2)		301 (A1)	5:12–13	148, 150 (A3)
		3:22b–28	42–45 (A3)	5:12–14	25, 33 (A2)
Romans	58 (A1); 32–34,	3:23	76 (A3)	**5:12–19**	11, 26, 32–35 (A2)
	49, 238 (A2); 43,	3:23–24	218 (A3)	5:12–21	94–95, 237,
	165, 291 (A3)	3:26	9 (A1)		255 (A3)
1–4	59 (A3)	3:28–30	218 (A3)	5:15	33 (A2)
1–5	290 (A3)	3:31	48 (A2)	5:16	33 (A2)
1–8	149, 200, 218 (A3)	4	26 (A1); 32, 47,	5:17	255 (A3)
1:1	183 (A3)		67 (A2); 166, 237 (A3)	5:18	37 (A2); 236 (A3)
1:1–7	**50, 56–60** (A1)	4:1	47, 67 (A2)	5:21	255 (A3)
1:7	111 (A3)	**4:1–5**	42, **47–51** (A2)	6	95, 98 (A3)
1:9	57 (A1)	4:1–12	58–60 (A3)	6:1	96 (A3)
1:15	57 (A1)	4:2	47, 49 (A2)	6:1–11	295 (A1)
1:16	56, 294 (A1); 48 (A2);	4:3	76 (A3)	6:1–15	94 (A3)
	76, 219 (A3)	4:3–5	76 (A3)	**6:1b–11**	**94–97** (A3)
1:16–17	8, **288**, 290,	4:9	67 (A2)	6:2	165 (A1)
	294–99 (A1);	4:9–18	67 (A2)	6:4	255 (A3)
	42–45, 218 (A3)	4:13–15	67 (A2)	6:4–5	93 (A3)
1:17	96, 112 (A3)	**4:13–17**	42, **47–51** (A2)	6:7	165 (A1)
1:17–18	57 (A1)	**4:13–25**	51, **58–62**, 65 (A3)	6:12–13	9 (A1)
1:18	68 (A2)	4:15	76 (A3)	6:12–19	255 (A3)
1:18–32	76–77, 94 (A3)	4:16	43 (A2)	**6:12–23**	**111–15** (A3)
1:18–2:16	58 (A3)	4:16–17	61 (A3)	6:16–19	45 (A3)
1:18–8:39	236 (A3)	4:17	48 (A2)	6:16–23	94 (A3)
1:19–20	272 (A3)	4:17–25	281 (A1)	6:18	117, 232 (A3)
1:19–21	290 (A3)	4:17b	48 (A2)	6:22	117 (A3)
1:28	255 (A3)	4:18	57 (A3)	7	95, 237 (A3)
2	3, 7 (A1)	4:21	57 (A3)	7:7	100 (A2)
2–3	237 (A3)	4:21–25	295 (A1)	7:7–13	100 (A2)
2:1	186 (A3)	4:22	67 (A2)	7:13	101 (A2)
2:1–5	9 (A1)	4:23–25	68 (A2); 76–77 (A3)	7:14	166 (A3)
2:1–29	76 (A3)	4:24–25	161 (A2)	7:14–25	101 (A2)
2:2	7 (A1)	5	78, 183 (A3)	**7:15–25a**	**130–34** (A3)
2:6	280 (A3)	5–6	255 (A3)	7:18	166 (A3)
2:9–11	294 (A1)	5:1	32, 67, 68, 70 (A2)	7:21–25	148 (A3)
2:16	57, 280–81 (A1);	**5:1–8**	69, **76–79**,	7:23	136 (A3)
	182 (A3)		**82–83** (A3)	7:24	100, 101 (A2)
2:17–3:31	58 (A3)	**5:1–11**	**67–70** (A2);	7:25	100 (A2)
3	68 (A2); 43 (A3)		60, 94 (A3)	8	102 (A2); 148, 150,
3:1	47 (A2)	5:2	32, 167 (A2)		166, 168 (A3)
3:3	47 (A2)	5:2–5	256 (A3)	8:1	100, 101, 102 (A2)
3:8	294 (A2); 94 (A3)	5:3–5	68 (A2)	**8:1–11**	100 (A2); **148–51**,
3:9	47 (A2)	5:3–10	77 (A3)		153 (A3)
3:9–23	77 (A3)	5:5	32 (A2)	8:1–12	9 (A1)
3:10–18	47 (A2)	5:6–9	67 (A2); 232 (A3)	8:1–17	250 (A1)
3:21	9 (A1)	5:7–8	119 (A2)	8:3	100, 101 (A2)
3:21–26	68 (A2); 94 (A3)	5:8	68, 70, 280 (A2);	8:4	294 (A2)
3:21–30	218 (A3)		74, 290 (A3)	8:5	100 (A2)
3:22	76 (A3)	5:9	67, 68, 70 (A2)	8:5–14	170 (A3)
3:22–28	290 (A1)	5:9–11	77, 95 (A3)	8:6–8	100, 102 (A2)

Romans (*continued*)

8:6–11	**100–103** (A2)
8:7–8	100 (A2)
8:9	100 (A2)
8:9–11	100 (A2)
8:11	101, 102, 103 (A2)
8:12	101 (A2)
8:12–17	101 (A2)
8:12–25	**165–68**, 170 (A3)
8:12–39	188 (A3)
8:15	101 (A2); 201 (A3)
8:15–17	101 (A2)
8:17	101 (A2)
8:18	9 (A1); 168n5 (A3)
8:18–39	150 (A3)
8:19–21	149 (A3)
8:22	44 (A3)
8:23	201 (A3)
8:23–25	18 (A1)
8:26–39	**182–86** (A3)
8:29	184n2 (A3)
8:31	117, 120 (A2)
8:31–39	161, 185 (A2); 236 (A3)
8:33–34	117 (A2)
8:34	288 (A2)
8:35–36	365 (A3)
8:37–39	200 (A3)
8:38–39	275 (A1); 105, 175–76 (A2)
8:39	33 (A2)
9	184 (A3)
9–11	200, 218, 236–37, 363 (A3)
9:1–5	**200–204**, 236 (A3)
9:1–13	217 (A3)
9:1–11:35	236 (A3)
9:6–18	237 (A3)
9:7	236 (A3)
9:11–17	183 (A3)
9:15–18	254 (A3)
9:17	290 (A3)
9:23–24	254 (A3)
9:24–25	217 (A3)
9:30–33	217 (A3)
9:30–10:13	218 (A3)
9:33	218–19 (A3)
10	57 (A1)
10:1	217 (A3)
10:1–5	217 (A3)
10:1–13	218 (A3)
10:1–15	218–19 (A3)
10:5–15	**217–21** (A3)
10:6	288 (A2)
10:8–10	218 (A3)
10:9	325 (A2)
10:11	218 (A3)
10:12–13	218 (A3)
10:14–15	99 (A1)
10:14–17	57 (A1)
10:15	57 (A1)
10:16	57 (A1)
10:17	218 (A3)
10:18–21	236 (A3)
10:34–43	272 (A2)
11	237 (A3)
11:1–2a	**236–39** (A3)
11:2–28	236 (A3)
11:5	9 (A1)
11:11–32	218 (A3)
11:15	237 (A3)
11:17–21	48 (A2)
11:17–24	28 (A1)
11:22	295 (A1)
11:28	57 (A1); 202–3, 236 (A3)
11:29	256 (A3)
11:29–32	**236–39** (A3)
11:32	202 (A3)
11:33	237 (A3)
11:33–36	256, 272 (A3)
11:35	236 (A3)
11:36	236 (A3)
12–14	85 (A2)
12–16	8 (A1); 200 (A3)
12:1	9, 295 (A1); 325 (A2); 236, 277 (A3)
12:1–2	301 (A1); 233 (A2); 289–90 (A3)
12:1–8	252, **254–57**, 272 (A3)
12:1–21	237 (A3)
12:1–15:13	47, 218, 236 (A3)
12:3–13	410 (A3)
12:3–21	295 (A1)
12:4–8	325 (A2)
12:6–8	325, 326 (A2)
12:9	25 (A1)
12:9–21	168, 255, **272–75**, 278 (A3)
12:13	25 (A1)
12:16	8, 25 (A1)
12:17	8 (A1)
12:21	8 (A1)
13	3, 57 (A1); 248 (A3)
13:1–7	290 (A3)
13:1–11	8 (A1)
13:4b	290 (A3)
13:8–10	266 (A1); 255 (A3)
13:8–14	287, **289–93** (A3)
13:9	24, 255 (A1); 48 (A3)
13:11	9 (A1)
13:12	7 (A1)
13:12–13	9 (A1)
13:13	9 (A1)
13:14	9 (A1)
14	308 (A3)
14:1	255 (A3)
14:1–12	**307–10** (A3)
14:1–15:6	56 (A1); 165 (A3)
14:1–15:7	237 (A3)
14:1–15:13	25 (A1)
14:4	255 (A3)
14:10	255 (A3)
14:13	255 (A3)
14:14	308 (A3)
14:15	255 (A3)
14:17	57 (A1)
15	19 (A1)
15:1	56 (A1); 308n1 (A3)
15:1–2	57 (A1)
15:1–6	27 (A1)
15:2–3	24 (A1)
15:3	24 (A1)
15:4–13	**17, 24–28** (A1)
15:5	8, 25 (A1)
15:5–6	237 (A3)
15:5–7	237 (A3)
15:6	218 (A3)
15:7	255 (A3)
15:7–13	236 (A3)
15:13	237 (A3)
15:14–15	417 (A3)
15:16	57, 295 (A1)
15:18	295 (A1)
15:20	57 (A1)
15:24	57 (A1)
15:25–28	166 (A3)
16:1–7	337 (A2)
16:18	111 (A3)
16:25	57 (A1)

16:25–26	56 (A1)	3:13	281 (A1)	12	217 (A1); 324, 325,
16:25–27	57 (A1)	3:15	280 (A1)		330 (A2); 256 (A3)
17:14–25	100 (A2)	3:16–17	250, 266n1 (A1)	12–13	295 (A3)
		3:16–23	**258, 265–68** (A1)	12–14	381 (A3)
1 Corinthians	187n2, 200,	3:17	280 (A1)	12:1	324 (A2); 325,
	235 (A1); 148,	3:21	260 (A1)		335 (A2)
	325, 335 (A2)	3:23	186 (A1)	**12:3b–13**	**324–27**,
1:1	183 (A3)	4:1	27 (A3)		339 (A2)
1:1–9	189, 201 (A1)	**4:1–5**	**273, 280–83**,	12:4	325 (A2)
1:3–6	189 (A1)		285 (A1);	12:4–11	250 (A1)
1:10	217 (A1)		**25–28** (A3)	12:7	326, 330 (A2)
1:10–12	280 (A1)	4:4–5	280 (A1)	12:8–9	325 (A2)
1:10–13	265 (A1)	4:5	275 (A1); 182 (A3)	12:11	325 (A2)
1:10–17	148, 324 (A2);	4:6	280 (A1)	12:12	186 (A1); 330 (A2)
	14 (A3)	4:10	218 (A1)	12:12–13	502 (A3)
1:10–18	**193,**	4:12	218 (A1)	12:12–27	266 (A1)
	200–203 (A1)	4:13	218 (A1)	12:12–31	94 (A2)
1:11	186, 280 (A1)	4:16	454 (A3)	12:13	325, 330 (A2)
1:12	217, 251, 265 (A1);	4:17	186 (A1)	12:25b–26	365 (A3)
	324 (A2); 381 (A3)	4:21	280 (A1)	12:26	327 (A3)
1:13	324 (A2)	5:1–8	381 (A3)	12:27	186 (A1)
1:14–17	95 (A3)	5:7	282 (A3)	12:31	272 (A1)
1:17	201, 217, 233 (A1)	6:1–11	381 (A3)	13	201, 217, 234 (A1);
1:18	187 (A1)	6:15	186 (A1)		325 (A2); 12,
1:18–31	**209, 216–20**,	7:21	73 (A1)		168 (A3)
	222 (A1)	8	201, 217 (A1)	13:1	335 (A2)
1:23	131 (A2)	8:1–13	200 (A3)	13:2	27 (A3)
1:27	224 (A1)	8:1–11:1	308 (A3)	13:4	325 (A2)
1:27–28	141 (A3)	8:6	186, 218 (A1);	13:5	325 (A2)
1:28	365 (A3)		325 (A2)	**13:11–14**	**2, 8–11** (A1)
1:31	224 (A1)	10:1–2	307 (A1)	13:12	284 (A2); 432 (A3)
2	217 (A1)	10:4	61 (A2)	14	324, 325 (A2)
2:1	234 (A1); 27 (A3)	10:6	254 (A1)	14:2	335 (A2)
2:1–5	218 (A1)	10:14	400 (A3)	14:7	324 (A2)
2:1–16	**225, 233–237** (A1)	10:16–18	149 (A2)	14:13	335 (A2)
2:2	327 (A2)	10:23–11:1	308 (A3)	14:14–15	324, 335 (A2)
2:3	218 (A1); 345 (A3)	11	217 (A1)	14:18	324 (A2)
2:7	27 (A3)	11:1	454 (A3)	14:23	324 (A2)
2:12	241 (A1)	11:2	28 (A3)	15	217 (A1); 191,
2:16	255 (A3)	11:2–16	292, 381 (A3)		280 (A2); 469 (A3)
3	234, 259 (A1)	11:17	28 (A3)	15:1	417 (A3)
3:1–4	265 (A1)	11:17–18	266 (A1)	15:3–5	280 (A2)
3:1–9	**242, 249–52** (A1)	11:17–34	280 (A1); 381 (A3)	15:8	225 (A2)
3:2	262, 284 (A2);	11:22–29	28 (A3)	15:13	207 (A2)
	419 (A3)	11:24	147 (A2)	15:22	236 (A3)
3:9	256, 265 (A1)	11:24–25	143 (A2)	15:23	186 (A1)
3:10	250 (A1)	11:25	231 (A2)	15:24	148 (A2)
3:10–11	**258, 265–68** (A1)	11:26	143, 144, 149 (A2)	15:42–44	100 (A2)
3:10–13	280 (A1)	11:27–34	149 (A2)	15:51	234 (A1)
3:10–15	280 (A1)	11:28–29	149 (A2)	15:51–57	95 (A3)
3:11	261 (A3)	11:29	266 (A1)	15:54	379 (A3)
3:11–15	265 (A1)	11:33	149 (A2)	16:19	324 (A2)

2 Corinthians	200 (A1); 324 (A2)	1:11–12	154 (A1)	1:23	289 (A2)
1:1	183 (A3)	2	187n2 (A1)	2:1	294 (A2)
1:1–9	**177, 184–87** (A1)	2:1–10	294 (A2)	2:1–2	294 (A2)
1:3–7	294 (A2)	2:11–14	236 (A1); 308 (A3)	2:2	85 (A2)
1:18–22	281 (A1)	2:12	362 (A3)	2:4–5	85 (A2)
2:4–11	312 (A3)	2:15–21	59, 111, 362 (A3)	2:4–7	295 (A2)
3:7–18	312 (A1)	2:16	76 (A3)	2:8	69 (A2)
4	13, 469 (A3)	3–4	69 (A2)	2:8–9	232 (A2)
4:1–2	12 (A3)	3:6–9	76 (A3)	2:10	138 (A1)
4:5	325 (A2)	3:6–18	183 (A3)	2:11–13	294 (A2)
4:6	143, 312 (A1)	3:19	59, 76 (A3)	2:13–14	153 (A1)
5	11 (A2)	3:24	59 (A3)	2:14	139, 155 (A1)
5:1	11, 201 (A2)	3:26–28	365 (A3)	2:14–16	295 (A2)
5:2	11 (A2)	3:27–28	9 (A1)	2:15	139 (A1)
5:10	281 (A1)	3:27–29	95 (A3)	2:15–16	140 (A1)
5:14	280 (A2)	3:28	8, 155 (A1); 75, 337 (A2); 242 (A3)	2:16	502 (A3)
5:14–15	11 (A2)			2:17	294 (A2)
5:16–17	11 (A2)	3:28–29	502 (A3)	2:19	153 (A1); 294 (A2)
5:16–6:13	312 (A3)	4:5–7	166 (A3)	2:21	153 (A1)
5:17	186 (A1); 95, 365 (A3)	4:9–10	308 (A3)	3	157 (A1)
		5:2–12	362 (A3)	3:1	294 (A2)
5:18	12 (A2)	5:13–15	266 (A1)	**3:1–12**	**146, 152–56** (A1)
5:18–19	184 (A2)	5:16	95, 97 (A3)	3:2	148 (A1); 191 (A2)
5:18–21	77 (A3)	5:16–26	92 (A1)	3:4	295 (A2)
5:20–21	5 (A2)	5:19–21	9, 252 (A1)	3:4–6	295 (A2)
5:20b–6:10	**11–14** (A2)	5:22	43 (A1)	3:7–8	148 (A1)
5:21	12, 167 (A2)	5:22–23	283 (A2)	3:14	294 (A2)
6:1	12, 14n5 (A2)	5:22–26	168 (A3)	3:14–19	294 (A2)
6:1b	13 (A2)	6:6–16	294 (A2)	3:18	54 (A2)
6:2	12 (A2)	6:7–9	170 (A3)	3:18–19	54 (A2)
6:5	12 (A2)	6:17	119 (A2)	3:20–21	294 (A2)
6:6–7	12 (A2)			4:1–3	295 (A2)
6:7	12 (A2)	**Ephesians**	85, 294–96 (A2); 503–4 (A3)	4:1–6	327 (A3)
6:16	131 (A1)			4:2–3	381 (A3)
6:17	85 (A2)	1	93 (A2)	4:3	382 (A3)
7:15	345 (A3)	1–3	294 (A2)	4:4	501 (A3)
10–13	218 (A1)	1:3	137 (A1); 503 (A3)	4:4–6	252 (A1)
10:10	234 (A1)	**1:3–14**	**130, 137–40**, 143 (A1)	4:6	295 (A2)
11:5	234 (A1)			4:11	325 (A2)
11:12–19	363 (A3)	1:4	153 (A1)	4:14	501 (A3)
11:16–30	154 (A1)	1:5	153 (A1)	4:15–16	502 (A3)
11:16–33	218 (A1)	1:6	161 (A2)	4:22	84 (A2)
11:24–25	82 (A3)	1:7	131 (A1)	4:24	84 (A2)
12	234 (A1)	1:9–10	235 (A1)	4:25	84 (A2)
12:2–7	234 (A1)	1:10	153 (A1)	4:25–27	84 (A2)
13	12 (A3)	1:14	501 (A3)	4:25–32	84 (A2)
13:11–13	**10–13, 14** (A3)	1:15	294, 296, 297 (A2)	4:25–5:5	84 (A2)
12:14	218 (A1)	**1:15–23**	**294–97** (A2); **501–5**, 509 (A3)	4:26–27	84 (A2)
				4:28	84 (A2)
Galatians	185 (A1); 294 (A2)	1:17	296 (A2)	4:31–32	84 (A2)
1:1	183 (A3)	1:21	296, 297 (A2)	5:1	84 (A2)
		1:22–23	295 (A2)	5:1–2	84, 295 (A2)

5:2	84, 85 (A2)	2:1–5	168 (A3)	1:26–27	138 (A1)
5:3	84 (A2)	**2:1–13**	**343–47** (A3)	2:2	190 (A2)
5:4	84 (A2)	2:2	25 (A1); 123, 124 (A2)	2:7	250 (A1)
5:5	84 (A2)			3	192 (A2)
5:6	86 (A2); 501–2 (A3)	2:4	123, 124 (A2)	3–4	85 (A2)
5:6–7	84 (A2)	2:5	25 (A1); 123 (A2)	3:1	188, 191, 192 (A2)
5:7	86 (A2)	2:5–8	121, 294 (A1); 77 (A3)	**3:1–4**	**190–94** (A2)
5:8	84, 85, 86 (A2)			3:2	190 (A2)
5:8–9	84, 90 (A2)	**2:5–11**	**122–27**, 138, 288, 315 (A2); 381 (A3)	3:5	256 (A1); 400 (A3)
5:8–14	**84–87** (A2)			3:5–11	191 (A2)
5:9	85 (A2)	2:6	124 (A2)	3:10	92 (A1)
5:10	86 (A2)	2:6–7	335 (A3)	3:12–4:5	190 (A2)
5:10–14	84 (A2)	2:6–8	118 (A2)	3:27–29	410 (A3)
5:11	86 (A2)	2:7	126 (A2); 25 (A3)	4:1	72 (A1)
5:12	86 (A2)	2:7–8	124 (A2)		
5:13	86 (A2)	2:8	127 (A1)	**1 Thessalonians**	13 (A1); 449, 484 (A3)
5:13–14	84 (A2)	2:9	122, 288 (A2)		
5:14	84, 85, 87 (A2)	2:9–10	393 (A3)	**1:1–10**	392–93, **399–402**, 404 (A3)
5:15–20	85 (A2)	2:9–11	124 (A2)		
5:15–6:9	138 (A1)	2:11	311 (A1); 335 (A2)	1:3	391, 484–85 (A3)
5:21–6:9	85 (A2)	2:12–13	335, 342 (A3)	1:6	391, 450–51 (A3)
5:22–33	85 (A2)	2:14–15	124 (A2)	1:6–9	449 (A3)
5:29–30	502 (A3)	2:21	123 (A2)	1:8	484 (A3)
5:31	254 (A1)	3:1–4:3	380 (A3)	1:10	468 (A3)
6:4	455 (A3)	3:1b–3	362 (A3)	**2:1–8**	409–10, **416–19** (A3)
6:5	345 (A3)	3:2–4	123 (A2)		
6:5–9	85 (A2)	3:2b	363 (A3)	2:2	409 (A3)
6:9	72 (A1)	**3:4b–14**	**362–66** (A3)	2:9	81, 417, 452 (A3)
6:10–17	12 (A2)	3:10–11	125 (A2)	2:9–11	442 (A3)
6:11–17	85 (A2)	3:12–14	361 (A3)	**2:9–13**	**449–53** (A3)
6:12	138, 140, 154 (A1); 85 (A2)	3:15	123 (A2)	2:10	454 (A3)
		3:17–19	123, 124 (A2)	2:14	450 (A3)
		3:20	401 (A3)	3:2	449 (A3)
Philippians		3:20–21	125 (A2)	3:6–8	400 (A3)
1	327 (A3)	3:20–4:1	124 (A2)	3:12–13	449 (A3)
1:5	325 (A3)	3:21	255 (A3)	3:13	42 (A1)
1:5–6	124 (A2)	4:1–2	123 (A2)	4:1–12	85 (A2); 468, 470 (A3)
1:6	125 (A2); 325 (A3)	**4:1–9**	376, **380–84** (A3)		
1:7	330 (A3)	4:2	217 (A1); 123 (A2)	4:5	470 (A3)
1:8	325 (A3)	4:4a	364 (A3)	4:6	468 (A3)
1:10–11	124, 125 (A2)	4:5	375 (A3)	4:9–10	468 (A3)
1:14	326 (A3)	4:7	182 (A3)	4:11	450 (A3)
1:20	326 (A3)	4:18	123 (A2)	4:13	487 (A3)
1:21–30	**325–28** (A3)			4:13–18	401, **467–70** (A3)
1:27	123 (A2); 324, 343, 345 (A3)	**Colossians**	192 (A2)	**5:1–11**	468, 477, **484–87**, 489, 490 (A3)
		1	191 (A2)		
1:27–30	123 (A2)	1:15	123 (A1)	5:2	472 (A3)
1:28	124 (A2); 326 (A3)	1:15–16	121 (A1)	5:4–5	473 (A3)
1:30	331 (A3)	1:15–20	105 (A1); 168, 190, 192 (A2)	5:4–6	480 (A3)
2	159 (A2); 335, 350 (A3)			5:5	469 (A3)
		1:19–20	161 (A2)	5:5–10	9 (A1)
2:1–4	381 (A3)	1:24	190 (A1); 119 (A2)	5:6	472 (A3)

1 Thessalonians (*continued*)		2	125 (A1)	10:19–20	181 (A2)
5:9	480, 483 (A3)	2:1	105 (A1)	10:19–22	178–79 (A2)
5:9–10	468 (A3)	2:1–4	177 (A2)	10:21	180 (A2)
5:11	480, 491 (A3)	2:3–4	120 (A1)	10:22	120 (A1); 179 (A2)
5:12–13	280 (A1)	2:5–3:6	177 (A2)	10:23–24	167 (A2)
5:14	308n1 (A3)	2:6–7	121 (A1)	10:23–25	177, 179 (A2)
5:18–24	468 (A3)	2:9–18	107 (A1)	10:24	179, 181 (A2)
5:24	280 (A1)	2:10	115 (A1)	10:25	121 (A1); 181 (A2)
		2:10–18	**114, 120–24** (A1)	10:32–33	105 (A1)
2 Thessalonians		2:11	167 (A2)	10:32–34	122 (A1); 178 (A2)
3:8	81 (A3)	2:14	167 (A2)	10:34	121 (A1)
		3:7–19	177 (A2)	11	436 (A3)
1 Timothy	74 (A1)	3:12–15	105 (A1)	11:1	175 (A2); 470 (A3)
2	25 (A2)	4	166 (A2)	11:2	117 (A3)
2:2–10	72 (A1)	4:13	281 (A1)	11:8	51 (A3)
2:14	25 (A2)	4:14	288 (A2)	11:23–24	248 (A3)
3:1	254 (A1)	**4:14–16**	**166–69** (A2)	11:39	436 (A3)
3:2	253 (A2)	4:15	119, 166 (A2)	12:1–2	433 (A3)
3:5	72 (A1)	5	166 (A2)	12:2	94 (A1)
6:14	18 (A2)	5:5	63 (A1)	12:3	121 (A1); 178 (A2)
		5:7	167 (A2)	12:4	94 (A1)
2 Timothy	74 (A1)	5:7–8	105 (A1)	12:7–11	178 (A2)
1:5	417 (A3)	**5:7–9**	**164, 166–69** (A2)	12:12	121 (A1); 178 (A2)
1:7	417 (A3)	5:8	166, 167 (A2)	12:12–13	346 (A3)
2:12	99 (A3)	5:11	276 (A3)	12:29	281 (A1)
3:12	400 (A3)	5:12	121 (A1)	13:1–4	108 (A1)
		6:1	167 (A2)	13:2	69 (A3)
Titus	74 (A1)	6:1–2	120 (A1)	13:3	105, 121 (A1)
1:12	89–90 (A1)	6:1–3	178 (A2)	13:8	200–201 (A2)
2:2–6	89 (A1)	6:4–5	120 (A1)	13:22	105, 107 (A1); 178 (A2)
2:9–10	89 (A1)	6:4–8	121 (A1)		
2:10	73 (A1)	6:10	121 (A1)		
2:11–14	**65**, 68, **72–75** (A1)	6:18	470 (A3)	**James**	
		6:19–20	470 (A3)	1:1	16 (A1)
2:13	401 (A3)	7:1–10:18	107 (A1)	1:1–2	42 (A1)
2:14	89 (A1)	7:14	425 (A3)	1:2–3	42 (A1)
3:1–3	92 (A1)	7:26	288 (A2)	1:6–7	42 (A1)
3:2–3	90 (A1)	9–10	178 (A2)	1:8	255 (A1)
3:4–7	74, **81, 89–92** (A1)	9:1–10:18	177 (A2)	1:9	42 (A1)
3:8	89 (A1)	9:4	318 (A3)	1:9–10	43 (A1)
3:9–11	89 (A1)	9:24	288 (A2)	1:9–11	43 (A1)
		10	178, 179 (A2)	1:12	42–43 (A1)
Hebrews	164, 166, 177 (A2)	10:2	179, 180, 181 (A2)	1:13–14	42 (A1)
		10:12	178 (A2)	1:17	147 (A1)
1:1	132 (A1)	10:16	178, 181 (A2)	1:18	43 (A1)
1:1–4	167 (A2)	10:16–17	178 (A2)	1:19–20	254 (A1)
1:1–12	**98, 104–8** (A1)	10:16–18	178 (A2)	1:20	42 (A1)
1:2–3	121 (A1)	10:16–22	177 (A2)	1:22–2:26	48 (A3)
1:4–13	106 (A1)	**10:16–25**	172, **177–81** (A2)	1:26	42 (A1)
1:5	63 (A1)	10:17–18	178 (A2)	2	421 (A3)
1:8	166 (A2)	10:19	180, 181 (A2)	2:1–13	43 (A1)

2:2–6	42 (A1)	1:13	217 (A2)	3:1	217, 247, 248 (A2)
2:5	43 (A1)	1:14	233 (A2)	3:2	280 (A2)
2:8–13	43 (A1)	1:16	85, 235, 248 (A2)	3:4	224 (A1)
2:9	255 (A1)	1:17	232, 234, 235, 238, 248 (A2)	3:6	248 (A2)
2:11	255 (A1)			3:8	217, 233 (A2); 381 (A3)
2:15	42 (A1)	**1:17–23**	**232–35** (A2)	3:13	279 (A2)
2:22	43 (A1)	1:18	227, 232, 233, 235 (A2)	3:13–17	279 (A2)
3:13–18	381 (A3)			**3:13–22**	**279–82** (A2)
3:13–4:17	48 (A3)	1:19	144, 232, 233, 238 (A2)	3:14	282 (A2)
3:18	43 (A1)			3:15	271, 281 (A2)
4:1–10	43 (A1)	1:21	227, 233 (A2)	3:17	279 (A2)
4:1–12	295 (A3)	1:22	217, 227, 233, 235, 238, 248 (A2)	3:18	280 (A2)
4:2	254 (A1)			3:18–22	279, 280 (A2)
4:6	42–43 (A1)	1:22–23	227 (A2)	3:19	280 (A2)
4:8	255 (A1)	1:23	233, 234, 235, 248 (A2)	3:21	281, 282 (A2)
4:10	43 (A1)			3:21-22	288 (A2)
4:11–12	42 (A1)	1:24	233 (A2)	4:3	216, 232 (A2)
5:1	43 (A1)	2	217, 233, 234, 249, 257 (A2)	4:4	216 (A2)
5:2	18 (A2)			4:7	217, 310 (A2)
5:4	42 (A1)	2–11	281 (A2)	4:12	217, 248, 310 (A2)
5:7	43 (A1); 401 (A3)	2:1	233, 262, 263, 264, 266 (A2)	**4:12–14**	**309–13** (A2)
5:7–10	**34**, 36, **42–45** (A1)			4:12–16	400 (A3)
5:9	42 (A1)	2:2	248, 249, 250, 262 (A2)	4:13	310 (A2)
5:11	42–43 (A1)			4:13–14	312 (A2)
5:12	43 (A1)	**2:2–10**	**262–66** (A2)	4:14	310, 313, 315 (A2)
5:13–14	42 (A1)	2:4	248, 263, 264 (A2)	4:16	279 (A2)
5:16–18	43 (A1)	2:4–10	263 (A2)	4:17	232 (A2)
5:17–18	43 (A1)	2:5	233, 248, 263, 264 (A2)	4:17–18	248 (A2)
5:20	295 (A3)			4:19	248 (A2)
		2:6–8	263 (A2)	5:1	217, 309, 310 (A2)
1 Peter	216–18, 232–34, 242, 249, 262–65, 280, 309, 311–13 (A2)	2:7	264 (A2)	5:2	253 (A2)
		2:9	248, 263, 264, 266 (A2); 451 (A3)	5:4	248 (A2)
				5:6	310 (A2)
1	217, 234 (A2)	2:9–10	263 (A2)	5:6–8	310 (A2)
1:1	216, 232, 262 (A2)	2:11	216, 233, 238 (A2)	5:6–9	313 (A2)
1:1–5	248 (A2)	2:11–4:11	120 (A2)	**5:6–11**	**309–13** (A2)
1:3	216, 217, 219, 222, 234 (A2)	2:12	217 (A2)	5:7	310 (A2)
		2:13	217 (A2)	5:8	310 (A2)
1:3–5	232 (A2)	2:16	247 (A2)	5:9	217, 310, 312 (A2)
1:3–9	**216–19**, 222 (A2)	2:18	217, 247, 249 (A2)	5:11	262, 311 (A2)
1:4	216 (A2)	2:19	247 (A2)	5:13	309 (A2)
1:5	217, 219 (A2)	2:19–21	247 (A2)		
1:6	218, 310 (A2)	**2:19–25**	**247–50** (A2)	**2 Peter**	
1:6–7	217 (A2)	2:21	248, 249, 252, 281 (A2)	1	317 (A1)
1:7	217, 218, 219, 310 (A2)			1:1	50 (A2)
		2:21–25	161, 248 (A2)	1:3–7	311 (A1)
1:8	210, 217, 218, 219, 222, 310 (A2)	2:23	248, 249, 250, 252 (A2)	1:6–7	313 (A1)
				1:12	313 (A1); 417n2 (A3)
1:8–9	217 (A2)	2:24	249, 250, 252 (A2)	**1:16–21**	**304**, 305–6, **311–14** (A1)
1:9	219 (A2)	2:25	248, 250, 252 (A2)		
1:12	254 (A1); 233 (A2)	3	217, 233, 234 (A2)	2:1–3	311–12 (A1)

2 Peter (continued)
2:15–19	311 (A1)
3:1	417n2 (A3)
3:10–13	477 (A3)
3:13	48 (A1)
3:15–17	311 (A1)

1 John
	431–32 (A3)
1:5	85 (A2)
2:1	224 (A1)
2:1–2	433 (A3)
2:9	85 (A2)
2:18	434 (A3)
2:18–26	431 (A3)
3	432 (A3)
3:1–3	**431–34 (A3)**
3:6	433 (A3)
3:11–22	381 (A3)
3:15	254 (A1)
3:24	329 (A2)
4	421 (A3)
4:1–3	341 (A2)
4:7	147 (A2)
4:8	155 (A2)
4:18	285, 329 (A2); 346 (A3)
4:19	147 (A2)
5:21	400 (A3)

2 John
	431 (A3)

3 John
	431 (A3)

Jude
1:5	417n2 (A3)

Revelation
	265 (A3)
1:1	188 (A2)
1:3	425 (A3)
1:7	307 (A1)
2–3	425–26 (A3)
2:9–11	426 (A3)
2:17	318 (A3)
3:10–12	426 (A3)
4:1	425 (A3)
4:1–11	425–26 (A3)
5:1–7:8	425 (A3)
5:6	144 (A2)
6	425 (A3)
6–7	425 (A3)
7	432 (A3)
7–15	430 (A3)
7:1	430 (A3)
7:1–8	425 (A3)
7:4	436 (A3)
7:9	425, 429–30, 470 (A3)
7:9–17	**424–28**, 432, 436 (A3)
7:10–12	430 (A3)
7:11	428 (A3)
7:14	144 (A2); 429 (A3)
7:14–15	430 (A3)
7:15b–16a	430 (A3)
7:17	379, 429 (A3)
8–9	426 (A3)
8:1–2	460 (A3)
12:11	144 (A2)
15:3	57 (A1)
17:13–14	436 (A3)
19:1–2	99 (A3)
19:9	141 (A2); 472 (A3)
19:19–20	436 (A3)
20–22	436 (A3)
21	310 (A2)
21–22	167 (A2); 426 (A3)
21:1–4	376 (A3)
21:1–6	394 (A3)
21:3	131, 190 (A1)
21:4	379 (A3)
21:6	274 (A1)
22:1–2	340 (A2)

APOCRYPHA

Tobit
4:15	273 (A3)
12:8–9	18 (A2)
14:4	317 (A3)

Judith
13	205 (A2)

Wisdom
	471 (A3)
6:17–20	471 (A3)
6:18–20	471 (A3)
7:26	121 (A1)
10:15	137 (A1)
10:20	137 (A1)
12:13	168 (A3)
12:16–19	168 (A3)
16:20	318 (A3)

Sirach   Ecclesiasticus/Sirach
7:34	273 (A3)
11:27	15 (A1)
15:17	255 (A1)
18:23	66 (A1)
24:1	137 (A1)
24:10	137 (A1)
24:12	137 (A1)
24:18–20	194 (A3)
25:24	25 (A2)

2 Maccabees
6–7	205 (A2)
7:25	205 (A2)

3 Maccabees
2:22	48–49 (A1)

TARGUMIC TEXTS

Targum Jonathan   61 (A2)

Apostolic Fathers

Didache
1:5	18 (A2)

Polycarp

To the Philippians
3.3-5.1	18 (A2)